THE CHURCH OF ENGLAND

YEAR BOOK

127TH EDITION

2011

A directory of local and national
structures and organizations
and the Churches and Provinces
of the Anglican Communion

SINCE 1883

CHURCH HOUSE PUBLISHING

Church House Publishing
Church House
Great Smith Street
London
SW1P 3AZ

ISBN 978–0–7151–1047–8
ISSN 0069 3987

Typeset by RefineCatch Ltd,
Bungay, Suffolk

Printed by Anthony Rowe,
Chippenham, Wilts

The Church of England Year Book
The official Year Book of the
Church of England

*127th edition © The Archbishops'
Council 2010*

Contents

INDEX TO ADVERTISEMENTS

Advertisements can be found on the following pages

The inclusion of an advertisement is for the purposes of information and is not to be taken as implying acceptance of the objects of the advertiser by the publisher.

  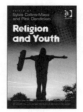 

Heythrop College
University of London

Heythrop College:

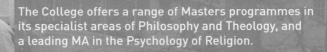

- is a College of the University of London, specialising in Philosophy, Theology and Psychology
- has a larger number of academic faculty in these subjects than most universities
- offers degrees of the University of London, with a worldwide reputation for academic excellence

The College offers a range of Masters programmes in its specialist areas of Philosophy and Theology, and a leading MA in the Psychology of Religion.

All programmes can be studied either full- or part-time.

MA Philosophy
MA Philosophy and Religion
MA Psychology of Religion
MA Contemporary Ethics
MA Biblical Studies
MA Canon Law
MA Abrahamic Studies
MA Christianity and Interreligious
   Relations
MA Christian Spirituality
MA Christian Theology
MA Pastoral Theology

Heythrop College, University of London
Kensington Square   London W8 5HN   020 7795 6600
www.heythrop.ac.uk

A YEAR IN REVIEW 2009/10

NOVEMBER
In a keynote address to the TUC Economics Conference, the Archbishop of Canterbury emphasised that economics was only one aspect of human existence and needed to be kept in perspective. Three new videocasts were released through the Church of England website, with money-saving tips and a budgeting spreadsheet to help people enjoy Christmas without getting into debt.

Dr Williams invited faith leaders and Trustees of the Inter Faith Network to Lambeth Palace to launch 'Inter Faith Week', where they signed a statement of common commitment to continue building good inter-religious relations and to contribute to the common good from different religious perspectives. The Archbishop of York brought regional religious leaders together at Bishopthorpe Palace. Representatives from the Yorkshire & Humber Faith Forum discussed how the organisation had developed since its creation in 2005 and reflected on the current economic situation.

On Armistice Day the BBC broadcast live from Westminster Abbey a Service to mark the Passing of the First World War Generation, during which the Archbishop of Canterbury preached. The service followed the deaths of the last remaining UK veterans of World War One, but marked the passing not only of the veterans but also the whole generation whose lives spanned the twentieth century. The congregation from across the UK included Her Majesty The Queen, The Duke of Edinburgh and a large number of other members of the Royal Family.

Students and staff at many of the Church of England's 4,500 primary and 220 secondary schools joined in the UK's first inter-faith week, facilitated by the Inter Faith Network for the UK and the Department for Communities and Local Government. An independent academic study of recent Ofsted inspection data showed that 'faith schools' promoted community cohesion and equality significantly and substantially more than other schools.

On the centenary of the Great Congo Demonstration led by the then Archbishop of Canterbury, Dr Randall Davidson, to protest against violence and oppression in the Congo Free State, the Archbishop of Canterbury, the Archbishop of the Anglican Province of Congo and the Bishop of Winchester voiced their concerns over the continuing conflict in the Democratic Republic of Congo.

Dr Williams addressed the Pontifical Council for Promoting Christian Unity in Rome as part of a symposium at the Gregorian University to celebrate the centenary of the birth of Cardinal Willebrands, the first president of the Council. He and the Pope reaffirmed their desire to strengthen ecumenical relations between Anglicans and Roman Catholics, and a preparatory committee met to prepare the third phase of the Anglican-Roman Catholic International Commission (ARCIC). The Bishop of Guildford responded, as Chairman of the Council for Christian Unity, to the publication of the Apostolic Constitution and its complementary norms by the Vatican.

In response to the DPP's consultation on policy on assisted suicide the Archbishops' Council's Mission and Public Affairs Council (MPA) released its own draft policy, proposing changes to strengthen the presumption in favour of prosecution and stressing the importance of never viewing assisted suicide as acceptable or commendable.

The Archbishop of Canterbury paid tribute to the work of the Mothers' Union, describing it as the most influential and widespread lay movement in the Churches of the Anglican Communion. Dr Williams released a 2009 World Aids Day video, highlighting the plight of expectant mothers who are HIV positive and the support they need to prevent the transmission of HIV to their babies.

Returns from churches participating in Back to Church Sunday 2009 suggested that they had welcomed back 53,000 people that Sunday, a 71 per cent increase on 2008, an average of 19 people returning to each church after receiving a personal invitation.

The Pensions Board rebutted as misconceived a *Financial Times* article about the clergy pension scheme's investment strategy: it had at all times accorded with mainstream actuarial and investment advice from professional advisors.

Archbishop Desmond Tutu launched the online Advent calendar, with 'tread gently' challenges and video stories behind each window.

The Archbishops of Canterbury and York formally advised the College of Bishops that the normal administration of Holy Communion ought to resume, subject to the June guidelines on good hygiene practice and allowing for local discretion in the event of outbreaks of pandemic flu in particular centres of population.

Appointments The Ven Donald Allister, Archdeacon of Chester, was appointed Bishop of Peterborough. Canon Martin Warner, Canon Treasurer of St Paul's Cathedral, was appointed Bishop of Whitby. The Ven Danny Kajumba, Archdeacon of Reigate, was appointed Chair of the Archbishops' Council's Committee for Minority Ethnic Anglican Concerns. Simon Baynes, the Revd Richard Billinghurst, the Revd Paul Boughton, the Revd Nigel Bourne, Graham Campbell and John Ferguson were elected to the Pensions Board.

DECEMBER

The Archbishop of Canterbury warned that the Revd Mary Glasspool's election as suffragan bishop by the Diocese of Los Angeles raised very serious questions not just for the Episcopal Church and its place in the Anglican Communion, but for the Communion as a whole. As the final version of the Anglican Communion Covenant was sent to member Churches, the Archbishop explained its purpose and the processes surrounding its adoption.

New statistics showed that tax-efficient planned giving in 2007 had averaged more than £9 a week for the first time, while the total income of parishes had increased by £70 million to £898 million, well above inflation. Total voluntary income rose to £485 million and total parish expenditure to £838 million, with £50 million of this donated by parishes to external charities. 574 new clergy were ordained in 2008, 19 more than in 2007 and 87 more than in 2006. Another 490 ordinands were accepted for training in 2008, bringing the total in training at the end of the year to 1,411. Clergy numbers were buoyant, but the number of retirements also remained high.

The Archbishop of Canterbury preached in Copenhagen Cathedral at the midpoint of the critical UN Climate Change talks. The Church of England had earlier launched its environmental strategy for the next seven years, as global faith leaders and UN Secretary-General, Ban Ki-moon, gathered to discuss commitments on climate change before the world's political leaders met in Copenhagen.

Twelve finalists from rural churches across the country were guests of the Archbishop of Canterbury, Dr Rowan Williams, at Lambeth Palace as he announced the overall winner and the two runners-up in the *Country Life* 'Unsung Heroes of the Rural Church' competition.

In its response to a BBC Trust consultation on BBC Television, the Church argued for a proper portrayal of religion, reflecting and exploring the factors giving people's lives purpose, as an explicit part of the BBC's requirement to "sustain citizenship and civil society". The long-standing ban on branded goods appearing on television programmes should be maintained, said the Church in a submission to the Department for Culture, Media and Sport's review of 'product placement' on TV.

The Archbishops of Canterbury and York condemned the resurgence of police intimidation of Anglicans in Zimbabwe, where churchgoers, including clergy and local bishops, had been barred from entering their churches and threatened with arrest and violence. Pakistan's Prime Minister, Syed Yousuf Raza Gilani, assured a Church of England delegation led by the Bishop of Bradford that his government was fully committed to upholding the rights and equal status of all the country's minorities. He also highlighted measures being taken to stop the misuse of the so-called blasphemy laws which had led to the recent fatal violence against Christian communities in the Punjab. The Rt Revd Stephen Venner, Bishop to the Forces, emphasised the importance of working with the Afghan government to bring stability, democracy and an enduring peace, clarifying that talks could be held only with former Taliban militants who had forsaken the path of war.

Society's rush to create independent citizens was crushing and narrowing children's experiences of childhood, the Archbishop of Canterbury said in his Christmas Sermon in Canterbury Cathedral: Christmas taught us that a truly fulfilled existence meant accepting joyfully our dependence on one another. The Archbishop of York spoke out on asylum, describing asylum seekers who find themselves destitute and struggling to survive with little or no means of support as society's "living ghosts". He posted a Christmas message on YouTube, calling on people to be like the innkeeper from the Nativity story, encouraging them to be a similar presence in their community, showing the love of God to others.

Appointments Canon Dr David Hoyle, Gloucester Diocesan Officer for Ministry, was appointed Dean of Bristol. James Archer and Sandra Newton were elected to the Pensions Board.

JANUARY
In his New Year Message the Archbishop of Canterbury set out that, in this global society we now inhabit, "risk and suffering are everybody's problem, the needs of our neighbours are the needs of the whole human family."

MPA welcomed the report on Alcohol published by the Commons Select Committee on Health as an immensely significant landmark report, bringing into focus what practitioners and researchers had been saying for years. The Church joined more than 1,000 organisations in the national Dying Matters Coalition. Led by the National Council for Palliative Care, working closely with the Department of Health and other key stakeholders, the coalition's aim was to promote public awareness around death, dying and bereavement. It also joined an industry-led campaign to press Government to provide adequate compensation for groups – including hundreds of churches – affected by changes to the way that radio frequencies are allocated and "evicted" from special events frequencies. Warm welcomes were given both to a recommendation from the House of Commons Public Accounts Committee that cathedrals should receive direct funding from Government; and to the announcement that the Department for Business Innovation and Skills had accepted the Competition Commission's recommendation of a body to enforce the Groceries Supply Code of Practice.

As Peers met to consider the Government's Equality Bill, three bishops, including the Bishop of Exeter as Chair of the Churches Legislation Advisory Service, emphasised the importance of striking the right balance between the rights and responsibilities of different groups to be protected from harassment and unfair discrimination and the rights of churches and religious organisations to appoint and employ people consistently with their guiding doctrine and ethos. The House of Bishops Europe Panel told the EU that its plans for the next decade failed to reflect the needs of both the most disadvantaged and those 'ordinary citizens who indirectly contribute to its financial and political viability'.

The Archbishop of Canterbury offered a message of support to the people of Haiti affected by the devastation caused by the earthquake, and the Archbishop of York urged support for the Christian Aid appeal. Dr Williams met the UN Secretary General, Ban Ki-Moon, in New York following a day of consultations with heads and senior staff from a range of UN agencies and UN Ambassadors. Dr Williams also led the Closing Session of the World Economic Forum Annual Meeting 2010 in Davos, Switzerland, with a discussion on "Being Responsible for the Future".

The latest church attendance figures showed that around 1.7 million people continued to attend services each month, with around 1.1 million attending church as part of a typical week – and not just on a Sunday. The total regularly attending had dropped two per cent overall in the six years since 2002, with the 2008 figures showing a drop of one per cent against 2007. But the number of under 16s had increased by three per cent over the year, returning to two per cent below their 2002 level. On Education Sunday, churches across the country considered what it meant to be 'called to serve', the theme of 2010's annual day of prayer and celebration for all those involved in the world of education.

The Archbishop of Canterbury marked National Holocaust Memorial Day by asking whether the legacy of Holocaust survivors "will . . . be a world in which such things no longer happen because we and our children have learned the lessons and acted on them? Or will their generation, with all its suffering, its tenacity and its offering of hope pass from us like a nightmare best forgotten?"

'Manage, don't mow, your churchyard and give space to endangered plant species', was the message from the Church's national environmental campaign Shrinking the Footprint as it signed up to the United Nations International Year of Biodiversity.

FEBRUARY
Debates on children and young people, mission, TV coverage of religion, science and religious belief, church buildings, relations with the Anglican Church in North America, clergy pensions and legislation all featured in sessions of the General Synod, held in London. In a wide-ranging Presidential Address, the Archbishop of Canterbury discussed the nature of human freedom and the value of listening and learning from one another, in both national and international debates, as well as those occurring during Synod.

Marking one year since the launch of the Archbishops' Appeal for Zimbabwe, the Archbishop of Canterbury launched an exhibition of photographs at Southwark Cathedral to showcase the work of the Anglican Church in Zimbabwe. The Appeal had surpassed all expectations in raising almost half a million pounds. Dr Williams expressed his regret at the decision of the Most Revd Dr Mouneer Anis, Bishop of the Anglican Diocese of Egypt with North Africa and the Horn of Africa, and President Bishop of the Province of Jerusalem and the Middle East, to resign from the Standing Committee of the Anglican Communion.

MPA updated its guidance note on countering far right political parties, extremist groups and racist politics. The Bishop of Ripon & Leeds, representing the Urban Bishops' Panel, condemned the detention of the children of asylum seekers as "a shameful practice" which must be halted.

The Church's three national investing bodies sold their shares in Vedanta Resources plc on the advice of the Church's Ethical Investment Advisory Group

(EIAG), whose engagement with the company had produced no substantive results. MPA also welcomed the backing given by the Government for the proposals on mandatory labelling of alcoholic products in the latest Select Committee Report on Alcohol. Acknowledging the difficult task given to the DPP by the Law Lords, MPA also expressed its appreciation of the manner in which he had undertaken his task, but continued to oppose any change in the law with regard to assisted suicide. "Assisted suicide remains a crime and, as with all crimes, there remains a presumption in favour of prosecution."

Accompanied by the Rt Rev Michael Jackson, the Anglican chair to the Anglican Jewish Commission, the Archbishop of Canterbury paid a four-day visit to Jordan, Israel and Palestine, meeting Christians in the Holy Land, and also local Heads of State and Government. The Archbishop received the Woolf Institute of Abrahamic Faiths 'Building Bridges Award' in recognition of his 'commitment to addressing contemporary cultural and inter faith issues'.

A new web-based service, launched to mark the beginning of Lent, let people across the country share their hopes and concerns anonymously in the form of a prayer – and also have those thoughts offered to God by a bishop. Prayers received during Lent were displayed on the site and shared with a number of bishops who had undertaken to remember the submissions in their own prayers. The Archbishop of York supported 'Say One For Me' by spending the day in York meeting shoppers and collecting prayer requests.

Churches around England invited couples to celebrate marriage on Valentine's Day – which in 2010 fell on a Sunday.

An extensive review of the outcomes of the Church's handling of past concerns about child protection was completed. The review – believed to be the most comprehensive of its type – involved analysis of more than 40,000 diocesan files dating back more than 30 years.

Appointments The Rt Revd Christopher Foster, Bishop of Hertford, was appointed Bishop of Portsmouth. Giles Mandelbrote was appointed Librarian and Archivist, Lambeth Palace Library.

MARCH

Visiting the Diocese of Guildford, the Archbishop of Canterbury examined the role of Christ in a pluralist society. He also took part in a public conversation with Professor Jim Al-Khalili at the University of Surrey, during which they discussed a range of contemporary issues, including science and religion. On a four-day pastoral visit to the Diocese of Lincoln, Dr Williams led the celebrations of the life of Bishop Edward King, marking 100 years since his death. The Archbishop of York's visit to New Zealand began with a powhiri (Maori welcome) in front of Holy Trinity Cathedral in Parnell, where Dr Sentamu went on to preach on the theme of 'Crisis'. At Taranaki in New Plymouth he celebrated the inauguration of St Mary's Pro Cathedral to full cathedral status.

The Church of England warned that basic human rights cannot be made contingent on the exercise of responsibilities. In a response to the Ministry of Justice Green Paper on Rights and Responsibilities, MPA argued that connecting rights too closely with responsibilities risks undermining the inalienable nature of fundamental human rights. To mark the Dying Matters Coalition's first Awareness Week, churchgoers were encouraged to talk openly about dying and death, in a new podcast suitable for sermon and housegroup use.

The Archbishop of Canterbury welcomed the official announcement that His Holiness Pope Benedict XVI was to visit the UK in September at the invitation of Her

Majesty The Queen. Dr Williams was presented with the Russian Order of Friendship, for his "outstanding contribution to the cooperation and friendly relations between Russia and the UK". Both archbishops preached at ecumenical services to commemorate the 30th anniversary of the martyrdom of Archbishop Oscar Romero – Archbishop Sentamu in York, and Archbishop Williams in Westminster Abbey. Dr Williams wrote to Patriarch Kyrill of Moscow, offering prayers in the aftermath of the bombings on the Moscow Metro.

Government and the third sector will work together over the next five years to tackle key environmental issues such as climate change and sustainable development, according to the vision set out in *Shaping our future*, a new report by the joint Ministerial and Third Sector Task Force, involving ministers and officials from Defra, the Office of the Third Sector, the Department for Energy and Climate Change, the Department for Communities and Local Government and 16 third sector organisations.

New figures showed that the number of worshippers attending cathedral services across the average week had increased by 24 per cent since 2000; cathedrals were expected to welcome almost 50,000 worshippers to Easter services.

In his ecumenical Easter Letter to fellow Church leaders, the Archbishop of Canterbury urged those living in politically secure environments to offer practical support as well as prayers for suffering Christians around the world, particularly in Zimbabwe, Mosul, Egypt and Nigeria.

Appointments The Rt Reverend Stephen Cottrell, Bishop of Reading, was appointed Bishop of Chelmsford.

APRIL

In his Easter sermon, the Archbishop of Canterbury urged Christians to keep a proper sense of proportion when they felt they were experiencing opposition to their faith and to remember both the physical suffering of Christian minorities in other countries and call to mind what exactly the Cross stands for in their faith. The Archbishop of York baptised 11 Christians from different denominations by total immersion outside York Minster. The theme of his Easter sermon was 'The Wrong Place To Look' – "Why do you look for the living among the dead? He is not here, but has risen."

A campaign was launched to encourage "people with a very big heart" to stand for election to the General Synod. Under the slogan 'Be Part of the Big Picture', new resources included a five-minute DVD filmed at General Synod in February 2010, featuring contributions from the Archbishops of Canterbury and York, Business Committee chair Preb Kay Garlick, outgoing members of the Houses of Laity and Clergy, and national journalists.

To mark the 60th anniversary of the Schuman Declaration, the founding document of the European Coal and Steel Community, and to stimulate wider debate about Europe's future in a turbulent and troubled world, the House of Bishops' Europe Panel commissioned a pamphlet to examine afresh this declaration and the Christian values that shaped and influenced Robert Schuman's vision for Europe. MPA welcomed the Ministry of Defence's Green Paper ahead of the Strategic Defence Review as a healthy stimulant to a long overdue national conversation about the identity of our country, its nature, its interests, its duties and its direction in a dark, volatile and troubled new world.

New resources for Vocations Sunday 2010 were made available to help congregations, church groups, and website visitors explore the theme of responding to God's calling, in the world and in the Church.

The Archbishop of Canterbury used his video address to the Fourth Global South to South Encounter meeting in Singapore to emphasise that it was the work of God's Spirit that can heal the tensions within the Anglican family.

To mark World Malaria Day, the Archbishop of Canterbury for the first time recorded a message to demonstrate his support and to urge others to unite in the fight against malaria.

Ministering to children's spirituality was a core function for the Church rather than a luxury add-on, argued a new book by Dr Rebecca Nye: local churches had a crucial role in listening to children's verbal and non-verbal expressions of spiritual searching and wonder.

At a Forum entitled 'Make a Difference' held at Bishopthorpe Palace, the Archbishop of York cross-questioned teenagers from across the North East as they shared their nine-point Manifesto with him and encouraged them to apply their Christian beliefs to political issues and draw up their own Manifesto, to be presented to the next Prime Minister. The Church had earlier published prayers to help voters considering their options in the forthcoming General Election, reminding them that they can make a difference and seeking protection from despair and cynicism.

The Church Commissioners' 2009 results showed that the fund had outperformed its comparator group over that year as well as over the past five, 10 and 20 years, meaning that the Commissioners' current level of support to the Church – including increased pensions costs – could be maintained, in cash terms, for a further three-year period, from 2011 to 2013.

Appointments The Revd Canon Catherine Ogle, Vicar of Huddersfield St Peter, and Rural Dean of Huddersfield Deanery, was appointed Dean of Birmingham. The Rt Revd Tim Thornton, Bishop of Truro, was appointed Chair of The Children's Society.

MAY
The Church published the 142-page report of the Revision Committee that had been considering in detail the draft legislation to enable women to become bishops. The Committee had met on 16 occasions over the past 12 months and considered 114 submissions from members of the General Synod and a further 183 submissions from others. The House of Bishops discussed the report, noting that the Synod would be helped in its task by the clarity and thoroughness of the Committee's analysis.

The Archbishop of Canterbury chaired the 9th Annual Building Bridges Seminar in Washington DC, bringing together leading Muslim and Christian scholars to explore issues at the heart of the two traditions. During two days of inter-faith visits, Dr Williams visited the Dawoodi Bohra Mosque, Northolt, and the Jain Temple at the Oshwal Centre, Potters Bar.

The Archbishop of York spent two days in the Diocese of Bradford, visiting many projects and meeting inspirational people working tirelessly in their communities. Dr Sentamu also visited the Diocese of Ripon & Leeds, seeing pioneering youth and children's projects and meeting a wide variety of local people in both North Yorkshire and West Yorkshire. The Archbishop criticised the scandal of hundreds of people being prevented from exercising their right to vote because polling stations closed as people queued and in one case owing to a lack of ballot papers. He later welcomed to Bishopthorpe Palace the Destiny Africa Children's Choir, made up of children who had been rescued from horrific situations and who now lived together at Kampala Children's Centre in Uganda.

The BBC's proposed return to its core public service mission was a welcome 'homecoming' that should herald output appealing to the broadest possible range of audiences, according to the Church of England's response to the Director-General's proposals for the future strategy of the corporation.

The Church of England published three prayers for the World Cup: two for the teams, the hosts and the fans – and one for those not interested. The prayers asked for blessings on all those involved, for generous sportsmanship and for the competition to be a source of celebration.

In his Pentecost letter to the Anglican Communion, the Archbishop of Canterbury encouraged Anglicans to pray for renewal in the Spirit and focus on the priority of mission, so that 'we may indeed do what God asks of us and let all people know that new and forgiven life in Christ is possible'.

Appointments The Archbishops of Canterbury and York appointed the Rt Revd Christopher Chessun, Bishop of Woolwich, as Bishop for Urban Life and Faith. Elizabeth Hall was appointed as Safeguarding Adviser for the C of E and the Methodist Church in Britain.

JUNE

The Archbishop of York issued a reminder about the crucial importance of Christian Witness as he addressed over 300 delegates who had attended the Edinburgh 2010 World Missionary Conference. The House of Bishops commended a report on "their understanding of the uniqueness of Christ in Britain's multi-faith society", produced as requested by the General Synod in 2009. A new Church of England teaching document, *Living thankfully before God: Living fairly before each other*, aimed to help Christians examine some key contemporary social issues, highlighting the Biblical foundations for life. More locally, the Bishop of St Albans swapped snacks for seeds at a Church of England secondary school with a summer challenge to learn what it took to grow their own crops – and do without their own snacks: five portions of fresh fruit and veg was not an option for children in the developing world most affected by climate change.

The Church of England's national investing bodies agreed an ethical investment policy on investments in the defence sector recommended by the EIAG, involving a complete bar on investment in companies involved in the production of indiscriminate weapons and a 10% turnover threshold for companies involved in conventional weaponry.

Preparations for celebrating the 200th anniversary of the Church of England's opening the first free schools in England and Wales began with the launch of a website aimed at inspiring and supporting today's 5,000 Church of England and Church in Wales schools, and their associated churches, to mark the landmark birthday in creative ways.

The Church, which maintains more of this country's architectural heritage than any other organisation, backed English Heritage's call on Government to support local efforts to maintain England's architectural heritage. Thousands of growing churches celebrated Cherishing Churchyards Week as part of the UN's International Year of Biodiversity, with the nationwide project supported by the Church's national environmental campaign, Shrinking the Footprint.

Appointments The Rt Revd James Langstaff, Bishop of Lynn, was appointed Bishop of Rochester. Canon Geoffrey Annas, Vicar of Southampton Thornhill St Christopher, was appointed Bishop of Stafford; and the Ven Peter Hancock, Archdeacon of The Meon, was appointed Bishop of Basingstoke. The Revd Dr John Davies, Vicar of Melbourne St Michael and Chairman of Industrial Mission in Derbyshire was appointed Dean of Derby.

JULY

The July General Synod at York University was the last before the five-yearly elections to and inauguration of the new Synod in November. Key debates centred on the women bishops legislation, while other subjects included clergy pensions, clergy terms of service, relations with the Church of Scotland, the status of deaneries and resources for Fresh Expressions. The Synod also saw the national launch by the Archbishop of York of the Acts 435 charity, which helps churches to make a practical difference in their local communities helping those who are going through tough times financially.

The Pensions Board entered into a £50m loan agreement with Santander Corporate Banking to provide the finance needed over the next 3–4 years to assist clergy with their retirement accommodation, thus enabling the Board to continue to provide assistance to clergy through the existing CHARM (Church Housing Assistance for Retired Ministry) scheme.

Following the publication of Common Worship on the Church of England website, the Archbishops' Council added the full text of The Book of Common Prayer, thus completing the project to make all the Church of England's official liturgy available online. And an innovative way of planning a church wedding by web, provided by the Weddings Project, had proved a surprise hit with couples.

The Cathedrals Fabric Commission for England welcomed a new fund of £500,000 for cathedral fabric repairs thanks to the Wolfson Foundation, a charity supporting excellence in the fields of science and medicine, health, education and the arts and humanities.

The Bishop of Lincoln, Chairman of the Board of Education, wrote to the new Education Secretary to express his serious concern at the cancellation of the Building Schools for the Future programme in secondary schools. As the House of Commons began to debate the Academies Bill, the Church signalled its deep disappointment at the recent announcement in another area of education policy that, it said, will see the fate of the learning environment of at least 30,000 young people doomed to dilapidation for the medium term.

The Archbishop of Canterbury hosted an event at Lambeth Palace which brought together 50 imams and clergy from 25 local areas to encourage and strengthen local inter faith relationships. Then, together with the Chief Rabbi, the Archbishop of Westminster and leaders of other faiths, Dr Williams hosted a discussion with the Secretary of State and the Minister for Decentralisation focussing on the government's approach to the 'Big Society' and the government's willingness to see Church and faith communities as providing a model to be appreciated.

The Archbishop of Canterbury delivered the keynote address at the 11th Assembly of the Lutheran World Federation in Stuttgart, Germany, reflecting on the Assembly's theme of 'Give Us Today Our Daily Bread', in which he explored a number of interpretations of this line from the Lord's Prayer.

Appointments Canon Paul Bayes, National Mission and Evangelism Adviser, was appointed Bishop of Hertford. Canon Jonathan Frost, Residentiary Canon of Guildford Cathedral and Bishop's Adviser for Interfaith Relations, was appointed Bishop of Southampton.

AUGUST

In Uganda for the All Africa Bishops' Conference, the Archbishop of Canterbury visited the Mildmay Centre near Kampala, describing his time with the staff and the children in the paediatric ward as "inspirational".

In the Church's submission to the BBC Trust, the Rt Revd Nigel McCulloch, Bishop of Manchester and the Church of England's lead spokesman on communications, praised the religious programming offered by some of the BBC's best-loved radio stations, while joining calls for a Religion Editor to work across the corporation's news and current affairs output to strengthen further its role in boosting religious literacy as a key tool for understanding today's world.

A-level and GCSE results respectively saw the seventh and twelfth consecutive year-on-year increases in the number of students taking Religious Studies and Religious Education exams, interpreted as further evidence that young people are interested in exploring religious perspectives on the big questions in life, and in studying how different moral and cultural frameworks shape people's understanding of the world around them.

In a joint bid to welcome more weddings in church, the Archbishops' Council's Weddings Project and the Royal School of Church Music teamed up to offer fresh advice for churches, including answers to brides' biggest questions about wedding music and money.

Appointments The Rt Revd Stephen Conway, Bishop of Ramsbury, was appointed Bishop of Ely.

SEPTEMBER
50 years after the first meeting of a Pope and an Archbishop of Canterbury in modern times – that of Pope John XXIII and Archbishop Geoffrey Fisher, in December 1960 – Pope Benedict XVI paid a fraternal visit to Archbishop Rowan Williams. Following the Pope's Address to Civil Society at Westminster Hall, the Archbishop and the Pope shared Evening Prayer in Westminster Abbey with a wide representative cross-section of the Churches of Britain and Ireland. His Holiness later visited Dr Williams at his London home, Lambeth Palace.

The Archbishop sent a greeting to Jewish communities at the start of the festival of Rosh Hashanah, marking the start of the Jewish New Year. In his message, the Archbishop expressed the hope that religious communities could pray together for peace and justice. Dr Williams also sent his annual greetings to Muslim communities for the festival of Eid Al-Fitr, marking the end of Ramadan. His greeting celebrated the many positive examples of Christian-Muslim encounter, including collaborative relief work in response to the recent flooding in Pakistan.

In his Prisoners Education Trust Annual Lecture *Human Responsibilities, Independent of Circumstances* the Archbishop of York questioned the deterrent effect of imprisonment and severity of sentencing, the pivotal role of communities and the need for restorative justice. Dr Sentamu said, "We should be pained and troubled by the size of our prison population in Britain. We need to show love and compassion while ensuring justice is served and seen to be served". The Archbishop also called for individuals to join him in prayer on the International Prayer Day for Zimbabwe.

The seventh Back to Church Sunday used two popular radio stations to deliver a message of welcome over the airwaves straight into the homes of 1.3 million people. The adverts supported an estimated 400,000 personal invitations that members of more than 4,000 churches sent to their friends. Speaking at churches in Canterbury diocese, the Archbishop said that desire for God was 'undimmed' in 21st Century Britain.

Dr Williams issued a video message to mark the opening of the United Nations Summit on the Millennium Development Goals in New York. The Church was one of the official partners in the UK of the UN 2010 International Year of Biodiversity, and bell ringers from small parish churches to large cathedrals and minsters joined in to ring in tune with the United Nations to mark crucial international talks on biodiversity. The Church's national investing bodies become signatories to the UN Principles for Responsible Investment.

At a private meeting at Lambeth Palace, Dr Williams and the Pakistan Minister for Minorities Affairs, Mr Shahbaz Bhatti, discussed a number of issues currently facing Pakistan including interfaith relations, the recent floods and an escalating sense of insecurity amongst minority religious communities.

Church schools across the country were invited to showcase examples of how they help foster strong community relations with the launch of the Church School Awards for inspiring citizens and transforming communities. Regional prizes will be awarded at both primary and secondary level, with overall national winners for both levels drawn from these regional winners.

The Bishop of Manchester welcomed the launch of The Real Easter Egg, the UK's first and only Easter egg to mention Jesus on the box, and asked Church schools to put in an order before Christmas to demonstrate to supermarket chains the demand for such an egg.

OCTOBER

The Archbishop of Canterbury and the Archbishop of Sudan, Dr Daniel Deng, warned that Sudan risked a return to civil war and poverty unless the international community stepped in to ensure that a referendum on independence for the south went ahead as planned. Dr Williams also expressed his concerns about the protection of refugees in the UK during a visit to the Refugee Council, the leading charity working with asylum seekers and refugees in the UK. The Archbishop visited the Zoroastrian Centre in Harrow, the first time that an Archbishop of Canterbury had made an official visit to a Zoroastrian place of worship.

Young people had not inherited the rebellious hostility to the Church of their parents' generation, although for many of them religion was irrelevant for day-to-day living. These were two of the findings of *The Faith of Generation Y*, by Sylvia Collins-Mayo, Bob Mayo and Sally Nash, with the Bishop of Coventry (who has five Generation Y children). The Archbishop of York, President of the YMCA, visited the YMCA in West London and presented YMCA volunteers with the Jack Petchey Young Achievers Award, highlighting the crucial difference the YMCA was making in young lives. The Church and Community Fund launched a new website, www.ccfund.org.uk, to promote its work and share the many good news stories of parish-linked community projects around the country securing the £½ million in grants each year.

The Archbishop of Canterbury embarked on a 16-day visit to India at the invitation of the Communion of Churches in India, travelling to eight major cities across the country. On the first Sunday of his visit, Dr Williams preached at a service of thanksgiving to mark the Global Day of Prayer for the Millennium Development Goals at St Paul's Cathedral in Kolkata. Among dozens of sermons and talks by the Archbishop during his stay, the keynote lecture of his visit was the Chevening Lecture, given in New Delhi at the invitation of the High Commissioner, Sir Richard Stagg, and hosted by the British Council.

The Standing Committee of the House of Bishops announced the membership of a working group under the chairmanship of the Rt Revd Nigel Stock, Bishop of St Edmundsbury & Ipswich, to advise the House on the preparation of a draft statutory code of practice. This followed the reference to dioceses late the previous month of the draft legislation to enable women to become bishops; dioceses had until 14 November 2011 to debate and vote on it.

MPA published its response to the White Paper *Equity and Excellence: Liberating the NHS*.

The response welcomed the ongoing commitment of the White Paper to "a comprehensive service, available to all, free at the point of use and based on clinical need, not the ability to pay", but also listed a number of criticisms, maintaining that 'patient-centred' care ought not to be interpreted as 'self-centred' care.

Church leaders were encouraged to attend one of a series of briefings touring the UK in October and November organised by *More Than Gold*, an ecumenical organisation aiming to support, enthuse and resource churches of all denominations in the way they used the 2012 Olympics as a catalyst to mission. The call came as the C of E launched a special Olympics section and podcast on its website at www.cofe.anglican.org/olympics.

Appointments The Rt Revd Christopher Chessun, Bishop of Woolwich, was appointed Bishop of Southwark. The Rt Revd John Pritchard, Bishop of Oxford, was appointed Chairman of the Board of Education and the National Society Council. In changes to the Archbishop of Canterbury's personal staff, Tim Livesey took on a new role as Secretary for International Affairs, with the Revd George Pitcher succeeding him as Secretary for Public Affairs.

CALENDAR 2011–2012

According to the Calendar, Lectionary and Collects authorized pursuant to Canon B 2 of the Canons of the Church of England for use from 30 November 1997 until further resolution of the General Synod of the Church of England.

Key
BOLD UPPER CASE – Principal Feasts and other Principal Holy Days
Bold Roman – Sundays and Festivals
Roman – Lesser Festivals
Small Italic – Commemorations
Italic – Other Observances

JANUARY (Year A)
1 **The Naming and Circumcision of Jesus**
2 **The Second Sunday of Christmas**
6 **THE EPIPHANY**
9 **The Baptism of Christ** – *The First Sunday of Epiphany*
10 *William Laud, archbishop, 1645*
11 *Mary Slessor, missionary, 1915*
12 Aelred of Hexham, Abbot of Rievaulx, 1167
   Benedict Biscop, Abbot of Wearmouth, scholar, 689
13 Hilary, Bishop of Poitiers, teacher of the faith, 367
16 **The Second Sunday of Epiphany**
17 Anthony of Egypt, hermit, abbot, 356
   Charles Gore, bishop, founder of the Community of the Resurrection, 1932
18–25 *Week of Prayer for Christian Unity*
19 Wulfstan, Bishop of Worcester, 1095
20 *Richard Rolle of Hampole, Spiritual Writer, 1349*
21 Agnes, child martyr at Rome, 304
22 *Vincent of Saragossa, deacon, first Martyr of Spain, 304*
23 **The Third Sunday of Epiphany**
24 Francis de Sales, bishop, teacher of the faith, 1622
25 **The Conversion of Paul**
26 Timothy and Titus, companions of Paul
28 Thomas Aquinas, priest, philosopher, teacher of the faith, 1274
30 **The Fourth Sunday of Epiphany**
31 *John Bosco, priest, founder of the Salesian Teaching Order, 1888*

FEBRUARY
1 *Brigid, abbess, c. 525*
2 **THE PRESENTATION OF CHRIST IN THE TEMPLE** (Candlemas)
3 Anskar, Archbishop of Hamburg, missionary in Denmark and Sweden, 865
4 *Gilbert of Sempringham, founder of the Gilbertine Order, 1189*
6 **The Fifth Sunday before Lent** – *Accession of Queen Elizabeth II, 1952*
10 *Scholastica, sister of Benedict, Abbess of Plombariola, c.543*
13 **The Fourth Sunday before Lent**
14 Cyril and Methodius, missionaries, 869 and 885
15 *Sigfrid, Bishop, 1045*
   Thomas Bray, priest, founder of SPCK and SPG, 1730

17 *Janani Luwum, archbishop, martyr, 1977*
20 **The Third Sunday before Lent**
23 Polycarp, Bishop of Smyrna, martyr, c.155
27 **The Second Sunday before Lent**

MARCH
1 David, bishop, patron of Wales, c.601
2 Chad, Bishop of Lichfield, missionary, 672
6 **Sunday next before Lent**
7 Perpetua, Felicity and companions, martyrs, 203
8 Edward King, bishop. 1910
   Felix, bishop, 647
   Geoffrey Studdert Kennedy, priest, poet, 1929
9 **ASH WEDNESDAY**
13 **The First Sunday of Lent**
17 Patrick, bishop, missionary, patron of Ireland, c.460
18 *Cyril, Bishop of Jerusalem, teacher of the faith, 386*
19 **Joseph of Nazareth**
20 **The Second Sunday of Lent**
21 Thomas Cranmer, archbishop, reformation martyr, 1556
24 *Walter Hilton of Thurgarton, Augustinian canon, mystic, 1396*
   Oscar Romero, Archbishop of San Salvador, martyr, 1980
25 **THE ANNUNCIATION OF OUR LORD TO THE BLESSED VIRGIN MARY**
26 *Harriet Monsell, founder of the Community of St John the Baptist, 1883*
27 **The Third Sunday of Lent**
31 *John Donne, priest, poet, 1631*

APRIL
1 *Frederick Denison Maurice, priest, teacher of the faith, 1872*
3 **The Fourth Sunday of Lent** – *Mothering Sunday*
9 *Dietrich Bonhoeffer, Lutheran pastor, martyr, 1945*
10 **The Fifth Sunday of Lent**
11 *Gewirge Selwyn, bishop, 1878*
16 *Isabella Gilmore, deaconess, 1923*
17 **Palm Sunday**
18 Monday of Holy week
19 Tuesday of Holy Week
20 Wednesday of Holy Week
21 **Maundy Thursday**
22 **Good Friday**

23 Easter Eve
24 **EASTER DAY**
25 Monday of Easter Week
26 Tuesday of Easter Week
27 Wednesday of Easter Week
28 Thursday of Easter Week
29 Friday of Easter Week
30 Saturday of Easter Week

MAY
1 **The Second Sunday of Easter**
2 **George, martyr, patron of England, c.304** *(transferred from 23 April)*
3 **Mark the Evangelist**
4 **Philip and James, Apostles** *(transferred from 1 May)*
8 **The Third Sunday of Easter**
14 **Matthias the Apostle**
15 **The Fourth Sunday of Easter**
16 *Carline Chisholm, social reformer, 1877*
19 Dunstan, Archbishop of Canterbury, restorer of monastic life, 988
20 Alcuin of York, deacon, Abbot of Tours, 804
21 *Helena, protector of the Holy Places, 330*
22 **The Fifth Sunday of Easter**
24 John and Charles Wesley, evangelists, hymn writers 1791 and 1788
25 The Venerable Bede, monk at Jarrow, scholar, historian, 735
   Aldhelm, bishop 709
26 Augustine, first Archbishop of Canterbury, 605
   John Calvin, reformer 1564
   Philip Neri, founder of the Oratorians, spiritual guide, 1595
28 *Lanfranc, Prior of Le Bec, Archbishop of Canterbury, scholar, 1089*
29 **The Sixth Sunday of Easter**
30 Josephine Butler, social reformer, 1906
   Joan of Arc, visionary, 1431
   Apolo Kivebulaya, priest, evangelist, 1933
31 **The Visit of the Blessed Virgin Mary to Elizabeth**

JUNE
1 Justin, martyr, c.165
2 **ASCENSION DAY**
3 *Martyrs of Uganda, 1885–7, 1977*
4 *Petroc, Abbot of Padstow, 6th century*
5 **The Seventh Sunday of Easter**
6 *Ini Kapuria, founder of the Melanesian Brotherhood, 1945*
8 Thomas Ken, Bishop of Bath and Wells, nonjuror, hymn writer, 1711
9 Columba, Abbot of Iona, missionary, 597
   Ephrem of Syria, deacon, hymn writer, teacher of the faith, 373
11 **Barnabas the Apostle**
12 **PENTECOST**
14 *Richard Baxter, puritan divibe, 1691*
15 *Evelyn Underhill, spiritual writer, 1941*
16 Richard, Bishop of Chichester, 1253
   Joseph Butler, Bishop of Durham, philosopher, 1752
17 *Samuel and Henrietta Barnett, social reformers, 1913 and 1936*

18 *Bernard Mizeki, apostle of the MaShona, martyr, 1896*
19 **TRINITY SUNDAY**
22 Alban, first martyr of Britain, c.250
23 **Day of Thanksgiving for the Institution of the Holy Communion (Corpus Christi)**
24 **The Birth of John the Baptist**
26 **The First Sunday after Trinity**
27 *Cyril, bishop, teacher of the faith, 444*
28 Irenaeus, bishop, teacher of the faith, c.200
29 **Peter and Paul, Apostles** *or* **Peter the Apostle**

JULY
1 *Henry, John and Henry Venn the younger, priests, evangelical divines, 1797, 1813 and 1873*
3 **Thomas the Apostle** – *The Second Sunday after Trinity*
6 *Thomas More, scholar, and John Fisher, Bishop of Rochester, Reformation martyrs, 1535*
10 **The Third Sunday after Trinity**
11 Benedict, abbot, c.550
14 John Keble, priest, Tractarian, poet, 1866
15 Swithun, Bishop of Winchester, c.862
   Bonaventure, friar, bishop, teacher of the faith, 1274
16 *Osmund, Bishop of Salisbury, 1099*
17 **The Fourth Sunday after Trinity**
18 *Elizabeth Ferard, deaconess, founder of the Community of St Andrew, 1883*
19 Gregory, bishop and his sister Macrina, deaconess, teachers of the faith, c.394 and c.379
20 *Margaret of Antioch, martyr, 4th century*
   Bartolomé de las Casas, apostle to the Indies, 1566
22 **Mary Magdalene**
23 *Bridget of Sweden, Abbess of Vadstena, 1373*
24 **The Fifth Sunday after Trinity**
25 **James the Apostle**
26 Anne and Joachim, parents of the Blessed Virgin Mary
27 *Brooke Foss Westcott, Bishop of Durham, teacher of the faith, 1901*
29 Mary, Martha and Lazarus, Companions of Our Lord
30 William Wilberforce, social reformer, 1833
31 **The Sixth Sunday after Trinity**

AUGUST
4 *Jean-Baptiste Vianney, Curé d'Ars, spiritual guide, 1859*
5 Oswald, King of Northumbria, martyr, 642
6 **The Transfiguration of Our Lord**
7 **The Seventh Sunday after Trinity**
8 Dominic, priest, founder of the Order of Preachers, 1221
9 Mary Sumner, founder of the Mothers' Union, 1921
10 Laurence, deacon at Rome, martyr, 258
11 Clare of Assisi, founder of the Minoresses (Poor Clares), 1253
   John Henry Newman, priest, Tractarian, 1890
13 Jeremy Taylor, Bishop of Down and Connor, teacher of the faith, 1667
   Florence Nightingale, nurse, social reformer, 1910
   Octavia Hill, social reformer, 1912

14 **The Eighth Sunday after Trinity**
15 **The Blessed Virgin Mary**
20 **Bernard, Abbot of Clairvaux, teacher of the faith, 1153**
   William and Catherine Booth, founders of the Salvation Army, 1912 and 1890
21 **The Ninth Sunday after Trinity**
24 **Bartholomew the Apostle**
27 Monica, mother of Augustine of Hippo, 387
28 **The Tenth Sunday after Trinity**
29 Beheading of John the Baptist
30 John Bunyan, spiritual writer, 1688
31 Aidan, Bishop of Lindisfarne, missionary, 651

SEPTEMBER
 1 *Giles of Provence, hermit, c.710*
 2 *The Martyrs of Papua New Guinea, 1901 and 1942*
 3 Gregory the Great, Bishop of Rome, teacher of the faith, 604
 4 **The Eleventh Sunday after Trinity**
 6 *Allen Gardiner, missionary, founder of the South American Missionary Society, 1851*
 8 The Birth of the Blessed Virgin Mary
 9 *Charles Fuge Lowder, priest, 1880*
11 **The Twelfth Sunday after Trinity**
13 John Chrysostom, bishop, teacher of the faith, 407
14 **Holy Cross Day**
15 Cyprian, Bishop of Carthage, martyr, 258
16 Ninian, Bishop of Galloway, apostle of the Picts, c.432
   Edward Bouverie Pusey, priest, tractarian, 1882
17 Hildegard, Abbess of Bingen, visionary, 1179
18 **The Thirteenth Sunday after Trinity**
19 *Theodore, archbishop, 690*
20 John Coleridge Patteson, bishop and companions, martyrs, 1871
21 **Matthew, Apostle and Evangelist**
25 **The Fourteenth Sunday after Trinity**
26 *Wilson Carlile, founder of the Church Army, 1942*
27 Vincent de Paul, founder of the Lazarists, 1660
29 **Michael and All Angels**
30 *Jerome, translator of the Scriptures, teacher of the faith, 420*

OCTOBER
 1 *Remigius, Bishop of Rheims, apostle of the Franks, 533*
   Anthony Ashley Cooper, Earl of Shaftesbury, social reformer, 1885
 2 **The Fifteenth Sunday after Trinity**
 4 Francis of Assisi, friar, deacon, 1226
 6 William Tyndale, translator of the Scriptures, Reformation martyr, 1536
 9 **The Sixteenth Sunday after Trinity**
10 Paulinus, bishop, missionary, 644
11 *Ethelburga, abbess, 675*
   James the Deacon, companion of Paulinus, 7th cent.
12 Wilfrid of Ripon, bishop, missionary, 709
   Elizabeth Fry, prison reformer, 1845
   Edith Cavell, nurse, 1915
13 Edward the Confessor, King of England, 1066
15 Teresa of Avila, teacher of the faith, 1582

16 **The Seventeenth Sunday after Trinity**
17 Ignatius, bishop, martyr, c.107
18 **Luke the Evangelist**
19 Henry Martyn, translator of the Scriptures, missionary in India and Persia, 1812
23 **The Last Sunday after Trinity** – *Bible Sunday*
25 *Crispin and Crispian, martyrs, c.287*
26 Alfred, king, scholar, 899
   Cedd, abbot, bishop, 664
28 **Simon and Jude, Apostles**
29 James Hannington, Bishop of Eastern Equatorial Africa, martyr in Uganda, 1885
30 **The Fourth Sunday before Advent**

NOVEMBER
 1 **ALL SAINTS' DAY**
 2 Commemoration of the Faithful Departed (All Souls' Day)
 3 Richard Hooker, priest, Anglican apologist, teacher of the faith, 1600
   Martin de Porres, friar, 1639
 6 **The Third Sunday before Advent**
 7 Willibrord, bishop, 739
 8 Saints and martyrs of England
 9 *Margery Kempe, mystic, c.1440*
10 Leo the Great, Bishop of Rome, teacher of the faith, 461
11 Martin, Bishop of Tours, c.397
13 **The Second Sunday before Advent** – *Remembrance Sunday*
14 *Samuel Seabury, bishop, 1796*
16 Margaret, Queen of Scotland, philanthropist, reformer of the Church, 1093
   Edmund Rich of Abingdon, Archbishop of Canterbury, 1240
17 Hugh, Bishop of Lincoln, 1200
18 Elizabeth of Hungary, Princess of Thuringia, philanthropist, 1231
19 Hilda, Abbess of Whitby, 680
   Mechtild, béguine of Magdeburg, mystic, 1280
20 **Christ the King** – *The Sunday next before Advent*
22 *Celia, martyr, c.230*
23 Clement, Bishop of Rome, martyr, c.100
25 *Catherine of Alexandria, martyr, 4th century*
   Isaac Watts, hymn writer, 1748
27 **The First Sunday of Advent** – *Year B begins today*
29 *Day of Intercession and Thanksgiving for the missionary work of the Church*
30 **Andrew the Apostle**

DECEMBER
 1 *Charles de Foucauld, hermit in the Sahara, 1916*
 3 *Francis Xavier, missionary, apostle of the Indies, 1552*
 4 **The Second Sunday of Advent**
 6 Nicholas, bishop, c.326
 7 Ambrose, Bishop of Milan, teacher of the faith, 397
 8 The Conception of the Blessed Virgin Mary
11 **The Third Sunday of Advent**
13 Lucy, martyr, 304
   Samuel Johnson, moralist, 1784

14 John of the Cross, poet, teacher of the faith, 1591
17 *O Sapientia*
   Eglantyne Jebb, social reformer, founder of 'Save The Children', 1928
18 **The Fourth Sunday of Advent**
24 Christmas Eve
25 **CHRISTMAS DAY**
26 **Stephen, deacon, first martyr**
27 **John, Apostle and Evangelist**
28 **The Holy Innocents**
29 Thomas Becket, Archbishop of Canterbury, martyr, 1170
31 *John Wyclif, reformer, 1384*

JANUARY 2012
1 **The Naming and Circumcision of Jesus –** *First Sunday of Christmas*
2 Basil the Great and Gregory of Nazianzus, bishops, teachers of the faith, 379 and 389
6 **THE EPIPHANY**
8 **The Baptism of Christ** – *The First Sunday of Epiphany*
10 *William laud, Archbishop of Canterbury, 1645*
11 *Mary Slessor, Missionary in West Africa, 1915*
12 Aelred of Hexham, Abbot of Rievaulx, 1167
   Benedict Biscop, Abbot of Wearmouth, scholar, 689
13 Hilary, Bishop of Poitiers, teacher of the faith, 367
   Kentigern (Mungo), missionary Bishop in Strathclyde and Cumbria, 603
   George Fox, founder of the Society of Friends (the Quakers), 1691
15 **The Second Sunday of Epiphany**
17 Anthony of Egypt, hermit, abbot, 356
   Charles Gore, bishop, founder of the Community of the Resurrection, 1932

18–25 *Week of Prayer for Christian Unity*
19 Wulfstan, Bishop of Worcester, 1095
20 *Richard Rolle of Hampole, spiritual writer, 1349*
21 Agnes, child martyr at Rome, 304
22 **The Third Sunday of Epiphany**
24 Francis de Sales, Bishop of Geneva, teacher of the Faith, 1662
25 **The Conversion of Paul**
26 Timothy and Titus, companions of Paul
28 Thomas Aquinas, priest, philosopher, teacher of the faith, 1274
29 **The Fourth Sunday of Epiphany**
31 **John Bosco, Priest, Founder of the Salesian Teaching Order, 1888**

Other dates

6 February	Accession Day
7 February	General Synod meets until 11 February
20 February	Education Sunday
6 March	Unemployment Sunday
15 May	Christian Aid Week until 21st
8 July	General Synod meets in York until 12th
10 July	Sea Sunday
24 July	Day of Prayer for Vocations to Religious Life
11 September	Racial Justice Sunday
2 October	Animal Welfare Sunday
16 October	Hospital Sunday
24 October	United Nations Day
13 November	Prisoners Sunday
14 November	General Synod meets until 16th (if required)
1 December	World AIDS Day
4 December	Human Rights Day

SELECTED CHURCH STATISTICS

The Church of England today

The Church of England plays a vital role in the life of the nation, proclaiming the Christian gospel in words and actions and providing services of Christian worship and praise.

Its network of parishes covers the country, bringing a vital Christian dimension to the nation as well as strengthening community life in numerous urban, suburban and rural settings. Its cathedrals are centres of spirituality and service, and its network of chaplaincies across continental Europe meets important local needs.

The Church of England plays an active role in national life with its members involved in a wide range of public bodies. Twenty-six bishops are members of the House of Lords and are engaged in debates about legislation and national and international affairs.

The Church of England is part of the worldwide Anglican Communion.

There are a number of interviews relating to the Church of England on Premier Christian Radio, under the title 'Work in Progress'.

Key facts about the Church of England

Church attendance and visits
- **1.7 million** people take part in a Church of England service each month, a level that has been maintained since the turn of the millennium. Around one million participate each Sunday.
- Over **2.6 million** participate in a Church of England service on Christmas Day or Christmas Eve. **Thirty five per cent** of the population attend a church service around Christmas, including 22 per cent among those of non-Christian faiths and 13 per cent of those with no religious alignment.
- In 2009, **43 per cent** of adults attended a church or place of worship for a memorial service for someone who has died and **17 per cent** were seeking a quiet space. Both these proportions are increases on 22 per cent and 12 per cent respectively in 2001.
- **Eighty-five per cent** of the population visit a church or place of worship in the course of a year, for reasons ranging from participating in worship to attending social events or simply wanting a quiet space.
- Every year, around **12 million** people visit Church of England cathedrals, including almost **300,000** pupils on school visits. Three of England's top five historic 'visitor attractions' are York Minster, Canterbury Cathedral and Westminster Abbey.

Education
- **Seven in ten** (70 per cent) of the population agree that Church of England schools have a positive role in educating the nation's children.
- **One in four** primary schools and **one in 16** secondary schools in England are Church of England schools. Approaching **one million pupils** are educated in more than 4,600 Church of England schools.

Ministers
- At the end of 2009, there were **19,504** ministers licensed by Church of England dioceses, including clergy, Readers and Church Army officers: one minister for every 2,600 people in England. The total does not include almost **1,600** chaplains to prisons, hospitals, the armed forces and in education, nor over **6,000** retired ministers with permission to officiate.

Community involvement
- **More people do unpaid work for church organizations than any other organization.** Eight per cent of adults undertake voluntary work for church organizations while 16 per cent belong to religious or church organizations.
- A quarter of regular churchgoers (among both Anglicans and other Christians separately) are involved in voluntary community service outside the church. Churchgoers overall contribute **23.2 million hours** voluntary service each month in their local communities outside the church.

- The Church of England provides activities outside church worship in the local community for **407,000 children and young people** (aged under 16 years) and 32,900 young people (aged 16 to 25 years). **More than 116,460 volunteers** run children/young people activity groups sponsored by the Church of England outside church worship.

Church buildings
- **Nearly half the population** (46 per cent) think that central taxation, local taxation, the National Lottery or English Heritage should be 'primarily' responsible for providing money to maintain churches and chapels. In fact, these churches and cathedrals are largely supported by the efforts and financial support of local communities. Often, they are the focus of community life and service.
- There are 14,500 places of worship in England listed for their special architectural or historic interest, **85 per cent of which belong to and are maintained by the Church of England.**
- Necessary repairs to all listed places of worship in England have been valued at £925m over the next five years, or £185m a year.

Sources: *Church Statistics* 2004/5, 2006/7 and 2007/8.
Opinion Research Business national polls 2001 to 2009.
English Heritage and Church of England Cathedral and Church Buildings Division joint research.
Church Life Survey 2001.

Tables

The following pages contain a selection of tables as available at the Church of England web site, www.cofe.anglican.org

Table K
New measures of church attendance have been employed:

Average weekly attendance – the average number of attenders at church services throughout the week typically over a four-week period in October.

Average Sunday attendance – the average number of attenders at Sunday church services typically over a four-week period in October.

Tables N to T
The following definitions apply:

Income

Unrestricted income	income that may be used by the PCC for general church expenses.
Restricted income	income which may not be used for any purpose other than as specified by the donor. (Income which a PCC designates for a specified purpose is considered to be unrestricted, since the PCC and not the donor is determining how it is to be used.)
Recurring income	includes direct giving, other voluntary income and any other recurring income. It may be unrestricted or restricted.
One-off income	includes non-recurring grants, legacies, special appeals, insurance claims and the sale of fixed assets. It may be unrestricted or restricted.
Total voluntary income	direct giving plus income tax on gift aid plus other voluntary income.
Total direct giving	planned giving plus church collections and boxes.
Other voluntary income	all other voluntary income for ordinary expenditure excluding direct giving and income tax on gift aid, e.g. fund-raising events, net profit on magazine/bookstall, sundry donations.

Expenditure
Total charitable donations includes payments to:

the recognized missionary societies, or other overseas missions, diocesan associations, Diocesan Mission Councils; Christian organizations primarily concerned with relief and development; home missions and other Church societies and organizations (including the Church Urban Fund); other charities – payments to other charities which are secularly based.

Recurring expenditure	includes donations to charities, parish share/quota, clergy expenses, church running costs, costs relating to trading, salaries and support costs.
Capital expenditure	includes major repairs, redecoration and new building work.

Notes on tables N to T
1. Figures for cathedrals are not included.
2. *i.e. adjusted by the Retail Price Index to reflect 2008 purchasing power.
3. The Diocese in Europe is not included in these tables.
Please also note that:
1.   Whilst many figures in these tables have been rounded, totals, percentages and averages were

calculated before rounding. Hence row and column totals will not always agree exactly with the sum of the stated amounts.

2. Among the 13,000 parishes of the Church of England there are around 600 Local Ecumenical Projects in roughly half of which there is a congregation and a ministry shared between the Church of England and certain other churches. In such circumstances it is not always possible (or indeed desirable) to isolate the Anglican component of the congregation. The parochial statistics will therefore include a small element which may appear also in the statistics of other churches.

3. Where figures are not available for any reason, 'N/A' appears in these tables.

A   Church of England Licensed Ministries 2009

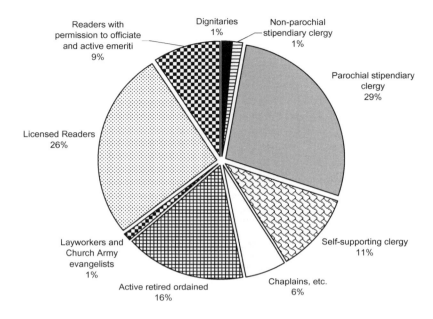

Licensed stipendiary clergy	8,591	Active retired ordained	4,610
Licensed self-supporting clergy	3,100	Licensed Readers	7,472
Chaplains and other ministries	1,627	Readers with permission to	2,584
Licensed layworkers and lay Church Army	341	officiate and active emeriti	
evangelists			

The figures for stipendiary clergy (full-time, part-time and including those outside the clergy share system) and for lay workers above are based on statistics derived from the central Church payroll. Details of chaplains and other ministers working outside the parish framework, and of non-stipendiary clergy, are based on statistics derived from the database used to compile *Crockford's Clerical Directory*. Where possible, they have been cross-referenced with material produced by organizing bodies (Church Army, the Home Office for prison chaplains, and the Hospital Chaplaincies Council for hospital chaplains).

The figure shown for active retired ordained clergy is an estimate of the number of licensed retired clergy who take an active part in ministry. It is based on the number of retired clergy known to have either permission to officiate, licence to officiate or actual appointments. Pension Board records indicated a total of 8,954 retired stipendiary clergy in 2009.

B Summary of Diocesan Licensed Ministers 2009

Ref. No.	Diocese		Full-time stipendiary clergy			Part-time stipendiary clergy			Self-supporting clergy, except ordained local ministers		
			men	women	Total	men	women	Total	men	women	Total
1	Bath & Wells	C	158	42	200	8	8	16	23	27	50
2	Birmingham	C	115	44	159	3	3	6	20	21	41
3	Blackburn	Y	156	17	173	4	2	6	21	22	43
4	Bradford	Y	84	13	97	3	6	9	20	18	38
5	Bristol	C	100	24	124	1	5	6	18	22	40
6	Canterbury	C	116	24	140	2	3	5	23	27	50
7	Carlisle	Y	109	28	137	0	2	2	21	21	42
8	Chelmsford	C	300	76	376	7	6	13	43	50	93
9	Chester	Y	202	48	250	12	6	18	18	32	50
10	Chichester	C	274	19	293	9	3	12	49	28	77
11	Coventry	C	91	19	110	6	3	9	11	21	32
12	Derby	C	119	28	147	0	0	0	24	30	54
13	Durham	Y	147	42	189	6	2	8	17	24	41
14	Ely	C	101	39	140	6	5	11	23	26	49
15	Exeter	C	174	35	209	15	6	21	23	21	44
16	Gloucester	C	102	36	138	3	2	5	44	43	87
17	Guildford	C	138	32	170	4	12	16	32	36	68
18	Hereford	C	68	24	92	0	3	3	14	30	44
19	Leicester	C	104	36	140	4	3	7	18	21	39
20	Lichfield	C	244	59	303	12	11	23	24	33	57
21	Lincoln	C	138	36	174	3	1	4	9	21	30
22	Liverpool	Y	158	51	209	0	2	2	12	13	25
23	London	C	453	72	525	6	9	15	106	45	151
24	Manchester	Y	179	56	235	4	4	8	26	17	43
25	Newcastle	Y	101	34	135	3	3	6	13	18	31
26	Norwich	C	156	34	190	2	8	10	17	16	33
27	Oxford	C	293	92	385	6	2	8	109	91	200
28	Peterborough	C	108	27	135	2	1	3	19	21	40
29	Portsmouth	C	87	19	106	0	3	3	22	37	59
30	Ripon & Leeds	Y	89	38	127	2	0	2	22	15	37
31	Rochester	C	179	27	206	3	9	12	22	29	51
32	St Albans	C	179	73	252	3	6	9	43	45	88
33	St Edms & Ipswich	C	107	31	138	4	5	9	19	17	36
34	Salisbury	C	162	50	212	1	0	1	26	43	69
35	Sheffield	Y	115	37	152	1	4	5	17	6	23
36	Sodor & Man	Y	12	1	13	0	0	0	6	2	8
37	Southwark	C	267	80	347	2	5	7	96	104	200
38	Southwell	Y	108	43	151	3	6	9	15	14	29
39	Truro	C	90	17	107	3	0	3	22	24	46
40	Wakefield	Y	103	39	142	0	3	3	19	22	41
41	Winchester	C	179	21	200	5	3	8	41	44	85
42	Worcester	C	108	29	137	1	0	1	10	22	32
43	York	Y	178	44	222	5	1	6	42	37	79
44	Europe	C	128	13	141	0	0	0	33	14	47
Totals Province of Canterbury (C)			**4,838**	**1,158**	**5,996**	**121**	**125**	**246**	**983**	**1,009**	**1,992**
Totals Province of York (Y)			**1,741**	**491**	**2,232**	**43**	**41**	**84**	**269**	**261**	**530**
Totals CHURCH OF ENGLAND			**6,579**	**1,649**	**8,228**	**164**	**166**	**330**	**1,252**	**1,270**	**2,522**

Notes:
1. The above figures include only those ministers who were working within the diocesan framework as at 31st December 2009.
2. The Archbishop of Canterbury and ordained members of his staff at Lambeth Palace are classed as extra-diocesan and are not included in these figures.

Ordained local ministers among self-supporting clergy			Total clergy (stipendiary and self-supporting)	Readers and Church Army	Total clergy, readers and Church Army	Diocese ref. no.
men	women	Total				
0	0	0	266	284	550	1
0	0	0	206	166	372	2
0	0	0	222	171	393	3
0	0	0	144	104	248	4
5	4	9	179	167	346	5
12	14	26	221	108	329	6
2	2	4	185	115	300	7
1	0	1	483	384	867	8
0	0	0	318	375	693	9
0	0	0	382	154	536	10
3	8	11	162	160	322	11
0	0	0	201	246	447	12
1	4	5	243	149	392	13
0	0	0	200	144	344	14
0	0	0	274	180	454	15
3	6	9	239	145	384	16
28	26	54	308	127	435	17
3	6	9	148	87	235	18
0	0	0	186	145	331	19
33	31	64	447	313	760	20
14	17	31	239	151	390	21
12	18	30	266	273	539	22
0	0	0	691	211	902	23
41	45	86	372	155	527	24
9	8	17	189	103	292	25
23	23	46	279	184	463	26
19	30	49	642	230	872	27
0	0	0	178	131	309	28
0	0	0	168	91	259	29
0	0	0	166	103	269	30
0	0	0	269	256	525	31
0	1	1	350	214	564	32
15	25	40	223	130	353	33
23	27	50	332	105	437	34
0	0	0	180	196	376	35
2	0	2	23	28	51	36
0	0	0	554	191	745	37
0	0	0	189	287	476	38
5	4	9	165	80	245	39
8	16	24	210	136	346	40
0	0	0	293	284	577	41
0	0	0	170	124	294	42
0	1	1	308	222	530	43
0	0	0	188	73	261	44
187	222	409	8,643	5,265	13,908	
75	94	169	3,015	2,417	5,432	
262	316	578	11,658	7,682	19,340	

3. Reader and Church Army figures do not include Readers with PTO or emeriti, or ordained Church Army evangelists.

C   Licensed Readers and Church Army 2009

Ref. No.	Diocese		Reader admissions during year — men	Reader admissions during year — women	Licensed Readers at 31 December 2009 — men		Licensed Readers at 31 December 2009 — women		Readers in training at 31 December 2009 — men	Readers in training at 31 December 2009 — women	Church Army (lay evangelists) at 31 December 2009 — men	Church Army (lay evangelists) at 31 December 2009 — women
1	Bath & Wells	C	7	10	143	(56)	136	(18)	3	2	4	1
2	Birmingham	C	4	8	78	(20)	87	(23)	7	11	1	0
3	Blackburn	Y	3	7	72	(42)	97	(19)	6	3	2	0
4	Bradford	Y	0	3	39	(25)	59	(15)	6	14	5	1
5	Bristol	C	4	11	69	(27)	98	(30)	12	17	0	0
6	Canterbury	C	2	3	38	(29)	64	(20)	7	6	6	0
7	Carlisle	Y	1	5	57	(29)	56	(20)	4	6	2	0
8	Chelmsford	C	1	10	181	(48)	196	(35)	2	18	3	4
9	Chester	Y	6	10	189	(93)	181	(29)	21	23	3	2
10	Chichester	C	5	2	85	(80)	63	(38)	11	10	6	0
11	Coventry	C	7	3	79	(28)	75	(14)	3	7	4	2
12	Derby	C	4	3	123	(40)	121	(30)	1	7	2	0
13	Durham	Y	1	7	61	(34)	85	(16)	7	15	1	2
14	Ely	C	1	4	74	(27)	67	(12)	6	16	3	0
15	Exeter	C	4	3	89	(54)	86	(46)	14	23	4	1
16	Gloucester	C	4	3	82	(29)	61	(20)	6	15	1	1
17	Guildford	C	3	4	70	(38)	49	(21)	11	5	5	3
18	Hereford	C	0	5	45	(10)	38	(7)	3	5	2	2
19	Leicester	C	0	8	66	(20)	76	(11)	1	2	2	1
20	Lichfield	C	2	11	156	(60)	145	(48)	11	28	8	4
21	Lincoln	C	4	2	52	(28)	95	(17)	8	22	4	0
22	Liverpool	Y	2	9	123	(33)	142	(26)	22	25	5	3
23	London	C	4	3	111	(26)	92	(26)	6	19	5	3
24	Manchester *	Y	3	6	78	(51)	71	(23)	5	10	4	2
25	Newcastle	Y	2	5	45	(19)	53	(20)	5	6	2	3
26	Norwich	C	1	6	84	(53)	96	(43)	2	14	3	1
27	Oxford	C	3	8	120	(40)	103	(26)	8	14	4	3
28	Peterborough	C	2	7	69	(22)	58	(10)	11	16	2	2
29	Portsmouth	C	0	5	44	(19)	47	(17)	6	6	0	0
30	Ripon & Leeds	Y	3	4	51	(19)	45	(28)	3	13	4	3
31	Rochester	C	8	7	131	(70)	120	(36)	14	8	3	2
32	St Albans	C	3	3	111	(41)	98	(34)	19	31	5	0
33	St Edms & Ipswich	C	3	1	72	(34)	54	(37)	5	6	3	1
34	Salisbury	C	1	3	67	(63)	37	(30)	5	7	1	0
35	Sheffield	Y	0	5	92	(17)	81	(17)	13	11	14	9
36	Sodor & Man	Y	2	1	17	(7)	11	(3)	1	2	0	0
37	Southwark	C	4	10	96	(48)	89	(27)	16	24	3	3
38	Southwell & Nottingham	Y	6	3	132	(21)	150	(19)	8	13	4	1
39	Truro	C	0	2	40	(29)	37	(13)	5	9	1	2
40	Wakefield	Y	1	5	59	(25)	73	(16)	9	7	4	0
41	Winchester	C	5	4	154	(47)	123	(14)	20	19	5	2
42	Worcester	C	3	2	52	(26)	71	(13)	5	7	1	0
43	York	Y	6	7	109	(47)	108	(24)	14	15	2	3
44	Europe	C	4	1	44	(14)	29	(5)	17	20	0	0
	Totals Province of Canterbury (C)		**93**	**152**	**2,625**	**(1,126)**	**2,511**	**(721)**	**245**	**394**	**91**	**38**
	Totals Province of York (Y)		**36**	**77**	**1,124**	**(462)**	**1,212**	**(275)**	**124**	**163**	**52**	**29**
	Totals CHURCH OF ENGLAND		**129**	**229**	**3,749**	**(1,588)**	**3,723**	**(996)**	**369**	**557**	**143**	**67**

Comparable figures for 2008											
Totals Province of Canterbury (C)	113	145	2,741	(1,127)	2,543	(697)	245	405	85	35
Totals Province of York (Y)	50	67	1,155	(472)	1,214	(241)	126	177	55	29
Totals CHURCH OF ENGLAND	163	212	3,896	(1,599)	3,757	(938)	371	582	140	64

Notes: * Readers data for Manchester are for 2008

Readers figures in brackets refer to the additional number of Readers with Permission to Officiate and active Emeriti.
These figures have been revised since the publication of 'The Annual Report of the Central Readers Council of the Church of England 2009'.

There are a further six Church Army evangelists who are nationally deployed.
Ordained Church Army evangelists are counted in the 'Chaplaincy and other ministries' table.

Selected Church Statistics

D   Distribution of FTE Stipendiary Diocesan Clergy 2009

Actual and according to the clergy deployment formula

Ref. No.	Diocese		December 31st 2009 Actual	December 31st 2009 Share	Number over under (-) share	Percent over under (-) share
1	Bath and Wells	C	208	197	11	5.6%
2	Birmingham	C	162	172	-10	-5.9%
3	Blackburn	Y	176	197	-21	-10.8%
4	Bradford	Y	102	102	0	0.3%
5	Bristol	C	128	128	0	-0.3%
6	Canterbury	C	142	150	-8	-5.2%
7	Carlisle	Y	138	130	8	6.0%
8	Chelmsford	C	382	383	-1	-0.2%
9	Chester	Y	257	240	17	7.2%
10	Chichester	C	299	271	28	10.3%
11	Coventry	C	116	124	-8	-6.8%
12	Derby	C	147	156	-9	-5.8%
13	Durham	Y	195	195	0	-0.2%
14	Ely	C	146	138	8	5.6%
15	Exeter	C	214	228	-14	-6.2%
16	Gloucester	C	141	138	3	1.8%
17	Guildford	C	178	154	24	15.8%
18	Hereford	C	94	108	-14	-13.3%
19	Leicester	C	144	146	-2	-1.6%
20	Lichfield	C	314	306	8	2.7%
21	Lincoln	C	176	219	-43	-19.5%
22	Liverpool	Y	210	201	9	4.5%
23	London	C	532	490	42	8.6%
24	Manchester	C	239	257	-18	-7.0%
25	Newcastle	C	138	136	2	1.7%
26	Norwich	C	196	190	5	2.9%
27	Oxford	C	389	376	13	3.5%
28	Peterborough	C	137	151	-14	-9.5%
29	Portsmouth	C	108	108	-1	-0.5%
30	Ripon and Leeds	Y	128	136	-8	-5.9%
31	Rochester	C	213	181	32	17.8%
32	St. Albans	C	257	258	-1	-0.5%
33	St. Edms and Ipswich	C	143	149	-7	-4.4%
34	Salisbury	C	213	207	6	2.7%
35	Sheffield	Y	155	157	-2	-1.2%
36	Sodor and Man	Y	13	18	-5	-27.8%
37	Southwark	C	351	322	29	8.9%
38	Southwell	Y	156	160	-5	-2.8%
39	Truro	C	109	113	-5	-4.0%
40	Wakefield	Y	144	152	-9	-5.6%
41	Winchester	C	205	217	-12	-5.7%
42	Worcester	C	138	133	5	3.4%
43	York	Y	225	258	-33	-12.7%
Province of Canterbury (C)			**5,976**	**5,913**	**63**	**1.1%**
Province of York (Y)			**2,276**	**2,339**	**-63**	**-2.7%**
CHURCH OF ENGLAND			**8,252**	**8,252**	**0**	**0.0%**

Note: The 'Actual' is the number of full-time stipendiary clergy plus the whole-time equivalent of the part-time clergy. Shares are allocated as whole posts.

E   Ordinations 1998 to 2009

Proportion of ordinations by gender 1999, 2004 and 2009

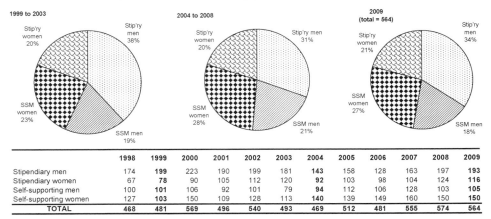

	1998	1999	2000	2001	2002	2003	2004	2005	2006	2007	2008	2009
Stipendiary men	174	199	223	190	199	181	143	158	128	163	197	193
Stipendiary women	67	78	90	105	112	120	92	103	98	104	124	116
Self-supporting men	100	101	106	92	101	79	94	112	106	128	103	105
Self-supporting women	127	103	150	109	128	113	140	139	149	160	150	150
TOTAL	468	481	569	496	540	493	469	512	481	555	574	564

Notes:
1. Stipendiary figures are compiled from information supplied by the Church Commissioners.
2. Self-supporting (including OLM) figures are compiled from information supplied by the Ministry Division.
3. Stipendiary figures from 2005 onwards treat ordinations to part-time ministry as whole ordinations, not full-time equivalents.

E (cont'd)   Ordinations & Reader Admissions 1995 to 2009

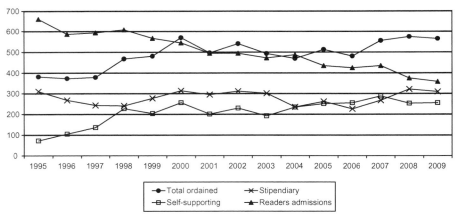

Notes:
1. Stipendiary figures are compiled from information supplied by the Church Commissioners.
2. Self-supporting (including OLM) figures are compiled from information supplied by the Ministry Division.
3. Readers figures are compiled from information supplied by the dioceses.

F   Parochial Baptisms and Thanksgivings 2008

Ref. No.	Diocese	Live births	Baptisms: Infants under one year of age	Baptisms: Infant baptism rates per 1,000 live births	Children aged 1 to 12 years	All other persons	Thanksgivings: Infants	Thanksgivings: Child	Baptisms and Thanksgivings Total
1	Bath & Wells	9,639	1,840	191	870	210	70	25	3,015
2	Birmingham	22,538	1,520	67	860	230	75	25	2,710
3	Blackburn	16,310	2,850	175	1,240	260	65	35	4,450
4	Bradford	10,416	920	88	340	90	35	10	1,395
5	Bristol	13,051	1,330	102	570	220	65	10	2,195
6	Canterbury	10,421	1,680	161	980	230	55	25	2,970
7	Carlisle	5,081	1,720	339	370	100	25	0	2,215
8	Chelmsford	41,645	2,860	69	1,860	540	225	135	5,620
9	Chester	18,834	3,540	188	1,460	310	130	75	5,515
10	Chichester	17,329	2,400	138	1,400	310	105	60	4,275
11	Coventry	10,436	1,030	99	590	120	110	30	1,880
12	Derby	12,060	1,680	139	740	190	145	40	2,795
13	Durham	17,125	3,650	213	1,270	210	135	50	5,315
14	Ely	8,775	1,430	163	600	160	70	35	2,295
15	Exeter	11,794	1,920	163	1,020	220	45	15	3,220
16	Gloucester	7,053	1,560	221	700	200	25	15	2,500
17	Guildford	12,470	1,690	136	1,040	200	60	40	3,030
18	Hereford	2,982	860	288	340	60	85	35	1,380
19	Leicester	12,091	980	81	540	160	35	20	1,735
20	Lichfield	25,680	3,900	152	1,840	410	245	140	6,535
21	Lincoln	11,501	2,960	257	1,250	240	70	10	4,530
22	Liverpool	18,599	3,220	173	1,480	240	130	75	5,145
23	London	61,193	2,500	41	1,970	660	105	40	5,275
24	Manchester	29,258	3,270	112	1,530	410	270	115	5,595
25	Newcastle	8,811	1,560	177	510	90	10	5	2,175
26	Norwich	9,334	1,490	160	650	190	40	10	2,380
27	Oxford	30,542	3,690	121	2,070	430	140	60	6,390
28	Peterborough	11,681	1,370	117	820	220	45	15	2,470
29	Portsmouth	8,423	1,090	129	620	140	25	5	1,880
30	Ripon & Leeds	10,355	1,290	125	600	130	40	5	2,065
31	Rochester	16,044	1,770	110	1,230	280	265	160	3,705
32	St. Albans	24,320	2,430	100	1,460	350	100	55	4,395
33	St. Edms & Ipswich	7,302	1,150	157	640	160	50	20	2,020
34	Salisbury	9,711	2,130	219	900	230	120	40	3,420
35	Sheffield	15,213	2,180	143	840	310	280	70	3,680
36	Sodor & Man	979	210	215	70	20	0	0	300
37	Southwark	42,232	2,360	56	1,730	440	105	55	4,690
38	Southwell & Nottingham	13,062	1,460	112	590	230	95	25	2,400
39	Truro	5,448	1,080	198	410	100	35	15	1,640
40	Wakefield	14,817	2,000	135	800	240	205	20	3,265
41	Winchester	15,018	2,460	164	1,120	230	105	35	3,950
42	Worcester	9,825	1,570	160	770	190	90	40	2,660
43	York	16,176	3,500	216	1,400	340	220	45	5,505
44	Europe		350		200	80	35	10	675
	Totals Province of Canterbury	480,538	55,080	115	29,790	7,400	2,745	1,220	96,235
	Totals Province of York	195,036	31,370	161	12,500	2,980	1,640	530	49,020
	Totals CHURCH OF ENGLAND	675,574	86,450	128	42,290	10,380	4,385	1,750	145,255

Comparable figures for 2007:

	Totals Province of Canterbury	468,267	55,980	120	28,190	7,290	2,855	1,110	95,400
	Totals Province of York	189,780	32,440	171	12,150	2,895	1,890	580	49,900
	Totals CHURCH OF ENGLAND	658,047	88,400	134	40,300	10,200	4,700	1,700	145,400

Notes: 1. Figures for cathedrals are included.
2. Live births per diocese are estimates based on statistics obtained from the Office for National Statistics (ONS).

G Parochial Marriages and Funerals 2008

Ref. No.	Diocese	Marriages	Blessings of civil marriage	Total	Held in church	Held in crematoria /cemeteries	Total	Number of deaths	% with C of E funeral
		Marriages			**Funerals**				
1	Bath & Wells	1,430	130	1,560	2,430	1,710	4,140	9,453	44%
2	Birmingham	1,080	50	1,130	1,320	3,020	4,340	12,563	35%
3	Blackburn	1,080	80	1,160	2,380	2,510	4,890	13,970	35%
4	Bradford	610	40	650	840	770	1,610	6,301	26%
5	Bristol	820	40	860	1,110	1,420	2,530	7,583	33%
6	Canterbury	1,110	90	1,200	1,260	2,210	3,470	9,014	38%
7	Carlisle	740	50	790	1,810	970	2,780	5,452	51%
8	Chelmsford	2,700	210	2,910	3,020	4,900	7,920	24,558	32%
9	Chester	1,630	70	1,700	3,890	3,080	6,970	16,023	43%
10	Chichester	1,800	170	1,970	2,560	3,540	6,100	17,380	35%
11	Coventry	890	60	950	1,690	920	2,610	7,463	35%
12	Derby	1,180	100	1,280	2,560	1,900	4,460	10,212	44%
13	Durham	1,130	60	1,190	3,780	2,580	6,360	15,697	41%
14	Ely	1,050	90	1,140	1,840	1,220	3,060	5,793	53%
15	Exeter	1,450	140	1,590	2,910	2,060	4,970	12,370	40%
16	Gloucester	1,070	100	1,170	2,150	1,420	3,570	6,090	59%
17	Guildford	1,230	90	1,320	1,360	2,020	3,380	8,112	42%
18	Hereford	610	40	650	1,430	690	2,120	3,402	62%
19	Leicester	900	50	950	1,590	1,410	3,000	8,256	36%
20	Lichfield	2,230	140	2,370	5,640	4,660	10,300	20,278	51%
21	Lincoln	1,600	130	1,730	3,030	2,510	5,540	11,028	50%
22	Liverpool	1,060	60	1,120	3,570	1,930	5,500	16,023	34%
23	London	1,610	170	1,780	1,470	2,960	4,430	22,664	20%
24	Manchester	1,250	70	1,320	2,550	3,200	5,750	19,146	30%
25	Newcastle	640	60	700	1,350	1,750	3,100	8,371	37%
26	Norwich	1,210	90	1,300	2,490	2,500	4,990	9,430	53%
27	Oxford	2,680	210	2,890	3,580	3,690	7,270	16,404	44%
28	Peterborough	1,040	100	1,140	1,580	870	2,450	7,156	34%
29	Portsmouth	920	70	990	1,210	1,700	2,910	7,378	39%
30	Ripon & Leeds	810	50	860	1,370	1,220	2,590	7,402	35%
31	Rochester	1,050	100	1,150	1,590	3,960	5,550	10,672	52%
32	St. Albans	1,670	110	1,780	2,710	3,210	5,920	14,437	41%
33	St. Edms & Ipswich	920	100	1,020	2,000	1,120	3,120	6,244	50%
34	Salisbury	1,440	130	1,570	2,470	1,960	4,430	9,687	46%
35	Sheffield	1,080	60	1,140	2,410	2,700	5,110	12,028	42%
36	Sodor & Man	110	20	130	330	170	500	843	59%
37	Southwark	1,740	140	1,880	1,350	3,180	4,530	17,481	26%
38	Southwell & Nottingham	1,210	70	1,280	2,380	1,690	4,070	10,301	40%
39	Truro	930	70	1,000	1,610	880	2,500	5,938	42%
40	Wakefield	930	70	1,000	2,230	2,050	4,280	10,873	39%
41	Winchester	1,740	140	1,880	2,240	2,020	4,260	12,046	35%
42	Worcester	1,000	60	1,070	1,930	1,930	3,860	8,407	46%
43	York	1,620	100	1,730	3,120	2,750	5,870	14,036	42%
44	Europe	160	360	520	280	680	960		
	Totals Province of Canterbury	**39,260**	**3,480**	**42,740**	**62,410**	**66,250**	**128,660**	**321,499**	**40%**
	Totals Province of York	**13,890**	**870**	**14,760**	**32,020**	**27,380**	**59,400**	**156,466**	**38%**
	Totals CHURCH OF ENGLAND	**53,150**	**4,350**	**57,500**	**94,430**	**93,630**	**188,060**	**477,965**	**39%**
	Comparable figures for 2007:*								
	Totals Province of Canterbury	**39,870**	**3,480**	**43,350**	**61,680**	**68,590**	**130,280**	**317,430**	**41%**
	Totals Province of York	**14,750**	**1,000**	**15,750**	**33,920**	**30,120**	**64,040**	**155,497**	**41%**
	Totals CHURCH OF ENGLAND	**54,620**	**4,480**	**59,110**	**95,600**	**98,710**	**194,320**	**472,927**	**41%**

Notes: 1. Figures for cathedrals are included.

2. The number of deaths are estimates based on statistics obtained from the Office for National Statistics (ONS)

3. * The comparable 2007 figures have been revised since the publication of ' *Church Statistics 2007/8* '

H   Confirmations 2008

Ref. No.	Diocese	Males	Females	Total	Number of Services
1	Bath and Wells	166	268	434	43
2	Birmingham	185	297	482	92
3	Blackburn	653	816	1,469	86
4	Bradford	67	98	165	22
5	Bristol	130	250	380	24
6	Canterbury	200	322	522	34
7	Carlisle	157	243	400	53
8	Chelmsford	412	716	1,128	82
9	Chester	313	544	857	106
10	Chichester	479	598	1,077	61
11	Coventry	114	167	281	11
12	Derby	154	257	411	33
13	Durham	208	386	594	34
14	Ely	143	224	367	37
15	Exeter	242	374	616	59
16	Gloucester	112	228	340	41
17	Guildford	251	364	615	42
18	Hereford	99	172	271	33
19	Leicester	106	120	226	20
20	Lichfield	453	734	1,187	117
21	Lincoln	170	223	393	42
22	Liverpool	363	587	950	75
23	London	660	1020	1,680	191
24	Manchester	452	709	1,161	73
25	Newcastle	115	198	313	64
26	Norwich	116	233	349	48
27	Oxford	654	852	1,506	126
28	Peterborough	253	360	613	50
29	Portsmouth	61	107	168	14
30	Ripon & Leeds	194	285	479	50
31	Rochester*	426	562	988	63
32	St. Albans	379	557	936	73
33	St. Edms & Ipswich	156	250	406	38
34	Salisbury	215	434	649	34
35	Sheffield	108	182	290	29
36	Sodor and Man	11	22	33	2
37	Southwark	483	737	1,220	95
38	Southwell	182	304	486	27
39	Truro	69	105	174	36
40	Wakefield	151	224	375	76
41	Winchester	241	349	590	70
42	Worcester	119	216	335	37
43	York	280	505	785	108
44	Europe	129	142	271	44
	Totals Province of Canterbury	**7,377**	**11,238**	**18,615**	**1,690**
	Totals Province of York	**3,254**	**5,103**	**8,357**	**805**
	Totals CHURCH OF ENGLAND	**10,631**	**16,341**	**26,972**	**2,495**
	Comparable figures for 2007:				
	Totals Province of Canterbury	7,722	11,633	19,355	1,823
	Totals Province of York	3,409	5,152	8,561	815
	Totals CHURCH OF ENGLAND	11,131	16,785	27,916	2,638

Note: Confirmations in the Armed Forces are not included.

* Number of services in Rochester are for 2007

I Parochial Church Electoral Rolls 1990 to 2008

Ref. No.	Diocese	Church Electoral Rolls				
		2008	2007[1]	2002[1]	1996[1]	1990[1]
1	Bath & Wells	35,400	36,000	38,000	42,700	47,300
2	Birmingham	17,200	17,500	18,200	19,300	19,900
3	Blackburn	33,400	34,700	34,300	37,400	47,000
4	Bradford	11,300	11,300	12,300	12,700	14,900
5	Bristol	15,000	15,400	16,600	19,000	22,200
6	Canterbury	20,500	20,600	21,000	21,000	21,000
7	Carlisle	20,000	20,400	21,600	24,900	25,700
8	Chelmsford	46,100	45,300	48,600	50,800	51,100
9	Chester	43,700	42,600	45,700	48,600	50,500
10	Chichester	53,000	54,100	51,800	58,200	62,700
11	Coventry	16,600	17,300	16,300	17,700	19,800
12	Derby	18,100	17,800	20,700	20,100	24,100
13	Durham	21,900	22,800	24,000	27,400	30,900
14	Ely	18,600	18,300	19,100	20,900	23,800
15	Exeter	30,900	30,800	30,500	33,900	38,000
16	Gloucester	23,000	22,100	23,600	26,300	28,400
17	Guildford	28,800	28,100	29,500	30,600	33,100
18	Hereford	17,400	17,600	18,100	18,900	20,000
19	Leicester	16,000	16,400	17,000	16,100	19,300
20	Lichfield	43,300	44,600	45,000	52,200	58,400
21	Lincoln	26,500	28,400	27,800	31,300	35,900
22	Liverpool	27,500	26,800	28,800	32,500	36,900
23	London	68,700	64,400	59,600	52,500	45,100
24	Manchester	32,300	32,600	34,500	38,000	39,300
25	Newcastle	16,100	16,000	16,700	17,500	19,500
26	Norwich	20,000	19,800	23,900	25,900	31,100
27	Oxford	53,600	52,700	54,600	60,600	58,700
28	Peterborough	18,800	18,300	18,000	19,500	21,700
29	Portsmouth	16,800	16,400	17,500	18,000	19,500
30	Ripon & Leeds	16,800	15,300	17,600	19,300	24,600
31	Rochester	29,500	28,500	29,900	31,300	34,100
32	St. Albans	38,000	36,900	39,400	43,100	50,000
33	St. Edms & Ipswich	23,000	23,300	24,100	25,300	26,900
34	Salisbury	40,500	40,700	42,500	45,900	48,200
35	Sheffield	17,400	17,400	18,600	20,700	22,600
36	Sodor & Man	2,600	2,700	2,400	2,800	3,300
37	Southwark	45,800	44,800	44,200	45,400	46,100
38	Southwell & Nottingham	18,600	18,800	18,300	18,700	20,800
39	Truro	15,600	15,700	16,900	17,600	21,900
40	Wakefield	19,500	19,800	20,300	23,200	24,900
41	Winchester	38,300	37,000	38,500	42,100	44,400
42	Worcester	18,600	19,200	20,300	22,400	21,200
43	York	33,700	33,600	35,000	38,200	41,100
44	Europe	10,700	10,300	9,300	N/A	N/A
	Totals Province of Canterbury	**864,400**	**858,400**	**880,300**	**929,000**	**994,000**
	Totals Province of York	**314,700**	**315,000**	**330,000**	**362,000**	**402,000**
	Totals CHURCH OF ENGLAND	**1,179,100**	**1,173,400**	**1,210,000**	**1,290,400**	**1,396,000**

Notes: 1. Electoral Rolls are revised annually and new rolls are compiled every six years. Thus in 1990, 1996, 2002 and 2007 new electoral rolls were compiled.
2. Figures for cathedrals are included from 2002 onwards.
3. N/A These figures are not available so national electoral roll totals for 1990 and 1996 do not include the Diocese of Europe.

Selected Church Statistics

J Average Weekly Attendances 2008
Adults, Children and Young People

Ref. No.	Diocese	Average attendances Weekly 2008 Adults	Average attendances Weekly 2008 Children & young people	Average attendances Sunday 2008 Adults	Average attendances Sunday 2008 Children & young people	Usual Sunday attendance 2008 Adults	Usual Sunday attendance 2008 Children & young people
1	Bath & Wells	22,700	5,100	20,900	2,800	18,400	2,500
2	Birmingham	15,500	3,700	13,800	2,400	12,600	2,100
3	Blackburn	24,600	7,700	22,100	5,700	18,400	4,000
4	Bradford	9,600	2,600	8,700	1,500	7,500	1,200
5	Bristol	12,600	3,400	11,400	2,000	10,400	1,900
6	Canterbury	18,100	4,500	15,700	3,200	13,700	2,600
7	Carlisle	14,000	2,800	12,300	1,600	10,100	1,100
8	Chelmsford	33,800	8,400	30,200	6,000	27,400	5,100
9	Chester	31,700	7,500	27,700	4,800	23,500	4,100
10	Chichester	38,500	8,900	33,400	5,700	30,600	5,600
11	Coventry	13,400	2,800	12,100	2,100	11,300	1,900
12	Derby	15,300	2,900	13,800	2,300	12,000	2,000
13	Durham	17,900	3,300	15,200	2,300	13,300	2,000
14	Ely	16,200	3,900	14,900	2,300	12,800	2,000
15	Exeter	22,200	2,800	20,300	2,400	19,400	2,300
16	Gloucester	17,700	4,000	15,500	2,500	13,600	1,900
17	Guildford	22,700	6,600	20,400	4,800	18,600	4,100
18	Hereford	11,000	1,700	10,000	1,100	7,200	800
19	Leicester	13,500	2,400	12,500	1,800	10,900	1,700
20	Lichfield	29,800	8,300	26,100	4,300	23,900	3,700
21	Lincoln	20,800	4,700	18,400	2,600	15,700	1,700
22	Liverpool	22,800	6,200	20,000	4,500	16,900	3,500
23	London	61,400	17,500	49,600	11,100	47,200	10,900
24	Manchester	26,900	8,700	23,600	6,100	19,600	5,100
25	Newcastle	12,100	2,200	10,500	1,400	8,800	1,000
26	Norwich	18,800	2,700	17,500	1,700	14,700	1,300
27	Oxford	46,800	11,500	42,200	8,300	37,200	7,500
28	Peterborough	15,900	4,100	13,700	2,500	12,100	2,300
29	Portsmouth	11,900	2,200	10,700	1,700	10,000	1,500
30	Ripon & Leeds	13,400	3,700	11,800	2,400	10,400	1,900
31	Rochester	23,300	7,000	21,000	4,900	19,000	4,400
32	St. Albans	30,100	9,100	25,600	5,300	21,900	4,400
33	St. Edms & Ipswich	17,100	3,300	15,500	2,100	13,400	1,800
34	Salisbury	26,800	5,300	23,500	3,300	20,600	2,800
35	Sheffield	15,100	3,900	13,000	2,400	11,100	2,000
36	Sodor & Man	2,100	400	1,900	300	1,500	200
37	Southwark	35,000	11,900	32,400	9,400	28,300	7,800
38	Southwell & Nottingham	15,000	4,400	13,400	2,200	11,700	1,800
39	Truro	11,900	1,800	10,600	1,000	9,200	1,000
40	Wakefield	14,300	3,000	12,400	2,100	11,000	1,600
41	Winchester	27,200	7,700	24,100	4,500	22,400	4,300
42	Worcester	12,900	3,000	11,400	1,600	10,500	1,400
43	York	26,200	6,000	22,300	3,200	19,200	2,500
44	Europe	10,900	1,700	10,300	1,600	9,900	1,600
	Totals Province of Canterbury	**673,600**	**162,900**	**597,300**	**107,300**	**534,900**	**94,800**
	Totals Province of York	**245,700**	**62,400**	**214,800**	**40,500**	**182,900**	**32,000**
	Totals CHURCH OF ENGLAND	**919,300**	**225,300**	**812,000**	**147,800**	**717,800**	**126,800**
	Comparable figures for 2007:*						
	Totals Province of Canterbury	**689,500**	**157,800**	**610,500**	**107,200**	**544,900**	**97,700**
	Totals Province of York	**250,900**	**61,400**	**219,400**	**40,900**	**191,200**	**34,500**
	Totals CHURCH OF ENGLAND	**940,400**	**219,200**	**829,900**	**148,100**	**736,100**	**132,200**

Notes: 1. Children and young people are for the majority of dioceses defined as under the age of 16.
2. Figures for cathedrals are included.
3.* The comparable 2007 figures have been revised since the publication of 'Church Statistics 2007/8'

K All Age Church Attendance 2000 to 2008

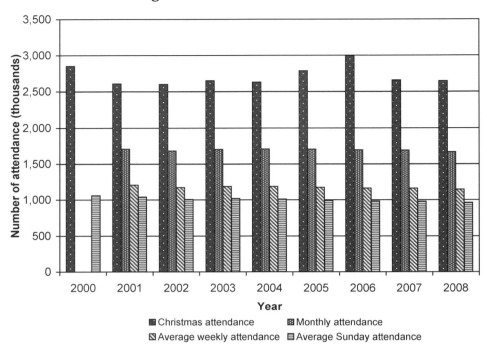

Parochial Church Attendance 2000 to 2008

L   Weekly Church Attendance

	Weekly attendance								
	Adult			Children and young people			All age		
Year	Highest attendance 000s	Average attendance 000s	Lowest attendance 000s	Highest attendance 000s	Average attendance 000s	Lowest attendance 000s	Highest attendance 000s	Average attendance 000s	Lowest attendance 000s
2000*	1,451	1,031	742	455	243	120	1,855	1,274	885
2001	1,332	976	727	416	229	113	1,708	1,205	862
2002	1,296	941	693	424	229	111	1,682	1,170	825
2003	1,312	957	714	430	230	110	1,704	1,187	844
2004	1,308	951	706	437	235	111	1,707	1,186	839
2005	1,302	942	696	444	232	107	1,706	1,174	823
2006	1,294	937	690	442	228	103	1,694	1,163	812
2007	1,303	940	691	424	219	99	1,690	1,160	811
2008	1,267	919	679	438	225	100	1,667	1,145	800

M   Sunday Church Attendance

	Sunday attendance								
	Adult			Children and young people			All age		
Year	Highest attendance 000s	Average attendance 000s	Lowest attendance 000s	Highest attendance 000s	Average attendance 000s	Lowest attendance 000s	Highest attendance 000s	Average attendance 000s	Lowest attendance 000s
2000	1,191	878	660	300	180	103	1,464	1,058	781
2001	1,170	868	657	285	173	99	1,425	1,041	774
2002	1,143	838	623	278	167	94	1,395	1,005	733
2003	1,156	853	645	272	164	92	1,401	1,017	755
2004	1,147	846	638	272	164	91	1,394	1,010	746
2005	1,136	836	629	264	158	87	1,374	993	733
2006	1,123	828	622	262	155	84	1,361	983	722
2007	1,129	830	622	252	148	79	1,357	978	718
2008	1,099	812	611	249	148	80	1,322	960	707

Notes:
1. Figures for cathedrals are included.
2. Children and young people are under 16 years of age while adults are 16 years of age or over.
3. From 2000 church attendance figures are calculated typically from a four-week count in October.
4. * In 2000 attendance at midweek weddings and funerals was included.
5. An approximation to monthly attendance can be taken from the highest weekly attendance counted over a typical month.

Selected Financial Comparisons 1964 to 2008

N Tax-efficient Planned Giving to Parochial Church Councils: Contributors, Amounts and Average Weekly Rates

		Actual		In real terms of 2008*	
	Subscribers	Tax-efficient** planned giving, net, £ 000s	Weekly average per subscriber	Tax-efficient** planned giving, net, £ 000s	Weekly average per subscriber
Year	000s		£		£
1964	126	2,113	0.32	31,963	4.88
1970	168	3,325	0.38	38,606	4.42
1980	362	17,692	0.94	56,805	3.02
1990	405	71,130	3.38	121,164	5.75
1995	404	111,045	5.28	159,976	7.61
1996	404	118,111	5.62	166,144	7.90
1997	401	124,439	5.96	169,711	8.13
1998	399	132,114	6.37	174,206	8.40
1999	412	145,752	6.86	189,284	8.91
2000	451	157,922	6.73	199,188	8.49
2001	491	179,669	7.03	222,566	8.71
2002	504	189,904	7.25	231,506	8.83
2003	513	201,272	7.55	238,462	8.95
2004	517	215,085	8.00	247,457	9.20
2005	523	224,636	8.26	251,312	9.24
2006	527	236,625	8.64	256,573	9.37
2007	514	247,822	9.28	257,658	9.65
2008	514	261,354	9.77	261,354	9.77

O Weekly Average Tax-efficient Planned Giving Per Subscriber 1990 to 2008**

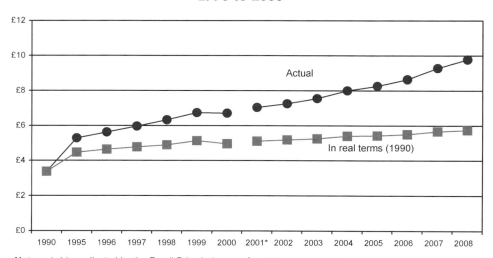

Notes: 1. * i.e. adjusted by the Retail Price Index to reflect 2008 purchasing power.

2. ** 2001 onwards include unrestricted and restricted giving, earlier years are primarily unrestricted tax-efficient planned giving.

Selected Church Statistics

P Direct Unrestricted Giving to Parochial Church Councils

		Actual		In real terms of 2008**	
Year	Church Electoral Roll 000s	Total direct giving £ 000s	Weekly average per Electoral Roll member £	Total direct giving £ 000s	Weekly average per Electoral Roll member £
1964	2,739	14,961	0.11	226,311	1.61
1970	2,559	15,847	0.12	183,997	1.40
1980	1,815	51,521	0.55	165,422	1.75
*1990	1,396	141,076	1.94	240,310	3.31
1995	1,468	197,163	2.58	284,042	3.72
*1996	1,290	205,417	3.06	288,956	4.31
1997	1,325	215,599	3.15	294,036	4.30
1998	1,347	244,338	3.51	322,184	4.63
1999	1,357	253,000	3.61	328,563	4.69
2000	1,377	268,541	3.78	338,712	4.77
2001	1,372	282,244	3.98	349,631	4.93
*2002	1,210	296,382	4.75	361,311	5.79
2003	1,235	306,667	4.81	363,332	5.70
2004	1,254	323,403	5.00	372,078	5.75
2005	1,269	335,095	5.08	374,888	5.68
2006	1,266	348,716	5.34	378,113	5.79
*2007	1,173	368,713	6.10	383,347	6.34
2008	1,179	383,862	6.32	383,862	6.32

Q Total Unrestricted Voluntary and Recurring Income of PCCs

Year	Total voluntary income £ 000s Actual	Weekly average per Electoral Roll member £ Actual	Total voluntary income £ 000s In real terms (2008)	Weekly average per Electoral Roll member £ In real terms (2008)	Recurring income Actual £000s	Recurring income In real terms (2008) £000s
1964	20,033	0.14	303,034	2.12	22,108	334,422
1970	22,110	0.17	256,715	1.97	26,396	306,479
1980	72,798	0.77	233,737	2.47	85,880	275,740
*1990	195,193	2.69	332,494	4.58	237,385	404,364
1995	275,388	3.61	396,736	5.20	327,531	471,856
*1996	288,358	4.30	405,627	6.05	344,897	485,160
1997	305,345	4.46	416,432	6.08	374,324	510,507
1998	314,933	4.52	415,271	5.96	403,801	532,452
1999	326,377	4.66	423,856	6.05	418,557	543,567
2000	346,856	4.88	437,491	6.16	442,477	558,098
2001	365,851	5.16	453,200	6.39	462,664	573,127
*2002	385,861	6.18	470,392	7.53	486,597	593,196
2003	401,600	6.30	475,806	7.46	506,838	600,490
2004	423,452	6.55	487,185	7.54	538,031	619,009
2005	440,574	6.68	492,892	7.47	561,141	627,776
2006	459,800	7.04	498,562	7.63	585,399	634,749
*2007	485,131	8.02	504,386	8.34	619,327	643,908
2008	504,818	8.31	504,818	8.31	650,940	650,940

Notes: 1. Figures for cathedrals and their daughter churches are not included.
2. Explanations of composite items and totals are given in the Definitions.
3. * Electoral Rolls are revised annually and new rolls are compiled every six years. Thus in 1990, 1996, 2002 and 2007 new electoral rolls were compiled.
4. ** i.e. adjusted by the Retail Price Index to reflect 2008 purchasing power.
5. The Diocese in Europe is not included in these tables.

Selected Church Statistics

R Total Income of Parochial Church Councils
1998 to 2008, £ millions

Year	Unrestricted			Restricted			Total (unrestricted & restricted)		
	Recurring	One-off	Total	Recurring	One-off	Total	Recurring	One-off	Total
1998	404	36	440	54	63	117	457	100	557
1999	419	37	456	55	69	123	473	106	579
2000	442	39	482	57	86	143	499	126	625
2001	463	40	503	61	88	149	523	128	652
2002	487	46	533	61	81	142	547	128	675
2003	507	54	561	63	92	155	570	146	716
2004	538	53	591	67	101	168	605	154	759
2005	561	55	616	73	103	176	635	158	792
2006	585	59	644	75	107	182	661	166	826
2007	619	73	692	122	84	206	741	157	898
2008	651	70	721	117	87	204	768	158	925

S Chart of Income From 1998 to 2008

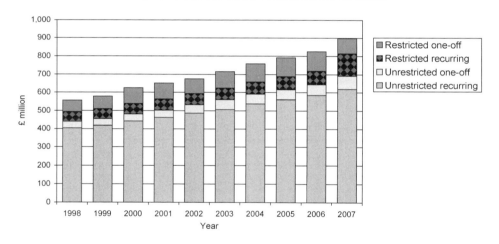

T Total Expenditure of Parochial Church Councils 1998 to 2008, £ millions

Year	Recurring expenditure	Capital expenditure	Total expenditure
1998	415	103	518
1999	437	127	564
2000	458	145	603
2001	483	145	628
2002	514	149	663
2003	535	162	697
2004	568	159	726
2005	601	178	779
2006	618	175	792
2007	654	184	838
2008	680	194	874

U Growth in Income and Expenditure

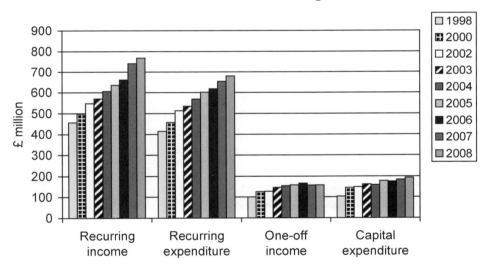

In the 10 year span between 1998 and 2008 recurring income increased by 68% compared with a rise in the Retail Prices Index of 32%.
Over the same period recurring expenditure increased by 64%, one-off income increased by 58%, and capital expenditure increased by 88%.

Proposed TABLE OF PAROCHIAL FEES From 1 January 2011 As approved by the General Synod July 2010. The Fees Order still needs to be approved by Parliament.	Fee Payable Towards Stipend of Incumbent (See Note 2)	Fee Payable To Parochial Church Council	Total Fee payable
BAPTISMS	£	£	£
Certificate issued at time of baptism	12.00	—	**12.00**
Short certificate of baptism given under section 2, Baptismal Registers Measure 1961	9.00	—	**9.00**
MARRIAGES			
Publication of banns of marriage	15.00	7.00	**22.00**
Certificate of banns issued at time of publication	12.00	—	**12.00**
Marriage Service (Marriage certificate – See Note 6)	126.00	136.00	**262.00**
FUNERALS AND BURIALS			
Service in Church			
Funeral service in church	57.00	45.00	**102.00**
Burial in churchyard following on from service in church	—	196.00	**196.00**
Burial in cemetery or cremation following on from service in church (See Note 3(ii))	—	—	**NIL**
Burial of body in churchyard on separate occasion (See Note 3(iii))	36.00	196.00	**232.00**
Burial of cremated remains in churchyard on separate occasion	36.00	80.00	**116.00**
Burial in cemetery on separate occasion (See Note 3(ii))	36.00	—	**36.00**
No Service in Church			
Service in crematorium or cemetery (See Note 3(ii))	102.00	—	**102.00**
Burial of body in churchyard (See Note 3(iv))	36.00	196.00	**232.00**
Burial of cremated remains in churchyard (See Note 3(iv))	36.00	80.00	**116.00**
Certificate issued at time of burial (See Note 3(v))	12.00	—	**12.00**
MONUMENTS IN CHURCHYARDS			
Permitted in accordance with rules, regulations or directions made by the Chancellor of the diocese, including those relating to a particular churchyard or part of a churchyard (but excluding a monument authorized by a particular faculty, the fee for which is set by the Chancellor)			
Small cross of wood	9.00	12.00	**21.00**
Small vase not exceeding 305mm × 203mm × 203mm (approx. 12" × 8" × 8")	36.00	45.00	**81.00**
Tablet, plaque or other marker commemorating a person whose remains have been cremated	36.00	45.00	**81.00**
Any other monument	54.00	104.00	**158.00**
(the above fees to include the original inscription)			
Additional inscription on existing monument (See Note 4)	36.00	—	**36.00**
SEARCHES IN CHURCH REGISTERS			
Searching registers of marriages for period before 1 July 1837 (See Note 5)			
(for up to one hour)	12.00	7.00	**19.00**
(for each subsequent hour or part of an hour)	9.00	7.00	**16.00**
Searching registers of baptisms or burials (See Note 5) (including the provision of one copy of any entry therein) (for up to one hour)	12.00	7.00	**19.00**
(for each subsequent hour or part of an hour)	9.00	7.00	**16.00**
Each additional copy of an entry in a register of baptisms or burials	12.00	7.00	**19.00**
Inspection of instrument of apportionment or agreement for exchange of land for tithes deposited under the Tithe Act 1836	9.00	—	**9.00**
Furnishing copies of above (for every 72 words)	9.00	—	**9.00**
EXTRAS The fees shown in this table are the statutory fees payable. It is stressed that the figures do not include any charges for extras such as music (e.g. organist, choir), bells, and flowers, which are fixed by the Parochial Church Council.	**Published by** **The Archbishops' Council** **Church House, Great Smith Street,** **London. SW1P 3AZ**		

NOTES

1. DEFINITIONS
'Burial' includes deposit in a vault or brick grave and the interment or deposit of cremated remains.

'Churchyard' includes the curtilage of a church and a burial ground of a church whether or not immediately adjoining such church.

(NOTE: This includes any area used for the interment of cremated remains within such a curtilage or burial ground, whether consecrated or not.)

'Cemetery' means a burial ground maintained by a burial authority.

'Monument' includes headstone, cross, kerb, border, vase, chain, railing, tablet, plaque, marker, flatstone, tombstone or monument or tomb of any other kind.

2. INCUMBENT'S FEE
Incumbents declare their fees to the Diocese, which takes them into account in determining the stipend paid to the incumbent.

3. FUNERALS AND BURIALS
i)   No fee is payable in respect of a burial of a still-born infant, or for the funeral or burial of an infant dying within one year after birth.

ii) The fees prescribed by this table for a funeral service in any cemetery or crematorium are mandatory except where a cemetery or crematorium authority has itself fixed different charges for these services, in which case the authority's charges apply.

iii) The fee for a burial in a churchyard on a separate occasion applies when burial does not follow on from a service in church.

iv) If a full funeral service is held at the graveside in a churchyard, the incumbent's fee is increased to that payable where the service is held in church.

v)   The certificate issued at the time of burial is a copy of the entry in the register of burials kept under the Parochial Registers and Records Measure 1978.

4. MONUMENTS IN CHURCHYARDS
The fee for an additional inscription on a small cross of wood, or a small vase, shall not exceed the current fee payable to the incumbent for the erection of such a monument.

5. SEARCHES IN CHURCH REGISTERS
The search fee relates to a particular search where the approximate date of the baptism, marriage or burial is known. The fee for a more general search of a church register would be negotiable.

6. FEE FOR MARRIAGE CERTIFICATE
The following fees are currently payable to the incumbent under the Registration of Births, Deaths and Marriages (Fees) Order 2010: certificate of marriage at registration £3.50; subsequently £9.00.

These fees may be increased from 1 April 2011.

Dioceses

PART 1

PART 1 CONTENTS

Every effort has been made to ensure that all details are accurate at the time of going to press.

Provinces of Canterbury and York

The dioceses in the respective Provinces of Canterbury and York are as below:

The Province of Canterbury Bath and Wells, Birmingham, Bristol, Canterbury, Chelmsford, Chichester, Coventry, Derby, Ely, Europe, Exeter, Gloucester, Guildford, Hereford, Leicester, Lichfield, Lincoln, London, Norwich, Oxford, Peterborough, Portsmouth, Rochester, St Albans, St Edmundsbury and Ipswich, Salisbury, Southwark, Truro, Winchester, Worcester.

The Province of York Blackburn, Bradford, Carlisle, Chester, Durham, Liverpool, Manchester, Newcastle, Ripon and Leeds, Sheffield, Sodor and Man, Southwell and Nottingham, Wakefield, York.

The entry for each diocese is preceded by a territorial description and a few vital statistics:

Population Derived from the 2008 mid-year estimates published by the Office for National Statistics (source: ONS web site www.statistics.gov.uk). Calculations are based on diocesan proportions of Ward and Civil Parish populations.

Area in square miles, as calculated from material supplied by the Office of National Statistics and the Church Commissioners.

Stipendiary clergy Full-time parochial clergy, men and women, working within the diocesan framework in parishes as at 31 December 2009 and counted under the current deployment formula.

Benefices Figures as at December 2009, compiled from information provided by the Church Commissioners. The figure does not include cathedrals or conventional districts.

Parishes / **Churches** as listed at 31 December 2009 (with later additions) in the Parish Register maintained by the Research and Statistics Department of the Archbishops' Council.

In most cases, the Diocesan Secretary/Chief Executive is also the Secretary of the Diocesan Synod.

PROVINCIAL LAY OFFICERS

Canterbury
Dean of the Court of Arches Rt Worshipful Charles George QC

Vicar-General Rt Worshipful Timothy Briden

Registrar Canon John Rees, 16 Beaumont St, Oxford OX1 2LZ
Tel: 01865 297200
Fax: 01865 726274
email: jrees@wslaw.co.uk

York
Official Principal and Auditor of Chancery Court of York Rt Worshipful Charles George QC

Vicar-General of the Province and Official Principal of the Consistory Court Rt Worshipful Peter Collier QC

Registrar Mr Lionel Lennox, Provincial Registry, Stamford House, Piccadilly, York YO1 9PP
Tel: 01904 623487
Fax: 01904 561470
email: lpml@denisontill.com

Joint Registrar (Provincial Elections) Mr Stephen Slack, The Legal Office, Church House, Great Smith St, London SW1P 3AZ   Tel: 020 7898 1366
email: stephen.slack@c-of-e.org.uk

Archbishop of Canterbury's Personal Staff

Lambeth Palace, London SE1 7JU
Tel: 020 7898 1200   *Fax:* 020 7401 9886
Web: www.archbishopofcanterbury.org

CHIEF OF STAFF
Mr Christopher Smith

Archbishop's Personal Assistant
Mrs Mary Whitticase

Secretary for Public Affairs
Mr Tim Livesey

Deputy Secretary for Public Affairs
Revd Helen Dawes

Press Secretary
Ms Marie Papworth

Press Officer
Mr David Brownlie-Marshall

Patronage Secretary
Mr Derek Fullarton

Premises and Administration Secretary
Mr Andrew Nunn

Secretary for Anglican Communion Affairs
Canon Joanna Udal

Anglican Communion Liaison Officer
Miss Fiona Millican

Secretary for Anglican Relations
Canon Flora Winfield

Secretary for International Development
Revd Rachel Carnegie

Director of Programmes and Advocacy
Miss Helen Stawski

Ecumenical Officer and Personal Chaplain
Canon Jonathan Goodall

Deputy Secretary for Ecumenism
Revd Dr Leslie Nathaniel

Chaplain
Canon Anthony Ball

Secretary for Inter Religious Affairs
Canon Guy Wilkinson

International Inter Faith Dialogues Assistant
Rev Rana Youab Khan

Archbishops' Missioner and Team Leader of Fresh Expressions
Rt Revd Graham Cray

Steward
Colonel Malcolm Croft

Finance Officer
Miss Rebecca Pashley

Archbishop of York's Personal Staff

Bishopthorpe Palace, Bishopthorpe, York YO23 2GE
Tel: 01904 707021   *Fax:* 01904 709204
email: office@archbishopofyork.org
Web: www.archbishopofyork.org

Chief of Staff
Revd Malcolm Macnaughton
email:
   malcolm.macnaughton@archbishopofyork.org

Chaplain/Researcher to the Archbishop
Revd Dr Daphne Green
   email: daphne.green@archbishopofyork.org

Executive Officer / Researcher
Mrs Margaret Pattinson
   email: margaret.pattinson@archbishopofyork.org

Director of Communications
Mr Kerron Cross
   email: kerron.cross@archbishopofyork.org

Domestic Chaplain to the Archbishop
Revd Richard Carew
   email: richard.carew@archbishopofyork.org

Senior Secretary
Miss Alison Cundiff
   email: alison.cundiff@archbishopofyork.org

DIOCESE OF BATH AND WELLS

Founded in 909. Somerset; north Somerset; Bath;
north-east Somerset; a few parishes in Dorset.

Population 911,000   Area 1,614 sq m
Full-time Stipendiary Parochial Clergy 187   Benefices 198
Parishes 470   Churches 566
www. bathandwells.org.uk
Overseas link dioceses: Luapula, Lusaka, Central Zambia,
Northern Zambia and Eastern Zambia.

BISHOP (78th)
Rt Revd Peter Price, The Palace, Wells BA5 2PD
[2002]   *Tel:* 01749 672341
Fax: 01749 679355
email: bishop@bathwells.anglican.org

SUFFRAGAN BISHOP
TAUNTON Rt Revd Peter Maurice, The Palace,
Wells BA5 2PD (*Office*) [2006]   *Tel:* 01749 672341
Fax: 01749 679355
email: bishop.taunton@bathwells.anglican.org
Bishops' Senior Chaplain and Adviser Preb Stephen
Lynas (*same address, tel and fax nos*)
email: chaplain@bathwells.anglican.org
Bishop's Domestic Chaplain Revd Julia Hedley
(*same address, tel and fax nos*)
email: julia.hedley@bathwells.anglican.org

ASSISTANT BISHOPS
Rt Revd Richard Third, 25 Church Close,
Martock, Yeovil TA12 6DS   *Tel:* 01935 825519
Rt Revd William Persson, Ryalls Cottage, Burton
St, Marnhull, Sturminster Newton DT10 1PS
Tel: 01258 820452
Rt Revd Paul Barber, Hillside, 41 Somerton Rd,
Street BA16 0DR   *Tel:* 01458 442916
Rt Revd Barry Rogerson, Flat 2, 30 Albert Rd,
Clevedon BS21 7RR   *Tel:* 01275 541964
email: barry.rogerson@blueyonder.co.uk
Rt Revd Roger Sainsbury, Abbey Lodge, Battery
Lane, Portishead BS20 7JD   *Tel:* 01275 847082
email: bishoproger@talktalk.net
Rt Revd Andrew Burnham, Bishop's House,
Church Lane, Dry Sandford, Abingdon OX13 6JP
Tel: 01865 390746
email: bishop.andrew@ebbsfleet.org.uk
Rt Revd George Cassidy, Darch House, 17 St
Andrew Road, Stogursey, Bridgwater TA5 1TE
Tel: 01278 732625
email: georgecassidy123@btinternet.com

**CATHEDRAL CHURCH OF ST ANDREW
IN WELLS**
Dean of Wells Very Revd John Clarke, The Dean's
Lodging, 25 The Liberty, Wells BA5 2SZ [2004]
Tel: 01749 670278
email: dean@wellscathedral.uk.net

Cathedral Offices Chain Gate, Cathedral Green,
Wells BA5 2UE   *Tel:* 01749 674483
Fax: 01749 832210
email: office@wellscathedral.uk.net
Web: www.wellscathedral.org.uk
Canons Residentiary
Chancellor Canon Andrew Featherstone, 8 The
Liberty, Wells BA5 2SU [2005]   *Tel:* 01749 679587
email: andrew.featherstone@btinternet.com
Precentor Canon Patrick Woodhouse, 4 The
Liberty, Wells BA5 2SU [2000]   *Tel:* 01749 673188
email: pwoodhouse@liberty4.fsnet.co.uk
Treasurer Canon Dr Graham Dodds, 2 The
Liberty, Wells BA5 2SU [2010]   *Tel:* 01749 674702
email: Graham.Dodds@bathwells.anglican.org
Archdeacon Ven Nicola Sullivan, 6 The Liberty,
Wells BA5 2SU [2007]   *Tel:* 01749 685147
email: adwells@bathwells.anglican.org
Lay Members
Cathedral Administrator Dr Paul Richards,
Cathedral Offices
email: administrator@wellscathedral.uk.net
Preb Adrian I'Anson, Cathedral Offices
Preb Barbara Bates, Cathedral Offices
Preb Gill Hawkings, Cathedral Offices
Registrar Preb Mr Tim Berry, Diocesan Registry,
14 Market Place, Wells BA5 2RE
Tel: 01749 674747
Fax: 01749 834060
email: tim.berry@harris-harris.co.uk
Cathedral Organist Mr Matthew Owens (*based at
Cathedral Offices*)
email: musicoffice@wellscathedral.uk.net

ARCHDEACONS
WELLS Ven Nicola Sullivan, 6 The Liberty, Wells
BA5 2SU [2007]   *Tel:* 01749 685147
Fax: 01749 679755
email: adwells@bathwells.anglican.org
BATH Ven Andy Piggott, 56 Grange Rd, Saltford,
Bristol BS31 3AG [2005]   *Tel:* 01225 873609
Fax: 01225 874110
email: adbath@bathwells.anglican.org
TAUNTON Ven John Reed, 2 Monkton Heights,
West Monkton, Taunton TA2 8LU [1999]
Tel: 01823 413315
Fax: 01823 413384
email: adtaunton@bathwells.anglican.org

CONVOCATION (MEMBERS OF THE
HOUSE OF CLERGY OF THE GENERAL
SYNOD)
Proctors for Clergy
Ven Andy Piggott
Preb Stephen Lynas
Revd James Dudley-Smith
Revd Sue Rose

MEMBERS OF THE HOUSE OF LAITY OF THE GENERAL SYNOD
Mr Edward Armitstead
Mr Tim Hind
Mrs Jenny Humphreys
Dr Cherida Stobart
Miss Fay Wilson Rudd

DIOCESAN OFFICERS
Dioc Secretary Mr Nicholas Denison, Dioc Office,
The Old Deanery, Wells BA5 2UG
Tel: 01749 670777
Fax: 01749 674240
email: nick.denison@bathwells.anglican.org
Chancellor of Diocese The Worshipful Timothy
Briden, 1 Temple Gardens, Temple, London
EC4Y 9BB
Registrar of Diocese and Bishop's Legal Secretary
Preb Mr Tim Berry, Diocesan Registry, 14
Market Place, Wells BA5 2RE   *Tel:* 01749 674747
Fax: 01749 834060
email: tim.berry@harris-harris.co.uk

DIOCESAN ORGANIZATIONS
Diocesan Office The Old Deanery, Wells BA5 2UG
Tel: 01749 670777
Fax: 01749 674240
email: general@bathwells.anglican.org

ADMINISTRATION
Dioc Synod (*Chairman, House of Clergy*)   Preb
Colin Randall, The Rectory, 72 High St,
Wellington TA21 8RF   *Tel:* 01823 662248
email: colinms.randall@virgin.net
(*Chairman, House of Laity*) Ms Christina Baron,
The Old Vicarage, St Thomas Street, Wells
BA5 2UZ   *Tel:* 01749 675071
email: baron.christina@googlemail.com
(*Secretary*) Mr Nicholas Denison, Dioc Office (*as
above*)
Board of Finance (*Chairman*) Mr Harry
Musselwhite, Highfields, 207 Bailbrook Lane,
Bath BA1 7AB   *Tel:* 01225 858913
email: harry.musselwhite@btopenworld.com
(*Secretary*) Mr Nicholas Denison, Dioc Office
Finance Group Mr Nicholas Denison (*as above*)
Board of Patronage Mr Philip Nokes, Dioc Office
email: philip.nokes@bathwells.anglican.org
Mission and Pastoral Committee Mr Philip Nokes
(*as above*)
Designated Officer Mr Philip Nokes (*as above*)
Deputy Dioc Secretary Mr Philip Nokes (*as above*)
Accountant Mr Nick May, Dioc Office
email: nick.may@bathwells.anglican.org

Property Officer Mrs Penny Cooke, Dioc Office
email: penny.cooke@bathwells.anglican.org
Dioc Surveyor Mr Paul Toseland, Dioc Office
email: paul.toseland@bathwells.anglican.org

CHURCHES
Advisory Committee for the Care of Churches
(*Chairman*) Mr Hugh Playfair, Blackford House,
Blackford, Yeovil BA22 7EE   *Tel:* 01963 440611
(*Secretary*) Preb Mr Tim Berry, Dioc Registry,
14 Market Place, Wells BA5 2RE
Tel: 01749 674747
Fax: 01749 834060
email: tim.berry@harris-harris.co.uk
(*Assistant Secretary*) Mrs Sarah Davis, Dioc
Registry (*as above*)
email: sarah.davis@harris-harris.co.uk
Association of Change Ringers Revd Tim
Hawkings, The Rectory, Cheddar Rd, Axbridge
BS26 2DL   *Tel:* 01934 732261
email: revhawkings@googlemail.com

EDUCATION
Board of Education Diocesan Office, The Old
Deanery, Wells BA5 2UG   *Tel:* 01749 670777
Fax: 01749 674240
email: education@bathwells.anglican.org
Dioc Director of Education Mrs Maureen Bollard,
Dioc Office
email: maureen.bollard@bathwells.anglican.org
School Improvement Advisers
Mrs Pauline Dodds, Dioc Office
email: pauline.dodds@bathwells.anglican.org
Mr David Williams, Dioc Office
email: david.williams@bathwells.anglican.org
School Development Advisers
Mrs Tess Robinson, Dioc Office
email: tess.robinson@bathwells.anglican.org
Mrs Suzanne McDonald, Dioc Office
email: suzanne.mcdonald@
bathwells.anglican.org
Parish Adviser for Young People Mr Tony Cook,
Dioc Office
email: tony.cook@bathwells.anglican.org
Parish Adviser for Children Mrs Jane Tibbs, Dioc
Office   *email:* jane.tibbs@bathwells.anglican.org
Safeguarding Children Adviser Vacancy

MINISTRY FORUM
Chairman The Bishop of Taunton
Principal of the School of Formation Preb Dr
Graham Dodds, Dioc Office
email: graham.dodds@bathwells.anglican.org
Ministry Development Consultant Mr Steve
Annandale, Dioc Office
email: steve.annandale@bathwells.anglican.org
Director of Continuing Ministerial Development
Revd Simon Hill, Dioc Office
email: simon.hill@bathwells.anglican.org
Education for Discipleship Officer Revd Jennifer
Cole, Dioc Office
email: jennifer.cole@bathwells.anglican.org

Diocesan Director of Ordinands Preb Peter Rapsey, The Vicarage, Church Lane, Evercreech BA4 6HU
Tel: 01749 830322
email: peter.rapsey@btinternet.com
Diocesan Director of Vocations Preb Dr Catherine Wright, The Rectory, West Monkton, Taunton TA2 8QT
Tel: 01823 413380
email: catherine.wright@bathwells.anglican.org
Adviser in Prayer and Spirituality Revd Jane Eastell, Meadowside, Wild Oak Lane, Trull, Taunton TA3 7JT
Tel: 01823 321069
email: jane.eastell@bathwells.anglican.org
Adviser in Care and Counselling of the Clergy and their Families Mr John Careswell, The Coach House, Cork Street, Frome BA11 1BL
Tel: 01373 471317
email: john.careswell@fromecounselling.co.uk
Chaplain to the Deaf Mrs Pamela Grottick, 9 Chestnut Close, Baltonsborough, Glastonbury BA6 8PH
Tel: 01458 851401
email: pamg@wpci.org.uk
Warden of Readers Ven John Reed, 2 Monkton Heights, West Monkton, Taunton TA2 8LU
Tel: 01823 413315
email: adtaunton@bathwells.anglican.org
Director of Reader Studies Preb Dr Graham Dodds (as above)
Dean of Women Clergy Preb Dr Catherine Wright (as above)

MISSION FORUM

Chairman The Archdeacon of Bath
Executive Officer/Diocesan Missioner Canon Roger Medley, Dioc Office
email: roger.medley@bathwells.anglican.org
Ecumenical Mission Enabler Revd Annie Naish, Dioc Office
email: annie.naish@bathwells.anglican.org
Social Justice and Environment Adviser Mr David Maggs, Dioc Office
email: david.maggs@bathwells.anglican.org
World Mission Adviser & Exec Sec Zambia Link Mrs Jenny Humphreys, Dioc Office
email: jenny.humphreys@bathwells.anglican.org
Rural Life Adviser Revd Robert Widdowson, The Rectory, Fosse Rd, Oakhill, Radstock BA3 5HU
Tel: 01749 841688
email: ruralrobert@fsmail.net
Healing Adviser Revd Matthew Thomson, The Vicarage, Station Road, Congresbury, Bristol BS49 5DX
Tel: 01934 833126
email: revmattthomson@hotmail.com
Renewal Adviser Revd Keith Powell, Homefields House, Paynes Lane, Othery, Bridgwater TA7 0QB
Tel: 01823 698619
email: jill.powell3@googlemail.com

STEWARDSHIP GROUP

Chairman The Archdeacon of Bath
Stewardship Adviser Mr Andrew Rainsford, Dioc Office
email: andrew.rainsford@bathwells.anglican.org

BISHOP'S LITURGY GROUP

Chairman Revd Robin Lodge, St Andrew's Vicarage, 118 Kingston Road, Taunton TA2 7SR
Tel: 01823 352471
email: robin.lodge1@btinternet.com

PRESS AND PUBLICATIONS

Diocesan Communications Officer (Press and Media)/Bishops' Press Officer Preb John Andrews
Tel: 01934 830208
07976 554962 (Mobile)
email: john.andrews@bathwells.anglican.org
Diocesan Communications Officers (Internal) Miss Gillian Buzzard, Dioc Office
email: gillian.buzzard@bathwells.anglican.org
Mrs Helen Hawthorne, Dioc Office
email: helen.hawthorne@bathwells.anglican.org
Editor of Directory/Database Manager Mrs Gill Davey, Dioc Office
email: gill.davey@bathwells.anglican.org

WIDOWS' OFFICER

Revd Dan Richards, 1 Quaperlake St, Bruton BA10 0HA
Tel: 01749 812386
email: revdanrich@mbzonline.net

RETREAT HOUSE

Abbey House, Glastonbury (*Warden* Liz Pearson)
Tel: 01458 831112
Fax: 01458 831893
email: info@abbeyhouse.org

DIOCESAN RECORD OFFICE

Somerset County Record Office, Obridge Rd, Taunton, Som. TA2 7PU *County and Diocesan Archivist* Mr Tom Mayberry
Tel: 01823 278805
Fax: 01823 325402
email: archives@somerset.gov.uk

DIOCESAN RESOURCE CENTRE

Old Deanery, Wells BA5 2UG
Tel: 01749 685129
Fax: 01749 674240
email: resourcecentre@bathwells.anglican.org

RURAL DEANS
ARCHDEACONRY OF WELLS

Axbridge Revd Tim Hawkings, The Rectory, Cheddar Rd, Axbridge BS26 2DL
Tel: 01934 732261
email: revhawkings@googlemail.com
Bruton Preb Rose Hoskins, Springfields, Weston Bampfylde, Yeovil BA22 7HZ
Tel: 01963 440026
email: revrose@weston-ampfylde.freeserve.co.uk
Cary Preb Rose Hoskins (*as above*)
Frome Revd David Barge, St Mary's House, 40 Innox Hill, Frome, BA11 2LN
Tel: 01373 455996
email: dbarge@btinternet.com
Glastonbury Revd Robin Ray, Leigholt Farm, Somerton Road, Street BA16 0SU
Tel: 01458 841281
email: robinray@btinternet.com

Ivelchester Revd Peter Thomas, Rectory, Cat St, Chiselborough, Stoke-sub-Hamdon TA14 6TT
Tel: 01935 881202
email: PThomas5@aol.com
Yeovil Revd Anthony Perris, St James Vicarage, 1 Old School Close, Yeovil BA21 3UB
Tel: 01935 429398
email: antonyperris@yahoo.com
Shepton Mallet Canon Tony Birbeck, Beeches, Cannards Grave Rd, Shepton Mallet BA4 4LX
Tel: 01749 330382
email: tonybirkbeck@hotmail.co.uk

ARCHDEACONRY OF BATH
Bath Revd Patrick Whitworth, Rectory, Weston, Bath BA1 4BU
Tel: 01225 421159
email: pwhitworth@metronet.co.uk
Chew Magna Preb Jan Knott, Rectory, Church Lane, Farmborough, Bath BA3 1AN
Tel: 01761 479311
email: jpknott@btinternet.com
Locking Revd Richard Taylor, The Rectory, Cecil Rd, Weston Super Mare BS23 2NF
Tel: 01934 623399
email: revrjtaylor@hotmail.com
Midsomer Norton Revd Christopher Hare, Rectory, South Rd, Timsbury BA2 0EJ
Tel: 01761 479660
email: chrishare@stmarystimsbury.org

Portishead Revd Ian Hubbard, Rectory, 1 Well Lane, Yatton, Bristol BS49 4HT   *Tel:* 01934 832184
email: ian@hubbardi.freeserve.co.uk

ARCHDEACONRY OF TAUNTON
Sedgemoor Revd Will Lane, The Rectory, 7 Vicarage Road, Woolavington TA7 8DX
Tel: 01278 683408
email: reverend.lane@googlemail.com
Crewkerne and Ilminster Revd Andrew Tatham, Rectory, Broadway, Ilminster TA19 9RE
Tel: 01460 52559
email: aftatham@ukonline.co.uk
Exmoor Revd Stephen Stuckes, The Vicarage, Manor Road, Alcombe, Minehead TA24 6EJ
Tel: 01643 703285
email: sstuckes24@btinternet.com
Quantock Revd Stephen Campbell, Hodderscombe Lodge, Holford, Bridgwater TA5 1SA
email: campbell1sa@btinternet.com
Taunton Revd Geoff Boucher, The Rectory, West Monkton, Taunton TA2 8QT   *Tel:* 01823 412226
email: geoffboucher@btinternet.com
Tone Revd Christopher Rowley, Vicarage, 62 Rockwell Green, Wellington TA21 9BX
Tel: 01823 662742
email: christopherrowley@uwclub.net

DIOCESE OF BIRMINGHAM

Founded in 1905. Birmingham; Sandwell, except for an area in the north (LICHFIELD); Solihull, except for an area in the east (COVENTRY); an area of Warwickshire; a few parishes in Worcestershire.

Population 1,436,000   Area 292 sq m
Full-time Stipendiary Parochial Clergy 144   Benefices 142
Parishes 149   Churches 195
www.birmingham.anglican.org
Overseas link dioceses: Lake Malawi, Southern Malawi, Northern Malawi (Malawi).

BISHOP (9th)
Rt Revd David Andrew Urquhart, Bishop's Croft, Old Church Rd, Harborne, Birmingham, B17 0BG [2006]   *Tel:* 0121 427 1163
    Fax: 0121 426 1322
email: bishop@birmingham.anglican.org
Domestic Chaplain Canon Andrew Gorham, East Wing, Bishop's Croft, Old Church Rd, Birmingham B17 0BE   *Tel:* 0121 427 2295 (Home)
    0121 427 1163 (Office)
email:
    bishopschaplain@birmingham.anglican.org

SUFFRAGAN BISHOP
ASTON Rt Revd Andrew Watson [2008], 16 Coleshill St, Sutton, Coldfield B72 1SH
    Tel: 0121 426 0448 (Office)
    Fax: 0121 428 1114
email: bishopofaston@birmingham.anglican.org

HONORARY ASSISTANT BISHOPS
Rt Revd Anthony Charles Dumper, 117 Berberry Close, Bournville, Birmingham B30 1TB [1993]
    Tel: 0121 458 3011
Rt Revd Michael Humphrey Dickens Whinney, 3 Moor Green Lane, Moseley, Birmingham B13 8NE [1989]   *Tel:* 0121 249 2856
Rt Revd Peter Hall, 27 Jacey Rd, Edgbaston, Birmingham B16 0LL [1998]   *Tel:* 0121 455 9240
Rt Revd Maurice Walker Sinclair, 55 Selly Wick Drive, Selly Park, Birmingham B29 7JQ [2002]
    Tel: 0121 4712617
email: mauricewsinclair@blueyonder.co.uk
Rt Revd Mark Santer, 81 Clarence Rd, Moseley, Birmingham B13 9UH [2003]
Rt Revd Iraj Mottadeheh, 2 Highland Rd, Newport TF10 7AE [2005]   *Tel:* 01952 813615

CATHEDRAL CHURCH OF ST PHILIP
Dean Very Revd Catherine Ogle, 38 Goodby Road, Moseley, Birmingham B13 8NJ
    Tel: 0121 262 1840
email: dean@birminghamcathedral.com
Assistant Dean Canon Peter Howell-Jones, 172 Station Rd, Sutton Coldfield B73 5LE
    Tel: 0121 321 2493
email: assistantdean@birminghamcathedral.com

Cathedral Office Birmingham Cathedral, Colmore Row, Birmingham B3 2QB   *Tel:* 0121 262 1840
    Fax: 0121 262 1860
email: enquiries@birminghamcathedral.com
Canons Residentiary
Canon Missioner Canon Nigel Hand, 12 Nursery Drive, Handsworth, Birmingham B20 2SW [2008]
    Tel: 0121 262 1840
email:
    canonmissioner@birminghamcathedral.com
Canon Liturgist Revd Canon Janet Chapman, 4 Nursery Drive, Handsworth, Birmingham B20 2SW   *Tel:* 0121 262 1840
email: canonliturgist@birminghamcathedral.com
Bursar Administrator Ruth Harvey, Cathedral Office   *Tel:* 0121 262 1847
email: administrator@birminghamcathedral.com
Director of Music Mr Marcus Huxley, Cathedral Office   *Tel:* 0121 262 1846
email: music@birminghamcathedral.com

ARCHDEACONS
ASTON Ven Dr Brian Russell, c/o Dioc Office [2005]   *Tel:* 0121 426 0400
    Fax: 0121 428 1114
    email: archdeaconofaston@
    birmingham.anglican.org
BIRMINGHAM Ven Hayward Osborne, c/o Dioc Office [2001]   *Tel:* 0121 426 0441
    Fax: 0121 428 1114
email:
    archdeaconofbham@birmingham.anglican.org

CONVOCATION (MEMBERS OF THE HOUSE OF CLERGY OF THE GENERAL SYNOD)
Proctors for Clergy
Revd Catherine Grylls
Revd Canon Nigel Hand
Ven Hayward Osborne

MEMBERS OF THE HOUSE OF LAITY OF THE GENERAL SYNOD
Canon Dr Paula Gooder
Dr Rachel Jepson
Mr Robert Holgate

Birmingham   9

DIOCESAN OFFICERS

Dioc Secretary Mr Jim Drennan, 175 Harborne Park Rd, Harborne, Birmingham B17 0BH
Tel: 0121 426 0400
Fax: 0121 428 1114
email: j.d.drennan@birmingham.anglican.org
Chancellor of Diocese His Honour Judge Martin Cardinal, c/o Diocesan Registrar, Martineau, No. 1 Colmore Square, Birmingham B4 6AA
Registrar of Diocese and Bishop's Legal Secretary Mr Hugh Carslake, Martineau, No. 1 Colmore Square, Birmingham B4 6AA   Tel: 0800 763 2000
Fax: 0800 763 2001
email: lawyers@martineau-uk.com
Web: www.martineau-uk.co.uk
Dioc Surveyor Mr Alan Broadway, Dioc Office
Tel: 0121 426 0400
email: alan.broadway@birmingham.anglican.org

DIOCESAN ORGANIZATIONS

Diocesan Office 175 Harborne Park Rd, Harborne, Birmingham B17 0BH   Tel: 0121 426 0400
Fax: 0121 428 1114
Web: www.birmingham.anglican.org

ADMINISTRATION

Dioc Synod (*Chair, House of Clergy*) Canon Peter Howell-Jones, 172 Station Rd, Sutton Coldfield B73 5LE   Tel: 0121 321 2493 (Home)
0121 262 1840 (Office)
email: assistantdean@birminghamcathedral.com
(*Chair, House of Laity*) Mr Stephen Fraser, 47 Wroxton Rd, Yardley, Birmingham B26 1SH
email: stevef_bham@btinternet.com
(*Secretary*) Mr Jim Drennan, Dioc Office
Board of Finance (*Chair*) Mr Phil Nunnerley
(*Secretary*) Mr Jim Drennan (*as above*)
Deputy Secretary (*Finance*) Canon Paul Wilson, Dioc Office
Parsonages Committee Mr Jim Drennan (*as above*)
Dioc Trustees (*Secretary*) Canon Paul Wilson (*as above*)
Pastoral Committee Mr Jim Drennan, Dioc Office
Designated Officer Mr Hugh Carslake, Martineau (*as above*)   Tel: 0800 763 2000
Fax: 0800 763 2001
email: lawyers@martineau-uk.com

CHURCHES

Advisory Committee for the Care of Churches (*Chair*) Dr Jim Berrow, c/o Dioc Office; (*Secretary*) Mr Tim Clayton, Dioc Office
email: t.clayton@birmingham.anglican.org

EDUCATION

Dioc Director of Education Revd Jackie Hughes, Dioc Office
email: j.hughes@birmingham.anglican.org
Schools Support Officer Revd Peter French, Dioc Office
email: p.french@birmingham.anglican.org
RE Adviser Mrs Jill Stolberg, Dioc Office
email: j.stolberg@birmingham.anglican.org

MINISTRY

Director of Ordinands and Women's Ministry Canon Faith Claringbull, Dioc Office
email: f.claringbull@birmingham.anglican.org

MINISTRIES

Chair Ven Dr Brian Russell, Dioc Office
Bishop's Adviser for Continuing Clergy Ministerial Education Revd Mark Pryce, Dioc Office
email: m.pryce@birmingham.anglican.org
Bishop's Adviser for Lay Adult Education and Training Revd Liz Howlett, Dioc Office
email: l.howlett@birmingham.anglican.org
Bishop's Adviser for Minority Ethnic Anglicans Dr Mukti Barton, Dioc Office
email: m.barton@birmingham.anglican.org
Bishop's Adviser for Children's Ministry Ms Claire Wesley, Dioc Office
email: claire@birmingham.anglican.org
Bishop's Adviser for Youth Ministry Miss Helen Tomblin, Dioc Office
email: helen@birmingham.anglican.org
Assistant Adviser for Youth Ministry/Digital Youth Adviser Mr Craig Gilman, Dioc Office
email: craig@birmingham.anglican.org
Dioc Music Adviser Mr Mick Perrier, c/o Dioc Office   *email:* mick@mperrier.freeserve.co.uk
Readers' Board (*Secretary*) Mr Michael Lynch, 57 Fairholme Rd, Hodge Hill, Birmingham B36 8HN
Tel: 0121 242 0534
email: mike4jeannie@blueyonder.co.uk

LITURGICAL

Bishop's Liturgical Advisory Committee Chair Revd Peter Babington, Parish Office, St Francis Centre, Sycamore Rd, Bournville, Birmingham B30 2AA
Tel: 0121 472 7215
email: pgbabington@gmail.com

MISSION AND EVANGELISM

Chair The Bishop of Aston
Bishop's Director for Mission Canon Peter Howell-Jones, Birmingham Cathedral, Colmore Row, Birmingham B3 2QB   Tel: 0121 262 1840
Fax: 0121 262 1860
email: assistantdean@birminghamcathedral.com
Mission Development Adviser Vacancy, Dioc Office
Tel: 0121 426 0420
email: sally@birmingham.anglican.org
Ecumenical Officer with Responsibility for LEPs Revd David James, 160a New Road, Rubery, Birmingham B45 9JA   Tel: 0121 460 1278
email: david.james5@btinternet.com
Stewardship and Income Generation Officer Mrs Jayne Grunnill, Dioc Office   Tel: 0121 426 0424
email: jayne@birmingham.anglican.org

HEALTHCARE CHAPLAINCIES

Bishop's Adviser Ven Hayward Osborne, Dioc Office

PRESS AND PUBLICATIONS
Bishop's Director of Communications Vacancy, Dioc Office   *Tel:* 0121 426 0438 (Office)
                          07973 173195 (Mobile)
Editor of Dioc Newsletter Vacancy
Editor of Dioc Directory Vacancy
Assistant to the Director of Communications Mrs Cara Butowski   *Tel:* 0121 426 0439
      email: c.butowski@birmingham.anglican.org

INDUSTRIAL RELATIONS
Industrial Chaplain (CIGB) Mrs Barbara Hayes, Dioc Office   *Tel:* 0121 426 0425
      email: b.hayes@birmingham.anglican.org

DIOCESAN RECORD OFFICES
Birmingham Archives and Heritage, Central Library, Chamberlain Square, Birmingham B3 3HQ, Archives Dept, *Tel:* 0121 303 4549 (*For parish records in the City and Diocese of Birmingham*)
      email: archives.heritage@birmingham.gov.uk
Warwick County Record Office, Priory Park, Cape Rd, Warwick CV34 4JS, *Head of Heritage & Culture* (*Archives*) Ms Caroline Sampson, *Tel:* 01926 738959 (*For parish records in the Metropolitan Borough of Solihull, together with those still in the County of Warwick*)
      email: recordoffice@warwickshire.gov.uk
Sandwell Community History and Archives Service, Smethwick Library, High St, Smethwick, Warley, W Midlands B66 1AA *Borough Archivist* Sarah Chubb, *Tel:* 0121 558 2561 (*For parish records in the Warley deanery*)
      email: archives_service@sandwell.gov.uk

CHURCH AND WORLD
Chair Vacancy, Dioc Office

CHRISTIAN STEWARDSHIP
see Mission and Evangelism

COMMUNITY REGENERATION
Chair Vacancy
Vice-Chair Mr Frank Joyce, c/o Dioc Office
Director Fred Rattley, Dioc Office
                          Tel: 0121 426 0442
      email: f.rattley@birmingham.anglican.org

COMMUNITY PROJECTS COMMITTEE
Chair Revd Nigel Traynor

AREA DEANS
ARCHDEACONRY OF ASTON
Aston Revd Dr Andrew Jolley, Aston Vicarage, Sycamore Rd, Aston, Birmingham B6 5UH
                          Tel: 0121 327 5856
      email: andy@astonnechellscofe.org.uk

Coleshill Revd Brian Castle, Vicarage, Haywood Rd, Tile Cross, Birmingham B33 0LH
                          Tel: 0121 779 2739
      email: revbcastle@aol.com
Polesworth Revd Michael Harris, Vicarage, 224 Tamworth Rd, Amington, Tamworth B77 3DE
                          Tel: 01827 62573
      email: mike.harris26@ntlworld.com
Solihull Canon Tim Pilkington, Rectory, St Alphege Close, Church Hill Rd, Solihull B91 3RQ   *Tel:* 0121 705 0069
      email: rector@solihullparish.org.uk
Sutton Coldfield Revd Dr Matthew Rhodes, Rectory, Glebe Fields, Curdworth, Sutton Coldfield B76 9ES   *Tel:* 01675 470384
      email: catmat30@hotmail.com
Yardley and Bordesley Revd Peter Smith, Vicarage, Burney Lane, Alum Rock, Birmingham B8 2AS
                          Tel: 0121 783 7455
      email: peter@ccbl.org.uk

ARCHDEACONRY OF BIRMINGHAM
Central Birmingham Revd Andrew Lenox-Conyngham, 29 Bradshaw Close, Park Central, Attwood Green, Birmingham B15 2DD
                          Tel: 0121 666 6089
      email: lenox@birm.eclipse.co.uk
Edgbaston Revd Priscilla White, 115 Balden Road, Harborne, Birmingham B32 2EL
                          Tel: 0121 427 2410
      email: priscillawhite.harborne@btinternet.com
Handsworth Revd Helen Hingley, 147 Hamstead Rd, Great Barr, Birmingham B43 5BB
                          Tel: 0121 358 1286
      email: h.hingley@btinternet.com
King's Norton Revd Colin Corke, 220 Longbridge Lane, Longbridge, Birmingham B31 4JT
                          Tel: 0121 475 3484
      email: colin@ado67.freeserve.co.uk
Moseley Revd Peter Babington, Parish Office, St Francis Centre, Sycamore Rd, Bournville, Birmingham B30 2AA   *Tel:* 0121 472 7215 (Office)
                          Tel: 0121 472 1209 (Home)
      email: pgbabington@gmail.com
Shirley Revd David Senior CBE, Vicarage, 592 Fox Hollies Road, Hall Green, Birmingham B28 9DX   *Tel:* 0121 777 3689
      email: david@ascensionhallgreen.fsnet.co.uk
Warley Revd Anthony Perry, Vicarage, 27 Poplar Ave, Edgbaston, Birmingham B17 8EG
                          Tel: 0121 429 2165
      email: trinity20@hotmail.co.uk

DIOCESE OF BLACKBURN

Founded in 1926. Lancashire, except for areas in the east (BRADFORD) and in the south (LIVERPOOL, MANCHESTER); a few parishes in Wigan.

Population 1,306,000   Area 878 sq m
Full-time Stipendiary Parochial Clergy 159   Benefices 189
Parishes 225   Churches 281
www.blackburn.anglican.org
Overseas link dioceses: Free State (South Africa),
Braunschweig (Germany) (Evangelical Lutheran Landeskirche).

BISHOP (8th)
Rt Revd Nicholas Reade, Bishop's House, Ribchester Rd, Clayton-le-Dale, Blackburn BB1 9EF [2004]   *Tel:* 01254 248234
Fax: 01254 246668
email: bishop@bishopofblackburn.org.uk
Domestic Chaplain Revd David Arnold, Bishop's House
email: chaplain@bishopofblackburn.org.uk
Bishop's Secretary Mrs Sue Taylor, Bishop's House
email: secretary@bishopofblackburn.org.uk
Assistant Secretary Mrs Hilary Wilby, Bishop's House
email: asstsecretary@bishopofblackburn.org.uk

SUFFRAGAN BISHOPS
LANCASTER Rt Revd Geoffrey S. Pearson, Shireshead Vicarage, Whinney Brow, Forton, Preston PR3 0AE [2006]   *Tel:* 01524 799900
Fax: 01524 799901
email: bishoplancaster@btconnect.com
BURNLEY Rt Revd John Goddard, All Saints House, Padiham Rd, Burnley BB12 6PA [2000]
Tel: 01282 688060
email: bishop.burnley@googlemail.com

HONORARY ASSISTANT BISHOPS
Rt Revd Gordon Bates, Caedman House, 2 Loyne Park, Whittington, Carnforth LA6 2NX
Tel: 01524 848492
Rt Revd Michael Vickers, 2 Collingham Park, Lancaster LA1 4PD   *Tel:* 01524 848492
Rt Revd Alan Winstanley, Vicarage, Preston Rd, Whittle-le-Woods, Chorley PR6 7PS
Tel: 01257 241291
Rt Revd and Rt Hon Lord Hope of Thornes, 2 Aspinall Rise, Hellifield, Skipton BD23 4JT

CATHEDRAL CHURCH OF ST MARY THE VIRGIN
Dean Very Revd Christopher Armstrong, The Deanery, Preston New Rd, Blackburn BB2 6PS [2001]   *Tel:* 01254 52502 (Home)
email: dean@blackburn.anglican.org
Cathedral Office Cathedral Close, Blackburn BB1 5AA   *Tel:* 01254 503090 (Office)
Fax: 01254 689666
email: cathedral@blackburn.anglican.org

Canons Residentiary
Sacrist Canon Andrew Hindley, 22 Billinge Ave, Blackburn BB2 6SD [1996]
Tel: 01254 261152 (Home)
01254 503099 (Office)
email: andrew.hindley@blackburn.anglican.org
Chancellor Vacancy
Canon Dr Susan Penfold, The Vicarage, Church Lane, Great Harwood BB6 7PU
Tel: 01254 884039 (Home)
01254 503090 ext. 245 (Office)
email: sue.penfold@blackburn.anglican.org
Administrator Vacancy
Director of Music Mr Richard Tanner, 8 West Park Rd, Blackburn BB2 6DG *Tel:* 01254 56752 (Home)
01254 503090 ext. 251 (Office)
email: richard.tanner@blackburn.anglican.org

ARCHDEACONS
BLACKBURN Ven John Hawley, 19 Clarence Park, Blackburn BB2 7FA [2002]   *Tel:* 01254 262571
Fax: 01254 263394
email: archdeacon.blackburn@milestonet.co.uk
LANCASTER Vacancy

CONVOCATION (MEMBERS OF THE HOUSE OF CLERGY OF THE GENERAL SYNOD)
Proctors for Clergy
Revd Canon Susan Penfold
Revd Paul Benfield
Canon Dr Simon Cox
Revd Peter Law-Jones

MEMBERS OF THE HOUSE OF LAITY OF THE GENERAL SYNOD
Mrs Rosemary Lyon
Mr Gerald Burrows
Mrs Susan Witts
Mrs Vivienne Goddard
Prof Helen Leathard
Mrs Alison Wynne

DIOCESAN OFFICERS
Dioc Secretary Mr Graeme Pollard, Church House, Cathedral Close, Blackburn BB1 5AA
Tel: 01254 503070
Fax: 01254 667309
email: graeme.pollard@blackburn.anglican.org

Chancellor of Diocese His Honour Judge John Bullimore, Rectory, 14 Grange Drive, Emley, Huddersfield HD8 9SF   Tel: 01484 849161
Registrar of Diocese and Bishop's Legal Secretary Mr Thomas Hoyle, Diocesan Registry, Cathedral Close, Blackburn BB1 5AA   Tel: 01254 503070
Fax: 01254 667309
email: registry@blackburn.anglican.org

DIOCESAN ORGANIZATIONS
Diocesan Office Church House, Cathedral Close, Blackburn BB1 5AA   Tel: 01254 503070
Fax: 01254 667309
email: diocese@blackburn.anglican.org

ADMINISTRATION
Dioc Synod (Chairman, House of Clergy) Canon John Hall, The Vicarage, 49 Mount Road, Fleetwood FY7 6QZ   email: johnbloem@aol.com
(Chairman, House of Laity) Mr Jeff Warburton, 6 Chapel Street, Longridge, Preston PR3 3JH
email: jeffpne@aol.com
(Secretary) Mr Graeme Pollard, Church House (as above)
Board of Finance (Chairman) Mr John Dell, 66 Moseley Rd, Burnley BB11 2RF
(Secretary) Mr Graeme Pollard (as above)
Property Committee (Chairman) Canon Andrew Sage; (Secretary) Mr Graeme Pollard (as above)
Mission and Pastoral Committee Mr Graeme Pollard (as above)
Designated Officer Mr Thomas Hoyle, Dioc Registry, Cathedral Close, Blackburn BB1 5AA
Tel: 01254 503070
Funding and Stewardship Officer Ms Mary Smith, St Mary's House, Cathedral Close, Blackburn BB1 5AA   Tel: 01254 503070
email: mary.smith@blackburn.anglican.org

CHURCHES
Advisory Committee for the Care of Churches (Chairman) Mr John Tillotson, Bonds Farm, Horns Lane, Goosnargh, Preston PR3 2NE
Tel: 01772 783436
(Secretary) Mr Graeme Pollard (as above)

EDUCATION
Board of Education (Dioc Director) Canon Peter Ballard, Church House
email: education@blackburn.anglican.org
Principal Adviser Lisa Fenton, Church House
email: lisa.fenton@blackburn.anglican.org
Diocesan Youth Officer Mr Craig Abbott, Church House
email: craig.abbott@blackburn.anglican.org
Children's Work Adviser Mrs Susan Witts, Church House
email: susan.witts@blackburn.anglican.org

MINISTRY
Director of Ordinands Revd Dr John Darch, 24 Bosburn Drive, Mellor Brook, Blackburn BB2 7PA   Tel: 01254 813544

Director of Ministry Canon Dr Susan Penfold, Church House
email: sue.penfold@blackburn.anglican.org
Director of IME 1–4 Revd Dr John Darch (as above)
Adviser in Women's Ministry Revd Rachel Watts, St James' Vicarage, Brierncliffe, Burnley BB10 2HU
Tel: 01282 423700
Mothers' Union Mrs P. Rothwell, 7 Aldon Grove, Longton, Preston PR4 5PJ   Tel: 01772 614045
Warden of Readers and Pastoral Assistants Revd Sue Williams, St Leonard's House, Potter Lane, Samlesbury PR5 0UE   Tel: 01772 877930

LITURGICAL
Chairman Very Revd Christopher Armstrong (as above)
Secretary Revd Michael Gisbourne, St Thomas' Vicarage, Church St, Garstang, Preston PR3 1PA
Tel: 01995 602162
email: revgis@fish.co.uk

MISSIONARY AND ECUMENICAL
Board for Mission and Unity (Chairman) Bishop of Lancaster
Ecumenical Officer Revd Mike Hartley, Vicarage, Church Rd, Warton, Preston PR4 1BD
Tel: 01772 632227

PRESS AND PUBLICATIONS
Dioc Communications Officer Mr Martyn Halsall, Vicarage, Bridekirk, Cockermouth CA13 0PE
Tel and Fax: 01900 824555
07790 253909 (Mobile)
email: martyn.halsall@ukonline.co.uk

DIOCESAN RECORD OFFICES
Diocesan Registry, Cathedral Close, Blackburn BB1 5AB   Tel: 01254 503070
Lancashire Record Office, Bow Lane, Preston PR1 8ND County Archivist Mr Bruce Jackson
Tel: 01772 254868

SOCIAL RESPONSIBILITY
Lead Officer Revd Ed Saville, St Mary's House, Cathedral Close, Blackburn BB1 5AA
Tel: 01254 503070
email: ed.saville@blackburn.anglican.org
Racial Justice and Cohesion Officer Revd Ed Saville, St Mary's House, Cathedral Close, Blackburn BB1 5AA   Tel: 01254 503070
email: ed.saville@blackburn.anglican.org
Officer for People with Sensory, Physical and Learning Difficulties Ms Sheron Hall, St Mary's House
email: sheron.hall@blackburn.anglican.org
Rural Areas Officer Revd Tim Horobin, St Mary's House
email: tim.horobin@blackburn.anglican.org
Urban Areas Officer The Archdeacon of Blackburn (as above)

ARCHDEACONRY OF BLACKBURN

Accrington Canon Roger Smith, St James' Vicarage, Church Lane, Haslingden, Rossendale BB4 5QZ   *Tel:* 01706 215533
email: Rsmith9456@aol.com
Blackburn with Darwen Revd Andrew Raynes, Christ Church with St Matthew's Vicarage, Brandy House Brow, Blackburn BB2 3EY
Tel: 01254 56292
Burnley Revd Mark Jones, Vicarage, 1 Arbory Drive, Padiham, Burnley BB12 8JS
Tel: 01282 772442
email: jones.padiham@btinternet.co.uk
Chorley Revd Michael Everitt, Rectory, 13 Rectory Lane, Standish, Wigan WN6 0XA
Tel: 01257 421396
email: rector@standish.org.uk
Leyland Revd Chris Nelson, St Mary's Vicarage, 14 Cop Lane, Penwortham, Preston PR1 0SR
Tel: 01772 743143
email: kitnel@btinternet.com
Pendle Revd Tony Rindl, Vicarage, Skipton Rd, Foulridge, Colne BB8 7NP *Tel:* 01282 870959
email: rindl-@fish.co.uk
Whalley Revd John Hartley, St Peter's Vicarage, 49a Ribchester Rd, Blackburn BB1 9HU
Tel: 01254 248072

ARCHDEACONRY OF LANCASTER

Blackpool Canon Dr Simon Cox, All Hallows Rectory, 86 All Hallows Rd, Bispham, Blackpool FY2 0AY   *Tel:* 01253 351886
email: drsjcox@yahoo.co.uk
Garstang Revd Andrew Wilkinson, Vicarage, Vicarage Lane, Churchtown, Garstang, Preston PR3 0HW   *Tel and Fax:* 01995 602294
email: vic.garstang@virgin.net
Kirkham Revd Peter Law-Jones, Vicarage, St Thomas Rd, Lytham St Annes
Tel: 01253 722725
email: peter.lawjones@tesco.net
Lancaster Revd Mike Peatman, Rectory, Church Walk, Morecambe LA4 5PR   *Tel:* 01524 410941
email: mikepeat@sky.com
Poulton Revd Martin Keighley, Vicarage, 7 Vicarage Rd, Poulton-le-Fylde FY6 3NA
Tel: 01253 883086
email: martinkeighley@btconnect.com
Preston Revd Timothy Lipscomb, Rectory, 13 Ribblesdale Place, Preston PR1 3NA
Tel: 01772 252528
email: lavish@ermine2.fsnet.co.uk
Tunstall Canon Paul Warren, Vicarage, St John's Grove, Silverdale, Carnforth LA5 0RH
Tel: 01524 701268

DIOCESE OF BRADFORD

Founded in 1919. Bradford; the western quarter of North Yorkshire; areas of east Lancashire, south-east Cumbria and Leeds.

Population 683,000   Area 920 sq m
Full-time Stipendiary Parochial Clergy 84   Benefices 104
Parishes 128   Churches 163
www.bradford.anglican.org
Overseas link dioceses: South Western Virginia, Khartoum and other northern dioceses (Sudan), Erfurt (Germany).

BISHOP (9th)
Vacancy
Bishop's Chaplain Canon Denise Poole, Bishops-croft, Ashwell Rd, Bradford BD9 4AU
Tel: 01274 545414
Fax: 01274 544831
email: denise.poole@bradford.anglican.org

HONORARY ASSISTANT BISHOP
Rt Revd Colin Buchanan, 21 The Drive, Alwoodley, Leeds LS17 7QB [2004]   *Tel:* 0113 267 7721
Rt Revd and Rt Hon David M. Hope, 2 Aspinall Rise, Hellifield BD23 4JT [2005]
Rt Revd Martyn William Jarrett, 3 North Lane, Roundhay, Leeds LS8 2QJ   *Tel:* 0113 265 4280
Fax: 0113 265 4281
bishop-of-beverley@3-north-lane.fsnet.co.uk

CATHEDRAL CHURCH OF ST PETER
Dean Very Revd Dr David Ison, The Deanery, 1 Cathedral Close, Bradford BD1 4EG [2005]
Tel: 01274 777722 (Office)
01274 777727 (Home)
Fax: 01274 777730
email: dean@bradford.anglican.org
Canons Residentiary
Canon Frances Ward, 3 Cathedral Close, Bradford BD1 4EG [2006]   *Tel:* 01274 777733
Fax: 01274 777730
email: fefward@btinternet.com
Canon Andrew Williams, 2 Cathedral Close, Bradford BD1 4EG [2006]
Tel: 01274 777721 (Office)
01274 735707 (Home)
Fax: 01274 777730
email: andy.williams@
cathedral.bradford.anglican.org
Cathedral Office 1 Stott Hill, Bradford BD1 4EH
Tel: 01274 777720
Fax: 01274 777730
email: secretary@cathedral.bradford.anglican.org
Administrator Mr Chris Aldred, Bradford Cathedral, 1 Stott Hill, Bradford BD1 4EH
Tel: 01274 777726
Fax: 01274 777730
email:
administrator@cathedral.bradford.anglican.org

Education Officer Mrs Caroline Moore, Bradford Cathedral, 1 Stott Hill, Bradford BD1 4EH
Tel: 01274 777734
Fax: 01274 777730
email: caroline.moore@
cathedral.bradford.anglican.org
Cathedral Organist Mr Andrew Teague, Bradford Cathedral, 1 Stott Hill, Bradford BD1 4EH
Tel: 01274 777725
Fax: 01274 777730
email: choirmaster@
cathedral.bradford.anglican.org
Head Verger Mr Jon Howard, Bradford Cathedral, 1 Stott Hill, Bradford BD1 4EH
Tel: 01274 777724
Fax: 01274 777730
email: vergers@cathedral.bradford.anglican.org
Publicity Officer Mrs Sandra Howard, Bradford Cathedral, 1 Stott Hill, Bradford BD1 4EH
Tel: 01274 777723
Fax: 01274 777730
email: sandra.howard@
cathedral.bradford.anglican.org

ARCHDEACONS
CRAVEN Ven Paul Slater, Woodlands, Netherghyll Lane, Cononley, Keighley BD20 8PB [2005]
Tel: 01535 635113 (Home)
01535 650533 (Office)
email: paulj.slater@dial.pipex.com
BRADFORD Ven Dr David Lee, 47 Kirkgate, Shipley, West Yorkshire BD18 3EH [2004]
Tel: 01274 200698
Fax: 01274 200698
email: david.lee@bradford.anglican.org

CONVOCATION (MEMBERS OF THE HOUSE OF CLERGY OF THE GENERAL SYNOD)
Proctors for Clergy
Revd Paul Ayers
Revd Canon Samuel Randall
Revd Ruth Yeoman

MEMBERS OF THE HOUSE OF LAITY OF THE GENERAL SYNOD
Mr Malcolm Halliday
Mr Ian Fletcher
Mrs Zahida Mallard

DIOCESAN OFFICERS

Dioc Secretary (acting) Mrs Debbie Child, Kadugli House, Elmsley St, Steeton, Keighley BD20 6SE
Tel: 01535 650521
Fax: 01535 650550
email: debbie@kadugli.org.uk
Human Resources Manager Mrs Debbie Child, Kadugli House
Tel: 01535 650521
Fax: 01535 650550
email: debbie@kadugli.org.uk
Chancellor of Diocese His Honour John de G. Walford, Ingerthorpe Cottage, Thwaites Lane, Markington HG3 3PF
Tel: 01765 677449
Registrar of Diocese and Bishop's Legal Secretary Mr Peter William Foskett, Diocesan Registry, Forward House, 8 Duke St, Bradford BD1 3QX
Tel: 01274 202132
Fax: 01274 202107
email: peter.foskett@gordonsllp.com
Dioc Insurance Adviser Mr John Watts, Towergate Risk Solutions, Towergate House, Five Airport West, Lancaster Way, Yeadon, Leeds LS19 7ZA
Tel: 0113 391 9317
Fax: 0113 391 9334
Child Protection Adviser Mrs Jenny Price, Church House, 1 South Parade, Wakefield WF1 1LP
Tel: 01924 371802
email: jenny.price@bradford.anglican.org
Vulnerable Adults Protection Adviser Dr Tony Wellsteed
Tel: 01274 587558

DIOCESAN ORGANIZATIONS

Diocesan Office Kadugli House, Elmsley St Steeton, Keighley BD20 6SE   *Tel:* 01535 650555
Fax: 01535 650550
email: office@kadugli.org.uk

ADMINISTRATION

Dioc Synod (Chairman, House of Clergy) Canon John Nowell, Church House, Baildon, Shipley BD17 6NE   *Tel and Fax:* 01274 594941
email: john.nowell@bradford.anglican.org
(Chairman, House of Laity) Ms Sallie Bassham, Winshaw Barn, Chapel-le-Dale, Carnforth LA6 3AT
email: sallie.bassham@bradford.anglican.org
(Secretary) Mrs Debbie Child, Dioc Office
Board of Finance (Chairman) Mrs Sharron Arnold, 42 Effingham Rd, Harden, Bingley BD16 1LQ
Tel: 01274 272894
email: sharron.arnold@talktalk.net
(Secretary) Mrs Debbie Child *(as above)*
(Accountant) Mr Peter Capel-Cure, Dioc Office
Tel: 01535 650525
email: peter@kadugli.org.uk
Property Committee (Chairman) Mr David Nelson, Old Gledstone, West Marton, Skipton BD23 3JR
Tel: 01282 843476
Fax: 01282 843554
Property Officer Mr David Meadows, Dioc Office
Tel: 01535 650524
email: david@kadugli.org.uk

Pastoral Committee (Chairman) Mr Raymond Edwards, Crosslands, Stanbury, Keighley BD22 0HB   *Tel:* 01535 642883
Designated Officer Mrs Debbie Child *(as above)*
Diocesan Advisory Committee (Chairman) Vacancy
(Secretary) Mrs Sylvia Johnson, Dioc Office
Tel: 01535 650523
email: Sylvia@kadugli.org.uk
Redundant Churches Uses Committee Revd Alan Fell, Vicarage, Loftus Hill, Sedburgh, Cumbria LA10 5SQ   *Tel:* 01539 620283 (Office)
01539 620559 (Home)
email: alan.fell@bradford.anglican.org
(Secretary) Mrs Sylvia Johnson , Dioc Office
Tel: 01535 650523
email: Sylvia@kadugli.org.uk
Redundant Churches Uses Committee Vacancy
(Secretary) Mrs Sylvia Johnson *(as above)*

CHURCH IN THE WORLD

Bishop's Officer Canon Sam Randall, Vicarage, Morton Lane, East Morton, Keighley BD20 5RS
Tel: 01274 561640
email: sam.randall@bradford.anglican.org
Interfaith Adviser Dr Philip Lewis, 9 Garden Lane, Heaton, Bradford BD9 5QJ
Tel: 01274 543891
Ecumenical Officer Revd Peter Mott, Rectory, 13 Westview Grove, Keighley BD20 6JJ
Tel: 01535 601499
email: peter.mott@live.co.uk
Social Responsibility see Bishop's Officer
Urban Adviser see Bishop's Officer
World Church Links
Northern Sudan Ven Dr David Lee *(as above)*
Southwestern Virginia Mrs Jill Wright, 15 Walker Close, Glusburn, Keighley BD20 8PW
Tel: 01535 634526
email: jill@woodchipcomputers.co.uk
Erfurt Mrs Rosie Tudge, St John's Vicarage, 9 St John's Avenue, Farsley, Pudsey LS28 5DN
Tel: 0113 2570059

COMMUNICATIONS

Chairman Mr Michael Moss, 4 Ashfield Rd, Shipley BD18 4JX   *Tel:* 01274 823133
email: mikemoss@blueyonder.co.uk
Media Relations Officer Ms Alison Bogle, 59 Hookstone Drive, Harrogate HG2 8PR
Tel: 01423 812995
07768 110175 (Mobile)
email: alison@bogle.force9.co.uk
Dioc News/Diocesan Office (as above)
Newsround Mr David Markham, 29 Ashley Rd, Bingley BD16 1DZ   *Tel:* 01274 567180
Webkeeper Mr Chris Wright, 15 Walker Close, Glusburn, Keighley BD20 8PW
Tel: 01535 636981
email: chris@woodchipcomputers.co.uk

EDUCATION

Chairman Mrs Diana Chambers, Romille Lodge, 4 Ridgeway, Skipton BD23 1LX
Tel: 01756 798389

Director of Education Revd Clive Sedgewick, Windsor House, Cornwall Rd, Harrogate HG1 2PW *Tel:* 01423 817553
Fax: 01423 817051
07903 326053 (Mobile)
email: clives@brleducationteam.org.uk

MINISTRY AND MISSION
Bishop's Officer Ven Paul Slater (*as above*)
Administrator Mrs Suzanne Evans, Dioc Office
Tel: 01535 650532
email: suzanne@kadugli.org.uk
Director of In-Service Training see Bishop's Officer
Director of Post-Ordination Training Revd Andrew Tawn, Rectory, Low Mill Lane, Addingham. Ilkley LS29 0QP *Tel:* 01943 830276
Director of Ordinands Canon Ann Turner, Rectory, Broughton, Skipton BD23 3AN
Tel: 01282 842332
email: ann.turner@bradford.anglican.org
Associate Directors of Ordinands Revd Michael Burley, Vicarage, 21 Southfield Rd, Burley-in-Wharfedale, Ilkley LS29 7PB *Tel:* 01943 863216
email: michael.burley@btinternet.com
Revd Ruth Yeoman, Vicarage, 12 Fairfax Gardens, Menston, Ilkley LS29 6ET *Tel:* 01943 877739
email: vicar@stjohnmenston.org.uk
Stewardship for Parishes Revd Uell Kennedy, Dioc Office *Tel:* 01535 650531
email: uell@kadugli.org.uk
Ministry Development Officer Vacancy
Adult Education Canon Steve Allen, 48 Toller Grove, Heaton, Bradford BD9 5NP
Tel: 01274 482059
email: steve.allen@bradford.anglican.org
Training Canon Steve Allen (*Lay*); Bishop's Officer Ven Paul Slater (*Clergy*)
Evangelism Revd Robin Gamble, Vicarage, 470 Leeds Rd, Thackley, Bradford BD10 9AA
Tel: 01274 419574
email: robinp.gamble@blueyonder.co.uk
Revd Sue Hope, 31 South Edge, Moorhead, Shipley BD18 4RA *Tel:* 01274 583652
email: shope12443@aol.com
Warden of Readers Revd Christine Shedd, Holy Trinity Vicarage, Park House Road, Low Moor, Bradford BD12 0HR *Tel:* 01274 678859
email: c.shedd@btinternet.com
Retired Clergy and Widows Officer (Bradford Archdeaconry) Canon Chris Hayward, 12 Ron Lawton Crescent, Burley-in-Wharfedale, Ilkley LS29 7ST *Tel:* 01943 865261
(*Craven Archdeaconry*) Canon John Bearpark, 31 Northfields Crescent, Settle BD24 9JP
Tel: 01729 822712
Children's Work Ven Dr David Lee (*as above*)
Healing Revd Gill Mack, Vicarage, Shire Lane, Hurst Green, Clitheroe BB7 9QR
Tel: 01254 826686
email: gillmack@tiscali.co.uk

Liturgy Chairman Dr Chris Clough, Brier Meade, 4 Scarborough Rd, Shipley BD18 3DR
Tel: 01274 778053
email: c.m.i.clough@blueyonder.co.uk
Youth Bradford Ms June Hopkinson, 20 Ravenscliffe Rd, Calverley, Leeds LS28 5RZ
Tel: 01274 310234
email: junehopkinson@localhost.bfd.uk
Craven Mr Steve Grasham, 12 Railway St, Beechcliffe, Keighley BD20 6AQ *Tel:* 01535 609293
email: steve.grasham@btinternet.com

DIOCESAN RECORD OFFICES
Diocesan Records Officers Mrs Mary Creaser, Rose Cottage, Austwick, Lancaster LA2 8BH
Tel: 01524 251536
email: mary.creaser@bradford.anglican.org
Mrs Margaret Barker, 2 Farnham Close, Baildon, Shipley BD17 6SF *Tel:* 01274 595750
West Yorkshire Archives Service, Bradford Central Library, Princes Way, Bradford BD1 1NN *Archivist* Ms Letitia Lawson, *Tel:* 01274 735099 (*For parishes in Bradford Metropolitan District*)
Archives Dept, Central Library, Northgate House, Halifax HX1 1UN *Archivist* Ms P. Sewell, *Tel:* 01422 392636 (*For parishes in Calderdale Metropolitan District*)
Record Office, County Offices, Kendal LA9 4RQ *County Archivist* Ms A. Rowe, *Tel:* 01539 773540 (*For parishes in the County of Cumbria*)
County Record Office, Bow Lane, Preston PR1 2RE *County Archivist* Mr B. Jackson, *Tel:* 01772 533039 (*For parishes in the County of Lancashire*)
Archives Dept, Leeds District Archives, Chapeltown Rd, Sheepscar, Leeds LS7 3AP *Archivist* S. Davidson, *Tel:* 0113 214 5814 (*For parishes in Leeds Metropolitan District*)
County Record Office, Malpas Rd, Northallerton DL7 8AF *County Archivist* Mr M. K. Sweetmore, *Tel:* 01609 777585 (*For parishes in the County of North Yorkshire*)

RURAL DEANS
ARCHDEACONRY OF BRADFORD
Airedale Revd Gary Hodgson, St Michael's Vicarage, Littlelands, Cottingley BD16 1AL
Tel: 01274 560761
email: gshodgson@sky.com
Bowling and Horton Canon Paul Bilton, St Wilfrid's Vicarage, St Wilfrid's Rd, Lidget Green, Bradford BD7 2LU *Tel:* 01274 572504
email: paul@bunghiu.freeserve.co.uk
Calverley Revd Paul Tudge, St John's Vicarage, 9 St John's Avenue, Farsley, Pudsey LS28 5DN
Tel: 01274 611631
email: paultudge@btinternet.com
Otley Revd Cayte Norman, Vicarage, Layton Avenue, Rawdon, Leeds LS19 6QQ
Tel: 0113 2503263
email: office@stpetersrawdon.co.uk

Bradford 17

ARCHDEACONRY OF CRAVEN

Bowland Revd Roger Wood, Vicarage, Stainforth, Settle BD24 9PG   *Tel:* 01729 823010
            email: roger.wood@bradford.anglican.org
Ewecross Revd Ian Greenhalgh, Vicarage, Austwick, Lancaster LA2 8BE   *Tel:* 01524 251313
            email: ian.greenhalgh@bradford.anglican.org

Skipton Canon Ann Turner, Rectory, 7 Roundell Drive, Dairy Meadow, West Marton, Skipton BD23 3UL   *Tel:* 01282 842332
            email: ann.turner@bradford.anglican.org
South Craven Revd Susan Griffiths, The Vicarage, Briggate, Silsden, Keighley BD20 9JS
                    Tel: 01535 652204
            email: susan.griffiths@bradford.anglican.org

DIOCESE OF BRISTOL

Founded in 1542. Bristol; the southern two-thirds of South Gloucestershire; the northern quarter of Wiltshire, except for two parishes in the north (GLOUCESTER); Swindon, except for a few parishes in the north (GLOUCESTER) and in the south (SALISBURY); a few parishes in Gloucestershire.

Population 935,000   Area 474 sq m
Full-time Stipendiary Parochial Clergy 103   Benefices 111
Parishes 161   Churches 207
www.bristol.anglican.org
Overseas link province: Uganda.

BISHOP (55th)
Rt Revd Michael Hill, 58a High St, Winterbourne, Bristol BS36 1JQ [2003] *Tel:* 01454 777728
Fax: 01454 777814
email: bishop@bristoldiocese.org

SUFFRAGAN BISHOP
SWINDON Rt Revd Dr Lee Rayfield, Mark House, Field Rise, Swindon SN1 4HP [2005]
Tel: 01793 538654
Fax: 01793 525181
email: bishop.swindon@bristoldiocese.org

CATHEDRAL CHURCH OF THE HOLY AND UNDIVIDED TRINITY
Dean Very Revd Dr David Michael Hoyle [2010]
Cathedral Office Bristol Cathedral, Abbey Gatehouse, College Green, Bristol BS1 5TJ
Tel: 0117 926 4879
Fax: 0117 925 3678
email: dean@bristol-cathedral.co.uk
Canons Residentiary
Theologian Vacancy
City Canon Canon Timothy Higgins, City Rectory, Apt 8, 10 Unity St, Bristol BS1 5HH [2006]
Tel: 0117 927 7977
email: canon@bristol-cathedral.co.uk
Precentor Canon Wendy Wilby, 55 Salisbury Rd, Redland, Bristol BS6 7AS [2007]
Tel: 0117 904 6903
email: precentor@bristol-cathedral.co.uk
Development
Canon Andrew Tremlett, 41 Salisbury Rd, Redland, Bristol BS6 7AR [2008]   *Tel:* 0117 909 9479
email: canon.development@
bristol-cathedral.co.uk
Capitular Canons
Canon Caro Barker-Bennett, Canon Tim Harle, Canon Richard Outhwaite, Canon Sue Topalian
Minor Canons
Revd Catherine Coster, Revd Gwyn Owen, Revd Dr Berj Topalian
Chapter Clerk Mr Andrew Phillips, Cathedral Office   *Tel:* 0117 946 8172
email: andrew.phillips@bristol-cathedral.co.uk
Cathedral Organist Mr Mark Lee, Cathedral Office
Tel: 0117 946 8177
email: organist@bristol-cathedral.co.uk

ARCHDEACONS
BRISTOL Ven Tim McClure, 10 Great Brockeridge, Westbury-on-Trym, Bristol BS9 3TY [1999]
Tel: 0117 962 1433
Fax: 0117 962 9438
email: tim.mcclure@bristoldiocese.org
MALMESBURY Vacancy

CONVOCATION (MEMBERS OF THE HOUSE OF CLERGY OF THE GENERAL SYNOD)
Proctors for Clergy
Revd Christopher Dobson
Revd Dr Emma Ineson
Canon Mark Pilgrim

MEMBERS OF THE HOUSE OF LAITY OF THE GENERAL SYNOD
Prof Glynn Harrison
Miss Jacqueline Humphreys
Canon David Froude

DIOCESAN OFFICERS
Dioc Secretary Mrs Lesley Farrall, Diocesan Church House, 23 Great George St, Bristol BS1 5QZ   *Tel:* 0117 906 0100
Fax: 0117 925 0460
email: lesley.farrall@bristoldiocese.org
Chancellor of Diocese Dr James Behrens, Searle Court, 6 New Square, London WC2A 3QS
Tel: 020 7242 6105
Registrar of Diocese and Bishop's Legal Secretary Mr Tim Berry, Harris and Harris, 14 Market Place, Wells BA5 2RE   *Tel:* 01749 674747
Fax: 01749 676585
email: tim.berry@harris-harris.co.uk

DIOCESAN ORGANIZATIONS
Diocesan Office Diocesan Church House, 23 Great George St, Bristol BS1 5QZ   *Tel:* 0117 906 0100
Fax: 0117 925 0460
email: any.name@bristoldiocese.org

ADMINISTRATION
Assistant Dioc Secretary Mrs Sally Moody, Dioc Church House

Dioc Synod (*Chairman, House of Clergy*) Canon David Harrex, The Rectory, 97 Canterbury Close, Yate, Bristol BS37 5TU   *Tel:* 01454 311483 (*Chairman, House of Laity*) Prof. Gordon Stirrat, Malpas Lodge, 24 Henbury Rd, Bristol BS9 3HJ
Tel: 0117 950 5310
Board of Finance (*Chairman*) Mr David Froude, c/o Dioc Church House; (*Secretary*) Mrs Lesley Farrall, Dioc Church House
Finance Manager Mr David Hargrave, Dioc Church House
Mission and Pastoral Committee (*Secretary*) Mrs Lesley Farrall (*as above*)
Dioc Electoral Registration Officer Ms Lynette Cox (*as above*)
Designated Officer Mr Tim Berry, Harris and Harris, 14 Market Place, Wells BA5 2RE
Tel: 01749 674747
Fax: 01749 676585
Child Protection Officer Mrs Carolyn Buckeridge
Tel: 0844 892 0104
Safeguarding Vulnerable Adults Officer Mrs Jeanette Plumb   *Tel:* 07866 495802
0117 906 0100

CHURCHES

Advisory Committee for the Care of Churches (*Chairman*) Revd James Wilson, St Gregory's Vicarage, Filton Rd, Horfield, Bristol BS7 0PD
Tel: 0117 969 2839
email: revjameswilson@aol.com
(*Secretary*) Mr Tim Berry
(*Asst Secretary*) Mrs Jane Holmes, c/o Harris and Harris, 14 Market Place, Wells BA5 2RE
Tel: 01749 674747
Fax: 01749 676585

EDUCATION

Board of Education (*Director*) Mrs J. Waters-Dewhurst, All Saints RE Centre, 1 All Saints Court, Bristol BS1 1JN   *Tel:* 0117 906 0100
Fax: 0117 925 0404
email: allsaints@bristoldiocese.org

DIOCESAN LAY MINISTERS' COUNCIL

Secretary Mrs Anne Iles, 119 Monks Park Ave, Horfield, Bristol BS7 0UA   *Tel:* 0117 969 2371

DIOCESAN ECUMENICAL AND GLOBAL DEVELOPMENT OFFICER

Revd Chris Dobson, Dioc Church House

MINISTRY DEVELOPMENT

Adviser for Initial Ministerial Education (*DDO*) Revd Derek Chedzey, Dioc Church House
Adviser for Licensed Ministry (*DDO*) Revd Samantha Rushton, Dioc Church House
Asst Adviser for Licensed Ministry (*DDO*) Canon Ray Brazier   *Tel:* 0117 952 3209
email: rayvb@tiscali.co.uk
Administrators Miss Rachel Williams, Mrs Stella O'Brien, Dioc Church House

STRATEGY SUPPORT

Director of Strategy Support Canon Douglas Holt, Dioc Church House
Vacancy Development Adviser Mr George Rendell, Dioc Church House
Vacancy Development Adviser Mrs Melanie Griffiths, Dioc Church House
Adviser on Growth Revd Paul Rush, 5 Gold View, Rushy Platt, Swindon SN5 8ZG
Tel: 01793 872 853
email: rev.paul.rush@ntlworld.com
Department Administrator Miss Clare Franklin, Dioc Church House

ADVISER FOR MINISTERIAL SUPPORT

Vacancy, Dioc Church House

DEAN OF WOMEN'S MINISTRY

Canon Christine Froude, St Mary's Vicarage, 8 Priory Gardens, Shirehampton, Bristol BS11 0BZ
Tel: 0117 985 5450
email: christinefroude@lineone.net

BISHOP'S ADVISORY GROUP ON HEALING

Chairman Revd Ros Wilson, 10 Druid Stoke Avenue, Stoke Bishop, Bristol BS9 1DD
Tel: 0117 330 1610
email: rosw@another.com

DIOCESAN WORSHIP AND LITURGY COMMITTEE

Chairman Preb Gill Behenna, 1 Saxon Way, Bradley Stoke, Bristol BS32 9AR
Tel: 01454 202483
email: gill@signsofgod.org

PRESS, PUBLICITY AND PUBLICATIONS

Communications Officer and Press Officer Mr Oliver Home   *Tel:* 01454 777728
email: oliver.home@bristoldiocese.org
Editor of Dioc Directory Ms Lynette Cox, Dioc Church House

DIOCESAN RECORD OFFICES

Bristol Record Office, 'B' Bond, Smeaton Rd, Bristol BS1 6XN *County Archivist* Mr J. S. Williams, *Tel:* 0117 922 4224 (*For parish records in the archdeaconry of Bristol*)
Wiltshire and Swindon History Centre, Cocklebury Rd, Chippenham SN15 3QN *County Archivist* Mr John Darcy, *Tel:* 01249 705500 (*For parish records in the archdeaconry of Malmesbury*)

DIOCESAN RESOURCE CENTRE

All Saints Centre, 1 All Saints Court, Bristol BS1 1JN   *Tel:* 0117 906 0100
Fax: 0117 925 0404
email: allsaints@bristoldiocese.org

THE CHURCHES' COUNCIL FOR INDUSTRY AND SOCIAL RESPONSIBILITY

Director Revd Jon Doble, 162 Pennywell Rd, Bristol BS5 0TX   *Tel:* 0117 955 7430
Fax: 0117 955 7436
email: jon@ccisr.org.uk

The Pilgrim Centre, Regents Circus, Swindon SN1 1PX *Tel* and *Fax:* 01793 491454
email: isrswindon@btconnect.com
Administrators Mrs Alison Paginton, Mrs Christine Durant (Swindon, part-time), Mrs Vena Prater (part-time)
Industrial Chaplain Revd Tim Harrison
Chaplain for Economic Life (*Swindon*) Revd Angela Overton-Benge
Social Responsibility Officer (*Swindon and Wiltshire*) Revd Dr Simon Topping (part-time)
Social Responsibility Officer (*Bristol*) Dr Simon Bale
Inter-Faith Adviser Vacancy
Church Urban Fund Officer Revd Jon Doble
Senior Chaplain Avon and Somerset Constabulary Pastor Andy Paget (part-time)
Senior Chaplain Wiltshire Constabulary Revd Dr Richard Armitage (part-time)
Chaplain to the City Centre (*Bristol*) Canon Timothy Higgins (part-time)
Marriage and Family Life Adviser Mrs Alison Paginton
Community Ministry Adviser Mrs Sandra O'Shea
Major Emergency Plan Administrator Mrs Sheila Tubey (volunteer)

AREA DEANS
ARCHDEACONRY OF BRISTOL
Bristol South Revd Gwyn Owen, Vicarage, Goslet Rd, Stockwood, Bristol BS14 8SP
Tel: 01275 831138
email: christtheservant@blueyonder.co.uk

Bristol West Canon Mark Pilgrim, St Peter's Vicarage, 17 The Drive, Henleaze, Bristol BS9 4LD
Tel: 0117 962 0636
email: markpilgrimis@aol.com
City Revd Mat Ineson, St Matthew's Vicarage, 11 Glentworth Road, Redland, Bristol BS6 7EG
Tel: 0117 942 4186
email: mat.ineson@bristol.anglican.org

ARCHDEACONRY OF MALMESBURY
Chippenham Revd Simon Tyndall, The Rectory, 9 Greenway Park, Chippenham SN15 1QG
Tel and *Fax:* 01249 657216
email: simon@tyndall.plus.com
Kingswood and South Gloucestershire Revd David Adams, Vicarage, 85 Bath Rd, Longwell Green, Bristol BS30 9DF
Tel: 0117 932 3714
email: djaadams@surfaid.org
North Wiltshire Revd Neill Archer, Abbey Vicarage, Holloway, Malmesbury SN16 9BA
Tel: 01666 837187
email: andrew@evansa63.fsnet.co.uk
Swindon Canon Rob Burles, Rectory, Verwood Close, Park North, Swindon SN3 2LE
Tel: 01793 611473
Fax: 01793 574924
email: rob@burles.org.uk

DIOCESE OF CANTERBURY

Founded in 597. Kent east of the Medway, excluding
the Medway Towns (ROCHESTER).

Population 875,000   Area 970 sq m
Full-time Stipendiary Parochial Clergy 127   Benefices 155
Parishes 262   Churches 329
www.canterburydiocese.org
Overseas link dioceses: Antananarivo, Antsiranana,
Toamasina, Mahajanga (Madagascar), Arras (Pas-de-Calais), Basel.

ARCHBISHOP (104th)
Most Revd and Rt Hon Rowan Douglas Williams,
Primate of all England and Metropolitan, Lambeth
Palace, London SE1 7JU *Tel:* 020 7898 1200;
Fax: 020 7261 9836 and Old Palace, Canterbury,
Kent CT1 2EE. *Tel:* 01227 459382, *Fax:* 01227
784985 [2003]
[Rowan Cantuar:]
Dioc Chaplain Revd Martin Short

*Matters relating to the Diocese of Canterbury should
be referred to the* **Bishop of Dover** *(see below)*
For the **Archbishop of Canterbury's Personal
Staff** *see page* 4

PRO-DIOCESAN BISHOP
DOVER: Rt Revd Trevor Willmott, Old Palace,
Canterbury, Kent CT1 2EE, *Tel:* 01227 459382,
Fax: 01227 784985 [2010]
Chaplain Revd Martin Short, Old Palace,
Canterbury, Kent CT1 2EE, *Tel:* 01227 459382,
Fax: 01227 784985
Hon Chaplains Canon Alan Duke, Roundways,
Derringstone Hill, Barham, Canterbury CT4 6QD,
Tel: 01227 831812, *email:* mail@alanaduke.com
Canon Ron Diss, 35 Castle Row, Canterbury
CT1 2QY, *Tel:* 01227 462410

SUFFRAGAN BISHOPS
MAIDSTONE Vacancy

PROVINCIAL EPISCOPAL VISITORS
EBBSFLEET Vacancy
RICHBOROUGH Vacancy

HONORARY ASSISTANT BISHOPS
Rt Revd Graham Cray, Rectory, Church Rd,
Harrietsham, Maidstone ME17 1AP
Tel: 01622 851170
email: grahamcray@btconnect.com
Rt Revd Michael Gear, 10 Acott Fields, Yalding,
Maidstone ME18 6DQ   *Tel:* 01622 817388
email: bp_mikegear@yahoo.com
Rt Revd Richard Llewellin, 193 Ashford Rd,
Thanington, Canterbury CT1 3XS
Tel: 01227 789515
email: rllewellin@clara.co.uk

Rt Revd Anthony Michael Turnbull, 67 Strand St,
Sandwich CT13 9HN   *Tel:* 01304 611389
email: bstmt@btopenworld.com

**CATHEDRAL AND METROPOLITICAL
CHURCH OF CHRIST**
Dean Very Revd Dr Robert Willis, The Deanery,
The Precincts, Canterbury CT1 2EP [2001]
Tel: 01227 865200 (Office)
email: dean@canterbury-cathedral.org
Cathedral Office Cathedral House, 11 The
Precincts, Canterbury CT1 2EH
Tel: 01227 762862
Fax: 01227 865222
Canons Residentiary
Canon Treasurer and Director of Education Canon
Dr Edward Condry, 15 The Precincts, Canter-
bury CT1 2EP [2002]   *Tel:* 01227 865228
email: edwardc@canterbury-cathedral.org
*Canon Librarian and Director of Post Ordination
Training* Canon Christopher Irvine, 19 The
Precincts, Canterbury CT1 2EP [2007]
Tel: 01227 865226
email: canon.irvine@canterbury-cathedral.org
Canon Pastor Canon Clare Edwards, 22 The
Precincts, Canterbury CT1 2EP [2004]
Tel: 01227 865227
email: canonclare@canterbury-cathedral.org
Archdeacon Ven Sheila Watson, 29 The Precincts,
Canterbury CT1 2EP [2007]   *Tel:* 01227 865238
Fax: 01227 785209
email: archdeacon@canterbury-cathedral.org
Precentor and Sacrist David Mackenzie Mills,
2 Starrs House, Canterbury CT1 2EH
Tel: 01227 876225
email: precentor@canterbury-cathedral.org
Receiver General Brigadier M. J. Meardon,
Cathedral House   *Tel:* 01227 865212
email: ReceiverGeneral@canterbury-cathedral.org
Cathedral organist Dr David Flood, 6 The Pre-
cincts, Canterbury CT1 2EE   *Tel:* 01227 865242
email: organist@canterbury-cathedral.org

ARCHDEACONS
CANTERBURY Ven Sheila Watson, 29 The Precincts,
Canterbury CT1 2EP [2007]   *Tel:* 01227 865238
Fax: 01227 785209
email: archdeacon@canterbury-cathedral.org

MAIDSTONE Ven Philip Down, The Old Rectory, The Street, Pluckley TN27 0QT [2002]
Tel: 01233 840291
Fax: 01233 840759
email: pdown@archdeacmaid.org

CONVOCATION (MEMBERS OF THE HOUSE OF CLERGY OF THE GENERAL SYNOD)
Dignitaries in Convocation
The Dean of Canterbury
Proctors for Clergy
Revd Canon Clare Edwards
Ven Philip Down
Canon Mark Roberts

MEMBERS OF THE HOUSE OF LAITY OF THE GENERAL SYNOD
Mr David Kemp
Mrs Caroline Spencer
Miss Sara Muggeridge

DIOCESAN OFFICERS
Diocesan House, Lady Wootton's Green, Canterbury CT1 1NQ
Tel: 01227 459401
Fax: 01227 450964
Please note that individual Diocesan Officers may be emailed on initialsurname@diocant.org (e.g. jhills@diocant.org)
Dioc Secretary Mr Julian Hills   *Fax:* 01227 787073
email: jhills@diocant.org
Commissary General His Honour Judge Richard Walker, c/o The Registry, Minerva House, 5 Montague Close, London SE1 9BB
Tel: 020 7593 5000
Dioc Registrar and Legal Adviser to the Diocese Mr Owen Carew-Jones, Minerva House, 5 Montague Close, London SE1 9BB
Tel: 020 7593 5110

DIOCESAN ORGANIZATIONS
Diocesan House, Lady Wootton's Green, Canterbury CT1 1NQ
Tel: 01227 459401
Fax: 01227 450964
email: reception@diocant.org

ADMINISTRATION
Dioc Synod (Chairman, House of Clergy) Canon Mark Roberts, Rectory, Knightrider St, Sandwich CT13 9ER
Tel: 01304 613138
email: revdmarkroberts@supanet.com
(Chairman, House of Laity) Mrs Caroline Spencer, Little Eggarton, Godmersham, Canterbury CT4 7DY
Tel: 01227 731170
email: caroline@eggarton.eclipse.co.uk
(Secretary) Mr Julian Hills, Dioc House
Board of Finance (Chairman) Mr Raymond Harris
(Secretary) Mr Julian Hills *(as above)*
Designated Officer Ms Gillian Marsh, Dioc House
Dioc Accountant Mr Rob Trice, Dioc House

Director of Property Services Mr Philip Bell, Old Palace, The Precincts, Canterbury CT1 2EE
Tel: 01227 478390
email: pbell@diocant.org
Chairman Mr Brian Marshall

CHURCHES
Advisory Committee for the Care of Churches (Secretary) Mr Ian Dodd, Old Palace, The Precincts, Canterbury CT1 2EE
Tel: 01227 478390
email: idodd@diocant.org
Chairman Dr Richard Morrice, 3 Stafford Rd, Tunbridge Wells TN25 4QZ

EDUCATION
Chairman Professor Michael Wright CBE
Director of Education Revd Nigel Genders, Dioc House

MINISTRY
Chair Ven Philip Down *(see* Archdeacon of Maidstone)
Director of Training Canon Rob Mackintosh, Dioc House
Director of Ordinands Revd Clive Todd, Dioc House
Assistant Directors of Ordinands
Revd Mark Ball   *Tel:* 01227 472557,
email: mark@canterburycityparish.org.uk
Revd Marian Bond   *Tel:* 01622 858251,
email: mnhbond@googlemail.com
Revd Philip Brown   *Tel:* 01227 730141,
email: filbrown@btinternet.com
Revd Sheila Cox   *Tel:* 01233 501193,
email: sheila.m.cox@btopenworld.com
Revd Jacqui Cray   *Tel:* 01622 673068,
email: jackiecray@hotmail.co.uk
Revd Steven Wilson   *Tel:* 01795 536801,
email: revdscwilson@tiscali.co.uk
Adviser for Women's Ministry Revd Hilary Jones, St Martin's Rectory, Horn St, Cheriton, Folkestone CT20 3JJ   *Tel:* 01303 238509
email: revhilaryjones@btinternet.com
Local Ministry Training Scheme Principal Dr Ivan Khovacs, Dioc House
Local Ministry Training Scheme Director of Studies Dr Wendy Dackson, Dioc House
Local Ministry Officer Revd Peter Ingrams, Dioc House
Ministry Development Officer Mr Neville Emslie, Dioc House
Association of Readers (Warden) Mrs Hilary Richter, Dioc House
Deputy Wardens of Readers Mrs Pat Tatchell, *Tel:* 01795 471 956, *email:* tatch@blueyonder.co.uk, Canon Rosemary Walters, *Tel:* 01227 768891, *email:* rosemary.walters@canterbury.ac.uk
(Hon Secretary) Mr Nigel Collins, 79 Alfred Rd, Dover CT16 2AD   *Tel:* 01304 204737
email: nigelcollins@cross-links.org.uk

Clergy Retirement Officer
Canterbury Archdeaconery (*minus Dover and Elham Deaneries*), Revd Grahame Whittlesea
Tel: 01227 472536
email: gandawhittlesea@tiscali.co.uk
Maidstone Archdeaconery (*plus Dover and Elham Deaneries*), Revd Ron Gamble
email: r-gamble@sky.com

LITURGICAL COMMITTEE
Bishop's Advisor Revd Liz Hawkes
Tel: 01227 360948
email: lizhawkes@tiscali.co.uk
Secretary Vacancy

MISSION AND ECUMENICAL
Chairman Vacancy
Secretary Revd Andrew Sewell   Tel: 01622 861470
email: andrew@asewell.plus.com
Diocesan Missioners
Fresh Expressions of Church Canon Kerry Thorpe
Tel: 01843 871183
email: Kerrythorpe@harvestnac.freeserve.co.uk
Inherited Models of Church Revd Richard King
Tel: 01233 712598
email: richarddking@hotmail.com
Children's Missioner Captain Graham Nunn, CA
Tel: 01622 672088

COMMUNICATONS
Communications Director and Deputy Diocesan Secretary Mrs Emily Shepherd, Dioc House
Editor of Dioc Directory, ICT Administrator: Mr Mark Binns, Dioc House
HR Adviser Mrs Sarah Carruthers, Dioc House

DIOCESAN RECORD OFFICES
Cathedral Archives and Library, The Precincts, Canterbury CT1 2EH *Tel:* 01227 865330 (*For parish records in the archdeaconry of Canterbury*)
Centre for Kentish Studies, County Hall, Maidstone ME14 1XQ *Tel:* 01622 754321 (*For parish records in the archdeaconry of Maidstone*)

STEWARDSHIP
Adviser Mrs Liz Marsh, Dioc House
Part-time Adviser Mrs Jenny Hunt, Dioc House

AREA DEANS
ARCHDEACONRY OF CANTERBURY
Canterbury Canon Noelle Hall, Rectory, 13 Ersham Rd, Canterbury CT1 3AR
Tel: 01227 462686
Fax: noelle@thinker117.freeserve.co.uk

Dover Revd David Ridley, St Mary's Vicarage, Taswell St, Dover CT16 1SE   Tel: 01304 206842
email: davidridley@btopenworld.com
East Bridge Revd John Sweatman, Vicarage, Queens Rd, Ash, Canterbury CT3 2BG
Tel: 01304 812296
email: thevicar@s8nicholas.org.uk
Elham Revd Hilary Jones, St Martin's Rectory, Horn St, Cheriton CT20 3JJ   Tel: 01303 238509
email: revhilaryjones@btinternet.com
Ospringe Canon Tony Oehring, Vicarage, 16 Newton Rd, Faversham ME13 8DY
Tel: 01795 532592
email: vicar@stmaryofcharity.org
Reculver Revd Ron Hawkes, Vicarage, 25 Dence Park, Herne Bay CT6 6BQ   Tel: 01227 360948
email: reverendronald@tiscali.co.uk
Sandwich Vacancy
Thanet Revd Paul Worledge, St Luke's Vicarage, St Luke's Avenue, Ramsgate CT11 7JX
Tel: 01843 592562
email: vicar@stlukesramsgate.org
West Bridge Revd Margi Walker, Rectory, Curtis Lane, Stelling Minnis, Canterbury CT4 6BT
Tel: 01233 709318
email: margiwalker@uwclub.net

ARCHDEACONRY OF MAIDSTONE
Ashford Canon Lindsay Hammond, Vicarage, Westwell, Ashford TN25 4LQ   Tel: 01233 712576
email: lindsayhammond@hotmail.co.uk
Maidstone Revd Andrew Sewell, St Paul's Vicarage, 130 Boxley Road, Maidstone ME14 2AH   *email:* andrew@asewell@plus.com
North Downs Revd Susan Hollins, Vicarage, The Street, Boxley, Maidstone ME14 3DX
Tel: 01622 600440
email: s.hollins540@btinternet.com
Romney Revd Neville Gallagher, Vicarage, Old Way, Appledore TN26 2DB   Tel: 01233 758250
email: nrwg45@aol.com
Sittingbourne Revd John Lewis, Vicarage, School Lane, Borden, Sittingbourne ME9 8JS
Tel: 01795 472986
email: fr.johnlewis@tiscali.co.uk
Tenterden Revd Jacques Desrosiers, Vicarage, Rolvenden TN17 4ND   Tel: 01580 241235
email: vicarage1965@btinternet.com
The Weald Revd Bill Hornsby, Vicarage, Back Lane, Goudhurst, Cranbrook TN17 1AN
Tel: 01580 211739
email: billhornsby@btinternet.com

DIOCESE OF CARLISLE

Founded in 1133. Cumbria, except for small areas in
the east (NEWCASTLE, BRADFORD).

Population 491,000   Area 2,477 sq m
Full-time Stipendiary Parochial Clergy 124   Benefices 123
Parishes 263   Churches 344
www.carlisle.anglican.org
Overseas link dioceses: Madras (CSI), Zululand (South Africa),
Stavanger (Norway), Northern Argentina.

BISHOP (67th)
Rt Revd James Newcome, [2009], Holm Croft,
13 Castle Road, Kendal LA9 7AU
Tel: 01539 727836
email: bishop.carlisle@carlislediocese.org.uk
[James Carliol]
Bishop's Chaplain Vacancy
email: bishop.chaplain@carlislediocese.org.uk

SUFFRAGAN BISHOP
PENRITH Vacancy

HONORARY ASSISTANT BISHOPS
Rt Revd Ian Macdonald Griggs, Rookings,
Patterdale, Penrith CA11 0NP [1994]
Tel: 01768 482064
email: ian.griggs@virgin.net
Rt Revd George Lanyon Hacker, Keld House,
Milburn, Penrith CA10 1TW [1994]
Tel: 01768 361506
email: bishhack@mypostoffice.co.uk
Rt Revd Andrew Alexander Kenny Graham, Fell
End, Butterwick, Penrith CA10 2QQ [1997]
Tel: 01931 713147
Rt Revd Hewlett Thompson, Low Broomrigg,
Warcop, Appleby CA16 6PT [2000]
Tel: 01768 341281
Rt Revd Robert Hardy, Carleton House, Back
Lane, Langwathby, Penrith CA10 1NB [2002]
Tel: 01768 881210
Rt Revd John Richardson, The Old Rectory, Bew-
castle, Carlisle CA6 6PS [2003]   *Tel:* 01697 748389

CATHEDRAL CHURCH OF THE HOLY AND UNDIVIDED TRINITY
Dean Very Revd Mark Boyling, The Deanery,
Carlisle CA3 8TZ [2004]   *Tel:* 01228 523335
Fax: 01228 547049
email: dean@carlislecathedral.org.uk
Cathedral Office 7 The Abbey, Carlisle CA3 8TZ
Tel: 01228 548151
Fax: 01228 547049
email: office@carlislecathedral.org.uk
Web: www.carlislecathedral.org.uk
Canons Residentiary
Canon Brian Roy McConnell, 3 The Abbey,
Carlisle CA3 8TZ [2006]   *Tel:* 01228 521834
email: canonwarden@carlislecathedral.org.uk

Ven Kevin Thomas Roberts, 2 The Abbey, Carlisle,
CA3 8TZ [2009]   *Tel:* 01228 523026
email: archdeacon.north@carlislediocese.org.uk
Canon Michael Alan Manley, 14 The Abbey,
Carlisle CA3 8TZ [2007]   *Tel:* 01228 542790
email: canonmissioner@carlislecathedral.org.uk

Lay Members of Chapter
Dr Philip Herrick, Fircroft, Houghton, Carlisle
CA6 4HZ [2001]
Two vacancies
Bursar and Chapter Clerk Mr Ian Burns, Cathedral
Office
Administrative Officer Mrs Carolyne Baines,
Cathedral Office
Cathedral Organist Mr Jeremy Suter, 6 The Abbey,
Carlisle CA3 8TZ   *Tel:* 01228 526646
Fax: 01228 547049
email: jeremysuter@hotmail.com

ARCHDEACONS
CARLISLE Ven Kevin Roberts, 2 The Abbey,
Carlisle CA3 8TZ [2009]   *Tel:* 01228 523026
email: archdeacon.north@carlislediocese.org.uk
WEST CUMBERLAND Ven Richard Pratt, 50 Stain-
burn Rd, Workington CA14 1SN [2009]
Tel: 01900 66190
email: archdeacon.west@carlislediocese.org.uk
WESTMORLAND AND FURNESS Ven George Howe,
Vicarage, Windermere Rd, Lindale, Grange over
Sands LA11 6LB [2000]   *Tel:* 01539 534717
Fax: 01539 535090
email: archdeacon.south@carlislediocese.org.uk

CONVOCATION (MEMBERS OF THE HOUSE OF CLERGY OF THE GENERAL SYNOD)
Proctors for Clergy
Revd Ferial Etherington
Ven George Howe
Canon Nigel Davies
Revd Simon Austen

MEMBERS OF THE HOUSE OF LAITY OF THE GENERAL SYNOD
Dr Christopher Angus
Dr Charles Hanson
Mr Peter Hine
Mr David Mills

Carlisle

DIOCESAN OFFICERS

Dioc Secretary Mr Derek Hurton, Church House, West Walls, Carlisle CA3 8UE   *Tel:* 01228 522573
01228 815402 (Direct Line)
Fax: 01228 815400
email: diocesan.secretary@carlislediocese.org.uk
Chancellor of Diocese Mr Geoffrey Tattersall, 2 The Woodlands, Lostock, Bolton BL6 4JD
Registrar of Diocese and Bishop's Legal Secretary Mrs Jane Lowdon, Sintons Solicitors, The Cube, Barrack Rd, Newcastle-upon-Tyne NE4 6DB
Tel: 0191 226 7878
Fax: 0191 226 7852
email: j.lowdon@sintons.co.uk

DIOCESAN ORGANIZATIONS

Diocesan Office Church House, West Walls, Carlisle CA3 8UE   *Tel:* 01228 522573
Fax: 01228 815400
email: enquiries@carlislediocese.org.uk
Web: www.carlislediocese.org.uk

ADMINISTRATION

Dioc Synod (*Chairman, House of Clergy*) Revd Dr Peter Tiplady, Meadow Croft, Wetheral, Carlisle CA4 8JG   *Tel:* 01228 561611
email: petertiplady@mac.com
(*Chairman, House of Laity*) Mr Michael Bonner, 1 Fell View, Branthwaite, Workington CA14 4SY
Tel: 01900 605536
email: mimbonner@talktalk.net
(*Secretary*) Mr Derek Hurton, Dioc Office
Board of Finance (*Chairman*) Mr John Lee, Millersholme, Lanercost, Brampton CA8 2HL
Tel: 016977 2515
(*Secretary*) Mr Derek Hurton (*as above*)
Assistant Dioc Secretary (*Finance*) Mr Neil Barrett, Dioc Office   *Tel:* 01228 815404
Assistant Dioc Secretary (*Property*) Mr Brian Cook, Dioc Office   *Tel:* 01228 815403
Finance Resources Officer Mr Geoffrey Hine, Dioc Office   *Tel:* 01228 815401
Pastoral Committee Vacancy   *Tel:* 01228 815408
Designated Officer Mrs Jane Lowdon (*as above*)

CHURCHES

Advisory Committee for the Care of Churches (*Chairman*) Lord Hothfield, Drybeck Hall, Appleby in Westmorland CA16 6TF; (*Secretary*) Mr Derek Hurton, Dioc Office; (*Administrative Secretary*) Mr Brian Cook (*as above*)

EDUCATION

Board of Education, Church Centre, West Walls, Carlisle CA3 8UE   *Tel:* 01228 538086
Fax: 01228 815409
email: education@carlislediocese.org.uk
Director of Education Vacancy
Senior Schools Officer Revd Bert Thomas, Church Centre   *Tel:* 0845 395 0646
RE Officer Mr Stephen Mott, Church Centre
Diocesan Youth Officer Vacancy

MINISTRY AND TRAINING

Ministry Development Adviser Canon Amiel Osmaston, Dioc Office   *Tel:* 01228 815406
email: ministry.dev@carlislediocese.org.uk
Principal Lancashire and Cumbria Theological Partnership and Adviser for Ministry and Training Canon Tim Herbert, Dioc Office
Tel: 01228 815405
email: admin@lctp.co.uk
Adviser for Clergy Training Revd Ruth Crossley, Vicarage, Levens, Kendal LA8 8PY
Tel: 01539 560233
email: cme@carlislediocese.org.uk
Director of Ordinands Vacancy, Church House, West Walls, Carlisle, CA3 8UE
email: bishop.chaplain@carlislediocese.org.uk
Adviser for Women's Ministry Canon Mary Day, Vicarage, Cross Canonby, Maryport CA15 6SJ
Tel: 01900 814192
email: vicarmary@talktalk.net

SOCIAL RESPONSIBILITY

Churches Social Action Network Ven Richard Pratt, 50 Stainburn Road, Workington CA14 1SN
Tel: 01900 66190
email: archdeacon.west@carlislediocese.org.uk
Industrial Mission Ven Richard Pratt (*as above*)

ECUMENICAL AFFAIRS

Diocesan Ecumenical Officer Ven George Howe, Vicarage, Windermere Rd, Lindale, Grange over Sands LA11 6LB [2000]   *Tel:* 01539 534717
Fax: 01539 535090
email: archdeacon.south@carlislediocese.org.uk
Churches Together in Cumbria (*Ecumenical Development Officer*) Revd Ruth Harvey, Croslands, Beacon Street, Penrith CA11 7TZ
Tel: 07882 259631
email: rctic@phonecoop.coop
Rural Officer Revd Sarah Lunn, Rectory, Long Marton, Appleby in Westmorland CA16 6BN
Tel: 01768 361269
email: sarahlunn@care4free.net

EVANGELISM

Diocesan Officer Revd John Reeves, Vicarage, Irthington, Carlisle CA6 9NJ   *Tel:* 01697 741864

PARTNERSHIP IN WORLD MISSION

Officer Mrs Lynne Tembey, Holm Cultram. Vicarage, Abbeytown, Wigton CA7 4SP
Tel: 01697 361246
Fax: 01697 61506

PRESS AND PUBLICATIONS

Communications Officer Mrs Hannah Horton
Tel: 07809 613531
email: communications@carlislediocese.org.uk
Editor of Dioc News Mrs Hannah Horton
Dioc Directory Mrs Jean Hardman, Dioc Office
Tel: 01228 815408
email: jean.hardman@carlislediocese.org.uk

DIOCESAN ARCHIVIST
County Archivist Ms A. Rowe   *Tel:* 01228 226477

DIOCESAN RECORD OFFICES
Cumbria Record Office, The Castle, Carlisle CA3
8UR   *Tel:* 01228 227285
    email: carlisle.record.office@cumbriacc.gov.uk
Cumbria Record Office, County Offices, Kendal
LA9 4RQ   *Tel:* 01539 773540
    email: kendal.record.office@cumbriacc.gov.uk
Cumbria Record Office & Local Studies Library,
140 Duke St, Barrow-in-Furness LA14 1XW
    Tel: 01229 894363
    email: barrow.record.office@cumbriacc.gov.uk
Cumbria Record Office and Local Studies
Library, Scotch St, Whitehaven CA28 7BJ
    Tel: 01946 506420
email:
    whitehaven.record.office@cumbriacc.gov.uk

RURAL DEANS
ARCHDEACONRY OF CARLISLE
Appleby Revd Carole Marsden, Fairfield, Faraday
Road, Kirkby Stephen, CA17 4QL
    Tel: 017683 71279
    email: carole.sam@hotmail.co.uk
Brampton Revd Gary Cregeen, Vicarage,
Lambley Bank, Scotby, Carlisle CA4 8BX
    Tel: 01228 513205
    email: gary@CandJCregeen.co.uk
Carlisle Canon John Libby, St James Vicarage,
Goschen Rd, Carlisle CA2 5PF   *Tel:* 01228 515639
    Fax: 01228 524569
    email: john.libby@btinternet.com

Penrith Revd Richard Moatt, Vicarage, 1 Low
Farm, Langwathby, Penrith CA10 1NH
    Tel: 01768 881212
    email: moatt@btinternet.com

**ARCHDEACONRY OF WESTMORLAND AND
FURNESS**
Barrow Revd Ian Hook, St Mark's Vicarage,
Rawlinson St, Barrow in Furness LA14 1BX
    Tel: 01229 820405
    email: ianhook@dsl.pipex.com
Furness Canon Gary Wemyss, Vicarage, Penny
Bridge, Ulverston LA12 7RQ   *Tel:* 01229 861285
    email: gwemyss@clara.co.uk
Kendal Revd Tim Harmer, Sunnybank, Under-
barrow, Kendal, Cumbria LA8 8HG
    Tel: 01539 568865
    email: ruraldean_kendal@hotmail.com
Windermere Canon Robert Coke, Vicarage, Mil-
lans Park, Ambleside LA22 9AD
    Tel: 01539 433205
    email: vicar@amblesidechurch.org.uk

ARCHDEACONRY OF WEST CUMBERLAND
Calder Revd John Woolcock, Vicarage, Seascale,
Cumbria CA20 1QT   *Tel:* 01946 728217
    email: john.woolcock@btinternet.com
Derwent Revd Stephen Walker, Vicarage,
Torpenhow, Wigton CA7 1HT   *Tel:* 016973 71541
    email: rector@binsey.org.uk
Solway Canon Mary Day, Vicarage, Cross
Canonby, Maryport CA15 6SJ   *Tel:* 01900 814192
    email: vicarmary@talktalk.net

DIOCESE OF CHELMSFORD

Founded in 1914. Essex, except for a few parishes in the north (ELY, ST EDMUNDSBURY AND IPSWICH); five East London boroughs north of the Thames; three parishes in south Cambridgeshire.

Population 2,840,000   Area 1,531 sq m
Full-time Stipendiary Parochial Clergy 352   Benefices 328
Parishes 466   Churches 600
www.chelmsford.anglican.org

Overseas link dioceses: Embu, Mbeere, Kirinyaga, Meru (Kenya); Trinidad and Tobago; Karlstad; Iasi (Romania)

BISHOP

Rt Revd Stephen Cottrell, Bishopscourt, Margaretting, Ingatestone CM4 0HD
Tel: 01277 352001
Fax: 01277 355374
email: bishopscourt@chelmsford.anglican.org
Bishop's Chaplain Vacancy (*same address*)
Tel: 01277 352001
Fax: 01277 355374
email: @chelmsford.anglican.org
Director of Communications and Bishop's Press Officer Ralph Meloy   *Tel:* 01245 294424 (Office)
07654 382674 (Pager)
email: rmeloy@chelmsford.anglican.org

AREA BISHOPS

BARKING Rt Revd David John Leader Hawkins, Barking Lodge, Verulam Ave, London E17 8ES [2003]   *Tel:* 020 8509 7377
email: b.barking@chelmsford.anglican.org
BRADWELL Rt Revd Laurence Alexander Green, Bishop's House, Orsett Rd, Horndon-on-the-Hill SS17 8NS [1993]   *Tel:* 01375 673806
Fax: 01375 674222
email: b.bradwell@chelmsford.anglican.org
COLCHESTER Rt Revd Christopher Heudebourck Morgan, 1 Fitzwalter Rd, Lexden, Colchester CO3 3SS [2001]   *Tel:* 01206 576648
Fax: 01206 763868
email: b.colchester@chelmsford.anglican.org

HONORARY ASSISTANT BISHOPS

Rt Revd Keith Newton, Richborough House, 6 Mellish Gardens, Woodford Green IG8 0BH
Tel: 020 8505 7259
email: keith@newtonfam.freeserve.co.uk
Rt Revd Charles Derek Bond, 52 Horn Brook, Saffron Walden, Essex CB11 3JW
Tel: 01799 521308
email: bondd@aol.com
Rt Revd John Martin Ball, 5 Hillview Rd, Chelmsford CM1 7RS   *Tel:* 01245 268296
email: ball_john@onetel.com

CATHEDRAL CHURCH OF ST MARY THE VIRGIN, ST PETER AND ST CEDD

Dean Very Revd Peter Judd, The Dean's House, 3 Harlings Grove, Chelmsford CM1 1YQ [1997]
Tel: 01245 354318 (Home)
01245 294492 (Office)
email: dean@chelmsfordcathedral.org.uk
Cathedral Office 53 New St, Chelmsford CM1 1TY
Tel: 01245 294489
Fax: 01245 294499
Web: www.chelmsfordcathedral.org.uk

Canons Residentiary
Vice-Dean Canon Ivor Moody, 4 Bishopscourt Gardens, Springfield, Chelmsford CM2 6AZ
Tel: 01245 294493 (Office)
01245 267773 (Home)
email: vicedean@chelmsfordcathedral.org.uk

Canon Theologian Canon Andrew Knowles, 2 Harlings Grove, Chelmsford CM1 1YQ [1998]
Tel: 01245 355041 (Home)
01245 294484 (Office)
email: theologian@chelmsfordcathedral.org.uk

Canon Precentor Canon Simon Pothen, 1a Harlings Grove, Chelmsford CM1 1YQ [2007]
Tel: 01245 491599 (Home)
Tel: 01245 294482 (Office)
email: precentor@chelmsfordcathedral.org.uk

Hon Associate Chaplain Vacancy

Hon Associate Chaplain and Bishop's Chaplain Vacancy

Hon Associate Chaplain and Diocesan Director of Ordinands Canon Richard More, 25 Roxwell Rd, Chelmsford CM1 2LY   *Tel:* 01245 264187
email: ddo@chelmsford.anglican.org

Cathedral Administrator and Chapter Clerk Revd Philip Tarris, Cathedral Office
Tel: 01245 294488
email: administrator@chelmsfordcathedral.org.uk

28   Dioceses

Director of Music Mr Peter Nardone, 1 Harlings Grove, Chelmsford CM1 1YQ
Tel: 01245 262006 (Home)
01245 252429 (Office)
email: dom@chelmsfordcathedral.org.uk

Assistant Director of Music Mr Oliver Waterer
Tel: 01245 252429
email: adom@chelmsfordcathedral.org.uk

ARCHDEACONS
COLCHESTER Ven Annette Cooper, 63 Powers Hall End, Witham CM8 1NH [2004]
Tel: 01376 513130
Fax: 01376 500789
email: a.colchester@chelmsford.anglican.org
HARLOW Ven Martin Webster, Glebe House, Church Lane, Sheering CM22 7NR [2009]
Tel: 01279 734524
Fax: 01279 734426
email: a.harlow@chelmsford.anglican.org
SOUTHEND Ven David Lowman, The Archdeacon's Lodge, 136 Broomfield Road, Chelmsford CM1 1RN [2001]
Tel: 01245 258257
Fax: 01245 250845
email: a.southend@chelmsford.anglican.org
WEST HAM Ven Elwin Cockett, 86 Aldersbrook Rd, Manor Park, London E12 5DH [2007]
Tel: 020 8989 8557
Fax: 020 8530 1311
email: a.westham@chelmsford.anglican.org

CONVOCATION (MEMBERS OF THE HOUSE OF CLERGY OF THE GENERAL SYNOD)
Proctors for Clergy
Ven Annette Cooper
Revd John Dunnett
Revd Tim Bull
Revd Canon Martin Wood
Revd David Banting
Revd Jenny Tomlinson

MEMBERS OF THE HOUSE OF LAITY OF THE GENERAL SYNOD
Mrs Isabel Adcock
Mr Robert Hammond
Mrs Mary Durlacher
Ms Kathleen Playle
Mr David G Llewelyn Morgan
Mrs Ruth Whitworth
Mr Robin Stevens

DIOCESAN OFFICERS
Chief Executive Steven Webb, Diocesan Office, 53 New St, Chelmsford CM1 1AT
Tel: 01245 294400
Chancellor of Diocese Chancellor George Pulman QC, Diocesan Registry, 53a New St, Chelmsford CM1 1NE
Tel: 01245 259470
Registrar of Diocese and Bishop's Legal Secretary Mr Brian Hood, Diocesan Registry, 53a New St, Chelmsford CM1 1NE
Tel: 01245 259470

Legal Advisers to the Board of Finance Winckworth Sherwood, 53a New St, Chelmsford CM1 1NE
Tel: 01245 262212

DIOCESAN ORGANIZATIONS
Diocesan Office 53 New St, Chelmsford CM1 1AT
Tel: 01245 294400
Fax: 01245 294477
email: mail@chelmsford.anglican.org

ADMINISTRATION
Dioc Synod (Chairman, House of Clergy) Canon Martin D Webster, *Tel:* 01992 672115; *(Chairman, House of Laity)* Canon Dr Susan Atkin, *Tel:* 01206 854976; *(Secretary)* Steve Webb, Dioc Office *Tel:* 01245 294400
Board of Finance (Chairman) Canon John Spence OBE
(Company Secretary) Steven Webb, Dioc Office
Tel: 01245 294400
email: swebb@chelmsford.anglican.org
Senior Property Manager Richard Smith, Dioc Office
Tel: 01245 294420
Designated Officer Mr Brian Hood, Dioc Registry, 53a New St, Chelmsford CM1 1NG
Tel: 01245 259470
Dioc Mission and Pastoral Committee (Chairman) Rt Revd Stephen Cottrell, Bishopscourt, Margaretting, Ingatestone CM4 0HD; *(Secretary)* Mr Nathan Whitehead, Dioc Office
email: nwhitehead@chelmsford.anglican.org

CHURCHES
Advisory Committee for the Care of Churches (Chairman) Dr James Bettley, The Old Vicarage, Church Rd, Malden CM9 8NP *Tel:* 01612 892450; *(Secretary)* Mrs Sandra Turner, Dioc Office
email: sturnerj@chelmsford.anglican.org
Redundant Churches Committee (Secretary) Kevin Quinlan, Dioc Office
Essex Association of Change Ringers Mary Bone, 11 Bullfields, Sawbridgeworth, Herts CM21 9BD
Tel: 01279 726159

CHILD PROTECTION
Child Protection Adviser Revd Jean Halliday, Dioc Office
Tel: 01245 294457
07903 831965 (Mobile)
email: jhalliday@chelmsford.anglican.org

EDUCATION
Director of Education Rob Fox, Dioc Office
email: rfox@chelmsford.anglican.org
Early Years Adviser Vacancy, Dioc Office
Tel: 01245 294440
RE Adviser Mrs Alison Seaman, Dioc Office
Tel: 01245 294440
email: aseaman@chelmsford.anglican.org
School and RE Advisers Ann Bard, Revd Lyn Hillier, Rosemary Privett Dioc Office
email: abard@chelmsford.anglican.org
l.hillier@chelmsford.anglican.org
rprivett@chelmsford.anglican.org

Children's Work Adviser Mr Stephen Kersys, Dioc Office   *email:* skersys@chelmsford.anglican.org

MISSION AND MINISTRY
Dioc Director of Ordinands and NSM Officer Canon Richard More, 25 Roxwell Rd, Chelmsford CM1 2LY   *Tel:* 01245 264187
Fax: 01245 348789
email: ddo@chelmsford.anglican.org
Director of Mission and Ministry Canon Roger Matthews, Dioc Office   *Tel:* 01245 294455
email: rmatthews@chelmsford.anglican.org
Lay Ministry Education Coordinator Canon Philip Ritchie, Dioc Office   *Tel:* 01245 294449
email: pritchie@chelmsford.anglican.org
Adviser for Women's Ministry Revd Jenny Tomlinson, 17 Borough Lane, Saffron Waldon CB11 4AG   *Tel:* 01799 500947
Interfaith Adviser Vacancy

COMMUNICATIONS
Communications Director Ralph Meloy, Dioc Office   *Tel:* 01245 294424
07654 382674 (Pager)
email: rmeloy@chelmsford.anglican.org

OTHER COMMITTEES
Readers' Committee Revd Dr Martin Kitchen, Rectory, Strotford Road, Leaden Roding, Dunmow CM6 1GY   *Tel:* 01279 876147
email: martinx.kitchen@btinternet.com
Liturgical Committee (Chairman) Ven Elwin Cockett, 86 Aldersbrook Rd, Manor Park, London E12 5DH   *Tel:* 020 8989 8557
email: a.westham@chelmsford.anglican.org

DIOCESAN RECORD OFFICE
Essex Records Office, Wharf Rd, Chelmsford CM2 6YT   *Tel:* 01245 244644
email: ero.enquiry@essexcc.gov.uk

DIOCESAN HOUSE OF RETREAT
Pleshey, Chelmsford CM3 1HA (*Warden* Revd Sheila Coughtrey)   *Tel:* 01245 237251
Fax: 01245 237594
email: retreathouse.pleshey@virgin.net
Web: www.retreathousepleshey.com

RURAL DEANS
ARCHDEACONRY OF WEST HAM
Barking and Dagenham Revd Roger Gayler, St Mark's Vicarage, 187 Rose Lane, Marks Gate, Romford RM6 5NR   *Tel:* 020 8599 0414
Havering Revd David Marshall, St James's Vicarage, 24 Lower Bedfords Rd, Romford RM1 4DG   *Tel:* 01708 746614
email: revdave@dsl.pipex.com
Newham Canon Dave Wade, Vicarage, 16a Ruscoe Rd, Canning Town, London E16 1JB
Tel: 020 7476 2076
email: ann@renewalprogramme.freeserve.co.uk
Redbridge Revd Paul Harcourt, All Saints Vicarage, 4 Inmans Row, Woodford Green IG8 0NH   *Tel:* 020 8504 0266
email: paul@asww.org.uk

Waltham Forest Revd Steven Saxby, 121 Forest Rise, Walthamstow, London E17 3PW
Tel: 020 8520 3854
email: stevensaxby@btinternet.com

ARCHDEACONRY OF HARLOW
Epping Forest Dr Joyce Smith, St Lawrence House, 46 Mallion Court, Ninefields, Waltham Abbey EN9 3EQ   *Tel:* 01992 767916
email: joyce@smith2767.fsnet.co.uk
Harlow Revd Martin Harris, 43 Upper Park, Harlow CM20 1TW   *Tel:* 01279 411100
email: martin.harris@messages.co.uk
Ongar Revd Toni Smith, Vicarage, Church Street, Ingatestone, Essex CM4 0RN   *Tel:* 01277 821464
email: blackmore.vicarage@btinternet.com

ARCHDEACONRY OF SOUTHEND
Brentwood Revd Dr Ian Herbert Jorysz, The Vicarage, Wigley Bush Lane, Brentwood CM14 5QP   *Tel:* 01277 212054
email: ian@jorysz.com
Basildon Revd Margaret Shaw, St Andrew's Vicarage, 3 The Fremnells, Basildon, Essex SS14 2QX   *Tel:* 01268 520516
email: sh.ma@btinternet.com
Chelmsford North Canon Carla I Hampton, The New Vicarage, 1 Glebe Meadow, Chelmsford CM3 1EX   *Tel:* 01245 364081
email: carla@hamptonc.freeserve.co.uk
Chelmsford South Revd Andrew T Griffiths, 450 Beehive Lane, Chelmsford CM2 8RN
Tel: 01245 353922
email: andy.griffiths@yahoo.co.uk
Hadleigh Revd David Tudor, St Nicholas' House, Canvey Island SS8 0JR   *Tel:* 01268 682586
email: dstudor@tiscali.co.uk
Maldon and Dengie Revd Gordon Anderson, Vicarage, Burnham Rd, Southminster CM0 7ES
Tel: 01621 772300
email: gandr42@btinternet.com
Rochford Revd Mike Lodge, Rectory, Hockley Rd, Rayleigh SS6 8BA   *Tel:* 01268 742151
email: mike.lodge@btinternet.com
Southend Canon Stephen Burdett, Southend Rectory, 144 Alexandra Road, Southend-on-Sea SS1 1HB   *Tel:* 01702 342687
email: stephenburdett@btinternet.com
Thurrock Revd Ed W Hanson, The Rectory, School Lane, Orsett RM16 3JS   *Tel:* 01375 891254
email: rector@hobnob.org.uk

ARCHDEACONRY OF COLCHESTER
Braintree Very Revd Canon Philip Need, The Deanery, Bocking, Braintree CM7 5SR
Tel: 01376 324887
email: thedeanofbocking@tiscali.co.uk
Colchester Revd Ian A Hilton, The Rectory, New Town Rd, Colchester CO1 2EF   *Tel:* 01206 530320
email: ian.hilton@talktalk.net *Dedham and Tey* Revd Philip Banks, Vicarage, 4 Church Green, Coggeshall, Colchester CO6 1UD
Tel: 01376 561234
email: fr-philip@st-peter-ad-vincul.org.uk

Dunmow and Stansted Revd Cilla Hawkes, Greenfields, Felstead, Dunmow CM6 3LF
Tel: 01371 856480
email: cilla@hawkesfarming.co.uk
Harwich Revd Peter Mann, Rectory, 51 Highfield Avenue, Dovercourt, Harwich CO12 4DR
Tel: 01255 502033
email: cookbird@gmail.com
Hinckford Revd Laurie Bond, Vicarage, Queen St, Castle Hedingham, Halstead CO9 3EZ
Tel: 01787 460274
email: revlbond@hotmail.com

Saffron Walden and Newport Revd David R Tomlinson, St John's Vicarage, 8a Victoria Avenue, Grays RM16 2RP
Tel: 01375 372101
email: dtjtgrays@btinternet.com
St Osyth Revd Guy Douglas A Thorburn, St John's Vicarage, Valley Avenue, Great Clacton CO15 4AR
Tel: 01255 423435
*email:*revguy.thorburn@virgin.net
Witham Revd John Martin Suddards, The Rectory, 7 Chipping Dell, Witham CM8 2JX
Tel: 01376 513509
email: suddards@suddards.plus.com

DIOCESE OF CHESTER

Founded in 1541. Cheshire; Wirral; Halton, south of the Mersey; Warrington, south of the Mersey; Trafford, except for an area in the north (MANCHESTER); Stockport, except for a few parishes in the north (MANCHESTER) and in the east (DERBY); the eastern half of Tameside; a few parishes in Derbyshire; a few parishes in Manchester; a few parishes in Flintshire.

Population 1,565,000   Area 1,017 sq m
Full-time Stipendiary Parochial Clergy 234   Benefices 226
Parishes 276   Churches 370
www.chester.anglican.org
Overseas link province: Aru and Boga Congo, Melanesia.

BISHOP (40th)
Rt Revd Dr Peter Robert Forster, Bishop's House, Abbey Square, Chester CH1 2JD [1996]
Tel: 01244 350864
Fax: 01244 314187
email: bpchester@chester.anglican.org
[Peter Cestr:]
Bishop's Chaplain Vacancy (same address)
Tel: 01244 350864

SUFFRAGAN BISHOPS
BIRKENHEAD Rt Revd (Gordon) Keith Sinclair, Bishop's Lodge, 67 Bidston Rd, Prenton CH43 6TR [2007]
Tel: 0151 652 2741
Fax: 0151 651 2330
email: bpbirkenhead@chester.anglican.org
STOCKPORT Rt Revd Robert Atwell, Bishop's Lodge, Back Lane, Dunham Town, Altrincham WA14 4SG [2008]
Tel: 0161 928 5611
Fax: 0161 929 0692
email: bpstockport@chester.anglican.org

HONORARY ASSISTANT BISHOPS
Rt Revd William Alaha Pwaisiho, Rectory, Church Lane, Gawsworth, Macclesfield, SK11 9RJ
Tel: 01260 223201
Rt Revd Colin Frederick Bazley, 121 Brackenwood Rd, Higher Bebington, Wirral CH63 2LU
Tel: 0151 608 1193
Rt Revd Geoffrey Turner, 23 Lang Lane, West Kirby, Wirral CH48 5HG
Tel: 0151 625 8504
Rt Revd Alan Chesters, 64 Hallfields Rd, Tarvin, Chester CH3 8ET
Tel: 01829 740825
Rt Revd John Hayden, 45 Birkenhead Rd, Hoylake, Wirral CH47 5AF
Tel: 0151 632 0448
Rt Revd Graham Dow, 34 Kimberley Ave, Romiley SK6 4AB
Tel: 0161 494 9148

CATHEDRAL CHURCH OF CHRIST AND THE BLESSED VIRGIN MARY
Dean Very Revd Professor Gordon Ferguson McPhate, Deanery, 7 Abbey St, Chester CH1 2JF [2002]
Tel: 01244 500971
email: dean@chestercathedral.com
Cathedral Office 12 Abbey Square, Chester CH1 2HU
Tel: 01244 324756
email: office@chestercathedral.com
Web: www.chestercathedral.com

Vice-Dean Vacancy
Canon Chancellor
Canon Jane Brooke, 12 Abbey Square, Chester CH1 2HU
Tel: 01244 324756
email: canon.brooke@chestercathedral.com
Canon Precentor
Canon Christopher Humphries, 9 Abbey St, Chester CH1 2JF [2005]
Tel: 01244 500967
email: canon.humphries@chestercathedral.com
Chief Executive, Administrator and Chapter Clerk
Ms Annette Moor, Cathedral Office
Tel: 01244 500962
email: chief.executive@chestercathedral.com
Director of Music Mr Philip Rushforth, Cathedral Office
Tel: 01244 500974
email: philip.rushforth@chestercathedral.com
Interim Cathedral Architect Mr James Sanderson, Cathedral Office

ARCHDEACONS
CHESTER Ven Michael Gilbertson, Church House, Lower Lane, Aldford, Chester CH3 6HP [2010]
Tel: 01244 681937 ext 253
Fax: 01244 620456
email: michael.gilbertson@chester.anglican.org
MACCLESFIELD Ven Ian Bishop
email: ian.bishop@chester.anglican.org

CONVOCATION (MEMBERS OF THE HOUSE OF CLERGY OF THE GENERAL SYNOD)
Proctors for Clergy
Revd Ian Bishop
Canon David Felix
Revd Robert Munro
Revd Alison Cox
Revd Dr Jonathan Gibbs
Revd Charles Razzall

MEMBERS OF THE HOUSE OF LAITY OF THE GENERAL SYNOD
Prof Tony Berry
Mr Peter Hart
Dr Graham Campbell
Mrs Jenny Dunlop
Mr John Freeman
Mrs Lois Haslam
Dr John Mason
Mrs Elizabeth Renshaw

DIOCESAN OFFICERS

Dioc Secretary Mr George Colville, Church House, Lower Lane, Aldford, Chester CH3 6HP
Tel: 01244 681973
Fax: 01244 620456
email: george.colville@chester.anglican.org
Chancellor of Diocese His Honour Judge David Turner, c/o Friars, White Friars, Chester CH1 1XS
Registrar of Diocese and Bishop's Legal Secretary Mrs Helen McFall, Friars, White Friars, Chester CH1 1XS
Tel: 01244 321066
Fax: 01244 312582
email: helen.mcfall@cullimoredutton.co.uk

DIOCESAN ORGANIZATIONS

Diocesan Office Church House, Lower Lane, Aldford, Chester CH3 6HP
Tel: 01244 681973
Fax: 01244 620456
email: churchhouse@chester.anglican.org

ADMINISTRATION

Dioc Synod (*Vice-President, House of Clergy*) Revd Dr Jonathan Gibbs
(*Vice-President, House of Laity*) Canon Dr David Blackmore
(*Secretary*) George Colville, Church House
Board of Finance (*Chairman*) Canon Elizabeth Renshaw MBE
(*Secretary*) George Colville (*as above*)
Diocesan Surveyor Mr Peter Gowrley, Church House
Diocesan Accountant Mr Nigel Strange, Church House
Designated Officer and Director of HR Elizabeth Squires (*as above*)
Head of HR Mrs Liz Geddes, Church House

CHURCHES

Advisory Committee for the Care of Churches (*Chairman*) Prof Robert Munn; (*Director of Property*) Mr Paul Broadhurst, Church House

EDUCATION

Director of Education Mr Jeff Turnbull, Church House
Children Mr David Bell, Church House
Youth Mr Mark Montgomery, Church House

MISSION AND MINISTRY

Director of Ministry Canon Dr Christopher Burkett, Church House
email: christopher.burkett@chester.anglican.org
Director of Ordinands Revd Ray Samuels, Bishop's House, Abbey Square, Chester CH1 2JD
Tel: 01244 346945
email: ray.samuels@chester.anglican.org
Assistant Director of Ordinands Revd John Lees, 110 Grove Park, Knutsford WA16 8QB
Tel: 01565 654755
email: johnlees@dslpipex.com

Director of Studies for Ordinands Revd Gary O'Neill, 10 Neston Close, Helsby WA6 0FH
Tel: 01928 723327
email: gary.oneill@chester.anglican.org
Bishop's Officer for NSMs Canon Prof Roger Yates, 3 Racecourse Park, Wilmslow SK9 5LU
Tel: 01625 520246
Diocesan Dean of Women in Ministry Revd Libby Lane, St Peter's Vicarage, 1 Harrop Rd, Hale, Antrincham WA15 9BU
Tel: 0161 928 4182
Director of Studies for Readers Liz Shercliff, Church House
email: liz.shercliff@chester.anglican.org
Warden of Readers Revd John Knowles, Vicarage, 531 Chester Rd, Woodford, Stockport SK7 1PR
Tel: 0161 439 2286
email: john.knowles2@virgin.net
Clergy Development Officer Revd David Herbert, Church House
email: david.herbert@chester.anglican.org
Warden of Pastoral Workers Mrs Veronica Johnston, 66 Overleigh Rd, Handbridge, Chester CH4 8AB
Tel: 01244 671216
email: veronica.johnston@chester.anglican.org
Pastoral Worker Training Officer Revd Maureen Pickering, Curzon Cottage, 2A Curzon Park South, Chester CH4 8AB
Tel: 01244 677352
email: mapickering@btinternet.com
Adviser in Christian Spirituality Revd Donald Brockbank, 1 Plover Avenue, Winsford CW7 1LA
Tel: 01606 593651
email: donald@brockbankrev.freeserve.co.uk

PARISH DEVELOPMENT TEAM

Parish Development Officers Revd Richard Burton, Church House
email: richard.burton@chester.anglican.org
Revd Steve Wilcockson, Church House
email: steve.wilcockson@chester.anglican.org
Adviser in Christian Giving Mr Martin Smith, Church House
email: martin.smith@chester.anglican.org
Diocesan Worship Adviser Revd Colin Randall
email: colinrandall@mac.com

MISSIONARY AND ECUMENICAL

Partners in World Mission Mr John Freeman, Stable Court, 20A Leigh Way, Weaverham, Northwich CW8 3PR
Tel: 01606 852872
County Ecumenical Officer Mr Mark Thompson, 81 Forge Fields, Sandbach CW11 3RD
Tel: 01270 750431
email: ceo.ctic@googlemail.com
Dioc Ecumenical Officer Canon Mike Lowe, 4 Greenway Rd, Heald Green, Cheadle SK8 3NR
Tel: 0161 419 5889
email: mike.lowe@chester.anglican.org

PRESS AND PUBLICATIONS

Dioc Director of Communications Mr Stephen Regan, Church House or 07764 615069 (Mobile)
email: stephen.regan@chester.anglican.org

Design and Communications Officer Mr Stephen Freeman (*as above*)
  email: stephen.freeman@chester.anglican.org
Editor of Dioc Year Book Canon Dr John Mason (*as above*)

DIOCESAN RECORD OFFICE
Cheshire Records Office, Duke St, Chester CH1 2DN *County Archivist* Mr J. Pepler
  Tel: 01244 603391

SOCIAL RESPONSIBILITY
Director of Social Responsibility
Mrs Janice Mason, Church House
  email: janice.mason@chester.anglican.org

RURAL DEANS
ARCHDEACONRY OF CHESTER
Birkenhead Vacancy
Chester Revd Dr Mark Hart, Vicarage, Wicker Lane, Guilden Sutton, Chester CH3 7EL
  Tel: 01244 300306
  email: markhart61@googlemail.com
Frodsham Revd Sue Wilkins, Vicarage, 6 Kirkstone Crescent, Beechwood, Runcorn WA7 3JQ
  Tel: 01928 713101
  email: suewilkins@hallwoodlep.fsnet.co.uk
Great Budworth Vacancy
Malpas Vacancy
Middlewich Vacancy
Wallasey Rt Revd Colin Bazley, 121 Brackenwood Rd, Higher Bebington, Wirral CH63 2LU
  Tel: 0151 608 1193
  email: cbazley@gmail.com
Wirral North Gillian Rossiter, St John's Vicarage, 142 Birkenhead Rd, Meols, Wirral CH47 0LF
  Tel: 0151 632 1661
  email: johnsthebaptistchurch@btinternet.com

Wirral South Revd Dr Gordon Welch, 6 St James Ave, Upton, Chester CH2 1NA
  Tel: 01244 382196
  email: gordonwelch@btinternet.com

ARCHDEACONRY OF MACCLESFIELD
Bowden Canon John Sutton, Vicarage, 12 Thorley Lane Timperley, Altrincham, Cheshire WA15 7AZ
  Tel: 0161 980 4330
  email: jfsuttontimp@aol.com
Chadkirk Revd Dr Peter Jenner, Vicarage, Church Rd, Mellor, Stockport SK6 5LX
  Tel: 0161 484 5079
  email: jennerfamily@btinternet.com
Cheadle Revd Rob McLaren, Vicarage, 41 London Road North, Poynton, Stockport SK12 1AF
  Tel: 01625 856877
Congleton Canon David Taylor, Mossley Vicarage, 2 Hartley Gardens, Congleton CW12 3WA
  Tel: 01260 273182
  email: revdtaylor@hotmail.com
Knutsford Canon Prof Roger Yates, 3 Racecourse Park, Wilmslow SK9 5LU
  Tel: 01625 520246
  email: raycandoc@yahoo.co.uk
Macclesfield Revd Taffy Davies, St James's Vicarage, Sutton, Macclesfield SK11 0DS
  Tel: 01260 252228
  email: taffy@parishpump.co.uk
Mottram Revd Richard Lamey, St Mary's Vicarage, 39 Bradley Green Rd, Newton, Hyde SK14 4NA
  Tel: 0161 368 1489
  email: richardlamey@btinternet.com
Nantwich Canon Bill Baker, Vicarage, 14 Dane Bank Ave, Crewe CW2 8AA
  Tel: 01270 569000
  email: canonbillbaker@uwclub.net
Stockport Canon Alan Bell, 7 Corbar Rd, Mile End, Stockport SK2 6EP
  Tel: 0161 456 0918
  email: vicaralanbell@aol.com

DIOCESE OF CHICHESTER

Founded in 1070, formerly called Selsey (AD 681). West Sussex, except for one parish in the north (GUILDFORD); East Sussex, except for one parish in the north (ROCHESTER); one parish in Kent.

Population 1,546,000   Area 1,459 sq m
Full-time Stipendiary Parochial Clergy 276   Benefices 298
Parishes 374   Churches 505
www.diochi.org.uk
Overseas link dioceses: IDWAL (Inter-Diocesan West Africa Link) –
Ghana, Sierra Leone, Cameroon, Guinea (West Africa).

BISHOP (103rd)
Rt Revd John William Hind, The Palace, Chichester PO19 1PY [2001]   *Tel:* 01243 782161
Fax: 01243 531332
email: bishop.chichester@diochi.org.uk
[John Cicestr:]
Senior Chaplain & Episcopal Vicar for Ministry
Canon Ian Gibson, The Palace (*as above*)
email: ian.gibson@diochi.org.uk

AREA BISHOPS
HORSHAM Rt Revd Mark Sowerby, Bishop's House, 21 Guildford Rd, Horsham RH12 1LU [2009]   *Tel:* 01403 211139
Fax: 01403 217349
email: bishop.horsham@diochi.org.uk
Chaplains Revd Clay Knowles, 32 Livingstone Road, Burgess Hill, West Sussex RH15 8QP *Tel:* 01444 254429 & Revd Stephen Merriman, St James House, 12 Cornwall Road, Littlehampton, West Sussex BN17 6EE *Tel:* 01903 724311
LEWES Rt Revd Wallace Benn, Bishop's Lodge, 16a Prideaux Rd, Eastbourne BN21 2NB [1997]
Tel: 01323 648462
Fax: 01323 641514
email: bishop.lewes@diochi.org.uk
Chaplain Vacancy

HONORARY ASSISTANT BISHOPS
Rt Revd Christopher Charles Luxmoore, 42 Willowbed Drive, Chichester PO19 2JB [1991]
Tel: 01243 784680
Rt Revd Michael Marshall, Upper Chelsea Rectory, 97a Cadogan Lane, London SW1X 9DU [1992]   *Tel:* 020 7730 7270
Rt Revd Michael Manktelow, 14 Little London, Chichester PO19 1NZ [1994]   *Tel:* 01243 531096
Rt Revd David Wilcox, 4 The Court, Hoo Gardens, Willingdon, Eastbourne BN20 9AX [1996]   *Tel:* 01323 506108
Rt Revd Kenneth Barham, Rosewood, Canadia Rd, Battle TN33 0LR [2007]   *Tel:* 01424 773073
Rt Revd David Farrer, Vicarage, 26 Maltravers, Arundel, West Sussex BN18 9BU
Tel: 01903 885209
Rt Revd Lindsay Urwin, OGS, Baverstock House, Bridewell Street, Walsingham, Norfolk NR22 6EE
Tel: 01328 820323

CATHEDRAL CHURCH OF THE HOLY TRINITY
Dean Very Revd Nicholas Frayling, The Deanery, Chichester PO19 1PX [2002]
Tel: 01243 812484 (Office)
01243 812494 (Home)
Fax: 01243 812499
email: dean@chichestercathedral.org.uk
Cathedral Office The Royal Chantry, Cathedral Cloisters, Chichester PO19 1PX
Tel: 01243 782595
Fax: 01243 812499
email: reception@chichestercathedral.org.uk
Precentor Canon Timothy Schofield, 4 Vicars' Close, Chichester PO19 1PT [2006]
Tel: 01243 813589
Fax: 01243 812499
email: precentor@chichestercathedral.org.uk
Chancellor Canon Dr Anthony Cane, The Residentiary, 2 Canon Lane, Chichester PO19 1PX [2007]   *Tel:* 01243 813594
Fax: 01243 812499
email: chancellor@chichestercathedral.org.uk
Treasurer Canon Ian Gibson, Caigers Cottage, Woodgate, Chichester PO20 3SQ [2009]
Tel: 01243 782161
Fax: 01243 812499
email: ian.gibson@diochi.org.uk
Priest-Vicar Canon David Nason, 1 St Richard's Walk, Chichester PO19 1QA   *Tel:* 01243 775615
Fax: 01243 812499
Communar Vacancy, Cathedral Office
Tel: 01243 812489
Fax: 01243 812499
email: communar@chichestercathedral.org.uk
Cathedral Organist and Master of the Choristers
Miss Sarah Baldock, 2 St Richard's Walk, Chichester PO19 1QA   *Tel:* 01243 812486
Fax: 01243 812499
email: organist@chichestercathedral.org.uk

ARCHDEACONS
CHICHESTER Ven Douglas McKittrick, 2 Yorklands, Dyke Rd Ave, Hove BN3 6RW [2002]
Tel: 01273 505330
Fax: 01273 421041
email: archchichester@diochi.org.uk

HORSHAM Ven Roger Combes, 3 Danehurst Crescent, Horsham RH13 5HS [2003]
Tel: 01403 262710
Fax: 01403 210778
email: archhorsham@diochi.org.uk
LEWES AND HASTINGS Ven Philip Hugh Jones, 27 The Avenue, Lewes BN7 1QT [2005]
Tel: 01273 479530
Fax: 01273 476529
email: archlandh@diochi.org.uk

CONVOCATION (MEMBERS OF THE HOUSE OF CLERGY OF THE GENERAL SYNOD)
Proctors for Clergy
Revd Jonathan Frais
Revd Stephen France
Revd Alastair Cutting
Revd Richard Jackson
Ven Douglas McKittrick
Revd Rebecca Swyer

MEMBERS OF THE HOUSE OF LAITY OF THE GENERAL SYNOD
Mr John Ashwin
Mrs Lorna Ashworth
Mr John Booth
Mr Justin Brett
Mrs Mary Nagel
Miss Joy Gilliver
Ms Andrea Williams
Mr Jacob Vince

DIOCESAN OFFICERS
Dioc Secretary Vacancy, Diocesan Church House, 211 New Church Rd, Hove BN3 4ED
Tel: 01273 421021
Fax: 01273 421041
email: diocsec@diochi.org.uk
Chancellor of Diocese Chancellor Mark Hill, Pump Court Chambers, 3 Pump Court, Temple, London EC4Y 7AJ
Registrar of Diocese and Bishop's Legal Secretary Mr John Stapleton, Thomas Eggar, The Corn Exchange, Baffins Lane, Chichester PO19 4GE
Tel: 01243 813238
Fax: 01243 775640
email: john.stapleton@thomaseggar.com

DIOCESAN ORGANIZATIONS
Diocesan Office Diocesan Church House, 211 New Church Rd, Hove BN3 4ED
Tel: 01273 421021
Fax: 01273 421041
email: enquiry@diochi.org.uk

ADMINISTRATION
Dioc Synod (Chairman, House of Clergy) Revd Alastair Cutting
(Chairman, House of Laity) Dr B. Hanson
Dioc Fund and Board of Finance (Incorporated) (Chairman) Dr Clive Dilloway; *(Secretary)* Vacancy *(as above)*

Finance Committee Vacancy
Stipends Committee (Secretary) Vacancy
Parsonages Committee (Property Director) Mr Andrew Craft, Dioc Church House
Pastoral Committee (Secretary) Mr Steven Sleight, Dioc Church House

CHURCHES
Advisory Committee for the Care of Churches (Chairman) Mr John Ebdon, c/o Dioc Church House; *(Secretary)* Mr Steven Sleight *(as above)*
email: steven.sleight@diochi.org.uk

EDUCATION AND TRAINING
Schools
Director of Education Mr Mike Wilson, Dioc Church House
email: mike.wilson@diochi.org.uk
Schools Administration Mrs Elizabeth Yates, Dioc Church House
Schools Support Mr Martin Lloyd, Mrs Lesley Mason, Mr Nigel Sarjudeen, Dioc Church House
Children and Young People
Adviser for Work with Children and Youth Mr Alistair Campbell, Dioc Church House
Tel: 01273 425694
Youth Officer Vacancy, Dioc Church House

MINISTRY AND ADULT CHRISTIAN EDUCATION
Adviser for Ministry and Adult Christian Education Miss Joy Gilliver, Dioc Church House
Tel: 01273 421021
email: joy.gilliver@diochi.org.uk
Readers Committee (Hon Secretary) Mrs Patricia Deane
Diocesan Director of Ordinands Canon Dr Philip Bourne, 6 Patcham Grange, Brighton BN1 8UR
Tel: 01273 564057
email: philip.bourne@diochi.org.uk
Vocations Officer Revd Moira Wickens, Kingston Buci Rectory, Shoreham-by-Sea BN43 6EB
Tel: 01273 592591
email: moirawickens@aol.com
Ministry Development Officer Revd Rebecca Swyer, Dioc Church House
email: rebecca.swyer@diochi.org.uk
Programme Co-ordinator, Initial Ministerial Education 4–7 Revd Rebecca Swyer, Dioc Church House email: rebecca.swyer@diochi.org.uk
Adult Education Officer: Revd Beverley Miles, Dioc Church House
email: Beverley.miles@diochi.org.uk
Episcopal Vicar for Ministry (Clergy Terms of Service) Canon Ian Gibson

MISSION AND RENEWAL
Adviser Revd Richard Jackson, Dioc Church House
Diocesan Evangelist Captain Gordon Banks, Dioc Church House
Christian Stewardship Officer Mr Ian Clark, Dioc Church House

Overseas Council (*Secretary*) Revd M. Payne, Vicarage, Vicarage Lane, Scaynes Hill, Haywards Heath RH17 7PB   *Tel:* 01444 831265

ECUMENICAL
European Ecumenical Committee (*Chairman*) The Dean of Chichester
(*Secretary*) Mr Jeffrey Stanbridge
                              Tel: 01243 789305
Dioc Ecumenical Co-ordinator Mr Ian Chisnall
                    Tel: 07976 811654 (Mobile)
              email: ianpchisnall@aol.com

LITURGICAL
Liturgy Consultant Revd Ian Forrester, Dioc Church House
Music Consultant Revd Ian Forrester (*as above*)

CHURCH IN SOCIETY
Adviser Revd Barry North, Dioc Church House
Association for Family Support Work, Central Office, c/o Dioc Church House

PRESS AND PUBLICATIONS
Communications Officer Mrs Lisa Williamson & Revd David Farey, Dioc Church House
                              Tel: 01273 425691
              Out of Hours *Tel:* 07775 022461
              email: media@diochi.org.uk

DIOCESAN RECORD OFFICES
East Sussex Mrs Elizabeth Hughes, *County Archivist*, The Maltings, Castle Precincts, Lewes BN7 1YT   *Tel:* 01273 482356
West Sussex Mr R. Childs *County Archivist*, County Records Office, County Hall, Chichester PO19 1RN   *Tel:* 01243 533911

RURAL DEANS
ARCHDEACONRY OF CHICHESTER
Arundel and Bognor Canon Mark Standen, Rectory, Rectory Lane, Angmering BN16 4JU
                              Tel: 01903 784979
              email: standens@angmering.org.uk
Brighton Revd Andrew Manson-Brailsford, St George's House, 6 Sussex Mews, Kemp Town, Brighton BN2 1GZ   *Tel:* 01273 625538
        email: revmanson-brailsford@hotmail.co.uk
Chichester Revd Richard Hunt, Rectory, Tower House, Chichester PO19 1QN   *Tel:* 01243 531624
Hove Revd Keith Perkinton, 127 Hangleton Way, Hove BN3 8ER   *Tel:* 01273 413044
              email: keithperkinton1@hotmail.co.uk
Worthing (*Acting*) Revd Colin Kassell, Park House, 3 Madeira Avenue, Worthing BN11 2AT
                              Tel: 01903 205111
              email: colin.kassell@ntlworld.com

ARCHDEACONRY OF HORSHAM
Cuckfield Revd Christopher Breeds, Vicarage, Wivelsfield, Haywards Heath RH17 7RD
                              Tel: 01444 471783
East Grinstead (*Acting*) Canon Julia Peaty, 15 Overton Shaw, East Grinstead RH19 2HN
                              Tel: 01342 322386
              email: julia@peaty.net
Horsham Canon Guy Bridgewater, Vicarage, Causeway, Horsham RH12 1HE
                              Tel: 01403 272919
              email: bridgewaters@tiscali.co.uk
Hurst Revd Peter Sills, The Coach House, Keymer Rd BN6 8JR   *Tel:* 01273 842670
Midhurst Revd Martin Lane, The Rectory, Harting, Petersfield GU31 5QB
                              Tel: 01730 825234
              email: martinjlane@btinternet.com
Petworth (*Acting*) Revd David Twinley, Vicarage, Church Lane, Bury, Pulborough RH20 1PB
                              Tel: 01798 839057
              email: frdavid@twinley.me.uk
Storrington Revd Paul Welch, Rectory, 2 London Rd, Pulborough RH20 1AP   *Tel:* 01798 875773
              email: paul.welch@virgin.net
Westbourne Ven Mervyn Banting, Furzend, 38a Bosham Hoe PO18 8ET   *Tel:* 01243 572340
              email: merlinbanting@f2s.com

ARCHDEACONRY OF LEWES AND HASTINGS
Battle and Bexhill Revd David R. Frost, Vicarage, 67 Woodsgate Park, Bexhill-on-Sea TN39 4DL
                              Tel: 01424 211186
        email: david@drfrost.worldonline.co.uk
Dallington Revd Stan Tomalin, 1 Barn Close, Hailsham, BN27 1TL   *Tel:* 01323 846680
              email: stantomalin@googlemail.com
Eastbourne Very Revd Jeffery Gunn, Vicarage, Spencer Road, Eastbourne BN21 4PA
                              Tel: 01323 722317
              email: jtgunn@tiscali.co.uk

Hastings Revd Chris H. Key, St Helen's Rectory, 266 Elphinstone Rd, Hastings TN34 2AG
                              Tel: 01424 425012
        email: chriskey@st-helens-ore.freeserve.co.uk

Lewes and Seaford Revd Geoffrey Daw, The Rectory, 14 Lockitt Way, Lewes Kingston
                              Tel: 01273 473665
              email: Geoffrey.Daw@btinternet.com

Rotherfield Revd Jeremy James, Vicarage, High St, Wadhurst TN5 6AA   *Tel:* 01892 782083
              email: jeremy@jrjames.freeserve.co.uk

Rye Revd Lucy Murdoch, Vicarage, 39 Lydd Road, Camber TN31 7RJ   *Tel:* 01797 225386
              email: dog.home@virgin.net

Uckfield Revd Phil Hodgins, Rectory, East Hoathly, Lewes BN8 6EG   *Tel:* 01825 840270

DIOCESE OF COVENTRY

Re-founded in 1918. Coventry; Warwickshire, except for small areas in the north (BIRMINGHAM) and south-west (GLOUCESTER) and one parish in the south (OXFORD); an area of Solihull.

Population 797,000   Area 686 sq m
Full-time Stipendiary Parochial Clergy 99   Benefices 134
Parishes 198   Churches 241
www.coventry.anglican.org

BISHOP
Rt Revd Dr Christopher John Cocksworth, Bishop's House, 23 Davenport Rd, Coventry CV5 6PW [2008]   *Tel:* 024 7667 2244
Fax: 024 7671 3271
email: bishcov@btconnect.com
Personal Assistant Christine Camfield (*same address*)
email: christine.camfield@btconnect.com
Secretary Mrs Maureen Prett (*same address*)
email: maureen.prett@btconnect.com

SUFFRAGAN BISHOP
WARWICK Rt Revd John Ronald Angus Stroyan, Warwick House, 139 Kenilworth Rd, Coventry CV4 7AP [2005]   *Tel:* 024 7641 2627
email: Bishop.Warwick@covcofe.org
Personal Assistant Mrs Kerry Vanston-Rumney
email: kerry.rumney@covcofe.org

CATHEDRAL CHURCH OF ST MICHAEL
Dean Very Revd John Dudley Irvine, Coventry Cathedral, 1 Hill Top, Coventry CV1 5AB [2001]
Tel: 024 7652 1227
email: john.irvine@coventrycathedral.org.uk
Cathedral Offices 1 Hill Top, Coventry CV1 5AB
Tel: 024 7652 1200
Fax: 024 7652 1220
Web: www.coventrycathedral.org.uk
Canons Residentiary and Senior Staff
Canon Pastor Canon Timothy John Pullen (*same address*) [2008]   *Tel:* 024 7652 1223
email: tim.pullen@coventrycathedral.org.uk
Canon Precentor Canon Dr David Stone (*same address*) [2010]   *Tel:* 024 7652 1212
email: david.stone@coventrycathedral.org.uk
Canon Director of Reconciliation Ministry Canon David Porter (*same address*) [2008]
Tel: 024 7652 1262
email: david.porter@coventrycathedral.org.uk
Cathedral Executive Director Mrs Jane Woodward (*same address*)   *Tel:* 024 7652 1242
email: jane.woodward@coventrycathedral.org.uk
Curate Revd Becky Welch (*same address*)
email: becky.welch@coventrycathedral.org.uk

Canons Theologian
Canon Dr Christopher Lamb, Brookside Avenue, Wellesbourne, Warwick CV35 9RZ [1992]
Tel: 01789 842060
Canon Tim Dakin, Church Mission Society, Partnership House, 157 Waterloo Rd, London SE1 8BU [2001]   *Tel:* 020 7928 8681
Canon Professor Ben Quash, Department of Theology and Religious Studies, King's College London, Strand, London WC2R 2LS [2004]
Tel: 020 7848 2339/2073
Canon Professor Richard Farnell, Coventry University, Priory St, Coventry CV1 5FB [2006]
Tel: 024 7688 7688
Clerk to the College of Canons Mr Roger Pascall, 1 The Quadrant, Coventry CV1 2DW
Tel: 024 7663 1212
Director of Music Mr Kerry Beaumont (*same address*)   *Tel:* 024 7652 1219
email: kerry.beaumont@coventrycathedral.org.uk

ARCHDEACONS
COVENTRY Ven Ian Watson, Cathedral and Diocesan Offices, 1 Hill Top, Coventry CV1 5AB [2007]   *Tel:* 024 7652 1337 (Office)
024 7641 7750 (Home)
email: ian.watson@covcofe.org
Archdeacon Missioner Ven Morris Rodham, Cathedral & Diocesan Offices, 1 Hill Top, Coventry CV1 5AB [2010]   *Tel:* 024 7652 1337
email: morris.rodham@covcofe.org
Dean of Women's Ministry Canon Katrina Scott, Willenhall Vicarage, Robin Hood Rd, Coventry CV3 3AY   *Tel:* 024 7630 3266
email: krgscott@hotmail.com

CONVOCATION (MEMBERS OF THE HOUSE OF CLERGY OF THE GENERAL SYNOD)
Proctors for Clergy
Revd Martin Saxby
Revd Ruth Walker
Revd Mark Beach

MEMBERS OF THE HOUSE OF LAITY OF THE GENERAL SYNOD
Mrs Kay Dyer
Mr Samuel Margrave
Dr Yvonne Warren

DIOCESAN OFFICERS

Diocesan Secretary Mr Simon Lloyd, Cathedral and Diocesan Offices, 1 Hill Top, Coventry CV1 5AB   *Tel:* 024 7652 1307
Fax: 024 7652 1330
email: simon.lloyd@covcofe.org
Chancellor of Diocese Chancellor Stephen Eyre, St Phillip's Chambers, 55 Temple Row, Birmingham B2 5LS
Deputy Chancellor Glyn Samuel, St Phillip's Chambers, 55 Temple Row, Birmingham B2 5LS
Registrar of Diocese and Bishop's Legal Secretary Mrs Mary Allanson, Rotherham & Co, 8 The Quadrant, Coventry CV1 2EL   *Tel:* 024 7622 7331

DIOCESAN ORGANIZATIONS

Diocesan Office Cathedral and Diocesan Offices, 1 Hill Top, Coventry CV1 5AB   *Tel:* 024 7652 1200
Fax: 024 7652 1330
Web: www.coventry.anglican.org

ADMINISTRATION

Diocesan Synod (*Chairman, House of Clergy*) Revd Canon Richard Williams
(*Chairman, House of Laity*) Mr Graham Wright
(*Secretary*) Mr Simon Lloyd, Cathedral & Diocesan Offices
Board of Finance (*Chairman*) Canon Ian Francis, The Firs, Main St, Frankton, Rugby CV23 9NZ
Tel: 01926 632918
email: ian@frankton.org
(*Secretary*) Mr Simon Lloyd (*as above*)
(*Assistant Secretary*) Mr Andrew Roberts
email: andrew.roberts@covlec.org
Systems Development Manager Mr Phil Ash
email: phil.ash@covlec.org
Director of Finance & Administration Mr David Oglethorpe
email: david.oglethorpe@covcofe.org
Parsonages Committee Mrs Nicky Caunt, Cathedral & Diocesan Offices
email: nicky.caunt@covlec.org
Trustees Mr David Dumbleton, Rotherham & Co, 8 The Quadrant, Coventry CV1 2EL
Tel: 024 7622 7331
Pastoral Committee Mr Andrew Roberts (*as above*)
Designated Officer Christine Camfield (*as above*)
Diocesan Directory Editor Mr Phil Ash (*as above*)

CHURCHES

Advisory Committee for the Care of Churches Dr Claire Strachan, Cathedral and Diocesan Offices   *email:* claire.strachan@covlec.org

EDUCATION

Diocesan Director Mrs Linda Wainscot, 1 Hill Top, Coventry CV1 5AB   *Tel:* 024 7652 1250
email: linda.wainscot@covcofe.org
Religious Education and Spirituality and Schools Officer Mrs Lizzie McWhirter, 1 Hill Top, Coventry CV1 5AB   *Tel:* 024 7652 1250

MINISTRY

Principal of the Diocesan Training Partnership Revd Dr Richard Cooke, Cathedral & Diocesan Offices, 1 Hill Top, Coventry CV1 5AB
Tel: 024 7652 1316
email: richard.cooke@covcofe.org
Diocesan Director of Ordinands Canon Roger Spiller, Cathedral & Diocesan Offices, 1 Hill Top, Coventry CV1 5AB   *Tel:* 024 7652 1316
Initial Ministerial Education Revd Paul Wignall, Cathedral & Diocesan Offices, 1 Hill Top, Coventry CV1 5AB   *Tel:* 024 7652 1316
email: paul.wignall@covcofe.org
Readers (*Hon Registrar*) Mr Paul Mileham
Tel: 01926 426250
email: paul@mileham.net

PARISH DEVELOPMENT AND EVANGELISM

Contact *Archdeacon Missioner*, Cathedral & Diocesan Offices, 1 Hill Top, Coventry CV1 5AB
Tel: 024 7652 1337
email: morris.rodham@covcofe.org

STEWARDSHIP

Dioc Adviser Mr Graham Wright, 1 Mayfield Drive, Kenilworth CV8 2SW   *Tel:* 01926 864991
email: grahampjw@aol.com

PRESS AND PUBLICATIONS

Dioc Communications Officer Vacancy, all enquiries to the Diocesan Secretary   *Tel:* 024 7652 1307

DIOCESAN RECORD OFFICE

Warwickshire County Record Office, Priory Park, Cape Rd, Warwick CV34 4JS *Head of Heritage and Culture (Archives) Services* Ms Caroline Sampson
Tel: 01926 738959
Fax: 01926 738969
email: recordoffice@warwickshire.gov.uk

SOCIAL RESPONSIBILITY

Contact *Archdeacon Missioner*, Cathedral and Diocesan Offices, 1 Hill Top, Coventry CV1 5AB
Tel: 024 7652 1337
email: morris.rodham@covcofe.org

RURAL DEANS
ARCHDEACONRY OF COVENTRY

Coventry North Vacancy
Coventry South Revd Stephen Burch, St James Vicarage, 395 Tile Hill Lane, Coventry CV4 9DP
Tel: 024 7646 6262
email: stephen.burch@btinternet.com
Coventry East Revd Malcolm Tyler, Walsgrave Vicarage, 4 Faber Rd, Coventry CV2 2BG
Tel: 024 7661 5152
email: stmaryssowe@aol.com
Kenilworth Canon Roy Brown 3 Margetts Close, Kenilworth CV8 1EN   *Tel:* 01926 850638
email: brownphilips5@sky.com
Nuneaton Revd Peter Allan, Ansley Vicarage, Birmingham Rd, Ansley, Nuneaton CV10 9PS
Tel: 024 7639 9070
email: peter@ansleychurch.org

Rugby Revd Martin Saxby, St Matthew's Vicarage, 7 Vicarage Rd, Rugby CV22 7AJ
Tel: 01788 330442
email: martinPA@stmatthews.org.uk

ARCHDEACONRY OF WARWICK
Alcester Vacancy
Fosse Revd John Burrell, The Rectory, Church Lane, Lighthorne, Warwick CV35 0AR
Tel: 01926 651279
email: gjburrell@btinternet.com

Shipston Revd Dr Jill Tucker, The Old House, Oxhill, Warwick CV35 0QN *Tel:* 01295 680663
email: revjill.tucker@tiscali.co.uk
Southam Revd John Armstrong, The Rectory, Park Lane, Southam CV47 0JA
Tel: 01926 812413
email: revarmstrong@gmail.com
Warwick and Leamington Revd Paul Manuel, St Mark's Vicarage, 2 St Mark's Road, Leamington Spa CV32 6DL *Tel:* 01926 421004
email: paul.manuel14@ntlworld.com

DIOCESE OF DERBY

Founded in 1927. Derbyshire, except for a small area in the north (CHESTER);
a small area of Stockport; a few parishes in Staffordshire.

Population 1,010,000   Area 997 sq m
Full-time Stipendiary Parochial Clergy 136   Benefices 159
Parishes 253   Churches 332
www.derby.anglican.org
Overseas link of Derbyshire Churches (Baptist, Methodist, URC and Anglican):
Church of North India.

BISHOP (7th)
Rt Revd Dr Alastair Redfern, The Bishop's House,
6 King St, Duffield, Derby DE56 4EU [2005]
Tel: 01332 840132
Fax: 01332 840397
email: bishop@bishopofderby.org
[Alastair Derby]

SUFFRAGAN BISHOP
REPTON Rt Revd Humphrey Southern, Repton
House, Lea, Matlock DE4 5JP [2007]
Tel: 01629 534644
Fax: 01629 534003
email: bishop@repton.free-online.co.uk

HONORARY ASSISTANT BISHOPS
Rt Revd Robert Beak OBE, Ashcroft Cottage,
Butts Rd, Ashover, Chesterfield S45 0AX [1991]
Tel: 01246 590048
Rt Revd Jack Nicholls, 77 Rowton Grange Rd,
Chapel-en-le-Frith, High Peak SK23 0LD
Tel: 01298 812462
email: jnseraphim@gmx.com

CATHEDRAL CHURCH OF ALL SAINTS
Dean Very Revd Dr John Davies, Derby
Cathedral Centre, 18–19 Iron Gate, Derby DE1
3GP [2010]
Tel: 01332 341201
Fax: 01332 203991
email: dean@derbycathedral.org
Cathedral Office Derby Cathedral Centre, 18–19
Iron Gate, Derby DE1 3GP
email: office@derbycathedral.org
Canons Residentiary
Canon Precentor Canon David Perkins, 24
Kedlerton Rd, Derby DE22 1GU
Tel: 01332 341201
Canon Theologian Canon Andie Brown, Vicarage,
149 Church Rd, Quarndon, Derby DE22 5JA
[2003]
Tel: 01332 553424
Fax: 01332 292969
email: andie.brown@derby.anglican.org
Canon Pastor Canon Elaine Jones, 22 Kedleston
Rd, Derby DE22 1GU [2004]   Tel: 01332 208995
Fax: 01332 203991
email: elainejones@derbycathedral.org
Chaplains Revd Richenda Leigh, University of
Derby, Kedleston Rd, Derby DE22 1GB
01332 591878 (University)
email: chaplaincy@derby.ac.uk

Lay Chapter Members
Mrs Janet Love, Mrs Christine McMullen, Canon
Richard Powell, Mr Mark Titterton
Senior Executive Officer and Chapter Clerk Mr
David Stanbridge, Cathedral Office
email: davidstanbridgeseo@derbycathedral.org
Finance Officer Mr Peter Holdridge, Cathedral
Office   email: peterh@derbycathedral.org
Visitors' Officer Canon Elaine Jones, Cathedral
Office   email: visitors@derbycathedral.org
Master of Music and Organist Mr Peter Gould,
Cathedral Office   Tel: 01332 345848
email: pdgould@derbycathedral.org
Sub Organist Mr Tom Corfield, Cathedral Office
Tel: 01332 345848

ARCHDEACONS
CHESTERFIELD Ven Christine Wilson, The Old
Vicarage, Church St, Baslow, Derby DE45 1RY
Tel: 01246 583023
email: archchesterfield@derby.anglican.org

DERBY Ven Christopher Cunliffe, Derby Church
House, Full St, Derby DE1 3DR [2006]
Tel: 01332 388676 (Office)
Fax: 01332 292969
email: archderby@derby.anglican.org

CONVOCATION (MEMBERS OF THE HOUSE OF CLERGY OF THE GENERAL SYNOD)
Proctors for Clergy
Revd Neil Barber
Revd Jacqueline Searle
Revd Christine Wilson

MEMBERS OF THE HOUSE OF LAITY OF THE GENERAL SYNOD
Mrs Madelaine Goddard
Mrs Christine McMullen
Mr Peter Collard

DIOCESAN OFFICERS
Dioc Secretary Mr Bob Carey, Derby Church
House, 1 Full St, Derby DE1 3DR
Tel: 01332 388650
Fax: 01332 292969
email: finance@derby.anglican.org

Derby   41

Chancellor of Diocese His Honour Judge John W. M. Bullimore, Rectory, 14 Grange Drive, Emley, Huddersfield HD8 9SF
Tel: 01924 849161
Registrar of Diocese and Bishop's Legal Secretary Mrs Nadine Waldron, Eddowes Waldron Solicitors, 12 St Peter's Churchyard, Derby DE1 1TZ
Tel: 01332 348484
email: gedward@btconnect.com

DIOCESAN ORGANIZATIONS
Diocesan Office Derby Church House, 1 Full St, Derby DE1 3DR
Tel: 01332 388650
Fax: 01332 292969
email: finance@derby.anglican.org
Web: www.derby.anglican.org

ADMINISTRATION
Dioc Synod (Chairman, House of Clergy) Revd Paul Sandford, St Stephen's Vicarage, 313 Sinfin Lane, Sinfin, Derby DE24 9GP
email: prsandford@ntlworld.com
(Chairman, House of Laity) Mr Bill Bryant, Church House, North Church St, Bakewell DE45 1DB
Tel: 01629 815225
email: bryban@msn.com
(Secretary) Mr Bob Carey, Derby Church House
Board of Finance (Chairman) Mr Brian Dollamore, Castle House, Castle Square, Melbourne, Derby DE73 8DY
(Secretary) Mr Bob Carey (as above)
Parsonages Secretary Nigel Sherratt, Derby Church House
Tel: 01332 388672
Dioc Surveyors
Derby Archdeaconry Bob Spencer, Sir William Baird & Partners, St Michael's House, Queen St, Derby DE1 3DT
Tel: 01332 347203
Fax: 01332 347708
email: mail@sirwilliambaird.co.uk
Chesterfield Archdeaconry Mr G. Steel, Barlow & Associates Ltd, 7 Vernon St, Derby DE1 1FR
Tel: 01332 603000
email: gary@barlow-associates.co.uk
Pastoral Committee Vacancy
Designated Officer Mrs Nadine Waldron (as above)

CHURCHES
Advisory Committee for the Care of Churches (Chairman) Canon Michael Knight
(Secretary) Mrs Virginia Davis, Derby Church House
Tel: 01332 388683
Fax: 01332 292969

EDUCATION
Dioc Education Office Derby Church House, 1 Full St, Derby DE1 3DR
Tel: 01332 388660
Fax: 01332 381909
email: nettarussell@ddbe.org
Director Phil Moncur
email: philmoncur@ddbe.org
Deputy Director and Schools Adviser Mrs Alison Brown
email: alisonbrown@ddbe.org

Finance Officer Mrs Lizzie Walker
Tel: 01332 388662
email: lizziewalker@ddbe.org
Children's Work Adviser Mrs Helen Proudfoot
email: helenproudfoot@ddbe.org
Youth Adviser Mr Alistair Langton
email: alistairlangton@ddbe.org
Warden, Peak Centre Champion House Revd Adrian Murray-Leslie, Champion House, Edale, Hope Valley S33 7ZA
Tel: 01433 670254
email: warden@peakcentre.org.uk

TOURISM OFFICERS
Derby North Mr Roger Harvey, Wella Cottage, 3 Main St, Newthorpe NG16 2EX
Tel: 01773 717067
Derby South Mr Les Allen, 17 South St, Littleover, Derby DE23 6BA
Tel: 01332 766642

DEVELOPING DISCIPLESHIP AND MINISTRY
CME (Clergy and Laity) Adviser Canon Andie Brown, Derby Church House
Tel: 01332 388671
email: andie.brown@tiscali.co.uk
Director of Ordinands Revd Geraldine Pond, Vicarage, Bellevue Rd, Ashbourne DE6 1AT
Tel: 01335 343129
email: geraldine@geraldinepond.com
Bishop's Convenor for NSMs and MSEs Canon Keith Orford, 27 Lums Hill Rise, Matlock DE4 3FX
Tel: 01629 55349
email: keith.orford@btinternet.com
Dean of Women Priests Revd Jackie Searle, Vicarage, 35 Church St, Littleover, Derby DE23 6GF
Tel: 01332 767802
email: jackie@stpeterlitteover.org.uk
Warden of Readers Dr Esther Elliott, Derby Church House
(Secretary) Revd Karen Padley
Worship Advisory Group (Chairman) Revd Karen Padley
Tel: 01773 712097

MISSION AND UNITY
Ecumenical Officer Revd Tony Kaunhoven, Bakewell Vicarage, South Church St, Bakewell DE45 1FD
Tel: 01629 814462
email: jazzyrector@aol.com
World Development Officer Vacancy
Dioc Mission Adviser Revd Lakshmi Jeffreys, Derby Church House
Tel: 01332 388687
email: lakshmi.jeffreys@derby.anglican.org
Bishops' Interfaith Adviser Vacancy

PRESS AND COMMUNICATIONS
Office Derby Church House, Full St, Derby DE1 3DR
Tel: 01332 388680
Fax: 01332 292969
Communications Officer Revd Rob Marshall, Derby Church House
Tel: 01332 388680
email: communications@derby.anglican.org
Editor of 'Our Diocese' Contact Mrs V Alexander (Secretary)

DIOCESAN RECORD OFFICE

Derbyshire Record Office, County Offices, Matlock DE4 3AG *County Archivist* Dr Margaret O'Sullivan   *Tel:* 0845 605 8058
          email: record.office@derbyshire.gov.uk

SOCIAL RESPONSIBILITY

Community Action Officers
Ms Stella Collishaw, Derby Church House
          Tel: 01332 388685
          email: stella.collishaw@derby.anglican.org
Mrs Joy Bates, Derby Church House
          Tel: 01332 388686
          email: joy.bates@derby.anglican.org
Church and Society Officer Revd Richard Jordan
          Tel: 01332 388668
          email: richard.jordan@derby.anglican.org

RURAL DEANS
ARCHDEACONRY OF DERBY

Ashbourne Revd Chris Mitchell, Rectory, 16 Eaton Close, Hulland Ward, Ashbourne DE6 3EX
          Tel: 01335 372138
          email: pennychris@tiscali.co.uk
Derby North Revd Julian Hollywell, St Werburghs Vicarage, Gascoigne Drive, Spondon, Derby DE21 76L   *Tel:* 01332 673573
          email: fatherjulian@btinternet.com
Derby South Revd Paul Sandford, St Stephen's Vicarage, 313 Sinfin Lane, Derby DE24 9GP
          Tel: 01332 760135
          email: prsandford@ntlworld.com
Duffield Revd William Bates, 4 Lawn Avenue, Allestree, Derby DE22 2PE   *Tel:* 01332 550224
          email: williambates@btinternet.com
Erewash Canon Ian Gooding, Rectory, Stanton-by-Dale, Ilkeston DE7 4QA
          Tel: 0115 932 4584
          Fax: 0115 944 0299
          email: ian.e.gooding@gmail.com

Heanor Revd Mike Alexander, 80 Main Rd, Smalley, Derby DE7 6EF   *Tel:* 01332 880380
          email: mikealexander@ticvic.fsnet.co.uk
Longford Revd Andy Murphie, Vicarage, 28 Back Lane, Hilton, Derby DE65 5GJ
          Tel: 01283 733433
          email: andymurphie@btinternet.com
Melbourne Revd Tony Luke, Rectory, Rectory Gardens, Aston-on-Trent, Derby DE72 2AZ
          Tel: 01332 792658
          email: tonyluketenor@aol.com
Repton Revd Lesley de Pomerai, Rectory, 2 Station Lane, Walton on Trent, Swadlincote, Derby DE12 8NA

ARCHDEACONRY OF CHESTERFIELD

Alfreton Revd Philip Brooks, Vicarage, 19 Coasthill, Crich, Matlock DE4 5DS
          Tel: 01773 852449
          email: philipdbro@aol.com
Bakewell and Eyam Revd Andrew Montgomerie, Rectory, Eyam, Hope Valley S32 5QH
          Tel: 01433 630821
          email: asmontgomerie@hotmail.co.uk
Bolsover and Staveley Vacancy
Buxton Revd John Goldsmith, Vicarage, Monyash, Bakewell DE45 1JH
          Tel: 01629 812234
          email: goldsmith681@btinternet.com
Chesterfield Revd Nigel Johnson, Newbold Rectory, St John's Rd, Chesterfield S41 8QN
          Tel: 01246 450374
          email: nvjohnson@tiscali.co.uk
Glossop Revd John Baines, St George's Vicarage, Church Lane, New Mills, High Peak SK22 4NP
          Tel: 01663 743225
          email: vicar@newmillschurch.co.uk
Wirksworth Canon David Truby, Rectory, Coldwell St, Wirksworth, Matlock DE4 4FB
          Tel: 01629 822858
          email: david.truby@btinternet.com

Founded in 635. Durham, except for an area in the south-west (RIPON AND LEEDS), and four parishes in the north (NEWCASTLE); Gateshead; South Tyneside; Sunderland; Hartlepool; Darlington; Stockton-on-Tees, north of the Tees.

Population 1,456,000   Area 987 sq m
Full-time Stipendiary Parochial Clergy 169   Benefices 192
Parishes 230   Churches 281
www.durham.anglican.org
Overseas link diocese: Lesotho.

BISHOP (71st)
Vacancy, Auckland Castle, Bishop Auckland DL14 7NR   *Tel:* 01388 602576
                                    Fax: 01388 605264
        email: bishop@bishopdunelm.co.uk
Senior Chaplain, Executive Officer and Press Officer to the Bishop of Durham Canon Jon Bell (*same address*)   *email:* chaplain@bishopdunelm.co.uk

SUFFRAGAN BISHOP
JARROW Rt Revd Mark Watts Bryant, Bishop's House, 25 Ivy Lane, Low Fell, Gateshead, NE9 6QD [2007]   *Tel:* 0191 491 0917
                                    Fax: 0191 491 5116
    email: bishop.of.jarrow@durham.anglican.org

HONORARY ASSISTANT BISHOPS
Rt Revd Martyn William Jarrett, 3 North Lane, Roundhay, Leeds LS8 2QJ [2000]
(Bishop of Beverley and Provincial Episcopal Visitor)
                                    Tel: 0113 265 4280
                                    Fax: 0113 265 4281
email:
        bishop-of-beverley@3-north-lane.fsnet.co.uk
Rt Revd Prof Stephen Whitefield Sykes, Ingleside, Whinney Hill, Durham DH1 3BE [1999]
                                    Tel: 0191 384 6465
        email: S.W.Sykes@durham.ac.uk

CATHEDRAL CHURCH OF CHRIST, BLESSED MARY THE VIRGIN AND ST CUTHBERT OF DURHAM
Dean Very Revd Michael Sadgrove, The Deanery, Durham DH1 3EQ [2003]
                            Tel: 0191 386 4266 (Office)
                                0191 384 7500 (Home)
Canons Residentiary
Canon Dr David Kennedy, 7 The College, Durham DH1 3EQ [2001]   *Tel:* 0191 375 0242
    email: canon.precentor@durhamcathedral.co.uk
Canon Rosalind Brown, 6a The College, Durham DH1 3EQ [2005]   *Tel:* 0191 384 2415
    email: rosalind.brown@durhamcathedral.co.uk

Canon Dr Stephen Cherry, Carter House, Pelaw Leazes Lane, Durham DH1 1TB [2006]
                                    Tel: 0191 374 6012
        email: stephen.cherry@durham.anglican.org
Ven Ian Jagger, 15 The College, Durham DH1 3EQ [2006]   *Tel:* 0191 384 7534
                                    Fax: 0191 386 6915
email:
    archdeacon.of.durham@durham.anglican.org
Canon Prof Mark McIntosh [2009], 14 The College, Durham DH1 3EQ   *Tel:* 0191 386 4657
        email: mark.mcintosh@durham.ac.uk
Lay Members
Vacancy (*Chapter Office*)
Mr Adrian Beney (*Chapter Office*) [2007]
Succentor Revd David Sudron, 3 The College, Durham DH1 3EQ   *Tel:* 0191 384 2481(Home)
                                0191 386 4266 (Office)
                                    Fax: 0191 386 4267
    email: succentor@durhamcathedral.co.uk
Chapter Clerk Mr Philip Davies [2009], Chapter Office, The College, Durham DH1 3EH
                                    Tel: 0191 386 4266
                                    Fax: 0191 386 4267
    email: philip.davies@durhamcathedral.co.uk
Cathedral Organist (Lay Canon) Canon James Lancelot, 6 The College, Durham DH1 3EQ
                                    Tel: 0191 386 4766
        email: organist@durhamcathedral.co.uk

ARCHDEACONS
DURHAM Ven Ian Jagger, 15 The College, Durham DH1 3EQ [2006]   *Tel:* 0191 384 7534
                                    Fax: 0191 386 6915
email:
    archdeacon.of.durham@durham.anglican.org
AUCKLAND Ven Nick Barker, Vicarage, 45 Milbank Rd, Darlington DL3 9NL [2007]
                                    Tel: 01325 480444
                                    Fax: 01325 354027
email:
    archdeacon.of.auckland@durham.anglican.org
SUNDERLAND Ven Stuart Bain, St Nicholas Vicarage, Hedworth Lane, Boldon Colliery NE35 9JA [2002]   *Tel:* 0191 536 2300
                                    Fax: 0191 519 3369
email:
    archdeacon.of.sunderland@durham.anglican.org

CONVOCATION (MEMBERS OF THE HOUSE OF CLERGY OF THE GENERAL SYNOD)

Dignitaries in Convocation
The Dean of Durham
Proctors in Convocation
Revd David Brooke
Revd Graeme Buttery
Revd Dr Margaret Gilley
Ven Ian Jagger

MEMBERS OF THE HOUSE OF LAITY OF THE GENERAL SYNOD

Dr Richard Goudie
Mrs Frances Wood
Dr James Harrison
Sister Anne Williams

DIOCESAN OFFICERS

Dioc Secretary Mr Ian Boothroyd, Dioc Office, Auckland Castle, Bishop Auckland DL14 7QJ
Tel: 01388 660010
Fax: 01388 603695
email: Diocesan.Secretary@durham.anglican.org
Chancellor of Diocese The Worshipful the Revd Canon Rupert Bursell, Diocesan Registry, Messrs Smith Roddam, 56 North Bondgate, Bishop Auckland DL14 7PG *Tel:* 01388 603073
Fax: 01388 450483
Deputy Chancellor Mr J. D. C. Harte, The Law School, Newcastle University, 21–24 Windsor Terrace, Newcastle-upon-Tyne NE1 7RU
Tel: 0191 222 7614 *or* 222 7624
Registrar of Diocese and Bishop's Legal Secretary Ms H. Monckton-Milnes, Dioc Registry *(as above)*
Deputy Registrar Mr D. Harris, Dioc Registry
Property Manager, Dioc Surveyor and Secretary to Houses Committee Mr M. Galley, Dioc Office
Tel: 01388 660006
email: mike.galley@durham.anglican.org

DIOCESAN ORGANIZATIONS

Diocesan Office Auckland Castle, Bishop Auckland DL14 7QJ *Tel:* 01388 604515
Fax: 01388 603695
email: diocesan.office@durham.anglican.org

ADMINISTRATION

Dioc Synod (Chairman, House of Clergy) Canon John Dobson, Vicarage, 104 Blackwell Lane, Darlington DL3 8QQ *Tel:* 01325 354503
email: john.dobson@durham.anglican.org
(Chairman, House of Laity) Dr Jamie Harrison, 5 Dunelm Court, South Street, Durham DH1 4QX
Tel: 0191 384 8643
(Secretary) Mr Ian Boothroyd, Dioc Office
email: ian.boothroyd@durham.anglican.org
Board of Finance (Chairman) Dr Julian Chadwick, 31 Wearside Drive, The Sands, Durham DH1 1LE *Tel:* 0191 384 3135
email: julian.chadwick@btinternet.com
(Secretary) Mr Ian Boothroyd *(as above)*

Glebe Committee (Chairman) Dr Julian Chadwick *(as above); (Secretary)* Mr Paul Stringer, Dioc Office *Tel:* 01388 660002
Houses Committee (Chairman) Revd S Pinnington, Rectory, 5 Lingfield, Houghton le Spring DH5 8QA *Tel:* 0191 584 3487
email: rectorstmichaels@btinternet.com
(Secretary) Mr M. Galley, Dioc Office
Mission and Pastoral Committee (Chairman) Ven Ian Jagger; *(Secretary)* Mr Paul Stringer, Dioc Office *Tel:* 01388 660002 (Direct line)
email: paul.stringer@durham.anglican.org
Church Buildings Committee (Chairman) Vacancy *(Secretary)* Mr Bill Heslop, Dioc Office
Tel: 01388 660001 (Direct line)
email: bill.heslop@durham.anglican.org
Closed Churches Uses Committee (Chairman) Mr W Grant, 6 Sunniside Terrace, Cleadon, Sunderland SR6 7XE *Tel:* 0191 536 4140; *(Secretary)* Mr Bill Heslop, Dioc Office *(as above)*
Designated Officer Mr Paul Stringer, Dioc Office *(as above)*
Administrative Secretary Mr Paul Stringer, Dioc Office *(as above)*
Officer Manager Mrs Mandy Blackett, Dioc Office
Tel: 01388 660010
email: mandy.blackett@durham.anglican.org
Pensions Officers Canon Keith Woodhouse, 85 Baulkham Hills, Penshaw, Houghton le Spring DH4 7RZ *Tel:* and *Fax:* 0191 584 3977
email: keith.woodhouse@durham.anglican.org
Woman Adviser in Ministry Revd Jane Grieve, Rectory, 107 Front Street, Cockfield, Bishop Auckland DL13 5AA *Tel:* 01388 718447
email: jane.grieve@durham.anglican.org

CHURCHES

Advisory Committee for the Care of Churches (Chairman) Very Revd Michael Sadgrove, The Deanery, Durham DH1 3EQ *Tel:* 0191 384 7500
Fax: 0191 386 4267
email:
Michael.sadgrove@durhamcathedral.co.uk
(Secretary) Mr G. W. Heslop, Dioc Office *(as above)* *Tel:* 01388 660001

EDUCATION

Director of Education for Durham and Newcastle Vacancy, Church House, St John's Terrace, North Shields NE29 6HS *Tel:* 0191 270 4100
Assistant Director (Primary) Mr Brian Hedley, Church House, St John's Terrace, North Shields NE29 6HS
Assistant Director (Secondary and FE) Mr Mike Davison, Church House, St John's Terrace, North Shields NE29 6HS

DIOCESAN RESOURCE TEAM

Director of Ministerial Development and Parish Support (also CMD Officer) Canon Dr Stephen Cherry, Carter House, Pelaw Leazes Lane, Durham DH1 1TB *Tel:* 0191 374 6004
email: stephen.cherry@durham.anglican.org

Director of Ordinands Revd Richard Collins, Carter House, Pelaw Leazes Lane, Durham DH1 1TB *Tel:* 0191 374 6015 *email:* ddo@durham.anglican.org
Adviser in Pastoral Care and Counselling Mrs Alison Moore, Carter House, Pelaw Leazes Lane, Durham DH1 1TB *Tel:* 0191 374 6021 *email:* alison.moore@durham.anglican.org
Adviser for Youth Ministry Mr Nicholas Rowark, Carter House, Pelaw Leazes Lane, Durham DH1 1TB *Tel:* 0191 374 6008 *email:* nick.rowark@durham.anglican.org
Ecumenism Resources Officer Revd Sheelagh White, 37 Brancepeth Road, Oxclose, Washington NE38 0LA *Tel:* 0191 415 9468
Liturgical Committee Chairman Canon David Kennedy, 7 The College, Durham DH1 3EQ *Tel:* 0191 375 0242 *email:* canon.precentor@durhamcathedral.co.uk
Secretary Revd Dr Gareth Lloyd, 6 Ruskin Rd, Birtley, Chester-le-Street DH3 1AD *Tel:* 0191 410 2115 *email:* Gareth@dunelm.org.uk
Missioner Vacancy Carter House, Pelaw Leazes Lane, Durham DH1 1TB
Shared Ministry Development Officer Revd Judy Hirst, Carter House, Pelaw Leazes Lane, Durham DH1 1TB *Tel:* 0191 374 6014 *email:* judy.hirst@durham.anglican.org
Social Responsibility Officer Vacant
Stewardship Development Officer Mr Alistair Jenkins, Carter House, Pelaw Leazes Lane, Durham DH1 1TB *Tel:* 0191 374 6016 *email:* alistair.jenkins@ddemt.co.uk
Warden of Readers Bishop of Jarrow, Bishop's House, 25 Ivy Lane, Low Fell, Gateshead. NE9 6QD *Tel:* 0191 491 0917 *email:* bishop.of.jarrow@durham.anglican.org
(Registrar) Mr David Talbot, 66 Wheatall Drive, Whitburn, Sunderland SR6 7HQ *Tel:* 0191 529 2265 *email:* talbot886@btinternet.com

LINDISFARNE REGIONAL TRAINING PARTNERSHIP
Principal Revd Canon Cathy Rowling, Church House, St John's Terrace, North Shields NE29 6HS *Tel:* 0191 270 4143 *email:* cathyrowling@lindisfarnertp.org
Director of Studies and Tutor for Ordination Training Revd Richard Bryant, Church House, St John's Terrace, North Shields NE29 6HS *Tel:* 0191 270 4150 *email:* richardbryant@lindisfarnertp.org
Developing Discipleship Officer Revd Alastair Macnaughton, Church House, St John's Terrace, North Shields NE29 6HS *Tel:* 0191 234 0371 *email:* alastairmacnaughton@lindisfarnertp.org
IME 4–7 Director Revd Rick Simpson, The Rectory, Brancepeth, Durham DH7 8EL *Tel:* 0191 380 0440 *email:* ricksimpson@lindisfarnertp.org

Tutor for Reader Training Revd Dr Michael Beck, Church House, St John's Terrace, North Shields NE29 6HS *Tel:* 0191 270 4138 *email:* michaelbeck@lindisfarnertp.org
Administrator Miss Jenny Crawford, Church House, St John's Terrace, North Shields NE29 6HS *Tel:* 0191 270 4144 *email:* jennycrawford@lindisfarnertp.org

PARTNERSHIP BODIES
DFW Adoption (Chairman) Ven Stuart Bain (as above); (Director) Ms Margaret Bell, Agriculture House, Stonebridge, Durham DH1 3RY *Tel:* 0191 386 3719 *email:* office@dfw.org.uk
Durham-Lesotho Link Executive Officers Revds Rob and Margaret Bianchi, 8 Lindisfarne, Biddick, Washington NE38 7JR *Tel:* 0191 417 0852 *email:* dleo.bianchi@tiscali.co.uk
Northumbrian Industrial Mission (Chairman) Mr Paul Southgate, NIM Office, Sunderland Minster Church, High St West, Sunderland SR1 3ET *Tel:* 0191 373 5453 *email:* chiefofficer-crc@btconnect.com; (Secretary) Mrs Joan Smith, 64 Cornmoor Rd, Whickham, Newcastle-upon-Tyne NE16 4PY *Tel:* 0191 420 1238
Tees Valley Ministry (Chairman) Dr D. Hall, c/o Churches Regional Commission in the North-East, Ushaw College, Durham DH7 9RH; (Secretary) Mr P. Etwell (same address) *Tel:* 0191 373 5453 *Fax:* 0191 373 7804
Chaplaincy to the Arts and Recreation (Chairman) Canon Dr J P Cassidy, St Chad's College, University of Durham, 18 North Bailey, Durham DH1 3RH *Tel:* 0191 334 3345 *email:* j.p.cassidy@dur.ac.uk
Secretary Mr C Porter, 18 Chelsea Gardens, Norton, Stockton on Tees TS20 1RZ *email:* charles.porter@ntlworld.com

PRESS AND PUBLICATIONS
Editor of Dioc Directory Mr Ian Boothroyd (as above)
Director of Communications and Editor of Dioc News Revd Paul Judson, St Luke's Vicarage, 5 Tunstall Rd, Hartlepool TS26 8NF *Tel:* 01429 293111 *email:* Director.of.Communications@durham.anglican.org Durham.Newslink@durham.anglican.org

DIOCESAN RECORD OFFICE
Archives and Special Collections, University Library (Palace Green Section), University of Durham, Palace Green, Durham DH1 3RN
Archivist Mr Andrew Gray *Tel:* 0191 334 2972 *email:* pg.library@durham.ac.uk (For diocesan records)
County Record Office, County Hall, Durham DH1 5UL *Tel:* 0191 383 3253 *email:* record.office@durham.gov.uk (For parochial records for the whole diocese)

AREA DEANS

ARCHDEACONRY OF SUNDERLAND

Chester-le-Street Revd David Glover, 27 Wroxton, Biddick, Washington NE38 7NU
Tel: 0191 418 7911
email: htcwashington@tiscali.co.uk
Gateshead Revd Alan Raine, St Andrew's Vicarage, Whinbrooke, Gateshead NE10 8HR
Tel: 0191 469 3257
email: alanraine@virginmedia.com
Gateshead West (Acting) Revd Tom Jamieson, Barmoor House, 64 Main Road, Ryton NE40 3AJ
Tel: 0191 413 4592
email: tomjamieson@hotmail.com
Houghton-le-Spring (Acting) Revd E. Wilkinson, The Vicarage, Front St. Newbottle, Houghton le Spring DH4 4EP
Tel: 0191 584 3244
email: wilkinson.edward.rev@googlemail.com
Jarrow Revd Bill Braviner, St Peter's House, York Ave, Jarrow NE32 5LP
Tel: 0191 489 3279
email: bill@braviner.com
email: bill.braviner@durham.anglican.org
Wearmouth Revd Dick Bradshaw, St Matthew's Vicarage, Silksworth Rd, New Silksworth, Sunderland SR3 2AA
Tel: 0191 523 9124
email: jenanddick@tiscali.co.uk

ARCHDEACONRY OF DURHAM

Durham Revd Dr Rod Allon-Smith, Crossgate Centre, Alexandria Crescent, Durham DH1 4HF
Tel: 0191 384 4330
email: rod.allon-smith@durham.anglican.org

Easington Revd Alan Milne, Vicarage, Church Lane, Murton, Seaham SR7 9RD
Tel and *Fax:* 0191 526 2410
email: alanmilne_41@hotmail.com
Hartlepool Vacancy
Lanchester Revd Gary Birchall, Vicarage, Front St, Burnopfield, Newcastle-upon-Tyne NE16 6HQ
Tel: 01207 270261
email: gary.birchall@dsl.pipex.com
Sedgefield Revd Keith Lumsdon, St Luke's Vicarage, Church Lane, Ferryhill DL17 8LT
Tel: 01740 651438
email: keithlumsdon@hotmail.com

ARCHDEACONRY OF AUCKLAND

Auckland Canon Neville Vine, 4 Conway Grove, Bishop Auckland DL14 6AF
Tel: 01388 604397
email: neville.vine@btinternet.com
Barnard Castle Revd Alec Harding, Vicarage, Parsons Lonnen, Newgate, Barnard Castle DL12 8ST
Tel: 01833 637018
email: alec.harding@durham.anglican.org
Darlington Canon John Dobson, Vicarage, 104 Blackwell Lane, Darlington DL3 8QQ
Tel and *Fax:* 01325 354503
email: john.dobson@durham.anglican.org
Stanhope Revd Vince Fenton, Rectory, 14 Hartside Close, Crook DL15 9NH
Tel: 01388 760939
email: vincent.fenton@durham.anglican.org
Stockton Revd David Brooke, Rectory, Church Lane, Redmarshall, Stockton-on-Tees TS21 1ES
Tel: 01740 630810
email: david@revd.co.uk

DIOCESE OF ELY

Founded in 1109. Cambridgeshire, except for an area in the north-west (PETERBOROUGH) and three parishes in the south (CHELMSFORD); the western quarter of Norfolk; one parish in Bedfordshire.

Population 705,000   Area 1,507 sq m
Full-time Stipendiary Parochial Clergy 124   Benefices 192
Parishes 307   Churches 334
www.ely.anglican.org
Overseas link dioceses: Vellore (Church of South India) (Ecumenical),
Church of North Elbe.

BISHOP (68th)
The Bishop's House, Ely CB7 4DW Vacancy
Tel: 01353 662749
Fax: 01353 669477
email: bishop@ely.anglican.org
Bishop's Lay Chaplain Dr Bridget Nichols (*same address and tel. no.*)
email: bridget.nichols@ely.anglican.org
Bishop's Personal Assistant (*same address and tel. no.*) Vacancy
Bishop's Secretary Mrs Sarah King (*same address and tel. no.*)   *email:* sarah.king@ely.anglican.org

SUFFRAGAN BISHOP
HUNTINGDON Rt Revd Dr David Thomson, 14 Lynn Rd, Ely CB6 1DA [2008]   *Tel:* 01353 662137
Fax: 01353 669357
email: suffragan@ely.anglican.org
Bishop's Secretary Mrs Jane Baker (*same address, tel. no. and email*)

CATHEDRAL CHURCH OF THE HOLY AND UNDIVIDED TRINITY
Dean Very Revd Dr Michael Chandler, The Deanery, The College, Ely CB7 4DN [2003]
Tel: 01353 667735
Fax: 01353 665658
Vice Dean and Canon Pastor Canon David Pritchard, The Black Hostelry, The College, Ely CB7 4DL [2004]   *Tel:* 01353 660302
Canons Residentiary
Canon Missioner Canon Dr Alan Hargrave, The Chapter House, The College, Ely CB7 4DL [2004]
Tel: 01353 660304
Canon Precentor Canon Dr James Garrard, The Precentor's House, High St, Ely CB7 4JU [2008]
Tel: 01353 660335
Administrator Mrs Carol Campbell, The Chapter House, The College, Ely CB7 4DL
Tel: 01353 660321
Director of Music Mr Paul Trepte, The Chapter House, The College, Ely CB7 4DL
Tel: 01353 667735

ARCHDEACONS
CAMBRIDGE Ven John Stuart Beer, St Botolph's Rectory, 1a Summerfield, Cambridge CB3 9HE [2004]   *Tel* 01223 350424
Fax: 01223 360929
email: archdeacon.cambridge@ely.anglican.org
HUNTINGDON AND WISBECH Ven Hugh Kyle McCurdy, Whitgift House, The College, Ely CB7 4DL [2005]   *Tel:* 01353 658404 (Home)
Tel: 01353 652709 (Office)
Fax: 01353 652745
email: archdeacon.handw@ely.anglican.org

CONVOCATION (MEMBERS OF THE HOUSE OF CLERGY OF THE GENERAL SYNOD)
Proctors for Clergy
Revd Timothy Alban-Jones
Revd Michael Booker
Ven Hugh McCurdy

MEMBERS OF THE HOUSE OF LAITY OF THE GENERAL SYNOD
Mrs Janet Perrett
Mr Stephen Tooke
Dr Elaine Storkey

DIOCESAN OFFICERS
Dioc Secretary Dr Matthew Lavis, Bishop Woodford House, Barton Rd, Ely CB7 4DX
Tel: 01353 652701
01353 652702 (Direct Line)
Fax: 01353 652745
email: d.secretary@office.ely.anglican.org
Chancellor of Diocese The Hon Mr Justice William Gage, The Royal Courts of Justice, The Strand, London WC2 2LL
Registrar of Diocese Mr Peter Beesley, 1 The Sanctuary, London SW1P 3JT   *Tel:* 020 7222 5381

DIOCESAN ORGANIZATIONS
Diocesan Office Bishop Woodford House, Barton Rd, Ely CB7 4DX   *Tel:* 01353 652701
Fax: 01353 652745
email: jackie.cox@office.ely.anglican.org

ADMINISTRATION

Dioc Synod (*Chairman, House of Clergy*) Canon Jonathan Young, Rectory, Parsons Drive, Ellington, Huntingdon PE28 0AU
Tel: 01480 891695
(*Chairman, House of Laity*) Mrs Janet Perrett, 38 Beachampstead Road, Great Staughton PE19 5DX   *email:* jrperrett@talktalk.net
(*Secretary*) Dr Matthew Lavis, Dioc Office
Assistant Secretary (*Pastoral*) Miss Jane Logan, Dioc Office
Finance Committee (*Chairman*) Mr Hugh Duberly; (*Secretary*) Dr Matthew Lavis (*as above*)
Accounts Administrator Mrs Janice Sulman, Dioc Office
Dioc Surveyor Mr Stephen Layton, Dioc Office
Board of Patronage (*Secretary*) Miss Jane Logan, Dioc Office
Designated Officer Dr Matthew Lavis (*as above*)

CHURCHES

Advisory Committee for the Care of Churches (*Secretary*) Miss Jane Logan, Dioc Office
Archdeaconry of Cambridge Church Music Society (*Secretary*) Mrs. S. Barton, 239 Lichfield Road, Cambridge CB1 3SH   *Tel:* 01223 505764
email: suzanne_barton@yahoo.com
Ely RSCM Committee (*Secretary*) Mrs K. M. Coutts, 74 Barton Road, Ely, Cambs. CB7 4HZ
Tel: 01353 614141

EDUCATION AND TRAINING

email: ed&t@office.ely.anglican.org
web: www.ely.anglican.org/education
Dioc Board of Education and Training (*Secretary*) Canon Tim Elbourne, Dioc Office
Director of Education and Training Canon Tim Elbourne (*as above*)
Children's Adviser Mrs Julia Chamberlin
Youth Officer Capt David Waters
RE Adviser (*Schools*) Dr Shirley Hall, Dioc Office
Schools Buildings and Finance Officer Mr David Hicks
Director of Ministerial and Adult Learning Canon Les Oglesby, Dioc Office
Ministry and Adult Learning Officer Revd Christine Worsley
Reader Ministry Contact The Bishop of Huntingdon

MINISTRY

Director of Ministry and Vocation and Diocesan Director of Ordinands Canon Vanessa Herrick, 2 Cromwell Rd, Ely CB6 1AS   *Tel:* 01353 662909
Fax: 01353 662056
Readers' Board (*Chair*) Mrs Elaine Levitt, 23 Oberon Close, Hartford, Huntingdon, Cambs PE29 1TB   *Tel:* 01480 455225
email: Elaine@hartford.eclipse.co.uk
Warden The Bishop of Huntingdon

LITURGICAL COMMITTEE

Secretary Mr Simon Kershaw, 5 Sharp Close, St Ives, Cambs PE27 6UN   *Tel:* 01480 381471
email: simon@kershaw.org.uk

MISSIONARY AND ECUMENICAL

Council for Mission and Ministry (*Chair*) The Bishop of Huntingdon   *Tel:* 01353 662137
Ecumenical Officer Vacancy

PRESS AND PUBLICATIONS

Bishop's Press Officer Canon Owen Spencer-Thomas, 52 Windsor Rd, Cambridge CB4 3JN
Tel: 01223 358446
Communications Officer Mrs Val Robson, Dioc Office
Editor of Dioc Directory Dr Matthew Lavis, Dioc Office

DIOCESAN RECORD OFFICES

Dioc Archivist P. M. Meadows, c/o University Library, West Rd, Cambridge CB3 9DR
Tel: 01223 333141
Cambridgeshire Archives, Shire Hall, Castle Hill, Cambridge CB3 0AP *Principal Archivist* Mr P. C. Saunders *Tel:* 01223 699487/ 699399 (*For parishes in the archdeaconry of Cambridge and the deaneries of Ely and March*)
Huntingdonshire Archives, Grammar School Walk, Huntingdon PE29 3LF *Senior Archivist* Mrs L. S. Akeroyd *Tel:* 01480 375842 (*For parishes in the former archdeaconry of Huntingdon*)
Cambridge Record Office, Shire Hall, Cambridge (*see above*) (*For parishes in the deaneries of Ely and March*)
Norfolk Record Office, Central Library, Norwich NR2 1NJ *City and County Archivist* Dr John Alban *Tel:* 01603 22233 (*For parishes in the deaneries of Feltwell and Fincham*)
Wisbech and Fenland Museum, Museum Square, Wisbech PE13 1ES *Assistant Curator* Mr J. R. Bell *Tel:* 01945 583817 (*For parishes in the deanery of Wisbech Lynn Marshland*)

DIOCESAN RESOURCE CENTRE

Contact Dioc Resource Centre, Dioc Office

SOCIAL RESPONSIBILITY

Board for Church in Society (*Chairman*) Canon Alan Hargrave (*see above*)
(*Secretary*) Dr Hilary Lavis, Dioc Office
Tel: 01353 652720
Committee for Family and Social Welfare (*Chairman*) Mr Adrian Wright, 5 Lode Ave, Waterbeach, Cambridge CB5 9PX   *Tel:* 01223 861846
Cambridgeshire Deaf Association (*Ely Dioc Association for the Deaf*) (*Chairman*) Mr R. Holland, 8 Romsey Terrace, Cambridge
Mothers' Union (*President*) Mrs Joan Cameron, 5 St Catherine's, Ely CB6 1AP   *Tel:* 01353 614467

RURAL AND AREA DEANS
ARCHDEACONRY OF CAMBRIDGE

Bourn Revd Michael Matthews, Vicarage, Broad Lane, Haslingfield, Cambs CB23 1JF
Tel: 01223 870285

Cambridge North Canon Dr John Binns, Great St Mary's Vicarage, 39 Madingley Rd, Cambridge CB3 0EL   *Tel:* 01223 355285

Cambridge South Canon Andrew Greany, Little St Mary's Vicarage, 4 Newnham Terrace, Cambridge CB3 9EX   *Tel:* 01223 350733

Fordham and Quy Revd Tim Alban-Jones, The Vicarage, Cross Green, Soham, Ely, Cambs CB7 5DU   *Tel:* 01353 720423

North Stowe Revd James Blandford-Baker, St Andrew's Vicarage, Church St, Histon CB4 9EP   *Tel:* 01223 233456

Granta Canon Michael Goater, Vicarage, 12 Church St, Great Shelford CB2 5EL   *Tel:* 01223 843654

Shingay Canon Shamus Williams, Vicarage, Church St, Guilden Morden, Royston SG8 0JP   *Tel:* 01763 853067

ARCHDEACONRY OF HUNTINGDON AND WISBECH

Ely Revd Peter Taylor, Gravel Head Farm, Downham Common, Lt Downham, Ely CB6 2TY   *Tel:* 01353 698714

Fincham and Feltwell Revd David Evans, Rectory, Church Road, Hilgay, Downham Market PE38 0JL   *Tel:* 01366 384418

Huntingdon Canon Brian Atling, Blue Cedars, Common Lane, Hemingford Abbots, Huntingdon PE28 9AW   *Tel:* 01480 493975

March Revd Nigel Whitehouse, Rectory, 9a St Mary's St, Whittlesey, Peterborough PE7 1BG   *Tel:* 01733 203676

St Ives Revd Chris Barter, Rectory, Rectory Lane, Somersham, Huntingdon PE28 3EL   *Tel:* 01487 840676

St Neots Revd Annette Reed, Vicarage, 24 St James Rd, Little Paxton, Huntingdon PE19 6QW   *Tel:* 01480 211048

Wisbech Lynn Marshland Revd John Penny, Vicarage, 37 Church Rd, Tilney St Lawrence, King's Lynn, Norfolk PE34 4QQ   *Tel:* 01945 880259

Yaxley Canon Malcolm Griffith, Rectory, Church Causeway, Sawtry, Huntingdon PE28 5TD   *Tel:* 01487 830215

DIOCESE IN EUROPE

Founded 1980 by union of the Diocese of Gibraltar (founded 1842) and the (Fulham) Jurisdiction of North and Central Europe. Area, Europe, except Great Britain and Ireland; Morocco; Turkey; the Asian countries of the former Soviet Union.

Licensed Clergy 155 Churches and Congregations 295
www.europe.anglican.org

BISHOP OF GIBRALTAR IN EUROPE (3rd)
Rt Revd Dr (Douglas) Geoffrey Rowell, Bishop's Lodge, Church Rd, Worth, Crawley, W Sussex RH10 7RT [2001]   *Tel:* 01293 883051
Fax: 01293 884479
email: bishop@dioceseineurope.org.uk
Bishop's Chaplain Revd Kevin O'Brien
Bishop's Personal Assistant Mrs Margaret Gibson

SUFFRAGAN BISHOP
IN EUROPE Rt Revd Dr David Hamid, 14 Tufton St, London SW1P 3QZ [2002]   *Tel:* 020 7898 1160
Fax: 020 7898 1166
email: david.hamid@europe.c-of-e.org.uk
Bishop's Chaplain and PA Revd Deacon Frances Hiller

HONORARY ASSISTANT BISHOPS
Rt Revd Eric Devenport, 6 Damocles Court, Pottergate, Norwich NR2 1HN [1993]
Tel: 01603 664121
email: eric@edevenport.orangehome.co.uk
The Rt Revd John Flack, The Vicarage, 34 Station Road, Nassington, Peterborough PE8 6QB [2003]
Tel: 01780 782271 / 00 44 (0)7810 714056
email: johnrobertflack@hotmail.com
Rt Revd Richard Garrard, 26 Carol Close, Stoke Holy Cross, Norwich NR14 8NN [2001]
Tel: 01508 494165
email: garrard.r.a@btinternet.com
Rt Revd Patrick Harris, Apartment B, Ireton House, Pavillion Gardens, The Park, Cheltenham GL50 2SP [1999]   *Tel:* 01242 231376
email: pandvharris@blueyonder.co.uk
Rt Revd Edward Holland, 37 Palfrey St, London W6 9EW [2002]   *Tel:* 020 8746 3636
email: ed.holland@btopenworld.com
Rt Revd Michael Manktelow, 14 Little London, Chichester, W Sussex PO19 1NZ [1994]
Tel: 01243 531096
Rt Revd Fernando Soares, Centro Diocesano, Rua de Afonso Albuquerque No 86, Apartado 392, 4431–905 Vila Nova de Gaia, Portugal [1995]
Tel: 00 351 223 754018
Fax: 00 351 223 752016
email: bisposoares@igreja-lusitana.org

Rt Revd John Taylor, 22 Conduit Head Rd, Cambridge CB3 0EY [1998]   *Tel:* 01223 313783
email: john.taylor6529@ntlworld.com
Rt Revd David Smith, 34 Cedar Glade, Dunnington, York YO19 5QZ [2002]   *Tel:* 01904 481225
email: david@djmhs.force9.co.uk
Rt Revd Pierre Whalon, American Cathedral, 23 Avenue George V, 75008 Paris, France [2001]
Tel: 00 33 1 53 23 84 00 (Cathedral)
Fax: 00 33 1 47 23 95 30 (Cathedral)
Tel: 00 33 1 47 20 02 23 (Direct)
Fax: 00 33 1 40 27 03 53 (Home)
email: office@tec-europe.org
The Rt Revd and Rt Hon Lord Hope of Thorns (David Michael), 2 Aspinall Rise, Hellifield, Skipton BD23 4JT
Rt Revd Michael Turnbull, 67 Strand St, Sandwich CT13 9HN [2003]   *Tel:* 01304 611389
email: bstmt@btopenworld.com

CATHEDRAL CHURCH OF THE HOLY TRINITY, GIBRALTAR
Dean Very Revd Dr John Paddock, The Deanery, Bomb House Lane, Gibraltar [2008]
Tel: 00 350 200 78377 (Deanery)
Fax: 00 350 200 78463
email: deangib@gibraltar.gi

PRO-CATHEDRAL OF ST PAUL, VALLETTA, MALTA
Chancellor Canon Simon Godfrey, Chancellor's Lodge, St Paul's Anglican Pro-Cathedral, Independence Square, Valletta VLT12, Malta [2009]   *Tel:* 00 356 21 22 57 14
Fax: 00 356 21 22 58 67
email: anglican@onvol.net / simonhmgodfrey@googlemail.com

PRO-CATHEDRAL OF THE HOLY TRINITY, BRUSSELS, BELGIUM
Chancellor Canon Dr Robert Innes, Pro-Cathedral of the Holy Trinity, 29 rue Capitaine Crespel, 1050 Brussels [2005]   *Tel:* 00 32 2 511 71 83
Fax: 00 32 2 511 10 28
email: chaplain@holytrinity.be

ARCHDEACONS

THE EASTERN ARCHDEACONRY Ven Patrick Curran, c/o British Embassy, Jaurèsgasse 12, 1030 Vienna, Austria [2002]   *Tel:* 00 43 1 718 5902 (Home)
Tel: and *Fax:* 00 43 1 714 8900 (Office)
email: office@christchurchvienna.org
NORTH WEST EUROPE Ven John de Wit, V Hogendorpstraat 26, 3581 KE Utrecht, The Netherlands [2008]   *Tel:* 00 31 30 251 34 24
email: chaplain@holytrinityutrecht.nl
FRANCE Ven Kenneth Letts, Presbytère Anglican, 11 rue de la Buffa, 06000 Nice, France [2007]
Tel: 00 33 4 93 87 19 83
Fax: 00 33 4 93 82 25 09
email: kletts@mac.com /
anglican.nice@gmail.com
GIBRALTAR Ven David Sutch St Andrew, Oficina 1, Edificio Jupiter, Avenida Nuestro Padre Jesus Cautivo 74, Los Boliches, 29640 Fuengirola (Malaga), Spain [2008]
Tel: 00 34 952 580 600 (Office)
+34 952 472 140 (Home)
Fax: 00 34 952 580 600 (Office)
+34 952 472 140 (Home)
email: frdavid@standrews-cofe-spain.com
ITALY AND MALTA Ven Jonathan Boardman, All Saint's Church, Via del Babuino 153, 00187 Rome, Italy [2009]   *Tel & Fax:* 39 06 3600 1881
email: j.boardman@allsaintsrome.org (Personal)
office@allsaintsrome.org (Office)
GERMANY AND NORTHERN EUROPE Ven Jonathan LLoyd, Tuborgvej 82, 2900 Hellerup, Copenhagen, Denmark [2010]   *Tel:* 00 45 39 62 77 36
Fax: 00 45 39 62 77 35
email: chaplain@st-albans.dk
SWITZERLAND Ven Peter Potter, Jubiläumsplatz 2, CH-3005 Berne, Switzerland [2009]
Tel: 41 31 351 03 43 (Home)
41 31 352 85 67 (Office)
Fax: 41 31 351 05 48
email: berne@anglican.ch

CONVOCATION (MEMBERS OF THE HOUSE OF CLERGY OF THE GENERAL SYNOD)

Revd Canon Ian Hutchinson-Cervantes
Canon Debbie Flach

MEMBERS OF THE HOUSE OF LAITY OF THE GENERAL SYNOD

Lay Canon Mrs Ann Turner
Mrs Madeleine Holmes

DIOCESAN OFFICERS

Dioc Secretary Mr Adrian Mumford, Dioc Office
Assistant Dioc Secretary Mrs Jeanne French, Dioc Office
Chancellor of Diocese The Worshipful Mark Hill, 3 Pump Court, Temple, London EC4Y 7AJ (contact via Dioc Office)
Registrar of Diocese and Bishop's Legal Secretary Mr Aiden Hargreaves-Smith, Winkworth

Sherwood, 5 Montague Close, London SE1 9BB
(contact via the Diocesan Office)
Tel: 020 7898 1155
Fax: 020 7898 1166
email: diocesan.office@europe.c-of-e.org.uk

DIOCESAN ORGANIZATIONS

Diocesan Office 14 Tufton St, London SW1P 3QZ
Tel: 020 7898 1155
Fax: 020 7898 1166
email: diocesan.office@europe.c-of-e.org.uk
Web: www.europe.anglican.org

ADMINISTRATION

Dioc Synod (Clerical Vice-President) Canon Debbie Flach, 7 rue Leonard de Vinci, 59700 Marcq en Baroeul, France   *Tel:* 00 33 3 28 52 66 36
email: chaplain@christchurchlille.com
(Lay Vice-President) Lay Canon Mrs Ann Turner, Grotesteenweg 47, bus 42, 2600 Berchem, Antwerp, Belgium
Tel and *Fax:* 00 32 3 440 25 81
email: ann@turner.be
(Secretary) Mr Adrian Mumford, Dioc Office
Board of Finance (Chairman) Mr Michael Hart, c/o Dioc Office; *(Secretary)* Mr Adrian Mumford, Dioc Office

CHURCHES

Faculty Committee (Secretary) Mr Adrian Mumford *(as above)*

MINISTRY AND TRAINING

Warden of Readers Rt Revd Dr David Hamid, Dioc Office
Director of Ordinands Revd William Gulliford, Dioc Office
email: william.gulliford@europe.c-of-e.org.uk
or william.gulliford@london.anglican.org
Director of Training Revd Ulla Monberg, Borgmester Jensens Allé 9, 2th, 2100 Copenhagen Ø Denmark   *Tel:* 00 45 3526 0660
email: ullamonberg@msn.com

LITURGY

Enquiries to Canon Prof Paul Bradshaw, Notre Dame London Centre, 1 Suffolk St, London SW1Y 4HG   *Tel:* 020 7484 7811
Fax: 020 7484 7853
email: bradshaw.1@nd.edu

MEDITERRANEAN MISSIONS TO SEAMEN

Administrator Mr Adrian Mumford *(as above)*

PRESS AND PUBLICATIONS

Press and Communications Officer Revd Paul Needle, Dioc Office
Tel: 00 34 662 482944 (Mobile)
email: paul.needle@europe.c-of-e.org.uk
Editor of 'The European Anglican' Revd Paul Needle *(as above)*

DIOCESAN RECORD OFFICE
London Metropolitan Archives, 40 Northampton
Road, London EC1R 0HB   *Tel:* 020 7332 3820
              email: ask.lma@cityoflondon.gov.uk

**ARCHBISHOP'S APOKRISARIOI AND
REPRESENTATIVES**
To the Holy See Very Revd David Richardson,
Palazzo Doria Pamphilj, Piazza dei Collegio
Romano 2 – Int 7, 00186 Rome, Italy
                      Tel: 39 06 678 0302
                      Fax: 39 06 678 0674
          email: anglican.centre.rome@flashnet.it
*To the Patriarch of Romania, and the Patriarch of
Bulgaria* Vacancy
To the Archbishop of Athens and All Greece Canon
Malcolm Bradshaw, c/o British Embassy,
Ploutarchou 1, Athens 106 75
         Tel and *Fax:* 00 30 210 721 4906 (Home)
                 email: anglican@otenet.gr

To the Patriarch of Moscow and All Russia Canon
Dr Simon Stephens, British Embassy Moscow,
Sofiiskaya Naberezhnaya, Moscow 109702
             Tel and *Fax:* 007 495 629 0990
          email: chaplain@standrewsmoscow.org
To the Patriarch of Serbia Revd Robin Fox,
St Mary's Anglican Church, Visegradska 23,
11000 Belgrade, Serbia and Montenegro
                      Tel: 00 381 11 3232 948
                 email: robin.fox@sbb.co.yu

DEANERIES
The archdeaconry of Germany and Northern
Europe has Deanery Synods rather than a single
Archdeaconry Synod. The names and addresses
of the officers are available from the Diocesan
Office.

DIOCESE OF EXETER

Transferred to Exeter in 1050, formerly at Crediton in 909. Devon, except for one parish in the south-east (SALISBURY) and one parish in the west (TRURO); Plymouth; Torbay.

Population 1,139,000   Area 2,575 sq m
Full-time Stipendiary Parochial Clergy 196   Benefices 189
Parishes 492   Churches 617
www.exeter.anglican.org
Overseas link diocese: Cyprus and the Gulf; Thika (Kenya).

BISHOP (70th)
Rt Revd Michael Laurence Langrish, The Palace, Exeter EX1 1HY [2000]   *Tel:* 01392 272362
Fax: 01392 430923
email: bishop.of.exeter@exeter.anglican.org
[Michael Exon:]
Chaplain and Assistant to the Bishop Revd Dr Adrian Hough (*same address*)
email: adrian.hough@exeter.anglican.org
Personal Assistant Miss Sarah Johnson
email: sarah.johnson@exeter.anglican.org
Administrative Secretary Mrs Tracey Watson
email: tracey.watson@exeter.anglican.org

SUFFRAGAN BISHOPS
CREDITON Rt Revd Robert John Scott Evens, 32 The Avenue, Tiverton EX16 4HW [2004]
Tel: 01884 250002
Fax: 01884 257454
email: bishop.of.crediton@exeter.anglican.org
PLYMOUTH Rt Revd John Ford, 31 Riverside Walk, Tamerton Foliot, Plymouth PL5 4AQ [2006]
Tel: 01752 769836
email: bishop.of.plymouth@exeter.anglican.org

HONORARY ASSISTANT BISHOPS
Rt Revd Andrew Burnham, Bishop's House, Dry Sandford, Abingdon OX13 6JP [2001]
Tel: 01865 390746
email: bishop.Andrew@ebbsfleet.org.uk
Rt Revd Richard Fox Cartwright, Royal Masonic Benevolent Institute, Cadogan Court, Barley Lane, Exeter EX4 1TA [1988]   *Tel:* 01392 251017
Rt Revd Ivor Colin Docker, Braemar, Bradley Rd, Bovey Tracey, Newton Abbot TQ13 9EU [1991]
Tel: 01626 832468
Rt Revd Robert David Silk, 1 Centenary Way, Torquay TQ2 7SB [2005]   *Tel:* 01803 614458
Rt Revd Richard Hawkins, 3 Westbrook Close, Whipton, Exeter EX4 8BS [2005]
Tel: 01392 462622
Rt Revd Michael Robert Westall, St Luke's Vicarage, 1 Mead Rd, Livermead, Torquay TQ2 6TE [2007]   *Tel:* 01803 605437
Rt Revd James Philip Mason, St Maurice's Rectory, 31 Wain Park, Plympton, Plymouth PL7 2HX [2006]   *Tel:* 01752 346114

Rt Revd Martin Shaw, 11 Russell Terrace, Exeter EX4 4HX [2010]   *Tel:* 01392 663511
*email:*amartinshaw@gmail.com

CATHEDRAL CHURCH OF ST PETER
Dean Very Revd Jonathan Meyrick, The Deanery, 10 Cathedral Close, Exeter EX1 1EZ [2005]
Tel: 01392 273509
email: dean@exeter-cathedral.org.uk
Canons Residentiary
Precentor Canon Carl Turner, 6 Cathedral Close, Exeter EX1 1EZ [2001]   *Tel:* 01392 272498
email: precentor@exeter-cathedral.org.uk
Missioner Vacancy
Chancellor Canon Andrew Godsall, 12 Cathedral Close, Exeter EX1 1EZ [2006]   *Tel:* 01392 275756
email: andrew.godsall@exeter.anglican.org
Treasurer and Pastor Vacancy
Chapter Canons Mrs Hannah Foster, Mrs Elsa Wakefield, Mr Jonathan Harris, one vacancy
Priest Vicars Revd Alison Turner, Revd David Walford, Revd Philip Darby
Cathedral Offices 1 The Cloisters, Exeter EX1 1HS
Tel: 01392 255573
Fax: 01392 285986
email: admin@exeter-cathedral.org.uk
Web: www.exeter-cathedral.org.uk
Administrator Mr Paul Snell   *Tel:* 01392 285973
email: prs@exeter-cathedral.org.uk
Clerk to the Chapter Mr Tony Le Riche
Tel: 01392 285971
email: admin@exeter-cathedral.org.uk
Liturgy and Music Dept   *Tel:* 01392 285984
email: liturgy@exeter-cathedral.org.uk
Director of Music Mr Andrew Millington, 11 Cathedral Close, Exeter EX1 1EZ
Tel: 01392 277521
email: music@exeter-cathedral.org.uk
Third Millennium Campaign Director Mrs Jill Taylor, Cathedral Campaign Office
Tel: 01392 285974
email:
campaigndirector@exeter-cathedral.org.uk
Head of Visitor Services Mrs Catherine Escott
Tel: 01392 285983
email: visitors@exeter-cathedral.org.uk

ARCHDEACONS

EXETER Ven Penny Driver, Emmanuel House, Station Rd, Ide, Exeter EX2 9RS [2006]
Tel: 01392 425577
email: archdeacon.of.exeter@exeter.anglican.org
TOTNES Ven John Rawlings, Blue Hills, Bradley Rd, Bovey Tracey, Newton Abbot TQ13 9EU [2006]
Tel: 01626 832064
Fax: 01626 834947
email: archdeacon.of.totnes@exeter.anglican.org
BARNSTAPLE Ven David Gunn-Johnson, Stage Cross, Sanders Lane, Bishop's Tawton, Barnstaple EX32 0BE [2003]
Tel: 01271 375475
Fax: 01271 377934
email:
archdeacon.of.barnstaple@exeter.anglican.org
PLYMOUTH Ven Ian Chandler, St Mark's House, 46a Cambridge Road, Ford, Plymouth PL2 1PU
Tel: 01752 793397
email:
archdeacon.of.plymouth@exeter.anglican.org

CONVOCATION (MEMBERS OF THE HOUSE OF CLERGY OF THE GENERAL SYNOD)

Proctors for Clergy
Preb Samuel Philpott
Revd Roderick Thomas
Ven Penny Driver
Revd Canon Andrew Godsall
Revd Caroline Ralph

MEMBERS OF THE HOUSE OF LAITY OF THE GENERAL SYNOD

Mrs Anneliese Barrell
Mr Jack Shelley
Miss Emma Forward
Mrs Anne Foreman

Dioc Synod (Chairman, House of Clergy) Revd Douglas Dettmer, Rectory, Thorverton, Exeter EX5 5NR
Tel: 01392 860332
(Secretary, House of Clergy) Revd Gilly Maude, Vicarage, 17 Seafields, Dartmouth Road, Goodrington, Paignton TQ4 6NY
Tel: 01803 846335
email: gillian.maude@btinternet.com
(Chairman, House of Laity) Mr Charles Hodgson, The Smithy, East Worlington, Crediton EX17 4SY
Tel: 01884 861571
email: catherine-charles.hodgson@virgin.net
(Secretary, House of Laity) Mr Graham Lea, 2 Thornyville Close, Oreston, Plymouth PL9 7LE
Tel: 01752 403392
Synod Secretary Mr Mark Beedell, The Old Deanery

DIOCESAN OFFICERS

Dioc Secretary Mr Mark Beedell, The Old Deanery, The Cloisters, Exeter EX1 1HS
Tel: 01392 272686
Fax: 01392 499594
email: dsec@exeter.anglican.org

Chancellor of Diocese Hon Sir Andrew McFarlane, Royal Courts of Justice, Strand, London WC2A 2LL
Tel: 020 7947 6008
Deputy Chancellor of Diocese Mr Gregory Percy Jones, Francis Taylor Building, Inner Temple, London EC4Y 7BY
Tel: 020 7353 8415
Registrar of Diocese and Bishop's Legal Secretary Mr Martin Follett, Michelmores, Woodwater House, Pynes Hill, Exeter EX2 5WR
Tel: 01392 687421
email: mjf@michelmores.com
Deputy Registrar Mr Christopher Butcher, Michelmores
Tel: 01392 687419
email: cnb@michelmores.com

THE DEPARTMENT FOR SUPPORT SERVICES

Director and Dioc Secretary Mr Mark Beedell (*as above*)
Asst Dioc Secretary Dr Ed Moffatt, The Old Deanery
Tel: 01392 294928
Fax: 01392 499594
email: ed.moffatt@exeter.anglican.org
Diocesan Office The Old Deanery, The Cloisters, Exeter EX1 1HS
Tel: 01392 272686
Fax: 01392 499594
email: admin@exeter.anglican.org

ADMINISTRATION

Board of Finance (Chairman) David Cain, Venn Farm, Kingsnympton, Umberleigh EX37 9TR
Tel: 01769 572448
email: twelvetwentyfive@msn.com
(Secretary) Mr Mark Beedell (*as above*)
Parsonages Committee (Secretary) Mr Graham Davies, The Old Deanery
Tel: 01392 294954
Fax: 01392 499594
email: graham.davies@exeter.anglican.org
Dioc Surveyors Mr Peter Stanton and Mr Mark Lewis, The Old Deanery
Tel: 01392 294952
Fax: 01392 499594
email: peter.stanton@exeter.anglican.org *or* mark.lewis@exeter.anglican.org
Smith & Dunn, Alliance House, Cross St, Barnstaple EX31 1BA (*for Barnstaple Archdeaconry*)
Tel: 01271 327878
Fax: 01271 328288
Mission and Pastoral Committee (Secretary) Vacancy
Tel: 01392 294943
email: pastoral@exeter.anglican.org
Board of Patronage (Chairman) Mrs Shirley-Ann Williams, 2 Katherine's Lane, Ridgeway, Ottery St Mary EX11 1FB
Tel: 01404 811064
Trusts Mrs Jane Scriven, The Old Deanery
Tel: 01392 294913
email: jane.scriven@exeter.anglican.org
Designated Officer Mr Mark Beedell (*as above*)

SAFEGUARDING UNIT

Mrs Sue Chamberlain, The Old Deanery
Tel: 01392 294912
email: sue.chamberlain@exeter.anglican.org

CHURCHES

Dioc Advisory Committee for the Care and Maintenance of Churches (Chairman) Revd Nigel Freathy; *(Secretary)* Miss Louise Skinner, The Old Deanery; *Tel:* 01392 294944; *email:* dac@exeter.anglican.org
Redundant Churches Uses Committee (Secretary) Miss Pru Williams *(as above)*

COMMUNICATIONS

Communications Officer Mrs Rebecca Paveley
The Church of England, Devon (Diocesan News)
Tel: 01392 294905
07812 110636 (Mobile)
email: communications@exeter.anglican.org
Web: www.exeter.anglican.org

THE COUNCIL FOR WORK WITH CHILDREN AND YOUNG PEOPLE

Diocesan Director of Education Mrs Alyson Sheldrake, The Old Deanery, The Cloisters, Exeter EX1 1HS   *Tel:* 01392 294950
Fax: 01392 294966
email: dde@exeter.anglican.org
Executive Assistant Mrs Marilyn Pearce
Tel: 01392 294950
email: marilyn.pearce@exeter.anglican.org
Diocesan Education Officer Mrs Tatiana Wilson
Tel: 01392 294941
email: tatiana.wilson@exeter.anglican.org
Revd Richard Maudsley   *Tel:* 01392 294961
email: richard.maudsley@exeter.anglican.org
Mrs Penny Burnside   *Tel:* 01392 294942
email: penny.burnside@exeter.anglican.org
Dioc Church Schools Liaison Officer Mrs Christina Mabin   *Tel:* 01392 294939
Dioc Consultant for SIAS, RE and Collective Worship Mrs Tricia Martin   *Tel:* 01392 294950
email: ress.pmartin26@btopenworld.com
Children's Work Adviser Miss Katherine Lyddon
Tel: 01392 294936
email: katherine.lyddon@exeter.anglican.org
Dioc Youth Work Adviser Martin Thompson
Tel: 01392 294932
email: martin.thompson@exeter.anglican.org
Dioc Youth Church Adviser Revd James Grier
Tel: 01392 294934
email: james.grier@exeter.anglican.org
Church Schools Surveyors Richard Power and Jason Down   *Tel:* 01392 294952
Fax: 01392 294967
email: school.premises@exeter.anglican.org *or* richard.power@exeter.anglican.org *or* jason.down@exeter.anglican.org
Church Schools Funding Adviser Raymond Twohig
Tel: 01392 294952
email: raymond.twohig@exeter.anglican.org

THE COUNCIL FOR WORSHIP AND MINISTRY

Director, Officer for Non-Stipendiary Ministry and Continuing Ministerial Education Canon Andrew Godsall, The Old Deanery   *Tel:* 01392 294902

Council Administrator Mrs Alyson Moore, The Old Deanery   *Tel:* 01392 294920
email: alyson.moore@exeter.anglican.org
Director of Ordinands, Adviser for Vocations Revd Becky Totterdell, The Palace, Exeter EX1 1HY
Tel: 01392 477702
email: ddo@exeter.anglican.org
Adviser for Women's Ministry Vacancy
Administrator Mrs Sandra Brown, The Palace, Exeter EX1 1HY   *Tel:* 01392 477702
email: sandra.brown@exeter.anglican.org
Local Stewardship Adviser, North Devon Mr Paul Mason   *Tel:* 01409 281548
email: paulgidcott@aol.com
Local Stewardship Adviser, South Devon Preb Mark Bate   *Tel:* 01392 833485
email: morleybate@freeuk.com
Board of Readers (Secretary) Mr Ronald Edinborough, The Old Deanery
Tel: 01392 294907
email: ron.edinborough@exeter.anglican.org
Adult Education Adviser Vacancy
Warden of Readers Ven David Gunn-Johnson, Stage Cross, Sanders Lane, Bishop's Tawton, Barnstaple EX32 0BE   *Tel:* 01271 375475
Fax: 01271 377934
email:
archdeacon.of.barnstaple@exeter.anglican.org
Co-ordinator Spiritual Direction Mrs Wendy Pezzey, 7 De la Hay Avenue, Stoke, Plymouth PL3 4HS   *Tel:* 01752 218432
*email:*wspezzey2@live.co.uk
Mission Community Teams Adviser Preb David Rudman, Rectory, Kingsnympton, Umberleigh EX37 9ST   *Tel:* 01769 580457
email: david.rudman@exeter.anglican.org
Local Ministry Teams Adviser Preb David Rudman, Rectory, Kingsnympton, Umberleigh EX37 9ST
Tel: 01769 580457
email: david.rudman@exeter.anglican.org
Dioc Consultant for Worship and Music Mr Andrew Maries   *Tel:* 01884 34389
email: maries@keynotetrust.org.uk
Web: www.exeterdlc.org.uk

THE COUNCIL FOR MISSION AND UNITY

Director and Diocesan Missioner Vacancy
Administrator Vacancy
Chaplain with Deaf People Revd Catherine Carlyon, The Old Deanery
Tel: 01392 294909 (voice and text)
Fax: 01392 294965
07855 098953 (Mobile)
email: catherinecarlyon@btopenworld.com
Dioc Ecumenical Adviser Revd Simon Crittall, The Old Deanery   *Tel:* 01392 294960
email: simon.crittall@exeter.anglican.org
County Ecumenical Officer Revd Sabrina Groeschel, 1 Furze Road, Woodbury, Exeter EX5 1PF
Tel: 01395 239116

Cyprus and the Gulf Link (*Chairman*) Mr Oliver Mayfield, Bank House, Market Square, Colyton EX24 6JS   *Tel* and *Fax:* 01297 552942
          email: oliver.colyton@tiscali.co.uk
Ministry of Healing and Deliverance The Archdeacon of Totnes
Thika Link Mrs Kate Bray (parish links), The Old Deanery   *Tel:* 01392 294930
          email: thika.link@exeter.anglican.org
World Development Adviser Vacancy
FRED (Fresh Expressions Devon) Canon Mark Rylands (*as above*)
Nightchurch Laura McAdam, c/o Cathedral Office, 1 The Cloisters, Exeter EX1 1HS
          Tel: 07971 242256
          e-mail: laura@nightchurch.org.uk

THE COUNCIL FOR CHURCH AND SOCIETY
Director Mr Martyn Goss, The Old Deanery
          Tel: 01392 294924
          Fax: 01392 499594
          email: martyn@exeter.anglican.org
Social Responsibility Officer Miss Sally Farrant, The Old Deanery   *Tel:* 01392 294918
          email: sally.farrant@exeter.anglican.org
Family Life and Marriage Education Coordinator Mrs Susie Ursell, The Old Deanery
          Tel: 01392 294919
          email: susie.ursell@exeter.anglican.org
Rural Officer Mrs Sue Tucker, Quither Farm, Quither, Milton Abbot, Tavistock PL19 0PZ
          Tel: 01822 860177 (Work)
          01392 294921 (Office)
          email: sue.tucker@exeter.anglican.org

MISCELLANEOUS ORGANIZATIONS
Widows and Dependants (*Exeter Archdeaconry*) Revd Tony Mortimer, 97 Egremont Road, Exmouth EX8 1SA   *Tel:* 01395 271390
          *email:*tpmortimer@googlemail.com
(*Totnes Archdeaconry*) Revd Tony Meek, The Willows, Orley Rd, Ipplepen, Newton Abbot TQ12 5SA   *Tel:* 01803 814370
          Fax: 01803 814369
          email: FrTonyMeek@aol.com
(*Plymouth Archdeaconry*) Preb John Richards, 24 Trewithy Drive, Crownhill, Plymouth PL6 5TY
          Tel: 01752 214442
          email: jfr-sjr@fish.co.uk
(*Barnstaple Archdeaconry*) Preb Dr Kenneth Moss, 3 Mondeville Way, Northam, Bideford EX39 1DQ

DIOCESAN RECORD OFFICE
Devon Record Office, Great Moor House, Bittern Rd, Sowton Industrial Estate, Exeter EX2 7NL
Archivist Mr John Draisey   *Tel:* 01392 384253
          email: devrc@devon.gov.uk

RURAL DEANS
ARCHDEACONRY OF EXETER
Aylesbeare Preb Ian Morter, Rectory, 1 Maer Lane, Exmouth EX8 2DA   *Tel:* 01395 272227
          email: ian.c.morter@lineone.net

Cadbury Revd Douglas Dettmer, Rectory, Thorverton, Exeter EX5 5NR   *Tel:* 01392 860332
Christianity Preb Stephen Bessent, Rectory, Alphington, Exeter EX2 8XJ   *Tel:* 01392 437662
          email: rectory6ssmgi@btinternet.com
Cullompton Revd Alan MacDonald, Rectory, 21a King St, Silverton, Exeter EX5 4JG
          Tel: 01392 860350
          email: almac1@talktalk.net
Assistant Rural Dean Revd Anna Norman-Walker, Rectory, Willand, Cullompton EX15 2RH
          Tel: 01884 32509
          email: anna@norman-walker.fsnet.co.uk
Honiton Preb Sue Roberts, Rectory, Rookwood Close, Honiton EX14 1BH   *Tel:* 01404 42925
          email: revdsue@btinternet.com
Kenn Revd Graham Mayer, Rectory, Dry Lane, Christow, Exeter EX6 7PE
          Tel: 01647 252845
          email: rivertide@btinternet.com
Ottery Revd Robert Wilkinson, The Rectory, Grove Rd, Whimple, Exeter EX5 2TP
          Tel: 01404 822521
          email: robwilkinson@lineone.net
Tiverton Revd Alan MacDonald, Rectory, 21a King St, Silverton, Exeter EX5 4JG
          Tel: 01392 860350
          email: almac1@talktalk.net
Assistant Rural Dean Revd Anna Norman-Walker, Rectory, Willand, Cullompton EX15 2RH
          Tel: 01884 32509
          email: anna@norman-walker.fsnet.co.uk

ARCHDEACONRY OF TOTNES
Moreton Revd Paul Wimsett, Vicarage, The Parade, Chudleigh, Newton Abbot TQ13 0JF
          Tel: 01626 853241
          email: wimsett@tesco.net
Newton Abbot and Ipplepen Revd Ian Eglin, Rectory, Paternoster Lane, Ipplepen, Newton Abbot TQ12 5RY   *Tel:* 01803 812215
          email: ian@eglins.co.uk
Okehampton Revd Stephen Cook, Rectory, 1 Church Path, Okehampton EX20 1LW
          Tel: 01837 659297
          email: scook9673@aol.com
Torbay Revd Gillian Maude, Vicarage, 17 Seafields, Dartmouth Rd, Paignton TQ4 6NY
          Tel: 01803 846335
          email: gillian.maude@btinternet.com
Totnes Revd John Rowland, Vicarage, Glebelands, Buckfastleigh TQ11 0BH
          Tel: 01364 644228
          email: djrowland@btconnect.com
Woodleigh Vacancy

ARCHDEACONRY OF BARNSTAPLE
Barnstaple Revd Paul Hockey, Vicarage, Fremington, Barnstaple EX31 2NX
          Tel: 01271 373879
          email: paulhockey@talktalk.net

Hartland Shirley Henderson, Vicarage, North Road, Hartland, Bideford EX39 6BP
Tel: 01237 440229
email: shirely.1949@hotmail.co.uk
Holsworthy The Archdeacon of Barnstaple
Shirwell Revd Leslie Austin, Parsonage, 1 The Glebe, Bratton Fleming, Barnstaple EX31 4RE
Tel: 01598 710807
email: leslie@laustin4.wanadoo.co.uk
South Molton Revd Peter Attwood, Vicarage, East St, South Molton EX36 3HX   *Tel:* 01598 740235
email: rev@podlea.co.uk
Torrington Revd Kim Mathers, Rectory, Newton Tracey, Barnstaple EX31 3PL   *Tel:* 01271 858292
email: revkimmathers@btinterent.com

ARCHDEACONRY OF PLYMOUTH
Ivybridge Preb David Arnott, Vicarage, Bowden Hill, Yealmpton, Plymouth PL8 2JX
Tel and *Fax:* 01752 880979
email: revdavidarnott@virgin.net

Devonport Revd Stephen Beach, Vicarage, Agaton Rd, St Budeaux, Plymouth PL5 2EW
Tel: 01752 361019
email: stephenbeach@btinternet.com
Moorside Revd David Gill, Vicarage, 53 Whitsoncross Lane, Tamerton Foliot, Plymouth PL5 4NT   *Tel:* 01752 771033
email: dbmgill@tiscali.co.uk
Sutton Revd Karl Freeman, Rectory, 9 Seymour Drive, Mannamead, Plymouth PL3 5BG
Tel: 01752 248601
email: karldesk@blueyonder.co.uk
Tavistock Revd Geoff Lloyd, Rectory, Sampford Spiney, Horrabridge, Yelverton PL20 7RE
Tel: 01822 854682
email: stjohnshorrabridge@tiscali.co.uk

DIOCESE OF GLOUCESTER

Founded in 1541. Gloucestershire except for a few parishes in the north (WORCESTER); a few parishes in the south (BRISTOL) and one parish in the east (OXFORD); the northern third of South Gloucestershire; two parishes in Wiltshire; a small area in south-west Warwickshire; a few parishes in the southern part of Worcestershire.

Population 619,000   Area 1,140 sq m
Full-time Stipendiary Parochial Clergy 125   Benefices 115
Parishes 306   Churches 394
www.gloucester.anglican.org

BISHOP (40th)
Rt Revd Michael Francis Perham, The Bishop of Gloucester's Office, 2 College Green, Gloucester GL1 2LR [2004]   *Tel:* 01452 410022 ext. 270
Fax: 01452 308324
email: bshpglos@glosdioc.org.uk
Home address: Bishopscourt, Pitt St, Gloucester GL1 2BQ   *Tel:* 01452 524598
[Michael Gloucester]
Bishop's Chaplain Vacancy (*same address and fax no.; tel. no. as above, ext. 268*)
Bishop's Secretary Mrs Diane Best (*same address and tel. no.*)   *email:* dbest@glosdioc.org.uk

SUFFRAGAN BISHOP
TEWKESBURY Rt Revd John Stewart Went, Bishop's House, Staverton, Cheltenham GL51 0TW [1995]   *Tel:* 01242 680188
Fax: 01242 680233
email: bshptewk@star.co.uk

HONORARY ASSISTANT BISHOPS
Rt Revd Peter Vaughan, Willowbrook, Downington, Lechlade GL7 3DL [2002]
Tel: 01367 252216
Rt Revd Humphrey Taylor, 10 High St, Honeybourne, Evesham WR11 7PQ [2003]
Tel: 01386 834846
Rt Revd Patrick Harris, Apartment B, Ireton House, Pavilion Gardens, The Park, Cheltenham GL50 2SP [2005]   *Tel:* 01242 231376
Rt Revd David Jennings, Laurel Cottage, East End, Northleach, Cheltenham GL54 3ET
Tel: 01451 860743

CATHEDRAL CHURCH OF ST PETER AND THE HOLY AND INDIVISIBLE TRINITY
Dean Vacancy, The Deanery, 1 Miller's Green, Gloucester GL1 2BP [1997]   *Tel:* 01452 524167
email: thedean@gloucestercathedral.org.uk
Dean's Secretary Mrs Fiona Price, The Cathedral Office, 12 College Green, Gloucester GL1 2LX
Tel: 01452 508217
email: fiona@gloucestercathedral.org.uk
Cathedral Office, 12 College Green, Gloucester GL1 2LX   *Tel:* 01452 528095
Fax: 01452 300469
Web: www.gloucestercathedral.org.uk

Canons Residentiary
Precentor Canon Neil Heavisides, 7 College Green, Gloucester GL1 2LX [1993]
Tel: 01452 523987
email: nheavisides@gloucestercathedral.org.uk
Canon Pastor Canon Celia Thomson, 3 Miller's Green, Gloucester GL1 2BN [2003]
Tel: 01452 415824
email: cthomson@gloucestercathedral.org.uk
Ven Geoffrey Sidaway, Glebe House, Church Lane, Maisemore, Gloucester GL2 8EY [2007]
Tel: 01452 528500
Fax: 01452 381528
email: archdglos@star.co.uk
Canon Nikki Arthy, The Rectory, Hempsted, Gloucester GL2 5LW   *Tel:* 01452 523808
email: nikkiarthy@btinternet.com
Chapter Steward Mr Mark Beckett, Cathedral Office (*as above*)   *Tel:* 01452 508216
email: mbeckett@gloucestercathedral.org.uk
Director of Music Mr Adrian Partington, 7 Miller's Green, Gloucester GL1 2BN
Tel: 01452 508212
email: a.partington@gloucestercathedral.org.uk
Assistant Director of Music Mr Ashley Grote, 14 College Green, Gloucester GL1 2LX
Tel: 01452 508212
email: ashley@gloucestercathedral.org.uk
Music and Liturgy Administrator Mrs Helen Sims, The Cathedral Office (*as above*)   *Tel:* 01452 508212
email: helen@gloucestercathedral.org.uk

ARCHDEACONS
GLOUCESTER Ven Geoffrey Sidaway, Glebe House, Church Lane, Maisemore, Gloucester GL2 8EY [2000]   *Tel:* 01452 528500
Fax: 01452 381528
email: archdglos@star.co.uk
CHELTENHAM Ven Robert Springett, 2 College Green, Gloucester GL1 2LY [2010]
Tel: 01452 835594
Fax: 01452 410022 ext 224
email: archdchelt@glosdioc.org.uk

CONVOCATION (MEMBERS OF THE HOUSE OF CLERGY OF THE GENERAL SYNOD)
Proctors for Clergy
Revd Dr Sandra Millar

Revd Canon Michael Parsons
Canon Celia Thomson
Revd Canon John Witcombe

MEMBERS OF THE HOUSE OF LAITY OF THE GENERAL SYNOD
Dr William Belcher
Prof Jenny Tann
Mr Graham Smith

DIOCESAN OFFICERS
Dioc Secretary Dr Kevin Brown, Church House, College Green, Gloucester GL1 2LY
Tel: 01452 410022 ext. 223
Fax: 01452 308324
Executive Assistant Ms Andrea Goodman (same address)
Tel: 01452 410022 ext. 223
email: agoodman@glosdioc.org.uk
Chancellor of Diocese Chancellor June Rodgers, 2 Harcourt Buildings, The Temple, London EC4Y 9DB
Registrar of Diocese and Bishop's Legal Secretary Mr Chris Peak, Dioc Registry, 34 Brunswick Rd, Gloucester GL1 1JW
Tel: 01452 520224
Fax: 01452 306866
email: chris.peak@madgelloyd.com

DIOCESAN ORGANIZATIONS
Diocesan Office Church House, College Green, Gloucester GL1 2LY
Tel: 01452 410022
Fax: 01452 308324
email: church.house@glosdioc.org.uk
Web: www.gloucester.anglican.org

ADMINISTRATION
Dioc Synod (*Vice President, House of Clergy*) Canon Dr Jeni Parsons, Rectory, Matson Lane, Matson, Gloucester GL4 6DX
Tel: 01452 522598
email: jeni@hencity.fsnet.co.uk
(*Vice-President, House of Laity*) Canon Ian Marsh, Mynd House, The Highlands, Painswick GL6 6SL
Tel: 01452 812829
email: ian@marshfamily.eclipse.co.uk
(*Secretary*) Dr Kevin Brown, Church House
Board of Finance (*Chairman*) Revd John Wright, Vicarage, 6 The Green, Tetbury GL8 8DN
Tel: 01666 502333
email: sheba.wright@virgin.net
(*Secretary*) Dr Kevin Brown (*as above*)
Director of Finance Mr Benjamin Preece-Smith, Church House
Houses Committee (*Secretary*) Ms Juliet Weston, Church House
Pastoral Committee (*Secretary*) Dr Kevin Brown (*as above*)
Board of Patronage (*Secretary*) Canon Jonathan MacKechnie-Jarvis, Church House
Designated Officer Dr Kevin Brown (*as above*)
Trust (*Secretary*) Canon Jonathan MacKechnie-Jarvis (*as above*)
Redundant Churches Uses Committee (*Secretary*) Canon Jonathan MacKechnie-Jarvis (*as above*)
Glebe Committee (*Secretary*) Ms Juliet Weston (*as above*)
HR Manager Mrs Judith Knight, Church House

CHURCHES
Advisory Committee for the Care of Churches (*Chairman*) Mr Henry Russell, Ley Mary Farmhouse, Windrush, Burford, Oxon OX18 4TS
Tel: 01451 844397
(*Secretary*) Canon Jonathan MacKechnie-Jarvis (*as above*)

CHILDREN AND YOUNG PEOPLE DEPARTMENT
Director of Children and Young People Department Mrs Helena Arnold, 4 College Green, Gloucester GL1 2LR
Tel: 01452 410022 ext. 272
email: harnold@glosdioc.org.uk
Adviser to Schools Mrs Shahne Vickery (*same address*)
Tel: 01452 410022 ext. 259
email: svickery@glosdioc.org.uk
Buildings and Admissions Adviser Mr Rob Stephens (*same address*)
Tel: 01452 410022 ext. 242
email: rstephens@glosdioc.org.uk
Dioc Youth Officer Vacancy (*same address*)
Tel: 01452 410022 ext. 245
email: sbullock@glosdioc.org.uk
Dioc Children's Officer Revd Dr Sandra Millar (*same address*)
Tel: 01452 410022 ext. 246
email: smillar@glosdioc.org.uk

MINISTRY
Acting Director of Ministry Canon John Witcombe, 4 College Green, Gloucester GL1 2LR
Tel: 01452 410022 ext. 249
email: dhoyle@glosdioc.org.uk
Acting Officer for Ministry Canon Kathy Lawrence, 4 College Green, Gloucester GL1 2LR
Tel: 01452 410022 ext. 263
email: klawrence@glosdioc.org.uk
Associate Director of Ordinands Revd Stephen Ware (*same address*)
Tel: 01452 410022 ext. 241
Vocations Officer Revd Catherine Williams (*same address*)
Tel: 01452 410022
Dean of Women Clergy Canon Dr Jeni Parsons, Rectory, Matson Lane, Matson, Gloucester GL4 6DX
Tel: 01452 522598
email: jeni@hencity.fsnet.co.uk
NSM Officer Canon Michael Tucker, Rectory, Amberley, Stroud GL5 5JG
Tel: 01453 878515
Chaplain for Deaf and Hard of Hearing People Revd Steve Morris, The Vicarage, 27a Barnwood Avenue, Gloucester GL4 3AB
Tel: 01452 619531
email: spadework@fsmail.net
Warden of Readers Revd Stephen Ware, 4 College Green, Gloucester GL1 2LR
Tel: 01452 410022 ext. 261
email: sware@glosdioc.org.uk
West of England Ministerial Training Course (*Principal*) Canon Dr Michael Parsons, University of Gloucestershire, Francis Close Hall, Swindon Rd, Cheltenham GL50 4AZ
Tel and Fax: 01242 543382
email: office@wemtc.freeserve.co.uk
Local Ministry Officers Revd Grahame Humphries, Vicarage, The Square, Blockley, Moreton-in-Marsh GL56 9ES
Tel: 01386 700283

Canon Kathy Lawrence (*as above*)
Revd Brian Parfitt (*same address*)
Tel: 01452 410022 ext. 238
email: bparfitt@glosdioc.org.uk
Diocesan Ecumenical Officer Revd David Ackerman, Vicarage, Windrush, Burford, Oxon OX18 4TS *Tel:* 01451 844276
Diocesan Worship Officer Revd Tom Clammer, 4 College Green, Gloucester GL1 2LR
Tel: 01452 410022 ext 280
email: tclammer@glosdioc.org.uk

BISHOP'S WORSHIP, PRAYER AND SPIRITUALITY GROUP
Chair Revd Susan Bailey, 28 Burleigh Way, Wickwar, Wotton-under-Edge GL12 8LR
Tel: 01454 294112
email: susan.m.bailey@gmail.com
Secretary Revd Tom Clammer (*as above*)

PRESS AND PUBLICATIONS
Communications Officer Mrs Lucy Taylor, Church House *Tel:* 01452 410022 ext. 250
07811 174125 (Mobile)
email: ltaylor@glosdioc.org.uk

DIOCESAN RECORD OFFICE
Gloucestershire Records Office, Clarence Row, Gloucester GL1 3DW *Dioc Archivist* Ms Heather Forbes *Tel:* 01452 425295
email: records@gloscc.gov.uk (Office)
email: heather.forbes@gloucestershire.gov.uk

DIOCESAN RESOURCE CENTRE
Warden Mrs Carolyn Wright, 9 College Green, Gloucester GL1 2LX *Tel:* 01452 385217
email: glosrerc@star.co.uk

SOCIAL RESPONSIBILITY
Director of Social Responsibility Canon Adrian Slade, St Peter's House 2 College Street, Gloucester GL1 2NE *Tel:* 01452 521438
email: glossr@star.co.uk
Assistant Dioc Officer for Social Responsibility Mrs Fran Tolond, 1 Mickle Mead, Highnam, Gloucester GL2 8NF *Tel:* 01452 383441
email: glosasro@star.co.uk
County Ecumenical Officer Revd Dr Alison Evans, Elm Farm House, High St, Kings Stanley, Stonehouse GL10 3JF *Tel:* 01453 824034
email: malcolm.alison@btinternet.com
Accord Canon Dr Michael Tucker, Rectory, Amberley, Stroud GL5 5GJ *Tel:* 01453 878515
email: mike@tuckers.org.uk

Rural Adviser Vacancy
Environmental Development Officer Vacancy
Ecumenical Adviser Vacancy Contact Church House 01452 410022

AREA DEANS
ARCHDEACONRY OF CHELTENHAM
Cheltenham Acting Area Dean Revd Michael Garland, St Mary's Vicarage, 63 Church St, Charlton Kings, Cheltenham GL53 8AT
Tel: 01242 253402
email: michael.garland50@tiscali.co.uk
Cirencester Revd John Jessop, Rectory, Daglingworth, Cirencester GL7 7AG *Tel:* 01285 640782
email: jjessop@onetel.net
Fairford Revd Brian Atkinson, Vicarage, The Croft, Fairford GL7 4BB *Tel:* 01285 712467
email: Katkio1225@aol.com
North Cotswolds: Revd Veronica James, Rectory, Copse Hill Road, Lower Slaughter, Cheltenham GL54 2HY *Tel:* 01451 821777
email: flojoefred@hotmail.com
Tewkesbury and Winchcombe Canon Paul Williams, Abbey House, Abbey Precinct, Church Street, Tewkesbury GL20 5SR *Tel:* 01684 856144
email: vicar@tewkesburyabbey.org.uk

ARCHDEACONRY OF GLOUCESTER
Forest South Canon Philippa Brunt, Tidenham Vicarage, Gloucester Rd, Tutshill, Chepstow, Monmouthshire NP16 7DH *Tel:* 01594 562828
email: pabrunt@btinternet.com
Gloucester City Canon Robert Simpson, St James' Vicarage, 1 The Conifers, Upton St, Gloucester GL1 3JQ *Tel and Fax:* 01452 422349
email: revrobertcsimpson@blueyonder.co.uk
Assistant Area Dean Canon Tim Newcombe, Holy Trinity Vicarage, Church Rd, Longlevens, Gloucester GL2 0AJ *Tel:* 01452 524129
email: tnewco@tiscali.co.uk
Severn Vale Revd Richard Mitchell, Vicarage, School Lane, Shurdington, Cheltenham GL51 4TF
Tel: 01242 702911
email: richard.mitchell@talk21.com
Stroud Canon Stephen Bowen, Vicarage, Brimscombe, Stroud GL5 2PA *Tel:* 01453 882204
email: sabowen75@gmail.com
Wotton Revd Rob Axford, Vicarage, Culverhay, Wotton-Under-Edge GL12 7LS
Tel: 01453 842175
email: rob.axford@metronet.co.uk

DIOCESE OF GUILDFORD

Founded in 1927. The western two-thirds of Surrey south of the Thames, except for a small area in the north-east (SOUTHWARK); areas of north-east Hampshire; a few parishes in Greater London; one parish in West Sussex.

Population 995,000   Area 538 sq m
Full-time Stipendiary Parochial Clergy 160   Benefices 141
Parishes 164   Churches 217
www.cofeguildford.org.uk
Overseas link diocese: IDWAL (Inter-Diocesan West Africa Link) – Nigeria.

BISHOP (9th)
Rt Revd Christopher Hill, Willow Grange, Woking Rd, Guildford GU4 7QS [2004]
Tel: 01483 590500
Fax: 01483 590501
Bishop's Personal Assistant Mary Morris
email: mary.morris@cofeguildford.org.uk

SUFFRAGAN BISHOP
DORKING Rt Revd Ian James Brackley, Dayspring, 13 Pilgrim's Way, Guildford GU4 8AD [1996]
Tel: 01483 570829
Fax: 01483 567268
email: bishop.ian@cofeguildford.org.uk
Bishop's Personal Assistant Muriel Mulvany
email: muriel.mulvany@cofeguildford.org.uk

CATHEDRAL CHURCH OF THE HOLY SPIRIT
Dean Very Revd Victor Stock, The Deanery, 1 Cathedral Close, Guildford GU2 7TL [2002]
Tel: 01483 547861 (Office)
01483 560328 (Home)
email: dean@guildford-cathedral.org
Dean's Personal Assistant Mrs Cathy Mansell
Tel: 01483 547862 (Office)
email: cathy@guildford-cathedral.org
Cathedral Office Guildford Cathedral, Stag Hill, Guildford, Surrey GU2 7UP   *Tel:* 01483 547860
Fax: 01483 303350
email: reception@guildford-cathedral.org
Canons Residentiary
Sub-Dean and Precentor Canon Nicholas Thistlethwaite, 3 Cathedral Close, Guildford GU2 7TL [1999]   *Tel:* 01483 547865
email: precentor@guildford-cathedral.org
Canon Pastor Canon Angela Weaver, 4 Cathedral Close, Guildford GU2 7TL [2006]
Tel: 01483 547863
email: angela@guildford-cathedral.org
University Chaplain Vacancy
Cathedral Administrator Commodore Tony Lyddon RN, Cathedral Office   *Tel:* 01483 547864
email: administrator@guildford-cathedral.org
Cathedral Organist and Master of the Choristers Mrs Katherine Dienes-Williams, 5 Cathedral Close, Guildford GU2 7TL   *Tel:* 01483 547866
email: organist@guildford-cathedral.org

ARCHDEACONS
SURREY Ven Stuart Beake, Dioc House, Quarry St, Guildford GU1 3XG [2005]   *Tel:* 01483 790350
email: stuart.beake@cofeguildford.org.uk
DORKING Ven Julian Henderson, The Old Cricketers, Portsmouth Rd, Ripley, Woking, Surrey GU23 6ER [2005]   *Tel:* 01483 479300
Fax: 01483 479568
email: julian.henderson@cofeguildford.org.uk

CONVOCATION (MEMBERS OF THE HOUSE OF CLERGY OF THE GENERAL SYNOD)
Dignitaries in Convocation
The Bishop of Dorking
Proctors for Clergy
Revd Robert Cotton
Ven Julian Henderson
Revd Barbara Messham
Revd Philip Plyming
Canon Hazel Whitehead

MEMBERS OF THE HOUSE OF LAITY OF THE GENERAL SYNOD
Canon Peter Bruinvels
Mr Keith Malcouronne
Anne Martin
Mr Adrian Vincent

DIOCESAN OFFICERS
Dioc Secretary Mr Stephen Marriott, Diocesan House, Quarry St, Guildford GU1 3XG
Tel: 01483 790300
Fax: 01483 790333
Chancellor of Diocese Mr Andrew Jordan, 11 Fairlawn Avenue, Chiswick, London W4 5EF
Registrar of Diocese and Bishop's Legal Secretary Mr Peter Beesley, 1 The Sanctuary, London SW1P 3JT   *Tel:* 020 7222 5381
Fax: 020 7222 7502
Deputy Registrar Mr Howard Dellar

DIOCESAN ORGANIZATIONS
Diocesan Office Diocesan House, Quarry St, Guildford GU1 3XG   *Tel:* 01483 571826
Fax: 01483 790333

ADMINISTRATION

President The Bishop of Guildford
Dioc Synod (*Vice-President, House of Clergy*) Revd Robert Cotton, Holy Trinity Rectory, 9 Eastgate Gardens, Guildford GU1 4AZ   *Tel:* 01483 505816
(*Vice-President, House of Laity*) Canon Peter Bruinvels, 14 High Meadow Close, St Paul's Rd West, Dorking RH4 2LG   *Tel:* 01306 887082
(*Secretary*) Mr Stephen Marriott, Dioc House
      email: stephen.marriott@cofeguildford.org.uk
Deputy Secretary Mr Michael Bishop, Dioc House
      email: mike.bishop@cofeguildford.org.uk
Board of Finance (*Chairman*) Mr Nigel Lewis, Dioc House
Accountant Mr Stephen Collyer
Asst Secretary Revd Ruth Walker, Dioc House
Pastoral Committee Mr Michael Bishop (*as above*)
Designated Officer Mr Peter Beesley, 1 The Sanctuary, London SW1P 3JT   *Tel:* 020 7222 5381
                        Fax: 020 7222 7502

CHURCHES

Advisory Committee for the Care of Churches (*Chairman*) Mr Hamish Donaldson, Edgecombe, Hill Rd, Haslemere GU27 2JN; (*Secretary*) Revd Ruth Walker, Dioc House
      email: ruth.walker@cofeguildford.org.uk

EDUCATION

Education Centre Diocesan Education Centre, Stag Hill, Guildford GU2 7UP
                        Tel: 01483 450423
                        Fax: 01483 450424
Director of Education and Secretary Dioc Board of Education Mr Derek Holbird
      email: derek.holbird@cofeguildford.org.uk
Senior Education Officer – Children and Parish Education Mrs Heather Henderson
Assistant Children's Education Officer Mrs Alison Hendy
Youth Adviser Mr David Welch
Adviser in Adult Education Mrs Joanna Walker
Further Education Adviser Mr Bob Linnell
Centre Administrator Mrs Jane Baker
Schools' Officer Development and Personnel and Finance Carole Dunscombe, David Hallam
Deputy Director of Education – Schools Michael Hall

MINISTRY

Director of Ministerial Training and CME Director Canon Hazel Whitehead, Dioc House
                        Tel: 01483 790307
      email: hazel.whitehead@cofeguildford.org.uk
Director of Ordinands Revd William Challis, Dioc House   *Tel:* 01483 571826
      email: william.challis@cofeguildford.org.uk
Guildford Local Ministry Programme (*Principal*) Revd Dr Steve Summers   *Tel:* 01483 790319
Warden of Licensed Lay Ministers Mrs Liz Lang, Rectory, Thursley Rd, Elstead GU8 6DG
                        Tel: 01252 703251
      email: lizlang@connectfree.co.uk

Senior Tutor for Pastoral Assistant's Foundation Course Mrs Sue Lawrence, Dioc House
                        Tel: 01483 790321
      email: sue.lawrence@cofeguildford.org.uk
CMD Tutor for Readers and Pastoral Assistants and Vocations Officer Revd Liz Boughton, Dioc House
                        Tel: 01483 790321
      email: liz.boughton@cofeguildford.org.uk
CMD Tutor for Readers Revd Richard Hay
      email: richard.hay3@btinternet.com
Readers' Board (*Registrar*) Dr Anthony Metcalfe, Peterstone, 15 The Mead, Ashtead KT21 2LZ
                        Tel: 01372 274162
      email: ar_metcalfe@yahoo.co.uk

MISSION, EVANGELISM AND PARISH DEVELOPMENT

Director
Revd John Gooding, Dioc House
      email: john.gooding@cofeguildford.org.uk
Stewardship & Parish Funding Adviser Mr Tony Hennessey-Brown, Dioc House
email:
      tony.hennessey-brown@cofeguildford.org.uk
Local Mission Adviser Revd Stephen Cox, Dioc House
      email: stephen.cox@cofeguildford.org.uk
Spirituality Adviser Revd Alan Elkins
                email: alan-elkins@lineone.net
Spiritual Direction Co-ordinator Mrs Christina Chaplin   *email:* chris.chaplin@virgin.ne
Bishop's Adviser on Hospital Chaplaincy Revd Chris Vallins   *email:* chrisvallins@yahoo.com
Healing Adviser Revd Elizabeth Knifton
      email: eknifton@acornchristian.org
World Mission Adviser Revd Andrew Wheeler
      email: andrew.wheeler@st-saviours.org.uk
Nigeria Link Officer Revd David Minns
      email: dkminns@btinternet.com
Sports Ministry Adviser Revd Clive Potter
      email: milfordvicarage@gmail.com

PRESS AND PUBLICATIONS

Director of Communications Revd Mark Rudall, Dioc House   *Tel:* 01483 790310
                        07779 654975 (Mobile)
      email: mark.rudall@cofeguildford.org.uk
Media Officers Mrs Emma Nutbrown-Hughes, David Green   *Tel:* 01483 790345
Editor of Dioc Newspaper Mrs Emma Nutbrown-Hughes (*as above*)   *Tel:* 01483 790347
      email: editorial@cofeguildford.org.uk
Information Administrator Mrs Mary Peters
                        Tel: 01483 790335
      email: mary.peters@cofeguildford.org

DIOCESAN RECORD OFFICE

Surrey History Centre, 130 Goldsworth Rd, Woking GU2 1ND *Team Leader, Heritage Public Services* Dr Patricia Reynolds; *Special Collections Archivist* Diana Stiff   *Tel:* 01483 518737

SOCIAL RESPONSIBILITY

Director Canon Chris Rich, Dioc House
Tel: 01483 790353
email: chris.rich@cofeguildford.org.uk
Church's Community Care Adviser Tony Oakden, Dioc House Tel: 01483 790325
email: tony.oakden@cofeguildford.org.uk
Partnership Development Adviser Canon David Tonkinson, Dioc House Tel: 01483 790334
email: david.tonkinson@cofeguildford.org.uk
Open to All Adviser Suzette Jones, Dioc House
Tel: 01483 790335
email: suzette.jones@cofeguildford.org.uk

RURAL DEANS

ARCHDEACONRY OF SURREY

Aldershot Revd David Willey, Rectory, 66 Church Ave, Farnborough GU14 7AP   Tel: 01252 544754
email: rector@stpetersfarnborough.org.uk
Cranleigh Revd John Bundock, Vicarage, Birtley Rise, Bramley, Guildford GU5 0HZ
Tel: 01483 892109
email: jnebundock@tiscali.co.uk
Farnham Revd Anne Gell, Vicarage, 2 Kings Lane, Wrecclesham GU10 4QB   Tel: 01252 716431
email: annegell@lineone.net
Godalming Revd J. M. Fellows, Rectory, Compton, Guildford GU3 1ED   Tel: 01428 810328
email: csph.office@virgin.net
Guildford Revd Barbara Messham, All Saints Vicarage, 18 Vicarage Gate, Onslow Village, Guildford GU24 7QJ   Tel: 01483 572006
email: barbaramessham@googlemail.com

Surrey Heath Revd A. Body, Chobham Vicarage, Bagshot Rd, Chobham, Woking GU24 8BY
Tel: 01276 858197
email: ab@tasoma.orangehome.co.uk

ARCHDEACONRY OF DORKING

Dorking Revd Paul Bryer, St Paul's Vicarage, 7 South Terrace, Dorking RH4 2AB
Tel: 01306 881998
email: paul@stpaulsdorking.org.uk
Emly Revd Carole Bourne, The Vicarage, St Mary's Road, East Molesey KT8 0ST
Tel: 020 8979 0677
email: cbmole@msn.com
Epsom Revd Stuart Thomas, The Minister's House, 71 Ruxley Lane, Ewell KT19 9FF
Tel: 020 8311 127
email: revstuart.thomas@btinternet.com
Leatherhead Revd Robert Jenkins, Vicarage, St Andrew's Walk, Cobham, Surrey KT11 3EQ
Tel: 01932 862109
email: er.jenkins@btinternet.com
Runnymede Revd T. J. Hillier, Vicarage, London St, Chertsey KT16 8AA   Tel: 01932 563141
email: tim.hillier@o2.co.uk
Woking Revd Cathy Blair, St Paul's Vicarage, Pembroke Road, Woking GU22 7ED
Tel: 01483 850489
email: cathy@stpaulswoking.org.uk

DIOCESE OF HEREFORD

Founded *c* 676. Herefordshire; the southern half of Shropshire; a few parishes in Powys and Monmouthshire.

Population 309,000   Area 1,660 sq m
Full-time Stipendiary Parochial Clergy 82   Benefices 115
Parishes 343   Churches 417
www.hereford.anglican.org
Overseas link dioceses: Masasi and Tanga with Zanzibar,
Dar es Salaam (Tanzania), Kirchenkreis of Nurnberg.

DIOCESES

BISHOP (104th)
Rt Revd Anthony Priddis, The Bishop's House, Hereford HR4 9BN [2004]   *Tel:* 01432 271355
Fax: 01432 373346
email: bishop@hereford.anglican.org

SUFFRAGAN BISHOP
LUDLOW Rt Revd Alistair J Magowan, Bishop's House, Corvedale Rd, Craven Arms, Shropshire SY7 9BT [2009]   *Tel* and *Fax:* 01588 673571
email: bishopofludlow@btinternet.com

CATHEDRAL CHURCH OF THE BLESSED VIRGIN MARY AND ST ETHELBERT
Dean Very Revd Michael Tavinor, The Deanery, College Cloisters, Hereford HR1 2NG [2002]
Tel: 01432 374203
email: dean@herefordcathedral.org
Cathedral Office 5 College Cloisters, Hereford HR1 2NG   *Tel:* 01432 374200
Fax: 01432 374220
email: office@herefordcathedral.org
Web: www.herefordcathedral.org
Canons Residentiary
Chancellor Canon Christopher Pullin, 2 Cathedral Close, Hereford HR1 2NG [2008]
Tel: 01432 341905
chancellor@herefordcathedral.org
Precentor Canon Andrew Piper, 1 Cathedral Close, Hereford HR1 2NG [2003]   *Tel:* 01432 266193
email: precentor@herefordcathedral.org
Cathedral Chaplain Pred Kay Garlick, c/o Cathedral Office   *Tel:* 01432 374214
email: kay.garlick@herefordcathedral.org

Additional Members
Miss Sandra Elliott, c/o Cathedral Office
Mr Richard Price, c/o Cathedral Office
Chapter Clerk Lt Col Andrew Eames, Cathedral Office   *Tel:* 01432 374231
email: clerk@herefordcathedral.org
Head of Administration and Finance Mr Steven Kent, Cathedral Office   *Tel:* 01432 374205
email: accounts@herefordcathedral.org
Cathedral Organist Mr Geraint Bowen, 7 College Cloisters, Hereford HR1 2NG   *Tel:* 01432 374238
email: organist@herefordcathedral.org

Assistant Organist Mr Peter Dyke, 1a Cathedral Close, Hereford HR1 2NG   *Tel:* 01432 374215
email: peter.dyke@herefordcathedral.org

ARCHDEACONS
HEREFORD Ven Paddy Benson, Dioc Office
Tel: 01432 373316
email: archdeacon@hereford.anglican.org
LUDLOW Rt Revd Alistair J Magowan, Bishop's House, Corvedale Rd, Craven Arms, Shropshire SY7 9BT   *Tel* and *Fax:* 01588 673571
email: bishopofludlow@btinternet.com

CONVOCATION (MEMBERS OF THE HOUSE OF CLERGY OF THE GENERAL SYNOD)
Proctors for Clergy
Preb Brian Chave
Revd Simon Cawdell
Revd Clare Sykes

MEMBERS OF THE HOUSE OF LAITY OF THE GENERAL SYNOD
Dr John Dinnen
Dr Martin Elcock
Mrs Rosemary Lording

DIOCESAN OFFICERS
Dioc Secretary Mr John Clark, Diocesan Office, The Palace, Hereford HR4 9BL
Tel: 01432 373300
Fax: 01432 352952
email: diosec@hereford.anglican.org
Chancellor of Diocese Chancellor R. Kaye, Leeds Combined Court Centre, The Court House, 1 Oxford Row, Leeds LS1 3BG   *Tel:* 0113 306 2800
Registrar of Diocese and Bishop's Legal Secretary Mr Peter Beesley, Dioc Registry, 1 The Sanctuary, Westminster, London SW1P 3JT
Tel: 020 7222 5381
Dioc Surveyors Hook Mason Partnership, 41 Widemarch St, Hereford HR4 9EA   *Tel:* 01432 352299

DIOCESAN ORGANIZATIONS
Dioc Office The Palace, Hereford HR4 9BL
Tel: 01432 373300
Fax: 01432 352952
email: diooffice@hereford.anglican.org

Bishop's Office The Palace, Hereford HR4 9BN
Tel: 01432 271355
Fax: 01432 373346

ADMINISTRATION

Dioc Synod (Chairman, House of Clergy) Preb B. Chave, Vicarage, Vowles Close, Hereford HR4 0DF Tel: 01432 273086
(Chairman, House of Laity) Mrs Diana George, Greenway, Walterstone, Hereford HR2 0DT
Tel: 01873 890259
(Secretary) Mr John Clark, Dioc Office
Board of Finance (Chairman) Mr Charles Hunter, Upper Grange, Bacton, Hereford HR2 0AR
Tel: 01981 240561
(Secretary) Mr John Clark (as above)
Financial Secretary Mr Gordon Powell, Dioc Office
Benefice Buildings Committee Mr John Clark (as above)
Glebe Committee Mr Stephen Challenger, Dioc Office
Board of Patronage Mr John Clark, Dioc Office
Designated Officer Mr Peter Beesley, 1 The Sanctuary, Westminster, London SW1P 3JT
Tel: 020 7222 5381
Pastoral Secretary & Personnel Manager Mr Graham Hamer, Dioc Office
Trusts Mr John Clark (as above)

CHURCHES

Advisory Committee for the Care of Churches (Chairman) The Archdeacon of Hereford (as above)
(Secretary) Mr Stephen Challenger (as above)

EDUCATION

Director of Education Vacancy, Dioc Office (Ludlow), Units 8 & 9, The Business Quarter, Ludlow Eco Park, Sheet Rd, Ludlow, Shropshire SY88 1FD Tel: 01584 871080
email: education@hereford.anglican.org
Schools Officer Vacancy
Young Peoples Officer Miss Esther Gregory
Tel: 01584 871078
email: e.gregory@hereford.anglican.org

LUDLOW CONFERENCE CENTRE

Tel: 01584 873882
Fax: 01584 877945

MINISTRY AND TRAINING

Director of Ordinands Revd Mary Lou Toop, Vicarage, Minsterley, Shropshire SY5 0AA
Tel: 01743 790399
email: maryloutoop@lineone.net
Continuing Ministerial Development Officer Revd Nicholas Helm, c/o Dioc Office (Ludlow)
Lay Development Officer Revd Caroline Pascoe, c/o Dioc Office (Ludlow)
Local Ministry Officer Revd Dr John Daniels, c/o Dioc Office (Ludlow) Tel: 01584 871081
Advisers for Non-Stipendiary Ministry Revd M. D. Vockins, Birchwood Lodge, Storridge, Malvern WR13 5EZ Tel: 01886 884366
Revd J. Edwards, 2 Madeley Wood View, Madeley, Telford TF7 5TF Tel: 01952 583254

Adviser on Women in Ministry Revd Jill Talbot-Ponsonby, The Old Barn, Cleeve Lane, Ross-on-Wye, Herefordshire HR9 7TB Tel: 01989 565003
email: jill@talbot-ponsonby.org
Readers' Association (Warden) Preb Andrew Talbot-Ponsonby, The Old Barn (as above)
Tel: 01989 565003
email: andrew@talbot-ponsonby.org
Widows and Dependants (Hereford Diocese Clerical Charity) Mr John Clark (as above)

WORSHIP

Chairman Canon Andrew Piper (as above)
Secretary Vacancy

MISSIONARY AND ECUMENICAL

Ecumenical Committee Vacancy
Council for World Partnership and Development (Chairman) Mrs Hazel Gould; (Secretary) Revd C. Fletcher, Rectory, Bredenbury, Bromyard, Herefordshire HR7 4TF Tel: 01885 482236
Evangelism Committee (Chairman) The Bishop of Ludlow

AGRICULTURE

Chaplain Revd Nick Read, Rectory, Pembridge, Hereford HR6 9EB Tel: 01544 388998
email: agchap@tiscali.co.uk

PRESS, PUBLICITY AND PUBLICATIONS

Dioc Communications Officer Ms Anni Holden, The Palace, Hereford HR4 9BL
Tel: 01432 373342
email: a.holden@hereford.anglican.org
Editor of Dioc Newspaper Mr R. Calver, The Palace (as above)

DIOCESAN RECORD OFFICE

Hereford Records Office, The Old Barracks, Harold St, Hereford HR1 2QX Tel: 01432 260750
(For diocesan records and parish records for Hereford Archdeaconry)
Shrewsbury Records and Research Centre, Castle Gates, Shrewsbury SY1 2AQ Tel: 01743 255350
Head of Records and Research Mary McKenzie (For parish records for Ludlow Archdeaconry)

SOCIAL RESPONSIBILITY

Social Responsibility Officer Miss Jackie Boys, The Gateway Office (as above) Tel: 01432 373311
email: j.boys@hereford.anglican.org
Council for Social Responsibility (Chairman) Mrs Caroline Bond, 25 Cartway, Bridgnorth, Shropshire WV16 4BG
(Secretary) Miss Jackie Boys (as above)

STEWARDSHIP

Community Partnership and Funding Officer Mrs Wendy Coombey, Dioc Office Tel: 01432 373313
email: w.coombey@hereford.anglican.org

RURAL DEANS

ARCHDEACONRY OF HEREFORD

Abbeydore Revd A. F. Evans, Rectory, Ewyas Harold, Herefordshire HR2 0EZ
Tel: 01981 871088

Bromyard Revd C. Sykes, Vicarage, 28 Church Lane, Bromyard HR7 4DZ   *Tel:* 01885 482438

Hereford Preb P. Towner, The Vicarage, 102 Green St, Hereford HR1 2QW   *Tel:* 01432 273676

Kington and Weobley Preb S. Hollinghurst, The Rectory, Presteigne, Powys LD8 2BP
Tel: 01544 267777

Ledbury Revd M. D. Vockins, Birchwood Lodge, Storridge, Malvern WR13 5EZ   *Tel:* 01886 884366

Leominster Preb M. C. Cluett, Vicarage, Brookside, Caon Pyon, Hereford HR4 8NY
Tel: 01432 830802

Ross and Archenfield Revd E C Goddard, The Vicarage, St Weonards, Herefordshire HR2 8NN
Tel: 01981 580307

ARCHDEACONRY OF LUDLOW

Bridgnorth Revd S. H. Cawdell, Vicarage, Lodge Park, Claverley, Nr Wolverhampton WV5 7DP
Tel: 01746 710268

Clun Forest Preb R. T. Shaw, Vicarage, Clun, Craven Arms, Shropshire SY7 8JG
Tel: 01588 640809

Condover Revd S. Lowe, Rectory, 1 New Rd, Much Wenlock TF13 6EQ   *Tel:* 01952 727396

Ludlow Revd M. J. Stewart, The Vicarage, Bromfield, Ludlow SY8 2JP   *Tel:* 01584 856625

Pontesbury Revd M. G. Whittock, Rectory, Longden, Shrewsbury, Shropshire SY5 8ET
Tel: 01743 861003

Telford Severn Gorge
Preb M. Kinna, Rectory, Broseley TF12 5DA
Tel: 01952 882647

DIOCESES

DIOCESE OF LEICESTER

Restored in 1926. Leicestershire, except the former county of Rutland
(PETERBOROUGH); one parish in Northamptonshire.

Population 945,000   Area 835 sq m
Full-time Stipendiary Parochial Clergy 122   Benefices 111
Parishes 236   Churches 321
www.leicester.anglican.org
Overseas link dioceses: Yokohama, Mount Kilimanjaro (Tanzania)
and Trichy, Tanjore (India).

BISHOP (6th)
Rt Revd Timothy John Stevens, Bishop's Lodge
Annexe, 12 Springfield Rd, Leicester LE2 3BD
[1999]   *Tel:* 0116 270 8985
                             Fax: 0116 270 3288
[Timothy Leicester]
Bishop's PA Melanie Glover
        email: Melanie.Glover@LecCofE.org
Bishop's Chaplain Revd Michael Smith (*same
address*)   *Tel:* 0116 270 3390
                             Fax: 0116 270 3288
        email: Mike.Smith@LecCofE.org
Executive Assistant to the Bishop Revd. Gill Jackson
                             Tel: 0116 270 8985
        email: Gill.Jackson@LecCofE.org

CATHEDRAL CHURCH OF ST MARTIN
Dean Very Revd Vivienne Faull, Cathedral Centre,
21 St Martin's, Leicester LE1 5DE [2000]
                             Tel: 0116 248 7456
                             Fax: 0116 248 7470
        email: Viv.Faull@LecCofE.org
Cathedral Centre 21 St Martin's, Leicester LE1 5DE
                             Tel: 0116 248 7400
                             Fax: 0116 248 7470
        email: LeicesterCathedral@LecCofE.org
        Web: www.cathedral.leicester.anglican.org
Canons Residentiary
Pastor Canon Chancellor Canon David Monteith
                             Tel: 0116 248 7463
        email: David.Monteith@LecCofE.org
Precentor Vacancy
                             Tel: 0116 248 7464
                             email:
Urban Canon Barry Naylor [2002]
                             Tel: 0116 248 7471
        email: Barry.Naylor@LecCofE.org
Canon Paul Hackwood (NSM) [2007]
                             Tel: 0116 239 6533
        email: Paul.Hackwood@me.com
Cathedral Chaplain Vacancy
Cathedral Administrator Mr Francis Brown
                             Tel: 0116 248 7459
        email: Francis.Brown@LecCofE.org
Marketing and Development Manager Ms Claire
Recordon   *Tel:* 0116 248 7468
        email: Claire.Recordon@LecCofE.org
Cathedral Solicitor Mr Trevor Kirkman, Latham &

Co., Charnwood House, 2 Forest Rd,
Loughborough LE11 3NP   *Tel:* 01509 238822
Director of Music Dr Christopher Johns (Jan 2011)
                             Tel: 0116 248 7476
Asst Director Master of Music Mr Simon Headley
The cathedral offices will be moving to St Martins
House, 7 Peacock Lane, Leicester LE1 5PZ in
January 2011. Email addresses will remain the
same but new telephone numbers will be
allocated.

ARCHDEACONS
LEICESTER Ven Richard Atkinson, Church House,
St Martin's East, Leicester LE1 5FX [2002]
                             Tel: 0116 248 7419
                             Fax: 0116 253 2889
        email: Richard.Atkinson@LecCofE.org
LOUGHBOROUGH Ven David Newman, Church
House, St Martin's East, Leicester LE1 5FX [2009]
                             Tel: 0116 248 7421
                             Fax: 0116 253 2889
        email: David.Newman@LecCofE.org

**CONVOCATION (MEMBERS OF THE
HOUSE OF CLERGY OF THE GENERAL
SYNOD)**
Dignitaries in Convocation
The Dean of Leicester
Proctors for Clergy
Ven Richard Atkinson
Revd Amanda Ford
Revd John McGinley

**MEMBERS OF THE HOUSE OF LAITY OF
THE GENERAL SYNOD**
Mr Stephen Barney
Yvonne Shayne Ardron
Anne Bloor

DIOCESAN OFFICERS
Dioc Secretary Vacancy
Assistant Dioc Secretary Mr Andrew Roberts,
Church House, St Martin's East, Leicester LE1 5FX
        email: Andrew.Roberts@CovLec.org
PA to Dioc Secretary Vacancy   *Tel:* 0116 248 7426
Chancellor of Diocese Dr James Behrens, Serle
Court, 6 New Square, Lincoln's Inn, London
WC2A 3QS   *Tel:* 020 7242 6105
                             Fax: 020 7405 4004

Registrar of Diocese and Bishop's Legal Secretary Mr Trevor Kirkman, Latham and Co., Charnwood House, 2 Forest Rd, Loughborough LE11 3NP
Tel: 01509 238822
Fax: 01509 238833
email: TrevorKirkman@lathamlawyers.co.uk

DIOCESAN ORGANIZATIONS
Diocesan Office St Martin's House, 7 Peacock Lane, Leicester LE1 5PZ (from 31 January 2011)
Tel: 0116 248 7400
Fax: 0116 253 2889
email: ChurchHouse@LecCofE.org

ADMINISTRATION
Director of Finance Mr John Orridge, Dioc Office
email: John.Orridge@LecCofE.org
Management Accountant Miss Caroline Berry, Dioc Office email: Caroline.Berry@CovLec.org
Finance Officer Mr Paul Wilson, Dioc Office
email: Paul.Wilson@CovLec.org
Accounts Officer Vacancy
Accounts Assistant Mrs Karen Issitt, Dioc Office
email: Karen.Issitt@LecCofE.org
Senior Property Manager Mrs Nicky Caunt, Dioc Office email: Nicky.Caunt@CovLec.org
Clergy Housing Officer Mrs Dinta Chauhan, Dioc Office email: Dinta.Chauhan@CovLec.org
Property Officer Miss Lesley Whitwell, Dioc Office
email: Lesley.Whitwell@CovLec.org
IT Manager Mr Phil Ash, Dioc Office
email: Phil.Ash@CovLec.org
Dioc Synod (Chairman, House of Clergy) Revd Amanda Ford, 10 Parkside Close, Beaumont Leys, Leicster, LE4 1EP Tel: 0116 235 2667
email:mandyford@btinternet.com
Dioc Synod (Chairman, House of Laity) Prof David Wilson, 56 Grangefield Drive, Rothley, Leicester LE7 7NB Tel: 0116 230 3402
email: djwilson@dmu.ac.uk
Dioc Synod and Bishop's Council (Secretary) Dioc Secretary, Dioc Office
Mission and Pastoral Committee Dioc Secretary (as above)
Stipends Officer Mrs Jill Benn, Dioc Office
email: Jill.Benn@CovLec.org
Board of Finance (Chairman) Mr Stephen Barney, 77 Brook St, Wymeswold, Loughborough LE12 6TT Tel: 01509 881160
email: stephen4747@live.co.uk
Board of Finance (Secretary) Dioc Secretary (as above)
Finance Committee Mr Andrew Roberts (as above)
Property and Glebe Committee Mr Andrew Roberts (as above)
Designated Officer Mrs Jane Easton (as above)
Director of Parish Funding and Fundraising Mr Andrew Nutter, Dioc Office Tel: 0116 248 7422
email: Andrew.Nutter@LecCofE.org
Parish Funding Director
Mrs Maxine Johnson, Brook House, Stonton Rd, Church Langton, Market Harborough LE16 7SZ
Tel: 01858 545745
email: mjohnson@resort-solutions.co.uk

Child Protection Officer Mr Andrew Roberts (as above)

CHURCHES
Advisory Committee for the Care of Churches (Acting Chairman) Revd Richard Curtis, Vicarage, Oakham Road, Tilton on the Hill LE7 9LB
Tel: 07855 746041
Church Buildings Development Officer Dr Claire Strachan, Coventry Cathedral and Diocesan Offices, 1 Hill Top, Coventry CV1 5AB
Tel: 024 7652 1200
email: Claire.Strachan@CovLec.org
Assistant Church Buildings Development Officer Mr Rupert Allen, Coventry Cathedral and Diocesan Offices, 1 Hill Top, Coventry CV1 5AB
Tel: 024 7652 1200
email: Rupert.Allen@CovLec.org

EDUCATION
Diocesan Board of Education Church House, St Martin's East, Leicester LE1 5FX
Tel: 0116 248 7450
Fax: 0116 251 1638
Director Mrs Mary Lawson (same address)
email: Mary.Lawson@LecCofE.org
Chairman The Venerable David Newman (as above)
Religious Education Adviser Mrs Janet Ingram (as above) email: Janet.Ingram@LecCofE.org
Religious Education Administration Mrs Helen Van Roose, Dioc Office
email: Helen.VanRoose@LecCofE.org
Schools Officer Mrs Kerry Miller (same address)
email: Kerry.Miller@LecCofE.org

INTERFAITH
Director of Interfaith Relations and of the St Philip's Centre for Study and Engagement in a Multi Faith Society Canon Dr John Hall, St Philip's House, 2a Stoughton Drive North, Leicester LE5 5UB
Tel: 0116 273 3459
email: john.hall@stphilipscentre.co.uk
Administrator Mrs Kathy Morrison (same address)

MINISTRY
Director of Mission and Ministry Canon Dr Mike Harrison, Dioc Office Tel: 0116 248 7417
Fax: 0116 253 2889
email: Mike.Harrison@LecCofE.org
Head of the School for Ministry Revd Dr Stuart Burns, Dioc Office Tel: 0116 248 7417
email: Stuart.Burns@LecCofE.org
Director of Youth Ministry Vacancy
Dioc Director of Ordinands Canon Sue Field, 134 Valley Rd, Loughborough LE11 3QA
Tel: 01509 234472
email: sue.field1@tesco.net
Under 25s Children's Officer Canon Dr Mike Harrison Tel: 0116 248 7428
email: Mike.Harrison@LecCofE.org
Officer for Non-Stipendary Ministry Vacancy

Warden of Evangelists Revd John McGinley
Tel: 01455 442750
email: john.mcginley1@ntlworld.com
Warden of Readers Revd Simon Harvey, St Paul's
House, Hamble Rd, Oadby, Leicester LE2 4NX
Tel: 0116 271 0519
email: simon@sjharvey.org.uk
Reader Training Officer Revd Amos Kasibante, 290
Victoria Park Rd, Leicester LE2 1XE
Tel: 0116 285 6493
email: ask11@leicester.ac.uk
Pastoral Assistants Adviser Canon Jane Curtis,
Vicarage, Oakham Road, Tilton on the Hill
LE7 9LB
Tel: 0116 2597244
email: jcurtis@leicester.anglican.org
Officer for NSM Vacancy
Director of Post-Ordination Training Revd Chris
Oxley, St Anne's Vicarage, 76 Letchworth Rd,
Leicester LE3 6FH
Tel: 0116 285 8452
email: oxleycr@btopenworld.com
Director of Women's Ministry Canon Jane Curtis
(*as above*)
Retired Clergy and Widows Officer Anthony
Wessel Esq, The Old Forge, 16 High St, Desford,
Leicester LE9 9JF
Tel: 01455 822404
Fax: 01455 823545
email: anthony.wessel@dial.pipex.com

LITURGICAL
Chairman Canon Dr Stephen Foster, Cathedral
Centre, 21 St Martin's, Leicester LE1 5DE
Tel: 0116 248 7400
email: Stephen.Foster@LecCofE.org
Secretary Revd Richard Curtis, (*as above*)

SOCIAL RESPONSIBILITY
Director of Social Responsibility Mr Peter Yates,
Church House, St Martin's East, Leicester LE1
5FX
Tel: 0116 248 7404
Fax: 0116 248 7446
Fax: 01455 250833
email: Peter.Yates@LecCofE.org
Chaplain to People Affected by HIV Revd Trevor
Thurston-Smith, The Lodge, Margaret Rd, Off
Gwendolen Rd, Leicester LE5 5FW
Tel: 0116 273 3377
email: trevor@faithinpeople.org.uk
Rural Officer
Canon Ken Baker, Homestead, 9 The Green,
Lilbourne, nr Rugby CV23 0SR
Tel: 01788 860409
email: kw.baker@btinternet.com
Environment Officer Revd Andrew Quigley, The
Vicarage, 49 Ashley Way, Market Harborough,
LE16 7XD
Tel: 01858 410253
email: andrew@aquigley.wanadoo.co.uk

ECUMENICAL
Ecumenical Officer Mr Vic Allsop, Clematis
Cottage, 14 Church Lane, Hoby, Melton
Mowbray, Leics LE14 3DR
Tel: 0116 248 7404
Fax: 0116 248 7446
email: Peter.Yates@LecCofE.org

PRESS AND PUBLICATIONS
Communications Officer Ms Liz Hudson-Oliff,
Dioc Office
Tel: 0116 248 7402
07967 388861 (Mobile)
email: Liz.Jepson@LecCofE.org
Editor of Dioc Directory Ms Liz Hudson-Oliff (*as
above*)
Editor of 'News and Views' Ms Liz Hudson-Oliff (*as
above*)

DIOCESAN RECORD OFFICE
Leicestershire Records Office, Long Street,
Wigston, Leicester LE18 2AH   Tel: 0116 257 1080
Fax: 0116 257 1120

AREA DEANS
ARCHDEACONRY OF LEICESTER
City of Leicester Canon Chris Burch, St Peter's
Vicarage, Braunstone Lane, Leicester LE3
3AL
Tel: 0116 289 3377
email: chris@burches.co.uk
Framland Revd Beverley Stark, Rectory, 23 Melton
Rd, Waltham-on-the-Wolds, Melton Mowbray
LE14 4AJ
Tel: 01664 464600
email: beverley.stark@btinternet.com
Gartree I and Gartree II Canon Michael Rusk,
Rectory, 31 Hill Field, Oadby, Leicester LE2 4RW
Tel: 0116 271 2135
email: m.f.rusk@leicester.anglican.org
Goscote Revd Rob Gladstone, Rothley Vicarage,
128 Hallfields Lane, Rothley, Leicester LE7 7NG
Tel: 0116 230 2241
email: rob@rgladstone.wanadoo.co.uk

ARCHDEACONRY OF LOUGHBOROUGH
Akeley East Revd Cynthia Hebden, Vicarage,
30a Brick Kiln Lane, Shepshed, Loughborough
LE12 9EL
Tel: 01509 508550 (Home)
01509 502255 (Office)
email: cynthia.hebden@btopenworld.com
North West Leicestershire Revd Brian Robertson,
The Rectory, 4 Upper Packington Rd, Ashby-de-
la-Zouch LE65 1EF
Tel: 01530 414 404
email: b-robertson@sthelens.ashby.co.uk
Guthlaxton Canon Ken Baker, Homestead, 9 The
Green, Lilbourne, Nr Rugby CV23 0SR
Tel: 01788 860409
email: kw.baker@btinternet.com
Sparkenhoe West Revd Tom Meyrick, Rectory,
6 The Paddock, Newbold Verdon, Leicester
LE9 9NW
Tel: 01455 824986
email: meyrick@ekit.com
Sparkenhoe East Revd John Sharpe, Rectory, Main St,
Glenfield, Leicester LE3 8DG   Tel: 0116 287 1604
email: jesharpe@leicester.anglican.org

DIOCESE OF LICHFIELD

Founded in 664, formerly Mercia (AD 656). Staffordshire, except for a few parishes in the south-east (BIRMINGHAM, DERBY); a few parishes in the south-west (HEREFORD); the northern half of Shropshire; Wolverhampton; Walsall; the northern half of Sandwell.

Population 2,003,000   Area 1,744 sq m
Full-time Stipendiary Parochial Clergy 280   Benefices 275
Parishes 423   Churches 572
www.lichfield.anglican.org
Overseas link dioceses: W. Malaysia, Kuching, Singapore,
Qu'Appelle (Canada), Mecklenburg.

BISHOP (98th)
Rt Revd Jonathan Gledhill, Bishop's House, 22 The Close, Lichfield WS13 7LG [2003]
Tel: 01543 306000
Fax: 01543 306009
email: bishop.lichfield@lichfield.anglican.org
Bishop's Chaplain Revd Peter Walley (*same address*)
email: peter.walley@lichfield.anglican.org
Bishop's Press Officer Mr Gavin Drake, St Saviour's House, High Mount St Hednesford, Cannock WS12 4BN
Tel: 01543 425425
Fax: 01543 425589
07699 730404 (Pager)
ISDN (G722): 01543 871152
email: gavin.drake@lichfield.anglican.org

AREA BISHOPS
SHREWSBURY Rt Revd Mark Rylands, 68 London Rd, Shrewsbury SY2 6PG [2009]
Tel: 01743 235867
Fax: 01743 243296
email: bishop.shrewsbury@lichfield.anglican.org
STAFFORD Rt Revd Geoff Annas, Ash Garth, Broughton Crescent, Barlaston, Stoke-on-Trent ST12 9DD [2005]
Tel: 01782 373308
Fax: 01782 373705
email: bishop.stafford@lichfield.anglican.org
WOLVERHAMPTON Rt Revd Clive Gregory, 61 Richmond Rd, Merridale, Wolverhampton WV3 9JH [2007]
Tel: 01902 824503
Fax: 01902 824504
email:
bishop.wolverhampton@lichfield.anglican.org

HONORARY ASSISTANT BISHOPS
Rt Revd David Bentley, 19 Gable Croft, Lichfield, WS14 9RY [2004]
Tel: 01543 419376
Rt Revd Iraj Mottahedeh, 2 Highland Rd, Newport, TF10 7AE [2005]
Tel: 01952 813615

CATHEDRAL CHURCH OF THE BLESSED VIRGIN MARY AND ST CHAD
Dean Very Revd Adrian Dorber, The Deanery, 16 The Close, Lichfield WS13 7LD [2005]
Tel: 01543 306250 (Office)
01543 306294 (Home)
email: adrian.dorber@lichfield-cathedral.org
Chapter Office 19a The Close, Lichfield WS13 7LD
Tel: 01543 306100
Fax: 01543 306109

email: enquiries@lichfield-cathedral.org
Web: www.lichfield-cathedral.org
Canons Residentiary
Treasurer Ven Christopher Liley, 24 The Close, Lichfield WS13 7LD [2001]
Tel: 01543 306145
Fax: 01543 306147
email: chris.liley@lichfield.anglican.org
Chancellor Canon Dr Pete Wilcox, 13 The Close, Lichfield WS13 7LD [2006]
Tel: 01543 306101 (Office)
email: canon.chancellor@lichfield-cathedral.org
Precentor Canon Wealands Bell, 23 The Close, Lichfield WS13 7LD
Tel: 01543 306101 (Office)
email: wealands.bell@lichfield-cathedral.org
Administrator, Vacancy, Chapter Office, 19a The Close, Lichfield WS13 7LD
Tel: 01543 306105 (Office)
email: ann.lakin@lichfield-cathedral.org (PA)
Lay Members of Chapter
Mrs Mithra Tonking
Mrs Margaret Harding
Mr Peter Durrant
Mr Bryan Ramsell
Bursar's Office Chapter Office, 19a The Close, Lichfield WS13 7LD
Tel: 01543 306103
email: nici.danaher@lichfield-cathedral.org
Organist and Master of the Choristers Mr Philip Scriven, 11 The Close, Lichfield WS13 7LD
Tel: 01543 306200
email: philip.scriven@lichfield-cathedral.org
Visits Officer Mrs Sue Evans, Visitors' Study Centre, The Close, Lichfield WS13 7LD
Tel: 01543 306240
email: sue.evans@lichfield-cathedral.org
Communications and Marketing Officer Mrs Claire Lamplugh, Visitors' Study Centre, The Close, Lichfield WS13 7LD
Tel: 01543 306121
email: claire.lamplugh@lichfield-cathedral.org
Fundraising Administrator Mrs Tracy Withers, Visitors Study Centre, The Close, Lichfield WS13 7LD
Tel: 01543 306120
email: tracy.withers@lichfield-cathedral.org

ARCHDEACONS
LICHFIELD Ven Christopher Liley, 24 The Close, Lichfield WS13 7LD [2001]
Tel: 01543 306145
Fax: 01543 306147
email: archdeacon.lichfield@lichfield.anglican.org

SALOP Ven John Hall, Tong Vicarage, Shifnal TF11 8PW [1998] Tel: 01902 372622
Fax: 01902 374021
email: john.hall@lichfield.anglican.org
STOKE-UPON-TRENT Ven Godfrey Stone, 39 The Brackens, Clayton, Newcastle-under-Lyme ST5 4JL [2002] Tel: 01782 663066
Fax: 01782 711165
email: archdeacon.stoke@lichfield.anglican.org
WALSALL Ven Christopher Sims, 55b Highgate Rd, Walsall WS1 3JE [2005] Tel: 01922 620153
Fax: 01922 445354
email: archdeacon.walsall@lichfield.anglican.org

CONVOCATION (MEMBERS OF THE HOUSE OF CLERGY OF THE GENERAL SYNOD)
Proctors for Clergy
Revd Paul Farthing
Revd Patricia Hawkins
Revd Stephen Pratt
Revd Maureen Hobbs
Revd Mark Ireland
Ven Christopher Sims

MEMBERS OF THE HOUSE OF LAITY OF THE GENERAL SYNOD
Mr David Beswick
Mrs Penelope Allen
Mr Christopher Corbet
Mrs Joanna Monckton
Mr John Shand
Dr Chik Kaw Tan
Mr John Wilson

DIOCESAN OFFICERS
Dioc Synod (Chairman, House of Clergy) Revd John Allan, Vicarage, Church Rd, Alrewas, Burton-on-Trent DE13 7BT Tel: 01283 790486
email: revdjohnallan@revdjohnallan.plus.com
(Chairman, House of Laity) Mr John Wilson, 49 Oakhurst, Lichfield WS14 9AL
Tel: 01543 268678
email: charity.services@btclick.com
Dioc Secretary Mrs Julie Jones, St Mary's House, The Close, Lichfield, Staffs. WS13 7LD
Tel: 01543 306030
Fax: 01543 306039
email: julie.jones@lichfield.anglican.org
Mission and Pastoral Committee (Secretary) Revd David Wright, Rectory, 42 Park Road East, Wolverhampton WV1 4QA Tel: 01902 423388
email: david.wright@lichfield.anglican.org
Chancellor of Diocese Judge Marten Coates, St Mary's House
Diocesan Registrar and Bishop's Legal Secretary Mr Niall Blackie, Manby Bowdler LLP, Routh House, Hall Court, Hall Park Way, Telford, Shropshire TF3 4NJ Tel: 01952 292129
Fax: 01952 291716
email: n.blackie@fbcmb.co.uk

DIOCESAN ORGANIZATIONS
Diocesan Office, see individual addresses below

ADMINISTRATION
Chairman Mr Peter Sharpe
Team Leader Mrs Julie Jones, St Mary's House, The Close, Lichfield WS13 7LD Tel: 01543 306030
Fax: 01543 306039
Finance Director Mr Jonathan R. L. Hill, St Mary's House
Benefice Buildings and Glebe Committee (Secretary) Mr Andrew Mason, St Mary's House
Diocesan Surveyor Mr Charles Glenn, St Mary's House
Trust (Secretary) Mrs Diane Holt, St Mary's House
Designated Officer Mr Niall Blackie, St Mary's House
Manager Christian Giving Mr Neil Bradley, 32 Aitken Close, Tamworth B78 3LR
Tel: 01827 704444
email: bradnsj@aol.com
Dioc Director of Communications Mr Gavin Drake *(Bishop's Press Officer, as above)*
Child Protection Officer Revd Charmian Beech, Rectory, Abbots Way, Hodnet, Market Drayton TF9 3NQ Tel: 01630 685491
email: charmian.beech@virgin.net
Head of Internal Communications Mr Ian Law, 19 Lincoln Croft, Shenstone, Lichfield WS14 0ND
Tel: 01543 480308
email: ianl@eclipse.co.uk
Editor of Dioc Newspaper 'Spotlight' Mrs Carol Law, 19 Lincoln Croft, Shenstone, Lichfield WS14 0ND Tel: 01543 480308

ECUMENISM
Area Ecumenical Adviser (Black Country) Revd Simon Mansfield, St Gregory's Vicarage, 112 Long Knowle Lane, Wednesfield, Wolverhampton WV11 1JQ Tel: 01902 731667
email: smansfield@toucansurf.com
Area Ecumenical Adviser (Shropshire) Mrs Veronica Fletcher, 67 Derwent Drive, Priorslee, Telford TF2 9QR Tel: 01952 299318
email: veronica.fletcher@telford.gov.uk
Area Ecumenical Adviser (Staffordshire) Miss Sue Booth, 6 Fairoak Flats, Harrowby Drive, Newcastle-under-Lyme ST5 3JR
Tel: 01782 613855
email: soobooth1@googlemail.com

CHURCHES
Advisory Committee for the Care of Churches (Chairman) Mr Kevin Hartley, 8 Hanbury Hill, Stourbridge DY8 1BE Tel: 01384 440868;
(Secretary) Mrs Katie Brown, DAC Office, Admaston Farmhouse, Admaston, Rugeley WS15 3NJ Tel: 01889 500304 (Office);
email: katie.brown@lichfield.anglican.org

EDUCATION
Chair of Board of Education Mrs Elaine Townsend, 2 The Old Rectory, Rectory Drive, Weston-under-Lizard, Shifnal TF11 8QG
Tel: 01952 850534
Fax: 01952 850626
email: e.townsend@btinternet.com

Director of Education and Team Leader Mr Colin Hopkins, St Mary's House
   email: colin.hopkins@lichfield.anglican.org
Schools Advisers Mrs Joan Furlong, 46 Gravelly Drive, Newport TF10 7QS
   Tel and *Fax:* 01952 404381
   email: joan.furlong@lichfield.anglican.org
Mrs Sue Blackmore, 153 Hockley Rd, Wilnecote, Tamworth B77 5EF   *Tel:* 01827 707638
   email: sue.blackmore@lichfield.anglican.org
Mrs Rosemary Woodward, 151 Porlock Ave, Stafford ST17 0XY   *Tel:* 01785 665883
email:
   rosemary.woodward@lichfield.anglican.org
Warden of Diocesan Youth Centre Revd Arthur Hack, Dovedale House, Ilam, Ashbourne DE6 2AZ   *Tel:* 01335 350365
   Fax: 01335 350441
   email: warden@dovedale-house.org.uk

MINISTRY MISSION AND TRANSFORMING COMMUNITIES
MINISTRY

Director of Ministry (Ministry Team Leader, also responsible for Ministry Development Review, Continuing Ministerial Development and IME 4–7). Revd Lesley Bentley, St Mary's House, Lichfield
   Tel: 01889 508066 (Home)
   01543 306227 (Office)
   email: lesley.bentley@lichfield.anglican.org
Ministry Development Dept PA Mrs Janet Wallis
   Tel: 01653 306227
   email: janet.wallis@lichfield.anglican.org
Ministry Development Dept Administrator (with responsibility for Ministry Development Review Mrs Jane Instone
   Tel: 01543 306228
   email: jane.instone@lichfield.anglican.org
Director of Ordinands Revd David Newsome, St Mary's House, Lichfield
   Tel: 01543 306192 (Home)
   01543 306220 (Office)
   email: david.newsome@lichfield.anglican.org
PA to the Director of Ordinands and Vocations Dept Mrs Sue Jackson   *Tel:* 01543 306220 (Office)
   email: sue.jackson@lichfield.anglican.org
Vocational Education Officer Revd Deborah Sheridan, 45 High Grange, Lichfield WS13 7DU
   Tel: 01543 264363
   email: d.sheridan@postman.org.uk
Vocations and Ministry Development Officer for Minority Ethnic Anglicans, Wolverhampton Revd Pamela Daniel, 33 Reform Street, West Bromwich B70 7PF   *Tel:* 0121 525 1985
   email: pamdaniel@hotmail.com
Director of Lay Development Vacancy St Mary's House   *Tel:* 01543 306225 (Office)
St Mary's House
Principal, OLM and Reader Training Revd Pauline Shelton, Dray Cottage, Cheadle Road, Draycott in the Moors, Stoke on Trent ST11 9RQ (home)

St Mary's House, Lichfield (Office)
   Tel: 01782 388834 (Home)
   01543 306224 (Office)
   email: pauline.shelton@lichfield.anglican.org
Local Ministry Scheme Administrator Mrs Sheila Walker   *Tel:* 01543 306223 (Office)
   email: sheila.walker@lichfield.anglican.org
Warden of Readers Mr John Addison, 19 Woodland Avenue, Wolstanton, Newcastle-under-Lyme ST5 8AZ   *Tel:* 01782 853169
   email: john.maddison@lichfield.anglican.org
Chaplain to Deaf People Revd Dr Leonie Wheeler, St Andrew's Rectory, 7 Wallshead Way, Church Aston, Newport TF10 9JG   *Tel:* 01952 810942
   email: leonie.wheeler@btinternet.com
Bishop's Adviser in Pastoral Care and Counselling Revd Dr Jeff Leonardi, The New Rectory, Bellamour Way, Colton, Rugeley WS14 3JW
   Tel: and *Fax:* 01889 570897
   email: jeff.leonardi@btinternet.com

MISSION

Director of Parish Mission Revd George Fisher, The Parish Mission Office, The Small Street Centre, 1a Small Street, Walsall WS1 3PR
   Tel: 01922 650063 (Home)
   01922 707863 (Office)
   email: george.fisher@lichfield.anglican.org
Director of World Mission Revd Philip Swan, The World Mission Office, The Small Street Centre, 1a Small Street, Walsall WS1 3PR
   Tel: 01902 621148 (Home)
   01922 707860 (Office)
   email: philip.swan@lichfield.anglican.org
Parish Mission Research Assistant Mr Richard Barrett, The Parish Mission Office, The Small Street, Centre, 1a Small Street, Walsall WS1 3PR
   Tel: 01922 707863 (Office)
   email: richard.barrett@lichfield.anglican.org
PA to the Director of World Mission Miss Clare Spooner, The World Mission Office, The Small Street Centre, 1a Small Street, Walsall WS1 3PR
   Tel: 01922 707861 (Office)
   email: worldmission@lichfield.anglican.org
Youth and Children's Adviser Mr Mark Hatcher, Hillcroft, Stoney Lane, Endon, Stoke-on-Trent, ST9 9BX   *Tel:* 01782 502822
   email: mark.hatcher@lichfield.anglican.org
Spirituality Adviser in the Lichfield and Rugeley Deaneries Revd Christine Polhill, Little Hayes, Beaudesert Park, Cannock Wood, Rugeley WS5 4JJ   *Tel:* 01543 674474
   email: christine@refectiongardens.org.uk

TRANSFORMING COMMUNITIES

Transforming Communities Director Revd David Primrose, The Social Responsibility Office, The Small Street Centre, 1a Small Street, Walsall WS1 3PR   *Tel:* 01922 707864 (Office)
Transforming Communities Assistant Miss Joy Roxborough   *Tel:* 01922 707864 (Office)
   email: joy.roxborough@lichfield.anglican.org

DIOCESAN RECORD OFFICES

Staffordshire Record Office, Eastgate St, Stafford ST16 2LZ *Tel:* 01785 278379, *email:* staffordshire.record.office@staffordshire.gov.uk *Head of Archive Service* Mrs Thea Randall (*For parishes in the archdeaconries of Lichfield and Stoke-on-Trent*)
Lichfield Record Office, The Library, The Friary, Lichfield WS13 6QG *Tel:* 01543 510720, *email:* lichfield.record.office@staffordshire.gov.uk *Archivist* Mr Andrew George (*For diocesan records and parishes within the City of Lichfield*)
Shropshire Archives, Castle Gates, Shrewsbury SY1 2AQ *Tel:* 01743 255350, *email:* archives@shropshire.gov.uk *Head of Records and Research* Dr Mary McKenzie (*For parishes in the archdeaconry of Salop*)

RURAL DEANS
ARCHDEACONRY OF LICHFIELD

Lichfield Revd John Allan, Vicarage, Church Rd, Alrewas, Burton-on-Trent DE13 7BT
Tel: 01283 790486
email: revdjohnallan@tiscali.co.uk
Penkridge Preb Ian Cook, 4 Orams Lane, Brewood, Stafford ST19 9EA   *Tel:* 01902 850960
email: prebyxkel@btopenworld.com
Rugeley Preb Michael Newman, Rugeley Rectory, 20 Church St, Rugeley WS15 2AB
Tel: 01889 582149
email: eileennewman20@aol.com
Tamworth Revd Jim Trood, 6 Bamforth St, Glascote, Tamworth B77 2AS   *Tel:* 01827 305313
email: jimtrood@btinternet.com

ARCHDEACONRY OF STOKE-ON-TRENT

Alstonfield Revd Paul Skillings, Vicarage, Waterfall Lane, Waterhouses, Stoke-on-Trent ST10 3HT   *Tel:* 01538 308506
email: paul_skillings@talktalk.net
Cheadle Revd Steve Osbourne, Vicarage, 8 Vicarage Crescent, Caverswall, Stoke-on-Trent ST11 9EW   *Tel:* 01782 388037
email: steve.osbourne@btopenworld.com
Eccleshall Revd Nigel Clemas, Whitmore Rectory, Snape Hall Rd, Whitmore Heath, Newcastle-under-Lyme ST5 5HZ
Tel: 01782 680258
email: nclemas@hotmail.com
Leek Revd Matthew Parker, St Edward's Vicarage, 6 Church St, Leek ST13 6AB
Tel: 01538 382515
email: matpark01@aol.com
Newcastle-under-Lyme Revd Gerald Gardiner, St Andrew's Vicarage, 50 Kingsway West, Westlands, Newcastle-under-Lyme ST5 3PU
Tel: 01782 619594
Stafford Revd Paul Thomas, St Thomas' Vicarage, Doxey, Stafford ST16 1EQ   *Tel:* 01785 258796
email: paul@wyndhamthomas.freeserve.co.uk

Stoke (*North*) Revd Rod Clark, Christchurch Vicarage, 10 Emery St, Cobridge, Stoke-on-Trent ST6 2JT   *Tel:* 01782 212639
email: revrod@tiscali.co.uk
Stoke-upon-Trent Preb David Lingwood, Stoke Rectory, 172 Smithpool Rd, Stoke-on-Trent ST4 4PP   *Tel:* 01782 747737
email: dp.lingwood@btinternet.com
Stone Revd Peter Dakin, 20 Tudor Hollow, Fulford, Stoke-on-Trent ST11 9NP
Tel: 01782 397073
email: pdakin@waitrose.com
Tutbury Revd Anthony Wood, Vicarage, 3 Church Lane, Barton-under-Needwood, Burton-on-Trent DE13 8HU   *Tel:* 01283 712359
email: tonywood@surefish.co.uk
Uttoxeter Revd Ted Whittaker, The Rectory, 12 Orchard Close, Uttoxeter ST14 7DZ
Tel: 01889 563644
email: tedwhittaker@orange.net

ARCHDEACONRY OF SALOP

Edgmond and Shifnal Revd Keith Hodson, Rectory, Beckbury, Shifnal TF11 9DG
Tel: 01952 750774
email: keithhodson@talk21.com
Ellesmere Revd Les Foster, Vicarage, Little Ness Rd, Ruyton-XI-Towns, Shrewsbury SY4 1LQ
Tel: 01939 261234
email: lesfoster@lunevic.freeserve.co.uk
Hodnet Revd Jeremy Stagg, Vicarage, Childs Ercall, Market Drayton TF9 2DA
Tel: 01952 840229
email: jerome@fish.co.uk
Oswestry Revd Adrian Bailey, Vicarage, Old Chirk Road, Gobowen, Oswestry SY11 3LL
Tel: 01691 661226
email: arb2@totalise.co.uk
Shrewsbury Revd Mark Thomas, 25 The Crescent, Town Walls, Shrewsbury SY1 1TH
Tel: 01743 343761
email: vicar@stchadschurchshrewsbury.com
Telford Revd Vaughan Sweet, The Vicarage, 180 Holyhead Rd, Wellington, Telford TF1 2DW
Tel and Fax: 01952 254251
email: v.sweet@virgin.net
Wem and Whitchurch Revd Rob Haarhoff, Vicarage, Shrewsbury Rd, Hadnall, Shrewsbury SY4 4AG   *Tel:* 01939 210241
email: rob.haarhoff@gmail.com
Wrockwardine Preb David Chantrey, The Rectory, Wrockwardine, Telford TF6 5DD
Tel: 01952 251857
email: david.chantrey@surefish.co.uk

ARCHDEACONRY OF WALSALL

Trysull Revd Maureen Hobbs, Vicarage, 20 Dartmouth Avenue, Pattingham, Wolverhampton WV6 7DP   *Tel:* 01902 700257
email: hobbsmaureen@yahoo.co.uk
Walsall Revd Martin Rutter, St Margaret's Vicarage, Chapel Lane, Great Barr, Birmingham B43 7BD   *Tel:* 0121 357 5813
email: mcrutter@tesco.net

Wednesbury Revd Richard Inglesby, 5 Sutton Rd, Moxley, Wednesbury WS10 8SG
Tel: 01902 653084
email: ringlesby@hotmail.com

West Bromwich Revd Andrew Smith, All Saints Vicarage, 90 Hall Green Rd, West Bromwich B71 3LB
Tel: 01215 883698
email: vicar.allsaintswestbrom@googlemail.com

DIOCESE OF LINCOLN

Founded in 1072, formerly Dorchester (AD 886), formerly Leicester (AD 680), originally Lindine (AD 678). Lincolnshire; North East Lincolnshire; North Lincolnshire, except for an area in the west (SHEFFIELD).

Population 1,013,000   Area 2,673 sq m
Full-time Stipendiary Parochial Clergy 155   Benefices 215
Parishes 507   Churches 640
www.lincoln.anglican.org
Overseas link dioceses: RC Diocese of Brugge, Härnösands (Sweden), Tirunelveli (CSI).

BISHOP (70th)
Rt Revd Dr John Charles Saxbee, Bishop's House, Eastgate, Lincoln LN2 1QQ [2001]
Tel: 01522 534701
Fax: 01522 511095
email: bishop.lincoln@lincoln.anglican.org
[John Lincoln]
Bishop's Chaplain Canon Michael Silley (*same address*)

SUFFRAGAN BISHOPS
GRIMSBY Rt Revd David Douglas James Rossdale, Bishop's House, Church Lane, Irby-on-Humber, Grimsby DN37 7JR [2000]   *Tel:* 01472 371715
Fax: 01472 371716
email: bishop.grimsby@lincoln.anglican.org
GRANTHAM Rt Revd Dr Timothy William Ellis, Saxonwell Vicarage, Church St, Long Bennington, Newark NG23 5ES [2006]
Tel: 01400 283344
Fax: 01400 283321
email: bishop.grantham@lincoln.anglican.org

HONORARY ASSISTANT BISHOPS
Rt Revd Donald Snelgrove, Kingston House, 8 Park View, Barton-on-Humber DN18 6AX [1994]
Rt Revd John Brown, 130 Oxford Rd, Cleethorpes DN35 0BP [1995]   *Tel:* 01472 698840
Rt Revd David Tustin, The Ashes, Tunnel Rd, Wrawby, Brigg DN20 8SF [2001]
Tel: 01652 655584

CATHEDRAL CHURCH OF THE BLESSED VIRGIN MARY
Dean Very Revd Philip Buckler, The Deanery, 11 Minster Yard, Lincoln LN12 1PJ [2007]
Tel: 01522 561611
email: dean@lincolncathedral.com
Communications Office (main switchboard)
Tel: 01522 561600
Fax: 01522 561634
Web: www.lincolncathedral.com
Canons Residentiary
Precentor Canon Gavin Kirk, The Precentory, 16 Minster Yard, Lincoln LN2 1PX [2003]
Tel: 01522 561633
email: precentor@lincolncathedral.com

Chancellor Canon Mark Hocknull, The Chancery, 12 Eastgate, Lincoln LN2 1QG [2009]
Tel: 01522 561633
email: chancellor@lincolncathedral.com
Subdean Canon Alan Nugent, The Subdeanery, 18 Minster Yard, Lincoln LN2 1PX [2003]
Tel: 01522 561631
email: subdean@lincolncathedral.com
Chapter Clerk and Chief Executive Mr Roy Bentham, Chapter Office, 4 Priorygate, Lincoln LN2 1PL   *Tel:* 01522 561601
Fax: 01522 561603
email: chiefexecutive@lincolncathedral.com
Director of Music and Organist and Master of the Choristers Mr Aric Prentice, Lincoln Minster School, Prior Building, Upper Lindum St, Lincoln LN2 5RW   *Tel:* 01522 551300
email: aric.prentice@church-schools.com
Assistant Director of Music and Sub-Organist Mr Charles Harrison, 2a Vicars' Court, Minster Yard, Lincoln LN2 1PT   *Tel:* 01522 561647
email: charles-harrison@gmx.co.uk
Organist Laureate Mr Colin Walsh, Graveley Place, 12 Minster Yard, Lincoln LN2 1PJ
Tel: 01522 561646
email: colinwalsh1@btinternet.com

ARCHDEACONS
LINCOLN Ven Timothy Barker, The Archdeacon's House, Northfield Rd, Quarrington, Sleaford NG34 8RT   *Tel:* 01529 304348
email: archdeacon.lincoln@lincoln.anglican.org
STOW and LINDSEY Ven Jane Sinclair, Sanderlings, Willingham Rd, Market Rasen, Lincoln LN8 3RE [2007]   *Tel:* 01673 849896
email:
archdeacon.stowlindsey@lincoln.anglican.org

CONVOCATION (MEMBERS OF THE HOUSE OF CLERGY OF THE GENERAL SYNOD)
Revd Christopher Lilley
Canon Gavin Kirk
Canon Timothy R. Barker

MEMBERS OF THE HOUSE OF LAITY OF THE GENERAL SYNOD
Miss Rachel Beck
Mrs Sylvia Pounds

Mrs Susan Slater
Mrs Carol Ticehurst

DIOCESAN OFFICERS

Chief Executive Mr Maximilian Manin, The Old Palace, Minster Yard, Lincoln LN2 1PU
Tel: 01522 504030
Fax: 01522 504051
email: chief.executive@lincoln.anglican.org
Chancellor of Diocese HHJ Revd Mark Bishop QC, c/o Dioc Office
Registrar of Diocese and Bishop's Legal Secretary Miss Caroline Mockford, The Diocesan Registry, Chattertons, Low Moor Rd, Doddington Rd, Lincoln LN6 3JY
Tel: 01522 814600
Fax: 01522 814601
email: caroline.mockford@chattertons.com

DIOCESAN ORGANIZATIONS

Diocesan Office The Old Palace, Minster Yard, Lincoln LN2 1PU
Tel: 01522 504050
Fax: 01522 504051
email: reception@lincoln.anglican.org
Web: www.lincoln.anglican.org

ADMINISTRATION

Diocesan Synod (*Chairman, House of Clergy*) Canon J. A. Patrick
Tel: 01522 504050
(*Chairman, House of Laity*) Mr J. C. Watt
Tel: 01522 504050
(*Secretary*) Mr Richard Wilkinson, Diocesan Office
Diocesan Council (*Chairman*) Rt Revd Dr John Saxbee, Bishop of Lincoln
(*Secretary*) Mr Richard Wilkinson (*as above*)
Finance Executive (*Chairman*) Mr Hugh Drake, Diocesan Office
Human Resources Mr Richard Wilkinson (*as above*)
Trusts Committee Mr Andrew Gosling, Dioc Office
Assets (and Glebe) Committee Mr Peter Gaskell
Clergy Housing and Board Property Committee Vacancy
Board of Patronage Mr Richard Wilkinson (*as above*)
Designated Officer Miss Caroline Mockford, Chattertons, Low Moor Rd, Doddington Rd, Lincoln LN6 3JY
Tel: 01522 814600
email: caroline.mockford@chattertons.com
Dioc Electoral Registration Officer Mr Richard Wilkinson, Diocesan Office

CHURCHES

Advisory Committee for the Care of Churches (*Chairman*) Revd Nick Buck, Dioc Office
(*Secretary*) Mr Keith Halliday, Diocesan Office
Church Buildings Revd Neil Brunning, 11 Cavendish Drive, Lea, Gainsborough, Lincolnshire DN21 5HU
Tel: 01427 617938
Church Extension Committee Mr Richard Wilkinson (*as above*)
Redundant Churches Uses Committee (*Secretary*) Mrs Judith Crowe, Diocesan Office

EDUCATION

Director of Education Mr Peter Staves, Diocesan Office
Tel: 01522 504010
email: education@lincoln.anglican.org
Diocesan Board of Education (*Chair*) Rt Revd David Douglas James Rossdale, Bishop's House, Church Lane, Irby-on-Humber, Grimsby DN37 7JR
Tel: 01472 371715
email: bishop.grimsby@lincoln.anglican.org
Church School Buildings Manager Mr Simon Hardy (*same address*)
Schools Adviser Mr David Clements (*same address*)
Technical Asst, Buildings Mr Michael Pues (*same address*)

FORMATION IN DISCIPLESHIP AND MINISTRY

Head of School of Theology Revd Dr Mark Hocknull, Diocesan Office
Tel: 01522 504025
email: mark.hocknull@lincoln.anglican.org
Director of Studies Revd Sally Myers, Diocesan Office
Tel: 01522 504021
Head of Clergy Development Revd David Mc Cormick, Diocesan Office
Tel: 01522 504022
Discipleship and Lay Ministry Development Officer Revd Andrew Tyler, Diocesan Office
Tel: 01522 504024
Diocesan Director of Ordinands and Vocations Adviser Revd Dr Jeffrey Heskins, Diocesan Office
Tel: 01522 504029
Adviser on Women's Ministry Revd K. Windslow, Rectory, Vicarage Lane, Wellingore, Lincoln LN5 0JF
Tel: 01522 810246
email: kathryn.windslow@btinternet.com
Ordinands' Grants Mr Peter Gaskell, Diocesan Office
Warden of Readers Canon Alex Whitehead, 77 Yarborough Rd, Lincoln LN2 1HS
Tel: 01427 788251
Readers (*Secretary*) Mr J. Marshall, 73 Sentance Crescent, Kirton, Boston PE20 1XF
Tel: 01205 723097
Clergy Widows Officers Canon and Mrs Michael Boughton, 45 Albion Crescent, Lincoln LN1 1EB
Tel: 01522 569653
Clergy Retirement Officer Canon Brian Osborne, 3 Newlands Rd, Hacconby, Bourne PE10 0UT
Tel: 01778 570818
email: brian-ruth.osborne@tiscali.co.uk

PRESS, PUBLICITY AND PUBLICATIONS

Communications and Press Officer Mr Will Harrison, Diocesan Office
Editor of Crosslincs and ebulletin Mr Will Harrison, Diocesan Office

LITURGICAL COMMITTEE

Secretary Vacancy

MISSION AND ECUMENICAL CONCERNS

Churches Together in all Lincolnshire Mr Simon Dean, c/o Diocesan Office
Tel: 01522 504071
Lincolnshire Chaplaincy Services (Company No. 6491058)

Chair of Board Rt Revd D. D. J. Rossdale (Bishop of Grimsby) Tel: 01472 371715
Chaplaincy Director Ven Jane Sinclair (Archdeacon of Stow and Lindsay) Tel: 01637 849896
email: archdeacon.stowlindsay@lincoln.anglican.org
Business Manager Miss A. J. McNish, Diocesan Office Tel: 01522 504070
Industrial Chaplains
Lincoln Canon Andrew Vaughan, 4 Grange Close, Canwick, Lincoln LN4 2RH
Tel: 01522 528266
Lincoln Revd Lynne Ward, 9 Bellwood Grange, Cherry Willingham, Lincoln LN3 4JD
North Lincs Canon Mike Cooney, 16 Neap House Rd, Gunness, Scunthorpe DN15 8TT
Tel: 01724 784245
North East Lincs Vacancy
Rural Chaplains
Chaplain for Environmental Issues and Sustainable Development Mr Terry Miller, Diocesan Office
Tel: 01522 504072
Agricultural Chaplain Canon Alan Robson, The Manse, 1 Manor Drive, Wragby, Market Rasen LN8 5SL Tel: 01673 857871
Waterways Chaplain Revd Maurice Perry, Silver Birches, Stockwell Gate, Whaplode, Spalding PE12 6UE
Further and Higher Education
Lincoln University Chaplain Revd Les Acklam, 14 Nettleham Close, Lincoln LN2 1SJ
Tel: 01522 886079
Scunthorpe Colleges Chaplain Revd Susan Walker, St Andrew's Rectory, 16 Belton Rd, Epworth, Doncaster DN9 1JL Tel: 01724 407004
Grimsby Institute Chaplain Vacancy
Grantham College and Stamford New College Mr Peter Weeks, 64 Roman Bank, Stamford PE9 2ST
Tel: 07853 097671
Lincoln College Revd David Edgar, 1 St Giles' Avenue, Lincoln LN2 4PE Tel: 01522 528199
Other Chaplains – Non Lincolnshire Chaplaincy Services
Chaplain to the Deaf Community Revd Simon Bishop, 220 Boultham Park Rd, Lincoln LN6 7SU
Tel: 01522 787136
Work with Young People Capt D. Rose CA, Diocesan Office Tel: 01522 504066
Youth Animator/U2charist Vacancy
Parish Support & Project Worker Suzanne Starbuck, Diocesan Office

STEWARDSHIP AND RESOURCES
Director, Resources Consultancy Mr Andrew Wright, Diocesan Office Tel: 01522 504060
Resources Consultants Mr Simon Bland, Diocesan Office

DIOCESAN RECORD OFFICE
Lincolnshire Archives Office, St Rumbold St, Lincoln LN2 5AB Tel: 01522 526204

RURAL DEANS
ARCHDEACONRY OF STOW
Isle of Axholme Canon Michael Cooney, 16 Neap House Rd, Gunness, Scunthorpe DN15 8TT
Tel: 01724 784245
email: mike.cooney@btinternet.com
Corringham Canon Rhys Prosser, Vicarage, 69 Mill Lane, Saxilby, Lincoln LN1 2HN
Tel: 01522 702427
email: rs.prosser@virgin.net
Lawres Revd Peter Godden, Rectory, Hackthorn, Lincoln LN2 3PF Tel: 01673 860856
email: peter@owmbygroup.co.uk
Manlake Revd Canon Michael Cooney, 16 Neap House Rd, Gunness, Scunthorpe DN15 8TT
Tel: 01724 784245
email: mike.cooney@btinternet.com
West Wold Canon Ian Robinson, Vicarage, 3 Spa Top, Caistor, Lincoln LN7 6UH
Tel: 01472 851339
email: revianrobinson@tiscali.co.uk
Yarborough Ven Jane Sinclair, Sanderlings, Willingham Road, Market Rasen LN8 3RE
Tel: 01673 849896
email: archdeacon.stowlindsey@lincoln.anglican.org

ARCHDEACONRY OF LINDSEY
Bolingbroke Canon Peter Coates, Vicarage, Church St, Spilsby PE23 5DU Tel: 01790 752526
email: peter.coates@onetel.net
Calcewaithe & Candleshoe Canon Terry Steele, Rectory, Glebe Rise, Burgh le Marsh, Skegness PE24 5BL Tel: 01754 810216
email: father.terry@btclick.com
Grimsby & Cleethorpes Canon Peter Mullins, Rectory, 23 Littlecoates Rd, Grimsby DN34 4NG
Tel: 01472 346986
email: p.m.mullins@virgin.net
Haverstoe Canon Ian Shelton, Rectory, 95 High St, Waltham, Grimsby DN37 0PN Tel: 01472 822172
email: robertshelton954@hotmail.com
Horncastle Revd Alec Boyd, Rectory, Fieldside, Mareham le Fen, Boston PE22 7QU
Tel: 01507 568215
email: alec@ajboyd.wanadoo.co.uk
Louthesk Canon Stephen Holdaway, Rectory, 49 Westgate, Louth LN11 9YE Tel: 01507 610247
email: stephen.holdaway@btinternet.com

ARCHDEACONRY OF LINCOLN
Stamford (Formerly Aveland and, Ness with Stamford) Mark Warrick, All Saints Vicarage, Casterton Road, Stamford PE9 2YL
Tel: 01780 756942
email: mark.warrick@stamfordallsaints.org.uk
Beltisloe Revd Canon Andrew Hawes, Vicarage, Church Lane, Edenham, Bourne PE10 0LS
Tel: 01778 591358
email: athawes@tiscali.co.uk

Dioceses

Christianity Revd David Osbourne, Rectory, 2A St Helen's Avenue, Boultham, Lincoln LN6 7RA
Tel: 01522 682026
email: davidosbourne@tiscali.co.uk
Elloe East and West Revd Rosamund Seal, Vicarage, 34 Church Lane, Moulton, Spalding PE12 6NP
Tel: 01406 370791
email: rosamund@sealatmoulton.co.uk
Graffoe Revd Nicholas John Buck, Rectory, 11 Torgate Lane, Bassingham LN5 9HF
Tel: 01522 788383
email: nick_buck@tiscali.co.uk
Grantham Canon Christopher Andrews, The Rectory, 4 Church St, Grantham NG31 6RR
Tel: 01476 561342
email: chris@stwulframs.com

Holland Revd Robin Whitehead, Vicarage, Wormgate, Boston PE21 6NP   *Tel:* 01205 354670
email: robin.whitehead@virgin.net
Lafford Canon John Patrick, Vicarage, Market Place, Sleaford NG34 7SH   *Tel:* 01529 302117
email: japatrick@btinternet.com
Loveden Revd Dr Alan Megahey, Rectory, Church End, Leadenham LN5 0PX
Tel: 01400 273987
email: rector.leadenham@btopenworld.com

BISHOP (7th)
Rt Revd James Stuart Jones, Bishop's Lodge, Woolton Park, Woolton, Liverpool L25 6DT [1998]   *Tel:* 0151 421 0831
[James Liverpool]
Bishop's Personal Assistant Mrs Margaret Funnell *(same address)*   *Tel:* 0151 421 0831 (Office)
                              Fax: 0151 428 3055
email: bishopslodge@liverpool.anglican.org

SUFFRAGAN BISHOP
WARRINGTON   Rt Revd Richard Blackburn, St James' House, 20 St James' Rd, Liverpool L1 7BY   *Tel:* 0151 709 9722
email:
    bishopofwarrington@liverpool.anglican.org
Bishop's Personal Assistant Mrs Nerys Cooke, St James' House, 20 St James' Rd, Liverpool L1 7BY   *Tel:* 0151 705 2140
    email: Nerys.cooke@liverpool.anglican.org

HONORARY ASSISTANT BISHOPS
Rt Revd Frank Sergeant, 32 Brotherton Drive, Trinity Gardens, Salford M3 6BN [2008]
                              Tel: 0161 839 7045
Rt Revd Ian Stuart, Provost's Office, Liverpool Hope, Hope Park, Liverpool L16 9JD [1999]
                              Tel: 0151 291 3547
Rt Revd Martyn William Jarrett (Provisional Episcopal Visitor), 3 North Lane, Roundhay, Leeds LS8 2QJ [2005]   *Tel:* 0113 265 4280
                              Fax: 0113 265 4281
email:
    bishop-of-beverley@3-north-lane.fsnet.co.uk

CATHEDRAL CHURCH OF CHRIST
Dean Very Revd Justin Welby, The Cathedral, St James's Mount, Liverpool L1 7AZ [2007]
                              Tel: 0151 702 7202
                              Fax: 0151 702 7292
    email: dean@liverpoolcathedral.org.uk
Canons Residentiary
Treasurer Canon Anthony Hawley, The Cathedral [2002]   *Tel:* 0151 702 7204
                              Fax: 0151 702 7292
    email: canon.hawley@liverpoolcathedral.org.uk
Precentor Canon Myles Davies [2008]
    Tel: 0151 702 7203 / 0151 228 5252
    email: canon.davies@liverpoolcathedral.org.uk

Dwelly Raven: Canon Dr Jules Gomes [2010]
                              Tel: 0151 702 7201
                              Fax: 0151 702 7292
Chancellor: Canon Cynthia Dowdle [2008]
                              Tel: 0151 702 7287
    email: cynthia.dowdle@hotmail.com
Canon for Mission and Evangelism: Canon Richard White [2009]   *Tel:* 0151 702 7243
    email: richard.white@liverpoolcathedral.org.uk
Director of Operations Mike Eastwood, St James' House, 20 St James' Rd, Liverpool L1 7BY
                              Tel: 0151 709 9722 /
                              0151 705 2117
    email: mike.eastwood@liverpool.anglican.org
Director of Music David Poulter, The Cathedral
                              Tel: 0151 702 7291
    email: david.poulter@liverpoolcathedral.org.uk
Organist Titulaire: Prof Dr Ian Tracey, The Cathedral
    email: ian.tracey@liverpoolcathedral.org.uk

ARCHDEACONS
LIVERPOOL   Ven Ricky Panter, 2a Monfa Rd, Bootle, Merseyside L20 6BQ [2002]
                        Tel and Fax: 0151 922 3758
    email: archdeaconricky@blueyonder.co.uk
WARRINGTON   Ven Peter Bradley, Rectory, 1A College Rd, Upholland, Skelmersdale WN8 0PY [2001]   *Tel:* 01695 622936
                              Fax: 01695 625865
    email: archdeacon@peterbradley.fsnet.co.uk

CONVOCATION (MEMBERS OF THE HOUSE OF CLERGY OF THE GENERAL SYNOD)
Proctors for Clergy
Revd Canon James Cook
Revd Canon Roger Driver
Revd Brenda Stober
Revd Peter Spiers
Revd Timothy Stratford

MEMBERS OF THE HOUSE OF LAITY OF THE GENERAL SYNOD
Mr Paul Hancock
Mr Mark Stafford
Mrs Debra Walker
Christopher Pye
Canon Margaret Swinson

DIOCESAN OFFICERS

Dioc Secretary Mike Eastwood, St James' House, 20 St James Rd, Liverpool L1 7BY
Tel: 0151 709 9722
Fax: 0151 709 2885
Chancellor of Diocese Sir Mark Hedley
Registrar of Diocese and Bishop's Legal Secretary Roger Arden, St James' House
Tel: 0151 709 2222

DIOCESAN ORGANIZATIONS

Diocesan Office St James' House, 20 St James Rd, Liverpool L1 7BY
Tel: 0151 709 9722
Fax: 0151 709 2885
Web: www.liverpool.anglican.org

ADMINISTRATION

Dioc Synod (*Chair, House of Clergy*) Revd Nicholas Anderson, The Vicarage, 1 View Rd, Rainhill, Merseyside L35 0LE
Tel: 0151 426 4666
(*Chair, House of Laity*) Canon Margaret Swinson, 46 Glenmore Ave, Liverpool L18 4QF
Tel: 0151 724 3533
(*Secretary*) Mike Eastwood, Dioc Office
(*Asst Secretary*) Ultan Russell, Dioc Office
Board of Finance (*Chair*) David Greensmith, Dioc Office
(*Secretary*) Mike Eastwood (*as above*)
Pastoral Committee (*Chair*) Vacancy; (*Secretary*) Sandra Holmes; (*Bishop's Planning Officer*) Revd David Burrows, Dioc Office
email: david.burrows@liverpool.anglican.org
Clergy Housing and Glebe Committee (*Chair*) Joy Mills, Dioc Office; (*Surveyor*) Alan Gayner, Dioc Office
Support Claire Evans, Dioc Office
Designated Officer Revd David Burrows, Dioc Office

CHURCHES

Advisory Committee for the Care of Churches (*Chair*) Revd Stephen Parish, 1a Fitzherbert St, Warrington WA2 7QG
Tel: 01925 631781

EDUCATION

Chair Bishop of Warrington
Director of Education Jon Richardson, Dioc Office
Asst Director Stuart Harrison, Dioc Office
Senior Diocesan Schools Adviser Joan O'Rourke Dioc Office
Diocesan Schools Adviser Joan Stein, Dioc Office

MINISTRY

Director of Ordinands Revd David Parry, Vicarage, St Michael's Church Rd, Liverpool L17 7BD
Tel: 0151 286 2422
Dean of Women's Ministries Canon Cynthia Dowdle, Vicarage, Tithebarn Rd, Knowsley Village, Merseyside L34 0JA
Tel: 0151 546 4266

LEARNING AND STEWARDSHIP

Director Steve Pierce
Readers' Association (Warden) Ms Jean Todd

Learning Manager Karen Dooley
email: karen.dooley@liverpool.anglican.org
Learning Manager Suzanne Matthews
Resources Officer Gordon Fath
email: gordon.fath@liverpool.anglican.org
Resources/Church Urban Fund Carolyn Spittle, Dioc Office

CHURCH GROWTH AND ECUMENISM

Team Leader Linda Jones, Dioc Office
Tel: 0151 705 2109
email: linda.jones@liverpool.anglican.org
Youth Adviser Missioner Frank Hinds
Tel: 0151 705 2147
email: frank.hinds@liverpool.anglican.org
Diocesan Adviser on Liturgy and Worship Revd Neil Kelley, Dioc Office
Tel: 0151 928 3342
Diocesan Ecumenical Adviser Linda Jones, Dioc Office
Director of Pioneer Ministry Canon Philip Potter, Dioc Office

COMMUNICATIONS

Media Manager Stuart Haynes, Dioc Office
Tel: 0151 705 2150
email: stuart.haynes@liverpool.anglican.org
Communications Officer Andrea Young, Dioc Office
Tel: 0151 705 2131
email: andrea.young@liverpool.anglican.org

DIOCESAN RECORD OFFICE

For further information apply to Registrar, St James' House, 20 St James Rd, Liverpool L1 7BY *Tel:* 0151 709 9722 *or* The Lancashire Record Office, Bow Lane, Preston PR1 8ND *Archivist* Mr K. Hall *Tel:* 01772 254868

CHURCH AND SOCIETY

Tel: 0151 705 2130
Fax: 0151 705 2215
email: churchandsociety@liverpool.anglican.org
Senior Officer Ultan Russell
email: ultan.russell@liverpool.anglican.org
Disability Awareness and Vulnerable Adults Officer Sister Ruth Reed
email: ruth.reed@liverpool.anglican.org
Racial Justice Officer Hyacinth Sweeney Dixon *email:*
hyacinth.sweeney-dixon@liverpool.anglican.org
Adviser on Older People's Issues Mary Kessler
Tel: 01704 530660
Relationship Adviser Revd Joyce Weaver
Tel: 01925 634993
Rural Issues Adviser Vacancy
Church and World Adviser Revd Julie Fleming
Tel: 0151 263 2518
Akure Link Adviser Revd Roy Doran
Tel: 01744 23601
email: revroydoran@ravenhead.fsnet.co.uk
Team Leader, Pastoral Services for the Deaf Community Revd Dr Hannah Lewis
email: hannah.lewis@liverpool.anglican.org

MERSEYSIDE AND REGION CHURCHES ECUMENICAL ASSEMBLY
Ecumenical Development Officer Revd Ian Smith (URC), Quaker Meeting House, 22 School Lane, Liverpool L1 3BT   *Tel:* 0151 709 0125

MISSION IN THE ECONOMY (MitE)
Team Coordinator Revd Fran Lovett, Liverpool Cathedral, St James' Mount, Liverpool L1 7AZ
Tel: 0151 702 7208

AREA DEANS
ARCHDEACONRY OF LIVERPOOL
Bootle Canon Roger Driver, The Vicarage, 70 Merton Rd, Bootle L20 7AT   *Tel:* 0151 922 3316
email: rogerdriver@btinternet.com
Huyton Canon John Taylor, Vicarage, Vicarage Place, Prescot L34 1LA   *Tel:* 0151 426 6719
email: the-revd-john-taylor@supanet.com
Liverpool North Canon Henry Corbett, St Peter's Vicarage, Shrewsbury House, Langrove St, Liverpool L5 3PE   *Tel:* 0151 207 1948
email: henry-corbett@btinternet.com
Liverpool South – Childwall Canon Christopher John Crooks, Rectory, 67 Church Rd, Woolton, Liverpool L25 6DA   *Tel:* 0151 428 1853
email: kipcrooks@blueyonder.co.uk
Sefton Canon Peter Spiers, St Luke's Vicarage, Liverpool Road, Crosby, Liverpool L23 5SE
Tel: 01519 241737
email: pete@spiersfamily.eclipse.co.uk
Toxteth and Wavertree Canon Mark Stanford, Vicarage, 40 Devonshire Rd, Toxteth, Liverpool L8 3TZ   *Tel:* 0151 727 1248
email: mark@stphilemons.org.uk

Walton Canon Ray Bridson, St Columba's Vicarage, Pinehurst Ave, Liverpool L4 2TZ
Tel: 0151 474 7231
email: frray@blueyonder.co.uk
West Derby Canon Steve McGanity, St Andrew's Vicarage, 176 Queen's Drive, Liverpool L13 0AL
Tel: 0151 287 2887

ARCHDEACONRY OF WARRINGTON
North Meols Canon Phil Green, Vicarage, Rufford Road, Crossens, Southport PR9 8JH
Tel: 01704 227662
email: revphilgreen@talktalk.net
Ormskirk Canon Nick Wells, Vicarage, 20 Damfield Lane, Maghull, Liverpool L31 6DD
Tel: 0151 531 8972
email: nick.the-vic@blueyonder.co.uk
St Helens Canon Mark Cockayne, St Mark's Vicarage, 2 Stanley Bank Rd, Haydock, St Helens WA11 0UW   *Tel:* 01744 602641
email: markcockayne@eplusmail.com
Warrington Canon Stephen Attwater, Rectory, Station Rd, Padgate, Warrington WA2 0PD
Tel: 01925 821555
email: attwater292@btinternet.com
Widnes Canon David Gait, St John's House, Greenway Rd, Widnes WA8 6HA
Tel: 0151 424 3134
email: dave.gait@btinternet.com
Wigan Canon Margaret Sherwin, 3 Green Lane, Hindley Green, Wigan WN2 4HN
Tel: 01942 255833
email: mjsherwin@btinternet.com
Winwick Canon Joan Matthews, 8 Parchments, Newton-le-Willows WA12 9SR
Tel: 01925 270795
email: revjoan@hotmail.com

DIOCESE OF LONDON

Founded in 314. The City of London; Greater London north of the Thames, except five East London boroughs (CHELMSFORD) and an area in the north (ST ALBANS); Surrey north of the Thames; a small area of southern Hertfordshire.

Population 3,717,000   Area 277 sq m
Full-time Stipendiary Parochial Clergy 481   Benefices 404
Parishes 395   Churches 475
www.london.anglican.org
Overseas link dioceses: Niassa and Lebombo (Mozambique), Angola;
(Willesden): Hong Kong and Macao.

BISHOP (132nd)
Rt Revd and Rt Hon Dr Richard John Carew Chartres KCVO, The Old Deanery, Dean's Court, London EC4V 5AA [1995]   *Tel:* 020 7248 6233
Fax: 020 7248 9721
email: bishop@londin.clara.co.uk
[Richard Londin:]
Personal Jurisdiction Cities of London and Westminster (*Archdeaconries of London and Charing Cross*)
Matters relating to the other Areas should be referred to the appropriate Area Bishop
Personal Assistant Janet Laws
Diary Secretary Frances Charlesworth

AREA BISHOPS
STEPNEY Vacancy   *Tel:* 020 8981 2323
Fax: 020 8981 8015
email: bishop.stepney@london.anglican.org
KENSINGTON Rt Revd Paul Williams, Dial House, Riverside, Twickenham, Middx TW1 3DT [2009]
Tel: 020 8892 7781
email: bishop.kensington@london.anglican.org
EDMONTON Rt Revd Peter Wheatley, 27 Thurlow Rd, London NW3 5PP [1999]
Tel: 020 7435 5890
Fax: 020 7435 6049
email: bishop.edmonton@london.anglican.org
WILLESDEN Rt Revd Peter Broadbent, 173 Willesden Lane, London NW6 7YN [2001]
Tel: 020 8451 0189
07957 144674 (Mobile)
Fax: 020 8451 4606
email: bishop.willesden@btinternet.com

SUFFRAGAN BISHOP
FULHAM Vacancy
Assists the Diocesan in all matters not delegated to the Areas and pastoral care of parishes operating under the London Plan.

HONORARY ASSISTANT BISHOPS
Rt Revd Donald Arden, 6 Frobisher Close, Pinner HA5 1NN   *Tel:* 020 8866 6009
Fax: 020 8868 8013
email: ardendj@yahoo.co.uk
Rt Revd Michael Colclough, 2 Amen Court, London EC4M 7BU   *Tel:* 020 7236 0199
email: canonpastor@stpaulscathedral.org.uk
Rt Revd Edward Holland, 37 Parfrey St, London W6 9EW   *Tel:* 020 8746 3636
email: ed.holland@btopenworld.com
Rt Revd Graeme Knowles, 9 Amen Court, London EC4M 7BU   *Tel:* 020 7236 2827
Fax: 020 7332 0298
email: thedean@stpaulscathedral.org.uk
Rt Revd Robert Ladds, Christ Church House, 76 Brent Street, London NW4 2ES
Tel: 020 8202 8123
email: episcopus@ntworld.com
Most Revd Walter Makhulu, Cheyne House, 10 Crondace Rd, London SW6 4BB
Tel: 020 7371 9419
email: makhulu@btinternet.com
Rt Revd Michael Marshall, 53 Oakley Gardens, London SW3 5QQ [1984]   *Tel:* 020 7351 0928
email: sebastian97@hotmail.co.uk
Rt Revd Preb Sandy Millar, St Mark's Vicarage, 1 Moray Rd, London N4 3LD   *Tel:* 020 7561 5462
email: sandy.millar@tollingtonparish.org.uk

CATHEDRAL CHURCH OF ST PAUL
Dean Rt Revd Graeme Knowles, 9 Amen Court, London EC4M 7BU [2007]   *Tel:* 020 7236 2827
Fax: 020 7332 0298
email: thedean@stpaulscathedral.org.uk
Canons Residentiary
Treasurer Canon Mark Oakley, 6 Amen Court, EC4M 7BU [2010]   *Tel:* 020 7248 8572
Fax: 020 7489 8579
email: treasurer@stpaulscathedral.org.uk
Precentor Vacancy
Canon Pastor Rt Revd Michael Colclough, 2 Amen Court, EC4M 7BU [2008]   *Tel:* 020 7236 0199
Fax: 020 7489 8579
email: pastor@stpaulscathedral.org.uk

Chancellor Canon Giles Fraser, 6 Amen Court, EC4M 7BU [2009]   *Tel/Fax:* 020 7248 2559
email: chancellor@stpaulscathedral.org.uk
Lay Canons
Ms Lucrezia Walker, Chapter House, St Paul's Churchyard, London EC4M 8AD
Tel: 020 7246 8350
Fax: 020 7248 3104
email: lucreziawalker@aol.com
Mr Gavin Ralston, Chapter House, St Paul's Churchyard, London EC4M 8AD
Tel: 020 7246 8350
Fax: 020 7248 3104
email: gavin@stpaulscathedral.org.uk
Dr Peter McCullough, The Chapter House, St Paul's Churchyard, London EC4M 8AD
Tel: 020 7246 8350
Fax: 020 7248 3104
email: peter@stpaulscathedral.org.uk
The College of Minor Canons
Sacrist Revd Jason Rendell, 8a Amen Court, EC4M 7BU [2007]   *Tel:* 020 7246 8331
Fax: 020 7246 8336
email: sacrist@stpaulscathedral.org.uk
Chaplain Revd Sarah Eynstone, 7b Amen Court, London EC4M 7BU [2009]   *Tel:* 020 7246 8323
Fax: 020 7246 8336
email: chaplain@stpaulscathedral.org.uk
Succentor Revd Andrew Hammond, 7a Amen Court, London EC4M 7BU   *Tel:* 020 7246 8338
email: succentor@stpaulscathedral.org.uk
Headmaster of the School Mr Neil Chippington, St Paul's Cathedral School, New Change, London EC4M 9AD   *Tel:* 020 7248 5156
Fax: 020 7329 6568
email: admissions@spcs.london.sch.uk
Registrar Mr Nicholas Cottam, Chapter House, St Paul's Churchyard, EC4M 8AD
Tel: 020 7246 8311
Fax: 020 7248 3104
email: registrar@stpaulscathedral.org.uk
Dean's Virger Mr Michael Page, 4b Amen Court, EC4M 7BU   *Tel:* 020 7246 8320
Fax: 020 7248 3104
email: virgers@stpaulscathedral.org.uk
Solicitor to the Foundation at St Paul's Cathedral Mr Owen Carew-Jones, Winckworth Sherwood, Minerva House, 5 Montague Close, London SE1 9BB   *Tel:* 020 7593 5034
Fax: 020 7248 3221
email: ocj@winckworths.co.uk
Surveyor Mr Martin Stancliffe, The Chapter House, St Paul's Churchyard, EC4M 8AD
Tel: 020 7236 4128 and 01904 644001 (York)
Director of Music Mr Andrew Carwood, 5 Amen Court, EC4M 7BU   *Tel:* 020 7651 0899
Fax: 020 7248 2817
email: andrewc@stpaulscathedral.org.uk
Organist Mr Simon Johnson, 4a Amen Court, EC4M 7BU   *Tel:* 020 7236 6883
email: simon@stpaulscathedral.org.uk

Sub-Organist Mr Tim Wakerell, Chapter House, St Paul's Churchyard, EC4M 8AD
Tel: 020 7236 6883
Fax: 020 7248 2871
email: suborganist@stpaulscathedral.org.uk

ARCHDEACONS
LONDON Ven David Meara, The Archdeacon of London's Office, The Old Deanery, Dean's Court, London EC4V 5AA [2009]   *Tel:* 020 7236 7891
Fax: 020 7248 7455
email: archdeacon.london@london.anglican.org
CHARING CROSS Ven Dr William Jacob, 15A Gower St, London WC1E 6HW [1996]
Tel: 020 7323 1992
Fax: 020 7323 4102
email:
archdeacon.charingcross@london.anglican.org
HACKNEY Vacancy
email: archdeacon.hackney@london.anglican.org
MIDDLESEX Ven Stephan Welch, 98 Dukes Ave, London W4 2AF [2006]   *Tel:* 020 8742 8308
email:
archdeacon.middlesex@london.anglican.org
HAMPSTEAD Vacancy
email:
archdeacon.hampstead@london.anglican.org
NORTHOLT Ven Rachel Treweek, 16 Baldwyn Gardens, Acton, London W3 6HL [2006]
Tel and *Fax:* 020 8993 6415
email: archdeacon.northolt@london.anglican.org

CONVOCATION (MEMBERS OF THE HOUSE OF CLERGY OF THE GENERAL SYNOD)
Dignitaries in Convocation
The Bishop of Willesden
Revd Dr Richard Burridge
Ven William Noblett
Proctors for Clergy
Preb Philippa Boardman
Revd Christopher Hobbs
Revd Clare Herbert
Revd Jane Morris
Revd Stephen Coles
Preb David Houlding
Revd Philip Noah
Revd Charles Marnham
Revd Alan Moses
Ven Rachel Treweek

MEMBERS OF THE HOUSE OF LAITY OF THE GENERAL SYNOD
Ms Susan Cooper
Mrs Sarah Finch
Mr Aiden Hargreaves-Smith
Mrs Mary Johnston
Dr Lindsay Newcombe
Mr Anirban Roy
Mrs Alison Ruoff
Mr Clive Scowen
Mr John Ward
Dr Phillip Rice

DIOCESAN OFFICERS

Dioc Secretary Mr Andy Brookes, London Diocesan House, 36 Causton St, London SW1P 4AU
        Tel: 020 7932 1100
        Fax: 020 7932 1114
Chancellor of Diocese Chancellor Nigel Seed, Winckworth Sherwood, Minerva House, 5 Montague Close, London SE1 9BB
        Tel: 020 7593 5110
        Fax: 020 7248 3221
Registrar of Diocese and Bishop's Legal Secretary Mr Paul Morris (*same address*)
Official Principal of the Archdeaconry of Hackney His Honour David Smith QC, Beachcroft, Beach, Bitton, Bristol BS30 6NP
Official Principal of the Archdeaconry of Hampstead Dean Sheila Cameron, 2 Harcourt Bldgs, Temple, London EC4Y 9DB
Official Principal of the Archdeaconry of Northolt Mr Paul Morris (*as above*)

DIOCESAN ORGANIZATIONS
CHAIRMEN
London Dioc Fund (*Dioc Board of Finance*) The Bishop of London
Vice Chairmen Mr David Loftus and Preb David Houlding
Finance Committee Ven Dr William Jacob
Dioc Synod (*House of Clergy*) Preb David Houlding (*House of Laity*) Mr David Loftus
Dioc Board for Schools Ven Stephan Welch

ADMINISTRATION
Diocesan Office London Diocesan House, 36 Causton St, London SW1P 4AU
        Tel: 020 7932 1100
        Fax: 020 7932 1112
        Web: www.london.anglican.org
Director of Finance and Operations Ms Helen Verney
Human Resources Manager Ms Paula Bailey
Director of Property Mr Michael Bye
Synodical Secretary Mrs Monica Bolley
Communications Manager Mr Robert Hargrave
Dioc Advisory Committee (*Chair*) Ven Peter Delaney; (*Secretary*) Mr Geoffrey Hunter

EDUCATION
Senior Chaplain for Higher Education Revd Stephen Williams, University Chaplaincy Office, 30B Torrington Square, London WC1E 7JL
        Tel: 020 7580 9812
        Fax: 020 7631 3219
        email: chaplaincy@lon.ac.uk
Director, Board for Schools Revd Dr Howard Worsley, London Dioc House   *Tel:* 020 7932 1161
        Fax: 020 7932 1111
     email: howard.worsley@london.anglican.org

MINISTRY
Vicar General to the London College of Bishops, Dioc Director of Ordinands, Preb Nick Mercer,

The Old Deanery, Dean's Court, London EC4V 5AA   *Tel:* 020 7489 4274
     email: nick.mercer@london.anglican.org
Director of Professional Development, Readers and Licensed Lay Ministry Revd Neil Evans, Willesden Area Office, 268a Kenton Rd, Kenton, Harrow HA3 8DB   *Tel:* 020 8907 5993
     email: neil.evans@london.anglican.org
Two Cities
Dean of Women's Ministry Revd Rosemary Lain-Priestley, 13d Hyde Park Mansions, Cabell St, London NW1 5BD   *Tel:* 020 7723 5352
     email: rosemarylainpriestley@btopenworld.com
Stepney
Area Director of Training and Development Preb Andy Windross, Centre for Training and Development (Stepney Episcopal Area), St Anne's Community Hall, Hemsworth St, London N1 5LF   *Tel and Fax:* 020 7254 7440
     email: andy.windross@london.anglican.org
Dean of Women's Ministry Revd Irena Edgcumbe, St Anne's Vicarage, 37 Hemsworh St, London N1 5LF   *Tel:* 020 7729 1243
     email: irena.edgcumbe@london.anglican.org
Kensington
Area Director of Ministry Revd Martin Breadmore, 207 London Road, Twickenham TW1 1EJ
        Tel: 020 8891 0324
     email: martin.breadmore@london.anglican.org
Dean of Women's Ministry Revd Rosemary Hoad, St Mary's Vicarage, Osterley Rd, Isleworth TW7 4PW   *Tel:* 020 8560 3555
     email: rosemary.hoad@dsl.pipex.com
Willesden
Area Director of Training and Development Revd Neil Evans (*as above*)
Edmonton
Area Director of Training and Development Caulene Herbert, 27 Thurlow Rd, Hampstead, London NW3 5PP   *Tel:* 020 7431 6827
     email: caulene.herbert@london.anglican.org

MISSION
Children's Ministry Adviser Samuel Donoghue, London Dioc House   *Tel:* 020 7932 1255
     email: sam.donoghue@london.anglican.org
Diocesan Community Ministry Adviser Jack Maple   *Tel:* 020 7932 1122
     email: jack.maple@london.anglican.org

LITURGICAL
Chairman Rt Revd Graeme Knowles (*as above*)
Convener Revd Keith Robus, St Gabriel's Vicarage, 15 Balfour Rd, North Acton, London, W3 0DG   *Tel:* 020 8992 5938
     email: keith@robus.demon.co.uk

PRESS AND COMMUNICATIONS
Communications Manager Mr Robert Hargrave, London Dioc House   *Tel:* 020 7932 1227
     email: robert.hargrave@london.anglican.org
Press, media and public affairs
        Tel: 020 7618 9106 (24 hours)
     email: dioceseoflondon@luther.co.uk

DIOCESAN RECORD OFFICES

London Metropolitan Archive, 40 Northampton Rd, London EC1R 0HB *Head Archivist* Dr Deborah Jenkins *Tel:* 020 7332 3824 (*All parishes except City and Westminster*)
Guildhall Library, Aldermanbury, London EC2P 2EJ *Archivist* Mr S. G. H. Freeth *Tel:* 020 7606 3030, Ext 1862/3 (*City parishes*)
Westminster Archives Dept, 10 St Ann's St, London SW1P 2XR *Archivist* Mr Jerome Farrell *Tel:* 020 7798 2180 (*Westminster parishes*)

AREA DEANS
ARCHDEACONRY OF LONDON
City Revd Oliver Ross, St Olave's Rectory, 8 Hart St, London EC3R 7NB   *Tel:* 020 7488 4318
          email: rector.stolave@mac.com

ARCHDEACONRY OF CHARING CROSS
Westminster (*Paddington*) Revd Alastair Thom, Vicarage, 19 Macroom Rd, London W9 3HY
          Tel: 020 8962 0294
          email: alastairthom@yahoo.co.uk
Westminster (*St Margaret*) Revd Philip Chester, St Matthew's House, 20 Great Peter St, London SW1P 2BU   *Tel:* 020 7222 3704
          email: office@stmw.org
Westminster (*St Marylebone*) Preb Alan Moses, 7 Margaret St, London W1W 8JG
          Tel: 020 7636 1788
          Fax: 020 7436 4470
          email: alanmoses@blackberry.orange.co.uk

ARCHDEACONRY OF HACKNEY
Hackney Revd Julia Porter-Pryce, St Peter's Vicarage, 86 De Beauvoir Rd, London N1 5AT
          Tel: 020 7254 5670
          email: juliap@freeuk.com
Islington Revd Michael Learmouth, The Rectory, 10 Thornhill Square, London N1 1BQ
          Tel: 020 7607 9039
          email: michaelwlearmouth@gmail.com
Tower Hamlets Preb Alan Green, St John's Rectory, 30 Victoria Park Square, Bethnal Green, London E2 9PB   *Tel:* 020 8980 1742
          email: alan.green@virgin.net

ARCHDEACONRY OF MIDDLESEX
Hammersmith and Fulham Revd Gary Piper, St Matthew's Vicarage, 2 Clancarty Rd, London SW6 3AB   *Tel:* 020 7731 3272
          email: revgarypiper@hotmail.com
Hampton Revd Derek Winterburn, Vicarage, 7 Church St, Hampton, Middlesex TW12 2EB   *Tel:* 020 8979 3071
          email: vicar@winterburn.me.uk
Hounslow Revd Derek Simpson, Rectory, 3 The Butts, Brentford TW8 8BJ
          Tel: 020 8568 7442 (Office)
          email: derek.simpson@parishofbrentford.org.uk

Kensington Revd Dr Mark Hargreaves, 59a Portobello Rd, London W11 3DB
          Tel: 020 7229 6774
          email: mark@nottinghillchurch.org.uk
Chelsea Revd Rob Gillion, Rectory, 97a Cadogan Lane, London SW1X 9DU   *Tel:* 020 7823 2009
          email: rector@holytrinitysloanesquare.co.uk
Spelthorne Revd David McDougall, St Saviour's Vicarage, 205 Vicarage Road, Sunbury on Thames, Middx TW16 7TP
          Tel: 01932 782 800 (Office)
          email: david@st-saviours-sunbury.org.uk

ARCHDEACONRY OF HAMPSTEAD
Central Barnet Revd Paul Walmsley-McLeod, The Rectory, 147 Friern Barnet Lane, London N20 0NP   *Tel:* 020 0445 7844
          email: pawm_friernbarnet@hotmail.com
West Barnet Revd Gwyn Clement, The Vicarage, 34 Parson Street, London NW4 1QR
          Tel: 020 8203 2884
          email: fr.gwyn@btinternet.com
North Camden (*Hampstead*) Revd Andrew Cain, 134a Abbey Rd, London NW6 4SN
          Tel and Fax: 020 7624 5434
          email: vicaragekilburn@btopenworld.com
South Camden (*Holborn and St Pancras*) Revd Andrew Meldrum, St Anne's Vicarage, 106 Highgate West Hill, London NW6 6AP
          Tel and Fax: 020 8340 5190
          email: javintner@aol.com
Enfield Revd Dr Richard James, Christ Church Vicarage, 2A Chalk Lane, Cockfosters, Herts EN4 9QJ   *Tel:* 020 8441 1230
          email: richard.j.ccc@btconnect.com
East Haringey Revd Luke Miller, St Mary's Vicarage, Lansdowne Rd, London N17 9XE
          Tel: 020 8808 6644
          email: frmiller@stmarystottenham.org
West Haringey Revd Timothy Pike, 99 Hillfield Ave, Crouch End, London N8 7DG
          Tel: 020 8340 1300
          email: fathertimpike@hotmail.com

ARCHDEACONRY OF NORTHOLT
Brent Revd Felicity Scroggie, St Andrew's Vicarage, 956 Harrow Road, Wembley, Middx HA0 2QA   *Tel:* 020 8904 4016
          email: felicity.scroggie@london.anglican.org
Ealing Revd Andrew Corsie, Perivale Rectory, Federal Rd, Greenford UB6 7AP
          Tel: 020 8997 1948
          email: andrew.corsie@perivalechurch.org.uk
Harrow Canon Richard Bartlett, Holy Trinity Vicarage, Gateway Close, Northwood, Middlesex HA6 2RP   *Tel:* 01923 825732
          email: richard.bartlett@london.anglican.org
Hillingdon Canon Simon Evans, The Vicarage, 13 Eastcote Rd, Ruislip, Middlesex HA4 8BE
          Tel: 01895 633040
          email: frsimon@waitrose.com

DIOCESE OF MANCHESTER

Founded in 1847. Manchester, except for a few parishes in the south (CHESTER); Salford; Bolton; Bury; Rochdale; Oldham; the western half of Tameside; an area of Wigan; an area of Trafford; an area of Stockport; an area of southern Lancashire.

Population 1,980,000   Area 415 sq m
Full-time Stipendiary Parochial Clergy 217   Benefices 215
Parishes 269   Churches 344
www.manchester.anglican.org
Overseas link dioceses: Lahore, Namibia.

BISHOP (11th)
Rt Revd Nigel Simeon McCulloch, Bishopscourt, Bury New Rd, Manchester M7 4LE [2002]
Tel: 0161 792 2096 (Office)
Fax: 0161 792 6826
email:
bishop@bishopscourt.manchester.anglican.org
[Nigel Manchester]
Chaplain Canon Christopher Bracegirdle (*same address*)
email:
chaplain@bishopscourt.manchester.anglican.org
Bishop's Missioner Canon Roger Hill (*same address*)

SUFFRAGAN BISHOPS
BOLTON Rt Revd Chris Edmonson, Bishop's Lodge, Walkden Rd, Worsley, Manchester M28 2WH [2008]
Tel: 0161 790 8289
Fax: 0161 703 9157
email: bishopchris@manchester.anglican.org
MIDDLETON Rt Revd Mark Davies, The Hollies, Manchester Rd, Rochdale OL11 3QY [2008]
Tel: 01706 358550
Fax: 01706 354851
email: bishopmark@manchester.anglican.org

CATHEDRAL AND COLLEGIATE CHURCH OF ST MARY, ST DENYS AND ST GEORGE
Dean Very Revd Rogers Govender, Manchester Cathedral, Victoria St, Manchester M3 1SX [2006]
Tel: 0161 833 2220
email: dean@manchestercathedral.org
Cathedral Office Manchester Cathedral, Victoria St, Manchester M3 1SX   *Tel:* 0161 833 2220
Fax: 0161 839 6218
email: office@manchestercathedral.org
Web: www.manchestercathedral.org
Canons Residentiary
Sub Dean & Theologian Canon Andrew Shanks, 3 Booth Clibborn Court, Park Lane, Manchester M7 4PJ [2004]
Tel: 0161 792 8820
Fax: 0161 839 6218
email: canon.shanks@manchestercathedral.org
Evangelist Canon Tony Hardy, 30 Rathen Rd, Withington, Manchester M20 4GH [2009]
Tel: 0161 446 1099
email:
canon.evangelist@manchestercathedral.org

Bishop's Chaplain Canon Christopher Bracegirdle, Bishopscourt, Bury New Road, Manchester M7 4LE   *Tel:* 0161 788 8461
email:
chaplain@bishopscourt.manchester.anglican.org
Canon Precentor Canon Gilly Myers, Manchester Cathedral, Victoria St, Manchester M3 1SX [2008]
Tel: 0161 833 2220
email: precentor@manchestercathedral.org
Archdeacon of Manchester
Ven Mark Ashcroft (*Archdeacon of Manchester*), 14 Moorgate Avenue, Withington, Manchester M20 1HE   *email:* archdeaconmanchester@manchester.anglican.org
Cathedral Chaplains
Revd Peter Bellamy-Knights; Canon Adrian Rhodes
Lay Members of Chapter
Mr David Howe
Cllr Roy Walters
Mrs Jennifer Curtis
Mr Barrie Cheshire
Chapter Clerk   Mr Peter Mellor, c/o Cathedral Office (tel. ext. 229)
email: administrator@manchestercathedral.org
Cathedral Education Officer Mrs Pam Elliott, c/o Cathedral Office (tel. ext. 236)
email: pam.elliott@manchestercathedral.org
Visitor Centre Manager Mr Peter Mellor (c/o Cathedral Office)   *Tel:* 0161 835 4030
email: peter.mellor@manchestercathedral.org
Cathedral Organist and Master of the Choristers Mr Christopher Stokes, c/o Cathedral Office (tel. ext. 225)
email:
christopherstokes@manchestercathedral.org
Sub-Organist Mr Jeffrey Makinson, c/o Cathedral Office (tel. ext. 225)
email: jeffrey.makinson@manchestercathedral.org
Worship and Music Administrator Miss Katy Leese, c/o Cathedral Office (tel. ext. 238)   *email:* worship-music.admin@manchestercathedral.org
Cathedral Administrator Mr Peter Mellor, c/o Cathedral Office (tel. ext. 229)
email: administrator@manchestercathedral.org
Cathedral Administrative Secretary: Miss Joanne Hooper, c/o Cathedral Office (tel. ext. 221)
email: joanne.hooper@manchestercathedral.org

Dean's PA Alison Rowland, c/o Cathedral Office (tel. ext. 220)
email: alison.rowland@manchestercathedral.org
Cathedral Office Assistant Karen Scott, c/o Cathedral Office (tel. ext. 235)
email: karen.scott@manchestercathedral.org
Junior Office Assistant Helen Boulton, c/o Cathedral Office (tel. ext. 222)
email: helen.boulton@manchestercathedral.org
Head Verger Mr Michael Scott, c/o Cathedral Office
email: michael.scott@manchestercathedral.org
Cathedral Accountant Mr John Atherden, c/o Cathedral Office (tel. ext 234)
accountant@manchestercathedral.com
Finance Assistant Joanne Hodkin, c/o Cathedral Office (tel. ext. 224)
email: joanne.hodkin@manchestercathedral.org
Director of Fundraising & Development Anthony O'Connor, c/o Cathedral Office (tel. ext. 233)
email: anthony.o'connor@manchestercathedral.org

ARCHDEACONS

MANCHESTER Ven Mark Ashcroft, 14 Moorgate Avenue, Withington, Manchester M20 1HE
Tel: 0161 448 1976
email:
archdeaconmanchester@manchester.anglican.org
ROCHDALE Ven Cherry Vann, 57 Melling Rd, Oldham OL4 1PN [2008] *Tel:* 0161 678 1454
Fax: 0161 678 1455
email: archrochdale@manchester.anglican.org
SALFORD Ven David Sharples, 2 The Walled Gardens, Ewhurst Avenue, Swinton M7 0FR
Tel: 0161 794 2331 / 0161 708 9366
Fax: 0161 794 2411
email:
archdeaconsalford@manchester.anglican.org
BOLTON Ven David Bailey, 14 Springside Road, Bury BL9 5JE *Tel:* 0161 761 6117
Fax: 0161 763 7973
email: archbolton@btinternet.com

CONVOCATION (MEMBERS OF THE HOUSE OF CLERGY OF THE GENERAL SYNOD)
Dignitaries in Convocation
The Bishop of Hulme
Proctors for Clergy
Ven Dr John Applegate
Canon Sarah Bullock
Revd Sharon Jones
Canon Simon Killwick
Revd Andrew Salmon
Ven Cherry Vann

MEMBERS OF THE HOUSE OF LAITY OF THE GENERAL SYNOD
Dr Peter Capon
Mr John Barber
Mrs Christine Sandiford
Mr Geoffrey Tattersall
Mr Michael Heppleston
Mr James Townsend

DIOCESAN OFFICERS
Chief Executive Mr John Beck, Diocesan Church House, 90 Deansgate, Manchester M3 2GH
Tel: 0161 828 1402
Fax: 0161 828 1480
Chancellor of Diocese G. F. Tattersall, Dioc Registry, Dioc Church House
Deputy Chancellor Ms C. Otton-Goulder, Dioc Registry, Dioc Church House *Tel:* 0161 834 7545
Registrar of Diocese and Bishop's Legal Secretary Ms Jane Monks (*same address*)
Dioc Surveyor for Parsonage Houses Mr John Prichard, The Lloyd Evans Partnership, 5 The Parsonage, Manchester M3 2HS
Tel: 0161 834 6251

DIOCESAN ORGANIZATIONS
Diocesan Office Diocesan Church House, 90 Deansgate, Manchester M3 2GH
Tel: 0161 828 1400
Fax: 0161 828 1480
email: manchesterdbf@manchester.anglican.org

ADMINISTRATION
Dioc Synod (Chairman, House of Clergy) Revd Andy Salmon
(Chairman, House of Laity) Mr Phillip Blinkhorn
Board of Finance (Chairman) Mr Alan Cooper, 11 Ravensdale Gdns, Eccles, Manchester M30 9JD
Tel: 0161 789 1514
(Secretary) Mr John Beck; *(Head of Finance and IT)* Mrs Janet Bury, Dioc Office; *(Legal Secretary)* Miss Jane Monks, Dioc Registry, Dioc Church House
Tel: 0161 834 7545
Property Committee (Property Secretary) Mr Geoff Hutchinson, Dioc Office *(Secretary)* Ven David Bailey
Mission Pastoral Committee (Secretary) Mr John Beck *(Chairman)* Very Revd Roger Govender
Designated Officer Miss Jane Monks, Dioc Registry, Dioc Church House *Tel:* 0161 834 7545

CHURCHES
Advisory Committee for the Care of Churches (Chairman) Mr Adrian Golland, Peel House, 29 Higher Dunscar, Egerton, Bolton BL7 9TE; *(DAC Secretary)* Ms Christine Hart, Dioc Office

EDUCATION
Chairman Rt Revd Mark Davies
Director of Education Mr Maurice Smith, Diocesan Church House, 90 Deansgate, Manchester M3 2GH
Tel: 0161 828 1400
Fax: 0161 828 1484
Education Officers
(Buildings) Miss Tracy Squirrell (*same address*)
(Governor Training) Mr Wil Leeson
((Asst Director of Education and Section 23/RE) Mr John Wilson (*same address*)
Children's Work Revd Steve Dixon (*same address*)
Youth Work Miss Susie Mapledoram (*same address*)
Deputy Director of Education and Training and Development Mrs Janet Cowley (*same address*)

CHURCH AND SOCIETY

Chairman Rt Revd Mark Davies
Director and Partnership Development Officer Mr Martin Miller, Dioc Office   *Tel:* 0161 828 1400
Training Officer (Church and Community Engagement) Mr Mike France, Dioc Office
International Officer Vacancy, Dioc Office
Mission Planning Officer Ms Alison Peacock, Dioc Office
Parish Resource Officer Canon Dian Leppington, Dioc Office
Hon European Adviser Revd Dr Keith Archer, Dioc Office

DISCIPLESHIP AND MINISTRY TRAINING

Chairman Revd Canon Sarah Bullock
Director of Ministry Training and OLM Principal Revd Peter Reiss, Dioc Office
Training Officer (CME and LD) Revd David Foster
Training Officer (Reader Training) Revd Jayne Prestwood, Dioc Office   *Tel:* 0161 828 1400
Dioc Director of Ordinands and OLM Officer Ven David Sharples, Bishopscourt, Bury New Rd, Manchester M4 4LE   *Tel:* 0161 708 9366

PRESS AND PUBLICATIONS

Director of Communications David Marshall, Dioc Office   *Tel:* 0161 828 1400
07836 224444 (Mobile)
email: dmarshall@manchester.anglican.org
Editor of Dioc Year Book c/o Dioc Office
Editor of Dioc Magazine Mrs Ann Mummery
email: amummery@manchester.anglican.org

DIOCESAN RECORD OFFICE

For further information apply to The Archivist, The Central Library, St Peter's Square, Manchester M2 5PD   *Tel:* 0161 234 1980

AREA DEANS

ARCHDEACONRY OF MANCHESTER

Ardwick Revd Ian Gomersall, St Chrysostom's Rectory, 38 Park Range, Manchester M14 5HQ
Tel: 0161 224 6971
Fax: 0161 870 6197
email: ian.gomersall@btinternet.com
Heaton Revd Les Ireland, St Andrew's Rectory, 27 Errwood Rd, Manchester M19 2PN
Tel: 0161 224 5877
email: LesIreland@ntlworld.com
Hulme Revd Simon Killwick, Christ Church Rectory, Monton St, Manchester M14 4LT
Tel: 0161 226 2476
email: frskillwick@btinternet.com
North Manchester Revd Daniel Burton, The Vicarage, 105 Brideoak St, Cheetham Hill M8 0AY   *Tel:* 0161 205 1734
email: daniel.burton100@ntlworld.com
Stretford Revd John Hughes, St John's Rectory, 1 Lindum Ave, Old Trafford, Manchester M16 9NQ   *Tel:* 0161 872 0500
email: john_dhughes@yahoo.co.uk

Withington Revd Ian McVeety, St John's Vicarage, 186 Brooklands Rd, Sale M33 3PB
Tel: 0161 973 5947
email: ian@stjohnsvicarage.fsnet.co.uk

ARCHDEACONRY OF BOLTON

Bolton Canon Rodger Petch, 101 Cloister St, Bolton BL1 3HA   *Tel:* 01204 842627
email: rodgerpetch@yahoo.co.uk
Bury Revd Stuart Millington, All Saints Vicarage, 10 Kirkburn View, Brandlesholme, Bury BL8 1DL   *Tel:* 0161 797 1595
email: stuart@revmillington.wanadoo.co.uk
Deane Revd Roger Cooper, St Katharine's Vicarage, Blackhorse St. Blackrod, Bolton BL6 5EN   *Tel:* 01204 468150
email: revrog17@hotmail.com
Radcliffe and Prestwich Revd Debby Plummer, St Margaret's Vicarage, St Margaret's Rd, Prestwich M25 2QB   *Tel:* 0161 773 2698
email: prestwichplummers@btinternet.com
Rossendale Revd Susan Davies, Rectory, 539 Newchurch Rd, Rossendale BB4 9HH
Tel and *Fax:* 01706 219708
email: susanannedavies@aol.com
Walmsley Revd Wendy Oliver, Harwood Vicarage, Stitch-mi-Lane, Bolton BL2 4HU
Tel: 01204 525196
email: wendyloliver@googlemail.com

ARCHDEACONRY OF ROCHDALE

Ashton-under-Lyne Revd Roger Farnworth, St James Vicarage, Union St, Ashton-under-Lyne OL6 9NQ   *Tel:* 0161 330 2771
email: rogerfarnworth@aol.com
Heywood and Middleton Revd Ian Butterworth, St Martin's Vicarage, Vicarage Rd North, Castleton OL11 2TE   *Tel:* 01706 632363
email: i.butterworth@tesco.net
Rochdale Revd Sharon Jones, St Andrew's Vicarage, Arm Rd, Dearnley, Littleborough OL15 8NJ   *Tel:* 01706 378466
email: sharon@dearnleyvicarage.plus.com
Oldham East Revd Alan Butler, St Mary's Vicarage, 18 Rushcroft Road, High Crompton, Shaw OL2 7PP   *Tel:* 01706 847455
email: alanbutler@ntlworld.com
Oldham West Revd David Penny, St Matthew's Vicarage, Mill Brow, Chadderton OL1 2RT
Tel: 0161 624 8600
email: revdpenny@btinternet.com

ARCHDEACONRY OF SALFORD

Eccles Revd Ted Crofton, Rectory, 12b Westminster Rd, Eccles, Manchester M30 9EB
Tel: 0161 281 5739
email: ea_crofton@msn.com
Salford Revd Andy Salmon, 6 Encombe Place, Salford M3 6FJ   *Tel:* 0161 834 2041
email: rev.andy@btinternet.com
Leigh Revd Canon Dr Robert Buckley, Howe Bridge Rectory, Leigh Rd, Atherton, Manchester M46 0PH   *Tel:* 01942 883359
email: revrobert@athertonparish.co.uk

DIOCESE OF NEWCASTLE

Founded in 1882. Northumberland; Newcastle upon Tyne; North Tyneside;
a small area of eastern Cumbria; four parishes in northern County Durham.

Population 784,000   Area 2,110 sq m
Full-time Stipendiary Parochial Clergy 119   Benefices 134
Parishes 174   Churches 241
www.newcastle.anglican.org
Companion link dioceses: Winchester, More (Norway), Botswana (Africa).

BISHOP (11th)
Rt Revd (John) Martin Wharton, Bishop's House,
29 Moor Rd South, Gosforth, Newcastle upon
Tyne NE3 1PA [1998]   *Tel:* 0191 285 2220
          email: bishop@newcastle.anglican.org
[Martin Newcastle]
Bishop's Chaplain Canon Dr Audrey Anne
Elkington (*same address*)

ASSISTANT BISHOP
Rt Revd Frank White, (Home) 83 Kenton Road,
Kenton, Newcastle upon Tyne NE3 4NL [2010]
          Tel: 0191 285 1502
          email: f.white@newcastle.anglican.org
(Office) Bishop's House, 29 Moor Rd South,
Gosforth, Newcastle upon Tyne NE3 1PA
          Tel: 0191 285 2220

HONORARY ASSISTANT BISHOPS
Rt Revd Kenneth Edward Gill, Kingfisher Lodge,
41 Long Cram, Haddington, East Lothian EH41
4NS [1999]   *Tel:* 01620 822113
          email: k.gill@newcastle.anglican.org
Rt Revd Stephen Pedley, The Blue House,
Newbrough NE47 5AN [2005]   *Tel:* 01434 674238
Rt Revd John Henry Richardson, Old Rectory,
Bewcastle, Carlisle, Cumbria CA6 6PS [2003]
          Tel: 01697 748389

CATHEDRAL CHURCH OF ST NICHOLAS
Dean Very Revd Christopher Charles Dalliston,
26 Mitchell Ave, Jesmond, Newcastle upon Tyne
NE2 3LA [2003]   *Tel:* 0191 281 6554
          0191 232 1939
          email: dean@stnicnewcastle.co.uk
Chapter Office Cathedral House, 42/44 Mosley
Street, Newcastle upon Tyne NE1 1DF
          Tel: 0191 232 1939
          Fax: 0191 230 0735
          email: office@stnicnewcastle.co.uk
Canons Residentiary
Canon Peter Robert Strange, 55 Queens Terrace,
Jesmond, Newcastle upon Tyne NE2 2PL [1986]
          Tel: 0191 281 0181
          0191 232 1939
          email: peterstrange@stnicnewcastle.co.uk

Ven Geoffrey Vincent Miller, 80 Moorside North,
Fenham, Newcastle upon Tyne NE4 9DU [1999]
          Tel: 0191 273 8245
          Fax: 0191 226 0286
          email: g.miller@newcastle.anglican.org
Canon David John Elkington, 16 Towers Ave,
Jesmond, Newcastle upon Tyne NE2 3QE [2002]
          Tel: 0191 281 0714
          email: djelk@tiscali.co.uk
Canon Sheila Bamber, 2a Holly Avenue,
Jesmond, Newcastle upon Tyne NE2 2PY [2010]
          Tel: 0191 281 4329
          email: sheilabamber@stnicnewcastle.co.uk
Director of Music Mr Michael Stoddart
          Tel: 0191 261 4505
          email: directorofmusic@stnicnewcastle.co.uk
Director of Girl's Choir David Stevens
          email: stnicsgirlschoir@btconnect.com
Cathedral Secretary Ms Elspeth Robertson,
Cathedral House   *Tel:* 0191 232 1939
          email: office@stnicnewcastle.co.uk
Cathedral Administrator Mr Julian Haynes,
Cathedral House   *Tel:* 0191 232 1939
          email: julianhaynes@stnicnewcastle.co.uk
Finance Administrator Ian Clough, Cathedral
House   *Tel:* 0191 232 1939
          email: ianclough@stnicnewcastle.co.uk

ARCHDEACONS
LINDISFARNE Ven Peter John Alan Robinson,
4 Acomb Close, Stobhill Manor, Morpeth NE61
2YH [2008]   *Tel:* 01670 503810
          Fax: 01670 503 469
          email: p.robinson@newcastle.anglican.org
NORTHUMBERLAND Ven Geoffrey Vincent Miller,
80 Moorside North, Fenham, Newcastle upon
Tyne NE4 9DU [2005]   *Tel:* 0191 273 8245
          Fax: 0191 226 0286
          email: g.miller@newcastle.anglican.org

**CONVOCATION (MEMBERS OF THE
HOUSE OF CLERGY OF THE GENERAL
SYNOD)**
Proctors for Clergy
Revd Janet Appleby
Canon John Sinclair
Revd Dr Dagmar Winter

MEMBERS OF THE HOUSE OF LAITY OF THE GENERAL SYNOD
Dr John Bull
Mrs Margaret White
Miss Carol Wolstenholme

DIOCESAN OFFICERS
Dioc Secretary Mr Graham Barnard, Church House, St John's Terrace, North Shields NE29 6HS
Tel: 0191 270 4100
Fax: 0191 270 4101
Chancellor of Diocese His Honour Judge David Hodson, The Law Courts, Quayside, Newcastle upon Tyne NE1 3LA
Tel: 0191 201 2000
Registrar of Diocese and Bishop's Legal Secretary Mrs Jane Lowdon, Sintons Solicitors, The Cube, Barrack Rd, Newcastle upon Tyne NE4 6DB
Tel: 0191 226 7878
Fax: 0191 226 7850
email: j.lowdon@sintons.co.uk

DIOCESAN ORGANIZATIONS
Diocesan Office Church House, St John's Terrace, North Shields NE29 6HS
Tel: 0191 270 4100
Fax: 0191 270 4101
email: church_house@newcastle.anglican.org

ADMINISTRATION
Dioc Synod (*Chairman, House of Clergy*) Canon John Robert Sinclair, The Vicarage, Newburn, Newcastle upon Tyne NE15 8LQ
Tel: 0191 229 0522
email: johnsinclair247@aol.com
(*Chairman, House of Laity*) Mr Michael Stoker, 51 Hastings Avenue, Whitley Bay NE26 4AG
Tel: 0191 252 0250
email: mike.stoker@talk21.com
(*Secretary*) Mr Graham Barnard, Church House
Office Manager and Assistant to Diocesan Secretary Mrs Vanessa Ward, Church House
Finance Board (*Chairman*) Mr Simon Harper, Church House
(*Secretary*) Mr Graham Barnard (*as above*)
Director of Finance and IT Mr Kevin Scott
Accountant Mr John Hall, Church House
Property Manager Mr Ian Beswick, Church House
Dioc Society (*Trusts*) Mr Graham Barnard (*as above*)
Mission and Pastoral Committee Mr Nigel Foxon, Church House

CHURCHES
Advisory Committee for the Care of Churches (*Chairman*) Canon Dr Geoffrey Purves, Hawthorn House, Kirkwhelpington, Northumberland NE19 2RT
Tel: 01830 540395
(*Secretary*) Mr Nigel Foxon (*as above*)
Closed Churches Committee Mr Nigel Foxon (*as above*)

EDUCATION
Director of Education Vacancy
Assistant Director of Education Primary Mr Brian Hedley, Church House

Assistant Director of Education Secondary/FE Mr Mike Davison
Bursar Mrs Eileen Bell, Church House
PA to Directors Mrs Coleen Miller, Church House
Administrator Mrs Ann Adiguzel, Church House

MINISTRY AND TRAINING
Director of Ordinands Canon Dr Audrey Anne Elkington, Bishop's House, 29 Moor Rd South, Gosforth, Newcastle upon Tyne NE3 1PA
Tel: 0191 285 2220
Continuing Ministerial Education Adviser Vacancy
Bishop's Adviser for Women's Ministry Canon Dr Audrey Anne Elkington, Bishop's House
Development Officer for Children's Work Sandra Doore, Church House
Lindisfarne Regional Training Partnership
Principal Canon Cathy Rowling, Church House
Director of Studies and Formational Tutor for Clergy IME 1–3 Canon Richard Bryant, Church House
Formational Tutor for Clergy IME 4–7 Revd Rick Simpson, Church House
Formational Tutor for Readers, Revd Dr Michael Beck, Church House
Director of Discipleship Development Revd Alastair Macnaughton, Church House
Administrator Jenny Crawford, Church House
Secretary, Association of Readers Mrs Sue Hart, 73 Monkseaton Drive, Whitley Bay NE26 3DQ
Tel: 0191 2523941
Retreat House Mr George Hepburn, Shepherds Dene Retreat House, Riding Mill, Hexham, Northumberland NE44 6AF *Tel:* 01434 682212
email: enquiry@shepherdsdene.co.uk
Sons of Clergy Society Mrs Gwenda Gofton, 4 Crossfell, Ponteland NE20 9EA
Tel: 01661 820344
Diocesan Widows Officer Mrs Marjorie Craig, 5 Springwell Meadow, Alnwick NE66 2NY
Tel: 01665 602806

LITURGICAL
Chairman Revd Christopher Clinch, 8 Blenkinsopp Mews, Newcastle-upon-Tyne NE3 5RN
Tel: 0191 258 9167
email: CClinch@kings-tynemouth.co.uk

MISSION, SOCIAL RESPONSIBILITY AND ECUMENISM
Adviser in Local Evangelism Canon David John Elkington, 16 Towers Ave, Jesmond, Newcastle upon Tyne NE2 3QE *Tel:* 0191 281 0714
email: djelk@tiscali.co.uk
Ecumenical Officer Revd David Cant, Vicarage, Wylam, Northumberland NE41 8AT
Tel: 01661 853254
email: david_stoswins@hotmail.co.uk

PRESS, PUBLICITY AND PUBLICATIONS
Dioc Communications Officer Mrs Sue Scott, Church House
Editor of 'Link' Mrs Sue Scott (*as above*)
Editor of Dioc Year Book Mr Graham Barnard (*as above*)

Newcastle

DIOCESAN RECORD OFFICE

For further information apply to Northumberland Collections Service, Queen Elizabeth II Country Park, Ashington NE63 9YF   *Tel:* 01670 528080

DIOCESAN RESOURCE CENTRE

Contact Karenza Passmore, Church House, St John's Terrace, North Shields NE29 6HS
Tel: 0191 270 4161
Fax: 0191 270 4101
email: k.passmore@resourcescentreonline.co.uk

STEWARDSHIP

Parish Giving Officer Mr Richard Gascoyne, Church House   *Tel:* 0191 270 3136
email: r.gascoyne@newcastle.anglican.org

AREA DEANS
ARCHDEACONRY OF NORTHUMBERLAND

Bedlington Revd Derry Twomey, 21 Church Lane, Bedlington, Northumberland NE22 5EL
Tel: 01670 823453
email: derrytwomey@aol.com
Newcastle Central Revd Philip Cunningham, 17 Rectory Rd, Gosforth, Newcastle-upon-Tyne NE3 1XR   *Tel:* 0191 285 1326
email: philipcunningham@hotmail.com
Newcastle East Canon Kevin Hunt, Walker Vicarage, Middle St, Newcastle upon Tyne NE6 4DB   *Tel:* 0191 262 3666
email: kevin@hunt10.plus.com
Newcastle West Canon John Robert Sinclair, The Vicarage, Newburn, Newcastle upon Tyne NE15 8LQ   *Tel:* 0191 229 0522
email: johnsinclair247@aol.com

Tynemouth Canon Adrian John Hughes, St George's Vicarage, Beverley Terrace, Cullercoats, North Shields NE30 4NS   *Tel:* 0191 252 1817
email: revajh@btinternet.com

ARCHDEACONRY OF LINDISFARNE

Alnwick Vacancy
Bamburgh and Glendale Canon Brian Hurst, Vicarage, 7 The Wynding, Bamburgh, Northumberland NE69 7DB   *Tel:* 01668 214748
email: brian.hurst1@btopenworld.com
Bellingham Revd Dr Susan Ramsaran, Rectory, Bellingham, Hexham NE48 2JS
Tel: 01434 220019
email: SMRamsaran@aol.com
Corbridge Revd David Hewlett, Vicarage, Greencroft Avenue, Corbridge NE45 5DW
Tel: 01434 632128
email: david.hewlett3@btinternet.com
Hexham Canon Graham Usher, Rectory, Eilansgate, Hexham NE46 3EW
Tel: 01434 603121
email: rector@hexhamabbey.org.uk
Morpeth Revd Dr Dagmar Winter, Vicarage, Kirkwhelpington, Newcastle upon Tyne NE19 2RT   *Tel:* 01830 540260
email: dagmar.winter@btinternet.com
Norham Revd Dr George Robert Joseph (Rob) Kelsey, Vicarage, Norham Berwick upon Tweed TD15 2LF   *Tel:* 01289 382325
email: Robert@josephkelsey.fsnet.co.uk

DIOCESE OF NORWICH

Founded in 1094, formerly Thetford (AD 1070), originally Dunwich (AD 630) and Elmham (AD 673). Norfolk, except for the western quarter (ELY); an area of north-east Suffolk.

Population 867,000   Area 1,804 sq m
Full-time Stipendiary Parochial Clergy 173   Benefices 186
Parishes 563   Churches 632
Overseas link province: Papua New Guinea.

BISHOP (71st)
Rt Revd Graham Richard James, Bishop's House, Norwich NR3 1SB [1999]   *Tel:* 01603 629001
Fax: 01603 761613
email: bishop@bishopofnorwich.org
[Graham Norvic:]
Bishop's Chaplain Revd Simon Ward (*same address*)   *Tel:* 01603 614172
email: bishopschaplain@bishopofnorwich.org
Bishop's Secretary Mrs Coralie Nichols (*same address*)   *Tel:* 01603 629001
email: secretary@bishopofnorwich.org

SUFFRAGAN BISHOPS
THETFORD Rt Revd Dr Alan Winton, The Red House, 53 Norwich Rd, Stoke Holy Cross, Norwich NR14 8AB [2009]   *Tel:* 01508 491014
Fax: 01508 492105
email: bishop.thetford@norwich.anglican.org
Bishop's Secretary Mrs Jane Hazell (*same address*)
email: jane.hazell@norwich.anglican.org
LYNN Vacancy
email: bishoplynn@norwich.anglican.org
Bishop's Secretary Mrs Carolyn Vincent (*same address*)
email: carolyn.vincent@norwich.anglican.org

HONORARY ASSISTANT BISHOPS
Rt Revd E. Devenport, 6 Damocles Court, Pottergate, Norwich NR2 1HN [2000]
Tel: 01603 664121
email: eric@edevenport.orangehome.co.uk
Rt Revd A. C. Foottit, Ivy House, Whitwell St, Reepham NR10 4RA [2004]   *Tel:* 01603 870340
email: acfoottit@hotmail.com
Rt Revd P. J. Fox, Vicarage, Harwood Rd, Norwich NR1 2NG [2008]   *Tel:* 01603 625679
email: peterandangiefox@yahoo.co.uk
Rt Revd R. Garrard, 26 Carol Close, Stoke Holy Cross, Norwich NR14 8NN [2003]
Tel: 01508 494165
email: garrard.r.a@btinternet.com
Rt Revd D. Gillett, 10 Burton Close, Diss IP22 4YJ [2008]   *Tel:* 01379 640309
email: dkgillett@btinternet.com

Rt Revd D. Leake, The Anchorage, Lower Common, East Runton, Cromer NR27 9PG [2003]   *Tel:* 01263 513536
email: david@leake8.wanadoo.co.uk
Rt Revd M. Menin, 32c Bracondale, Norwich NR1 2AN [2000]   *Tel:* 01603 627987
Rt Revd L. Urwin, The College, Walsingham NR22 6EF [2009]   *Tel:* 01328 824204
email: pr.adm@olw-shrine.org.uk

CATHEDRAL CHURCH OF THE HOLY AND UNDIVIDED TRINITY
Dean Very Revd Graham Smith, The Deanery, The Close, Norwich NR1 4EG [2004]
Tel: 01603 218308 (Office)
email: dean@cathedral.org.uk
Cathedral Office 12 The Close, Norwich NR1 4DH
Tel: 01603 218300
Fax: 01603 766032
Web: www.cathedral.org.uk
Canons Residentiary
Canon Pastor and Custos Canon Richard Capper, 52 The Close, Norwich NR1 4EG [2005]
Tel: 01603 665210 (Home)
01603 218331 (Office)
email: canonpastor@cathedral.org.uk
Precentor and Vice-Dean Canon Jeremy Haselock, 34 The Close, Norwich NR1 4DZ [1998]
Tel: 01603 218314 (Home)
01603 218306 (Office)
email: precentor@cathedral.org.uk
Canon Librarian Canon Dr Peter Doll, 56 The Close, Norwich NR1 4EG [2009]
Tel: 01603 666758 (Home)
01603 218336 (Office)
email: canonlibrarian@cathedral.org.uk
Chapter Steward Mr Alan Kefford, 12 The Close, Norwich NR1 4DH
Tel: 01603 218303
email: akefford@cathedral.org.uk
Master of the Music Mr David Lowe, 12 The Close, Norwich NR1 4DH   *Tel:* 01603 626589
email: dlowe@cathedral.org.uk
Organist Mr David Dunnett, 12 The Close, Norwich NR1 4DH   *Tel:* 01603 218315
email: organist@cathedral.org.uk

Sacrist Mr Roger Lee, 12 The Close, Norwich NR1 4DH   *Tel:* 01603 218325
            email: sacrist@cathedral.org.uk

ARCHDEACONS

NORWICH Ven Jan McFarlane, 31 Bracondale, Norwich NR1 2AT [2009]   *Tel:* 01603 620007
email: archdeacon.norwich@norwich.anglican.org
LYNN Ven John Ashe, Holly Tree House, Whitwell Rd, Sparham, Norwich NR9 5PN [2009]
                          Tel: 01362 688032
email: archdeacon.lynn@norwich.anglican.org
NORFOLK Ven David Hayden, Vicarage, 8 Boulton Rd, Thorpe St Andrew, Norwich NR7 0DF [2002]
            Tel and *Fax:* 01603 702477
email: archdeacon.norfolk@norwich.anglican.org

CONVOCATION (MEMBERS OF THE HOUSE OF CLERGY OF THE GENERAL SYNOD)
Proctors for Clergy
Canon Steven Betts
Ven Jan McFarlane
Revd Charles Read
Revd Dr Patrick Richmond

MEMBERS OF THE HOUSE OF LAITY OF THE GENERAL SYNOD
Mr Robin Back
Mrs Susan Johns
Mr James Wortley

DIOCESAN OFFICERS
Dioc Secretary Mr Richard Butler, Diocesan House, 109 Dereham Rd, Easton, Norwich NR9 5ES   *Tel:* 01603 880853
     email: richard.butler@norwich.anglican.org
Deputy Dioc Secretary Mr David Broom, Dioc House   *Tel:* 01603 882367
     email: david.broom@norwich.anglican.org
Chancellor of Diocese His Honour Judge Paul Downes, 44 The Close, Norwich NR1 4EQ
Registrar of Diocese and Bishop's Legal Secretary Mr Stuart Jones, Birketts LLP, Kingfisher House, 1 Gilders Way, Norwich NR3 1UB
                          Tel: 01603 756501
                          Fax: 01603 626147
     email: stuart.jones@norwich.anglican.org

DIOCESAN ORGANIZATIONS
Diocesan Office Diocesan House, 109 Dereham Rd, Easton, Norwich NR9 5ES
                          Tel: 01603 880853
                          Fax: 01603 881083
            Web: www.norwich.anglican.org

ADMINISTRATION
Dioc Synod (*Chairman, House of Clergy*) Canon Steven Betts, Emmaus House, 6 The Close, Norwich NR1 4DH   *Tel:* 01603 729811
     email: steven.betts@norwich.anglican.org
(*Chairman, House of Laity*) Mr Geoff Wortley, c/o Dioc House   *email:* jamesgwortley@aol.com

(*Secretary*) Mr David Broom, Dioc House
Designated Officer Canon Richard Bowett (*as above*)
Dioc Electoral Registration Officer Mr David Brom (*as above*)
Board of Finance (*President*) The Bishop of Norwich (*as above*)
(*Chairman*) Mr Kit Cator, c/o Dioc House
                          email: kit.cator@afiweb.net
(*Secretary*) Diocesan Secretary, Dioc House
Property Committee (*Chairman*) Mr David Richardson, c/o Dioc House
     email: david.richardson@arnolds.uk.com
Surveyor Mr Michael Marshall, Dioc House
                          Tel: 01603 882364
     email: michael.marshall@norwich.anglican.org

DIOCESAN MISSION AND PASTORAL COMMITTEE
Chairman Mrs Sue Johns, c/o Dioc House
            email: sue.johns@hse.gsi.gov.uk
Secretary Mr David Broom, Dioc House
Board of Patronage (*Chairman*) Canon Stuart Nairn, Rectory, Main Rd, Narborough, King's Lynn PE32 1TE   *Tel:* 01760 338552
     email: nairn.nvgrectory@btinternet.com
(*Secretary*) Mrs Jennifer Vere, Southlands, Church Corner, North Lopham, Diss IP22 2LP
                          Tel: 01379 687679
DAC (*Diocesan Advisory Committee for the Care of Churches*) (*Chairman*) Mr Chris Brown, c/o Dioc House   *email:* chris@clb47.waitrose.com
(*Secretary*) Mrs Jean Gosling, Dioc House
                          Tel: 01603 882350
     email: jean.gosling@norwich.anglican.org

EDUCATION
Board of Education (*Chairman*) Canon Peter Hartley, c/o Dioc House
            email: peter.hartley49@btinternet.com
Director of Education Mr Andy Mash, Dioc House
                          Tel: 01603 881352
     email: andy.mash@norwich.anglican.org
Diocesan Project Manager Mrs Jenny Daynes, Dioc House   *Tel:* 01603 881358
     email: jenny.daynes@norwich.anglican.org
Schools' Adviser Mrs Gill Hipwell, Dioc House
                          Tel: 01603 882346
     email: gill.hipwell@norwich.anglican.org
The Horstead Centre (*Residential Centre and Youth and Children's Work*), Rectory Rd, Horstead, Norwich NR12 7EP
            Web: www.horsteadcentre.org.uk
(*Warden*) Mr Mark Heybourne, c/o Dioc House
                          Tel: 01603 737215
                               01603 882362
     email: mark.heybourne@norwich.anglican.org
(*Manager*) Mr Alex Willimott, c/o Horstead Centre   *Tel:* 01603 737215
     email: alex@horsteadcentre.org.uk
Youth and Children's Administrator Mrs Tricia Elson, c/o Horstead Centre   *Tel:* 01603 266316
     email: tricia.elson@horsteadcentre.org.uk

DISCIPLESHIP & MINISTRY FORUM
(and Governing Board of the Ordained Local Ministry Scheme)
Chairman Rt Revd Dr Alan Winton (*as above*)
Bishop's Officer for Ordinands and Initial Training Canon Steven Betts (*as above*)
Principal of Dioc Ministry Course Revd Sue Woan, Emmaus House   *Tel:* 01603 729812
          email: sue.woan@norwich.anglican.org
Vice-Principal of Dioc Ministry Course and Director of Studies Revd Charles Read, Emmaus House
          Tel: 01603 729813
          email: charles.read@norwich.anglican.org
Director of Reader Training Revd Clive Blackman, Emmaus House   *Tel:* 01603 729814
          email: clive.blackman@norwich.anglican.org
Director of Continuing Ministerial Education Revd Cathy Nicholls, Emmaus House
          Tel: 01603 729817
          cathy.nicholls@norwich.anglican.org
Lay Development Co-ordinator Revd Susanna Gunner, Emmaus House (as above)
          Tel: 01603 729815
          email: susanna.gunner@norwich.anglican.org
Dioc Officer for NSMs Revd Roger MacPhee, 8 Lawn Close, Knapton, North Walsham NR28 0SD   *Tel:* 01263 720045
          email: rmacphee4@aol.com
Readers' Committee (*Chairman and Warden of Readers*) Ven John Ashe (*as above*)
(*Secretary*) Mr John Pountain, Brambles, Briar Lane, Swainsthorpe, Norwich NR14 8PX
          Tel: 01508 470567
County Ecumenical Officer Revd Dale Gingrich, Church Bungalow, Gayton Rd, Gaywood, King's Lynn PE30 4DZ   *Tel:* 01508 765167
          email: dale.gingrich@norwich.anglican.org
Bishop's Officer for Retired Clergy and Widows Canon Patrick Foreman, Seorah, 7 Mallard's Close, Fakenham NR21 8PU   *Tel:* 01328 853691
          email: patrick@pandmforeman.eclipse.co.uk
Evangelism Resources Group (*Chairman*) Ven David Hayden (*as above*)

LITURGICAL
Liturgical Adviser Canon Jeremy Haselock (*as above*)
Chairman of DLC Revd Charles Read (*as above*)

PRESS, PUBLICITY AND PUBLICATIONS
Communications Committee (*Chairman*) The Dean of Norwich (*as above*)
Communications Officer Ven J. McFarlane (*as above*)
          Tel: 07818 422395 (mobile)
Internal Communications Officer Mr Gordon Darley, Dioc House   *Tel:* 01603 882349
          email: gordon.darley@norwich.anglican.org
Magazine Editor Revd Barry Furness, Dioc House   *Tel:* 01603 882348
          email: barry.furness@norwich.anglican.org

DIOCESAN RECORD OFFICE
Norfolk Record Office, Archive Centre, County Hall, Martineau Lane, Norwich NR1 2DO *County Archivist* Dr John Alban   *Tel:* 01603 222599
          Fax: 01603 761885

SOCIAL AND COMMUNITY CONCERNS
Forum Chairman Vacancy
Coordinator Revd Simon Wilson, Rectory, Guist Rd, Foulsham, Dereham NR20 5RZ
          Tel: 01362 683275
          email: simon.wilson@norwich.anglican.org
Urban Affairs and Church Urban Fund Canon Peter Howard, St Francis Vicarage, Rider Haggard Rd, Norwich NR7 9UQ   *Tel:* 01603 702799
          email: plhoward@btinternet.com
Tourism Ven David Hayden (*as above*)

RURAL DEANS
ARCHDEACONRY OF NORWICH
Norwich East Canon Peter Howard, St Francis Vicarage, Rider Haggard Rd, Norwich NR7 9UQ
          Tel: 01603 702799
          email: plhoward@btinternet.com
Norwich North Revd Paul Mackay, St Catherine's Vicarage, Aylsham Road, Mile Cross, Norwich NR3 2RJ   *Tel:* 01603 426767
          email: vicar@stcatherinesmilecross.org.uk
Norwich South Canon Alan Strange, Rectory, 17 Essex Street, Norwich NR2 5BL
          Tel: 01603 622225
          email: rector@trinitynorwich.org

ARCHDEACONRY OF NORFOLK
Blofield Revd Paul Cubitt, The Rectory, 10 Oak Wood, Blofield, Norwich NR13 4JQ
          Tel: 01603 713160
          email: revp@cubitt.karoo.co.uk
Depwade Revd David Sochon, The Bungalow, Wolfer Green, Shotesham, Norwich NR15 1YP
          Tel: 01508 558495
          email: davids@tasvalley.org
Great Yarmouth Revd Irene Knowles, 18 Royal Ave, Great Yarmouth NR30 4EB
          Tel: 01493 857292
          email: revmik@hotmail.co.uk
Humbleyard Revd Christopher Davies, Vicarage, 5 Vicar St, Wymondham, NR18 0PL
          Tel: 01953 602269
          email: vicar@wymondhamabbey.org.uk
Loddon Revd Robert Parsonage, Rectory, Rectory Lane, Poringland, Norwich NR14 7SL
          Tel: 01508 492215
          email: rector@poringland-benefice.org.uk
Lothingland Canon Ian Bentley, St Mark's Vicarage, 212 Bridge Road, Oulton Broad, Lowestoft NR33 9JX   *Tel:* 01502 572563
          email: ian@revbentley.freeserve.co.uk
Redenhall Canon Tony Billett, Rectory, 26 Mount St, Diss IP22 3QG   *Tel:* 01379 642072
          email: disschurch2@btconnect.com

Saint Benet at Waxham and Tunstead Revd William Hill, Grange Farm House, Yarmouth Rd, Worstead, North Walsham NR28 9LX
Tel: 01692 404917
email: revd.william.hill@btinternet.com
Thetford and Rockland Revd Kenneth Reeve, The Rectory, Rectory Lane, Great Ellingham, Attleborough NR17 1LD *Tel:* 01953 457644

ARCHDEACONRY OF LYNN

Breckland Canon Stuart Nairn, Rectory, Main Rd, Narborough, King's Lynn PE32 1TE
Tel: 01760 338552
email: nairn.nvgrectory@btinternet.com
Burnham and Walsingham Revd Norman Banks, Vicarage, Church Street, Walsingham NR22 6BL
Tel: 01328 821316
email: nabwalsingham@lineone.net
Dereham in Mitford Canon Sally Theakston, Rectory, Vicarage Meadows, Dereham NR19 1TW
Tel: 01362 693680
email: stheakston@aol.com

Heacham and Rising Revd Michael Brock, Vicarage, Shernborne Rd, Dersingham, King's Lynn PE31 6JA *Tel:* 01485 520214
email: vicar@stndersingham.co.uk
Holt Revd Howard Stoker, Rectory, 11 Church St, Holt NR25 6BB *Tel:* 01263 712048
email: holtrectory@tiscali.co.uk
Ingworth Revd Brian Faulkner, Rectory, School Road, Erpingham, Norwich NR11 7QX
Tel: 01263 768073
email: brian-faulkner@lineone.net
Lynn Revd Christopher Ivory, St Margaret's Vicarage, St Margaret's Place, King's Lynn PE30 5DL
email: vicar@stmargaretskingslynn.org.uk
Repps Revd Michael Langan, Rectory, 22a Harbord Rd, Overstrand, Cromer NR27 0PN
Tel: 01263 759350
email: ml@netcom.co.uk
Sparham Revd Selwyn Tillett, The Rectory, Ringland Lane, Weston Longville, Norwich NR9 5JU *Tel:* 01603 880563
email: selwyn@tillett.org.uk

DIOCESE OF OXFORD

Founded in 1542. Oxfordshire; Berkshire; Buckinghamshire; one parish in each of Bedfordshire, Gloucestershire, Hampshire, Hertfordshire and Warwickshire.

Population 2,198,000   Area 2,221 sq m
Full-time Stipendiary Parochial Clergy 362   Benefices 302
Parishes 622   Churches 816
www.oxford.anglican.org
Overseas link dioceses: Vaxjo (Sweden), Kimberley and Kuruman (Southern Africa).

BISHOP (42nd)
Rt Revd John Pritchard, Diocesan Church House, North Hinksey, Oxford OX2 0NB [2007]
Tel: 01865 208200 (Office)
Fax: 01865 790470
email: bishopoxon@oxford.anglican.org
Bishop's Domestic Chaplain Revd Amanda Bloor (*same address*)   Tel: 01865 208200 (Office)
Fax: 01865 790470

AREA BISHOPS
READING Vacancy   Tel: 0118 984 1216
Fax: 0118 984 1218
email: bishopreading@oxford.anglican.org
BUCKINGHAM Rt Revd Dr Alan Wilson, Sheridan, Grimms Hill, Gt Missenden HP16 9BG [2003]
Tel: 01494 862173
Fax: 01494 890508
email: bishopbucks@oxford.anglican.org
DORCHESTER Rt Revd Colin Fletcher, Arran House, Sandy Lane, Yarnton, Oxford OX5 1PB [2000]   Tel: 01865 375541
Fax: 01865 379890
email: bishopdorchester@oxford.anglican.org

PROVINCIAL EPISCOPAL VISITOR
Rt Revd Andrew Burnham (Bishop of Ebbsfleet), Bishop's House, Dry Sandford, Abingdon OX13 6JP   Tel: 01865 390746
email: bishop.andrew@ebbsfleet.org.uk

HONORARY ASSISTANT BISHOPS
Rt Revd Keith Arnold, 9 Dinglederry, Olney MK46 5ES [1997]   Tel: 01234 713044
Rt Revd John Bone, 4 Grove Rd, Henley-on-Thames RG9 1DH [1997]   Tel: 01491 413482
Rt Revd Dr Kenneth Cragg, 3 Goring Lodge, White House Rd, Oxford OX1 4QE [1982]
Tel: 01865 249895
Rt Revd William Down, 54 Dark Lane, Witney OX28 6LX [2001]   Tel: 01993 706615
Rt Revd Ronald Gordon, 16 East St Helen St, Abingdon OX14 5EA [1991]   Tel: 01235 526956
Rt Revd James Johnson, St Helena, 28 Molyneux Drive, Bodicote, Banbury OX15 4AP [2005]
Tel: 01295 255357
Rt Revd Peter Nott, 3 Valance Court, Aston Rd, Bampton OX18 2AF [1999]   Tel: 01993 850688

Rt Revd Henry Richmond, 39 Hodges Court, Marlborough Rd, Oxford OX1 4NZ [1999]
Tel: 01865 790466
Rt Revd Henry Scriven, 16 East St Helens St, Abingdon, Oxford, Oxon OX14 5EA
Tel: 01235 536607
Rt Revd Andrew Burnham, Bishop's House, Dry Sandford, Abingdon, Oxon OX13 6BP
Tel: 01865 390746

CATHEDRAL CHURCH OF CHRIST
Dean Very Revd Christopher Lewis, The Deanery, Christ Church, Oxford OX1 1DP [2003]
Tel: 01865 276161
Fax: 01865 276238
Dean's Secretary Ms Rachel Perham (*same address*)
Tel: 01865 276161
email: rachel.perham@chch.ox.ac.uk
Sub-Dean Revd Dr Edmund Newell, Christ Church, Oxford OX1 1DP [2008]
Tel: 01865 276278
email: subdean@chch.ox.ac.uk
Sub Dean's PA Ms Hannah Clegg (*same address*)
Tel: 01865 276278
email: hannah.clegg@chch.ox.ac.uk
Canons Residentiary
Ven Julian Hubbard, Archdeacon's Lodging, Christ Church, Oxford OX1 1DP [2005]
Tel: 01865 276185
email: archdoxf@oxford.anglican.org
Canon Dr Marilyn Parry, Diocesan Church House, North Hinksey Lane, Oxford OX2 0NB [2001]   Tel: 01865 208291
email: marilyn.parry@oxford.anglican.org
Canon Prof. George Pattison, Priory House, Christ Church, Oxford OX1 1DP [2004]
Tel: 01865 276247
email: george.pattison@chch.ox.ac.uk
Canon Prof Sarah Foot, Christ Church, Oxford OX1 1DP [2007]   Tel: 01865 286078
email: sarah.foot@chch.ox.ac.uk
Canon Prof Nigel Biggar, Christ Church, Oxford OX1 1DP [2007]   Tel: 01865 276219
email: nigel.biggar@chch.ox.ac.uk
Precentor Revd John Paton, Christ Church, Oxford OX1 1DP [2003]   Tel: 01865 276214
email: john.paton@chch.ox.ac.uk

Liturgy and Publicity Assistant David Bannister, Christ Church, Oxford OX1 1DP
Tel: 01865 276214
email: david.bannister@chch.ox.ac.uk
Cathedral Registrar Mr Millius Palayiwa, Christ Church, Oxford OX1 1DP   *Tel:* 01865 276277
email: millius.palayiwa@chch.ox.ac.uk
Cathedral Bursar Mr John Briggs, Christ Church, Oxford OX1 1DP   *Tel:* 01865 286846
email: john.briggs@chch.ox.ac.uk
Office and Financial Administrator Mrs Eileen Head, Christ Church, Oxford OX1 1DP
Tel: 01865 276155
Fax: 01865 276277
email: eileen.head@chch.ox.ac.uk
Cathedral Organist Dr Stephen Darlington, Christ Church, Oxford OX1 1DP   *Tel:* 01865 276195
email: stephen.darlington@chch.ox.ac.uk
Organist's Secretary Mrs Anthea Madden, Christ Church, Oxford OX1 1DP   *Tel:* 01865 276195
Dean's Verger Mr Matthew Power, Christ Church, Oxford OX1 1DP   *Tel:* 01865 276154
email: matthew.power@chch.ox.ac.uk
Canon's Verger Miss Jessica Hallion, Christ Church, Oxford OX1 1DP
Cathedral Verger Mr Charles Gibb, Christ Church, Oxford OX1 1DP   *Tel:* 01865 276154
Education & Visitor's Officer, Cathedral Verger Mr Jim Godfrey, Christ Church, Oxford OX1 1DP
Tel: 01865 276154
email: jim.godfrey@chch.ox.ac.uk

ARCHDEACONS

OXFORD Ven Julian Hubbard, Archdeacon's Lodging, Christ Church, Oxford OX1 1DP [2005]
Tel and *Fax:* 01865 208245
email: archdoxf@oxford.anglican.org
BERKSHIRE Ven Norman Russell, Foxglove House, Love Lane, Donnington, Newbury RG14 2JG [1998]   *Tel:* 01635 552820
Fax: 01635 522165
email: archdber@oxford.anglican.org
BUCKINGHAM Ven Karen Gorham, Rectory, Stone, Aylesbury HP17 8RZ [2007]   *Tel:* 01865 208264
email: archdbuc@oxford.anglican.org

CONVOCATION (MEMBERS OF THE HOUSE OF CLERGY OF THE GENERAL SYNOD)

Proctors for Clergy
The Bishop of Oxford
Revd Moira Astin
Revd Jonathan Baker
Revd Susan Booys
Revd Mark Chapman
Canon Timothy Dakin
Revd Hugh Lee
Revd John Cook
Ven Karen Gorham
Revd Rosie Harper

MEMBERS OF THE HOUSE OF LAITY OF THE GENERAL SYNOD

Jule Dziegiel
Mr Robert Hurley
Miss Prudence Dailey
Dr Philip Giddings
Mrs Victoria Russell
Mr Brian Newey
Mr Gavin Oldham
Dr Anna Thomas-Betts

DIOCESAN OFFICERS

Dioc Secretary Mrs Rosemary Pearce, Diocesan Church House, North Hinksey Lane, Oxford OX2 0NB   *Tel:* 01865 208200
Fax: 01865 790470
email: diosec@oxford.anglican.org
Chancellor of Diocese Revd Dr Rupert Bursell QC, Diocesan Registry, 16 Beaumont St, Oxford OX1 2LZ   *Tel:* 01865 297200
Fax: 01865 726274
email: oxford@winckworths.co.uk
Registrar of Diocese and Bishop's Legal Secretary Canon John Rees (*same address*)
Registrar of the Archdeaconries Canon John Rees (*as above*)

DIOCESAN ORGANIZATIONS

Diocesan Office Diocesan Church House, North Hinksey Lane, Oxford OX2 0NB
Tel: 01865 208200
Fax: 01865 790470

ADMINISTRATION

Dioc Synod (*Vice-President, House of Clergy*) Revd Dr Andrew Bunch, Vicarage, Church Walk, Oxford OX2 6LY   *Tel:* 01865 510460
email: vicar@churchwalk.eclipse.co.uk
(*Vice-President, House of Laity*) Mrs Judith Scott, 4 Crescent Rd, Wokingham RG40 2DB
Tel: 0118 977 1656
email: jscott@bcs.org.uk
(*Secretary*) Mrs Rosemary Pearce, Dioc Church House
Board of Finance (*Chairman*) Mr Brian Newey, Chestnut Cottage, The Green South, Warborough, Wallingford OX10 7DN   *Tel:* 01865 858322
Fax: 01865 858043
(*Secretary*) Mrs Rosemary Pearce (*as above*)
Director of Glebe and Buildings Mr Roger Harwood, Dioc Church House   *Tel:* 01865 208230
email: roger.harwood@oxford.anglican.org
Dioc Trustees (*Oxford*) Ltd Mrs Rosemary Pearce (*as above*)
Pastoral Committee (*Secretary*) and Electoral Roll Officer Mr Howard Cattermole, Dioc Church House   *Tel:* 01865 208243
email: howard.cattermole@oxford.anglican.org
Designated Officer Canon John Rees (*as above*)

CHURCHES

Advisory Committee for the Care of Churches (*Chairman*) Mr David Jefferson, The Vyne, Deep

Field, Datchet SL3 9JS; (*Secretary*) Miss Natalie Merry, Dioc Church House   *Tel:* 01865 208229
email: natalie.merry@oxford.anglican.org
Sites Advisory Committee (*Secretary*) Miss Natalie Merry (*as above*)

MISSION
Director Revd Dr Michael Beasley, Dioc Church House   *Tel:* 01865 208251
Fax: 01865 790470
email: michael.beasley@oxford.anglican.org
Parish Development Advisers
Buckingham Mr Andrew Gear, Dioc Church House   *Tel* 01865 208256
Fax: 01865 790470
email: andrew.gear@oxford.anglican.org
Oxford Revd Olivia Graham, Dioc Church House
Tel: 01865 208246
Fax: 01865 790470
email: olivia.graham@oxford.anglican.org
Berkshire Revd Janet Russell, Dioc Church House
Tel: 01865 208296
email: janet.russell@oxford.anglican.org
Children's Work Yvonne Morris, Dioc Church House   *Tel:* 01865 208255
email: yvonne.morris@oxford.anglican.org
Child Protection Officer Stephen Barber, Dioc Church House   *Tel:* 01865 208290
email: stephen.barber@oxford.anglican.org
Christian Giving and Funding Adviser Robin Brunner-Ellis, Dioc Church House
Tel: 01865 208254
email: robin.brunner-ellis@oxford.anglican.org
Director of Studies Revd Dr Keith Beech-Gruneberg, Dioc Church House
Tel: 01865 208282
email: director.of.studies@oxford.anglican.org
Training Officer and Director of LLM Training Revd Phillip Tovey, 20 Palmer Place, Abingdon, OX14 5LZ   *Tel:* 01235 527077
email: phillip.tovey@oxford.anglican.org
Youth Work Ian Macdonald, Dioc Church House
Tel: 01865 208253
email: ian.macdonald@oxford.anglican.org
Ordained Local Ministry (OLM) Principal Revd Beren Hartless   *Tel:* 01865 208258
email: beren.hartless@oxford.anglican.org
Licensed Lay Ministry (LLM) Adviser Mrs Sheila Lloyd   *Tel:* 01865 208731
email: sheila.lloyd@oxford.anglican.org
Diocesan Director of Ordinands Revd Jules Cave Bergquist, Diocesan Church House, North Hinksey Lane, Oxford OX2 0NB
Tel: 01865 208200
Directors of Ordinands
Oxfordshire and Berkshire Vacancy
Buckingham Revd Caroline Windley, 1 Cavalry Path, Aylesbury HP19 9RP
Tel and Fax: 01296 432921
email: caroline.windley@oxford.anglican.org
City of Oxford Revd Jules Cave Bergquist (*as above*)
Vocation Network Chair Revd Jules Cave Bergquist (*as above*)

Accredited Lay Ministry Adviser Vacancy
Women in Ordained Ministry Adviser Vacancy

EDUCATION
Director of Education Leslie Stephen, Dioc Church House   *Tel:* 01865 208236
email: leslie.stephen@oxford.anglican.org

MISSIONARY AND ECUMENICAL
Partnership in World Mission (*Secretary*) Revd Dr Tim Naish, 307 London Rd, Headington, Oxford OX3 9EJ   *Tel:* 01865 766627
email: tim.naish@ripon-cuddlesdon.ac.uk
Ecumenical Officers
Oxford Vacancy
Berkshire Revd Moira Astin, St James Vicarage, 23 Kingfisher Drive, Woodley, Reading RG5 3LG
Tel: 0118 954 5669
email: moira.astin@ntlworld.com
Buckingham Canon Tony Dickinson, St Francis' Vicarage, Amersham Rd, Terriers, High Wycombe HP13 5AB   *Tel:* 01494 520676
email: tony.dickinson@oxford.anglican.org
Milton Keynes Revd Chris Collinge, St James' Vicarage, 29 Bradwell Rd, Bradville, Milton Keynes MK13 7AX   *Tel:* 01908 314224
email: chriscollinge@hotmail.com

COMMUNICATIONS
Director of Communications Ms Sarah Meyrick, Dioc Church House   *Tel:* 01865 208224
Editor of Dioc Newspaper 'The Door' Miss Joanne Duckles, Dioc Church House   *Tel:* 01865 208227
email: joanne.duckles@oxford.anglican.org

DIOCESAN RECORD OFFICES
County Archivist, St Luke's Church, Temple Rd, Cowley, Oxford OX4 2EN   *Tel:* 01865 398200
email: archives@oxfordshire.gov.uk (*For records of the diocese, and parish records in the archdeaconry of Oxford*)
Berkshire Record Office, 9 Coley Ave, Reading RG1 6AF *Tel:* 0118 901 5132 (*For parish records in the archdeaconry of Berkshire*)
Buckinghamshire Record Office, County Hall, Aylesbury, Bucks. HP20 1UA *Tel:* 01296 382587 (*For parish records in the archdeaconry of Buckingham*)

SOCIAL RESPONSIBILITY
Social Responsibility Adviser (*Secretary*) Ms Alison Webster, Dioc Church House
Tel: 01865 208213
email: alison.webster@oxford.anglican.org
PACT (Parents and Children Together) Council for Social Work Mrs Jan Fishwick, 7 Southern Court, South St, Reading RG1 4QS   *Tel:* 0118 938 7600
email: pactcharity@compuserve.com
Council for the Deaf (*Chairman*) Mrs Jo Saunders, Dioc Church House

AREA DEANS

ARCHDEACONRY OF OXFORD

Aston and Cuddesdon Revd Sue Booys, Rectory, Manor Farm Rd, Dorchester OX10 7HZ
Tel: 01865 340007
email: rector@dorchester-abbey.org.uk
Bicester and Islip Revd Charles Masheder, Rectory, Church Walk, Ambrosden, Oxon OX25 2UJ
Tel: 01869 247813
email: chasmash@ic24.net
Chipping Norton Revd Judy French, Vicarage, Church Lane, Charlbury OX7 3PX
Tel: 01608 810286
email: vicar@stmaryscharlbury.co.uk
Cowley Revd Bruce Gillingham, St Clement's Rectory, 58 Rectory Rd, Oxford OX4 1BW
Tel: 01865 246674
email: bruce@stclements.org.uk
Deddington Revd Patricia Freeth, Vicarage, High St, Cropredy, Oxon OX17 1NG
Tel: 01295 750980
email: pfreeth@toucansurf.com
Henley Revd Graham Foulis Brown, Vicarage, Kidmore End, Reading RG4 9AY
Tel: 0118 972 3987
email: gdfb.vicarage@lineone.net
Oxford Revd Anthony Ellis, St Mary's Rectory, 19 Mill St, Kidlington OX5 2EE
Tel and *Fax:* 01865 372230
email: anthony.churchkid@talktalk.net
Witney Revd William Blakey, St John's Rectory, 6 Burford Rd, Caterton, Oxon OX18 3AA
Tel: 01993 846996
email: rector@theblakeys.co.uk
Woodstock Revd Ernest Jones, Rectory, 22 Castle Road, Wootton, Woodstock, OX20 1EG
Tel: 01993 812543
email: threechurches@virgin.net

ARCHDEACONRY OF BERKSHIRE

Abingdon Revd Pam McKellen, Vicarage, Radley, Abingdon OX14 2JN
Tel: 01235 554739
email: p.mckellen@btinternet.com
Bracknell Canon Nick Parish, 1 Old Lands Hill, Bracknell RG12 2QX
Tel: 01344 641498
email: nick.parish@ntlworld.com
Bradfield Revd Peter Steele, Vicarage, Wasing Lane, Aldermarston, RG7 4LX
Tel: 0118 9712281
email: petesteele@btinternet.com
Maidenhead Revd Dr Jeremy Hyde, 2a Belmont Park Rd, Maidenhead SL6 6HT
Tel: 01628 621651
email: jeremy.hyde@btinternet.com
Newbury Revd Rita Ball, Rectory, High Street, Hermitage, Berks RG18 9ST
Tel: 01635 202967
email: rita.e.ball@btinternet.com

Reading Canon Brian Shenton, Hamelsham, Downshire Square, Reading RG1 6NJ
Tel: 0118 956 8163
Fax: 0118 958 7041
email: stmaryshouserdg@waitrose.com
Sonning Revd David Hodgson, Rectory, 2a Norreys Ave, Wokingham RG40 1TU
Tel: 0118 979 2999
email: david@allsaintswokingham.org.uk
Vale of White Horse Revd Richard Hancock, St Andrew's Vicarage, High St, Shrivenham, Swindon SN6 8AN
Tel: 01793 780183
email: vicar@standrews-shrivenham.fsnet.co.uk
Wallingford Revd Edward Carter, St Peter's Vicarage, 47a Newlands Avenue, Didcot OX11 8QA
Tel: 01235 812114
email: priest-in-charge@stpeters-didcot.org
Wantage Revd John Robertson, Vicarage, Main St, Grove, Wantage, Oxon OX12 7LQ
Tel: 01235 766484
email: vicargrove@tiscali.co.uk

ARCHDEACONRY OF BUCKINGHAM

Amersham Revd Derrick Carr, 52 Warren Wood Drive, High Wycombe, Bucks HP11 1EA
Tel: 05602 158514
email: carrd@btopenworld.com
Aylesbury, Revd Andrew Blyth, The Rectory, 42 Redwood Drive, Aylesbury HP21 9RJ
Tel: 01296 394906
email: andrew.blyth@htaylesbury.org
Buckingham Revd Philip Derbyshire, Rectory, Chapel Lane, Thornborough MK18 2DJ
Tel: 01280 812515
email: philjoydot@btinternet.com
Burnham Revd Allen Walker, New Vicarage, Mill St, Colnbrook, Slough SL3 0JJ *Tel:* 01753 684181
email: mrawalker@aol.com
Claydon Revd David Hiscock, Rectory, Castle St, Marsh Gibbon, Bicester OX27 0HJ
Tel: 01869 277297
email: david@s3d.co.uk
Milton Keynes Revd Tim Norwood, 3 Daubeney Gate, Shenley Church End, Milton Keynes MK5 6EH
Tel: 01908 505812
email: tim@mkdeanery.org
Mursley Revd John Waller, Rectory, 10 Pound Hill, Great Brickhill, Milton Keynes MK17 9AS
Tel: 01525 261062
email: rector@brickhillchurches.org.uk
Newport Revd Christa Pumfrey, New Rectory, 7a Northampton Rd, Lavendon, Olney MK46 4EY
Tel: 01234 240013
email: christa.pumfrey@btinternet.com
Wendover Revd Mark Dearnley, Vicarage, 34a Dobbins Lane, Wendover HP22 6HP
Tel: 01296 622230
email: areadeansofficewendover@virgin.net
Wycombe Revd David Picken, Vicarage, 6 Priory Avenue, High Wycombe HP13 6SH
Tel: 01494 525602
email: dap@dircon.co.uk

DIOCESE OF PETERBOROUGH

Founded in 1541. Northamptonshire, except for one parish in the west (LEICESTER); Rutland; Peterborough, except for an area in the south-east; one parish in Lincolnshire.

Population 840,000   Area 1,149 sq m
Full-time Stipendiary Parochial Clergy 123   Benefices 146
Parishes 348   Churches 385
www.peterborough-diocese.org.uk
Overseas link diocese: Bungoma (Kenya).

BISHOP (37th)
Rt Revd Donald Spargo Allister, Bishop's Lodging, The Palace, Peterborough PE1 1YA
Tel: 01733 562492
Fax: 01733 890077
email: bishop@peterborough-diocese.org.uk
Bishop's Private Secretary Miss Alex Low (*same address*)
email: alex.low@peterborough-diocese.org.uk
Bishop's Administrator and Press Officer Revd Derek Williams (*same address*)
Tel: 01733 887014 (Office)
01604 843881 (Home)
077770 981172 (Mobile)
Fax: 01733 890077 (Office)
email:
derek.williams@peterborough-diocese.org.uk

SUFFRAGAN BISHOP
Vacancy

HONORARY ASSISTANT BISHOP
Rt Revd John Robert Flack, The Vicarage, 34 Station Road, Nassington, Peterborough PE8 6QB [2003]
Tel: 01780 782271
07810 714056 (Mobile)

CATHEDRAL CHURCH OF ST PETER, ST PAUL AND ST ANDREW
Dean Very Revd Charles Taylor, The Deanery, Minster Precincts, Peterborough PE1 1XS [2007]
Tel: 01733 562780
Fax: 01733 897874
email: DeanPetOffice@aol.com
Precentor Canon R. Bruce Ruddock, Precentor's Lodging, 14A Minster Precincts, Peterborough PE1 1XX [2004]
Tel: 01733 355310
email:
bruce.ruddock@peterborough-cathedral.org.uk
Canons Residentiary
Missioner Canon Jonathan Baker, Canonry House, Minster Precincts, Peterborough PE1 1XX [2004]
Tel: 01733 897335 (Home)
01733 355310 (Office)
email:
jonathan.baker@peterborough-cathedral.org.uk

Ven David Painter (*Archdeacon of Oakham*), Diocesan Office, Peterborough PE1 1YB [2000]
Tel: 01733 887019 (Office)
01733 891360 (Home)
Fax: 01733 555271
email:
david.painter@peterborough.diocese.org.uk
Lay Members of Chapter
Mr John Martin, Manor Cottage, Main St, Woodnewton, Peterborough PE8 5EB
Tel: 01780 470298
email: nassington_house@hotmail.com
Hon Treasurer Sir John Parsons, Old Rectory, Eydon, Daventry NN11 3QE   *Tel:* 01327 260745
email: jparsoneydon@btopenworld.com
Mr Mike Opperman, Littleworth Mission, Main Rd, Deeping St Nicholas, Spalding, Lincs PE11 3EN
Tel: 01775 630497
email: jenny@littleworthmission.com
Mrs Sally Trotman, 2 High St, Maxey, Peterborough PE6 9EB
Tel: 01778 344022
email: sally_trotman@yahoo.co.uk
Chapter Administrator Elizabeth Knight, Cathedral Office, Minster Precincts, Peterborough PE1 1XS
Tel: 01733 562780
Fax: 01733 897874
email: DeanPetOffice@aol.com
Director of Music Mr Andrew Reid, Cathedral Office, Minster Precincts, Peterborough PE1 1XX
Tel: 01733 355319
email:
andrew.reid@peterborough-cathedral.org.uk

ARCHDEACONS
NORTHAMPTON Ven Christine Allsopp, Westbrook, 11 The Drive, Northampton NN1 4RZ [2005]
Tel: 01604 714015
Fax: 01604 792016
email: archdeacon@aofn.wanadoo.co.uk
OAKHAM Ven David Painter, Diocesan Office, Peterborough PE1 1YB [1999]
Tel: 01733 891360 (Home)
01733 887019 (Office)
Fax: 01733 555271
email:
david.painter@peterborough-diocese.org.uk

CONVOCATION (MEMBERS OF THE HOUSE OF CLERGY OF THE GENERAL SYNOD)
Proctors for Clergy
Ven Christine Allsopp
Canon William Croft
Revd Stephen Trott

MEMBERS OF THE HOUSE OF LAITY OF THE GENERAL SYNOD
Mr Dennis Allsopp
Mrs Veronica Heald
Mr Andrew Presland

DIOCESAN OFFICERS
Dioc Secretary Mr Richard Pestell, Diocesan Office, The Palace, Peterborough PE1 1YB
Tel: 01733 887000
Fax: 01733 555271
email: diosec@peterborough-diocese.org.uk
Deputy Dioc Secretary and Financial Controller Mr Graham Cuthbert, Dioc Office
email: depsec@peterborough-diocese.org.uk
Chancellor of Diocese Chancellor David Pittaway QC, c/o Diocesan Registrar, 4 Holywell Way, Longthorpe, Peterborough PE3 6SS
Deputy Chancellor Mr George Pulman, c/o Diocesan Registrar (*as above*)
Registrar of Diocese and Bishop's Legal Secretary Revd Raymond Hemingray, 4 Holywell Way (*as above*)
Tel and *Fax:* 01733 262523
email: rh@raymondhemingray.co.uk

DIOCESAN ORGANIZATIONS
Diocesan Office The Palace, Peterborough PE1 1YB
Tel: 01733 887000
Fax: 01733 555271
email: office@peterborough-diocese.org.uk
Web: www.peterborough-diocese.org.uk

ADMINISTRATION
Dioc Synod (*Vice-President, Clergy*) Canon Gordon Steele, 26 Minster Precincts, Peterborough PE1 1XZ
Tel: 01733 566265
email: gordonsteele@fish.co.uk
(*Vice-President, Laity*) Mrs Anne Toms, The Old Nurseries, 1A Ivydene Terrace, Broughton, Kettering NN14 1NJ
Tel: 01536 791095
email: acbl@mrc-lmb.cam.ac.uk
(*Secretary*) Mr Richard Pestell, The Palace, Peterborough PE1 1YB
Board of Finance (*Chairman*) Mr Paul Stothard, 38A Watling St East, Towcester, Northants NN12 6AF
Tel: 01327 351983
email: stothy@live.co.uk
(*Secretary*) Mr Richard Pestell (*as above*)
Houses Committee (*Chairman*) Mr Michael Duerden, 21 South Rd, Oundle, Peterborough PE8 4BU
Tel: 01832 273383
Property Officer Mrs Sandra Allen, Dioc Office
Safeguarding Officer Mr Garry Johnson, Dioc Office
Pastoral Committee Mr Richard Pestell (*as above*)
Board of Patronage Mr Richard Pestell (*as above*)

Designated Officer Revd Raymond Hemingray, 4 Holywell Way, Longthorpe, Peterborough PE3 6SS
Tel and *Fax:* 01733 262523
email: rh@raymondhemingray.co.uk

CHURCHES
Advisory Committee for the Care of Churches (*Chairman*) Vacancy, c/o DAC, Diocesan Office, The Palace, Peterborough PE1 1YB
Tel: 01733 887007
Fax: 01733 555271
email: dac@peterborough-diocese.org.uk
(*Secretary*) Mr Paul Middleton, Dioc Office
Redundant Churches Uses Committee (*Chairman*) Mr Roy Atkinson, c/o DAC, Diocesan Office, The Palace, Peterborough PE1 1YB
Tel: 01733 887007
Fax: 01733 555271
email: dac@peterborough-diocese.org.uk
(*Secretary*) Mr Paul Middleton, Dioc Office

EDUCATION
Board of Education (*Schools*) (*Director of Education* (*Schools*) *and Secretary*) Dr Stephen Partridge, Bouverie Court, The Lakes, Bedford Rd, Northampton NN4 7YD
Tel: 01604 887006
Fax: 01604 887077
email: education@peterborough-diocese.org.uk
Deputy Director of Education (*Schools*) Peter Goringe, Bouverie Court, The Lakes, Bedford Rd, Northampton NN4 7YD
Tel: 01604 887006
email: education@peterborough-diocese.org.uk
Schools Officer Revd Philip Davies, Rectory, 3 Hall Yard, King's Cliffe, Peterborough PE8 6XQ
Tel: 01780 470314
email: P.J.Davies.@tesco.net

MINISTRY
Dioc Vocations Adviser and Director of Ordinands Canon Julie Hutchinson, New Rectory, Stanwick, Wellingborough NN9 6PP
Tel: 01933 626203
email: stanwick@fish.co.uk
Coordinator of Adult Education and Training Mr Chris Peck, Bouverie Court, The Lakes, Bedford Rd, Northampton NN4 7YD
Tel: 01604 887042
Fax: 01604 887077
email: chris.peck@peterborough-diocese.org.uk
Continuing Ministerial Education Officer (*CME*) Revd Dr Andrew Rayment, Bouverie Court (*as above*)
Tel: 01604 887047
Fax: 01604 887077
email: andrew.rayment@peterborough-diocese.org.uk
Curates' Training Coordinator Revd Alison White, 4 The Avenue, Dallington, Northampton NN4 7AN
Tel: 01604 581400
email: alisonmarywhite@btinternet.com
NSM Officer Vacancy
Adviser in Women's Ministry Vacancy
Warden of Readers Canon Phillip E. Nixon, St James's Vicarage, Vicarage Rd, Northampton NN5 7AX
Tel: 01604 751164
email: phillipn@btinternet.com

Warden of Pastoral Assistants Revd David Kirby, Rectory, Church Way, Weston Favell, Northampton NN3 3BX   *Tel:* 01604 413218
          email: kirbydg@gmail.com
Warden of Parish Evangelists Revd Melvyn Pereira, 20 Ribble Close, Wellingborough, Northants NN8 5XJ   *Tel:* 01933 673437
          email: melvyn.pereira@gleneagleschurch.co.uk

MISSION

Diocesan Mission Enabler Revd Miles Baker, Bouverie Court, The Lakes, Bedford Rd, Northampton NN4 7YD   *Tel:* 01604 887043
          Fax: 01604 887077
email: miles.baker@peterborough-diocese.org.uk
Children's Missioner Rona Orme, Bouverie Court (*as above*)   *Tel:* 01604 887045
          Fax: 01604 887077
email: rona.orme@peterborough-diocese.org.uk
Youth Officer Vacancy   *Tel:* 01604 887044
          Fax: 01604 887077
Urban Priority Areas Link Officer and Church Urban Fund Officer Mr Roger Poolman, 13 Curtis Mews, Wellingborough NN8 5PE   *Tel:* 01933 676544
          email: roger.poolman@ntlworld.com
Social Responsibility Adviser Revd Robert Hill, Bouverie Court, The Lakes, Bedford Rd, Northampton NN4 7YD   *Tel:* 01604 887046
          Fax: 01604 887077
email: robert.hill@peterborough-diocese.org.uk
Ecumenical Officer Canon Giles Godber, Vicarage, 25 West St, Geddington, Kettering NN14 1BD
          Tel: 01536 742200
          email: gilbar@telco4u.net
Hospital Chaplaincy Adviser Canon Lesley McCormack, Barnbrook, Water Lane, Chelveston, Wellingborough NN9 6SP
          Tel: 01933 492609
          email: lesley.mccormack@kgh.nhs.uk
Rural Officer Vacancy

LITURGICAL

Officer Canon R. Bruce Ruddock, Precentor's Lodging, 14A Minster Precincts, Peterborough PE1 1XX   *Tel:* 01733 343389

PRESS, PUBLICITY AND PUBLICATIONS

Bishop's Press Officer Revd Derek Williams, c/o Dioc Office   *Tel:* 01733 887014 (Office)
          01604 843881 (Home)
          07770 981172 (Mobile)
email:
    derek.williams@peterborough-diocese.org.uk
Dioc Publications and Communications Mrs Liz Hurst (c/o Dioc Office)   *Tel:* 01733 887012
          Fax: 01733 555271
email:
    communications@peterborough-diocese.org.uk

DIOCESAN RECORD OFFICES

Wootton Park, Northampton NN4 9BQ *County Archivist* Miss Sarah Bridges
          Tel: 01604 762129
          email: archivist@northamptonshire.gov.uk
(*For all parishes in Northants. and the former Soke of Peterborough*)
Leicestershire Record Office, Long St, Wigston Magna, Leicester LE18 2AH *County Archivist* Mr Carl Harrison *Tel:* 0116 257 1080 (*For all parishes in Rutland*)

RURAL DEANS
ARCHDEACONRY OF NORTHAMPTON

Brackley Revd M. Roger H. Bellamy, Vicarage, Church Ave, Kings Sutton, Banbury OX17 3RD
          Tel: 01295 811364
          email: rogerbellamy@hotmail.co.uk
Brixworth Revd Mary Garbutt, Rectory, 35 Main St, Great Oxenden, Market Harborough LE16 8NE   *Tel:* 01858 461992
          email: mary@familygarbutt.plus.com
Daventry Revd Ann Slater, The Rectory, Church Lane, Nether Heyford, Northants NN7 3LQ
          Tel: 01327 342201
          email: ann.slater@btinternet.com
Northampton Revd David Wiseman, Christ Church Vicarage, 3 Christ Church Rd, Northampton NN3 2LE   *Tel:* 01604 633254
Towcester Revd John Hall, Vicarage, 154 Midland Rd, Wellingborough NN8 1NF
          Tel: 01327 860507
          email: fr-john@lambfold.org
Wellingborough Revd Tony Lynett, Vicarage, 154 Midland Rd, Wellingborough NN8 1NF
          Tel: 01933 227101
          email: tartleknock@aol.com

ARCHDEACONRY OF OAKHAM

Corby Revd Rod Lee, St Columba's Vicarage, 157 Studfall Ave, Corby NN17 1LG
          Tel: 01536 204158
          email: rlee103400@aol.com
Higham Revd Grant Brockhouse, Vicarage, Wood St, Higham Ferrers, Wellingborough NN10 8DL
          Tel: 01933 312433
          email: grantbrockhouse@care4free.net
Kettering Revd Brian Withington, Rectory, Gate Lane, Broughton, Kettering NN14 1ND
          Tel: 01536 791373
          email: brian.andco@virgin.net
Oundle Canon Richard Ormston, Vicarage, 12 New St, Oundle, Peterborough PE8 4EA
          Tel: 01832 273595
          email: Ormston4@aol.com
Peterborough Vacancy
Rutland Revd Lee Francis-Dehqani, Vicarage, Vicarage Rd, Oakham, Rutland LE15 6EG
          Tel: 01572 722108
          email: lee.fd@btinternet.com

DIOCESE OF PORTSMOUTH

Founded in 1927. The south-eastern third of Hampshire; the Isle of Wight.

Population 748,000   Area 408 sq m
Full-time Stipendiary Parochial Clergy 97   Benefices 128
Parishes 142   Churches 173
www.portsmouth.anglican.org
Overseas link diocese: IDWAL (Inter-Diocesan West Africa Link) – Ghana,
Gambia, Liberia (West Africa).

BISHOP (8th)
Rt Revd Christopher Foster   *Tel:* 01329 280247
Fax: 01329 231538
email: bishports@portsmouth.anglican.org
Bishop's Chaplain Vacancy
Secretaries Ms Judy Couzens, Ms Yvonne Collins

HONORARY ASSISTANT BISHOPS
Rt Revd Michael Adie, Greenslade, Froxfield,
Petersfield GU32 1EB [2005]   *Tel:* 01730 827266
Revd Dr Peter Selby, Afton Cottage, Afton Rd,
Freshwater, Isle of Wight PO40 9TP [2008]
Tel: 01983 759216
Rt Revd Godfrey Ashby, 12 Jay Close, Horndean,
Portsmouth PO8 9DJ [2008]   *Tel:* 023 9235 9914

CATHEDRAL CHURCH OF ST THOMAS OF CANTERBURY
Dean Very Revd David Brindley, The Deanery,
13 Pembroke Rd, Portsmouth PO1 2NS [2002]
Tel: 023 9282 4400 (Home)
email:
david.brindley@portsmouthcathedral.org.uk
023 9289 2963 (Personal Asst)
email: liz.snowball@portsmouthcathedral.org.uk
Cathedral Office Cathedral House, 63–67 St
Thomas's St, Old Portsmouth PO1 2HA
Tel: 023 9282 3300
Fax: 023 9289 2964
Web: www.portsmouthcathedral.org.uk
Canons Residentiary
Canon David T. Isaac, 1 Pembroke Close, Old
Portsmouth PO1 2NX [1990]
Tel: 023 9289 9654 (Office)
email: david.isaac@portsmouth.anglican.org
Pastor Canon Michael Tristram, 51 High St, Old
Portsmouth PO1 2LU [2003]
Tel: 023 9273 1282 (Home)
023 9282 3300 (Office)
email:
michael.tristram@portsmouthcathedral.org.uk
Canon Nick Ralph, 101 St Thomas's Street, Old
Portsmouth PO1 2HE [2009]
Tel: 023 9289 9674 (Office)
email: nick.ralph@portsmouth.anglican.org

Precentor Canon Nicholas Biddle, 32 Woodville
Drive, Pembroke Park, Portsmouth PO1 2TG
[2010]   *Tel:* 023 9282 3300 ext 225 (Office)
Tel: 023 9234 8139 (Home)
email:
nicholas.biddle@portsmouthcathedral.org.uk
*Cathedral Administrator, Chapter Clerk and Clerk to
Cathedral Council* Colonel (Rtd) Jonathan Lloyd
MBE   *Tel:* 023 9289 2961
email:
jonathan.lloyd@portsmouthcathedral.org.uk
Cathedral Organist and Master of Choristers Dr
David Price, Audley House, St James's Street,
Southseat PO1 4JA
Tel: 023 9282 3300 ext 228 (Office)
email: david.price@portsmouthcathedral.org.uk
Cathedral Sub-Organist
Marcus Wibberley, Flat 1, Cathedral House,
St Thomas' St, Old Portsmouth PO1 2EZ
Tel: 023 9289 2966 (Office)
023 9229 3565 (Home)
email:
marcus.wibberley@portsmouthcathedral.org.uk

ARCHDEACONS
PORTSDOWN Ven Dr Trevor Reader, 5 Brading Ave,
Southsea PO4 9QJ [2006]   *Tel:* 023 9243 2693
Fax: 023 9229 8788
email: adportsdown@portsmouth.anglican.org
THE MEON Vacancy   *Tel:* 01329 280101
Fax: 01329 281603
email: admeon@portsmouth.anglican.org
ISLE OF WIGHT Ven Caroline Baston, 5 The
Boltons, Kite Hill, Wootton Bridge, Isle of Wight
PO33 4PB [2006]   *Tel and Fax:* 01983 884432
email: adiow@portsmouth.anglican.org

CONVOCATION (MEMBERS OF THE HOUSE OF CLERGY OF THE GENERAL SYNOD)
Proctors for Clergy
Revd Philip Cochrane
Revd Timothy Jessiman
Canon Bob White

MEMBERS OF THE HOUSE OF LAITY OF THE GENERAL SYNOD
Mrs Lucy Docherty

104   **Dioceses**

Mrs Susan Rodgers
Mrs Deborah Sutton

DIOCESAN OFFICERS
Dioc Secretary Revd Wendy Kennedy, First Floor, Peninsular House, Wharf Rd, Portsmouth PO2 8HB
Tel: 023 9289 9664
Fax: 023 9289 9651
email: wendy.kennedy@portsmouth.anglican.org
Deputy Dioc Secretary Mr Paul Tizzard
Tel: 023 9282 9664
Fax: 023 9289 9651
email: paul.tizzard@portsmouth.anglican.org
PA to Dioc and Deputy Dioc Secretaries Mrs Jane Dobbs
Tel: 023 9282 9664
Fax: 023 9289 9651
email: jane.dobbs@portsmouth.anglican.org
Chancellor of Diocese The Worshipful C. Clark QC, Upper Croft, Goodworth, Clatford, Andover SP11 7QX
Tel: 01962 868161
Fax: 01962 867645
email: cc@3pumpcourt.com
Deputy Chancellor His Honour Judge Keith Cutler, Woodacre, West Gomeldon, Salisbury SP4 6LS
Tel: 01980 611710
Registrar of Diocese and Bishop's Legal Secretary Miss Hilary Tyler, Messrs Brutton & Co., West End House, 288 West St, Fareham PO16 0AJ
Tel: 01329 236171
Fax: 01329 289915
email: hilary.tyler@brutton.co.uk
Bishop's Council/Board of Finance/Pastoral Committee (*Chairman*) Rt Revd Christopher Foster (*as above*)
(*Secretary*) Revd Wendy Kennedy (*as above*)

DIOCESAN ORGANIZATION
Diocesan Office First Floor, Peninsular House, Wharf Rd, Portsmouth PO2 8HB
Tel: 023 9289 9650
Fax: 023 9289 9651
email: admin@portsmouth.anglican.org
Dioc Synod (*Secretary*) Revd Wendy Kennedy (*as above*)
Dioc Synod (*Chairman House of Clergy*) Canon Robert White, St Mary's Vicarage, Portsmouth PO1 5PA
Tel: 023 9282 2687 (Home)
023 9282 2990 (Office)
email: revrcwhite@aol.com
(*Chairman, House of Laity*) Mrs Lucy Docherty, 33 Southampton Rd, Fareham PO16 7DZ
Tel: 01329 233602
07952 780108 (Mobile)
email: lucy@docherty1.co.uk

MISSION AND DISCIPLESHIP
Head of Department Canon David Isaac, Dioc Office
Tel: 023 9289 9654
Fax: 023 9289 9651
email: david.isaac@portsmouth.anglican.org
Mission Resources Adviser Revd Dr Dennis Lloyd, Dioc Office
Tel: 023 9289 9676 (Office)
023 9241 2605 (Home)
email: dennis.lloyd@portsmouth.anglican.org

Dioc Director of Ordinands Revd Robin Coutts, Vicarage, Church Lane, Hambledon, Waterlooville PO7 4RT
Tel: 023 9263 2717
email: robin.coutts@portsmouth.anglican.org
Dioc Continuing Ministerial Education Officer Revd Karina Green, Vicarage, 8 Queen St, Portsmouth PO1 3HL
Tel: 023 9283 8713
email: karina.green@portsmouth.anglican.org
Bishop's Adviser on Women's Ministry Vacancy
Youth and Children's Work Adviser Ben Mizen, Dioc Office
Tel: 023 9289 9652
email: ben.mizen@portsmouth.anglican.org
Spirituality Adviser Vacancy

MISSION AND EDUCATION
Director of Education, Portsmouth and Winchester Mr Tony Blackshaw, Dioc Office
Tel: 023 9289 9658
Fax: 023 9289 9651
email: tony.blackshaw@portsmouth.anglican.org
Head of Department Mr Tony Blackshaw (*as above*)
Deputy Director of Education, Portsmouth and Winchester Miss Emily Fletcher, Dioc Office
Tel: 023 9289 9680
Fax: 023 9289 9651
email: emily.fletcher@portsmouth.anglican.org
Diocesan Further Education Adviser Vacancy

MISSION AND RESOURCES
Head of Department Mr Paul Tizzard, Dioc Office
Senior Finance Officer Ms Yvette Hoyland, Dioc Office
Tel: 023 9289 9683
email: yvette.hoyland@portsmouth.anglican.org
Diocesan Property Manager and Surveyor and Secretary to Property Committee Mr Barry Fryer, Dioc Office
Tel: 023 9289 9663
email: B.Fryer@portsmouth.anglican.org
Central Services Manager and Secretary to Dioc Advisory Committee Mrs Sherry Sherrington, Dioc. Office
Tel: 023 9289 9660
email:
sherry.sherrington@portsmouth.anglican.org
Safeguarding Officer Mr John Marshman, Dioc Office
Tel: 023 9289 9665
email: john.marshman@portsmouth.anglican.org
Parish Finance Adviser Mr Christopher Malone, Dioc Office
Tel: 023 9289 9655
email:
christopher.malone@portsmouth.anglican.org

MISSION AND SOCIETY
Chair (*appointed by the Bishop*) Ven Caroline Baston, Archdeacon of the Isle of Wight, 5 The Boltons, Kite Hill, Wootton Bridge IOW PO33 4PB
Tel: 01983 884432
email: adiow@portsmouth.anglican.org
Diocesan Secretary Revd Wendy Kennedy
Head of Mission and Society Section and Social Responsibility Adviser Canon Nick Ralph, First Floor, Peninsular House, Wharf Rd, Portsmouth, Hants PO2 8HB
Tel: 023 9289 9674
email: nick.ralph@portsmouth.anglican.org
Chair of the Council for Social Responsibility Steering Group Mrs Lucy Docherty

Chaplain to the Deaf and Hard of Hearing Revd Robert Sanday, 3 Wheat Close, Knightwood, Chandlers Ford, Hants SO53 4HA
Tel: 023 8026 5897
email: robertsanday@aol.com
Church Tourism Adviser Revd Chris Etherton, 19 Station Avenue, Sandown, Isle of Wight PO36 9BW
Tel: 07906 238368
email: chrisetherton@tiscali.co.uk
Committee for Minority Ethnic Anglican Concerns (CMEAC) Representative Mr Apollo Tutesigensi, 38 Cornwall Rd, Fratton, Portsmouth PO1 5BW
Tel: 023 9273 7058
email: atutessigensi@hotmail.com
Communications Adviser Mr Neil Pugmire, First Floor, Peninsular House, Wharf Rd, Portsmouth, Hants PO2 8HB
Tel: 023 9289 9673
email: neil.pugmire@portsmouth.anglican.org
Communications Assistant Mrs Caroline Challender, First Floor, Peninsular House, Wharf Rd, Portsmouth, Hants PO2 8HB
Tel: 023 9289 9675
email: caroline.challender@portsmouth.anglican.org
Disability Adviser Revd Mary Tillman, 3 Fareham Rd, Gosport, Hants PO13 0XL   Tel: 01329 232589
07718 762323 (Mobile)
email: met@tillman.freeserve.co.uk
Environment Adviser Revd Andy Norris, Vicarage, 113 Church Rd, Warsash, Southampton SO31 9GF
Tel: 01489 570046
email: environment@portsmouth.anglican.org
Ecumenical Adviser Revd Simon Sayers, Rectory, 20 Church Path, Emsworth PO10 7DP
Tel: 01243 372428
email: simonsayers@hotmail.com
Good Neighbours Support Service (Co-Ordinator) Mrs Mary Mitchell GNSS, Peninsular House, Wharf Rd, Portsmouth PO2 8HB
Tel: 023 9289 9671
email: mary.mitchell@goodneighbours.org.uk
(North Adviser: Local Authority - Basingstoke, Hart, Rushmore, East Hants) Mrs Elizabeth Foulds (as above)   Tel: 07827 925326 (Mobile)
email: Elizabeth.foulds@neighbourcare.org.uk
(South West Adviser: Local Authority - New Forest, Test Valley, Eastleigh) Mrs Angela Smith (as above)
Tel: 07827 925327 (Mobile)
email: angela.smith@goodneighbourcare.org.uk
(South East Adviser: Local Authority - Winchester, Havant, Fareham, Gosport) Mrs Sandra Osborne (as above)   Tel: 07827 925328 (Mobile)
email: sandra.osborne@goodneighbourcare.org.uk
Hospital Chaplaincy Canon Nick Fennemore, Chaplaincy Office, Queen Alexandra Hospital, Cosham, Portsmouth PO6 3LY
Tel: 023 9228 6408
email: nick.fennemore@porthosp.nhs.uk
Interdiocesan West Africa Link (Chair) Canon Terry Louden, Vicarage, East Meon, Petersfield GU32 1NH
Tel: 01730 823221
email: terrylouden@btinternet.com

Industrial Chaplaincy (Qinetiq Chaplain) Canon Roger Devonshire, 4 Chiltern Court, Florence Rd, Southsea PO5 2NX   Tel: 023 9287 6339
email: rdevonshire@btinternet.com
Interfaith Adviser Vacancy
Isle of Wight Social Responsibility Co-ordinator Revd Nick Wallace, Rectory, Pitts Lane, Binstead Ryde IOW   Tel: 01983 562890
email: rewallace@hotmail.com
New Religious Movements Adviser Revd Andy Norris, Vicarage, 113 Church Rd, Warsash, Southampton SO31 9GF   Tel: 01489 570846
Port Chaplain Revd Philip Hiscock, 36 Gomer Lane, Alverstoke, Gosport, Hants PO12 2SA
Tel: 02392 346881
email: philip.hiscock@ntlworld.com
Porvoo Adviser Revd Philip Cochrane, 12 Greenwood Close, Fareham PO16 7UF
Tel: 01329 232688
email: philip@htscf.com
Diocesan Rural Officer and Rural Affairs Adviser (Mainland) Revd D H Heatley, Vicarage, Hawkley, Liss, Hants GU33 6NF
Tel: 01730 827459
email: dhheatley@aol.com
Rural Affairs Adviser (IOW) Revd Graham Morris, Vicarage, Maples Drive, Bonchurch, Isle of Wight PO38 1NR   Tel: 01983 853729
email graham.morris@btinternet.com
Urban Ministry Adviser Canon Bob White, St Mary's Vicarage, Fratton Rd, Portsmouth PO1 5PA   Tel: 023 9282 2990
email: revrcwhite@aol.com
World Development Adviser Canon Marion Mort, Rivendell, High St, Shirrell Heath, Southampton SO32 3JN   Tel: 01329 832178
email: marion.mort@portsmouth.anglican.org

AREAS OF CONCERN

Evangelism Revd Tim Jessiman, Vicarage, 61 Hart Plane Avenue, Waterlooville, Hants PO8 8RG
Tel: 023 9226 4551
email: tim.jessiman@ntlworld.com
The Mother's Union Mrs Alison Hubbard, Holmwood, West St, Hambledon PO7 4SN
Tel: 023 9263 2314
email: alisonhubbard1@gmail.com

CHURCHES

Dioc Advisory Committee for the Care of Churches (Chair) Very Revd David Brindley; (Secretary) Mrs Susan Hodge
email: susan.hodge@portsmouth.anglican.org
Redundant Churches Uses Committee (Chair) Revd Wendy Kennedy (as above); (Secretary) Mrs Sherry Sherrington

MINISTRY

Widows Officers (Mainland) The Archdeacon of Portsdown; The Archdeacon of the Meon (Isle of Wight); The Archdeacon of the Isle of Wight

DIOCESAN RECORD OFFICES

Portsmouth City Records Office, 3 Museum Rd, Portsmouth PO1 2LE *Archivist* Miss Alison Drew
Tel: 023 9282 7261
email: alison.drew@portsmouth.gov.uk
(For Gosport, Fareham, Havant and Portsmouth deaneries)
Hampshire Record Office, Sussex St, Winchester SO23 8TH *County Archivist* Miss Janet Smith *Tel:* 01962 846154; *Fax:* 01962 878681; *email:* enquiries.archives@hants.gov.uk *(For Bishop's Waltham and Petersfield deaneries)*
Isle of Wight County Record Office, 26 Hillside, Newport, Isle of Wight PO30 2EB *Archivist* Mr R. Smout
Tel: 01983 823821
email: record.office @iow.gov.uk
(For the Isle of Wight deaneries)

AREA DEANS
ARCHDEACONRY OF THE MEON

Bishop's Waltham Revd Stuart Holt, Rectory, Rectory Lane, Meonstoke SO32 3NF
Tel: 01489 877512
email: revstuartholt@btinternet.com
Fareham Revd Stephen Girling, Crofton Vicarage, 40 Vicarage Lane, Stubbington, Fareham PO14 2JX
Tel: 01329 661154
email: stephengirling@f2s.com

Gosport Revd Peter Sutton, Vicarage, Victoria Square, Lee-on-the-Solent PO13 9NF
Tel: 023 9255 0269 (Home)
023 9255 6445 (Office)
email: peter.sutton4@virgin.net
Petersfield Revd Rob Dewing, Sheet Vicarage, 2 Pullens Lane, Sheet, Petersfield GU31 4DB
Tel: 01730 263673
email: robdewing@stmaryssheet.org.uk

ARCHDEACONRY OF PORTSDOWN

Havant Revd Dr Paul Moore, Vicarage, Padnell Rd, Cowplain, Waterlooville PO8 8DZ
Tel: 023 9226 2295
email: p.h.moore@btinternet.com
Portsmouth Revd Michael Lewis, Vicarage, 26 Victoria Grove, Southsea PO5 1NE
Tel: 023 9287 3535 (Home)
023 9282 9038 (Office)

ARCHDEACONRY OF THE ISLE OF WIGHT

East Wight Revd Graham Morris, Vicarage, Maples Drive, Bonchurch, Isle of Wight PO38 1NR
Tel: 01983 853729
email: graham.morris@btinternet.com
West Wight Revd Jonathan Hall, Rectory, 69 Victoria Grove, East Cowes, Isle of Wight PO32 6DL
Tel: 01983 200107
email: jel.victoriahall@btinternet.com

Re-constituted in 1836. The central third of North Yorkshire; Leeds, except for an area in the west (BRADFORD), an area in the east (YORK) and an area in the south (WAKEFIELD); an area of south-western County Durham.

Population 837,000   Area 1,359 sq m
Full-time Stipendiary Parochial Clergy 115   Benefices 111
Parishes 166   Churches 261
www.ripon.anglican.org
Overseas link diocese: Colombo and Kurunagala (Sri Lanka).

BISHOP (12th)
Rt Revd John Richard Packer, Hollins House, Weetwood Avenue, Leeds, LS16 5NG [2000]
Tel: 0113 224 2789
Fax: 0113 230 5471
email: bishop@riponleeds-diocese.org.uk
[John Ripon and Leeds]
Bishop's Personal Assistant Mrs Janet Slater (*same address*)

SUFFRAGAN BISHOP
KNARESBOROUGH Rt Revd James Harold Bell, Thistledown, Main St, Exelby, Bedale DL8 2HD [2004]
Tel: 01677 423525
Fax: 01677 427515
email: bishop.knaresb@btinternet.com

HONORARY ASSISTANT BISHOPS
Rt Revd David Jenkins, Ashbourne, Cotherstone, Barnard Castle DL12 9PR [1994]
Tel: 01833 650804
Rt Revd Martyn Jarrett, 3 North Lane, Roundhay, Leeds LS8 2QJ [2002]
Tel: 0113 265 4280
Fax: 0113 265 4281
email:
bishop-of-beverley@3-north-lane.fsnet.co.uk
Rt Revd Clive Handford, Wayside, 1 The Terrace, Kirkby Hill, Boroughbridge YO51 9DQ
Tel: 01423 325406
email: gchandford@gmail.com

CATHEDRAL CHURCH OF ST PETER AND ST WILFRID
Dean Very Revd Keith Jukes, Minster House, Bedern Bank, Ripon HG4 1PE [2007]
Tel: 01765 602609
email: deankeith@riponcathedral.org.uk
Dean's Secretary Mrs Judith Bustard
Cathedral Office Liberty Courthouse, Minster Rd, Ripon HG4 1QS
Tel: 01765 603462
Fax: 01765 690530
email: postmaster@riponcathedral.org.uk
Web: www.riponcathedral.org.uk
Canon Precentor: Canon Paul Greenwell, St Wilfrid's House, Minster Close, Ripon HG4 1QR
Tel: 01765 600211
email: canonpaul@riponcathedral.org
Canons Residentiary

Canon Keith Punshon, St Peter's House, Minster Close, Ripon HG4 1QR [1996]   *Tel:* 01765 604108
email: canonkeith@riponcathedral.org.uk
Canon Janet Henderson, Hoppus House, Smith Lane, Hutton Conyers, Ripon HG4 5DX
Tel: 01765 601316
email: janeth@riponleeds-diocese.org.uk
Cathedral Administrator Lt Col Ian Horsford, Cathedral Office
Tel: 01765 603462
email: ianhorsford@riponcathedral.org.uk
Director of Music Mr Andrew Bryden, c/o Ripon Cathedral, Ripon HG4 1QT   *Tel:* 01765 603496
email: andrewbryden@riponcathedral.org.uk

ARCHDEACONS
LEEDS Ven Peter Burrows, 3 West Park Grove, Leeds LS8 2HQ [2005] *Tel* and *Fax:* 0113 269 0594
email: peterb@riponleeds-diocese.org.uk
RICHMOND Ven Janet Henderson, Hoppus House, Smith Lane, Hutton Conyers, Ripon HG4 5DX [2007]
Tel: 01765 601316
email: janeth@riponleeds-diocese.org.uk

CONVOCATION (MEMBERS OF THE HOUSE OF CLERGY OF THE GENERAL SYNOD)
Proctors for Clergy
Canon Kathryn Fitzsimons
Ven Peter Burrows
Revd Jonathan Clark

MEMBERS OF THE HOUSE OF LAITY OF THE GENERAL SYNOD
Dr John Beal
Mr Nigel Greenwood
Dr Richard Mantle

DIOCESAN OFFICERS
Dioc Secretary Dr Sue Proctor   *Tel:* 0113 200 0540
email: suep@riponleeds-diocese.org.uk
Chancellor of Diocese The Worshipful Simon Grenfell, St John's House, Sharow Lane, Ripon, N Yorks. HG4 5BN
email: sgrenfell@lix.compulink.co.uk
Joint Registrars of Diocese and Bishop's Legal Secretaries Mr Christopher Tunnard and Mrs Nicola Harding, Ripon and Leeds Diocesan

Registry, Cathedral Chambers, 4 Kirkgate, Ripon HG4 1PA　　　　Tel: 01765 600755
　　　　　　　　　　　　Fax: 01765 690523
　　email: registry@tunnardsolicitors.com
Dioc Surveyor Mr Michael Lindley, Dioc Office
　　email: michaell@riponleeds-diocese.org.uk

DIOCESAN ORGANIZATIONS

Diocesan Office Ripon and Leeds Diocesan Office, St Mary's St, Leeds LS9 7DP　　Tel: 0113 200 0540
　　　　　　　　　　　　Fax: 0113 249 1129

ADMINISTRATION

Dioc Synod (Chairman, House of Clergy) Canon Anthony Shepherd, St Peter's Vicarage, 13 Beech Grove, Harrogate HG2 0ET　　Tel: 01423 500901
　　　　email: ashepherd@talktalk.net
(Chairman, House of Laity) Mrs Ann Nicholl, 17 Parkland Terrace, Leeds LS6 4PW
　　　　　　　　　　Tel: 0113 269 4045
　　email: anicholl@parkland17.freeserve.co.uk
(Secretary) Dr Sue Proctor, Dioc Office
　　email: philipa@riponleeds-diocese.org.uk
Board of Finance (Chairman) Mr Alastair Thompson, Woodlands Cottage, 15 Wyncroft Grove, Bramhope, Leeds LS16 9DG
　　　　　　　　　　Tel: 0113 267 8496
　　email: alastair_thompson@btopenworld.com
(Secretary) Dr Sue Proctor (as above); (Administrative and Deputy Secretary) Mr Peter Mojsa, Dioc Office　email: peterm@riponleeds-diocese.org.uk
(Financial Secretary) Mr Norman Gardner, Dioc Office
　　email: Normang@riponleeds-diocese.org.uk
Parsonages Board Dr Sue Proctor (as above); (Parsonages Officer) Mr Michael Lindley, Dioc Office
　　email: michaell@riponleeds-diocese.org.uk
Pastoral Committee Mr Peter Mojsa (as above)
Board of Patronage Mr Peter Mojsa (as above)
Designated Officer Dr Sue Proctor (as above)
Dioc Electoral Registration Officer Dr Sue Proctor (as above)
Widows and Dependants (Widows' Officer) Dr Sue Proctor (as above)

CHURCHES

Advisory Committee for the Care of Churches (Chairman) Mr C. Brown, 40 Leeds Rd, Harrogate HG4 8AY　　　　Tel: 01423 567587
　　email: coljanbrown@talktalk.net
(Secretary) Mr Peter Mojsa, Dioc Office
Church Buildings Committee Mr Peter Mojsa (as above)
Redundant Churches Uses Committee Mr Peter Mojsa (as above)

EDUCATION

Director of Education, Bradford, Ripon and Leeds Revd Clive Sedgewick, The Diocesan Education Team, Windsor House, Cornwall St, Harrogate HG1 2PW　　　　Tel: 01423 817553
　　　　　　　　　　Fax: 01423 817051
　　email: clives@brleducationteam.org.uk

Schools Advisers Fiona Beevers and Eileen Bellett (same address)
　　email: fionab@brleducationteam.org.uk and eileenb@brleducationteam.org.uk
Buildings Advisers Helen Williams (same address)
　　email: helenw@brleducationteam.org.uk
Phillip Smith (same address)
　　email: peters@brleducationteam.org.uk
Development Education Worker Mrs Sarah Fishwick, Diocese of Ripon and Leeds Global Education Project, 233–237 Roundhay Rd, Leeds LS8 4HS　　　　Tel: 0113 380 5661
　　　　email: sarah@leedsdec.org

COUNCIL FOR MISSION

Chair Revd C. J. Swift
Director of Mission Resourcing Revd Adrian Alker, Dioc Office　　　　Tel: 0113 200 0559
　　email: adriana@riponleeds-diocese.org.uk
Diocesan Director of Lay Training Mrs Liz Williams, Dioc Office　　Tel: 0113 200 0556
　　email: lizw@riponleeds-diocese.org.uk
Diocesan Director of Clergy Training Canon Paul Hooper, Dioc Office　　Tel: 0113 200 0557
　　email: Paulh@riponleeds-diocese.org.uk
Director of Ordinands Revd Peter Clement, The Parish House, 16 Orchard Close, Sharow, Ripon HG4 5BE　　　　Tel: 01765 607017
　　email: peterc@riponleeds-diocese.org.uk
Adviser for Women's Ministry Canon Alison Montgomery, Washington House, Littlethorpe, Ripon HG4 3LJ　　　　Tel: 01765 605276
email:
　　Montgomery@littlethorpe97.freeserve.co.uk
Youth Work Adviser Capt Nic Sheppard, 7 Loxley Grove, Wetherby LS22 7YG　　Tel: 01937 585440
　　email: nic.Sheppard@churcharmy.net
Warden of Readers Miss Ann Hemsworth, 12 Kelmscott Grove, Cross Gates, Leeds LS15 8HH
　　　　　　　　　　Tel: 0113 293 7494
　　email: ann@elancama.co.uk
Adviser for Non-Stipendiary Ministry Ven Simon Golding, Arlanza, Hornby Rd, Appleton Wiske, Northallerton DL6 2AF　　Tel: 01609 881185
　　　　email: perce2000@virgin.net
Convenor of Advisory Group on Christian Healing Revd Tom Lusty, Sue Ryder Care, Wheatfield Hospice, Grove Rd, Leeds LS6 2AE
　　　　　　　　　　Tel: 0113 278 7249
　　email: tom.lusty@suerydercare.org
World Church Officer Vacancy
Ecumenical Officer Revd Colin Cheeseman, 2a Ryder Gardens, Leeds, LS8 1JS
　　　　　　　　　　Tel: 0113 266 9747
　　email: colin.cheeseman@ntlworld.com
Social Responsibility Officer Vacancy
Community Chaplain for People with Learning Difficulties Vacancy
Racial Justice Officer Revd Ade Lawal, Wyther Vicarage, Houghley Lane, Leeds LS13 4RU
　　　　　　　　　　Tel: 0113 279 8614
　　email: vicar.bede@btinternet.com

Rural Ministry Officer Vacancy
Urban Ministry Officer Canon Kathryn Fitzsimons,
52 Newton Court, Leeds LS8 2PH
Tel: 0113 248 5011
email: kathrynfitzsimons@hotmail.com

LITURGICAL
Chairman Vacancy
Secretary Revd Stuart Lewis, Rectory, Kirkby
Overblow, Harrogate HG3 1HD
Tel: 01423 872314

COMMUNICATIONS
Communications Committee Canon John Carter, 7
Blenheim Court, Harrogate HG2 9DT
Tel: 01423 530369
Fax: 01423 538557
email: jhgcarter@aol.com
Press Officer Revd John Carter (*as above*)
Editor of 'Together' (*monthly*) Revd John Carter (*as
above*)

DIOCESAN RECORD OFFICES
County Record Office, County Hall, Northaller-
ton DL7 8DF *Senior Archivist* (*Collections*)
Margaret Boustead *Tel:* 01609 777585
Leeds Archives Department, Chapeltown Rd,
Sheepscar, Leeds LS7 3AP *Leeds City Archivist*
Stephanie Davidson *Tel:* 0113 214 5814
Fax: 0113 214 5815

STEWARDSHIP
Stewardship Adviser Mr Paul Winstanley, Dioc
Office *email:* Paulw@riponleeds-diocese.co.uk

AREA DEANS
ARCHDEACONRY OF RICHMOND
Harrogate Revd Nigel Sinclair, St Robert's
Vicarage, 21 Crimple Meadows, Pannal,
Harrogate HG3 1EL *Tel:* 01423 870202
email: nigelsinclair@btinternet.com
Richmond Revd Stan Howarth, The Rectory, 1
Appleby Close, Aldbrough St John, Richmond
DL11 7TT *Tel:* 01325 374634
email: stantherevman@hotmail.com
Ripon Revd Mark Tanner, Holy Trinity Vicarage,
3 College Road, Ripon HG4 2AE
Tel: 01765 690930
email: mark.tanner@holytrinityripon.org.uk
Wensley Revd Brendan Giblin, Rectory, Wensley,
Leyburn DL8 4HS *Tel:* 01969 622276
email: bgiblin@toucansurf.com

ARCHDEACONRY OF LEEDS
Allerton Canon Alan Taylor, Vicarage, Elford Place
West, Leeds LS8 5QD *Tel:* 0113 248 6992
email: alan.taylor@leeds.gov.uk
Armley Revd Kingsley Dowling, Wortley
Vicarage, Dixon Lane Rd, Leeds LS12 4RU
Headingley Revd David Calder, 2 Halcyon Hill,
Leeds LS7 3PU *Tel:* 0113 263 8867
email: kingsleydowling@talktalk.net
Headingley Vacancy
Whitkirk Revd Mike Benwell, St Luke's Vicarage,
Stanks Lane North, Leeds LS14 5AS
Tel: 0113 273 1302
email: Benwell@ndirect.co.uk

DIOCESE OF ROCHESTER

Founded in 604. Kent west of the Medway, except for one parish in the south-west (CHICHESTER); the Medway Towns; the London boroughs of Bromley and Bexley, except for a few parishes (SOUTHWARK); one parish in East Sussex.

Population 1,239,000   Area 542 sq m
Full-time Stipendiary Parochial Clergy 196   Benefices 189
Parishes 215   Churches 265
www.rochester.anglican.org
Overseas link diocese: Harare (Zimbabwe).

BISHOP (106th)
Rt Revd James Langstaff, Bishopscourt, St Margaret's St, Rochester ME1 1TS
Tel: 01634 842471
Fax: 01634 831136
email: bishop.rochester@rochester.anglican.org
Chaplain Canon Alan Vousden   Tel: 01634 814439
email: bishops.chaplain@rochester.anglican.org

SUFFRAGAN BISHOP
TONBRIDGE Rt Revd Dr Brian Castle, Bishop's Lodge, 48 St Botolph's Rd, Sevenoaks TN13 3AG [2002]
Tel: 01732 456070
Fax: 01732 741449
email: bishop.tonbridge@rochester.anglican.org

HONORARY ASSISTANT BISHOP
Rt Revd Michael Gear, 10 Acott Fields, Yalding, Maidstone ME18 6DQ [1999]   Tel: 01622 817388
email: mike.gear@rochester.anglican.org

CATHEDRAL CHURCH OF CHRIST AND THE BLESSED VIRGIN MARY
Dean Very Revd Adrian Newman, The Deanery, The Precinct, Rochester ME1 1SR [2005]
Tel: 01634 202183 (Home)
01634 843366 (Office)
email: dean@rochestercathedral.org
Chapter Office Garth House, The Precinct, Rochester ME1 1SX   Tel: 01634 843366
Fax: 01634 401410
Canons Residentiary
Canon Philip Hesketh, East Canonry, The Precinct, Rochester ME1 1TG [2005]
Tel: 01634 202898 (Home)
01634 810073 (Office)
email: canonpastor@rochestercathedral.org
Ven Simon Burton-Jones, The Archdeaconry, The Precinct, Rochester ME1 1TG [2010]
Tel: 01634 813533 (Home)
01634 560000 (Office)
email: archdeacon@rochestercathedral.org
Canon Neil Thompson, Easter Garth, The Precinct, Rochester ME1 1TG [2008]
Tel: 01634 405265 (Home)
01634 810063 (Office)
email: precentor@rochestercathedral.org

Canon Jean Kerr, Prebendal House, King's Orchard, The Precinct, Rochester ME1 1TG [2005]
Tel: 01634 844508 (Home)
email: jean.kerr@rochester.anglican.org
Director of Operations Dr Edwina Bell, Chapter Office   Tel: 01634 810060 (Office)
email: administrator@rochestercathedral.org
Cathedral Organist and Director of Music Mr Scott Farrell, Chapter Office   Tel: 01634 810061
email: dom@rochestercathedral.org

ARCHDEACONS
BROMLEY AND BEXLEY Ven Dr Paul Wright, The Archdeaconry, The Glebe, Chislehurst BR7 5PX [2004]   Tel: 020 8467 8743
email:
archdeacon.bromley@rochester.anglican.org
ROCHESTER Ven Simon Burton-Jones, The Archdeaconry, The Precinct, Rochester ME1 1TG [2010]
Tel: 01643 560000
email:
archdeacon.rochester@rochester.anglican.org
TONBRIDGE Ven Clive Mansell, 3 The Ridings, Blackhurst Lane, Tunbridge Wells TN2 4RU [2002]   Tel: 01892 520660
email:
archdeacon.tonbridge@rochester.anglican.org

CONVOCATION (MEMBERS OF THE HOUSE OF CLERGY OF THE GENERAL SYNOD)
Proctors for Clergy
Revd Dr John Perumbalath
Revd Angus MacLeay
Ven Clive Mansell
Canon Gordon Oliver

MEMBERS OF THE HOUSE OF LAITY OF THE GENERAL SYNOD
Mr James Cheeseman
Brig Ian Dobbie
Mr Philip French
Mr Gerald O'Brien
Mrs Angela Scott

DIOCESAN OFFICERS
Dioc Secretary and Bishop's Officer Canon Louise Gilbert, St Nicholas Church, Boley Hill, Rochester ME1 1SL   Tel: 01634 560000
Fax: 01634 408942
email: louise.gilbert@rochester.anglican.org

Chancellor of Diocese Mr John Gallagher, Hardwicke Building, New Square, Lincoln's Inn, London WC2A 3SB   *Tel:* 020 7242 2523
Registrar of Diocese and Bishop's Legal Secretary Mr Owen Carew-Jones, Minerva House, 5 Montague Close, London SE1 9BB
Tel: 020 7593 5110
Fax: 020 7248 3221
email: a.harrison@winckworths.co.uk

DIOCESAN ORGANIZATIONS

Diocesan Office St Nicholas Church, Boley Hill, Rochester ME1 1SL   *Tel:* 01634 560000
Fax: 01634 408942
email: enquiries@rochester.anglican.org
Web: www.rochester.anglican.org

ADMINISTRATION

Deputy Diocesan Secretary Mr Geoff Marsh, Dioc Office
email: geoff.marsh@rochester.anglican.org
Dioc Synod (Chairman, House of Clergy) Canon Jim Stewart
(Chairman, House of Laity) Mrs Angela Scott
(Secretary) Canon Louise Gilbert, Dioc Office
Board of Finance (Chairman) Mr Graeme King, Strath Darent House, Shoreham Rd, Otford, Sevenoaks TN14 5RW   *Tel:* 01959 522118; *(Secretary)* Canon Louise Gilbert *(as above)*; *(Dioc Treasurer)* Mr Martyn Burt, Dioc Office
email: martyn.burt@rochester.anglican.org
Pastoral Committee Mrs Suzanne Rogers, Dioc Office
email: suzanne.rogers@rochester.anglican.org
Board of Patronage Mrs Suzanne Rogers *(as above)*
Designated Officer Mr Owen Carew-Jones, Minerva House, 5 Montague Close, London SE1 9BB   *Tel:* 020 7593 5110
Trusts Mrs Nikki McVeagh (Legal), Dioc Office
email: nikki.mcveagh@rochester.anglican.org

CHURCHES

Advisory Committee for the Care of Churches (Chair) Mr Derek Shilling, Ivy Bank, Shoreham Rd, Otford, Sevenoaks TN14 5RP   *Tel:* 01959 522059
(DAC Secretary) Mark Trevett, Dioc Office
Redundant Churches Mr Geoff Marsh *(as above)*

EDUCATION

Education Office Diocesan Office
email: education@rochester.anglican.org
Board of Education (Chair) Christopher Thornton, Kettleshill House, Underriver, Sevenoaks TN15 0RX
Secretary, Director of Education and Bishop's Officer Vacancy, Educ Office
Assistant Director of Education (Schools) Ms Jan Thompson, Educ Office
Assistant Director of Education (Voluntary Education) Mr Richard Thomas, Educ Office
Assistant Director of Education (Finance) Mr John Constanti, Educ Office

MINISTRY AND TRAINING

Advisory Council for Ministry and Training (Chairman) The Bishop of Tonbridge *(as above)*; *(Secretary, Director of Ministry and Training and Bishop's Officer)* Revd Christopher Dench, Dioc Office
email: chris.dench@rochester.anglican.org
Director of Ordinands Revd Glynn Ackerley, Vicarage, Butchers Hill, Shorne, Gravesend DA12 3EB   *Tel:* 01474 822239
Associate Director of Ordinands Canon Elizabeth Walker, Vicarage, Comp Lane, Platt, Sevenoaks TN15 8NR   *Tel:* 01732 885482
Readers' Association (Warden) Mrs Karen Senior, Dioc Office
email: readers@rochester.anglican.org
Clerical Registry, Dioc Retirement Officer and Widows Officer Revd Colin Terry, The Chaplain's House, Bromley College, London Rd, Bromley BR1 1PE   *Tel:* 020 8460 4712
email: bromcoll@aol.com
Evangelists (Warden) Canon Jean Kerr *(as above)*
Pastoral Assistants (Warden) Revd Bryan Knapp, Vicarage, 169 Maidstone Rd, Paddock Wood, Tonbridge TN12 6DZ   *Tel:* 01892 833917

WORSHIP IN MISSION

Chair Revd David Graham, Rectory, Hayes St, Hayes, Bromley BR2 7LH   *Tel:* 020 8462 1373

MISSION AND UNITY

Advisory Council for Mission and Unity (Chairman) The Archdeacon of Bromley and Bexley *(as above)*
(Secretary and Bishop's Officer for Mission and Unity) Canon Jean Kerr *(as above)*
(Mission Growth Team Leader) Revd Ross Garner, St Barnabas Vicarage, 1 St Barnabas Close, Oxford Rd, Gillingham ME7 4BU
Interfaith (Chairman) Revd Malcolm Cooper, 1 Crest View, Greenhithe DA9 9QU
Tel: 01322 381213
Local Evangelism (Chairman) Canon Jean Kerr *(as above)*

PRESS, PUBLICITY AND COMMUNICATIONS

Advisory Council for Communications (Chairman) Ven Simon Burton-Jones, Archdeacon of Rochester *(as above)*
(Bishop's Officer for Communications) Ms Lindy Mackenzie, Dioc Office   *Tel:* 01634 560000
07500 837416 (Mobile)
email: lindy.mackenzie@rochester.anglican.org
Communications Assistant Ms Lou Whiffin, Dioc Office   *Tel:* 07827 157330 (Mobile)
email: lou.whiffin@rochester.anglican.org
Editor of 'Link' Newspaper Ms Lindy Mackenzie, Dioc Office   *Tel:* 01634 560000
07500 837416 (Mobile)
email: linknews@rochester.anglican.org

DIOCESAN RECORD OFFICES

Centre for Kentish Studies, County Hall, Maidstone ME14 1XQ *Tel:* 01622 694363; Medway Archives and Local Studies Centre, Civic Centre, Strood, Rochester ME2 4AW *Tel:* 01634 732714; Bexley Local Studies and Archive Centre, Central Library, Townley Rd, Bexleyheath DA6 7HJ *Tel:* 020 8301 1545 (*For the deaneries of Erith and Sidcup in the archdeaconry of Bromley*)

Bromley Local Studies and Archives, Central Library, High St, Bromley, Kent BR1 1EX *Tel:* 020 8460 9955 (*For the deaneries of Beckenham, Bromley and Orpington in the archdeaconry of Bromley*)

CHURCH IN SOCIETY (SOCIAL RESPONSIBILITY)

Rural Issues Revd Caroline Pinchbeck, Rectory, Newnham Lane, Eastling, Faversham ME13 0AS
Urban Priorities Revd Dr John Perumbalath, St Mark's Vicarage, 123 London Rd, Northfleet, Gravesend DA11 9NH   *Tel:* 01474 535814
    email: john.perumbalath@diocese-rochester.org
Poverty and Hope (*Director*) Mr Chris Weller, 9 Calverley Park, Tunbridge Wells TN1 2SH

STEWARDSHIP

Mr Alan Strachan, Dioc Office

AREA/RURAL DEANS

ARCHDEACONRY OF BROMLEY AND BEXLEY

Beckenham Canon Paul Miller, Vicarage, 37 Kingswood Rd, Shortlands, Bromley BR2 0HG
    Tel: 020 8460 4989
    email: paul.miller@diocese-rochester.org
Bromley Revd Michael Camp, Vicarage, 9 St Paul's Square, Bromley BR2 0XH
    Tel: 020 8460 6275
    email: michael.camp@diocese-rochester.org
Erith Revd Antony Lane, Rectory, 1 Claremont Crescent, Dartford DA1 4RJ   *Tel:* 020 8301 5086
    email: antony.lane@diocese-rochester.org
Orpington Revd Jay Colwill, The Vicarage, 165 Charterhouse Road, Orpington, BR6 9EP
    Tel: 01689 870923
    email: jay.colwill@diocese-rochester.org
Sidcup Revd Stephen Sealy, St John's Vicarage, 13 Church Avenue, Sidcup DA14 6BU
    Tel: 020 8300 0383
email: stephen.sealy@diocese-rochester.org

ARCHDEACONRY OF ROCHESTER

Cobham Revd John Peal, The New Rectory, The Street, Ash, Sevenoaks TN15 7HA
    Tel: 04747 872209
    email: john.peal@diocese-rochester.org
Dartford Revd Richard Arding, Vicarage, 1 Curate's Walk, Wilmington, Dartford DA2 7BJ   *Tel:* 01322 220561
Gillingham Revd Jonathan Jennings, St Augustine's Vicarage, Rock Avenue, Gillingham ME7 5PW   *Tel:* 01634 850288
    email: jonathan.jennings@diocese-rochester.org
Gravesend Revd Ruth Oates, Vicarage, 57 New House Lane, Gravesend DA11 7HJ
    Tel: 01474 740565
    email: ruth.oates@diocese-rochester.org
Rochester Revd Paul Kerr, Vicarage, 1 Binnacle Rd, Rochester ME1 2XR   *Tel:* 01634 841183
    email: office@stjustuschurch.freeserve.co.uk
Strood Revd James Southward, Vicarage, Hermitage Rd, Higha, Rochester ME3 7NE
    Tel: 01634 717360
    email: jfsouthward@yahoo.co.uk

ARCHDEACONRY OF TONBRIDGE

Malling Revd Jim Brown, Vicarage, 2 The Grange, East Malling ME19 6AH
    Tel: 01732 843282
    email: jim.brown@diocese-rochester.org
Paddock Wood Revd Gwen Smith, Vicarage, Maidstone Rd, Hadlow, Tonbridge TN11 0DJ
    Tel: 01732 850238
    email: vicar@stmaryshadlow.org.uk
Sevenoaks Canon Paul Francis, St Mary's Vicarage, The Glebe Field, Shoreham Lane, Riverhead, Sevenoaks TN13 3DR   *Tel:* 01732 455736
    email: paul.francis@diocese-rochester.org
Shoreham Canon Brenda Hurd, Rectory, Borough Green Rd, Wrotham, Sevenoaks TN15 7RA
    Tel: 01732 882211
    email: brenda.hurd@diocese-rochester.org
Tonbridge Canon M. E. Brown, Vicarage, Church St, Tonbridge TN9 1HD   *Tel:* 01732 770962
    email: mark@tonbridgeparishchurch.org.uk
Tunbridge Wells Revd Brian Senior, St Philip's Vicarage, Birken Rd, Tunbridge Wells TN2 3TE
    Tel: 01892 512071
    email: brian@bsenior.fsnet.co.uk

Founded in 1877. Hertfordshire, except for a small area in the south (LONDON) and one parish in the west (OXFORD); Bedfordshire, except for one parish in the north (ELY) and one parish in the west (OXFORD); an area of Greater London.

Population 1,752,000   Area 1,116 sq m
Full-time Stipendiary Parochial Clergy 235   Benefices 203
Parishes 336   Churches 407
www.stalbansdioc.org.uk
Overseas link dioceses: Jamaica, Guyana, NE Caribbean and Aruba (West Indies).

BISHOP (10th)
Rt Revd Dr Alan Gregory Clayton Smith, Abbey Gate House, Abbey Mill Lane, St Albans AL3 4HD   *Tel:* 01727 853305
                    Fax: 01727 846715
                    email: bishop@stalbans.anglican.org
Chaplain Capt Andrew Crooks, CA
                    Tel: 01727 853305
                    email: chaplain@stalbans.anglican.org
Secretaries Mrs Mary Handford, Mrs Claire Wood
                    email: bishop@stalbans.anglican.org

SUFFRAGAN BISHOPS
BEDFORD Rt Revd Richard Inwood, Bishop's Lodge, Bedford Rd, Cardington MK44 3SS [2003]
                    Tel: 01234 831432
                    Fax: 01234 831484
                    email: bishopbedford@stalbans.anglican.org
HERTFORD Rt Revd Paul Bayes, Bishopswood, 3 Stobarts Close, Knebworth SG3 6ND [2010]
                    email: bishophertford@stalbans.anglican.org

HONORARY ASSISTANT BISHOP
Rt Revd David John Farmbrough, St Michael Mead, 110 Village Rd, Bromham MK43 8HU [1993]   *Tel:* 01234 825042
Rt Revd Robin J. N. Smith, 7 Aysgarth Rd, Redbourn, St Albans AL3 7PJ [2002]
                    Tel: 01582 791964
Rt Revd J. W. Gladwin, The White House, 131A Marford Road, Wheathampstead, St Albans AL4 8NH   *Tel:* 01582 834223

CATHEDRAL AND ABBEY CHURCH OF SAINT ALBAN
Dean Very Revd Jeffrey John, The Deanery, Sumpter Yard, St Albans AL1 1BY [2004]
                    Tel: 01727 890202
                    Fax: 01727 890227
                    email: dean@stalbanscathedral.org.uk
Cathedral Office The Chapter House, Sumpter Yard, St Albans AL1 1BY   *Tel:* 01727 860780
                    Fax: 01727 850944
                    email: mail@stalbanscathedral.org.uk
                    Web: www.stalbanscathedral.org.uk
Canons Residentiary
Canon Stephen Lake (*Sub-Dean*), The Old Rectory, Sumpter Yard, St Albans AL1 1BY [2001]
                    Tel: 01727 890201
                    email: subdean@stalbanscathedral.org.uk

Canon Kevin Walton (*Canon Chancellor*), 2 Sumpter Yard, St Albans AL1 1BY [2008]
                    Tel: 01727 890242
                    email: canon@stalbanscathedral.org.uk
Canon John Kiddle (Officer for Mission and Development), 19 Stanbury Avenue, Watford WD17 3HW [2010]   *Tel:* 01923 460083
                    email: john.kiddle@stalbans.anglican.org
Canon Dennis Stamps (*Ministerial Development Officer*), 7 Corder Close, St Albans AL3 4NH [2002]   *Tel:* 01727 841116
                    email: dstamps@stalbans.anglican.org
Minor Canons
Young People Revd Darren Collins, Deanery Barn, Sumpter Yard, St Albans AL1 1BY [2007]
                    Tel: 01727 890206
                    email: mcyp@stalbanscathedral.org.uk
Liturgy Revd Anna Matthews, 1 The Deanery, Sumpter Yard, St Albans AL1 1BY [2006]
                    Tel: 01727 890207
                    email: mcl@stalbanscathedral.org.uk
Cathedral Administrator and Clerk to the Chapter Mr Justin Cross, Cathedral Office   *Tel:* 01727 890208
                    email: admin@stalbanscathedral.org.uk
Master of the Music Mr Andrew Lucas, 31 Abbey Mill Lane, St Albans AL3 4HA
                    Tel: 01727 890242
                    email: music@stalbanscathedral.org.uk
Assistant Master of the Music and Director of the St Albans Abbey Girls Choir Mr Tom Winpenny, 34 Orchard St, St Albans AL3 4HL
                    Tel: 01727 890245
                    email: amom@stalbanscathedral.org.uk
Cathedral Education Officer Annette Cranston, Education Centre, Sumpter Yard, St Albans AL1 1BY   *Tel:* 01727 890262
                    email: education@stalbanscathedral.org.uk
Cathedral Architect Mr Richard Griffiths
Archaeological Consultant Prof Martin Biddle

ARCHDEACONS
ST ALBANS Ven Jonathan Smith, 6 Sopwell Lane, St Albans AL1 1RR [2002]   *Tel:* 01727 847212
                    Fax: 01727 848311
                    email: archdstalbans@stalbans.anglican.org
BEDFORD Ven Paul Hughes, 17 Lansdowne Rd, Luton LU3 1EE [2003]   *Tel:* 01582 730722
                    Fax: 01582 877354
                    email: archdbedf@stalbans.anglican.org

HERTFORD Ven Trevor Jones, Glebe House, St Mary's Lane, Hertingfordbury, Hertford SG14 2LE [1997]   Tel: 01992 581629
Fax: 01992 558745
email: archdhert@stalbans.anglican.org

CONVOCATION (MEMBERS OF THE HOUSE OF CLERGY OF THE GENERAL SYNOD)
Proctors for Clergy
Revd Canon John Kiddle
Revd Richard Hibbert
Ven Jonathan Smith
Canon Stephen Lake
Revd Dr Joan Spreadbury

MEMBERS OF THE HOUSE OF LAITY OF THE GENERAL SYNOD
Mr Samuel Follett
Mr Simon Baynes
Dr Edmund Marshall
Mr William Seddon
Mr Philip McDonough
Mrs Christina Rees

DIOCESAN OFFICERS
Dioc Secretary Miss Susan Pope, Holywell Lodge, 41 Holywell Hill, St Albans AL1 1HE
Tel: 01727 854532
Fax: 01727 844469
email: mail@stalbans.anglican.org
Chancellor of Diocese His Honour the Worshipful Roger G. Kaye QC, Holywell Lodge, 41 Holywell Hill, St Albans AL1 1HD   Tel: 01727 865765
Registrar of Diocese and Bishop's Legal Secretary Mr David Cheetham (*same address*)
Surveyor Mr Alastair Woodgate, c/o 41 Holywell Hill, St Albans AL1 1HE
Tel: 01727 854516

DIOCESAN ORGANIZATIONS
Diocesan Office Holywell Lodge, 41 Holywell Hill, St Albans AL1 1HE   Tel: 01727 854532
Fax: 01727 844469
email: mail@stalbans.anglican.org
Web: www.stalbans.anglican.org

ADMINISTRATION
Dioc Synod (*Chairman, House of Clergy*) Revd Geoffrey Tickner, The Vicarage, 18 Letchmore Road, Stevenage SG1 3JD   Tel: 01438 353229
(*Chairman, House of Laity*) Mr John Wallace, 14 Church St, Leighton Buzzard LU7 7BT
Tel: 01525 375133
(*Secretary*) Miss Susan Pope, Dioc Office
Board of Finance (*Chairman*) Mr David Nye
(*Secretary*) Miss Susan Pope (*as above*)
Financial Secretary Mr Martin Bishop, Dioc Office
Estates Secretary Mrs Michèle Manders, Dioc Office
Board of Patronage Mr Jim May, Dioc Office

Designated Officers (*Joint*) Mr David Cheetham and Miss Susan Pope, Dioc Office
Mission and Pastoral Committee Mr Jim May (*as above*)
Trusts Mr Nigel Benger, Dioc Office

CHURCHES
Advisory Committee for the Care of Churches (*Chairman*) Dr Christopher Green, Dioc Office; (*Secretary*) Mr Jim May (*as above*)

EDUCATION
Dioc Education and Resources Centre Dioc Office
Tel: 01727 854532
Fax: 01727 844469
Director of Education Mr Jon Reynolds (*as above*)
School Buildings Officer Mrs Julia Creasey (*as above*)
RE Adviser Mrs Jane Chipperton (*as above*)

MINISTRY
Director of Ordinands Vacancy   Tel: 01727 833777
Ministerial Development Officer Canon Dr Dennis Stamps (*Ministerial Development Officer*), 7 Corder Close, St Albans AL3 4NH   Tel: 01727 841116
Local Ministry Officer Vacancy
Continuing Ministerial Education Officer Revd Ysmena Pentalow, Dioc Office   Tel: 01727 818154
Reader Ministry Officer Ms Lauryn Awbrey, Dioc Office   Tel: 01727 818154
Assistant Director of Ordinands Revd Sue Groom, The Vicarage, 65 Church Street, Langford, Biggleswade SG18 9QT   Tel: 01462 700248
Board of Readers' Work Mrs Margaret Tinsley, 145 The Ridgeway, St Albans AL4 9XA
Tel: 01727 859528
Mr Richard Osborn, 41 Tiverton Rd, Potters Bar EN6 5HX   Tel: 01707 657491
Mr Ron Upton, 65 Nunnery Lane, Luton LU3 1XB   Tel: 01582 596208
Youth Officer Mr David Green, Dioc Office
Children's Work Adviser, Bedfordshire Revd Ruth Pyke, Dioc Office
Hertfordshire Revd Vanessa Cato, Dioc Office

MISSIONARY AND ECUMENICAL
Ecumenical Officers
Bedfordshire Vacancy
Hertfordshire Revd Christopher Futcher, Rectory, 9 Rothamsted Ave, Harpenden AL5 2DD
Tel: 01582 712202
Board for Church and Society Mr Simon Best (*Chairman*), The Hollies, Kimpton Rd, Peters Green LU2 9QW
Council for Partnership in World Mission Revd Christopher Briggs, Lawrence Cottage, 2 Hailey Lane, Hertford SG13 7NX   Tel: 01992 462922
Workplace Ministry Revd Michael Shaw, 41 Holywell Hill, St Albans AL1 1HE
Tel: 01727 869461

PRESS AND PUBLICATIONS

Dioc Communications Officer Mr Arun Kataria, Dioc Office   *Tel:* 01727 818110
Fax: 01727 844469
email: comms@stalbans.anglican.org
Editor of Dioc Directory Miss Susan Pope (*as above*)
Dioc Leaflet Mrs Claudia Brown (*as above*)

DIOCESAN RECORD OFFICES

County Hall, Hertford SG13 8DE *Tel:* 01992 555105 (*For diocesan records and parish records for St Albans and Hertford archdeaconries*)
County Hall, Bedford MK42 9AP *County Archivist* Mr Kevin Ward *Tel:* 01234 63222 Ext 277 (*For parish records for Bedford archdeaconry*)

SOCIAL RESPONSIBILITY

Officer for Mission and Development Canon John Kiddle, Dioc Office   *Tel:* 01727 851748
Social Responsibility Officer Revd Dr Andrew Coleby, Dioc Office   *Tel:* 01727 851748

STEWARDSHIP

Stewardship Development Officer Mr Geoff Fletcher, Dioc Office   *Tel:* 01727 854532

RURAL DEANS
ARCHDEACONRY OF ST ALBANS

Aldenham (*Provisional date for dissolution of Aldenham Deanery January 1 2011*) Revd Geoff Buckler, The Rectory, High St, Bushey, WD23 1BD   *Tel:* 020 8950 1546
Berkhamsted Revd Dr M Bowie, The Rectory, Rectory Lane, Berkhamsted HP4 2DH
Tel: 01442 864194
Hemel Hempstead Revd David Lawson, St Mary's Vicarage, 7 Belswain's Lane, Hemel Hempstead HP3 9PN   *Tel:* 01442 261610
Hitchin Revd Michael Roden, Church House, Churchyard, Hitchen SH5 1HP
Tel: 01462 451758
Rickmansworth Revd Gavin Collins, Christ Church Vicarage, Chorleywood Common, Rickmansworth WD3 5SG   *Tel:* 01923 282149
St Albans Revd David Ridgeway, St Stephen's Vicarage, 14 Watling Rd, St Albans AL1 2PX
Tel: 01727 862598
Watford Revd D J Middlebrook, St Luke's Vicarage, Devereux Drive, Watford WD17 3DD
Tel: 01923 246161
Wheathampstead Revd John Green, Vicarage, 50 Trowley Hill Rd, Flamstead, St Albans AL3 8EE
Tel: 01582 842040

ARCHDEACONRY OF BEDFORD

Ampthill Revd M. F. J. Bradley, 26 Dew Pond Rd, Flitwick, Bedford MK45 1RT   *Tel:* 01525 712369
Bedford Canon Dr C. Dent, St Andrew's Vicarage, 1 St Edmond Rd, Bedford MK40 2NQ
Tel: 01234 354234
Biggleswade Revd D. G. Williams, Rectory, High St, Sandy SG19 1AQ   *Tel:* 01767 680512
Dunstable Revd R. J. Andrews, Rectory, 8 Furness Avenue, Dunstable LU6 3BN   *Tel:* 01582 703271
Elstow Revd S. Liley, Vicarage, Green Lane, Clapham, Bedford MK41 6ER
Tel and *Fax:* 01234 352814
Luton Canon Stephen Purvis, St Luke's Vicarage, High St, Leagrave, Luton LU4 9JY
Tel: 01582 572737
Sharnbrook Revd David Mason, 2a Devon Rd, Bedford MK40 3DF   *Tel:* 01234 309737
Shefford Revd J. A. Harper, Rectory, Church Rd, Meppershall, Shefford SG17 5NA
Tel: 01462 813334

ARCHDEACONRY OF HERTFORD

Barnet Revd Richard Watson, Rectory, 136 Church Hill Rd, East Barnet EN4 8XD
Tel: 020 8383 3840
Bishop's Stortford Revd Christopher Boulton, The Rectory, High St, Much Hadham SG10 6DA
Tel: 01279 842609
Buntingford Revd Lady Carol Kimberley, Vicarage, Great Hormead, Buntingford SG9 0NT
Tel: 01763 289258
Cheshunt Revd Carol Selby, St Clement's House, 44 Hillview Gardens, Cheshunt EN8 0PE
Tel: 01992 625098
Welwyn and Hatfield (*Joint Rural Dean*) Revd Richard E. Pyke, Rectory, 1 Fore St, Hatfield AL9 5AN   *Tel* and *Fax:* 01707 262072
Welwyn and Hatfield (*Joint Rural Dean*) Canon Carl Garner, Rectory, 354 Knightsfield, Welwyn Garden City AL8 7NG   *Tel:* 01707 326677
Hertford and Ware (*Joint Rural Dean*) Canon Pauline Higham, Hertford Hundred House, 1 Little Berkhamsted Lane, Little Berkhamsted Hertford SG13 8LU   *Tel:* 01707 875940
Hertford and Ware (*Joint Rural Dean*) Revd N. L. Sharp, Little Amwell Vicarage, 17 Barclay Close, Hertford Heath, Hertford SG13 7RW
Tel: 01992 589147
Stevenage Revd Geoffrey Tickner, Vicarage, 18 Letchmore Rd, Stevenage SG1 3JD
Tel: 01438 353229

DIOCESE OF ST EDMUNDSBURY AND IPSWICH

Founded in 1914. Suffolk, except for a small area in the north-east (NORWICH); one parish in Essex.

Population 635,000   Area 1,439 sq m
Full-time Stipendiary Parochial Clergy 127   Benefices 130
Parishes 446   Churches 477
www.stedmundsbury.anglican.org
Overseas link dioceses: Hassalt (Belgium),
Kagera (Tanzania).

BISHOP (9th)
Rt Revd Nigel Stock, Bishop's House, 4 Park Rd, Ipswich IP1 3ST [2007]   *Tel:* 01473 252829
Fax: 01473 232552
email:
bishop.nigel@stedmundsbury.anglican.org
[Nigel St Edm and Ipswich]
Bishop's Chaplain Revd Mary Sokanovic (*same address and telephone*)
email: mary@stedmundsbury.anglican.org
Bishop's Secretary Mrs Denise Rudland (*same address and telephone*)
email: denise@stedmundsbury.anglican.org
Assistant Secretary Mrs Julia Venmore-Rowland (*same address and telephone*)
email: julia@stedmundsbury.anglican.org

SUFFRAGAN BISHOP
DUNWICH Rt Revd Clive Young, 28 Westerfield Rd, Ipswich IP4 2UJ [1999]   *Tel:* 01473 222276
Fax: 01473 210303
email: bishop.clive@stedmundsbury.anglican.org
Bishop's Secretary Mrs Sheila Burnham (*same address*)
email: sheila@stedmundsbury.anglican.org

CATHEDRAL CHURCH OF ST JAMES AND ST EDMUND, BURY ST EDMUNDS
Dean Very Revd Dr Frances Ward, The Deanery, Bury St Edmunds IP33 1RS [2010]
Tel: 01284 748722
email: dean@stedscathedral.org
Cathedral Office Abbey House, Angel Hill, Bury St Edmunds IP33 1LS   *Tel:* 01284 748720
Fax: 01284 768655
email: cathedral.secretary@stedscathedral.org
Canons Residentiary
Precentor Canon Michael Hampel, 1 Abbey Precincts, Bury St Edmunds IP33 1RS [2004]
Tel: 01284 748724
email: precentor@stedscathedral.org
Canon Pastor Canon Matthew Vernon, Cathedral Office [2009]   *Tel:* 01284 701472
email: canon.pastor@stedscathedral.org
Canon Theologian Canon Christopher Burdon, 3 Crown St, Bury St Edmunds IP33 1QX [2007]
Tel: 01284 706813
email: canon.theologian@stedscathedral.org

Administrator Mr Keith Huddart, Cathedral Office   *Tel:* 01284 748728
email:
cathedral.administrator@stedscathedral.org
Visitor Officer Mrs Margaret Lambeth, Cathedral Office   *Tel:* 01284 748721
email: visitor.officer@stedscathedral.org
Public Relations Manager Mrs Sarah Friswell, Cathedral Office   *Tel:* 01284 748726
email: pr.manager@stedscathedral.org
Children's Education Officer Mrs Helen Woodroffe, Cathedral Office   *Tel:* 01284 747467
email: discoverycentre@stedscathedral.org
Director of Music Mr James Thomas, Cathedral Office   *Tel:* 01284 748379
email: dom@stedscathedral.org
Assistant Director of Music and Arts Officer Mr David Humphreys, Cathedral Office
Tel: 01284 748737
email: adom@stedscathedral.org
Head Verger Mr Duncan Withers, Cathedral Office
Tel: 01284 748729
email: head.verger@stedscathedral.org

ARCHDEACONS
SUDBURY Ven David Jenkins, Sudbury Lodge, Stanningfield Rd, Great Whelnetham, Bury St Edmunds IP30 0TL [2006]
Tel and *Fax:* 01284 386942
email:
archdeacon.david@stedmundsbury.anglican.org
SUFFOLK Ven Judy Hunt, Glebe House, The Street, Ashfield cum Thorpe, Stowmarket IP14 6LX [1994]   *Tel:* 01728 685497
Fax: 01728 685969
email: archdeacon.judy@
stedmundsbury.anglican.org

CONVOCATION (MEMBERS OF THE HOUSE OF CLERGY OF THE GENERAL SYNOD)
Proctors for Clergy
Revd Canon Jonathan Alderton-Ford
Revd Andrew Dotchin
Revd Tony Redman

MEMBERS OF THE HOUSE OF LAITY OF THE GENERAL SYNOD
Mr Tim Allen

Mrs Margaret Condick
Mr Peter Smith

DIOCESAN OFFICERS

Dioc Secretary Mr Nicholas Edgell, Diocesan Office, St Nicholas Centre, 4 Cutler St, Ipswich IP1 1UQ   *Tel:* 01473 298500
Fax: 01473 298501
email: dbf@stedmundsbury.anglican.org
Chancellor of Diocese The Honourable Sir Justice Blofeld, 20–32 Museum St, Ipswich IP1 1HZ
Registrar of Diocese and Bishop's Legal Secretary Mr James Hall, 20–32 Museum St, Ipswich IP1 1HZ
Tel: 01473 232300
Fax: 01473 230524
email: james-hall@birketts.co.uk

DIOCESAN ORGANIZATIONS

Diocesan Office St Nicholas Centre, 4 Cutler St, Ipswich IP1 1UQ   *Tel:* 01473 298500
Fax: 01473 298501
email: dbf@stedmundsbury.anglican.org

ADMINISTRATION

Dioc Secretary Mr Nicholas Edgell, Dioc Office
Deputy Dioc Secretary Miss Nicola Andrews, Dioc Office
Assistant Dicoesan Secretary Mr Gavin Stone, Dioc Office
Assistant Diocesan Secretary Canon Graham Hedger, Dioc Office
Dioc Synod (*Chairman, House of Clergy*) Revd Ian Morgan, The Rectory, 74 Ancaster Road, Ipswich IP2 9AJ   *Tel:* 01473 601895
(*Chairman, House of Laity*) Canon Barbara Rowe, The Maltings, Honey Lane, Leavenheath, Colchester CO6 4NY   *Tel:* 01206 262875
(*Secretary*) Mr Nicholas Edgell, Dioc Office
(*Diocesan Secretary and Chief Executive*) Mr Nicholas Edgell (*as above*)
Deputy Secretary Miss Nicola Andrews
Pastoral and DAC Secretary Mr James Halsall
Diocesan Accountant Mrs Katy Reade
Dioc Surveyor Mr Christopher Clarke, Clarke & Simpson, Well Close Square, Framlingham IP13 9DU   *Tel:* 01728 724200
Designated Officer Canon Graham Hedger (*as above*)

CHURCHES

Advisory Committee for the Care of Churches (*Chairman*) Mr Tim Allen, Bell House, Quay St, Orford, Woodbridge IP12 2NU   *Tel:* 01394 450789
(*Secretary*) Mr James Halsall (*as above*)

COUNSELLING

Adviser in Pastoral Care and Counselling Canon Harry Edwards, Rectory, Marlesford, Woodbridge IP13 0AT   *Tel:* 01728 746747
email: harry@psalm23.demon.co.uk
Bishop's Adviser on Exorcism and Deliverance The Bishop of Dunwich

MINISTRY

Accredited Ministry Group (*Chairman*) The Bishop of Dunwich (*as above*)
Vocations Adviser (*Sudbury*) Revd Katharine King, Vicarage, Bures CO8 5AA   *Tel:* 01787 227315
email: katharine@rlcking.freeserve.co.uk
Vocations Adviser (*Suffolk*) Revd Betty Mockford, 10 Castle Brooks, Framlingham IP13 9SF
Tel: 01728 724193
Dioc Director of Ordinands Canon Mark Sanders, Rectory, Woodbridge Rd, Grundisburgh, Woodbridge, IP13 6UF   *Tel:* 01473 735182
Dioc Director of Continuing Ministerial Education 1–4 Canon Mark Sanders (*as above*)
Continuing Ministerial Education Officer Revd Chris Burdon
Principal of Dioc Ministry Scheme Ms Christine Amjad-Ali, Abbey House, 30 Angel Hill, Bury St Edmunds IP33 1LS   *Tel:* 01284 749435
email: christine@stedmundsbury.anglican.org
Vice-Principal, Dioc Ministry Scheme Revd David Herrick, Abbey House, 30 Angel Hill, Bury St Edmunds IP33 1LS   *Tel:* 01284 749435
email: davidh@stedmundsbury.anglican.org
Lay Education and Training Adviser Miss Elizabeth Moore, 7 Maltings Garth, Thurston, Bury St Edmunds IP31 3PP   *Tel:* 01359 233050
email: elizabeth@stedmundsbury.anglican.org
Warden of Readers Canon Lionel Simpkins, St Augustine's Vicarage, 2 Bucklesham Rd, Ipswich IP3 8TJ   *Tel:* 01473 728654
Dioc Youth Development Adviser Mr Neil Williams, Dioc Office   *Tel and Fax*: 01473 298522
email: neil@stedmundsbury.anglican.org
Dioc Children's Officer and Educational Officer of the Cathedral Mrs Helen Woodroffe, The Discovery Centre, St Edmundsbury Cathedral, Angel Hill, Bury St Edmunds IP33 1LS
Tel and Fax: 01284 748731
email: helen@discoveryc.fsnet.co.uk
Dioc Widows Officers Revd John and Mrs Helen Elliston, 27 Wyvern Rd, Ravenswood, Ipswich IP3 9TJ   *Tel:* 01473 726617
Clergy Retirement Officer Canon Cedric Catton, 60 Sexton Meadows, Bury St Edmunds IP33 2SB
Tel: 01284 749429
email: moretee@vicar1.freeserve.co.uk

SCHOOLS

Dioc Director of Education and Schools Officer Mrs Jane Sheat, Dioc Office   *Tel:* 01473 298570
Dioc Schools Adviser Mrs Helen Matter, Dioc Office

LITURGICAL

Chairman The Bishop of St Edmundsbury and Ipswich
Secretary Canon David Lowe, New Vicarage, 54 Princess Rd, Felixstowe IP11 7PL
Tel: 01394 284226

MISSION AND PUBLIC AFFAIRS

Bishop's Policy and Liaison Officer Canon Graham Hedger, Dioc Office   *Tel:* 01473 277042
email: graham@stedmundsbury.anglican.org

Community Affairs Adviser Mrs Kathleen Ben Rabha, Dioc Office
Agricultural Chaplain Canon Sally Fogden, Meadow Farm, Sapiston, Bury St Edmunds IP31 1RX   Tel: 01359 268923
          email: sallyfogden@tiscali.co.uk
Church Buildings & Tourism Officer Ms Marion Welham Dioc Office   Tel: 01502 578154
          email: marion@stedmundsbury.anglican.org
Bishop's Ecumenical Adviser and Inter-Faith Adviser Canon Peter Mortimer, 20 Leggart Drive, Bramford, Ipswich IP8 4ET   Tel: 01473 747419
          email: revpeter@fish.co.uk
Chaplain to the Deaf Community Vacancy
Parish Resources Adviser Canon Jim Pendorf, Dioc Office   Tel: 01473 298504
          email: jim@stedmundsbury.anglican.org

COMMUNICATIONS

Dioc Communications Director Mr Nick Clarke, Dioc Office   Tel: 01473 298521
          07779 780030 (Mobile)
          email: nick@stedmundsbury.anglican.org

DIOCESAN RECORD OFFICES

77 Raingate St, Bury St Edmunds IP33 2AR Tel: 01284 352352 Ext 2352 (For parish records for Sudbury and Hadleigh deaneries)
Gatacre Rd, Ipswich IP1 2LQ Tel: 01473 264541 (For parish records for Ipswich and Suffolk archdeaconries)
The Central Library, Lowestoft NR32 1DR Tel: 01502 405357 (For parish records for NE Suffolk parishes)

SPIRITUALITY

Dioc Spiritual Director for Cursillo Revd Mary Sokanovic, Side View, School Rd, Coddenham, Ipswich IP6 9PS   Tel: 01449 760527
          email: marysok@tiscali.co.uk
Lay Director for Cursillo Mr Paul Thacker, Chapel Cottage, 79 Chedburgh Rd, Chevington, Bury St Edmunds IP29 5QU   Tel: 01284 850384
          email: pa.thacker@btinternet.com

RURAL DEANS
ARCHDEACONRY OF IPSWICH

Bosmere Revd Diane Williams, 10 Meadow View, Needham Market, Ipswich IP6 8RH
          Tel: 01449 720316
          email: diane.rev@btinternet.com
Colneys Canon Geoffrey Grant, Rectory, Nacton, Ipswich IP10 0HY   Tel: 01473 659232
          email: canon@nildram.co.uk
Hadleigh Very Revd Martin Thrower, The Deanery, Church Street, Hadleigh IP7 5DT
          Tel: 01473 822218
          email: martin.thrower@btinternet.com
Ipswich Revd Ian Morgan, Rectory, 74 Ancaster Rd, Ipswich IP2 2LE   Tel: 01473 601895
          email: ianmorgan@aol.com

Samford Revd Brin Singleton, The Rectory, Days Road, Capel St Mary, Ipswich IP9 2LE
          Tel: 01473 310759
          email: reverend.singleton@tiscali.co.uk
Stowmarket Revd Barbara Bilston, Boy's Hall, Ward Green, Old Newton, Stowmarket IP14 4EY
          Tel: 01449 781253
          email: b.b.bilston@open.ac.uk
Woodbridge Revd Pauline Stentiford, Sheepstor, The Street, Boyton, Woodbridge IP12 3LH
          Tel: 01394 411469
          email: pauline.stentiford@btopenworld.com

ARCHDEACONRY OF SUDBURY

Clare Revd Ian Finn, Vicarage, 10 Hopton Rise, Haverhill CB9 7FS   Tel: 01440 708768
          email: ian.finn1@btinternet.com
Ixworth Revd John Fulton, Rectory, Church Lane, Hepworth, Diss IP22 2PU   Tel: 01359 250285
          email: jwfulton@ukonline.co.uk
Lavenham Revd Simon Hill, Rectory, Howe Lane, Cockfield, Bury St Edmunds IP30 0HA
          Tel: 01284 828599
          email: mlima001@btinternet.com
Mildenhall Revd Stephen Mitchell, All Saints Vicarage, The Street, Gazeley, Newmarket CB8 8RB   Tel: 01638 552630
          email: smitch4517@aol.com
Sudbury Revd Robin King, Vicarage, Bures CO8 5AA   Tel: 01787 227315
          email: robin@ricking.freeserve.co.uk
Thingoe Revd Alan Gates, The Vicarage, Church Rd, Great Barton, Bury St Edmunds IP31 2QR
          Tel: 01284 787274
          email: alan.gates@virgin.net

ARCHDEACONRY OF SUFFOLK

Beccles and South Elmham Revd Paul Nelson, Rectory, Molls Lane, Brampton, Beccles NR34 8DB   Tel: 01502 575859
          email: hedgeparson@tiscali.co.uk
Halesworth Revd Paul Nelson, Rectory, Molls Lane, Brampton, Beccles NR34 8DB
          Tel: 01502 575859
          email: hedgeparson@tiscali.co.uk
Hartismere Revd Andrew Mitcham, Vicarage, 41 Castle Street, Eye IP23 7AW   Tel: 01379 870277
          email: andrew@redmail.co.uk
Hoxne Revd Fiona Newton, The Vicarage, 15 Noyes Avenue, Laxfield, Woodbridge IP13 8EB
          Tel: 01986 798266
          email: fionanewton@rmplc.co.uk
Loes Revd Graham Owen, Rectory, Framlingham, Woodbridge IP13 9BJ
          Tel: 01728 621082
          email: gowen.mowen@talktalk.net
Saxmundham Revd Nigel Hartley, Vicarage, Church Walk, Aldeburgh, Saxmundham IP15 5DU   Tel: 01728 452223
          email: nigel.hartley@btinternet.com

DIOCESE OF SALISBURY

Founded in 1075, formerly Sherborne (AD 705) and Ramsbury (AD 909). Wiltshire, except for the northern quarter (BRISTOL); Dorset, except for an area in the east (WINCHESTER); a small area of Hampshire; a parish in Devon.

Population 893,000   Area 2,046 sq m
Full-time Stipendiary Parochial Clergy 193   Benefices 161
Parishes 453   Churches 575
www.salisbury.anglican.org
Overseas link provinces and dioceses: Episcopal Church of the Sudan, Evreux (France).

BISHOP (77th)
Vacancy South Canonry, 71 The Close, Salisbury
SP1 2ER [1993]   *Tel:* 01722 334031
Fax: 01722 413112
email: dsarum@salisbury.anglican.org
[David Sarum]

AREA BISHOPS
SHERBORNE Rt Revd Dr Graham Kings, Sherborne
Office, St Nicholas' Church Centre, 30 Wareham
Road, Corfe Mullen, Wimborne BH21 3LE
Tel: 01202 659427
Fax: 01202 691418
email: sherborne.office@salisbury.anglican.org
RAMSBURY Rt Revd Stephen David Conway,
Ramsbury Office, Southbroom House, London
Rd, Devizes SN10 1LT [2006]   *Tel:* 01380 729808
Fax: 01380 848247
email: ramsbury.office@salisbury.anglican.org

CATHEDRAL CHURCH OF THE BLESSED VIRGIN MARY
Dean Very Revd June Osborne, The Deanery, 7
The Close, Salisbury SP1 2EF [2004]
Dean's Office 6 The Close, Salisbury SP1 2EF
Tel: 01722 555110
Fax: 01722 555155
email: thedean@salcath.co.uk
Web: www.salisburycathedral.org.uk
Canons Residentiary
Precentor Canon Jeremy Davies, Hungerford
Chantry, 54 The Close, Salisbury, SP1 2EL [1985]
Tel: 01722 555179 (Home)
Office Dept of Liturgy and Music, Ladywell, 33
The Close, Salisbury, SP1 2EJ   *Tel:* 01722 555125
Fax: 01722 555117
email: precentor@salcath.co.uk
Chancellor Canon Edward Probert, 24 The Close,
Salisbury SP1 2EH [2004]   *Tel:* 01722 555193
Office: Chapter Office, 6 The Close, Salisbury SP1
2EF   *Tel:* 01722 555189
Fax: 01722 555109
email: chancellor@salcath.co.uk
Treasurer Canon Mark Bonney, 23 The Close,
Salisbury SP1 2EH [2004]   *Tel:* 01722 555177
Office: Chapter Office, 6 The Close (*as above*)
Tel: 01722 555186
Fax: 01722 555109
email: treasurer@salcath.co.uk

Vicar of the Close Revd Charles Mitchell-Innes, 32
The Close, Salisbury SP1 2EH   *Tel:* 01722 555192
email: voc@salcath.co.uk
Cathedral Associate Priest Revd Maggie
Guillebaud   *Tel:* 01722 555198
email: m.guillebaud@salcath.co.uk
Chapter Clerk Brigadier Mark Elcomb, Chapter
Office, 6 The Close, Salisbury SP1 2EF
Tel: 01722 555105
Fax: 01722 555109
email: chapterclerk@salcath.co.uk
Visitors Dept Mr David Coulthard, Ladywell, 33
The Close, Salisbury SP1 2EJ   *Tel:* 01722 555120
Fax: 01722 555116
email: d.coulthard@salcath.co.uk
Education Centre Mrs Susan Hayter (*Administrator*), Wren Hall, 56c The Close, Salisbury SP1
2EL   *Tel:* 01722 555180
email: wrenhall@salcath.co.uk
Director of Music Mr David Halls, Dept of
Liturgy and Music (*as above*)   *Tel:* 01722 555127
email: d.halls@salcath.co.uk

ARCHDEACONS
SHERBORNE Ven Paul Taylor, Aldhelm House,
West Stafford, Dorchester DT2 8AB [2004]
Tel: 01305 269751
email: adsherborne@salisbury.anglican.org
DORSET Ven Stephen Waine, 28 Merriefield Drive,
Broadstone, BH18 8BP   *Tel:* 01202 659427
Fax: 01202 691418
email: addorset@salisbury.anglican.org
WILTS Ven John Wraw, Southbroom House, London
Rd, Devizes SN10 1LT [2004]
Tel: 01380 729808
Fax: 01380 848247
email: adwilts@salisbury.anglican.org
SARUM Ven Alan Jeans, Herbert House, 118 Lower
Rd, Lower Bemerton, Salisbury SP2 9NW [2003]
Tel: 01380 729808
Fax: 01380 828247
email: adsarum@salisbury.anglican.org

CONVOCATION (MEMBERS OF THE HOUSE OF CLERGY OF THE GENERAL SYNOD)
Proctors for Clergy
Canon Jane Charman
Canon Richard Franklin

Canon Nigel LLoyd
Ven Alan Jeans
Revd Christopher Strain

MEMBERS OF THE HOUSE OF LAITY OF THE GENERAL SYNOD
Mr Paul Boyd-Lee
Dr Ian Bromilow
Mrs Christine Corteen
Mr Christopher Fielden
Mr Robert Key
Mrs Deborah Isaac

DIOCESAN OFFICERS
Dioc Secretary Mrs Lucinda Herklots, Church House, Crane St, Salisbury SP1 2QB
Tel: 01722 411922
Fax: 01722 411990
Chancellor of Diocese His Honour Judge Samuel Wiggs, c/o Dioc Office
Registrar of Diocese and Bishop's Legal Secretary Mr Andrew Johnson, Minster Chambers, 42–44 Castle St, Salisbury SP1 3TX
Tel: 01722 411141
Fax: 01722 411566

DIOCESAN ORGANIZATIONS
Diocesan Office Church House, Crane St, Salisbury SP1 2QB
Tel: 01722 411922
Fax: 01722 411990
email: enquiries@salisbury.anglican.org
Web: www.salisbury.anglican.org

ADMINISTRATION
Dioc Secretary Mrs Lucinda Herklots, Dioc Office
Deputy Dioc Secretary Mr Richard Trahair, Dioc Office
Dioc Synod (Chairman, House of Clergy) Canon Paul Richardson, Vicarage, Bitham Lane, Westbury BA13 3BU
Tel: 01373 822209
(Chairman, House of Laity) Vacancy
(Secretary) Mrs Lucinda Herklots, Dioc Office
Stewardship and Resources Officer Mr Geoff Taylor, Dioc Office
Board of Finance (Chairman) Mr Gil Williams, Princes Farm, Ryme Intrinseca, Sherborne DT9 6JX
Tel: 01935 873580
(Secretary) Mrs Lucinda Herklots, Dioc Office
Diocesan Surveyor Mr John Carley, Dioc Office
Tel: 01722 411933
Pastoral Committee (Secretary) Mrs Christine Romano, Dioc Office
Designated Officer Mr Andrew Johnson, Minster Chambers, 42–44 Castle St, Salisbury SP1 3TX
Tel: 01722 411141

CHURCHES
Advisory Committee for the Care of Churches (Chairman) Cathedral Treasurer; *(Secretary)* Mrs Sue Cannings, Dioc Office
Tel: 01722 438654
Re-Use of Closed Churches Working Group and Furnishings Officer Mr Richard Trahair *(as above)*
Tel: 01722 411933

Ringers' Association Mr Anthony Lovell-Wood, 11 Brook Close, Tisbury, Salisbury
Tel: 01747 871121

EDUCATION
Director of Education Mr Chris Shepperd, Diocesan Education Centre, Devizes Rd, Salisbury SP2 9LY
Tel: 01722 428420
Fax: 01722 328010
Finance Mr Peter Kidman *(same address)*
Tel: 01722 428421
Buildings Officer Mrs Catherine Hannell *(same address) Tel:* 01722 428426
Advisers for School Development Mrs Carole McCormack, Mrs Anne Davey, Mr Mark Stratta *(same address)*
Youth and Children's Officers Youth and Children's Ministry Team *(same address)*
Tel: 01722 428427

MINISTRY
Director of Learning for Discipleship and Ministry Canon Jane Charman, Dioc Office
Tel: 01722 411944
email: ministry@salisbury.anglican.org
Co-ordinator for Vocations and Spirituality, Revd Ian Cowley, Dioc Office
Director of Ordinands Ven Alan Jeans, Dioc Office
Co-ordinator for Learning for Discipleship Revd Dr Stella Wood, Dioc Office
Co-ordinator of Locally Deployable Ordained Ministry Vacancy, Dioc Office
Adviser for Women's Ministry Revd Vanda Perrett
Tel: 01672 851746

AREA RESOURCE TEAMS
Liturgical Canon Mark Bonney, Loders, 23 The Close, Salisbury SP1 2EH
Tel: 01722 444177
Social Responsibility (Wilts.) Vacancy *(Dorset) (also Ecumenical)* Mr Colin Brady, 23 Bagber Farm Cottages, Milton Rd, Milborne St Andrew, Blandford Forum DT11 0LB
Tel: 01258 839140
Ecumenical Officer Vacancy
County Ecumenical Officer (Wiltshire) Revd Kate Sax, The Former Vicarage, 1a The Weir, Edington, Westbury BA13 4PX
Tel: 01380 831239
(Dorset) Mrs Val Potter, 22 Durbeville Close, Dorchester DT1 2JT
Tel: 01305 264416
Urban Priority Officer Revd Dick Saunders, St Philip's Vicarage, 41 Moores Ave, Kinson, Bournemouth BH11 8AT
Tel: 01202 581135
Officers for Rural Areas (Ramsbury Episcopal Area) Vacancy
(Sherborne Episcopal Area) (also Dioc Environmental Officer) Revd Dr Jean Coates, Rectory, Main St, Broadmayne, Dorchester CT2 8EB
Tel: 01305 852435
European Affairs Officer Canon Richard Franklin, Holy Trinity Vicarage, 7 Glebe Close, Weymouth, DT44 9RL
Tel: 01305 760354
Chaplain to Travelling People Revd Roger Redding, Vicarage, Ebbesbourne Wake, Salisbury SP5 5JL
Tel: 01722 780408

International Development and World Mission
Canon Ian Woodward, Vicarage, West St, Bere
Regis, Wareham BH20 7HQ   *Tel:* 01929 471262

PRESS AND PUBLICATIONS
Communications Coordinator Mr Michael Ford,
Dioc Office   *Tel:* 01722 438650
                                        07770 961629 (Mobile)
        email: comms@salisbury.anglican.org
Editor of 'The Sarum Link' Mrs Mary Tapping,
Dioc Office   *Tel:* 01722 438652
Editor of Dioc Directory Mrs Miriam Darke, Dioc
Office   *Tel:* 01722 411922
Editor of Dioc Handbook Dioc Secretary (*as above*)

DIOCESAN RECORD OFFICES
Diocesan Record Office and Wiltshire Parochial
Records, Wiltshire and Swindon History
Centre, Cocklebury Rd, Chippenham SN15 3QN
Tel: 01249 705500 and ask for the Duty Archivist
(*For diocesan records and parishes in the arch-
deaconries of Wiltshire and Sarum*)
Dorset History Centre, Bridport Rd, Dorchester
DT1 1RP *County Archivist* Mr Hugh Jacques
Tel: 01305 250550 (*For parishes in the County of
Dorset*)
Hampshire Record Office, Sussex Street, Win-
chester SO23 8TH *Tel:* 01962 846154 (*For the few
Salisbury diocesan parishes situated in the County
of Hampshire*)

RURAL DEANS
ARCHDEACONRY OF SHERBORNE
Dorchester Revd Janet Smith, Vicarage, Mill Lane,
Charminster, Dorchester DT2 9QP
                                        Tel: 01305 262477
Lyme Bay Revd Bob Thorn, Rectory, Church
Street, Burton Bradstock, Bridport DT6 4QS
                                        Tel: 01308 898799
Sherborne Canon Henry Pearson, Rectory, Trent,
Sherborne DT9 4SL   *Tel:* 01935 851049
Weymouth Revd Ian Hobbs, 39 Icen Rd,
Weymouth DT3 5JL   *Tel:* 01305 785553

ARCHDEACONRY OF DORSET
Blackmore Vale Revd David Seymour, Vicarage,
Church St, Sturminster, Newton DT10 1DB
                                        Tel: 01258 471276
Milton and Blandford Revd Simon Everett,
Vicarage, Iwerne Minster, Blandford Forum
DT11 8NF   *Tel:* 01747 811291
Poole Revd Jean de Garis, Vicarage, Lytchett
Minster, Poole BH16 6JQ   *Tel:* 01202 622253
Purbeck Revd John Wood, Rectory, 12 Church
Hill, Swanage BH19 1HU   *Tel:* 01929 422916
Wimborne Canon John Holbrook, Rectory, 17
King St, Wimborne BH21 1DZ *Tel:* 01202 882340

ARCHDEACONRY OF SARUM
Alderbury Revd Vanda Perrett, Rectory, High St,
Porton, Salisbury SP4 0LH *Tel:* 01980 610305
Chalke Canon David Henley, Rectory, Broad
Chalke, Salisbury SP5 5DS *Tel:* 01722 780262
Salisbury Revd David Linaker, Little Bower,
Campbell Rd, Salisbury SP1 3BG
                                        Tel: 01722 322537
Stonehenge Revd Mark Zammitt, Rectory, Church
Street, Durrington, Salisbury SP4 8AL
                                        Tel: 01980 653953

ARCHDEACONRY OF WILTS
Bradford Revd Andrew Evans, Rectory, Ham
Green, Holt, Trowbridge BA14 6PZ
                                        Tel: 01225 782289
Calne Revd Thomas Woodhouse, Vicarage, Glebe
Rd, Wootton Bassett SN4 7DU
                                        Tel: 01793 854302
Devizes Canon Paul Richardson, Rectory, 39 Long
Street, Devizes SN10 1NS   *Tel:* 01380 723705
Heytesbury Revd John Tomlinson, Rectory, 1
Bests Lane, Sutton Veny, Warminster BA12 7AU
                                        Tel: 01985 840014
Marlborough Revd Andrew Studdert-Kennedy,
Rectory, Rawlingswell Lane, Marlborough SN8
1AU   *Tel:* 01672 512357
Pewsey Revd Nicolas Leigh-Hunt, Rectory, 5
Eastcourt, Burbage, Marlborough SN8 3AG
                                        Tel: 01672 810258

DIOCESE OF SHEFFIELD

Founded in 1914. Sheffield; Rotherham; Doncaster, except for a few parishes in the south-east (SOUTHWELL AND NOTTINGHAM); an area of North Lincolnshire; an area of south-eastern Barnsley; a small area of the East Riding of Yorkshire.

Population 1,196,000   Area 576 sq m
Full-time Stipendiary Parochial Clergy 141   Benefices 153
Parishes 173   Churches 212
www.sheffield.anglican.org
Overseas link dioceses: Argentina, Hattingen Witten (Germany).

BISHOP
Rt Revd Dr Steven Croft
Bishopscroft, Snaithing Lane, Sheffield S10 3LG
Tel: 0114 230 2170
Fax: 0114 263 0110
email: bishop@bishopofsheffield.anglican.org
Domestic Chaplain Revd Canon Geoffrey Harbord, Bishopscroft   *Tel:* 0114 230 2170
Fax: 0114 263 0110
email: geoffrey.harbord@sheffield.anglican.org

SUFFRAGAN BISHOP
DONCASTER Rt Revd Cyril Ashton, 3 Farrington Court, Wickersley, Rotherham S66 1JQ [1999]
Tel: 01709 730130
Fax: 01709 730230
email: bishop.cyril@sheffield.anglican.org

HONORARY ASSISTANT BISHOPS
Rt Revd Kenneth Harold Pillar, 75 Dobcroft Rd, Millhouses, Sheffield S7 2LS [1989]
Tel: 0114 236 7902
Rt Revd Martyn William Jarrett, 3 North Lane, Roundhay, Leeds LS8 2QJ [2002]
Tel: 0113 265 4280
Fax: 0113 265 4281
email: bishop-of-beverley@aol
3-north-lane.fsnet.co.uk

CATHEDRAL CHURCH OF ST PETER AND ST PAUL
Dean Very Revd Peter Bradley, The Cathedral, Church St, Sheffield S1 1HA   *Tel:* 0114 263 6063
email: dean@sheffield-cathedral.org.uk
Cathedral Office Sheffield Cathedral, Church St, Sheffield S1 1HA   *Tel:* 0114 275 3434
Fax: 0114 279 7412
email: enquiries@sheffield-cathedral.org.uk
Web: www.sheffield-cathedral.org.uk
Canons Residentiary
Precentor Canon Simon Cowling, The Cathedral [2007]   *Tel:* 0114 263 6065
email: precentor@sheffield-cathedral.org.uk
Dioc Director of Ordinands and Dean of Women's Ministry Canon Dr Joanne Grenfell, The Cathedral [2006]   *Tel:* 0114 263 6064
email: joanne.grenfell@sheffield-cathedral.org.uk

CAP Project Manager Revd Tim Renshaw, The Cathedral   *Tel:* 0114 263 6974
email: CBAOffice@sheffield-cathedral.org.uk
Canon Residentiary and Anglican Chaplain to the University of Sheffield Vacancy   *Tel:* 0114 222 8923
email: w.lamb@sheffield.ac.uk
Canon for Learning & Development Canon Chris Burke, The Cathedral [2010]   *Tel:* 0114 263 6066
email: chris.burke@sheffield-cathedral.org.uk
General Manager Mr Carl Hutton
Tel: 0114 236 6079
email: carl.hutton@sheffield-cathedral.org.uk
Director of Music Mr Neil Taylor, The Cathedral
Tel: 0114 263 6069
email: musicians@sheffield-cathedral.org.uk
Asst Director of Music Mr Anthony Gowing, The Cathedral   *Tel:* 0114 275 3434
email: musicians@sheffield-cathedral.org.uk

ARCHDEACONS
SHEFFIELD AND ROTHERHAM Ven Martyn Snow, 34 Wilson Rd, Sheffield S11 8RN [1999]
Tel: 0114 266 6099
Fax: 0114 267 9782
email: archdeacons.office@sheffield.anglican.org
Office Diocesan Church House, 95–99 Effingham St, Rotherham S65 1BL
DONCASTER Ven Robert Fitzharris, Fairview House, 14 Armthorpe Lane, Doncaster DN2 5LZ [2001]   *Tel:* 01302 325787
Fax: 01302 760493
email: archdeacons.office@sheffield.anglican.org
Office Diocesan Church House (*as above*)

CONVOCATION (MEMBERS OF THE HOUSE OF CLERGY OF THE GENERAL SYNOD)
Proctors for Clergy
Revd Canon Simon Bessant
Revd Canon Geoffrey Harbord
Revd Jeffrey Stokoe

MEMBERS OF THE HOUSE OF LAITY OF THE GENERAL SYNOD
Dr Jacqueline Butcher
Canon Elizabeth Paver
Jane Patterson

DIOCESAN OFFICERS

Dioc Secretary Mr Malcolm Fair, Diocesan Church House, 95–99 Effingham St, Rotherham S65 1BL   *Tel:* 01709 309117
Fax: 01709 512550
email: malcolm.fair@sheffield.anglican.org
Chancellor of Diocese Worshipful David McClean, 6 Burnt Stones Close, Sheffield S10 5TS
Tel: 0114 230 5794
email: j.d.mcclean@sheffield.ac.uk
Registrar of Diocese and Bishop's Legal Secretary Mr Andrew Vidler, Wake Smith and Tofields, 68 Clarkehouse Road, Sheffield S10 2LJ
Tel: 0114 266 6660
email: andrew.vidler@wake-smith.com

DIOCESAN ORGANIZATIONS

Diocesan Office Diocesan Church House, 95–99 Effingham St, Rotherham S65 1BL
Tel: 01709 309100
Fax: 01709 512550
email: reception@sheffield.anglican.org
Web: www.sheffield.anglican.org

ADMINISTRATION

Dioc Secretary Mr Malcolm Fair, Dioc Office
Tel: 01709 309117
Deputy Secretary/Finance Officer Mr Roger Pinchbeck, Dioc Office   *Tel:* 01709 309142
Property Manager Mr Paul Beckett, Dioc Office
Tel: 01709 309122
Board of Finance (*Chair*) Lay Canon Sandra Newton, 50 Broomgrove Rd, Sheffield S10 2NA
Tel: 0114 266 1079
Diocesan Mission and Pastoral Committee (*Chair*) Rt Revd Steven Croft, Bishopscroft, Snaithing Lane, Sheffield S10 3LG   *Tel:* 0114 230 2170
(*Secretary*) Mr Malcolm Fair, Dioc Office
Tel: 01709 309117
Redundant Churches Uses Committee (*Chair*) Ven Martyn Snow (*as above*)
(*Secretary*) Mr Paul Beckett (*as above*)
Parsonages Committee (*Chair*) Ven Robert Fitzharris (*as above*)
(*Secretary*) Mr Paul Beckett (*as above*)
Board of Patronages (*Chair*) Prof David McClean, 6 Burnt Stones Close, Sheffield S10 5TS
Tel: 0114 230 5794
(*Secretary*) Mr Malcolm Fair Dioc Office
Tel: 01709 309117
DAC Chair Revd Canon Peter Ingram, The Vicarage, 80 Millhouses Lane, Sheffield S7 2HB
Tel: 0114 236 2838
DAC Secretary Mr Graham Williams, Dioc Office
01709 309 121
Administration Supervisor Mrs Christine Brocklebank, Dioc Office   *Tel:* 01709 309 128
Designated Officer Revd Canon Geoffrey Harbord, Bishopscroft, Snaithing Lane, Sheffield S10 3LG
Tel: 0114 230 2170
Fax: 0114 263 0110
email:
geoffrey.harbord@sheffield.anglican.org.uk

Communications Officer The Revd Rob Marshall, Media 33, 5 Brampton Court, Brough HU15 1DZ
Tel: 01482 562455
email: rob@media33.co.uk

DIOCESAN SYNOD

(*Chair, House of Clergy*) Revd Ian Smith, St Paul's Vicarage, Wheata Road, Sheffield S5 9FP
Tel: 0114 246 8494
(*Chair, House of Laity*) Canon Elizabeth Paver, 113 Warning Tongue Lane, Bessacarr, Doncaster DN4 6TB   *Tel:* 01302 530706
(*Secretary*) Mr Malcolm Fair (*as above*)

CHURCHES

Advisory Committee for the Care of Churches (*Chair*) Canon Peter Ingram, Holy Trinity Vicarage, 80 Millhouses Rd, Sheffield S7 2LL
Tel and Fax: 0114 236 2838
(*Secretary*) Mr Graham Williams, Dioc Office
Tel: 01709 309120

EDUCATION

Dioc Board of Education (*Chair*) Ven Robert Fitzharris (*as above*); (*Secretary*) Miss Heather Morris BEd Hons MSc, Dioc Office
Tel: 01709 309124
Director of Education Miss Heather Morris BEd Hons MSc, Dioc Office

TOURISM

Malcolm Fair, Dioc Office

BOARD OF MINISTRY AND MISSION

Board of Ministry and Mission (*Chair*) The Bishop of Doncaster; (*Secretary*) Canon Dr John Thomson, Dioc Office   *Tel:* 01709 309143
Director of Ministry and Mission Canon Dr John Thomson, Dioc Office
Director of Ordinands Canon Dr Joanne Grenfell, The Cathedral Church of St Peter and St Paul, Church St, Sheffield S1 1HA   *Tel:* 0114 275 3434
Director of Youth Ministries Mr Mike North
Tel: 01709 309146
Children's and Youth Officer Mrs Jennie Lambourne, Dioc Office   *Tel:* 01709 309144
Director of IME4–7 Revd Chris Stebbing, St John's Vicarage, 91 Manor Oakes Rd, Sheffield S2 5EA   *Tel:* 0114 274 7423
Asst POT Officers Revd Lydia Wells, The Vicarage, Kingston Rd, Intake, Doncaster DN2 6LS (SMs)
Tel: 01302 343 119
Revd Gary Schofield, The Vicarage, Manor Rd, Wales, Sheffield S26 5PD (SMs)
Tel: 01909 771 111
Revd Jan Foden, The Vicarage, Stainforth Rd, Barnby Dun, Doncaster DN3 1AA (NSM)
Tel: 01302 882 835
Discipleship Development Officer Revd Alan Isaacson, The Rectory, High Bradfield, Sheffield S6 6LG   *Tel:* 0114 285 1225
Diocesan Missioner and Warden of Evangelism Revd Ian Smith, St Paul's Vicarage, Wheata Rd, Sheffield S5 9FP   *Tel:* 0114 246 8494

Bishop's Adviser on Women in Ministry Canon Dr Joanne Grenfell, The Cathedral Church of St Peter and St Paul, Church St, Sheffield S1 1HA
Tel: 0114 275 3434
Bishop's Adviser on Parish Development Vacancy
Bishop's Adviser on Music and Worship Revd Helen Bent, The Vicarage, 61 Whitehill Lane, Brinsworth, Rotherham S60 5JR
Tel: 01709 363 850
Bishop's Adviser on Spirituality and Chaplain of Whirlow Grange Conference Centre Revd Philip Roderick, Whirlow Grange Conference Centre, Ecclesall Rd South, Sheffield S11 9PZ
Tel: 0114 235 3704
Bishop's Adviser on Non-Stipendiary Ministry Vacancy
Bishop's Adviser on Church Army Ministry Revd Jane Truman
Tel: 0114 246 8811
Warden of Readers Vacancy
Readers' Board (Secretary) Mr Stuart Carey, Corben House, 3 Station Rd, Hatfield, Doncaster DN7 6PQ
Tel: Tel: 01302 844936
Ecumenical Officer Revd Frances Ecclestone, The Vicarage, 1 Barnfield Road, Crosspool, Sheffield S10 5TD
Tel: 0114 230 2531

PRESS AND PUBLICATIONS
Director of Communications Revd Rob Marshall, 33rpm public relations, 5 Brampton Court, Brough HU15 1DZ
Tel: 01482 562455
Fax: 0870 286 3348
email: rob@media.33.co.uk
Editor of Dioc Directory Mrs Christine Brocklebank, Dioc Office
Tel: 01709 309128

DIOCESAN RECORD OFFICES
Sheffield City Archives, 52 Shoreham St, Sheffield S1 4SP
Tel: 0114 273 4756
(For parishes in the archdeaconry of Sheffield)
Doncaster Archives, King Edward Rd, Balby, Doncaster DN4 0NA
Tel: 01302 859811
(For parishes in the archdeaconry of Doncaster)

FAITH AND JUSTICE
Director of Faith and Justice and Secretary Ms Kate Plant, Dioc Office
Tel: 01709 309136
South Yorkshire Workplace Chaplaincy Capt Christopher Chesters CA, 9 The Copse, Bramley, Rotherham S66 0TP
Tel: 0114 275 5865
Fax: 0114 272 6767
Office South Yorkshire Workplace Chaplaincy, Cemetery Rd Baptist Church, Napier St Entrance, Sheffield S11 8HA
Tel: 0114 275 5865
Bishop's Adviser on Black Concerns Mrs Carmen Franklin
Tel: 0114 245 7160

Bishop's Representative for Child Protection Ms Sue Booth
Tel: 0113 275 5266
Bishop's Rural Adviser Revd Keith Hale, Tankersley Rectory, 9 Chapel Road, Pilley, Barnsley S75 3AR
Tel: 01226 744140
European Link Officer Ven Robert Fitzharris, *(Archdeacon of Doncaster)*, Dioc Office

STEWARDSHIP
Christian Giving Director Mr Nicholas Hutton, Dioc Office
Tel: 01709 309151

AREA DEANS
ARCHDEACONRY OF SHEFFIELD
Attercliffe Revd Steve Willett, Vicarage, 63 Sheffield Rd, Sheffield S12 4LR
Tel: 0114 248 4486
Ecclesall Canon Peter Ingram, Vicarage, 80 Millhouses Lane, Sheffield S7 2HB
Tel: 0114 236 2838
Ecclesfield Revd Rick Stordy, St John's Vicarage, 23 Housley Park, Chapeltown, Sheffield S35 2UE
Tel: 0114 257 0966
Hallam Revd Phillip Townsend, St Timothy's Vicarage, 152 Slinn St, Sheffield S10 1NZ
Tel: 0114 266 1745
Laughton Revd Jane Bolton, The Rectory, 217 Nursery Road, Dinnington, Sheffield S25 2QU
Tel: 01909 562 335
Rotherham Canon David Bliss, 51 Hallam Rd, Moorgate, Rotherham S60 3ED
Tel: 01709 364 341

ARCHDEACONRY OF DONCASTER
Adwick-le-Street Revd Mark Wigglesworth, Vicarage, Church St, Askern, Doncaster DN6 0PH
Tel: 01302 700404
Doncaster Canon John Willett, St Wilfrid's Vicarage, Cantley Lane, Cantley, Doncaster DN4 6PA
Tel: 01302 535133
Hickleton Revd Richard Parker, 104 Hawshaw Lane, Hoyland, Barnsley S74 0HH
Tel: 01226 749 231
Snaith and Hatfield Canon Cyril Roberts, The Orchard, Pontefract Rd, Snaith, Goole DN14 9JS
Tel: 01405 860866
Tankersley Revd Keith Hale, Tankersley Rectory, 9 Chapel Rd, Pilley, Barnsley S75 3AR
Tel: 01226 744 140
Wath Revd Nigel Elliott, Vicarage, Highthorne Rd, Kilnhurst, Mexborough S64 5UU
Tel: 01709 589674
West Doncaster Revd Brian Inston, The Vicarage, 6 Greenfield Lane, Balby, Doncaster DN4 0PY
Tel: 01302 853 278

DIOCESE OF SODOR AND MAN

Founded in 447. The Isle of Man.

Population 80,000   Area 221 sq m
Full-time Stipendiary Parochial Clergy 10   Benefices 28
Parishes 28   Churches 45
www.sodorandman.im
Overseas link dioceses: Cashel (Ireland), Pretoria (Southern Africa).

BISHOP
The Rt Revd Robert M.E. Paterson, Thie Yn Aspick, 4 The Falls, Tromode Rd, Douglas, Isle of Man IM4 4PZ [2008] *Tel:* 01624 622108
email: bishop@sodorandman.im
[+Robert Sodor as Mannin]
Bishop's Chaplain and Mission Adviser Miss Gillian Poole   *email:* mission@sodorandman.im
Bishop's Secretary Miss Rosemary Bannan
email: secretary@sodorandman.im

CATHEDRAL CHURCH OF ST GERMAN, PEEL
Dean The Bishop
Vice Dean Revd Canon Nigel Godfrey, St German's Cathedral Office, Peel, Isle of Man IM5 1HH   *Tel:* 01624 842608
email: vice-dean@sodorandman.im
Canons
Canon Duncan Whitworth, St Matthew's Vicarage, Alexander Drive, Douglas, Isle of Man IM2 3QN [1996]   *Tel:* 01624 676310
Canon David Green, Vicarage, Maughold, Isle of Man IM7 1AS [2005]   *Tel:* 01624 812070
Canon Philip Frear, Vicarage, Saddle Rd, Braddan, Isle of Man IM4 4LB [2005]
Tel: 01624 675523
Canon Malcolm Convery, 50 Faaie ny Cabbal, Kirk Michael, Isle of Man IM6 2HU [1999]
Tel: 01624 878855

ARCHDEACON
Ven Brian Smith, St George's Vicarage, 16 Devonshire Rd, Douglas, Isle of Man IM2 3RB [2005]   *Tel:* 01624 675430
email: archdeacon@sodorandman.im

MANX CONVOCATION
(*Secretary*) Revd Canon David Greenwood, St Paul's Vicarage, Walpole Drive, Ramsey, Isle of Man IM8 1NA   *Tel:* 01624 812275
email: davidgreenwood@manx.net

YORK CONVOCATION
Proctor for the Clergy

(MEMBER OF THE HOUSE OF CLERGY OF THE GENERAL SYNOD)
Proctor for the Clergy
Ven Brian Smith

MEMBER OF THE HOUSE OF LAITY OF THE GENERAL SYNOD
Miss Laura Davenport

DIOCESAN OFFICERS
Vicar-General and Chancellor of Diocese The Worshipful Clare Faulds, The Lynague, German, IM5 2AQ   *Tel:* 01624 842045
Diocesan Registrar and Bishop's Legal Secretary Mr Timothy Mann, MannBenham, 49 Victoria Street, Douglas, Isle of Man IM1 2LD
Tel: 01624 639359
email: TimothyMann@mannbenham.com
Diocesan Synod Secretary Mrs Sylvia Lawrinson, Apt 8, Hillary Wharf, South Quay, Douglas, Isle of Man IM1 5BL   *Tel:* 01624 627664
email: synod@sodorandman.im
Bishop's Legal Adviser Mr Kenneth Gumbley, 37 Farmhill Park, Braddan, Isle of Man IM2 2ED
email: kfwg@gumbley.net

CHURCH COMMISSIONERS FOR THE ISLE OF MAN
The Bishop (*Chair*)
The Archdeacon
Mr Peter Cowell
Mr Henry Dawson
Mrs Jacqueline Frear
Mr Stephen Hamer
Revd Margaret Burrow
Revd Canon David Greenwood
Revd Canon Duncan Whitworth
(*Secretary*) Mrs Sylvia Lawrinson (*as above*)

DIOCESAN ORGANIZATIONS
DIOCESAN SYNOD
Chairman, House of Clergy Revd Canon David Greenwood (*as above*)
Chairman, House of Laity Mr Nigel Cretney, Yn Balley, Lhergy Cripperty, Union Mills, Isle of Man IM4 4NH   *Tel:* 01624 851060
email: nigelcretney@manx.net
(*Secretary*) Mrs Sylvia Lawrinson (*as above*)

BOARD OF FINANCE
Chairman Ven Brian Smith (*as above*)
(*Secretary*) Mrs Sylvia Lawrinson (*as above*)

Diocesan Treasurer Mrs Suzanne Ellis, Reayrt House, Andreas, Isle of Man IM7 4HH
Tel: 01624 880610
email: treasurer@sodorandman.im

CHURCH BUILDINGS
Advisory Committee for the Care of Churches (Secretary) Mrs Sylvia Lawrinson (*as above*)

SECTOR MINISTERS AND ADVISERS
Contact via the Bishop's Office, Thie yn Aspick, 4 The Falls, Tromode Road, Douglas, Isle of Man IM4 4PZ *Tel:* 01624 622108
email: secretary@sodorandman.im
Access & Disability Mr Guy Thompson
Bishop's Visitors Dr Paul & Mrs Barbara Bregazzi
Children's Work Adviser Revd Ian Davies & Mrs Nancy Clague
Youth Work Adviser Miss Laura Davenport
Education Officer Revd Ian Davies
Christian Giving Adviser Mrs Diane Marchment
Media & Communications Officer Revd John Coldwell *Tel:* 01624 621694
email: media@sodorandman.im
Webmaster Vacancy – *via Bishop's Chaplain and Media Officer*
Church & Society Adviser Revd Cyril Rogers
C.M.E.A.C. Link Revd Marc Wolverson
Data Protection Officer Mr Charles Flynn
Ecumenical Adviser Mr Howard Connell
email: ecumenism@sodorandman.im
Environment Advisers Revd Brian & Mrs Mary Evans-Smith
Healing & Deliverance Adviser Revd Canon Philip Frear (*as above*)
Leisure, Sport & Tourism Advisers Mrs Maria Coldwell, Mr Ray Platt, Mrs Julie Wolverson
Director of Vocation & Training (DDO.) Revd Canon Nigel Godfrey (*as above*)
C.M.D (lay & ordained) Convener Revd Canon David Greenwood (*as above*)

Training Officer Vacancy
Warden of Readers Mr Colin Finney
email: readers@sodorandman.im
Chaplain to P.T.O. Ministers (lay & ordained) Revd Leslie Lawrinson (*as S. Lawrinson above*)
Pastor to Ministers' Widows & Widowers Mrs Brenda Willoughby
Rural Life Adviser Vacancy
Safeguarding Officer Mrs Margaret Galloway
Spiritual Life Adviser Revd Canon Peter Robinson (*as below*)
World Mission Co-ordinators Revd Canon Malcolm & Mrs Valerie Convery (*as above*)
Diocesan Links Co-ordinator Mr Colin Gurney

CHAPLAINCIES
The Isle of Man College Revd Marc Wolverson
Noble's General Hospital Revd Canon Philip Frear (*as above*)
Hospice Isle of Man Revd Lynda Brady
Ramsey Cottage Hospital Mrs Anne Kean (*temporary*)
H.M. Prison, Jurby Revd Canon David Green (*as above*)

ARCHIVED DIOCESAN RECORDS
Archivist Miss Wendy Thirkettle, The Manx Museum Library, Kingswood Grove, Douglas Isle of Man IM1 3LY *Tel:* 01624 64800

RURAL DEANS
Castletown and Peel Revd Canon Peter Robinson, The Vicarage, Arbory Road, Castletown, Isle of Man IM9 1ND *Tel:* 01624 823509
Douglas Canon Duncan Whitworth (*as above*)
Ramsey Canon David Greenwood (*as above*)
The three Rural Deaneries are being replaced by four **MISSION PARTNERSHIPS**: *North, South East and West.*

Founded in 1905. Greater London south of the Thames, except for most of the London Boroughs of Bromley and Bexley (ROCHESTER), and a few parishes in the south-west (GUILDFORD); the eastern third of Surrey.

Population 2,537,000   Area 317 sq m
Full-time Stipendiary Parochial Clergy 320   Benefices 267
Parishes 291   Churches 365
www.southwark.anglican.org
Overseas link dioceses: Manicaland, Central Zimbabwe, Matabeleland, Masvingo (Zimbabwe).

BISHOP
Until 17 January 2011
Acting Diocesan Bishop Rt Revd Dr Richard Cheetham (see Kingston Area below)
After 17 January 2011
Rt Rev Christopher Chessun, Bishop's House, 38 Tooting Bec Gardens London SW16 1QZ
Tel: 020 8769 3256
Fax 020 8769 4126
email: bishop.christopher@southwark.anglican.org
Personal Assistant and Lay Chaplain Capt Terry Drummond CA (*same address*)
email: terry.drummond@southwark.anglican.org
Bishop's Personal Secretary Ms Winsome Thomas (*same address*)
email: winsome.thomas@southwark.anglican.org
Secretary Mrs Penny Lochead (*same address*)
email: penny.lochead@southwark.anglican.org

AREA BISHOPS
CROYDON Rt Revd Nicholas Baines, St Matthew's House, 100 George St, Croydon CR0 1PE [2003]
Tel: 020 8256 9634
Fax: 020 8256 9631
email: bishop.nick@southwark.anglican.org
KINGSTON Rt Revd Dr Richard Cheetham, Kingston Episcopal Area Office, 620 Kingston Rd, Raynes Park, London SW20 8DN [2002]
Tel: 020 8545 2440
Fax; 020 8545 2441
email: bishop.richard@southwark.anglican.org
WOOLWICH Rt Revd Christopher Chessun, Dioc Office [2005]
After 17 January 2011 Vacancy
Tel: 020 7939 9407

HONORARY ASSISTANT BISHOPS
Rt Revd Mark Wood, College of St Barnabas, Blackberry Lane, Lingfield RH7 6NJ [2002]
Tel: 01342 870260
Rt Revd Michael Doe, General Secretary, USPG, Anglicans in World Mission, 200 Great Dover St, London SE1 4YB [2006]   Tel: 0845 273 1701
Rt Revd and Rt Hon Lord Harries of Pentregarth, 41 Melville Rd, Barnes, London SW19 9RH [2006]
Tel: 020 8288 6053

CATHEDRAL AND COLLEGIATE CHURCH OF ST SAVIOUR AND ST MARY OVERIE
Dean Very Revd Colin Slee OBE, Provost's Lodging, Bankside, London SE1 9JE [1994] (*All correspondence to be addressed to the Cathedral Office*)
Tel: 020 7367 6731 (Office)
Fax: 020 7367 6725 (Office)
Tel: 020 7928 6414 (Home)
Fax: 020 7928 9404 (Home)
email: colin.slee@southwark.anglican.org
Cathedral Office Montague Chambers, London Bridge, London SE1 9DA   Tel: 020 7367 6700
Fax: 020 7367 6725/6730
email: cathedral@southwark.anglican.org
Canons Residentiary
Sub-Dean Canon Andrew Nunn, Cathedral Office [1999]   Tel: 020 7367 6727 (Office)
020 7735 8322 (Home)
email: andrew.nunn@southwark.anglican.org
Pastor Canon Bruce Saunders, Cathedral Office [2003]   Tel: 020 7367 6706 (Office)
020 7820 8376 (Home)
email: bruce.saunders@southwark.anglican.org
Chancellor and Theologian Canon Jane Steen, Dioc Office [2005]   Tel: 020 7939 9409
email: jane.steen@southwark.anglican.org
Missioner Ven Dr Michael Ipgrave [2010]
Tel: 020 7939 9409
email: michael.ipgrave@southwark.anglican.org
Treasurer Vacancy
Succentor Revd Anna Macham, [2007] Cathedral Office   Tel: 020 7367 6705
email: anna.macham@southwark.anglican.org
Priest Assistant Canon Wendy Robins [2002]
Tel: 020 7939 9436
email: wendy.robins@southwark.anglican.org
Administrator Mr Matthew Knight, Cathedral Office   Tel: 020 7367 6726
email: matthew.knight@southwark.anglican.org
Education Officer Ms Alexandra Carton, Cathedral Office   Tel: 020 7367 6715
email: edcentre@southwark.anglican.org
Visitors' Officer Mr David Payne, Cathedral Office
Tel: 020 7367 6734
email: david.payne@southwark.anglican.org
Cathedral Organist Mr Peter Wright, Cathedral Office   Tel: 020 7367 6703
email: peter.wright@southwark.anglican.org

ARCHDEACONS

CROYDON Ven Anthony Davies, St Matthew's House, 100 George St, Croydon CR0 1PE [1994]
Tel: 020 8256 9630
Fax: 020 8256 9631
email: tony.davies@southwark.anglican.org

LAMBETH Ven Christopher Skilton, Kingston Episcopal Area Office, 620 Kingston Rd, Raynes Park, London SW20 8DN [2003]
Tel: 020 8545 2440
Fax: 020 8545 2441
email: chris.skilton@southwark.anglican.org

LEWISHAM Ven Christine Hardman, Dioc Office [2001]
Tel: 020 7939 9408
email:
christine.hardman@southwark.anglican.org

REIGATE Ven Daniel Kajumba, St Matthew's House (*as above*)
Tel: 020 8256 9630
email: daniel.kajumba@southwark.anglican.org

SOUTHWARK Ven Michael Ipgrave, Dioc Office (*as above*) [2004]
Tel: 020 7939 9409
email: michael.ipgrave@southwark.anglican.org

WANDSWORTH Ven Stephen Roberts, Kingston Episcopal Area Office (*as above*) [2005]
Tel: 020 8545 2440
Fax: 020 8545 2441
email: stephen.roberts@southwark.anglican.org

CONVOCATION (MEMBERS OF THE HOUSE OF CLERGY OF THE GENERAL SYNOD)

Dignitaries in Convocation
The Dean of Southwark
Proctors for Clergy
Revd Canon Simon Butler
Revd Canon Giles Goddard
Ven Christine Hardman
Revd Canon Gary Jenkins
Revd Rosemarie Mallett
Revd Canon Andrew Nunn
Revd Mark Steadman
Revd Canon Anne Stevens

MEMBERS OF THE HOUSE OF LAITY OF THE GENERAL SYNOD

Mrs April Alexander
Miss Vasantha Gnanadoss
Mr Adrian Greenwood
Mr Peter Haddock
Mr Robin Hall
Mr Tom Sutcliffe
Mr Brian Wilson

DIOCESAN OFFICERS

Dioc Secretary Mr Simon Parton, Diocesan Office, Trinity House, 4 Chapel Court, Borough High St, London SE1 1HW
Tel: 020 7939 9400
Fax: 020 7939 9468
email: simon.parton@southwark.anglican.org

Deputy Dioc Secretary Mr Andrew Lane, Dioc Office (*as above*)
email: andrew.lane@southwark.anglican.org

Chancellor of Diocese Mr Philip Petchey, 2 Harcourt Buildings, Temple, London EC4Y 9DB
Tel: 020 7353 8415
Registrar of Diocese and Bishop's Legal Secretary Mr Paul Morris, Minerva House, 5 Montague Close, London SE1 9BB
Tel: 020 7593 5000
Fax: 020 7593 5099

DIOCESAN ORGANIZATIONS

Diocesan Office Trinity House, 4 Chapel Court, Borough High St, London SE1 1HW
Tel: 020 7939 9400
Fax: 020 7939 9468
email: trinity@southwark.anglican.org
Web: www. southwark.anglican.org

ADMINISTRATION

Dioc Synod (*Chairman, House of Clergy*) Canon Graham Shaw
(*Chairman, House of Laity*) Mr Adrian Greenwood;
(*Secretary*) Mr Simon Parton, Dioc Office
South London Church Fund and Diocesan Board of Finance (*Chairman*) Mr John Kempsell;
(*Secretary*) Mr Simon Parton, Dioc Office
Parsonages Board (*Secretary*) Mr Eric Greber, Dioc Office
email: eric.greber@southwark.anglican.org
Mission & Pastoral Committee (*Secretary*) Mr Andrew Lane, Dioc Office
email: andrew.lane@southwark.anglican.org
Redundant Churches Uses Committee (*Secretary*) Mr Eric Greber, Dioc Office
Designated Officer Mr Paul Morris, Minerva House, 5 Montague Close, London SE1 9BB
Tel: 020 7593 5000
Fax: 020 7593 5099

CHURCHES

Advisory Committee for the Care of Churches (*Chairman*) Dr Cyril Young c/o Trinity House (*as above*); (*Secretary*) Mr Andrew Lane (*as above*)

ECUMENICAL

Chair of Ecumenical Sub-Group Revd Peter Hart, Vicarage, 70 Marksbury Ave, Richmond TW9 4JF
Tel: 020 8392 1425
email: Pwhart1@aol.com

EDUCATION

Board of Education (*Director*) Mrs Barbara Lane, 48 Union St, London SE1 1TD
Tel: 020 7234 9200
email: barbara.lane@southwark.anglican.org

MISSION WORKING GROUP

Acting Chair The Archdeacon of Lambeth (*as above*)
Canon Missioner Ven Dr Michael Ipgrave (*as above*)
Mission Theologian Revd Dr Sharon Moughtin-Mumby
Tel: 020 7939 9416
email: sharon.mm@btinternet.com

Officer for Lay Mission and Ministry Revd Lu Gale Croydon Episcopal Area Office
Tel: 020 8256 9630
Spiritual Formation Adviser Mr Chris Chapman, Dioc Office
Inter Faith Relations Co-ordinator Siriol Davies
Tel: 020 7201 4854
email: sirioldavies@yahoo.co.uk
Parish Development Adviser Rev Ruth Worsley
Tel: 020 7939 9417
email: ruth.worsley@southwark.anglican.org
Ecumenical Projects Officer John Richardson
Tel: 01462 422502
email: john@ctslondon.org.uk
Groups Support Worker John Beaumont
Tel: 020 7939 9414
Fax: 020 7939 9467
email: john.beaumont @southwark.anglican.org

PUBLIC POLICY GROUP
Chair Terry Drummond CA, Bishop's House (as above)
Public Policy/Environment Officer Rev Dr Barry Goodwin, Croydon Episcopal Area Office
Tel: 020 8256 9637
email: barry.goodwin@southwark.anglican.org
Groups Support Worker John Beaumont, Dioc Office (as above)

CHILDREN AND YOUTH DEVELOPMENT GROUP
Chair The Rev Canon Tim Marwood
Tel: 020 8940 8435
email: timmarwood@yahoo.co.uk
Research and Administrative Officer Caroline Gibson
Tel: 020 7939 9412
Fax: 020 7939 9467
email: caroline.gibson@southwark.anglican.org

OTHER OFFICERS
Dioc Safeguarding and Child Protection Adviser Jill Sandham, c/o Dioc Office
Tel: 020 7939 9400
email: jill.sandham@southwark.anglican.org
Adviser in Women's Ministry Canon Dianna Gwilliams
Tel: 020 8693 1524
email: dianna.gwilliams@btopenworld.com
Minority Ethnic Anglican Concerns Officer Ms Lola Brown, Dioc Office
Tel: 020 7939 9418
Interfaith Group Chair Siriol Davies
Tel: 020 7201 4854
email: sirioldavies@yahoo.co.uk
Liturgical Committee Revd Dr John Thewlis (Secretary), Rectory, 2 Talbot Rd, Carshalton SM5 3BS
Tel: 020 8647 2366
Retirement Officer Canon Nicky Tredennick
Tel: 01342 843570
email: rev.nicky.hello@amserve.com
Rural Ministry Adviser Revd Dr Barry Goodwin, c/o Croydon Episcopal Area Office
Tel: 020 8256 9637
Southwark Dioc WelCare Revd Anne-Marie Garton (Director), St John's Community Centre, 19 Frederick Crescent, London SW9 6XN

Tel: 020 7939 9424
email: anne-marie.garton@southwark.anglican.org

MINISTRY AND TRAINING COMMITTEE
Canon Theologian and Director of Ministerial Education Canon Dr Jane Steen, Dioc Office
Tel: 020 7939 9449
Acting Diocesan Director of Ordinands Revd Margaret E Jackson
Tel: 020 7939 9458
email: margaret.jackson@southwark.anglican.org
Reader Training Revd Anne Stevens, St Michael's Vicarage, 93 Bolingbroke Grove, London SW11 6HA
Tel: 020 7228 1990
email: anne.stevens@southwark.anglican.org
Warden of Readers Canon Andrew Nunn, Southwark Cathedral (as above)
Southwark Pastoral Auxiliary Training Officer Mr Chris Chapman, Dioc Office
Tel: 020 7939 9474
email: chris.chapman@southwark.anglican.org
Southwark Pastoral Auxiliary Co-ordinator Revd Lu Gale, Croydon Episcopal Area Office (as above)

COMMUNICATIONS
Director of Communications and Resources and Bishop's Press Officer Wendy Robins, Dioc Office
Tel: 020 7939 9400 (Office)
email: wendy.s.robins@southwark.anglican.org
Communications Officer Steve Harris, Dioc Office
Tel: 020 7939 9437
email: steve.harris@southwark.anglican.org

DIOCESAN RECORD OFFICES
London Metropolitan Archives, 40 Northampton Rd, London EC1R 0HB
Tel: 020 7332 3820
Fax: 020 7833 9136 (Parish records for Inner London Boroughs except Lewisham)
Lewisham Local Studies and Archives Centre, Lewisham Library, 199–201 Lewisham High St, London SE13 6LG
Tel: 020 8297 0682
Fax: 020 8297 1169 (Parish records for East and West Lewisham deaneries)
Bexley Local Studies and Archive Centre, Central Library, Townley Road, Bexleyheath DA6 7HJ
Tel: 020 8301 1545 (For Parishes in the London Borough of Bexley)
Surrey History Centre, 130 Goldsworth Rd, Woking GU21 1ND
Tel: 01483 594594
Fax: 01483 594595 (County of Surrey and Surrey London Boroughs)
London Borough of Sutton Local Studies Centre, St Nicholas Way, Sutton SM1 1JN
Tel: 020 8770 5000 (London Borough of Sutton)

STEWARDSHIP
Director of Communications and Resources Wendy Robins, Dioc Office
email:
wendy.s.robins@southwark.anglican.org.uk
Stewardship Resources Officer Jackie Pontin, Dioc Office
Tel: 020 7939 9435
email: jackie.pontin@southwark.anglican.org

AREA DEANS

ARCHDEACONRY OF SOUTHWARK
Bermondsey Revd Mark Steadman, St Philip's Vicarage, Avondale Square, London SE1 5PD
Tel: 020 7237 3239
email: frmark.steadman@yahoo.co.uk
Camberwell Acting Area Dean Revd Mark Steadman (*as above*)
Dulwich Canon Dianna Gwilliams, St Barnabas Vicarage, 38 Calton Ave, London SE21 7DG
Tel: 020 8693 1524
email: dianna.gwilliams@btopenworld.com
Southwark and Newington Revd Andrew Dodd, Rectory, 57 Kennington Park Rd, London SE11 4JQ
Tel: 020 7735 1894
email: rector@stmarynewington.org.uk

ARCHDEACONRY OF LAMBETH
Merton Revd Canon Stephen Coulson St Mark's Vicarage Locks Lane Mitcham Surrey CR4 2JX
Tel: 020 8648 2397
email: steve@scoulson.freeserve.co.uk
Lambeth North Revd Stephen Sichel St Matthew's Vicarage 5 St Matthew's Road London SW2 1ND
Tel: 020 7733 9605
email: sichel@tiscali.co.uk
Lambeth South Revd Simon P. Gates, Vicarage, 2 Thornton Rd, Balham, London SW12 0JU
Tel: 020 8671 8276
email: simon.gates@stwss.org.uk

ARCHDEACONRY OF REIGATE
Caterham Revd Alan Middleton, Rectory, 35 Dane Rd, Warlingham CR6 9NP
Tel: 01883 624125
email: alan.middleton@southwark.anglican.org
Godstone Revd Graham Paddick, St John's Vicarage, The Platt, Dormansland, Lingfield, Surrey RH7 6QU
Tel: 01342 832391
email: stjohndor@btinternet.com
Reigate Revd Garth Barber, Vicarage, Woodland Way, Kingswood, Tadworth KT20 6NW
Tel: 01737 832164
email: garth.barber@virgin.net

ARCHDEACONRY OF LEWISHAM
Charlton Revd Kim Hitch, St James Rectory, 62 Kidbrooke Park Rd, London SE3 0DU
Tel: 020 8856 3438
email: kim@hitchoffice.org.uk
Deptford Revd Neil Nicholls, St James Vicarage, St James, New Cross, London SE14 6AD
Tel: 020 8691 2167
email: revn@hotmail.co.uk
East Lewisham Revd Richard D. Bainbridge, Vicarage, 47 Handen Rd, London SE12 8NR
Tel: 020 8318 2363
email: revrdb@yahoo.com
Eltham and Mottingham Revd Elaine Cranmer, St Luke's Vicarage, 107 Westmount Rd, Eltham, London SE9 1XX
Tel: 020 8850 3030
email: rev.elaine@virgin.net

Plumstead Revd Harry Owen, All Saints Vicarage, 106 Herbert Rd, Plumstead, London SE18 3PU
Tel: 020 8854 2995
email: h.d.owen@talk21.com
West Lewisham Revd Michael Kingston, St Bartholomew's Vicarage, 4 Westwood Hill, Sydenham, London SE26 6QR
Tel: 020 8778 5290
email: michaelkingston@btinternet.com

ARCHDEACONRY OF WANDSWORTH
Battersea Revd Geoffrey Vevers, St Saviour's Vicarage, 351a Battersea Park Rd, London SW11 4LH
Tel: 020 7498 1642
email: g.m.vevers@btinternet.com
Kingston Revd David Houghton, 14 The Ridge, Surbiton, Surrey KT5 8HX
Tel: 020 8399 6053
email: davidj.houghton@tiscali.co.uk
Richmond and Barnes Revd Canon Tim Marwood, The Vicarage, Bute Avenue, Petersham, Richmond, TW10 7AX
Tel: 020 8940 8435
email: timmarwood@yahoo.co.uk
Tooting Revd Wilma Roest, St Mary's Vicarage, 35 Elmfield Road, London, SW17 8AG
Tel: 020 8673 1188
email: vicar@stmarybalham.org.uk
Wandsworth Revd Heinz Toller, St Paul's Vicarage, 116 Augustus Rd, London SW19 6EW
Tel: 020 8788 2024
email: vicar@stpaulswimbledonpark.org.uk

ARCHDEACONRY OF CROYDON
Croydon Addington Revd Mervyn McKinney, Vicarage, The Avenue, West Wickham, Kent BR4 0DX
Tel: 020 8777 5034
email: mervmckinney@btinternet.com
Croydon Central Revd Trevor Mapstone, 33 Hurst Way, South Croydon, Surrey, CR2 7AP
Tel: 020 8688 6676
email: tmapstone@emmanuelcroydon.org.uk
Croydon North Revd Beverley Mason, St John's Vicarage, 2 Sylvan Road, Upper Norwood, London, SE19 2RX
Tel: 020 8653 0378
email: revdbev@tiscali.co.uk
Croydon South Revd Christine Spurway, St James' Vicarage, 1b St James' Rd, Purley CR8 2DL
Tel: 020 8660 5436
email: christine@christinespurway.orange.com
Sutton Revd Christopher Wheaton, Vicarage, 38 Beeches Ave, Carshalton SM5 3LW
Tel: 020 8647 6056
email: good.shepherd432@btinternet.com

CHAPTER OF MINISTERS IN SECULAR EMPLOYMENT
Chapter Dean for Kingston Revd Peter King, 49 Leinster Ave, East Sheen, London SW14 7JW
Tel: 020 8876 8997

DIOCESE OF SOUTHWELL AND NOTTINGHAM

Founded in 1884. Nottinghamshire; a few parishes in South Yorkshire.

Population 1,081,000   Area 847 sq m
Full-time Stipendiary Parochial Clergy 133   Benefices 168
Parishes 260   Churches 307
www.southwell.anglican.org
Overseas link diocese: Natal (South Africa)

BISHOP
Rt Revd Paul Butler, Bishop's Manor, Southwell
NG25 0JR [2009]   *Tel:* 01636 812112
                                   Fax: 01636 815401
email: bishop@southwell.anglican.org
[Paul Southwell and Nottingham]
Chaplain Canon Anthony Evans
      email: chaplain@southwell.anglican.org
Personal Assistant Mrs Jackie Davies
      email: jackie@southwell.anglican.org

SUFFRAGAN BISHOP
SHERWOOD Rt Revd Anthony Porter, Dunham
House, 8 Westgate, Southwell NG25 0JL [2006]
                                   Tel: 01636 819133
                                   Fax: 01636 819085
Personal Assistant Miss Jenny Andrews
      email: jenny@southwell.anglican.org

PROVINCIAL EPISCOPAL VISITOR
Rt Revd Martyn Jarrett, 3 North Lane, Roundhay,
Leeds LS8 2QJ   *Tel:* 0113 265 4280
email:
      bishop-of-beverley@3-north-lane.fsnet.co.uk

HONORARY ASSISTANT BISHOPS
Rt Revd John Finney, Greenacre, Crow Lane,
South Muskham, Newark NG23 6DZ [1998]
                                   Tel: 01636 679791
Rt Revd Ronald Milner, 7 Crafts Way, Southwell
NG25 0BL [1994]   *Tel:* 01636 816256
Rt Revd Roy Williamson, 30 Sidney Rd, Beeston,
Nottingham NG9 1AN [1998]   *Tel:* 0115 925 4901

**CATHEDRAL AND PARISH CHURCH OF
THE BLESSED VIRGIN MARY**
Dean Very Revd John Arthur Guille, The
Residence, 1 Vicars' Court, Southwell NG25 0HP
[2007]   *Tel:* 01636 812782
      email: dean@southwellminster.org.uk
Office The Minster Office, The Minster Centre,
Church St, Southwell NG25 0HD
                         Tel: 01636 812649/817810
                                   Fax: 01636 817284
      email: office@southwellminster.org.uk
      Web: www.southwellminster.org.uk

Canons Residentiary
Precentor Canon Jacqueline D. Jones, 2 Vicars'
Court, Southwell NG25 0HP [2003]
                                   Tel: 01636 817295
      email: jacquijones@southwellminster.org.uk
Canon Pastor Canon Nigel Coates, 3 Vicars'
Court, Southwell NG25 0HP [2005]
                                   Tel: 01636 817296
      email: nigelcoates@southwellminster.org.uk
*Canon with Responsibility for Education and
Learning* Canon Edward (Ed) Pruen, 5 Vicars'
Court, Southwell NG25 0HD   *Tel:* 01636 819848
      email: canoned@southwellminster.org.uk
Chapter Clerk Mrs Caroline Jarvis, The Minster
Office, The Minster Centre, Church St, Southwell
NG25 0HD   *Tel:* 01636 817285
      email: chapterclerk@southwellminster.org.uk
Rector Chori Mr Paul Hale, 4 Vicars' Court,
Southwell NG25 0HP   *Tel:* 01636 812228/817297
      email: rectorchori@southwellminster.org.uk
Head Verger Mr Andrew Todd, Vestry, Southwell
Cathedral   *Tel:* 01636 817290
      email: vergers@southwellminster.org.uk

ARCHDEACONS
NOTTINGHAM Ven Peter Hill, 4 Victoria Crescent,
Sherwood, Nottingham NG5 4DA [2007]
                         Tel: 0115 985 8641 (Home)
                              01636 817206 (Office)
                              07771 778182 (Mobile)
                         Fax: 01636 815882 (Office)
email: archdeacon-nottm@southwell.anglican.org
NEWARK Ven Dr Nigel Peyton, 4 The Woodwards,
Newark NG24 3GG [1999]
                              Tel: 01636 817206 (Office)
                              01636 612249 (Home)
                              07917 690576 (Mobile)
                         Fax: 01636 815882 (Office)
email:
      archdeacon-newark@southwell.anglican.org

**CONVOCATION (MEMBERS OF THE
HOUSE OF CLERGY OF THE GENERAL
SYNOD)**
Proctors for Clergy
Ven Peter Hill
Canon Tony Walker
Revd Sally Baylis

MEMBERS OF THE HOUSE OF LAITY OF THE GENERAL SYNOD

Mrs Pamela Bishop
Mr Nick Harding
Mr Colin Slater

DIOCESAN OFFICERS

Chief Executive Mr Nigel Spraggins, Dunham House, 8 Westgate, Southwell NG25 0JL
Tel: 01636 817205 (Office)
07887 538682 (Mobile)
01636 816445 (Home)
Fax: 01636 815084
email: ce@southwell.anglican.org
PA to the Chief Executive Mrs Barbara Wilds
Tel: 01636 817205
email: barbara@southwell.anglican.org
Chancellor of Diocese The Worshipful Mrs Linda Mary Box, Diocesan Office *Tel:* 01636 817209
Deputy Chancellor Mr Stephen Eyre
Registrar of Diocese and Bishop's Legal Secretary Canon Christopher Hodson, Diocesan Office
Tel: 01636 817209
Deputy Registrar Amanda Redgate

DIOCESAN ORGANIZATIONS

Diocesan Office Dunham House, 8 Westgate, Southwell NG25 0JL *Tel:* 01636 814331
Fax: 01636 815084
email: mail@southwell.anglican.org
Web: www.southwell.anglican.org

ADMINISTRATION

Diocesan Synod (*Vice-president and Chair, House of Clergy*) Canon Mark Tanner
(*Chair, House of Laity*) Mrs Pam Bishop
(*Secretary*) Chief Executive, c/o Diocesan Office
Tel: 01636 817204
Synod Administrator Mrs Caroline Todd, c/o Diocesan Office *Tel:* 01636 817222

FINANCE AND ADMINISTRATION

Director of Finance and Administration Mr David Meredith, Diocesan Office *Tel:* 01636 817202

PARISH SUPPORT

(*Includes Property, DAC and Stewardship*)
Director of Parish Support and Stewardship Advice Canon Carole Park *Tel:* 01636 817242
*email:*carolepark@southwell.anglican.org

PARISH SUPPORT (PROPERTY)

Building Surveyor Mr Ian Greaves (*as above*)
Tel: 01636 817214

PARISH SUPPORT (STEWARDSHIP)

Director of Funding Canon Carole Park
Tel: 01636 817242
email: carolepark@southwell.anglican.org

CHURCHES

Advisory Committee for the Care of Churches (*Chairman*) Canon Keith Turner, Rectory, Main St, Linby, Nottingham NG15 8AE *Tel:* 0115 963 2346
email: k.h.turner@btopenworld.com
Web: www.southwellchurches.nottingham.ac.uk

EDUCATION

Director of Education Mrs Claire Meese
Tel: 01636 817238
01636 814504 (General Office)
Diocesan School Advisers Mrs Jane Lewis *and* Mrs Anne Lumb (*same address*) *Tel:* 01636 817236
email: jane.lewis@southwell.anglican.org /
anne.lumb@southwell.anglican.org
Youth Ministry Adviser Angela Brymer
Tel: 01636 817233
email: angela.heywood@southwell.anglican.org
Children's Ministry Adviser Mr Nick Harding (*same address*) *Tel:* 01636 817234
email: nick@southwell.anglican.org

DEPARTMENT FOR DEVELOPMENT

Diocesan Office, 8 Westgate, Southwell NG25 0JL
Director, Ministry & Mission Canon Dr Nigel Rooms *Tel:* 01636 817231
email: nigel.rooms@southwell.anglican.org
Director, Partnerships & Mission Revd David McCoulough *Tel:* 01636 817987
email: davidmcc@southwell.anglican.org
Diocesan Director of Ordinands and Curate Training Canon Terry Joyce, Dioc Office, Department for Development *Tel:* 01636 817212
email: tjoyce@southwell.anglican.org
Dean of Women's Ministry Vacancy
Clergy Training Officer Revd Con Apokis
Tel: 01636 817208
email: kon@southwell.anglican.org
Lay Training Officer Revd Alison Cox
Tel: 01636 817985
Warden of Readers and Director of Studies Mr Christopher Perrett, Harvest Barn, Grassthorpe, Newark, Nottingham NG23 5QZ
Tel: 01636 822426
email: chris.perrett@southwell.anglican.org
Sport Ministry
Sport Ambassador Mr Tim Friend
Tel: 07887 530751
email: tim@southwell.anglican.org
Chaplain to Retired Clergy/Clergy Widows Officer Revd David Edinborough *Tel:* 0115 9251066
email: davidedinborough@btinternet.com
Bishop's Adviser on Rural Affairs Revd Derek Hollis, Diocesan Office *Tel:* 01636 817229
email: rural.adviser@southwell.anglican.org
Officer for Urban Life and Mission Vacancy
Workplace Chaplain Revd Alison Maddocks
Tel: 0115 983 1553
email:
alison.maddocks@nottinghamchurches.org

Equality and Diversity Officer and Rainbow Project Leader Ms Dianne Skerritt   *Tel:* 0115 948 3658
01636 817229
email: dskerritt@southwell.anglican.org
Chaplain for Sector Chaplaincies Venerable Robin Turner CB, DL   *Tel:* 01636 812250
email: pr.turner@lineone.net
Diocesan Ecumenical Officer Revd Stephen Morris
Tel: 0115 960 4477
email: stephen.morris@nottinghamchurches.org
Natal Link Officer Revd Barbara Holbrook, The Rectory, 1 Eastwood Road, Kimberley, Nottingham NG16 2HX   *Tel:* 0115 938 3565

PRESS AND PUBLICATIONS
Director of Communications Mrs Rachel Farmer, Diocesan Office   *Tel:* 01636 817218 (Office)
Tel: and *Fax:* 01636 816276 (Home)
07712 196381 (Mobile)
email: rachel@southwell.anglican.org
Editor of Diocesan Magazine 'C' Mrs Rachel Farmer (*as above*)

DIOCESAN RECORDS OFFICE
Nottinghamshire Archives, County House, Castle Meadow Rd, Nottingham NG1 1AG *Principal Archivist* Mr Mark Dorrington
Tel: 0115 950 4524

AREA DEANS
ARCHDEACONRY OF NEWARK
Bassetlaw and Bawtry Revd Jonathan Smithurst, The Rectory, Abbey Road, Mattersey, Doncaster, DN10 5DX   *Tel:* 01777 817364
email: j.smithurst@ctmail.co.uk

Mansfield Revd George Butler, St Mark's Vicarage, Nottingham Rd, Mansfield NG18 1BP
Tel: 01623 655548
email: revgib@tiscali.co.uk
Newark and Southwell Canon Tony Tucker, Vicarage, Main St, Balderton, Newark NG24 3NN   *Tel:* 01636 704811
07976 953068 (Mobile)
email: tonytucker57@googlemail.com
Newstead Revd Dr Richard Kellett, Vicarage, Mansfield Rd, Skegby, Sutton-in-Ashfield NG17 3ED   *Tel:* 01623 558800
email: richard@kellett.com

ARCHDEACONRY OF NOTTINGHAM
East Bingham Canon Jim Wellington, The Rectory, Nottingham Rd, Keyworth, Nottingham NG12 0UB   *Tel:* 0115 937 2017
email: jhcwelli@btinternet.com
West Bingham Revd John Bentham, 51 Chatsworth Rd, West Bridgford, Nottingham NG2 7AE
Tel: 0115 846 1054
email: john.bentham@nottingham.ac.uk
Gedling Revd Philip Williams, St James' Vicarage, Marshall Hill Drive, Mapperley, Nottingham NG3 6FY   *Tel:* 0115 960 6185
email: phil.stjames@virgin.net
Nottingham North Revd Jerry Lepine, The Rectory, 143 Russell Drive, Nottingham NG8 2BD   *Tel:* 0115 928 1798
email: jerry.lepine@btopenworld.com
Nottingham South Vacancy

DIOCESE OF TRURO

Founded in 1877. Cornwall; the Isles of Scilly; one parish in Devon.

Population 535,000   Area 1,390 sq m
Full-time Stipendiary Parochial Clergy 100   Benefices 129
Parishes 221   Churches 307
www.truro.anglican.org
Overseas link diocese: Strängnas, Sweden and Umzimvubu, South Africa.

BISHOP (15th)
Rt Revd Tim Thornton, Lis Escop, Feock, Truro TR3 6QQ [2008]   *Tel:* 01872 862657
Fax: 01872 862037
email: bishop@truro.anglican.org
[Timothy Truro]
Domestic Chaplain Vacancy
Bishop's Personal Assistant Mrs Lesley Rogers, Lis Escop   *email:* lesley.r@truro.anglican.org

SUFFRAGAN BISHOP
ST GERMANS Rt Revd Royden Screech, 32 Falmouth Rd, Truro TR1 2HX [2000]
Tel: 01872 273190
Fax: 01872 277883
email: bishop@stgermans.truro.anglican.org

CATHEDRAL CHURCH OF THE BLESSED VIRGIN MARY IN TRURO
Dean Very Revd Dr Christopher Hardwick, The Deanery, The Avenue, Truro TR1 1HR [2005]
Tel: 01872 272661
Cathedral Office 14 St Mary's St, Truro TR1 2AF
Tel: 01872 245006
Fax: 01872 277788
email: dean@trurocathedral.org.uk
Canons Residentiary
Precentor Canon Perran Gay, St Michael's House, 52 Daniell Rd, Truro TR1 2DA [1994]
Tel: 01872 245003
email: perran@trurocathedral.org.uk
Missioner Canon Philip Lambert, Foxhayes, 3 Knights Hill, Kenwyn, Truro TR1 3UY [2006]
Tel: 01872 245018
email: philip@trurocathedral.org.uk
Pastor Canon Peter Walker, The Vicarage, Feock, Truro TR3 6SD [2001]   *Tel:* 01872 862534
Tel: 01872 245016
email: peter@trurocathedral.org.uk
Chapter Canons
Ven Roger Bush [2006]
Mr Robert Foulkes [2001]
Mrs Bridget Hugh-Jones [2001]
Chief Executive Mr Neil Parsons
email: chiefexecutive@trurocathedral.org.uk
Director of Music Chris Gray, Cathedral Office
email: chris@trurocathedral.org.uk

ARCHDEACONS
BODMIN Ven Clive Cohen, Archdeacon's House, Cardynham, Bodmin PL30 4BL [2000]
Tel and *Fax:* 01208 821614
email: clive@truro.anglican.org
CORNWALL Ven Roger Bush, Westwood House, Tremorvah Crescent, Truro TR1 1NL [2006]
Tel and *Fax:* 01872 225630
email: roger@truro.anglican.org

CONVOCATION (MEMBERS OF THE HOUSE OF CLERGY OF THE GENERAL SYNOD)
Proctors for Clergy
Revd Alan Bashforth
Ven Roger Bush
Revd Canon Perran Gay

MEMBERS OF THE HOUSE OF LAITY OF THE GENERAL SYNOD
Mrs Susannah Leafe
Mrs Sheri Sturgess
Gp Capt Paul Terrett

DIOCESAN OFFICERS
Dioc Secretary Vacancy   *Tel:* 01872 274351
Fax: 01872 222510
Web: www.truro.anglican.org
Interim Managing Director Ven Clive Cohen Diocesan House, Kenwyn, Truro TR1 1JQ
Tel: 01872 274351
email: diosec@truro.anglican.org
Deputy Dioc Secretary Mrs Esther Pollard, Diocesan House, Kenwyn, Truro TR1 1JQ
Tel: 01872 274351
email: esther.pollard@truro.anglican.org
Chancellor of Diocese The Worshipful Timothy Briden, Lamb Chambers, Lamb Building, Temple, London EC4Y 7AS   *Tel:* 020 7797 8300
Fax: 020 7707 8308
email: info@lambchambers.co.uk
Registrar of Diocese and Bishop's Legal Secretary Mr Martin Follett, Truro Diocesan Registry, MichelmoresLLP, Woodwater House, Pynes Hill, Exeter EX2 5WR   *Tel:* 01392 687415
Fax: 01392 360563
email: mjf@michelmores.com

Dioc Surveyor Mr Matthew Williams, Dioc House, Kenwyn, Truro TR1 1JQ   *Tel:* 01872 241507
Fax: 01872 222510
email: matthew.williams@truro.anglican.org

DIOCESAN ORGANIZATIONS
Diocesan Office Diocesan House, Kenwyn, Truro TR1 1JQ   *Tel:* 01872 274351
Fax: 01872 222510
email: info@truro.anglican.org

ADMINISTRATION
Dioc Synod and Bishop's Council (Acting Secretary) Mrs Esther Pollard, Dioc Office
Dioc Synod (Chairman, House of Clergy) Revd Alan Bashforth, Vicarage, 6 Penwinnick Parc, St Agnes TR5 0UQ   *Tel:* 01872 553391
(Chairman, House of Laity) Dr Mike Todd
Board of Finance (Chairman) Mr David Bishop; *(Secretary)* Mrs Esther Pollard *(as above)*
Parsonages Committee Mrs Esther Pollard *(as above)*
Mission & Pastoral Committee Revd Julie Millar, Dioc Office
Glebe Committee Mrs Lyn Poole, Dioc Office
Board of Patronage Revd Paul Arthur, Rectory, 16 Trelavour Rd, St Dennis, St Austell PL26 8AH   *Tel:* 01726 822317
email: kpaularthur@googlemail.com
Designated Officer Mrs Esther Pollard *(as above)*

CHURCHES
Advisory Committee for the Care of Churches (Chairman) Mrs Christine Edwards, Garden Place, Camels, Veryan, Truro TR2 5PJ *Tel:* 01872 501727
(Secretary) Mrs Lyn Poole, Dioc Office
email: lyn.poole@truro.anglican.org
Truro Diocesan Guild of Ringers (President) Mr Michael Wycherley, 34 St Gluvias St, Penryn TR10 8BJ *Tel:* 01326 374119; *(Gen Secretary)* Mr Robert Perry, 11 Trevaylor Close, Truro TR1 1RP, *Tel:* 01872 277117
Churches Uses Committee (Secretary) Mrs Lyn Poole *(as above)*

EDUCATION AND TRAINING
Director and Secretary of Education Mrs Sue Green, Dioc Office   *Tel:* 01872 247214
email: sue.green@truro.anglican.org
Diocesan Deanery Development Facilitator Mrs Sarah Welply *(same address)*
email: sarah.welply@truro.anglican.org
Diocesan Deanery Development Facilitator Mrs Shelley Porter *(same address)*
email: shelley.porter@truro.anglican.org

MINISTRY
Director of Ministerial Formation & Development Revd Paul Arthur, Rectory, 16 Trelavour Rd, St Dennis, St Austell PL26 8AH   *Tel:* 01726 822317
email: kpaularthur@googlemail.com
Co-Directors of Ordinands The Bishop of St Germans *(as above)*; Canon Julia Wilkinson, Rectory, St Issey, Wadebridge PL27 7HJ
Tel and Fax: 01841 540314
email: canjulia@btinternet.com

South-west Ministry Training Course (Principal) Revd David Moss, Amory Building, University of Exeter, Rennes Drive, Exeter EX4 4RJ
Tel: 01392 264403
email: principal@swmtc.org.uk
Web: www.swmtc.org.uk
Warden of Readers Rt Revd Royden Screech *(as above)*
Deputy Warden of Readers Revd Paul Arthur *(as above)*
Clergy Retirement and Widows Officer Revd Owen Blatchly, 1 Rose Cottages, East Rd, Stithians, Truro TR3 7BD   *Tel:* 01209 860845

EVANGELISM AND UNITY
Chairman Revd Angela Butler, 22 Esplanade Road, Pentire, Newquay TR7 1QB
Tel: 01637 859238
email: angelambutler@btinternet.com
Officer for Unity Revd Elizabeth Foot, Godrevy House, Penpol Ave, Hayle TR27 4NG
Tel: 01736 757151
email: godrevyvic@hotmail.co.uk
World Church Committee (Chairman) Bishop of St Germans

KINGDOM GROUP
Social Responsibility Officer Revd Andrew Yates, Dioc Office
email: andrew.yates@truro.anglican.org

PRESS AND PUBLICATIONS
Dioc Communications Officer Mr David Watson, Dioc Office   *Tel:* 01872 274351
email: david.watson@truro.anglican.org
Editor of Dioc News Leaflet Mr David Watson *(as above)*
Editor of Dioc Directory Mrs Clare Jones *(as above)*

DIOCESAN RECORDS
Diocesan Records Officer Mr Paul Brough, County Archivist, County Hall, Truro TR1 3AY
Tel: 01872 323127

STEWARDSHIP
Revd Julie Millar, Dioc House   *Tel:* 01872 274351

RURAL DEANS
ARCHDEACONRY OF CORNWALL
St Austell Revd Paul Arthur, Rectory, 16 Trelavour Rd, St Dennis, St Austell PL26 8AH
Tel: 01726 822317
email: kpaularthur@googlemail.com
Carnmarth North Revd Olive Stevens, Hideaway, The Square, Portreath, Redruth TR16 4LA
Tel: 01209 842372
email: olivestevens@aol.com
Carnmarth South Canon John Harris, St Gluvias Vicarage, Penryn TR10 9LQ   *Tel:* 01326 373356
email: john.harris@stgluvias.org.uk
Kerrier Revd Lesley Walker, Rectory, St Martin, Helston TR12 6BU   *Tel:* 01326 231971
email: walker53@btopenworld.com

Penwith Revd Howard Peskett, 7 North Parade, Penzance TR18 4SH   *Tel:* 01736 362913
email: howard.peskett@btinternet.com
Powder Revd Alan Bashforth, Vicarage, 6 Penwinnick Parc, St Agnes, Truro TR5 0UG
Tel: 01872 553391
email: onepaw@btinternet.com
Pydar Revd Christopher Malkinson, Vicarage, 46 Treverbyn Rd, Padstow PL28 8DN
Tel: 01841 533776
email: chrismalk@hotmail.com

ARCHDEACONRY OF BODMIN

East Wivelshire (*Acting*) Revd Peter Sharpe, Rectory, Liskeard Road, Callington PL17 7JD
Tel: 01579 383341
email: rector.callington@gmail.com

Stratton Canon Rob Dickenson, Rectory, The Glebe, Week St Mary, Holsworthy EX22 6UY
Tel: 01288 341134
email: parsonrob@aol.com

Trigg Major Vacancy

Trigg Minor and Bodmin Canon Sherry Bryan, Rectory, Green Briar, Coombe Lane, St Breward PL30 4LT   *Tel* and *Fax:* 01208 851829
email: sherrybryan4@aol.com

West Wivelshire Canon Tony Ingleby, The Rectory, Church St, Liskeard PL24 3AQ
Tel: 01579 342178
email: revtonyingleby@gmail.com

DIOCESE OF WAKEFIELD

Founded in 1888. Wakefield; Kirklees; Calderdale; Barnsley, except for an area in the south-east (SHEFFIELD); an area of Leeds; a few parishes in North Yorkshire.

Population 1,118,000   Area 557 sq m
Full-time Stipendiary Parochial Clergy 130   Benefices 148
Parishes 184   Churches 239
Overseas link dioceses: Adelaide (Australia), Faisalabad (Pakistan),
Mara (Tanzania) and Skara (Sweden).

BISHOP (12th)
Rt Revd Stephen Platten, Bishop's Lodge, Woodthorpe Lane, Wakefield WF2 6JL [2003]
Tel: 01924 255349
Fax: 01924 250202
email: bishop@bishopofwakefield.org.uk
Bishop's Domestic Chaplain and Communications Officer Revd Matthew Bullimore, Bishops Lodge, Woodthorpe Lane, Sandal, Wakefield WF2 6JL
Tel: 01924 255349
Tel: 01924 250574 (Direct Line)
email: mbullimore@bishopofwakefield.org.uk

SUFFRAGAN BISHOP
PONTEFRACT Rt Revd Anthony Robinson, Pontefract House, 181A Manygates Lane, Sandal Wakefield WF2 7DR [1998]   Tel: 01924 250781
Fax: 01924 240490
email: bishop.pontefract@wakefield.anglican.org

CATHEDRAL CHURCH OF ALL SAINTS
Cathedral Centre 8–10 Westmorland St, Wakefield WF1 1PJ   Tel: 01924 373923
Fax: 01924 215054
email: admin@wakefield-cathedral.org.uk
Web: www.wakefield-cathedral.org.uk
Dean Very Revd Jonathan Greener, The Deanery, 1 Cathedral Close, Margaret St, Wakefield WF1 2DP   Tel: 01924 373923 (Office)
01924 239308 (Home)
email:
jonathan.greener@wakefield-cathedral.org.uk
Administrator and Chapter Clerk Dr Nigel Russell
Tel: 01924 434482 (Direct line)
email: nigel.russell@wakefield-cathedral.org.uk
Dean's PA Mr Neil Holland   Tel: 01924 373923
email: neil.holland@wakefield-cathedral.org.uk
Cathedral Secretary Roz Cochrane
Tel: 01924 373923
email: roz.cochrane@wakefield-cathedral.org.uk
Head Verger Mrs Julie Lovell
Tel: 01924 373923 (Direct Line)

Canons Residentiary
Sub Dean and Canon Pastor Canon Michael Rawson, 3 Cathedral Close, Margaret St, Wakefield WF1 2DP [2007]
Tel: 01924 373923 (Office)
01924 379743 (Home)
email:
michael.rawson@wakefield-cathedral.org.uk
Canon Precentor Canon Andrea Hofbauer, 4 Cathedral Close, Margaret St, Wakefield WF1 2DP [2009]   Tel: 01924 373923 (Office)
01924 200191 (Home)
email: andi.hofbauer@wakefield-cathedral.org.uk
Rt Revd Anthony Robinson, Pontefract House, 181A Manygates Lane, Sandal, Wakefield WF2 7DR [2005]   Tel: 01924 250781
email: bishop.pontefract@wakefield.anglican.org
Canon Dr John Lawson, 7 Belgravia Rd, St John's, Wakefield WF1 3JP [2005]   Tel: 01924 380182
email: john.lawson@wakefield.anglican.org
Canon Tony Macpherson, 14 Belgravia Rd, St John's, Wakefield WF1 3JP [2007]
Tel: 01924 275274
email: canontonymac@gmail.com
Honorary Chaplains Revd Prof Roger Grainger, Revd George Midgley, Canon Stuart Ramsden, Revd Derek Birch
Ecumenical Canons Bishop Malkaz Songulashvili (Baptist Church of Georgia) [2006], Bishop Arthur Roche (Roman Catholic Bishop of Leeds) [2006], Revd Peter Whittaker (Chair, W. Yorkshire District of Methodist Churches) [2006]
Honorary Assistant Priest Revd June Lawson
email: jlawson@mirfield.org.uk
Lay Canons
Arthur Mauya, Dr Juliet Barker, Mrs Linda Box, Mrs Angela Byram, Dr Keith Judkins, Mrs Celia Kilner, Prof Michael Clarke, Mr Yaqub Masih, Hon Judge John Bullimore, Mr Barry Sheerman MP, Ms Kate Taylor
Clerk to the College of Canons Mrs Linda Box, Bank House, Burton St, Wakefield WF1 2DA
Tel: 01924 373467
Fax: 01924 366234
email: info@dixon-coles-gill.co.uk
Education Officer Ms Ali Bullivent
email: ali.bullivent@wakefield-cathedral.org.uk

Director of Music Mr Tom Moore, Cathedral Office   email: music@wakefield-cathedral.org.uk
Assistant Director of Music Vacancy

ARCHDEACONS
HALIFAX Ven Robert Freeman, 2 Vicarage Gardens, Rastrick, Brighouse HD6 3HD
Tel: 01484 714553
Fax: 01484 711897
email: archdeacon.halifax@wakefield.anglican.org
PONTEFRACT Ven Peter Townley, The Vicarage, Kirkthorpe, Wakefield WF1 5SZ
Tel: 01924 896327
Tel: 01924 434459 (Church House Direct Line)
Fax: 01924 364834 (Church House)
email:
archdeacon.pontefract@wakefield.anglican.org

CONVOCATION (MEMBERS OF THE HOUSE OF CLERGY OF THE GENERAL SYNOD)
Dignitaries in Convocation
The Dean of Wakefield
Proctors for Clergy
Revd Canon Joyce Jones
Ven Robert Freeman
Revd Maggie McLean
Revd Paul Cartwright

MEMBERS OF THE HOUSE OF LAITY OF THE GENERAL SYNOD
Mr David Ashton
Mrs Alison Fisher
Mrs Mary Judkins
Mr Paul Neville

DIOCESAN OFFICERS
Dioc Secretary Mr Ashley Ellis, Church House, 1 South Parade, Wakefield WF1 1LP
Tel: 01924 371802
Fax: 01924 364834
email: diocesan.secretary@wakefield.anglican.org
Chancellor of Diocese Worshipful Chancellor His Honour Judge Paul Downes, Norwich Combined Court, Law Courts, Bishopgate, Norwich NR3 1UR   Tel: 01603 728200
email: hhjudge.downes@judiciary.gsi.gov.uk
Joint Registrars of Diocese and Bishop's Legal Secretaries Mr Julian Gill and Mrs Julia Wilding, Bank House, Burton St, Wakefield WF1 2DA
Tel: 01924 373467
Fax: 01924 366234
email: info@dixon-coles-gill.com

DIOCESAN ORGANIZATIONS
Diocesan Office Church House, 1 South Parade, Wakefield WF1 1LP   Tel: 01924 371802
Fax: 01924 364834
email: church.house@wakefield.anglican.org

ADMINISTRATION
Dioc Secretary Mr Ashley Ellis, Church House
Finance Manager and Deputy Secretary Mr Bryan Lewis, Church House

Dioc Synod (Chair, House of Clergy) Canon Tony Macpherson, 14 Belgravia Rd, St John's, Wakefield WF1 3JP   Tel: 01924 378360
email: canontonymac@gmail.com
(Chair, House of Laity) Mrs Mary Judkins, The Old Vicarage, 3 Church Lane, East Ardsley, Wakefield WF3 2LJ   Tel: 01924 826802
email: elephantmj@aol.com
(Secretary) Mr Ashley Ellis (as above)
Dioc Communications Officer Mrs Jane Bower, Church House   Tel: 01924 371802
email: jane.bower@wakefield.anglican.org
Board of Finance (Chairman) Ven Robert Freeman, Church House; (Secretary) Mr Ashley Ellis (as above)
Finance Manager Mr Bryan Lewis, Church House
Dioc Property Manager Ms Helen Price, Church House
Assistant Property Manager Mr Kevin Smith
Mission and Pastoral Committee Mr Ashley Ellis (as above)
Dioc Trust Mr Bryan Lewis (as above)
Giving and Resources Adviser Mrs Jo Beacroft-Mitchell, Church House
Board of Patronage Mrs Linda Box, Bank House, Burton St, Wakefield WF1 2DA
Tel: 01924 373467
Fax: 01924 366234
email: info@dixon-coles-gill.com
Designated Officer Mrs Julia Wilding (as above)

CHURCHES
Advisory Committee for the Care of Churches Mrs Julia Wilding (as above)

EDUCATION
Director of Education Canon Ian Wildey, Church House
Board of Education (Chairman) Ven Peter Townley; (Secretary) Revd Canon Ian Wildey

RESOURCING CHILDREN, YOUTH AND FAMILIES TEAM
Team Co-ordinator and Children's Adviser (5–11) Vacancy
Under 5s Adviser Mrs Ellie Wilson, Church House
11–18s Adviser Mrs Liz Morton, Church House

MINISTRY
Dioc Director of Ordinands Revd Stephen Race, St John's Vicarage, Green Rd, Dodworth, Barnsley S75 3R   Tel: 01226 206276
email: stephen.race@wakefield.anglican.org
Asst Directors of Ordinands Revd Calvert Prentis, 132 Trinity Street, Huddersfield HD1 4DT
Tel: 01484 422998
email: holytvicar@btinternet.com
Revd Joy Cousans, The Rectory, Church Lane, Clayton West, Huddersfield HD8 9LY
Tel: 01484 862321
email: joy@daveandjoy.plus.com

Wakefield   **139**

Canon Owen Page, Vicarage, 7 Fern Valley Chase, Todmorden OL14 7BS   Tel: 01706 813180
email: owen@opage.freeserve.co.uk
Dioc Director of Training Revd Dr John Lawson, Church House   email: jal@bh-cc.co.uk
Warden of Readers Revd John Hellewell, Vicarage, Church Lane, Mount Pellon, Halifax HX2 0EF
Tel: 01422 365027
email: john@revjhell.freeserve.co.uk
Adviser for Women's Ministry Revd June Lawson
Vocations Officer Revd Matthew Pollard, 1 Vicarage Gardens, Rastrick, Brighouse HD6 3HD
Tel: 01484 713386
Coordinator for Local Ministry Vacancy
Wakefield Ministry Consultancy Team, Church House
Continuing Ministerial Education Officer Canon Stephen Kelly, Vicarage, Woolley, Wakefield WF4 2JU   Tel: 01226 382550
email: stephen.kelly@wakefield.anglican.org
Bishop's Adviser for Pastoral Care and Counselling Canon Revd Christine Bullimore, Rectory, 14 Grange Drive, Emley, Huddersfield HD8 9SF
Tel: 01924 849161
email: chrisbullimore@talktalk.net

SOCIAL RESPONSIBILITY

Development Officer Susan Parker, Church House
Diocesan Co-ordinator for Social Responsibility Revd Maureen Browell, 150 Fleminghouse Lane, Huddersfield HD5 8UD   Tel: 01484 545085
email: Maureenbrowell@talktalk.net
Diocesan Rural Officer (Farming) Revd Dennis Handley, Vicarage, Ripponden, Sowerby Bridge HX6 4DF   Tel: 01422 822239
email:dennisandcatherine@ripponden.fslife.co.uk
Diocesan Rural Officer (Broader Rural Issues) Revd Hugh Baker, Vicarage, 2 Netherton Hall Gardens, Netherton, Wakefield WF4 4JA
Tel: 01924 278384
email: hugh.baker@tesco.net
Advisers on Urban Issues The Revd David Fletcher, 37 Hops Lane, Wheatley, Halifax HX3 5FB
Tel: 01422 349844
email: de.fletcher@btinternet.com
The Revd David Nicholson, The Vicarage, St John's Road, Cudworth, Barnsley S72 8DE
Tel: 01226 710279
email: fr_d_pp_cudworth@hotmail.com
Diocesan Environmental Issues Adviser Revd Bill Halling, 56 Westborough Drive, Highroad Well, Halifax HX2 7QL   Tel: 01422 320829
email: halling@uwclub.net
Diocesan Theology and Society Advisers Revd Maggie McLean, The Vicarage, 107a Stocksbank Road, Mirfield WF4 9QT   Tel: 01924 493277
email: m.a.mclean@btinternet.com
Revd Keith Griffin, The Vicarage, 3 Vicarage Meadows, Holmfirth HD9 1DZ
Tel: 01484 682644
email: revdkg@tiscali.co.uk

Adviser on Disability Vacancy
Canon Missioner Canon Tony Macpherson (as above)

OTHER OFFICERS

Safeguarding and Child Protection Adviser Mrs Jenny Price, Church House
email: jenny.price@wakefield.anglican.org
Bishop's Adviser for Ecumenical Affairs (for West Yorkshire) Revd Glenn Coggins, The Vicarage, 1 Church Lane, East Ardsley, Wakefield WF3 2LJ
Tel: 01924 822184
email: glenn@cogginsg.freeserve.co.uk
Ecumenical Affairs Officer (for South Yorkshire) Revd Simon Moor, The Vicarage, 12 High Street, Silkstone, Barnsley S75 4JN   Tel: 01226 790232
email: samoor@talktalk.net
Chaplain Among Deaf People Revd Bob Shrine, Vicarage, 80 Carr House Rd, Shelf, Halifax HX3 5LS   Typetalk: 18002 01274 677693
Fax: 01274 677693
email: bob.shrine@ukonline.co.uk
Interfaith Relations The Revd Leslie Pinfield, The Vicarage, 17 Cross Church St, Paddock, Huddersfield HD1 4SN   Tel: 01484 530814
email:frleslie@btopenworld.com
Retired Clergy and Widows Officers Revd John Wilkinson, 29 Pontefract Rd, Ferrybridge, Knottingley WF11 8PN   Tel: 01977 607250
Revd Dick Bradnum, 4 Southlands Drive, Huddersfield HD2 2LT   Tel: 01484 420721

PRESS AND PUBLICATIONS

Dioc Year Book (Editor) Mr Ashley Ellis, Church House

DIOCESAN RECORD OFFICE

County Archivist Lisa Broadest, West Yorkshire Archive Service, Registry of Deeds, Newstead Rd, Wakefield WF1 2DE   Tel: 01924 305980
email: wakefield@wyjs.org.uk

DIOCESAN RESOURCES CENTRE

Wakefield Centre Manager: Resourcing Children, Youth and Families Team
Mirfield Centre Manager: Canon John Lawson
Assistant Manager (Wakefield and Mirfield) Mrs Sheila Crosby, Church House

RURAL DEANS
ARCHDEACONRY OF HALIFAX

Almondbury Revd Richard Steel, Rectory, Church Lane, Kirkheaton, Huddersfield HD5 0BH
Tel: 01484 532410
email: richard.steel@ntlworld.com
Brighouse and Elland Revd David Burrows, All Saints' Vicarage, Charles St, Elland HX5 0JF
Tel: 01422 373184
email: rectorofelland@btinternet.com
Calder Valley Canon James Allison, Vicarage, Brier Hey Lane, Mytholmroyd, Hebden Bridge HX7 5PJ   Tel: 01422 883130
email: erringden@aol.com

Halifax Revd Stephen Bradberry, 129 Paddock Lane, Norton Tower, Halifax HX2 0NT
Tel: 01422 358282
email: sbradberry@tiscali.co.uk
Huddersfield Revd Mary Railton-Crowder, The Vicarage, 4 Brendon Drive, Birkby, Huddersfield HD2 2DF
Tel: 01484 546966
email: revmrc@yahoo.com
Kirkburton Canon Christine Bullimore, Rectory, 14 Grange Drive, Emley, Huddersfield HD8 9SF
Tel: 01924 849161
Fax: 01924 849219
email: chrisbullimore@talktalk.net

ARCHDEACONRY OF PONTEFRACT
Barnsley Revd Stephen Race, St John's Vicarage, Green Road, Dodworth, Barnsley S75 3RT
Tel: 01226 206276
email: stephen.race@wakefield.anglican.org

Birstall Canon Felicity Lawson, St Peter's House, 2a Church Street, Gildersome LS27 7AS
Tel: 0113 253 3339
email: felicity.lawson@tiscali.co.uk
Dewsbury Revd Paul Maybury, Vicarage, 12 Fearnley Avenue, Ossett WF5 9ET
Tel: 01924 217379
Fax: 0870 137 5994
email: paul@trinityossett.org.uk
Pontefract Canon Bob Cooper, St Giles Vicarage, 9 The Mount, Pontefract WF8 1NE
Tel: 01977 706803
email: robert.cooper@onetel.net
Wakefield Canon Patricia Maguire, St George's Vicarage, 23c Broadway, Wakefield WF2 8AA
Tel: 01924 373088
email: revmaguire@tiscali.co.uk

DIOCESE OF WINCHESTER

Founded in 676. Hampshire, except for the south-eastern quarter (PORTSMOUTH), an area in the north-east (GUILDFORD), a small area in the west (SALISBURY) and one parish in the north (OXFORD); an area of eastern Dorset; the Channel Islands.

Population 1,291,000   Area 1,216 sq m
Full-time Stipendiary Parochial Clergy 186   Benefices 189
Parishes 259   Churches 406
www.winchester.anglican.org
Overseas link provinces: Province of Uganda, Province of Myanmar, Provinces of Rwanda, Burundi and Republic of Congo (formerly Zaïre).

BISHOP (96th)
Rt Revd Michael Charles Scott-Joynt, Wolvesey, Winchester. SO23 9ND [1995]   *Tel:* 01962 854050
Fax: 01962 897088
email: michael.scott-joynt@dsl.pipex.com
[Michael Winton]
Bishop's Lay Assistant Vacancy (*same address*)
Tel: 01962 897082
Bishop's Secretary Miss Joyce Cockell (*same address*)   *Tel:* 01962 854050
email: joyce.cockell@winchester.anglican.org

SUFFRAGAN BISHOPS
SOUTHAMPTON Vacancy
BASINGSTOKE Rt Revd Peter Hancock, Bishop's Lodge, Colden Lane, Old Alresford SO24 9DH
Tel: 01962 737330
email: bishop.peter@winchester.anglican.org

HONORARY ASSISTANT BISHOPS
Rt Revd John Austin Baker, Norman Corner, 4 Mede Villas, Kingsgate Rd, Winchester SO23 9QQ [1994]   *Tel:* 01962 861388
Rt Revd Simon Hedley Burrows, 8 Quarry Rd, Winchester, SO23 0JF [1994]   *Tel:* 01962 853332
Rt Revd John Dennis, 7 Conifer Close, Winchester SO22 6SH [1999]   *Tel:* 01962 868881
Rt Revd Edwin Barnes, 1 Queen Elizabeth Ave, Lymington SO41 9HN [2001]   *Tel:* 01590 610133
Rt Revd John Ellison, The Furrow, Evingar Rd, Whitchurch RG28 7EU [2008]   *Tel:* 01256 892126
Rt Revd Christopher Herbert, 1 Beacon Close, Boundstone, Farnham GU10 4PA [2010]
Tel: 01252 795600

CATHEDRAL CHURCH OF THE HOLY TRINITY, AND OF ST PETER, ST PAUL AND OF ST SWITHUN
Dean Very Revd James Edgar Atwell, Cathedral Office, 9 The Close, Winchester SO23 9LS [2006]
Tel: 01962 857203
Fax: 01962 857264
email: the.dean@winchester-cathedral.org.uk

Cathedral Office 9 The Close, Winchester SO23 9LS
Tel: 01962 857200
Fax: 01962 857201
email:
cathedral.office@winchester-cathedral.org.uk
Web: www.winchester–cathedral.org.uk

Canons Residentiary
Canon Roland Riem, Cathedral Office, 9 The Close, Winchester SO23 9LS [2005]
Tel: 01962 857216
email: roland.riem@winchester-cathedral.org.uk
Canon Michael St John-Channell, 8 The Close, Winchester SO23 9LS [2006]   *Tel:* 01962 857211
email: precentor@winchester-cathedral.org.uk
Canon Missioner Canon Steve Pittis, Cathedral Office, 9 The Close, Winchester SO23 9LS [2008]
Tel: 01962 857241
email: pittisinc@virginmedia.com

Lay Canons
Receiver General Mrs Annabelle Boyes Cathedral Office, 9 The Close, Winchester SO23 9LS
Tel: 01962 857206
Fax: 01962 857201
email: annabelle.boyes@
winchester-cathedral.org.uk
Professor Lord Raymond Plant, Cathedral Office, 9 The Close, Winchester SO23 9LS
Tel: 01962 857200
Mr John Pringle, Cathedral Office, 9 The Close, Winchester SO23 9LS   *Tel:* 01962 857200
Pastoral Assistant Canon Jacqueline Browning, Cathedral Office, 9 The Close, Winchester SO23 9LS   *Tel:* 01962 857237
email:
jackie.browning@winchester-cathedral.org.uk
Clerk at Law Mr Julian Hartwell, Martyrwell, Cheriton, Alresford SO24 0QA
Tel: 01962 857200
Director of Music Mr Andrew Lumsden, Cathedral Office, 9 The Close, Winchester SO23 9LS   *Tel:* 01962 857218
email:
andrew.lumsden@winchester-cathedral.org.uk
Assistant Director of Music Mr Simon Bell, Cathedral Office, 9 The Close, Winchester SO23 9LS   *Tel:* 01962 857213
email: simon.bell@winchester-cathedral.org.uk

ARCHDEACONS
WINCHESTER Ven Michael Harley, 22 St John's St, Winchester SO23 0HF [2009]   *Tel:* 01962 869442
email: michael.harley@winchester.anglican.org
BOURNEMOUTH Vacancy

CONVOCATION (MEMBERS OF THE HOUSE OF CLERGY OF THE GENERAL SYNOD)
Dignitaries in Convocation
The Bishop of Basingstoke
Proctors for Clergy
The Very Revd Bob Key
Revd David Williams
Ven Michael Harley
Canon Clive Hawkins
Revd Rosalind Rutherford

MEMBERS OF THE HOUSE OF LAITY OF THE GENERAL SYNOD
Mr John Davies
Dr Tony Bennett
Mrs Christine Fry
Mr Ken Shorey
Dr Brian Walker
Channel Islands
Mrs Jane Bisson
Mr David Robilliard

DIOCESAN OFFICERS
Dioc Secretary Mr Andrew Robinson, Old Alresford Place, Alresford SO24 9DH
Tel: 01962 737305
Fax: 01962 737358
email: andrew.robinson@winchester.anglican.org
Chancellor of Diocese Worshipful His Honour Christopher Clark QC, c/o Dioc Office
Registrar of Diocese and Bishop's Legal Secretary Mr Andrew Johnson, Batt Broadbent, Minster Chambers, 42/44 Castle Street, Salisbury SP1 3TX
Tel: 01722 411141
email: aj@battbroadbent.co.uk

DIOCESAN ORGANIZATIONS
Diocesan Office Old Alresford Place, Alresford SO24 9DH   *Tel:* 01962 737300
Fax: 01962 737358
Web: www.winchester.anglican.org

ADMINISTRATION
Assistant Dioc Secretary Mr Colin Harbidge, Old Alresford Place   *Tel:* 01962 737307
email: colin.harbidge@winchester.anglican.org
Director of Finance Mr Stephen Collyer, Old Alresford Place   *Tel:* 01962 737336
email: stephen.collyer@winchester.anglican.org
Dioc Synod (*Chairman, House of Clergy*) Canon Ian Tomlinson, Rectory, Ragged Appleshaw, Andover SP11 9HX   *Tel:* 01264 772414
email: ian@raggedappleshaw.freeserve.co.uk
(*Chairman, House of Laity*) Mr Ian Newman, Meadow View, 15 Bowerwood Rd, Fordingbridge SP6 1BL   *Tel:* 01425 653269
email: ian@innewman.co.uk

(*Secretary*) Mr Andrew Robinson, (*as above*)
Board of Finance (*Chairman*) Mr Arthur Binns, Nil-Des, Ashley Lane, New Milton BH25 5AQ
Tel: 01425 611379
email: dustyakjb@aol.com
(*Secretary*) Mr Andrew Robinson (*as above*)
Director of Property Mr Rolf Hawkins, Old Alresford Place   *Tel:* 01962 737330
email: rolf.hawkins@winchester.anglican.org
Mission and Pastoral Committee (*Secretary*) Canon Simon Baker, Old Alresford Place
Electoral Registration Officer Miss Jayne Tarry, Old Alresford Place   *Tel:* 01962 737348
email: jayne.tarry@winchester.anglican.org
Editor of Dioc Directory Miss Jayne Tarry (*as above*)

CHURCHES
Advisory Committee for the Care of Churches (*Chairman*) Canon Michael Anderson, Old Alresford Place
(*Secretary*) Mrs Catherine Roberts
Tel: 01962 737306
email: catherine.roberts@winchester.anglican.org

EDUCATION
Director of Education Mr Tony Blackshaw (*Joint working with Diocese of Portsmouth*), First Floor, Peninsular House, Wharf Rd, Portsmouth PO2 8HB   *Tel:* 023 9289 9681
email: tony.blackshaw@portsmouth.anglican.org

DISCIPLESHIP AND MINISTRY
Director of Discipleship & Ministry Canon Simon Baker (*as above*)
Vocations, Recruitment and Selection Officer (*including ordinands*) Revd Julia Mourant
Tel: 01962 737316
email: julia.mourant@winchester.anglican.org
Ministry Training Officer (*including ordinands*) Revd Duncan Strathie   *Tel:* 01962 737314
email: duncan.strathie@winchester.anglican.org
Continuing Ministerial Development Officer Revd Norman Boakes   *Tel:* 01962 737314
email: norman.boakes@winchester.anglican.org
Adult Evangelism and Discipleship Adviser Revd Mike Powis, Old Alresford Place
Tel: 01962 737354
email: mike.powis@winchester.anglican.org
Diocesan Children & Families Adviser Mr Andy Saunders, Old Alresford Place   *Tel:* 01962 737321
email: andy.saunders@winchester.anglican.org
Diocesan Youth Oficer Mr Pete Maidment
Tel: 01962 737320
email: pete.maidment@winchester.anglican.org
Rural Officer Revd Robert Stapleton, New Vicarage, Romsey Rd, King's Sombourne, Stockbridge SO20 6PR   *Tel:* 01974 388223
email: robertstapleton@hotmail.com

ADVISERS
Stewardship Adviser Mr Gordon Randall, Old Alresford Place   *Tel:* 01962 737232
email: gordon.randall@winchester.anglican.org

Communications Adviser Ms Abha Thakor, Old Alresford Place   Tel: 01962 737325
email: abha.thakor@winchester.anglican.org
Clergy HR Adviser Ms Susan Beckett, Old Alresford Place   Tel: 01962 737353
email: susan.beckett@winchester.anglican.org

DIOCESAN RECORD OFFICES
Hants. Record Office, Sussex St, Winchester SO23 8TH Archivist Janet Smith Tel: 01962 846154; email: enquiries.archives@hants.gov.uk (For diocesan records and parishes in Hampshire [except Southampton], Bournemouth and Christchurch)
Southampton City Record Office, Civic Centre, Southampton SO14 7LY Archivist Mrs Sue Woolgar   Tel: 023 8083 2251
email: city.archives@southampton.gov.uk (For parishes in Southampton)
Guernsey Island Archives, St Barnabas, Cornet St, St Peter Port, Guernsey GY1 1LF
Tel: 01481 724512
Fax: 01481 715814
email: archives@gov.gg
Jersey Archive Service, Clarence Rd, St Helier, Jersey JE2 4JY Archivist Linda Romeril
Tel: 01534 833300
Fax: 01534 833301
email: archives@jerseyheritagetrust.org

SAFEGUARDING AND INCLUSION
Director for Safeguarding and Inclusion Ms Jane Fisher, Old Alresford Place   Tel: 01962 737347
email: jane.fisher@winchester.anglican.org

TOURISM
Churches and Tourism Adviser Vacancy

AREA & RURAL DEANS
ARCHDEACONRY OF BOURNEMOUTH
Bournemouth Revd Andy McPherson, Vicarage, 53a Holdenhurst Avenue, Iford, Bournemouth BH7 6RB   Tel: 01202 425978
email: parish.office@stsaviours.f2s.com
Christchurch Revd Mark Godson, The Vicarage, 71 Church Street, Fordingbridge SP6 1BB
Tel: 01425 650855
email: team.rector@gmail.com
Eastleigh Canon Peter Vargeson, The Vicarage, School Road, Bursledon, Southampton SO31 8BW   Tel: 023 8040 2821
email: peter.vargeson@bursledonparish.org

Lyndhurst Revd Dominic Furness, The Vicarage, Lymington Rd, Milford-on-Sea, Lymington SO41 0QN   Tel: 01590 643289
email: dominic.furness@tiscali.co.uk
Romsey Revd Ron Corne, Broughton Rectory, Rectory Lane, Broughton, Stockbridge SO20 8AB
Tel: 01794 301287
email: cronandrew@aol.com
Southampton Revd Gary Philbrick, The Vicarage, 357 Burgess Rd, Southampton SO16 3BD
Tel: 023 8055 4231
email: gary.philbrick@dsl.pipex.com

ARCHDEACONRY OF WINCHESTER
Alresford Revd Phil Collins, The Rectory, 37 Jacklyns Lane, Alresford SO24 9LF
Tel: 01962 732105
email: nortoncollins@yahoo.co.uk
Alton Revd Howard Wright, The Vicarage, 22 Lymington Bottom, Four Marks, Alton GU34 5AA   Tel: 01420 563344
email: howardwright@xalt.co.uk
Andover Revd Jill Bentall, Rectory, Penton Mewsey, Andover SP11 0RD   Tel: 01264 773554
Basingstoke Revd Andrew Bishop, The Vicarage, Church Lane, Old Basing, Basingstoke RG24 7DJ
Tel: 01256 473762
email: as.bishop@tiscali.co.uk
Odiham Canon Robin Ewbank, Vicarage, Church Lane, Hartley Wintney, Hook RG27 8DZ
Tel: 01252 842670
email: robin.ewbank@stjohnshw.co.uk
Whitchurch Revd Christine Dale, The Rectory, Mount Rd, Woolton Hill, Newbury RG20 9QZ
Tel: 01635 253323
email: cdale001@btinternet.com
Winchester Revd Alan Gordon, Rectory, 4 Campion Way, King's Worthy, Winchester SO23 7QP   Tel: 01962 882166
email: rector@worthyparishes.org.uk

CHANNEL ISLANDS
Dean of Jersey Very Revd Bob Key, The Deanery, David Place, St Helier, Jersey, CI JE2 4TE
Tel: 01534 720001
email: robert_f_key@yahoo.com
Dean of Guernsey Very Revd Paul Mellor, Deanery, Cornet St, St Peter Port, Guernsey, CI GY1 1BZ   Tel: 01481 720036
Fax: 01481 722948
email: paul@townchurch.org.gg

DIOCESE OF WORCESTER

Founded in 679. Worcestershire, except for a few parishes in the south (GLOUCESTER) and in the north (BIRMINGHAM). Dudley; a few parishes in Wolverhampton, Sandwell and in northern Gloucestershire.

Population 845,000   Area 671 sq m
Full-time Stipendiary Parochial Clergy 120   Benefices 103
Parishes 175   Churches 286
www.cofe-worcester.org.uk
Overseas link diocese: Peru (Province of Southern Cone).

BISHOP (113th)
Rt Revd John Geoffrey Inge, The Bishop's Office, The Old Palace, Deansway, Worcester WR1 2JE [2007]   *Tel:* 01905 731599
                            Fax: 01905 739382
email: bishop.worcester@cofe-worcester.org.uk
[John Wigorn]

SUFFRAGAN BISHOP
DUDLEY Rt Revd David Stuart Walker, Bishop's House, Bishop's Walk, Cradley Heath B64 7RH [2000]   *Tel:* 0121 550 3407
                            Fax: 0121 550 7340
email: bishop.david@cofe-worcester.org.uk

HONORARY ASSISTANT BISHOPS
Rt Revd Christopher Mayfield, Harwood House, 54 Primrose Crescent, St Peter's, Worcester WR5 3HT [2002]   *Tel:* 01905 764822
Rt Revd Mark Santer, 81 Clarence Rd, Moseley, Birmingham B13 9UH [2002]   *Tel:* 0121 441 2194
Rt Revd Humphrey Taylor, 10 High St, Honey-bourne, Evesham WR10 7PQ [2003]
                            Tel: 01386 934846
Rt Revd Andrew Burnham, Bishop's House, Dry Sandford, Abingdon, Oxford OX13 6JP
                            Tel: 01865 390746

CATHEDRAL CHURCH OF CHRIST AND THE BLESSED MARY THE VIRGIN OF WORCESTER
Dean Very Revd Peter Gordon Atkinson, The Deanery, 10 College Green, Worcester WR1 2LH [2007]   *Tel:* 01905 732939
                            Tel: 01905 732909 (Office)
email: PeterAtkinson@worcestercathedral.org.uk
Canons Residentiary
Canon Dr Alvyn Pettersen, 2 College Green, Worcester WR1 2LH [2002]   *Tel:* 01905 732942
email: AlvynPettersen@worcestercathedral.org.uk
Canon David Stanton, 15A College Green, Worcester WR1 2LH [2005]   *Tel:* 01905 732940
     email: DavidStanton@worcestercathedral.org.uk
Canon Dr Georgina Byrne, 15B College Green, Worcester WR1 2LH [2009]   *Tel:* 01905 732900
email:
     GeorginaByrne@worcestercathedral.org.uk

Lay Canons
Vacancy
Cathedral Steward Mr Les West, Chapter Office
                            Tel: 01905 732907
Master of Choristers and Cathedral Organist Mr Adrian Lucas, Chapter Office   *Tel:* 01905 732916

ARCHDEACONS
WORCESTER Ven Roger Morris, The Archdeacon's House, Walker's Lane, Whittington, Worcester WR5 2RE [2008]   *Tel:* 01905 20537 (Dioc Office)
                            email: jhinds@cofe-worcester.org.uk
DUDLEY Ven Fred Trethewey, 15 Worcester Rd, Droitwich WR9 8AA [2001]   *Tel:* 01905 773301
                            Fax: 0871 813 3256

CONVOCATION (MEMBERS OF THE HOUSE OF CLERGY OF THE GENERAL SYNOD)
Dignitaries in Convocation
The Bishop of Dudley
Proctors for Clergy
Revd Stuart Currie
Revd Canon Matthew Baynes
Revd Eva McIntyre

MEMBERS OF THE HOUSE OF LAITY OF THE GENERAL SYNOD
Canon Prof Michael Clarke
Mrs Jennifer Barton
Mr Robin Lunn

DIOCESAN OFFICERS
Dioc Secretary Mr Robert Higham, The Old Palace, Deansway, Worcester WR1 2JE
                            Tel: 01905 20537
Chancellor of Diocese Mr Charles Mynors, Francis Taylor Building, Inner Temple, London EC4Y 7BD   *Tel:* 020 7353 8415
Registrar of Diocese and Bishop's Legal Secretary Mr Michael Huskinson, Messrs March & Edwards, 8 Sansome Walk, Worcester WR1 1LN
                            Tel: 01905 723561
                            Fax: 01905 723812
Deputy Diocesan Registrar Mr Robert Sprake, Messrs March & Edwards, 8 Sansome Walk, Worcester WR1 1LN
Dioc Surveyor Mr Mark Wild, Dioc Office
                            Tel: 01905 20537

Worcester   **145**

DIOCESAN ORGANIZATIONS

Diocesan Office The Old Palace, Deansway, Worcester WR1 2JE   *Tel:* 01905 20537
                                                                               Fax: 01905 612302

ADMINISTRATION

Asst Dioc Secretary (Finance) Mr Stephen Lindner, Dioc Office
DAC Secretary Mr John Dentith, Dioc Office
Dioc Synod (Chairman, House of Clergy) Revd Stuart W. Currie, St Stephen's Vicarage, 1 Beech Ave, Worcester WR3 8PZ   *Tel:* 01905 452169
                                        email: sw.currie@virgin.net
(Chairman, House of Laity) Mr David Hawkins, Dioc Office
(Secretary) Mr Robert Higham, Dioc Office

DIOCESAN MISSION, PASTORAL & RESOURCES COMMITTEE

(being the Diocesan Mission Pastoral Committee)
(Chairman) Mr Alastair Findlay; *(Secretary)* Mr Robert Higham *(as above)*
Parsonages Board (Chairman) Mr Robert Pearce, Dioc Office
(Secretary) Mr Stephen Lindner *(as above)*
Investment and Glebe Committee (Chairman) Mr Peter Seward *(as above)*
(Secretary) Mr Stephen Lindner *(as above)*
Glebe Agent Mr Anthony Champion, Halls, 4 Foregate St, Worcester WR1 1DB
                                        Tel: 01905 611066
Stewardship Committee (Chairman) Mr Alan Hughes, Dioc Office
Stewardship and Resources Officer Vacant
Mission & Pastoral Committee Mr Robert Higham *(as above)*
Board of Patronage Mr Robert Higham *(as above)*
Designated Officer Mr Robert Higham *(as above)*
Diocesan Trustees Mr Michael Huskinson, Messrs March & Edwards, 8 Sansome Walk, Worcester WR1 1LN   *Tel:* 01905 723561
                                        Fax: 01905 723812

CHURCHES

Advisory Committee for the Care of Churches (Chairman) Mr John Bailey, Dioc Office; *(Secretary)* Mr John Dentith, Dioc Office
Change Ringers Association Mr D. Andrews

EDUCATION

Board of Education (Chair) Revd Stuart W. Currie, St Stephen's Vicarage, 1 Beech Ave, Worcester WR3 8PZ   *Tel:* 01905 452169
Director of Education Revd David Morphy, Dioc Office
Associate Director of Education Mr Bernard Peters, Dioc Office
Deputy Director of Education Mrs Ann Mundy
Tertiary Education Officer Revd David Morphy *(as above)*
Schools Improvement Officer Mr Jonathan Rendall, Dioc Office
Children's Officer Emma Pettifer, Dioc Office
Youth Officer Dr Sarah Brush, Dioc Office

TRAINING AND MINISTRY

Director of Development Canon Robert Jones, Dioc Office   *email:* rjones@cofe-worcester.org.uk
Dioc Director of Ordinands Revd Canon Georgina Byrne, from 13/09/09
Dean of Women's Ministry Revd Georgina Byrne, Rectory, Dioc Office
Asst Director of Development (Discipleship) Revd Stephen Winter, Dioc Office
Chaplain to MENCAP Canon Hazel Hughes, Wribbenhall Vicarage, Trimpley Lane, Bewdley DY12 1JJ   *Tel:* 01299 402196
Association of Readers
Secretary Miss E. R. Tomlin, 4 Lambourne Avenue, Malvern Link, Worcestershire WR14 1NL
                                        Tel: 01684 578500
Registrar Dr M. J. Robinson, 5 Park Dingle, Bewdley DY12 2JY   *Tel:* 01299 403080
                                        email: mikejrobinson@fsmail.net
Retired Clergy
Dean of Retired Clergy The Rt Revd Christopher Mayfield *(as above)*
Non-Stipendiary Ministers/Ministers in Secular Employment
Dean of NSMs/MSEs Revd Canon Jane Fraser Dioc Office

LITURGICAL

Secretary Revd D. Chaplin, Vicarage, 29 Old Coach Rd, Droitwich WR9 8BB
                                        Tel: 01905 798929
                                        email: doug@archy.clara.co.uk

MISSION AND UNITY

Board for Mission (Chairman) Revd Stephen G. F. Owens, Vicarage, Far Forest, Kidderminster DY14 9TT   *Tel:* 01299 266580
Mission Administrator Margaret Rutter, Dioc Office
Ecumenical Officer – Worcestershire Revd David Ryan, Vicarage, 4 Daty Croft, Home Meadow, Warndon, Worcester WR4 0JB
                                        Tel: 01905 616109
Ecumenical Officer – Black Country Churches Engaged Revd Barry Gilbert, Rectory, 2 Church Hill, Brierley Hill DY5 3PX   *Tel:* 01384 78146

PRESS AND PUBLICATIONS

Dioc Communications Officer and Bishop's Press Office Samantha Setchell, Dioc Office
                                        Tel: 07852 302516
Editor of the Dioc Directory Mrs Alison Vincent
Editor of Dioc News Samantha Setchell

DIOCESAN RECORD OFFICES

County Archivist, Record Office, County Hall, Spetchley Rd, Worcester WR5 2NP *County Archivist* Mr R. Whittaker *Tel:* 01905 766530; *Fax:* 01905 766363 *(For diocesan records and most parish records)*
Dudley Archives and Local History Dept, Mount Pleasant St, Coseley WV14 9JR *Archivist* Mrs K. H. Atkins *Tel:* 01384 812770 *(For parish records for the deaneries of Kingswinford (formerly Himley), Dudley and Stourbridge)*

SOCIAL RESPONSIBILITY
Church Action Within Society (Chairman) Professor Michael Taylor, Dioc Office
Social Responsibility Officer and Secretary Revd John Paxton
Faith at Work in Worcestershire: Team Leader Revd Phillip Jones, 7 Egremont Gardens, Worcester WR4 0QH   *Tel* and *Fax:* 01905 755037
        email: phillipjones@faithatwork.org.uk
Chaplaincy to Agriculture and Rural Life Vacancy

RURAL DEANS
ARCHDEACONRY OF WORCESTER
Evesham Revd Terry M. Mason, Vicarage, Church St, Broadway, Worcester WR12 7AE
        Tel: 01386 852352
        email: broadwayvicarage@tesco.net
Malvern Revd W. David Nichol, Holy Trinity Vicarage, 2 North Malvern Rd, Malvern WR14 4LR   *Tel:* 01684 561126
email: david@trinityandthewest.wanadoo.co.uk
Martley and Worcester West Revd David Sherwin, The Rectory, Martley, Worcester WR6 6QA
        Tel: 01886 888664
Pershore Revd Matthew Baynes, Bredon Rectory, Tewkesbury, GL20 7LT   *Tel:* 01684 7772237
        email: matthew@tcbaynes.fsnet.co.uk
Upton Canon Frances A. Wookey, Vicarage, 5 Westmere, Hanley Swan, Worcester WR8 0DG
        Tel: 01684 310321
        email: fwookey@fides.demon.co.uk

Worcester East Revd S. Agnew, The Vicarage, Claines Lane, Worcester WR3 7RN
        Tel: 01905 754772
        email: revsagnew@yahoo.com

ARCHDEACONRY OF DUDLEY
Bromsgrove Revd R. M. Johnson, 120 Carthorse Lane, Brockhill, Redditch B97 6SZ
        Tel: 01527 61936
        email: dickim@globalnet.co.uk
Droitwich Canon Sheila Banyard, Rectory, 205 Worcester Road, Droitwich, Worcs WR9 8AS
        Tel: 01905 773134
        email: sk.banyard@virgin.net
Dudley Canon Hilary Hanke, St Luke's Vicarage, Upper High St, Cradley Heath B64 5HX
        Tel: 01384 569940
Kidderminster Revd Keith James, The Rectory, 57 Park Lane, Bewdley, Worcs. DY12 2HA
        Tel: 01299 402275
        email: keith.james2@btconnect.com
Kingswinford Vacancy
Stourbridge Revd Andrew Hazlewood, The Rectory, Pedmore Lane, Stourbridge, West Midlands DY9 0SW   *Tel:* 01562 887287
        email: andrewhazlewood@gmail.com
Stourport Revd Louise Grace, The Rectory, Lindridge, Tenbury Wells, Worcs. WR15 8JQ
        Tel: 01584 881331
        email: revgrace@hotmail.co.uk

Founded in 627. York; East Riding of Yorkshire, except for an area in the south-west (SHEFFIELD); Kingston-upon-Hull; Redcar and Cleveland; Middlesbrough; the eastern half of North Yorkshire; Stockton-on-Tees, south of the Tees; an area of Leeds.

Population 1,416,000   Area 2,661 sq m
Full-time Stipendiary Parochial Clergy 201   Benefices 263
Parishes 454   Churches 610
www.dioceseofyork.org.uk
Overseas link dioceses: Cape Town (South Africa), Mechelen-Brussels (Belgium).

ARCHBISHOP (97th)
Most Revd and Rt Hon Dr John Tucker Mugabi Sentamu, *Primate of England and Metropolitan*, Bishopthorpe Palace, Bishopthorpe, York YO23 2GE [2005]   *Tel:* 01904 707021/2
Fax: 01904 709204
email: office@archbishopofyork.org
Web: www.bishopthorpepalace.co.uk
[Sentamu Ebor]
Chaplain and Researcher Revd Dr Daphne Green
email: daphne.green@archbishopofyork.org
Domestic Chaplain Revd Richard Carew
email: Richard.carew@archbishopofyork.org
Chief of Staff Revd Malcolm Macnaughton
Tel: 01904 772362
email:
malcolm.macnaughton@archbishopofyork.org

SUFFRAGAN BISHOPS
SELBY Rt Revd Martin Wallace, Bishop's House, Barton-le-Street, Malton YO17 6PL [2004]
Tel: 01653 627191
Fax: 01653 627193
email: bishselby@clara.net
HULL Rt Revd Richard Frith, Hullen House, Woodfield Lane, Hessle HU13 0ES [1998]
Tel: 01482 649019
Fax: 01482 647449
email: richard@bishop.karoo.co.uk
WHITBY Rt Revd Martin Warner, 60 West Green, Stokesley, Middlesbrough TS9 5BD [1999]
Tel: 01642 714475
Fax: 01642 714472
email: bishopofwhitby@yorkdiocese.org

PROVINCIAL EPISCOPAL VISITOR
BEVERLEY Rt Revd Martyn William Jarrett, 3 North Lane, Roundhay, Leeds LS8 2QJ [2000]
Tel: 0113 265 4280
Fax: 0113 265 4281
email:
bishop-of-beverley@3-north-lane.fsnet.co.uk

HONORARY ASSISTANT BISHOPS
Rt Revd Clifford Condor Barker, Flat 29 Dulverton Hall, The Esplanade, Scarborough YO11 2AR [1991]   *Tel:* 01723 340129

Rt Revd Michael Henshall, Brackenfield, 28 Hermitage Way, Eskdaleside, Sleights, Whitby YO22 5HG [1996]   *Tel:* 01947 811233
Rt Revd David George Galliford, 10 St Mary's Mews, Wigginton, York YO32 2SE [1995]
Tel: 01904 761489
Rt Revd David Lunn, Rivendell, 28 Southfield Rd, Wetwang, Driffield YO25 9XX [1997]
Rt Revd David Smith, 34 Cedar Glade, Dunnington, York YO19 5QZ [2002]
Tel: 01904 481225

CATHEDRAL CHURCH OF ST PETER
Dean Very Revd Keith Jones, The Deanery, York YO1 7JQ [2004]   *Tel:* 01904 623608 (Home)
01904 557202 (Office)
Fax: 01904 557204 (Office)
email: dean@yorkminster.org
Dean and Chapter Office Church House, Ogleforth, York YO1 7JN   *Tel:* 01904 557200
Fax: 01904 557201
email: reception@yorkminster.org
Chancellor Canon Glyn Webster, 4 Minster Yard, York YO1 7JD [1999]   *Tel:* 01904 620877 (Home)
01904 557207 (Office)
Fax: 01904 557204
email: chancellor@yorkminster.org
Theologian Canon Dr Jonathan Draper, 3 Minster Court, York YO1 7JJ [2000]
Tel: 01904 625599 (Home)
01904 557211 (Office)
email: theologian@yorkminster.org
Precentor Revd Peter Moger, 2 Minster Court, York YO1 7JJ   *Tel:* 01904 557205 (Office)
Fax: 01904 557204
email: precentor@yorkminster.org
Chapter Steward Mr John Morris, Dean and Chapter Office   *Tel:* 01904 557212
Fax: 01904 557204
email: chapter.steward@yorkminster.org
Lay Canons
Canon Maureen Loffill, Wedgwood House, Heslington, York YO10 5DP   *Tel:* 01904 430246
Fax: 01904 421481
email: maureen@maureenloffill.demon.co.uk
Canon Dr Ann Lees, Diocesan House, Aviator Court, Clifton Moor, York YO30 4WJ
Tel: 01904 699511
email: alees@yorkdiocese.org

Canon Dr Andrew Green, Juniper House, The Nookin, Husthwaite, York YO61 4PY
Tel: 07770 321564
email: andrewgreen@bpipoly.com
Chapter Clerk Mr Andrew Oates, Dean and Chapter Office
Tel: 01904 557210
Fax: 01904 557204
email: chapterclerk@yorkminster.org
Head Verger Mr Alex Carberry, York Minster Vestry
Tel: 01904 557221
email: alexc@yorkminster.org
Director of Music Mr Robert Sharpe, Dean and Chapter Office
Tel: 01904 557206
Fax: 01904 557204
email: roberts@yorkminster.org
Chief Accountant Mrs Sue Pace, Dean and Chapter Office
Tel: 01904 557213
Fax: 01904 557215
email: suep@yorkminster.org
Chamberlain and Director of Development Dr Richard Shephard, Dean and Chapter Office
Tel: 01904 557245
Fax: 01904 557246
email: richards@yorkminster.org
High Steward The Earl of Halifax, Garrowby, York YO41 1QD
Tel: 01759 368236
Fax: 01759 368154
email: halifax@garrowby.plus.com

ARCHDEACONS
YORK Ven Richard Seed, Holy Trinity Rectory, Micklegate, York YO1 6LE [1999]
Tel: 01904 623798
Fax: 01904 628155
email: archdeacon.of.york@yorkdiocese.org
EAST RIDING Ven David Butterfield, Brimley Lodge, 27 Molescroft Rd, Beverley HU17 7DX [2007]
Tel and Fax: 01482 881659
email: archdeacon.of.eastriding@yorkdiocese.org
CLEVELAND Ven Paul Ferguson, 2 Langbaurgh Rd, Hutton Rudby, Yarm TS15 0HL [2001]
Tel: 01642 706095
Fax: 01642 706097
email: archdeacon.of.cleveland@yorkdiocese.org

CONVOCATION (MEMBERS OF THE HOUSE OF CLERGY OF THE GENERAL SYNOD)
Dignitaries in Convocation
The Bishop of Beverley
Proctors for Clergy
Revd Jeremy Fletcher
Ven Paul Ferguson
Revd Andrew Howard
Revd Christian Selvaratnam
Canon Suzanne Sheriff
Canon Glyn Webster

MEMBERS OF THE HOUSE OF LAITY OF THE GENERAL SYNOD
Canon Linda Ali
Mr Martin Dales

Mrs Jennifer Reid
Mrs Rosalind Brewer
Mr Richard Brown
Mr Jon Steel

DIOCESAN OFFICERS
Dioc Secretary Canon Peter Warry, Diocesan House, Aviator Court, Clifton Moor, York YO30 4WJ
Tel: 01904 699500
Fax: 01904 699501
Chancellor of Diocese The Worshipful Peter Collier QC, 12 St Helen's Rd, Dringhouses, York YO24 1HP
Registrar of Diocese and Archbishop's Legal Secretary Mr Lionel Lennox, The Registry, Stamford House, Piccadilly, York YO1 9PP
Tel: 01904 623487
Fax: 01904 611458

DIOCESAN ORGANIZATIONS
Diocesan Office Diocesan House, Aviator Court, Clifton Moor, York YO30 4WJ   *Tel:* 01904 699500
Fax: 01904 699501
email: office@yorkdiocese.org
Web: www.dioceseofyork.org.uk

ADMINISTRATION
Dioc Synod (Chairman, House of Clergy) Canon John Harrison, Vicarage, Easingwold, York YO61 3JT
Tel: 01347 821394
email: vicar.easingwold@hotmail.co.uk
(Chairman, House of Laity) Canon Richard Liversedge, 1 Caledonia Park, Victoria Dock, Hull HU9 1TE
Tel: 01482 588357
email: r.liversedge@hulldrypool.freeserve.co.uk
(Secretary) Canon Peter Warry, Dioc Office
Assistant Dioc Secretary Ms Shirley Davies, Dioc Office
Board of Finance (Chairman) Mr Robin Clough, Dioc Office; *(Secretary)* Canon Peter Warry
Finance Manager Mrs Catherine Evans, Dioc Office
Diocesan Surveyor and Estates Manager Mr Graham Andrews, Dioc Office
Pastoral & Mission Committee Ms Shirley Davies *(as above)*
Designated Officer Canon Peter Warry, Dioc Office
Property Sub-Committee Mrs Linda Crackles, Dioc Office
Dioc Communications Officer Eleanor Course, Dioc Office

CHURCHES
Advisory Committee for the Care of Churches (Chairman) Canon David Hodgson, The Ascension Vicarage, Penrith Rd, Berwick Hills, Middlesbrough TS3 7JR
Tel: 01642 244857
(Secretary) Mr Philip Thomas, Dioc Office
Furnishings Officer Mr David Haddon-Reece, Vicarage, Egton, Whitby YO21 1UT
Tel: 01947 895315
Closed Churches Ms Shirley Davies *(as above)*

EDUCATION

Board of Education (*Director*) Canon Dr R. Ann Lees, Dioc Office
email: ann.lees@yorkdiocese.org
Asst Director of Education Mrs Viv Todd (*Educational Services and Schools Support*)
School Buildings Officer Simon Quartermaine
Religious Education and Collective Worship Mrs Celia Roberts and Mrs Olivia Seymour
Adviser for Children and Youth Work (*East Riding*) Jon Steel, 2 Appin Close, Bransholme, Hull HU7 5BB   *Tel:* 01482 828805
                        07736 378051 (Mobile)
Adviser in Children's and Youth Work (*York*) Revd Nigel Chapman, Vicarage, Coxwold, York YO61 4AD   *Tel:* 01347 868287
        email: nigel.chapman@yorkdiocese.org
Children's & Youth Officer (*Cleveland*) Vacancy

MINISTRY AND MISSION

Training, Mission & Ministry Directory Revd Dr Gavin Wakefield, Dioc Office   *Tel:* 01904 699504
        email: gavin.wakefield@yorkdiocese.org
Diocesan Adviser on Vocations Revd David Mann, 3 Glebe Close, Bolton Percy, York YO23 7HB
                        Tel: 01904 744619
        email: david.mann@yorkdiocese.org
Dean of Self Supporting Ministry Revd Dr Julie Watson, 20 Talisker Gardens, Highcliffe View, Redcar TS10 2TG   *Tel:* 01624 478147
        email: dssm@yorkdiocese.org
Dean of Women's Ministry Canon Elaine Bielby, St Helen's Vicarage, Welton, Brough HU15 1ND
                        Tel: 01482 666677
        email: ebielby@ebielby.karoo.co.uk
Warden of Readers Ven Paul Ferguson, 2 Langbaurgh Rd, Hutton Rudby, Yarm TS15 0HL
                        Tel: 01642 706095
                        Fax: 01642 706097
email: archdeacon.of.cleveland@yorkdiocese.org
Ecumenical Advisers
York Archdeaconry Revd Andrew Clements, Vicarage, 80 Osbaldwick Lane, York YO10 3AX
                        Tel: 01904 416763
        email: andrew@ozmurt.freeserve.co.uk
East Riding Archdeaconry Vacancy
Cleveland Archdeaconry Revd Dr Michael Hazelton, Vicarage, Danby, Whitby YO21 2NQ
                        Tel: 01287 660388

LITURGICAL

York Diocesan Liturgical Group (*Chairman*) Rt Revd Richard Frith, Bishop of Hull

PRESS AND PUBLICATIONS

Archbishop's Media Adviser (*National*) Kerron Cross   *Tel:* 01904 707021
Communications Officer (*Diocese*) Eleanor Course, Dioc Office   *Tel:* 01904 699530
                        07946 748702 (Mobile)
        email: comms@yorkdiocese.org
Editor of Dioc Magazine (*as above*)

DIOCESAN RECORD OFFICES

The Borthwick Institute of Historical Research, University of York, Heslington, York YO10 5DD
Director and Diocesan Archivist Christopher C. Webb   *Tel:* 01904 321166
        Web: www.york.ac.uk/inst/bihr
(*For parish records in the Archdeaconry of York*)
East Riding of Yorkshire Archive Office, County Hall, Beverley HU17 9BA *Archivist* Mr Ian Mason
Tel: 01482 392790
email: ian.mason@eastriding.gov
Web: www.eastriding.gov.uk/learning
(*For parish records in the Archdeaconry of the East Riding*)
North Yorkshire County Record Office, Malpas Rd, Northallerton DL7 8PB *Acting County Archivist* Mrs Judith A. Smeaton *Tel:* 01609 777585 (*For parish records in the Archdeaconry of Cleveland**)
*Parishes within the present county boundaries of Cleveland may, if they so wish, deposit their records in the Cleveland County Archives Dept, Exchange House, 6 Marton Rd, Middlesbrough TS1 1DB *Archivist* Mr D. Tyrell   *Tel:* 01642 248321

SOCIAL RESPONSIBILITY

Social Responsibility Council Bishop of Whitby (*Chair*) (*as above*)

RURAL DEANS
ARCHDEACONRY OF YORK

Derwent Revd Richard Kirkman, Rectory, York Rd, Escrick, York YO19 6EY   *Tel:* 01904 728406
        email: rmkquanta@onetel.net
Easingwold Revd John Harrison, Vicarage, Easingwold, York YO61 3JT   *Tel:* 01347 821394
        email: vicar.easingwold@hotmail.co.uk
New Ainsty Revd Peter Bristow, Vicarage, 86 High St, Boston Spa, Wetherby LS23 6EA
                        Tel: 01937 842454
        email: peterbristow1@ntlworld.com
Selby Revd Chris Wilton, Vicarage, 2 Sir John's Lane, Sherburn in Elmet, Leeds LS25 6BJ
                        Tel: 01977 682122
South Wold Revd James Finnemore ogs, Rectory, Bishop Wilton, York YO42 1SA
                        Tel: 01759 368230
Southern Ryedale Revd Quentin Wilson, The Coach House, East Heslerton, Malton YO17 8RN
                        Tel: 01944 728060
York Revd Martin Baldock, Vicarage, Dringhouses, York YO24 1QG   *Tel:* 01904 706120
        email: parishoffice@care4free.net

ARCHDEACONRY OF THE EAST RIDING

Beverley Revd Angela Bailey, The Rectory, 31 Old Village Rd, Little Weighton Cottingham HU20 3US   *Tel:* 01482 843317
Bridlington Revd Dr Peter Pike, The Vicarage, Church St, Flamborough YO15 1PE
                        Tel: 01262 851370
        email: revpeterpike@hotmail.com
Central and North Hull Revd Paul Smith, The Rectory, Hallgate, Cottingham HU16 4DD
                        Tel: 01482 847668

Harthill Revd Ruth Hind, 5 Howl Lane, Hutton, Driffield YO25 9QA   *Tel:* 01377 270402
Holderness North Revd Chris Simmons, New Rectory, 105 Main St, Brandesbourne, Driffield YO25 8RG   *Tel:* 01964 541593
        email: chris@csimmons.plus.com
Holderness South Revd Anthony Burdon, Vicarage, Main Rd, Thorngumbald, Hull HU12 9NA   *Tel:* 01964 601381
        email: tony@tonyburdon.karoo.co.uk
Howden Revd James Little, The Minster Rectory, Market Place, Howden DN14 7BL
        Tel: 01430 432056
        email: RevJLittle@aol.com
Scarborough Revd Martyn Dunning, St Mary's Vicarage, 1 North Cliffe Gardens, Scarborough YO12 6PR   *Tel:* 01723 371354
    email: enquiries.stmaryschurch@btinternet.com
East Hull Revd Mick Fryer, St Aidan's Vicarage, 139 Southcoates Ave, Hull HU9 3HF
        Tel: 01482 374403
        email: mick@staidans.org.uk
West Hull Revd Tim Boyns, All Saints Vicarage, 4 Chestnut Avenue, Hessle HU13 0RH
        Tel: 01482 648555
        email: timboyns@timboyns.karoo.co.uk

ARCHDEACONRY OF CLEVELAND
Guisborough Canon John Weetman, St Peter's Vicarage, 66 Aske Rd, Redcar TS10 2BP
        Tel: 01642 490700
Middlesbrough Canon Erik Wilson, St Barnabas Vicarage, 8 The Crescent, Linthorpe, Middlesbrough TS5 6SQ   *Tel:* 01642 817306
        email: erik.wilson@ntlworld.com
Mowbray Revd Richard Rowling, Rectory, Cemetery Rd, Thirsk YO7 1PR
        Tel: 01845 523183
        email: rfrowling@aol.com
Northern Ryedale Revd Paul Mothersdale, Rectory, Thornton Dale, Pickering YO18 7QW
        Tel: 01751 474244
        email: paulmothersdale@bigfoot.com
Stokesley Revd John Ford, Vicarage, 21 Thornton Rd, Stainton, Middlesbrough TS8 9DS
        Tel: 01642 288131
        email: revjohn.ford@ntlworld.com
Whitby Revd David Cook, The Vicarage, 22 Eskdaleside, Sleights, Whitby YO22 5EP
        Tel: 01947 810349

National Structures

PART 2

PART 2 CONTENTS

Every effort has been made to ensure that all details are accurate at the time of going to press.

NATIONAL STRUCTURES

THE GENERAL SYNOD OF THE CHURCH OF ENGLAND

Office

Church House, Great Smith St, London SW1P 3AZ
Tel: 020 7898 1000 *Fax:* 020 7898 1369
email: synod@c-of-e.org.uk
Web: www.cofe.anglican.org

Dates of Sessions

The following periods have been set aside for Groups of Sessions of the General Synod:

2011: 7 February – 11 February, London
8 July – 12 July, York
14 November – 16 November, London (if required)

2012: 6 February – 10 February, London
6 July – 10 July, York
19 November – 21 November (if required)

Composition of the General Synod

	Canterbury	York	Either	Totals
House of Bishops				
Diocesan Bishops	30	14		44
Suffragan Bishops ... including the Bishop of Dover *ex officio*	6	3		9
	36	17		53
House of Clergy				
Deans	3	2		5
Service Chaplains and Chaplain-General of Prisons	4			4
Elected Proctors and the Dean of Guernsey or Jersey	129	55		184
University Proctors ..	4	2		6
Religious Communities			2	2
Co-opted places (maximum)	3	2		5
	143	61	2	206

	Canterbury	York	Either	Totals
House of Laity				
Elected Laity	136	59		195
Religious Communities			2	2
Lay Armed Services .			3	3
Co-opted places (maximum)			5	5
Ex officio (First and Second Church Estates Commissioners) ..			2	2
	136	59	12	207
House of Bishops, House of Clergy or House of Laity				
Ex officio (Dean of the Arches, the two Vicars General, the Third Church Estates Commissioner, the Chairman of the Pensions Board and six Appointed Members of the Archbishops' Council)			11	11
Maximum totals	315	137	25	477

The General Synod consists of the Convocations of Canterbury and York, joined together in a House of Bishops and a House of Clergy, and having added to them a House of Laity.

The House of Bishops is made up of the Upper Houses of the Convocations of Canterbury and York. It consists of the archbishops and all other diocesan bishops and the Bishop of Dover as *ex officio* members, four bishops elected by and from the suffragan bishops (and certain other bishops) of the Province of Canterbury (other than the Bishop of Dover), three bishops elected by and from the suffragan bishops (and certain other bishops) of the Province of York, and any other bishops residing in either Province who are members of the Archbishops' Council.

The House of Clergy is made up of the Lower Houses of the Convocations of Canterbury and York. It consists of clergy (other than bishops) who have been elected, appointed or chosen in accordance with Canon H 2 and the rules made under it (including deans, proctors from the dioceses and university constituencies and clerical members of religious communities) together with *ex officio* members.

The House of Laity consists of members from each diocese of the two Provinces elected by lay members of the deanery synods (or annual meetings of the chaplaincies in the case of the Diocese in Europe) or chosen by and from the lay members of religious communities, together with *ex officio* members.

Representatives of other Churches, the Church of England Youth Council, and Deaf Anglicans Together are invited to attend the Synod and under its Standing Orders enjoy speaking but not voting rights.

OFFICERS OF THE GENERAL SYNOD
Presidents
The Archbishop of Canterbury
The Archbishop of York

Prolocutor of the Lower House of the Convocation of Canterbury Not known at time of going to press

Prolocutor of the Lower House of the Convocation of York Not known at time of going to press

Chair of the House of Laity Not known at time of going to press

Vice-Chair of the House of Laity Dr Philip Giddings

Secretary General Mr William Fittall

Clerk to the Synod Revd David Williams

Chief Legal Adviser and *Joint Registrar of the Provinces of Canterbury and York (Registrar of the General Synod)* Mr Stephen Slack

Deputy Legal Adviser Revd Alexander McGregor

Standing Counsel Sir Anthony Hammond

OFFICERS OF THE CONVOCATIONS
Synodical Secretary of the Convocation of Canterbury
Revd Stephen Trott, Rectory, 41 Humfrey Lane, Boughton, Northampton NN28RQ
                    email: revstrott@sky.com

Synodal Secretary of the Convocation of York
Ven Alan Wolstencroft, The Bakehouse, 1 Latham Row, Horwich, Bolton
                    email: alanchrisw@tiscali.co.uk

NON-DIOCESAN MEMBERS
The following are non-diocesan members of General Synod:

Suffragan Bishops in Convocation
CANTERBURY
The Bishop of Dover (*ex officio*)
The Bishop of Dorchester
The Bishop of Dudley
The Bishop of Grimsby
The Bishop of Willesden

YORK
The Bishop of Beverley
The Bishop of Hull
The Bishop of Knaresborough

Deans in Convocation
CANTERBURY
The Dean of Canterbury
The Dean of Leicester
The Dean of Southwark

YORK
The Dean of Bradford
The Dean of Carlisle

Chaplain-General of Prisons and Archdeacon of Prisons Ven William Noblett

Armed Forces Synod
Ven Martin Poll
Ven Stephen Robbins
Ven Ray Pentland
Major-General Patrick Marriott
Lt Cdr Philippa Sargent
Mrs Lynn Hayler

University Representatives in Convocation
CANTERBURY
Oxford
Canon Dr Judith Maltby

Cambridge
Revd Duncan Dormor

London
Revd Dr Richard Burridge

Other Universities (Southern)
Vacancy

YORK
Durham and Newcastle
Revd Miranda Threlfall-Holmes

Other Universities (Northern)
Vacancy

Representatives of Religious Communities in Convocation
CANTERBURY
Revd Sister Rosemary Howorth CHN

YORK
Revd Thomas Seville CR

Lay Representatives of Religious Communities
Sister Anita Smith OHP
Brother Thomas Quin

Ex officio Members of the House of Laity
Dean of the Arches
Rt Worshipful Charles George QC
Vicar-General of the Province of Canterbury
Chancellor Timothy Briden
Vicar-General of the Province of York
His Honour Peter Collier
First Church Estates Commissioner Mr Andreas Whittam Smith

Second Church Estates Commissioner Mr Tony Baldry MP

Third Church Estates Commissioner Mr Timothy Walker

Chairman of the Church of England Pensions Board
Mr Jonathan Spencer

Representatives who have been appointed to the Synod under its Standing Orders with speaking but not voting rights

Ecumenical Representatives
Very Revd Dr Alan McDonald (Church of Scotland)
Very Revd Archimandrite Ephrem Lash (Orthodox Church)
Revd Graham Maskery (United Reformed Church)
Revd Jan Mullin (Moravian Church)
Revd Dr Roger Walton (Methodist Church)
Revd Prof Paul Fiddes (Baptist Union)
Bishop Dr Joe Aldred (Black-led Churches)
Revd Mgr Andrew Faley (Roman Catholic Church)

Church of England Youth Council Representatives
Not known at time of going to press

Deaf Anglicans Together Representatives
Revd Catherine Nightingale
Mrs Patricia Callaghan
Susan Myatt

Appointed Members of the Archbishops' Council
Mr Andrew Britton
Prof John Craven
Mr Philip Fletcher
Mrs Mary Chapman
Mr Mark Russell
Revd Dr Rosalyn Murphy

House of Bishops

Chairman The Archbishop of Canterbury

Vice-Chairman The Archbishop of York

Secretary Mr Jonathan Neil-Smith
Tel: 020 7898 1373
email: jonathan.neil-smith@c-of-e.org.uk

Theological Consultant Dr Martin Davie
Tel: 020 7898 1488
email: martin.davie@c-of-e.org.uk

The House of Bishops meets separately from sessions of the General Synod twice a year, in private session. It has a special responsibility for matters relating to doctrine and liturgy under

Article 7 of the Constitution of General Synod. Its agendas nevertheless range more widely, reflecting matters relating to the exercise of *episcope* in the Church. Each year the College of Bishops – consisting of all diocesan and suffragan bishops – also meet; as do diocesan bishops with the archbishops.

The following committees or panels work under the umbrella of the House:

THE STANDING COMMITTEE OF THE HOUSE OF BISHOPS
Chairman Most Revd and Rt Hon John Sentamu
(*Archbishop of York*)

Secretary Mr Jonathan Neil-Smith

The Standing Committee consists of the Archbishops of Canterbury and York, the bishop elected by the House to serve on the Archbishops' Council who serves as Chair of the Ministry Council, one bishop appointed jointly by the Archbishops from amongst those elected by the House to serve on the Church Commissioners' Board of Governors, the bishop appointed by the Archbishops to chair the Faith & Order Commission, the member elected by the House to serve on the Business Committee, one member elected by the House, and one member appointed by the Archbishops acting jointly. Its principal role is to prepare the agendas for the House's meetings, but it also deals with other matters on the House's behalf.

THE HOUSE'S CONTINUING MINISTERIAL EDUCATION COMMITTEE
Chairman Rt Revd Martin Wharton (*Bishop of Newcastle*)

Secretary Mr Alasdair Cameron
Tel: 020 7898 1878
email: alasdair.cameron@c-of-e.org.uk

THE RURAL BISHOPS' PANEL
Chairman Rt Revd Anthony Priddis (*Bishop of Hereford*)

Secretary Dr Jill Hopkinson   *Tel:* 02476 853073
email: jill@rase.org.uk

THE URBAN BISHOPS' PANEL
Chairman Rt Revd John Packer (*Bishop of Ripon & Leeds*)

Secretary Revd Dr Andrew Davey
Tel: 020 7898 1448
email: andrew.davey@c-of-e.org.uk

House of Clergy

Joint Chairmen The Prolocutors of the Convocations

Secretary Dr Colin Podmore   *Tel:* 020 7898 1385
email: colin.podmore@c-of-e.org.uk

Membership of the House of Clergy comprises the Lower House of the Convocation of Canterbury and the Lower House of the Convocation of York joined into one House.

The Standing Committee of the House of Clergy consists of the Prolocutors of the Convocations, the two persons elected by the House to serve on the Archbishops' Council, the two Pro-Prolocutors of the Convocation of Canterbury and four other persons elected by and from the Lower House of the Convocation of Canterbury, the two Deputy Prolocutors of Convocation of York and two other persons elected by and from the Convocation of York.

House of Laity

Chair Vacancy

Vice-Chair Dr Philip Giddings

Secretary Mr Nicholas Hills   *Tel:* 020 7898 1363
email: nicholas.hills@c-of-e.org.uk

The Standing Committee of the House of Laity consists of the Chair and Vice-Chair, the members of the Business and Appointments Committees elected by the House and the members of the Archbishops' Council elected by the House.

Principal Committees

THE BUSINESS COMMITTEE
Chair Vacancy

Secretary Revd David Williams (*Clerk to the Synod*)
Tel: 020 7898 1559
email: david.williams@c-of-e.org.uk

Following elections to the General Synod in October 2010, membership of this body is uncertain at the time of going to press. Please refer to the Secretary for current membership.

The Committee is responsible for organizing the business of the Synod, enabling it to fulfil its role as a legislative and deliberative body.

THE LEGISLATIVE COMMITTEE
Ex officio Members
The Archbishop of Canterbury
The Archbishop of York
The Prolocutors of the Convocations
The Chair and Vice-Chair of the House of Laity
The Dean of the Arches
The Second Church Estates Commissioner

Elected Members
Following elections to the General Synod in October 2010, the elected membership of this body is uncertain at the time of going to press. Please refer to the Secretary for current membership.

Secretary Mr Stephen Slack   *Tel:* 020 7898 1367
                    email: stephen.slack@c-of-e.org.uk

THE STANDING ORDERS COMMITTEE
Chair Mr Geoffrey Tattersall QC

Ex officio Members
The Prolocutors of the Convocations
The Chair and Vice-Chair of the House of Laity

Appointed Members
Following elections to the General Synod in October 2010, membership of this body is uncertain at the time of going to press. Please refer to the Secretary for current membership.

Secretary Miss Sarah Clemenson

PRINCIPAL COMMISSIONS
The Clergy Discipline Commission

Chair Rt Hon Lord Justice Mummery
Deputy Chair His Honour Judge John Bullimore

Secretary Miss Sarah Clemenson

Office Church House, Great Smith St, London
SW1P 3AZ   *Tel:* 020 7898 1371
                    Fax: 020 7898 1718/1721

MEMBERS
Following elections to the General Synod in October 2010, membership of this body is uncertain at the time of going to press. Please refer to the Secretary for current membership.

The Clergy Discipline Commission is constituted under the Clergy Discipline Measure 2003. Under that Measure the Commission is required to give general advice to disciplinary tribunals, the courts of the Vicars-General, bishops and arch-bishops as to the penalties which are appropriate in particular circumstances; to issue codes of

practice and general policy guidance to persons exercising functions in connection with clergy discipline; and to make annually to the General Synod through the House of Bishops a report on the exercise of its functions during the previous year.

Under the 2003 Measure the Commission is also required to compile and maintain 'provincial panels' of persons available for appointment as members of a disciplinary tribunal or a Vicar-General's Court for the purposes of dealing with cases under it and to formulate guidance for the purposes of the 2003 Measure generally and to promulgate it in a Code of Practice approved by the Dean of the Arches and the General Synod.

The Commission also monitors the exercise of discipline, highlights and encourages best practice, and builds up casework experience in disciplinary matters.

The Crown Nominations Commission

Secretary to the Commission Ms Caroline Boddington, Archbishops' Secretary for Appointments

Office The Wash House, Lambeth Palace, London
SE1 7JU   *Tel:* 020 7898 1876/7
                    Fax: 020 7898 1899

MEMBERS

Ex officio
The Archbishop of Canterbury
The Archbishop of York
Elected Members

Three members of the House of Clergy
Very Revd Colin Slee
Revd Canon Peter Spiers
Revd Canon Glyn Webster

Three members of the House of Laity
Mr Aiden Hargreaves-Smith
Professor Glynn Harrison
Mrs Mary Johnston
Six members of the Vacancy-in-See Committee of the diocese whose bishopric is to become, or has become, vacant

Ex officio non-voting members
Sir Paul Britton (*The Prime Minister's Appointments Secretary*)

Ms Caroline Boddington (*Archbishops' Secretary for Appointments*)

The Commission was established by the General Synod in February 1977. Its function is to consider vacancies in diocesan bishoprics in the Provinces of Canterbury and York, and candidates for appointments to them. At each meeting the Chair is taken by the Archbishop in whose Province the vacancy has arisen. The Commission agrees upon two names for nomination to the Prime Minister by the appropriate Archbishop or, in the case of the Archbishopric of Canterbury or York, by the chairman of the Commission. The names submitted are given in an order of preference voted upon by the Commission. The Prime Minister accepts the first name and reverts to the second name should the first be unable to take up the post.

The Dioceses Commission

Chairman Vacancy

Vice-Chair Professor Michael Clarke

Secretary Dr Colin Podmore

Office Church House, Great Smith St, London SW1P 3AZ   *Tel:* 020 7898 1385
          email: colin.podmore@c-of-e.org.uk

MEMBERS
Canon Jonathan Alderton-Ford (St Edmundsbury and Ipswich), Revd Paul Benfield (Blackburn), Prof Michael Clarke (Worcester), Mrs Lucinda Herklots, Revd Dame Sarah Mullally, Prof Hilary Russell, Rt Revd Nigel Stock (Bishop of St Edmundsbury and Ipswich).

A Dioceses Commission was set up in 1978 under the Dioceses Measure 1978. In 2008 it was replaced by a new body of the same name, established under the Dioceses, Mission and Pastoral Measure 2007. Part II of that Measure makes provision for such matters as the reorganization of diocesan boundaries, the creation and revival of suffragan sees, and the delegation of episcopal functions by diocesan bishops to suffragan and assistant bishops.

The Commission's duties are laid down by the Measure. Its primary duty is to keep under review the provincial and diocesan structure of the Church of England and in particular the size, boundaries and number of provinces; the size, boundaries and number of dioceses and their distribution between the provinces; the number and distribution of bishops and the arrangements for episcopal oversight. The Commission may make reorganization schemes either of its own volition or in response to proposals from diocesan bishops. Schemes require the approval of the diocesan synods concerned (other than in exceptional circumstances) and that of the General Synod. The Commission also gives advice on good practice regarding diocesan administration and responds to requests for advice on particular issues. It comments on proposals to change the names of episcopal sees. When a diocesan bishop proposes to fill a vacant suffragan see the Commission may require the process for creating a new see to be followed if it is not convinced that the need for a suffragan bishop has been demonstrated.

Further information about the Commission and its work may be found on the Church of England website at www.cofe.anglican.org/about/gensynod/commissions.html/diocom

The Fees Advisory Commission

Chair His Honour Judge Andrew Rutherford

Secretary Miss Sarah Clemenson

Office Church House, Great Smith St, London SW1P 3AZ   *Tel:* 020 7898 1371
          Fax: 020 7898 1718/1721
          email: sarah.clemenson@c-of-e.org.uk

MEMBERS
Following elections to the General Synod in October 2010, membership of this body is uncertain at the time of going to press. Please refer to the Secretary for current membership.

The Fees Advisory Commission is constituted under Part II of the Ecclesiastical Fees Measure 1986, as amended by the Church of England (Miscellaneous Provisions) Measure 2000 and other legislation. It makes recommendations as to certain fees to be paid to ecclesiastical judges, legal officers and others, and embodies those recommendations in Orders which are laid before the General Synod for approval. If approved, the Orders take effect unless annulled by either House of Parliament, and are published as Statutory Instruments.

The Legal Advisory Commission

Chair Chancellor Rupert Bursell

Secretary Vacancy

Office Church House, Great Smith St, London
SW1P 3AZ   *Tel:* 020 7898 1367
                          Fax: 020 7898 1718/1721

MEMBERS
Ex officio members
The Dean of the Arches and Auditor
The Vicar-General of Canterbury
The Vicar-General of York
The Provincial Registrar of Canterbury
The Provincial Registrar of York
The Chief Legal Adviser to the Archbishops'
    Council and the General Synod
Standing Counsel to the General Synod
The Official Solicitor to the Church
    Commissioners

Appointed and co-opted members
The Commission has up to 17 appointed
members and up to 3 co-opted members.
Following elections to the General Synod in
October 2010, this element of the membership of
this body is uncertain at the time of going to
press. Please refer to the Secretary for current
membership.

The Legal Advisory Commission gives advice
on legal matters of general interest to the
Church which are referred to it by the Archbishops' Council and its Divisions, Boards,
Councils and Commissions, by the General
Synod and its Houses and Commissions, by
the Church Commissioners and the Church of
England Pensions Board, and by diocesan clerical
and lay office holders. The Commission cannot
accept requests for advice from private individuals or secular bodies. In addition, the
Commission cannot normally give opinions on
contentious matters, but it may be able to do so
(depending on the circumstances) if the facts are
agreed by all parties to the dispute, all parties
join in referring the matter to the Commission for
an opinion and it is not (and is not expected to
become) the subject-matter of proceedings in the
courts.

The opinions of the Commission and its pre-
decessor, the Legal Board, on matters of general
interest are published by Church House Publishing in a loose-leaf form under the title *Legal Opinions Concerning the Church of England*. The 8th
edition was published in May 2007. Opinions
issued by the Commission since that date can
be accessed at www.cofe.anglican.org/about/
churchlawlegis/guidance/

The Legal Aid Commission

Chairman Mr Richard Bowman

Secretary Mr Stephen York

Office Church House, Great Smith St, London
SW1P 3AZ   *Tel:* 020 7898 1703
                          Fax: 020 7898 1718/1721

MEMBERS
*Following elections to the General Synod in October
2010, membership of this body is uncertain at the
time of going to press. Please refer to the Secretary for
current membership.*

The Legal Aid Commission operates under the
Church of England (Legal Aid) Measure 1994,

and administers the Legal Aid Fund which was
originally set up under the Ecclesiastical Jurisdiction Measure 1963 and is continued by the 1994
Measure.

Legal aid under the 1994 Measure may be
granted, subject to various conditions, for certain
types of proceedings before Ecclesiastical Courts
and tribunals; details of eligibility for legal
aid and the Commission's procedures, together
with an application form for legal aid, are
obtainable from the Secretary, on request, or at
www.cofe.anglican.org/about/churchlawlegis/
clergydisclipline/legalaid.html

The Liturgical Commission

Chair Rt Revd Stephen Platten (*Bishop of
Wakefield*)

Secretary and Worship Development Officer
(Vacancy)   *Tel:* 020 7898 1365
                email: sue.moore@c-of-e.org.uk

Office Church House, Great Smith St, London
SW1P 3AZ   *Tel:* 020 7898 1376

MEMBERS
*Following elections to the General Synod in October
2010, membership of the Commission is uncertain at
the time of going to press. Please refer to the office for
current membership.*

In response to resolutions by the Convocations
in October 1954, the Archbishops of Canterbury
and York appointed a standing Liturgical Commission 'to consider questions of a liturgical

character submitted to them from time to time by the Archbishops of Canterbury and York and to report thereon to the Archbishops'. In 1971 the Commission became a permanent Commission of the General Synod. Its functions are:

1 to prepare forms of service at the request of the House of Bishops for submission to that House in the first instance;

2 to advise on the experimental use of forms of service and the development of liturgy;

3 to exchange information and advice on liturgical matters with other Churches both in the Anglican Communion and elsewhere;

4 to promote the development and understanding of liturgy and its use in the Church.

Further information about the Commission's work and its Transforming Worship initiative may be found on the Transforming Worship website at www.transformingworship.org.uk

General Synod Publications

Printed copies of General Synod publications can be purchased from Church House Bookshop. The *Report of Proceedings* is now only available in electronic format and is available to download, along with the texts of many other papers, on the General Synod section of the Church of England website.

THE CONVOCATIONS OF CANTERBURY AND YORK

CONSTITUTION

Each of the Convocations consists of two Houses, an Upper House and a Lower House. The Upper House consists of all the diocesan bishops in the Province, the Bishop of Dover (in the case of the Convocation of Canterbury), bishops elected by and from amongst suffragan bishops of the Province, and any other bishops residing in the Province who are members of the Archbishops' Council. The Archbishop presides. The Lower House comprises clergy (other than bishops) who have been elected, appointed or chosen in accordance with Canon H 2 and the rules made under it (including deans, proctors from the dioceses and university constituencies and clerical members of religious communities) together with *ex-officio* members. The Prolocutor is the chair and spokesperson of the House.

MEMBERS OF THE CONVOCATIONS

	Canterbury	York	Either Province
Upper House			
Diocesan Bishops.....	30	14	
Suffragan Bishops....	6	3	
	36	17	
Lower House			
Deans.................	3	2	
Dean of Jersey or Guernsey	1		
Armed Services.......	3		
Chaplain-General of Prisons.............	1		
Elected Proctors	128	55	
University Proctors ..	4	2	
Religious			2
Co-opted Clergy......	0	0	
	140	59	2

OFFICERS

Convocation of Canterbury
President The Archbishop of Canterbury

Prolocutor of the Lower House Not known at the time of going to press

Other Officers
Pro-Prolocutors
Not known at the time of going to press.

Standing Committee of the Lower House
The Prolocutor
The Pro-Prolocutors
Remaining members not known at the time of going to press.

Following elections to the General Synod in October 2010, these positions are not known at the time of going to press. Please refer to the Registrar for information.

Registrar Mr Stephen Slack

Synodical Secretary, Actuary and Editor of the Chronicle of Convocation
Revd Stephen Trott, Rectory, 41 Humfrey Lane, Boughton, Northampton NN2 8RQ
Tel: 01604 845655
email: revstrott@sky.com

Ostiarius Mr Clive McCleester, Hospital of St Cross, St Cross Rd, Winchester SO23 9SD

Convocation of York
President The Archbishop of York

Prolocutor of the Lower House Not known at the time of going to press

Other Officers
Deputy Prolocutors
Not known at the time of going to press

Assessors (Standing Committee)
Not known at the time of going to press
Following elections to the General Synod in October 2010, these positions are not known at the time of going to press. Please refer to the Registrar for information.

Registrar Mr Lionel Lennox

Synodal Secretary and Treasurer and Editor of the Journal of Convocation
Ven Alan Wolstencroft, The Bakehouse, 1 Latham Row, Horwich, Bolton BL6 6QZ
Tel and Fax: 01204 469985
email: alanchrisw@tiscali.co.uk

Apparitor Mr Alex Carberry, Head Verger of York Minster

ACTS AND PROCEEDINGS

For the Acts and Proceedings of the Convocations, readers are referred to *The Chronicle of the Convocation of Canterbury* and to the *York Journal of Convocation*. Back numbers are available from Wm Dawson & Sons Ltd, Cannon House, Folkestone, Kent.

THE ARCHBISHOPS' COUNCIL

The Archbishops' Council
Charity Registration no: 1074857

Tel: 020 7898 1000
Fax: 020 7898 1369

The Turnbull Report

In 1994, a Commission was established by the Archbishops of Canterbury and York 'to review the machinery for central policy and resource direction in the Church of England, and to make recommendations for improving its effectiveness in supporting the ministry and mission of the Church to the nation as a whole'. The following year, the Commission, chaired by the Rt Revd Michael Turnbull, the then Bishop of Durham, produced a report entitled *Working as One Body*.

The need for change

The Commission looked at the constituent parts of the central structures of the Church of England – essentially the Offices of the Archbishops of Canterbury and York, the House of Bishops, the General Synod and its Boards and Councils, the Central Board of Finance, the Church Commissioners and the Church of England Pensions Board. Its conclusion was that more coherence and coordination were needed in order to give the Church an enhanced capacity to consider policy and resource issues together.

The Archbishops' Council

Amongst the Commission's recommendations was the establishment of a new Council to provide a focus for leadership and executive responsibility and a forum for strategic thinking and planning. Within an overall vision for the Church set by the House of Bishops, the Council would propose an ordering of priorities in consultation with the House of Bishops and the General Synod and take an overview of the Church's financial needs and resources. Not all of the details of the Turnbull model were accepted, but the General Synod endorsed the main thrust and agreed to the creation of the Archbishops' Council. It came into being at the beginning of 1999 under the terms of the National Institutions Measure 1998.

Purpose and work

The objects of the Archbishops' Council under the National Institutions Measure 1998 are to '*co-ordinate, promote, aid and further the work and mission of the Church of England*'. The Council seeks to do this by:

- giving a clear strategic sense of direction to the national work of the Church of England,

within an overall vision set by the House of Bishops and informed by an understanding of the Church's opportunities, needs and resources;
- encouraging and resourcing the Church in parishes and dioceses;
- promoting close collaborative working between the Church's national bodies, including through the management of a number of common services (Communications, Human Resources, IT etc)
- supporting the Archbishops with their diverse ministries and responsibilities; and
- engaging confidently with Government and other bodies.

The Archbishops' Council works closely with the Offices of the Archbishops of Canterbury and York, the House of Bishops and the General Synod, the Church Commissioners and the Church of England Pensions Board. It is supported in its wide-ranging brief by the staff and members of its Divisions:

- Education
- Cathedral and Church Buildings – which includes the Church Buildings Council and the Cathedrals Fabric Commission for England
- Central Secretariat – which includes the Council for Christian Unity and Research and Statistics
- Communications – which includes Church House Publishing
- Human Resources
- Legal
- Ministry
- Mission and Public Affairs – which includes the Committee for Minority Ethnic Anglican Concerns

The work of the Council is described in more detail in its annual report, but briefly includes the following:

- the promotion of the Church's mission and evangelism to all parts of society;
- the monitoring of Government policy where proposed legislative and other changes may bear directly on the Church of England;
- the expression of a Church of England view on social and ethical issues of importance to the nation, such as marriage and family life, penal policy or the needs of urban and rural priority areas;
- the development of educational policy and provision of advice and support services in

relation to primary, secondary and further and higher education, with particular regard to Church colleges and schools;

- the encouragement of the Church's ministry among children and young people and enabling lifelong learning within the Church;
- developing more effective and equitable financial arrangements within the Church nationally;
- proposing an annual budget for the work undertaken at Church House, funding ordination training, and grants for other purposes for approval by the General Synod;
- distributing selective stipend support and parish mission funding funded by the Church Commissioners;
- working closely with the House of Bishops, the Council has a role in developing policy over the selection, training, deployment and conditions of service of clergy and Readers, including recommending stipend levels;
- enhancing relations with other Christian Churches;
- nurturing relations with other faiths;
- encouraging the care and effective use of church buildings;
- supporting hospital chaplains and hospital chaplaincy generally;
- monitoring and making recommendations about issues with policy implications for minority ethnic groups within the Church and the wider community.

It engages on behalf of the Church with Government on a wide range of issues of concern to the Church of England and its mission to the nation.

Its programme of work for the new quinquennium, in collaboration with the Church Commissioners and the House of Bishops, is set out in GS 1607, *Into the New Quinquennium and its updates.*

MEMBERS
Joint Presidents
Most Revd and Rt Hon Dr Rowan Williams, Archbishop of Canterbury
Most Revd and Rt Hon Dr John Sentamu, Archbishop of York

Following elections to the General Synod in October 2010, membership of these bodies is uncertain at the time of going to press. Please refer to the Secretary of the body in question for current membership.

A Church Estates Commissioner
Mr Andreas Whittam Smith, First Church Estates Commissioner

Appointed by the Archbishops
Mr Andrew Britton, former Director, National Institute of Economic and Social Research
Mrs Mary Chapman, former Chief Executive, the Chartered Institute of Management
Professor John Craven, Vice-Chancellor, University of Portsmouth
Mr Philip Fletcher, Chairman, Water Services Regulation Authority
Revd Dr Rosalyn Murphy, priest-in-charge of St Thomas's Church, Blackpool
Mr Mark Russell, Chief Executive, Church Army

Staff
William Fittall, *Secretary General*
Tel: 020 7898 1360
email: william.fittall@c-of-e.org.uk

Revd Janina Ainsworth, *Education/National Society*
Tel: 020 7898 1500
email: janina.ainsworth@c-of-e.org.uk

Revd Dr Malcolm Brown, *Mission and Public Affairs*
Tel: 020 7898 1468
email: malcolm.brown@c-of-e.org.uk

Peter Crumpler, *Communications*
Tel: 020 7898 1462
email: peter.crumpler@c-of-e.org.uk

Janet Gough, *Cathedral and Church Buildings*
Tel: 020 7898 1887
email: janet.gough@c-of-e.org.uk

Ven Christopher Lowson, *Ministry*
Tel: 020 7898 1390
email: christopher.lowson@c-of-e.org.uk

Su Morgan, *Human Resources*
Tel: 020 7898 1565
email: su.morgan@c-of-e.org.uk

Stephen Slack, *Legal Adviser*
Tel: 020 7898 0366
email: stephen.slack@c-of-e.org.uk

Revd David Williams, *Central Secretariat/Clerk to the Synod*
Tel: 020 7898 1559
email: david.williams@c-of-e.org.uk

Nicholas Hills, *Assistant Secretary*
Tel: 020 7898 1363
email: nicholas.hills@c-of-e.org.uk

Archbishops' Council: key working relationships

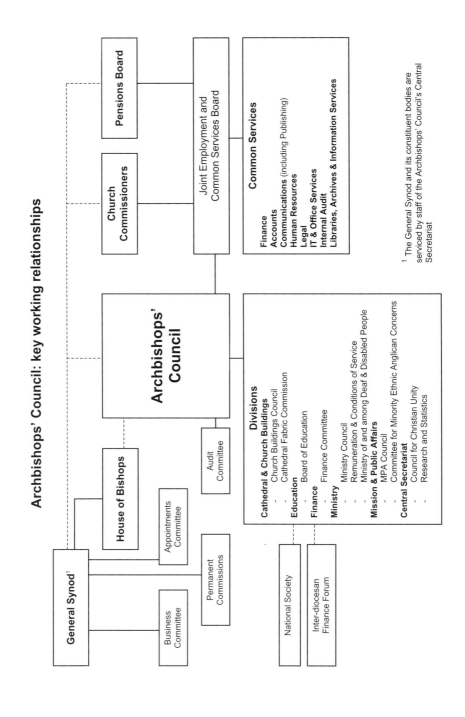

General Synod[1]

Business Committee

Permanent Commissions

Appointments Committee

House of Bishops

Audit Committee

Pensions Board

Church Commissioners

Joint Employment and Common Services Board

Common Services

Finance
Accounts
Communications (including Publishing)
Human Resources
Legal
IT & Office Services
Internal Audit
Libraries, Archives & Information Services

Archbishops' Council

National Society

Inter-diocesan Finance Forum

Divisions

Cathedral & Church Buildings
- Church Buildings Council
- Cathedral Fabric Commission
Education
- Board of Education
Finance
- Finance Committee
Ministry
- Ministry Council
- Remuneration & Conditions of Service
- Ministry of and among Deaf & Disabled People
Mission & Public Affairs
- MPA Council
- Committee for Minority Ethnic Anglican Concerns
Central Secretariat
- Council for Christian Unity
- Research and Statistics

[1] The General Synod and its constituent bodies are serviced by staff of the Archbishops' Council's Central Secretariat

National Structures

ARCHBISHOPS' COUNCIL BUDGET

The Budget covers five areas, each of which is separately approved by the General Synod annually. These are Training for Ministry, National Church Responsibilities, grants, mission agencies pensions support and revenue costs relating to the Church's Housing Assistance for the Retired Ministry (CHARM).

The vote 1 apportionment for 2011 represents an increase of 3.7 per cent from the previous year and provides a top-up of £175,000 to the relatively low levels of **Training for Ministry** reserves. The budget for **National Church Responsibilities** covers the costs of work in support of the Church's ministry and mission to the nation that needs to be undertaken, or is most effectively and/or efficiently carried out, at national level. The 2011 budget represents a reduction of 1.5% against the 2010 level. The **Grants** budget, which mainly funds the Church of England's contributions to the Inter Anglican budget and to ecumenical bodies, shows an increase of 1.3% on 2010.

The budget for **Mission Agencies Pensions Contributions** covers payments in respect of the pension contributions of clergy serving with the Partnership for World Mission agencies. Budgeted expenditure in 2011 is 2.0% above 2010 budget levels.

The final part of the budget comprises the revenue costs relating to the **Church's Housing Assistance for the Retired Ministry** (CHARM), which provides assistance to ensure that all clergy have access to housing upon retirement. The 2011 budget provides for an increase of 5.0 per cent.

The detailed 2011 budget as agreed by the General Synod in July 2010 (and set out more fully in GS 1781) is summarized in the table below. The overall picture is an increase in the apportionment of 1.5 per cent.

The Appointments Committee of the Church of England

Chairman Revd Prebendary David Houlding

Secretary Mr Nicholas Hills   *Tel:* 020 7898 1363

Four members appointed by the Archbishops' Council

Seven elected Members
Following elections to the General Synod in October 2010, membership of these bodies is uncertain at the time of going to press. Please refer to the Secretary of the body in question for current membership.

A joint committee of the General Synod and the Archbishops' Council, the Appointments Committee is responsible for making appointments and/or recommendations on appointments to synodical and other bodies as the Archbishops, the Synod or the Archbishops' Council require. It published its guidelines for best practice in the making of such appointments in 2005 as GS Misc 802, copies of which can be obtained from its Secretary.

Audit Committee

MEMBERS
Chair Mr Anthony Hesselwood

Secretary Michael Cole
Following elections to the General Synod in October 2010, membership of these bodies is uncertain at the time of going to press. Please refer to the Secretary of the body in question for current membership.

The Committee provides independent oversight of the Archbishops' Council's framework of corporate governance, risk management and internal control. It oversees the discharge of the Council's responsibilities relating to financial statements, external and internal audit and internal control systems, and reports to the Council thereon with recommendations as appropriate.

2011 Budget

	2011	
	£	£
TRAINING FOR MINISTRY (Vote 1)		
Expenditure	12,095,500	
Movement to Reserves	175,000	**12,270,500**
Financed by:		
Income	(30,000)	
Diocesan apportionment	(12,240,500)	**(12,270,500)**
NATIONAL CHURCH RESPONSIBILITIES (Vote 2)		
Central Secretariat		
(including Christian Unity/Research & Statistics)	1,815,587	
Ministry	1,389,660	
Education	681,646	
Mission & Public Affairs	1,245,368	
Cathedral and Church Buildings	828,430	
Church House Publishing	(44,106)	
Communications	463,301	
Human Resources	280,084	
Legal	668,421	
Finance & Resources	798,032	
Information Technology & Office Services	502,638	
Records	197,996	
Internal Audit	78,237	
Accommodation	1,253,035	
Depreciation	187,135	
Contingency	100,000	
		10,445,735
Financed by:		
Income	(305,000)	
Diocesan apportionment	(10,140,735)	
		(10,445,735)
GRANTS (Vote 3)		
Anglican Communion	455,600	
British ecumenical bodies	260,000	
Conference of European Churches	85,700	
World Council of Churches	108,000	
Church Urban Fund	203,000	
Legal Costs (including Legal Aid Fund)	400,000	
Other grants and expenses	42,400	
		1,554,700
Financed by:		
Diocesan apportionment		**(1,554,700)**
MISSION AGENCY CLERGY PENSIONS (Vote 4)		
Expenditure		**847,250**
Financed by:		
Diocesan apportionment	(800,000)	
Use of reserves	(47,250)	**(847,250)**
CHARM COSTS (Vote 5)		
Expenditure		**3,415,550**
Financed by:		
Diocesan apportionment		**(3,415,550)**
TOTAL EXPENDITURE (net of income)		**(28,023,735)**
Movement to reserves		127,750
TOTAL DIOCESAN APPOINTMENT		**(28.151.485)**

FINANCE COMMITTEE

MEMBERS
Chair appointed by Archbishops' Council
Mr Andrew Britton

Note: Following elections to the General Synod in October 2010, membership of the Finance Committee in respect of members elected by the General Synod is uncertain at the time of going to press. Please refer to the Secretary of the body in question for current membership.

Secretary David White   *Tel:* 020 7898 1684
      email: david.white@c-of-e.org.uk

Terms of reference
1 To advise the Archbishops' Council and the dioceses on all financial aspects of the Council's work, including its investment and trustee responsibilities, and on the overall financial needs and resources of the Church.
2 To make recommendations to the Archbishops' Council as to its annual budget and on mechanisms for monitoring and controlling the expenditure of the Council.

3 To consult with dioceses on financial matters, and to make recommendations thereon as appropriate to the Archbishops' Council and the dioceses.
4 To assess and seek to rationalize and simplify the systems for cash flow within the Church.
5 To provide a central forum for the development and promotion of Christian stewardship and fundraising.
6 To provide and coordinate research and guidance on financial, accounting and related matters.
7 To provide a channel for communicating on financial matters with Her Majesty's Government, financial regulators and other appropriate enforcement bodies, both directly and through the Churches Main Committee.
8 To work in collaboration with ecumenical partners on matters within the Committee's terms of reference.
9 To carry out such other work as may be entrusted to it by the Archbishops' Council.

CENTRAL SECRETARIAT

Under the direction of the Clerk to the Synod and Head of Central Secretariat, staff of the Central Secretariat provide the secretariat for the General Synod, its three Houses (House of Bishops, House of Clergy and House of Laity), the Archbishops' Council and the Business and Appointments Committees. Members of staff of the Secretariat serve as secretaries to a number of the Synod's principal commissions and committees and also as secretaries of *ad hoc* committees and working parties as required. They also serve various other groups, such as the Churches' Funerals Group. The Clerk to the Synod acts as Secretary to the Business Committee and provides advice and assistance as necessary to synodical bodies and members of Synod.
The Central Secretariat includes the Council for Christian Unity and Research and Statistics.

Clerk to the Synod/Head of Central Secretariat
Revd David Williams   *Tel:* 020 7898 1559
      email: david.williams@c-of-e.org.uk

Secretary, Council for Christian Unity
Canon Dr Paul Avis   *Tel:* 020 7898 1470
      email: paul.avis@c-of-e.org.uk

Head of Research and Statistics
Revd Lynda Barley   *Tel:* 020 7898 1542
      email: lynda.barley@c-of-e.org.uk

Senior Administrative Staff
Nicholas Hills
(*Secretary*: Appointments Committee, House of Laity, Standing Committee of the House of Laity; *Assistant Secretary*: Archbishops' Council)
      Tel: 020 7898 1363
      email: nicholas.hills@c-of-e.org.uk
David Pertaub
(*Head of Synod Support*)   *Tel:* 020 7898 1374
      email: david.pertaub@c-of-e.org.uk
Jonathan Neil-Smith
(*Secretary*: House of Bishops and Standing Committee of the House of Bishops)
      Tel: 020 7898 1373
      email: jonathan.neil-smith@c-of-e.org.uk
Revd Frances Arnold
(*Secretary*: House of Bishops' Theological Group; *Executive Officer*: House of Bishops)
      Tel: 020 7898 1372
      email: frances.arnold@c-of-e.org.uk
Dr Colin Podmore
(*Secretary*: House of Clergy, Standing Committee of the House of Clergy, Dioceses Commission)
      Tel: 020 7898 1385
      email: colin.podmore@c-of-e.org.uk
Secretary of the Liturgical Commission and Worship Development Officer Vacancy

Sue Moore
(*Secretary*:   Churches'   Funerals   Group
[www.christianfunerals.org]; *Assistant to Colin Podmore*)   *Tel:* 020 7898 1376
      email: sue.moore@c-of-e.org.uk

Frances Arnold
(*Executive Officer*, House of Bishops; *Secretary*:
House of Bishops' Theological Group))
Tel: 020 7898 1372
email: frances.arnold@c-of-e.org.uk

Elizabeth Hall
(*Safeguarding Adviser – Child and Adult Protection*:
Church of England and Methodist Church)
Tel: 020 7898 1330
email: elizabeth.hall@c-of-e.org.u

The Council for Christian Unity

General Secretary Canon Dr Paul Avis
Tel: 020 7898 1470
email: paul.avis@c-of-e.org.uk

European Secretary Revd Dr Leslie Nathaniel
Tel: 020 7898 1474
email: leslie.nathaniel@c-of-e.org.uk

National Adviser (Unity-in-Mission) Revd Dr
Roger Paul
Tel: 020 7898 1479
email: roger.paul@c-of-e.org.uk

Assistant Secretary Mr Francis Bassett
Tel: 020 7898 1481
email: francis.bassett@c-of-e.org.uk

Theological Secretary Dr Martin Davie
Tel: 020 7898 1488
email: martin.davie@c-of-e.org.uk

Office Church House, Great Smith St, London
SW1P 3AZ
Tel: 020 7898 1470
Fax: 020 7898 1483
Web: www.cofe.anglican.org/ccu

MEMBERS
Chairman Rt Revd Christopher Hill (*Bishop of
Guildford*)

*Following elections to the General Synod in October
2010, membership of these bodies is uncertain at the
time of going to press. Please refer to the Secretary of
the body in question for current membership.*

The Council was established as an advisory
committee of the General Synod on 1 April 1991
to continue and develop the ecumenical work
formerly undertaken by the Board for Mission
and Unity. That Board, set up on 1 January
1972, had inherited the responsibilities of the
Missionary and Ecumenical Council of the
Church Assembly (MECCA) and the Church
of England Council on Foreign Relations
(CFR).

FUNCTIONS OF THE COUNCIL
(*Adapted from the Constitution*)
(a) To stimulate and encourage theological
reflection in consultation with the Doctrine
Commission and the Faith and Order

Advisory Group and to advise the Archbishops' Council and the General Synod on
unity issues and proposals in the light of the
Christian understanding of God's purposes
for the world.

(b) To advise the House of Bishops on matters
referred to it by the House.

(c) To foster ecumenical work in the Church
nationally and in the dioceses.

(d) In conjunction with the Archbishops' Council to promote unity and ecumenical concerns in the work of all the Boards, Councils,
Divisions, etc.

(e) In ecumenical concerns on behalf of the
Archbishops' Council to be the principal link
between the General Synod and

(i) The Anglican Consultative Council;
(ii) individual provinces and dioceses
of the Anglican Communion and
the United Churches incorporating
former Anglican dioceses.

(f) On behalf of the Archbishops' Council to be
the principal channel of communication
between the General Synod and

(i) The World Council of Churches;
(ii) The Conference of European
Churches;
(iii) Churches Together in Britain and
Ireland;
(iv) Churches Together in England;
(v) all other Christian Churches in the
British Isles and abroad.

(g) To service committees and commissions
engaged in ecumenical discussions with
other Churches.

THE FAITH AND ORDER COMMISSION
Chairman Rt Revd John Hind (Bishop of
Chichester)

The newly formed Faith and Order Commission
consists of not more than sixteen persons
appointed by the Archbishops. The Commission
advises the Archbishops, House of Bishops and
the Council on matters of ecumenical, theological
and doctrinal concern.

COMMITTEE FOR ROMAN CATHOLIC RELATIONS
Chairman Rt Revd Tim Thornton (Bishop of Truro)

The Committee for Roman Catholic Relations consists of not more than fifteen persons appointed by the Archbishops after consultation with the Council. This Committee promotes relations between the Church of England and the Roman Catholic Church in this country and it meets twice a year with the equivalent Roman Catholic body. The two bodies form the English Anglican Roman Catholic Committee.

MEISSEN COMMISSION – ANGLICAN COMMITTEE
Chairman Rt Revd Nicholas Baines (*Bishop of Croydon*)
The Meissen Commission (the Sponsoring Body for Church of England EKD Relations) was established in 1991 to oversee the implementation of the Meissen Declaration and encourage relationships with the Evangelical Church in Germany. It comprises Anglican and German committees.

CHURCH OF ENGLAND MORAVIAN CONTACT GROUP
Chairman Vacancy
The Church of England Moravian Contact Group consists of four representatives, ordained and lay, from each Church, together with ecumenical observers and staff. The Church of England representatives are appointed by the Archbishops. The Contact Group works to make real in the lives of the two Churches the commitments of the Fetter Lane Declaration overseeing the implementation of those developments that are already possible, ensuring that further consideration is given to those areas where convergence is still required and nurturing growth in communion.

ECUMENICAL INSTRUMENTS
Contact is maintained with the World Council of Churches, the Conference of European Churches, Churches Together in Britain and Ireland, and Churches Together in England, where members and staff represent the Church of England at various levels. The Council is particularly concerned with helping the Church of England to relate effectively at every level to the ecumenical instruments.

PANELS OF THE CCU
The CCU has two subsidiary panels:

Methodist-Anglican Panel for Unity in Mission
Co-Chairman (*Anglican*) Rt Revd Nigel Stock (*Bishop of St Edmundsbury and Ipswich*)
Porvoo Panel
Chairman Rt Revd David Hamid (*Suffragan Bishop in Europe*)

Research and Statistics

Head of Research and Statistics Revd Preb Lynda Barley
Tel: 020 7898 1592
Fax: 020 7898 1532
email: statistics.unit@c-of-e.org.uk
Web: www.cofe.anglican.org/info/statistics
Office: Church House, Great Smith St, London SW1P 3AZ

While the gathering of parochial statistics remains at the heart of the Research and Statistics department's work, the department has broadened the range of statistics it maintains and diversified so that it is now providing a statistical and research service to the central Church and beyond. A new series of research-based parish booklets, *Time to Listen*, has been established and the department's role as a central resource is continuing to develop within the Archbishops' Council where it forms part of the Central Secretariat.

The Research and Statistics department is responsible (through the dioceses) for the annual collection, collation and analysis of parochial finance and membership *Church Statistics*. The department is seeking to improve the efficiency of the processing of these statistics, so that more of its resources can be devoted to researching underlying trends and evaluating the merits of the statistics collected. Working closely with the Mission and Public Affairs Division, the department continues to develop the church attendance and membership statistics that are collected annually, with the aim of providing a range of statistics and research resources which will be a tool for mission. It is also developing an ongoing mechanism for monitoring diversity across the Church. Continued efforts are being made, in conjunction with the Communications Unit, to improve and develop systems for the communication of research and statistical information, particularly focusing on new national survey findings concerning people's use of and attitudes towards local churches.

The department maintains a national parish database, which is being enhanced with new parish profile information and coordinated with the Geographical Information System mapping of parish boundaries. Some of the information presently held on the department's database concerns social deprivation, and the department is responsible for the coordination and, where appropriate, the mapping of census and other government statistics across the Church. The department maintains strong links with the Cathedral and Church Buildings Division regarding the use of cathedral and church buildings, with the Ministry Division in the preparation and production of *Statistics of Licensed Ministers*, and with the Church Commissioners in the development of the *Crockford* database.

The department provides a professional consultancy service to the NCIs and particular research support for the national Church Wedding project and future development of ministry

deployment. It maintains links with other denominations on statistical and research matters and reports on an annual basis local and national mission statistics to the Methodist Church. It is developing its role across the Church as a source of reliable research information regarding the place of the Church in modern society.

MINISTRY DIVISION

Chairman of Ministry Division Rt Revd Graham James, (*Bishop of Norwich*)   *Tel:* 01603 629001
email: bishop@bishopofnorwich.org

Director of Ministry Ven Christopher Lowson
Tel: 020 7898 1390
email: christopher.lowson@c-of-e.org.uk

Finance and Administration Vacancy
Tel: 020 7898 1392

Senior Selection Secretary Revd Stephen Ferns
Tel: 020 7898 1399
email: stephen.ferns@c-of-e.org.uk

Theological Education and Training Dr David Way
Tel: 020 7898 1405
email: david.way@c-of-e.org.uk

Adviser for Ministry of and among Deaf and Disabled People Revd Philip Maddock   *Tel:* 01543 306085
email: philip.maddock@c-of-e.org.uk

Secretary of the Central Readers' Council Dr Alan Wakely   *Tel:* 020 7898 1417
email: crcsec@hallarn.com
Web: www.readers.cofe.anglican.org

Selection Secretaries
Mr Kevin Diamond   *Tel:* 020 7898 1402
email: kevin.diamond@c-of-e.org.uk

Mrs Carys Walsh   *Tel:* 020 7898 1406
email: carys.walsh@c-of-e.org.uk

Revd Jules Cave Bergquist (*Vocations Officer*)
Tel: 020 7898 1395
email: jules.cavebergquist@c-of-e.org.uk

Revd Hilary Ison   *Tel:* 020 7898 1424
email: hilary.ison@c-of-e.org.uk

Revd Catherine Williams   *Tel:* 0207 898 1593
email: catherine.williams@c-of-e.org.uk

National Continuing Ministerial Education Officer Dr Tim Ling   *Tel:* 020 7898 1408
email: tim.ling@c-of-e.org.uk

Grants Officer Dr Mark Hodge   *Tel:* 020 7898 1396
email: mark.hodge@c-of-e.org.uk

National Adviser for Quality in Reader Education Mrs Sue Hart   *Tel:* 020 7898 1419
email: susan.hart@c-of-e.org.uk

National Consultant for Reader Selection Mr Nick Daunt   *Tel:* 01695 632326
email: nickdaunt@lineone.net

Office Church House, Great Smith St, London SW1P 3AZ   *Tel:* 020 7898 1412
Fax: 020 7898 1421

MINISTRY COUNCIL
Chair Rt Revd Graham James (*Bishop of Norwich*)

Revd Prof Loveday Alexander, Mr Andrew Britton, Mrs Mary Chapman, Revd Vanessa Herrick, Mr David Mills, Rt Revd John Packer, Rt Revd John Pritchard, Rt Revd Nigel Stock.

The provision of a properly trained and supported ministry is critical to the Church's mission. The division brings together policy on the selection, training, deployment and remuneration of the Church of England's ministry

The Ministry Council oversees the work of the Division. The committee meets four times a year under the chairmanship of the Bishop of Norwich (Chairman of the Division) and consists of members appointed by the House of Bishops, the Appointments Committee of the Church of England and elected by the General Synod.

The Ministry Council is supported by panels looking after Candidates, Research Degrees, Reader Education, Quality in Formation, and Finance. In addition the work of the Deployment, Remuneration and Conditions of Service, and Ministry of and Among Deaf and Disabled People committees are represented on the Council. The Central Readers' Council continues to fulfil its role in enhancing the contribution of Readers to the overall ministry of the Church, and its secretary is a valued honorary member of the staff team.

QUALITY in FORMATION PANEL
Chair Professor Michael Wright

Revd Dr Ruth Ackroyd, Ven Sheila Watson, Dr Paula Gooder, Revd Paul Goodliff, Mr Sion Evans, Revd Fiona Thomas, one vacancy

Terms of reference
1 To oversee the transition to a single quality framework for inspection, validation, moderation and Reader moderation and to carry out the current processes of inspection, validation, moderation and Reader moderation as required.
2 To provide training and support for reviewers involved in the current and future processes.

FINANCE PANEL
Chair Prof John Craven

Mr Tim Allen, Mr John Butler, Mr Richard Finlinson, Mrs Judith Nash

Terms of reference
The responsibility of the Finance Panel is to advise the Ministry Council on all aspects of its financial responsibility regarding the cost of ordinand training funded from Central Church Funds. Specifically:
1 To advise on policy concerning the location, establishment, inspection and financial support of theological colleges and courses;
2 To prepare and administer the Training Budget, and to advise on the financial support of candidates.

CANDIDATES PANEL
Chair Rt Revd Mark Bryant (*Bishop of Jarrow*)

Canon Katrina Barnes, Canon Christine Bullimore, Canon Jane Curtis, Revd Dr James Gardom, Miss Caulene Herbert, Mrs Susan Knowles, Revd Gary Renison, Sister Edith Margaret CHN, Ven Stephen Roberts, Revd Tim Sledge, Canon James Stewart, Dr Yvonne Warren, Canon Brian Watchom, Mr Hugh Wright

Terms of reference
1 To advise sponsoring bishops on:
(1) the reduction or lengthening of candidates' training
(2) the transferral of candidates from one training institution to another
(3) the return of candidates to training after a break of more than three months
(4) the suitability of candidates for transfer of category of ministry or change of focus of ministry
(5) the suitability of ministers from other denominations to be ministers in the Church of England
(6) candidates' potential to be theological educators
2 To undertake other work in relation to recruitment and selection

RESEARCH DEGREES PANEL
Chair Canon Dr Judith Maltby

Revd Prof William Horbury, Revd Prof Ben Quash, Prof Andrew Wright

Terms of reference
1 To give permission to ordinands seen as potential theological educators to study for research degrees (MPhil, PhD etc) outside of Bishops' Regulations for Training as part of pre-ordination training.
2 To allocate its budget to pay for, or contribute to, the additional costs of such training.

DEPLOYMENT, REMUNERATION AND CONDITIONS OF SERVICE COMMITTEE
Chair Rt Revd John Packer (*Bishop of Ripon and Leeds*)

Following elections to the General Synod in October 2010, membership of these bodies is uncertain at the time of going to press. Please refer to the Secretary of the body in question for current membership.

Terms of reference
1 To advise the House of Bishops and the Archbishops' Council on a strategy for ministry, with particular reference to the deployment, remuneration and conditions of service of those in authorized ministry, working in collaboration with dioceses, the Church Commissioners and the Church of England Pensions Board and with ecumenical partners.
2 To produce, in partnership with dioceses, a framework of national policy for stipends and other related matters, and to advise dioceses as appropriate on such matters.
3 To produce, in partnership with dioceses, a framework of national policy for the deployment of all ministerial resources, ordained and lay, available to the Church.
4 To monitor and advise in consultation with interested parties on sector and chaplaincy ministries within the total ministry of the Church.
5 To report regularly through the Ministry Council to the Archbishops' Council on the work of the Committee.

COMMITTEE FOR MINISTRY OF AND AMONG DEAF AND DISABLED PEOPLE
Chair Rt Revd Nicholas Reade (*Bishop of Blackburn*)

Following elections to the General Synod in October 2010, membership of these bodies is uncertain at the time of going to press. Please refer to the Secretary of the body in question for current membership.

The functions of the Committee include:
1 To monitor and advise on the progress of sector and chaplaincy ministries among deaf and disabled people within the total ministry of the Church, in consultation with those responsible for specific areas.
2 To encourage and strengthen the participation of deaf people in the life and witness of the Church, to represent the views of deaf people to

the Church and of the Church to deaf people, and to support the work of the chaplains.
3 To report regularly through the Ministry Council to the Archbishops' Council on the work of the Committee.
4 To advise the Central Bodies and the dioceses on matters related to general disability issues, especially the implementation of the Disability Discrimination Act as it applies to the Church.

Following elections to the General Synod in October 2010, membership of these bodies is uncertain at the time of going to press. Please refer to the Secretary of the body in question for current membership.

RECENT MINISTRY DIVISION PUBLICATIONS
Ministry in the Church of England

Shaping the Future: New Patterns of Training for Lay and Ordained, CHP 2006

In association with The Ecclesiastical Law Society
Canon Law for the Newly Ordained (2nd Ed)

Supporting the Ministry of Retired Clergy

The 37th Report of the Central Stipends Authority Dignity at Work: Working to reduce incidents of bullying and harassment

Drawn Together: The formation of the Yorkshire Regional Training Partnership

Reader Upbeat: revised report

Opening Doors: Guidelines and introductory DVD – Ministry with people with learning difficulties and people on the autistic spectrum

Clergy Couples Guidance

BISHOPS' REGULATIONS FOR TRAINING SELECTION FOR ORDAINED MINISTRY
1 Candidates should be commended in the first place by someone who has pastoral responsibility for them to the Diocesan Director of Ordinands. Before being accepted for training, they are required:
  i)   to have the necessary educational qualifications for or show that they have the potential to benefit from a formal course of training;
  ii) to satisfy medical requirements;
  iii) to be sponsored by their bishop for attendance at a Bishops' Advisory Panel.

2 Candidates for ordained ministry will be sponsored for a Bishops' Advisory Panel under the single category of 'ordained ministry'.
3 Central Church funds for pre-ordination/licensing training will be available for the pre-ordination phase of training:

(1) to those candidates who have attended a Bishops' Advisory Panel
(2) where the training pathway lies within the parameters of these regulations
(3) where the pathway comprises either (a) an approved route or combination of routes approved by the Ministry Division or (b) where an individual training plan for a candidate which has been approved by the Ministry Division, through the Candidate's Panel or the Research Degrees Panel.

4 If sponsoring papers envisage an incumbent status post in the future then the candidate's training may include access to college, course or a combination of these. Where candidates can demonstrate a high level of academic aptitude (normally through having a 2.1 in a first degree or equivalent), the pathway can include the departmental theology degrees in theological faculties where these are part of routes approved by the Ministry Division.
5 If an assistant ministry is envisaged then the candidate's training will normally be in course-type training. In addition there will be the option for the negotiation for elements of college-type or OLM-type training where this can be negotiated and financed within the RTP or region.
6 If the envisaged focus of ministry is OLM/locally deployed, then normally the candidate will train on the diocese's OLM scheme or local ministry pathway. In addition there will be an option for the negotiation for elements of college-type or course-type training where this can be negotiated and financed within the RTP or region.
7 The expected levels of attainment are set out in the Learning Outcomes at the point of ordination, on completion of IME and, where appropriate, for those seeking a post of incumbent status or equivalent.
8 In Higher Education terms, the normal minimum level of attainment at the point of ordination is diploma level. In this context 'diploma level' means attainment in both ministerial formation and theological learning. OLM/locally deployed ministry candidates should be working towards or complete Level 2 or equivalent.
9 Two years full-time and three years part-time for formation and education will act as a starting point in terms of expectation about training in the pre-ordination phase.
10 The normal expectation will be that candidates will make the maximum use of both prior learning and IME4–7 to ensure they reach the highest appropriate level of attainment appropriate for them (normal minimum of diploma level but also higher levels as appropriate).
11 This approach to choice of pathways applies to all candidates irrespective of age. However, where candidates are 55 or over at the point of entry into training, the ordaining bishop has discretion over the final form of the training.

National Structures

12 Access to types and length of training should normally fall within the bands set out in the points system the current version of which is available from the Ministry Division.
13 Where a diocese wishes for a candidate to train outside Bishops' Regulations, it should make a case to the Ministry Division (see 3. (3) above).

GRANTS
Candidates who have been recommended for training are eligible for financial help from Church funds. Details about grants can be obtained from the Grants Officer, Ministry Division, Church House, Great Smith St, London SW1P 3AZ.

For **Theological Colleges** *and* **Regional Courses** *see also* pages 235–237.

The Central Readers' Council

Patron HRH The Duke of Edinburgh

Presidents The Archbishops of Canterbury and York

Chair Rt Revd Robert Paterson (*Bishop of Sodor and Man*)

Vice-Chair Canon Chrysogon Bamber

Secretary Dr Alan Wakely   *Tel:* 01353 775132
                    email: crcsec@hallarn.com

Associate Secretary Jenny Macpherson
                    Tel: 020 7898 1401
          email: jennie.macpherson@c-of-e.org.uk

National Consultant for Quality in Reader Education
Mrs Sue Hart   *Tel:* 0191 252 3941
                    email: harts@sky.com

National Consultant for Reader Selection Mr Nick Daunt   *Tel:* 01695 632326
          email: nickdaunt@lineone.net

National Consultant for Reader CMD Mrs Wendy Sargeant   *Tel:* 01760 440152
          email: wendy.sargeant@virgin.net

Editor of 'The Reader' Revd Heather Fenton
          email: reader.editor@btconnect.com

MEMBERS
The CRC Executive Committee is elected for a five-year term co-terminous with General Synod. In addition to the Chair, Vice-Chair and all the officers listed above, the Committee consists of:

Two Wardens
Ven John Reed, Mrs Christine Haines
Reader representatives
Dr Marion Gray, Mrs Jennifer Williams, Miss Gloria Cadman, Mr Andy Lie

Treasurer
Mrs Carol Lidgett
(Those appointed to chair sub-committees of the Executive also serve *ex officio* on the Executive itself.)
The Central Readers' Council (CRC) works to enhance the contribution of Readers to the overall ministry of the Church, particularly to encourage the most effective integration with other forms of ministry, ordained and lay. It works in cooperation with the Ministry Division which moderates and coordinates the training of Reader candidates. CRC arranges national conferences for Readers, provides a forum for the exchange of ideas between dioceses on Reader matters and publishes a quarterly magazine, *The Reader*.
CRC is a registered charity, which derives its income mostly from capitation grants made by diocesan Readers' boards. It has its origins in the revival of Reader ministry in the Church of England in 1866 and particularly in the Central Readers' Board, which was granted a constitution by the Archbishops in 1921. CRC today is the immediate successor to the Central Readers' Conference, under a new constitution adopted in 2002, and revised in 2007 and 2010.
CRC has three representatives from each diocese, including the Warden and Secretary of Readers, and one representative from each of the Armed Forces. Any Reader appointed to a Ministry Division committee is *ex officio* a member of CRC. A non-voting observer is invited from the Deaf Readers and Pastoral Assistants Association, the Church of Ireland, the Scottish Episcopal Church and each of the dioceses of the Church in Wales. The annual general meeting is held in March/April each year.

MISSION AND PUBLIC AFFAIRS DIVISION
Mission and Public Affairs Council

Chairman   Dr Philip Giddings

Vice-Chairs: Public Affairs Mission Rt Revd Michael Hill (*Bishop of Bristol*); *Hospital Chaplaincy* Rt Revd Michael Perham (*Bishop of Gloucester*)

Director Revd Dr Malcolm Brown
Tel: 020 7898 1468
email: malcolm.brown@c-of-e.org.uk
MISSION AND PUBLIC AFFAIRS COUNCIL

FUNCTIONS OF THE COUNCIL
The functions of the Council shall be:
(a) To advise the Archbishops' Council, the General Synod and the House of Bishops on matters within the Council's remit;
(b) To work with dioceses, relevant diocesan networks and the Church's voluntary societies on matters within its remit;
(c) To relate to and cooperate with appropriate bodies within the churches of Britain and Ireland and the ecumenical instruments of CTBI and CTE;
(d) To take lead responsibility in relating to other Churches of the Anglican Communion and the Anglican Consultative Council, its Commissions and Networks, on issues relating to the Church's mission and role in public life;
(e) To relate to government departments and voluntary bodies relevant to its work.

In discharging its functions, the MPA Council shall include within its remit the following areas:
(i) the Church's engagement with social, ethical, political, environmental issues and work for justice and peace at local, national and international levels;
(ii) mission and evangelism; the Church of England's responsibilities for world mission and development; inter faith relations; and theological and missiological reflection on them;
(iii) the Church's mission and ministry (in liaison with Ministry Division) in urban and rural areas;
(iv) the Church's responsibility to confront the reality of racism in its own life and in society;
(v) the support of minority ethnic Christians in the Church of England, and their contribution to its life and witness;
(vi) the work of Hospital Chaplaincy and the Church's relation to the Department of Health, the National Health Service and Trusts and the provision of professional training and Continuing Professional Education for Chaplains.

MEMBERS
Following elections to the General Synod in October 2010, membership of these bodies is uncertain at the time of going to press. Please refer to the Secretary of the body in question for current membership.

STAFF
Director Revd Dr Malcolm Brown
Tel: 020 7898 1468
email: malcolm.brown@c-of-e.org.uk
Parliamentary Secretary Mr Richard Chapman
Tel: 020 7898 1438
email: richard.chapman@c-of-e.org.uk

Deputy Parliamentary Secretary Mr Simon Stanley
Tel: 020 7898 1478
email: simon.stanley@c-of-e.org.uk

Home Affairs Revd Christopher Jones
Tel: 020 7898 1531
email: christopher.jones@c-of-e.org.uk

International and Development Affairs Dr Charles Reed
Tel: 020 7898 1533
email: charles.reed@c-of-e.org.uk

Marriage and Family Policy Mrs Sue Burridge
Tel: 020 7898 1535
email: sue.burridge@c-of-e.org.uk

Medical Ethics, Health and Social Care Policy Rev Dr Brendan McCarthy
Tel: 020 7898 1523
*email:*brendan.maccarthy@c-of-e.org.uk

Community and Urban Affairs Revd Dr Andrew Davey
Tel: 020 7898 1446
email: andrew.davey@c-of-e.org.uk

Adviser for Minority Ethnic Anglican Concerns Mrs Sonia Barron
Tel: 020 7898 1442
Fax: 020 7898 1431
email: sonia.barron@c-of-e.org.uk

World Mission Policy Adviser Canon Janice Price
Tel: 020 7898 1328
email: janice.price@c-of-e.org.uk

Adviser for Mission Theology, Alternative Spiritualities and New Religious Movements Dr Anne Richards
Tel: 020 7898 1444
email: anne.richards@c-of-e.org.uk

National Adviser for Mission and Evangelism Vacancy

Associate Adviser: Mission and Evangelism Dr Rachel Jordan
Tel: 020 7898 1436
email: Rachel.jordan@c-of-e.org.uk

National Inter Faith Relations Adviser Canon Guy Wilkinson   *Tel:* 020 7898 1477
          email: guy.wilkinson@c-of-e.org.uk

National Rural Officer Dr Jill Hopkinson
          Tel: 024 7685 3073
          Fax: 024 7669 6460
          email: jillh@rase.org.uk

Hospital Chaplaincies Administrator Miss Mary Ingledew   *Tel:* 020 7898 1895
          email: mary.ingledew@c-of-e.org.uk

All staff are based in Church House, Westminster with the following exception: the office of the National Rural Officer is at the Arthur Rank Centre, Stoneleigh Park, Warwickshire CV8 2LZ. The National Inter Faith Relations Adviser is based at Lambeth Palace.

COMMITTEE FOR MINORITY ETHNIC ANGLICAN CONCERNS
Chair Ven Danny Kajumba
Adviser Mrs Sonia Barron
The principal tasks of the Committee are to monitor and make recommendations about issues which arise or which ought to arise in the context of the work of the Archbishops' Council and its Divisions and of the General Synod itself, as far as they have policy implications for minority ethnic groups within the Church and the wider community; and to assist the Bishops and their dioceses in developing diocesan-wide strategies for combating racial bias within the Church, encouraging them to make the problem of racism a priority concern in their programmes and to circulate the best analyses of racism, including theological analyses.

GROUPS AND PANELS OF THE MPA COUNCIL
The Council currently has the following working groups or panels. Those which are ecumenical or formally constituted with other agencies, are described in greater detail.

CofE: World Mission and Anglican Communion Panel
Chairman Rt Revd Michael Hill (*Bishop of Bristol*)

Secretary Canon Janice Price   *Tel:* 020 7898 1328
          email: janice.price@c-of-e.org.uk

The CofE: World Mission and Anglican Communion Panel is a partnership between the General Synod and the World Mission Agencies of the Church of England drawing its members from the General Synod, the Mission Agencies, representatives of Diocesan Companion Links, Associate Members and our ecumenical partners. There are eleven full partner Agencies: Church Army, the Church's Ministry among Jewish People (CMJ), Church Mission Society (CMS), Church Pastoral Aid Society (CPAS), Crosslinks, Intercontinental Church Society (ICS), The Mission to Seafarers, The Mothers' Union, South American Mission Society (SAMS), the Society for Promoting Christian Knowledge (SPCK) and the United Society for the Propagation of the Gospel (USPG). There are over 20 Associate Members.

Its main tasks are concerned with the Church of England's role in furthering partnership in mission within the Anglican Communion; supporting the work of Diocesan Companion Links; and with coordinating the policies and selected tasks of the Church of England's World Mission Agencies. It has an advisory role in enabling English dioceses and General Synod to see their way more clearly towards their participation in world mission as members of the Anglican Communion and ecumenically.

Mission Theological Advisory Group (MTAG)
Co-Chairman (with Revd Prof John Drane) Rt Revd Dr Brian Castle (*Bishop of Tonbridge)*
Secretary Dr Anne Richards   *Tel:* 020 7898 1444
          email: anne.richards@c-of-e.org.uk

The ecumenical Mission Theological Advisory Group is composed of nominees from the Mission and Public Affairs Division of the Archbishops' Council and the Global Mission Network (GMN) of Churches Together in Britain and Ireland (CTBI). It is concerned with the theology of mission and deals with theological issues referred to it by the participating bodies.

Presence and Engagement Task Group
Chairman Rt Revd David James (*Bishop of Bradford*)
Secretary Canon Guy Wilkinson
          Tel: 020 7898 1477
          email: guy.wilkinson@c-of-e.org.uk
Rural Advisory Group
Chair Rt Revd James Bell (*Bishop of Knaresborough*)

Secretary Dr Jill Hopkinson
Office The Arthur Rank Centre, Stoneleigh Park, Warwickshire CV8 2LZ   *Tel:* 024 7685 3073
          Fax: 024 7669 6460
          email: jillh@rase.org.uk

EDUCATION DIVISION
Transforming Church and Community through Education and Learning

The Education Division staff work in three teams: Lifelong Learning; Schools Strategy; Training and Development.

THE BOARD OF EDUCATION

The Board of Education's Constitution (as laid down by General Synod) sets out three main functions: to advise the General Synod and the Archbishops' Council on all matters relating to education; to advise the dioceses similarly; to take action in the field of education (in the name of the Church of England, the Archbishops' Council and the General Synod) on such occasion as is required.

The Board of Education meets twice a year, in April and October. Panels of Board members, supplemented by a small number of non-Board members, oversee the various aspects of the work. Board and panel members receive a weekly electronic bulletin about the issues being addressed by the Education Division staff; these bulletins frequently invite guidance from Board members and from diocesan education staff and Church of England secondary schools who also receive the bulletins.

Chair
Rt Revd John Saxbee (*Bishop of Lincoln*); (From 1 February) The Rt Revd John Pritchard (*Bishop of Oxford*)

Following elections to the General Synod in October 2010, membership of these bodies is uncertain at the time of going to press. Please refer to the Secretary of the body in question for current membership.

EDUCATION DIVISION STAFF
Chief Education Officer and Head of the Education Division Revd Janina Ainsworth
Tel: 020 7898 1500

Lifelong Learning team
National Adviser for Higher Education and Chaplaincy Revd Dr Stephen Heap   Tel: 020 7898 1513
email: stephen.heap@c-of-e.org.uk

National Further Education Adviser Revd Dr John Breadon   Tel: 020 7898 1517
email: john.breadon@c-of-e.org.uk

Schools Strategy team
Head of School Improvement Mr Nick McKemey
Tel: 020 7898 1490
email: nick.mckemey@c-of-e.org.uk

Head of School Development Dr Rob Gwynne
Tel: 020 7898 1789
email: rob.gwynne@c-of-e.org.uk

National Schools Support Officer Mrs Liz Carter
Tel: 020 7898 1515
email: liz.carter@c-of-e.org.uk

Training and development team
National Children's Adviser Ms Mary Hawes
Tel: 020 7898 1504
email: mary.hawes@c-of-e.org.uk

National Adviser in Lay Discipleship and Shared Ministry Miss Joanna Cox   Tel: 020 7898 1511
email: joanna.cox@c-of-e.org.uk

National Youth Adviser Mr Peter Ball
Tel: 020 7898 1506
email: peter.ball@c-of-e.org.uk

Office Church House, Great Smith St, London SW1P 3AZ   Tel: 020 7898 1501
Fax: 020 7898 1520

THE WORK OF THE EDUCATION DIVISION
The work of the Education Division embraces four main aspects which support activity at national, diocesan, parish and school level. The four aspects are:
- **Engaging with national institutions** through ensuring a high profile and working closely with Government and key organisations.
- **Growing the Church's mission** by increasing the opportunities for children, young people and students to encounter the Christian faith. In part this is achieved by increasing the number of designated schools and organisations and developing their Christian distinctiveness.
- **Professional support and nurture** by supporting high professional standards, providing high quality support and advice and achieving the best quality outcomes for the people the Division serves.
- **Research, development and evaluation** through a co-ordinated research programme and maintaining databases which inform the work.

The Division operates in three teams, with overall leadership provided by the Chief Education Officer. The three teams are:

Lifelong Learning Team

This team focuses on the Church's involvement in education beyond statutory school leaving age.

For **higher education** the team aims to develop the Church's presence and witness by:
• monitoring developments and extending reach and contacts
• stimulating and developing practical concern in student and university affairs – a concern both for the life of higher education institutions, their ethical, social, spiritual and religious concerns, and for the individuals who work and study in the sector
• liaison and partnership with national bodies, including the Department for Business, Innovation, and Skills, the Higher Education Funding Council, representative university groups, ecumenical and other faith bodies;
• helping ministry in Higher Education through advisory, liaison and representative services to chaplaincy work already established, and to reflect upon that ministry.

For **further education** the key role is strategic thinking and planning with the aim of developing the Church's presence and witness within FE colleges and the wider Learning and Skills sector by:
• engaging with the Government's programme of reform by monitoring policy and contributing to improvement strategies
• increasing the Church's involvement through establishing and supporting chaplaincy and college/faith partnerships
• helping to shape the sector's understanding of spiritual and moral development for staff and students, fostering shared human values and dialogue and promoting a more holistic educational experience for all students
• working with a range of ecumenical and interfaith partners.

The team is involved in the work of the 11 **Church Colleges and Universities** founded as a direct result of the Church's role as first provider of mass schooling. All are highly diverse organisations which retain a commitment to teacher education alongside a wide portfolio of courses, including (for most) significant departments of theology and religious studies. In 2009 all bar one of the 11 institutions, along with 3 Roman Catholic institutions, signed a Memorandum of Understanding committing them to the outworking of the Christian foundation in the 21st century.

Training and Development Team

This team supports the voluntary aspects of education and training for children, young people, adult learning and lay discipleship. By resourcing diocesan networks and supporting work in parishes and local communities, it aims to promote effective Christian nurture, discipleship and outreach and to encourage training and best practice. Much of the work at national level involves developing effective collaborations with key diocesan personnel, government, voluntary agencies, ecumenical and denominational partnerships and other divisions of the National Church Institutions.

The work with children and young people is guided by **'Going for Growth'** which is the formally adopted national strategy for work with Children and Young People. It is now being implemented. The strategy also offers a framework for these aspects of the Church's ministry which honours the absolute value of each child and young person, the importance of relationships, and the establishment of the Kingdom of God here on earth.

Work with and for **young people** focuses on:
• Collaboration with a range of organisations including central and local government, the National Youth Agency, and the National Council for Voluntary Youth Services, as well as those key partnerships with National Ecumenical bodies, Anglican voluntary societies, and other Christian agencies.
• The participation of young people in the life of the church through the work of the Church of England Youth Council and also through a range of different approaches to young people's participation in dioceses.
• Provision of training opportunities and resources for both voluntary and paid youth workers through partnership with key training providers (including The Centre for Youth Ministry, University of Chester and Oasis) as well as the Church's own provision of training in Dioceses and nationally (including the Equipping competency framework for voluntary youth workers).
• Young people's involvement in mission, especially through the provision of the Youth Evangelism Fund which has involved groups of young people delivering peer evangelism projects and events in their own localities.

Work in supporting the Church's ministry with, for and by **children** up to the age of 11 involves:
• Advocacy of the place and value of children in the Church, particularly in the areas of the church as a worshipping community.
• Collaborative working with the network of Diocesan Children's Advisers and Ecumenical partners.
• Initiating in-service training where appropriate, in order to equip laity and clergy with the necessary resources and skills for nurturing the faith of children and their families.
• Developing and creating partnerships with Christian and secular agencies including the Consultative Group on Children's Ministry, the Children's Workforce Development Council and VCS Engage.

- Keeping a watching brief on current government polices under the Every Child Matters agenda, with particular regard to their application in the voluntary and faith sector.

The work with **lay discipleship and shared ministry** involves consultancy, support, research and development to enhance the capacity and provision of adult Christian formation and lifelong leaning in the Church. The work seeks to:
- promote the development of theological education for lay people
- provide guidance on developing volunteer, lay and shared ministry, and to resource new diocesan developments in formal lay ministry and patterns of integrated training, in association with the Ministry Division
- improve the quality of adult and lifelong learning through training the trainers, promoting partnerships, researching and disseminating good practice and developing new initiatives encouraging Christian discipleship in the Church and the world.

School Strategy Team
The School Strategy team incorporates work done by both the National Society and the Church in furthering the development and effectiveness of the Church's academies, primary and secondary schools. The team is involved in:

- monitoring the impact of legislation, capital programmes and the various programmes for expanding and changing the school system
- increasing the number of Church of England schools especially through the Academies programme
- enabling DBEs to grow their provision through professional support and guidance, releasing and accessing funds for new developments
- support for governors and employers of the school workforce
- supporting the implementation of succession strategies for school leadership and research into the performance and characteristics of church schools
- identifying, disseminating and sharing the best practice within the diverse national family of Anglican schools
- developing and maintaining the Statutory Inspection of Anglican Schools (SIAS) Section 48 framework, training and quality assuring inspectors
- providing training and research for school improvement in church schools
- resourcing high quality Religious Education and collective worship
- developing the whole curriculum for church schools and for the spiritual, moral, social and cultural development and wellbeing of children and young people.

CATHEDRAL AND CHURCH BUILDINGS DIVISION

This area of the Archbishops' Council's responsibilities relates to the Church's concern with cathedral and church buildings and related matters.

Cathedral and Church Buildings Divisional Group

Chairman Rt Revd and Rt Hon Dr Richard Chartres KCVO DD FSA

Members
Chair of the Cathedrals Fabric Commission
Chair of the Church Buildings Council
4 other Members (appointed by the Appointments Committee from within the Synodical members of the CCC and CFCE)

Head of Division Miss Janet Gough
The Division was formed in 2002 from the staff formerly serving the Cathedral Fabric Commission and the Council for the Care of Churches, and supporting the work of the Archbishops' Council in relation to cathedral and church buildings. In 2008, the Division was joined by the staff formerly serving the Advisory Board for Redundant Churches, the independent statutory adviser to the Church Commissioners on churches proposed for closure, and former

Anglican churches subject to the Pastoral Measure. At the same time, the CCC and ABRC were dissolved and their functions transferred to the newly constituted Church Buildings Council. The CBC is the Church's national advisory, grant-making and educational body supporting dioceses and parishes with the care, use and development of parish churches and their contents and churchyards. Through its Statutory Advisory Committee, it also advises the Commissioners and others on churches proposed for closure and closed for regular public worship. The CFCE is the central planning body with advisory and regulatory functions relating to the fabric, contents, setting and archaeology of the Church of England's cathedrals and their precincts. The Head of Division is Secretary of the CBC and CFCE.

The Division is responsible for developing and maintaining relations between Church and State, national and local bodies on church buildings matters, and for the development of the Church's vision of how the Church of England may (in partnership with the State and local communities) best meet its responsibilities for its church buildings.

Overall the Church of England is responsible for 16,000 parish churches and 41 cathedrals that form the centres for the Church's worship and its mission in the community. These buildings and their contents represent 14 centuries of religious architecture, art and history, which have continuously developed up to the present day, and are still developing. Some 13,000 are listed buildings (including 45 per cent of all the country's Grade I buildings), while many churchyards are an important ecological resource.

Building Faith in our Future, a strategy for church buildings was issued in 2004 outlining the achievements carried out within church buildings and the potential fragility of these achievements, and calling for greater partnerships from public bodies of all kinds to help sustain them for the future. Since then the Division has continued to develop and support a range of capacity building initiatives and took a major step forward in winning fair access to public funds for churches in the launch in March 2009 of

the report *Churches and Faith Buildings: Realising the Potential.* Resulting from a collaboration between the Church and five Government departments, it acknowledges the huge engagement of the Church at local and regional level and the potential that churches have to help Government meet its various agendas, addresses the issue of 'squeamishness' in allocating public funds to faith groups, and identifies existing funding and support which will enable churches to be adapted for community use. In 2009/10 the Division launched the programme *Crossing the Threshold,* a series of events and resources aimed at training the trainers within diocesan structures and in partnership with others. It is about providing churches with the resources they need to open up their buildings to the wider community. The Division also shares responsibility for managing *Shrinking the Footprint,* the Church of England's national environmental campaign.

The Division maintains a library of books and other material dedicated solely to ecclesiastical architecture, art, design and liturgy available for readers interested in those areas.

The Church Buildings Council

Chairman Mrs Anne Sloman OBE

MEMBERS
Following elections to the General Synod in October 2010, membership of these bodies is uncertain at the time of going to press. Please refer to the Secretary of the body in question for current membership.

The Church Buildings Council (CBC) carries out the functions formerly of the Council for the Care of Churches (CCC) and the Advisory Board for Redundant Churches (ABRC). The CCC was formed in 1921 to coordinate the work of the Diocesan Advisory Committees for the Care of Churches, which advise diocesan chancellors on faculty applications, and clergy, churchwardens, architects and others responsible for church buildings and their contents on their care, use and development. The ABRC was formed in 1969 as the independent statutory advisor to the Church Commissioners on churches proposed for closure for regular worship and former Anglican churches subject to the Pastoral Measure.

The CBC's priority is to enable parishes to release through responsible stewardship the mission and worship potential of church buildings. We seek to encourage and assist parishes in the care and conservation, use and development of the Church's buildings including their contents and churchyards.

The CBC advises the Archbishops' Council on all matters relating to the use, care and planning or design of places of worship, their curtilages and contents; acts on the Council's behalf in contacts with government departments and other bodies and in negotiations with professional bodies over church inspection and repair; and assists in the review or revision of legislation relating to church buildings and their contents.

The CBC, through its Statutory Advisory Committee, advises the Church Commissioners and others on the interest, quality and importance of churches and their contents, and the alteration and conversion of churches to alternative use, working closely with the central and local authorities of Church and State.

The CBC provides Diocesan Pastoral Committees with detailed reports about the architectural and historic qualities of churches likely to be closed for regular worship. It also submits specialist advice to diocesan chancellors, Diocesan Advisory Committees and parishes on proposals that are or may become the subject of faculty applications, e.g. the construction of church extensions, re-ordering schemes, the sale of church furnishings, the partial demolition of churches, the conservation of significant furnishings, and related archaeological work.

The CBC maintains contact with Diocesan

Advisory Committees through regular circulation of information, by an annual meeting for Chairmen, Secretaries and other members and by visits. The membership of DACs is varied: it includes both clergy and lay, some with professional expertise in architecture, art history and archaeology, and others of no specialist knowledge but of sound judgement and experience, or representing the views of English Heritage, the local planning authority and the amenity societies. Every diocese has specialist advisers on organs, bells, clocks, archaeology, as well as on heating and lighting.

The CBC administers funds (generously provided by charitable bodies) for the conservation of furnishings and works of art in churches, and collaborates closely with English Heritage, the Heritage Lottery Fund, National and other Lottery distributors and other grant-making bodies. Advice is available from the Council on specific conservation problems.

The Council's specialist committees offer expert advice on conservation matters and administer grants from charitable foundations for the care and conservation of significant or historic furnishings and works of art in churches and churchyards. Churches in England, Scotland and Wales, of any denomination, are eligible for these grants. In addition, under an agreement reached with the Wolfson Foundation, the Council considers applications for grant aid towards fabric repairs for Grade I and Grade II* Anglican churches in England, Scotland and Wales. More information about these grants and applications can be made online at www.churchcare.co.uk.

The CBC is not only concerned with the care and conservation of ancient buildings and their contents, but also with the development of places of worship as community resources. It runs three websites: www.churchcare.co.uk, which provides advice on matters related to the use, development, care and conservation of church buildings for churchwardens and other volunteers who look after church buildings; www.churchart.co.uk, which gives advice on commissioning new works of art and includes details of nearly 200 individual artists and craftspeople and www.shrinkingthefootprint.org, which is the website of the Church of England's environmental campaign providing practical guidance and advice on best practice.

The Cathedrals Fabric Commission for England

Chairman Rt Hon Frank Field MP

Vice-Chairman Miss Jennie Page OBE

Following elections to the General Synod in October 2010 there will be some changes in the membership of the Commission during 2011. Please refer to our web page or the Secretary for current membership.

MEMBERS
Very Revd James Atwell (*Dean of Winchester*), Miss Sarah Brown, Canon Peter Bruinvels (Guildford), Mr Richard Carr-Archer, Mr Geoffrey Clifton, Canon Jeremy Davies, Mr Peter Draper, Mr Michael Drury, Dr Richard Hall, Canon Jeremy Haselock (Norwich), Canon David Isaac (Portsmouth), Very Revd Peter Judd (*Dean of Chelmsford*), Mrs Judith Leigh, Mr John Maine, Rt Revd Stephen Platten (*Bishop of Wakefield*), Mr Nicholas Rank, Mr Dickon Robinson, Ven Jane Sinclair, Canon Peter Smith (St Edmundsbury & Ipswich), Mr Tom Sutcliffe (Southwark), Canon Dr Nicholas Thistlethwaite, Mr Paul Velluet.

In 1949, at the request of Deans and Chapters, the Cathedrals Advisory Committee was set up to give help and advice on places and problems affecting the fabric, furnishings, fittings and precincts of cathedrals.

In 1981, the Committee was reconstituted as a permanent Commission of the General Synod, under the title The Cathedrals Advisory Commission for England.

In 1991, the Commission was further reconstituted as a statutory body under the Care of Cathedrals Measure and renamed The Cathedrals Fabric Commission.

The Commission oversees the Church's own system of controls under the Care of Cathedrals Measure as amended by the Care of Cathedrals (Amendment) Measure 2005. Before implementing any proposals which would affect the character of a cathedral building, its setting, or archaeological remains within its precinct, or an object of artistic, archaeological, architectural or historic interest owned by the Chapter, in its possession or to the possession of which it is entitled, the Dean and Chapter are required to get approval under the Measure, either from the Fabric Advisory Committee serving the cathedral or from the Commission itself. The Commission also offers advice on matters relating to the architecture, archaeology, art and history of cathedrals and their precincts, landscape and environment, and publishes a range of guidance and advisory note (available on www.cofe.anglican.org) and also run seminars and conferences for Fabric Advisory Committees and cathedral chapters and their professional advisers.

The Commission administers grant schemes for cathedrals including: The English Cathedrals Repair Fund and The Cathedrals Amenities Fund. Details of these can be found on www.churchcare.co.uk.
Staff of the Cathedral and Church Buildings Division
Head of Division Miss Janet Gough
Tel: 020 7898 1887
email: janet.gough@c-of-e.org.uk

Depuy Secretary CFCE Ms Maggie Goodall
Tel: 020 7898 1888
email: maggie.goodall@c-of-e.org.uk

Cathedrals Officer Ms Allie Nickell
Tel: 020 7898 1862
email: allie.nickell@c-of-e.org.uk

Senior Adviser, Closed Churches Dr Jeffrey West
Tel: 020 7898 1872
email: jeffrey.west@c-of-e.org.uk

Casework Officer, Closed Churches Ms Anne McNair
Tel: 020 7898 1871
email: anne.mcnair@c-of-e.org.uk

Casework and Law Officer Mr Jonathan Goodchild
Tel: 020 7898 1883
email: jonathan.goodchild@c-of-e.org.uk

Archaeology Officer Dr Joseph Elders
Tel: 020 7898 1875
email: joseph.elders@c-of-e.org.uk

Casework Officer Mrs Jude Johncock (on maternity leave)
Tel: 020 7898 1864
email: jude.johncock@c-of-e.org.uk

Casework Officer Mrs Diana Coulter (to cover maternity leave)
email: diana.coulter@c-of-e.org.uk

Senior Conservation Officer Mr Andrew Argyrakis
Tel: 020 7898 1885
email: andrew.argyrakis @c-of-e.org.uk

Conservation & Grants Officer Dr David Knight
Tel: 020 7898 1886
email: david.knight@c-of-e.org.uk

Conservation & Grants Officer Dr Pedro Gaspar
Tel: 020 7898 1889
email: pedro.gaspar@c-of-e.org.uk

Policy Officer Ms Rebecca Payne
Tel: 020 7898 1886
email: rebecca.payne@c-of-e.org.uk

Project Manager Ms Ruth Watkinson
Tel: 020 7898 1865
email: ruth.watkinson@c-of-e.org.uk

SHARED SERVICES
Finance and Resources

Chief Finance Officer: Mr Ian Theodoreson
Tel: 020 7898 1795
email: ian.theodoreson@c-of-e.org.uk

Finance and Resources is a shared service function providing five levels of support to the NCIs and wider Church generally:

1. The Accounting Services Section is responsible for processing, recording and maintaining the prime books of account, banking, payments, payroll, (including Clergy Pay), management reporting, statutory financial reporting, budgeting and forecasting, securing assets and ensuring the bodies are legally compliant in terms of statutory reporting, tax and charity law.
2. The Financial Policy and Planning section provides financial information to help inform management decisions, including the production of financial policy advice and analysis.
3. The SAP support team is responsible for managing the use of and controls within the NCIs SAP system.
4. The Strategy and Development Unit advises on resource allocation, evaluating the effectiveness of spending plans and measuring impact.
5. The work of the National Stewardship & Resources Officer involves supporting parishes and dioceses in developing mechanisms for effective giving and looking at better ways to manage expenditure through common working.

Accounting Services

Director of Accounting Services: Mr Paul Burrage
Tel: 020 7898 1677
email: paul.burrage@c-of-e.org.uk

The Accounting Services Section provides accounting services principally for (the three largest NCIs) the Archbishops' Council, the Church Commissioners and the Church of England Pensions Board, and also for the National Society. It is responsible for payroll, cash and treasury, processing, tax expertise (principally property and VAT related), and through three 'client-facing' teams, for the largest NCIs, provides statutory financial accounting, management accounting, and support for budget setting and forecasts.

Financial Policy and Planning

Head of Financial Policy & Planning: Mr David White
Tel: 020 7898 1684
email: david.white@c-of-e.org.uk

The Financial Policy Section supports the Archbishops' Council and the Church Commissioners in the development of financial policy and analysis, and in the monitoring and management of its finances. It works in close partnership with dioceses as well as departments across the Archbishops' Council and Commissioners. It calculates and communicates the apportionment of the Council's budget to dioceses.

The section supports the development of spending plans from the Church Commissioners' fund, including liaison with their actuaries. It seeks to ensure that the General Synod (through a Financial Memorandum) is aware of the significant financial implications of proposals before decisions are taken and contributes to the development of policy on financial matters across the Church.

The department provides secretariat support for the Council's Finance Committee (which meets around five times a year) which is responsible for the management of the Council's financial business and advice and coordination on financial matters over the Church as a whole, the Inter-Diocesan Finance Forum (which meets twice a year and comprises three representatives of each diocese) and the Consultative Group of DBF Chairs and Diocesan Secretaries (comprising one DBF Chair and one Diocesan Secretary from each region). The Forum and the Consultative Group provide an opportunity for consultation on remuneration policy, conditions of service, pensions policy, the national Church budget and apportionment, allocations to dioceses for the support of ministry in poorer areas and other issues with a financial perspective

The section supports the work of the Church Commissioners by supporting the work of its Assets Committee and staff level Assets Management Group. Key roles include the production of coordinated investment performance statistics and financial forecasts in respect of income and expenditure, cashflow and longer term actuarial projection.

SAP Support

Systems Accountant: Sarah Jowett
Tel: 020 7898 1600
email: sarah.jowett@c-of-e.org.uk

The SAP support team is responsible for managing the use of the NCIs SAP system, supporting the core modules of finance, real estate, purchasing, loans management and plant maintenance. The team works to ensure that users obtain maximum benefit from the opportunities SAP provides whilst at the same time maintaining the integrity of controls within the system.

The SAP team provides a helpdesk service for the Archbishops' Council, Church Commissioners, Pensions Board and National Society dealing with technical changes to the system and user queries in relation to all modules.

Strategy and Development unit

Head of Unit Mr Philip James

The role of the (Resource) Strategy and Development Unit is to undertake research and strategy development on behalf of the Church in respect of its mission resourcing (principally relating to those resources held at national level).

A key part of the role is to ensure that the funds of the Church Commissioners are being used effectively to advance the spiritual and numerical growth of the Church. The Unit is also responsible for administering the Church and Community Fund.

Christian Stewardship

National Stewardship & Resources Officer Dr John Preston *Tel:* 020 7898 1540
email: john.preston@c-of-e.org.uk

Through its Christian Stewardship Committee, the Archbishops' Council affirms the principles and practice of Christian stewardship as a part of discipleship. Stewardship advisers encourage church people to respond to God's love and generosity and resource God's mission through the Church by the discovery and use of human and financial resources. This is often focused on the giving of money – regularly, tax-effectively and in proportion to income.

Initiatives are promoted, support given and ideas exchanged between the diocesan members of the Christian stewardship network. There is a particular focus on identifying, documenting and resourcing elements of good practice, so that other dioceses and parishes can benefit from what is proven to be effective. Current areas of good practice include:

- resourcing parishes to encourage giving through the appointment of a Parish Giving Officer;
- the key tasks promoted in the recent report GS 1723 'Giving for Life';
- promoting legacy giving as part of our holistic stewardship;
- supporting parishes engaging with a capital fundraising programme.

Church people, through their giving, are rightly the providers of the largest part of the Church's income but the Committee is reviewing how it can best help the Church at all levels to seek additional income streams.

A national website to resource all those concerned with Christian giving, stewardship and parish finances is available at www.parishresources.org.uk. This contains a wide range of resources for parish-giving officers, treasurers, gift-aid secretaries and those who preach and teach on stewardship and generosity.

INTERNAL AUDITING DEPARTMENT

Director of Risk Management and Internal Audit: Mr Michael Cole *Tel:* 020 7898 1658
email: michael.cole@c-of-e.org.uk

The Internal Auditing Department provides internal audit services to the Church Commissioners, the Church of England Pensions Board, the Archbishops' Council and the other National Church Institutions.

The department carries out regular departmental and process reviews in accordance with a programme agreed each year with each Audit Committee, and also investigates particular issues that might arise from time to time.

The Internal Auditing Department provides consultancy support to managers on matters of governance, risk management and internal control.

INFORMATION TECHNOLOGY AND OFFICE SERVICES

Head of Information Technology and Office Services Andy Budge *Tel:* 020 7898 1640

Office Church House, Great Smith St, London SW1P 3AZ
The Information Technology department provides and maintains the IT infrastructure for the National Church Institutions, including IT

systems development and integration, as well as all aspects of PC desktop and network support and training. The department also provides central purchasing of IT equipment for the NCIs and some bishops' offices. Office Services includes reprographics, telephony, some central buying facilities across the NCIs and coordinates central meeting room bookings and catering

LIBRARIES AND ARCHIVES

Director of Libraries, Archives and IT Mr Declan
Kelly   *Tel:* 020 7898 1432

Address Church of England Record Centre, 15
Galleywall Rd, South Bermondsey, London SE16
3PB   *Tel:* 020 7898 1030
                                            Fax: 020 7898 1043
                          email: archivist@c-of-e.org.uk
                          Web: www.cofe.anglican.org/about/
                                            librariesandarchives/

The Centre, which is a central service operated
by the Church Commissioners, houses the non-
current records of the Church Commissioners,
the Archbishops' Council, the Church of England
Pensions Board, the General Synod and the
National Society, together with those of some
ecumenical bodies. Its main purpose is to provide
low-cost off-site storage and records management advice for the business records of the
Central Church Bodies. The Centre also serves as
an advisory point for queries concerning the
archives of the Church of England. Enquiries are
welcome; archive material can be seen at the
Reading Room at Lambeth Palace Library by
prior appointment.

THE LEGAL OFFICE

The Legal Office of the National Institutions of
the Church of England is responsible for providing legal advice and other services to the National
Church Institutions. Its principal functions are:

- responsibility for the legislative programme
  of the General Synod;
- giving advice to the National Church Institutions and their respective committees and
  staff; and
- undertaking some transactional work for the
  National Church Institutions, especially the
  Church Commissioners and the Pensions
  Board.

*Head of the Legal Office, Chief Legal Adviser to the
Archbishops' Council, Registrar and Chief Legal
Adviser to the General Synod and Official Solicitor to
the Church Commissioners*
Mr Stephen Slack   *Tel:* 020 7898 1366
                email: stephen.slack@c-of-e.org.uk

Secretary Miss Judith Gracias   *Tel:* 020 7898 1367
                email: judith.gracias@c-of-e.org.uk

*Deputy Legal Adviser to the Archbishops' Council
and the General Synod* Revd Alexander McGregor
                                            Tel: 020 7898 1748
           email: alexander.mcgregor@c-of-e.org.uk

Deputy Official Solicitor Mr Tim Crow
                                            Tel: 020 7898 1717
                          email: tim.crow@c-of-e.org.uk

Standing Counsel to the General Synod Sir
Anthony Hammond QC   *Tel:* 020 7898 1799
           email: anthony.hammond@c-of-e.org.uk

Secretary Miss Judith Gracias   *Tel:* 020 7898 1367
                email: judith.gracias@c-of-e.org.uk
Office Church House, Great Smith St, London,
SW1P 3AZ   *Fax:* 020 7898 1718/1721
                          email: legal@c-of-e.org.uk
                          DX: 148403 WESTMINSTER 5
           Web: www.cofe.anglican.org/legal/about/
                                            churchlawlegis/

COMMUNICATIONS OFFICE

Communication is central to the mission of the
Church as a Christian presence in every community. The Communications Office serves the
Church at every level, seeking to convey the
vibrant life of the Church, and its vital role at the
heart of society.

The Office serves all the National Church
Institutions, General Synod and the House of
Bishops, works closely with Lambeth Palace
and Bishopthorpe, and supports the activities of
diocesan communicators around the country.

Working to a 'mission-shaped communications' agenda, the Office seeks to ensure all
its activities are mission-oriented, proactive,
professional and integrated.

It works with all sections of the media, issuing
information, assisting them in their coverage
of the Church and providing a 24-hour media
response service throughout the year. It also
produces information to improve communications within the Church, including a monthly
Communications Update available via email
across the Church.

The focus for the Church's role in public discussions involving media policy, the office liaises
with the BBC, commercial broadcasters, and
various government bodies. It also supports
the Church's role in other public affairs issues,
ensuring that the Church of England's voice is
heard on key issues. In addition, it presents
information to Parliament and other audiences
on issues of concern, such as the cost of maintaining and extending the use of the Church's listed
buildings, embryology laws and climate change.

It also promotes the Church's national environmental campaign Shrinking the Footprint (www.shrinkingthefootprint.org).

A communications training programme offers a range of skills to equip the Church to communicate using the latest technologies. The full schedule and range of expert tutors can be seen at www.commstraining.cofe.anglican.org. The Office oversees development of the Church of England's popular website, www.cofe.anglican.org, one of the first 'entry points' for information about the Church.

The Office is increasingly involved in promoting key mission opportunities such as major festivals, life's special occasions, especially weddings, and projects like Love Life Live Lent and Back to Church Sunday.

The Communications Office also runs an enquiry service answering questions from the public.

Director of Communications Peter Crumpler
Tel: 020 7898 1462
email: peter.crumpler@c-of-e.org.uk

Head of Media Relations Steve Jenkins
Tel: 020 7898 1457
email: steve.jenkins@c-of-e.org.uk

Senior Media Officer Louis Henderson
*Tel:*020 7898 1621
email: lou.henderson@c-of-e.org.uk

Senior Media Officer Vacancy *Tel:* 020 7898 1464
email: ben.wilson@c-of-e.org.uk

Head of Communications Development Gillian Oliver *Tel:* 020 7898 1458
email: gillian.oliver@c-of-e.org.uk

Senior Communications Officer Rachel Harden
Tel: 020 7898 1459
email: rachel.harden@c-of-e.org.uk

Office Church House, Great Smith St, London SW1P 3AZ *Tel:* 020 7898 1000
Fax: 020 7222 6672
Web: www.cofe.anglican.org

*Seconded to the Archibishops' Council Wedding Project until October 2011

Diocesan Communicators Panel

Chairman Rt Revd Nicholas Baines (*Bishop of Croydon*)

Executive Officer Peter Crumpler
Tel: 020 7898 1462
email: peter.crumpler@c-of-e.org.uk

Members Canon John Carter, Nick Clarke, Rachel Farmer, Anni Holden, Rachel Harden, Revd Mark Rudall, Revd David Marshall, Marie Papworth

Church House Publishing

Church House Publishing (CHP) is the official publisher to the Archbishops' Council and the General Synod. In addition to publishing *Common Worship*, CHP publishes resources to further the mission and enhance the reputation of the Church of England. Reference publications include *Crockford's Clerical Directory* and *The Church of England Year Book*. Both these publications are continually updated and you are welcome to send corrections to the addresses below. For up-to-date information visit our online catalogue at www.chpublishing.co.uk

On 30 June 2009, the Archbishops' Council signed an outsourcing agreement with Anglican charity Hymns Ancient & Modern Ltd. Under the agreement, the Council continues to publish a range of titles to support the ministry and mission of the Church under its Church House Publishing imprint, with Hymns Ancient & Modern (HA&M) acting as its production and marketing arm.

Director of Communications Peter Crumpler
Tel: 020 7898 1462
email: peter.crumpler@c-of-e.org.uk

Publishing Manager Dr Thomas Allain-Chapman
Tel: 020 7898 1450
email: thomas.allain-chapman@c-of-e.org.uk

General Enquiries *Tel:* 01603 612914
Fax: 01603 624483
email: publishing@c-of-e.org.uk
Web: www.chpublishing.co.uk

The Church of England Year Book
email: yearbook@c-of-e.org.uk

Crockford's Clerical Directory
The Compiler, Crockford, Church House, Great Smith St, London SW1P 3AZ *Tel:* 020 7898 1012
Fax: 020 7898 1769
email: crockford@c-of-e.org.uk

HUMAN RESOURCES DEPARTMENT

The Human Resources (HR) department aims to support the National Church Institutions (NCIs) and diocesan bishops achieve their mission and business objectives by delivering efficient and cost effective HR services, including support for recruitment, in relation to the 497* staff employed by the NCIs and the 108 staff of diocesan bishops. It also contracts with the Corporation of Church House for services in relation to their 31 staff. Additionally, health, safety and welfare advice and services are provided to the 206 staff employed directly by the Church Commissioners on their estates and the Pensions Board in their residential schemes. It works with the Ministry Division, the Legal Office and dioceses to design, develop and implement the Church's strategy to give ecclesiastical office holders improved terms and conditions of service.

The department now provides HR services under service level agreements, for 2210 ecclesiastical office holders and 66 DBF staff in 7 southern dioceses.

It does this, within the NCIs, through

- creating a high performance working environment where staff have role clarity and focus on delivery, learning and development is actively pursued, and career pathways are well defined within the limits of small organizations;
- establishing a 'partnership' culture between employers, staff and trade unions through effective consultation and negotiation mechanisms;
- promoting joint employer initiatives and improved cultural alignment between the NCIs;

- developing a diverse workforce and a just workplace;
- pursuing the optimum deployment of staff through strategic resourcing, reward and HR information systems;
- developing a safe and healthy working environment;
- enabling, with others, bishops and dioceses to better support and to develop their parish clergy.

* This figure includes 50 staff employed on 'as and when' contracts who do not form part of the permanent workforce establishment of the NCIs.

STAFF

Director of Human Resources Ms Su Morgan
Tel: 020 7898 1565
email: su.morgan@c-of-e.org.uk
HR Senior Staff
Ms Julia Hudson *HR Manager – Clergy Terms of Service Implementation and Bishops*
Tel: 020 7898 1589
email: julia.hudson@c-of-e.org.uk
Mr Peter Cunningham *HR Manager – Operation*
Tel: 020 7898 1182
email: peter.cunningham@c-of-e.org.uk
Miss Leann Dawson *HR Manager – Clergy deployment and remuneration/Secretary to Remuneration and Conditions of Service Committee*
Tel: 020 7898 1751
email: leann.dawson@c-of-e.org.uk
Ms Poli Shajko, *HR Manager/Diocesan Team Leader* (*based in Oxford Diocese*) *Tel:* 01865 208770
email: poli.shajko@c-of-e.org.uk

Office Church House, Great Smith St, London SW1P 3AZ

THE CHURCH COMMISSIONERS FOR ENGLAND

Office Church House, Great Smith St, London SW1P 3AZ   *Tel:* 020 7898 1000
Fax: 020 7898 1131
email: commissioners.enquiry@c-of-e.org.uk

Chairman The Archbishop of Canterbury

Secretary Mr Andrew Brown   *Tel:* 020 7898 1134
email: andrew.brown@c-of-e.org.uk

Chief Finance Officer for the National Church Institutions Mr Ian Theodoreson
Tel: 020 7898 1795
email: ian.theodoreson@c-of-e.org.uk

Director of Investments Mr Tom Joy
Tel: 020 7898 1115
email: tom.joy@c-of-e.org.uk

Chief Investment Officer Mr Mark Chaloner (Stock Exchange portfolio and ethical policy monitoring)   *Tel:* 020 7898 1126
email: mark.chaloner@c-of-e.org.uk

Chief Surveyor Mr Joseph Cannon (Property portfolio)   *Tel:* 020 7898 1759
email: joseph.cannon@c-of-e.org.uk

Pastoral and Closed Churches Secretary and Acting Bishoprics and Cathedrals Secretary Mr Paul Lewis (Pastoral reorganization, closed churches, clergy housing and glebe)   *Tel:* 020 7898 1741
email: paul.lewis@c-of-e.org.uk

Director of Libraries, Archives and Information Services Mr Declan Kelly   *Tel:* 020 7898 1432
email: declan.kelly@c-of-e.org.uk

LEGAL DEPARTMENT
Official Solicitor Mr Stephen Slack
Tel: 020 7898 1704
email: stephen.slack@c-of-e.org.uk
Deputy Official Solicitor Mr Timothy Crow
Tel: 020 7898 1717
email: tim.crow@c-of-e.org.uk
Web: www.cofe.anglican.org/legal

MEMBERS
Following elections to the General Synod in October 2010, membership of these bodies is uncertain at the time of going to press. Please refer to the Secretary of the body in question for current membership.

The Archbishops of Canterbury and York

First Church Estates Commissioner Mr Andrew Whittam Smith

Second Church Estates Commissioner Mr Tony Baldry MP

Third Church Estates Commissioner Mr Timothy Walker

Four bishops elected by the House of Bishops of the General Synod Rt Revd and Rt Hon Richard Chartres (*Bishop of London*), Rt Revd David Urquhart (*Bishop of Birmingham*), Rt Revd Michael Hill (*Bishop of Bristol*), Rt Revd Peter Forster (*Bishop of Chester*)

Two deans or provosts elected by all the deans and provosts Very Revd Adrian Newman (*Dean of Rochester*), Very Revd Christopher Hardwick (*Dean of Truro*)

Three clergy elected by the House of Clergy of the General Synod Canon Bob Baker, Revd Jeremy Crocker, Revd Stephen Trott

Four lay persons elected by the House of Laity of the General Synod Mrs April Alexander, Canon Peter Bruinvels, Mr Gavin Oldham, Mr Jacob Vince

Three persons nominated by Her Majesty the Queen Mr Richard Powers, Canon John Spence, Mr John Wythe

Three persons nominated by the Archbishops of Canterbury and of York acting jointly Mr Nicholas Sykes, Mr Peter Parker, Mr Peter Harrison QC

Three persons nominated by the Archbishops acting jointly after consultation with others including the Lord Mayors of the cities of London and York and the Vice-Chancellors of Oxford and Cambridge Mr Brian Carroll, Mrs Emma Osborne, Mr Hywel Rees-Jones

Six State Office Holders The First Lord of the Treasury; the Lord President of the Council; the Secretary of State for the Home Department; the Speaker of the House of Lords; the Secretary of State for Culture, Media and Sport; and the Speaker of the House of Commons.

FUNCTIONS
The Church Commissioners' main tasks are to manage their assets, and make money available in accordance with the duties laid upon them by Acts of Parliament and Measures of the General Synod and former Church Assembly, and to

discharge other administrative duties entrusted to them.

These duties include financial support for mission and ministry in parishes, particularly in areas of need and opportunity, clergy pensions for service before 1998 and other legal commitments such as those in relation to bishops and cathedrals, and the administration of the legal framework for pastoral reorganization and settling the future of churches closed for worship.

CONSTITUTION
The Church Commissioners were formed on 1 April 1948, when Queen Anne's Bounty (1704) and the Ecclesiastical Commissioners (1836) were united.

The full body of Commissioners meets once a year to consider the Report and Accounts and the allocation of available money. The management of the Commissioners' affairs is shared between the Board of Governors, the Assets Committee, the Bishoprics and Cathedrals Committee, the Nominations and Governance Committee, the Pastoral Committee, the Church Buildings (Uses and Disposals) Committee and the Audit Committee.

The National Institutions Measure 1998 created the Archbishops' Council, with consequential amendment to the Church Commissioners' functions and working relationships. The Measure also transferred their former function and powers as Central Stipends Authority to the Council on 1 January 1999.

As from 2010 the Church Commissioners are a registered charity and regulated by the Charity Commission.

Functions of the Board of Governors and the Commissioners' Committees

BOARD OF GOVERNORS
The Board is responsible for overall policy matters and there are individual committees covering policy in the following specific areas. All Commissioners are Board Members except for the six Officers of State.

ASSETS COMMITTEE
Chairman Mr Andreas Whittam Smith
Deputy Chairman Mr Nicholas Sykes
Rt Revd Michael Hill (*Bishop of Bristol*), Canon Bob Baker, Mr Brian Carroll, Mr Gavin Oldham, Mrs Emma Osborne, Mr Richard Powers, Mr John Wythe
Secretary Mr Andrew Brown

Exclusive responsibility for managing the Commissioners' assets, for investment policy and for advising the Board on the maximum amount of money available for distribution each year. The Committee is assisted by two sub-groups working on the Commissioners' stock exchange and property portfolios.

AUDIT COMMITTEE
Chairman Canon John Spence
Mrs April Alexander, Mr Peter Morriss*, Mr Chris Daykin*, Mr Hywel Rees-Jones, Mr Hugh Shields*
Secretary Mr Michael Cole

Responsible for all matters relating to the audit of the Commissioners' accounts and related matters.

BISHOPRICS AND CATHEDRALS COMMITTEE
Chairman Mr Timothy Walker
Deputy Chairman Very Revd Christopher Hardwick (*Dean of Truro*)

Rt Revd David Urquhart (*Bishop of Birmingham*), Rt Revd David Rossdale* (*Bishop of Grimsby*), Very Revd Adrian Newman (*Dean of Rochester*), Revd Mary Bide*, Mr Peter Parker, Revd Canon Jeremy Haselock*, Ms Sallie Bassham*, Mrs Hilary Hill†
Acting Secretary Mr Paul Lewis

Responsible for the costs of episcopal administration, the provision and management of suitable housing for diocesan bishops, assisting by grants and loans with the housing of suffragan and assistant bishops, and some assistance in respect of cathedral clergy and lay staff.

NOMINATIONS AND GOVERNANCE COMMITTEE
Chairman Mr Brian Carroll
Deputy Chairman Canon Peter Bruinvels
Mr Andreas Whittam Smith, Mr Timothy Walker, Rt Revd and Rt Hon Richard Chartres (*Bishop of London*), Revd Stephen Trott, Canon John Spence
Secretary Mr Andrew Brown

Advises the Board of Governors on appointments, use of trustees' skills and best practice in governance.

PASTORAL COMMITTEE
Chairman Mr Timothy Walker
Deputy Chairman Rt Revd Peter Forster (*Bishop of Chester*)
Rt Revd John Pritchard* (*Bishop of Oxford*), Ven Rachel Treweek* (*Archdeacon of Northolt*), Revd Jeremy Crocker, Revd Canon Stephen Evans*, Revd Stephen Trott, Canon Peter Bruinvels, Mrs Julia Flack*, Mr Peter Harrison, Mrs Christine McMullen*

Secretary Mr Paul Lewis
Responsible for matters concerning pastoral reorganization, parsonages and glebe property.

CHURCH BUILDINGS (USES AND DISPOSALS) COMMITTEE
Chairman Mr Timothy Walker
Deputy Chairman Revd Stephen Trott
Ven John Duncan*, Canon Bob Baker, Revd John Swanton*, Mr Brian Carroll, Mrs Emma Osborne, Mr Christopher Perrett*, Mr Jacob Vince, Mr Charles Wilson*
Secretary Mr Paul Lewis

Responsible for the Commissioners' work relating to closed church buildings.

The Commissioners draw no income from the State.

The asterisks in the above lists indicate non-Commissioner committee members.

The dagger symbol (†) in one of the above lists indicates consultant.

CHARITABLE EXPENDITURE IN 2009
The Commissioners' charitable expenditure falls under two main headings:
1 Provision of non-pensions support – £79.8 million in 2009 – to the Church including parish mission and ministry support of £42 million which was mainly targeted towards areas of greatest financial need.
2 Payment of clergy pensions and pensions to their widows – £111 million in 2009. The Church of England Pensions Board authorizes pensions, but much of the money is provided and paid by the Church Commissioners. The Commissioners are responsible for pensions earned on service before 1 January 1998 and dioceses and parishes for pensions earned after that date.

MANAGEMENT OF ASSETS
The total return on the Commissioners' assets in 2009 was 15.6% and their return over the ten years to 2009 averaged 5.1% per annum (industry benchmark 3.1% per annum).

PASTORAL MEASURE RESPONSIBILITIES
The Commissioners are responsible for preparing schemes for pastoral reorganization based on proposals put forward by Bishops under the Pastoral Measure 1983. This includes the consideration of any representations made in response to consultation on draft schemes. Those making representations have the opportunity to address the relevant Commissioners' Committee.

The Commissioners also deal with objections to certain personage and glebe transactions.

CLOSED CHURCH BUILDINGS
The Pastoral Measure 1983 sets out the process for closing a church building which is no longer needed for public worship. The Commissioners will prepare a draft scheme to give effect to the proposals, consult locally and hear any representations received in respect of them.

The Commissioners also determine the future use of closed church buildings. Under the Pastoral Measure, dioceses are charged with the seeking of a suitable use for the buildings and reporting to the Commissioners who will then publish a draft scheme to facilitate that use and its sale for that purpose.

Buildings of high heritage value for which no suitable alternative use can be found may be vested in the Churches Conservation Trust, an independent body jointly funded by the Church and State to care for such closed church buildings.

FURTHER INFORMATION
Further information is available in the Commissioners' Annual Report and Accounts which, together with other information leaflets, is available free of charge from the Commissioners and *via* the Church of England web site at http://www.cofe.anglican.org/about/church commissioners/annualreport/. Requests for speakers to give talks about the Commissioners' work are welcome.

THE CHURCH OF ENGLAND PENSIONS BOARD

Secretary and Chief Executive Mr M. G. Shaun Farrell

Pensions Manager Mr Tony Williams

Chief Finance Officer Mr Ian Theodoreson

Housing Manager Ms Loraine Miller

Policy and Resources Mr Lee Marshall

Office 29 Great Smith St, London SW1P 3PS
Tel: 020 7898 1800
Fax: 020 7898 1801
email: cepb.enquiries@c-of-e.org.uk

Hon Medical Adviser Dr Trevor Hudson

MEMBERS
The current constitution of the Board was adopted by the General Synod with effect from 1 January 1998 having regard both to the Pensions Act 1995 and to the changes made to the financial arrangements for providing pensions for those in the stipendiary ministry. There are 20 members.

Appointed Chairman by the Archbishops with the approval of the General Synod
Dr Jonathan Spencer

Nominated by the Archbishops of Canterbury and York
Mr Philip Hamlyn Williams (*Chairman of the Audit Committee*), Mr David Froude

Elected by the House of Bishops
Rt Revd David Walker (*Chairman of the Housing Committee*)

Elected by the House of Clergy
Revd Richard Billinghurst, Revd P Boughton, Revd N. Bourne

Elected by members of the Church Workers Pension Fund
Mr Ian Clark, Mr Colin Peters

Elected by members of the Church Administrators Pension Fund
Mr J. Ferguson

Elected by the House of Laity
Mr J. Archer, Mr S. Baynes, Dr Graham Campbell, Mr Alan Fletcher, Mr Tim Hind (*Deputy Vice-Chair*), Canon Harry Marsh

Elected by the employers participating in the Church Workers Pension Fund and Church Administrators Pension Fund
Mr Clive Hawkins (*Chair of the Investment Committee*), Canon S. Newton

Nominated by the Church Commissioners
Mr Peter Parker

RESPONSIBILITIES
The Pensions Board was established by the Church Assembly in 1926 as the Church of England's pensions authority and to administer the pension scheme for the clergy. Subsequently it has been given wider powers, in respect of discretionary benefits and the provision of accommodation both for those retired from stipendiary ministry and for the spouses of those who have served in that ministry, and to administer pension schemes for lay employees of Church organizations.

The Board, which reports to the General Synod, is trustee of a number of pension funds and charitable funds. Whilst the Church has drawn together under the Board its central responsibilities for retirement welfare, the Board works in close cooperation both with the Archbishops' Council and with the Church Commissioners. There is also a partnership between the Board and dioceses in financial commitments towards discretionary grants and housing, and at the level of personal pastoral service through Widows Officers, archdeacons and Retirement Officers.

PENSIONS
The Board is administrator of the pension arrangements for clergy, deaconesses and licensed lay workers, and for their widows and widowers, keeping records of pensionable service and corresponding about pensions matters both with pensioners and with those not yet retired. It is corporate trustee of the Church of England Funded Pensions Scheme, which has assets of £617.6 million and to which contributions are currently being paid at the rate of some £71 million a year to provide for pensions and associated benefits arising from service after the end of 1997. The Church Commissioners continue to meet the cost of benefits arising from service prior to 1 January 1998.

The Clergy (Widows and Dependants) Pensions Fund was closed to new entrants after widows' pensions were introduced under the main scheme. It has assets of £23.4 million and provides an additional benefit to widows and other dependants of those who made contributions to it. The benefits payable are reviewed following each triennial actuarial valuation. The next valuation will be carried out as at 31 December 2012.

The Board is also corporate trustee of the

Church Workers Pension Fund, through which over 200 Church organizations make pension provision for their lay employees, and the Church Administrators Pension Fund (for staff of the National Church bodies). It is responsible for all the activities of these funds including the administration and keeping of records, payment of benefits, collection of contributions and investment of monies currently held in the funds; these now total approximately £259 million.

RETIREMENT HOUSING SCHEMES

The purpose of the retirement housing scheme – the Church Housing Assistance for the Retired Ministry, or CHARM – is to assist those vacating 'tied' accommodation with the provision of somewhere to live. It is intended to support those who would not be able to make their own provision for retirement housing. Approximately 3,000 retired clergy and their dependants are currently assisted through CHARM.

CHARM is a discretionary facility and the Board specifies a number of parameters relating to the size and type of property which is available, as well as the form and amount of assistance which is available.

The rental housing has mostly been purchased with finance from the Church Commissioners. For investment reasons, the Commissioners decided to withdraw their funding of new CHARM properties with effect from 30 June 2010. The Board is in the course of arranging an alternative finance source for the scheme, so that it will be able to continue meeting the needs of those who call on it for housing support.

There are two sections to the scheme; (a) a rental section in excess of 1,200 properties available for occupation under licence and (b) a shared ownership scheme for retiring clergy who wish to acquire an equity interest in their retirement accommodation. A value linked mortgage scheme, covering some 1,250 loans, remains in place but is closed to new loans having been replaced by the Shared Ownership scheme, introduced in April 2008. The Board has funded approximately 484 of the rental properties and some mortgage loans from its own charitable funds. Some of the properties have been received as gifts, and it continues to add to its stock further properties acquired in this way. Others have been purchased or built using monetary gifts in trust for that purpose.

SUPPORTED HOUSING AND NURSING CARE

The Board owns and manages supported housing schemes in seven locations, and one nursing home. All of these provisions were purpose-designed. The Board's charitable resources provide the capital for purchasing or building the homes and for their subsequent maintenance and operation.

Each is run by a professional resident manager who reports to the Board's Supported Housing Manager. Occupation costs are set having regard to the costs of running the scheme and increases in clergy pensions. Each resident and patient is, however, charged a cost which, with available State support, is affordable having regard to their financial resources. As total occupation charges are insufficient to cover the operating costs, the shortfall is met from the Board's charitable funds.

Early in 2010 the Board decided to explore the possibility of converting part of its Manormead Nursing Home into a specialist dementia care unit with places for six beneficiaries. The unit is being designed with features which can aid those with dementia including a secure, sensory garden area promoting interest and stimulation. Subject to formal Board approval, it is hoped that the unit will open by the end of 2010.

THE BOARD AS A CHARITY

The care of the more elderly of its pensioners is an activity of the Board which attracts considerable regular support, voluntarily from within the Church at parochial and diocesan level, and from churchgoers and other people of goodwill everywhere. Money and other property given or bequeathed to the Board has averaged slightly under £1 million per annum in recent years. The Pensions Board is registered as a charity. The charitable funds currently have a total net value of some £91 million (including the Board's own stake in the retirement housing scheme).

PUBLICATIONS

Your Pension Questions Answered
Information about the Pension Scheme for clergy, deaconesses and licensed lay workers, including an outline of the arrangements for paying voluntary contributions to increase retirement benefits.

Retirement Housing
Explains the assistance that the Board is able to make (with financial support from the Church Commissioners) to clergy, their spouses and widow(er)s, and also to deaconesses and licensed lay workers for their retirement housing.

Providing for Housing in Retirement
A handbook of sources of finance for the clergy to acquire property on a buy-to-let basis.

Christian Care in Retirement
Information about the Board's supported housing schemes and its nursing home.

The Church of England Pensions Board – Our Work is Caring . . .
Describes the discretionary assistance made available to its beneficiaries through the Board's charitable funds and explains how contributions may be made to support that work.

Pensions Administration for Church of England Employers
A guide to the services and schemes offered by the Board.

The Church Workers Pension Fund
An explanation of the retirement benefits available to church workers whose employers participate in the Fund.

Report and Accounts for the year 2008
Contains information about all the Board's activities during the year. Also available on our web site, www.cofe.anglican.org/about/cepb

OTHER BOARDS, COUNCILS, COMMISSIONS, ETC. OF THE CHURCH OF ENGLAND

The Advisory Board for Redundant Churches

Function transferred to the Statutory Advisory Committee of the Church Buildings Council.

The Churches Conservation Trust
(formerly the Redundant Churches Fund)

Chief Executive Mr Crispin Truman, 1 West Smithfield, London EC1A 9EE   *Tel:* 020 7213 0660
Fax: 020 7213 0678
email: central@tcct.org.uk
Web: www.visitchurches.org.uk

Director of Conservation Ms Sarah Robinson

Director of Regions Mr Colin Shearer

Director of Finance and Resources Mr Vipan Narang

Head of Development and Communications Mr Paul Stephenson

BOARD OF TRUSTEES
Mr Loyd Grossman OBE FSA (*Chairman*), Mrs Jenny Baker OBE, Mrs Deborah Dance, Mr Alec Forshaw, Mr Matthew Girt, The Very Revd Peter Judd, Revd Brian McHenry CBE, Mr Nick Thompson, Ms Jane Weeks, Mr Duncan Wilson OBE.

The Churches Conservation Trust is the national charity protecting historic churches at risk. We've saved over 340 unique buildings which attract more than a million visitors a year. With our help and your support they are kept open, in use and free to all – living once again at the heart of their communities.

Trust churches host occasional services as well as concerts, exhibitions and lectures. The Trust, which is a registered charity, depends upon statutory funding from the Church Commissioners (24 per cent) and the Department for Culture, Media and Sport (55 per cent) and charitable grants and voluntary donations (21 per cent).

CCLA Investment Management Limited

Registered Office 80 Cheapside, London EC2V 6DZ
Company Registration No 2183088
Authorized and regulated by the Financial Services Authority   *Tel:* 0844 561 5000
Fax: 0844 561 5128
Web: www.ccla.co.uk

Executive Directors
Chief Executive Mr Michael Quicke
email: michael.quicke@ccla.co.uk

Chief Investment Officer Mr James Bevan
email: james.bevan@ccla.co.uk
Director of Market Development Mr Andrew Robinson   *email:* andrew.robinson@ccla.co.uk
Investment Director Mr Colin Peters
email: colin.peters@ccla.co.uk

Chief Operating Officer Mr Sean Curran
email: sean.curran@ccla.co.uk

Non Executive Directors
Mr James Dawnay (*Chairman*), Mr Miles Roberts, Mr John Galbraith, Mr Richard Fitzalan Howard, Mr Rodney Dennis
Company Secretary Mrs Jacqueline Fox

CCLA Investment Management Limited (CCLA) is a specialist investment management company serving charities, churches and local authorities. It is the largest manager of charitable funds in the UK, both by the value of funds managed and the number of individual investing charities. It aims to provide good quality investment management services at reasonable cost. It is the manager, registrar and administrator of the CBF Church of England Funds, the trustee of which is CBF Funds Trustee Limited and to which CCLA is accountable. Six Funds are offered to Church of England investors: the Investment Fund, a mixed fund invested mainly in equities, the UK Equity Fund, the Global Equity Income Fund, the Fixed Interest Securities Fund, the Deposit Fund and the Property Fund. CCLA also manages several segregated charity portfolios. CCLA is owned 60 per cent by the CBF Church of England Investment Fund, 25 per cent by the COIF Charities Investment Fund (part of which is non voting) and 15 per cent by the Local Authorities Mutual Investment Trust. CCLA is authorized and regulated by the Financial Services Authority (FSA) under the Financial Services and Markets Act 2000 (FSMA). Under the FSMA, the CBF, in its role as Trustee, is not considered to be operating the Funds 'by way of business'. In consequence, it is not required to be regulated by the FSA. Deposits taken by the CBF Church of England Deposit Fund are exempted from the FSMA by virtue of the Financial Services and Markets Act (Exemption) Order 2001.

The CBF Church of England Funds

Established under the Church Funds Investment Measure 1958, these open ended funds aim to meet most of the investment needs of a church trust and are used by diocesan boards of finance and trusts, cathedrals, diocesan boards of education, theological colleges, church schools and educational endowments, church societies, the Church Commissioners and many PCCs.

Investment Fund
The main CBF Church of England Fund for capital that can be invested for the long term. A widely spread portfolio mainly of UK and overseas equities but also including some bond and property investments. Aims to provide steady and rising income and capital growth. Weekly share dealings. The Fund targets an attractive and rising level of income.

UK Equity Fund
This Fund provides church trustees with a means of obtaining investment solely in a specialist UK equity portfolio. Weekly share dealings. The Fund targets an attractive and rising level of income.

Fixed Interest Securities Fund
Invested only in UK fixed interest stocks. Intended to supplement where necessary the initial lower income yield on the Investment Fund. Recommended only for a small proportion of long term capital as it offers little protection from inflation over the longer term. Weekly share dealings.

Deposit Fund
This money Fund is for cash balances which need to be available at short notice and with minimal risk of capital loss. Accounts in the Fund obtain a rate of interest close to money market rates even on small sums. Daily deposit and withdrawal facilities. The Fund is rated AAA/VI by Fitch Ratings.

Property Fund
Invests directly in UK commercial property. Fund is intended primarily for long term investment by large church trusts. Month end share dealings but periods of notice may be imposed. The Fund provides a high level of income.

Global Equity Income Fund
This fund targets a high and growing income from a portfolio of international shares. Weekly share dealings.

Risk Warnings: The value of the Investment, UK Equity, Fixed Interest Securities and Property Funds and their income can fall as well as rise and an investor may not get back the amount invested. Past performance is no guarantee of future returns. The Funds are intended for long term investment and are not suitable for money liable to be spent in the near future. Guarantees regarding repayment of deposits in the Deposit Fund cannot be given.

Brochures and Reports and Accounts are available from CCLA Investment Management Limited at the address above and on its web site, www.ccla.co.uk

31 May 2009	Investment Fund	Fixed Interest Securities Fund	Deposit Fund	Property Fund	UK Equity Fund	Global Equity Income Fund
Value of Fund	£781 million	£81 million	£926 million	£94 million	£110 million	£49 million
Net Asset Value per share	999.64p	155.94p	–	120.05p	102.11p	116.19p
Income Yield %	4.64	5.64	0.50	6.66	4.95	5.33
Gross Redemption Yield %	–	2.92	–	–	–	–

The Church and Community Fund

Chairman: Ven George Howe
Secretary: Mr Kevin Norris

Formerly known as the Central Church Fund, the CCF changed its name to the Church and Community Fund (CCF) in June 2006. The CCF supports the Church of England's mission by awarding grants to community projects run by parish churches, deaneries, dioceses and other regional or national bodies.

The Archbishops' Council (registered charity number 1074857) is trustee of the CCF but has delegated management to a CCF Committee whose members are the administrative trustees of the Fund.

CCF-funded projects should seek to take the church out into the community, bring the community into the church and strengthen the relationship between the two. The CCF trustees welcome applications that show imagination in responding to needs. They are likely to be particularly sympathetic to applications from those areas least able to raise funds themselves.

The CCF awarded a total of £449,047 to 128 church community projects in 2009 (2008: £593,600 to 143 projects). It also gave £320,000 as a direct grant to the Archbishops' Council in support of the national work of the Church and £20,000 to the Archbishops' Discretionary Funds.

The CCF relies on legacies and donations to increase the number of grants awarded so that more churches can reach out to their communities and respond to real local needs. Please contact the Secretary to find out more about how to make a donation, leave a legacy or apply for a grant.

The Church and Community Fund, Church House, Great Smith St, London SW1P 3AZ
Tel: 020 7898 1541/1767
Fax: 020 7898 1558
*email:*kevin.norris@c-of-e.org.uk
Web: www.churchandcommunityfund.org.uk

The Corporation of the Church House

Presidents The Archbishop of Canterbury; The Archbishop of York

Chairman of Council Michael Chamberlain OBE

Treasurer David Barnett

Secretary Chris Palmer   *Tel:* 020 7898 1311
email: chris.palmer@c-of-e.org.uk

Office Church House, Great Smith St, London SW1P 3AZ
Tel: 020 7898 1311
Fax: 020 7898 1321

The Corporation owns and maintains Church House, Westminster which is the administrative headquarters of the national institutions of the Church of England

The original Church House was built in the early 1890s as the Church's memorial of Queen Victoria's Jubilee, to be the administrative headquarters of the Church of England, and was replaced by the present building to a design by Sir Herbert Baker. The foundation stone was laid in 1937 by Queen Mary and on 10 June 1940 King George VI, accompanied by the Queen, formally opened the new House and attended the first Session of the Church Assembly in the great circular hall. The building was almost immediately requisitioned by the Government and for the rest of the war became the alternative meeting place of both Houses of Parliament; the Lords sat in the Convocation Hall and the Commons in the Hoare Memorial Hall. Oak panels in these halls commemorate this use.

Other Boards, Councils, Commissions, etc.   **199**

By October 1946 some administrative offices of the Church Assembly returned to Church House and the Church Assembly was able to return for its Autumn Session in 1950. The building is now the headquarters of the Archbishops' Council, the Church Commissioners and the Church of England Pensions Board, as well as being the venue for the General Synod in the spring and (if it meets) in the autumn. A large-scale refurbishment carried out in 2006 has provided sufficient open-plan office space to accommodate nearly all staff of the Central Church Institutions, who moved into Church House during the early part of 2007.

Church House has also become an important national centre for conferences and meetings, the income from which contributes significantly to the maintenance costs of the building.

The business of the Corporation is vested in its Council of 9 (of whom 3 are nominated by the Appointments Committee, 2 are elected by the membership of the Corporation and 4 are co-opted by the Council).

The National Society (Church of England) for Promoting Religious Education
Leading Education with Christian Purpose

Patron Her Majesty The Queen

President The Archbishop of Canterbury

Vice Presidents The Archbishop of York and the Archbishop of Wales

Chairman of the Council Rt Revd Dr John Saxbee (*Bishop of Lincoln*); (From 1 February) The Rt Revd John Pritchard (*Bishop of Oxford*)

General Secretary Revd Janina Ainsworth

Treasurer Maurice Sharples

Deputy Secretary Mr Nick McKemey
Tel: 020 7898 1490
email: nick.mckemey@c-of-e.org.uk

Deputy Secretary Dr Rob Gwynne
Tel: 020 7898 1789
email: rob.gwynne@c-of-e.org.uk

National Schools Support Office: Mrs Liz Carter
Tel: 020 7898 1515
email: liz.carter@c-of-e.org.uk

Interim Business Manager Mrs Cheryl Payne
Tel: 020 7898 1501
email: cheryl.payne@c-of-e.org.uk

Information Manager Mr Peter Churchill
Tel: 020 7898 1518
email: peter.churchill@c-of-e.org.uk

RE Development Officers Revd Canon Jane Brooke, Mrs Cathy Davie *Web:* www.natsoc.org.uk

The National Society will be celebrating its **bicentenary in 2011** with a programme of events in schools and dioceses, culminating in a Service of Thanksgiving in Westminster Abbey in October.

The original purpose of the Society was '*The Promotion of the Education of the Poor in the Principles of the Established Church*'. It works in close association with the Education Division (*see* page 180), sharing the main objectives focused particularly on schools work.

Founded in 1811, the Society was chiefly responsible for setting up, in cooperation with local clergy and others, the **nationwide network** of **Church schools** in England and Wales; it was also, through the Church colleges, a pioneer in teacher education

A concern for Church schools is still at the heart of the Society's work. It provides

- a legal and advisory service for dioceses and schools
- support for RE and collective worship in dioceses and schools through the work of the RE Development Officers
- training and accreditation for inspectors for Church schools under Section 48 of the Education Act 2005 (Statutory Inspection of Anglican Schools)
- sample contracts and application forms and associated policies for appointment of staff in church schools
- funded developmental work in recruitment and training of leaders in church schools
- grants to assist in costs of school building projects
- links to courses accredited by the church universities and university colleges

The Society represents the Church of England in planning and promoting Education Sunday, an ecumenical observation that takes place every year on the ninth Sunday before Easter.

After nearly two centuries of close association with Church schools and colleges, the National Society has built up an impressive collection of documents in its archives. These include about 15,000 files of correspondence with schools throughout England and Wales founded in association with the National Society and many published works, including the Society's own. Access is available to *bona fide* researchers by appointment at the Church of England Record Centre.

Applications for membership and donations to The National Society from individuals, schools and other bodies wishing to support the Society's work and share its resources are welcomed (*see membership form on the website or contact Cheryl Payne*).

THE ECCLESIASTICAL COURTS

The Ecclesiastical Courts consist of (1) the Diocesan or Consistory Courts, (2) the Provincial Courts, and for both Provinces (3) the Court of Ecclesiastical Causes Reserved and, when required, (4) a Commission of Review. In certain faculty cases an appeal lies from the Provincial Courts to the Judicial Committee of the Privy Council. The jurisdiction of the Archdeacons' Courts is now confined to the visitations of archdeacons. The Ecclesiastical Courts are in the main now regulated by the Ecclesiastical Jurisdiction Measure 1963. The Court of Faculties is the Court of the Archbishop of Canterbury through which the legatine powers transferred to the Archbishop of Canterbury by the Ecclesiastical Licences Act 1533 are exercised.

The personnel of the Diocesan Courts is given in the diocesan lists. The personnel of the Court of Faculties and of the Provincial and some of the other Courts is as follows:

THE COURT OF ARCHES
Dean of the Arches Rt Worshipful Charles George QC

Registrar Canon John Rees
16 Beaumont St, Oxford OX1 2LZ
Tel: 01865 297200
Fax: 01865 726274
email: jrees@wslaw.co.uk

THE COURT OF THE VICAR-GENERAL OF THE PROVINCE OF CANTERBURY
Vicar-General Rt Worshipful Timothy Briden

Registrar
Canon John Rees (*as above*)

THE CHANCERY COURT OF YORK
Auditor Rt Worshipful Charles George QC

Registrar Mr Lionel Lennox
The Provincial Registry, Stamford House, Piccadilly, York YO1 9PP *Tel:* 01904 623487
Fax: 01904 561470
email: lpml@denisontill.com

THE COURT OF THE VICAR-GENERAL OF THE PROVINCE OF YORK
Vicar-General Rt Worshipful Peter Collier QC

Registrar Mr Lionel Lennox (*as above*)

THE COURT OF ECCLESIASTICAL CAUSES RESERVED
Judges

Rt Revd David Hope

Rt Revd Richard Harries
Rt Revd Thomas Wright
Dame Elizabeth Butler-Sloss
Sir John Mummery

Registrar for the Province of Canterbury Canon John Rees (*as above*)

Registrar for the Province of York Mr Lionel Lennox (*as above*)

THE COURT OF FACULTIES
Master of the Faculties Rt Worshipful Charles George QC

Registrar Mr Peter Beesley
1 The Sanctuary, London SW1P 3JT
Tel: 020 7222 5381
Fax: 020 7222 7502
email: faculty.office@1Thesanctuary.com

Disciplinary Tribunals constituted under the Clergy Discipline Measure 2003

President of Tribunals Rt Hon Lord Justice Mummery

Deputy President of Tribunals His Honour Judge John Bullimore
c/o The Legal Office, Church House, Great Smith St, London SW1P 3AZ

'Legally qualified' members of the provincial panels of Canterbury and York (the same ten are appointed to each panel) from which the chair of a disciplinary tribunal will be appointed by the President of Tribunals if the President or Deputy President is not to chair the tribunal.

His Honour Judge Dr Rupert Bursell QC
Mr David Cheetham
Mr Peter Collier QC
His Honour Judge Simon Grenfell
Revd Raymond Hemingray
Canon Christopher Hodson
His Honour the Worshipful Roger Kaye QC
Mr Geoffrey Tattersall QC
His Honour Judge David Turner QC
His Honour Judge Samuel Wiggs

Registrar of Tribunals for the Province of Canterbury Canon John Rees (*as above*)

Registrar of Tribunals for the Province of York Mr Lionel Lennox (*as above*)

Designated Officer Mr Adrian Iles, The Legal Office, Church House, Great Smith St, London SW1P 3AZ

Appeal Panels

APPEAL PANEL CONSTITUTED UNDER SCHEDULE 4 THE PASTORAL MEASURE 1983
(Tribunals to settle compensation claims of clergy dispossessed under a Pastoral Scheme)

Chair The Dean of the Arches

Deputy Chairs
The Vicar-General of Canterbury
The Vicar-General of York

In addition to the Chair, a tribunal comprises four members of the Lower House of the relevant Province and two members of the House of Laity drawn from the following panels:

Convocation of Canterbury, Lower House
Following elections to the General Synod in October 2010, membership of this panel is uncertain at the time of going to press. Please refer to the Secretary for current membership.

Convocation of York, Lower House
Following elections to the General Synod in October 2010, membership of this panel is uncertain at the time of going to press. Please refer to the Secretary for current membership.

House of Laity of the General Synod
Following elections to the General Synod in October 2010, membership of this panel is uncertain at the time of going to press. Please refer to the Secretary for current membership.

Secretary Vacancy

APPEAL PANEL CONSTITUTED UNDER STANDING ORDER 120(d)(i)
(Tribunals to hear appeals in internal General Synod elections)

House of Bishops
Following elections to the General Synod in October 2010, membership of this panel is uncertain at the time of going to press. Please refer to the Secretary for current membership.

House of Clergy
Following elections to the General Synod in October 2010, membership of this panel is uncertain at the time of going to press. Please refer to the Secretary for current membership.

House of Laity
Following elections to the General Synod in October 2010, membership of this panel is uncertain at the time of going to press. Please refer to the Secretary for current membership.

Secretary Vacancy

APPEAL PANEL APPOINTED PURSUANT TO RULE 44(8) OF THE CHURCH REPRESENTATION RULES AS AMENDED BY THE NATIONAL INSTITUTIONS MEASURE 1998 (SCHEDULE 5, PARAGRAPH 2(c))
(Tribunals to hear appeals in elections to the House of Laity of the General Synod)

The Dean of the Arches
The Vicar-General of Canterbury
The Vicar-General of York
Following elections to the General Synod in October 2010, the remaining membership of this panel is uncertain at the time of going to press. Please refer to the Secretary for current membership.

Secretary Vacancy

APPEAL PANEL APPOINTED PURSUANT TO RULE 25(5) OF THE CLERGY REPRESENTATION RULES 1975 TO 2004
(Tribunals to hear appeals in elections to the Convocations)

The Dean of the Arches
The Vicar-General of Canterbury
The Vicar-General of York
Following elections to the General Synod in October 2010, the remaining membership of this panel is uncertain at the time of going to press. Please refer to the Secretary for current membership

Secretary Vacancy

GENERAL SYNOD LEGISLATION, CONSTITUTION AND BUSINESS

Legislation passed 2003–2010 together with commencement dates

Dates in brackets are the dates of legislation coming into force. Items of legislation no longer in force are omitted.

MEASURES

Synodical Government (Amendment) Measure 2003 (1 January 2004)

Church of England (Pensions) Measure 2003 (1 May 2003)

Clergy Discipline Measure 2003 (in force 1 October 2003: sections 3, 39, 45 and 48; in force 1 June 2005: sections 44(3) and (4); in force 8 September 2005: sections 4, 5 and 21; remainder in force 1 January 2006)

Stipends (Cessation of Special Payments) Measure 2005 (1 July and 31 December 2005)

Care of Cathedrals (Amendment) Measure 2005 (in force 6 June 2005: section 19 so far as it relates to paragraph 6 of Schedule 3, section 20 and paragraph 6 of Schedule 3; in force 7 February 2006: sections 8(4)(a), 12(1), 17 (so far as it relates to paragraphs 1–8 and 12 of Schedule 1), 18 and 19 (so far as it relates to the provisions of Schedule 3 specified below) and paragraphs 1–8 and 12 of Schedule 1, Schedule 2, sub-paragraphs (b), (e), (g) and (i) of paragraph 4 of Schedule 3 and paragraph 7 of Schedule 3; remainder in force 1 January 2008

Church of England (Miscellaneous Provisions) Measure 2005 (1 June and 1 September 2005)

Church of England (Miscellaneous Provisions) Measure 2006 (all in force 1 October 2006 except section 1 and Schedule 1; section 1 and schedule 1 in force 1 December 2007)

Pastoral (Amendment) Measure 2006 (1 January 2007)

Dioceses, Pastoral and Mission Measure 2007 (in force 1 January 2008: sections 1, 51, 62(1)–(3), 63(1) (so far as it relates to paragraph 7(b) of Schedule 5), 63(5) and 66 and paragraph 7(b) of Schedule 5; in force 1 February 2008: sections 52, 61, 62(5), 64 and 65 (so far as it relates to the repeals in Schedule 7 coming into force on the same date), Schedules 3 and 6 and the repeals in Schedule 7 of section 1 and Schedules 1 and 5 of the Pastoral Measure 1983, section 11(e) of the Church of England (Miscellaneous Provisions) Measure 1995 and sections 2(4) and (5) of the Synodical Government (Amendment) Measure

2003; in force 31 March 2008: sections 47–50 and 63(4); in force 1 May 2008: sections 13–16, 22, 63(7) and 65 (so far as it relates to the repeals in Schedule 7 coming into force on the same date) and the repeals in Schedule 7 of sections 10–15 of the Dioceses Measure 1978, sections 8 and 10 of the Church of England (Miscellaneous Provisions) Measure 1983, section 11(2) of the Bishops (Retirement) Measure 1986, section 2 of the Clergy (Ordination) Measure 1990 and section 12 of the Church of England (Miscellaenous Provisions) Measure 1995; in force 11 June 2008: sections 23–46, 53–60, 62(4) and (6), 63(1) (so far as it is not already in force), (2) and (3) and 65 (so far as it relates to the repeals in Schedule 7 coming into force on the same date) and Schedules 4 and 5 (so far as it is not already in force) and the repeals in Schedule 7 of section 15 of the Faculty Jurisdiction Measure 1964, sections 2, 41, 45 and 87(1) of and paragraphs 1–4 of Schedule 5 to the Pastoral Measure 1983, section 20(1) of the Care of Cathedrals Measure 1990, section 31(1) of the Care of Churches and Ecclesiastical Jurisdiction Measure 1991, section 1 of the Pastoral (Amendment) Measure 1994, section 6(1) of the Care of Places of Worship Measure 1999, section 2(3) of the Synodical Government (Amendment) Measure 2003 and paragraphs 10 and 13 to Schedule 4 to the Church of England (Miscellaneous Provisions) Measure 2005; in force 1 September 2008: section 2, 3(5) and (6), 4, 5, 6((1)–(2) and (4)–(8), 7–11, 18–21, 63(6) and 65 (so far as it relates to the repeals in Schedule 7 coming into force on the same date) and the repeals in Schedule 7 of the words after "being" to "any other diocese" in rule 34(1)(c) in Schedule 3 to the Synodical Government Measure 1969, rules 1–9, 16–17 and 18(1)(a) and (2)–(4), the words "and the report of the Commission thereon" in sections 18(5) and (7) and sections 19–25 of and the Schedule to the Dioceses Measure 1978, section 6 of the Church of England (Legal Aid and Miscellaneous Provisions) Measure 1988, paragraph 18 of Schedule 3 to the Church of England (Miscellaneous Provisions) Measure 1992, paragraph 7 of Schedule 2 to the Cathedrals Measure 1999 and section 18 of the Church of England (Miscellaneous Provisions) Measure 2000; in force 1 February 2009: sections 3(1) to (4) and section 6(3); the remainder to come into force on 1 January 2011)

Church of England Marriage Measure 2008 (1 October 2008)

Ecclesiastical Offices (Terms of Service) Measure 2009 (in force 1 July 2009: sections 2, 10 and 13; in force 24 November 2009: section 8; the remainder to come into force on a date or dates yet to be determined)

Church of England Pensions (Amendment) Measure 2009 (2 April 2009)

Vacancies in Suffragan Sees and Other Ecclesiastical Offices Measure 2010 (in force 1 June 2010: sections 1 and 3; the remainder to come into force on a date or dates yet to be determined)

Church of England (Miscellaneous Provisions) Measure 2010 (in force 1 July 2010: sections 3, 4, 9, 10(1) and (3), and 13; in force 1 September 2010: all remaining provisions except section 8 (to come into force on a date yet to be determined))

Crown Benefices (Parish Representatives) Measure 2010 (to come into force on a date or dates yet to be determined)

STATUTORY INSTRUMENTS

Church Representation Rules (Amendment) Resolution 2004 SI 2004 No. 1889 (1 August 2004, 1 January 2005 and 15 February 2005)

Clergy Discipline Rules 2005 SI 2005 No 2022 (1 January 2006)

Clergy Discipline Appeal Rules 2005 SI 2005 No 3201 (1 January 2006)

Church of England (Legal Aid) (Amendment) Rules 2006 SI 2006 No 1939 (1 August 2006)

Care of Cathedrals Rules 2006 SI 2006 No 1941 (1 January 2008)

Parsonages Measure (Amendment) Rules 2007 SI 2007 No 862 (1 May 2007)

National Institutions of the Church of England (Transfer of Functions) Order 2007 SI 2007 No 1556 (1 January 2008)

Payments to the Churches Conservation Trust Order 2008 SI 2008 No 1968 (1 April 2009)

Ecclesiastical Offices (Terms of Service) Regulations 2009 SI 2009 No 2108 (1 January 2011)

Church of England Pensions (Amendment) Regulations 2009 SI 2009 No 2109 (1 January 2010)

Church Representation Rules (Amendment) Resolution 2009 SI 2009 No 2129 (1 January 2010)

Legal Officers (Annual Fees) Order 2010 (1 January 2011)

Ecclesiastical Judges, Legal Officers and Others (Fees) Order 2010 (1 January 2011)

Parochial Fees Order 2010 (1 January 2011)

Ecclesiastical Offices (Terms of Service) Directions 2010 (1 January 2011)

Church of England Pensions (Amendment) Regulations (1 January 2011)

Copies of the above legislation as originally enacted may be obtained from TSO (details below) or from the Office of Public Sector Information website: www.opsi.gov.uk/uk-church-measures. The consolidated text of the Church Representation Rules (as at July 2010) is published by Church House Publishing (£7.99).

Further Details

Lists of Church of England Measures which have received the Royal Assent from 1920 onwards and of Statutory Instruments to date which are still in force are available the Legal Office web site at: www.cofe.anglican.org/about/churchlawlegis. Recently passed Measures and Rules made pursuant to Measures are sold by TSO and may be obtained from (TSO) Orders, PO Box 29, Norwich NR3 1GN (*telephone enquiries:* 0870 600 5522, *email:* customer.services@tso.co.uk *online ordering:* www.tsoshop.co.uk). TSO or the Legal Office will advise on obtaining copies of Measures that are out of print. All requests should quote as a reference the title and year of the Measure. Church of England legislation in up to date form may also be found on the UK Statute Law Database at: www.statutelaw.gov.uk.

Constitution

1 The General Synod shall consist of the Convocations of Canterbury and York joined together in a House of Bishops and a House of Clergy and having added to them a House of Laity.

2 The House of Bishops and the House of Clergy shall accordingly comprise the Upper and the Lower Houses respectively of the said Convocations, and the House of Laity shall be elected and otherwise constituted in accordance with the Church Representation Rules.

3 (1) The General Synod shall meet in sessions at least twice a year, and at such times and places as it may provide, or, in the absence of such provision, as the Joint Presidents of the Synod may direct.

(2) The General Synod shall, on the dissolution of the Convocations, itself be automatically dissolved, and shall come into being on the calling together of the new Convocations.

(3) Business pending at the dissolution of the General Synod shall not abate, but may be resumed by the new Synod at the stage reached before the dissolution, and any Boards, Commissions, Committees or other bodies of the Synod may, so far as may be appropriate and subject to any Standing Orders or any directions of the Synod or of the Archbishops of Canterbury and York, continue their proceedings during the period of the dissolution, and all things may be done by the Archbishops or any such bodies or any officers of the General Synod as may be

necessary or expedient for conducting the affairs of the Synod during the period of dissolution and for making arrangements for the resumption of business by the new Synod.

(4) A member of the General Synod may continue to act during the period of the dissolution as a member of any such Board, Commission, Committee or body:

Provided that, if a member of the Synod who is an elected Proctor of the clergy or an elected member of the House of Laity does not stand for re-election or is not re-elected, this paragraph shall cease to apply to him with effect from the date on which the election of his successor is announced by the presiding officer.

4 (1) The Archbishops of Canterbury and York shall be joint Presidents of the General Synod, and they shall determine the occasions on which it is desirable that one of the Presidents shall be the chairman of a meeting of the General Synod, and shall arrange between them which of them is to take the chair on any such occasion:

Provided that one of the Presidents shall be the chairman when any motion is taken for the final approval of a provision to which Article 7 of this Constitution applies and in such other cases as may be provided in Standing Orders.

(2) The Presidents shall, after consultation with the Appointments Committee of the Church of England, appoint from among the members of the Synod a panel of no fewer than three or more than eight chairmen, who shall be chosen for their experience and ability as chairmen of meetings and may be members of any House; and it shall be the duty of one of the chairmen on the panel, in accordance with arrangements approved by the Presidents and subject to any special directions of the Presidents, to take the chair at meetings of the General Synod at which neither of the Presidents takes the chair.

[(3) Under the Synodical Government Measure the Provincial Registrars are Joint Registrars of the General Synod but since 1980 the responsibility has been exercised by the Legal Adviser to the General Synod whom each Archbishop appointed as his Joint Registrar for this purpose.]

5 (1) A motion for the final approval of any Measure or Canon shall not be deemed to be carried unless, on a division by Houses, it receives the assent of the majority of the members of each House present and voting:

Provided that by permission of the chairman and with the leave of the General Synod given in accordance with Standing Orders this requirement may be dispensed with.

(2) All other motions of the General Synod shall, subject as hereinafter provided, be determined by a majority of the members of the Synod present and voting, and the vote may be taken by a show of hands or a division:

Provided that, except in the case of a motion relating solely to the course of business or procedure, any 25 members present may demand a division by Houses and in that case the motion shall not be deemed to be carried unless, on such a division, it receives the assent of the majority of the members of each House present and voting.

(3) This Article shall be subject to any provision of this Constitution or of any Measure with respect to special majorities of the Synod or of each House thereof, and where a special majority of each House is required the vote shall be taken on a division by Houses, and where a special majority of the whole Synod is required, the motion shall, for the purposes of this Article, be one relating solely to procedure.

(4) Where a vote is to be taken on a division by Houses, it may be taken by an actual division or in such other manner as Standing Orders may provide.

6 The functions of the General Synod shall be as follows:

(*a*) to consider matters concerning the Church of England and to make provision in respect thereof –

(1) by Measure intended to be given, in the manner prescribed by the Church of England Assembly (Powers) Act 1919, the force and effect of an Act of Parliament, or

(2) by Canon made, promulged and executed in accordance with the like provisions and subject to the like restrictions and having the like legislative force as Canons heretofore made, promulged and executed by the Convocations of Canterbury and York, or

(3) by such order, regulation or other subordinate instrument as may be authorized by Measure or Canon, or

(4) by such Act of Synod, regulation or other instrument or proceeding as may be appropriate in cases where provision by or under a Measure or Canon is not required;

(*b*) to consider and express their opinion on any other matters of religious or public interest.

7 (1) A provision touching doctrinal formulae or the services or ceremonies of the Church of England or the administration of the Sacraments or sacred rites thereof shall, before it is finally approved by the General Synod, be referred to the House of Bishops, and shall be submitted for such final approval in terms proposed by the House of Bishops and not otherwise.

(2) A provision touching any of the matters aforesaid shall, if the Convocations or either of them or the House of Laity so require, be referred, in the terms proposed by the House of Bishops for final approval by the General Synod, to the two Convocations sitting separately for their provinces and to the House of Laity; and no provision so referred shall be submitted for final approval by the General Synod unless it has been approved, in the terms so proposed, by each House of the two Convocations sitting as aforesaid and by the House of Laity.

(3) The question whether such a reference is required by a Convocation shall be decided by the President and Prolocutor of the Houses of that Convocation, and the Prolocutor shall consult the Standing Committee of the Lower House of Canterbury or, as the case may be, the Assessors of the Lower House of York, and the decision of the President and Prolocutor shall be conclusive:

Provided that if, before such a decision is taken, either House of a Convocation resolves that the provision concerned shall be so referred or both Houses resolve that it shall not be so referred, the resolution or resolutions shall be a conclusive decision that the reference is or is not required by that Convocation.

(4) The question whether such a reference is required by the House of Laity shall be decided by the Prolocutor and Pro-Prolocutor of that House who shall consult the Standing Committee of that House, and the decision of the Prolocutor and the Pro-Prolocutor shall be conclusive:

Provided that if, before such a decision is taken, the House of Laity resolves that the reference is or is not required, the resolution shall be a conclusive decision of that question.

(5) Standing Orders of the General Synod shall provide for ensuring that a provision which fails to secure approval on a reference under this Article by each of the four Houses of the Convocations or by the House of Laity of the General Synod is not proposed again in the same or a similar form until a new General Synod comes into being, except that, in the case of objection by one House of one Convocation only, provision may be made for a second reference to the Convocations and, in the case of a second objection by one House only, for reference to the Houses of Bishops and Clergy of the General Synod for approval by a two-thirds majority of the members of each House present and voting, in lieu of such approval by the four Houses aforesaid.

(6) If any question arises whether the requirements of this Article or Standing Orders made thereunder apply to any provision, or whether those requirements have been complied with, it shall be conclusively determined by the Presidents and Prolocutors of the Houses of the Convocations and the Prolocutor and Pro-Prolocutor of the House of Laity of the General Synod.

8 (1) A Measure or Canon providing for permanent changes in the Services of Baptism or Holy Communion or in the Ordinal, or a scheme for a constitutional union or a permanent and substantial change of relationship between the Church of England and another Christian body, being a body a substantial number of whose members reside in Great Britain, shall not be finally approved by the General Synod unless, at a stage determined by the Archbishops, the Measure or Canon or scheme, or the substance of the proposals embodied therein, has been approved by a majority of the dioceses at meetings of their Diocesan Synods, or, in the case of the Diocese in Europe, of the Bishop's Council and Standing Committee of that diocese.

(1a) If the Archbishops consider that this Article should apply to a scheme which affects the Church of England and another Christian body but does not fall within paragraph (1) of this Article, they may direct that this Article shall apply to that scheme, and where such a direction is given this Article shall apply accordingly.

(1b) The General Synod may by resolution provide that final approval of any such scheme as aforesaid, being a scheme specified in the resolution, shall require the assent of such special majorities of the members present and voting as may be specified in the resolution, and the resolution may specify a special majority of each House or of the whole Synod or of both, and in the latter case the majorities may be different.

(1c) A motion for the final approval of a Measure providing for permanent changes in any such Service or in the Ordinal shall not be deemed to be carried unless it receives the assent of a majority in each House of the General Synod of not less than two-thirds of those present and voting.

(2) Any question whether this Article applies to any Measure or Canon or scheme, or whether its requirements have been complied with, shall be conclusively determined by the Archbishops, the Prolocutors of the Lower Houses of the Convocations and the Prolocutor and Pro-Prolocutor of the House of Laity of the General Synod.

9 (1) Standing Orders of the General Synod may provide for separate sittings of any of the three Houses or joint sittings of any two Houses and as to who is to take the chair at any such separate or joint sitting.

(2) The House of Laity shall elect a Chairman and Vice-Chairman of that House who shall also discharge the functions assigned by this Constitution and the Standing Orders and by or under any Measure or Canon to the Prolocutor and Pro-Prolocutor of that House.

10 (1) The General Synod shall appoint a Legislative Committee from members of all three

Houses, to whom shall be referred all Measures passed by the General Synod which it is desired should be given, in accordance with the procedure prescribed by the Church of England Assembly (Powers) Act 1919, the force of an Act of Parliament; and it shall be the duty of the Legislative Committee to take such steps with respect to any such Measure as may be so prescribed.

(2) The General Synod may appoint or provide by their Standing Orders for the appointment of such Committees, Commissions and bodies (in addition to the Committees mentioned in Section 10 of the National Institutions Measure 1998), which may include persons who are not members of the Synod, and such officers as they think fit.

(3) Each House may appoint or provide by their Standing Orders for the appointment of such Committees of their members as they think fit.

11 (1) The General Synod may make, amend and revoke Standing Orders providing for any of the matters for which such provision is required or authorized by this Constitution to be made, and consistently with this Constitution, for the meetings, business and procedure of the General Synod.

(1a) Provision may be made by Standing Order that the exercise of any power of the General Synod to suspend the Standing Orders or any of them shall require the assent of such a majority of the members of the whole Synod present and voting as may be specified in the Standing Order.

(2) Each House may make, amend and revoke Standing Orders for the matter referred to in Article 10 (3) hereof and consistently with this Constitution and with any Standing Orders of the General Synod, for the separate sittings, business and procedure of that House.

(3) Subject to this Constitution and to any Standing Orders, the business and procedure at any meeting of the General Synod or any House or Houses thereof shall be regulated by the chairman of the meeting.

12 (1) References to final approval shall, in relation to a Canon or Act of Synod, be construed as referring to the final approval by the General Synod of the contents of the Canon or Act, and not to the formal promulgation thereof:

Provided that the proviso to Article 4 (1) shall apply both to the final approval and to the formal promulgation of a Canon or Act of Synod.

(2) Any question concerning the interpretation of this Constitution, other than questions for the determination of which express provision is otherwise made, shall be referred to and determined by the Archbishops of Canterbury and York.

(3) No proceedings of the General Synod or any House or Houses thereof, or any Board, Commission, Committee or body thereof, shall be invalidated by any vacancy in the membership of the body concerned or by any defect in the qualification, election or appointment of any member thereof.

13 Any functions exercisable under this Constitution by the Archbishops of Canterbury and York, whether described as such or as Presidents of the General Synod, may, during the absence abroad or incapacity through illness of one Archbishop or a vacancy in one of the Sees, be exercised by the other Archbishop alone.

General Synod Business

FEBRUARY 2010 GROUP OF SESSIONS

LEGISLATIVE BUSINESS
The Synod
Took note of a report by the Steering Committee (GS 1639Z) on draft Amending Canon No 29 (GS 1639B) and gave the draft Amending Canon Final Approval. The voting on Final Approval was as follows: *Bishops In Favour 25, Against 0, Recorded abstentions 0; Clergy In Favour 98, Against 2, Recorded abstentions 0; Laity in Favour 108, Against 2, Recorded abstentions 1.* The motion 'That the petition for Her Majesty's Royal Assent and Licence (GS 1639C) be adopted' was subsequently carried.

Took note of a report by the Steering Committee (GS 1715Z) on the draft Ecclesiastical Fees (Amendment) Measure (GS 1715B), amended the draft Measure and gave it Final Approval. The voting on Final Approval was as follows: *Bishops*

In Favour 22, Against 0, Recorded abstentions 1; Clergy In Favour 99, Against 10, Recorded abstentions 11; Laity In Favour 115, Against 9, Recorded abstentions 4.

Took note of a report by the Revision Committee (GS 1727Y) on the draft Care of Cathedrals Measure (GS 1727A), considered the draft Measure clause by clause and subsequently gave it Final Approval. The voting on Final Approval was as follows: *Bishops In Favour 14, Against 0, Recorded abstentions 0; Clergy In Favour 72, Against 0, Recorded abstentions 0; Laity In Favour 97, Laity 0, Laity Recorded abstentions 0.*

Took note of a report by the Revision Committee (GS 1740Y) on the draft Mission and Pastoral Measure (GS 1740A), considered the draft Measure clause by clause and subsequently gave it Final Approval. The voting was as follows: *Bishops In Favour 13, Against 0, Recorded* abstentions 1; *Clergy In Favour 72, Against 1, Recorded abstentions 1; Laity In Favour 78, Against 0, Recorded abstentions 2.*

Approved two Codes of Practice (GS 1774 and GS 1775) issued under section 8 of the Ecclesiastical Offices (Terms of Service) Measure 2009 for the purposes of Regulations 31 and 32 respectively of the Ecclesiastical Offices (Terms of Service) Regulations 2009.

LITURGICAL BUSINESS
The Synod
Took note of a report by the Revision Committee (GS 1724Y) on the liturgical business entitled 'Additional Weekday Lectionary and Amendments to Calendar, Lectionary and Collects' (GS 1724A). Synod subsequently re-committed the liturgical business to the Revision Committee for further revision. The voting was as follows: *In Favour 110, Against 108, Recorded abstentions 10.*

OTHER BUSINESS
The Synod
Received a presidential address from the Archbishop of Canterbury.

Heard an address from the Revd David Gamble (President of the Methodist Conference) and Dr Richard Vautrey (Vice-President), and asked questions of them.

Heard a presentation by the Rt Revd Graham Cray (Bishop of Maidstone) on *Fresh Expressions* (GS 1766), and asked questions of him.

Heard a presentation by the Rt Revd Richard Chartres (Bishop of London) and Mrs Anne Sloman (Chair of the Church Buildings Committee) on *Realising the Missionary Potential of Church Buildings* (GS 1767).

Took note of the *Forty-fourth Report of the Standing Orders Committee* (GS 1763) and approved various amendments to the Standing Orders.

Heard a presentation on *Clergy Pensions: Proposed Scheme Changes: A Report from the Archbishops' Council* (GS 1758) by Mr Shaun Farrell (Secretary and Chief Executive of the Pensions Board) and subsequently debated and carried the amended motion: 'That this Synod: (a) endorse the recommendations at paragraph 2 of GS 1758 subject to the necessary statutory and other consultations that the Archbishops' Council now needs to conduct; (b) in the light of those consultations invite the Archbishops' Council to submit to the Synod in July final proposals, including such changes as are necessary to the funded scheme rules; and (c) ask the Archbishops' Council to consider the preparation of a report which describes and explores the overall clergy remuneration

package.' The voting was: *In Favour 273, Against 14, Recorded abstentions 8.*

Carried the motion on *Clergy Pensions: Ill-health Retirement: A Report from the Archbishops' Council* (GS 1759): 'That this Synod: (a) endorse the recommendations at paragraph 1 of GS 1759; (b) subject to consultation with scheme members, invite the Pensions Board to submit to the Synod in July such changes as are necessary to the funded scheme rules; and (c) ask the Archbishops' Council to report to the Synod in 2011 on progress with arrangements for implementing national occupational health standards.'

Carried the motion on *General Synod Elections 2010: Report by the Business Committee* (GS 1760): 'That this Synod approve the recommendations set out in paragraphs (i) and (ii) on page 4 of GS 1760.'

Carried the motion on *Mission-Shaped Church: Report from the Mission and Public Affairs Council* (GS 1761):

'That this Synod:
(a) affirm the mixed economy of traditional churches and fresh expressions of church, working in partnership, as the most promising mission strategy in a fast changing culture;
(b) encourage those responsible for vocations and training in dioceses and parishes to promote the imaginative recruitment, training and deployment of ordained and lay pioneer ministers in and beyond title posts;
(c) commend the making of Bishops' Mission Orders to integrate suitable fresh expressions of church in the life of the dioceses; and
(d) request the Mission and Public Affairs Division and the Research and Statistics Unit to gather evidence on the spiritual and numerical growth of the mixed economy church in general and fresh expressions of church in particular, and to bring a further report or reports to Synod in the next quinquennium.'

Debated a Private Members' Motion from Mr Nigel Holmes (Carlisle) on *TV Coverage of Religious and Ethical Issues* (GS 1762A and GS 1762B) and carried the amended motion:

'That this Synod:
(a) express its appreciation of the vital role played by those engaged in communicating religious belief and practice through the media, at a time of major changes within the industry; and
(b) express its deep concern about the overall reduction in religious broadcasting across

British television in recent years, and call upon mainstream broadcasters to nurture and develop the expertise to create and commission high quality religious content across the full range of their output, particularly material that imaginatively marks major festivals and portrays acts of worship.'

The voting was: *In Favour 267, Against 4, Recorded abstentions 2.*

Debated a Private Members' Motion from Lorna Ashworth (Chichester) on the *Anglican Church in North America* (GS 1764A and GS 1764B) and carried the amended motion:

'That this Synod, aware of the distress caused by recent divisions within the Anglican churches of the United States of America and Canada:
(a) recognise and affirm the desire of those who have formed the Anglican Church in North America to remain within the Anglican family;
(b) acknowledge that this aspiration, in respect both of relations with the Church of England and membership of the Anglican Communion, raises issues which the relevant authorities of each need to explore further; and
(c) invite the Archbishops to report further to the Synod in 2011.'

The voting was as follows: *In Favour 309, Against 69, Recorded abstentions 17.*

Debated a Diocesan Synod Motion from the diocese of Ripon and Leeds on *Repair of Church Buildings* (GS 1768) and carried the amended motion:

'That this Synod, recognizing that:
(a) church buildings are an important part of our national heritage and provide not only a spiritual focus for worship and pilgrimage but in many cases also play a vital role as community meeting places, visitor centres and spaces for the wider celebration of the arts;
(a) many volunteers raise large sums of money to help sustain this heritage;
(b) English Heritage, the Heritage Lottery Fund and grant making trusts make a valuable contribution towards the cost of repairing church buildings; but
(c) the national backlog of church building repairs is still of great magnitude, welcome the contribution made to church building repairs by the Listed Places of Worship Grant Scheme, and call on HM Government to:

(i) substantially increase the amount of money available for the repair of listed church buildings; and
(ii) give an early commitment to continuing beyond March 2011 the Listed Places of Worship Grant Scheme.'

The voting was as follows: *In Favour 248, Against 0, Recorded abstentions 0.*

Took note of the report *Going for Growth: Transformation for Children, Young People and the Church* (GS 1769) from the Board of Education/National Society Council.

Debated and carried a Private Members' Motion by Mark Bratton (Coventry) on *Parity of Provision for Surviving Civil Partners* (GS 1770A and GS 1770B): 'That this Synod request the Archbishops' Council and the Church of England Pensions Board to bring forward changes to the rules governing the clergy pension scheme in order to go beyond the requirements of the Civil Partnership Act 2004 and provide for pension benefits to be paid to the surviving civil partners of deceased clergy on the same basis as they are currently paid to surviving spouses.' The voting was as follows: *Bishops In Favour: 12, Against 2, Recorded abstentions 3; Clergy In Favour 98, Clergy 23, Recorded abstentions 10; Laity In Favour 77, Against 59, Recorded abstentions 9.*

Debated a Private Members' Motion from Mr Thomas Benyon (Oxford) on *Violent Computer Games* (GS 1771A and GS 1771B) and carried the amended motion:

'That this Synod
(a) express concern about the potentially desensitising and damaging effect upon children, young people and vulnerable adults of computer games containing gratuitous violent and sexual content;
(b) congratulate HM Government on the action it has taken to date in response to the Byron Review;
(c) call upon HM Government to continue to keep under review the regulatory system for advertising video games to prevent the targeting of children, young people and vulnerable adults with unsuitable material;
(d) declare its support for all those, especially carers, working through research, education and public information, to prevent children, young people and vulnerable adults from being damaged by video and computer games and similar material; and
(e) request the MPA Division to continue to monitor developments in this area.'

The voting was as follows: *In Favour 168, Against 0, Recorded abstentions 0.*

Debated and carried a Diocesan Synod Motion from the diocese of Manchester on *Compatibility of Science and Christian Belief* (GS 1772A and GS 1772B): 'That this Synod, concerned at the promotion of a perceived need to choose between the claims of science and belief in God: (a) affirm the compatibility of belief in God and an understanding of science; and (b) urge the House of Bishops and all dioceses robustly to promote a better public understanding of the compatibility of science and Christian belief.' The voting was as follows: *In Favour 241, Against 2, Recorded abstentions 2.*

Debated a Diocesan Synod Motion from the diocese of Chelmsford on *Confidence in the Bible* (GS 1765A and GS 1765B) and carried the amended motion:

'That this Synod
(a) believe that the 400th anniversary in 2011 of the King James Version of the Bible is an obvious opportunity to celebrate the exceptional contribution which that translation has made to shaping the life, language and culture of this and other nations;
(b) commend the King James Version and other translations of the Bible as relevant and authoritative for personal and public instruction, reiterating the importance of continuing Biblical translation, scholarship and teaching;
(c) note with enthusiasm the events throughout the year being organised by the 2011 Trust and other bodies, details of which are to be warmly commended to Church and local communities; and
(d) request that dioceses, deaneries and parishes undertake local initiatives to celebrate and teach the Bible both within the Church and throughout wider society.'

The voting was as follows: *In Favour 244, Against 0, Recorded abstentions 0.*

Heard a presentation on Military Chaplaincy by Brigadier General Patrick Marriott (Commandant, RMAS), Ven Stephen Robbins (Chaplain General from HM Land Forces), Ven John Green (Chaplain of the Fleet) and Ven Ray Pentland (Chaplain in Chief (RAF)), and asked questions of them.

JULY 2010 GROUP OF SESSIONS

LEGISLATIVE BUSINESS
The Synod
Resolved that the Canon entitled 'Amending Canon No 29' (GS 1639D) be promulged and executed.

Took note of a report by the Revision Committee (GS1708–09Y) on Women in the Episcopate:

draft Bishops and Priests (Consecration and Ordination of Women) Measure (GS 1708A) and draft Amending Canon No 30 (GS 1709A) and considered the draft Measure and draft Amending Canon clause by clause.

Approved the Legal Officers (Annual Fees) Order 2010 (GS 1796), the Ecclesiastical Judges, Legal Officers and Others (Fees) Order 2010 (GS 1797), the Parochial Fees Order 2010 (GS 1798), the Ecclesiastical Offices (Terms of Service) (Amendment) Regulations 2010 (GS 1783) and the Ecclesiastical Offices (Terms of Service) Directions 2010 (GS 1784).

Approved the Church of England Funded Pensions Scheme (Cessation of Contracting Out etc.) (Amendment) Rules 2010 (GS 1785), the Church of England Funded Pensions Scheme (Retirement Age etc.) (Amendment) Rules 2010 (GS 1786), the Church of England Funded Pensions Scheme (Accrual Rate) (Amendment) Rules 2010 (GS 1787), the Church of England Funded Pensions Scheme (Health and Disability)(Amendment) Rules 2010 (GS 1788), the Church of England Funded Pensions Scheme (Civil Partners' Benefits)(Amendment) Rules 2010 (GS 1789), the Church of England Pensions Scheme (Miscellaneous Provisions)(Amendment) Rules 2010 (GS 1790) and the Church of England Pensions (Amendment) Regulations 2010 (GS 1791).

LITURGICAL BUSINESS
The Synod
Took note of a further report from the Revision Committee (GS1724Z) and gave Final Approval to the Liturgical Business entitled 'Additional Weekday Lectionary and Amendments to Calendar, Lectionary and Collects' (GS 1724A (as amended) and GS 1724B) for a period from 14 July 2010 until further resolution of the Synod. The voting on Final Approval was as follows: *Bishops In Favour (21), Against (0), Recorded abstentions (0); Clergy In Favour (101), Against (0), Recorded abstentions (0); Laity In Favour (125), Against (0), Recorded abstentions (2).*

FINANCIAL BUSINESS
The Synod
Took note of a report on the Archbishops' Council's draft Budget and Proposals for Apportionment for 2011 (GS 1781); approved the proposed expenditure for: training for ministry; the work of the Council generally; grants and provisions; inter-diocesan support/mission agencies clergy pension contributions; and CHARM; and approved the Council's proposals for apportionment amongst the dioceses.

OTHER BUSINESS
The Synod
Received a presidential address by the Archbishop of Canterbury.

Received an address by Archbishop Andres Poder of the Estonian Evangelical-Lutheran Church.

Approved changes to the Standing Orders of the General Synod as set out in the *Forty-Fifth Report of the Standing Orders Committee* (Annex B of GS 1782).

Approved the establishment of the Faith and Order Commission, as proposed in GS 1782, and approved its constitution (as set out in Annex A of GS 1782).

Approved the recommendations set out in GS 1779 concerning the *Term of Office of Archbishops' Council Elected Members in the next Quinquennium*.

Took note of the report entitled *Review of Constitutions* (GS 1793).

Heard a presentation from the Archbishop of York on the *Archbishops' Council's Annual Report* (GS 1794) and asked questions of three members of the Archbishops' Council.

Heard a presentation from the First Church Estates Commissioner, Mr Andreas Whittam Smith, on the *Church Commissioner's Annual Report* and asked questions of him and the Third Church Estates Commissioner, Mr Timothy Walker.

Debated the motion on *Clergy Pensions: Change to the Pensions Shceme: Report from the Archbishops' Council* (GS 1780) and carried the amended motion:

'That this Synod:
(a) endorse the recommendations contained in paragraph 31 of GS 1780;
(b) invite the Archbishops' Council's Deployment. Remuneration and Conditions of Service Committee (i) to convene a small working group to consider the effect that these recommendations will have on the performance, deployment and morale of the clergy and on the wider mission of the Church and (ii) in the light of the group's findings, to offer guidance on these matters to bishops and archdeacons within the next two years.'

Debated a Diocesan Synod Motion from the diocese of Coventry on *Deanery Synods* (GS 1773A and GS 1773B) and carried the amended motion:

'That this Synod:
(a) welcome the wide measure of discretion

that each diocese has to determine the extent of any delegation of functions to deaneries;
(b) note the increasing range of legal vehicles available to deaneries where it is agreed that a more executive role may help in promoting the mission of the Church; and
(c) invite the Archbishops' Council, in consultation with the House of Bishops, to produce updated guidance on available options, with examples of how recent practice has been developing.'

Debated a Diocesan Synod Motion from the diocese of Bath and Wells on *Job Sharing in Ordained Parochial Ministry* (GS 1799A and GS 1799B) and carried the motion:

'That this Synod, having regard to:
(a) the benefits of be gained from job sharing arrangements in the parochial deployment of ordained ministers, in particular married couples where both parties are ordained;
(b) the absence at present of any effective provision for job sharing in the ordained parochial ministry;

Request the Archbishops' Council to bring forward legislative proposals for the making of such job sharing arrangements.'

Debated a Private Members' Motion from Richard Moy (Lichfield) on *Fresh Expressions Resources* (GS1795A and GS1795B) and carried the amended motion:

'That this Synod request the Archbishops' Council to identify sources of funding for the publication of an on-line library of visual and video resources for worship, so that hard-pressed local worship leaders may access and use them in both mission and congregational contexts.'

Debated a Diocesan Synod Motion from the diocese of Ripon and Leeds on *Qualifying Connection* (GS 1800A and GS 1800B) and carried the motion:

'That this Synod request the Archbishops' Council to introduce legislation which would enable the Bishop to give directions allowing those who have a "qualifying connection" with a particular parish (under the Church of England Marriage Measure 2008) to marry in any church within the benefice of which that parish forms a part'.

I

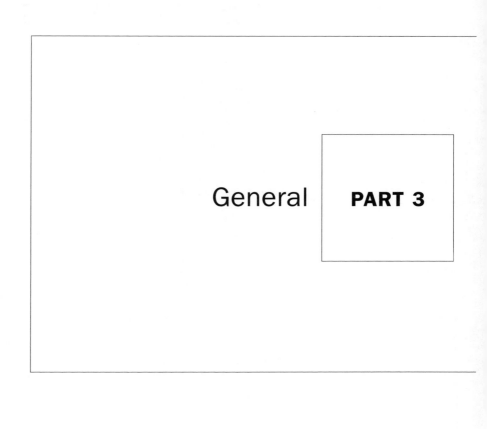

General   **PART 3**

PART 3   CONTENTS

GENERAL INFORMATION

Addressing the Clergy

Since the Lambeth Conference of 1968, at which styles of address were debated, there has been a trend towards simpler forms of address. Resolution 14 stated: 'The Conference recommends that the bishops, as leaders and representatives of a servant Church, should radically examine the honours paid to them in the course of divine worship, in titles and customary address, and in style of living, while having the necessary facilities for the efficient carrying on of their work.'

Whereas formerly a bishop would have been addressed as 'My Lord' and a dean as 'Mr Dean', it has become more usual to address a bishop in speech as 'Bishop' and a dean as 'Dean'. There is, however, a correct way to address clergy on an envelope, which is normally as follows:

Archbishop of Canterbury or York	The Most Revd and Rt Hon the Lord Archbishop of
Archbishop of another Province	The Most Revd the Lord Archbishop of
Bishop of London	The Rt Revd and Rt Hon the Lord Bishop of
Diocesan/Suffragan Bishop	*Either* The Rt Revd the Lord Bishop of *or* The Rt Revd the Bishop of
Assistant/Retired Bishop	The Rt Revd J. D. Smith (*or* John Smith)
Dean	The Very Revd the Dean of
Provost	The Very Revd the Provost of
Archdeacon	The Ven the Archdeacon of
Canon	The Revd Canon J. D. Smith (*or* John or Jane Smith)
Prebendary	The Revd Prebendary J. D. Smith (*or* John or Jane Smith)
Rural Dean	No special form of address (The Revd, the Revd Canon, etc.)
Dean of Oxford/Cambridge College	No special form of address
Cleric also Professor	*Either* The Revd Professor J. D. Smith *or* Professor the Revd J. D. Smith
Canon also Professor	*Either* The Revd Canon Professor J. D. Smith *or* Professor the Revd Canon J. D. Smith
Cleric also Doctor	*Either* The Revd Dr J. D. Smith *or* The Revd J. D. Smith (degree)
Canon also Doctor	The Revd Canon J. D. Smith (degree)
Other Clergy/Priest/Deacon	The Revd J. D. Smith (*or* John or Jane Smith)

The following points should be noted particularly:

1 A diocesan or suffragan bishop has a title conferred on him by his consecration or subsequent translation, which he is entitled to hold until he resigns. He then reverts to his personal name, retaining the title 'Right Reverend'.
2 A dean, provost or archdeacon has a territorial title until he resigns. He then reverts to his personal name, and his title is 'Reverend' unless the rank of dean, provost or archdeacon emeritus has been awarded.
3 Retired archbishops properly go back to the status of a bishop but may be given as a courtesy the style of an archbishop.
4 A bishop holding office as a dean or archdeacon is addressed as The Rt Revd the Dean/Archdeacon of.
5 If a cleric's name or initials are unknown, he or she should be addressed as The Revd — Smith or the Revd Mr/Mrs/Miss/Ms Smith. It is never correct to refer to a cleric as 'The Reverend Smith' or 'Revd Smith'.
6 There is no universally accepted way of addressing an envelope to a married couple of whom both are in holy orders. We recommend the style 'The Revd A. B. and the Revd C. D. Smith'.

Archbishops of Canterbury and York

CANTERBURY

597 Augustine
604 Laurentius
619 Mellitus
624 Justus
627 Honorius
655 Deusdedit
668 Theodore
693 Beorhtweald
731 Tatwine
735 Nothelm
740 Cuthbeorht
761 Breguwine
765 Jaenbeorht
793 Æthelheard
805 Wulfred
832 Feologild
833 Ceolnoth
870 Æthelred
890 Plegmund
914 Æthelhelm
923 Wulfhelm
942 Oda
959 Ælfsige
959 Beorhthelm
960 Dunstan
c988 Athelgar
990 Sigeric Serio
995 Ælfric
1005 Ælfheath
1013 Lyfing
1020 Æthelnoth
1038 Eadsige
1051 Robert of Jumièges
1052 Stigand
1070 Lanfranc
1093 Anselm
1114 Ralph d'Escures
1123 William de Corbeil
1139 Theobald
1162 Thomas Becket
1174 Richard [of Dover]
1185 Baldwin
1193 Hubert Walter
1207 Stephen Langton
1229 Richard le Grant
1234 Edmund Rich
1245 Boniface of Savoy
1273 Robert Kilwardby
1279 John Peckham
1294 Robert Winchelsey
1313 Walter Reynolds
1328 Simon Mepeham
1333 John Stratford
1349 Thomas Bradwardine
1349 Simon Islip
1366 Simon Langham
1368 William Whittlesey

1375 Simon Sudbury
1381 William Courtenay
1396 Thomas Arundel[†]
1398 Roger Walden
1414 Henry Chichele
1443 John Stafford
1452 John Kemp
1454 Thomas Bourchier
1486 John Morton
1501 Henry Dean
1503 William Warham
1533 Thomas Cranmer
1556 Reginald Pole
1559 Matthew Parker
1576 Edmund Grindal
1583 John Whitgift
1604 Richard Bancroft
1611 George Abbot
1633 William Laud
1660 William Juxon
1663 Gilbert Sheldon
1678 William Sancroft
1691 John Tillotson
1695 Thomas Tenison
1716 William Wake
1737 John Potter
1747 Thomas Herring
1757 Matthew Hutton
1758 Thomas Secker
1768 Frederick Cornwallis
1783 John Moore
1805 Charles Manners Sutton
1828 William Howley
1848 John Bird Sumner
1862 Charles Thomas Longley
1868 Archibald Campbell Tait
1883 Edward White Benson
1896 Frederick Temple
1903 Randall Thomas Davidson
1928 Cosmo Gordon Lang
1942 William Temple
1945 Geoffrey Francis Fisher
1961 Arthur Michael Ramsey
1974 Frederick Donald Coggan
1980 Robert Alexander Kennedy Runcie
1991 George Leonard Carey
2002 Rowan Douglas Williams

YORK

BISHOPS

625 Paulinus
[vacancy for 30 years]
664 Ceadda
669 Wilfrith I
678 Bosa[‡]
705 John of Beverley
718 Wilfrith II

ARCHBISHOPS

c734 Ecgbeorht
767 Æthelbeorht
780 Eanbald I
796 Eanbald II
c812 Wulfsige
837 Wigmund
854 Wulfhere
900 Æthelbeald
c928 Hrothweard
931 Wulfstan I
958 Oscytel
971 Edwaldus
972 Osweald
992 Ealdwulf
1003 Wulfstan II
1023 Ælfric Puttoc
1041 Æthelric[§]
1051 Cynesige
1061 Ealdred
1070 Thomas I
1100 Gerard
1109 Thomas II
1119 Thurstan
1143 William Fitzherbert
1147 Henry Murdac[*]
1154 Roger of Pont l'Eveque
1191 Geoffrey Plantagenet
1215 Walter de Gray
1256 Sewal de Bovill
1258 Godfrey Ludham
1266 Walter Giffard
1279 William Wickwane
1286 John le Romeyn
1298 Henry Newark
1300 Thomas Corbridge
1306 William Greenfield
1317 William Melton
1342 William Zouche
1352 John Thoresby
1374 Alexander Neville
1388 Thomas Arundel
1396 Robert Waldby
1398 Richard le Scrope
1407 Henry Bowet
1426 John Kemp
1452 William Booth

1465 George Nevill
1476 Lawrence Booth
1480 Thomas Rotherham (or Scot)
1501 Thomas Savage
1508 Christopher Bainbridge
1514 Thomas Wolsey
1531 Edward Lee
1545 Robert Holgate
1555 Nicholas Heath
1561 Thomas Young
1570 Edmund Grindal
1577 Edwin Sandys
1589 John Piers
1595 Matthew Hutton
1606 Tobias Matthew
1628 George Montaigne
1629 Samuel Harsnett
1632 Richard Neile
1641 John Williams
1660 Accepted Frewen
1664 Richard Sterne
1683 John Dolben
1688 Thomas Lamplugh
1691 John Sharp
1714 William Dawes
1724 Lancelot Blackburn
1743 Thomas Herring
1747 Matthew Hutton
1757 John Gilbert
1761 Robert Hay Drummond
1777 William Markham
1808 Edward Venables Vernon Harcourt
1847 Thomas Musgrave
1860 Charles Thomas Longley
1863 William Thomson
1891 William Connor Magee
1891 William Dalrymple Maclagan
1909 Cosmo Gordon Lang
1929 William Temple
1942 Cyril Foster Garbett
1956 Arthur Michael Ramsey
1961 Frederick Donald Coggan
1975 Stuart Yarworth Blanch
1983 John Stapylton Habgood
1995 David Michael Hope
2005 John Tucker Mugabi Sentamu

[†] On 19 October 1399 Boniface IX annulled Arundel's translation to St Andrews and confirmed him in the see of Canterbury.
[‡] Wilfrith was restored to office in 686 and Bosa in 691.
[§] Ælfric Puttoc was restored in 1042.
[*] William Fitzherbert was restored in 1153.

Bishops in the House of Lords

The Archbishops of Canterbury and York and the Bishops of London, Durham and Winchester always have seats in the House of Lords. The twenty-one other seats are filled by diocesan bishops in order of seniority. In the case of bishops awaiting seats, the order of seniority is shown (1), (2), (3), etc.

The Bishop of Sodor and Man and the Bishop of Gibraltar in Europe are not eligible to sit in the House of Lords.

	Election as Diocesan Bishop confirmed	Translated to present See	Entered House of Lords
Canterbury (Most Revd & Rt Hon R. D. Williams)	1992*	2002	2003
York (Most Revd & Rt Hon J. T. M. Sentamu)	2002	2005	2006
London (Rt Revd & Rt Hon R. J. C. Chartres)	1995		1996
Durham (Vacancy)			
Winchester (Rt Revd M. C. Scott-Joynt)	1995		1996
Bath and Wells (Rt Revd P. B. Price)	2002		2008
Birmingham (Rt Revd D. Urquhart)	2006		(1)
Blackburn (Rt Revd N. S. Reade)	2004		2009
Bradford (Vacancy)			
Bristol (Rt Revd M. Hill)	2003		2009
Carlisle (Rt Revd J. Newcome)	2009		(9)
Chelmsford (Rt Revd S. Cottrell)	2010		(13)
Chester (Rt Revd P. R. Forster)	1996		2001
Chichester (Rt Revd J. W. Hind)	2001		2008
Coventry (Rt Revd C. J. Cocksworth)	2008		(5)
Derby (Rt Revd A. L. J. Redfern)	2005		2010
Ely (Vacancy)			
Exeter (Rt Revd M. L. Langrish)	2000		2005
Gloucester (Rt Revd M. F. Perham)	2004		2009
Guildford (Rt Revd C. J. Hill)	2004		2010
Hereford (Rt Revd A. M. Priddis)	2004		2009
Leicester (Rt Revd T. J. Stevens)	1999		2003
Lichfield (Rt Revd J. M. Gledhill)	2003		2009
Lincoln (Rt Revd J. C. Saxbee)	2001		2008
Liverpool (Rt Revd J. S. Jones)	1998		2003
Manchester (Rt Revd N. S. McCulloch)	1992	2002	1997
Newcastle (Rt Revd J. M. Wharton)	1997		2003
Norwich (Rt Revd G. R. James)	1999		2004
Oxford (Rt Revd J. L. Pritchard)	2007		(2)
Peterborough (Rt Revd D. Allister)	2010		(11)
Portsmouth (Rt Revd C. Foster)	2010		(12)
Ripon and Leeds (Rt Revd J. R. Packer)	2000		2006
Rochester (Rt Revd James Langstaff)	2010		(14)
St Albans (Rt Revd A. G. C. Smith)	2009		(8)
St Edmundsbury and Ipswich (Rt Revd W. N. Stock)	2007		(3)
Salisbury (Vacancy)			
Sheffield (Rt Revd S. J. L. Croft)	2009		(7)
Southwark (Vacancy)			
Southwell and Nottingham (Rt Revd P. Butler)	2009		(10)
Truro (Rt Revd T. M. Thornton)	2008		(6)
Wakefield (Rt Revd S. G. Platten)	2003		2009
Worcester (Rt Revd J. G. Inge)	2008		(4)

* As Bishop of Monmouth in the Church in Wales, the bishops of which do not have seats in the House of Lords.

Chaplains

Chaplains in Her Majesty's Services

ROYAL NAVY

Chaplains of all denominations are employed in many parts of the world, ashore and afloat in capital ships, frigates and destroyers, Royal Marine Commando Units, hospitals, Royal Naval Air Stations, HM Naval Bases and Training Establishments. Apart from conducting the customary services in their ships, units or establishments, for which all the necessary facilities are provided, chaplains find numerous opportunities for extending the work of the Church through pastoral contacts with families and dependants, as well as being 'friend and adviser of all on board'. They are given particular opportunity to teach the Christian faith to young people in Training Establishments. In-Service training for all Royal Naval Chaplains is carried out at the Armed Forces Chaplaincy Centre, Amport House, Andover, Hants. SP11 8BG. Christian Leadership Courses for all service personnel are provided at the centre during the year. The Anglican Church in the Royal Navy is served by 45 priests and is very much a part of the Church of England with the Single Service and Tri-Service Synodical structures. The Senior Anglican Chaplain in the Royal Navy is granted the ecclesiastical dignity of Archdeacon by the Archbishop of Canterbury. The Archbishop is the Ordinary for all service chaplains and grants ecclesiastical licences to all Anglican chaplains on the Active List. The Royal Navy is an Equal Opportunities employer and applications for entry from both male and female priests up to the age of 49 are always welcome. Full particulars concerning the entry of Anglican Chaplains can be obtained from DGNCS, Navy Command HQ, MP 1.2, Leach Building, Whale Island, Portsmouth PO2 8BY   *Tel:* 023 9262 5553
Fax: 023 9262 5134
email: lee.foley211@mod.uk

ARMY

Army chaplains serve wherever soldiers serve, including the front line in Afghanistan, providing spiritual, moral and pastoral support to soldiers and their families. Army chaplains are non-combatants and do not bear arms. They are ordained men and women recommended for this ministry by the Churches: Church of England, Church of Scotland, Roman Catholic, Methodist and United Board (United Reformed Church and Baptist), Elim Pentecostal and Assemblies of God. They provide an 'all-souls' ministry to all in their care but ensure that soldiers have access to a chaplain of a particular Church or faith group when required. Chaplains of all denominations are administered by the Chaplain General. The Chaplain General's post may be filled by a chaplain from any of the Churches. The appointment is currently held by an Anglican, the Venerable Stephen Robbins, who is also Archdeacon for the Army. *The Chaplain General* Ven Stephen Robbins QHC. Ministry of Defence Chaplains (Army), Headquarters Land Forces, Ramillies Building, Marlborough Lines, Monxton Road, Andover SP11 8HT   *Tel:* 01264 383374
Fax: 01264 381824

ROYAL AIR FORCE

From the foundation of the Royal Air Force, chaplains have been proud to minister to the needs of servicemen and women and their families, in peace and war. The Chaplains' Branch of the Royal Air Force offers a real challenge and a rewarding ministry to young priests who have the necessary qualities, initiative and enthusiasm. The Royal Air Force is a large body of men and women drawn from every corner of Britain and from every stratum of society. There is a continuing need for clergy to minister to these men and women and the Royal Air Force understands and supports this ministry. Chaplains are commissioned by Her Majesty the Queen to provide for the pastoral and spiritual needs of all Service personnel and their families. This care is unlimited, and extends wherever members of the Royal Air Force are called to serve. Clergy may apply for a position in either a full-time or reserve capacity. Further details concerning chaplaincy in the Royal Air Force can be obtained from: Chaplaincy Services (RAF), Valiant Block, RAF High Wycombe HP14 4UE
Tel: 01494 494469
Web: www.raf.mod.uk/chaplains
For a list of **Chaplains to Her Majesty's Services** *see Crockford.*

Forces Synodical Council

President The Archbishop of Canterbury

Senior Vice-President Rt Revd Stephen Venner (*The Archbishop of Canterbury's Episcopal Representative to Her Majesty's Forces*)

Lay Vice-President Lieutenant Commander Philippa Sargent RN

Secretary Fran Hall, c/o MCS, Air Cmd, RAF High Wycombe, Bucks HP14 4UP

On the direction of the Secretary of State for Defence and the Archbishop of Canterbury in the 1980s, the Forces Synodical Council was first convened in 1990 in London. Since 1997 it has had thirty-six elected members, six clergy and six lay members from the Royal Navy, Army and the Royal Air Force, and nine *ex officio* members.

The Council is chaired by the Bishop to HM Forces but has no fiscal or Armed Service command authority. It gives the Anglican clergy and laity of the whole Armed Services the opportunity to contribute to General Synod, to the Armed Services Chain of Command and to the Ministry of Defence. They can also make decisions pertinent to the life and ministry of the Anglican Church within the Armed Forces, and although members are not drawn exclusively from the Church of England, all ministers hold the Licence of the Archbishop of Canterbury.

Each Armed Service constitutes a separate Archdeaconry with elected representatives at chaplaincy level, forming what are known as Chaplaincy Councils and an elected Archdeaconry Synod. The three Archdeacons (one appointed by the Archbishop of Canterbury to each of the Armed Services) chair their respective Archdeaconry Synods, are *ex officio* members of the Forces Synodical Council and were, until 2005, *ex officio* members of General Synod. Under the changes in composition of General Synod that came into force in 2005, these *ex officio* posts lapsed and the Armed Forces received a total of seven representative seats on General Synod, divided between the laity and the clergy.

Chaplains in Higher Education

The Church of England supports chaplains in universities and colleges of higher education across the country including the Church Colleges and Universities. The National Adviser for Higher Education, based in the Education Division at Church House, Westminster, is the officer of the Board of Education leading on the Church's policy and ministry in higher education.

The National Adviser advises the Board on policy relating to HE; resources dioceses, universities and colleges and their chaplains, coordinates conferences, induction, and training for HE chaplains (with ecumenical cooperation through the Churches' Higher Education Liaison Group (CHELG)), acts as consultant to chaplains and ecumenical chaplaincy teams, and advises enquirers considering ministry in this sector of education. In general, organized events are open to chaplains throughout Great Britain as well as to ecumenical partners and diocesan staff. The National Adviser and the Board of Education's Higher Education Panel are available to advise the government and Church at all levels when required.

The role of chaplain includes ministry to staff and students, and to institutions as a whole, their leaders and structures. Chaplains are also a point of contact for people of other faiths. The university student experience has changed dramatically in recent years, and the Higher Education Act 2004 has emphasized both increased access for students from non-traditional backgrounds and also increased fees for many students, to be paid back after graduation. The next year will be one of further change, as new arrangements for the funding of universities and support of students are likely to be introduced. A key focus for chaplaincy is the promotion of a new understanding of the Church's ministry in the higher education sector. This is a challenging ministry in the context of mission, in the face of continuing change and increasing student numbers, with all the pressures on people, finance and structures that these bring. It is increasingly carried out in a multi-faith context and is seen as bringing a major contribution to community cohesion. It requires wisdom and understanding and is certainly not restricted to recent curates.

The Board of Education's report *Pillars of the Church: supporting chaplaincy in further and higher education* (GS Misc 667, 2002) and its report to the General Synod *Aiming Higher: Higher Education and the Church's Mission* (GS 1567, 2005) are available from www.chpublishing.co.uk. Also available is *The Church of England's Higher Education Strategy: Implementing Aiming Higher*, which sets out the strategy for work for the five years beginning 2007. Further enquiries may be made to: The National Adviser for Higher Education, Education Division, Church House, London SW1P 3NZ   *Tel:* 020 7898 1513
Web:
> www.cofe.anglican.org/info/education/hefe

For a list of **Educational Chaplains** *see Crockford.*
For **Church Universities and Colleges of Higher Education** *see* page 222.

Chaplains in Further Education

Chaplaincy to Further Education Colleges began in the 1970s and has from the beginning been ecumenical in character and funding. The Churches' National Adviser in Further Education is based at Church House, but is jointly managed and funded, in equal partnership, by the Methodist Church and the Church of England, and also works with the National Council of the National Ecumenical Agency in Further Education.

In July 2006 General Synod debated a report, *Pushing Further: from Strategy to Action*, which committed the Church to a five-year strategy and programme of action designed to develop chaplaincies in all 400 colleges and to ensure provision for spiritual and moral development of all students.

Most of the current 200 Further Education chaplaincies are organized as ecumenical teams, with a mix of ordained and lay members contributing time on a part-time and often voluntary basis to support a regular presence and activities in their local college: increasingly these teams are becoming multi-faith in organization and character. About 12 colleges support a full-time chaplain (who may have an additional role as a teacher or counsellor) and a larger and growing number fund a half-time chaplain, who also serves in a local church.

DfES, the Department for Education and Skills, published in 2006 a White Paper on FE, recognizing students' faith background as important and endorsing multi-faith chaplaincy as a means of meeting these needs. The Learning and Skills Council, the funding body for further education colleges and other further education providers, has become increasingly supportive of Further Education chaplaincy. It has funded conferences and a research study and has now published a national handbook on Further Education Chaplaincy. There are also strong partnerships and regular contact with QIA, QCA, Learn Direct, and NIACE (the National Association for Adult and Continuing Education).

Further Education Chaplaincy is concerned with providing for the spiritual and moral welfare of all students, of any faith or none. This is a vital, though challenging mission among today's young people, 43 per cent of whom are educated in further education colleges. This is more than those (40 per cent) who are in schools after the age of 16, and it includes higher proportions of young people from deprived areas, and especially, from ethnic minority backgrounds.

The National Adviser is working to implement the action programme proposed in *Pushing Further*, designed both to increase the number of colleges which support a chaplaincy and to strengthen existing chaplaincies, especially those where a single local minister is working in isolation. All who are interested in supporting or learning more about this work may order *Pushing Further*, the recently published report, or contact:

The National Further Education Adviser, Education Division, Church House, London SW1P 3NZ   *Tel:* 020 7898 1517

Web: www.cofe.anglican.org/about/education/hefe.html

Chaplains in the Prison Service

The Prison Service Chaplaincy, in partnership with the wider Church, provides chaplains for all HM Prisons in England and Wales. It works within the Prison Service which is part of the National Offender Management Service (NOMS) in the Ministry of Justice. The responsibilities of the Chaplain General and his headquarters colleagues include the giving of advice to ministers and officials about policy decisions with a religious or ethical dimension. In addition, chaplains are recruited, trained, deployed and supported in their work of providing for the religious needs of prisoners, giving opportunities for worship, formation and instruction, and offering a pastoral ministry at times of crisis and opportunity. Chaplains are also involved in enabling the observance of all faith traditions. Their ministry is always available to staff.

All prisons have an Anglican, a Roman Catholic and a Free Church chaplain, with chaplains from many different faiths; the headquarters team includes senior representatives of all three denominations, and the Muslim Adviser. The Chaplain General has responsibility for all faith traditions.

The Bishop to Prisons
Rt Revd James Jones (*Bishop of Liverpool*), Bishop's Lodge, Woolton Park, Liverpool L25 6DT
Tel: 0151 421 0831

Chaplain General
Ven William Noblett, Prison Service Chaplaincy, Room 310, Abell House, John Islip St, London SW1P 4LH   *Tel:* 020 7217 8997
Fax: 020 7217 8980
email: william.noblett@noms.gsi.gov.uk

Anglican Adviser to HMPs
Canon Michael Kavanagh (*as above*)
Tel: 020 7217 8667
07807 509720 (Mobile)

Fax: 020 7217 8980
email: michael.kavanagh@noms.gsi.gov.uk
For a list of **Prison Chaplains** see *Crockford*.

Chaplaincy in the National Health Service

Since the inception of the NHS, full- and part-time chaplains have been salaried members of staff. Their work in the various hospitals and healthcare institutions throughout the country furthers the mission and ministry of the Church in a secular setting. It also carries forward the Dominical command to care for the sick and dying and those who look after them.

Healthcare chaplaincy is at the cutting edge of ministry, often touching people's lives at times of great crisis and pain. The development in research techniques, the human genome project, etc. throw up new ethical challenges for chaplains, alongside other healthcare professionals. There are 508 full-time chaplains in the UK, of whom 280 are Anglican, and 3,000 part-time, of whom 1,700 are Anglican, not to mention the numerous volunteers involved to different degrees in chaplaincy (some 10,000 according to a recent survey). Together with Roman Catholic, Free Church and, increasingly, other World Faith colleagues, chaplains also minister to the 1.3 million staff employed by the NHS.

The Mission and Public Affairs Division, through the Hospital Chaplaincies Council, provides the interface between the Church of England, the Department of Health and the NHS. Following a major review of the HCC in 2010, this work is now more closely integrated with MPA's work on public policy and ethics so that the role of chaplains in healthcare can be better supported. Increasingly, this support is offered in partnership with ecumenical and multi-faith structures and chaplain-led bodies.

MPA's role in chaplaincy includes support for bishops (through their advisers for Hospital Chaplaincy) and individual chief executives and NHS trusts for guidance, advice and support in all matters relating to hospital/healthcare chaplaincy. Pastoral care of chaplains is an important part of the work. In conjunction with the Free Churches Group and the Roman Catholic Bishops' Conference, support is also given for the continuing professional development of new as well as serving chaplains. Introductory training courses are delivered through Cardiff University and attract academic points upon completion. There is also an innovative foundation degree in chaplaincy at St Mary's University College, Twickenham.

Hospital/healthcare chaplaincy presents an opportunity to minister to patients, staff and relatives and to be a prophetic voice within a secular institution. Please remember this work and ministry in your prayers.

Further particulars may be obtained from Miss Mary Ingledew, HCC Administrator, Mission & Public Affairs, Church House, Great Smith Street, London SW1P 3AZ.

Tel: 020 7898 1895
email: mary.ingledew@c-of-e.org.u
Web: www.nhs-chaplaincy-spiritualcare.org.uk

Chaplains to the Police

Apart from a handful of chaplains who are paid full-time or half-time with the Police, the majority of chaplains are ordinary clergy, both men and women working in parishes or local churches and giving their time and energy as volunteers. Most, but not all, chaplains are from the mainstream Christian denominations, but there are a growing number of chaplains of other faiths and belief systems. The services of police chaplains are available to all police officers and staff, and are not dependent upon membership of a faith community. Chaplains can be contacted at local police stations, or privately by telephone or email.

The National Association of Chaplains to the Police advances and supports the work of chaplains to the police in the United Kingdom. Further information is available through the website at www.police-chaplains.org.uk
President Baroness Harris of Richmond
Vice-President Matthew Baggott (*Chief Constable, Police Service in Northern Ireland*)
National Coordinator Revd David Wilbraham (*Force Chaplain, Thames Valley Police*)
Deputy National Co-ordinator Revd Viv Baldwin (*Volunteer Chaplain, West Midlands Police*)
National Secretary Revd Viv Baldwin, 20 Castle Rd, Woodford Halse, Northants NN11 3RS
email: secretary@police-chaplains.org.uk

GENERAL

Church Universities and Colleges of Higher Education

Bishop Grosseteste University College, Newport, Lincoln LN1 3DY   *Tel:* 01522 527347
Principal Professor Muriel Robinson
Chaplain Revd Carolyn James   *Tel:* 01522 583607
    email: Carolyn.james@bishopg.ac.uk
Lay Chaplain Tracey Byrne   *Tel:* 01522 583604
    email: tracey.byrne@bishopg.ac.uk

Canterbury Christ Church University, North Holmes Rd, Canterbury, Kent CT1 1QU
    Tel: 01227 767700

Vice Chancellor Dr Robin Baker
Dean of Chapel Revd Dr Jeremy Law
    Tel: 01227 782747
    email: jeremy.law@canterbury.ac.uk
Chaplains
Revd David Stroud
    email: david.stroud@canterbury.ac.uk
Revd Stephen Bould
    email: boldini@btopenworld.com

University of Chester, Parkgate Rd, Chester CH1 4BJ   *Tel:* 01244 511000
Vice Chancellor Professor Tim Wheeler
Chester Campus
Chaplain: Revd Ian Arch   *Tel:* 01244 513183
    email: i.arch@chester.ac.uk
Associate Chaplain Revd Andrew Buchanan
    Tel: 01244 382217
    email: a.buchanan@chester. ac.uk
Chaplaincy Assistants
Mr David Cowie   *Tel:* 01244 513083
    email: d.cowie@chester.ac.uk
Mrs Alison Upton   *email:* a.upton@chester.ac.uk
Warrington Campus
Assistant Chaplain Fr Ian Delinger
    email: i.delinger@chester.ac.uk

University of Chichester, Bishop Otter Campus, College Lane, Chichester PO19 4PE
    Tel: 01243 816000
Vice Chancellor (Acting) Professor Clive Behagg
Chaplain Revd John Dane   *Tel:* 01243 816036
    email: chaplain@chi.ac.uk

University of Gloucestershire, Francis Close Hall, Swindon Rd, Cheltenham, Gloucestershire GL50 2QF   *Tel:* 01242 532700
Vice Chancellor and Principal Dr Paul Hartley
Chaplains Revd Tamsin Merchant
    Tel: 01242 532735
    tmerchant@glos.ac.uk

Liverpool Hope University, Hope Park, Liverpool L16 9JD   *Tel:* 0151 291 3000
Vice Chancellor Professor Gerald Pillay

Chaplain Revd Philip Anderson *Tel:* 0151 291 3545
    email: andersonp@hope.ac.uk

Liverpool Hope is an ecumenical institution, fully Catholic and fully Anglican.

University College of St Mark and St John, Derriford Rd, Plymouth PL6 8BH
    Tel: 01752 636700
Principal Dr Margaret Noble
    Tel: 01752 636700 Ext 6528
    email: principal@marjon.ac.uk
Chaplain Revd Paul Thompson   *Tel:* 01542 384384
    email: chaplaincy@marjon.ac.uk

University of Cumbria, Brampton Rd, Carlisle, Cumbria CA3 9AY
Interim Vice Chancellor Professor Graham Upton
Lancaster Campus, University of Cumbria, Lancaster LA1 3JD   *Tel:* 01524 384260
Chaplain Revd Michael Gisbourne
    email: michael.gisbourne@cumbria.ac.uk
Chaplain Assistant Steven Kay
    email: steven.kay2@cumbria.ac.uk
Ambleside Campus, Rydal Rd, Ambleside, Cumbria LA22 8BB   *Tel:* 01539 430268
Chaplain Revd Paul Woodcock
    email: paul.woodcock@cumbria.ac.uk
Carlisle Campus, Fusehill St, Carlisle CA1 2HH   *Tel:* 01228 616204
Chaplain Vacancy
Penrith Campus, Newton Rigg, Penrith, Cumbria CA11 0AH   *Tel:* 01768 867053
Chaplain Revd Paul Woodcock
    email: paul.woodcock@cumbria.ac.uk

Whitelands College, Roehampton University, Parkstead House, Holybourne Avenue, Roehampton, London SW15 4JD   *Tel:* 020 8392 3500
Vice Chancellor Professor Paul O'Prey
Principal Revd Dr Geoffrey Walker
Chaplain Revd Dr Daniel Eshun
    Tel: 020 8392 3516
    email: d.eshun@roehampton.ac.uk

University of Winchester, Sparkford Rd, Winchester SO22 4NR   *Tel:* 01962 841515
Vice Chancellor Professor Joy Carter
Chaplain Revd Phil Dykes   *Tel:* 01962 827063
    email: phil.dykes@winchester.ac.uk

York St John University, Lord Mayor's Walk, York YO3 7EX   *Tel:* 01904 624624
Vice Chancellor Professor David Fleming
Chaplain Vacancy

Church Urban Fund

Office Church House, Great Smith St, London SW1P 3AZ
Tel: 020 7898 1647
Fax: 020 7898 1601
email: enquiries@cuf.org.uk
Web: www.cuf.org.uk

Church Urban Fund (CUF) raises money to change lives in the poorest communities in England. Working with the Church of England, CUF's mission is to serve people of faith who put their faith into action in the community. Working in collaboration with dioceses and partner organizations, CUF funds faith-based social action in the most economically and socially deprived areas of England, but its support also extends to advocacy and practical advice, working to create sustainable, relevant and local solutions to deep-rooted issues. The projects CUF partners with work in a broad range of areas, including community development, support for vulnerable and marginalized groups, housing and homeless, and interfaith dialogue. CUF is also closely involved in wider debate, both inside and outside the Church, representing faith-based social action and enabling the voices of faith communities and practitioners to be heard at a national level. Our vision is to see all local churches and Christians in England empowered to work to end poverty in their communities.

Established in 1987 following the landmark report *Faith in the City*, CUF has supported nearly 5.500 projects across England. Our experience over the last 23 years has been that a combination of money and capacity building is the best way to sustainably support projects. This explains CUF's shift from an endowed fund towards an active, fundraising foundation model. We are now a development organisation that provides advice, money and guidance to local churches and activists who share our passion to see lives changed. This change marks an important stage in the charity's development and maturation.

CUF's work has been made possible by the continuing support of individuals, parishes and dioceses, which have contributed to the Fund's work through time, money and prayers.
For further information on the resources available please visit our website.

Clergy Appointments Adviser

The adviser has been appointed by the Archbishops of Canterbury and York to assist clergy, in England and from overseas, to find suitable new appointments and to assist patrons and others responsible for making appointments to find suitable candidates. The adviser has a responsibility for beneficed and unbeneficed clergy, together with stipendiary deacons and accredited lay workers. A list of vacancies for incumbencies, team posts, assistant curates and specialized ministries is available on-line. For further information please contact: Revd John Lee, Clergy Appointments Adviser, The Wash House, Lambeth Palace, London SE1 7JU
Tel: 020 7898 1898
Fax: 020 7898 1899
email: admin.caa@c-of-e.org.uk
Web: www.cofe.anglican.org/info/caa

Conference Centres and Retreat Houses

CONFERENCE CENTRES

ASHBURNHAM PLACE	Ashburnham Place, Battle, E Sussex TN33 9NF (*Administrator:* Revd Andrew Wooding-Jones) *Tel:* 01424 892244 *Fax:* 01424 894200 *email:* bookings@ashburnham.org.uk *Web:* www.ashburnham.org.uk
BELSEY BRIDGE CONFERENCE CENTRE	Ditchingham, Bungay, Suffolk NR35 2DZ (*Manager:* Erica Strange) *Tel:* 01986 892133 *Fax:* 01986 895765 *email:* belseybridge@cct.org.uk
HAYES CONFERENCE CENTRE	Hayes Conference Centre, Swanwick, Derbyshire DE55 1AU (*Manager:* Mr Peter Anderson) *Tel:* 01773 526000 *Fax:* 01773 540841 *email:* office@cct.org.uk *Web:* www.cct.org.uk

HIGH LEIGH CONFERENCE CENTRE	High Leigh Conference Centre, Lord St, Hoddesdon, Herts EN11 8SG (*Manager:* Mr Ian Andrews) *Tel:* 01992 463016 *Fax:* 01992 446594 *email:* highleigh@cct.org.uk *Web:* www.cct.org.uk
LEE ABBEY	Lee Abbey Fellowship, Lynton, Devon EX35 6JJ (*Warden:* Chris Edmondson) *Tel:* 0800 389 1189 *Fax:* 01598 752619 *email:* relax@leeabbey.org.uk *Web:* www.leeabbey.org.uk

RETREAT HOUSES

The following is a list of diocesan conference centres and retreat houses including some run by religious communities. For details of accommodation for individual retreats *see* Religious Communities page 244, or contact the Retreat Association, Kerridge House, 42 Woodside Close, Amersham, Bucks HP6 5EF *Tel:* 01494 433004 *email:* info@retreats.org.uk, *Web:* www.retreats.org.uk

BATH AND WELLS	Abbey House, Chilkwell St, Glastonbury, Som. BA6 8DH (*Retreat House*) (*The Warden*) *Tel:* 01458 831112
BLACKBURN	Whalley Abbey, Whalley, Clitheroe, Lancs. BB7 9SS (*Warden*: Canon Andrew Sage) *Tel:* 01254 828400 *Fax:* 01254 825519
BRADFORD	Parcevall Hall, Appletreewick, Skipton, N Yorks. BD23 6DG (*Warden:* Beverley Seward) *Tel:* 01756 720213 *Fax:* 01756 720656
CARLISLE	Carlisle Diocesan Conference and Retreat Centre, Rydal Hall, Ambleside, Cumbria LA22 9LX (*General Manager:* Jonathan Green) *Tel:* 01539 432050 *Fax:* 01539 434887 *email:* bookings@rydalhall.org
CHELMSFORD	Diocesan House of Retreat, Pleshey, Chelmsford, Essex CM3 1HA (*Warden:* Revd Sheila Coughtrey) *Tel:* 01245 237251
CHESTER	Chester Diocesan Conference Centre, Foxhill, Tarvin Road, Frodsham, Cheshire WA6 6XB (*Wardens:* Mr & Mrs Ian Cameron) *Tel:* 01928 733777 *Fax:* 01928 731422 *email:* foxhillwarden@aol.com *Web:* foxhillconferences. co.uk
CHICHESTER	Monastery of the Holy Trinity, Crawley Down, Crawley, W Sussex RH10 4LH *Tel:* 01342 712074 St Margaret's Convent, Hooke Hall, 250 High St, Uckfield, East Sussex TN22 1EN *Tel:* 01825 766808
COVENTRY	Offa House (Coventry Diocesan Retreat House), Off-church, Leamington Spa, War. CV33 9AS (*Warden*: Ruth Godber) *Tel:* 01926 423309
DERBY	Morley Retreat and Conference House, Church Lane, Morley, Derby DE7 6DE *Tel:* 01332 831293
DURHAM	*See* entry for NEWCASTLE
ELY	Bishop Woodford House, Barton Road, Ely, Cambs. CB7 4DX (*Warden*: Peggie Banks) *Tel:* 01353 663039

GLOUCESTER	Glenfall House, Mill Lane, Charlton Kings, Cheltenham, Glos. GL54 4EP (*Warden:* Liz Palin) *Tel:* 01242 583654 *Fax:* 01242 251314
GUILDFORD	St Columba's House, Maybury Hill, Woking, Surrey GU22 8AB (*Director:* Fr Owen Murphy) *Tel:* 01483 766498
	House of Bethany, 7 Nelson Rd, Southsea, Hants. PO5 2AR *Tel:* 023 9283 3498
HEREFORD	Ludlow Conference Centre, Lower Galdeford, Ludlow, Shropshire SY8 1RZ *Tel:* 01584 873882 *Fax:* 01584 877945 *email:* info@theludlowconferencecentre.co.uk
LEICESTER	Launde Abbey, East Norton, Leicestershire LE7 9XB (*Warden*: Revd Tim Blewett) *Tel:* 01572 717254 *Fax:* 01572 717454 *email:* laundeabbey@leicester.anglican.org *Web:* www.launde.org.uk
LICHFIELD	Lichfield Diocesan Retreat and Conference Centre, Shallowford House, Shallowford, Stone, Staffs. ST15 0NZ (*Warden:* Liz Pearson) *Tel:* 01785 760233 *Fax:* 01785 760390
LONDON	The Royal Foundation of Saint Katharine, 2 Butcher Row, London E14 8DS (*Master:* Preb David Paton) *Tel:* 0845 4090135 *Fax:* 020 7702 7603 *email:* info@rfsk.org.uk
NEWCASTLE/DURHAM	Shepherd's Dene, Riding Mill, Northumberland NE44 6AF *Tel:* 01434 682212
NORWICH	Horstead Centre, Norwich NR12 7EP (*Manager:* Mark Heybourne) *Tel:* 01603 737215 (*Office*); 01603 737674 (*Guests*)
	All Hallows Convent, Ditchingham, Bungay NR35 2DT *Tel:* 01986 892840
OXFORD	St Mary's Convent, Wantage OX12 9DJ *Tel:* 01235 763141 / 01235 774075
SALISBURY	Sarum College, 19 The Close, Salisbury SP1 2EE *Tel:* 01722 424800 *Fax:* 01722 338508 *email:* hospitality@sarum.ac.uk
	Society of St Francis, The Friary, Hilfield, Dorchester DT2 7BE *Tel:* 01300 342313
	St Denys Retreat Centre, Ivy House, 2 Church St, Warminster BA12 8PG *Tel:* 01985 214824
SHEFFIELD	Whirlow Grange Conference Centre, Ecclesall Road South, Sheffield, S Yorks. S11 9PZ (*General Manager:* Graham Holland) *Tel:* 0114 236 3173 (*Office*); 236 1183 (*Visitors*) *email:* manager@whirlowgrange.co.uk
SOUTHWARK	Wychcroft, Bletchingley, Redhill, Surrey RH1 4NE *Tel:* 01883 743041

GENERAL

	The Community of Sisters of the Church, St Michael's Convent, 56 Ham Common, Richmond TW10 7JH *Tel:* 020 8940 8711/8948 2502
SOUTHWELL	Sacrista Prebend Retreat House, 4 Westgate, Southwell, Notts NG25 0JH *Tel:* 01636 816 833
TRURO	Epiphany House, Kenwyn, Church Rd, Truro, Cornwall TR1 3DR *Tel:* 01872 272249
WAKEFIELD	Community of the Resurrection, Mirfield, W Yorks. WF14 0BN *Tel:* 01924 494318 *Fax:* 01924 490489 *email:* community@mirfield.org.uk
	Community of St Peter, Horbury, W Yorks. WF4 6BB *Tel:* 01924 272181 *Fax:* 01924 261225
WINCHESTER	Old Alresford Place, Winchester Retreat and Conference Centre, Old Alresford, Hants. SO24 9DH (*Manager:* Isobel Chapman) *Tel:* 01962 732518 *Fax:* 01962 737358 *email:* enquiries@oldalresfordplace.co.uk
	Alton Abbey, King's Hill, Beech, Alton, Hants. GU34 4AP (*Abbot:* Rt Revd Dom Giles Hill osb) *Tel:* 01420 562145/563575
WORCESTER	Holland House, Cropthorne, nr Pershore, Worcs. WR10 3NB (*Warden:* Ian Spenser) *Tel:* 01386 860330 *email:* laycentre@hollandhouse.org
YORK	York Diocesan Retreat and Conference Centre, Wydale Hall, Brompton-by-Sawdon, Scarborough, N Yorks. YO13 9DG (*The Warden*) *Tel:* 01723 859270 *Fax:* 01723 859702 *email:* admin@wydale.org *Web:* www.wyedale.org
	St Oswald's Pastoral Centre, Woodlands Drive, Sleights, Whitby, N Yorks. YO21 1RY *Tel:* 01947 810496
	Sneaton Castle Centre, Whitby, N Yorks. YO21 3QN (*Centre Manager:* Linda Antill) *Tel:* 01947 600051 *Fax:* 01947 603490 *email:* sneaton@globalnet.co.uk *Web:* www.sneatoncastle.co.uk

Evangelism

The Mission and Public Affairs Division (MPA) seeks to help the Church of England to do its evangelism appropriately, courteously and clearly.

The MPA Council's report *Mission-shaped Church* has had substantial impact on the Church of England, with over 23,000 copies sold to date. The report was discussed at General Synod in February 2004 and was warmly commended to the Church; Synod is due to debate the report again in 2010. A number of follow-up volumes

have also been produced by Church House Publishing, covering practical subjects such as spirituality, the rural church, children and youth as well as exploring in depth the theological questions raised by today's missional initiatives.

Mission-shaped Church encourages dioceses to build an enabling framework for new ways of being church, alongside well-loved and traditional forms. The Dioceses, Pastoral and Mission Measure 2007 offers bishops the opportunity to make clear legal provision for new mission initiatives within the life of their dioceses. The House of Bishops has approved guidelines to identify, train and support pioneer ministers, both lay and ordained. Working alongside its partners MPA offers resource and support to dioceses as they make sense of this enabling framework in their own contexts.

Within MPA Dr Rachel Jordan is responsible for this area. Her work is done in close alliance with a number of partner organizations, in particular Fresh Expressions, the Archbishops' initiative presently led by the Rt Revd Graham Cray. MPA staff also work in partnership with colleagues in other denominations, the ACC, the Mission Agencies, Churches Together in England and other evangelistic agencies in this country.

The Archbishop of Canterbury's vision is of a mixed economy church, developing a spectrum of inherited and emerging forms of church and deploying these where each is most appropriate. The Mission and Evangelism desk works closely with Diocesan Missioners and Advisers on Evangelism to implement this vision and to identify and share good practice across the Church.

Fresh Expressions

Changing Church for Changing World

Fresh Expressions encourages new forms of church for a fast-changing world, working with Christians from a variety of denominations and traditions. It was initiated by the Archbishops of Canterbury and York with the Methodist Council and now includes the United Reformed Church. The initiative has resulted in hundreds of new congregations being formed alongside more traditional churches.
Fresh Expressions, Athena Drive, Tachbrook Park, Warwick CV34 6RQ   *Tel:* 03003 650563

email: contact@freshexpressions.org.uk
Web: www.freshexpressions.org.uk
Archbishops' Missioner and Team Leader of the Fresh Expressions Team Rt Revd Graham Cray, Rectory, Church Rd, Harrietsham, Kent ME17 1AP
Tel: 01622 851170
email: graham.cray@frashexpressions.org.uk

Names and contact details for other team members can be found on the website.

Faculty Office and Special Marriage Licences

The Faculty Office of the Archbishop of Canterbury, otherwise known as The Court of Faculties, exercises on behalf of the Archbishop the dispensing powers that he has by virtue of the Ecclesiastical Licences Act of 1533. These comprise the appointment of Notaries Public, the granting of degrees, and the granting of marriage licences. The right to grant a Special Licence for marriage at any convenient time or place in England or Wales is unique to the Archbishop, and this jurisdiction is sparingly exercised and good cause must always be shown why a more normal preliminary to Anglican marriage cannot be used. Marriage with any other preliminary must be solemnized between 8.00 a.m. and 6.00 p.m., and although a Special Licence could omit this requirement, that will only in practice be done in a case of serious illness.

The more common need for a Special Licence is the parties' desire to marry in a building not normally authorized for Anglican marriage, or in a parish where they do not have a legal qualification. Even in the last case cause must be shown, normally in the form of a real connection with the parish or church in question; the *Special Licence procedure is not intended to enable parties to choose a church building on aesthetic or sentimental grounds.*

More detailed guidance on the grounds that may be considered sufficient for the granting of a Special Licence may always be sought from the Faculty Office by letter or telephone.

Special arrangements may sometimes be made in a genuine emergency. In such cases the clergy or the couple concerned should first contact the Diocesan Registrar, archdeacon, or diocesan or area bishop. If unable to resolve the difficulty himself he will make arrangements for the Faculty Office to be approached.

Orders made by the Master of the Faculties prescribe from time to time fees which are to be charged for applications for Special Licences. The fee is currently £220.00.

The Faculty Office is open to telephone and personal callers between 10.00 a.m. and 4.00 p.m. Monday to Friday, except on certain days around Easter and Christmas.

Office 1 The Sanctuary, Westminster, London SW1P 3JT   *Tel:* 020 7222 5381 Ext 7162
Fax: 020 7222 7502
email: faculty.office@1Thesanctuary.com
Web: www.facultyoffice.org.uk

GENERAL

Hospice Movement

The word 'Hospice' was first used from the fourth century onwards when Christian orders welcomed travellers, the sick and those in need. It was first applied to the care of dying patients by Mme Jeanne Garnier who founded the Dames de Calvaire in Lyon, France in 1842. The modern hospice movement, however, with its twin emphases on medical and psychosocial intervention, dates from the founding of St Christopher's Hospice by Dame Cicely Saunders in 1967. Since 1967, 'hospice' has become a worldwide philosophy adapting to the needs of different cultures and settings – hospital, hospice and community – and is established in six continents.

Hospice and palliative care is the active, total care of patients whose disease no longer responds to curative treatment, and for whom the goal must be the best quality of life for them and their families. Palliative medicine is now a distinct medical speciality in the UK. It focuses on controlling pain and other symptoms, easing suffering and enhancing the life that remains. It integrates the psychological and spiritual aspects of care, to enable patients to live out their lives with dignity. It also offers support to families, both during the patient's illness and their bereavement. It offers a unique combination of care in hospices and at home.

Hospice and palliative care services mostly help people with cancer although increasingly patients with other life-threatening illnesses may also be supported; this includes HIV/AIDS, motor neurone disease, heart failure, kidney disease. Hospice and palliative care is free of charge to the patient regardless of whether it is provided by an independent charitable hospice, Macmillan Service, Marie Curie Cancer Care, Sue Ryder Palliative Care Centre or by an NHS service. The criteria for admission are based on medical, social and emotional need. Referral to a hospice or palliative care service (including inpatient and home care nursing services) is normally arranged by the patient's own GP or hospital doctor. Further information about hospice care in the UK and overseas, including the facility to find your local hospice and resources for health professionals, is available from The Hospice Information Service (*see below*). This is a partnership between Help the Hospices and St Christopher's Hospice and provides an enquiry service for the public and professionals. Publications include UK and International Directories of Hospice and Palliative Care.

Tel: 020 7520 8222
email: info@helpthehospices.org.uk
Web: www.helpthehospices.org.uk

Children's Hospices UK

Children's Hospices UK is the national charity that gives voice and support to all children's hospice services. We help children's hospices to keep improving the care and support they provide to children and young people who are not expected to reach adulthood and their families. We raise awareness of the range of support available both within hospices and at home. We also raise funds to help children's hospices to keep providing a free service. We campaign and lobby on behalf of children's hospices, ensuring their voice is heard by government.

Children's Hospice Services
It's every parent's worst nightmare to be told their child will die before them. But for an estimated 25,000 families across the UK, this is a reality. Some of these children will die when they're very young; others will deteriorate slowly over a number of years. In most cases, full-time care falls to the parents – 24 hours a day, seven days a week. The families affected are under huge emotional, physical and financial strain.

Children's hospice services help children and their families in these situations to deal with the emotional and physical challenges they face, helping them to make the most of life. They welcome the whole family for a break in friendly, homely surroundings and provide practical help in people's own homes. They offer a diverse range of services including specialist care, 24-hour telephone support, advice and information, and bereavement support for all family members. For more information please contact:

Children's Hospices UK, Fourth Floor, Bridge House, 48–52 Baldwin St, Bristol BS1 1QB

Tel: 0117 989 7820
Fax: 0117 929 1999
email: info@childhospice.org.uk
Web: www.childhospice.org.uk

For details of the **Association of Hospice and Palliative Care Chaplains** *see* page 269.

Marriage: Legal Aspects

The comprehensive statement of the law and information on related matters published by the Faculty Office of the Archbishop of Canterbury, *Anglican Marriage in England and Wales – A Guide to the Law for Clergy*, has recently been revised and updated and copies were sent to incumbents and licensed clergy of the Church of England and the Church in Wales in 2010. Further copies are available by post, price £7.50, from: The Faculty Office, 1 The Sanctuary, Westminster, London SW1P 3JT (cheques are to be made payable to 'The Faculty Office').

For details of **Special Marriage Licences** *see* the entry for the Faculty Office, page 227.

Press

CHURCH TIMES

Established 1863. The best-selling, award-winning independent weekly newspaper and website, reporting on the worldwide Christian Church and Anglicanism in particular. As well as its wide news coverage, the paper contains a full comment section on current affairs, general features, reviews of books, music and arts, a comprehensive gazette, and the biggest selection of church job advertisements. Goes to press on Wednesday; published on Friday; advertisements to be placed on Friday for the following week; price £1.40; subscription £65.

Editor Mr Paul Handley. *Office* 13–17 Long Lane, London EC1A 9PN *Tel:* 020 7776 1060
Fax: 020 7776 1086/1017
Subscriptions: *Tel:* 01603 612914
email: editor@churchtimes.co.uk
Web: www.churchtimes.co.uk

CHURCH OF ENGLAND NEWSPAPER

A weekly newspaper which aims to provide a full, objective and lively coverage of Christian news from Britain and overseas. Contents include general features, book, music, film and art reviews, the latest clergy appointments and an ongoing focus on how the Church can improve its mission. Goes to press on Tuesday; published Friday; deadline for advertisements 2.00 pm Monday; price £1.25 (annual subscription UK £65, Eur £90, Rest of world £110; Online £25; other rates on application). *Editor* C. M. Blakely. *Office* The Church of England Newspaper, 14 Great College St, London SW1P 3RX

Tel: 020 7878 1001
Fax: 020 7878 1031
email: cen@churchnewspaper.com
Web: www.churchnewspaper.com

ENGLISH CHURCHMAN

Church of England newspaper (established 1843), incorporating *St James's Chronicle* 1761. Protestant and evangelical. News, various features, book reviews, correspondence and church calendar. Published fortnightly, Fridays, price 40p. *Editor* Revd Peter Ratcliff.

Tel: 020 8417 0875
email: englishchurchman@aol.com

Services Authorized and Commended

Public worship in the Church of England is a matter governed by law.

Canon B 2 provides that the General Synod may approve forms of service with or without time limit. Services thus approved are alternative to those of *The Book of Common Prayer*. The power given to General Synod under Canon B 2 derives from the Worship and Doctrine Measure 1974.

Canon B 4 provides that the convocations, the archbishops in their provinces or the bishops in their dioceses may approve forms of service for use on occasions for which *The Book of Common Prayer* or *Authorized Alternative Services* do not provide.

Canon B 5 (paragraph 2) allows discretion to any minister where no other provision has been made under Canons B 1 or B 4, to use other forms of service that are considered suitable. If questions are raised as to whether such forms of service are suitable the decision rests with the bishop.

Authorized Alternative Services are those approved by the General Synod under Canon B 1 (for fuller details *see* below).

Commended Services are those that the bishops corporately have judged to be 'suitable' either for approval under Canon B 4 or for use in the contexts envisaged in Canon B 5 (for fuller details *see* page 231).

AUTHORIZED SERVICES ALTERNATIVE TO THE BOOK OF COMMON PRAYER
As at 1 January 2011

Published in *Common Worship: Services and Prayers for the Church of England* **and** *Common Worship: Collects and Post Communions*

1 Calendar
2 A Service of the Word
3 Schedule of permitted variations to *The Book of Common Prayer* Orders for Morning and Evening Prayer where these occur in *Common Worship*
4 Prayers for Various Occasions
5 The Litany
6 Authorized Forms of Confession and Absolution
7 Creeds and Authorized Affirmations of Faith
8 The Lord's Prayer
9 The Order for the Celebration of Holy Communion also called The Eucharist and The Lord's Supper
10 Collects and Post Communions
11 Rules for Regulating Authorized Forms of Service
12 The Lectionary
13 Opening Canticles at Morning and Evening Prayer; Gospel Canticles; Other Canticles; A Song of Praise (Epiphany); Te Deum Laudamus

Published in *Common Worship: Christian Initiation*
14 Holy Baptism
15 Emergency Baptism
16 Holy Baptism and Confirmation
17 Seasonal Provisions and Supplementary Texts
18 Affirmation of Baptismal Faith
19 Reception into the Communion of the Church of England

Published in *Common Worship: Pastoral Services*
20 Wholeness and Healing
21 The Marriage Service with prayers and other resources
22 Thanksgiving for the Gift of a Child
23 The Funeral Service with prayers and other resources
24 Series One Solemnization of Matrimony
25 Series One Burial Services

Published in *Common Worship: Ordination Services*
26 Ordination Services

Published separately
27 Public Worship with Communion by Extension (*NB explicit permission must be obtained from the bishop for the use of this rite.*)

28   Weekday Lectionary
29   An Order of Marriage for Christians from Different Churches

The above are all authorized by the General Synod for use until further resolution of the Synod.

Form of Service authorized by the Archbishops of Canterbury and York without time limit for use in their respective Provinces

A Service for Remembrance Sunday (included in *Common Worship: Times and Seasons – see* below)

COMMENDED SERVICES AND RESOURCES
As at 1 January 2011

Published in *Common Worship: Services and Prayers for the Church of England*
1   Introduction to Morning and Evening Prayer on Sunday
2   Introduction to Holy Baptism
3   Short Prefaces for the Sundays before Lent and after Trinity
4   Additional Canticles

Published in the President's Edition of *Common Worship*
5   Additional Blessings

Published in *Common Worship: Christian Initiation*
6   Rites Supporting Disciples on the Way of Christ
7   Admission of the Baptized to Communion
8   Celebration after an Initiation Service outside the Parish
9   Thanksgiving for Holy Baptism
10   A Corporate Service of Penitence
11   The Reconciliation of a Penitent

Published in *Common Worship: Pastoral Services*
12   An Order for Prayer and Dedication after a Civil Marriage
13   Thanksgiving for Marriage
14   Ministry at the Time of Death
15   Receiving the Coffin at Church before the Funeral
16   Funeral of a Child: Outline Orders and Resources
17   At Home after the Funeral
18   Memorial Services: Outline Orders and Sample Services
19   Prayers for Use with the Dying and at Funeral and Memorial Services
20   Canticles for Marriages, Funerals and Memorial Services

Published separately
21   Material contained in *New Patterns for Worship*
22   Material contained in *Common Worship: Times and Seasons*
23   Material contained in *Common Worship: Times and Seasons – President's Edition for Holy Communion*
24   Material contained in *Common Worship: Festivals*
25   *Common Worship: The Admission and Licensing of Readers*

SERVICES WHICH COMPLY WITH THE PROVISIONS OF A SERVICE OF THE WORD
(see Authorized Services, no. 2)
As at 1 January 2011

Published in *Common Worship: Services and Prayers for the Church of England*
1   An Order for Morning Prayer on Sunday
2   An Order for Evening Prayer on Sunday
3   An Order for Night Prayer (Compline)
4   An Order for Night Prayer (Compline) in Traditional Language

Published separately
5   Sample services contained in *New Patterns for Worship*
6   Services contained in *Common Worship: Daily Prayer*

PUBLICATIONS

The material is published in the following volumes:
•   *Common Worship: Services and Prayers for the Church of England*

- *Common Worship: President's Edition*
- *Common Worship: Collects and Post Communions*
- *Common Worship: Christian Initiation*
- *Common Worship: Pastoral Services*
- *Common Worship: Daily Prayer*
- *Common Worship: Times and Seasons*
- *Common Worship: Festivals*
- *Common Worship: Ordination Services (Study Edition)*
- *Common Worship: Times and Seasons – President's Edition for Holy Communion*
- *New Patterns for Worship*
- *Public Worship with Communion by Extension*
- *Common Worship: The Admission and Licensing of Readers*
- *An Order of Marriage for Christians from Different Churches*
- annual editions of the Common Worship Lectionary

It may also be found in the Common Worship area of the Church of England web site   at www.cofe.anglican.org/worship/liturgy/commonworship/

VERSIONS OF THE BIBLE AND OF THE PSALMS

The following may be used in Book of Common Prayer services (with the permission of the Parochial Church Council) instead of the Authorized Version of the Bible and the Psalter in *The Book of Common Prayer:*

Revised Version
Revised Standard Version
New English Bible
The Revised Psalter
The Liturgical Psalter (The Psalms
   in a new translation for worship)

Jerusalem Bible
Good News Bible
(Today's English Version)

Any version of the Bible or Psalter not prohibited by lawful authority may be used with Alternative Services and Commended Services.

A leaflet entitled *A Brief Guide to Liturgical Copyright* deals with the procedures for local reproduction. It provides guidance on preparing local texts and information about copyright requirements. The third edition (2000) is available at £1.50 from Church House Publishing and in the *Common Worship* area of the Church of England web site   at www.cofe.anglican.org/worship/liturgy/commonworship/copyright/

TV and Radio

BBC LOCAL RADIO
There are thirty-nine BBC local radio stations in counties and cities throughout England. Each station is responsible for its own religious broadcasting and some have religious advisory panels. Religious programmes are often presented and produced by local clergy and lay people who observe the editorial policy of the BBC. The BBC's Local Radio (and Local Online) coverage of religion is coordinated by the Editor for English Regions Religion, Canon Ashley Peatfield, *Tel:* 0113 224 7304, *email:* ashley.peatfield @bbc.co.uk. For details of stations, see *Web:* www.bbc.co.uk/england/radio/.

BBC RELIGION AND ETHICS DEPARTMENT
Produces a wide variety of religious broadcasts for transmission on BBC television, network radio and the World Service, including the Radio 4 'Thought for the Day' and Radio 2 'Pause for

Thought' slots. It also manages an extensive website at www.bbc.co.uk/religion. All BBC local radio stations produce their own religious programmes to cater for the particular needs of faith communities within their catchment areas. *Head of Religion and Ethics and Commissioning Editor for Religion TV* Aaqil Ahmed, BBC, PO Box 27, Oxford Rd, Manchester M60 1SJ
Executive Editor and Head of Religion Radio Christine Morgan, BBC, PO Box 27, Oxford Rd, Manchester M60 1SJ

STANDING CONFERENCE ON RELIGION AND BELIEF
The Standing Conference on Religion and Belief meets biannually to provide a forum for the BBC and its audience to discuss issues of religion and belief. Its membership is drawn from the major Christian traditions, along with other world faiths and humanist groups represented in the United Kingdom. The Standing Conference is

chaired by the Rt Revd Graham James, Bishop of Norwich, and the secretariat is provided by the Church and Media Network. Contact Andrew Graystone
Tel: 07772 710090
email: andrew.graystone1@btinternet.com

CHURCH AND MEDIA NETWORK

The Church and Media Network is an ecumenical body with charitable status. It was formed in 2009, succeeding the Churches' Media Council. The Network aims to build bridges of understanding between the Christian community and the media. The Church and Media Network also runs *theMediaNet*, which encourages vocations to the media and also offers support, encouragement and discipleship to Christians working in the media. *Chair* Dr Elaine Storkey *Director* Mr Andrew Graystone
Tel: 0845 6520027
07772 710090 (Mobile)
email: info@churchandmedia.net
Web: www.churchandmedia.net *or*
www.themedianet.org

FOUNDATION FOR CHRISTIAN COMMUNICATION LTD (CTVC)

Major television, radio and new media production company founded by the British film pioneer, Lord Rank, which specializes in making documentaries on religious, ethical and moral issues. CTVC have produced programmes for Channel 4 and ITV as well as radio programmes for BBC Radio 4 and The World Service. Some of Britain's leading presenters, such as Rageh Omaar, John McCarthy and Robert Beckford have presented several of CTVC's programmes. In the last few years CTVC has been awarded the prestigious religious broadcasting award – The Sandford St Martin. CTVC also hosts TrueTube – an interactive website which provides young people with an outlet to express their views on issues that matter to them, from teen crime to gangs to personal relationships, as well as hosting films young people have created. The site has been presented with a Jerusalem Award for best IPTV content. CTVC has one of the largest film and tape archive of any independent production company in Britain, covering the hundreds of films and programmes we have made over the past 80 years. *Chief Executive Officer* Mr Peter Weil, CTVC, 9–10 Copper Row, Tower Bridge Piazza, London SE1 2LH
Tel: 020 7940 8480
Fax: 020 7940 8490
email: info@ctvc.co.uk
Web: www.ctvc.co.uk and www.truetube.co.uk

OFFICE OF COMMUNICATIONS (Ofcom)

Ofcom is the independent regulator and competition authority for the UK communications industries, with responsibilities across television, radio, telecommunications and wireless communications services. *Chairman* Colette Bowe *Deputy Chairman* Philip Graf CBE *Chief Executive* Ed Richards Ofcom, Riverside House, 2a Southwark Bridge Rd, London SE1 9HA.
Tel: 0300 123 3000
Textphone: 0300 123 2024
Fax: 020 7981 3333
email: contact@ofcom.org.uk
Web: www.ofcom.org.uk

INDEPENDENT CHRISTIAN BROADCASTERS

A range of independent Christian broadcasters operate in the UK, including Premier Radio/Premier TV and United Christian Broadcasting.
Web: www.premier.org.uk
www.ucb.co.uk

SANDFORD ST MARTIN (CHURCH OF ENGLAND) TRUST

The Trust was established in 1978. From the beginning its purpose was to recognize and promote excellence in religious broadcasting, and to encourage Christian involvement in television and radio at both national and local levels. Founded through the generosity and vision of a distinguished Anglican layman, the late Sir David Wills, its origins were Anglican, but it operates ecumenically, seeking to promote high-quality programmes inspired by any of the major world religions as well as all Christian traditions. The Trust's principal activity is making annual awards for outstanding achievement in religious broadcasting. For the first 25 years of its existence awards were made at Lambeth Palace for radio and for television programmes in alternate years. In 1997 the Trust inaugurated a Religious Education award for an outstanding television programme, video or CD-rom in the field of religious education, and further awards were made in 1999, 2001 and 2003. Since 2003 the awards for television and radio programmes have been made annually, and this has allowed awards ceremonies to be held both at Lambeth Palace in London and also outside London, an innovation originally made for the Religious Education awards. Hence the 2003 television awards were made in Manchester, the 2004 radio awards in Glasgow, and the 2005 television awards in Bristol. 2006 saw the Trust sponsoring the first Readers of the Radio Times Award, which was presented at the annual television awards ceremony at Lambeth Palace. In 2007 the television awards were hosted by UTV in Belfast, with radio at Lambeth. In 2009, for the first time, the Trust hosted a single Awards Ceremony which combined awards for both radio and television programmes. In 2010 a joint awards ceremony was again held at Lambeth Palace and chaired by the Trust's Chairman, the Bishop of Croydon, the Rt Revd Nick Baines. The fifth RadioTimes Readers' Award was presented by the editor of Radio Times, Ben Preston, for programme one in

GENERAL

the series *A History of Christianity*, presented by Prof. Diarmaid MacCulloch (BBC Religion and Ethics for BBC 4). A personal award for services to religious broadcasting was made to Rabbi Dr Lionel Blue who among other programmes is best known for his contribution to *Thought for the Day* for over thirty years. The premier award for radio was won by *Two Sisters, Two Faiths,* a Ladbrook Production for BBC Radio 4; while *The Bible: A History; Episode 1 – Creation* (A Pioneer Production for Channel 4) won the premier award for television. *Chairman* Rt Revd Nicholas Baines, Bishop of Croydon. *Hon Secretary* Mr David Craig, Church House, Great Smith St, London SW1P 3AZ

> *Tel:* 020 7898 1796
> *Fax:* 020 7898 1797
> *email:* SandfordSMT@c-of-e.org.uk
> *Web:* www.sandfordawards.org.uk

WORLD ASSOCIATION FOR CHRISTIAN COMMUNICATION (WACC)

WACC is an organization of corporate and personal members who wish to give high priority to Christian values in the world's communication and development needs. It is not a council or federation of churches. The majority of members are communication professionals from all walks of life. Others include partners in different communication activities, and representatives of churches and agencies. It funds communication activities that reflect regional interests, and encourages ecumenical unity among communicators. As a professional organization, WACC serves the wider ecumenical movement by offering guidance on communication policies, interpreting developments in communications worldwide, discussing the consequences that such developments have for churches and communities everywhere but especially in the Third World, and assisting the training of Christian communicators. WACC publishes *Media Action*, an on-line newsletter; *Media Development*, a quarterly journal; *Media and Gender Monitor*, a bi-annual bulletin; and occasional books, monographs and brochures. It has 1500 members affiliates in 120 countries. UK members and affiliates include the Anglican Communion Office, Council for World Mission, Feed the Minds, and SPCK. *Gen Secretary* Revd Randy Naylor, 71 Lambeth Walk, London SE11 6DX

> *Tel:* 020 7735 2877
> *Fax:* 020 7735 2877
> *email:* info@waccglobal.org
> *Web:* www.waccglobal.org

Theological Colleges and Regional Courses

THEOLOGICAL COLLEGES

Address and Telephone Number	Diocese	Principal or Warden
Cranmer Hall (St John's College), Durham DH1 3RJ *Tel:* 0191 334 3866 *Fax:* 0191 334 3501 *email:* sj-cranmer-hall@durham.ac.uk	Durham	Revd Canon Anne Dyer
College of the Resurrection, Mirfield, W Yorks. WF14 0BW *Tel:* 01924 490441 *Fax:* 01924 492738 *email:* hscott@mirfield.org.uk	Wakefield	Revd Dr Joseph Kennedy
Oak Hill Theological College, Chase Side, Southgate, London N14 4PS *Tel:* 020 8449 0467 *Fax:* 020 8441 5996 *email:* mailbox@oakhill.ac.uk	London	Revd Dr Michael Ovey
Queen's Foundation for Ecumenical Theological Education, incorporating The Queen's College, Somerset Rd, Edgbaston, Birmingham B15 2QH (Ecumenical) *Tel:* 0121 454 1527 *Fax:* 0121 454 8171 *email:* enquire@ queens.ac.uk	Birmingham	Revd Dr David Hewlett
Ridley Hall, Cambridge CB3 9HG *Tel:* 01223 741080 *Fax:* 01223 741081 *email:* ridley-pa@lists.cam.ac.uk	Ely	Revd Andrew Norman
Ripon College, Cuddesdon, Oxford OX44 9EX *Tel:* 01865 874404 *Fax:* 01865 875431 *email:* enquiries@ripon-cuddesdon.ac.uk	Oxford	Revd Canon Dr Martyn Percy
St John's College, Chilwell Lane, Bramcote, Nottingham NG9 3DS *Tel:* 0115 925 1114 *Fax:* 0115 943 6438 *email:* principal@stjohns-nottm.ac.uk	Southwell	Canon Dr Christina Baxter
St Stephen's House, 16 Marston St, Oxford OX4 1JX *Tel:* 01865 613500 *Fax:* 01865 613513 *email:* enquiries@ssho.ox.ac.uk	Oxford	Revd Canon Dr Robin Ward
Trinity College, Stoke Hill, Bristol BS9 1JP *Tel:* 0117 968 2803 *Fax:* 0117 968 7470 *email:* principal@trinity-bris.ac.uk	Bristol	Revd Canon George Kovoor
Westcott House, Jesus Lane, Cambridge CB5 8BP *Tel:* 01223 741000 *Fax:* 01223 741002 *email:* general-enquiries@westcott.cam.ac.uk	Ely	Revd Martin Seeley
Wycliffe Hall, Oxford OX2 6PW *Tel:* 01865 274200 *Fax:* 01865 274215 *email:* enquiries@wycliffe.ox.ac.uk	Oxford	Revd Dr Richard Turnbull
Theological Institute of the Scottish Episcopal Church, TISEC General Synod Office, 21 Grosvenor Crescent, Edinburgh EH12 5EE *Tel:* 0131 225 6357 *Fax:* 0131 346 7247 *email:* tisec@scotland.anglican.org	Edinburgh	Revd Canon Dr Michael Fuller
St Michael's College, Llandaff, Cardiff CF5 2YJ *Tel:* 029 2056 3379 *Fax:* 029 2083 8008 *email:* ps@stmichaels.ac.uk	Llandaff	Revd Dr Peter Sedgwick

GENERAL

REGIONAL COURSES	
Address and Telephone Number	Principal or Director
Lancashire and Cumbria Diocesan Training Institute (CBDTI) Church House, West Walls, Carlisle, Cumbria CA3 8UE *Tel:* 01228 522573 *Fax:* 01228 815400 *email:* admin@lctp.co.uk	Revd Canon Tim Herbert
Eastern Region Ministry Course ERMC, Wesley House, Jesus Lane, Cambridge CB5 8BJ *Tel:* 01223 741026 *Fax:* 01223 741027 *email:* mcintosh@ermc.cam.ac.uk	Revd Dr Ian McIntosh
East Midlands Ministry Training Course Room C90, School of Education, University of Nottingham Jubilee Campus, Wollaton Rd NG8 1BB *Tel:* 0115 851 4853 *email:* francis.bridger@nottingham.ac.uk	Revd Dr Francis Bridger
Lindisfarne Regional Training Partnership Church House, St John's Terrace, North Shields NE29 6HS *Tel:* 0191 270 4144 *email:* enquiries@lindisfarnertp.org	Revd Canon Cathy Rowling
Ripon College, Cuddesdon, Incorporating Oxford Ministry Course OMC, Ripon College, Cuddesdon, Oxford OX44 9EX *email:* omc@ripon-cuddesdon.ac.uk	Revd Canon Prof Martyn Percy (*Associate Principal*)
St Mellitus College The Crypt, St George in the East, 16 Cannon St Rd, London E1 0HB *Tel:* 020 7481 9477 *Fax:* 020 7481 8907 *email:* info@stmelliluscollege.org.uk	Revd Dr Graham Tomlin
South East Institute for Theological Education Ground Floor, Sun Pier House, Medway St, Chatham, Kent ME4 4HF *Tel:* 01634 846683 *Fax:* 01634 819347 *email:* administrator@seite.co.uk (*office*); principal@seite.co.uk (*Principal*)	Revd Dr Jeremy Worthen
Southern North West Course St Werburgh's Rectory, 388 Wilbraham Rd, Chorlton-cum-Hardy, Manchester M21 0UH *email:* snwtpprincipal@chester.ac.uk	Ven John Applegate
Southern Theological Education and Training Scheme 19 The Close, Salisbury, Wilts. SP1 2EE *Tel:* 01722 424820 *Fax:* 01722 424811 *email:* swheway@stets.ac.uk	Revd Canon Vernon White
South West Ministry Training Course Amory Building, University of Exeter, Rennes Drive, Exeter EX4 4RJ *Tel:* 01392 264403 *email:* pauline@swmtc.org.uk	Revd Dr David Moss
Queen's Foundation for Ecumenical Theological Education, incorporating the West Midlands Ministerial Training Course The Queen's Foundation for Ecumenical Theological Education, Somerset Rd, Edgbaston, Birmingham B15 2QH *Tel:* 0121 454 1527 *Fax:* 0121 454 8171 *email:* enquire@queens.ac.uk	Revd Canon Dr David Hewlett
West of England Ministerial Training Course University of Gloucestershire, Francis Close Hall, Swindon Rd, Cheltenham GL50 4AZ *Tel:* 01242 532884 *email:* office@wemtc.freeserve.co.uk	Revd Canon Dr Michael Parsons
Yorkshire Ministry Course The Mirfield Centre, Stocksbank Rd, Mirfield, West Yorkshire WF14 0BW *Tel:* 01924 481 925 *email:* principal@ymc.org.uk	Dr Christine Grove

ORDAINED LOCAL MINISTRY SCHEMES RECOGNIZED BY THE HOUSE OF BISHOPS	
Address and Telephone Number	Principal or Director
Local Ministry Programme: Guildford, Diocesan House, Quarry St, Guildford GU1 3XG *Tel:* 01483 790319 *email:* steve.summers@cofeguildford.org.uk	Revd Dr Stephen Summers
Hereford OLM Scheme, Ludlow Diocesan Office, The Business Quarter, Ludlow Eco Park, Ludlow, Shropshire SY8 1FD *email:* j.daniels@hereford.anglican.org	Revd Dr John Daniels
Lichfield OLM Scheme, St Mary's House, The Close, Lichfield WS13 7LD *Tel:* 01543 306225 *email:* pauline.shelton@lichfield.anglican.org	Revd Pauline Shelton
Norwich OLM Scheme, Emmaus House, 65 The Close, Norwich NR1 4DH *Tel:* 01603 611196 *email:* suewoan@norwich.anglican.org	Miss Sue Woan
Oxford OLM Scheme, Diocesan Church House, North Hinksey, Oxford OX2 0NB *Tel:* 01865 208252 *email:* beren.hartless@oxford.anglican.org	Revd Beren Hartless
St Edmundsbury and Ipswich Diocesan Ministry Course, DMC Office, Abbey House, Angel Hill, Bury St Edmunds IP33 1LS *Tel:* 01284 749435 *email:* sheila@stedmundsbury.anglican.org	Mrs Christine Amjad-Ali
Salisbury OLM Scheme, Ministry Development Team, Church House, Crane St, Salisbury SP1 2QB *Tel:* 01722 411944 *Fax:* 01722 411990 *email:* paul.overend@salisbury.anglican.org	Revd Dr Paul Overend

GENERAL

ROYAL PECULIARS, THE CHAPELS ROYAL, ETC.

Westminster Abbey

Description of Arms. Azure, a cross patonce between five martlets or; on a chief or France and England quarterly on a pale, between two roses, gules, seeded and barbed proper.

COLLEGIATE CHURCH OF ST PETER

The Collegiate Church of St Peter in Westminster, usually called Westminster Abbey, is a Royal Peculiar, and, as such, it is extra-provincial as well as extra-diocesan and comes directly under the personal jurisdiction of Her Majesty The Queen, who is the Visitor.

Throughout medieval times it was the Abbey Church of a great Benedictine Monastery, which was in existence at Westminster before the Norman Conquest. After the dissolution of the monastery in 1540 it became increasingly a great national shrine, where famous writers, poets, statesmen and leaders in the Church and State are buried. It is the Coronation Church, and in it also take place from time to time Royal weddings and many services on great occasions of a National or Commonwealth character. Daily, the Holy Communion is celebrated and Morning and Evening Prayers are said or sung.

THE VISITOR
The Sovereign

DEAN
Very Revd Dr John R. Hall, The Deanery, Westminster SW1P 3PA [2006]   *Tel:* 020 7654 4801
Fax: 020 7654 4883
email: john.hall@westminster-abbey.org
Web: www.westminster-abbey.org

CANONS OF WESTMINSTER
Rector of St Margaret's Church, Revd Andrew Tremlett, 5 Little Cloister SW1P 3PL [2010]
Tel: 020 7654 4806
Fax: 020 7654 4811
email: andrew.tremlett@westminster-abbey.org

Canon Theologian (until January 2011) Revd Dr Nicholas Sagovsky, 3 Little Cloister, London SW1P 3PL [2004]   *Tel:* 020 7654 4808
Fax: 020 7654 4811
email: nicholas.sagovsky@westminster-abbey.org
Canon Theologian (post February 2011) Vacant (same address)

Canon Treasurer and Almoner Revd Robert P. Reiss, 1 Little Cloister, London SW1P 3PL [2005]
Tel: 020 7654 4804
Fax: 020 7654 4811
email: robert.reiss@westminster-abbey.org

Canon Steward Revd Dr Jane B. Hedges, 2 Little Cloister, London SW1P 3PL   *Tel:* 020 7654 4815
Fax: 020 7654 4811
email: jane.hedges@westminster-abbey.org

MINOR CANONS
Revd Dr James D. T. Hawkey, 6 Little Cloister, London SW1P 3PL [2010]   *Tel:* 020 7654 4850
email: james.hawkey@westminster-abbey.org

Revd Michael D. Macey, 7 Little Cloister, London SW1P 3PL [2008]   *Tel:* 020 7654 4855
email: michael.macey@westminster-abbey.org

CHAPLAIN
Sister Judith CSC, 3b Dean's Yard, London SW1P 3NY   *Tel:* 020 7654 4800
email: judith.csc@westminster-abbey.org

PRIESTS VICAR
Revd Paul Bagott
Revd Alan Boddy
Revd Laura Burgess
Revd Dr Paul Bradshaw
Revd Philip Chester
Revd Dr Alasdair Coles
Revd Dominic Fenton
Revd Ralph Godsall
Revd Jonathan Goodall
Revd Alan Gyle
Revd Dr Sarah Hartley
Revd Rose Hudson-Wilkin
Revd Edward Lewis
Revd Christopher Lowson
Revd Peter McGeary
Revd David Peters
Revd Garry Swinton
Revd Gavin Williams

LAY OFFICERS
Receiver General & Chapter Clerk   Sir Stephen Lamport KCVO DL, The Chapter Office, 20 Dean's Yard, London SW1P 3PA   *Tel:* 020 7654 4861
Fax: 020 7654 4914
email: stephen.lamport@westminster-abbey.org
Web: www.westminster-abbey.org

Organist and Master of the Choristers Mr James O'Donnell (*same address*)   *Tel:* 020 7654 4854
email: music@westminster-abbey.org

Registrar Mr Stuart Holmes (*same address*)
    Tel: 020 7654 4845
email: stuart.holmes@westminster-abbey.org

Press and Communications Office (*same address*)
    Tel: 020 7654 4923
email: press@westminster-abbey.org

Head of Communications Mr Duncan Jeffery (*same address*)   *Tel:* 020 7654 4888
    Fax: 020 7654 4891
email: duncan.jeffery@westminster-abbey.org

Surveyor of the Fabric Mr John Burton, 2b Little Cloister, London SW1P 3PL   *Tel:* 020 7654 4800
email: john.burton@westminster-abbey.org

Head of the Abbey Collections Dr Tony Trowles, The Muniment Room and Library, Westminster Abbey, London SW1P 3PL   *Tel:* 020 7654 4829
email: tony.trowles@westminster-abbey.org

Keeper of the Muniments Dr Richard Mortimer (*same address*)   *Tel:* 020 7654 4829
email: richard.mortimer@westminster-abbey.org

Headmaster of the Choir School Mr Jonathan Milton, Dean's Yard, London SW1P 3NY
    Tel: 020 7654 4918
email: jonathan.milton@westminster-abbey.org

Legal Secretary Mr Christopher Vyse, The Chapter Office, 20 Dean's Yard, London SW1P 3PA   *Tel:* 020 7654 4885
email: chris.vyse@westminster-abbey.org

Auditor Mr David Hunt, Smith & Williamson, 1 Riding House St, London W1A 3AS
    Tel: 020 7612 9194

Windsor

Description of Arms. The shield of St George, argent a cross gules, encircled by the Garter

THE QUEEN'S FREE CHAPEL OF ST GEORGE WITHIN HER CASTLE OF WINDSOR

A ROYAL PECULIAR
Founded by Edward III in 1348 and exempt from diocesan and provincial jurisdictions, the College of St George is a self-governing secular community of priests and laymen, the first duty of which is to celebrate Divine Service daily on behalf of the Sovereign, the Royal House and the Order of the Garter. Its present Chapel was founded by Edward IV in honour of Our Lady, St George and St Edward in 1475 and, with the cloisters and buildings annexed, is vested in the Dean and Canons. In it the Eucharist, Mattins and Evensong are sung or said daily and are open to all.

The Order of the Garter has its stalls and insignia in the Quire, where Knights and Ladies Companions are installed by the Sovereign. Beneath the Quire – the scene of many Royal funerals – are vaults in which lie the bodies of six monarchs. Elsewhere in the Chapel are the tombs of four others.

The College has its own school of 400 children, where it maintains twenty-four choristerships. It also awards an organ scholarship. A house for conferences has been established under the name of St George's House.

THE VISITOR
The Sovereign

DEAN
Rt Revd David Conner KCVO, The Deanery, Windsor Castle, Windsor, Berks. SL4 1NJ [1998]
    Tel: 01753 865561

CANONS
Vice-Dean and Treasurer Canon John White LVO, 4 The Cloisters, Windsor Castle [1982]
    Tel: 01753 848787

Precentor and Chaplain in the Great Park Canon John Ovenden LVO, Chaplain's Lodge, Windsor Great Park, Windsor, Berks. [1998]
    Tel: 01784 432434

Warden, St George's House Canon Dr Hueston Finlay, 8 The Cloisters, Windsor Castle, Windsor, Berkshire SL4 1NJ [2004]   *Tel:* 01753 848887

Steward Canon Dr James Woodward, 6 The Cloisters, Windsor Castle, Windsor, Berkshire SL4 1NJ [2009]   *Tel:* 01753 848709

MINOR CANONS
Succentor Revd Michael Boag, 5 The Cloisters, Windsor Castle [2003]   *Tel:* 01753 848737

Chaplain to St George's School Revd Andrew Zihni, 24 The Cloisters, Windsor Castle [2006]
    Tel: 01753 848710

LAY OFFICERS
Chapter Clerk Miss Charlotte Manley LVO OBE, Chapter Office, The Cloisters, Windsor Castle [2003]   *Tel:* 01753 848888

Director of Music Mr Timothy Byram-Wigfield, 23 The Cloisters, Windsor Castle [2004]
    Tel: 01753 848747

Assistant Director of Music Mr Richard Pinel, 3 The Cloisters, Windsor Castle, Windsor, Berkshire SL4 1NJ

Clerk of Accounts Mr Nick Grogan, 2 The Cloisters, Windsor Castle, Windsor, Berkshire SL4 1NJ   Tel: 01753 848720

Clerk of Works Mr Ian Poole, Clerk of Works Office, The Cloisters   Tel: 01753 848888

Archivist and Chapter Librarian Dr Clare Rider, The Vicars' Hall Undercroft, Windsor Castle, Windsor, Berkshire SL4 1NJ   Tel: 01753 848724

Virger Mr Vaughn Wright, 22 Horseshoe Cloister, Windsor Castle   Tel: 01753 848727

Headmaster, St George's School Mr Roger Jones, St George's School, Windsor Castle, Windsor, Berkshire SL4 1QF   Tel: 01753 865553

Domestic Chaplains to Her Majesty the Queen

Buckingham Palace Preb William Scott
Windsor Castle The Dean of Windsor

Sandringham Revd Jonathan Riviere

Chapels Royal

The Chapel Royal is the body of Clergy, Singers and Vestry Officers appointed to serve the spiritual needs of the Sovereign – in medieval days on Progresses through the Realm as well as upon the battlefields of Europe, as at Agincourt. Its ancient foundation is first century with the British Church: its latter day choral headquarters have been at St James's Palace since 1702 along with the Court of St James. Since 1312 the Chapel Royal has been governed by the Dean who, as the Ordinary, also exercises, along with the Sub-Dean, jurisdiction over the daughter establishments of Chapels Royal at the Tower of London and at Hampton Court Palace. Members of the public are welcome to attend Sunday and weekday services as advertised.

The Chapel Royal conducts the Service of Remembrance at the Cenotaph in Whitehall, with a Forces Chaplain in company, and combines with the choral establishment of the host abbey or cathedral on the occasion of Royal Maundy, under the governance of the Lord High Almoner and Sub-Almoner. Each Member of the College of thirty-six Chaplains to Her Majesty the Queen, headed by the Clerk and Deputy Clerk of the Closet, is required by Warrant to preach in the Chapel Royal once a year, and is visibly distinguished, along with the Chapel Royal, Forces and Mohawk Chaplains, by the wearing of a royal scarlet cassock.

Dean of the Chapels Royal
The Bishop of London

Sub-Dean
Preb William Scott
Chapel Royal, St James's Palace, London SW1A 1BL   Tel: 020 7024 5576

CHAPEL ROYAL AND THE QUEEN'S CHAPEL, ST JAMES'S PALACE
Priests in Ordinary
Revd Richard Bolton
Canon Paul Thomas
Revd Dr Stephen Young

Deputy Priests
Revd Roger Hall
Revd Dennis Mulliner
Canon Mark Oakley

HAMPTON COURT PALACE
Chapel Royal, Hampton Court, East Molesey, Surrey KT8 9AU   Tel: 020 3166 6515

Chaplain
Revd Denis Mulliner

HM TOWER OF LONDON
The Chaplain's Residence, London EC3N 4AP   Tel: 020 3166 6796
(includes the Chapels Royal of St John the Evangelist and St Peter ad Vincula)

Chaplain
Revd Roger Hall

THE ROYAL CHAPEL OF ALL SAINTS, WINDSOR GREAT PARK
This is a Private Chapel and the property of the Crown within the grounds of the Royal Lodge. Attendance is restricted to residents and employees of the Great Park.

Chaplain
Canon John Ovenden, Chaplain's Lodge, Windsor Great Park, Windsor, Berks SL4 2HP   Tel: 01784 432434

College of Chaplains

The position of Royal Chaplain is a very ancient one. The College of Chaplains, the members of which as such must not be confused with the Priests in Ordinary, preach according to a Rota of Waits in the Chapels Royal. The College comprises the Clerk of the Closet (who presides), the Deputy Clerk of the Closet, and thirty-six Chaplains. When a vacancy in the list of chaplains occurs, the Private Secretary to Her Majesty the Queen asks the Clerk of the Closet to suggest possible names to Her Majesty. The duties of the Clerk of the Closet include the presentation of bishops to Her Majesty when they do homage before taking possession of the revenues of their Sees; and he also examines theological books whose authors desire to present copies to Her Majesty the Queen. He preaches annually in the Chapel Royal, St James's Palace.

CLERK OF THE CLOSET
Rt Revd Christopher Hill (*Bishop of Guildford*)

DEPUTY CLERK OF THE CLOSET
Preb William Scott

CHAPLAINS TO HER MAJESTY THE QUEEN
Canon Gavin Ashenden
Preb Paul Avis
Revd Norman Banks
Revd Hugh Bearn
Canon Raymond Brazier

Canon John Byrne
Canon Gillian Calver
Canon Peter Calvert
Canon Andrew Clitherow
Canon Richard Cooper
Canon Ann Easter
Canon Christine Farrington
Canon Roger Hill
Revd Rose Hudson-Wilkin
Canon George Kovoor
Revd Edward Lewis
Canon Bill Matthews
Canon Paul Miller
Canon George Moffat
Revd William Mowll
Ven William Noblett
Canon John Ovenden
Canon Stephen Palmer
Revd Jonathan Riviere
Canon Bruce Ruddock
Canon Christopher Samuels
Canon Christopher Smith
Canon Eric Stephenson
Preb Pippa Thorneycroft
Canon Andrew Wingate
Canon Alison Woodhouse

Extra Chaplains
Canon Anthony Caesar
Canon Eric James
Canon Gerry Murphy
Revd John Robson
Revd John Stott

Royal Almonry

The Royal Almonry dispenses the Queen's charitable gifts and is responsible for the Royal Maundy Service each year, at which Her Majesty distributes Maundy money to as many men and as many women pensioners as the years of her own age.

HIGH ALMONER
Rt Revd Nigel McCulloch (*Bishop of Manchester*)

SUB-ALMONER
Preb William Scott
Chapel Royal, St James's Palace, London SW1A 1BL

The Queen's Chapel of the Savoy

Savoy Hill, Strand, London WC2R 0DA
Tel: 020 7379 8088 *or* 020 7836 7221
email: chapel@duchyoflancaster

CHAPEL OF THE ROYAL VICTORIAN ORDER
The Queen's Chapel of the Savoy was built as the principal chapel of a hospital for 'pouer, nedie people' founded by King Henry VII and finished in 1512 after his death. It is a private Chapel of Her Majesty the Queen in right of her Duchy of Lancaster, and Her Majesty appoints the chap-

lain. It is, therefore, a 'free' Chapel not falling within any diocesan jurisdiction.

On the occasion of his Coronation in 1937, King George VI commanded that the chapel of the Savoy should become the chapel of the Royal Victorian Order, an honour in the personal gift of the Sovereign, and the Chaplain of the Queen's Chapel is ex officio Chaplain of the Order. An ante-chapel, chaplain's office and robing room were constructed in 1958 to provide additional accommodation.

A new three-manual Walker organ was pre-sented to the Chapel by Her Majesty the Queen in 1965.

Members of the public are welcome to attend services which are held on Sundays (11 a.m.) and weekdays (except August and September) with the exception of those for special or official occasions. The Chapel has a particularly fine musical tradition with a choir of men and boys.

CHAPLAIN
Revd Prof Peter Galloway OBE

MASTER OF MUSIC
Mr Philip Berg FRCO, ARCM

VERGER
Mr Phillip Chancellor

HONORARY WARDENS
Mr Colin Brough
Dr Roy Palmer
Col Ronnie McCrum MVO

Royal Memorial Chapel Sandhurst

Camberley, Surrey GU15 4PQ   *Tel:* 01276 412543
                             Fax: 01276 412097
The Royal Memorial Chapel Sandhurst is the Chapel of the Royal Military Academy Sandhurst. It is also the Memorial Chapel of the officers of the British Army.

The present building was erected after the First World War as a memorial to those trained at Sandhurst who gave their lives in that conflict. Their names are inscribed on the Chapel's pillars. A memorial book contains the names of all officers of the Commonwealth Armies who died in the Second World War, and a page of this book is turned at the beginning of principal services.

A Book of Remembrance containing the names of all officers who have been killed in service since 1947 is kept in the South Africa Chapel.

The main Sunday service is at 1030. The forms of service include the Book of Common Prayer, Common Worship, and special services within the Academy's calendar. Services are open to the public, and passes may be obtained by contacting the Chapel Office.

CHAPLAIN
Canon J. R. B. Gough

ASSISTANT CHAPLAIN
Revd S. J. H. Dunwoody

CHOIRMASTER AND ORGANIST
Mr Peter Beaven

CONSTITUTION OF THE CHAPEL COUNCIL
Maj-Gen P. C. Marriot (*Chairman*); Canon J. R. B. Gough (*Deputy Chairman*); Maj. J. M. Watkinson (*Secretary*); Ven S. Robbins (*Chaplain General*); Maj-Gen Sir Simon Cooper; Maj Gen R. L. Kirkland; Brig M. Owen

The Royal Foundation of St Katharine

2 Butcher Row, London E14 8DS
                        Tel: 0300 111 1147
                        Fax: 020 7702 7603
                    email: info@rfsk.org.uk
                      Web: www.rfsk.org.uk
St Katharine's, founded by Queen Matilda in 1147 originally adjacent to the Tower of London, is a charitable conference and retreat house at Limehouse in East London, between the City and Canary Wharf. It serves the Church of England, other churches and charities, offering an attractive setting for day or residential group meetings, seminars or retreats. Individuals from home and overseas are also welcome to stay. There are excellent facilities with residential en suite accommodation for 44 people and a choice of 7 meeting rooms. Daily worship is held in the re-ordered chapel.

Her Majesty Queen Elizabeth II is Patron of the Foundation.

MEMBERS OF THE COURT
Mr Benjamin Hanbury (*Chairman*)
Revd John Tattersall (Treasurer)
The Viscount Churchill
Rt Revd and Rt Hon Richard Chartres (*Bishop of London*)
The Countess of Airlie
Sir Stephen Lamport
Mrs Elizabeth Marshall
Preb David Paton (*Master*)

MASTER
Preb David Paton

Deans of Peculiars

The few present-day Deans of Peculiars are the residue of some 300 such office-holders in the medieval period, when the granting of 'peculiar' status, fully or partially exempting a jurisdiction from episcopal control, was commonly employed by popes and others to advance the interests of a particular institution, or limit the power of the bishops. Unlike the Royal Peculiars, the deaneries had little in common, and the privileges and duties of the individual posts ranged from nominal to significant. Most of the special provisions were brought to an end in the nineteenth century. But each Peculiar has interesting light to throw on a phase of Anglican or national history.

Battle
Very Revd Dr John Edmondson, The Deanery, Caldbec Hill, Battle, E. Sussex TN33 0JY [2005]
Tel and *Fax:* 01424 772693

Bocking
Very Revd Philip Need, The Deanery, Bocking, Braintree, Essex CM7 5SR (Bocking, Essex) [1996]
Tel: 01376 324887
01376 553092 (Office)
email: thedeanofbocking@tiscali.co.uk
Very Revd Martin Thrower, The Deanery, Church St, Hadleigh, Ipswich IP7 5DT (Hadleigh, Suffolk) [2009]
Tel: 01473 822218
email: martin.thrower@btinternet.com

Stamford
Rt Revd Dr Timothy Ellis (*Bishop of Grantham*)

The Deans of Jersey and Guernsey
The Deans of Jersey and Guernsey are very senior members of insular society. The Dean of Jersey ranks next after the Lieutenant Governor, Bailiff and Deputy-Bailiff and is an ex officio member of the States. The Dean of Guernsey ranks third after the Lieutenant Governor and Bailiff, and though not a member of the States of Deliberation (the Island Parliament) he is a member of the States of Election (which appoints Jurats to the Royal Court). From their respective positions the Deans are expected to offer spiritual and moral leadership.

References to these offices go back to the tenth century in the case of Guernsey and 1135 in the case of Jersey; the names of the Deans of Guernsey since 1295 and almost all the Deans of Jersey since 1180 are known. Since 1495 the Dean of Jersey has been appointed by the Crown. Traditionally Rector of one of the twelve Jersey parishes, since 1875 the Dean of Jersey has always been Rector of St Helier. The Dean of Guernsey has usually been Rector of the Town Church in St Peter Port, but this has not always been the case.

The Channel Islands were formerly part of the Diocese of Coutances, Normandy, but were transferred to Winchester by Papal Bull in 1500. Their annexation to the Diocese of Winchester was confirmed by Queen Elizabeth I in 1568 (they continued to be 'annexed to' rather than being 'part of' that diocese), but, the reformation having reached the islands in an extreme Calvinist Presbyterian form, the authority of Winchester and the office of Dean were little regarded until the Restoration in 1660.

The Deans are presidents of their respective Ecclesiastical Courts and have the right to grant marriage licences, including special licences and faculties. The Guernsey Ecclesiastical Court also retains its jurisdiction in matters concerning probate of realty and issues Letters of Administration. As the Bishop's Commissaries, the Deans carry out many of the duties performed in England by suffragan bishops and archdeacons, including instituting and inducting new incumbents.

Jersey
Very Revd Robert Key, The Deanery, David Place, St Helier, Jersey JE2 4TE
Tel: 01534 720001
Fax: 01534 720001
email: robert_f_key@yahoo.com

Guernsey and Dependencies
Very Revd Paul Mellor, The Deanery, Cornet St, St Peter Port, Guernsey GY1 1BZ [2003]
Tel: 01481 720036
Fax: 01481 722948
email: paul@townchurch.org.gg

Preachers at the Inns of Court

THE TEMPLE
Master Revd Robin Griffith-Jones, The Master's House, Temple, London EC4Y 7BB
Tel: 020 7353 8559
email: master@templechurch.com

Reader Revd A. H. Mead, 11 Dungarvan Ave, London SW15 5QU   *Tel:* 020 8876 5833

LINCOLN'S INN
Very Revd Derek Watson, 29 The Precincts, Canterbury CT1 2EP   *Tel:* 01227 865238

GRAY'S INN
Revd Roger Holloway OBE, Flat 6, 2 Porchester Gardens, London W2 6JL   *Tel:* 020 7402 4937

RELIGIOUS COMMUNITIES

Anglican Religious Communities

The roots of the Religious Life can be traced back to the Early Church in Jerusalem, and the subsequent traditions such as the Benedictines, Franciscans, etc., were flourishing in England until the Reformation when all were suppressed.

Most Anglican Communities were founded in the nineteenth century as a result of the Oxford Movement. There are now over sixty different Communities in the British Isles and throughout the Anglican Communion. Some are very small. Some have over 80 members.

Religious Communities are formed by men and women who feel called to seek God and live out their baptismal vows in a particular way under vows. There are some 1,200 Anglican men and women living this life in the United Kingdom.

PRAYER AND WORK

Each Community has its own history and character; some follow one of the traditional Rules, and others those written by more recent founders, but all have one thing in common: their daily life based on the work of prayer and living together centred in their Daily Office and the Eucharist. The work grows from the prayer, depending on the particular Community and the gifts of its members.

Some Communities are 'enclosed'. The members do not normally go out, but remain within the convent or monastery and its grounds, seeking and serving God through silence and prayer, study and work. Other Communities share the basic life of prayer and fellowship and may also be involved in work outside the Community.

HOSPITALITY

Most Community houses offer a place where people can go for a time of Retreat, either alone or with a group, for a day, several days, or occasionally for longer periods of time. They offer a place of quiet to seek God, grow in prayer and find spiritual guidance.

THE CALLING

People who feel called to the Religious Life and who wish to apply to a Community are usually aged between 21 and 45. They normally need to be physically and psychologically robust. Academic qualifications are not essential. There is a training period of about three years before any vows are taken.

Those who are considering a vocation are advised to visit Community houses to experience their particular ethos: further information is available from the houses or general enquiries may be made to The Communities Consultative Council at the address below.

Advisory Council on the Relations of Bishops and Religious Communities

This Council, to serve the two Provinces, is responsible to the Archbishops and the House of Bishops. Its functions are (1) to advise bishops upon (*a*) questions arising about the charters, constitutions and rule of existing Communities, (*b*) the establishment of new Communities, (*c*) matters referred to it by a diocesan bishop; (2) to advise existing Communities or their Visitors in any matters that they refer to it; (3) to give guidance to those who wish to form Communities. The Chairman and Convenor of the Council must be a diocesan bishop appointed by the Archbishops of Canterbury and York. The Council consists of at least 13 members, 3 of whom are nominated by the bishops and 10 elected by the Communities. Up to 5 additional members may be co-opted. The present membership is: *Acting Chair* Rt Revd David Walker (*Bishop of Dudley*); *3 members nominated by the House of Bishops* Rt Revd John Pritchard (*Bishop of Oxford*), Rt Revd Anthony Robinson (*Bishop of Pontefract*), Rt Revd Humphrey Southern (*Bishop of Repton*); *10 members elected by the Communities* Sister Anita CSC, Father Colin CSWG, Brother Damian SSF, Sister Mary Julian Gough CHC, Father Peter Allan CR, Sister Rosemary CHN, Sister Mary Stephen OSB, Abbot Stuart Burns OSB, Mother Ann Verena CJGS, (*one vacancy*). *Co-opted* Rt Revd Andrew Burnham (*Bishop of Ebbsfleet*), Rt Revd Dominic Walker OGS (*Bishop of Monmouth*); Revd Christopher Neal CMS; *ARC Representative* Father Jonathan Ewer SSM. *Roman Catholic Observer* Sister Catherine McGovern OSF.

Correspondence in relation to the Advisory Council should be addressed to: The Bishop of Dudley, Bishop's House, Bishops Walk, Cradley Heath B64 7RH

Tel: 0121 550 3407
email: bishop.david@cofe-worcester.org.uk

Anglican Religious Communities in England

ARC is an umbrella body of all members of Anglican Religious Communities, Monks and Nuns, Brothers and Sisters living in community under vows of poverty, chastity and obedience. The communities range from large monastic houses to small groups of two or three brothers or sisters living and working in urban areas. It acts to support its members by encouraging cooperation and the exchange of ideas and experiences which are relevant to Religious Life. The ARC Committee has members elected from four constituent groups: Leaders, General Synod Representatives, Novice Guardians and Professed Religious. An annual conference is held in September. Details of Communities may be found in *Anglican Religious Life*, published by Canterbury Press, or, in an abbreviated form, via the following Web address: www.arcie.org.uk

Contact The Secretary, Anglican Religious Communities, c/o Mr Jonathan Neil-Smith, Church House, Great Smith St, London SW1P 3A
email: info@arcie.org.uk
Registered Charity no. 1097586

Communities for Men

BENEDICTINE COMMUNITY OF ST BENEDICT'S PRIORY
19a The Close, Salisbury, SP1 2EB
email: elmore.abbey@virgin.net

Conventual Prior Dom Simon Jarratt OSB

Visitor Rt Revd Dominic Walker OGS (*Bishop of Monmouth*)

Founded 1914. 1926–87 Nashdom Abbey, 1987–2010 Elmore Abbey, From 2010 St Benedict's Priory, Salisbury. Resident community 4 monks. Oblate confraternity of around 300. It is hoped to receive retreatants and day guests once building alterations at the Priory have been completed.

BENEDICTINE COMMUNITY AT BURFORD
See **Mixed Communities** page 254.

COMMUNITY OF OUR LADY AND ST JOHN
Alton Abbey, Abbey Road, Alton, Hants. GU34 4AP
Tel: 01420 562145/563575
email: abbey@domghill.mail1.co.uk

Abbot Rt Revd Dom Giles Hill OSB

Visitor Rt Revd Michael Scott-Joynt (*Bishop of Winchester*)

Founded 1884. A community of Benedictine monks which undertakes retreats. Guest accommodation for 18 people. Other work includes the manufacture of altar wafers and incense. The Seamen's Friendly Society of St Paul is managed from the Abbey. Day conference facilities and residential groups welcome: contact the Guestmaster.

COMMUNITY OF THE GLORIOUS ASCENSION
The Priory, Lamacraft Farm, Start Point, Kingsbridge, Devon TQ7 2NG   *Tel:* 01548 511474
email: ascensioncga@fsnet.com

Prior Bro Simon CGA

Visitor Rt Revd Edward Holland

Founded in 1960 – the brothers are based in Devon and continue the monastic pattern of a common-life, prayer and worship; together with their work of hospitality and ministry.

COMMUNITY OF THE RESURRECTION
House of the Resurrection, Mirfield, W Yorks. WF14 0BN   *Tel:* 01924 494318
Fax: 01924 490489
email: community@mirfield.org.uk

Superior Fr George Guiver CR   *Tel:* 01924 483301

Visitor Rt Revd Graham James (*Bishop of Norwich*)

Founded 1892, it undertakes teaching (theological college), retreats, missions and missionary works.

Theological College College of the Resurrection, Mirfield, W Yorks. WF14 0BW   *Tel:* 01924 481900
Fax: 01924 492738
email: registrar@mirfield.org.uk

The Mirfield Centre offers a programme of day and evening events and small conferences as well as offering a meeting place for about 50 people. *Address* Mirfield Centre, College of the Resurrection, Mirfield, W Yorks. WF14 0BW
Tel: 01924 481920
Fax: 01924 492738
email: centre@mirfield.org.uk

COMMUNITY OF THE SERVANTS OF THE WILL OF GOD

See **Mixed Communities** page 254.

COMPANY OF MISSION PRIESTS

Secretary Canon Peter Brown CMP, The Clergy House, Sawmill Lane, Durham DH7 8NS
Tel: 0191 378 0845

email:
peterandbrian@sawmill-lane.freeserve.co.uk

Visitor Bishop Lindsay Urwin OGS

Warden Father Pike CMP

Founded 1940. A society of apostolic life, a dispersed community of male priests of the Anglican Communion who, wishing to consecrate themselves wholly to the Church's mission, keep themselves free from the attachments of marriage and family, and endeavour to encourage and strengthen one another by mutual prayer and fellowship, sharing the vision of St Vincent de Paul of a priesthood dedicated to service, and in association with the whole Vincentian family.

ORATORY OF THE GOOD SHEPHERD

Web: www.ogs.net

European Provincial Revd Fr Peter Ford OGS, Calle Montevideo 2–7, 35007 Las Palmas de Gran Canaria, Gran Canaria, Canary Islands
email: pford@ogs.net

London-Cambridge College Prior Revd Nicholas Gandy OGS, Vicarage, Old Town, Brackley, Northamptonshire NN13 7BZ
Tel: 01280 702 767
email: ngandy@ogs.net

Founded in 1913 at Cambridge University. The Oratory is a society of professed priests and brothers working in four provinces: Europe, Australia, North America and Southern Africa. Members of the Oratory are bound together by a common Rule and discipline. They do not normally live together in community but meet for Chapter and are resident regularly for an annual Oratory Retreat and for Provincial Chapter (annual) and General Chapter (triennial). Members include bishops, parish priests, lecturers and missionaries. A two year period of probation precedes profession, and after ten years of annual profession, life vows may be taken. The Rule of the Oratory requires celibacy, the daily offices, where possible daily Eucharist, and a regular account of spending and direction of life. In addition, 'Labour of the Mind' is a characteristic of the Oratory and members are expected to spend time in study. Attached to the Oratory are Companions and Associates, lay, ordained, married and single, who keep a Rule of Life and are part of the Oratory family.

THE SOCIETY OF ST FRANCIS

The Society comprises a First Order for men (Society of St Francis) and women (*see* Community of St Francis, page 248), called to the Franciscan life under the vows of poverty, chastity and obedience; a Second Order of enclosed sisters (*see* Community of St Clare, page 248); and the Third Order for ordained and lay people, pledged to the spirit of the vows (*see* Third Order, Society of St Francis, page 255).

The Brothers of the First Order, founded in 1921, live a life of community centred on prayer and engage in active work especially in the areas of the poor and underprivileged. Three Friaries in this province (at Hilfield, Glasshampton and Alnmouth) have a ministry with guests and retreatants. The other centres of work are principally within a city context from which the brothers engage in various active ministries. Some work with educational institutions, conducting retreats and with parishes continues.

There are four Provinces: Europe, Australia/ New Zealand, the Pacific Islands, and the Americas.

Minister General Brother Clark Berge SSF, Little Portion Friary, PO Box 399, Mt Sinai, NY 11766/ 0399
Tel: (+1) 631 473 0553
email: clarke.berge@s-s-f.org

European Province

Minister Brother Samuel SSF, The Friary, Hilfield, Dorchester, Dorset DT2 7BE   Tel: 01300 341345
email: ministerssf@franciscans.org.uk
Web: www.franciscans.org.uk

Assistant Minister Brother Benedict SSF (Doncaster)

Bishop Protector Rt Revd Michael Perham (*Bishop of Gloucester*)

Houses
All SSF-UK houses can be emailed using [name of the house] ssf@franciscans.org.uk e.g. hilfieldssf@franciscans.org.uk
Alnmouth *Tel:* 01665 830213/830660
Fax: 01665 830580
Canterbury *Tel:* 01227 479364
Doncaster *Tel:* 01302 872240
Glasshampton *Tel:* 01299 896345
Fax: 01299 896083
Hilfield *Tel:* 01300 341345
Fax: 01300 341293
Holy Island *Tel:* 01289 389216
Fax: 07092 311104
Leeds *Tel:* 0113 226 0647
Plaistow: Divine Compassion *Tel:* 020 7476 5189
Plaistow: St Matthias' Vicarage *Tel:* 020 7511 7848
Walsingham *Tel:* 01328 820762

Australia and New Zealand Province
Minister Brother Alfred BoonKong SSF. *Houses:* Brisbane (QLD), Stroud (NSW), Kirikiriroa/Hamilton (NZ)

Papua New Guinea Province
Minister Brother Lawrence Hauje SSF. Houses: Haruro, Jimi, Katerada, Koki, Popondetta: Martyr's House, Popondetta: Newton College, Ukaka

Province of the Solomon Islands
Minister, Brother George SSF. *Houses:* Auki, Busa, Hautambu: La Verna, Hautambu: Little Portion, Honiara, Kira Kira, Kohimarama, Temotu, Vuru

Province of the Americas
Minister Brother Jude SSF. *Houses: Berkeley,* Long Island, San Francisco

SOCIETY OF ST JOHN THE EVANGELIST
St Edward's House, 22 Gt College St, Westminster, London SW1P 3QA
Tel: 020 7222 9234
Fax: 020 7799 2641
email: superior@ssje.org.uk
guestmaster@ssje.org.uk

Superior Revd Fr Peter Huckle SSJE
Assistant Superior Brother James Simon SSJE

Visitor Rt Revd Dominic Walker OGS (*Bishop of Monmouth*)

Founded 1866, for men, clerical and lay. Engaged in retreats, missions and educational work.

SOCIETY OF THE SACRED MISSION
See **Mixed Communities** page 254.

Communities for Women

EDGWARE ABBEY, BENEDICTINE COMMUNITY OF ST MARY AT THE CROSS
Priory Field Drive, Edgware, Middx HA8 9PU
Tel: 020 8958 7868
Fax: 020 8958 1920
email: info@edgwareabbey.org.uk

Abbess Mother Mary Thérèse Zelent OSB

Visitor Rt Revd Peter Wheatley (*Bishop of Edmonton*)

Founded in 1866 in Shoreditch, London, with the primary object of praying at the heart of the Church, through the offering of the Divine Office and the Eucharist, living under the Rule of St Benedict.

From the beginning, worship found expression in loving care as the sisters responded to the desperate needs of the sick, poor and disabled around them. This work grew, developing to meet the needs and demands of its time, and continues today with the provision of a Care Home, Henry Nihill House, adjacent to the Abbey.

Early in 2010 the small community made the decision to close the large convent building; this will take effect during 2011. Henry Nihill House, the Chapel, Cloisters and Gardens will remain in the Edgware Abbey Charitable Trust. Buildings near the chapel will be converted into a living area for the Sisters and Guest Accommodation for retreatants. Edgware Abbey, with its good transport links and accessibility from the M1 and A1, will continue in a smaller setting and the sisters will maintain their ministry of hospitality to those in need of rest and renewal.

BENEDICTINE COMMUNITY OF ST MARY'S ABBEY
52 Swan St, West Malling, Kent ME19 6JX
Tel: 01732 843309

Abbess Sister Mary David Best OSB

Visitor Rt Revd John Waine

We are a monastic community of women following the Rule of St Benedict. Our home is a Benedictine Abbey that flourished from c. 1090 to 1538. Our priorities are prayer, community life and hospitality to those who stay at our guest house and who wish to share in our worship and silence.

BENEDICTINE COMMUNITY AT BURFORD
See **Mixed Communities** page 254.

COMMUNITY OF ALL HALLOWS
All Hallows Convent, Ditchingham, Norfolk

Postal Address Bungay, Suffolk NR35 2DT
Tel: 01986 892749
Fax: 01986 895838
email: allhallowsconvent@btinternet.com

Leaders Sister Elizabeth and Sister Sheila CAH

Visitor Rt Revd Graham James (*Bishop of Norwich*)

Founded 1855. Augustinian Visitation Rule.

Work and Houses at Ditchingham:
The Convent (*as above*)
All Hallows House: Guests, retreats and spiritual direction
Tel: 01986 892840

Ditchingham Day Nursery – up to 30 children
Tel: 01986 895091

All Hallows Country Hospital and All Hallows Nursing Home: the hospital and nursing home have now been combined under the management of the All Hallows Health Care Trust

All Hallows House, Rouen Rd, Norwich NR1 1QT   Tel: 01603 624738

Guests, retreats and spiritual direction

COMMUNITY OF ST ANDREW
34 Reynard Court, Foxley Lane, Purley, Surrey CR8 3EN
Tel: 020 8668 4604 (Sr Teresa)   020 7221 8401
email: teresajoan@btinternet.com

Superior Revd Mother Lillian CSA

Visitor Rt Revd Richard Chartres (*Bishop of London*)

Founded 1861. Full membership of the Community consists of professed sisters who are Deaconesses or Distinctive Deacons or Priests. Present number is seven.
The fundamental ministry is the offering of prayer and worship, evangelism and pastoral work now through retirement ministries.

COMMUNITY OF ST CLARE
St Mary's Convent, Freeland, Witney, Oxon. OX29 8AJ   Tel: 01993 881225
Fax: 01993 882434
email: community@oscfreeland.co.uk

Abbess Sister Paula OSC

Bishop Protector Rt Revd Michael Perham (*Bishop of Gloucester*)

Founded 1950. Second Order of Society of St Francis. Contemplative and enclosed.

COMMUNITY OF ST DENYS
Ivy House, 2–3 Church St, Warminster, Wilts. BA12 8PG

Acting Leader Mrs June Watt (oblate)

Visitor Bishop of Salisbury

Christian mission through the operation of a day and residential Retreat Centre, prayer and intercession, and the award of small charitable grants for religious or educational purposes.

Tel: 01985 214824
email: stdenys@ivyhouse.org

COMMUNITY OF ST FRANCIS
Founded in 1905, the sisters of the First Order of the Society of St Francis, in the European Province and in the Province of the Americas, seek to live the gospel for today through lives of prayer, study and work. Prayer, together and alone, with the Eucharist having a central place, is the heart of each house and each sister's life. Four sisters are priests, and three live the solitary life. Study nurtures each sister's spiritual life and enables and enriches ministries. Work (voluntary or salaried) includes the practical running of the houses and a wide range of ministries, presently including hospitality, prison and hospital chaplaincy, spiritual direction, leading retreats and quiet days, parish work and missions, speaking and writing, counselling, caring for the homeless, providing support for families of those with a life-threatening illness, and nursing. In all this the sisters seek to follow Christ in the footsteps of Francis and Clare of Assisi, and in the spirit of humility, love and joy.

Minister General Sister Joyce CSF, Southwark
Tel 020 7898 8912
email: ministergeneralcsf@franciscans.org.uk

Minister Provincial, European Province Sister Helen Julian CSF, Freeland
Tel: 01993 358722
email: ministercsf@franciscans.org.uk
Web: www.franciscans.org.uk

Bishop Protector Rt Revd Michael Perham (*Bishop of Gloucester*)

Houses St Alphege Clergy House, Pocock St, London SE1 0BJ   Tel: 020 7898 8912
email: southwarkcsf@franciscans.org.uk

San Damiano, 38 Drury Street, Metheringham, Lincoln LN4 3EZ
Tel: 01526 321115
email: metheringhamcsf@franciscans.org.uk

The Vicarage, 11 St Mary's Rd, Plaistow, London E13 9AE   Tel: 020 8552 4019
email: stmaryscssf@franciscans.org.uk

St Francis House, 113 Gillott Rd, Birmingham B16 0ET   Tel: 0121 454 8302
email: birminghamcsf@franciscans.org.uk

St Matthew's House, 25 Kamloops Crescent, Leicester LE1 2HX   Tel: 0116 253 9158
email: leicestercsf@franciscans.org.uk

Korean Region: Box 1003, Gumi Post Office, Gumi, Gyeongbukdo 730–600, Republic of Korea
Tel: 054 451 2317; email: koreanfs@hotmail.com

Minister Provincial, Province of the Americas Sister Pamela Clare CSF, St Francis House, 3743 Cesar Chavez St, San Francisco CA 94110, USA
email: csfsfo@aol.com
Web: www.communitystfrancis.org

Bishop Protector Rt Revd Bevi Edna (Nedi) Rivera, Suffragan Bishop, Diocese of Olympia

COMMUNITY OF ST JOHN BAPTIST
Community of St John Baptist, The Priory, 2 Spring Hill Rd, Begbroke, Kidlington, Oxon. OX5 1RX
Tel: 01865 855320
Fax: 01865 855336
email: csjbteam@csjb.org.uk

Community Leader Sr Ann Verena CJGS

Visitor Rt Revd John Pritchard, Bishop of Oxford

Chaplain Revd Lister Tonge

Founded 1852 to honour and worship Almighty God and to serve him in works of charity. Undertakes mission and parish work, group quiet days, private retreats and spiritual direction.

COMMUNITY OF ST JOHN THE DIVINE
St John's House, 652 Alum Rock Rd, Birmingham, W Midlands B8 3NS
Tel: 0121 327 4174
email: csjdivine@btinternet.com
Web: www.csjd.org.uk

Leaders of the Community Sister Christine CSJD and Sister Margaret Angela CSJD

Visitor Rt Revd David Urquhart, Bishop of Birmingham

The Community was founded in 1848. The underpinning of our life and work is a spirituality based on St John the Apostle of Love. Today, as we continue to welcome people to test their vocation in the Religious Life, we have considered the challenge of change. The small core group of the Community has become the centre for a growing circle of Associates and Alongsiders who share much of our life. Our vision is to be a centre of prayer within the diocese, to exercise a ministry of hospitality to individuals and groups, to offer a ministry of spiritual accompaniment and to be open to new ways in which God might use us here, for example building friendships with our Muslim neighbours.

COMMUNITY OF ST LAURENCE
Convent of St Laurence, 4a Westgate, Southwell, Nottinghamshire NG25 0JH
Tel: 01636 814800

Warden Very Revd David Leaning

Founded 1874 in Norwich and moved to Belper in Derbyshire in 1877. Moved to Southwell in September 2001. Accommodation for visitors is available in the Sacrista Prebend Retreat House next door. (*See* **Retreat Houses** page 223.)

COMMUNITY OF ST MARY THE VIRGIN
St Mary's Convent, Challow Rd, Wantage, Oxon. OX12 9DJ
Tel: 01235 763141
email: conventsisters@csmv.co.uk
guestwing@csmv.co.uk
Web: www.csmvonline.org.uk

Superior Mother Winsome CSMV

Visitor The Bishop of Oxford, Rt Revd John Pritchard

The Community of St Mary the Virgin (CSMV) was founded in 1848. We are called to respond to our vocation in the spirit of the Blessed Virgin Mary: 'Behold, I am the handmaid of the Lord. Let it be to me according to your word.' Our common life is centred in the worship of God through the Eucharist, the daily Office and personal prayer, from which all else flows. The strong musical tradition of CSMV continues to enrich our worship. The work of the Community is inspired by Mary's words, 'Whatever He says to you, do it.' It may take the form of outgoing ministry in neighbourhood and parish, or in living alongside those in inner city areas. For others, it will be expressed in hospitality, spiritual direction, preaching and retreat giving, or in creative work in studio and press. Sisters also live and work among the elderly at St Katharine's House, a large Care Home for the elderly in Wantage. An extensive new area of mission has opened up for us since the launch of our interactive website in September 2009. In addition to a daily update, we offer weekly meditations and retreats on line. We are able to receive requests for prayer through our website, and we also stream all our Offices live. The Community has had a share in the nurturing and training of a small indigenous Community in Madagascar, and continues to maintain links with the sisters there. The Community also lived and worked in India and South Africa for many years. Involvement with both these countries remains through 'Wantage Overseas'. Our links with South Africa are also maintained by groups of Oblates and Associates living there. There are larger groups of Oblates and Associates in England. At St Mary's Convent there is a Guest Wing for those who wish to spend time in rest, retreat and silence within the setting of a religious community.

366 High St, Smethwick B66 3PD
Tel: 0121 558 0094
email: smethwick.sisters@btinternet.com

116 Seymour Rd, Harringay, London N8 0BG
Tel and *Fax:* 020 8348 3477
email: wanatage-os@fireflyuk.net

St Katharine's House, Ormond Rd, Wantage OX12 8EA (Home for the Elderly.)
Tel: 01235 767380
email: sisters.stkatharines@btconnect.com

COMMUNITY OF ST PETER
St Columba's House, Maybury Hill, Woking, Surrey GU22 8AB   *Tel:* 01483 750739
email: reverendmother@stpetersconvent.co.uk
Web: stcolumbashouse.org.uk

Superior Mother Lucy Clare CSP

Visitor Rt Revd David Walker (*Bishop of Dudley*)

Founded in 1861 for mission work and nursing. The Sisters are dispersed, but meet together at least monthly. Reverend Mother Lucy Clare, our Ordained Sister, and Sister Angela live in Woking and work within St Columba's House, the Sisterhood's retreat and conference centre. Sister Caroline Jane lives in Staines, is a community psychiatric nurse and also works in a local parish in Thorpe. Sister Rosamond and Sister Margaret Paul are at St Mary's Convent and Nursing Home in Chiswick. Sister Georgina Ruth lives in Croydon and works within a local parish.

COMMUNITY OF ST PETER, HORBURY
St Peter's Convent, Dovecote Lane, Horbury, Wakefield, W Yorks. WF4 6BD   *Tel:* 01924 272181
email: stpetersconvent@btconnect.com

Reverend Mother Mother Robina CSPH

Visitor The Bishop of Wakefield

Benedictine in spirit. Undertakes a variety of pastoral ministries and retreat work.

COMMUNITY OF THE COMPANIONS OF JESUS THE GOOD SHEPHERD
The Priory, 2 Spring Hill Rd, Begbroke, Kidlington, Oxon. OX5 1RX   *Tel:* 01865 855326
email: cjgs@csjb.org.uk

Superior Sister Ann Verena CJGS

Visitor Rt Revd Dominic Walker OGS (*Bishop of Monmouth*)

Founded 1920. Undertakes work with the elderly, lay and ordained ministry training, quiet days and retreats, spiritual direction.

COMMUNITY OF THE GLORIOUS ASCENSION
Prasada, 294 RD 37 Quartier Subrane, 83440 Montauroux, France   *Tel:* 00 334 94 47 74 26
email: cga.prasada@orange.fr
Web: www.cgaprasada.com

The Sisters are called to unite a monastic community life with work alongside other people.

At Prasada they welcome visitors who seek a peaceful environment in which to find refreshment. Guests and local English-speaking people have the opportunity to use the chapel for private prayer and to join the Sisters for Eucharist and Divine Office both on Sundays and weekdays.

COMMUNITY OF THE HOLY CROSS
Holy Cross Convent, Highfields, Nottingham Rd, Costock, Nr Loughborough LE12 6XE (from May 2011)   *Tel:* 01509 880336
Fax: 01509 881812
Web: www.holycrosschc.org.uk
email: chc.rempstone@webleicester.co.uk

Mother Superior Revd Mother Mary Luke CHC

Visitor Rt Revd Dr David Hope

Founded in 1857 for mission work but later adopted the Rule of St Benedict. All the work, centred on the daily celebration of the Divine Office and the Eucharist, is done within the Enclosure.

The Sisters contribute articles on spirituality and Christian unity to various publications and disseminate these via their web site. A variety of prayer and greeting cards are also produced by the Sisters. The Community provides for Quiet Days for individuals and groups, and there is limited residential accommodation for those wishing to make longer retreats.

COMMUNITY OF THE HOLY FAMILY
St Mary's Abbey, 52 Swan St, West Malling, Kent ME19 6JX   *Tel:* 01732 843309

Visitor Rt Revd John Hind (*Bishop of Chichester*)

The spirit of the educational work begun by the Foundress, Mother Agnes Mason, continues in the Diocese of Chichester through the operation of the Mother Agnes Trust. The Charity has enabled the creation of an extensive educational resource centre, incorporating a substantial and growing theological library, known as 'The Magnet', at St Leonard's-on-Sea. The remaining Sister lives gratefully with the Sisters at the Abbey.

COMMUNITY OF THE HOLY NAME
Convent of the Holy Name, Morley Rd, Oakwood, Derby DE21 4QZ   *Tel:* 01332 671716
Fax: 01332 669712
email: bursarsoffice@tiscali.co.uk
web: www.chnderby.org

Superior Sr Monica Jane CHN

Visitor Rt Revd John Inge

Founded 1865. Undertakes mission and retreat work. Guests received.

Branch Houses
Cottage 5, Lambeth Palace, London SE1 7JU
Tel: 020 7928 5407
64 Allexton Gardens, Welland Estate, Peterborough PE1 4UW   *Tel:* 01733 352077
St John's Rectory, St John's Rd, Longsight, Manchester M13 0WU   *Tel:* 0161 224 4336

Overseas
Lesotho Convent of the Holy Name, PO Box 22, Ficksburg 9730, RSA   *Tel:* 00266 22400249

Zululand Convent of the Holy Name, P/B 806, Melmoth 3835, RSA   *Tel:* 00273 54502892

COMMUNITY OF THE SACRED PASSION
Mother House: Convent of the Sacred Passion, 22 Buckingham Rd, Shoreham-by-Sea, W Sussex BN43 5UB   *Tel:* 01273 453807
email: communitysp@yahoo.co.uk
Superior Mother Philippa CSP

Visitor Rt Revd Ian Brackley (*Bishop of Dorking*)

Founded 1911. An order which combines prayer and mission work in varying forms. In England the sisters continue their life of prayer at the Mother House and a house in Clapham. Their active work is a response to the needs of the people among whom they live and so keeps developing. The Community withdrew from Tanzania in June 1991, leaving behind a community of more than ninety Tanzanian women known as the Community of St Mary. This community is still given support by CSP as is the Kwamkono Polio Hostel which was founded by CSP.

COMMUNITY OF THE SERVANTS OF THE CROSS
Green Willow Residential Home, 23 Vicarage Lane, East Preston, Littlehampton BN16 2SP
Tel: 01903 868761
Superior Mother Angela CSC
Visitor Rt Revd John Hind (*Bishop of Chichester*)
Warden and Chaplain Revd J. Lyon

Augustinian Rule. The sisters are now in retirement.

COMMUNITY OF THE SERVANTS OF THE WILL OF GOD
See **Mixed Communities** page 254.

COMMUNITY OF THE SISTERS OF THE CHURCH
St Michael's Convent, 56 Ham Common, Richmond, Surrey TW10 7JH
Tel: 020 8940 8711 and 020 8948 2502
Fax: 020 8948 5525
email: info@sistersofthechurch.org.uk
Web: www.sistersofthechurch.org.uk

UK Provincial Sister Susan CSC
email: susan@sistersofthechurch.org.uk

Visitor Rt Revd Christopher Chessun

Founded 1870 and has a modern rule, based on the original, expressing a life rooted in prayer and worship, which flows into an active ministry through hospitality, pastoral and social justice work, spiritual direction and counselling.
Other Houses in the UK
82 Ashley Rd, St Paul's Bristol BS6 5NT
Tel: 0117 941 3268
Fax: 0117 908 6620
112 St Andrew's Rd North, St Annes-on-Sea, Lancs. FY8 2JQ   *Tel:* 01253 728016
10 Furness Rd, West Harrow, Middx HA2 0RL
Tel and *Fax:* 020 8423 3780
Well Cottage, Upper Street, Kingsdown, Nr Deal, Kent CT14 8BH
Available for retreats and holidays
email: wellcottage@sistersofthechurch.org.uk

Novitiate
St Gabriel's, 27a Dial Hill Rd, Clevedon, North Somerset BS21 7HL   *Tel:* 01275 544 471

Main Houses of Overseas Provinces
Sister Linda Mary CSC, Mother Superior and Australian Provincial
29 Lika Drive, Kempsey, NSW 2440, Australia
send all correspondence to: PO Box 1105, Glebe, NSW2037, Australia
Sister Margaret CSC, Canadian Provincial
St Michael's House, 1392 Hazelton Boulevard, Burlington, Ontario L7P 4V3, Canada
Sister Phyllis CSC, Solomon Islands Provincial
Tetete ni Kolivuti, Box 510, Honiara, Solomon Islands

COMMUNITY OF THE SISTERS OF THE LOVE OF GOD
Convent of the Incarnation, Fairacres, Parker St, Oxford OX4 1TB   *Tel:* 01865 721301
Fax: 01865 250798
email: sisters@slg.org.uk
Guest Sister guests@slg.org.uk
Web: www.slg.org.uk

Reverend Mother Sister Margaret Theresa SLG

Visitor Rt Revd Michael Lewis (*Bishop of Cyprus and the Gulf*)

A contemplative community with a strong monastic tradition founded in 1906, which seeks to witness to the priority of God and to respond to the love of God – God's love for us and our love for God. We believe that we are called to live a substantial degree of withdrawal, in order to give ourselves to a spiritual work of prayer which, beginning and ending in the praise and worship of God, is essential for the peace and well-being of the world. Through offering our lives to God within the Community and through prayer and daily life together, we seek to deepen our relationship with Jesus Christ and one another. The Community has always drawn upon the spirituality of Carmel; life and prayer in silence and solitude is an important dimension in our vocation. The Community also draws from other traditions, and our Rule is not specifically Carmelite. Another important ingredient is an emphasis on the centrality of Divine Office and Eucharist together in choir, inspired partly by the Benedictine way of life.

SLG Press publishes pamphlets on spirituality and prayer.
SLG Press, Convent of the Incarnation, Fairacres, Parker St, Oxford OX4 1TB   *Tel:* 01865 241874
Fax: 01865 241889
email: editor@slgpress.co.uk
Web: www.slgpress.co.uk

ORDER OF THE HOLY PARACLETE
St Hilda's Priory, Sneaton Castle, Whitby, N Yorks. YO21 3QN   *Tel:* 01947 602079
Fax: 01947 820854
email: ohppriorywhitby@btinternet.com
Web: www.ohpwhitby.org

Superior Sister Dorothy Stella OHP

Visitor Most Revd John Sentamu

Founded in 1915 and based on the Rule of St Benedict. Main undertaking: prayer, pastoral work, retreats, conferences, missions, parish work.

Residential Conference Centre Sneaton Castle Centre, Whitby, N Yorks. YO21 3QN
Tel: 01947 600051
Fax: 01947 603490
email: sneaton@globalnet.co.uk
Web: www.sneatoncastle.co.uk
Accommodation and facilities for large and small groups for parish activities, conferences and educational courses.

Branch Houses
Beach Cliff, 14 North Promenade, Whitby, N Yorks. YO21 3JX   *Tel:* 01947 601968
St Oswald's Pastoral Centre, Woodlands Drive, Sleights, Whitby, N Yorks. YO21 1RY
Tel: 01947 810496
Fax: 01947 810759
email: ohpstos@globalnet.co.uk
9 Cranbourne St, Spring Bank, Hull HU3 1PP
Tel: 01482 586816
Fax: 01482 213114
email: ohphull@ohphull.karoo.co.uk

1A Minster Court, York YO1 7JD
Tel: 01904 5577276
email: ohpyork@onetel.net.uk

Working in York Minster and Library.
All Saints House, South Avenue, Dormanstown TS10 5II   *Tel:* 01642 486424
email: sisteranita@btinternet.com

Parish work
3 Acaster Rd, Bishopthorpe YO23 5SA
Tel: 01904 777294
email: ahpbishopthorpe@archbishopofyork.org

Chaplain Revd Simon J Lumby

Overseas
OHP Sisters, Box 523, Piggs Peak, Swaziland
Tel: 00 268 4371514
email: carole@bulembu.org
AIDS awareness, home for abused girls and AIDS orphans.

Convent of the Holy Spirit, PO Box AH 9375, Ahinsan, Kumasi, Ashanti, Ghana
Tel: 00233 242 203 432
email: ohpjac@yahoo.com

Fostering indigenous vocations, undertaking pastoral work and eye clinic ministry.

PRIORY OF OUR LADY, WALSINGHAM
Priory of Our Lady, Walsingham, Norfolk NR22 6ED   *Tel:* 01328 820340 (Reverend Mother); 01328 820901 (Sisters and Guest Sister)

Superior Mother Carolyne Joseph SSM
email: mothercarolyne@ssmargaret.com

Visitor Rt Revd Peter Wheatley (*Bishop of Edmonton*)

Autonomous house of the Society of St Margaret. Sisters are involved in the ministry of healing and reconciliation in the Shrine, the local parishes and the wider Church. They are also available to pilgrims and visitors and work in the Sacristy, the Shrine Shop and Education Department in the Shrine. A Guest House is available. Guests are welcome for short periods of rest, relaxation and retreat. All bookings to be made through the Guest Sister.

ST SAVIOUR'S PRIORY
18 Queensbridge Rd, London E2 8NS
Tel: 020 7739 6775 (Guest bookings) 020 7739 9976 (Sisters)
email: ssmpriory@aol.com
Web: www.stsaviourspriory.org.uk

Superior Revd Sr Helen Loder SSM

Visitor Rt Revd Dominic Walker OGS (*Bishop of Monmouth*)

Autonomous convent of the Society of St Margaret, working as staff members (lay or ordained) in various parishes, dance workshops, complementary therapy, with the homeless, etc.; retreats and individual spiritual direction. The Priory has a few guest rooms and facilities for individual private retreats as well as excellent facilities for small group meetings.

SISTERS OF BETHANY
7 Nelson Rd, Southsea, Hants. PO5 2AR
Tel: 023 9283 3498
email: ssb@sistersofbethany.org.uk
Web: www.sistersofbethany.org.uk

Superior Mother Rita-Elizabeth, ssB

Visitor Rt Revd Trevor Wilmott (*Bishop of Dover and Bishop in Canterbury*)

Founded 1866 for hospitality, retreat work and prayer for Christian Unity. The Sisters are available for leading quiet days and retreats, as spiritual directors, and also to give talks on prayer. People are welcome to come individually or as groups to spend time in silence and prayer. It is possible to accommodate a few residential guests, or groups of up to 24 for the day. A reference is required for guests applying to stay for the first time.

SISTERS OF CHARITY
237 Ridgeway, Plympton, Plymouth PL7 2HP
Tel: 01752 336112
email: plymptonsisters@tiscali.co.uk

Superior Revd Mother Elizabeth Mary sc

Visitor Rt Revd Robert Evens (*Bishop of Crediton*)

Founded 1869. The Rule is based on that of St Vincent de Paul. We assist as required in parish work and in intercessory prayer, and maintain a nursing home.

Branch Houses
St Vincent's Nursing Home, Plympton, Plymouth PL7 1NE   *Tel:* 01752 336205
Carmel, 7a Gress, Isle of Lewis HS2 0NB
Tel: 01851 820734

SOCIETY OF ALL SAINTS SISTERS OF THE POOR
All Saints Convent, St Mary's Rd, Oxford OX4 1RU   *Tel:* 01865 249127
Fax: 01865 726547
email: admin@socallss.co.uk
Guests' email: guestsister@socallss.co.uk

Community Leader Sister Helen Mary Assp

Visitor Rt Revd Bill Ind

Founded in London 1851. Works of the Society: St John's Residential Home for the Elderly, St Mary's Rd, Oxford OX4 1QE   *Tel:* 01865 247725
Fax: 01865 247920
email: admin@st-johns-home.org

Guest House (single, twin and double accommodation available). Also conference facilities for groups of up to about 12, weekdays, daytime only. Enquiries regarding visits, private retreats and conferences welcomed. Telephone and fax numbers as shown above for All Saints' Convent.

The Society is associated with:
Helen and Douglas House; The Porch Steppin' Stone Centre; All Saints Embroidery

SOCIETY OF ST MARGARET
St Margaret's Convent, Hooke Hall, 250 High St, Uckfield RN22 1EN   *Tel:* 01825 766808
Fax: 01825 763474
email: egmotherssm@hotmail.com

Superior Sister Cynthia Clare ssM

Visitor Rt Revd John Hind (*Bishop of Chichester*)

Founded 1855 and undertakes nursing work, runs guest and retreat accommodation, also parish work. Sisters available for spiritual guidance and quiet afternoons.

Branch House St Mary's Convent and Nursing Home, Burlington Lane, Chiswick, London W4 2QE (guest house for elderly ladies and nursing home for geriatric and handicapped ladies)
Tel: 020 8994 4641
Fax: 020 8995 9796

Superior Sister Jennifer Anne ssM

Visitor Rt Revd John Hind (*Bishop of Chichester*)

A Residential Home for elderly retired ladies; and Nursing Home for those needing full-time nursing care.

Overseas St Margaret's Convent (*semi-autonomous*), 157 St Michael's Rd, Polwatte, Colombo 3, Sri Lanka

A home for the aged, a retreat house and a children's home.

Sister Superior Sister Chandrani ssM
Tel: 00 94 11 2320692
Visitor Rt Revd Duleep de Chickera (Bishop of Colombo)

Branch House
St John's Home, 133 Galle Rd, Moratuwa, Sri Lanka.   *Tel:* 00 94 11 2645304

Independent Convents of the Society St Margaret
St Saviour's Priory, 18 Queensbridge Rd, London E2 8NS
Leader Sister Helen ssM   *Tel:* 020 7739 6775
email: ssmpriory@aol.com
Priory of Our Lady, Walsingham, Norfolk, NR22 6ED

Superior Mother Carolyn Joseph ssm
Tel: 01328 820340
email: mothercarolyne@ssmargaret.com
St Margaret's Convent, 17 Highland Park St,
Boston, MA 02119, USA
Superior Sister Carolyne ssm
Tel: 00 1 617 445 8961
Fax: 00 1 617 445 7120
email: ssmconvent@ssmbos.com

SOCIETY OF THE PRECIOUS BLOOD
Burnham Abbey, Lake End Rd, Taplow, Maiden-
head, Berks. SL6 0PW
Tel: 01628 604080
email: burnhamabbey@btinternet.com
Web: www.burnhamabbey.org

Superior The Revd Mother spb

Visitor Rt Revd Stephen Cottrell (*Bishop of Reading*)

Founded 1905 and based on Rule of St Augustine.
Contemplative and exists for the purpose of per-
petual intercession for the Church and for the
world.

Overseas Independent Daughter House Priory of
Our Lady Mother of Mercy, Masite, PO Box MS
7192, Maseru 100, Lesotho

Dependent House of the Overseas House St
Monica's House of Prayer, 46 Green St, West
End, Kimberley 8301, Cape, RSA

SOCIETY OF THE SACRED CROSS
Tymawr Convent, Lydart, Monmouth, Gwent
NP25 4RN
Tel: 01600 860244
email: tymawrconvent@btinternet.com
Web: www.churchinwales.org.uk/tymawr

Superior Sister Gillian Mary ssc

Visitor Rt Revd Dominic Walker ogs (*Bishop of
Monmouth*)

Founded in 1914 at St George's, Chichester; four
sisters felt called to the monastic, contemplative
life, which was established in Wales in 1923. The
community lives a life of prayer based on silence,
solitude and learning to live together, under
vows of poverty, chastity and obedience, with a
modern rule, Cistercian in spirit. It is possible for
women and men, married or single, to experience
our life of prayer by living alongside the community for periods longer than the usual guest
stay. There are facilities for retreatants and small
groups. The extended community consists of
companions, oblates and associates. The community is dedicated to the crucified and risen
Lord as the focus of its life and the source of the
power to live it. The setting in the unspoilt rural
border country of Wales plays a very real part in
the spirituality of the community.

SOCIETY OF THE SACRED MISSION
See **Mixed Communities** page 254.

Mixed Communities

BENEDICTINE COMMUNITY AT
MUCKNELL ABBEY
The Community of Benedictine nuns and monks
recently relocated from Burford to a new ecologic-
ally sustainable monastery in Worcestershire.
Mucknell Abbey, Mucknell Farm Lane, Stoulton,
Worcestershire WR7 9RB
Telephone not yet known
email: information@mucknellabbey.org.uk

Abbot Rt Revd Stuart Burns osb
email: abbot@mucknellabbey.org.uk

Visitor Rt Revd John Inge

By a common life of prayer, manual work
and study the Community tries to create an
atmosphere of stillness and silence in which the
Community and its guests are enabled to be open
and receptive to the presence of God.

While the recitation of the Office and celebration of the Eucharist constitute the principal
work of the Community, the ministry of hospitality, the care of the grounds (which comprise
a large organic kitchen garden in 40 acres of

orchard, meadow and woodland), and the
income-generating crafts of incense-making, icon
writing and block-mounting, and Chinese brush
painting provide a variety of manual work for
the members of the Community and those guests
who wish to share in it.

The monastery seeks to be a place of encounter
and reconciliation. The early concern of the Community was to pray for Christian unity, and the
Community enjoys links with Baptist, Lutheran,
Orthodox and Roman Catholic communities, and
is particularly committed to the furthering of the
Covenant between the Church of England and
the Methodist Church. This ecumenical concern
has broadened to include dialogue with people of
other faiths, particularly those with a monastic
tradition, and those who are seeking a spiritual
way, either within or outside an established
religious tradition.

COMMUNITY OF THE SERVANTS OF THE
WILL OF GOD
Monastery of the Holy Trinity, Crawley Down,
Crawley, W Sussex RH10 4LH
Tel: 01342 712074
email: brother.andrew@cswg.org.uk

Father Superior Revd Fr Colin cswg
Visitor Rt Revd John Hind (*Bishop of Chichester*)
Founded 1953 for men (clerical and lay). Women
are now received also. Contemplative. Retreats
and conferences. The Community has also
founded a charitable trust for promoting the
Christian tradition of contemplative life and
prayer within the Church.

SOCIETY OF ST FRANCIS, THIRD ORDER

One of the three Orders of the Society of St Fran-
cis (see also Communities for Men, page 246;
Communities for Women, page 248). The Third
Order is made up of women and men, lay and
ordained, single and married, seeking to live out
Franciscan ideals in the ordinary walks of life.
There are just under 2000 Tertiaries in the Euro-
pean Province; there are four other Provinces:
Africa, the Americas, Australia and New
Zealand.

Minister General Revd Dorothy Brooker TSSF, 16
Downing St, Pirimai, Napier, New Zealand
email: dmbrook@clear.net.nz

Minister Provincial European Province Revd Joanna
Coney, 4 Rowland Close, Wolvercote, Oxford
OX2 8PW
Tel: 01865 556456
email: ministertssf@franciscans.org.uk
Web: www.tssf.org.uk

SOCIETY OF THE SACRED MISSION

Founded 1893. A religious community engaged
in educational, pastoral and missionary work.
The Society is divided into Provinces:

Province of Europe
Visitor The Bishop of Oxford, Rt Revd John
Pritchard
Provincial Fr Colin Griffiths ssm
The Well, Newport Rd, Willen MK15 9AA
Tel: 01908 231 986
email: colin.griffiths@hotmail.com
Houses
St Antony's Priory, 74 Claypath, Durham DH1
1QT   *Tel:* 0191 384 3747
email: durham.ssm@which.net

1 Linford Lane, Milton Keynes, Bucks. MK15 9DL
Tel: 01908 663749
The Well, Newport Rd, Willen MK15 9AA

Southern Province
Visitor The Archbishop of Melbourne, Most Revd
Philip Freier
Provincial Fr Christopher Myers SSM
St John's Priory, 14 St John's Street, Adelaide,
South Australia 5000
email: ssm.s.province@esc.net.au
Houses St John's Priory, 14 St John's St, Adelaide,
S Australia 5000
St Michael's Priory, 75 Watsons Rd, Diggers Rest,
Victoria, Australia 3427

Southern African Province
Visitor The Archbishop of Cape Town, Most
Revd Thabo Makgoba
Provincial Fr Michael Lapsley ssm
SSM House, 33 Elgin Rd, Syband Park, Cape
Town 7700, RSA
email: michael.lapsley@attglobal.net
SSM Priory, PO Box 1579, Maseru 100, Lesotho,
Southern Africa   *email:* priorssm@ilesotho.com

Organizations

PART 4

Classified List of Organizations Included in this Section

Animal Welfare
Anglican Society for the Welfare of Animals

Art, Architecture
Art and Christianity Enquiry
Art and Sacred Places
Christian Arts
Church Monuments Society
Ecclesiological Society
Friends of Friendless Churches
York Glaziers' Trust

Bell-ringing
Ancient Society of College Youths
Central Council of Church Bell Ringers
Society of Royal Cumberland Youths

Bible Study
BRF
Bible Society
Lord Wharton's Charity
SASRA
Scripture Gift Mission International
Scripture Union
Vacation Term for Biblical Study

Blind People
Blind, Royal National Institute for the
Guild of Church Braillists
St John's Guild

Church Buildings
Friends of Friendless Churches
Greater Churches Group
Incorporated Church Building Society
Marshall's Charity
Vergers, Church of England Guild of

Church Societies – General
Additional Curates Society
Affirming Catholicism
Association of English Cathedrals
Cathedral and Church Shops Association
Cathedral Libraries and Archives Association
Cathedrals Administration and Finance
   Association
Catholic Group in General Synod
Church of England Flower Arrangers
   Association
CPAS (Church Pastoral Aid Society)
Church Society
Church Union
Churches' Advertising Network
Modern Churchpeople's Union
Open Synod Group
Parish and People
Society for the Maintenance of the Faith
Society of the Faith (Inc)
Unitas – The Catholic League

Church Societies – Specific
Anglican Fellowship in Scouting and Guiding
Anglican Mainstream
Association of Diocesan Registry Clerks
   (Southern Province)
Baptismal Integrity
Christian Evidence Society
CHRISM
Church House Deaneries Group
Church of England Record Society
College of Readers
Community of Aidan and Hilda
Day One Christian Ministries
Diocesan Clergy Chairs' Forum
Ecumenical Society of the Blessed Virgin
   Mary
Forward in Faith
Foundation for Church Leadership
Guild of St Leonard
Guild of Servants of the Sanctuary
Reform
Royal Martyr Church Union
Society of King Charles the Martyr
Society of Mary
Third Province Movement

Clergy Associations
Anglo-Catholic Ordination Candidates'
   Fund
Association of Black Clergy
Association of Hospice and Palliative Care
   Chaplains
Association of Ordinands and Candidates for
   Ministry
Clergy Consultation
College of Health Care Chaplains
English Clergy Association
Federation of Catholic Priests
Fellowship of Word and Spirit
Industrial Mission Association
Retired Clergy Association
School Chaplains' Conference
Society of Catholic Priests
Society of Ordained Scientists
Society of the Holy Cross
Unite Clergy and Faith Workers
See also **Professional Groups**

Consultancy
Christians Abroad
Grubb Institute
Living Stones

Coordinating Bodies
Church of England Evangelical Council
Churches' Funerals Group
Churches Main Committee
Evangelical Alliance

National Association of Diocesan Advisers for
Women's Ministry
Religious Education Council of England and
Wales
Universities and Colleges Christian Fellowship

Counselling
Anglican Association of Advisers in Pastoral
Care and Counselling
Lesbian and Gay Christian Movement
Relate
True Freedom Trust

Deaf People
British Deaf Association
Deaf People, Royal Association for
National Deaf Church Conference
RNID

Defence, Disarmament, Pacifism
Anglican Pacifist Fellowship
Commonwealth War Graves Commission
Council on Christian Approaches to Defence and
Disarmament

Diocesan Associations *see* pages 320–321

Drama
Actors' Church Union
Radius

Ecumenism
Anglican and Eastern Churches Association
Anglican–Lutheran Society
Churches' Group on Funeral Services
Fellowship of St Alban and St Sergius
Fellowship of St Thérèse of Lisieux
International Ecumenical Fellowship
Nikaean Club
Nikaean Ecumenical Trust
Order of Christian Unity
Society of Archbishop Justus Ltd
Society of St Willibrord

Education
Archbishop's Examination in Theology
Association of Church College Trusts
Bloxham Project
Christian Education
Culham Institute
Lincoln Theological Institute
Mirfield Centre
North of England Institute for Christian
Education
RE Today Services
Religious Education Council of England and
Wales
Royal Alexandra and Albert School
Royal Asylum of St Ann's Society
St George's College, Jerusalem
St Hild and St Bede Trust
Scripture Union in Schools
Trinity Foundation for Christianity and Culture

United Church Schools Trust
Woodard Corporation, the (Woodard Schools)

Evangelism
Church Army
College of Evangelists

Family
CARE
Family Action
Fellowship of St Nicholas
Mothers' Union
St Michael's Fellowship

Finance
Christian Ethical Investment Group
Ecclesiastical Insurance Office PLC
Ecumenical Council for Corporate
Responsibility
Number One Trust Fund

Grant-Making Bodies
All Saints Educational Trust
Bristol Clerical Education Society
Church of England Clergy Stipend Trust
Church Pastoral Aid Society Ministers in
Training Fund
Cleaver Ordination Candidates' Fund
Culham Educational Foundation
Elland Society Ordination Fund
Foundation of St Matthias
Hockerill Educational Foundation
Keswick Hall Charity
Newton's Trust
Ordination Candidate Funds (General)
Ordination Candidates Training Fund
Pilgrim Trust
Queen Victoria Clergy Fund
Revd Dr George Richards' Charity
Sarum St Michael Educational Charity
St Christopher's College Educational Trust
St Gabriel's Trust
St George's Trust
St Luke's College Foundation
St Mary's College Trust
St Peter's Saltley Trust
See also **Welfare**

Health, Healing and Medicine
Acorn Christian Healing Foundation
Association of Hospice and Palliative Care
Chaplains
Burrswood
Cautley House
Christian Healing Mission
Christian Medical Fellowship
College of Health Care Chaplains
Guild of Health
Guild of Pastoral Psychology
Guild of St Raphael
Harnhill Centre of Christian Healing
Pilsdon Community
Richmond Fellowship
St Luke's Hospital for the Clergy

Inter Faith, Religions
Council of Christians and Jews
INFORM
Inter Faith Network
World Congress of Faiths

Internet
COIN: Christians on the Internet
Society of Archbishop Justus Ltd

Libraries *see* pages 322–326

Marriage
Anglican Marriage Encounter
Broken Rites
Relate

Ministry
CHRISM
Diaconal Association of the Church of England
Diakonia
Distinctive Diaconate
MODEM
Royal Naval Licensed Readers' Society

Ministry, Women
Li Tim-Oi Foundation
Society for the Ministry of Women in the Church
WATCH

Mission
Aim International
Bible Society
Careforce
Christian Witness to Israel
CPAS (Church Pastoral Aid Society)
Church's Ministry Among Jewish People
Greenbelt Festivals
London City Mission
Mersey Mission to Seafarers
Mission to Seafarers, The
SASRA
Scripture Gift Mission
Scripture Union in Schools
Society for Promoting Christian Knowledge
Student Christian Movement
Trinitarian Bible Society
Universities and Colleges Christian Fellowship

Mission Overseas
All Nations Christian College
Church Mission Society
Crosslinks
Feed the Minds
Highbury Centre, The
Intercontinental Church Society
Interserve
Korean Mission Partnership
Leprosy Mission
Melanesian Mission
Mid-Africa Ministry
Mozambique and Angola Anglican Association
   (MANNA)

New England Company
OMF International (UK)
Overseas Bishoprics Fund
Oxford Mission
Papua New Guinea Church Partnership
Reader Missionary Studentship Association
Selly Oak Centre for Mission Studies
South American Mission Society
Southern Africa Church Development Trust
Tearfund
USPG: Anglicans in World Mission
World Vision

Music
Archbishops' Certificate in Church Music
Choir Benevolent Fund
Choir Schools Association
Church Music Society
Gregorian Association
Guild of Church Musicians
Hymn Society of Great Britain and Ireland
Jubilate Group
Morse-Boycott Bursary Fund
Plainsong and Medieval Music Society
Royal College of Organists
Royal School of Church Music

Overseas
Christian Aid
Christians Abroad
Farnham Castle, International Briefing and
   Conference Centre
United Nations Association (UNA–UK)
Womenaid International
World Vision

Patronage Trusts *see* pages 327–328

Prayer, Meditation, Retreats
Archway
Association for Promoting Retreats
Confraternity of the Blessed Sacrament
Friends of Little Gidding
Guild of All Souls
Guild of St Leonard
Julian Meetings, The
Julian of Norwich, Shrine of Lady
Pilsdon at Malling Community
Retreat Association
Sarum College
Servants of Christ the King
Society of Retreat Conductors
Women's World Day of Prayer

Professional Groups
Actors' Church Union
Association of Christian Teachers
Association of Christian Writers
Association of Ordinands and Candidates for
   Ministry
Christian Arts
Christians at Work
Church House Deaneries' Group

Church Schoolmasters' and School Mistresses'
  Benevolent Institution
Deans' Conference
Deans' Vergers' Conference
Ecclesiastical Law Society
Guild of Pastoral Psychology
Homes for Retired Clergy
Industrial Mission Association
Librarians' Christian Fellowship
National Association of Diocesan Advisers for
  Women's Ministry
Society of Retreat Conductors
Unite Clergy and Faith Workers
Vergers, Church of England Guild of
See also **Clergy Associations**

Publishing, Print Media
BRF
Book Aid
Feed the Minds
Rebecca Hussey's Book Charity
Scripture Union
Society for Promoting Christian Knowledge
Trinitarian Bible Society

Renewal
Keswick Convention
Sharing of Ministries Abroad (SOMA)

Research
Arthur Rank Centre
CARE
Centre for the Study of Christianity and
  Sexuality
Christian Research
Churches' Fellowship for Psychical and
  Spiritual Studies
Culham Institute
Latimer Trust
Rural Theology Association
St George's House, Windsor
Urban Theology Unit
William Temple Foundation

Rural Affairs
Arthur Rank Centre
Rural Theology Association

Scholarship and Science
Alcuin Club
Canterbury and York Society
Christian Evidence Society
Ecclesiastical Law Society
Faith and Thought
Henry Bradshaw Society
Latimer House
Liddon Trust
National Archives, The
Philip Usher Memorial Fund
Pusey House
Society for Liturgical Study
Society for Old Testament Study

Society of Ordained Scientists
Vacation Term for Biblical Study

Social Concern
Age Concern England
Careforce
Changing Attitude
Christian Socialist Movement
Church Action with the Unemployed
Church Housing Trust
English Churches Housing Group
Lesbian and Gay Christian Movement
Livability
mediawatch–uk
National Council for Social Concern
Order of Christian Unity
Pilsdon Community
St Pancras Housing
Samaritans

Training
Anglican Marriage Encounter
Association of Church Fellowships
Bridge Pastoral Foundation
Christian Education
Christians at Work
College of Preachers
GFS Platform for Young Women
Industrial Christian Fellowship
Paradox Ministries
RE Today Services
Student Christian Movement
William Temple Foundation

Travel, Pilgrimage
Accueil, Rencontre, Communauté UK
British Isles and Eire Airport Chaplains'
  Network
Pilgrim Adventure
Pilgrims' Association
Walsingham, Shrine of Our Lady of

Welfare
Almshouse Association
Beauchamp Community
Bromley and Sheppard's Colleges
Came's Charity
Church of England Soldiers', Sailors' and
  Airmen's Clubs
Church of England Soldiers', Sailors' and
  Airmen's Housing Association
Church Schoolmasters' and School Mistresses'
  Benevolent Institution
Church Welfare Association
College of St Barnabas
Community Housing and Therapy
Compassionate Friends, The
Corporation of the Sons of the Clergy
Diocesan Institutions of Chester, Manchester,
  Liverpool and Blackburn
Elizabeth Finn Care
Family Action
Frances Ashton's Charity

Friends of the Clergy Corporation
Friends of the Elderly
Homes for Retired Clergy
House of St Barnabas in Soho
Keychange
Langley House Trust
MACA – (Mental After Care Association)
Partis College
Pyncombe Charity
Revd Dr George Richards' Charity
Rainer
St Michael's Fellowship
Samaritans
Seamen's Friendly Society of St Paul
Shaftesbury Society
Society for the Assistance of Ladies in
    Reduced Circumstances
Society for the Relief of Poor Clergymen
Society of Mary and Martha
YMCA
YWCA England and Wales

Worship
Alcuin Club

Praxis
Prayer Book Society

Youth
Accueil, Rencontre, Communauté UK
Barnardo's
Boys' Brigade
Campaigner Ministries
Children's Society
Church Lads' and Church Girls'
    Brigade
Fellowship of St Nicholas
Frontier Youth Trust
GFS Platform for Young Women
Girlguiding UK
Girls' Brigade
Lee Abbey Household Communities
Lee Abbey International Students' Club
Rainer
St Christopher's Fellowship
Scout Association
Shaftesbury Homes and 'Arethusa'
Urban Saints (formerly Crusaders)
William Temple House

ORGANIZATIONS

The following list of societies and organizations with importance for the Church of England includes many that are specifically Anglican, others that are inter-denominational, and others without religious affiliation.

The inclusion of an organization is for the purposes of information and is not to be taken as implying acceptance of the objects of the organization by the Editor and Publishers of the *Year Book* or by the General Synod.

A classified list of organizations is provided in the preceding pages. **Diocesan Associations** (in support of overseas provinces and dioceses), **Libraries**, and **Patronage Trusts** are grouped together at the end of the section. *See also* Part 3 (General Information).

Accueil, Rencontre, Communaute UK (ARC UK)
ARC UK is a charity that organizes summer projects in which young people from across Europe give guided tours in their native language to visitors to churches. In so doing we seek to turn tourists into pilgrims through devotional tours in which visitors have the chance to engage, question and wonder. Our projects aim to enable churches in their ministry of welcome and education, ecumenical links and youth involvement. ARC UK is part of a network of associated organizations which organizes such projects throughout Europe. We are always interested to hear from those who might like to participate on one of our projects, or churches who might be interested in hosting a project. We are supported in our work by our Patron, the Bishop of Woolwich, the Rt Revd Christopher Chessun. *President:* Stephen Stavrou. *Secretary:* Anna Dorofeeva. *Recruitment Officer:* Christa Neudecker. *Treasurer:* Louise Lamb, Westcott House, Jesus Lane, Cambridge, CB5 8BP   *Tel:* 07528 930 966 (Mobile)
email: arc_england@yahoo.co.uk
Web: www.encounterarc.org.uk

Acorn Christian Foundation
Founded originally as the Acorn Christian Healing Trust in 1983 by Bishop Morris Maddocks and his wife Anne to see the Church and nation renewed in the service of Christ the Healer, believing that every person has the right to receive the best care and attention that will enable them to grow into wholeness. Acorn offers all Christian churches a variety of teaching and training resources in Christian healing. Many of these are conducted at Whitehill Chase, Acorn's resource centre in Hampshire, where a weekly open day is held every Tuesday (except August) in conjunction with a service of healing. Quiet Days are held bi-monthly, normally on Thursdays, and include three devotional talks and a midday service with the opportunity for personal prayer and reflection. 'Deeper Healing Days' are also run bi-monthly and these are days of prayer for inner healing concluding with a communion service. The well-established Christian Listener

courses range from a short introductory unit through to a twelve-session course, taught by trained tutors. There are 500 Acorn trained voluntary tutors throughout the country who teach listening skills to local church members. They in turn offer these resources in their church, home, workplace, local schools and wider community. Acorn has identified priority listening areas for rural and inner city deprived areas, a schools programme for youth, listening to Aids in Africa and reconciliation in Northern Ireland. Whitehill Chase is also available as a retreat centre and for church groups to hold meetings and conferences. Registered Charity no. 1080011. *Patron:* The Archbishop of Canterbury. *Director:* Revd Dr Russ Parker, Whitehill Chase, High St, Bordon, GU35 0AP   *Tel:* 01420 478121
Fax: 01420 478122
email: info@acornchristian.org
Web: www.acornchristian.org

Actors' Church Union
Founded 1899, members and associates serve those engaged in the performing arts through their interest, their action – often in association with other related bodies – and their prayers. Additionally, more than two hundred honorary chaplains serve all members of the profession in theatres, studios and schools at home and overseas. As well as spiritual counsel and practical advice, material help is given when possible. Through the Children's Charity, for example, funds are available for theatrical parents facing difficulties with the costs of their children's education. *President:* Rt Revd Jack Nicholls. *Senior Chaplain:* Revd Rob Gillion, St Paul's Church, Bedford St, Covent Garden, London, WC2E 9ED
Tel and Fax: 020 7240 0344
email: actors-church.union@tiscali.co.uk
Web: www.actorschurchunion.org

Additional Curates Society
Founded in 1837 to help maintain additional curates in poor and populous parishes and especially in new areas. The Society also fosters vocations to the priesthood. *General Secretary:* Revd Darren Smith. *Chairman:* Canon J. Winston.

Vice Chair: Rt Revd A. Robinson. *Treasurer:* Revd M. Lane, Gordon Browning House, 8 Spitfire Rd, Birmingham, B24 9PB   *Tel:* 0121 382 5533
Fax: 0121 382 6999
email: info@additionalcurates.co.uk
Web: www.additionalcurates.co.uk

Affirming Catholicism

A movement within the Church of England and the Anglican Communion, formed in 1990. 'The object of the Foundation shall be the advancement of education in the doctrines and the historical development of the Church of England and the Churches of the wider Anglican Communion, as held by those professing to stand within the catholic tradition' (extracted from the Trust Deed). Its purposes are to promote theological thinking about the contemporary implications of Catholic faith and order; to further the spiritual growth and development of clergy and laity; to organize or support lectures, conferences and seminars; to publish or support books, tracts, journals and other educational material; to provide resources for local groups meeting for purposes of study and discussion. *Chair:* Revd Jonathan Clark. *Administrator:* Mark Perrett, St Mary's Parish Office, Stoke Newington Church St, London, N19 9ES   *Tel:* 079 9185 1722
email: admin@affirmingcatholicism.org.uk
Web: www.affirmingcatholicism.org.uk

Age UK

(formerly Age Concern England)
Age UK cares about all older people and believes later life should be fulfilling and enjoyable. For too many this is impossible. As the leading charitable movement in the UK concerned with ageing and older people, Age UK finds effective ways to change that situation. Nationally, we take a lead role in campaigning, parliamentary work, policy analysis, research, specialist information and advice provision, publishing and training in the care of older people. Where possible we enable older people to solve problems themselves, providing as much or as little support as they need. Locally, Age UK provides community-based services such as lunch clubs, day centres and home visiting. These services are made possible through the work of many thousands of volunteers. Innovative programmes promote healthier lifestyles and provide older people with opportunities to give the experience of a lifetime back to their communities. Age UK is dependent on donations and legacies. The helpline is open seven days a week from 8 a.m. to 7 p.m. *Director General:* Mr Gordon Lishman CBE, Astral House, 1268 London Rd, London, SW16 4ER   *Tel:* 0800 169 6565 (Helpline)
020 8765 7200 (Reception)
email: contact@ageuk.org.uk
Web: www.ageuk.org.uk

Aim International

AIM International is an evangelical Christian mission agency serving in 20 countries in Africa and ministering to Africans living around the world. It was founded in 1895 and has over 900 members with the goal of seeing Christ-Centred churches established amongst all Africa's peoples. With priority for the unreached AIM is involved in church-planting, leadership training, education and health care. *International Director:* Revd Lanny Arenson. *UK Director:* Revd Andrew Chard, Aim International, Halifax Place, Nottingham, NG1 1QN   *Tel:* 0115 983 8120
Fax: 0115 8335156
email: ukadmin@aimeurope.net
Web: www.aimint.org/eu

Alcuin Club

Founded in 1897 to promote the study of liturgy, the Alcuin Club has a long and proud record of publishing both works of scholarship and practical manuals. Publications include collections, tracts and a new series of liturgy guides designed to accompany Common Worship. It also publishes, in conjunction with GROW, a series of Joint Liturgical Studies which has won wide acclaim. Members pay an annual subscription and receive new titles on publication. *President:* Rt Revd Michael Perham. *Chairman:* Canon Donald Gray. *Treasurer:* Mr John Collins. *Secretary:* Revd Gordon Jeanes. *Editorial Secretary:* Revd Dr Ben Gordon Taylor, 5 Saffron St, Royston, Herts, SG8 9TR   *Tel:* 01763 248678
email: alcuinclub@gmail.com
Web: www.alcuinclub.org.uk

All Nations Christian College

All Nations came into existence in 1971 following the merger of three Bible colleges. Whilst interdenominational in character, around twenty per cent of its students are members of the Anglican Communion. The College exists to train students primarily for cross-cultural ministries. With up to 120 international students of about 30 nationalities, as well as a respected international team of tutors, the community studying and socializing life is vibrant and challenging. Students can follow a ten-week (en route), one-year or two-year Biblical and Intercultural studies course with a profound missiological emphasis. In addition to the popular Cert HE, Dip HE and BA (Hons) programmes, there are now validated specialist pathways in the Arts, Leadership and Development Studies. The College also offers a thirteen week online programme (en route explore) and a five day short course for groups heading out on to short term mission trips (en route express).This can be accessed as a residential or on line course. The All Nations Masters programme in Contemporary Mission Studies was the first to be taught in the UK and has attracted leaders from around the world. There are five exit awards to choose from: MA in

Contemporary Mission Studies, MA in Development with Mission, MA in Leadership with Mission, MTh in Contextual Theology with Mission, MTh in Messianic Jewish Theology and Intercultural Studies. The College has a good mix of married and single students. There are number of facilities to help such as a crche on site, wifi access, multi-gym, sports ground and beautiful surroundings to name a few. All Nations, Easneye, Ware, SG12 8LX   Tel: 01920 443500
Fax: 01920 462997
email: info@allnations.ac.uk
Web: www.allnations.ac.uk

All Saints Educational Trust
Home/EU applicants: personal scholarships for intending teachers in degree-level education and/or professional training, particularly teachers of religious education, home economics and other subjects; those studying dietetics, food and nutrition, and public health promotion. Postgraduate qualifications relevant to continuing professional development may be considered. Financial constraint must in all cases be demonstrated. Not assisted: school pupils, students of counselling, engineering, law, medicine, ordination, social work, commercial hospitality. Commonwealth applicants: scholarships for full-time, taught postgraduate study in the UK only (taught Master's programmes favoured; doctorates and PGCE programmes will not normally be funded). Corporate awards: given for imaginative new projects that will support the classroom teacher and build up the profession, preference being given to those aimed at enhancing the Church's contribution to education. Closing dates for receipt of completed applications for 2011–12: Home/EU personal scholarships and Corporate Awards: 21 March 2011; Commonwealth Scholarships: 18 April 2011; Member of the Association of Church College Trusts (see separate entry). *Clerk to the Trust:* Mr S. P. Harrow, All Saints Educational Trust, Suite 8C, First Floor, Royal London House, 22–25 Finsbury Square, London, EC2A 1DX
Tel: 020 7920 6465
email: clerk@aset.org.uk
Web: www.aset.org.uk

Almshouse Association
(National Association of Almshouses)
Is concerned with the preservation and extension of over 1,750 member Almshouse Trusts. A number of major almshouses have a resident Anglican chaplain, or appoint Anglican clergy as Master or Custos of the foundation. It advises members on any matters concerning almshouses and the welfare of the elderly and aims to promote improvements in almshouses, to promote study and research into all matters affecting almshouses, and to make grants or loans to members. It also keeps under review existing and proposed legislation affecting almshouses and

when necessary takes action, and encourages the provision of almshouses. *Chairman:* Mr Simon Pott. *Director:* Mr Anthony De Ritter. *Deputy Director:* Mr Trevor Hargreaves. *Assistant Director:* Mr T. P. Wild, Billingbear Lodge, Maidenhead Rd, Wokingham, RG40 5RU   Tel: 01344 452922
Fax: 01344 862062
email: naa@almshouses.org
Web: www.almshouses.org

Ancient Society of College Youths
Established 1637. An international bell-ringing society based in the City of London, the College Youths seeks to recruit leading ringers from any part of the world in which English style change-ringing is practised. Members are active in supporting ringing for church services throughout the world. The Society maintains a charitable fund for the maintenance of bells, fittings and towers of churches where it has a historic association. *Secretary:* Mr John N. Hughes-D'Aeth, Boundary House, High St, Little Milton, Oxford, OX44 7PU   Tel: 020 3400 4660/01844 279965
Fax: 020 3400 1111
email: secretary@ascy.co.uk
Web: www.ascy.org.uk

Anglican and Eastern Churches Association
Founded 1864 to promote mutual understanding of, and closer relations between, the Orthodox, Oriental and Anglican Churches. Patrons: the Archbishop of Canterbury and the Patriarch of Constantinople. *Presidents:* The Lord Bishop of London and Archbishop Gregorios of Thyateira and Great Britain. *Chairman:* Revd William Taylor. *General Secretary:* Ms Janet Laws, c/o The Old Deanery, Dean's Court, London, EC4V 5AA
Tel: 020 7248 6233
email: janet.laws@btopenworld.com

Anglican Association of Advisers in Pastoral Care and Counselling
To support the work of Bishops' and Diocesan Advisers in Pastoral Care and Counselling or their equivalents; to encourage the appointment of an adviser in every diocese; to promote good practice in pastoral care and counselling of those in ministry, within the structures of the Church of England. Full membership is open to Bishops' and Diocesan Advisers or their equivalents. Associate membership is open to those holding similar appointments in other denominations and those interested in furthering the work of the Association. *Chair:* Canon Ian Tomlinson, Rectory, Ragged Appleshaw, Andover, SP11 9HX
Tel: 01264 772414
Web: www.aaapcc.org.uk

Anglican Fellowship in Scouting and Guiding
Founded in 1983 at the request of guiders, scouters and clergy. Its aims are to support leaders and clergy in the religious aspects of the Promise and Law and the training programme in

Scouting and Guiding, and to maintain links with other Guide/Scout religious guilds and fellowships in order to foster ecumenical understanding. Individual membership is open to persons aged 15 years or over who are members of the Scout and Guide movements, or others (e.g. clergy) who are sympathetic to the aims of Guiding and Scouting. Collective membership is available for Scout Groups and Guide Units (which do not have to be church sponsored), and for Anglican churches. *Chairman:* Mrs June Davies. *Vice-Chairman:* Vacancy. *Secretary:* Miss Joan Taylor. *Treasurer:* Miss Sandra Bendall, 31 Loseley Rd, Farncombe, Godalming, GU7 3RE
Tel: 01483 428876
email: nanniejune@btinternet.com
Web: www.anglicanfellowship.org.uk

Anglican Mainstream
Anglican Mainstream is a movement of organizations, churches, dioceses and individuals within the Anglican Communion worldwide, dedicated to teaching and preserving the Scriptural truths on which the Anglican Church was founded. It seeks to nurture, support and provide a network for orthodox Anglicans throughout the Communion. It published *Repair the Tear* as a response to the Windsor Report. *Convenor:* Dr Philip Giddings. *Episcopal Adviser:* Rt Revd Graham Cray. *Executive Secretary:* Canon Dr Chris Sugden, 21 High St, Eynsham, OX29 4HE
Tel and Fax: 01865 883388
email: csugden@anglican-mainstream.net
Web: www.anglican-mainstream.net

Anglican Marriage Encounter
Anglican Marriage Encounter is a voluntary organization which offers residential and non-residential programmes for married and engaged couples to review and deepen their relationship by developing a compelling vision for their marriage, and providing the communication skills to support this. *Episcopal Adviser:* Rt Revd Michael Scott-Joynt. *Lay Executive Couple:* David and Liz Percival, 11 Lamborne Close, Sandhurst, GU47 8JL
Tel: 01344 779658
email: mail@marriageencounter.freeserve.co.uk
Web: www.marriageencounter.org.uk

Anglican Pacifist Fellowship
Founded 1937. Members pledged to renounce war and all preparation to wage war and to work for the construction of Christian peace in the world. Quarterly newsletter 'The Anglican Peacemaker'. *Chairperson:* Mrs Mary Roe. *Hon Secretary:* Dr Tony Kempster, 11 Weavers End, Hanslope, Milton Keynes, MK19 7PA
Tel: 01908 510642
email: ajkempster@aol.com
Web: www.anglicanpeacemaker.org.uk

Anglican Society for the Welfare of Animals
Founded 1972, for the purpose of including the whole creation in the redemptive love of Christ and especially for prayer, study and action on behalf of animals. Registered Charity no. 1087270. Promotes Animal Welfare Sunday each October and offers a free information pack to all churches. *President:* Rt Revd Dominic Walker OGS. *Chairman:* Rt Revd Richard Llewellin. *Treasurer:* Mrs Jenny White, PO Box 7193, Hook, RG27 8GT
Tel and Fax: 01252 843093
email: AngSocWelAnimals@aol.com
Web: www.aswa.org.uk

Anglican–Lutheran Society
Founded in 1984 to pray for the unity of the Church and especially the Anglican and Lutheran Communions; to encourage opportunities for common worship, study, friendship and witness; to encourage a wider interest in and knowledge of the Anglican and Lutheran traditions and contemporary developments within them. The Society publishes a newsletter, 'The Window', organizes conferences, lectures and other events. *Co-Presidents:* Very Revd Dr John Arnold, Rt Revd Jrgen Johannesdotter. *Co-Moderators:* Rt Revd Jana Jeruma-Grinberga, Rt Revd Dr Rupert Hoare. *Secretary:* Revd Dr Roy Long, 15 Fishpond Close, Denton, Northants, NN7 1EE
Tel: 01604 891383 (Secretary)
email: Helen@ccwatford.u-net.com
Web: www.anglican-lutheran-society.org

Anglo-Catholic Ordination Candidates' Fund
Secretary: Revd J. F. H. Shead SSC, 57 Kenworthy Rd, Braintree, CM7 1JJ
Tel: 01376 321783
email: j.shead@tiscali.co.uk

Archbishop's Examination in Theology
Until 2007 the Archbishop's Examination in Theology comprised the Diploma of Student in Theology (the Lambeth Diploma) and the Degree of Master of Arts (the Lambeth MA). The Lambeth Diploma was instituted in 1905 by Archbishop Randall Davidson. It provided an opportunity for women to study theology, principally so that they could teach religious education in schools and churches. It was then extended to both men and women and the means of study was either by thesis or examination. The Lambeth MA was inaugurated by Dr Runcie in 1990 in order to provide an opportunity for theological study at a more advanced level. From 2007 the Archbishop's Examination in Theology was extended to offer an MPhil research degree, with the opportunity to extend to a PhD. In the last couple of years the Lambeth Diploma and Lambeth MA have ceased to be options. *For more information about the MPhil/PhD research degrees please contact:* The Administrator, Archbishop's Examination in Theology, Lambeth Palace, London, SE1 7JU
email: ruth.ruse@lambethpalace.org.uk

Archbishops' (Canterbury, Wales and Westminster) Certificate in Church Music
See Guild of Church Musicians, 292.

Archway

Anglican Retreat and Conference House Wardens' Association. Promotes the use of retreat and conference houses as a vital contribution to the life and development of Church and community. Is available to advise trustees/management committees and diocesan boards on issues concerning the running of retreat houses. *President:* Rt Rev Christopher Edmonson, Bishop of Bolton. *Chairperson:* Mrs Liz Palin. *Secretary:* Ms Eleanor Godber. *Treasurer:* Mr Jeff Witts, Glenfall House, Mill Lane, Charlton Kings, Cheltenham, Glos, GL54 4EP   *Tel:* 01242 583654
Fax: 01242 251314
email: liz@glenfallhouse.org
Web: www.archwaywardens.org.uk

Art and Christianity Enquiry (ACE)

ACE is the leading UK organisation in the field of visual arts and religion. ACE offers stimulating educational projects and publications, advice, information and skills. The ACE awards for religious art, architecture and literature are given biennially. The quarterly journal *Art and Christianity* is available by membership; complimentary copy available on request. *Director:* Laura Moffatt. *Art in Churches Officer:* Paul Bayley, All Hallows on the Wall, 83 London Wall, London, EC2M 5ND   *Tel and Fax:* 020 7374 0600
email: enquiries@acetrust.org
Web: www.acetrust.org

Art and Sacred Places (ASP)

ASP provides consultancy services nationally for permanent and temporary contemporary art commissions and interfaith projects in sacred places. Encouraging debate and understanding ASP promotes interaction between religion and art by exploring the relationship between art and spirituality. ASP believes that art and religion share fundamental concerns and explore similar territory, albeit in significantly different ways. ASP was founded under the auspices of Bishop John Gladwin in 1999 and became a charity in 2001. Charity Registration no. 1086739. *Contact for more information: Project Director:* Angela Peagram, Bakerswell, Meonstoke, Southampton, SO32 3NA   *Tel:* 01489 878725
Fax: 01489 878737
email: angela@artandsacredplaces.org
Web: www.artandsacredplaces.org

Arthur Rank Centre

Established 1972 as a collaborative venture between the churches, the Royal Agricultural Society of England and the Rank Foundation. The Arthur Rank Centre is now an independent Trust supported by the National Churches, the Royal Agricultural Society of England and the Rank Foundation. It is an ecumenical body and is recognized as the rural focus and resource centre for the churches nationally. It provides the secretariat for the Churches Rural Group, a representative ecumenical body which is a network of Churches Together in England. The Centre offers training for clergy recently appointed to rural areas and on multi-parish benefices. Members of staff are peripatetic and are available for consultations and conferences at local, diocesan and national levels. The Diocesan Rural Officers meet annually with the Church of England National Rural Officer, who is a member of staff at the Centre and who offers on-going advice, information and support. The Centre is also concerned with rural community issues and with farming and environmental matters. The Centre publishes the magazine *Country Way* – life and faith in rural Britain and a wide range of other resources and publications, including information on rural ministry and mission, worship, and the multi-parish benefice. Further information on the work of the Centre and the National Rural Officer will be found on the web site. *Director:* Revd Dr Gordon Gatward. *National Rural Officer, Mission and Public Affairs Division, Archbishops' Counci:* Dr Jill Hopkinson, Arthur Rank Centre, Stoneleigh Park, Warwickshire, CV8 2LG
Tel: 024 7685 3060
Fax: 024 7641 4808
email: info@arthurrankcentre.org.uk
Web: www.arthurrankcentre.org.uk

Association for Promoting Retreats

Founded in 1913 to foster the growth of the spiritual life in the Anglican Communion by the practice of retreats. Welcomes as members all Christians in sympathy with this aim. Membership by subscription for individuals, parishes and retreat houses. The APR is one of the six retreat groups which form the Retreat Association (see separate entry). *Administrator:* Paddy Lane, The Central Hall, 256 Bermondsey St, London, SE1 3UJ   *Tel:* 020 7357 7736
Fax: 0871 715 1917
email: apr@retreats.org.uk
Web: See 'member groups' at www.retreats.org.uk

Association of Black Clergy

Founded 1982 to bring together the minority ethnic clergy and lay ministers of the Christian Church in the United Kingdom, to provide support for all minority ethnic clergy and lay ministers, to encourage good practice and challenge racism individually, institutionally and structurally in particular in the Christian Church in the United Kingdom and to promote theological education and training that is relevant to minority ethnic Christian leadership. *Chairman:* Revd Jennifer Thomas. *Vice-Chair:* Revd Karowei Dorgu. *Facilitators (South):* Revd Yvonne Clarke, Revd Charles Lawrence. *Facilitator (North):* Very Revd Rogers Govender. *Secretary:* Revd Smitha Prasadam, Sherwood Park Vicarage, Sherwood Park Rd, Mitcham, CR4 1NJ   *Tel:* 020 8764 1258
Fax: 020 8764 8369
email: theascension@freeuk.com

Association of Christian Teachers

ACT is a non-denominational Christian membership organization which provides professional and spiritual support to Christians engaged in pre-school, primary, middle, secondary, special, college and university education in England. ACT encourages Christians to apply their faith to their work and provides opportunities for them to share together in prayer and fellowship. ACT strives to influence policy makers, politicians, the media and the Church by speaking from a professionally well-informed standpoint with a loving, Christian voice on behalf of Christians working in education. *Director (Strategy):* Mr Clive Ireson. *Office Manager:* Mrs Carol Horne, 94A London Rd, St Albans, AL1 1NX

Tel: 01727 840298
Fax: 01727 848966
email: act@christians-in-education.org.uk
Web: www.christians-in-education.org.uk

Association of Christian Writers

A group of Christians who wish to serve God in the field of writing. Some members are professional writers, others part-time and many are beginners in different areas of writing. Three writers' days a year are held and many local groups meet regularly. Members receive a quarterly magazine, and a manuscript criticism service is available. Applicants are asked to sign a declaration of faith. *Chairman:* Lin Ball. *Vice-Chairs:* Jan Greenough, Jan Clampett. *Treasurer:* Rosamund Rowe. *Company Secretary/ Administrator:* Jenn Bratt, 5 Cranston Close, Hounslow, TW3 3DQ   *Tel:* 020 8572 8349
email: admin@christianwriters.org.uk
Web: www.christianwriters.org.uk

Association of Church College Trusts

In 1979 the Association of Church College Trusts was established as a loosely knit organization to facilitate an exchange of information and cooperation. It meets every six months. The Church College Trusts were formed following the closure of their respective Colleges of Education. They are autonomous, answerable only to the Charity Commission; their financial management policies are such that they are required both to sponsor present work from their income and also to ensure that their capital is maintained at a level that can finance similar levels of work in the future. In the last 30 years they have been involved in helping individual teachers, students and others, sponsoring corporate projects in part or in total, and aiding school, college and church educational activities. The individual Trusts are: All Saints Educational Trust, Culham Educational Foundation, Foundation of St Matthias, Hockerill Educational Foundation, Keswick Hall Charity, St Christopher's College Trust, St Gabriel's Trust, St Hild and St Bede Trust, St Luke's College Foundation, St Mary's College Trust, St Peter's Saltley Trust, Sarum St Michael

Educational Charity (see separate entries). Please note that applications have to be made to the individual Trusts concerned and not centrally through the Association. *Secretary:* Revd Dr John Gay, Culham Institute, 15 Norham Gardens, Oxford, OX2 6PY   *Tel:* 01865 284885
Fax: 01865 284886
email: enquiries@culham.ac.uk
Web: www.culham.ac.uk

Association of Church Fellowships

Founded 1963. Sponsored by clergy and laity to meet a growing need in this country and overseas to encourage and enable the laity to take their full part in the life and work of the Church in open groups and in cooperation with existing groups. *National Chairman:* Revd Andrew Bullock, 34 Dudley Park Rd, Acocks Green, Birmingham, B27 6QR   *Tel:* 0121 706 9764
email: andrewbullock2@blueyonder.co.uk

Association of Diocesan Registry Clerks

The Association was established in 1999 to support and assist clerks and assistant staff in the furtherance of their professional roles in the diocesan and provincial registries and the Faculty Office of the Church of England by encouraging and sharing knowledge of ecclesiastical law, practice and procedures, imparting and exchanging information, and promoting discussion relevant to their roles.Because of the distances involved, there is usually only one meeting a year, a day meeting alternating with a two-day residential conference but a lively email correspondence and a semi-regular newsletter keeps members informed. *President:* Vacancy. *Chair:* Mrs Elisabeth Crouch. *Secretary:* Mr Ian Blaney, 1The Sanctuary, Westminster, London, SW1P 3JT   *Tel:* 020 7222 5381
DX: 145940 WESTMINSTER 4
Fax: 020 7222 7502
email: ian.blaney@1thesanctuary.com

Association of English Cathedrals

Established in 1990 and authorized by the Administrative Chapters of the Anglican Cathedrals as their representative organization, the AEC deals with governmental agencies, the General Synod and its constituent bodies and the Churches' Legislation Advisory Service on behalf of the English cathedrals, provided only that it cannot commit any individual cathedral chapter to a specific decision. Membership consists of one representative of each Administrative Chapter. *Chairman:* Very Revd Vivienne Faull. *Coordinator:* Mrs Sarah King, PO Box 53506, London, SE19 1ZL   *Tel:* 020 8761 5130
email: sarah.king@englishcathedrals.co.uk
Web: www.englishcathedrals.co.uk

Association of Hospice and Palliative Care Chaplains (AHPCC)

The AHPCC exists to promote good standards among Chaplains involved in the pastoral and spiritual care of people (including carers) facing death from a life threatening illness. Hospice and Palliative Care Chaplains seek to: meet spiritual and religious needs in hospice and palliative care units as a part of a multidisciplinary team that meets regularly; be proactive in assessing and addressing the complex spiritual and religious needs of patients and their families/carers that are an integral part of hospice and palliative care; discern, respect and meet the cultural, spiritual and religious needs, traditions and practices of all patients and their families/carers, including those of no faith; ensure that all spiritual and religious care is patient led and focused on the needs of the individual and their family/carers. The aims of the AHPCC are: to identify and promote good practice; to be an agent of professional development; to provide professional support and fellowship; to promote links with the constituency of palliative care; to promote links with relevant church bodies and faith communities. AHPCC offers training and support for clergy and lay people involved (whether on a full-time or part-time basis) by means of advice about appointments, induction, and training courses, keeps members up to date with current information by means of its website, and organises a three day conference/training event in May each year. St Christopher's Hospice, Sydenham, provides courses for chaplains newly appointed, and many hospices offer placements and courses which form part of pre- and post-ordination training. The AHPCC monitors professional developments within the constituency of palliative care, works to his own professional standards, and offers members support through regional groups. It works closely with the College of Health Care Chaplains, the Scottish Association of Chaplains in Healthcare, and the Chaplaincy Academic Accreditation Board to further the professionalism of healthcare chaplaincy throughout the UK. Membership fee is £30, and, in the first instance, prospective members should make contact with the membership secretary. The AHPCC is supported by 'Help the Hospices', and our link is Anne Garley at Help the Hospices, 33–44 Britannia St, London WC1X 9JG. *President:* Revd Tom Gordon. *Hon Secretary:* Revd Karen Murphy. *Treasurer:* Revd Judie Horrocks. *Webmaster and Newsletter Editor:* Ms Dawn Tierney, Tom Gordon, President AHPCC, 22 Gosford Rd, Port Seton, Port Seton, EH32 0HF

Tel: 01875 812262
email: president@ahpcc.org.uk
Web: www.ahpcc.org.uk

Association of Ordinands and Candidates for Ministry

Founded in 1968, AOCM represents ordinands from the Church of England, Church in Wales, Episcopal Church of Scotland and Church of Ireland as well as trainee Church Army evangelists. AOCM holds regional and national conferences during the year, to which every theological college, course and OLM scheme may send a representative. These conferences allow ordinands to share fellowship, and also for information and questions to pass between AOCM and the Ministry Division. AOCM publishes an annual handbook, *Together in Training,* which is provided free of charge to all ordinands, bishops and DDOs. *Chairman:* Alan Maxwell. *Treasurer:* Ian Robinson. *Secretary:* John Allister
email: secretary@aocm.org.uk
Web: www.aocm.org.uk

Baptismal Integrity (BI)

BI has four aims: to bring to an end the indiscriminate administration of infant baptism; to demonstrate that baptism is the sacrament instituted by Christ for those becoming members of the visible church; to seek the reform of the Canons and rules of the Church of England in line with the above stated aims; to promote within the Church of England debate and review of the biblical, theological, pastoral and evangelistic aspects of Christian initiation. BI affirms the propriety of baptising the infants of practising Christian believers and also of deferring baptism until later years. It also affirms the relevance and value of the Service of Thanksgiving for the Gift of a Child. BI publishes its magazine Update three times a year. Membership is £10 per annum (or concession) – more information via website or Chairman. *Acting Chairman:* Revd Steve Corbett. *Vice-Chairman:* Mr Roger Godin. *Secretary:* Mrs Carol Snipe. *Treasurer:* Ms Sallie Bassham, Winshaw Barn, Chapel-le-Dale, Ingleton, Camforth, LA6 3AT   *email:* roger.godin@baptism.org.uk
Web: www.baptism.org.uk

Barnardo's

Founded in 1866, Barnardo's is the UK's largest children's charity, whose inspiration and values derive from the Christian faith. It runs more than 400 projects nationwide and each year helps more than 100,000 children, young people and their families to overcome severe disadvantage. Barnardo's believes in children and works with them over the long term to tackle the effects of disadvantage and to ensure they can fulfil their potential. Children are helped to address problems such as abuse, homelessness and poverty and to tackle the challenges of disability. Barnardo's also campaigns for better care for children and their families in the community and champions the rights of every child. The charity no longer runs orphanages and now concentrates on working with children and their families in the community. *Chair of Council:* Geoffrey Barnett. *Chief Executive:* Ann Marie Carrie, Barnardo's, Tanners Lane, Barkingside, Ilford, IG6 1QG
Tel: 020 8550 8822
Fax: 020 8551 6870
email: dorothy.howes@barnardos.org.uk
Web: www.barnardos.org.uk

Beauchamp Community
Homes for retired people, clerical or lay, either sex. Unfurnished, single and double flats available from time to time. Applicants should be aged 60 – 74. Daily Eucharist. Apply to the Chaplain. Newland, Malvern, WR13 5AX

Tel: 01684 562100

Bible Reading Fellowship
BRF is a registered charity whose strapline is 'resourcing your spiritual journey'. BRF offers a wide range of resources designed to help adults and children on their journey of faith. Adults can choose from the wealth of books in BRF's spirituality, Bible reading, churches and leadership or gifts ranges. Also available for adults is BRF's online discipleship resource, Foundations21, which gives people the chance to work through 12 rooms in which they can explore aspects of the Christian faith at their own pace and at different depths. This popular resource is particularly helpful to those who are unable to regularly attend church, as well as those looking for something to complement the teaching they receive at church. Foundations21 is completely free, and is supported by donations. Barnabas is BRF's children's imprint and offers attractive colour books, Bibles for different ages, story books and activity books. There are also extensive resources available for children's workers in churches, and for teachers and those working with children in primary schools. BRF's Barnabas team are a group of trained professional story-tellers who visit schools and churches offering RE Days, INSET for teachers and ministry training for children's workers. The Barnabas team recently celebrated 10 years of their work. BRF also facilitates Messy Church, a fresh expression of church, helping churches reach out to families on the fringes of their community. Messy Church is as much for adults as it is for children, bringing people together for a mixture of crafts, food, fun and worship. Lucy Moore, author of the two bestselling Messy Church books, and a team of regional coordinators offer support and advice to Messy Churches around the country. BRF has a range of comprehensive, easy-to-use websites to help people find exactly what they are looking for, whether it is information on RE Days or INSET, free ideas to use with their children's group in church or shopping for resources on the brand-new BRF Online site, www.brfonline.org.uk. *Chair of Trustees:* Rt Revd Colin Fletcher, Bishop of Dorchester. *Chief Executive:* Mr Richard Fisher. *General Manager:* Mrs Karen Laister, 15 The Chambers, Vineyard, Abington, Oxfordshire OX14 3FE

Tel: 01865 319700
Fax: 01865 319701
email: enquiries@brf.org.uk
Web: www.brf.org.uk

Bible Society
Bible Society is working towards a day when the Bible's life-changing message is shaping lives and communities everywhere. We aim to show how the Bible connects with life. We make Scriptures available where there are none. And we work with the Church to help it live out the Bible's message in its daily life and witness. *Chief Executive:* James Catford. *Deputy Chief Executive:* Philip Poole. *Director of Programme:* Ann Holt. *Executive Director of Services:* Lesley Whelan, Stonehill Green, Westlea, Swindon, SN5 7DG

Tel: 01793 418100
Fax: 01793 418118
email: contactus@biblesociety.org.uk
Web: www.biblesociety.org.uk

Bloxham Project
Originating in 1967, the Project seeks to advance education and the Christian religion by promoting spiritual values in education and offering support and development for teachers, senior staff and chaplains. Offering a spiritual, inspirational and practical resource for schools and educators, the Project helps to develop spirituality, pastoral care, Christian leadership and school ethos and values. Providing a forum for debate and the exchange of best practice, the Project offers consultancy services and tailor-made training, day events, regional meetings, twice- termly newsletters, occasional publications and other materials. An ecumenical network of schools in all sectors, it is a resource for headteachers, leadership teams, chaplains, teaching and pastoral staff. *Chair of Trustees:* Mr David Exham. *Director:* Revd John Caperon, Ripon College, Cuddesdon, Oxford, OX44 9EX

Tel: 01865 877417
email: admin@bloxhamproject.org.uk
Web: www.bloxhamproject.org.uk

Book Aid Charitable Trust
Founded in 1988, Book Aid Charitable Trust supplies over one million handpicked new and used Christian books and Bibles to some of the poorest areas of the world each year. All these books and Bibles are donated by Christians in the UK from every denomination and background. The books are distributed mainly to Africa, Asia and the Caribbean, with smaller shipments sent to many other places. Book Aid is manned by volunteer workers and is funded by donations. Registered Charity no. 1039484. *Coordinator:* Ama Bamfo, Bromley House, Kangley Bridge Rd, London, SE26 5AQ

Tel: 020 8778 2145 (Admin)
020 8778 2247 (Bookshop)
Fax: 020 8778 2265
email: office@book-aid.org
Web: www.book-aid.org

Boys' Brigade
Founded 1883 for the advancement of Christ's kingdom among boys and the promotion of habits of obedience, reverence, discipline,

self-respect and all that tends towards a true Christian manliness. *Brigade Secretary:* Steve Dickinson, Felden Lodge, Felden Lane, Hemel Hempstead, HP3 0BL *Tel:* 01442 231681
Fax: 01442 235391
email: enquiries@boys-brigade.org.uk
Web: www.boys-brigade.org.uk

Bridge Pastoral Foundation
(formerly the Clinical Theology Association) Founded in 1962. The core activity of the Association is seminars in pastoral care and pastoral counselling, which are directed by authorized tutors and widely available in the UK. Seminars are designed to promote self-awareness, which is needed for effective pastoral work, and to teach the theory and practice of pastoral counselling with reference to the assumptions, values and meanings of the Christian faith. Further information about Bridge Pastoral Foundation education and training may be obtained from the Administrator. *Administrator:* Angela Ryan, 8 Kingsmead Rd North, Prenton, Birkenhead, CH43 6TB
Tel: 0151 652 0429
email: admin@bridgepastoral.org.uk
Web: www.bridgepastoral.org.uk

Bristol Clerical Education Society
Grants of up to £250 to ordinands and, occasionally, to clergy undertaking CME, for specific and practical needs. *Secretary:* Mrs S. J. Clover, Drummond House, Gosditch, Ashton Keynes, SN6 6NZ *Tel:* 01285 861199

British Deaf Association
The British Deaf Association (BDA) is the largest national organization run by deaf people, for deaf people. We represent the UK's deaf community and campaign for the official recognition of British Sign Language (BSL). Our vision is a world where deaf sign language users enjoy the same rights, responsibilities, opportunities and quality of life as everyone. Services include counselling, advocacy and youth services. BDA works with companies and organizations to make advice and information available in BSL on video or CD-ROM. We run the London Deaf Access Project and organize the annual Deaf Film and TV Festival. BDA Helpline is a national helpline giving information and advice on a range of subjects, such as the Disability Discrimination Act, welfare benefits, education and BSL; the line is open 9 a.m. to 5 p.m. Monday to Friday. *Patron:* HRH The Duke of York. *Chair:* Terry Riley. *Chief Exec:* Simon Wilkinson-Blake, Coventry Point 10th Floor, Market Way, Coventry, CV1 1EA
Tel: 02476 550936 (Voice)
02476 550393 (Text)
Fax: 02476 221541
email: helpline@bda.org.uk
Web: www.bda.org.uk

British Isles and Eire Airport Chaplains' Network
The British Isles and Eire Airport Chaplains' Network meets twice a year for a day or two-day conference and is working towards seeing airport chaplaincy established at every international or regional airport in the UK and Ireland. In 2005 there were chaplaincies at 35 airports, with others being negotiated. Of these, full-time chaplains or chaplaincy teams are at: Heathrow, Gatwick, Manchester, Luton and East Midlands. All airport chaplains are on call and are pleased to be able to assist those travelling through airports in any way. They can be contacted via the airport information desk. Some airport chaplaincies have web pages on their particular airport web sites; for a list of sites visit the address given below. (See also International Association of Civil Aviation Chaplains.) *Coordinator:* Revd Roy Monks. *General Secretary:* Vacancy, Building 34 Office 14, Nottingham E Midlands Airport, Derby, DE74 2SA
Tel: 01509 561955 01332 852990
Fax: 01332 810045
email: roy.monks@talk21.com
Web: www.aoa.org.uk/ourmem/index.asp

Broken Rites
Formed in 1983, Broken Rites is an interdenominational and independent association of divorced and separated wives of Anglican clergy, ministers and Church Army officers living in the United Kingdom, the Republic of Ireland and the geographical area covered by the Diocese in Europe. It affirms the Christian ideal of lifelong marriage. It welcomes the support of everyone who is in sympathy with its aims, which are to support one another with sympathy and understanding and practical help where possible; to continue to draw the attention of the Churches to the problems of ex-spouses of the clergy; and to promote a more vivid awareness among Christian people of the increasing incidence of clergy marriage breakdown and the implications for the witness of the Church and its teaching on marriage. *Hon Secretary:* Sue Atack, 13 Manse Avenue, Wrightington, Wigan, WN6 9RP
Tel: 01257 423893/07967 058114
email: secretary@brokenrites.org
Web: www.brokenrites.org

Bromley and Sheppard's Colleges
Bromley College was founded in 1666 to provide houses for clergy widows and Sheppard's College in 1840 to provide houses for unmarried daughters of clergy widows who had lived with their mothers at Bromley College. Houses in both colleges have been converted into flats and widows/widowers of clergy, retired clergymen and their spouses, divorced and separated spouses of clergy or retired clergy of the Church of England, the Church in Wales, the Scottish Episcopal Church or the Church of Ireland may

now be admitted. Contact the Chaplain/Clerk to the Trustees. *Clerk and Chaplain:* Revd Andrew Sangster, Chaplain's Office, Bromley & Sheppard's Colleges, London Rd, Bromley, BR1 1PE   *Tel:* 020 8460 4712 (Chaplain)
020 8464 3558 (Office)
Fax: 020 8464 3558
email: bromcoll@aol.com
Web: www./bromleycollege.org

Burrswood
Burrswood is a Christian hospital and place of healing founded in 1948 by Dorothy Kerin, who received a commission from God to 'heal the sick, comfort the sorrowing and give faith to the faithless'. The Dorothy Kerin Trust is a registered charity, administered by a board of trustees and has a non-surgical hospital with 40 beds for short-term inpatient care supported by an interdisciplinary team of resident doctors, nurses, physiotherapists and counsellors; a church with resident chaplains, which is fully integrated within the hospital and has healing services open to the public twice a week; a guest/retreat house with single and twin rooms, sleeping 9; a physio- and hydrotherapy complex for inpatients and outpatients and a medical and counselling outpatient facility. Additional public facilities include a Christian bookshop and tea room on-site and a charity shop in nearby Crowborough. Profits from these trading operations go into Burrswood's 'Access to Care' bursary fund which assists financially disadvantaged patients to receive care. *Chief Executive Officer:* Dr Gareth Tuckwell . *Senior Chaplain:* Revd Christine Garrard. *Senior Physician:* Dr Paul Worthley, Groombridge, Tunbridge Wells, TN3 9PY
Tel: 01892 863637 (Enquiries)
01892 863818 (Admissions)
Fax: 01892 863623; 01892 862597 (Admissions)
email: enquiries@burrswood.org.uk
Web: www.burrswood.org.uk

Came's Charity for Clergymen's Widows
Founded to provide small annual grants to benefit clergy widows who are wanting. Apply to the Clerk. Worshipful Company of Cordwainers, Dunster Court Mincing Lane, London, EC3R 7AH   *Tel:* 020 7929 1121
Fax: 020 7929 1124
email: office@cordwainers.org

Campaigner Ministries
Founded 1922, Campaigner Ministries is a national youth movement working in partnership with local churches. Campaigner Ministries trains and resources local leaders, enabling them to operate an exciting and relevant relational and holistic programme of evangelism and Christian discipleship for boys and girls between 4 and 18. It is recognized by UK government education departments and is a member of the Evangelical Alliance. *Executive Director:* Mr John Radcliffe. *Resources Director:* Mr Tony Etherington, 6 Eaton Court Rd Colmworth Business Park, Eaton Socon, St Neots, PE19 8ER   *Tel:* 01480 215622
Fax: 01480 405550
email: info@campaigners.org.uk
Web: www.campaigners.org.uk

Canterbury and York Society
Founded 1904 for the printing of bishops' registers and other ecclesiastical records. *Joint Presidents:* The Archbishops of Canterbury and York. *Chairman:* Vacancy. *Secretary:* Dr C. Fonge. *Treasurer:* Dr R. Hayes. *Editor:* Dr P. Hoskin, Borthwick Institute, University of York Heslington, York, YO10 5DD
Web: http://www.canterburyandyork.org

CARE (Christian Action Research and Education)
CARE is a registered charity seeking to combine practical caring initiatives, at national and community level, with public policy on social and ethical issues. CARE campaigns, provides resouces, undertakes caring work and helps to bring Christian insight and experience to matters of public policy, education and practical caring initiatives, particularly on the behalf of the needy. *Chairman:* Revd Lyndon Bowring. *Chief Executive:* Mrs Nola Leach. *Director of Parliamentary Affairs:* Dr Dan Boucher. *Operations Manager:* Mr Chris Nuttall, 53 Romney St, London, SW1P 3RF   *Tel:* 020 7233 0455/
08453 100 244 (supporter helpline)
Fax: 020 7233 0983
email: mail@care.org.uk
Web: www.care.org.uk

Careforce
Founded in 1980 to serve churches and Christian projects by recruiting British and international volunteers aged 17 to 30 to spend a year in the UK engaged in youth and outreach ministries in local churches, serving homeless people, the elderly, those with difficult family situations, those with addiction difficulties, and those with learning difficulties or physical disability. *Director:* Revd Ian Prior, 35 Elm Rd, New Malden, KT3 3HB   *Tel and Fax:* 020 8942 3331
email: enquiry@careforce.co.uk
Web: www.careforce.co.uk

Catch 22
(formerly Rainer)
A national voluntary organization, founded in 1788, working primarily with young people at risk, through over 60 community-based projects, some in partnership with local authorities and other voluntary organizations. Particular services include leaving care projects and bail support schemes, accommodation and support to young people on release from young offender

Organizations   **273**

institutions or who are homeless, youth training and employment schemes. *Chief Exec:* Mrs Joyce Moseley, Churchill House, 142–146 Old Street, London, EC1V 9BW   *Tel:* 020 7336 4800
Fax: 020 7336 4801
email: information@catch-22.org.uk
Web: www.catch-22.org.uk

Cathedral and Church Shops Association

The Association provides a forum for the exchange of information, arranges an annual conference and trade fair for its members. Sponsors meetings of shop staff in several areas of the country each spring giving advice and assistance for the setting up and running of church shops from experienced shop managers. Membership is open to any cathedral/church/abbey/religious house which is under sole control, or operated by a trading company for the sole benefit, of its chapter, parochial church council or religious house. *Chairman:* Mrs Alison Baker. *Treasurer:* Mr Bob Purssell. *Annual Conference and Trade Fair Organizer:* Revd Stuart M. Munns. *Hon Scretary:* Mrs Susan Kastner, Glastonbury Abbey Shop Ltd, Magdalene St, Glastonbury, Somerset, BA6 9EL   *Tel:* 01458 831631
email: shop@glastonburyabbey.com
Web: www.ccshops.org.uk

Cathedral Libraries and Archives Association

The CLAA supports the work of the cathedral and capitular libraries and archives in the Anglican churches of the United Kingdom and Ireland. It seeks to advance education by the promotion, preservation and protection of those collections and provides a forum for cooperation and the exchange of information among those who care for them. *Chairman:* Very Revd Peter Atkinson. *Hon Secretary:* Mrs Gudrun Warren. *Hon Treasurer:* Mr Jo Wisdom, c/o Norwich Cathedral Library, 12 The Close, Norwich, NR1 4DH
Tel: 01603 218327
Fax: 01603 766032
email: library@cathedral.org.uk
Web: http://www.cofe.anglican.org/about/ librariesandarchives/cathanddioceseslibs/

Cathedrals Administration and Finance Association (CAFA)

In 1975 cathedral administrators and treasurers began, as a body, to exchange information on all matters touching on best practice and the most effective administration of the English Anglican cathedrals. The association now enjoys a valued link with the Association of English Cathedrals for which organization it undertakes research as needed. There is an annual conference and regular regional meetings. *Chairman:* John Morris. *Admin Secretary:* Miss Casey Chick. *Treasurer:* Mrs Caroline Robinson, Church House, Great Smith St, London, SW1P 3NZ   *Tel:* 020 7898 1058
email: casey.chick@c-of-e.org.uk

Catholic Group in General Synod

The Catholic Group consists of those on General Synod committed to the catholic, traditional and orthodox voice in the Church of England. It seeks to make a positive contribution to all debates and especially where Catholic faith and order are involved. It welcomes both the ARCIC discussions and dialogue with the Orthodox churches. The group maintains that ethical teaching which scripture and tradition have consistently upheld. It is not averse to change where contemporary church life demands it, but stands firm on a gospel that is based on God's revelation of himself as Father, Son and Holy Spirit. Members represent a variety of practice within the doctrinal framework. *Chairman:* Canon Simon Killwick. *Secretary:* Mrs Mary Nagel, Aldwick Vicarage, 25 Gossamer Lane, Bognor Regis, PO21 3AT
Tel: 01243 262049
email: nagel@aldwick.demon.co.uk

Cautley House

A Christian centre for healing and wholeness, established in 1994. An Anglican foundation which seeks to be a resource for the whole Church. Individuals or groups (up to 24) are welcome to visit for up to two weeks. Daily services are held in the chapel and staff are available for confidential listening and prayer ministry. Non-residents are invited to attend the healing services which are held twice a week. *Director:* Revd Pat Vowles, 95 Seabrook Rd, Hythe, CT21 5QY   *Tel:* 01303 230762
Fax: 01303 237447
email: susan.evans@cautleyhouse.org.uk
admin@cautleyhouse.org.uk
Web: www.cautleyhouse.org.uk

Central Council of Church Bell Ringers

Founded 1891. Its aims are to promote the ringing of church bells, to represent the ringing exercise to the world at large and to provide expert information and advice to ringers, church authorities and the general public on all matters relating to bells and bell-ringing. *President:* Mr Anthony P. Smith. *Hon Secretary:* Mrs Mary Bone, 11 Bullfields, Sawbridgeworth, CM21 9DB
Tel: 01297 726159
email: secretary@cccbr.org.uk
Web: www.cccbr.org.uk

Centre for the Study of Christianity and Sexuality

Launched in 1996, CSCS aims to provide a safe platform to promote objective debate within the Christian Churches on matters concerning human sexuality, with a view to developing the spiritual teaching and doctrines of such Christian Churches. CSCS is associated with the international journal *Theology and Sexuality* and publishes the quarterly *CSCS News*. It also organizes a conference each year. Patrons and Matron: Rt Revd John Gladwin (Bishop of Chelmsford), Revd David Gamble (Co-ordinating Secretary,

Legal and Constitutional Practice, Methodist Church), Revd Roberta Rominger (Moderator, N Thames Synod of the URC). *Chair:* Canon Jane Fraser. *Secretary:* Vacancy. *Treasurer:* Mrs Daphne Cook. *Newsletter Editor:* Mr Anthony Woollard, The Campanile, Church Lane, Stoulton, Worcester WR7 4RE   *Tel:* 01905 840266/01789 762553
Fax: 01789 400040
email: cscs@revjane.demon.co.uk
Web: www.cscs.co.uk

Changing Attitude
Working for lesbian, gay, bisexual and transgender affirmation within the Anglican Communion, Changing Attitude is a network of lesbian, gay, bisexual, transgendered and heterosexual members of the Anglican churches of the UK, founded in 1995. Local groups meet regularly in 24 dioceses to offer encouragement and support and provide educational and training resources. We have a network of contacts in over 33 dioceses and supporters in every English diocese. We work alongside Integrity USA and Changing Attitude organizations in Nigeria, Australia, New Zealand, Ireland and Scotland. *Director:* Revd Colin Coward. *Hon Administrator:* Brenda Harrison, 6 Norney Bridge, Mill Rd, Marston, SN10 5SF   *Tel:* 01380 724908/07770 844302
email: info@changingattitude.org
Web: www.changingattitude.org.uk

Children's Society, The
Our Vision: We see a world where every child enjoys a good childhood; a world where everyone accepts their responsibility for ensuring that children are: valued and loved in caring relationships, surrounded by friends and family; are respected and supported in communities that recognize all children for their unique and vital contribution; are free to be children, encouraged to play, explore and use their imagination. We see a world where children have a safe place when they need one, are allowed to learn from their mistakes and where no child feels excluded, isolated or abandoned. Our Mission: We make childhood better for all children in the UK. Our direct action stops children feeling excluded, isolated or abandoned. We challenge injustice and influence the thinking of everyone – from the general public to politicians and decision makers – about what needs to change to improve the lives of children. We turn children's lives around, helping them to avoid crisis, overcome hardship and live their lives with hope, optmism and confidence. Our Values: Love, Justice and Forgiveness. *Chair of Trustees:* Rt Revd T. J. Stevens, Bishop of Leicester. *Chief Executive Officer:* Mr Bob Reitemeier, Edward Rudolf House, 69–85 Margery St, London, WC1X 0JL
Tel: 020 7841 4400 (Switchboard)
0845 300 1128 (Supporter Action Line)
Fax: 020 7841 4500
email: supporteraction@childrenssociety.org.uk
Web: www.childrenssociety.org.uk

Choir Benevolent Fund
Founded 1851. A registered Friendly Society for subscribing cathedral and collegiate lay clerks and organists. *Trustees:* The Deans of St Paul's, Westminster and Windsor. *Secretary:* Mr Roland Tatnell, Foxearth Cottage, Frittenden, Cranbrook, TN17 2AU   *Tel:* 01580 712825

Choir Schools Association
Founded 1919 to promote the welfare of cathedral, collegiate and parish church choir schools. In 1985 it set up a bursary trust to help children from low income families become choristers. *Chairman:* Mr Jonathan Milton. *Administrator:* Mrs Susan Rees, Wolvesey, College St, Winchester, SO23 9ND   *Tel:* 01962 890530
Fax: 01962 869978
email: info@choirschools.org.uk
Web: www.choirschools.org.uk

CHRISM
(CHRistians In Secular Ministry)
Formed in 1984, CHRISM is the national association for all Christians who see their secular employment as their primary Christian ministry and for those who support that vision. CHRISM welcomes members, both lay and ordained, from all Christian denominations, encourages them to be active within their own faith communities and to champion ministry in and through secular employment. A journal is published quarterly, together with occasional papers. There is an open annual conference and also a members' reflective weekend. *Treasurer:* Susan Cooper, 28 Headstone Lane, Harrow, HA2 6HG   *Tel:* 020 8863 2094
email: scooper@hedstone.demon.co.uk
Web: www.chrism.org.uk

Christian Aid
Christian Aid is an agency of the British and Irish churches and as such is one of the largest church-related international relief and development agencies in Europe. It works largely in the developing world providing support wherever the need is greatest, irrespective of race or religion. A substantial amount of its voluntary income is received through the annual Christian Aid Week collections led by churchgoers. It funds projects in more than 50 countries, standing by poor communities whether they are digging wells or fighting the consequences of debt, unfair trade or climate change, learning to read or articulating human rights abuses, healing the wounds of war or tackling the spread of preventable illnesses. Money spent overseas is passed to local partner organizations as Christian Aid believes that poor communities are best placed to devise and run their own projects and solve their own problems. Channelling money in this way is seen as an effective and respectful way of giving poor people the means to help themselves. Prevention of the causes of poverty is better than cure, but Christian Aid remains active in emergencies,

sending immediate help and capacity to cope with emergencies and disaster mitigation including food, shelter, medicine and transport when flood, famine, earthquake or war strike. The agency's charitable work includes campaigning and education work in the UK and Ireland, which accounts for up to eleven per cent of its income. This is because Christian Aid believes it must also tackle the structures and systems that keep people poor. It puts great emphasis on the involvement of individuals to address the root causes of poverty and encourage action by politicians and international institutions that will lead to their removal. *Director:* Dr Daleep Mukarji. *Chair of the Board:* Rt Revd John Gladwin, Inter-Church House, 35–41 Lower Marsh, London, SE1 7RL *Tel:* 020 7620 4444
Fax: 020 7620 0719
email: info@christian-aid.org.uk
Web: www.christian-aid.org.uk

Christian Arts
An association of artists, architects, designers, craftsmen and women all involved in the arts who are committed Christians and wish to explore and deepen the relationship between their faith and the arts. Its activities include holding exhibitions and an annual conference. An illustrated newsletter is published twice a year. Many members are available to accept commissions. Application may be made for the Christian Arts Directory of Artists. *Contact:* Paula Widdicombe, Little Morgrove, Perrymead, Bath, BA2 5AZ *Tel and Fax:* 01225 837868
email: widdicombebutton@btinternet.com

Christian Education
(Incorporating International Bible Reading Association and RE Today Services)
Christian Education provides advice, resources and opportunities for teaching and learning in the school, the church and the family group, carrying forward the work of the National Christian Education Council and the Christian Education Movement. *Chief Executive:* Peter Fishpool, 1020 Bristol Rd, Selly Oak, Birmingham, B29 6LB *Tel:* 0121 472 4242
Fax: 0121 472 7575
email: admin@christianeducation.org.uk
Web: www.christianeducation.org.uk

Christian Ethical Investment Group
Part of ECCR since 2008. For further details, see Ecumenical Council for Corporate Responsibility (ECCR) or contact info@eccr.org.uk/www.eccr.org.uk. *email:* info@eccr.org.uk
Web: www.eccr.org.uk

Christian Evidence Society
Founded in 1870 its principal object is 'to give instruction in evidences of Christianity'. Initially it produced tracts, sponsored lectures and arranged open-air work at Tower Hill and Hyde

Park Corner. Later it organised annual Drawbridge Lectures by distinguished names. Nowadays its literature is on its website, available for free download by all and it sponsors broadcasts on Premier Radio. To mark the Darwin anniversary, in 2009 the Revd Professor Alister McGrath delivered a Drawbridge Lecture on 'Belief in God'. *President:* The Archbishop of Canterbury. *Chairman:* Revd Prof Richard Burridge. *Administrator:* Canon Harry Marsh, 5 Vicarage Lane, Great Baddow, Chelmsford, CM2 8HY *Tel:* 01245 478038
email: harry.marsh@talktalk.net
Web: www.christianevidencesociety.org.uk

Christian Healing Mission
The Christian Healing Mission is a non-residential healing centre in London, dedicated to bringing healing to individuals and encouraging healing in churches. A number of link centres have been extablished throughout the country. The CHM has four main aims: to offer a place where people may come to receive prayer for healing; to visit churches to encourage them in the healing ministry; to provide training for individuals and groups wanting to learn more about praying for the sick; and finally to offer a prayer request service whereby people can request prayer for those known to them who are sick. Although rooted in the Church of England, the CHM is keen to work with people and churches of all denominations. The Director is an Anglican priest with many years' experience of parish ministry and is also the Bishop of Kensington's Adviser for Healing. *Director:* Revd John Ryeland, 8 Cambridge Court, 210 Shepherds Bush Rd, London, W6 7NJ *Tel:* 020 7603 8118 (Office)
Fax: 020 7603 5224
email: chm@healingmission.org
Web: www.healingmission.org

Christian Medical Fellowship
CMF aims (1) to unite Christian doctors and medical students in Christ, and to encourage them to deepen their faith, live like Christ, and serve him obediently, particularly through acting competently and with compassion in their medical practice; (2) to encourage Christian doctors and medical students to be witnesses for Christ among all those they meet; (3) to mobilize and support all Christian doctors, medical students and other healthcare professionals, especially members, in serving Christ throughout the world; (4) to promote Christian values, especially in bioethics and healthcare, among doctors and medical students, in the Church and in society. *Chief Executive:* Dr Peter Saunders. *Head of Finance and Administration:* Mr Marcus Watkins, 6 Marshalsea Rd, London, SE1 1HL *Tel:* 020 7234 9660
email: mail@cmf.org.uk
Web: www.cmf.org.uk

Christian Research

Christian Research works with Churches and Church leaders to help them 'turn the tide'. It identifies trends through its research programme, then interprets and publishes them in resources such as 'The Tide is Running Out', 'Religious Trends' and the UK Christian Handbook. Members receive 'Quadrant', a digest of trends in church and society. Forums and seminars help leaders apply the findings to their own context. Please ask for details. *Chairman:* Paul Sandham. *Exec Director:* Mrs Benita Hewitt, Vision Building, 4 Footscray Rd, Eltham, London, SE9 2TZ

Tel: 020 8294 1989
Fax: 020 8294 0014
email: admin@christian-research.org.uk
Web: www.ukchristianhandbook.org.uk
www.christian-research.org.uk

Christian Socialist Movement

The Christian Socialist Movement (CSM) seeks to be the Christian conscience of the Labour Party and a voice to churches on social and political issues. We have a tradition stretching back 150 years, believing that the teachings of Jesus; justice, equality and love for one another; are inextricably linked to the foundations and continuation of the Labour Party. Our magazine *The Common Good* is published twice a year. We also organize events, such as hustings for the leadership of the Labour Party, and have a presence at the Labour Conference; where we run fringe events with other major organisations, well known journalists and prominent political figures. Details of CSM membership rates is available on our web site. *Director:* Dr Andy Flannagan. *Chair:* Rt Hon Alun Michael MP, PO Box 65108, London, SW1P 9PQ

Tel: 020 7783 1590
email: info@thecsm.org.uk
Web: www.thecsm.org.uk

Christian Witness to Israel

To a people of promise – the message of Messiah. Working alongside local churches, Christian Witness to Israel has been sharing the message of Messiah with the Jewish people for over 150 years. It is a non-denominational, international and evangelical organization with workers in seven countries worldwide. We believe that the Jewish people's greatest need is to know Jesus their Messiah. In order to help meet this need, we provide appropriate literature and run an evangelistic website. We also host outreach events and provide training for Christians who wish to share the gospel with their Jewish friends, neighbours and colleagues. *General Secretary:* Mr Mike Moore, 166 Main Rd, Sundridge, Sevenoaks, TN14 6EL   *Tel:* 01959 565955
Fax: 01959 565966
email: hq@cwi.org.uk
Web: www.cwi.org.uk

Christians Abroad

Christians Abroad recruits skilled professionals and volunteers to serve overseas for partner Christian organizations in Britain and Ireland and overseas projects. It supplies support services to small NGOs and Christian agencies, including insurance and criminal records checks. Through 'World Service Enquiry' it gives advice and information about working in development and mission, publishes a monthly job list, an annual guide to volunteering and gives career advice through interview and on-line coaching. *World Service Enquiry:* Kevin Cusack. *Finance/Admin and Recruitment:* Colin South, Room 237 Bon Marche Centre, 241–251 Ferndale Rd, London, SW9 8BJ

Tel: 0870 770 7990 (Office)
0870 770 7991 (Admin and Recruitment Consultancy)
email: recruit@cabroad.org.uk
finance@cabroad.org.uk
wse@wse.org.uk
Web: www.cabroad.org.uk
www.wse.org.uk

Christians at Work

Christians at Work seeks to encourage, support and equip Christian fellowship, evangelism and witness in the workplace. It does this by seeking to unite Christian men and women at work in order tp promote a sense of unity in the gospel. The organisation produces resources, fact sheets and Bible study material; organizing conferences and seminars for local churches; and coordinating a network of around 150 workplace groups and around 200 individual members committed to the extension of Christ's kingdom in the working world. It was founded in 1942 to bring together Christians to pray and work for the extension of Christ's kingdom in the world of business and industry; to encourage active evangelism and fellowship; to provide information, literature and other facilities; to help Christians who stand alone in their place of work and to provide a means whereby young Christians starting work may be strengthened in their faith. *Director:* Revd Brian Allenby. *Administrator:* Miss Gail Alberts, 148 Railway Terrace, Rugby, CV21 3HN   *Tel:* 01788 579738
email: office@caw.uk.net
Web: www.caw.uk.net

Church Army

Church Army trains and equips around 300 Evangelists to share faith through words and action in a variety of contexts across the UK and Ireland. Evangelists are trained through a four year mission-based programme in which the trainee is based at a centre of mission alongside a Church Army team of experienced Evangelists. Church Army also runs Xplore, a global gap-year progamme for adults 18–24 years old. You can find more information and films about our work

and our Evangelists on our web site at www.churcharmy.org.uk *President:* The Most Revd Desmond Tutu. *Chief Secretary:* Mark Russell. *Candidates Secretary:* Vacancy, Wilson Carlile Centre, Cavendish St, Sheffield, S3 7RZ
Tel: 0300 1232113
email: info@churcharmy.org.uk
Web: www.churcharmy.org.uk
http://twitter.com/churcharmy

Church House Deaneries' Group – The National Deaneries Network
The Church House Deaneries' Group – The National Deaneries Network – exists to stimulate local and national consideration of the developing role of the deanery, to encourage an informal network for the exchange of information about deanery thinking and deanery initiatives through its web site and Deanery Exchange, published by Parish and People (see separate entry), and to promote the mission opportunities of deaneries. Every two years since 1988 it has held a national conference about deaneries. It has very close links with Parish and People, which resources deaneries with printed material (see separate entry). *Chairman:* Canon Robin Brown (St Alban's). *Secretary:* Mr David Maxwell (Rochester). *Treasurer:* Mr John Wilson (Lichfield), 14 Honeypot Close, Frindsbury, Rochester, ME2 3DU
Tel: 01634 722097
email: davel.maxwell@virgin.net

Church Housing Trust
Church Housing Trust is committed to changing the lives of homeless people, providing the help and services they would otherwise be denied. Our principal objective is to raise funds to benefit homeless people and those in housing need, and in particular those cared for by Riverside ECHG (formerly English Churches Housing Group). Our funds support residents in over 70 projects throughout England, including hostels, women's refuges, projects for young people, supported housing for the ex Services, accommodation for vulnerable young parents and children, specialist supported housing for people with drug, alcohol and mental health problems, and projects for ex offenders. Our funds help turn hostels into homes and prepare homeless people for independent living through life skills and education and training programmes. Charity no. 802801. PO Box 50296, London, EC1P 1WF
Tel: 020 7269 1630
Fax: 020 7404 2562
email: info@cht.dircon.co.uk
Web: www.churchhousingtrust.org.uk

Church Lads' and Church Girls' Brigade
The Brigade is the Anglican Church's only uniformed youth organisation, welcoming children and young people of all faiths and none, from ages 5 years to 21 years, engaging in 'fun, faith and friendship', equipping them to cope with the demands that society places upon them. The Brigade creates a caring and safe environment in which friendships between young people, children and adults can be established; helping children and young people to grow in confidence, developing their individual skills and abilities to work together, showing concern for others and the environment, exploring their spirituality and developing moral values. Operating in four age groups: 5–7 years, 7–10 years, 10–13 years and 13–21 years, there are appropriate training and activity programmes for all leaders and members to be engaged in. *Patron:* HM The Queen. *President:* The Archbishop of Canterbury. *Governor:* Anthony Baker. *Brigade Chaplain:* Rt Revd Jack Nicholls. *Brigade Secretary:* Alan Millward, National Headquarters, Saint Martin's House, 2 Barnsley Rd, Wath-Upon-Dearne, Rotherham, South Yorkshire S63 6PY
Tel: 01709 876535
Fax: 01709 878089
email: brigadesecretary@clcgb.org.uk
Web: www.clcgb.org.uk

Church Mission Society
CMS, founded in 1799, is committed to evangelistic mission, working to see our world transformed by the love of Jesus. It is a member of PWM and in 2008 was acknowledged as a mission community by the Advisory Council on the Relations of Bishops and Religious Communities. Early in 2010 CMS and the South American Mission Society (SAMS) integrated to form a new entity. CMS therefore now includes mission to and from Latin America. As a mission community, CMS is committed to Sharing Jesus, Changing Lives by making disciples, resourcing leaders and transforming communities. CMS works in over 35 countries, including the UK. It has over 2,000 members who commit to seven promises as they aspire to a whole lifestyle shaped by God's mission. It helped launch CMS Africa in 2009 and future plans include similar initiatives for Asia and Latin America. It networks with a large number of mission societies and projects, including sister CMS societies and through the Faith2Share Network. See the CMS website for full information about its promises, programmes, partners and publications. (See also Religious Communities: Church Mission Society.) Registered Charity no. 1131655. Company no. 6985330. *Patron:* The Archbishop of Canterbury. *Episcopal Visitor:* Rt Revd Dr Christopher Cocksworth, Bishop of Coventry. *Chair of Trustees:* John Ripley. *Community Leader/Executive Director:* Canon Tim Dakin, Watlington Rd, Oxford, OX4 6BZ
Tel: 01865 787 400 (Switchboard)
Fax: 01865 776 375
email: info@cms-uk.org
Web: www.cms-uk.org
www.wearesayingyes.org

Church Monuments Society
Founded in 1979 to encourage the appreciation, study and conservation of monuments. The Society promotes a biennial symposium, excursions, study days, a twice-yearly newsletter and an annual refereed journal. It also offers a programme of visits to locations throughout the country, a series of occasional lectures and an opportunity for people to meet and exchange views on a subject which spans many disciplines. It is the only society to cover all periods and all types of monument, and is the sponsor of the National Ledger Stone Survey. *President:* Dr Phillip G. Harris. *Secretary:* Dr Amy L. Harris. *Treasurer:* Dr John Brown. *Membership Secretary:* Mr Clive Easter. *Publicity:* Dr John Bromilow, c/o Society of Antiquaries of London, Burlington House, Piccadilly, London, W1J 0BE
Tel: 01752 773634 (Membership)
01837 851483 (Publicity)
Fax: 01837 851483
email: churchmonuments@aol.com
Web: www.churchmonumentssociety.org

Church Music Society
Founded 1906. The society is a leading publisher of all types of Church music, and has consistently served the Church of England by this means. An annual lecture and other events for members pursue further aims of advancing knowledge of the art and science of Church music. Although much of the society's focus is on music specifically for liturgy, CMS publications are also in world-wide use by choirs of all types for concerts, recitals and recordings. 'Te Deum Laudamus', a CD of CMS publications, is now available. Details of membership and activities are available from the Secretary. *President:* The Dean of Hereford. *Chairman:* Mr Ian Curror. *Hon Secretary:* Dr Simon Lindley. *Hon General Editor:* Mr Richard Lyne, 17 Fulneck, Pudsey, LS28 8NT
Tel and Fax: 0113 255 6143
email: cms@simonlindley.org.uk
Web: www.church-music.org.uk

Church of England Clergy Stipend Trust
Founded 1952 to augment stipends of parochial clergy, normally through Diocesan Boards of Finance. *Chairman:* Mr J. W. Parkinson FCA, Sceptre Court, 40 Tower Hill, London, EC3N 4DX
Tel: 020 7423 8000
Fax: 020 7423 8001

Church of England Evangelical Council
Founded 1960 to (1) bring together evangelical leaders of the Church of England for mutual counsel and discussion (2) seek to reach a common mind on the issues of the day and when appropriate to reveal their findings to the Church and nation (3) encourage those societies and individuals in a position to do so to increase the evangelical contribution to the Church of England (4) assist in such work throughout the Anglican Communion. It organizes an occasional National Evangelical Anglican Congress to help further its aims. *President:* Rt Revd Wallace Benn. *Chairman:* Ven Michael Lawson. *Secretary:* Canon Michael Walters. *Treasurer:* Dr Graham Campbell, 27 Alvanley Rise, Northwich, CW9 8AY
Tel: 01606 333126
email: executive.officer@ceec.info
Web: www.ceec.info

Church of England Flower Arrangers Association
The Church of England Flower Arrangers Association (CEFAA) was founded in 1981 to help and encourage all those who tend flowers in churches and link them in fellowship and friendship. It is open to all those baptized in the Christian faith. The aims are to expand interest in church flower arranging, to use talent to enrich places of worship and to support what theology and creation try to teach. CEFAA is a voluntary charity whose constitution covers the work members do in churches, church buildings and at church events. The Association is not sponsored and is non-competitive. Registered Charity no. 514372. *President:* Revd Noel Michell. *Chairman:* Mrs Hillary Brian. *Treasurer:* Mrs Naomi Hadden. *Secretary:* Mr Roger Brown, 25B Church Road, Hale Village, Liverpool, L24 4AY
Tel: 0151 425 2823
email: cefaa@btinternet.com
Web: www.cefaa.org.uk

Church of England Record Society
Founded in 1991 with the object of promoting interest in and knowledge of the history of the Church of England from the sixteenth century onwards, the Society publishes primary material of national significance for Church history. It aims to produce one volume each year, set against an annual subscription of £20 (individuals), and £30 (institutions). *Hon Secretary:* Dr Michael Snape, Dept of Modern History, University of Birmingham, Edgbaston, Birmingham, SE23 3XN
Tel: BI5 2TT
email: m.f.snape@bham.ac.uk
Web: www.coers.org

Church of England Soldiers', Sailors' and Airmen's Clubs (1891)
A registered charity which, since its foundation in 1891, has maintained clubs at home and abroad for HM Forces and their dependants, whatever their religious denomination. The work of the association now encompasses rented housing for elderly ex-Service people or their widows/widowers. The association also helps other charities to build sheltered housing for ex-Service people, working in parallel with its sister organization, CESSA Housing Association. Donations always welcomed. *General Secretary:* Cdr Martin Marks. *Assistant Secretary:* Cdr Mike

Pearce, CESSAC, 1 Shakespeare Terrace, 126 High St, Portsmouth, PO1 2RH
Tel: 023 9282 9319
Fax: 023 9282 4018
email: martin.marks@ntlbusiness.com

Church of England Soldiers', Sailors' and Airmen's Housing Association Ltd (1972)
A charitable Housing Association, registered with the Tenant Services Authority to provide low cost rented sheltered accommodation for retired ex-Service people and/or their partners of all denominations. Construction costs were provided partly by government grants, but donations are always welcome to help fund modernisation. *Chief Exec:* Cdr Mike Pearce. *Housing Manager:* Chris Wrenn, CESSA H. A., 1 Shakespeare Terrace, 126 High St, Portsmouth, PO1 2RH
Tel: 023 9282 9319
Fax: 023 9282 4018
email: mike.pearce@cessaha.co.uk
Web: www.cessaha.co.uk

Church Pastoral Aid Society Ministers in Training Fund
The Church Pastoral Aid Society administers the Ministers in Training Fund. This fund gives grants for personal maintenance (not fees) to evangelical men and women, married or single, who are facing financial hardship whilst training for ordained ministry. *Development Team Administrator:* Mrs Pauline Walden, Ministers in Training Fund, CPAS, Athena Drive, Tachbrook Park, Warwick, CV34 6NG
Tel: 01926 458480
Fax: 01926 458459
email: pwalden@cpas.org.uk
Web: www.cpas.org.uk

Church Schoolmasters and School Mistresses' Benevolent Institution
Founded in 1857 to provide assistance for Church of England teachers in England and Wales in times of temporary affliction or misfortune, or upon retirement or permanent disablement, and assistance towards the maintenance and education of their orphans. The CSSBI runs Glen Arun Care Home which has a strong Christian ethos and is set in a semi-rural location. The home provides residential and nursing care accomodation. It has 35 single rooms where residents can benefit from 24 hour nursing care. *Patron:* HM The Queen. *President:* The Bishop of London. *Chairman:* Miss Diana Bell. *Patient Care Manager:* Mrs Sue Green. *Company Secretary:* Mrs Marie di Cara, Glen Arun, 9 Athelstan Way, Horsham, RH13 6HA
Tel: 01403 253881 (Admin)
01403 255749 (Nursing Office)
Fax: 01403 254971
email: glenarun@hotmail.com

Church Society
Formed in 1950 by the amalgamation of the Church Association and National Church League, which was founded in 1835, continues to seek to maintain the evangelical and reformed faith of the Church of England, based upon the authority of Holy Scripture (see Canon A 5) and the foundational doctrines of the Thirty-nine Articles and the Book of Common Prayer. Publishes a journal, *Churchman*, and a quarterly broadsheet, *Cross+Way*. The Society publishes books, booklets and leaflets on current issues and organizes conferences and public meetings. Patronage is administered through the Church Society Trust. (See also Patronage Trusts.) *President:* The Viscount Brentford. *Chairman:* Mr James Crabtree. *General Secretary:* Revd David Phillips, Dean Wace House, 16 Rosslyn Rd, Watford, WD18 0NY
Tel: 01923 235111
Fax: 01923 800362
email: admin@churchsociety.org
Web: www.churchsociety.org

Church Union
Founded in 1859 at the time of the Oxford Movement, to promote catholic faith and order, it continues this work today by providing support and encouragement to those lay people and priests who wish to see catholic faith, order, morals and spirituality maintained and upheld, and who wish to promote catholic unity. The Union publishes books and tracts and produces an in-house magazine, the *Church Observer*. *President:* Rt Revd Edwin Barnes. *Chairman:* Mr David Morgan. *Treasurer:* Revd Richard Gomersall. *Membership Secretary:* Mrs Jenny Miller, 2a The Cloisters, Gordon Square, London, WC1H 0AG
Tel: 020 7388 3588 01884 34563 (Membership)
email: secretary@churchunion.co.uk
membership@churchunion.co.uk
Web: www.churchunion.co.uk

Church Welfare Association (Incorporated)
(formerly the Church Moral Aid Association) Founded 1851. Gives financial aid to Church projects assisting and supporting women and children in need of residential care and/or moral support. *Chairman:* Miss G. A. Reeve. *Secretary:* Mr D. J. Boddington, 15 Marina Court, Alfred St, Bow, London, E3 2BH
Tel: 020 8981 3341
Web: http://cwa.awardspace.co.uk

Church's Ministry Among Jewish People
Founded 1809 as London Society for Promoting Christianity Among the Jews, to take the Christian gospel to Jewish people. *President:* Rt Revd David Evans. *Chair:* Mr Ben Salter. *CEO:* Mr Robin Aldridge, Eagle Lodge, Hexgreave Hall Business Park, Farnsfield, Notts, NG22 8LS
Tel: 01623 883960
Fax: 01623 884295
email: enquiries@cmj.org.uk
Web: www.cmj.org.uk

Churches Tourism Association

A charitable ecumenical organisation committed to promoting the daily openness of church buildings to visitors and tourists as a contributory component of the Church's mission, and to the significance of church buildings as places of worship, repositories of architectural heritage and locations for community engagement. In addition to its own resources CTA, through its website, signposts organisations which specialise in offering literature and training in ministry to visitors and tourists. A newsletter is published approximately bi-monthly. Charity Registration No. 1101254. *Chair:* Canon John D. Brown. *Administrator:* Mr John Irving, The Churches Tourism Association, c/o The Churches Conservation Trust, 1 West Smithfield, London, EC1A 9EE   *Tel:* 020 7213 0660
email: canonjbrown@mac.com
jirving@tcct.org.uk
Web: www.churchestourismassociation.info

Churches' Advertising Network

A professional group of Christians from all traditions cooperating to develop the professional use of advertising as part of the Churches' communication and outreach. CAN seeks free or low cost poster space and radio airtime from leading media owners, which it uses on behalf of the Churches. All members give their services free. Charity Registration no. 1096868. *Chair:* Mr F. Goodwin. *Secretary & Treasurer:* Revd Tony Kinch. *Asst Treasurer:* Mrs Karen Gray. *Trustee:* Revd John Carter, The Methodist Centre, 24 School St, Wolverhampton, WV1 4LF
Tel: 01902 422100
Fax: 01902 313301
email: churchads@methodist.fsnet.co.uk
Web: www.churchads.org.uk

Churches' Fellowship for Psychical and Spiritual Studies

Founded 1953 to study the psychic and spiritual and their relevance to Christian faith and life. *President:* Very Revd Alexander Wedderspoon. *Chair:* Revd Nancy Walthew. *General Secretary:* Mr Julian Drewett, The Rural Workshop, South Rd, North Somercotes, Louth, LN11 7PT
Tel and Fax: 01507 358845
email: gensec@churchesfellowship.co.uk
Web: www.churchesfellowship.co.uk

Churches' Funerals Group

The Churches' Group on Funeral Services at Cemeteries and Crematoria was formed as an advisory group in 1980 by the mainstream Churches in England and Wales to co-ordinate their policies in connection with the pastoral and administrative aspects of funeral services at cemeteries and crematoria, and to represent the Churches at national level in joint discussions with public and private organizations on any matters relating to ministry at such funerals. The Group keeps in close touch with the main organizations concerned with funeral provision and bereavement counselling. To reflect its involvement in the wider aspects of all concerned with funerals and death in our society, the Group shortened its working title in 2002 to 'The Churches' Funerals Group'. Publications sponsored by the Group include *The Role of the Minister in Bereavement: Guidelines and Training Suggestions* (Church House Publishing, 1989); *Guidelines for Best Practice of Clergy at Funerals* (Church House Publishing, 1997); and two joint funeral service books (The Canterbury Press, Norwich), one for use in England (1986, 1994, 2001 and 2009), the other for use in Wales (1987). Three previous conference reports have been published: *The Role of a Minister at a Funeral* (1991), *Bereavement and Belief* (1993) and *Clergy and Cremation Today* (1995). An information leaflet entitled *Questions Commonly Asked about Funerals* (2nd edition, 2007) is also available free of charge from the Secretary. *Chairman:* Rt Revd Dr Geoffrey Rowell, Bp of Gibraltar in Europe. *Secretary:* Ms Sue Moore, Church House, Great Smith St, London, SW1P 3AZ
Tel: 020 7898 1376
Fax: 020 7898 1369
email: enquiries@christianfunerals.org
Web: www.christianfunerals.org

Churches' Legislation Advisory Service

Founded 1941, and registered as a charity in 1966, CLAS exists to advance the religious and other charitable work of its members by furthering their common interests in issues (such as those relating to property, finance, tax and charitable status) which help underpin and deliver that work. *Chairman:* Rt Revd Michael Langrish. *Secretary:* Frank Cranmer, Church House, Great Smith St, London, SW1P 3AZ
Tel: 020 7222 1265
email: frank.cranmer@centrallobby.com
Web: www.churcheslegislation.org.uk

Cleaver Ordination Candidates' Fund

An academic trust to assist ordinands, clergy pursuing recognized courses of postgraduate study, and parochial clergy on approved study leave. Candidates must belong to the Catholic tradition within the Anglican Communion. Preference may be given to graduates of British universities. There is no permanent office, the Clerk of the time being working from his home address. *Clerk to the Cleaver Trustees:* Revd Dr Peter Lynn, 119 Stanford Ave, Brighton, BN1 6FA   *Tel:* 01273 553361
email: clerk@cleaver.org.uk
Web: www.cleaver.org.uk

Clergy Consultation, The

(formerly known as Lesbian and Gay Clergy Consultation)
The Clergy Consultation is a confidential support organization for lesbian, gay, bisexual or

transgender clergy, religious, ordinands and their partners. There are over 200 members, mostly Anglican, but other denominations are welcome. Day conferences are organized twice a year, usually in London, as well as some social activities. The Consultation provides mutual support and advice, offers a forum for education and discussion, and responds to the professional and pastoral needs of homosexual clergy. It invites bishops, theologians and others who work in church structures to engage in dialogue. A newsletter is sent up to four times a year to all members. The Consultation operates a policy of strict confidentiality to protect the interests of its members. Details of meetings are given only to members and those invited to participate in meetings. There is an annual membership fee and a charge is made for attendance at each meeting. Reduced rates are available for the retired, for unemployed clergy, religious and ordinands who are studying full-time. 10 Wincott St, London, SE11 4NT   *email:* clergy.consultation@virgin.net

COIN: Christians on the Internet
An interdenominational group of Christians throughout Britain and Ireland working together since 1995 to advise, help and encourage the Church in its use of the Internet. It functions both as a group of individuals able to offer their particular expertise, and also, through email, as a lively online community discussing in depth a wide variety of issues affecting Christians, including specialist lists discussing Church of England issues, and Common Worship. Further details of COIN and its activities can be found on its web site. *Chair:* Revd Karen Spray. *Secretary:* Simon Kershaw. *Treasurer:* Revd Gordon Giles. *Membership Secretary:* Revd Alan Jesson
Tel: 01480 381471
email: secretary@coin.org.uk
membership@coin.org.uk
Web: www.coin.org.uk

College of Evangelists
The national College of Evangelists was founded in 1999 to support and give the accreditation of the Archbishops of Canterbury and York to evangelists in the Church of England. To be admitted as a member of the College, evangelists will be involved in active evangelistic ministry (not just training or teaching about evangelism) and will be operating nationally or regionally, beyond their diocesan boundaries. Potential candidates should contact their diocesan bishop in the first instance. *Chairman:* The Bishop of Worcester, The Bishop of Worcester's Office, Old Palace, Deansway, Worcester, WR1 2JE

College of Health Care Chaplains
Founded in 1992, the College is a multi-faith, interdenominational professional association open to all recognized health care chaplaincy staff, full-time and part-time, including volun-

tary and support workers, and others with an interest in health care chaplaincy. With around 1000 members throughout the United Kingdom, it provides peer support, advice and fellowship for members nationally and in 13 regional branches. A focus for professional development, good practice and training, the College publishes *The Journal of Health Care Chaplaincy* (available on subscription to non-members) and issues regular newsletters. As an autonomous section of the Unite trade union, terms and conditions are negotiated for all chaplains (irrespective of College membership) on a national basis, and members receive professional support on employment issues. *President:* Revd Mark Stobert. *Vice-President:* Revd Gareth Rowlands. *Registrar:* Revd William Sharpe, Unite Health Sector, 128 Theobald's Rd, London, WC1X 8TN
Tel: 020 3371 2004/020 3371 2013
Fax: 0870 731 5043
email: william.sharpe@unitetheunion.org
Web: www.healthcarechaplains.org

College of Preachers
An ecumenical network of preachers, ordained and lay, dedicated to preaching which is faithful and fresh, biblical and relevant, and to helping one another to develop preaching skills through seminars, conferences, a journal and guided study. *Chairman:* Revd Dr Leslie Griffiths. *Director:* Mr Paul Johns. *Administrator:* Miss Helen Skinner, 6th Floor, City Gate East, Tollhouse Hill, Nottingham, NG1 5FS
Tel: 0115 925 2025
Fax: 020 8883 0843
email: administrator@collegeofpreachers.org.uk
Web: www.collegeofpreachers.org.uk

College of Readers
An independent membership organization providing fellowship and support for Readers of the Anglican Communion in the British Isles, especially to those Readers who subscribe to the authority of scripture, the grace of the sacraments and the traditional understanding of the ordained ministry of the bishop, priest and deacon. The College is establishing a network of local circles and chaplains, and publishes a quarterly magazine, *Blue Scarf*, which keeps all members in touch. Distance learning packages are available, as are a series of publications on aspects of Reader ministry. Regional and national meetings are organized each year. *Patron:* Rt Revd Martyn Jarrett. *Secretary:* Mr John Mitchell, 6 The Chase, Penn, High Wycombe, HP10 8BA   *Tel:* 01494 813045
email: mesnape@yahoo.co.uk
Web: www.college-of-readers.org.uk

College of St Barnabas
Set in idyllic Surrey countryside, the College is a residential community of retired Anglican clergy, including married couples and widows.

Admission is also open to licensed Church Workers and Readers. There are facilities for visitors and guests, and occasional quiet days and private retreats can also be accommodated. Residents lead active, independent lives for as long as possible. There is a Nursing Wing providing residential and full nursing care for those who need it, enabling most residents to remain members of the College for the rest of their lives. Respite care is sometimes possible here. Sheltered flats in the Cloisters all have separate sitting rooms, bedrooms and en suite facilities. There are two chapels, daily Mass and Evensong, three libraries, a well equipped common room and refectory, a snooker table and a nine-hole putting green. The College is easily accessible by road and is also next to Dormans Station on the line from London to East Grinstead. For further details or to arrange a preliminary visit, please see our website or contact the Warden. *Warden:* Fr Howard Such. *Bursar:* Paul G. F. Wilkin, The College of St Barnabus, Blackberry Lane, Lingfield, Surrey RH7 6NJ   *Tel:* 01342 870260
Fax: 01342 871672
email: warden@collegeofstbarnabas.com
Web: www.st-barnabas.org.uk

Commonwealth War Graves Commission
Founded 1917. Responsible for marking and maintaining in perpetuity the graves of those of Commonwealth Forces who fell in the 1914–18 and 1939–45 Wars and for commemorating by name on memorials those with no known grave. *President:* HRH The Duke of Kent. *Chairman:* Secretary of State for Defence in the UK. *Enquiries:* Director Legal Services, 2 Marlow Rd, Maidenhead, Berkshire, SL6 7DX   *Tel:* 01628 507 138
Fax: 01628 507134
email: legal@cwgc.org
Web: www.cwgc.org

Community Housing and Therapy
CHT provides group and individual psychotherapy in residential settings to clients who are experiencing mental health and emotional difficulties. The care of each client is planned through an individual Care Plan which is reviewed every three to six months. Reviews are interdisciplinary and CHT therapists with social workers and psychiatrists, together with others, review progress and set goals together with the client. These goals focus on key areas in the life of each client, for example, housing needs, relationships, medication and re-training for work. *Chief Exec:* Mr John Gale. *Chief Operating Officer:* Ms Inma Vidana. *Deputy Director, Clinical Services:* Miss Beatriz Sanchez. *Senior Managers:* Mr Terry Saftis, Mrs Yin Ping Leung, 24/5–6 The Coda Centre, 189 Munster Rd, London, SW6 6AW
Tel: 020 7381 5888/0800 018 1261 (Freephone)
Fax: 020 7610 0608
email: co@cht.org.uk
Web: www.cht.org.uk

Community of Aidan and Hilda
A dispersed, ecumenical and international body of Christians who journey with God, and reconnect with the Spirit and the Scriptures, the saints and the streets, the seasons and the soil. The Community seeks to cradle a Christian spirituality for today which renews the Church and brings healing to fragmented people and communities. It welcomes people of all backgrounds and countries who wish to be wholly available to God the Holy Trinity, and to the way of Jesus as revealed in the Bible. In the earthing of that commitment members draw particular inspiration from Celtic saints such as Aidan and Hilda. Members follow a Way of Life based on a rhythm of prayer and study, simplicity, care for creation, and mission, seeking to weave together the separated strands of Christianity. Each shares their journey with a spiritual companion known as a Soul Friend. The work of the Community is the work of each member and can be expressed individually and corporately in many ways, such as through link houses, churches, monastic experiments, and indigenous national branches. Its mother house and spirituality centre is The Open Gate, Holy Island, Berwick-upon-Tweed, TD15 2SD. *Community Soul Friend (Episcopally endorsed visitor):* Canon Godfrey Butland. *International Guardian:* Revd Ray Simpson. *Secretary:* Naomi Ackland. *Retreat House Wardens:* Revd Graham and Dr Ruth Booth, Lindisfarne Retreat, Holy Island, Berwick-upon-Tweed, TD15 2SD
Tel: 01289 389249 (International Office)
01289 389222 (Holy Island Retreat House Bookings)
email: admin@aidanandhilda.org.uk
Web: www.aidanandhilda.org

Compassionate Friends, The
A nationwide charitable organisation run by bereaved parents offering support and understanding to parents whose child has died at any age and from any cause. Local Contacts and Support Groups, quarterly journal, leaflets and publications, postal library, website forum, retreats and a yearly gathering. The national helpline, which is always answered by a bereaved parent, is available for support and information daily from 10.00 – 16.00 and 19.00 – 22.00. *Office Manager:* Michael Brown, 53 North St, Bristol, BS3 1EN   *Tel:* 08451 23 23 04 (Helpline)
0845 120 3785 (Admin)
Fax: 0845 120 3786
email: helpline@tcf.org.uk
info@tcf.org.uk
Web: www.tcf.org.uk

Confraternity of the Blessed Sacrament
Founded 1862 to honour Jesus Christ our Lord in the Blessed Sacrament; to make mutual eucharistic intercession and to encourage eucharistic devotion. Registered Charity no. 1082897. *Superior-General:* Revd Christopher Pearson.

Secretary General: Canon Lawson Nagel, Aldwick Vicarage, 25 Gossamer Lane, Bognor Regis, PO21 3AT
Tel: 01243 262049
email: cbs@confraternity.org.uk
Web: www.confraternity.org.uk

Corporation of the Sons of the Clergy and Friends of the Clergy Corporation

The two charities work together and are able to assist Anglican clergy and their widows/widowers and dependants in times of financial need or distress. Grants are made for a wide range of purposes including holidays and resettlement, school clothing and school trips, university maintenance for undergraduate children, clerical clothing, heating and home maintenance for the retired, bereavement expenses and some of the expenses arising from separation and divorce. Book grants can be considered for ordinands in training. The Corporation of the Sons of the Clergy also administers the Clergy Orphan Corporation. 1 Dean Trench St, Westminster, London, SW1P 3HB
Tel: 020 7799 3696
Fax: 020 7222 3468
email: enquiries@clergycharities.org.uk
Web: www.clergycharities.org.uk

Council of Christians and Jews

Founded 1942 to combat all forms of religious and racial intolerance, to promote mutual understanding and goodwill between Christians and Jews, and to foster cooperation in educational activities and in social and community service. Forty local branches in the UK. Patron: HM The Queen. Presidents: Archbishop of Canterbury; Chief Rabbi; Cardinal Archibishop of Westminster; Moderator of the Free Churches; Rabbi Tony Bayfield; Head, Reform Movement; Archbishop of Thyatira and Great Britain; Moderator of the Church of Scotland. Chair: Rt Revd Nigel McCulloch, Bishop of Manchester. Chief Executive: David Gifford MA, 1st Floor, Camelford House, 87–89 Albert Embankment, London, SE1 7TP
Tel: 020 7820 0090
Fax: 020 7820 0504
email: cjrelations@ccj.org.uk
Web: www.ccj.org.uk

Council on Christian Approaches to Defence and Disarmament

CCADD was established in 1963 by the Rt Revd Robert Stopford, then Bishop of London, to study problems relating to defence and disarmament within a Christian context. The British Group of CCADD comprises Christians of different traditions, varying vocations and specializations and political views, with a range of responsibilities, governmental and non-governmental. CCADD seeks to bring an ethical viewpoint to bear on disarmament and arms control and related issues and to this end the British Group has always stressed the importance of dialogue between official and non-official bodies. President: Rt Revd Richard Harries. Chairman: Mr Brian Wicker. Admin Secretary: Mrs Liza Hamilton, 5 Cubitts Meadow, Buxton, Norwich, NR10 5EF
Tel and Fax: 01603 279939
email: ccadd@lineone.net
Web: http://website.lineone.net/ccadd

CPAS (Church Pastoral Aid Society) Ministers in Training Fund

CPAS administers the Ministers in Training Fund. This fund gives grants for personal maintenance (not fees) to evangelical men and women, married or single, who are facing financial hardship whilst training for ordained ministry. Leadership Development Adviser (Vocations): Revd Mark Norris, Ministers in Training Fund, CPAS, Atena Drive, Tachbrook Park, Warwick, CV34 6NG
Tel: 01926 458461
Fax: 01926 458459
email: vocations@cpas.org.uk
Web: www.cpas.org.uk

Crosslinks

Founded 1922 as the Bible Churchmen's Missionary Society (BCMS). Crosslinks is an international evangelical Anglican mission agency seeking to take God's Word to God's World in creative and entrepreneurial ways. A member of the Partnership for World Mission (PWM), it works in partnership with Anglican dioceses in the developing world primarily, through the provision of mission partners and student bursaries. Mission partners work in East, North and South Africa, Europe and Asia as well as among those of other faiths in the UK. President: Revd Dr C. Wright. General Secretary: Canon Andy Lines. Chairman: Revd M. Payne, 251 Lewisham Way, London, SE4 1XF
Tel: 020 8691 6111
Fax: 020 8694 8023
email: info@crosslinks.org
Web: www.crosslinks.org

Culham Educational Foundation

The Trust gives mainly personal grants not exceeding £1,500 to practising Anglicans who are pursuing personal study or undertaking projects or research primarily relating to RE in schools. Normally consideration will be given only to applicants who live or work in the Diocese of Oxford or who are former members of the old college at Culham. Member of the Association of Church College Trusts (see separate entry). Correspondent: Revd Dr John Gay, 15 Norham Gardens, Oxford, OX2 6PY
Tel: 01865 284885
Fax: 01865 284886
email: enquiries@culham.ac.uk
Web: www.culham.ac.uk

Culham Institute

This is a research, development and information agency working in the fields of Church schools,

Church colleges, RE and collective worship. It has established a national system of networking, collaborative activity and project management. Current collaboration includes work with the Jerusalem Trust, the St Gabriel's Trust, the All Saints Trust and the National Society. It is planning to establish a national Centre for Religious Education in the City of London. The Association of Church College Trusts and RE online have their bases at Culham. *Director:* Revd Dr John Gay, 15 Norham Gardens, Oxford, OX2 6PY
Tel: 01865 284885
Fax: 01865 284886
email: enquiries@culham.ac.uk
Web: www.culham.ac.uk

Day One Christian Ministries
Incorporating The Lord's Day Observance Society founded in 1831 to preserve Sunday as the national day of rest and to promote its observance as the Lord's Day for worship and Christian service, Day One Publications produces Christian books and cards, and Day One Prison Ministry works to supply prisons with evangelistic items. *President:* Revd Philip Hacking. *Managing Director:* Mr John Roberts. *Production:* Mr Jim Holmes, Ryelands Rd, Leominster, HR6 8NZ
Tel: 01568 613740
email: sales@dayone.co.uk
Web: www.docm.org.uk
www.dayone.co.uk

Deaf Anglicans Together (DAT)
(formerly National Deaf Church Conference)
This is the members' organization for Deaf People in the Church of England, and it welcomes members of other churches and hearing people as well. DAT provides fellowship and training through conferences (twice a year) and other events, and promotes British Sign Language and Deaf Culture by means of workshops and festivals, exploring the use of drama, storytelling. signed hymns and poems. DAT also acts as a forum for exploring relevant issues, and encourages the participation of Deaf people in the structures of the Church. DAT has three representatives on General Synod. *Contact:* Revd Bob Shrine, 7 Russell Hall Lane, Queensbury, Bradford, BD13 2AJ
Fax: 01274 889006
email: bob.shrine@btinternet.com

Deaf People, Royal Association for
RAD promotes the welfare and interests of deaf people, working with the Deaf Community, Deaf Clubs, deaf individuals and the parents of deaf children. Most of RAD's work is in London, Essex and the south-east of England. RAD is organized around the following services: Deaf Community Development; Advice and Advocacy; Learning Disability; Mental Health; Sign Language Interpreting; Training. *Chief Executive:*

Mr Tom Fenton, 18 Westside Centre, London Rd, Stanway, Colchester, CO3 8PH
Tel: 0845 688 2525/0845 688 2527 (Text)
Fax: 0845 688 2526
email: info@royaldeaf.org.uk
Web: www.royaldeaf.org.uk

Deans' Conference
The Deans' Conference is the meeting together (three times annually) of those who preside over their Cathedral Chapters to reflect upon cathedral issues of particular concern to Deans in their public and cathedral roles. *Chairman:* The Dean of Canterbury. *Treasurer:* The Dean of Exeter. *Secretary:* The Dean of Chelmsford, Cathedral Office, New St, Chelmsford, CM1 1TY *Tel:* 01245 294492
Fax: 01245 294499
email: dean@chelmsfordcathedral.org.uk

Deans' Vergers' Conference
Founded in 1989 to bring together Head Vergers who are employed in that capacity by a Dean and Chapter of the Church of England. The Conference enables members to communicate with one another, exchange and discuss ideas of common interest and to have regular contact with the Deans' Conference. The Head Vergers of the forty-two English cathedrals, Westminster Abbey and St George's Windsor are eligible for membership. *Chairman:* Alex Carberry . *Treasurer:* Clive McCleester . *Secretary:* Glynn Usher, Head Verger and Sub-Sacrist, Bristol Cathedral, College Green, Bristol BS1 5TJ
Tel: 0117 946 8179 (Direct)
0117 926 4879 (Cathedral Office)
Fax: 0117 925 3678
email: glynn.usher@bristol-cathedral.co.uk

Diaconal Association of the Church of England
DACE is a professional association for diaconal ministers (deacons, accredited lay workers and Church Army officers) working in the Church of England, established in 1988 to succeed the Deaconess Committee and the Anglican Accredited Lay Workers Federation. Associate membership is also open to those who support diaconal ministry, and diaconal ministers working in other provinces in the UK. DACE exists to promote the distinctive (permanent) diaconate and other diaconal ministries in the Church of England, support all nationally recognized diaconal ministers, and to consider the theological and practical implications of diaconal ministry within the total ministry of the Christian Church, in partnership with other agencies and denominations. DACE is a member of the Diakonia World Federation of Diaconal Associations and Diaconal Communities. A registered charity. *President:* Revd Kathryn Fitzsimons. *Secretary:* Revd Ann Wren. *Treasurer:* Revd Christopher Wren, 55 Vicarage Lane, Marton, Blackpool, Lancashire, FY4 4EF
Tel: 0870 321 3260
Web: www.dace.org

Diakonia

Founded in 1947 to link the various European deaconess associations, it is now a 'World Federation of Diaconal Associations'. It concerns itself with the nature and task of 'Diakonia' and encourages deaconesses, deacons, and lay people doing diaconal work. It also furthers ecumenical relations between the diaconal associations in other countries. The Diaconal Association of the Church of England is a member. There is a Diakonia 'UK Liaison Group' which also includes representatives from the Methodist Diaconal Order, the Church of Scotland Diaconate and the Deaconesses of the Presbyterian Church in Ireland. *President, DRAE:* Deacon Jackie Fowler, 82 Empress Road, Derby, DE23 6TE

Tel: 01332 361290
email: jackie.fowler@diakonia-world.org
Web: www.diakonia-world.org

Diocesan Clergy Chairs' Forum

The Forum is a voluntary group, allowing the elected chairs of the houses of clergy in each diocese to share ideas and experience, to address together various issues affecting the Church of England, to offer mutual support, and to develop principles of best practice in fulfilling this role in each diocese. Guidelines for best practice have been agreed with the House of Bishops. *Chair:* Canon Robert Cotton. *Hon. Secretary:* Revd Steve Parish, 1A Fitzherbert St, Warrington, WA2 7QG

Tel: 01925 631781
email: s.parish17@ntlworld.com

Diocesan Institutions of Chester, Manchester, Liverpool and Blackburn

For the relief of widows and orphans of clergymen who have officiated in their last sphere of duty in the Archdeaconries of Chester, Macclesfield, Manchester, Rochdale, Liverpool, Warrington or Blackburn. *Chair:* Canon Michael S. Finlay, Rectory, Warrington, WA1 2TL

Tel: 01925 635020
email: finlay289@btinternet.com

Distinctive Diaconate

An unofficial Church of England centre which serves to promote the diaconate as one of the historic orders of the Church's ministry with manifold potential for ministry today by sharing information about current developments through the newsletter *Distinctive Diaconate News*. It also produces *Distinctive News of Women in Ministry*. The *Mission and Ministry* report of Lambeth 1988 recommended the sharing of experiences with the diaconate within the Anglican Communion and suggested using Distinctive Diaconate. The editor was the convenor for the deacon/lay ministries group of Theological Education for the Anglican Communion. *Editor:* Revd Dr Sr Teresa CSA, St Andrew's House,

16 Tavistock Crescent, Westbourne Park, London, W11 1AP

Tel: 020 7221 4604
email: teresajoan@btinternet.com
Web: www.distinctive-diaconate.org.uk

Ecclesiastical Insurance Office PLC

Ecclesiastical is an independent UK-owned insurer and investment management organization that donates a significant proportion of its profits to charity. Ecclesiastical has been providing a range of personal insurances, financial advice and investment services for the Church and community for more than a century. Today Ecclesiastical provides a range of personal insurances and financial services including home, wedding and travel insurance, savings and investments, independent financial advice, life assurance and protection, mortgage advice, pensions and funeral plans through their partner company. They also offer a specialist commercial insurance for churches, church halls, charities, historic buildings and care sector organizations, plus clerical and church supplies through CPS. *Chairman:* Mr Will Samuel. *Group Chief Executive:* Mr Michael Tripp, Beaufort House, Brunswick Rd, Gloucester, GL1 1JZ

Tel: 0845 777 3322
Fax: 01452 304818
email: information@ecclesiastical.com
Web: www.ecclesiastical.com

Ecclesiastical Law Society

Founded in 1987 to promote the study of ecclesiastical law, through the education of office bearers and practitioners in the ecclesiastical courts, the enlargement of knowledge of ecclesiastical law among clergy and laity of the Anglican Communion, and assistance in matters of ecclesiastical law to the General Synod, Convocations, bishops and church dignitaries. *President:* Rt Revd Dr Eric Kemp. *Chairman:* The Bishop of Guildford. *Secretary:* Mr Peter Beesley. *Deputy Secretary:* Mr Howard Dellar, 1 The Sanctuary, London, SW1P 3JT

Tel: 020 7222 5381
Fax: 020 7799 2781
email: info@ecclawsoc.org.uk
Web: www.ecclawsoc.org.uk

Ecclesiological Society

For those who love churches. Studies the arts, architecture and liturgy of the Christian Church by meetings, tours and publications. *President:* Donald Buttress. *Chairman of the Council:* Trevor Cooper. *Honorary Membership Secretary:* Valerie Hitchman, PO Box 287, New Malden, KT3 4YT

Tel: 020 8942 2111/07718 155541
email: admin@ecclsoc.org
Web: www.ecclsoc.org

Ecumenical Council for Corporate Responsibility (ECCR)

ECCR, founded in 1989, is a church-based investor coalition and membership organization working for economic justice, human rights, environmental stewardship, and corporate and investor responsibility. It undertakes research, advocacy and dialogue with companies and investors and seeks to influence company policy and practice and to raise awareness of corporate and investor responsibility issues among the British and Irish churches, the investor community and the general public. It is a Body in Association with Churches Together in Britain and Ireland and a company limited by guarantee, registered in England and Wales. *Researcher:* Suzanne Ismail. *Coordinator:* Miles Litvinoff. *Administrator:* Binia Nightingale. *Church and Membership Relations Officer:* Helen Boothroyd, PO Box 500, Oxford, OX1 1ZL

> *Tel:* 01865 245 349 (Admin)
> 01325 580028 (Membership)
> *email:* info@eccr.org.uk
> *Web:* www.eccr.org.uk

Ecumenical Society of the Blessed Virgin Mary
Founded in London in 1967, 'to advance the study at various levels of the place of the Blessed Virgin Mary in the Church under Christ and to promote ecumenical devotion'. Patrons: the Archbishop of Canterbury, the Archbishop of Westminster, Archbishop Gregorios of Thyateira, Revd Dr John Newton. *General Secretary:* Fr W. McLoughlin. *Hon Treasurer:* Mr F. O'Brien. *Publications Secretary:* Mr D. Carter. *Constitution Secretary:* Revd V. Cassam. *Secretary:* Mr J. P. Farrelly, 11 Belmont Rd, Wallington, SM6 8TE

> *Tel:* 020 8647 5992
> *email:* gensec@esbvm.org.uk
> j.farrelly.123@btinternet.com
> *Web:* www.esbvm.org.uk

Elizabeth Finn Care
Elizabeth Finn Care gives grants and support to people struggling to cope with sudden or unexpected changes in their circumstances. We provide a financial and supportive safety net for people from over 120 occupations. Elizabeth Finn Care helps by providing both one-off and ongoing financial help, tailored to individual circumstances, as we as emotional support through our experienced caseworkers and national volunteer network. In 2007 we founded Turn2us, a charity offering website and helpline services designed to help people in financial need, and those who support them, access the welfare benefits and grants available to them. Turn2us and EFC joined together as a single charity with effect from October 2009. *Chief Exec:* Matthew Sykes. *Director of Income Generation and Communications:* Malcolm Tyndall, Hythe House, 200 Shepherds Bush Rd, London, W6 7NL

> *Tel:* 020 8834 9200/0800 413 220 (helpline)
> *Fax:* 020 7396 6739
> *email:* info@elizabethfinn.org.uk
> *Web:* www.elizabethfinncare.org.uk
> www.turn2us.org.uk

Elland Society Ordination Fund
Grants are made to applicants who are evangelical in conviction and who are in either residential or non-residential training for ordination in the Church of England. Priority is given to ordinands who are sponsored by dioceses in the Province of York or who intend to serve their title in that Province. Grants are usually to help those with unexpected or special financial needs which were not included in their main Church grant (if any). *Secretary/Treasurer:* Revd Colin Judd, 57 Grosvenor Road, Shipley, BD18 4RB

> *Tel:* 01274 584775
> *email:* thejudds@saltsvillage.wanadoo.co.uk
> *Web:* www.ellandsociety.co.uk

English Churches Housing Group
In 2006 ECMG merged with Riverside Housing to become their specialist provider of sheltered and supported housing services. ECMG has gone on to win national awards for its work and each year provides housing and support for over 10,000 people across 170 local authorities. *Chair:* Mr Philip Raw. *Managing Director:* Derek Caren, 49 Western Boulevard, Leicester, LE2 7HN

> *Tel:* 0845 155 9002 (customers)
> 0151 295 6518 (customers)
> *email:* enquiries@echg.org.uk
> *Web:* www.echg.org.uk

English Clergy Association
Founded 1938, the Association seeks to sustain in fellowship all Clerks in Holy Orders in their vocation and ministry within the Church of England, promoting in every available way the good of English parish and cathedral life and the welfare of clergy. Related Trustees give discretionary clergy holiday grants upon application to the Hon Almoner. The Association seeks to foster the independence within the Established Church of all clergy whether in freehold office or not, and broadly supports the patronage system. Publishes twice-yearly Parson and Parish magazine. Lay members may be admitted. Subscription £10 p.a. (£5 retired/ordinands). *Patron:* The Bishop of London. *Chairman:* Revd John Masding. *Deputy Chairman:* Mrs Margaret Laird. *Vice-Chairman:* Revd Jonathan Redvers Harris, Office Address: The Old School, Norton Hawkfield, Bristol, BS39 4HB

> *Tel:* 01275 830017/01983 565953
> *Fax:* 01275 830017
> *email:* benoporto-eca@yahoo.co.uk
> *Web:* www.clergyassoc.co.uk

Evangelical Alliance
Founded in 1846 as a representative body with denominational, congregational, organizational and individual supporters, its vision is to unite evangelicals and to provide an evangelical voice in the public square. Also aims to encourage action among evangelicals leading to spiritual and social transformation in the UK. Operates in

England, Northern Ireland, Scotland and Wales. *General Director:* Mr Steve Clifford, Whitefield House, 186 Kennington Park Rd, London, SE11 4BT   *Tel:* 020 7207 2100
Fax: 020 7210 2150
email: info@eauk.org
Web: www.eauk.org

Faith and Thought
(the operational name of the Victoria Institute or Philosophical Society of Great Britain)
Founded 1865 to enquire into the relationship between the Christian revelation and modern scientific research. Publishes *Faith and Thought new series* in succession to *The Journal of the Transactions of the Victoria Institute* (JTVI); from 1958 *Faith and Thought*; from 1989 *Faith&Thought Bulletin*. Jointly with Christians in Science, since 1989 it sponsors the publication of *Science and Christian Belief.* Charity Registration no. 285871. *President:* Sir John Houghton. *Chairman:* Revd Dr Robert Allaway. *Hon. Treasurer & Membership Secretary:* Revd John Buxton. *Editor & Meetings Secretary:* Reginald S. Luhman, 110 Flemming Avenue, Leigh on Sea, SS9 3AX
Tel: 01279 422661 (Hon Treasurer & Membership Secretary)
01702 475110 (Editor & Meeting Secretary)
Web: www.faithandthought.org.uk

Family Action
(formerly Family Welfare Association)
Founded 1869. Provides social work and social care services for families and individuals. Administers trust funds which give financial grants to individuals. Provides information to students through the Educational Grants Advisory Service. Assistance is primarily targeted at families and individuals with low incomes, particularly those living on benefits. See the web site for more information. *Contact:* Family Action, 501–505 Kingsland Rd, Dalston, London, E8 4AU
Tel: 020 7241 7459 (Tues-Thurs, 2–4pm only)
email: grantsenquiry@family-action.org.uk
Web: www.family-action.org.uk

Farnham Castle International Briefing and Conference Centre
Farnham Castle, the former palace of the bishops of Winchester, offers a unique and special location for church weekend retreats. Several London churches are regular visitors. The castle has 31 en suite bedrooms, including some family rooms, all with television. Facilities include two historic consecrated chapels, a wide choice of conference rooms and five acres of beautifully maintained gardens. Farnham Castle has an excellent dining room and bar. It overlooks the town of Farnham and is only seven minutes by taxi from the railway station. Farnham is 30 miles west of London, with good rail connections to Waterloo station (55 minutes). Special weekend rates are available for groups of over 30 adults. Please contact Teresa Clue, Events Manager, for further information. A video tour is available on the web site. *Chief Executive:* Mr James Twiss. *Director of Marketing & Client Services:* Mr Jeff Toms. *Conference Manager:* Mrs Barbara Milam. *Events Manager:* Teresa Clue, Farnham Castle, Farnham, GU9 0AG
Tel: 01252 721194
email: info@farnhamcastle.com
Web: www.farnhamcastle.com

Federation of Catholic Priests
A federation of priests in communion with the See of Canterbury who have undertaken to live in accordance with Catholic doctrine and practice. It exists for mutual support in propagating, maintaining and defending such doctrine and practice and for the deepening of the spiritual life of members. *Chairman:* Revd Stephen Bould. *Secretary General:* Preb Brian Tubbs, 58 Dorset Avenue, Exeter, EX4 1ND   *Tel:* 01392 200506
email: fathertubbs@aol.com
Web: www.priests.org.uk

Feed the Minds
Feed the Minds believes that education saves lives, reduces poverty and builds community. Working in partnership worldwide, Feed the Minds funds a wide variety of innovative, indigenous educational projects. By improving access to knowledge and learning, Feed the Minds helps give people the opportunity to experience life in all its fullness. Registered Charity no. 291333 *President:* Revd David Cornick. *Chair of Trustees:* Dr David Goodbourn. *Director:* Ms Josephine Carlsson, Feed the Minds, Park Place, 12 Lawn Lane, London, SW8 1UD
Tel: 08451 21 21 02
+44 (0)20 7582 3535 (International)
Fax: +44 (0)20 7735 7617
email: info@feedtheminds.org
Web: www.feedtheminds.org

Fellowship of St Alban and St Sergius
Founded 1928. An unofficial body which fosters understanding and friendship between Eastern Orthodox and Western Christians. *Patron:* The Archbishop of Canterbury. *Presidents:* The Bishop of London and Archbishop Gregorios of Thyateira and Great Britain. *General Secretary:* Revd Stephen Platt, 1 Canterbury Rd, Oxford, OX2 6LU   *Tel:* 01865 552991
email: gensec@sobornost.org
Web: www.sobornost.org

Fellowship of St Nicholas (FSN)
FSN uses its resources to offset the disadvantage, deprivation and abuse of children in need in Sussex. Our current services include 2 centre-based family support and day care services including mobile and outreach, UK on-line centres, youth clubs, nurseries, children's bereavement project and family support. *Chairman:* Mrs Mollie Green.

Chief Executive: Ms Christine Unsworth, The St Nicholas Centre, 66 London Rd, St Leonards-on-Sea, TN37 6AS   *Tel:* 01424 423683/01424 855222
Fax: 01424 460446
email: enquiries@fellowshipofstnicholas.org.uk
Web: www.fsncharity.co.uk

Fellowship of St Therese of Lisieux
Founded in 1997, the centenary year of St Therese's death and in anticipation of her being proclaimed a Doctor of the Church in 1998. Its purpose is to inform members of the Church of England about her teaching and its relevance to Christians of all denominations, and to gain an entry for her in the Anglican calendar of saints. Those who would like to know more about her approach to spirituality and Christian discipleship and share in the interest of others are welcome to join the fellowship. Members commit themselves to learn more about St Therese through reading, study and prayer; pray for other members regularly; take opportunities to spread her message within our churches; meet together once a year for a time of retreat, teaching or pilgrimage; and encourage one another by contact and correspondence as appropriate. *Contact:* Revds Graeme and Sue Parfitt, Brook End, Rectory Gardens, Henbury, Bristol, BS10 7AQ
Tel: 0117 959 0293
email: suegraeme@fish.co.uk
Web:
www.geocities.com/fellowship_of_st_therese/

Fellowship of Word and Spirit
Anglican evangelical organization comprising 300 clergy and lay people committed to empowering, equipping and encouraging evangelicals through the development of thoughtful biblical theology for the 21st century using publications, conferences and a network of supportive fellowship. *Honorary President:* Rt Revd Wallace Benn. *Chairman:* Revd Simon Vibert, c/o 86 All Hallows Rd, Bispham, Blackpool, FY2 0AY
email: admin@fows.org
Web: www.fows.org

Forward in Faith
Founded in November 1992, Forward in Faith exists to support all who in conscience are unable to accept the ordination of women to the priesthood or the episcopate. It seeks an ecclesial structure which will continue the orders of bishop and priest as the Church has received them. It offers support to all who need it via a national and local network. It is governed by a council elected by the members of its National Assembly, which meets annually. Through Forward in Faith International, it collaborates with its sister organizations in Australia and North America. It publishes the monthly journal *New Directions*, the quarterly newspaper *Forward/Plus*, the catechetical weekly Pew Sheet *Forward/* and the Sunday School course *Forward Teaching*.

Chairman: The Bishop of Fulham. *Director:* Mr Stephen Parkinson, 2A The Cloisters, Gordon Square, London, WC1H 0AG   *Tel:* 020 7388 3588
Fax: 020 7387 3539
email: FiF.UK@forwardinfaith.com
Web: www.forwardinfaith.com

Foundation for Church Leadership
The Foundation for Church Leadership (FCL) is an endowed charitable trust: its aims are to facilitate the support and development of emerging and senior church leaders, faith representatives and organizations for the benefit of leadership across the church. The Foundation primarily delivers its objectives through the provision of a series of consultancy and research initiatives. *Chair:* Dame Janet Trotter. *Director:* Julie Farrar, c/o Saxton Bampfylde, 35 Old Queen Street, London SW1H 9JA   *Tel:* 0845 1556338
email: info@churchleadershipfoundation.org
Web: www.churchleadershipfoundation.org

Foundation of St Matthias
Considers applications for personal and corporate grants with preference given to higher and further education; applicants from the dioceses of Bath and Wells, Bristol and Gloucester and from former students of the college. This does not preclude applicants from elsewhere. Applications should show how the chosen subject will contribute to the advancement of the Christian religion. Examples of personal study not considered: medicine, veterinary science, engineering, law. Corporate applications should promote projects for the educational training of others and show how the Church's contribution to higher and further education will be enhanced. Closing dates for applications: 31 January, 31 May and 30 September each year. The Trust is a member of the Association of Church College Trusts (see separate entry). *Correspondent:* Miss L. Cox, Diocesan Church House, 23 Great George St, Bristol, BS1 5QZ   *Tel:* 0117 906 0100
Fax: 0117 925 0460
Web: www.stmatthiastrust.org.uk

Frances Ashton's Charity
Supports serving or retired clergy of the Church England and the widows/widowers of clergy who have now passed away. The trustees will consider almost any kind of financial hardship with only few exceptions. The application deadline is 1st June annually for the main annual grant round, with decisions made in September. Where the applicant has an immediate or urgent need, please contact the Charities Aid Foundation for advice as the trustees may be able to support you quickly and at any time of the year if they agree the case is sufficiently urgent. Please contact Abigail Hiscock, Advisory and Consulting Manager at Charities Aid Foundation. *Contact:* Abigail Hiscock, Frances Ashton Charity,

c/o Advisory and Consulting, CAF, Kings Hill, West Malling, ME19 4TA   *Tel:* 03000 123 119
Fax: 03000 123 001
email: ahiscock@cafonline.org

Friends of Friendless Churches
Founded 1957 to preserve churches and chapels of architectural or historic interest. Now owns 43 redundant places of worship, half in England and half in Wales. Also administers the Cottam Will Trust, which gives grants for the introduction of works of art into ancient Gothic churches. *President:* The Marquess of Salisbury. *Chairman:* Mr Roger Evans. *Hon Secretary:* Mr John Bowles. *Hon Director:* Mr Matthew Saunders. *Asst Director:* Mrs Alison Du Cane, St Ann's Vestry Hall, 2 Church Entry, London, EC4V 5HB
Tel: 020 7236 3934
email: office@friendsoffriendlesschurches.org.uk
Web: www.friendsoffriendlesschurches.org.uk

Friends of Julian of Norwich
The cell of Julian of Norwich, a chapel attached to St Julian's Church, Norwich, stands on the site where the 14th-century anchoress wrote her book *Revelations of Divine Love.* The Julian Centre, beside the church, houses a small bookshop and a library of works on Julian and spirituality and welcomes visitors and pilgrims (open Monday to Saturday 10.30 a.m. to 3.30 p.m.). Large parties should book in advance (office hours as above). Accommodation is often available in the small convent beside the church. Quiet days can be arranged. Please contact the Sister in Charge, All Hallows House. The Julian Centre, Rouen Rd, Norwich, NR1 1QT
Tel: 01603 767380 (group bookings)
01603 624738 (accommodation, quiet days)
email: centre@friendsofjulian.org.uk
Web: www.friendsofjulian.org.uk

Friends of Little Gidding, The
Little Gidding is rightly called a 'thin place'. From the seventeenth-century Ferrar family community to T. S. Eliot's visit in 1936 and up to the present time, many have experienced the presence of God at Little Gidding. The Friends (founded in 1947) take a practical and active involvement in the care of the historic church and the old farmhouse – now a retreat centre. It co-ordinates, with the T. S. Eliot Society, an annual Eliot Festival; arranges an annual pilgrimage in July; commemorates Nicholas Ferrar's life on his feast day, 4 December; and supports the provision of accommodation and hospitality for visitors and pilgrims. *Chair:* Simon Kershaw. *Secretary:* Judith Hodgson, c/o Ferrar House, Little Gidding, Huntingdon, PE28 5RJ
Tel: 01832 275343
email: chair@littlegidding.org.uk
Web: www.littlegidding.org.uk

Friends of the Clergy Corporation
See Corporation of the Sons of the Clergy

Friends of the Elderly
Friends of the Elderly has been helping older people since 1905. Our vision is that all older people should retain their independence, dignity and peace of mind. We offer high quality residential and nursing care in 14 care homes, some with dementia units. We support older people to stay living in their own homes with a range of community services including welfare grants for those in financial need, day care, home support, home visiting and telephone befriending. Registered Charity no. 226064 *Patron:* HM The Queen. *Chief Executive:* Richard Furze, 40–42 Ebury St, London, SW1W 0LZ   *Tel:* 020 7730 8263
Fax: 020 7259 0154
email: enquiries@fote.co.uk
Web: www.fote.org.uk

Frontier Youth Trust
Founded 1964. Provides training, resources information, support and association for Christians working with disadvantaged young people in the community, whether church-based, unattached or within the youth and community service, particularly in urban/industrial areas. *Chief Executive:* Mr Dave Wiles, Unit 208B, The Big Peg, 120 Vyse St, Birmingham, B18 6NF
Tel: 0121 687 3505
email: frontier@fyt.org.uk
Web: www.fyt.org.uk

Fulcrum
A network for evangelical clergy and laity. Launched in 2003 at the National Evangelical Anglican Congress in Blackpool, Fulcrum seeks to renew the evangelical centre by giving a voice to a nourishing, generous orthodoxy. It provides support, theological exploration and encouragement for moderate evangelical Anglicans and creates a space in which genuine debate can take place in a spirit of non-defensiveness and gracious disagreement, acknowledging that the clash of ideas can be creative and worthwhile. It has a web site with regularly updated articles from leading evangelical theologians. *Chair:* Dr Elaine Storkey. *Theological Secretary:* Rt Revd Graham Kings. *General Secretary:* Revd Simon Cawdell. *Administrator:* Revd Stephen Kuhrt, The Vicarage, Lodge Park, Claverley, WV5 7DP
Tel: 01746 710268
email: admin@fulcrum-anglican.org.uk
Web: www.fulcrum-anglican.org.uk

Girlguiding UK
Founded 1910. Open to all girls and women between 5 and 65 years regardless of race, faith or any other circumstance. Its purpose is to enable girls to mature into confident, capable and caring women determined, as individuals, to realize their potential in their career, home and personal

life, and willing as citizens to contribute to their community and the wider world. Rainbows age 5–7; Brownies age 7–10; Guides age 10–14; Senior Section age 14–25; Leaders age 18 plus. *Chief Guide:* Mrs Liz Burnley. *Chief Executive:* Miss Denise King, 17/19 Buckingham Palace Rd, London, SW1W 0PT

> *Tel:* 0800 169 5901 / 020 7834 6242
> *Fax:* 020 7828 8317
> *email:* join.us@girlguiding.org.uk
> *Web:* www.girlguiding.org.uk

Girls Friendly Society in England and Wales, The (Campaign name GFS Platform)

Established in 1875, GFS Platform works with girls and young women aged 7+. The work focuses on two specific areas, namely four community projects that work with young women between the ages of 14 and 25 who are either pregnant or who have children, and 40 parish-based youth work branches throughout England and Wales that run voluntary youth groups for girls and young women aged 7+. Main activities include reducing social exclusion and building self-esteem by providing social, formal educational and health awareness sessions and generic support in a single gender and non-judgemental environment. GFS Platform offers young women and girls the opportunity to explore their own personal and social development. This enables them to acquire new skills and knowledge, gain confidence, make informed choices and take responsibility for their own lives. *Director:* Joy Lauezzari, Unit 2 Angel Gate, 326 City Rd, London, EC1V 2PT

> *Tel:* 020 7837 9669
> *Fax:* 020 7837 4107
> *email:* annualreport@gfsplatform.org.uk
> *Web:* www.gfsplatform.org.uk

Girls' Brigade England and Wales

An international interdenominational youth organization having as its aim 'to help girls to become followers of the Lord Jesus Christ and through self-control, reverence and sense of responsibility to find true enrichment of life'. *National Director:* Miss Ruth Gilson, PO Box 196, 129 Broadway, Didcot, OX11 8XN

> *Tel:* 01235 510425
> *Fax:* 01235 510429
> *email:* gbco@girlsbrigadeew.org.uk
> *Web:* www.girlsbrigadeew.org.uk

Greater Churches Network

The group was founded in 1991 as an informal association of large churches, which, by virtue of their great age, size and of their historical, architectural or ecclesiastical importance, display many of the characteristics of a cathedral and also fulfil a role which is additional to that of a normal parish church. The aims of the Greater Churches group are threefold: to provide help and mutual support in dealing with the special problems of running a "cathedral-like" church within the organisational and financial structure of a parish church; to enhance the quality of parish worship in such churches; and to promote wider recognition of the unique position and needs of churches in this category. The group also serves as a channel of communication for other organisations wishing to have contact with churches of this type. *Hon Secretary:* Ms Philippa Shaw, Tewkesbury Abbey Office, Church Street, Tewkesbury, Gloucestershire, GL20 5RZ

> *Tel:* 01684 856141
> *email:* philippa.shaw@tewkesburyabbey.org.uk

Greenbelt Festivals

Organizes an annual Christian arts festival which takes place at Cheltenham racecourse. Average audience figures are around 20,000, most of whom camp for the four-day event held over the August bank holiday weekend. There are tented and indoor venues for music, seminars, theatre, film, art galleries, workshops, visual arts, resources, cafes and shops. The event is inter-denominational. *Chair:* Jude Levermore. *Festival Manager:* Beki Bateson. *Development and Marketing Manager:* Paul Northup, All Hallows on the Wall, 83 London Wall, London, EC2M 5ND

> *Tel:* 020 7374 2755 (office)
> 020 7874 2760 (ticket line)
> *Fax:* 020 7374 2731
> *email:* info@greenbelt.org
> *Web:* www.greenbelt.org.uk

Gregorian Association

Founded 1870 to spread reliable information on Plainsong and to promote its use; to demonstrate its suitability to the English language by means of services and holding lectures and conferences; to provide expert advice and instruction on the use of Plainsong. *President:* The Archbishop of Canterbury. *Chairman:* Mr Grey Macartney. *Director of Music:* Dr Peter Wilton, 26 The Grove, Ealing, London, W5 5LH   *Tel:* 020 8840 5832

> *Fax:* 0870 055 3684
> *email:* pjsw@beaufort.demon.co.uk
> *Web:* www.beaufort.demon.co.uk/chant.htm

Grubb Institute, The

The Grubb Institute seeks to contribute to the repair, healing and transformation of the world, which we have all contributed to creating both consciously and unconsciously. It enables leaders to work with their experience of human systems, institutions and personal relations in the context of Christ's activity, using insights and concepts developed from the human sciences and Christian theology and values. It provides consultancy, action research and learning events for people of all faiths or of none, from voluntary organizations, education, health, social care, criminal justice agencies, and business. As a

Christian foundation, it has worked since 1969 with leaders in churches and dioceses, religious orders and agencies worldwide. *Executive Director:* Bruce Irvine. *Senior Organizational Analysts:* Jean Reed, Colin Quine, John Bazalgette, Vega Roberts. *Organizational Analyst:* Revd Rosy Fairhurst, The Grubb Institute, Cloudesley Street, London, N1 0HU   *Tel:* 020 7278 8061
Fax: 020 7278 0728
email: info@grubb.org.uk
Web: www.grubb.org.uk

Guild of All Souls

Founded 1873 as an intercessory guild, caring for the dying, the dead and the bereaved. Open to members of the Church of England and Churches in communion with her and any who share the objects of the Guild. Chantry chapel at Walsingham and at St Stephen's, Gloucester Rd, London. Patron of 41 livings of the Catholic tradition. *President:* The Bishop of Richborough. *General Secretary:* David Llewelyn Morgan. *Warden:* Louis A. Lewis. *Hon Treasurer:* Revd Paul E. Jones, Royal London House, 22–25 Finsbury Square, London, EC2A 1DX
Tel: 0207 920 6468 / 01371 830132
Fax: 01371 831430
Web: www.guildofallsouls.org.uk

Guild of Church Braillists

The Guild consists of a group of people who give their services to help blind readers by transcribing a variety of religious literature into Braille. Requests are welcome from individual readers for books, special services, etc. All other productions are sent to the National Library for the Blind or the Library of the RNIB. For further details contact the Secretary. *Secretary:* Mrs Mabel Owen, 321 Feltham Hill Rd, Ashford, TW15 1LP   *Tel:* 01727 845183

Guild of Church Musicians

Founded in 1888, but since 1961 has administered the Archbishops' Certificate in Church Music (ACert.CM) on behalf of the Archbishops of Canterbury and Westminster. This Certificate is a minimum qualification for church organists, choir trainers, cantors, choristers and leaders of instrumental groups and is fully ecumenical. The Archbishops' Award in Church Music is available for those who wish to be examined in practical skills only and the Guild's Preliminary Certificate in Church Music is aimed at young people and those starting in church music. Since 2002 the new qualification of Archbishops' Certificate in Public Worship (ACert.PW), for all who lead public worship, both clerical and lay, has been established. There is also a Fellowship examination (FGCM). *General Secretary:* Mr John Ewington OBE. *Warden:* Very Revd Dr Richard Fenwick. *President:* Dr Mary Archer. *Chairman*

Academic Board: Prof Peter Aston. *Examinations Secretary:* Dr Helen Burrows, St Katharine Cree Church, 86 Leadenhall St, London, EC3A 3DH
Tel: 01883 743168
email: JohnMusicsure@orbix.co.uk
Web: www.churchmusicians.org

Guild of Health

Founded in 1904 to further the Church's Ministry of Healing through prayer, teaching, sacrament and visiting the sick, and by cooperation with Christian doctors, nurses and other members of the healing team. It publishes a quarterly magazine *Way of Life* and organizes seminars on aspects of healing which are open to all. *President:* Rt Revd John Pritchard. *Chair:* Revd Roger Hoath. *Chaplain:* Revd Christopher MacKenna. *Administrator:* Ms Veronica Byrom, c/o St Marylebone Parish Church, 17 Marylebone Rd, London, NW1 5LT   *Tel:* 020 7563 1389
email: guildofhealth@stmarylebone.org
Web: www.gohealth.org.uk

Guild of Pastoral Psychology

The Guild offers a meeting ground for all interested in the relationship between religion and depth psychology, particularly the work of C. G. Jung and his followers. Depth psychology has contributed many new insights into the meaning of religion and its symbols and their relevance to everyday life. The Guild has monthly lectures in central London, a day conference in London in the spring and a three-day summer conference at Oxford. Further information and details of membership available from the Administrator. *Secretary:* Robert Macdonald, Flat 5, 75 Hatton St, London, NW8 0PL   *Tel:* 020 7724 7282
email: guild@macdonaldmedia.co.uk
Web: www.guildofpastoralpsychology.org.uk

Guild of Servants of the Sanctuary

Founded 1898 to raise the spiritual standard of Servers, to promote friendship among them and to encourage attendance at Holy Communion in addition to times of duty. *Warden:* Revd David Moore. *Secretary General:* Mr Terry Doughty, 7 Church Ave, Leicester, LE3 6AJ
Tel: 0116 262 0308
email: secretary.general@gssonline.org.uk
Web: www.gssonline.org.uk

Guild of St Leonard

The Guild was founded by the Revd John Sankey. Its object is to pray for all prisoners, those on licence or probation and for all who care for them. The Guild publishes a quarterly Intercession Paper. *Warden:* Rt Revd Lloyd Rees. *Chaplain and Secretary:* Revd Peter Walker, The Chaplain's Office, HMP Ford, Arundel, BN18 0BX
Tel: 01903 663000

Guild of St Raphael
Founded 1915 to work for the restoration of the Ministry of Healing as part of the normal function of the Church, by preparing the sick for all ministries of healing, by teaching the need of repentance and faith, by making use of the Sacraments of Healing and by Intercession. *Organizing Secretary:* Mrs Hanna Hart. *Warden:* Rt Revd N. Reade. *Sub-Warden:* Canon Paul Nener. *Editor of 'Chrism':* Prof Helen Leathard, 1a Snaetell Ave, Tuebrook, Liverpool, L13 7HA
Tel: 0151 228 3193/0151 228 2023
Fax: 0151 228 3193
email: office@guildofstraphael.org.uk
Web: www.guildofstraphael.org.uk

Harnhill Centre of Christian Healing
A resource centre for the ministry of Christian Healing through counselling, prayer, quiet days, teaching courses and Christian Healing Services. The Centre provides residential accommodation. *Chairman:* Dr David Wells. *Chaplain/Warden:* Revd Paul Springate, Harnhill Manor, Cirencester, GL7 5PX
Tel: 01285 850283
Fax: 01285 850519
email: office@harnhillcentre.org.uk
Web: www.harnhillcentre.org.uk

Henry Bradshaw Society
Founded 1890 for printing liturgical texts from manuscripts and rare editions of service books, etc. For available texts, please consult the Society's web site. *Secretary:* Dr Nicolas Bell, Music Collections, The British Library, 96 Euston Rd, London, NW1 2DB
email: nicolas.bell@bl.uk
Web: www.henrybradshawsociety.org

Hexthorpe Manor Community
Hexthorpe Manor Community works co-operatively with Holy Rood House. It is a long term Residential Therapeutic Community, for young adults between the ages of 18–30+. It now has its own Board of Directors. Hexthorpe Manor is a member of the Association of Therapeutic Communities and of the Community of Communities Project of the Royal College of Psychiatrists. *Patron:* The Archbishop of Canterbury. *Vice Patron:* Prof Mary Grey. *Chief Executive:* Revd Stanley Baxter. *Project Manager:* Beth Wood. *Chaplain:* Revd Elizabeth Baxter, Hexthorpe Manor, Old Hexthorpe, Doncaster, DN4 0HY
Tel: 01302 818184/01302 310133
email: hexthorpe.manor@yahoo.com

Highbury Centre
Christian guesthouse on quiet private road with ample free on-street parking. Reductions for missionaries/clergy. *Manager:* Mrs S. Scalora, 20–26 Aberdeen Park, Highbury, London, N5 2BJ
Tel: 020 7226 2663
Fax: 020 7704 1853
email: enquiries@thehighburycentre.org
Web: www.thehighburycentre.org

Hockerill Educational Foundation
Personal awards are made to teachers, intending teachers and others in further or higher education, with a priority to the teaching of RE. No awards to those training for ordination, mission, social work or counselling, or to children at school. Corporate grants to support the development of religious education, particularly in the Dioceses of Chelmsford and St Albans. Applications by 31 March each year. Member of the Association of Church College Trusts (see separate entry). *Correspondent:* Mr Derek J. Humphrey, 3 The Swallows, Harlow, Essex, CM17 0AR
Tel: 0560 3140931
Fax: 01992 425950
email: info@hockerillfoundation.org.uk
Web: www.hockerillfoundation.org.uk

Holy Rood House, Centre for Health and Pastoral Care
Opened in 1993, the Centre is a friendly house with a residential community. The house offers a gentle and holistic approach in a Christian environment where individuals or groups, of all ages and backgrounds, can work towards their own healing and explore their spiritual journey within an atmosphere of acceptance, love and openness. Professional counsellors and therapists, working closely with the medical profession, offer support at times of bereavement, abuse, addiction, relationship breakdown or illness, and creative arts and stress management play an important role in the healing process. Holy Rood House ministers within an awareness of justice and peace to daily or residential guests, and is also the home of the Centre for the Study of Theology and Health. *Patron:* The Archbishop of Canterbury. *Vice-Patron:* Prof Mary Grey. *Joint Exec Directors:* Revd Stanley and Revd Elizabeth Baxter. *Director,Therapeutic Care:* Jan Younger. *Director, Centre for Study of Theology & Health:* Revd Dr Jan Berry, 10 Sowerby Rd, Sowerby, Thirsk, YO7 1HX
Tel: 01845 522580/01845 522004
Fax: 01845 527300
email: enquiries@holyroodhouse.org.uk
Web: www.holyroodhouse.freeuk.com

Homes for Retired Clergy
See separate entries for Beauchamp Community and College of St Barnabas.

House of St Barnabas in Soho
Chief Executive: Andy Griffiths, 1 Greek St, Soho, London, W1D 4NQ
Tel: 020 7437 1894
Fax: 020 7434 1746
email: andy.griffiths@houseofstbarnabas.org.uk
Web: www.houseofstbarnabas.org.uk

Hymn Society of Great Britain and Ireland
Founded in 1936 to encourage study and research into hymns, both words and music; to promote good standards of hymn singing and to encourage the discerning use of hymns and songs in

worship. The Society publishes a quarterly magazine and there is a three-day annual conference. Further information and details of membership from the Secretary. *Secretary:* Revd Robert A. Canham, 99 Barton Rd, Lancaster, LA1 4EN   *Tel and Fax:* 01524 66740
email: robcanham@haystacks.fsnet.co.uk
Web: www.hymnsocietygbi.org.uk

Incorporated Church Building Society
Founded 1818. The Incorporated Church Building Society is managed by the National Churches Trust. Registered Charity no. 212752. *Patron:* HM The Queen. *Chairman:* Very Revd Henry Stapleton FSA. *Chief Executive:* Andrew Edwards. *Grants Manager:* Alison Pollard, 31 Newbury St, London, EC1A 7HU   *Tel:* 020 7600 6090
Fax: 020 7796 2442
email: info@nationalchurchestrust.org
Web: www.nationalchurchestrust.org

Industrial Christian Fellowship
Founded in 1918 as a successor to the Navvy Mission (1877) and incorporating the Christian Social Union, ICF is a nationwide ecumenical network that provides support for Christians who want to apply their faith in fresh and creative ways in the everyday working world. A recent new initiative to make links between the local church and working life is the 'Take your Minister to Work' project. ICF provides resources, including liturgy and prayers for personal and corporate use, reflections and services related to work; a newsletter and occasional papers; and the quarterly journal 'Faith in Business' (in association with the Ridley Hall Foundation). Close links with other groups and agencies involved with faith and work are maintained. Membership is open to individuals and organizations. *Chair:* Revd Carol Williams. *Secretary:* Mrs Ann Wright, PO Box 414, Horley, RH6 8WL   *Tel:* 01293 821322
email: wright@btinternet.com
Web: www.icf-online.org

Industrial Mission Association
The Industrial Mission Association (IMA) is a national and ecumenical association, mainly, though not exclusively, comprised of chaplains appointed to places of work throughout the UK. *Moderator:* Stephen Hazlett. *Membership Secretary:* Revd Crispin White. *Honorary Treasurer:* Adrian Thomas. *Hon Secretary:* David Wrighton, 34 Chalvington Rd, Chandlers Ford, Eastleigh, SO53 3DX   *Tel:* 0238 026 1146 (Secretary)
0190 383 0785 (Membership Secretary)
email: wrigdgshim@aol.com
Web:
http://www.industrialmission.org.uk/cms/

INFORM
Inform is an independent charity founded in 1988 with funding from the British Home Office and mainstream Churches with the aim of obtaining and making available accurate, balanced and up-to-date information about alternative spirituality and new religious movements or 'cults'. It has a large collection of data on computer and in various other forms (books, articles, cuttings, videos and cassettes), and is in touch with an international network of scholars and other specialists. People with questions or concerns about new religious movements or alternative spirituality should contact the Inform office, which is based at the London School of Economics, between 10 a.m. and 4.30 p.m., Mondays to Fridays. *Hon Director:* Prof Eileen Barker. *Deputy Director:* Amanda van Eck Duymaer van Twist. *Research Officers:* Sarah Harvey and Suzanne Newcombe. *Administrative Officer:* Jane Cooper, LSE, Houghton St, London, WC2A 2AE
Tel: 020 7955 7654 (Information line)
email: INFORM@LSE.ac.uk
Web: www.inform.ac

Inter Faith Network for the UK
Established in 1987 to encourage contact and dialogue between different faith communities in the United Kingdom. It aims to advance public knowledge and mutual understanding of the teaching, traditions and practices of the different faith communities in Britain, including an awareness of their distinctive features and of their common ground, and to promote good relations between persons of different faiths. Its member organizations include representative bodies from the Baha'i, Buddhist, Christian, Hindu, Jain, Jewish, Muslim, Sikh and Zoroastrian communities; national, regional and local inter faith bodies; and academic institutions and educational bodies concerned with inter faith issues. *Director:* Dr Harriet Crabtree. *Co-Chairs:* Rt Revd Dr Alastair Redfern and Dr Manazir Ahsan, 8A Lower Grosvenor Place, London, SW1W 0EN   *Tel:* 020 7931 7766
Fax: 020 7931 7722
email: ifnet@interfaith.org.uk
Web: www.interfaith.org.uk

Intercontinental Church Society
Founded 1823. ICS makes known the Christ of the Scriptures to people who speak English. It is a patronage society (nominating chaplains for international Anglican churches abroad), owns church buildings, and a mission agency engaged in church planting, growth and outreach to tourists, principally in Europe and around the Mediterranean; and publishes the *Directory of English-speaking Churches Abroad.* *President:* Viscount Brentford. *General Manager:* Mr David Healey, 1 Athena Drive, Tachbrook Park, Warwick, CV34 6NL   *Tel:* 01926 430347
Fax: 01926 888092
email: enquiries@ics-uk.org
Web: www.ics-uk.org

International Ecumenical Fellowship – British Region

IEF is a community of Christians both lay and ordained, with regional groups in Belgium, Czech Republic, France, Germany, Great Britain, Hungary, Poland, Romania, Slovak Republic and Spain. It also has individual members in various other countries. Through annual international gatherings and smaller regional groups, Christians from Catholic, Orthodox and Protestant traditions meet to worship, pray, study and enjoy fellowship together. IEF tries to strengthen the spirit of ecumenism and international friendship. IEF practises eucharistic hospitality as far as church discipline and individual conscience permit. *President of British Region:* Revd D. Hardiman. *Secretary:* Revd C. Hardiman. *Treasurer:* Mr P. Scribbins, 31 Okeley Lane, Tring, Hertfordshire, HP23 4HD   *Tel:* 0191 456 1943
email: davidhardiman@btinternet.com
Web: www.ief.info

Interserve

Interserve is an interdenominational, evangelical mission agency with over 800 full-time Christian professionals working across Asia, the Arab World, and among ethnic groups in England and Wales. Interservers work in many different ministries, seeking to share the love of Christ through everything they say and do. All Christians with a burden to respond to Jesus commission and make disciples of all nations are welcomed for both long and short term periods of service, with the aim of seeing lives and communities transformed through encounter with Jesus Christ. *Chairman:* Tim Baynes-Clarke. *National Director:* Steve Bell, 5/6 Walker Avenue, Wolverton Mills, Milton Keynes, MK12 5TW   *Tel:* 01908 552700
Fax: 01908 552779
email: enquiries@isewi.org
Web: www.interserveonline.org.uk

Jubilate Group

An association of authors and musicians formed in 1974 for the purpose of publishing material for contemporary worship: *Hymns for Today's Church, Church Family Worship, Carols for Today, Carol Praise, Let's Praise/ 1 and 2, Prayers for the People, Psalms for Today, Songs from the Psalms, The Dramatised Bible, The Wedding Book, Hymns for the People, World Praise 1 and 2 and Sing Glory. Chairman:* Revd Steve James. *Secretary:* David Peacock. *Copyright Managers:* Mrs M. Williams, Mr P. Williams, 4 Thorne Park Rd, Chelston, Torquay, TQ2 6RX   *Tel:* 01803 607754
Fax: 01803 605682
email: copyrightmanager@jubilate.co.uk
Web: www.jubilate.co.uk

Julian Meetings, The

A network of Christian contemplative prayer groups, begun in Britain in 1973. There are now about 350 groups in Great Britain and some in Australia, Canada, France, Ireland, Mexico, Southern Africa and the USA. Ecumenical. Magazine three times a year. *Contact:* Deidre Morris, 263 Park Lodge Lane, Wakefield, WF1 4HY   *Tel:* 01924 369437
email: gb@julianmeetings.org
Web: www.julianmeetings.org

Keswick Convention

The Keswick Convention is the main event organised annually by Keswick Ministries and has been taking place since 1875. It offers something for everyone – life-changing Bible teaching, uplifting worship and great fellowship combined with the chance to relax and enjoy a holiday in the wonderful setting of the Lake District. *Chairman:* Mr Jonathan Lamb. *General Director:* Mr David Bradley. *Operations Manager:* Mr Simon Overend, Keswick Convention Trust, Skiddaw St, Keswick, CA12 4BY   *Tel:* 01768 780075
Fax: 01768 775276
email: info@keswickministries.org
Web: www.keswickministries.org

Keswick Hall Trust Charity

The Trustees spending gives priority to their own local initiatives, but they also have limited funds and give grants in response to personal or corporate applicants for research or study in religious education. Within this field, they give priority to teachers or student teachers and to work in East Anglia. Member of the Association of Church College Trusts (see separate entry). Applications should be made online only at our website www.keswickhalltrust.org.uk *Executive Officer:* Malcolm Green, Keswick Hall Trust, PO Box 307, Woodbridge, IP13 6WL
Tel: 07760 433 409
email: admin@keswickhalltrust.org.uk
Web: www.keswickhalltrust.org.uk

Keychange Charity

(formerly Christian Alliance)
Established 1920. Offers care, acceptance and Christian community to people in need through the provision of residential care for frail elderly people and supported accommodation for young homeless people. *Chief Executive:* Graham Waters. *Operations Controller:* Barbara Barrett, 5 St George's Mews, 43 Westminster Bridge Rd, London, SE1 7JB   *Tel:* 020 7633 0533
Fax: 020 7928 1872
email: info@keychange.org.uk
Web: www.keychange.org.uk

Korean Mission Partnership

Founded in 1889 by Edward White Benson, Archbishop of Canterbury, as the Church of England Mission to Korea, the name was changed in 1993 when the Province of Korea was inaugurated. The name reflects the two-way nature of our mission today. Support goes to Korea by way of prayer, interest and funding. The Province has

sent a priest from Seoul to run the Korean Chaplaincy in the Diocese of London, ministering to Korean people who live mainly in and around the Home Counties. *President:* The Primate of Korea . *Chairman:* Revd Luke Lee. *Hon Admin Secretary:* Revd Martin Fletcher. *Hon Treasurer:* Mr Edwin Ward, The Rectory, Rectory Rd, Tiptree, CO5 0SX   *Tel:* 01621 815260/01296 423133
email: luke.gh.lee@googlemail.com
Web: www.koreanmission.org

Langley House Trust
Founded in 1958, the Langley House Trust, a national Christian charity, provides care and rehabilitation for ex-offenders (and those at risk of offending) as they work towards crime-free independence and reintegration into society. The Trust aims to help ex-offenders address their physical, emotional, mental and spiritual needs. It currently runs 16 residential projects and move-on accommodation across the UK (including a drug rehabilitation centre, and women's projects) providing bedspaces for ex-offenders, including those who are hard to place and those who have special needs, such as mental disorders. The Trust bases its services on Christian beliefs and values but is open to men and women of any or no faith. *Chairman:* Anthony Howlett-Bolton. *Chief Exec:* Steve Robinson. *Corporate Operations Director:* Tracy Wild. *Corporate Services Director:* Ken Brown. *Corporate Development Director:* Andrew Lerigo, PO Box 181, Witney, OX28 6WD   *Tel:* 01993 774075
Fax: 01993 772425
email: info@langleyhousetrust.org
Web: www.langleyhousetrust.org

Latimer Trust
The Latimer Trust is dedicated to providing a biblical and considered response to the issues facing today's Anglican Communion. Through a range of resources it is continuing and developing the work of Latimer House, founded in Oxford in the 1960s. *Chairman of the Council:* Revd Dr Mark Burkill. *Director of Research:* Revd Dr Gerald Bray, PO Box 26685, London, N14 4XQ
Tel: 020 8449 0467 ext. 227
email: administrator@latimertrust.org
Web: www.latimertrust.org

Lee Abbey Household Communities
There are two household communities based in Urban Priority Areas in Birmingham and Bristol. Community members live under a common rule of life and seek to be involved in their local community and church. *Contact:* Gill Arbuthnot, 101 Dorridge Rd, Dorridge, Solihull, B93 8BS
Tel: 0121 327 0095/01567 776558
Web: www.leeabbey.org.uk/households/

Lee Abbey International Students' Club
Founded in 1964 by the Lee Abbey Fellowship as a ministry to students of all nationalities, the Club provides long- and short-term hostel accommodation for students of all faiths or none and is served by a Christian community, which consists of young people from all over the world. Applications are invited from anyone interested in joining the community, residing as a student or staying as a holiday-maker. *Warden:* Canon Trevor Hubble, 57–67 Lexham Gardens, London, W8 6JJ   *Tel:* 020 7373 7242
Fax: 020 7244 8702
email: personnel@leeabbeylondon.com
accommodation@leeabbeylondon.com
Web: www.leeabbeylondon.com

Leprosy Mission, The
We are an international Christian development organisation, motivated by God's love and concern for people affected by leprosy. Our vision is a world without leprosy. We take a holistic view, addressing the physical, social, economic and spiritual needs of individuals and their communities. The Leprosy Mission works with partners in around 30 countries to bridge the gap of inequality. *National Director:* Rupert Haydock, Goldhay Way, Orton Goldhay, Peterborough, PE2 5GZ   *Tel:* 01733 370505
Fax: 01733 404880
email: post@tlmew.org.uk
Web: www.leprosymission.org.uk

Lesbian and Gay Christian Movement
LGCM has four principal aims: to encourage fellowship, friendship and support among lesbian and gay Christians through prayer, study and action; to help the whole Church examine its understanding of human sexuality and to work for positive acceptance of gay relationships; to encourage members to witness to their Christian faith within the gay community and to their convictions about human sexuality within the Church; to maintain and strengthen links with other lesbian and gay Christian groups both in Britain and elsewhere. An extensive network of local groups exists and a wide range of resources are available. *Chief Executive:* Revd Richard Kirker, Oxford House, Derbyshire St, Bethnal Green, London, E2 6HG
Tel and Fax: 020 7739 1249
email: lgcm@lgcm.org.uk
Web: www.lgcm.org.uk

Li Tim-Oi Foundation
The Foundation was launched on the 50th anniversary of the priesting of the first Anglican woman, Florence Li Tim-Oi, on 25 January 1944. On the centenary of her birth on 5 May 2007 the Foundation was relaunched with the mantra: 'It takes ONE woman'. The Foundation has allocated more than £550,000 in bursaries to empower over 275 Anglican women in the Two-thirds World of the 'South' to become agents for change in church and society. About 50 new requests for help a year, particularly from Africa, continue to outstrip available funds. Thus every

donation from parishes and individuals is put to effective use. Several have chosen the Foundation to benefit in lieu of presents at birthdays, weddings, anniversaries, Christmas and priesting, or of funeral flowers. Bequests, especially from women in gratitude for their own priesting, are particularly welcome. *Patrons:* The Archbishop of Canterbury, The Archbishop of Kenya, The Archbishop of the Congo, The Rt Rev Victoria Matthews, Bishop K. H. Ting, Baroness Perry of Southwark and Mrs Jane Williams.. *Chair:* Canon Pamela Wilding MBE. *Secretary:* Canon Christopher Hall, The Knowle, Deddington, Banbury, OX15 0TB   *Tel:* 01869 338225
email: achall@globalnet.co.uk
Web: www.ittakesonewoman.org
www.litim-oi.org

Librarians' Christian Fellowship
Constituted 1976 to provide opportunities for Christian librarians to consider issues in librarianship from a Christian standpoint, and to promote opportunities for presenting the Christian faith to people working in libraries of all kinds. *Hon Secretary:* Graham Hedges, 34 Thurlestone Ave, Ilford, IG3 9DU   *Tel:* 020 8599 1310
email: secretary@librarianscf.org.uk
Web: www.librarianscf.org.uk

Liddon Trust
See Society of the Faith (Incorporated).

Lincoln Theological Institute
Inaugurated in 1997 and now based at the University of Manchester, the Institute's primary aim is to undertake, promote and support theological enquiry into contemporary society and thereby to practise theology in the fullest sense. It focuses on postgraduate and postdoctoral research, working closely with colleagues in the Religions and Theology subject area. Core areas for research include modern ecclesiology; social, political and practical theologies; and religion in contemporary society. Its latest projects address the issues of climate change and the postcolonial. Students wishing to study under the auspices of the Institute may enrol through the University of Manchester for Master's and Doctoral degree programmes. Formal and informal enquiries from prospective students are encouraged. The Lincoln Theological Institute originated from Lincoln Theological College, founded in 1874 as an ordination training college. Since 2003 the Institute has been a fully integrated research unit within the University of Manchester.For further information please contact the Director. *Director:* Dr Peter M. Scott. *Research Associate:* Dr Stefan Skrimshire, School of Arts, Histories and Cultures, University of Manchester, Oxford Rd, Manchester, M13 9PL
Tel: 0161 275 3064/0161 275 3736
email: peter.scott@manchester.ac.uk
Web: http://www.arts.manchester.ac.uk/lti

Livability
(formerly know as the Shaftesbury Society)
Livability is a new charity, formed by the merger of the Shaftesbury Society and John Grooms. Livability creates choices for disabled people and brings life to local communities. We offer a wide range of services to around 8,000 disabled people and their families, including residential care, supported living, education and accessible holidays. We also provide community organizations with the resources, advice and confidence to transform their neighbourhoods. *Chief Executive:* Mary Bishop, 50 Scrutton St, London, EC2A 4XQ   *Tel:* 020 7452 2000
Fax: 020 7452 2001
email: info@livability.org.uk
Web: www.livability.org.uk

Living Stones
(formerly Church and Community Trust)
An independent organization that offers guidance and information to local churches concerning the more effective use of their resources – buildings, money, people – for worshipping God and serving the community. *Field Workers:* Roger Munday, Graham Ball, Quoin House, 11 East Park, Crawley, RH10 6AN
Tel and Fax: 01293 431899
email: info@living-stones.org.uk
Web: www.living-stones.org.uk

London City Mission
For over 175 years, LCM has been working with churches to bring the Christian message to the people of London. Today, in the workplace, out on the streets and in the various communities of London, over 300 workers and volunteers are actively seeking to bring Christian values and hope to those they meet. *Chairman:* Mark Harding. *Chief Executive:* Revd Dr John Nicholls, Nasmith House, 175 Tower Bridge Rd, London, SE1 2AH   *Tel:* 020 7407 7585
Fax: 020 7403 6711
email: enquiries@lcm.org.uk
Web: www.lcm.org.uk

Lord Wharton's Charity
Founded 1696 to distribute Bibles and other religious books to children and young people of all denominations in all counties of the United Kingdom and Northern Ireland. *Clerk to the Trustees:* Mrs B. Edwards, Magnolia Cottage, Harrowbeer Lane, Yelverton, PL20 6EA
Tel and Fax: 01822 852636
email: edwardsbobbarbara@btinternet.com

Marshall's Charity
Founded 1627. Makes grants for (1) building, purchasing or modernizing parsonages of the Church of England or the Church in Wales, (2) repairs to churches in Kent, Surrey and Lincolnshire. *Clerk to the Trustees:* Mr Richard Goatcher,

Marshall House, 66 Newcomen St, London, SE1 1YT   *Tel:* 020 7407 2979
Fax: 020 7403 3969
email: grantoffice@marshalls.org.uk
Web: www.marshalls.org.uk

Mediawatch-UK

(formerly the National Viewers' and Listeners' Association)

The association was founded in 1965 by Mrs Mary Whitehouse and her associates who felt that television was attacking and undermining family life. Mediawatch-UK is a voluntary association which campains for family values in the media. We believe that violence shown by the media contributes significantly to the increase of violence in society and should be curtailed in the public interest; that the use of swearing and blasphemy are unnecessary, offensive to many and destructive of our culture; that sexual innuendo and explicit sex trivialize and cheapen human relationships whilst undermining marriage and family life. We press for socially responsible broadcasting. Our other campaigns include fighting for meaningful protection for children from premature sexualisation by the media and from potentially harmful material online. Benefits of membership include regular newsletters and a list of media addresses to enable members to make their voices heard. After consulting members the name was changed to Mediawatch-UK from 1 March 2001. *Director:* Miss Vivienne Pattison, 3 Willow House, Kennington Rd, Ashford, TN24 0NR   *Tel:* 01233 633936
Fax: 01233 633836
email: info@mediawatchuk.org
Web: www.mediawatchuk.org

Melanesian Mission

The Melanesian Mission was established in 1854 to buy the first 'Southern Cross' ship for Bishop Selwyn to use for mission work in the islands of Melanesia. Today the Mission supports the Church of Melanesia (including the religious orders) through money, prayer and people – helping the church to fulfil its priorities and work through this vast and isolated region. *Chairman:* Vacancy. *Hon. Treasurer:* Mrs Helen Miller (Hon. Treas.). *Executive Officer:* David Friswell, 15 Covell Close, Bury St Edmunds, IP33 2HU
Tel: 01284 701988
email: mission@talktalk.net
Web: www.melanesia.anglican.org

Mersey Mission to Seafarers

Founded 1856 to 'promote the spiritual and temporal welfare of seafarers' from around the world who visit the ports of the River Mersey and the Isle of Man . *Chairman:* Sir Malcolm Thornton. *Chief Executive:* John P. Wilson, Liverpool

Seafarers Centre, 20 Crosby Rd South, Liverpool, L22 1RP
Tel: 0300 800 8080/07973 824154 (Mobile)
Fax: 0871 900 3223
email: admin@liverpoolseafarerscentre.org
Web: www.liverpoolsaefarerscentre.org

Mid-Africa Ministry (CMS)

Mid-Africa Ministry (MAM), founded in 1921, now forms part of the Church Mission Society. See separate entry for Church Mission Society.

Mirfield Centre

Offers a meeting place for about 60 people. Small residential conferences are possible in the summer vacation. Day and evening events are arranged by the Centre management team. *Director:* Revd June Lawson. *Centre Administrator:* Mrs Rachael Salmon. *Centre Brothers:* Father Oswin Gartside, Father Simon Holden, The Mirfield Centre, College of the Resurrection, Mirfield, WF14 0BWW   *Tel:* 01924 481920
Fax: 01924 481921
email: centre@mirfield.org.uk
Web: www.mirfieldcentre.org.uk

Mission to Seafarers, The

World mission agency which supports and links the Anglican Church's ministry to seafarers of all races and creeds in ports throughout the world. It has full-time staff and/or seafarers' centres in over 100 ports, honorary chaplains in over 120 others. In many ports it works in close cooperation with Christian societies of other denominations, and it is a member of the International Christian Maritime Association. *President:* HRH The Princess Royal. *Secretary General:* Revd Tom Heffer. *Director of Justice and Welfare:* Canon Ken Peters. *Director of Chaplaincy:* Vacancy, St Michael Paternoster Royal, College Hill, London, EC4R 2RL   *Tel:* 020 7248 5202
Fax: 020 7248 4761
email: general@missiontoseafarers.org
Web: www.missiontoseafarers.org

MODEM

MODEM is a network/association whose mission is to lead and enable authentic dialogue between exponents of Christian leadership, management and organization, and spirituality, theology and ministry. MODEM is an ecumenical membership organization, open to all Christians irrespective of age, gender, race, culture or nationality, and welcoming dialogue with all comers of all faiths. In association with SCM-/Canterbury Press, MODEM has published three ground-breaking books, *Management and Ministry* – appreciating contemporary issues; *Leading, Managing, Ministering* – challenging questions for church and society; and *Creative Church Leadership* – on the challenge of making a difference through leadership, the latter edited by Dr John Adair and John Nelson. The fourth and latest

book *How to Become a Creative Leader* was published in February 2008, and is essentially the 'how to' book following the previous three. See web site for further information and details of special introductory membership offer to include some or all of the books. *Chairman:* Revd Elizabeth Welch. *Secretary:* John Nelson. *Contact:* Peter J. Bates, Carselands, Woodmancote, Henfield, BN5 9SS   *Tel and Fax:* 01273 493172
email: info@modem-uk.org
membership@modem-uk.org
Web: www.modem-uk.org

Modern Church
(formerly Modern Churchpeople's Union)
An Anglican society which promotes liberal theology and offers Christian debate and discussion on religious issues. It embraces the spirit of freedom and informed enquiry and seeks to involve the Christian faith in an ongoing search for truth by interpreting traditional doctrine in the light of present day understanding. It holds an annual conference on contemporary issues. Membership includes subscription to the journal *Modern Believing*. *President:* Rt Revd John Saxbee. *General Secretary:* Revd Jonathan Clatworthy. *Administrator:* Mrs Christine Alker, MCU Office, 9 Westward View, Liverpool, L17 7EE   *Tel:* 0845 345 1909
email: office@modernchurch.org.uk
Web: www.modernchurch.org.uk

Montgomery Trust Lectures
This endowment by Sir Alexander Montgomery of Albury, Surrey supports public lectures particularly for theological societies and religious education teachers on the results of modern scholarship on the Bible, with an emphasis on Christian apologetics. Twenty eight lectures were provided in 2009–10. Hosts included: University departments; Further Education colleges; organizations providing ministerial support; ordinand and preacher training; theological societies; local groupings of Religious Education teachers; Standing Advisory Councils for Religious Education, churches and cathedrals. Host organizations should contact the Administrator to identify a lecturer/theme. An interactive catalogue is available on our website http://www.montgomerytrust.org.uk/. Printed copies of the catalogue are available by post. The Administrator arranges the booking with an available lecturer. The host organization gathers an audience in excess of 30 people and provides the venue. After the Lecture the host organization completes and returns to the Trust a straight forward report pro forma. Then the Trust provides the Lecturer direct with an honorarium and reimburses their travel expenses. The Advisory committee meets in the summer when amongst other duties they approve new additions to the list of Montgomery Lecturers. Suggestions for new additions to this list are invited to our Administrator Mark Clarke in Birmingham. *Advisers:* Revd Prof Richard

Burridge Dean of King's College London, Rt Revd Graeme Knowles Dean of St Paul's Cathedral and Very Revd Dr John Hall Dean of Westminster. *Administrator:* Mark Clarke, Christian Education, 1020 Bristol Road, Selly Oak, Birmingham, B29 6LB   *Tel:* 0121 472 4242
Fax: 0121 472 7575
email:
professionalservices@christianeducation.org.uk
Web: http://www.montgomerytrust.org.uk/

Morse-Boycott Bursary Fund
(formerly St Mary-of-the-Angels Song School Trust)
Founded in 1932 originally as a parochial Choir School but from 1935 to 1970 served the Church at large. Now provides financial assistance to the parents of boy choristers at cathedral choir schools throughout the UK. The Fund depends entirely on donations and legacies to build the capital from which bursaries can be provided to the needy. *Trustees:* Dean and Chapter of Chichester. *Administrator:* The Communar, The Royal Chantry, Cathedral Cloisters, Chichester, PO19 1PX   *Tel:* 01243 782595
Fax: 01243 812499
email: admin@chichestercathedral.org.uk
Web: www.chichestercathedral.org.uk

Mothers' Union
A Christian organization devoted to promoting marriage and the well-being of families worldwide. The Vision of Mothers Union is 'A world where Gods love is shown through loving, respectful and flourishing relationships'. This means that Mothers Union invests in relationship. Through programmes, policy work, community outreach, Christian fellowship and prayer, Mothers Union supports and nurtures relationships in the belief that this brings about stable families and benefits society. To do this, Mothers Union takes positives steps to encourage marriage and family life. Projects tackle the most urgent needs threatening relationships and communities, and work towards fostering strong families and independent, cohesive communities. Mothers Union is not a mission-sending organization, or a development charity, although mission and development are strong characteristics of its work. Rather, it is a network of 3.6 million people, each serving Christ in their local community at the grassroots level. It has a subscribers magazine, *Families First* and a magazine for members, Families Worldwide which includes the prayer diary material. Further information and resources are available from the charitys website. *Worldwide President:* Mrs Rosemary Kempnell. *Chief Exec:* Mr Reg Bailey, Mary Sumner House, 24 Tufton St, London, SW1P 3RB   *Tel:* 020 7222 5533
Fax: 020 7227 9737
email: mu@themothersunion.org
Web: www.themothersunion.org

Organizations   **299**

Mozambique and Angola Anglican Association (MANNA)

Founded by 1906, MANNA was formed to support the Diocese of Lebombo in southern Mozambique; it has now developed into supporting work within both the former Portuguese Territories, which are among the poorest in the world. While two world wars and lengthy civil wars hindered the work, since peace was established in both countries the church is growing at a great rate, predominantly by indigenous clergy who need support for their work. There are now three dioceses with well over 200 clergy. Registered Charity no. 262818. *Chair:* Ven Christopher Cunliffe, Archdeacon of Derby. *General Secretary:* Mr Ian Gordon, 16 Bayle Court, The Bayle, Folkestone, CT20 1SN   *Tel:* 01303 257248
email: n_grdn@yahoo.co.uk
Web: www.newportchurches.com/Manna

National Archives, The

Records of central government and courts of law from the Norman Conquest (Domesday Book) to the recent past (for example, the Suez Campaign). Kew, Richmond-upon-Thames, TW9 4DU   *Tel:* 020 8876 3444
email: enquiry@pro.gov.uk
Web: www.nationalarchives.gov.uk

National Association of Diocesan Advisers in Women's Ministry

NADAWM is a national network for monitoring, supporting and promoting the ministry of ordained women in the Church of England. It organizes an annual conference for diocesan representatives and provides consultancy and advice. *Chair:* Canon Rachel Watts. *Treasurer:* Revd Irena Edgcumbe. *Secretary:* Canon Georgina Byrne, 15b College Green, Worcester, WR1 2LH

National Churches Trust

The National Churches Trust, launched in 2007, is the successor to the Historic Churches Preservation Trust (HCPT) and administers the Incorporated Church Building Society (ICBS) funds. The National Churches Trust aims to fund, protect and support the built heritage of 47,000 churches, chapels and meeting houses throughout the UK. The Trust offers grants mainly for structural repairs, new facilities and improved access. Registered charity no. 1119845. *Patron:* HM The Queen. *Chairman of Trustees:* Michael Hoare. *Chief Executive:* Andrew Edwards. *Grants Manager:* Alison Pollard, 31 Newbury St, London, EC1A 7HU   *Tel:* 020 7600 6090
Fax: 020 7796 2442
email: info@nationalchurchestrust.org
Web: www.nationalchurchestrust.org

National Council for Social Concern

(formerly the Church of England National Council for Social Aid, Church of England Temperance Society and Police Court Missionaries)
The charity (also known by the short titles 'Concern' and 'Social Concern') has promoted a wide range of activities in connection with the Church of England, but in recent years has had a particular interest in aspects of the criminal justice system and in issues arising from addictions. It works closely with the Church of England Board for Social Responsibility. Details from the Secretary. *Presidents:* The Archbishops of Canterbury and York. *Chairman:* Rt Revd Colin Docker. *Secretary:* Mr Francis Mac Namara, 3 Vinson Rd, Liss, GU33 7NE
Tel: 01730 300974/07958 425927
email: info@social-concern.org
Web: www.social-concern.org

New England Company

A charity founded 1649. It is the senior English missionary society. *Governor:* Mr T. C. Stephenson. *Treasurer:* D. M. F. Scott. *Secretary:* Nikki Johnson, Flinders Cottage, The Street, Bolney, West Sussex RH17 5QW   *Tel:* 01444 882898
email: johnsonnikki@yahoo.co.uk
Web: www.newenglandcompany.org

Newton's Trust

Established to provide assistance to widows, widowers, separated or divorced spouses and unmarried children of deceased clergy and to divorced or separated wives of clergy of the Church of England, the Church in Wales and the Scottish Episcopal Church. Applications are considered by the Trustees, and one-off cash grants are made at their discretion. The Trustees meet four times a year. *Chairman:* Ven George Frost. *Treasurer:* Mr John Allen. *Secretary:* Mr D. E. Wallington, Secretary to Newton's Trust, 1 Tudor Close, Lichfield, Staffordshire WS14 9RX
Tel: 01543 302924 (Evenings)
email: d.wallington@ntlworld.com

Nikaean Club

Founded in 1925 is an association of Anglican clergy and laity. It provides the ecumenical ministry of the Archbishop of Canterbury with a network of ecumenical expertise and the capacity to offer hospitality to visiting Christian leaders, heads of non-Anglican churches and international ecumenical bodies. *Chair:* Dame Rosemary Spencer. *Guestmaster:* Canon Jonathan Gough. *Hon Secretary:* Mr Christopher Austen. *Hon Treasurer:* Revd Martin Macdonald, Lambeth Palace, London, SE1 7JU   *Tel:* 020 7898 1221
Fax: 020 7401 9886
email: christopher.austen@lambethpalace.org.uk

Nikaean Ecumenical Trust

Founded in 1992 and relaunched in 2002, the Trust exists to support ecumenical links between the Church of England and Christian churches overseas. It acts as the charitable wing of the Nikaean Club (see separate entry) and receives support from its members as well as from other Anglican bodies and individuals. It has also acquired the assets of the former Harold Buxton Trust, thanks to the generous co-operation of the SPCK. The Trust's principal activity at present is to provide grants to students from needy, non-Anglican Churches overseas (particularly the Orthodox and Oriental Orthodox Churches) who wish to study at colleges in the UK which are specifically Anglican or have strong Anglican connections. As the funds are still relatively modest, donations towards the work of the Trust are welcome. *Chair:* Rt Revd Dr Geoffrey Rowell. *Hon Secretary:* Mrs Margery Roberts, 7 Nunnery Stables, St Albans, AL1 2AS   *Tel:* 01727 856626

North of England Institute for Christian Education
Founded in 1981 as an ecumenical foundation managed by a board representing the educational interests of the Churches, universities and other educational institutions in the North East of England. Its primary objective is to create links, at both the theoretical and practical level, between Christian theology and education so as to contribute, mainly by research projects and publications, towards the further education of those with a responsibility for teaching the Christian faith. *Director:* Revd Prof Jeff Astley. *Secretary:* Mrs Evelyn Jackson, 18 North Bailey, Durham City, DH1 3RH   *Tel:* 0191 33 43331 (Director)
0191 33 43332 (Secretary)
email: Jeff.Astley@durham.ac.uk
Web: www.durham.ac.uk/neice

Number 1 Trust Fund
Founded 1909 for holding property and investments for the promotion of catholic practice and teaching within the Church of England, reformed by the Fidelity Trust Act 1977, and incorporated by the Charity Commissioners in 1996. One trustee is appointed by each of the Abbot of Elmore, the Superior of the Community of the Resurrection, the President of the Church Union, the President of the Society for the Maintenance of the Faith, the Master of the Guardians of the Shrine at Walsingham, the Principal of Pusey House, Oxford and the Principal of St Stephen's House, Oxford. *Chairman:* Rt Revd E. R. Barnes. *Trustees:* Revd J. M. R. Baker, Revd A. A. Mayass, Mr J. D. Hebblethwaite, Revd P. J. North, Revd R. Ward. *Secretary and Trustee:* Canon P. E. Ursell, Ascot Priory, Priory Rd, Ascot, SL5 8RT
Tel: 01344 885157
email: secretary@numberonetrust.org.uk

OMF International (UK)
(formerly China Inland Mission)
Founded 1865 to work in partnership with East Asia's churches through evangelism, church planting, discipling, theological training and professional services. *HR Director:* Mr Guido Braschi, Station Approach, Borough Green, Sevenoaks, TN15 8BG   *Tel:* 01732 887299
Fax: 01732 887224
email: omf@omf.org.uk
Web: www.omf.org.uk

Open Synod Group
The Open Synod Group provides a safe space in which Christians of all persuasions can meet and discuss any issues without fear of censure. The meetings are a mixture of interactive meetings about matters of concern and social events to foster friendships. The magazine attracts articles from a wide range of contributors of all shades of churchmanship. *President:* The Bishop of Ripon and Leeds. *Chairman:* Mr Tim Hind. *Secretary:* Mr Roy Thompson. *Treasurer and Membership Secretary:* Mr John Freeman. *Magazine Secretary:* Shirley-Ann Williams, May Rose Cottage, Sheriff Hutton, York, YO60 6SS   *Tel:* 01347 878644
07779 095273 (Mobile)
email: roythompson2@btinternet.com
Web: www.opensynodgroup.org.uk

Order of Christian Unity/Christian Projects
Christians from all denominations who care about Christian values in the family, medical ethics, Christian education and the media, and run an annual Schools Bible Project for secondary schools across Britain. *Chairman:* Mrs Joanna Bogle. *Treasurer:* Mr Andrew Pollock. *Vice-Chairman:* Lady Elizabeth Benyon, PO Box 44741, London, SW1P 2XA
email: auntiejoanna@yahoo.co.uk
Web: www.christianprojects.org.uk

Ordination Candidate Funds (General)
See separate entries for Anglo-Catholic Ordination Candidates' Fund, Bristol Clerical Education Society, Church Pastoral Aid Society Ministers in Training Fund, Cleaver Ordination Candidates' Fund, Elland Society Ordination Fund, Lady Peel Legacy Trust.

Ordination Candidates Training Fund
The Ordination Candidates Training Fund (OCTF) is a charity whose purpose is to assist in 'the training of candidates for Holy Orders in the Church of England ... and/or for foreign mission work holding distinctly ... evangelical views'.

The OCTF Trust was founded in 1937 to continue the work of the Revd Harold Salmon (Pa Salmon) who, as a Vicar, identified and fostered a vocation to the Ordained Ministry amongst people who, in those days, lacked the necessary formal education to be considered for training. The OCTF Trust has always sought to help those considering ordination to come to a place where the financial responsibility of their subsequent training will be undertaken by the Archbishops' Council's Ministry Division.

Financial assistance is given either through Salmon Bursaries or modest one-off awards. The Salmon Bursaries can offer significant financial assistance and are usually given to those pursuing relevant training but not yet formally recommended for ordination.

Further information is available from the website:
Web:
http://aocm.org.uk/ordination-candidates-fund
or from the Hon. Secretary.
Hon. Secretary: Edward Peacock, 24 Ferndale, Tunbridge Wells, Kent, TN2 3NS
Tel: 01892 543206
email: peacockedward@hotmail.com

Overseas Bishoprics' Fund
Founded 1841 to assist towards the endowment and maintenance of bishoprics in any part of the world and to act as trustees of episcopal endowment funds. *Chairman:* Mr John Broadley. *Secretary:* Mr Stephen Lyon. *Clerk:* Mr Paul Burrage, Church House, Great Smith St, London, SW1P 3NZ
Tel: 020 7803 3200
Fax: 020 7633 0185

Oxford Mission
Founded 1880. The Oxford Mission consists of two Religious Communities, the Brotherhood of St Paul and the Christa Sevika Sangha. Has houses in India and Bangladesh. Their work is pastoral, medical and educational and is carried on in the Dioceses of Kolkata and Dhaka. India: Col Subir Ghosh (Administrator); Bangladesh: Father Francis Pande SPB and the Revd Mother Susila CSS. *General Secretary:* Mrs Mary K. Marsh, PO Box 86, Romsey, SO51 8YD
Tel and Fax: 01794 515004
email: oxfordmission@aol.com
Web: www.oxford-mission.org

Papua New Guinea Church Partnership
PNGCP is the voluntary agency through which the Anglican Church of Papua New Guinea and the Church of England relate to each other. In 2007 ACPNG celebrated 30 years as an independent province in the Anglican Communion. Registered as a charity in 1960, the New Guinea Mission was founded in 1891 to give support to the then Diocese of New Guinea in prayer, by sending staff and raising money. In 1977, when the Province was inaugurated with five dioceses, the agency name was changed to Papua New Guinea Church Partnership in order to reflect the reciprocal nature of the work: giving and receiving. ACPNG continues to request people with skills and experience for governmentally approved support posts, mainly in health and administration. There are currently several in the country, including the Bishop of Port Moresby, the Rt Revd Peter Ramsden, for whom PNGCP acts as agent. Most years see a steady trickle of 'gap year' students and medical and nursing electives travelling to PNG to gain never-to-be-forgotten experience in the poorest, most populous Pacific nation. An annual grant goes to the provincial budget, money is raised for provincially approved projects, and audited accounts are sent to the UK. *President:* Rt Revd Dr David M. Hope. *Chairman:* Revd Paul Bagott. *General Secretary:* Miss Louise Ewington
Tel: 020 7313 3918
email: holyredeemerstmark@tiscali.co.uk
Web: www.pngcp.com

Paradox Ministries
Paradox Ministries encourages Christians to understand and pray about the Israeli–Palestinian Conflict, seeing it through the eyes of both people groups involved, and taking the needs, fear and pain of both sides seriously. Its director, who was Rector of a church in the Old City of Jerusalem for a number of years, circulates a free email newsletter, speaks at seminars and encourages support of indigenous reconciliation ministry in Jerusalem. The website contains background material, advice to clergy and regular news updates, together with a blog. *Directors (Chairman):* Revd Tony Higton. *(Executive):* Mrs Patricia Higton, 17 Church View, Marham, King's Lynn, PE33 9HW
Tel: 01760 338342
email: tony@higton.info
Web: www.prayerforpeace.org.uk

Parish and People
Parish and People was originally founded in 1949 and helped make the Parish Communion popular. In 1970 it was largely responsible for the formation of the ecumenical 'ONE for Christian Renewal'd5. P&P continues to promote new life in the Anglican Church, by publishing materials to enable parishes and deaneries to grow from the grass roots into a lively, open, people'd5s church in which lay ministry can blossom. The Deanery Resource Unit was launched in 1989. Over 250 deaneries throughout the Church of England now subscribe to its twice-a-year mailing. This includes *Deanery Exchange*, an A4 sheet sharing ideas and good practice, together with copies of booklets and briefings on matters of parish and deanery concern. P&P co-operates with the Church House Deaneries Group and other bodies enlivening deaneries. *Convenor:* Frank Harris. *Treasurer:* Revd John Cole . *Editor:* Peter Bates. *Orders to:* Canon Christopher Hall. *Secretary:* Revd Jimmy Hamilton-Brown, April Cottage, West St, Winterborne Stickland, Blandford, DT11 0NT
Tel: 01258 880627
email: secretary@parishandpeople.org.uk
Web: www.parishandpeople.org.uk

Partis College
Founded 1825 to provide accommodation (house) for ladies who are members of the Church of England with low incomes. The College was founded for the widows or daughters of

clergymen, HM forces and other professions. Patron: The Bishop of Bath and Wells. *Chairman:* Mrs J. Pepler. *Bursar:* Mrs Jill Harman. *Asst Bursar:* Mrs A. Kemp, No. 1 Partis College, Newbridge Hill, Bath, BA1 3QD

Tel: 01225 421532 07733 363713 (Mobile)
email: partiscoll@aol.com
Web: www.partiscollege.com

Philip Usher Memorial Fund

Founded 1948. Grants annual scholarships to Anglican priests, deacons or ordinands, preferably under 35 years of age, to study in a predominantly Orthodox country. Applications not later than 31 December for the following year. *Chairman:* Rt Revd Dr Geoffrey Rowell. *Administrator:* Janet Laws, c/o The Old Deanery, Dean's Court, London, EC4V 3AA   *Tel:* 020 7248 6233
Fax: 020 7248 9721
email: janet.laws@londin.clara.co.uk

Pilgrim Adventure

Founded in 1987, Pilgrim Adventure provides a selection of Christian Journeys inspired by the wanderings of the early Celtic saints. Hill walking, island hopping and worship in out-of-the-way places are all part of the experience. Pilgrim Adventure is Anglican-based and ecumenical in outlook. Enquiries to the Bookings Secretary. *Leader:* David Gleed. *Dep. Leader:* Paul Heppleston, South Winds, Culver Park, Tenby, SA70 7ED   *Tel:* 01834 844212
email: pilgrim.adventure@virgin.net
Web: www.pilgrim-adventure.org.uk

Pilgrim Trust, The

The Pilgrim Trust considers applications from charities and exempt public bodies. The Trust operates two programmes: Social Welfare and Preservation and Scholarship. More details on the programme themes can be found in the Trusts guidelines which are available on the website. The Pilgrim Trust makes large annual block grants to the Church Buildings Council and the National Churches Trust. Church of England churches seeking grants for the conservation of items of church furniture e.g. repairs to bells/ organs/monuments etc. should apply directly to the Church Buildings Council. Applications for repairs to the fabric of a building should be directed towards the National Churches Trust. *Director:* Miss Georgina Nayler, Clutha House, 10 Storeys Gate, London, SW1P 3AY

Tel: 020 7222 4723
email: info@thepilgrimtrust.org.uk
Web: www.thepilgrimtrust.org.uk

Pilgrims' Association, The

Founded in 1981, the Pilgrims' Association provides a forum in which those responsible for the care and welcome of pilgrims, visitors and tourists to our cathedrals, abbeys, churches, shrines and chapels can meet and exchange ideas and experiences. It is now also increasingly involved in bringing together those in cathedrals and churches who deliver education outside the classroom both to schools and adults. Originally a Trust, it is now a fully democratic institution governed by a Council of 15 members elected at the annual general meeting. Membership is both ecumenical and international, consisting of the great majority of Church of England cathedrals, three Roman Catholic cathedrals and several of the most visited parish churches, abbeys, priories and chapels from Anglican, Roman Catholic and Free Church denominations in England, Wales, the Republic of Ireland and Belgium. It operates mainly through an annual conference and periodic newsletters and through its web site. It is consulted regularly by government and VisitBritain on tourism and educational matters relating to cathedrals and churches. *Chairman:* Very Revd Jonathan Meyrick, Dean of Exeter. *Secretary:* Mrs Judy Davies. *Hon Treasurer:* Barry Palmer, 1 St John's Rd, Queen's Park, Chester, CH4 7AL   *Tel:* 01244 677991/
07767 675540 (Mobile)
Fax: 01244 677991
email: secretary@cathedralsplus.org.uk
Web: www.cathedralsplus.org.uk

Pilsdon at Malling Community

The Pilsdon Community established a new community in 2004, taking over the former Ewell Monastery site next to St Mary's Abbey, West Malling. The community is dedicated to the same ideals of the Christian Gospel as the original community in Dorset, offering community living, sustainable self-sufficient lifestyle and open hospitality. The community consists of 9 or 10 Community Members (leadership) and children, about 12 long stay residents and up to 2 visitors and wayfarers. The six acres of land and two large glasshouses are used for livestock and horticulture. The 16th-century barn chapel is used for daily offices, and the Eucharist is celebrated daily in either the barn or the Abbey chapel. Enquiries are always welcome. (See Pilsdon Community entry and website for more details.) Registered Charity no. 1123682. Company no. 6218667. *Guardian:* Revd Peter Barnett. *Treasurer:* Mr Albert Granville. *Admissions:* The Guardian. *Enquiries:* Any community member, 27 Water Lane, West Malling, ME19 6HH

Tel and Fax: 01732 870279
email: pilsdon.malling@tiscali.co.uk
Web: www.pilsdonatmalling.org.uk

Pilsdon Community

The Pilsdon Community is dedicated to the ideals of the Christian gospel in the context of community living and open hospitality. The Community at any one time will comprise between four to eight community members (leadership), between 15 and 20 guests (staying from one month to several years), up to six

visitors (staying one day to two weeks) and up to eight wayfarers (staying up to three days). Many of the guests have experienced a crisis in their lives (e.g. mental breakdown, alcoholism, drug addiction, marital breakdown, abuse, homelessness, prison, dropping out of college, asylum-seeking, etc.). Pilsdon provides an environment of communal living, manual work, recreation, worship and pastoral care, to rebuild peoples lives, self-respect, confidence and faith. Founded in 1958 by an Anglican priest, the Community occupies a Jacobean manor house and its outbuildings and smallholding of twelve acres, six miles from the sea near Lyme Regis. The community life is inspired by the monastic tradition and the Little Gidding Community built around families. The worship and spirituality is Anglican and sacramental, but ecumenical in membership, and all faiths and none as well as all races and cultures are welcome. Any enquiries should be made to the Warden or the Administrator. *Warden:* Revd Adam Dickens. *Admissions and Visitors:* Miss A. Plested. *Administrator:* Alan Frost, Pilsdon Manor, Pilsdon, Bridport, DT6 5NZ
Tel: 01308 868308
Fax: 01308 868161
email: pilsdon@btconnect.com
Web: www.pilsdon.org.uk

Plainsong and Medieval Music Society
Formed 1888 to promote the study and appreciation of plainsong and medieval music, especially through performance and publications; related journal, *Plainsong and Medieval Music.* *Administrator:* Anna Burson. *Chairman:* Prof John Harper, c/o RSCM, 19 The Close, Salisbury, SP1 2EB
Tel: 01722 424841
Fax: 01722 424849
email: pmms@rscm.com
Web: www.plainsong.org.uk

Praxis
Founded in 1990, Praxis was set up as a joint initiative of the Liturgical Commission, the Alcuin Club and the Grove Group for the Renewal of Worship. Its aims are to enrich the practice and understanding of worship in the Church of England; to serve congregations and clergy in their exploration of God's call to worship; and to provide a forum in which different worshipping traditions can meet and interact. Praxis events include day meetings, residential conferences and national consultations. *Chair:* Canon David Kennedy. *Secretary:* Canon Michael Rawson. *Administrator:* Mr Trevor Jarvis, c/o RSCM, 19 The Close, Salisbury, SP1 2EB *Tel:* 01722 424858
email: praxis@praxisworship.org.uk
Web: www.praxisworship.org.uk

Prayer Book Society
The Prayer Book Society exists to promote the use of the Book of Common Prayer and to defend the worship and doctrine contained therein. Dio-

cesan branches provide members with regular meetings, Prayer Book services and advice on church matters. It runs the yearly Cranmer Awards for young people. It has a popular mail order book company stocking a wide range of religious books and Christmas cards. Donations and memberships are appreciated and needed. Membership form from 011898 42582 or from any Secretary shown on the website. *Patron:* HRH The Prince of Wales. *Ecclesiastical Patron:* The Bishop of London. *Chairman:* Miss Prudence Dailey, The Studio, Copyhold Farm, Goring Heath, RG8 7RT
Tel: 0118 984 2582
Fax: 0118 984 5220
email: pbs.admin@pbs.org.uk *Web:* www.pbs.org.uk

Pusey House, Oxford
Founded 1884 to continue the work of Dr Pusey, academic and pastoral, in Oxford. *Principal:* Revd Jonathan Baker. *Custodian of the Library:* Revd William Davage. *Archivist:* Revd Barry Orford, Pusey House, Oxford, OX1 3LZ
Tel: 01865 278415
01865 288024
email: chapter@puseyhouse.org.uk
Web: www.puseyhouse.org.uk

Pyncombe Charity
Income about £10,000 p.a. applied to assist needy serving ordained clergy in financial difficulties due to illness, or occasionally other special circumstances, within the immediate family. Applications must be made through the diocesan bishop. *Secretary:* Mrs Rita Butterworth, Wingletye, Lawford, Crowcombe, Taunton, TA4 4AL
email: joeandrita@waitrose.com

Queen Victoria Clergy Fund
Founded 1897 to raise money towards the support of Church of England parochial clergy. All the Fund's income is disbursed annually in block grants to dioceses specifically for the help of the clergy. Requests for assistance should be directed to the diocese. *Chairman:* Alan Cooper OBE. *Secretary:* Chris Palmer, Church House, Great Smith St, London, SW1P 3AZ
Tel: 020 7898 1311
email: chris.palmer@c-of-e.org.uk

Radius
Radius (The Religious Drama Society of Great Britain). Founded in 1929 to promote drama which throws light on the human condition and to support people who create and use drama as a means of Christian understanding. Organizes training events, publishes a magazine and a small number of plays, offers a playwrights' assessment service and holds a collection of photocopiable typescripts suitable for use in churches and by church groups. *Patrons:* The Archbishop of Canterbury, Dame Judi Dench. *President:* Rt Revd Graeme Knowles. *Magazine-/General Enquiries/Council Vice-Chair:* Margaret

Hunt, 7 Lenton Rd, The Park, Nottingham, NG7 1DP   *Tel:* 0115 941 3922
email: office@radius.org.uk
Web: www.radius.org.uk

RE Today Services
RE Today Services is wholly owned by the charity Christian Education, and is committed to the teaching of the major world faiths in religious education, and to an accurate and fair representation of their beliefs, values and practices in all its teaching materials. It carries forward the work of the Christian Education Movement (CEM). *Chief Executive:* Peter Fishpool. *Professional Team Director:* Resemary Rivett, 1020 Bristol Rd, Selly Oak, Birmingham, B29 6LB   *Tel:* 0121 472 4242
Fax: 0121 472 7575
email: retoday@retoday.org.uk
Web: www.retoday.org.uk

Reader Missionary Studentship Association
Founded 1904 to offer financial assistance to Readers training as priests for service in the Church overseas. *Chairman:* Mr G. E. Crowley. *Hon Treasurer:* Mr Ron Edinborough. *Hon Secretary:* Ms Sally Pickersgill, 39 Abbey Gardens, Canterbury, CT2 7EU   *Tel:* 01227 459227
email: secretary@rmsa.org.uk
Web: www.rmsa.org.uk

Rebecca Hussey's Book Charity
Established 1714 to give grants of religious and useful books to institutions in the United Kingdom. 425 Bromyard House, Bromyard Avenue, London, W3 7BY   *Tel:* 020 8743 0181
email: carolinejdavis@aol.com

Reform
Established in 1993, Reform is a network of individuals and churches within the Church of England. We are committed to reforming the Church of England from within according to the Holy Scriptures. *Chairman:* Rod Thomas. *Administrators:* Jonathan and Fiona Lockwood, PO Box 1183, Sheffield, S10 3YA   *Tel:* 0114 230 9256
email: administrator@reform.org.uk
Web: www.reform.org.uk

Relate
Relate, the countrys largest relationship counselling organisation providing help and support for couples, singles, families and in schools. Also the national organisation for sex therapy and a leading source of information and advice online. Help is available at around 600 locations nationwide and by calling 0300 100 1234 or visit the website: www.relate.org.uk   *Chief Executive Officer:* Ms Claire Tyler, Premier House, Lakeside, Doncaster, DN4 5RA
Tel: 0300 100 1234 (Helpline)
Web: www.relate.org.uk

Religious Education Council of England and Wales
The Religious Education Council of England and Wales seeks to represent the collective interests of a wide variety of organizations and communities in deepening and strengthening provision for religious education in schools and colleges. The Council was formed in 1973 and is open to national organizations which have a special interest in the teaching of religious education. The present membership of more than 45 organizations includes representation from the main Christian denominations, the world faiths, the British Humanist Association and the main educational bodies with professional and academic RE interests. *Chair:* Prof Brian Gates. *Deputy Chair:* Joyce Miller. *Treasurer:* Dr Trevor Cooling, c/o CAN, 1 London Bridge, London, SE1 9BG   *Tel:* 020 7022 1833
email: info@religiouseducationcouncil.org.uk
Web: www.religiouseducationcouncil.org.uk

Retired Clergy Association
Founded 1927 to act as a bond of friendship in prayer and mutual help to retired clergy. Membership at 31 December 2006 was 3,400. There are local branches in Bexhill, Birmingham, Blackburn, Bournemouth, Bristol, Bury St Edmunds, Cambridge, Canterbury, Chester, Chichester, Eastbourne, East Devon, Ely, Harrogate, Henfield, Hereford, Huntingdonshire, Isle of Wight, Lancaster, Leigh-on-Sea, Ludlow, Manchester, Norwich, Oxford, Peterborough, Portsmouth (Mainland), Ripon, Rochester, Rugby, Salisbury, Scarborough and Filey, Shrewsbury, Southampton, Stockport, Wells, Weston-super-Mare, Winchester and Alresford, Worcester and York. *President:* The Bishop of Gloucester. *Chairman:* Rt Revd Richard Lewis. *Hon Secretary:* Canon John Sansom, Kiggon Cottage, St Clement, Truro, TR1 1TE   *Tel:* 01872 520471
email: johnandpauline@kiggoncottage.fsnet.co.uk

Retreat Association
Comprising these Christian retreat groups: Association for Promoting Retreats, Baptist Union Retreat Group, Catholic Network for Retreats and Spirituality, Methodist Retreat and Spirituality Network, Quaker Retreat Group, United Reformed Church Retreats Group. Offers information and resources about retreats to both would-be and seasoned retreatants, facilitates spiritual direction, promotes the work of retreat houses and coordinates training opportunities and regional activity. Retreats, an ecumenical journal listing retreat houses and their programmes in the UK and beyond, is published annually (2010 edition £8.50 incl p+p). Other literature available; send for publications list. *Director:* Alison MacTier, Kerridge House, 42 Woodside Close, Amersham, Bucks, HP6 5EF
Tel: 01494 433004
Fax: 0871 715 1917
email: info@retreats.org.uk
Web: www.retreats.org.uk

Revd Dr George Richards' Charity
Founded 1837 to provide financial assistance to clergy of the Church of England forced to retire early owing to ill-health. Widows, widowers and dependants can also apply for assistance. *Secretary:* Dr P. D. Simmons, 98 Thomas More House, Barbican, London, EC2Y 8BU
Tel: 020 7588 5583

Richmond Fellowship
Established in 1959, the Fellowship provides residential, supported housing, community services and employment services for people with mental health problems. It now operates more than 90 residential, supported housing, day care and employment services for people with mental health problems throughout the UK. For further information contact Richmond Fellowship. *PA to Chief Executive:* Marise Willis, 80 Holloway Rd, London, N7 8JG
Tel: 020 7697 3300
Fax: 020 7697 3301
email: marise.willis@richmondfellowship.org.uk
Web: www.richmondfellowship.org.uk

RNID
(formerly known as Royal National Institute for Deaf People)
RNID is the largest charity representing the 9 million deaf and hard of hearing people in the UK. It offers a range of services for deaf and hard of hearing people, and provides information and support on all aspects of deafness, hearing loss and tinnitus. As a membership charity, it aims to achieve a radically better quality of life for deaf and hard of hearing people. RNID's work involves campaigning and lobbying, providing services, training, products and equipment, and undertaking medical and technical research. It works throughout the UK. *Chairman:* Mr James Strachan. *Chief Executive:* Dr John Low, 19–23 Featherstone St, London, EC1Y 8SL
Tel: 0808 808 0123 (Voice)
0808 808 9000 (Textphone)
email: informationline@rnid.org.uk
Web: www.rnid.org.uk

Royal Alexandra and Albert School
Founded in 1758, a voluntary-aided junior and secondary school providing boarding education for boys and girls aged 7–18 who are without one or both parents or who would benefit from boarding education because of home circumstances. Only boarding fees payable and bursaries available. Bursaries for children of clergy are available for two thirds of the fees at this state boarding school where the full fees are only £3,655 per term for full boarding. In exceptional circumstances, further bursary support can be provided. Exceptional facilities. Contact: Headmaster for further details. *Patron:* HM the Queen. *President:* HRH the Duchess of Gloucester. *Headmaster:* Paul D. Spencer Ellis. *Foundation Secretary:*
Diana Bromley. *Admissions Secretary:* Sue Harrington, Gatton Park, Reigate, RH2 0TW
Tel: 01737 649000
Fax: 01737 649002
email: headmaster@gatton-park.org.uk
Web: www.gatton-park.org.uk

Royal Asylum of St Ann's Society
The Society, founded in 1702, offers grants towards the expenses of educating children, from the age of 11, at boarding or day schools. Most, but not all, of those aided are children of clergy of the Church of England; however, in the first instance clergy should approach the Corporation of the Sons of the Clergy. The Society welcomes collections, donations and legacies towards this purpose. *President:* The Dean of Westminster. *Chairman:* Mr Peter Ashby. *Secretary:* Mr David Hanson, King Edward's School, Witley, Petworth Rd, Wormley, GU8 5SG

Royal College of Organists
Founded 1864, incorporated by Royal Charter 1893, 'to promote the art of organ-playing and choir training. Holds lectures, recitals and master-classes nationwide. Examinations for Certificate, Associateship, Fellowship, Licentiateship in Teaching and Diploma in Choral Directing. Holds a large specialist library and archive, and publishes a scholarly journal every year. Membership open to all who take an interest in the work and profession of the organist and in organ music. *Patron:* HM The Queen. *President:* James O'Donnell. *General Manager:* Kim Gilbert, PO Box 56357, London, SE16 7XL
Tel: 05600 767208
email: admin@rco.org.uk
Web: www.rco.org.uk

Royal Martyr Church Union
Founded 1906: (1) Ever to cherish the sacred remembrance of Charles the First, King and Martyr, both in public worship and private devotion, and to this end to promote the restoration of his name to its proper place in the calendar of the worldwide Anglican Communion, and the observance of 30 January, the day of his martyrdom, by suitable services in the Book of Common Prayer and elsewhere. (2) To maintain the principles of faith, loyalty and liberty for which the King died – the faith of the Church, loyalty to the Crown, and the ancient liberties of the people. Holds annual commemorative eucharists in London and Edinburgh. Subscription £15.00 p.a.to include *Royal Martyr Annual. Chairman:* Tom Kerr. *Hon Secretary and Treasurer:* David Roberts, 7 Nunnery Stables, St Albans, AL1 2AS
Tel: 01727 856626

Royal National Institute of Blind People (RNIB)
Royal National Institute of Blind People (RNIB) is a charity which supports blind and partially

Organizations

sighted people to remain independent by: giving you free advice about your eye condition, the benefits you're entitled to, and the specialist and local support that's available; providing employment services and practical help for children and their families; suggesting ideas on how you can continue to enjoy your hobbies and leisure time; recommending everyday items and gadgets to make your life easier; offering a listening ear. *President:* His Grace the Duke of Westminster. *Chairman:* Lord Low of Dalston CBE. *Chief Executive:* Lesley-Anne Alexander, 105 Judd St, London, WC1H 9NE

> *Tel:* 0845 766 9999 (Helpline) 020 7391 2000
> *email:* helpline@rnib.org.uk
> *Web:* www.rnib.org.uk

Royal Naval Licensed Readers' Society

Founded 1860. Licensed Readers assist in the work of the Anglican Church amongst the men and women of the Royal Navy and their families. In ships at sea and in naval establishments ashore they work alongside Naval Chaplains in the furtherance of the Christian faith and the welfare of the Navy's people. The Society is dependent financially on voluntary contributions for the maintenance of its work. *Treasurer:* Mr Lee Foley, MP 1–2 Sir Henry Leach Building, Whale Island, Portsmouth, PO2 8BY   *Tel:* 023 9262 5508

> *Fax:* 023 9262 5134
> *email:* lee.foley211@mod.uk

Royal School of Church Music

The Royal School of Church Music (RSCM) is the leading organisation promoting and supporting church music. It is an educational charity dedicated to raising standards and promoting the best use of music in every style of Christian worship and in every denomination. It is funded through membership subscriptions, publication sales, course fees and the charitable support of individuals and institutions. It provides musical and educational resources to train, develop and inspire clergy, music leaders, musicians, singers and congregations. Its *Voice for Life* programme is a training scheme for singers of all ages that can be used by individual churches and schools, and *Church Music Skills* provides practical training for those leading music in worship. These programmes are complemented by workshops, festivals and short residential courses, and a network of volunteers runs events to meet local needs in the UK and five overseas branches. The RSCM publishes music through the RSCM Press, including musical resources for *Common Worship*, and RSCM Music Direct provides a fast and efficient mail-order service for music from all publishers. Affiliated churches and schools and individual members receive *Church Music Quarterly*, a highly informative and interesting magazine for all those concerned with church music, and *Sunday by Sunday*, an essential liturgy planner aiding those who plan and lead worship to enhance it through music appropriate to the day. Appointed the official music agency for the Church of England from April 1996. *President:* The Archbishop of Canterbury. *Chairman:* Lord Brian Gill. *Director:* Mr Lindsay Gray. *Bursar:* Miss Julia Harrison Place, 19 The Close, Salisbury, SP1 2EB   *Tel:* 01722 424848

> 01722 424841 (membership)
> *Fax:* 01722 424849
> *email:* enquiries@rscm.com
> *Web:* www.rscm.com

Rural Theology Association

Founded 1981 to provide a forum for the rural churches and to focus for the Church at large the distinctive ways and needs and contributions of the rural. Its aims are to study the gospel and develop theology in a rural setting, to encourage the development of patterns of ministry and mission appropriate to the countryside today, and to discover ways of living in the countryside which embody a Christian response to the world. It publishes the journal *Rural Theology* twice yearly. *President:* Revd Prof Leslie Francis. *Chairman:* Rt Revd Mark Rylands. *Secretary:* Canon Stephen Cope. *Treasurer:* Revd Christine Brewster, Vicarage, 28 Park Ave, Withernsea, HU19 2JU

> *Tel:* 01964 611426
> *email:* secretary@rural-theology.org.uk
> *Web:* www.rural-theology.org.uk

Saint George's Trust

The Trust exists to give grants to individuals to further the work of the Church of England. The Fellowship of Saint John (UK) Trust Association is the sole trustee. The funds at the Trust's disposal do not permit large grants for restoration projects, or any long-term financial support. The wide remit enables it to help a large number of individuals for sabbaticals, gap years and the like to a maximum of £350. All applications should be sent, together with a stamped addressed envelope, to the Trust with as much supporting documentation as possible. St Edward's House, 22 Great College St, London, SW1P 3QA

Samaritans

Samaritans exists to provide confidential emotional support to any person, irrespective of race, creed, age or status who is in emotional distress or at risk of suicide; and to increase public awareness of issues around suicide and depression. *Chief Exec:* Mr Dominic Rudd, The Upper Mill, Kingston Rd, Ewell, Surrey, KT17 2AF

> *Tel:* 020 8394 8300 (admin)
> 08457 909090 (helpline)
> *Fax:* 020 8394 8301
> *email:* Admin: admin@samaritans.org
> Helpline: jo@samaritans.org
> *Web:* www.samaritans.org

Sarum College

Sarum College is an ecumenical study and research centre based in Salisbury's Cathedral

Close. The College is housed in a Grade 1 listed building in Salisbury Cathedral Close and offers an extensive and varied programme of short residential and day courses, as well as academic programmes including the MA in Christian Spirituality and the MA in Christian Liturgy. Two new programmes, MA in Faith-based Leadership and MA in Theology, Imagination and Culture will begin in January 2011. The College has 47 bedrooms, many en suite, including 5 recently refurbished rooms in the 17th century Wren building overlooking the Cathedral. There are a range of meeting and conference rooms, a 19th century chapel, common room/bar, and a dining room seating up to 120. On-site parking is available. Bookings for residential conferences, parish groups, training events, board meetings are all welcome, as are individual guests who may wish to enjoy the Cathedral Close for leisure, study leave or sabbatical. The College houses a fine theological library of over 35,000 volumes, and an excellent independent theological bookshop, both of which offer postal/mail order facilities. *Principal:* Canon Keith Lamdin. *Residential Services Manager:* Linda Cooper. *Director of Central Services:* Mark Manterfield. *Director of Studies:* Dr Michael DeLashmutt. *Dicrector of Communications:* Christine Nielsen-Craig, 19 The Close, Salisbury, SP1 2EE *Tel:* 01722 424800/ *Fax:* 01722 338508 *email:* hospitality@sarum.ac.uk *Web:* www.sarum.ac.uk

Sarum St Michael Educational Charity
Personal grants may be awarded for further or higher education, to those who live, work or study within the Salisbury or adjacent dioceses (also to former students of the college). Bursaries may be awarded to those who live or study within the Salisbury diocese or adjoining dioceses, who intend to train to teach RE. Grants may be made to local schools, mainly for RE and worship resources. Grants may be made to parishes within the Salisbury diocese, for work with children and young people. Corporate grants may be made, where funds permit, to certain projects within the diocese. The governors meet four times a year to consider applications: please enquire about closing dates for applications, bearing in mind that grants are not awarded retrospectively. Applications should be made on forms available from the correspondent, submitted directly by the individual. Member of the Association of Church College Trusts (see separate entry). First Floor, 27A Castle St, Salisbury, SP1 1TT *Tel:* 01722 422296 *Fax:* 0870 135 9943 *email:* ssmsarum@waitrose.com

SASRA
(The Soldiers' and Airmen's Scripture Readers Association)

Founded 1838 to present the claims of Christ to the men and women serving in the Army and later the RAF, to promote interdenominational Christian fellowship among them and to encourage individual serving Christians to witness to their comrades. *Chairman:* Brigadier Ian Dobbie. *General Secretary:* Sqdn Ldr Colin Woodland, Havelock House, Barrack Rd, Aldershot, GU11 3NP *Tel:* 01252 310033 *Fax:* 01252 341804 *email:* admin@sasra.org.uk *Web:* www.sasra.org.uk

School Chaplains' Association
An association for all people, ordained and lay, involved in Christian ministry in state or independent schools. *President:* Rt Revd L. Urwin. *Chairman:* Revd John Thackeray. *Secretary:* Revd Jim Gascoigne. *Administrator:* Revd Robert Easton, c/o Kings's School, Rochester, ME1 1TE *Tel:* 01634 888555 *email:* treasurer@schoolchaplains.org.uk *Web:* www.schoolchaplains.org.uk

Scout Association, The
Founded in 1907 to promote the development of young people in achieving their full physical, intellectual, social and spiritual potential, as individuals, as responsible citizens and as members of their local, national and international communites. Membership 475,000. Tel: 0845 300 1818 (8 a.m. to 6 p.m. Mon to Fri) or 020 8433 7100. *Chief Scout:* Lt Cdr (Hons) Bear Grylls RN. *Chief Executive:* Derek Twine CBE, Gilwell Park, Bury Rd, Chingford, London, E4 7QW *Tel:* 020 8433 7100 *Fax:* 020 8433 7103 *email:* info.centre@scout.org.uk *Web:* www.scouts.org.uk

Scripture Union
Scripture Union seeks to make the Christian faith known to children, young people and families and to support the Church through resources, Bible reading and training. SU's work in Britain includes schools work, Bible ministries, publishing, training, evangelism, holidays, missions and family ministry. Scripture Union is active in more than 100 countries. *National Director:* Revd Tim Hastie-Smith. *Director of Ministry Delivery:* Mr Terry Clutterham. *Director of Ministry Support:* Mr David Thorpe, 207–209 Queensway, Bletchley, Milton Keynes, MK2 2EB *Tel:* 01908 856000 *Fax:* 01908 856111 *email:* info@scriptureunion.org.uk *Web:* www.scriptureunion.org.uk

Seamen's Friendly Society of St Paul
Trust administered by Alton Abbey, able to offer financial assistance to merchant sailors. *Contact:* Rt Revd Dom Giles Hill O.S.B., Alton Abbey, Abbey Rd, Beech, Alton, Hampshire, GU34 4AP *Tel:* 01420 562145/01420 563575 *email:* abbey@domghill.mail1.co.uk

Selly Oak Centre for Mission Studies (SOCMS)

The Centre is sponsored by USPG Anglicans in World Mission and the Methodist Church in Britain. It is the successor to the United College of the Ascension, Selly Oak and provides training, orientation and research in global mission. SOCMS is international in nature, attracting clergy and key leaders from churches worldwide for its Masters programme in Mission and Leadership Formation in the World Church. It offers formation and training for those crossing cultures in mission, long and short term, including the Experience Exchange Programme. It invites a Scholar in Residence and two Visiting Scholars each year to pursue research in global mission, and is part of an ever growing TransContinental Training Network of centres and institutions with similar aims across the world. As part of the Queen's Foundation for Ecumenical Theological Education in Birmingham, it infuses theological education and ordination training in Britain with the global mission perspectives, possibilities and personnel. *Director:* Deaconess Dr. Evie Vernon. *Tutor for Global Christianity and World Mission:* Revd Dr Joshva Raja. *Tutor for World Mission Education:* Revd George Wauchope. *Administrator:* Robert Bruce, The Queen's Foundation, Somerset Rd, Edgbaston, Birmingham, B15 2QH
Tel: 0121 454 1527
Fax: 0121 454 8171
email: socmsadmin@queens.ac.uk
Web: www.queens.ac.uk

Servants of Christ the King

Founded 1942 by Canon Roger Lloyd of Winchester. A movement of groups or 'Companies' of Christians who seek to develop a corporate life by praying together in silence, with disciplined discussion. They actively wait upon God to be led by the Holy Spirit, and undertake to do together any work which they are given by him to do. *Enquirers' Correspondent:* Dr Pauline Waters, Swallowdale, Wheelers Lane, Linton, Maidstone, ME17 4BN
Tel: 01622 743392
Web: www.sck.org.uk

SGM Lifewords

(formerly Scripture Gift Mission)
SGM creates Bible resources to help people communicate God's word to today's generation. A new, research-based range uses up-to-date Bible versions and contemporary graphics. SGM publishes materials in over 200 languages for use worldwide. 75 Westminster Bridge Rd, London, SE1 7HS
Tel: 020 7730 2155
Fax: 020 7401 9070
email: uk@sgmlifewords.com
Web: www.sgmlifewords.com

Shaftesbury Homes and 'Arethusa'

Founded 1843 to house and educate homeless children in London, the charity is now the leading voluntary sector provider of residential care for children in London. In London and Suffolk the charity also provides services for young people leaving care, and supported housing for the young homeless. Personal development is promoted through venture activities at the Arethusa Venture Centre on the Medway. *Chairman:* Gerri McAndrew. *Chief Exec:* Karen Wright, The Chapel, Royal Victoria Patriotic Building, Trinity Rd, London, SW18 3SX
Tel: 020 8875 1555 *Fax:* 020 8875 1954
email: info@shaftesbury.org.uk
Web: www.shaftesbury.org.uk

Sharing of Ministries Abroad (SOMA)

Founded in 1978 to serve the renewal of the Church throughout the world, particularly in the Anglican Communion, SOMA has eleven centres across the world. SOMA works for the transformation of individuals and churches, and the healing of communities and their lands through the renewing power of the Holy Spirit by sending and receiving teams worldwide on short-term mission within the Anglican Communion. A newsletter, *SHARING*, is published three times a year. *SOMA International Chairman:* The Most Revd Ben Kwashi. *SOMA UK National Director:* Revd Stephen Dinsmore. *SOMA UK Finance Administrator:* Steve Fincher, PO Box 69, Merriott, TA18 9AP
Tel: 01460 279737
email: info@somauk.org
Web: www.somauk.org

Social Responsibility Network, The

The Network (developed from the Anglican Association for Social Responsibility) aims to share good practice, ideas and information on a wide range of issues and provide peer support and encouragement for Christian practitioners in social responsibility and related fields in England and Wales. We do this by meeting together in local and regional groups, holding an annual conference on key issues, making resources available to one another, and sharing ideas, needs and resources via our discussion e-net. Open to all Christian practitioners. *Treasurer:* Canon Peter Williams. *Chair:* David Maggs, The Old Deanery, Wells, BA5 2UG
Tel: 01749 670777
email: wright@btinternet.com
Web: www.srnet.org.uk

Society for Liturgical Study

Founded 1978. The Society promotes liturgical study and research, and holds a conference in alternate years. Membership is interdenominational and is open to persons involved in teaching liturgy, or in research in this field, or holding official appointments with responsibility for liturgy and worship. *Secretary:* Revd Dr James Steven, Franklin-Wilkins Building, Waterloo Bridge Wing, Waterloo Bridge, London SE1 9NH
email: james.steven@kcl.ac.uk
Web: www.studyliturgy.org.uk

Society for Old Testament Study

Founded 1917 as a society for OT scholars in Britain and Ireland. Scholars not resident in the British Isles may also become members. Two meetings to hear and discuss papers are arranged annually. The Society also publishes its annual 'Book List' and is involved in other publishing activities. It maintains links with OT scholars throughout the world, particularly the Dutch-Flemish OT Society with which it holds joint meetings every three years. Candidates for membership must be proficient in biblical Hebrew and be proposed by two existing members. *Hon Secretary:* Dr John Jarick, St Stephen's House, 16 Marston Street, Oxford, OX4 1JX

Tel: 01865 613512
Fax: 01865 613513
email: john.jarick@theology.ox.ac.uk
Web: www.sots.ac.uk

Society for Promoting Christian Knowledge

SPCK was founded in 1698 to help people to understand – and to grow in – the Christian faith. It works to support and develop the knowledge of Christians and to interest and inform others. Throughout its history SPCK has been associated with the spread of education and informative literature in all its forms. It is an Anglican foundation but supports a diversity of Christian traditions. The Society has been involved in publishing since its foundation in 1698, and currently publishes around 100 new titles each year. Its output includes Christian books, websites and electronic products across a broad spectrum, from the catholic to the evangelical and from the conservative to the liberal. The range includes liturgy, theology, science and religion, biblical studies and spirituality, academic and student texts as well as stationery and books for a popular market, with resources for clergy, parishes and study groups. The International Study Guides series is aimed particularly at those training for ministry in the developing world, including many for whom English is not a first language. Under the Azure imprint are books for readers who are searching for faith but who might not ordinarily look to Christianity for help or guidance. The Assemblies website (www.assemblies.org.uk) provides teachers with regularly updated materials for school assemblies which they can download free of charge. SPCK Diffusion aims to produce innovative materials to resource a wide audience with information in a form relevant to their interests and experience. SPCK Worldwide supports the distribution of books and educational materials for Christians overseas, including in some of the poorest parts of the world. It depends entirely upon donations from individuals, churches and charitable trusts. *President:* The Archbishop of Canterbury. *Chairman of the Governing Body:* Rt Revd Michael Perham. *General Secretary:* Mr Simon Kingston.

Executive Administrator: Ms Pat Phillips, 36 Causton St, London, SW1P 4ST

Tel: 020 7592 3900
Fax: 020 7592 3939
email: spck@spck.org.uk
Web: www.spck.org.uk
www.assemblies.org.uk

Society for the Assistance of Ladies in Reduced Circumstances

Founded by the late Miss Edith Smallwood in 1886. Assistance is given to ladies living alone in their own home (either owned or rented) on a low income and domiciled in the United Kingdom, irrespective of age or social status. Registered Charity no. 205798. Enquiries welcome on freephone helpline. Donations and legacies gratefully received. *Patron:* HM The Queen. *Apply:* The Secretary, Lancaster House, 25 Hornyold Rd, Malvern, WR14 1QQ   *Tel:* 01684 574645/
0800 587 4696 (freephone helpline)
Fax: 01684 577212
email: info@salrc.org.uk
Web: www.salrc.org.uk

Society for the Maintenance of the Faith

Founded in 1873, the Society presents, or shares in the presentation of, priests to over 80 benefices. As well as its work as a patronage body the Society aims to promote Catholic teaching and practice in the Church of England at large. *President:* Dr Brian Hanson. *Secretary:* Revd Paul Conrad, Christ Church Vicarage, 10 Cannon Place, London, NW3 1EJ   *Tel and Fax:* 020 7435 6784

Society for the Relief of Poor Clergy (SRPC)

Founded 1788 to aid evangelical Anglican clergy and their dependants in times of financial distress due to sickness, bereavement or other difficulties. *Secretary:* Mrs Pauline Walden, c/o CPAS, Athena Drive, Tachbrook Park, Warwick, CV34 6NG   *Tel:* 01926 458458
Fax: 01926 458459
email: srpc@cpas.org.uk
Web: www.cpas.org.uk

Society of Archbishop Justus Ltd

The Society, named after the fourth Archbishop of Canterbury, was formed in 1996 and incorporated in 1997 as a non-profit corporation in New York, USA for the purpose of using the Internet to foster and further unity among Christians, especially Anglicans. It focuses on internet information services: web and email servers that help Anglicans to be one body. Members help install, operate and maintain the computers and networks that enable online communication, and help educate the Anglican public about how best to use those computers. Directors include both Church of England and ECUSA members. The Society sponsors the Anglicans Online web site and, on behalf of the International Anglican Domain Committee, administers the anglican.org

internet domain. More information is available on the web site. *Director:* Simon Sarmiento, PO Box 345, St Albans, AL1 5ZZ
email: directors@justus.anglican.org
Web: www.justus.anglican.org/soaj.html

Society of Catholic Priests
Founded in 1994, with now over 500 members, an inclusive society of priests who 'believe in one, holy, catholic and apostolic church ordaining men and women to serve as deacons, priests and bishops in the Church of God'. The objects of the Society are to promote the formation and support of priestly spirituality and catholic evangelism. *Patron:* The Archbishop of Canterbury. *Visitor General:* The Bishop of Manchester. *Rector General:* Canon Andrew Nunn. *Secretary General:* Revd Michael Skinner. *Membership Secretary:* Revd John Joyce, The Rectory, 21 Cuckfield Rd, Hurstpierpoint, Hassocks BN6 9RP
Tel: 01273 832203
Fax: 01689 823775
email: rector@hurstrectory.co.uk
Web: www.scp.org.uk

Society of King Charles the Martyr
Founded 1894 to promote observance of January 30, the day of the martyrdom of King Charles I in 1649, and uphold the traditional Anglican Catholic principles for which he died. Publishes various material including the journal *Church and King*. *Chairman:* Mr Robin Davies, 22 Tyning Rd, Winsley, Bradford on Avon, BA15 2JJ
Tel: 01225 862965
email: robinjbdavies@talktalk.net
Web: www.skcm.org

Society of Mary
Founded 1931 to promote devotion to Our Lady. Originally an Anglican Society and now an ecumenical Society welcoming all practising Catholics, and organizes pilgrimages to Marian Shrines, in particular Lourdes and Nettuno. *Superior General:* Rt Revd Robert Ladds. *Chaplain General:* Revd G. C. Rowlands. *Secretary:* Mrs Celia Bush, 169 Humber Doucy Lane, Ipswich, IP4 3PA

Society of Mary and Martha
An independent ecumenical charity run by a mixed lay Community providing confidential support for clergy and/or spouses, especially at times of stress, crisis, burnout or breakdown. Resources exclusively for people in ministry include the famous 12,000–mile Service weeks, Family Holiday week, and Linhay Lodges: well-appointed, self-contained accommodation for private retreats, sabbaticals, safe place, emergency bolt-hole or battery re-charge. Programme events open to everyone include retreats, reading weeks, pilgrimage, time out, MBTI, Enneagram and other resources for personal and spiritual growth. The Sheldon Centre is a beautifully converted farm with lovely views across the Teign Valley, just ten miles from the M5 and main line railway at Exeter. Major improvements during 2011 to replace the last of the smallest bedrooms with en-suite facilities. *Warden:* Carl Lee. *Administrator:* Sarah Horsman, Sheldon, Dunsford, Exeter, EX6 7LE *Tel:* 01647 252752
Fax: 01647 253900
email: smm@sheldon.uk.com
Web: www.sheldon.uk.com

Society of Ordained Scientists
Founded 1987. A dispersed order for ordained scientists, men and women. Members aim to offer to God, in their ordained role, the work of science in the exploration and stewardship of creation, to express the commitment of the Church to the scientific enterprise and their concern for its impact on the world, and to support each other in their vocation. Associate membership is available to those who are not ordained but are interested in the work of the Society. *Visitor:* Rt Revd David Walker, Bishop of Dudley. *Secretary:* Revd Dr Robin G. Harvey. *Warden:* Revd Richard Hills, Stamford Cottage, 47 Old Rd, Mottram, Hyde, Cheshire SK14 6LW
Tel: 01457 763104
email: rev.rlhills@talktalk.net
Web: www.ordainedscientists.org

Society of Retreat Conductors
Founded in 1923 for the training of retreat conductors, the running of retreat houses and the conducting of retreats. *Chairman:* Revd David Sutton. *Company Secretary:* Mrs Kathryn Redington. *Superior:* Canon Howard Such, c/o St Mary Woolnoth Vestry, Lombard St, London, EC3V 9AN *Tel:* 020 7929 0199
email: admin.src@btconnect.com

Society of Royal Cumberland Youths
Bell-ringing society founded in 1747. Its headquarters are at St Martin-in-the-Fields and the Society is responsible for ringing at a number of London churches. The society has a worldwide membership, promoting high standards among proficient change-ringers. *Master:* Ms Mary Holden. *Secretary:* Ms Penelope Sharpe, 62 Arthurdon Rd, London, SE4 1JU
Tel: 07734 960808
email: secretary@srcy.org.uk
Web: www.srcy.org.uk

Society of St Willibrord
(The Anglican and Old Catholic Society of St Willibrord)
Founded 1908 to promote friendly relations between the Anglican and Old Catholic Churches, including the fullest use of the full Communion established between them in 1931. Membership of the society is open to members of churches in full communion with Canterbury and/or Utrecht. *Presidents:* Rt Revd Geoffrey

ORGANIZATIONS

Rowell, Bishop of Gibraltar in Europe . *Patrons:* The Archbishops of Canterbury and Utrecht. *Hon Secretary:* Mthr Ariadne van den Hof. *Chairman:* Rt Revd J. Gledhill, Bishop of Lichfield, Y Rheithordy, Y Sgwr, Blaenau Ffestiniog, Gwynedd LL41 3UW   *Tel:* 01766 831536
email: honsecssw@gmail.com
Web: www.willibrord.org.uk

Society of the Faith (Incorporated)
The objects of the Society are to act as an Association of Christians in communion with the See of Canterbury for mutual assistance in the work of Christ's Church and for the furtherance of charitable undertakings, especially for the popularization of the Catholic Faith. We have occupied Faith House in Westminster since 1935 and formerly ran the Faith Press and Faithcraft. We manage Faith House as a resource for the Church, promote charitable activities, hold the annual Liddon Lecture and sponsor publications which promote the Society's objects. The restricted Liddon Fund provides two or three grants per year for young Anglicans (under 25 years old) who are engaged in advanced theological study, for example for a second degree. *Principal:* Dr Julian Litten. *Vice-principal:* Canon Robert Gage. *Secretary and Treasurer:* Mrs Margery Roberts, Faith House, 7 Tufton St, London, SW1P 3QB
Tel: 01727 856626

Society of the Holy Cross (SSC)
Founded 1855 for priests (1100 members) 'to maintain and extend the Catholic faith and discipline and to form a special bond of union between Catholic clergy'. Provinces: European Union, Australasia, Canada, Africa, USA. *Master General:* Preb Dr David Houlding SSC. *Provincial Master (for England):* Fr Kit Dunkeley SSC. *Secretary General:* Fr Richard Arnold SSC. *Treasurer General:* Fr David Lawson SSC. *Mission Director:* Fr Trevor Buxton SSC, All Hallows House, 52 Courthope Rd, London, NW3 2LD
Tel: 020 7267 7833/020 7263 6317
Fax: 020 7267 6317 *email:* sscmaster@lineone.net

South American Mission Society
(Incorporating the Spanish and Portuguese Church Aid Society)
Founded 1844 to make known the gospel of the Lord Jesus Christ to the people of Latin America and the Iberian Peninsula and continuing in active partnership now with the mission priorities of the Anglican churches in these regions. *Mission Director for South America:* Rt Revd Henry Scriven. *Mission Education Officer:* Mr Robert Lunt. *Finance Secretary:* Mr Philip Tadman, Allen Gardiner Cottage, Pembury Rd, Tunbridge Wells, TN2 3QU   *Tel:* 01892 538647/0114 269 2070
Fax: 01892 525797
email: finsec@samsgb.org
Web: www.samsgb.org

Southern Africa Church Development Trust
Founded 1960 to inform, encourage concern for and involvement in the Church in Southern Africa. Supports churches, community centres and schools, primary and secondary education through scholarships, clergy and lay training, and medical work. Publishes a quarterly bulletin of information and projects which is sent to all subscribers and supporters. *President:* Mr Martin Kenyon. *Director:* Dr Jack Mulder. *Chairperson:* Canon David Cook. *Hon Treasurer:* Mr Jim Wilkinson. *Secretary to the Board:* Mrs Susan Howden, 51 Heathside, Hinchley Wood, KT10 9TD   *Tel:* 020 8398 9638/020 8398 8699
email: jlerm2@hotmail.com
Web: www.sacdt.org

St Christopher's Educational Trust
Small grants to promote Christian religious education by improving practice in teaching, by developing new programmes of education and nurture for adults and young people and by support for individual study or research. The Trustees meet twice a year. Member of the Association of Church College Trusts (see separate entry). *Clerk to the Trustees:* Dr David Sellick, 23 Robin's Hill, St John's Road, Hitchin, SG4 9FE   *Tel:* 01462 440518
email: davidsellick@uk7.net
Web: www.natsoc.org.uk

St Christopher's Fellowship
St Christopher's is a charity and housing association providing care, accommodation, education, training and support to children, young people and vulnerable adults. We run children's homes, fostering services, supported housing and hostels, along with education, employment and outreach services. *Chairman:* Mr Anthony Hickinbotham. *Chief Exec:* Mr Jonathan Farrow, 1 Putney High St, London, SW15 1SZ
Tel: 020 8780 7800
Fax: 020 8780 7801
email: info@stchris.org.uk
Web: www.stchris.org.uk

St Gabriel's Trust
St Gabriel's is an Anglican teacher training foundation concerned with teacher training for school RE teachers; the Trust's main object is to further good practice in school RE. It is not able to make grants to clergy, theological students or 'Bible teachers' as such, but only to those who are actively involved in school RE; any study course must be school-related. Member of the Association of Church College Trusts (see separate entry). Owing to the overwhelming number of applications received, the Trustees have found it necessary to severely restrict funding for overseas students. Modest **personal grants** are made towards fees and expenses for Certificate, Diploma or MA courses, mainly to teachers studying part-time for further specialist RE qualifications

while continuing with their teaching jobs. The Trust makes a few grants for higher research. The Trustees will only consider applications from experienced RE teachers with QTS studying part-time and who are committed to a long term career in RE teaching. Applicants must be able to demonstrate that their research will be of practical benefit to classroom teaching and to RE. They should apply to the Trust well before they are due to start their proposed course, explaining their financial needs and other sources of funding anticipated. The Trust is not able to assist schools as such, as its objectives are **higher and further education**. A way in which individual schools can benefit from the Trust is usually when one of the teaching staff receives a personal grant towards the expenses of a part-time course of study for a further specialist qualification in RE. *Correspondent:* Mr P. M. Duffell. *Asst Clerk to Trustees:* Mrs B. Duffell, Ladykirk, 32 The Ridgeway, Enfield, EN2 8QH
Tel: 020 8363 6474

St George's College, Jerusalem
St George's College is a unique centre of continuing education in the Anglican Communion, offering short-term courses as well as facilities for individual reflection and study. It is open to both clergy and laity. Since its founding in 1962, the College has hosted participants from 92 countries and 96 Christian traditions. Course members engage with a wide range of biblical texts in the context of the land; encounter Jewish, Christian and Muslim faith as it is exercised today; and come to appreciate anew the rich fabric of faith and spirituality that this environment offers to the pilgrim. The College is situated 500 metres north of the Damascus Gate of the Old City of Jerusalem, and set in its own grounds adjacent to the Anglican Cathedral of St George the Martyr. Full details of courses can be obtained from the web site or the Secretary of the British Regional Committee. *Secretary of the British Regional Committee:* Revd Paul Conder, St. George's College Jerusalem, Post Office Box 1248, Jerusalem 91000, Israel
Tel: 1 972 2 626 4704
Fax: 1 972 2 626 4703
email: registrar@stgeorges.org.il
Web: www.sgcjerusalem.org

St George's House, Windsor Castle
Founded 1966. A residential consultation centre within Windsor Castle, and part of the 14th-century College of St George. Apart from ecumenical clergy conferences the House also hosts a range of other consultations. Some are internally organised, while others are instigated by external groups under the guidance of House staff. The range of themes is wide but all share a concern for greater human well-being. Accommodation for up to 33 people. *Chairman, Board of Trustees and Council:* Rt Revd David J. Conner, Dean of Windsor. *Warden:* Canon Dr Hueston Finlay.

Programme Director: Mr Gary McKeone. *Clergy Consultation Administrator:* Mrs Patricia Birdseye. *Warden's Administrator:* Mrs Sue Pendry, St George's House, Windsor Castle, Windsor, Berkshire SL4 1NJ
Tel: 01753 848848/
Fax: 01753 848849
email: sue.pendry@stgeorges-windsor.org
Web: www.stgeorgeshouse.org

St Hild and St Bede Trust
The Trust's annual income is restricted to the advancement of higher and further education in the Dioceses of Durham and Newcastle, and is presently committed to supporting the North of England Institute for Christian Education, the North East Religious Learning Resources Centre, several lectureships, chaplaincies (in particular the chaplaincy in the College of St Hild and St Bede), scholarships and a Church of England aided school. Member of the Association of Church College Trusts (see separate entry). *Correspondent:* Mr W. Hurworth. *Home:* 16 Tempest Court, Wynyard Park, Billingham TS22 5QF, c/o College of St Hild and St Bede, University of Durham, Durham, DH1 1SZ
Tel: 0191 334 8300/01740 644 274
email: w.hurworth@btinternet.com

St John's Guild
Founded in 1919 to assist the spiritual well-being of blind people, as well as to ease the isolation and loneliness in which some of them have lived. Since that time both needs and society have changed. St John's Guild has developed to meet those changes. The Guild supports 20 Branches, which are located in different parts of the country and meet to provide worship, fellowship and friendship. An important part of the Guild's work is a residential home for the visually impaired in St Albans. Regular publications in Braille and audio are produced and widely distributed. *Warden and Chairman:* Revd Graeme Hands. *Chief Officer:* Mr Richard McEwan. *Finance Officer:* Mrs Patricia Richards, Guild Office, 8 St Raphael's Court, Avenue Rd, St Albans, AL1 3EH
Tel: 01727 864076
email: stjohnsaccounts@btconnect.com
r.mcewan1@btinternet.com
Web: www.stjohnsguild.org

St Luke's College Foundation
The Foundation's object is the advancement of further and higher education in religious education and theology. Grants are awarded to individuals for research and taught postgraduate qualifications in these fields; and to eligible organizations for related initiatives and facilities. The Foundation does not finance buildings, or provide bursaries for institutions to administer; and it is precluded from the direct support of schools (although it supports teachers who are taking eligible studies). Member of the Association of Church College Trusts (see separate

Organizations   **313**

entry). *Correspondent:* Prof M. Bond, Heathayne, Colyton, EX24 6RS   *Tel and Fax:* 01297 552281

St Luke's Hospital for the Clergy
A surgical and medical hospital for the clergy, their spouses, widows, and dependent children, monks and nuns, deaconesses, ordinands, Church Army staff, and overseas missionaries. Over 150 leading London consultants give their services free of charge. Treatment is entirely free. The usual referral letter from a patient's doctor should be sent to the Medical Secretary at the Hospital. *President:* The Archbishop of Canterbury. *Chairman:* Mr Patrick Mitford-Slade. *Chief Executive:* Mr John Cherry, 14 Fitzroy Square, London, W1T 6AH   *Tel:* 020 7388 4954
Fax: 020 7383 4812
email: stluke@stlukeshospital.org.uk
Web: www.stlukeshospital.org.uk

St Mary's College Trust
The Trust's annual income is normally committed to supporting the Welsh National Centre for Religious Education, WNCRE at St Deiniol's Library, Hawarden, Flint, and the Anglican Chaplaincy at the University of Wales, Bangor. As a result, grants to individuals and other institutions are only awarded in very exceptional circumstances. Member of the Association of Church College Trusts (see separate entry). *Correspondent and Clerk:* Mr Gwilym Jones. *Treasurer:* Mr Dewy Williams. *Joint Chairmen:* The Bishops of Bangor and St Asaph, School of Education, Univ of Wales, Eifionydd, Normal Site, Holyhead Rd, Bangor, LL57 2PZ
Tel: 01248 382934 (Office) 01248 722738 (Home)
Fax: 01248 383092
email: g.t.jones@univ.bangor.ac.uk

St Michael's Fellowship
Runs four residential family assessment centres in South London working in partnership with parents to enable them to meet the needs of their child. Works with adolescent mothers, one- or two-parent families where parents may have learning disabilities, psychiatric illness, a history of abuse, domestic violence and where there are child protection concerns. Runs one supported housing scheme for vulnerable families, with self-contained flats and low support. Through Sure Start and Sure Start Plus offers community support to teenage parents and young fathers in the Borough of Lambeth. *Director:* Mrs Sue Pettigrew, 1F Gleneagle Rd, London, SW16 6AX   *Tel:* 020 8677 6888
Fax: 020 8677 5214
email: archangel@zetnet.co.uk
Web: www.stmichaelsfellowship.org.uk

St Pancras and Humanist Housing Association
Founded 1924 by the Revd Basil Jellicoe, this charitable association provides housing and support for families, single people and those with special needs in nearly 4,500 flats and houses in N London and Hertfordshire. *New Business Manager:* Gareth Jones, St Richard's House, 110 Eversholt St, London, NW1 1BS
Tel: 020 7209 9287
Fax: 020 7209 9223
Web: www.sph.org.uk

St Peter's Saltley Trust
The Trust exists to widen and advance the Church's work in adult Christian learning, further education and religious education in schools, for the benefit of Church and society. It offers grant funding and partnership working for creative projects in any of these three areas, within the region covered by the Anglican dioceses of Birmingham, Coventry, Hereford, Lichfield and Worcester. The Trust does not make grants for ongoing core costs, building improvements or for individual study/research. Member of the Association of Church College Trusts (see separate entry). *Director:* Dr Ian Jones. *Bursar and Acting Clerk to the Trustees:* Mrs Lin Brown, Grays Court, 3 Nursery Rd, Edgbaston, Birmingham, B15 3JX   *Tel:* 0121 427 6800
email: director@saltleytrust.entadsl.com
Web: www.saltleytrust.org.uk

Student Christian Movement
SCM is a student led community passionate about faith and justice. We have a long history of bringing students together to explore how to live out a radical faith in todays world. The national network is made up of university links, individual members, friends and subscribers. The movement holds regular conferences and produces a variety of resources, including the termly magazine *Movement*. It is affiliated to the World Student Christian Federation. *National Coordinator:* Hilary Topp. *Links Worker:* Rosie Venner. *Administrator:* Lisa Murphy, 308F The Big Peg, 120 Vyse St, Hockley, Birmingham, B18 6ND
Tel: 0121 200 3355
email: scm@movement.org.uk
Web: www.movement.org.uk

Tearfund
Tearfund is an evangelical Christian relief and development charity working with the local church around the world to bring physical, emotional and spiritual transformation to people living in poverty. Responding to natural disasters and emergencies, engaging in longer-term community development and speaking out to challenge injustice, Tearfund aims to make the fullness of life promised by Christ a reality for people in need. With support from individuals and churches in the UK and Ireland, Tearfund is in active partnership with local Christians in more than 60 countries. *Chief Executive:* Mr Matthew Frost, 100 Church Rd, Teddington, TW11 8QE   *Tel:* 0845 355 8355
Fax: 020 8943 3594
email: enquiry@tearfund.org
Web: www.tearfund.org

Third Province Movement

The object of the Third Province Movement, which was started in November 1992, is to advocate, and eventually secure, the establishment within the Church of England of an autonomous province for all those, whatever their churchmanship, who in conscience cannot accept the ordination of women to the priesthood, the episcopate and other liberal developments. It also advocates a realignment on the same principle within the whole Anglican Communion. *Chairman:* Mrs Margaret Brown, Luckhurst, Mayfield, TN20 6TY   *Tel:* 01435 873007
email: thirdprovince@aol.com
Web: www.thirdprovince.org.uk

Together (Mental After Care Association)

(formerly MACA)
Together is a leading national charity providing a wide range of quality community- and hospital-based services for people with mental health needs and their carers, including: advocacy, assertive outreach schemes, community support, employment schemes, forensic services, helplines/information, respite for carers, social clubs, supported accommodation with 24–hour care. *Chief Executive:* Liz Felton, 12 Old Street, London, EC1V 9BE   *Tel:* 020 7780 7300
Fax: 020 7780 7301
email: contact-us@together-uk.org
Web: www.together-uk.org

Traditional Choir Trust, The

The Traditional Choir Trust was started in 2002 by Dr John Sanders in Gloucester to: 'Give grants, bursaries and scholarships to boys otherwise unable to attend recognised choir schools. To encourage and financially assist choir schools, cathedrals, Chapels Royal, collegiate churches, university chapels, parish churches and other choral foundations to maintain the ancient tradition of the all male choir.' Upon Dr Sanders death in 2003, the Trusteeship was handed over to the Dean & Chapter of Chichester Cathedral. The Trust relies solely upon donations and legacies to build capital from which bursaries can be provided. *Trustees:* Dean and Chapter of Chichester. *Patron:* Very Revd Michael Tavinor, Dean of Hereford. *Administrator:* The Communar, The Royal Chantry, Cathedral Cloisters, Chichester. West Sussex, PO19 1PX
Tel: 01243 782595/01243 812492
Fax: 01243 812499
email: admin@chichestercathedral.org.uk
Web: www.chichestercathedral.org.uk

Trinitarian Bible Society

Founded in 1831 for the circulation of Protestant or uncorrupted versions of the Word of God. The Society will only circulate the Authorized Version in English, and foreign language scriptures translated from the same Greek and Hebrew texts with comparable accuracy. *Office Manager:* Mr J.

M. Wilson, Tyndale House, Dorset Rd, London, SW19 3NN   *Tel:* 020 8543 7857
Fax: 020 8543 6370
email: tbs@trinitarianbiblesociety.org
Web: www.trinitarianbiblesociety.org

Trinity Foundation for Christianity and Culture

TFCC is an international ecumenical institution committed to fostering community harmony through education. The Foundation's teaching programme, the TFCC Awareness Course, is designed and written by Bishop Michael Marshall and Revd Nadim Nassar to educate Christians for life in the twenty-first century. Each course module is written from a Christian viewpoint, teaching Christians about their own faith and that of their neighbours, so that they can respect the differences and live in a diverse society without fear and without compromising their faith. The Course considers Islamic and Jewish perspectives to build an awareness of 'the other' and to go deeper into the Christian faith. It is designed to be taught in churches, parish halls or any appropriate space, and is suitable for regular or occasional churchgoers, Christians outside the Church, seekers and the undecided. New courses are published each year. *President:* Rt Revd Michael Marshall. *Director:* Revd Nadim Nassar. *Chair of Trustees:* Charles Longbottom. *Chief Executive Officer:* Christopher Bunting. *Education Director:* St. John Wright, Holy Trinity Church, Sloane St, London, SW1X 9BZ
Tel: 020 7730 8830 (Office)
020 7259 0619 (Education)
Fax: 020 7730 9287
email: tfcc@tfccinternational.com
Web: www.tfccinternational.com

True Freedom Trust

An interdenominational support and teaching ministry on homosexuality and related issues, for the Church and people seeking Christian help. It believes that the Bible forbids homosexual acts. It supplies resources, speakers and organizes conferences to help the Church overcome fear and prejudice and act with understanding and love in a biblical and Christlike way. *Chairman:* Mr Stefan Cantore. *Director:* Mr Jonathan Berry, PO Box 13, Prenton, Wirral, CH43 6YB   *Tel:* 0151 653 0773
email: info@truefreedomtrust.co.uk
Web: www.truefreedomtrust.co.uk

Unitas – The Catholic League

Founded in 1913, its special objects are the reunion of all Christians with See of Rome, the spread of the catholic faith, the promotion of fellowship among Catholics and the deepening of the spiritual life. It is governed by a Priest Director and an Executive of elected members. Further details from the Secretary. *The Secretary:* Mr David Chapman, 293 Ordnance Rd, Enfield, EN3 6HB   *Tel:* 01992 763 893
email: nomadyane@btinternet.com
Web: www.unitas.org.uk

Unite Clergy and Faith Workers

Unite Faith Workers is the union for those who work for religious organizations as ministers, clergy and lay staff. Membership is open to all faiths and denominations. Set up in 1994, it is now part of Unite, which has more than 1.6 million members. Unite Faith Workers provides its members with a professional association of their own, with access to all the facilities and support of a modern union. Unite is recognized by the Church of England for staff in the National Church Institutions, and by some of the largest church-related charities, including Action for Children and The Children's Society. A growing number of diocesan office staff and others working for church organizations and agencies are members. Unite Faith Workers has its own Executive, and a national network of local representatives providing support for members, and belongs to the specialist Community, Youth Workers and Non-Profit Sector within Unite, in partnership with a number of national agencies, professional associations and charities. It works to bring about fairness and dignity at work for all its members, whatever their situation, and is currently leading the campaign for modern conditions of service for those who serve as ministers. A wide range of benefits is provided for members in good standing, including legal representation and professional advice on many issues affecting work and pensions, equal opportunities, harassment and bullying at work, and much more. *Chair of Church of England Section:* Revd David Chillman. *National Officer, Community, Youth Workers & Non-profit Sector:* Rachael Maskell. *Communications:* Maureen German, Community & Non-Profit Sector, 35 King St, London, WC2E 8JG   *Tel:* 020 7420 8978
Fax: 020 7420 8999
email: maureen.german@unitetheunion.org
Web: www.unitetheunion.org

United Church Schools Trust

(formerly Church Schools Company)
Founded as an educational charity in 1883 to create schools that offer pupils a good academic education based on Christian principles with particular reference to the Church of England. The Company's council has developed the concept of offering a broad and challenging education. To achieve this it has invested in the provision of excellent buildings and facilities including extensive ICT at each school. This ideal of strong schools embraces not just academic learning to high standards, but also the development of skills that will be essential throughout life both at work and socially. Teamwork, leadership, an enthusiastic response to challenge and an active concern for others are all attributes which are valued. Schools at Blackpool, Guildford, Surbiton, Caterham, Ashford, Hampshire near Romsey, Hull, Lincoln and Sunderland. Clergy bursaries available. A subsidiary charity,

the United Learning Trust, was founded in 2002 to manage a number of City Academies spread across the country. Thirteen Acadamies are currently open, mainly in inner city areas, with two more to be added during the academic year 2008–09. *Chairman:* Rt Revd and Rt Hon The Lord Carey of Clifton. *Chief Executive:* Sir Ewan Harper. *Deputy Chief Executive:* Charlotte Rendle-Short, Church Schools House, Titchmarsh, Kettering, NN14 3DA   *Tel:* 01832 735105
Fax: 01832 734760
email: admin@church-schools.com
Web: www.ucst.org.uk

United Nations Association of Great Britain and Northern Ireland (UNA-UK)

UNA-UK is the UK's leading independent policy authority on the UN. Through the work of our staff, volunteers and members, we campaign and educate to promote the principles of the UN Charter and to support the work of the UN and its agencies. UNA-UK is a non-party political organization that maintains an ongoing dialogue with UK government ministers, parliamentarians and the media on issues relating to the UN. We promote multilateralism and adherence to international law through four policy programmes: human rights and humanitarian action; peace and security; the Millennium Development Goals and climate change; and UN reform. Education lies at the heart of our work and to this end we provide support and materials for those interested in model UN events, as well as resources for people wanting to develop their knowledge. UNA-UK is proud to be a UK-wide membership organization encompassing individuals of diverse ages, backgrounds and interests. *Executive Director:* Mr Sam Daws. *Executive Assistant:* Miss Natalie Samarasinghe, 3 Whitehall Court, London, SW1A 2EL
Tel: 020 7766 3457/020 7766 3459
Fax: 020 7930 5893
email: samarasinghe@una.org.uk
Web: www.una.org.uk

Universities and Colleges Christian Fellowship

UCCF: The Christian Unions exists to give every student in Great Britain an opportunity to hear and respond to the gospel of Jesus. We are full time staff, volunteers, supporters and students all working together to make disciples of Christ in the student world. Visit www.uccf.org.uk to find out more. UCCF: The Christian Unions, 38 De Montfort Street, Leicester, LE1 7GP
Tel: 0116 255 1700
email: enquiries@uccf.org.uk
Web: www.uccf.org.uk

Urban Saints

Since 1906 Urban Saints (formerly known as Crusaders) has been reaching out to children and young people with the good news of Jesus Christ. We are passionate about working with all children and young people, helping them to realise their full God-given potential as they journey from childhood to adulthood. Young people (aged 5 to 18+) connect with the movement in a variety of ways, including weekly youth groups, special events, holidays, community projects and training programmes. These activities are led by thousands of volunteers who are comprehensively trained and supported in order to help them work effectively and achieve the highest possible standards of youth work practice. Whilst much of our work is in the UK and Ireland, increasingly we are helping indigenous churches within countries in the developing world to set up and run outreach work among un-churched children and young people. *Exec Director:* Matt Summerfield. *Volunteers Director:* Mark Arnold. *Marketing and Income Development Director:* Lorne Campbell. *Ministry Development Director:* John Fudge. *HR Manager:* Liz Dore, Kestin House, 45 Crescent Rd, Luton, LU2 0AH *Tel:* 01582 589850 *Fax:* 01582 721702 *email:* email@urbansaints.org *Web:* www.urbansaints.org www.crusadersreunited.org.uk www.urbansaints.org/energize

Urban Theology Unit
Ecumenical educational charity offering academic programmes engaging with contextual theology, ministerial practice, and urban realities. Academic programmes include Foundation Degree, MA in Theology and Ministry and MA in Urban Theology (York St John University), and M Phil/Ph D in Contextual, Urban and Liberation Theology and Ministerial Practice (University of Birmingham). There are UTU publications on British Liberation Theology, urban ministry, and contextual Bible readings. *Chairperson:* Revd Eileen Sanderson. *Acting Director:* Revd Dr Ian K Duffield. *Support Services Manager:* Mrs Kate Thompson, 210 Abbeyfield Rd, Sheffield, S4 7AZ *Tel:* 0114 243 5342 *Fax:* 0114 243 5356 *email:* office@utusheffield.org.uk *Web:* www.utusheffield.org.uk

USPG: Anglicans in World Mission
USPG works in direct partnership with Anglican churches in over 50 countries in Africa, Asia and Latin America. Founded in 1701 as the Society for the Propagation of the Gospel in Foreign Parts (SPG), we are one of the oldest Anglican mission agencies. In 1965 we merged with the Universities Mission to Central Africa (UMCA) and then the Cambridge Mission to Delhi to become USPG. The name was supplemented in 2007 to become USPG: Anglicans in World Mission. Today we are enabling churches to reach out to poor and marginalized communities in practical and life-changing ways. This means that we are helping churches to run schools, hospitals and clinics, build houses and wells, and provide agricultural training for subsistence farmers. We also support church outreach, theological training and youth work programmes. The vision is of holistic mission, and decision-making is shared in equal partnership with churches according to priorities which belong to the "local" church in the shape of Province or diocese. Where grants are provided, they are given so that churches may plan on a long-term basis for sustainability. We run a range of personnel programmes and we provide volunteers – clergy, ordinands and church workers from Britain and Ireland – with experience of the world church by sending them on short-term placements overseas. Churches and individuals in Britain and Ireland can get involved with USPG and world mission through prayer, fundraising (including a large Project Scheme) and speakers. We produce a range of publications – our regular newspaper, *Transmission*, which includes a *Prayer Diary*; a new study course for parish groups etc. every year; and a range of web-based resources for Advent, Lent and Harvest – as well as materials to provide for engagement with individual Projects. *President:* The Archbishop of Canterbury. *Chair:* Lay Canon Linda Ali. *General Secretary:* Rt Revd Michael Doe, 200 Great Dover St, London, SE1 4YB *Tel:* 020 7378 5678/0845 273 1701 *Fax:* 020 7378 5650 *email:* enquiries@uspg.org.uk *Web:* www.uspg.org.uk

Vacation Term for Biblical Study
The Vacation Term for Biblical Study is a Summer School held each summer at St Anne's College, Oxford, primarily devoted to the study of the Bible and related subjects. The aim is to enable people of all ages, occupations and denominations to become acquainted with contemporary scholarship. Further details are available from the Secretary. *Chairman:* Dr Barbara Spensley. *Secretary:* Revd Margaret Burrow. *Treasurer:* Mr Richard Garner, 1 Thorny Rd, Douglas, Isle of Man, IM2 5EF *Tel:* 01624 662173 *email:* margaret.burrow@mcb.net *Web:* www.vtbs.org.uk

Vergers, Church of England Guild of
Founded in 1932 to promote Christian fellowship and spiritual guidance among the vergers of the cathedrals and parish churches of England. The Guild is divided into branches which meet locally every month and nationally several times throughout the year. The Guild provides a comprehensive training course which students can study from home with the help of an area tutor and mentor. The course works alongside the well-established Annual Training Conference. The Guild Diploma is awarded to successful students. Advice concerning appointments, job descriptions and contracts is available through the Welfare Officer. Contact can be made through

the General Secretary. *General Secretary:* Miss Jeanne B. Scott, 309 Desborough Ave, High Wycombe, HP11 2TH *Tel:* 01494 438335
email: jeanne@jeannescott.wanadoo.co.uk
Web:
www.societies.anglican.org/guild-of-vergers

Walsingham, Shrine of Our Lady of
Founded in 1061 in response to a vision, destroyed in 1538, restored in 1922 by Revd A. Hope Patten, Vicar of Walsingham. Since 1931, when it was moved from the parish church, the Shrine has contained the image of Our Lady of Walsingham together with the Holy House, representing the house of the Annunciation and the home in Nazareth of the Holy Family. Nowadays Walsingham is England's premier place of pilgrimage. It is administered by a College of Guardians. Special facilities include accommodation for people of all ages and those with special needs, an Education Department for school visits, and retreat and conference facilities. Information is available from the Administrator. *Administrator:* Rt Revd Lindsay Urwin OGS. *Shrine Priest and Youth Missioner:* Revd S. Gallagher, The College, Walsingham, NR22 6EF *Tel:* 01328 820255
Fax: 01328 824206
email: pr.adm@olw-shrine.org.uk
Web: www.walsingham.org.uk

WATCH (Women and the Church)
Founded in 1996, WATCH promotes the ministry of women in the Church of England. It is based on a vision of the Church as a community of God's people where justice and equality prevail, regardless of gender. WATCH works for an inclusive church in which women will take their place alongside men at every level in the Church of England, including the episcopate. Other priorities shaping our work are to achieve honesty and openness in church appointments and better support for women in ministry, and to challenge barriers which impede the full expression of a woman's vocation and gifts. The ministry of both lay and ordained women is fostered through local diocesan WATCH branches, and members receive the magazine *Outlook. Chair:* Revd Rachel Weir. *Secretary:* Revd Kate Stacey, St John's Church, Waterloo Rd, London, SE1 8TY
Tel: 07815 729565/01635 247817
Fax: 020 8856 1023
email: angel.hughes@blueyonder.co.uk
Web: www.womenandthechurch.org

William Temple Foundation
Founded in 1947, as a research and training centre focusing on the links between theology, the economy and urban mission practice. The Foundation's current programme is to reflect theologically and strategically on the changing nature of urban space in Manchester, and the emerging patterns of church that are being created both to connect with these new spaces, and

with new understandings and definitions of local civil society. The Foundation is now also engaged in primary research into the work and identity of faith-based organizations in civil society, across the UK using the concept of religious and spiritual capital. This work is currently funded by the Leverhulme Trust (2007–2010). The Foundation is working with a wide variety of partners in this research, including the Northwest Development Agency, the Manchester Centre for Public Theology and the University of Manchester. It is also working with a wide variety of community and grassroots organizations. Emerging from this research, the Foundation is contributing teaching to the University of Manchester and the Partnership of Theological Education based in Manchester. It produces several publications on its research and regularly updates its work on its web site. Luther King House, Brighton Grove, Rusholme, Manchester, M14 5JP
Tel: 0161 249 2502
Fax: 0161 256 1142
email: temple@wtf.org.uk
Web: www.wtf.org.uk

William Temple House
William Temple House is a residence for 49/50 students from overseas and the United Kingdom in full-time education. The male and female students are of all faiths and nationalities. The House is under the management of The International Students' Club (C of E) Ltd, a registered charity. Enquiries to the Warden. International Students Club (C of E) Ltd, William Temple House, 29 Trebovir Rd, London, SW5 9NQ
Tel: 020 7373 6962/07958 726715 (Mobile)
Fax: 020 7341 0003
email: williamtemplehouse@btconnect.com
Web: www.williamtemplehouse.co.uk

Women's World Day of Prayer
Founded in America in 1887 (Britain 1930–34) to unite Christian women in prayer by means of services held on the first Friday in March each year, by fostering local interdenominational prayer groups meeting throughout the year and to assist financially or otherwise Christian projects throughout the World. *President:* Mrs Jean Hackett. *Chairperson:* Mrs Kathleen Skinner. *Administrator:* Mrs Mary Judd, WWDP, Commercial Rd, Tunbridge Wells, TN1 2RR
Tel: 01892 541411
Fax: 01892 541745
email: office@wwdp-natcomm.org
Web: www.wwdp-natcomm.org

Womenaid International
A humanitarian aid and development agency run by volunteers in the UK, which provides relief and assistance to women and children suffering distress caused by war, disasters or poverty. It seeks to empower women through education, training, provision of credit, and also campaigns against violations of women's human rights. An

implementing partner of the European Community Humanitarian Office (ECHO), the British Government and several UN agencies, it has provided over 30,000 tonnes of food, medical supplies and clothing to more than 1.5 million refugees in the former Yugoslavia, the Caucasus and Central Asia. Development assistance globally has ranged from building and repairing schools, supporting rescue centres for street children, repairing hospitals and providing medical equipment/supplies to micro-credit support and water/sanitation projects. *Founder:* Ms Pida Ripley, 3 Whitehall Court, London, SW1A 2EL
Tel: 020 7839 1790
Fax: 020 7839 2929
email: womenaid@womenaid.org
Web: www.womenaid.org

Woodard Schools
Founded by Canon Nathaniel Woodard in 1848 to promote education in the doctrines and principles of the Church of England. Woodard now owns some 19 schools and a further 23 schools are affiliated/associated *President:* Rt Revd Dr Anthony Russell (Bishop of Ely). *Registrar:* Mr Peter Beesley. *Senior Provost:* Canon Brendan Clover. *Director of Finance:* Mr Michael Corcoran. *Director of Education:* Mr Christopher Wright, High St, Abbots Bromley, Rugeley, WS15 3BW
Tel: 01283 840120
Fax: 01283 840893
email: jillshorthose@woodard.co.uk
Web: www.woodard.co.uk

World Congress of Faiths
Founded in 1936 to promote mutual understanding and a spirit of fellowship between people of different religious traditions. WCF works to explain and reconcile religious conflict and the tensions between the different communities. Conferences and lectures are arranged. The journal *Interreligious Insight* is published four times a year, jointly with the Interreligious Engagement Project and Common Ground, and has its own web site. A newsletter, *One Family*, is also published at least four times a year. *President:* Revd Marcus Braybrooke. *Chairman:* Rabbi Jacqueline Tabick. *Hon Treasurer:* Pejman Khojasteh. *Editor:* Revd Dr Alan Race. *Secretary:* Revd Feargus O'Connor, London Interfaith Centre, 125 Salusbury Rd, London, NW6 6RG
Tel: 01935 864055/020 8959 3129
Fax: 020 7604 3052
email: admin@worldfaiths.org
Web: www.worldfaiths.org

World Vision
Formed in London in 1979, World Vision UK is part of the international World Vision partnership and is a major UK relief and development agency. World Vision is at work in over 100 countries in Africa, Asia, Eastern Europe, Latin America and the Middle East. It is involved in partnering churches and other non-governmental organizations in projects which range from relief work in Africa to income generation projects in Bangladesh. *Chief Exec Officer:* Charles Badenoch. *Church Relations Manager:* Alistair Metcalfe, World Vision House, Opal Drive, Fox Milne, Milton Keynes, MK15 0ZR
Tel: 01908 841000
Fax: 01908 841001
email: church@worldvision.org.uk
Web: www.worldvision.org.uk/church

YMCA
Founded 1844 to promote the physical, intellectual and spiritual well-being of young people. *President:* The Archbishop of York. *National Secretary:* Angela Sarkis, National Council of YMCAs, 640 Forest Rd, London, E17 3DZ
Tel: 020 8520 5599
Fax: 020 8509 3190
email: national.secretary@england.ymca.org.uk
Web: www.ymca.org.uk

York Glaziers' Trust
Established 1967 by the Dean and Chapter of York and the Pilgrim Trust (1) to conserve and restore the stained glass of York Minster; (2) to conserve, restore and advise on all stained glass or glazing of historic or artistic importance, in any building whether religious or secular, public or private; (3) to establish and maintain within the City of York a stained glass workshop dedicated to the training and employment of conservators and craftsmen specializing in the preservation of glass of historic and artistic importance; and (4) to encourage public interest in the preservation of stained glass, to collaborate with educational institutions and to assist with scientific and art historical research into stained and painted glass. Advice should always be sought when considering treatment of glass of artistic or historic value. The Trust welcomes enquiries from all sources. It offers a full advisory service and will compile comprehensive condition reports. *Director:* Mrs Sarah E. Brown FSA. *Senior Conservator:* Nick Teed MA. *Business Manager:* Mr Peter M. Johnston, 6 Deangate, York, YO1 7JB
Tel: 01904 557228
email: info@yorkglaziers.org.uk
Web: www.york-glaziers.org.uk

YWCA England & Wales
YWCA England & Wales is a force for change for women facing discrimination and inequalities of all kinds. Our principal aims are to enable young women who are experiencing particular disadvantage to identify and realize their full potential, to influence public policy in order to achieve equality and social justice for young women, and to provide opportunities for participation in a worldwide women's movement. Clarendon House, 52 Cornmarket House, Oxford, OX1 3EJ
Tel: 01865 304200
Fax: 01865 204805
email: info@ywca.org.uk
Web: www.ywca.org.uk

Diocesan Associations

Association of the Dioceses of Singapore and West Malaysia

Revd Ann Bucknall
20 St Margaret's Rd
Lichfield
Staffs. WS13 7RA
Tel: 01543 257382
email: bucknall20ann
@talktalk.net

Belize Church Association

Mrs Barbara Harris
Honeysuckle Cottage
19 Whittall St
Kings Sutton
Banbury
Oxon. OX17 3RD
Tel: 01295 811310
email: bkayharris@
googlemail.com

Church of Ceylon Association

Canon Bob Campbell-
Smith
Even Keel
Pillory Hill
Noss Mayo
Devon PL8 1ED
Tel: 01752 872559
email: bobandlorna@
tiscali.co.uk

Congo Church Association

Mrs Rosemary Peirce
8 Burwell Meadow
Witney
Oxford OX28 5JQ
Tel: 01993 200103
email: rosemary.peirce@
ntlworld.com

Egypt Diocesan Association

MrsElspethMackinlay
The Horseshoes
The Green
Gressenhall
Dereham
Norfolk
NR20 4DT
Tel: 01362 860302
email: eda.egypt@
googlemail.com

Fellowship of the Maple Leaf
(*Provides grants to further mutual learning between the Church in Canada and the UK*)

Preb. David Sceats
St John's Rectory
Viewfield Park
Selkirk
TD7 4LH
Tel: 01750 213164
email: d-sceats@
sky.com
Web:
www.mapleleaf.org.uk

Friends of the Church in India

Revd Suresh Kumar
10 Park Hill Drive
Leicester
LE2 8HR
Tel: 0116 283 4031
email: suresh@
skumar.plus.com

Friends of the Diocese of Cyprus and the Gulf

Mrs Mary Banfield
Garden Corner
Old London Rd
Mickleham
Surrey RH5 6DL
Tel: 01372 373912
Fax: 01372 362770
email: mgbbmw@
aol.com

Friends of the Diocese of Iran

Mr John Clark
32 Weigall Rd
Lee
London SE12 8HE
email: john@mclark32.
freeserve.co.uk

Friends of the Diocese of Uruguay

N. J. Roberts
2 Upland Rise
Walton
Chesterfield
S40 2DD
Tel: 01246 233590
Mobile: 07896 162461
email: nick.roberts@
bcs.org
Web: www.friends-of-
the-diocese-of-
uruguay.org.uk

Guyana Diocesan Association

Revd Allan Buik
20 Cleaves Drive
Walsingham
Norfolk
NR22 6EQ
Tel: 01328 820030
email: allanbuik@
gmail.com

Jerusalem and the Middle East Church Association

Ms Shirley Eason
1 Hart House
The Hart
Farnham
Surrey GU9 7HJ
Tel and fax:
01252 726994
email: secretary@
jmeca.eclipse.co.uk
Web:
www.jmeca.org.uk

Kenya Church Association	Hon Secretary: Revd Bryan Wadland 55 Copthall Rd East Ickenham UB10 8SE Tel: 01895 613904 email: douglas087@ btinternet.com	St Helena Association	Canon Patricia Ann Turner 7 Roundell Drive West Marton Skipton BD23 3UL Tel: 01282 842332 email: ann.turner@ bradford.anglican.org
Lesotho Diocesan Association	Sister Jean Mary CHN Convent of the Holy Name Morley Road Oakwood Derby DE21 4QZ Tel: 01332 671 716 email: chnjmary@ yahoo.co.uk	Sudan Church Association	Mrs Sara Taffinder 69 Poynders Rd Clapham London SW4 8PL Tel and Fax: 020 8671 1974
MANNA Mozambique and Angola Anglican Association	General Secretary: Ian Gordon 16 Bayle Court The Bayle Folkestone Kent CT20 1SN Tel: 01303 257248 email: n_grdn@ yahoo.co.uk Web: www.newportchurches. com/manna	TZABA Transvaal, Zimbabwe and Botswana Association	Mrs Liz Martin 120 Church Lane East Aldershot Hampshire GU11 3SS Tel and Fax: 01252 320108 email: elizmmartin@ yahoo.co.uk
Nigeria Fellowship	Chair: Dr Anne Phillips 33 Cliffe Road Sheffield S6 5DR Tel: 0114 233 8529 email: annephillips2@ hotmail.co.uk	Uganda Church Association	Revd Dr Michael Hunter The Vicarage 51 Vicarage Lane Dore Sheffield S17 3GY Tel: 0114 236 3480 email: mutagwok@aol.com
Province of the Indian Ocean Support Association	Hon. Secretary: Vacancy Chair: Canon Hall Speers The Rectory 38 Manor Rd Barnet EN5 2JJ Tel: 020 8449 3894 email: hall.speers@ talk21.com Hon. Treasurer: Revd Hilary C. Jones St Martin's Rectory Horn St Folkestone CT20 3JJ Tel: 01303 238509 email: revhilaryjones@ btinternet.com	Zululand Swaziland Association	The Zululand Swaziland Association has ceased to exist as an independent charity. The Zululand Swaziland Trusteeship has now passed to the trustees of USPG, and donations to its ongoing work can be received by cheques made payable to 'USPG', earmarked 'Zululand Swaziland Trust'. USPG: Anglicans in World Mission 200 Great Dover St London SE1 4YB

Libraries

Canterbury

Cathedral Library
Cathedral House
The Precincts
Canterbury
Kent CT1 2EH

Cathedral Librarian (acting)
Mrs Karen Brayshaw

Cathedral Archivist
Mrs Cressida Williams

The archives and library at Canterbury are separate departments. Information about the archives is available on the archives pages of the Cathedral web site at www.canterbury-cathedral.org/history/archives.aspx or by telephoning 01227 865330. Information about the library can be found at www.canterbury-cathedral.org/history/libraries.aspx or by telephoning 01277 865287.

Tel: 01227 865330 (Archives)
01227 865287 (Library)
Fax: 01227 865222
email: library@canterbury-cathedral.org

Library collections: 52,000 printed volumes, 15th century to present. The Howley-Harrison Collection (16,000 books and pamphlets) includes anti-slavery and Oxford Movement material. Also cathedral printed music, and scores of Canterbury Catch Club. Mendham Collection of Catholic and anti-Catholic writings. Two parish libraries: Elham and Preston-next-Wingham, in a Dr Bray cabinet. The collections include substantial holdings on national and local history, including the English Civil War, travel, botany, English and foreign literature.

Archive collections: large collections of manuscript and archives, including the Cathedral archives; records of the Diocese of Canterbury; parish records; records of the City Council and other organizations, businesses, administrations and individuals in the Canterbury area.

Crowther Library

Crowther Centre for Mission Education
Church Mission Society
Watlington Rd
Oxford
OX4 6BZ

Librarian Ken Osborne

Tel: 01865 787552
Fax: 01865 776375
email: ken.osborne@cms-uk.org
Web: www.cms-uk.org/heritage/default.htm
Open: 0900–1700 hours Mon–Fri
Closed public holidays.

30,000 volumes, 250 current periodicals. Successor to the Partnership House Mission Studies Library that incorporated the post-1945 collections of the former Church Missionary Society and United Society for the Propagation of the Gospel Stock focuses on the work of the Church worldwide, missiology, history of mission, church history, African and Asian Christianity and interfaith relations. Also houses CMS's pre-1945 collection entitled the Max Warren Collection. Reference only.

Durham

Durham Cathedral Library
The College
Durham
DH1 3EH

Librarian Canon Rosalind Brown
Assistant Librarian Vacancy

Tel: 0191 386 2489
email: Library@
durhamcathedral.co.uk

Open: 0900–1300; 1400–1700 hours Mon–Fri; closed for first two full weeks in July.

Chapter Library of 40,000 printed books including 70 incunabula, 375 manuscripts 7th–16th centuries. Archival collections include Hunter, Sharp, Raine, Surtees, Ian Ramsey, J. B. Lightfoot, H. H. Henson, early music. Published catalogues of medieval manuscripts (1825, 1964, etc.), printed music (1968) and manuscript music (1986). An online guide to the archival collections is available at http://flambard.dur.ac.uk/ dynaweb/cld/.Small modern collection specializing in history of the north-east, church history, cathedrals and art. Meissen Library of theology in German of approx. 20,000 books donated by EKD inaugurated 1998. Catalogue at its website www.meissenlibrarydurham. co.uk. Archdeacon Sharp Library of modern theology of approx. 10,000 books in English. All Archdeacon Sharp Library books and many Chapter Library books are included in Durham University Library's online catalogue at http://library.dur.ac.uk (location 'Cathedral').

Exeter

Exeter Cathedral Library and Archives
West Wing
The Palace
Palace Gate
Exeter
EX1 1HX

Cathedral Librarian Peter Thomas
Assistant Librarian Stuart Macwilliam
Cathedral Archivist Angela Doughty

Tel: 01392 272894 (Library)
01392 495954 (Archives)
email: library@exeter-cathedral.org.uk
archive@exeter-cathedral.org.uk
Web: http://www.exeter-cathedral.org.uk/Admin/ Library/html

Open: 1400–1700 hours Mon–Fri (Library) Mon–Wed (Archives, by appointment only). Closed on public holidays.

20,000 items (Library); 50,000 (Archives), Manuscripts include Exeter Book and Exon Domesday; special collections include cathedral manuscripts and archives, early printed books in medicine and science, Cook Collection (16th–19th c., early linguistics), printed tracts (mainly Civil War period), Harington Collection (16th–19th c., theology, ecclesiastical history, history). Pre-2001 accessions included in online catalogue of Exeter University Library at www.ex.ac.uk/ library/. Medical and scientific collections also catalogued in *Medicine and science at Exeter Cathedral Library*, compiled by Peter W. Thomas (University of Exeter Press, 2003). See also *The library and archives of Exeter Cathedral*, by L. J. Lloyd and Audrey M. Erskine, 3rd edn (Exeter 2004).

Hereford

Hereford Cathedral Library and
Archives
Hereford Cathedral
Hereford
Herefordshire
HR1 2NG

Canon Chancellor Canon
Christopher Pullin
Archivist Mrs Rosalind Caird
Library and Archives Assistant
Miss Kirsty Clarke
Librarian Vacancy

Tel: 01432 374225/6
email: library@
herefordcathedral.org
Web:
www.herefordcathedral.org

Open: Tues and Thurs
1000–1600 hours. Other
times by prior appointment.
Closed in January for
essential conservation
and maintenance work.

The Library cares for the
Mappa Mundi (*c.* 1300),
Chained Library and All Saints'
Chained Library. The collection
includes 229 medieval
manuscripts from the 8th to the
early 16th centuries, over 3,000
pre-1801 printed books
including 56 incunabula, 10,000
books published post-1800
(many borrowable) and
manuscript and printed music
(18th to 20th centuries). There
are also 30,000 archives of the
Dean and Chapter, dating from
the 9th to 20th centuries.
Photographic service available.

Lambeth

Lambeth Palace Library
London
SE1 7JU

Librarian and Archivist
Giles Mandelbrote

Tel: 020 7898 1400
Fax: 020 7928 7932
email: lpl.staff@c-of-e.org.uk
Web: www.
lambethpalacelibrary.org

Open: 1000–1700 hours
Mon–Fri
Closed public holidays and
ten days at Christmas and
Easter.

Main library for the history of
the Church of England, open for
public use since 1610. 200,000
printed books, 4,900
manuscripts 9th–20th centuries.
Registers and correspondence of
Archbishops of Canterbury
12th–20th centuries. Records of
Province of Canterbury, the
Faculty Office, Lambeth
Conferences, Bishops of
London, and papers of
churchmen, statesmen and
organizations within the
Church of England.
Manuscripts and printed
books earlier than 1850 from
Sion College Library.

Pusey House

Pusey House
Oxford
OX1 3LZ

Custodian Revd William
Davage
Archivist Revd Dr Barry A.
Orford

Tel: 01865 278415
email: chapter@
puseyhouse.org.uk
Web:
www.puseyhouse.org.uk

Open: 0930–1230, 1400–1630
Mon–Fri; 0930–1230 Sat (by
appointment only) during
full term (weeks 0–8)
During vacation the library is
open Monday to Friday by
appointment only. The
library is closed during
August and at the beginning
of September until after the
St Giles' Fair.

Contact the Custodian for
vacation opening times

80,000 volumes. A theological
library specializing in
patristics, Church history and
liturgy. An extensive archive of
Oxford Movement and related
material.

St Deiniol's

St Deiniol's Residential
Library
Church Lane
Hawarden
Flintshire
CH5 3DF

Warden Revd Peter Francis

Tel: 01244 532350
Fax: 01244 520643
email: enquiries@
st-deiniols.org
Web:
    www.st-deiniols.org

Over 250,000 printed items
(books, journals and
pamphlets). Main subject areas:
theology, biblical studies,
spirituality, liturgy, church
history plus Bishop Moorman
Franciscan Collection and
excellent holdings in
nineteenth-century history, art
and literature. Thirty
bedrooms, two conference
rooms and chapel. Subsidised
rates for clergy and students.
Bursaries and scholarships
available.

St Paul's

The Library
St Paul's Cathedral
London
EC4M 8AE

Librarian Mr Jo Wisdom

Tel: 020 7246 8345
Fax: 020 7248 3104
email: library@
stpaulscathedral.org.uk

Re-established after the Great
Fire of 1666, the library is
strong in theology,
ecclesiastical history, and
sermons, especially of 17th and
18th centuries. Special
collections include early
printed Bibles; St Paul's Cross
sermons; 19th-century tracts.
The archive of Dean and
Chapter is deposited at
Guildhall Library,
Aldermanbury, London EC2P
2EJ.

Sarum College

Sarum College Library
19 The Close
Salisbury
Wilts.
SP1 2EE

*Librarian and Bookshop
Manager* Jennifer Monds
Assistant Librarian Jayne
Downey

Tel: 01722 424803
Fax: 01722 338508
email: library@sarum.ac.uk
web: www.sarum.ac.uk/
library

Open: 0900–1700 Mon–Fri
and some evenings during
term time
Fees: £30 per annum for
reading rights; £40 per
annum for reading and
borrowing rights; £5 per day
or £10 per week for visitors

Founded 1860. 36,000 volumes
mostly on academic theology,
church history, ethics and
Christian spirituality. Rare
book collection including 274
bound volumes of mainly
20th-century tracts, sermons,
charges and letters. About 1000
volumes are added each year.

Fifty journals are taken, with
back numbers available for
reference use. Inter-library loan
services offered. Internet, word
processing facilities and Wi-Fi
access available. Catalogue
accessible from the library
homepage at the above web
address. Accommodation
available. Researchers and
sabbaticals welcome. Quiet
space. Coffee, tea and lunches
may be purchased. There is also
a bookshop selling academic
theology.

ORGANIZATIONS

Sion College	The library has closed. The older books (–1850) were transferred to Lambeth Palace Library. The bulk of the balance of the collection is in the library of King's College, London.	Biblical studies, philosophy, Anglican theology, church history, biography and liturgy. Special collections include Sion College Port Royal Library, Industrial Christian Fellowship Library, and extensive pamphlet collections.
United Society for the Propagation of the Gospel Bodleian Library of Common-wealth and African Studies at Rhodes House South Parks Rd Oxford OX1 3RG	*Archivist* Miss Lucy McCann *Tel:* 01865 270908 *Fax:* 01865 270912 *email:* rhodes.house.library@bodleian.ox.ac.uk Bodleian reader's ticket required – details at www.bodleian.ox.ac.uk/bodley/services/admissions.	The Society's library to 1944 and archival material circa 1701–1965. Extensive collections from the 19th century, back holdings of missionary journals.
Westminster Abbey Westminster Abbey Muniment Room and Library London SW1P 3PA	*Head of the Abbey Collection and Librarian* Dr Tony Trowles *Keeper of the Muniments* Dr Richard Mortimer *Tel:* 020 7654 4830 *Fax:* 020 7654 4827 *email:* library@westminster-abbey.org *Web:* www.westminster-abbey.org Open: 1000–1300, 1400–1645 hours Mon–Fri; appointments required	20,000 volumes (16th–21st centuries), in excess of 70,000 archives (monastic history 8th–16th centuries, Abbey records to present day).
York Minster York Minster Library Dean's Park York YO1 7JQ	*Librarian* Ms Sarah Griffin *Archivist* Peter Young *Tel:* 0844 939 0021 ext 2501 (Library), ext 2530 (Archives) *email:* library@yorkminster.org archives@yorkminster.org *Web:* (Library catalogue) telnet://library.york.ac.uk (Library guide) http://www.yorkminster.org/learning/the-old-palace/ Open: 0900–1700 hours Mon–Fri Closed on public holidays	130,000 volumes. Theology; church history, art, architecture and stained glass; extensive collections of pre-1801 books; manuscripts; incunables; special collections of Yorkshire history, Yorkshire topographical prints, and Yorkshire Civil War tracts; music and photographic collections; archives of Dean and Chapter from medieval times.

See also main Organizations section

Patronage Trusts

Church Pastoral Aid Society Patronage Trust

Secretary Canon John Alderman
CPAS, Athena Drive
Tachbrook Park
Warwick CV34 6NG
Tel: 01926 458457
Fax: 01926 458459
email: jalderman@cpas.org.uk /
patronage@cpas.org.uk

A Trust holding Rights of Presentation to a number of benefices. Administered by the Church Pastoral Aid Society.

Church Patronage Trust

Secretary Canon Roger Salisbury
12 De Walden St
London W1G 8RN
Tel: 020 7935 9811
Fax: 020 7436 3019
email: roger.salisbury@allsouls.org

A Trust holding the Rights of Presentation to a number of benefices. Evangelical tradition.

Church Society Trust

Secretary Revd D. Phillips
Dean Wace House
16 Rosslyn Rd
Watford, Herts. WD18 0NY
Tel: 01923 235111
Fax: 01923 800362
email: admin@churchsociety.org

Patron of more than 100 livings.

Church Trust Fund Trust

Secretary Canon John Alderman
CPAS, Athena Drive
Tachbrook Park
Warwick CV34 6NG
Tel: 01926 458457
Fax: 01926 458459
email: jalderman@cpas.org.uk /
patronage@cpas.org.uk

A Trust holding Rights of Presentation to a number of benefices. Administered by the Church Pastoral Aid Society.

Guild of All Souls

General Secretary David G. Llewelyn Morgan
Guild of All Souls
Royal London House
22–25 Finsbury Square
London EC2A 1DX
Tel: 0207 920 6468
Fax: 01371 831430
Web: www.guildofallsouls.org.uk

Patron of 41 livings of Catholic tradition.

Hulme Trustees

Secretary Mr Jonathan Shelmerdine,
Butcher and Barlow
Solicitors
31 Middlewich Rd
Sandbach
Cheshire CW11 1HW
Tel: 01270 762521

A Trust holding the Rights of Presentation to a number of benefices.

Hyndman's (Miss) Trustees	*Administrative Secretary* Mrs Ann Brown 6 Angerford Ave Sheffield S8 9BG *Tel* and *Fax:* 0114 255 8522 *email:* ann.brown@hyndmans. org.uk *Web:* www.hyndmans.org.uk	Patronage Trust. Varied churchmanship.
Intercontinental Church Society	*General Manager* Mr David Healey 1 Athena Drive Tachbrook Park Warwick CV34 6NL *Tel:* 01926 430347 *Fax:* 01926 888092 *email:* enquiries@ics-uk.org	Manages the recruitment of clergy (especially as Patron) for many English-speaking churches abroad; evangelical.
Martyrs Memorial and Church of England Trust	*Secretary* Canon John Alderman CPAS, Athena Drive Tachbrook Park Warwick CV34 6NG *Tel:* 01926 458457 *Fax:* 01926 458459 *email:* jalderman@ cpas.org.uk / patronage@cpas.org.uk	A Trust holding Rights of Presentation to a number of benefices. Administered by the Church Pastoral Aid Society.
Peache Trustees	*Secretary* Revd Kenneth Habershon Truckers Ghyll Horsham Rd, Handcross W Sussex RH17 6DT *Tel:* 01444 400274 *email:* kandmhab@btopenworld.com	A Trust holding the Rights of Presentation to a number of benefices. Evangelical tradition.
Simeon's Trustees	*Administrative Secretary* Mrs Ann Brown 6 Angerford Ave Sheffield S8 9BG *Tel:* 0114 255 8522 *email:* ann.brown@ simeons.org.uk *Web:* www.simeons.org.uk	Holds and administers the patronage of those livings in the Church of England which belong to the Trust on the principles laid down in Charles Simeon's Charge.
Society for the Maintenance of the Faith	*Secretary* Revd Paul Conrad Christ Church Vicarage 10 Cannon Place London NW3 1EJ *Tel* and *Fax:* 020 7435 6784	Administers patronage and promotes Catholic teaching and practice.

Anglican and Porvoo Communions

PART 5

PART 5 CONTENTS

THE ANGLICAN COMMUNION

OUR FAITH

Anglican/Episcopal churches uphold and proclaim the Catholic and Apostolic faith, proclaimed in the Scriptures, interpreted in the light of tradition and reason. Following the teachings of Jesus Christ, Anglicans are committed to the proclamation of the good news of the Gospel to all creation. Our faith and ministry have been expressed through the *Book of Common Prayer*, received and adapted by the local churches, in the Services of Ordination (the Ordinal), and in the Chicago-Lambeth Quadrilateral, first expounded at the missionary Conference in Chicago, and revised by the Lambeth Conference of 1888. The Quadrilateral sets out four essential elements of the Christian faith:

1 The Holy Scriptures of the Old and New Testaments as 'containing all things necessary to salvation', and as being the rule and ultimate standard of faith.
2 The Apostles' Creed, as the baptismal symbol; and the Nicene Creed as the sufficient statement of the Christian Faith.
3 The two Sacraments ordained by Christ himself – Baptism and the Supper of the Lord – ministered with unfailing use of Christ's words of institution and of the elements ordained by Him.
4 The Historic Episcopate, locally adapted in the methods of its administration to the varying needs of the nations and peoples called of God into the unity of His Church.

Central to Anglican worship is the celebration of the Holy Eucharist (also called the Holy Communion, the Lord's Supper or the Mass). In this offering of prayer and praise, the life, death, resurrection and ascension of Jesus Christ are made a present reality through the proclamation of the Word and the celebration of the Sacrament. Anglicans celebrate the Sacrament of Baptism with water in the name of the Trinity, as the rite of entry into the Christian Church, and celebrate other Sacramental rites, including Confirmation, Reconciliation, Marriage, Anointing the sick and Ordination.

Common prayer is at the heart of Anglicanism. Its styles may vary from the simple to the elaborate, from evangelical to catholic, charismatic to traditional. The various Books of Common Prayer give expression to a comprehensiveness found within the churches, which seeks to chart a *via media* in relation to other Christian traditions.

OUR CHURCHES

Deriving from the ancient Celtic and Saxon churches of the British Isles, Anglicanism found its distinctive identity in the sixteenth and seventeenth century Reformation, when the separate Church of England came into being, together with the Church of Ireland, and the Scottish Episcopal Church. At the time of the American Revolution, an autonomous Episcopal Church was founded in the United States, and later Anglican or Episcopal churches were founded across the globe as a result of the missionary movements of the eighteenth and nineteenth centuries. Many of these were given autonomy as Provinces in the course of the nineteenth and twentieth centuries. In South Asia, the United Churches, formed between Anglican and several Protestant denominations, also joined the Anglican Communion, as did churches elsewhere such as the Spanish Episcopal Reformed Church and the Lusitanian Church of Portugal.

Today, the Anglican Communion Episcopal family consists of an estimated 78 million Christians, made up of 34 Provinces, 4 United Churches and 6 other Churches, spread across the globe.

THE INSTRUMENTS OF COMMUNION
The Archbishop of Canterbury

The churches are all in communion with the See of Canterbury in the Church of England, and thus the Archbishop of Canterbury, in his person and ministry, is the unique focus of Anglican unity. He calls the Lambeth Conference, and Primates' Meeting, and is President of the Anglican Consultative Council. The 104th Archbishop of Canterbury in succession to St. Augustine, the Most Revd and Rt Hon Rowan Williams, was enthroned in February 2003.

The Primates Meeting

Since 1979, the Archbishop of Canterbury has also invited the primates (the presiding bishop, archbishop or moderator) of each of the 38 Provinces to join him in regular meetings for consultation, prayer and reflection on theological, social and international matters. These meetings take place approximately every eighteen months to two years.

The Anglican Consultative Council

In 1968 the bishops of the Lambeth Conference requested the establishment of a body representative of all sections (bishops, clergy and laity) of the churches, which could co-ordinate aspects of international Anglican ecumenical and mission work. With the consent of the legislative bodies of all the Provinces, the Anglican Consultative Council was established, and has met regularly since.

ACC Meetings:
Limuru, Kenya (1971), Dublin, Eire (1973), Trinidad (1976), London, Ontario, (1979), Newcastle upon Tyne, England (1981), Badagry, Nigeria (1984), Singapore (1987), Lampeter, Wales (1990), Cape Town, South Africa (1993), Panama (1996), Dundee, Scotland (1999), Hong Kong (2002), Nottingham, England (2005), Jamaica (2009).

The Lambeth Conference

The Lambeth Conference is the longest-standing of the Instruments of Communion of the worldwide Anglican Communion. Its origins go back to 1865 when, on 20 September, the Provincial Synod of the Church of Canada unanimously agreed to urge the Archbishop of Canterbury and the Convocation of his Province to find a means by which the bishops consecrated within the Church of England and serving overseas could be brought together for a General Council to discuss issues facing them in North America, and elsewhere. Part of the background for this request was a serious dispute about the interpretation and authority of the Scriptures which had arisen in Southern Africa between Robert Gray, Archbishop of Cape Town, and Bishop Colenso, Bishop of Natal.

Notwithstanding the opposition of a significant number of the bishops in England, Archbishop Longley invited Anglican bishops to their first Conference together at Lambeth Palace on 24 September, 1867 and the three subsequent days. Seventy-six bishops finally accepted the invitation and the Conference was called to order and met in the Chapel of Lambeth Palace. A request to use Westminster Abbey for a service was not granted.

Of the 76 bishops attending the first Lambeth Conference the distribution was the following:

England	18 bishops
Ireland	5 bishops
Scotland	6 bishops
Colonial and Missionary	28 bishops
United States	19 bishops

It was made clear at the outset that the Conference would have no authority of itself as it was not competent to make declarations or lay down definitions on points of doctrine. But the Conference was useful in that it explored many aspects of possible inter-Anglican co-operation and by providing common counsel it inaugurated a practical way in which the unity of the faith of the Church could be maintained. The Conference did not take any effective action regarding the issues raised by Bishop Colenso but its far-reaching impact can be seen in the fact that it was the precursor of the Lambeth Conference that we know today.

Lambeth Conferences:
Lambeth Palace (1878, 1888, 1897, 1908, 1920,

1930, 1948 and 1958), Church House, Westminster (1968), University of Kent, Canterbury (1978, 1988), Canterbury (1998, 2008).

The Lambeth Conference hosted by Archbishop Williams in Canterbury in July 2008 was attended by 650 bishops. The model adopted by the Archbishop of Canterbury (indaba) was not oriented towards the passing of resolutions but rather towards respectful listening and the imperative that all bishops' voices be heard and valued; offering an open space for bishops to express their views knowing that they would be heard. This process generated honest interchange and mutual understanding and assisted bishops to respond to the concerns and mission imperatives of their colleagues across two broad themes: Equipping Bishops for God's Mission and Strengthening Anglican Identity. Reports and reflections can be found on the Lambeth Conference website (www.lambethconference.org)

THE ANGLICAN COMMUNION OFFICE

This is a permanent secretariat based in London under the leadership of the Anglican Communion's Secretary General the Revd Canon Dr Kenneth Kearon. The staff of the Anglican Communion Office (ACO) facilitate all meetings of the conciliar Instruments of Communion, as well as the Commissions and Networks of the Communion. They support the Secretary General in carrying out the decisions and resolutions of the Instruments.

ACO staff also act as guardians of Communion history, information and data; they co-ordinate Communion projects on church growth and evangelism, relief and development and theological studies; and they communicate Communion news and information worldwide. They maintain a presence at the United Nations and also facilitate meetings on ecumenical dialogues, interfaith dialogues and on Unity, Faith and Order issues.

Funding comes from a variety of sources, but mainly from the Inter-Anglican Provincial contributions as supported by all member Churches according to their membership and means. Member Churches are also invited to contribute to special projects, initiatives and emergencies as they arise.

More information and resources about the Communion and the work of the Anglican Communion Office can be found on at www.anglicancommunion.org. These include the official prayer cycle (daily prayer intentions for the dioceses of the Communion), full details of all member Churches, and the latest news from across the Communion via the Anglican Communion News Service (ACNS). ACNS is also available by subscribing online to the free email news service. A selection of Anglican Communion books and reports are also available from the online shop.

PROVINCES OF THE ANGLICAN COMMUNION

The Anglican Church in Aotearoa, New Zealand and Polynesia
The Anglican Church of Australia
The Church of Bangladesh
The Episcopal Anglican Church of Brazil
The Province of the Anglican Church of Burundi
The Anglican Church of Canada
The Church of the Province of Central Africa
The Anglican Church of the Central American Region
The Anglican Church of the Congo
The Church of England
Hong Kong Sheng Kung Hui
The Church of the Province of the Indian Ocean
The Church of Ireland
Nippon So Ko Kai – The Anglican Communion in Japan
The Episcopal Church in Jerusalem and the Middle East
The Anglican Church of Kenya
The Anglican Church of Korea
The Church of the Province of Melanesia
The Anglican Church of Mexico
The Church of the Province of Myanmar (Burma)
The Church of Nigeria (Anglican Communion)
The Church of North India
The Church of Pakistan
The Anglican Church of Papua New Guinea
The Episcopal Church in the Philippines
The Episcopal Church of Rwanda
The Scottish Episcopal Church
The Church of the Province of South East Asia
The Anglican Church of Southern Africa
The Anglican Church of the Southern Cone of America
The Church of South India
The Episcopal Church of the Sudan
The Anglican Church of Tanzania
The Church of the Province of Uganda
The Episcopal Church
Includes overseas dioceses in Taiwan, Haiti, Columbia, Honduras, Dominican Republic and Ecuador
The Church in Wales
The Church of the Province of West Africa
The Church of the Province of the West Indies

EXTRA PROVINCIAL DIOCESES AND OTHER CHURCHES

The Anglican Church of Bermuda
The Anglican Church of Ceylon (Sri Lanka)
The Episcopal Church of Cuba
The Lusitanian Church (Portugal)
The Spanish Reformed Episcopal Church
Falkland Islands

CHURCHES IN COMMUNION

The Mar Thoma Syrian Church
The Old Catholic Churches of the Union of Utrecht
The Philippine Independent Church
The Church in China is a 'post denominational' Church whose formation included Anglicans in the Holy Catholic Church in China.
Anglicans/Episcopalians, in certain parts of the Communion, are in full communion with some Lutheran Churches.

THE ANGLICAN COMMUNION OFFICE

Secretary General Canon Dr Kenneth Kearon, Anglican Communion Office, St Andrew's House, 16 Tavistock Crescent, London, W11 1AP.
Tel: 0207 313 3900
Fax 0207 313 3999
email: aco@anglicancommunion.org
Web: www.anglicancommunion.org

ANGLICAN AND PORVOO COMMUNIONS

Clerical Wear

Wippell's offer a wide range of clerical wear for men and women including cassocks, surplices, cottas, cassock albs, traditional albs, shirts and blouses.

For full details including fabric samples and prices call us now. Wippell's also make and sell vestments, hangings, stoles, frontals, silver and brass wear, stained glass and a range of church furnishings.

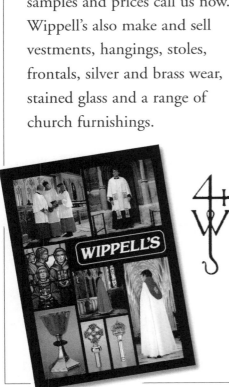

The Anglican Centre in Rome

The Anglican Centre in Rome was established in April 1966, endorsed by the Metropolitans of the Anglican Communion. This followed consultations among representatives of the several Churches of the Anglican Communion on action for the furtherance of Christian unity and the prospects for renewed fellowship and cooperation between Anglicans and Roman Catholics held out by the Second Vatican Council and by the historic visit of the Archbishop of Canterbury to Rome in March 1966. The Anglican Centre celebrated the fortieth anniversary of its foundation in 2006.

The Anglican Centre:

1. Provides a meeting place where clergy and laity, Anglican, Roman Catholic, and those of other Christian denominations, may come together for discussion, worship and prayer for the achievement of Christian unity.
2. Sponsors courses, lectures, seminars and discussions to enable a deeper understanding of the Roman Catholic Church, Anglicanism and the whole Western Christian tradition.
3. Is a welcoming reference point for visitors to Rome from member churches of the Anglican Communion, helping tourists in becoming pilgrims.
4. Holds a growing library of Anglican history, theology and liturgy, and of ecumenism, for the use of students and scholars of all Christian denominations.
5. Offers assistance to visiting Anglican scholars who wish to work in Rome, where possible putting them in touch with resident scholars in their field.
6. Offers a focal point for Anglican collaboration with the various agencies of the Roman Catholic Church and in particular the Pontifical Council for the Promotion of Christian Unity.
7. Supports the official dialogues for promoting unity between the Anglican Communion and the Roman Catholic Church.
8. Publishes a magazine, *CENTRO*, both online and in paper form, twice a year.

At the heart of the Centre's life is the chapel. Here the Eucharist is celebrated weekly on Tuesdays, at which the congregation is a microcosm of Christianity: Anglicans from around the world, Lutherans, Methodists, Roman Catholics and others. Visitors are welcome at the Eucharist and the lunch that follows.

The Centre's library is open from 9 a.m. to 1 p.m. Monday to Friday and by arrangement at other times. The Centre itself is normally open from 9 to 5 Monday to Friday, but it is advisable to ring ahead. It is closed in August and on public holidays. There is a governing body, and a director.

Director and Archbishop of Canterbury's Representative to the Holy See Very Revd Canon David Richardson, The Anglican Centre in Rome, Palazzo Doria Pamphilj, Piazza del Collegio Romano 2, 00186 Rome, Italy   *Tel:* 39 06 678 0302
Fax: 39 06 678 0674
(director) director@anglicancentre.it
Web: www.anglicancentreinrome.org

PA to the Director and Course Administrator Jan Hague
email: administrator@anglicancentre.it

Centre Receptionist and Librarian: Marcella Menna
email: anglican@anglicancentre.it

Development Officer UK Revd Bill Snelson
email: developmentUK@anglicancentre.it

FRIENDS OF THE ANGLICAN CENTRE IN ROME
Founded in 1984 to enlist support through both prayer and financial assistance for the work of the Centre.

President The Archbishop of Canterbury

Chairman Rt Revd Edward Holland

Chairman, English Friends Rt Revd Edward Holland, 37 Parfrey St, London W6 9EW

Secretary Miss Virginia Johnstone, 127 Cranmer Court, Whiteheads Grove, London SW3 3HE
Tel: 020 7589 0697

ANGLICAN AND PORVOO COMMUNIONS

CHURCHES AND PROVINCES OF THE ANGLICAN COMMUNION

AUTONOMOUS CHURCHES AND PROVINCES IN COMMUNION WITH THE SEE
OF CANTERBURY

Note: In the following directory section most provinces correspond to a specific country. In the postal addresses given, the name of the country is included only if some dioceses in the province are outside the country indicated by the name of the province.

Anglican Church in Aotearoa, New Zealand and Polynesia

Members 220,659

Formerly known as the Church of the Province of New Zealand, the Church covers 106,000 square miles and includes the countries of Aotearoa, New Zealand, Fiji, Tonga, Samoa and the Cook Islands. It was established as an autonomous Church in 1857. A revised constitution adopted in 1992 reflects a commitment to bicultural development that allows freedom and responsibility to implement worship and mission in accordance with the culture and social conditions of the Maori (Tikanga Maori), European (Tikanga Pakeha) and Polynesian (Tikanga Pasefika) membership. The Church has a strong and effective Anglican Missions Board.

Primate/Archbishops Most Revd Brown Turei (*Tikanga Maori*), PO Box 568, Gisborne 4040, New Zealand   *Tel:* 64 868 7028
Fax: 64 867 8859
email: browntmihi@xtra.co.nz
Web: www.anglican.org.nz

Most Revd Dr Winston Halapua (*Tikanga Pasefika*), PO Box 35, Suva, Fiji Islands   *Tel:* 679 330 4716
Fax: 679 330 2687
email: episcopus@connect.com.fj
Web: www.anglican.org.nz
Most Revd David Moxon (*Tikanga Pakeha*), PO Box 21, Hamilton 3240   *Tel:* 64 7 857 0020
Fax: 64 7 856 9975
email: bishop@hn-anglican.org.nz
Web: www.anglican.org.nz

General Secretary and *Treasurer* Revd Michael Hughes, PO Box 87188, Meadowbank, Auckland 1742, New Zealand   *Tel:* 64 9 521 4439
Fax: 64 9 521 4490
email: gensec@ang.org.nz/gensecpa@ang.org.nz
Web: www.anglican.org.nz

THEOLOGICAL COLLEGES
The College of St John the Evangelist, Private Bag 28–907, Remuera, Auckland 1541, New Zealand (serves both Anglicans and Methodists)
Tel: 64 9 521 2725
Fax: 64 9 521 2420
email: stjohnscollege@auckland.ac.nz
Web: www.stjohnscollege.ac.nz

Constituent Societies
College of the Southern Cross, (*Dean* Revd Canon J. White)

Te Rau Kahikatea, (*Te Ahorangi/Dean* Dr J. Plane-Te Paa)

College of the Diocese of Polynesia, (*Principal* Ven T. Tuatagaloa-Leota)

Theology House, 30 Church Lane, Merivale, Christchurch 8014, New Zealand (*Director* Revd Dr P. Carrell)   *Tel:* 64 3 355 9145
Fax: 64 3 355 6140
email: admin@theologyhouse.ac.nz
Web: www.theologyhouse.ac.nz
Selwyn College, 560 Castle St, Dunedin 9016, New Zealand (*Warden* Revd Dr D. Clark)
Tel: 64 3 477 3326
Fax: 64 3 477 9926
email: office.selwyn@otago.ac.nz
Web: www.selwyn.ac.nz

The two last named cater for pre-ordination or post-graduate studies.

AOTEAROA

Bishop in Te Tai Tokerau Rt Revd Te Kitohi Wiremu Pikaahu, PO Box 59103, Mangere Bridge, Manukau 2151, New Zealand
Tel: 64 9 278 2527
Fax: 64 9 278 2524
email: tkwp@xtra.co.nz

Bishop in Te Manawa o Te Wheke Rt Revd Ngarahu Katene, PO Box 146, Rotorua 3040
Tel and *Fax:* 64 7 348 4043
email: bishop @motw.org.nz

Bishop in Te Tairawhiti Most Revd William Brown Turei, PO Box 568, Gisborne 4040, New Zealand
Tel: 64 6 867 702
Fax: 64 6 867 8859
email: browntmihi@xtra.co.nz

Bishop in Te Upoko o Te Ika Rt Revd Muru Walters, 14 Amesbury Drive, Churton Park, Wellington 6037, New Zealand
Tel: 64 4 478 3549
Fax: 64 4 472 8863
email: muru.walters@xtra.co.nz

Bishop in Te Waipounamu Rt Revd John Robert Kuru Gray, PO Box 10086, Philipstown, Christchurch 8145, New Zealand
Tel: 64 3 389 1683
Fax: 64 3 389 0912
email: bishopgray@hawaipounamu.co.nz

AUCKLAND
Bishop Rt Revd Ross Bay, PO Box 37–242, Parnell, Auckland, 1151, New Zealand
Tel: 64 9 302 7201
Fax: 64 9 302 7217
email: bishop@auckanglican.org.nz
Web: www.auckanglican.org.nz

CHRISTCHURCH
Bishop Rt Revd Victoria Matthews, PO Box 4438, Christchurch 8140, New Zealand
Tel: 64 3 379 5950
Fax: 64 3 379 5954
email: bishop@anglicanlife.org.nz
Web: www.anglicanlife.org.nz

DUNEDIN
Bishop Rt Revd Dr Kelvin Wright, PO Box 13170, Green Island, Dunedin 9052, New Zealand
Tel: 64 3 488 0820
Fax: 64 3 488 2038
email: bishop@dn.anglican.org.nz
Web: www.dn.anglican.org.nz

NELSON
Bishop Rt Revd Richard Ellena, PO Box 100, Nelson 7040, New Zealand
Tel: 64 3 548 3124
Fax: 64 3 548 2125
email: bprichard@nelsonanglican.org.nz
Web: www.nelsonanglican.org.nz

POLYNESIA
Bishop Most Revd Dr Winston Halapua, Bishop's House, Box 35, Suva, Fiji
Tel: 679 330 4716
Fax: 679 330 2687
email: episcopus@connect.com.fj
Web: www.anglican.org.nz

Bishop for the Diocese of Polynesia in Aotearoa, New Zealand Vacancy

Bishop in Vanua Levu and Taveuni Rt Revd Apimeleki Nadoki Qiliho, Diocese of Polynesia, PO Box 29, Labasa, Fiji
Tel and *Fax:* 679 881 1420
email: minoff@connect.com.fj

Bishop in Viti Levu West Rt Revd Gabriel Mahesh Prasad Sharma, PO Box 117, Lautoka, Fiji
Tel and *Fax:* 679 666 0124
email: gabsharma@yahoo.com

WAIAPU
Bishop Rt Revd David Rice, PO Box 227, Napier 4140, New Zealand
Tel: 64 6 835 8230
Fax: 64 6 835 0680
email: deowaiapu@hb.ang.org.nz
Web: www.waiapu.anglican.org.nz

WAIKATO
Bishop Most Revd David John Moxon, PO Box 21, Hamilton 3240, New Zealand
Tel: 64 7 857 0020
Fax: 64 7 836 9975
email: bishop@hn-ang.org.nz
Web: www.waikato.anglican.org.nz

Bishop in Taranaki Rt Revd Philip Richardson, PO Box 547, Taranaki Mail Centre, New Plymouth 4340, New Zealand
Tel: 64 6 759 1178
Fax: 64 6 759 1180
email: bishop.pa@xtra.co.nz

WELLINGTON
Bishop Rt Revd Dr Thomas John Brown, PO Box 12–046, Wellington 6144, New Zealand
Tel: 64 4 472 1057
Fax: 64 4 449 1360
email: bishoptom@paradise.net.nz
Web: www.wn.ang.org.nz

Anglican Church of Australia

Members 3,881,162 (2001)
The Church came to Australia in 1788 with the 'First Fleet', which was made up primarily of convicts and military personnel. Free settlers soon followed. A General Synod held in 1872 formed the Australian Board of Missions. The Church became fully autonomous in 1962 and in 1978 published its first prayer book. A second Anglican prayer book was published in 1995.

Women were first ordained to the Diaconate in 1985 and to the Priesthood in 1992. There are 23 dioceses of which 19 ordain women as priests and chaplains. The Anglican Church of Australia is part of the Christian Conference of Asia and of the Council of the Church of East Asia. Links with Churches of New Guinea, Melanesia, and Polynesia are strong especially through the Anglican Board of Mission – Australia.

Primate of the Anglican Church of Australia Most Revd Dr Phillip John Aspinall (*Archbishop of Brisbane*)

General Secretary of the General Synod Mr Martin Drevikovsky

Hon Treasurer Mr John McKenzie

General Synod Office Suite 2, Level 9, 51 Druitt Street, Sydney, NSW 2000   *Tel:* 61 2 8267 2700
Fax: 61 2 8267 2727
email: gsoffice@anglican.org.au
Web: www.anglican.org.au

THE ANGLICAN THEOLOGICAL COLLEGES
Moore Theological College, 1 King St, Newtown, NSW 2042 (*Principal* Revd John Woodhouse)
Fax: 61 2 9577 9988
email: info@moore.usyd.edu.au
Web: www.moore.edu.au

Nungalinya College, PO Box 40371, Casuarina, NT 0811 (*Principal* Revd Dr L. Lee Levett-Olson)
Fax: 61 8 8927 2332
email: info@nungalinya.edu.au
Web: www.nungalinya.edu.au

Ridley College, 160 The Avenue, Parkville, VIC 3052 (*Principal* Revd Dr Peter Adam)
Fax: 61 3 9387 5099
email: registrar@ridley.unimelb.edu.au
Web: www.ridley.unimelb.edu.au

St Barnabas Theological College, 34 Lipsett Terrace, Brooklyn Park, SA 5032 (*Acting Principal* Right Revd Stephen Pickard)   *Fax:* 61 8 8416 8450
email: st.barnabas@flinders.edu.au
Web: http://ehlt.flinders.edu.au/theology/information

St Francis Theological College, 233 Milton Rd, PO Box 1261, Milton QLD 4064 (*Principal* The Revd Dr Steve Ogden)   *Fax:* 61 7 3369 4691
email: stfran@ministryeducation.org.au
Web: www.stfran.qld.edu.au

St Mark's National Theological Centre, 15 Blackall St, Barton, ACT 2600 (*Director* Professor Tom Frame)   *Fax:* 61 2 6273 4067
email: stmarks@csu.edu.au
Web: www.stmarksntc.org.au

Trinity College Theological School, Royal Parade, Parkville, VIC 3052 (*Dean* The Revd Dr Timothy Gaden)   *Fax:* 61 3 9348 7460
email: tcts@trinity.unimelb.edu.au
Web: www.trinity.unimelb.edu.au/theolog

The John Wollaston Theological College, Wollaston Rd, Mt Claremont, WA 6010 (*Dean and Warden* Revd Dr Nigel Leaves)
Fax: 61 8 9286 0260
email: info@wollastoncollege.com.au
Web: www.wollastoncollege.com.au

CHURCH PAPERS
The Adelaide Church Guardian Monthly newspaper containing wide news coverage from the diocese, province and nationally. *Editorial Offices* 26 King William Road, North Adelaide, SA 5006.
email: mstenberg@adelaide.anglican.com.au

The Melbourne Anglican Large monthly diocesan newspaper contains extensive news, comment locally and from around the world; with colour pictures. *Director/Editor* The Anglican Centre, 209 Flinders Lane, Melbourne, VIC 3000.
email: media@melbourne.anglican.com.au
Web: www.melbourne.anglican.com.au

Anglican Encounter Monthly newspaper of Newcastle Diocese, containing diocesan and Australian news. *Editorial Offices* PO Box 817, Newcastle, NSW 2302.
email: editor@angdon.com
Web: www.angdon.com

Tasmanian Anglican Monthly small newspaper format, from Tasmania Diocese, containing wide comment. *Editorial Offices* PO Box 748, Hobart, TAS 7001.   *email:* editor@anglicantas.org.au
Web: www.anglicantas.org.au

Southern Cross Large monthly newspaper of Sydney Diocese, containing diocesan, national, world news and comment, Archbishop's letter in both English and Chinese translation. Extensive use of colour. *Editorial Offices* PO Box W185 Parramatta Westfield NSW 2150.
email: newsroom@anglicanmedia.com.au
Web: www.anglicanmedia.com.au

Anglican Messenger Monthly newspaper of the Anglican Province of Western Australia, includes news from Perth, North West Australia and Bunbury. *Editorial Offices* GPO Box W2067, Perth, WA 6846.   *email:* messenger@perth.anglican.org
Web: www.anglicanmessenger.com.au

Market Place A monthly independent Anglican newspaper, includes national and international Anglican news and comment. *Editorial Offices* PO Box 335, Orange, NSW 2800.
email: market@ix.net.au

Focus Monthly newspaper based in Brisbane, containing diocesan and national news. *Editorial Offices* GPO Box 421, Brisbane, QLD 4001.
email: focus@anglicanbrisbane.org.au
Web: www.anglicanbrisbane.org.au

All diocesan newspapers contain a letter from the Archbishop or Bishop of the Diocese. The Dioceses of Armidale, Ballarat, Bathurst, Bendigo, Canberra and Goulburn, Gippsland, Grafton, Murray, Northern Territory, Riverina, Rockhampton, Wangaratta, and Willochra also produce magazines/Bishop's newsletters, with mainly diocesan and parochial news.

PROVINCE OF NEW SOUTH WALES
Metropolitan Most Revd Dr Peter Jensen
(*Archbishop of Sydney*)

ARMIDALE
Bishop Rt Revd Dr Peter Robert Brain, PO Box 198, Armidale, NSW 2350   *Tel:* 61 2 6772 4491
Fax: 61 2 6772 9261
email: diocarm@northnet.com.au
Web: www.armidaleanglicandiocese.com

BATHURST
Bishop Rt Revd Richard Hurford, PO Box 23, Bathurst, NSW 2795   *Tel:* 61 2 6331 1722
Fax: 61 2 6332 2772
email: bishop.hurford@bathurstanglican.org
Web: www.bathurstanglican.org.au

Assistant Bishop Rt Revd Peter Thomas Danaher, PO Box 619, Dubbo, NSW 2830   *Tel:* 02 6885 2670
Fax: 02 6881 6740
email: peterdanaher@bigpond.com

CANBERRA AND GOULBURN
Bishop Rt Revd Stuart Robinson, GPO Box 1981, Canberra, ACT   *Tel:* 61 2 6248 0811
Fax: 61 2 6247 6829
Web: www.canberragoulburn.anglican.org

Assistant Bishops
Rt Revd Allan B. Ewing, PO Box 8605, Wagga Wagga, NSW 2650   *Tel:* 61 2 6926 4226
Fax: 61 2 6926 4226
email: allan.ewing@anglicancg.com.au

Rt Revd Trevor W. Edwards, 28 McBryde Crescent, Wanniassa, ACT 2903   *Tel:* 61 2 6231 7347
Fax: 61 2 6231 7500
email: trevor@stmattswanniassa.org.au

GRAFTON
Bishop Rt Revd Keith Slater, Bishopsholme, PO Box 4, Grafton, NSW 2460   *Tel:* 61 2 6642 4122
Fax: 61 2 6643 1814
email: angdiog@nor.com.au
Web: http://graftondiocese.org.au

NEWCASTLE
Bishop Rt Revd Brian George Farran, Bishop's Registry, PO Box 817, Newcastle, NSW 2300
Tel: 61 2 4926 3733
Fax: 61 2 4926 1968
email: bishop@angdon.com
Web: www.angdon.com

Assistant Bishop Rt Revd Peter Stuart, PO Box 817, Newcastle, NSW 2300   *Tel:* 02 4926 3733
Fax: 02 4926 1968
email: BishopPeter@angdon.com

RIVERINA
Bishop Rt Revd Douglas R. Stephens, PO Box 10, Narrandera, NSW 2700   *Tel:* 61 2 6959 1648
Fax: 61 2 6959 2903
email: rivdio@dragnet.com.au
Web: www.anglicanriverina.com

SYDNEY
Archbishop Most Revd Dr Peter Jensen (*Metropolitan of the Province of NSW*), PO Box Q190, QVB Post Office, NSW 1230
Tel: 61 2 9265 1521
Fax: 61 2 9265 1504
email: archbishop@sydney.anglican.asn.au
Web: www.sydneyanglicans.net

Assistant Bishops
Rt Revd Peter Tasker (*Bishop of Liverpool & Georges River Region*) (*same address*)   *Tel:* 61 2 9265 1530
Fax: 61 2 9265 1543
email: ptasker@sydney.anglican.asn.au
Web: www.your.sydneyanglicans.net/
senior_clergy/bishop_tasker
Rt Revd Glenn Davies (*Bishop of Northern Region*) (*same address*)   *Tel:* 61 2 9265 1533
Fax: 61 2 9265 1543
email: gdavies@sydney.anglican.asn.au
Web: www.your.sydneyanglicans.net/
senior_clergy/ bishop_davies
Rt Revd Robert Charles Forsyth (*Bishop of South Sydney*) (*same address*)   *Tel:* 61 2 9265 1501
Fax: 61 2 9265 1543
email: robforsyth@sydney.anglican.asn.au
Web: www.your.sydneyanglicans.net/
senior_clergy/bishop_forsyth
Rt Revd Alan (Al) Stewart (*Bishop of Wollongong*), 74 Church St, Wollongong, NSW 2500
Tel: 61 2 4201 1800
Fax: 61 2 4228 4296
email: astewart@wollongong.anglican.asn.au
Web: www.your.sydneyanglicans.net/
senior_clergy/bishop_stewart
Rt Revd Ivan Yin Lee (*Bishop of Western Sydney*), PO Box 129, Parramatta, NSW 2124
Tel: 61 2 8023 6700
Fax: 61 2 9633 3636
email: ilee@westernsydney.anglican.asn.au
Web: www.your.sydneyanglicans.net/
senior_clergy/bishop_lee

PROVINCE OF QUEENSLAND
Metropolitan Most Revd Dr Phillip John Aspinall
(*Primate of the Anglican Church of Australia and Archbishop of Brisbane*)

BRISBANE
Archbishop Most Revd Dr Phillip John Aspinall (*Metropolitan of the Province of Queensland and Primate of the Anglican Church of Australia*), GPO Box 421, Brisbane, QLD 4001   *Tel:* 61 7 3835 2222
Fax: 61 7 3832 5030
email: archbishop@anglicanbrisbane.org.au
Web: www.anglicanbrisbane.org.au

Assistant Bishops
Rt Revd Geoff Smith (*Bishop of the Southern Region*) (*same address*)   *Tel:* 61 7 3420 6941
Fax: 61 7 3420 6216
Rt Revd Jonathan Charles Holland (*Bishop of the Northern Region*) (*same address*)   *Tel:* 61 7 3835 2213
Fax: 61 7 3831 1170
email: jholland@anglicanbrisbane.org.au
Rt Revd Robert William Nolan (*Bishop of the Western Region*), Box 2600, Toowoomba, QLD 4350
Tel: 61 7 4639 1875
Fax: 61 7 4632 6882
email: nolan@anglicanbrisbane.org.au

NORTH QUEENSLAND
Bishop Rt Revd William James (Bill) Ray, PO Box 1244, Townsville, QLD 4810
Tel: 61 7 4771 4175
Fax: 61 7 4721 1756
email: bishopnq@anglicannq.org
Web: www.anglicannq.org

Assistant Bishops
Rt Revd Saibo Mabo (*Assistant Bishop and National Torres Strait Islander Bishop*), PO Box 714, Thursday Island, QLD 4875
Tel and *Fax:* 61 7 4069 1960
email: bishopti@anglicannq.org
Rt Revd James Randolph Leftwich (*Assistant Bishop and National Aboriginal Bishop*), 14 Village Tce, Redlynch QLD 4870   *Tel:* 61 7 4051 1055
Fax: 61 7 4051 1033
email: diocesecairns@bigpond.com

THE NORTHERN TERRITORY
Bishop Rt Revd Gregory Edwin (Greg) Thompson, PO Box 2950, Darwin, NT 0801
Tel: 61 8 8941 7440
Fax: 61 8 8941 7446
email: ntdiocese@internode.on.net
Web: www.northernterritory.anglican.org

ROCKHAMPTON
Bishop Rt Revd Godfrey Charles Fryar, PO Box 6158, Central Queensland Mail Centre, Rockhampton, QLD 4702   *Tel:* 61 7 4927 3188
Fax: 61 7 4922 4562
email: bishop@anglicanrock.org.au
Web: www.anglicanrock.org.au

PROVINCE OF SOUTH AUSTRALIA
Metropolitan Most Reverend Jeffrey William Driver (*Archbishop of Adelaide*)

ADELAIDE
Archbishop Most Reverend Jeffrey William Driver (*Metropolitan of the Province of South Australia*), 26 King William Rd, N Adelaide, SA 5006
Tel: 61 8 8305 9350
Fax: 61 8 8305 9399
email: archbishop@adelaide.anglican.com.au
Web: www.adelaide.anglican.com.au

Assistant Bishop
Bishop Rt Revd Stephen Kim Pickard (*same address*)
email: spickard@adelaide.anglican.com.au

THE MURRAY
Bishop Rt Revd Ross Owen Davies, PO Box 394, Murray Bridge, SA 5253   *Tel:* 61 8 8532 2270
Fax: 61 8 8532 5760
email: registry@murray.anglican.org
Web: www.murray.anglican.org

WILLOCHRA
Bishop Rt Revd Garry Weatherill, Bishop's House, Main Road North, Gladstone, SA 5473
Tel: 61 8 8662 2249
Fax: 61 8 8662 2070
email: bishop@diowillochra.org.au
Web: www.diowillochra.org.au

PROVINCE OF VICTORIA
Metropolitan Most Revd Philip Leslie Freier (*Archbishop of Melbourne*)

BALLARAT
Bishop Rt Revd Michael George Hough, PO Box 89, Ballarat, VIC 3350   *Tel:* 61 3 5331 1183
Fax: 61 3 5333 2982
email: bpsec@ballaratanglican.org.au
Web: www.ballaratanglican.org.au/

BENDIGO
Bishop Rt Revd Andrew William Curnow, PO Box 2, Bendigo, VIC 3552   *Tel:* 61 3 5443 4711
Fax: 61 3 5441 2173
email: bishop@bendigoanglican.org.au
Web: www.bendigoanglican.org.au

GIPPSLAND
Bishop Rt Revd John Charles McIntyre, PO Box 928, Sale, VIC 3853   *Tel:* 61 3 5144 2044
Fax: 61 3 5144 7183
email: bishop@gippsanglican.org.au
Web: www.gippsanglican.org.au

MELBOURNE
Archbishop Most Revd Philip Leslie Freier (*Metropolitan of the Province of Victoria*), The Anglican Centre, 209 Flinders Lane, Melbourne, VIC 3000   *Tel:* 61 3 9653 4220
Fax: 61 3 9650 2184
email: archbishopsoffice@melbourne.anglican.com.au
Web: www.melbourne.anglican.org.au/

Assistant Bishops
Rt Revd Paul Raymond White (*Bishop of the Southern Region*) (*same address*)
Tel: 61 3 9653 4220
Fax: 61 3 9653 4268
email: sthregbishop@melbourne.anglican.com.au
Rt Revd Philip Huggins (*Bishop of the North-Western Region*) (*same address*)
email: phuggins@melbourne.anglican.com.au

Rt Revd Stephen Hale (*Bishop of the Eastern Region*) (*same address*)
email: shale@melbourne.anglican.com.au

WANGARATTA
Bishop Rt Revd Anthony John Parkes, Bishop's Lodge, PO Box 457, Wangaratta VIC 3676
Tel: 61 3 5721 3484
Fax: 61 3 5722 1427
email: bishop@wangaratta.anglican.org
Web: www.wangaratta.anglican.org

PROVINCE OF WESTERN AUSTRALIA
Metropolitan Most Revd Roger Adrian Herft (*Archbishop of Perth*)

BUNBURY
Bishop Rt Revd William David Hair McCall, PO Box 15, Bunbury, WA 6231   *Tel:* 61 8 9721 2100
Fax: 61 8 9791 2300
email: bishop@bunbury.org.au
Web: www.bunbury.org.au

NORTH WEST AUSTRALIA
Bishop Rt Revd David Mulready, PO Box 2783, Geraldton, WA 6531   *Tel:* 61 8 9921 7277
Fax: 61 8 9964 2220
email: bishop@anglicandnwa.org
Web: www.anglicandnwa.org

PERTH
Archbishop Most Revd Roger Adrian Herft (*Metropolitan of the Province of Western Australia*), GPO Box W2067, Perth, WA 6846
Tel: 61 8 9325 7455
Fax: 61 8 9325 6741
email: archbishop@perth.anglican.org
Web: www.perth.anglican.org

Assistant Bishops
Rt Revd Kay Goldsworthy (*same address*)
Rt Revd Tom Wilmot (*same address*)
email: twilmot@perth.anglican.org

TASMANIA
Bishop Rt Revd John Douglas Harrower, OAM, GPO 748, Hobart, TAS 7001   *Tel:* 61 3 6220 2015
Fax: 61 3 6223 8968
email: bishop@anglicantas.org.au
Web: www.anglicantas.org.au/

DEFENCE FORCE
Bishop Rt Revd Len Eacott (*Anglican Bishop to the Australian Defence Force and Bishop Assistant to the Primate*), Department of Defence, DSG-Duntroon, ACT 2600   *Tel:* 61 2 9265 9935
Fax: 61 2 9265 9959
email: dfc@anglican.org.au
Web: www.anglican.org.au/defence

The Episcopal Anglican Church of Brazil

(Igreja Episcopal Anglicana do Brasil)

Members 106,415
The Episcopal Anglican Church of Brazil is the 19th Province of the Anglican Communion, and its work began in 1890 as a result of the missionary work of two north American missionaries in Porto Alegre: James Watson Morris and Lucien Lee Kinsolving. Autonomy from the Episcopal Church in the United States was granted in 1965. The Episcopal Church now has more than a hundred thousand baptized members and a team of more than two hundred clergy, among whom are thirty women priests. It has established communities, and educational and social institutions, in the main urban areas of Brazil. The Brazilian province comprises nine dioceses: Southern, Southwestern, Rio de Janeiro, São Paulo, Recife, Brasília, Pelotas, Curitiba and Amazon. It also has one missionary district: Missionary District West.

Primate Most Revd Mauricio José Araújo Andrade (*Bishop of Brazília*)
email: mandrade@ieab.org.br
Web: www.ieab.org.br

Provincial Secretary Revd Canon Francisco de Assis da Silva

Provincial Offices PO Box 11.510, Teresópolis, CEP 90870–970, Porto Alegre, RS
Tel and Fax: 55 51 3318 6200
email: fassis@ieab.org.br

Provincial Treasurer Mrs Lucimara Feijó, Caixa Postal 11510, CEP 90841–970, Porto Alegre, RS
Tel and Fax: 55 51 3318 6200
email: lfieab@gmail.com

CHURCH PAPER
Estandarte Cristão, a bimonthly church journal in Portuguese, published since 1893, which contains general articles and news about the life of the Church at local, national and international level. This journal is the main channel of the Communication Department of the Church. *Editorial Offices:* Caixa Postal 11510, CEP 90870–970, Porto Alegre, RS   *Tel and Fax:* 55 51 3318 6200
email: comunicacao@ieab.org.br

AMAZON
Bishop Rt Revd Saulo Mauricio de Barros, Av. Sezerdelo Correia, 514, Batista Campos, 66025–240, Belem, PA   *Tel and Fax:* 55 91 3241 9720
email: saulomauricio@gmail.com

BRASÍLIA

Bishop Most Revd Maurício José Araújo de Andrade (*Primate of the Episcopal Anglican Church of Brazil*), EQS 309/310, sala 1 – Asa Sul, Caixa Postal 093, 70359–970, Brasília, DF
Tel: 55 61 3443 4305
Fax: 55 61 3443 4337
email: mandrade@ieab.org.br
Web: www.dab.ieab.org.br

CURITIBA

Bishop Rt Revd Naudal Alves Gomes, Rua Sete de Setembro, 3927 – Centro, 80250-010 Curitiba, PR
Tel: 55 41 3232 0917
email: naudal@yahoo.com.br

PELOTAS

Bishop Rt Revd Renato da Cruz Raatz, Rua Felix da Cunha, 425 – Centro, Caixa Postal 791, 96001–970 Pelotas, RS   *Tel* and *Fax:* 55 53 3227 7120
email: renatoraatz@bol.com.br
Web: www.dap.ieab.org.br

RECIFE

Bishop Rt Revd Sebastião Armando Gameleira Soares, Rua Virgílio Mota, 70, Parnamirim, 52060–582, Recife, PE   *Tel:* 55 81 3441 6843
email: sgameleira@gmail.com
Web: www.dar.ieab.org.br

RIO DE JANEIRO

Bishop Rt Revd Filadelfo Oliveira Neto, Rua Fonseca Guimarães, 12 Sta.Teresa, 20240–260, Rio de Janeiro, RJ   *Tel:* 55 21 2220 2148
Fax: 55 21 2252 9686
email: oliveira.ieab@gmail.com
Web: www.anglicana.com.br

SÃO PAULO

Bishop Rt Revd Douglas Bird, Rua Borges Lagoa, 172 – Vila Clementino, 04038–030 São Paulo, SP
Tel: 55 11 5549 9086/5579 9011
Fax: 55 11 5083 2619
email: roger@uol.com.br
Web: www.dasp.org.br

SOUTH WESTERN BRAZIL

Bishop Rt Revd Jubal Pereira Neves, Av. Rio Branco, 880/Sub-solo – Centro, Caixa Postal 116, 97010–970 Santa Maria, RS
Tel and *Fax:* 55 55 3221 4328
email: bispodso@via-rs.net
Web: www.swbrazil.anglican.org

SOUTHERN BRAZIL

Bishop Rt Revd Orlando Santos de Oliveira, Av. Eng. Ludolfo Boehl, 278, Teresópolis, 91720–150, Porto Alegre, RS   *Tel* and *Fax:* 55 51 318 6199
email: dmbispo@terra.com.br
Web: www.dm.ieab.org.br

Eglise Anglicane du Burundi

(The Province of the Anglican Church of Burundi)

Members 850,000
There are at least 850,000 Anglicans out of an estimated population of just over 8 million in Burundi. An Anglican presence was established through the work of the CMS in the 1930s and grew rapidly as a result of the East African revival. The former Ruanda Mission (now CMS) set up its first mission stations at Buhiga and Matana in 1935, and Buye in 1936. Activities were mainly focused on evangelism, education and medical work. The first national bishop was consecrated in 1965 and Buye diocese was created, covering the whole country. The Church of the Province of Burundi now consists of six dioceses, and it has been an independent province within the Anglican Communion since 1992. Among the Church's main concerns are peace and reconciliation, repatriation of returnees, community development, literacy, education, and health. It is committed to mission and evangelism with faith in the risen Christ as Lord and Saviour central to its preaching and teaching. It is concerned to support theological education and training for ministry, based on the authority of Scripture.

Primate Most Revd Bernard Ntahoturi (*Archbishop of Burundi and Bishop of Matana*)

Provincial Secretary Revd Pédaçuli Birakengana, BP 2098, Bujumbura   *Tel:* 257 22 224 389
Fax: 257 22 229 129
email: peab@cbinf.com
Provincial Accountant Christine Niyonkuru

THEOLOGICAL COLLEGES
Matana Theological Institute (Provincial)
Canon Warner Memorial College, EAB Buye, BP 94 Ngozi
Kosiya Shalita Bible College, EAB Matana, DS 13, Bujumbura *or* BP 447, Bujumbura
Buhiga College, EAB Gitega, BP 23 Gitega
Makamba College, EAB Makamba, BP 96 Makamba
Bujumbura Bible College, EAB Bujumbura, BP 1300 Bujumbura

BUJUMBURA

Bishop Rt Revd Pie Ntukamazina, BP 1300, Bujumbura   *Tel:* 257 22 249 104/5
Fax: 257 22 227 495
email: mgrpie@cbinf.com/bishoppie@yahoo.com

BUYE
Bishop Rt Revd Sixbert Macumi, BP 94, Ngozi
Tel: 257 22 302 210
Fax: 257 22 302 317
email: buyedioc@yahoo.fr

GITEGA
Bishop Rt Revd Jean Nduwayo, BP 23, Gitega
Tel: 257 22 402 247
email: eebgitega@cbinf.com

MAKAMBA
Bishop Rt Revd Martin Blaise Nyaboho, BP 96,
Makamba   Tel: 257 22 508 080
Fax: 257 22 229 129
email: eabdiocmak@yahoo.fr

MATANA
Bishop Most Revd Bernard Ntahoturi (*Archbishop of Burundi*), BP 447, Bujumbura
Tel: 257 79 924 595
Fax: 257 22 229 129
email: ntahober@cbinf.com/
ntahober@yahoo.co.uk

MUYINGA
Bishop Rt Revd Eraste Bigirimana, BP 55, Muyinga
Tel: 257 22 306 019
Fax: 257 22 306 152
email: bigirimanaeraste@yahoo.fr/
eabmuyinga@yahoo.fr

The Anglican Church of Canada

Members 641,845 (2001)

The Anglican witness in Canada started in the eighteenth century with the Church Missionary Society and the United Society for the Propagation of the Gospel. The Eucharist was first celebrated in Frobisher Bay (now Iqaluit) in 1578; the first church building was St Paul's, Halifax in 1750. The Church includes a large number of the original inhabitants of Canada (Indians, Inuit, and Metis) and has been a strong advocate of their rights. A book of alternative services was published in 1985. The Church has a strong international role in crisis assistance through the Primate's World Relief and Development Fund (PWRDF).

Primate of The Anglican Church of Canada Most Revd Fred J. Hiltz, 80 Hayden St, Toronto, ON, M4Y 3G2   Tel: 1 416 924 9192
Fax: 1 416 924 0211
email: primate@national.anglican.ca
Web: www.anglican.ca

General Secretary Ven. Dr Michael F. Pollesel
email: general.secretary@national.anglican.ca

General Treasurer Ms Michèle George
email: mgeorge@national.anglican.ca

Offices of the General Synod and of its Departments
80 Hayden St, Toronto ON, M4Y 3G2
Tel: 1 416 924 9192
Fax: 1 416 968 7983

National Indigenous Anglican Bishop Rt Revd Mark L. MacDonald (*same address*)
email: mmacdonald@national.anglican.ca
Web: http://www.anglican.ca/im/index.htm

UNIVERSITIES AND COLLEGES OF THE ANGLICAN CHURCH OF CANADA
British Columbia
Vancouver School of Theology*, 6000 Iona Dr, Vancouver, BC, V6T 1L4 (*Principal* Revd Dr Wendy Fletcher)   *email:* vstinfo@vst.edu

Manitoba
Henry Budd College for Ministry, Box 2518, The Pas MB, R9A IM3 (*Joint Co-ordinators* Ms Marion Jenkins and Revd Paul Sodtke)
email: hbcm@mts.net

St John's College, 92 Dysart Rd, Winnipeg, MB, R3T 2M5 (*Warden* Dr Janet Hoskins)
email: stjohns_college@umanitoba.ca

Newfoundland
Queen's College, 210 Prince Philip Dr (Q3000), St John's NF, A1B 3R6 (*Provost* Canon Dr John Mellis)   *email:* queens@mun.ca

Nova Scotia
Atlantic School of Theology*, 660 Francklyn St, Halifax, NS, B3H 3B5 (*Principal* Canon Dr Eric Beresford)
email: dmaclachlan@astheology.ns.ca

Nunavut
Arthur Turner Training School *Enquiries to* Diocese of the Arctic, Box 190, Yellowknife, NT X1A 2N2

Ontario
Canterbury College, 172 Patricia Rd, Windsor ON, N9B 3B9 (*Principal* Dr Gordon Drake)
email: canter@uwindsor.ca
Huron University College, 1349 Western Rd, London, ON, N6G 1H3 (*Principal* Dr Ramona Lumpkin)   *email:* rlumpkin@uwo.ca
Renison College, Westmount Rd N, Waterloo, ON, N2L 3G4 (*Principal* Dr John Crossley)
email: jecrossley@renison.uwaterloo.ca
Thorneloe College, Ramsey Lake Rd, Sudbury, ON, P3E 2C6 (*Provost* Revd Dr Robert Derrenbacker)
email: thorneprov@laurentian.ca

ANGLICAN AND PORVOO COMMUNIONS

Trinity College, 6 Hoskin Ave, Toronto, ON, M5S 1H8 (*Dean of Divinity* Revd Canon Dr David Neelands) *email:* divinity@trinity.utoronto.ca Wycliffe College, 5 Hoskin Ave, Toronto, ON, M5S 1H7 (*Principal* Revd Dr George Sumner) *email:* wycliffe.college@utoronto.ca

Quebec
Bishop's University, PO Box 5000, Lennoxville, QC, J1M 1Z7 *email:* amontgom@ubishops.ca Montreal Diocesan Theological College, 3473 University St, Montreal, QC, H3A 2A8 (*Principal* Canon Dr John Simons)
email: diocoll@netrover.com

Saskatchewan
College of Emmanuel and St Chad, 1337 College Dr, Saskatoon, SK, S7N OW6 (*Principal* Revd Dr William Richards)
email: emmanuel.stchad@usask.ca
*Ecumenical

CHURCH PAPERS
Anglican Journal/Journal anglican Tabloid format, national church paper under management of a Board of Trustees appointed by General Synod. It circulates as an insert for a number of diocesan publications. Issued monthly except July and August. *Editorial Offices:* 80 Hayden St, Toronto, ON M4Y 3G2.
email: anglican.journal@national.anglican.ca

Ministry Matters Published electronically three times a year by the Communication and Information Resources Dept of General Synod. Intended primarily for clergy and lay leaders. *Editorial Offices:* 80 Hayden St, Toronto, ON M4Y 3G2
email: ministry.matters@national.anglican.ca

PROVINCE OF BRITISH COLUMBIA AND YUKON
Metropolitan Most Revd John E. Privett (*Bishop of Kootenay*)

BRITISH COLUMBIA
Bishop Rt Revd James A. J. Cowan, 900 Vancouver St, Victoria, BC, V8V 3V7
Tel: 1 250 386 7781
Fax: 1 250 386 4013
email: synod@bc.anglican.ca
Web: www.bc.anglican.ca

CALEDONIA
Bishop Rt Revd William J. Anderson, PO Box 278, Prince Rupert, BC, V8J 3P6   *Tel:* 1 250 624 6013
Fax: 1 250 624 4299
email: synodofc@citytel.net
Web: www.caledonia.anglican.org

CENTRAL INTERIOR, ANGLICAN PARISHES OF
Bishop Rt Revd Barbara J. Andrews, 250–546 St Paul St, Kamloops BC V2C 5T1
Tel: 1 778 471 5573
Fax: 1 778 471 5586
email: apcioffice@shawbiz.ca
Web: www.apcionline.ca

KOOTENAY
Bishop Most Revd John E. Privett, 1876 Richter St, Kelowna, BC, V1Y 2M9   *Tel:* 1 250 762 3306
Fax: 1 250 762 4150
email: diocese_of_kootenay@telus.net
Web: www.kootenay.anglican.ca

NEW WESTMINSTER
Bishop Rt Revd Michael C. Ingham, Suite 580, 401 West Georgia St, Vancouver, BC, V6B 5A1
Tel: 1 604 684 6306
Fax: 1 604 684 7017
email: bishop@vancouver.anglican.ca
Web: www.vancouver.anglican.ca

YUKON
Bishop Rt Revd Larry D. Robertson, PO Box 31136, Whitehorse, Yukon Y1A 5P7
Tel: 1 867 667 7746
Fax: 1 867 667 6125
email: synodoffice@klondiker.com
Web: http://anglican.yukon.net

PROVINCE OF CANADA
Metropolitan Most Revd Claude E. W. Miller (*Bishop of Fredericton*)

CENTRAL NEWFOUNDLAND
Bishop Rt Revd F. David Torraville, 34 Fraser Rd, Gander, NL, A1V 2E8   *Tel:* 1 709 256 2372
Fax: 1 709 256 2396
email: bishopcentral@nfld.net
Web: www.centraldiocese.org

EASTERN NEWFOUNDLAND AND LABRADOR
Bishop Rt Revd Cyrus C. J. Pitman, 19 King's Bridge Rd, St John's, NL, A1C 3K4
Tel: 1 709 576 6697
Fax: 1 709 576 7122
email: cpitman@anglicanenl.nf.net
Web: www.nfol.ca

FREDERICTON
Bishop Rt Revd Claude E. W. Miller, 115 Church St, Fredericton, NB, E3B 4C8   *Tel:* 1 506 459 1801
Fax: 1 506 460 0520
email: diocese@anglican.nb.ca
Web: www.anglican.nb.ca

MONTREAL
Bishop Rt Revd Barry B. Clarke, 1444 Union Ave, Montreal, QC, H3A 2B8   *Tel:* 1 514 843 6577
Fax: 1 514 843 3221
email: bishops.office@montreal.anglican.org
Web: www.montreal.anglican.org

NOVA SCOTIA AND PRINCE EDWARD ISLAND
Bishop Rt Revd Susan Moxley, 6017, Quinpool Rd, Halifax, NS, B3K 5J6   *Tel:* 1 902 420 0717
Fax: 1 902 425 0717
email: office@nspeidiocese.ca
Web: www.nspeidiocese.ca
Suffragan Bishop Rt Revd Ronald W. Cutler (*same address*)

QUEBEC
Bishop Rt Revd Dennis P. Drainville, 31 rue des Jardins, Quebec, QC, G1R 4L6
Tel: 1 418 692 3858
Fax: 1 418 692 3876
email: synodoffice@quebec.anglican.ca
Web: www.quebec.anglican.org

WESTERN NEWFOUNDLAND
Bishop Rt Revd Percy D. Coffin, 25 Main St, Corner Brook, NF, A2H 1C2   *Tel:* 1 709 639 8712
Fax: 1 709 639 1636
email: dsown@nf.aibn.ca
Web: www.westernnewfoundland.anglican.org

PROVINCE OF ONTARIO
Metropolitan Most Revd Colin R. Johnson (*Archbishop of Toronto*)

ALGOMA
Bishop Rt Revd Stephen Andrews, Box 1168, Sault Ste Marie, ON, P6A 5N7   *Tel:* 1 705 256 5061
Fax: 1 705 946 1860
email: bishop@dioceseofalgoma.com
Web: www.dioceseofalgoma.com

HURON
Bishop Rt Revd Robert F. Bennett, 190 Queens Ave, London, ON N6A 6H7   *Tel:* 1 519 434 6893
Fax: 1 519 673 4151
email: bishops@huron.anglican.org
Web: www.diohuron.org
Suffragan Rt Revd Terrance A. Dance (*same address*)

MOOSONEE
Archbishop Rt Revd Thomas A. Corston, Box 841, Schumacher, ON, P0N 1G0   *Tel:* 1 705 360 1129
Fax: 1 705 360 1120
email: dmoose@domaa.ca
Web: http://moosonee.anglican.org

NIAGARA
Bishop Rt Revd Michael A. Bird, Cathedral Place, 252 James St North, Hamilton, ON, L8R 2L3
Tel: 1 905 527 1316
Fax: 1 905 527 1281
email: bishop@niagara.anglican.ca
Web: www.niagara.anglican.ca

ONTARIO
Bishop Rt Revd George L. R. Bruce, 90 Johnson St, Kingston, ON, K7L 1X7   *Tel:* 1 613 544 4774
Fax: 1 613 547 3745
email: gbruce@ontario.anglican.ca
Web: www.ontario.anglican.ca

OTTAWA
Bishop Rt Revd John H. Chapman, 71 Bronson Ave, Ottawa, ON, K1R 6G6   *Tel:* 1 613 232 7124
Fax: 1 613 232 3955
email: c/o ann-day@ottawa.anglican.ca
Web: www.ottawa.anglican.ca

TORONTO
Bishop Most Revd Colin R. Johnson, 135 Adelaide St East, Toronto, ON, M5C 1L8
Tel: 1 416 363 6021
Fax: 1 416 363 3683
email: cjohnson@toronto.anglican.ca
Web: www.toronto.anglican.ca

Area Bishops
Rt Revd Linda Nicholls (*Trent-Durham Area*), 965 Dundas St West, Suite 207, Whitby, ON, L1P 1G8
Tel: 1 905 668 1558
Fax: 1 905 688 8216
email: lnicholls@toronto.anglican.ca
Rt Revd M. George H. Elliott (*York-Simcoe Area*), 2174 King Rd, Suite 2, King City, ON, L7B 1L6
Tel: 1 905 833 8327
Fax: 1 905 833 8329
email: ysimcoe@neptune.on.ca
Rt Revd Patrick T. Yu (*York-Scarborough Area*), 135 Adelaide St East, Toronto, ON, M5C 1L8
Tel: 1 416 363 6021
Fax: 1 416 363 3683
email: patyu@toronto.anglican.ca
Rt Revd M. Philip Poole (*York Credit Valley*), 135 Adelaide St East, Toronto, ON, M5C 1L8
Tel: 1 416 363 6021
Fax: 1 416 363 3683
email: ppoole@toronto.anglican.ca

PROVINCE OF RUPERT'S LAND
Metropolitan Most Revd David N. Ashdown (*Archbishop of Keewatin*)

THE ARCTIC
Bishop Rt Revd Andrew P. Atagotaaluk, Box 190, Yellowknife, NT, X1A 2N2
Tel: 1 867 873 5432
Fax: 1 867 873 8478
email: diocese@arcticnet.org
Web: www.arctic.anglican.org

Suffragan Bishops
Rt Revd Benjamin T. Arreak (*Nunavik Region*), Box 154, Kuujjuaqq, QC, J0M 1C0
Tel: 1 819 964 2324
Fax: 1 819 964 2113
email: btarreak@sympatico.ca

Vacancy (*Mackenzie and Kitikmeot Region*), Box 190, Yellowknife, NT, X1A 2N2
Tel: 1 867 873 5432
Fax: 1 867 873 8478

ATHABASCA
Archbishop Rt Revd Fraser W. Lawton, Box 6868, Peace River, AB, T8S 1S6   *Tel:* 1 780 624 2767
Fax: 1 780 624 2365
email: bpath@telusplanet.net
Web: www.dioath.ca

BRANDON
Bishop Rt Revd James D. Njegovan, Box 21009, W.E.P.O., Brandon, MB, R7B 3W8
Tel: 1 204 727 7550
Fax: 1 204 727 4135
email: bishopbdn@mts.net
Web: www.dioceseofbrandon.org

CALGARY
Bishop Rt Revd Derek B. E. Hoskin, 560–1207 11th Ave SW, Calgary, AB, T3C 0M5
Tel: 1 403 243 3673
Fax: 1 403 243 2182
email: synod@calgary.anglican.ca
Web: www.calgary.anglican.ca

EDMONTON
Bishop Rt Revd Jane Alexander, 10035–103 St, Edmonton, AB, T5J 0X5   *Tel:* 1 780 439 7344
Fax: 1 780 439 6549
email: bishop@edmonton.anglican.ca
Web: www.edmonton.anglican.org

KEEWATIN
Archbishop Most Revd David N. Ashdown, 915 Ottawa St, Keewatin, ON, P0X 1C0

Tel: 1 807 547 3353
Fax: 1 807 547 3356
email: dioceseofkeewatin@shaw.ca
Web: www.gokenora.com/~dioceseofkeewatin

Area Bishop for Northern Ontario Region Rt Revd Lydia Mamakwa, Box 65, Kingfisher Lake, ON P0X 1Z0   *Tel:* 1 807 532 2067
Fax: 1 807 737 0731
email: lydiam@kingfisherlake.ca

QU'APPELLE
Bishop Rt Revd Gregory K. Kerr-Wilson, 1501 College Ave, Regina, SK, S4P 1B8
Tel: 1 306 522 1608
Fax: 1 306 352 6808
email: quappelle@sasktel.net
Web: http://diocse.sasktelwebsite.net

RUPERT'S LAND
Bishop Rt Revd Donald D. Phillips, 935 Nesbitt Bay, Winnipeg, MB, R3T 1W6   *Tel:* 1 204 922 4200
Fax: 1 204 922 4219
email: general@rupertsland.ca
Web: www.rupertsland.ca

SASKATCHEWAN
Bishop Rt Revd Michael W. Hawkins, 1308 5th Ave East, Prince Albert, SK, S6V 2H7
Tel: 1 306 763 2455
Fax: 1 306 764 5172
email: synod@sasktel.net
Web: www.saskatchewan.anglican.org

SASKATOON
Bishop Rt Revd David M. Irving, PO Box 1965, Saskatoon, SK, S7K 3S5   *Tel:* 1 306 244 5651
Fax: 1 306 933 4606
email: anglicansynod@sasktel.net
Web: www.saskatoon.anglican.org

The Church of the Province of Central Africa

Members 600,000
The province includes Botswana, Malawi, Zambia and Zimbabwe. The first Anglican missionary to Malawi was Bishop Charles Mackenzie who arrived with David Livingstone in 1861. The province was inaugurated in 1955 and has a movable bishopric. The countries forming the province are very different. Zambia and Botswana suffer the difficulties of rapid industrialization, along with underdevelopment and thinly populated areas. In Malawi 30% of the adult males are away as migrant labourers in other countries at any given time. Zimbabwe is experiencing problems of social adjustment after independence.

Archbishop of the Province Vacancy

Provincial Secretary Vacancy

Provincial Treasurer Mr R. Kanja, CPCA, PO Box 22317, Kitwe, Zambia   *Tel:* 260 351 081
260 9719 5368 (Mobile)
Fax: 267 351 668

ANGLICAN THEOLOGICAL COLLEGES
Leonard Kamungu (Anglican) Theological College, PO Box 959, Zomba. Malawi (*Dean* Revd Alinafe Kalemba)   *Tel:* 265 1 525 286
265 8 856 410 (Mobile)
National Anglican Theological College of Zimbabwe (Ecumenical Institute of Theology), 11 Thornburg Ave, Groom Bridge, Mount Pleasant, Harare, Zimbabwe
St John's Seminary, Mindolo, PO Box 20369, Kitwe, Zambia (*Rector* Rt Revd John Osmers)
Tel: 260 2 210960
email: josmers@zamnet.zm

CHURCH PAPER
Link Monthly newspaper for the Dioceses of Mashonaland and Matabeleland giving news and views of the dioceses. *Editorial Offices* Link Board of Management, PO Box UA7, Harare City.

BOTSWANA
Bishop Rt Revd Trevor Mwamba, PO Box 679, Gaborone, Botswana   *Tel:* 267 395 3779
Fax: 267 391 3015
email: angli_diocese@info.bw / musonda_mwamba@yahoo.com

CENTRAL ZAMBIA
Bishop Rt Revd Derek Gary Kamukwamba, PO Box 70172, Ndola, Zambia   *Tel:* 260 2 612 431
email: adcznla@zamnet.zm

CENTRAL ZIMBABWE
Bishop Rt Revd Ishmael Mukuwanda, PO Box 25, Gweru, Zimbabwe   *Tel:* 263 54 21 030
Fax: 263 54 21 097
email: diocent@telconet.co.zw / imukuwanda@gmail.com

EASTERN ZAMBIA
Bishop Rt Revd William Muchombo, PO Box 510154, Chipata, Zambia
Tel and *Fax:* 260 216 221 294
email: dioeastzm@zamnet.zm

HARARE
Bishop Rt Revd Chad Gandiya, Monmouth Rd, Avondale, Harare, Zimbabwe
Tel: 263 4 308 042
email: diohrecpca@ecoweb.co.zw

LAKE MALAWI
Bishop Rt Revd Francis Kaulanda, PO Box 30349, Lilongwe 3, Malawi   *Tel:* 265 797 858 (Office)
265 794 268 (Home)
Fax: 265 731 966
email: anglama@eomw.net

LUAPULA
Bishop Rt Revd Robert Mumbi, PO Box 710210, Mansa, Luapula, Zambia
emaill: diopula@zamtel.zm

LUSAKA
Bishop Rt Revd David Njovu, Bishop's Lodge, PO Box 30183, Lusaka, Zambia

Tel: 260 211 254 789 (Office)
260 211 252 449 (Home)
Fax: 260 1 254789
email: dnjovu@zamnet.zm

MANICALAND
Bishop Rt Revd Julius Makoni, 115 Herbert Chitepo St, Mutare, Zimbabwe
Tel: 263 20 64 194
Fax: 263 20 63 076
email: diomani@syscom.co.zw

MASVINGO
Bishop Rt Revd Godfrey Tawonezvi, PO Box 1421, Masvingo, Zambia   *Tel:* 263 39 362 536
email: bishopgodfreytawonezvi@gmail.com / anglicandiomsv@comone.co.zw

MATABELELAND
Bishop Rt Revd Wilson Sitshebo, PO Box 2422, Bulaweyo, Zimbabwe   *Tel:* 263 9 61 370
Fax: 263 9 68 353
email: angdiomat@telconet.co.zw / bishmat@mweb.co.zw

NORTHERN MALAWI
Bishop Rt Revd Leslie Mtekateka, Box 120, Mzuzu, Malawi, Central Africa   *Tel:* 265 331 486
Fax: 265 333 805
email: bishopboyle@sdnp.org.mw

NORTHERN ZAMBIA
Bishop Rt Revd Albert Chama, PO Box 20798, Kitwe, Zambia
Tel: 260 2 223 264 (Office) / 260 2 230 082 (Home)
Fax: 260 2 224 778
email: cpca@zamnet.zm

SOUTHERN MALAWI
Bishop Rt Revd James Tengatenga, PO Box 30220, Chichiri, Blantyre, 3, Malawi   *Tel:* 265 1 641 218
Tel: 265 1 641 218
Fax: 265 1 641 235
email: angsoma@sdnp.org.mw / jatenga@sdnp.org.mw

SOUTHERN MALAWI – UPPER SHIRE
Bishop Rt Revd Brighton Vitta Malasa, Private Bag 1, Chilema, Zomba, Malawi
Tel and *Fax:* 265 1 539 514
265 9545 609 (Mobile)
email: dionorth@zamnet.zm

The Anglican Church of the Central American Region

(Iglesia Anglicana de la Región Central de América)

Members 15,600
This province of the Anglican Communion is made up of the Dioceses of Guatemala, El Salvador, Nicaragua, Costa Rica and Panama. The Church was introduced by the Society for the

Propagation of the Gospel when England administered two colonies in Central America, Belize (1783–1982) and Miskitia (1740–1894). In the later years Afro-Antillean people brought their Anglican Christianity with them. The province is multicultural and multiracial and is committed to evangelization, social outreach, and community development.

Primate Most Revd Martin de Jesus Barahona Pascacio (*Bishop of El Salvador*)

Provincial Secretary Rt Revd Hector Monterroso (*Bishop of Costa Rica*)   *Tel:* 506 253 0790
Fax: 506 253 8331
email: iarca@amnet.co.cr

Provincial Treasurer Mr Harold Charles, Apt R, Balboa, Republic of Panama   *Tel:* 507 212 0062
Fax: 507 262 2097
email: iarcahch@sinfo.net

COSTA RICA
Bishop Rt Revd Hector Monterroso, Apt 10502, 1000 San José, Costa Rica   *Tel:* 506 225 0209/253 0790
Fax: 506 253 8331
email: anglicancr@racsa.co.cr/iarca@amnet.co.cr

EL SALVADOR
Bishop Most Revd Martin de Jesus Barahona Pascacio (*Primate of the Anglican Church of the Central American Region*), 47 Avenida Sur, 723 Col

Flor Blanca, Apt Postal (01), 274 San Salvador, El Salvador   *Tel:* 503 2223 2252
Fax: 503 2223 7952
email: anglican.sal@integra.com.sv

GUATEMALA
Bishop Rt Revd Armando Román Guerra-Soria, Apt 58A, Avenida La Castellana 40–06, Guatemala City, Guatemala   *Tel:* 502 2472 0852
Fax: 502 2472 0764
email: diocesis@terra.com.gt/
diocesis@infovia.com.gt

NICARAGUA
Bishop Rt Revd Sturdie Downs, Apt 1207, Managua, Nicaragua   *Tel:* 505 2225 174
Fax: 505 2226 701
email: episcnic@cablenet.com.ni/
episcnic@tmx.com.ni

PANAMA
Bishop Rt Revd Julio Murray, Box R, Balboa, Republic of Panama
Tel: 507 212 0062/507 262 2051
Fax: 507 262 2097
email: iepan@cwpanama.net/anglipan@sinfo.net
Web: www.episcopalpanama.org

The Church of the Province of Congo

Members 500,000
Ugandan evangelist Apolo Kivebulaya established an Anglican presence in the Democratic Republic of Congo (formerly Zaire) in 1896. The Church reached the Katanga (formerly Saba) region in 1955, but evangelization did not progress on a large scale until the 1970s. Following independence, the Church expanded and formed dioceses as part of the Province of Uganda, Burundi, Rwanda, and Boga-Zaire. The new province was inaugurated in 1992 and changed its name in 1997. On 17 September 2002 the then Archbishop Njojo and many other Congolese citizens had to flee to Uganda because of internal tribal warfare.

Archbishop Most Revd Dr Fidèle Dirokpa Balufuga (*Bishop of Kinshasa*)

Provincial Secretary Rt Revd Jean Molanga Botola (*Assistant Bishop of Kinshasa*)

Provincial Treasurer and Liaison Office in Kampala Mr Fréderick Ngadjole, PO Box 25586, Kampala, Uganda   *Tel:* 256 77264 7495
email: eac-mags@infocom.co.ug

Provincial Coordinator of Evangelism Ven Ise Somo Muhindo, PO Box 506, Bwera-Kasese, Uganda/ BP : 322, Butembo, DR Congo
Tel: 243 998548 601 (Mobile)
email: revd_isesomo@yahoo.fr

THEOLOGICAL COLLEGE
The Anglican Theological Seminary (Institut Supérieur Théologique Anglican, ISThA, *Principal* Canon Sabiti Tibafa), PO Box 25586, Kampala, Uganda   Tel: 243 99 779 1013
email: revdsabiti@yahoo.fr

ARU
Bishop Rt Revd Dr Georges Titre Ande, PO Box 25586 Kampala, Uganda   *or* c/o PO Box 226, Arua, Uganda   Tel: 243 81 039 30 71
email: revdande@yahoo.co.uk

BOGA (*formerly* BOGA-ZAIRE)
Bishop Rt Revd Henri Isingoma Kahwa, PO Box 25586, Kampala, Uganda   Tel: 243 99 333 090
email: peac_isingoma@yahoo.fr

BUKAVU
Bishop Rt Revd Sylvestre Bahati Bali-Busane, Av. Mgr Ndahura, No. Q/Nyalukemba, C/Ibanda, CAC-Bukavu, BP 2876, Bukavu, Democratic Republic of Congo / PO Box 134, Cyangugu, Rwanda   Tel: 243 99 401 3647
email: bahati_bali@yahoo.fr

KATANGA
Bishop Rt Revd Corneille Kasima Muno, PO Box 22037, Kitwe, Zambia   *Tel:* 243 97 047 173
Fax: 243 81 475 6075
email: kasimamuno@yahoo.fr

KINDU
Bishop Rt Revd Zacharie Masimango Katanda
(Dean of the Province), BP 5, Gisenyi, Rwanda
Tel: 243 99 891 6258
243 813 286 255 (Mobile)
email: angkindu@yahoo.fr

KINSHASA (Missionary diocese)
Bishop Vacancy, 11 Ave. Basalakala, Quartier
Immocongo Commune de Kalamu, Kinshasa 1,
B.P. 16482, DR Congo   *Tel:* 243 998 611 180
(Mobile)
email: dirokpa1@hotmail.com /
anglikin@yahoo.fr
Assistant Bishops
Rt Revd Jean Molanga Botola, EAC-Kinshasa, BP
16482, Kinshasa 1, DR Congo
Tel: 243 998 623 508 (Mobile)
email: molanga2k@yahoo.co.uk

Rt Revd Abiodun Olaoye *(same address)*
(Missionary in Kinsai)   *Tel:* 243 818 995 591
email: bishopolaoyeat@yahoo.com

KISANGANI
Bishop Rt Revd Lambert Funga Botolome, Av.
Bowane, N°10, Quartier des Musiciens,
C/Makiso, PO Box 86, Kisangani, DR Congo *or*
c/o PO Box 25586, Kampala, Uganda
Tel: 243 997 252 868 (Mobile)
email: lambertfunga@hotmail.com

NORD KIVU
Bishop Vacancy, PO Box 506, Bwera-Kasese,
Uganda
Assistant Bishop Rt Revd Enoch Kayeeye *(same address)*   *Tel:* 243 99 414 8579
email: email: bpkayeeye@hotmail.com

The Church of England

Baptized members 26,000,000
Covering all of England, the Isle of Man and the
Channel Islands; Europe except Great Britain and
Ireland; Morocco; Turkey; and the Asian countries of the former Soviet Union. The Church of
England is the ancient national Church of the
land. Its structures emerged from the missionary
work of St Augustine, sent from Rome in AD 597,
and from the work of Celtic missionaries in the
north. Throughout the Middle Ages, the Church
was in communion with the See of Rome, but in
the sixteenth century it separated from Rome and
rejected the authority of the Pope. The Church
of England is the established Church, with its
administration governed by a General Synod,
which meets twice a year.

Hong Kong Sheng Kung Hui

(Hong Kong Anglican Church)

Members 30,000
This dynamic province was inaugurated in 1998.
The history of the Church in China dates back to
the mid-nineteenth century; missionaries were
provided by the American Church, the Church of
England, the Church of England in Canada, etc.
The Province of Chung Hua Sheng Kung Hui (the
Holy Catholic Church in China) was established
in 1912 of which the Anglican Church in Hong
Kong and Macau was an integral part. Chung Hua
Sheng Kung Hui ceased to exist in the 1950s and
the diocese of Hong Kong and Macau was associated to other dioceses in South East Asia under the
custodianship of the Council of Churches of East
Asia, until the recent establishment of the diocese
as the 38th province of the Anglican Communion.
It has parishes in Hong Kong and Macau, which
returned to Chinese sovereignty in 1997 and 1999
respectively. It enjoys autonomy and independence as guaranteed by the Basic Law (the mini
constitution governing Hong Kong, the Special
Administrative Region of China).

Primate Most Revd Paul Kwong, Provincial
Office, Bishop's House, 1 Lower Albert Rd,
Central Hong Kong SAR   *Tel:* 852 2526 5355
Fax: 852 2521 2199
email: office1@hkskh.org
Web: www.hkskh.org

Provincial Secretary General Revd Peter Douglas
Koon *(same address)*
email: peter.koon@hkskh.org

Bishop of Hong Kong Island Most Revd Paul
Kwong, 25/F Wyndham Place, 40–44, Wyndham
Street, Central, Hong Kong SAR
Tel: 852 2526 5366
Fax: 852 2523 3344
email: do.dhk@hkskh.org
Web: http://dhk.hkskh.org

Bishop of Eastern Kowloon Rt Revd Louis
Tsui, Diocesan Office, 4/F Holy Trinity Bradbury

Centre, 139 Ma Tau Chung Rd, Kowloon City, Kowloon, Hong Kong SAR   *Tel:* 852 2713 9983
Fax: 852 2711 1609
email: ekoffice@ekhkskh.org.hk
Web: ekhkskh.org.hk

Bishop of Western Kowloon Rt Revd Thomas Soo, Diocesan Office, 15F, Ultragrace Commercial Building, 5 Jordon Rd, Kowloon, Hong Kong SAR   *Tel:* 852 2783 0811
Fax: 852 2783 0799
email: hkskhdwk@netvigator.com
Web: http://dwk.hkskh.org

Bishop of Macau Missionary Area Most Revd Paul Kwong, 1 andar A, Edf, HuaDu, No. 2 Trav. Do Pato, No. 49–51 Rua do Campo, Macau SAR
Tel: 853 2835 3867
Fax: 853 2832 5314
email: skhmma@macau.ctm.net
Web: www.hkskh.org

The Church of the Province of the Indian Ocean

Members 90,486

The Anglican mission was begun in Mauritius in 1812 by the Revd H. Shepherd, and the first Anglican church in the Seychelles was dedicated in January 1856. The growth of the church was fostered both by the Society for the Propagation of the Gospel and by the Church Missionary Society. The dioceses of Madagascar and Mauritius and Seychelles combined in 1973 to create the province, which now comprises seven dioceses.

Archbishop Most Revd Ian Gerald Ernest (*Bishop of Mauritius*)

Provincial Secretary Revd Samitiana Razafindralamo, Évêché Anglican, 12 rue Rabezavana, Ambodifilao, 101 TNR Antananarivo, Madagascar   *Tel:* 261 20 24 39162
Fax: 261 20 226 1331
email: eemtma@hotmail.com/eemdanta@dts.mg

Treasurer Mr Philip Tse Rai (*same address*)

Chancellor of the Province Mrs Hilda Yerriah, 4 rue Commerson, Beau Bassin
Tel: 230 20 80429 (Office)
230 46 75710 (Home)
email: hilda5885@hotmail.com

Dean of the Province Rt Revd Jean-Claude Andrianjafimanana (*Bishop of Mahajanga*)

THEOLOGICAL COLLEGES
St Paul's College, Ambatohararana, Merimandroso, Ambohidratrimo, Madagascar (*Warden* Revd Vincent Rakotoarisoa)

St Paul's College, Rose Hill, Mauritius (*Warden* Vacancy)

St Philip's Theological College, La Misère, Seychelles (*Diocesan Trainer* The Revd Peter Raath)

CHURCH PAPERS
Newsletters of the Province of the Indian Ocean Support Assn. *Editor* The Revd Philip Harbridge, Chaplain, Christ's College, Cambridge CB2 3BY, UK

Seychelles Diocesan Magazine A quarterly newspaper covering diocesan events and containing articles of theological and other interest.

Magazine du Diocèse de Maurice (Le Cordage) A quarterly newspaper covering diocesan events and containing articles of theological and ecumenical interest.

ANTANANARIVO
Bishop Rt Revd Samoela Jaona Ranarivelo, Évêché Anglican, Lot VK57 ter, Ambohimanoro, 101 Antananarivo, Madagascar   *Tel:* 261 20 222 0827
Fax: 261 20 226 1331
email: eemdanta@dts.mg
Assistant Bishop Rt Revd Todd MacGregor (*Tulear*) (*same address*)

ANTSIRANANA
Bishop Rt Revd Roger Chung Po Chuen, Évêché Anglican, BP 278, 4 rue Grandidier, 201 Antsiranana, Madagascar   *Tel:* 261 20 82 2 2650
email: mgrchungpo@blueline.mg

FIANARANTSOA
Bishop Rt Revd Gilbert Rateloson Rakotondravelo, Évêché Anglican Manantsara, BP 1418 Fianarantsoa, Madagascar
Tel: 261 20 75 51583
261 33 14 043 36 (Mobile)
email: eemdiofianara@yahoo.fr

MAHAJANGA
Bishop Rt Revd Jean-Claude Andrianjafimanana, BP 570, Rue de Temple Ziona, Mahajanga 401, Madagascar   *Tel:* 261 62 23611
261 32 04 55143 (Mobile)
email: andrianjajc@yahoo.fr/eemdmaha@dts.mg

MAURITIUS
Bishop Most Revd Ian Gerald Ernest (*Archbishop of the Province*), Bishop's House, Ave. Nallétamby, Phoenix, Mauritius
Tel: 230 686 5158
230 787 8131 (Mobile)
Fax: 230 697 1096
email: dioang@intnet.mu

SEYCHELLES
Bishop Rt Revd James Richard Wong Yin Song, PO Box 44, Victoria, Mahé, Seychelles
Tel: 248 32 1977/32 3879
248 52 7770 (Mobile)
Fax: 248 22 4043
email: angdio@seychelles.net
Web: www.seychelles.anglican.org

TOAMASINA
Bishop Rt Revd Jean Paul Solo, Évêché Anglican, Rue James Seth, BP 531, Toamasina 501, Madagascar
Tel: 261 20 533 1663
261 32 04 55143 (Mobile)
Fax: 261 20 533 1689
email: eemtoam@wanadoo.mg

The Church of Ireland

Members 410,000

Tracing its origins to St Patrick and his companions in the fifth century, the Irish Church has been marked by strong missionary efforts. In 1537 the English king was declared head of the Church, but most Irish Christians maintained loyalty to Rome. The Irish Church Act of 1869 provided that the statutory union between the Churches of England and Ireland be dissolved and that the Church of Ireland should cease to be established by law. A General Synod of the Church, established in 1871 and consisting of archbishops, bishops, and representatives of the clergy and laity, has legislative and administrative power. Irish Church leaders have played a key role in the work of reconciliation in the Northern Ireland conflict.

The Primate of All Ireland and Metropolitan Most Revd Alan Edwin Thomas Harper (*Archbishop of Armagh*)

The Primate of Ireland and Metropolitan: Most Revd John Robert Winder Neill (*Archbishop of Dublin & Bishop of Glendalough*)

Central Office of the Church of Ireland Church of Ireland House, Church Ave, Rathmines, Dublin 6, Republic of Ireland
Tel: 353 1 497 8422
Fax: 353 1 497 8821
email: office@rcbdub.org

Chief Officer and Secretary, Representative Church Body Mr Denis Reardon
email: chiefofficer@rcbdub.org

Head of Synod Services and Communications Mrs Janet Maxwell
email: comms@rcbdub.org

THEOLOGICAL INSTITUTE
The Church of Ireland Theological Institute, Braemor Park, Rathgar, Dublin 14, which conducts courses in conjunction with the School of Hebrew, Biblical and Theological Studies, Trinity College, Dublin, Republic of Ireland (*Director* Revd Dr Maurice Elliott)
Tel: 353 1 492 3506
Fax: 353 1 492 3082

CHURCH PAPER
Church of Ireland Gazette (weekly) Deals with items of general interest to the Church of Ireland in a national context and also contains news from the various dioceses and parishes together with articles of a more general nature. *Editor/Editorial Offices* 3 Wallace Ave, Lisburn, Co Antrim BT27 4AA
Tel: 44 28 9267 5743
Fax: 44 28 9266 7580
email: gazette@ireland.anglican.org

PROVINCE OF ARMAGH
ARMAGH
Archbishop Most Revd Alan Edwin Thomas Harper (*Primate of the Church of Ireland*), c/o Church House, 46 Abbey Street, Armagh BT61 7DZ
Tel: 44 28 3752 7144 (Office)
Fax: 44 28 3751 0596
email: archbishop@armagh.anglican.org
Web: www.ireland.anglican.org

CATHEDRAL CHURCH OF ST PATRICK, Armagh
Dean Very Revd Patrick Rooke, The Deanery, Library House, 43 Abbey Street, Armagh BT61 7DY
Tel: 44 28 3752 3142 (Office)
Tel: 44 28 3751 8447 (Home)
Fax: 44 28 3752 4177
email: dean@armagh.anglican.org

CLOGHER
Bishop Rt Revd Dr Michael Geoffrey St Aubyn Jackson, The See House, Fivemiletown, Co Tyrone BT75 0QP
Tel and Fax: 44 28 8952 2475
email: bishop@clogher.anglican.org

CATHEDRAL CHURCHES OF ST MACARTAN, Clogher, and ST MACARTIN, Enniskillen
Dean Very Revd Kenneth Robert James Hall, The Deanery, 13 Church Street, Enniskillen, Co Fermanagh BT74 7DW
Tel: 44 28 6632 2917 (Office)
Tel: 44 28 6632 2465 (Home)
email: dean@clogher.anglican.org

CONNOR
Bishop Rt Revd Alan Francis Abernethy, Diocesan Office, Church of Ireland House, 61–67 Donegall Street, Belfast BT1 2QH
Tel: 44 28 9032 2268
email: bishop@connor.anglican.org

CATHEDRAL CHURCH OF ST SAVIOUR, Lisburn
Dean Very Revd John Frederick Augustus Bond, The Rectory, 49 Rectory Gardens, Broughshane, Ballymena, Co Antrim, BT42 4LF
Tel and *Fax:* 44 28 2586 1215
email: skerry@connor.anglican.org

CATHEDRAL CHURCH OF ST ANNE, Belfast
(Cathedral of the United Dioceses of Down and Dromore and the Diocese of Connor)
Dean Very Revd Robert Samuel James Houston McKelvey, The Deanery, 5 Deramore Drive, Belfast BT9 5JQ
Tel: 44 28 9066 0980 (Home)
44 28 9032 8332 (Cathedral)
Fax: 44 28 9023 8855
email: dean@belfastcathedral.org

DERRY AND RAPHOE
Bishop Rt Revd Kenneth Raymond Good, The See House, 112 Culmore Rd, Londonderry, Co Derry BT48 8JF
Tel: 44 28 7126 2440
Fax: 44 28 7135 2554
email: bishop@derry.anglican.org

CATHEDRAL CHURCH OF ST COLUMB, Derry
Dean Very Revd William Wright Morton, The Deanery, 30 Bishop St, Londonderry, Co Derry BT48 6PP
Tel: 44 28 7126 2746
email: dean@derry.anglican.org

CATHEDRAL CHURCH OF ST EUNAN, Raphoe
Dean Very Revd John Hay, The Deanery, Raphoe, Co Donegal
Tel: 353 74 914 5226

DOWN AND DROMORE
Bishop Rt Revd Harold Creeth Miller, The See House, 32 Knockdene Park South, Belfast BT5 7AB
Tel: 44 28 9023 7602
Fax: 44 28 9023 1902
email: bishop@down.anglican.org
Web: www.ireland.anglican.org

CATHEDRAL CHURCH OF THE HOLY AND UNDIVIDED TRINITY, Down
Dean Very Revd Thomas Henry Hull, Lecale Rectory, 9 Quoile Road, Downpatrick, Co Down BT30 6SE
Tel: 44 28 4461 3101
Fax: 44 28 4461 4456

CATHEDRAL CHURCH OF CHRIST THE REDEEMER, Dromore
Dean Very Revd Stephen Harold Lowry, Dromore Cathedral Rectory, 28 Church Street, Dromore, Co Down BT25 1AA
Tel: 44 28 9269 2275 (Home)
44 28 9269 3968 (Office)
email: cathedral@dromore.anglican.org

KILMORE, ELPHIN AND ARDAGH
Bishop Rt Revd Kenneth Herbert Clarke, 48 Carrickfern, Cavan, Co Cavan, Republic of Ireland
Tel: 353 49 437 2759 (Home)
email: bishop@kilmore.anglican.org
Web: www.ireland.anglican.org

CATHEDRAL CHURCH OF ST FETHLIMIDH, Kilmore
Dean Very Revd W. R. Ferguson, Danesfort, Cavan, Co Cavan, Republic of Ireland
Tel and *Fax:* 353 49 433 1918
email: dean@kilmore.anglican.org

CATHEDRAL CHURCH OF ST MARY THE VIRGIN AND ST JOHN THE BAPTIST, Sligo, Republic of Ireland
Dean Very Revd Arfon Williams, The Deanery, Strandhill Road, Sligo, Co Sligo, Republic of Ireland
Tel: 353 71 915 7993

TUAM, KILLALA AND ACHONRY
Bishop Rt Revd Dr Richard Crosbie Aitken Henderson, Bishop's House, Knockglass, Crossmolina, Co Mayo, Republic of Ireland
Tel: 353 96 31317
Fax: 353 96 31775
email: bptuam@iol.ie
Web: www.ireland.anglican.org

CATHEDRAL CHURCH OF ST MARY, Tuam
Dean Very Revd Alastair John Grimason, Deanery Place, Cong, Co Mayo, Republic of Ireland
Tel: 353 94 954 6017
email: deantuam@hotmail.com

CATHEDRAL CHURCH OF ST PATRICK, Killala
Dean Vacancy

PROVINCE OF DUBLIN
CASHEL, WATERFORD, LISMORE, OSSORY, FERNS AND LEIGHLIN
Bishop Rt Revd Dr Michael Andrew James Burrows, Bishop's House, Troysgate, Co Kilkenny, Republic of Ireland
Tel: 353 56 77 86633 (Home)
email: cashelossorybishop@eircom.net
Web: www.ireland.anglican.org

CATHEDRAL CHURCH OF ST JOHN THE BAPTIST AND ST PATRICK'S ROCK, Cashel
Dean Very Revd Philip John Knowles, The Deanery, Cashel, Co Tipperary, Republic of Ireland
Tel: 353 62 61232 (Home)
353 62 61944 (Office)

CATHEDRAL CHURCH OF THE BLESSED TRINITY (CHRIST CHURCH), Waterford
Dean Very Revd Trevor Rashleigh Lester, The Deanery, 41 Grange Park Rd, Waterford, Co Waterford, Republic of Ireland
Tel: 353 51 874119
email: dean@waterford.anglican.org

CATHEDRAL CHURCH OF ST CARTHAGE, Lismore
Dean Very Revd Paul Richard Draper, The Deanery, The Mall, Lismore, Co Waterford, Republic of Ireland   *Tel:* 353 58 54105

CATHEDRAL CHURCH OF ST CANICE, Kilkenny
Dean Very Revd Katharine Margaret Poulton, The Deanery, Kilkenny, Republic of Ireland
Tel: 353 56 772 1516
Fax: 353 56 775 1817
email: dean@ossory.anglican.org

CATHEDRAL CHURCH OF ST EDAN, Ferns
Dean Very Revd Leslie David Arthur Forrest, The Deanery, Ferns, Enniscorthy, Co Wexford, Republic of Ireland   *Tel:* 353 53 936 6124
email: dean@ferns.anglican.org

CATHEDRAL CHURCH OF ST LASERIAN, Leighlin
Dean Very Revd Frederick John Gordon Wynne, The Deanery, Old Leighlin, Muine Bheag, Co. Carlow, Republic of Ireland

CORK, CLOYNE AND ROSS
Bishop Rt Revd William Paul Colton, St Nicholas' House, 14 Cove Street, Cork, Republic of Ireland
Tel: 353 21 500 5080 (Office)
email: bishop@ccrd.ie
Web: www.cork.anglican.org

CATHEDRAL CHURCH OF ST FIN BARRE, Cork
Dean Very Revd N. K. Dunne, The Deanery, Gilabbey St, Cork, Republic of Ireland
Tel: 353 21 500 5080 (Office)
email: revnigeldunne@eircom.net

CATHEDRAL CHURCH OF ST COLMAN, Cloyne
Dean Very Revd Alan Gordon Marley, The Deanery, Midleton, Co Cork, Republic of Ireland
Tel: 353 21 463 1449
email: dean@cloyne.anglican.org

CATHEDRAL CHURCH OF ST FACHTNA, Ross
Dean Very Revd Christopher Lind Peters, The Deanery, Rosscarbery, Co Cork, Republic of Ireland   *Tel:* 353 23 48166
email: candjpeters@eircom.net

DUBLIN AND GLENDALOUGH
Archbishop Most Revd John Robert Winder Neill, The See House, 17 Temple Rd, Dartry, Dublin 6, Republic of Ireland   *Tel:* 353 1 497 7849
Fax: 353 1 497 6355
email: archishop@dublin.anglican.org

CATHEDRAL CHURCH OF THE HOLY TRINITY
(COMMONLY CALLED CHRIST CHURCH)
Cathedral of the United Dioceses of Dublin and Glendalough, Metropolitan Cathedral of the United Provinces of Dublin and Cashel

Dean Very Revd Dermot Patrick Martin Dunne, 19 Mountainview Road, Ranelagh, Dublin 6
Tel: 353 1 677 8099 (Cathedral)
Fax: 353 1 679 8991
email: dean@cccdub.ie

THE NATIONAL CATHEDRAL AND COLLEGIATE CHURCH OF ST PATRICK, Dublin
(The 'National Cathedral of the Church of Ireland having a common relation to all the dioceses of Ireland')
Dean and Ordinary Very Revd Robert Brian MacCarthy, The Deanery, Upper Kevin St, Dublin 8, Republic of Ireland
Tel: 353 1 475 5449 (Home)
353 1 475 4817 (Cathedral)
353 1 453 9472 (Office)
Fax: 353 1 454 6374

LIMERICK, ARDFERT, AGHADOE, KILLALOE, KILFENORA, CLONFERT, KILMACDUAGH AND EMLY
Bishop Rt Revd Trevor Russell Williams, Rien Roe, Adare, Co Limerick, Republic of Ireland
Tel: 353 61 396 244
email: bishop@limerick.anglican.org
Web: www.ireland.anglican.org

CATHEDRAL CHURCH OF ST MARY, Limerick
Dean Very Revd John Maurice Glover Sirr, The Deanery, 7 Kilbane, Castletroy, Limerick, Republic of Ireland   *Tel and Fax:* 353 61 338 697
087 2541121 (Mobile)
email: dean@limerick.anglican.org

CATHEDRAL CHURCH OF ST FLANNAN, Killaloe
Dean Very Revd Stephen Ross White, The Deanery, Killaloe, Co Clare, Republic of Ireland
Tel: 353 61 376 687
email: dean@killaloe.anglican.org

CATHEDRAL CHURCH OF ST BRENDAN, Clonfert
Dean Very Revd Stephen Ross White (*as above*)

MEATH AND KILDARE
Bishop Most Revd Richard Lionel Clarke, Bishop's House, Moyglare, Maynooth, Co Kildare, Republic of Ireland
Tel: 353 1 628 9354 (Office)
email: bishop@meath.anglican.org
Web: www.ireland.anglican.org/meath/meath.html

CATHEDRAL CHURCH OF ST PATRICK, Trim
Dean of Clonmacnoise Very Revd Robert William Jones, St Patrick's Deanery, Loman St, Trim, Co Meath, Republic of Ireland   *Tel:* 353 46 943 6698

CATHEDRAL OF ST BRIGID, Kildare
Dean Very Revd John Joseph Marsden, The Deanery, Morristown, Newbridge, Co Kildare, Republic of Ireland   *Tel:* 353 45 438 158

ANGLICAN AND PORVOO COMMUNIONS

The Anglican Communion in Japan

(Nippon Sei Ko Kai)

Members 35,000

In 1859 the American Episcopal Church sent two missionaries to Japan, followed some years later by representatives of the Church of England and the Church in Canada. The first Anglican Synod took place in 1887. The first Japanese bishops were consecrated in 1923. The Church remained oppressed during the Second World War and assumed all church leadership after the war.

Primate Most Revd Nathaniel Makoto Uematsu (*Bishop of Hokkaido*)

Provincial Office Nippon Sei Ko Kai, 65–3 Yarai-cho, Shinjuku-ku, Tokyo 162–0805 (Please use this address for all correspondence)
Tel: 81 3 5228 3171
Fax: 81 3 5228 3175
email: province@nskk.org
Web: www.nskk.org

General Secretary Revd John Makito Aizawa
email: general-sec.po@nskk.org

Provincial Treasurer Mr Matthias Shigeo Ozaki

THEOLOGICAL TRAINING
Central Theological College, 1–12–31 Yoga, Setagaya-ku, Tokyo 158–0097, for clergy and lay workers
Bishop Williams Theological School, Shimotachiuri-agaru, Karasuma Dori, Kamikyo-ku, Kyoto 602–8332

CHURCH NEWSPAPERS
Sei Ko Kai Shimbun Published on the twentieth of each month in Japanese. Usually eight pages, tabloid format. Subscription through the Provincial Office. Each diocese also has its own monthly paper.

NSKK News English-language newsletter. Published quarterly. Available through the Provincial Office and also on the web page of Anglican Communion.

CHUBU
Bishop Rt Revd Peter Ichiro Shibusawa, 28–1 Meigetsu-cho, 2-chome, Showa-ku, Nagoya 466–0034
Tel: 81 52 858 1007
Fax: 81 52 858 1008
email: office.chubu@nskk.org
Web: www.nskk.org/chubu

HOKKAIDO
Bishop Most Revd Nathaniel Makoto Uematsu (*Archbishop of the Province*), Kita 15 jo, Nishi 5-20, Kita-Ku, Sapporo 001-0015   *Tel:* 81 11 717 8181

Fax: 81 11 736 8377
email: hokkaido@nskk.org
Web: www.nskk.org/hokkaido

KITA KANTO
Bishop Rt Revd Zerubbabel Katsuichi Hirota, 2–172 Sakuragi-cho, Omiya-ku, Saitama-shi, 331–0852
Tel: 81 48 642 2680
Fax: 81 48 648 0358
email: kitakanto@nskk.org
Web: www.nskk.org/kitakanto

KOBE
Bishop Rt Revd Andrew Yutaka Nakamura, 5–11–1 Yamatedori, Chuo-ku, Kobe-shi 650–0011
Tel: 81 78 351 5469
Fax: 81 78 382 1095
email: aao52850@syd.odn.ne.jp
Web: www.nskk.org/kobe

KYOTO
Bishop Rt Revd Stephen Takashi Kochi, 380 Okakuencho, Shimotachiuri-agaru, Karasuma-dori, Kamikyo-ku, Kyoto 602–8011
Tel: 81 75 431 7204
Fax: 81 75 441 4238
email: nskk-kyoto@mse.biglobe.ne.jp
Web: www.nskk.org/kyoto

KYUSHU
Bishop Rt Revd Gabriel Shoji Igarashi, 2–9–22 Kusakae, Chuo-ku, Fukuoka 810–0045
Tel: 81 92 771 2050
Fax: 81 92 771 9857
email: d-kyushu@try-net.or.jp
Web: http://www1.bbiq.jp/d-kyushu

OKINAWA
Bishop Rt Revd David Shoji Tani, 3–5–5 Meada, Urasoe-shi, Okinawa 910-2102   *Tel:* 81 98 942 1101
Fax: 81 98 942 1102
email: office.okinawa@nskk.org
Web: http://anglican-okinawa.jp

OSAKA
Bishop Rt Revd Samuel Osamu Ohnishi, 2–1–8 Matsuzaki-cho, Abeno-ku, Osaka 545–0053
Tel: 81 6 6621 2179
Fax: 81 6 6621 3097
email: office.osaka@nskk.org
Web: www.nskk.org/osaka

TOHOKU
Bishop Rt Revd John Hiromichi Kato, 2-13-15 Kokubun-cho, Aoba-ku, Sendai 980-0803
Tel: 81 22 223 2349
Fax: 81 22 223 2387
email: hayashi.tohoku@nskk.org
Web: www.nskk.org/tohoku

TOKYO
Bishop Rt Revd Peter Jintaro Ueda, 3-6-18 Shiba Koen, Minato-ku, Tokyo 105-0011
Tel: 81 3 3433 0987
Fax: 81 3 3433 8678
email: office.tko@nskk.org

YOKOHAMA
Bishop Rt Revd Laurence Yutaka Minabe, 14-57 Mitsuzawa Shimo-cho, Kanagawa-ku, Yokohama 221-0852
Tel: 81 45 321 4988
Fax: 81 45 321 4978
email: yokohama.kyouku@nskk.org
Web: anglican.jp/yokohama

The Episcopal Church in Jerusalem and the Middle East

Members 10,000
The Church comprises the dioceses of Jerusalem, Iran, Egypt, Cyprus, and the Gulf. The Jerusalem bishopric was founded in 1841 and became an archbishopric in 1957. Reorganization in January 1976 ended the archbishopric and combined the Diocese of Jordan, Lebanon and Syria with the Jerusalem bishopric after a 19-year separation. Around the same time, the new Diocese of Cyprus and the Gulf was formed and the Diocese of Egypt was revived. The Cathedral Church of St George the Martyr in Jerusalem is known for its ministry to pilgrims. St George's College, Jerusalem is in partnership with the Anglican Communion.

THE CENTRAL SYNOD
President-Bishop Most Revd Mouneer Hanna Anis (*Bishop in Egypt with North Africa and the Horn of Africa*)

Provincial Secretary The Revd Hanna Mansour, PO Box 3, Doha, Qatar
Tel and Fax: (Qatar) 974 442 4329
email: tianyoung@hotmail.com

Acting Provincial Treasurer Revd Canon William Schwartz, PO Box 87, Zamalek, Cairo 11211, Egypt
Tel: 202 738 0829
Fax: 202 735 8941
email: bishopmouneer@link.net

The Jerusalem and the Middle East Church Association acts in support of the Episcopal Church in Jerusalem and the Middle East, the Central Synod and all four dioceses. *Secretary* Mrs Vanessa Wells, 1 Hart House, The Hart, Farnham, Surrey GU9 7HA
Tel: 01252 726994
Fax: 01252 735558
*email:*secretary@jmeca.eclipse.co.uk

CYPRUS AND THE GULF
Bishop in Rt Revd Michael Augustine Owen Lewis, PO Box 22075, Nicosia 1517, Cyprus
Tel: 357 22 671220
Fax: 357 2 22 674553
email: bishop@spidernet.com.cy/
cygulf@spidernet.com.cy
Web: www.cyprusgulf.anglican.org

EGYPT WITH NORTH AFRICA AND THE HORN OF AFRICA
Bishop in Rt Revd Mouneer Hanna Anis (*President Bishop of the Episcopal Church of Jerusalem and the Middle East*), Diocesan Office, PO Box 87, Zamalek Distribution, 11211, Cairo, Egypt
Tel: 20 2 738 0829
Fax: 20 2 735 8941
email: bishopmouneer@gmail.com
Web: www.dioceseofegypt.org

Suffragan Rt Revd Andrew Proud (*Horn of Africa*) (*same address*)

Assistant Bishop Rt Revd Bill Musk (*North Africa*) (*same address*)
email: billamusk@googlemail.com

IRAN
Bishop in Rt Revd Azad Marshall, St Thomas Center, Raiwind Road, PO Box 688, Lohore, Punjab, 54000, Pakistan
Tel: 92 42 542 0452
email: bishop@saintthomascenter.org

JERUSALEM
Bishop in Rt Revd Suheil Dawani, St George's Close, PO Box 1278, Jerusalem 91 019, Israel
Tel: 972 2 627 1670
Fax: 972 2 627 3847
email: bishop@j-diocese.com
Web: www.j-diocese.org

The Anglican Church of Kenya

Members 3,500,000
Mombasa saw the arrival of Anglican missionaries in 1844, with the first African ordained to the priesthood in 1885. Mass conversions occurred as early as 1910. The first Kenyan bishops were consecrated in 1955. The Church became part of the Province of East Africa, established in 1960, but by 1970 Kenya and Tanzania were divided into separate provinces.

ANGLICAN AND PORVOO
COMMUNIONS

Primate Most Revd Benjamin M. Nzimbi (*Bishop of All Saints Cathedral Diocese*) PO Box 40502, 00100 Nairobi   *Tel:* 254 2 714 755
Fax: 254 2 718 442
email: archoffice@swiftkenya.com
Web: www.ackenya.org

Provincial Secretary Rt Revd Lawrence Dena (Assistant Bishop of Mombasa)
Tel: 254 2 271 4752/3/4
Fax: 254 2 271 4750
email: ackenya@insightkenya.com/ psd@akenya.org

Provincial Treasurer Dr William Ogara, Corat Africa, PO Box 42493, 00100 Nairobi
Tel: 254 2 890 165/6
Fax: 254 2 891 900/890 481

THEOLOGICAL COLLEGES
ACK Language School and Orientation School, PO Box 47429, Nairobi   *Tel:* 254 2 721893
email: c/o ackenya@insightkenya.com

ACK Guest House, PO Box 56292, Nairobi
Tel: 254 2 723200/2724780
email: ackghouse@insightkenya.com

ACK St Julian's Centre, PO Box 574, Village Market 00621   *Tel:* 254 66 76221
email: ackstjulians@swiftkenya.com

ACK Guest House Mombasa, PO Box 96170, Likoni, Mombasa
email: ackmsaghouse@swiftkenya.com

Carlile College for Theology & Business Studies, PO Box 72584, Nairobi   *Tel:* 254 2 558596/253
email: Williams@insightkenya.com

St Andrews College of Theology and Development Kabare, PO Box 6, Kerugoya
Tel: 254 60 21256
email: ackstandrewskabare@swiftkenya.com

Berea Theological College, PO Box 1945, Nakuru
Tel: 254 51 51295
email: berea-tc@africaonline.co.ke

St Paul's Theological College, Kapsabet, PO Box 18, Kapsabet   *Tel:* 254 53 2053
email: ackstpaulskapsabet@africaonline.co.ke

St Philip's Theological College Maseno, PO Box 1, Maseno   *Tel:* 254 57 51019

Bishop Hannington Institute Mombasa, PO Box 81150, Mombasa   *Tel:* 254 41 491396
email: ackbhanning-msa@swiftmombasa.com

Provincial TEE Programme (Trinity College), PO Box 72430, Nairobi   *Tel:* 254 2 558655/542607
email: acktrinitycollege@swiftkenya.com

Church Commissioners for Kenya, PO Box 30422, 00100 Nairobi   *Tel:* 254 20 717106
email: churchcom@insightkenya.com

Uzima Press, PO Box 48127, Nairobi
Tel: 254 20 220239/216836
email: uzima@nbnet.co.ke

ALL SAINTS CATHEDRAL DIOCESE
Bishop Most Revd Eliud Wabukala (*Archbishop of Kenya*), PO Box 40502, 00100 Nairobi   *Tel:* 254 20 714 755
Fax: 254 20 718 442/714 750
email: archoffice@swiftkenya.com

BONDO
Bishop Rt Revd Johannes Otieno Angela, PO Box 240, 40601 Bondo   *Tel:* 254 57 5 20415
email: ackbondo@swiftkenya.com

BUNGOMA
Bishop Vacancy, PO Box 2392, 50200 Bungoma
Tel and *Fax:* 254 337 30481
email: ackbungoma@swiftkenya.com

BUTERE
Bishop Rt Revd Michael Sande, PO Box 54, 50101 Butere   *Tel:* 254 56 620 412
Fax: 254 56 620 038
email: ackbutere@swiftkenya.com

ELDORET
Bishop Rt Revd Thomas Kogo, PO Box 3404, 30100 Eldoret   *Tel:* 254 53 62785
email: ackeldoret@africaonline.co.ke

EMBU
Bishop Rt Revd Henry Tiras Nyaga Kathii, PO Box 189, 60100 Embu   *Tel:* 254 68 30614
Fax: 254 68 30468
email: ackembu@swiftkenya.com

KAJIADO
Bishop Rt Revd John Mutua Taama, PO Box 203, 01100 Kajiado   *Tel:* 254 301 21201/05
Fax: 254 301 21106
email: ackajiado@swiftkenya.com

KATAKWA
Bishop Rt Revd Zakayo Iteba Epusi, PO Box 68, 50244 Amagoro   *Tel:* 254 55 54079
email: ackatakwa@swiftkenya.com

KERICHO
Bishop Rt Revd Jackson Ole Sapit, c/o PO Box 181, Kericho

KIRINYAGA
Bishop Rt Revd Daniel Munene Ngoru, PO Box 95, 10304 Kutus   *Tel:* 254 163 44221
Fax: 254 163 44 020
email: ackirinyaga@swiftkenya.com

KITALE
Bishop Rt Revd Stephen Kewasis Nyorsok, PO Box 4176, 30200 Kitale   *Tel:* 254 325 31631
email: ack.ktl@africaonline.co.ke

KITUI
Bishop Rt Revd Josephat Mule, PO Box 1054, 90200 Kitui
Tel: 254 141 22682
Fax: 254 141 22119
email: ackitui@swiftkenya.com

MACHAKOS
Bishop Rt Revd Mutie Kanuku, PO Box 282, 90100 Machakos
Tel: 254 145 21379
Fax: 254 145 20178
email: ackmachakos@swiftkenya.com

MASENO NORTH
Bishop Rt Revd Simon M. Oketch, PO Box 416, 50100 Kakemega
Tel and *Fax:* 254 331 30729
email: ackmnorth@swiftkenya.com

MASENO SOUTH
Bishop Rt Revd Francis Mwayi Abiero, PO Box 114, 40100 Kisumu
Tel: 254 35 21297
Fax: 254 35 21009
email: ackmsouth@swiftkenya.com

MASENO WEST
Bishop Rt Revd Joseph Otieno Wasonga, PO Box 793, 40600 Siaya
Tel: 254 334 21483
Fax: 254 334 21483
email: ackmwest@swiftkenya.com

MBEERE
Bishop Rt Revd Moses Masambe Nthuka, PO Box 122, 60104 Siakago
Tel: 254 162 21261
Fax: 254 162 21083
email: ackmbeere@swiftkenya.com

MERU
Bishop Rt Revd Charles Mwendwa, PO Box 427, 60200 Meru
Tel: 254 164 30719
email: ackmeru@swiftkenya.com

MOMBASA
Bishop Rt Revd Julius R. K. Kalu, PO Box 80072, 80100 Mombasa
Tel: 254 41 231 1105
Fax: 254 41 231 6361
email: ackmsa@swiftmombasa.com

Assistant Bishop Rt Revd Lawrence Dena (*same address*)

MOUNT KENYA CENTRAL
Bishop Rt Revd Isaac Maina Ng'ang'a, PO Box 121, 10200 Murang'a
Tel: 254 60 30560/30559
Fax: 254 60 30148
email: ackmkcentral@wananchi.com

Assistant Bishop Rt Revd Allan Waithaka (*same address*)

MOUNT KENYA SOUTH
Bishop Rt Revd Timothy Ranji, PO Box 886, 00900 Kiambu
Tel: 254 66 22521/22997
Fax: 254 66 22408
email: ackmtksouth@swiftkenya.com

MOUNT KENYA WEST
Bishop Rt Revd Joseph M. Kagunda, PO Box 229, 10100 Nyeri
Tel: 254 61 203 2281
email: ackmtkwest@wananchi.com

MUMIAS
Bishop Rt Revd Beneah Justin Okumu Salalah, PO Box 213, 50102 Mumias
Tel: 254 333 41476
Fax: 254 333 41232
email: ackmumias@swiftkenya.com

NAIROBI
Bishop Rt Revd Peter Njagi Njoka, PO Box 40502, 00100 Nairobi
Tel: 254 2 714 755
Fax: 254 2 226 259
email: acknairobi@swiftkenya.com

NAKURU
Bishop Rt Revd Stephen Njihia Mwangi, PO Box 56, 20100 Nakuru
Tel: 254 37 212 155/1
Fax: 254 37 44379
email: acknkudioc@net2000ke.com

NAMBALE
Bishop Rt Revd Josiah M. Were, PO Box 4, 50409 Nambale
Tel: 254 336 24040
Fax: 254 336 24040
email: acknambale@swiftkenya.com

NYAHURURU
Bishop Rt Revd Charles Gaikia Gaita, PO Box 926, 20300 Nyahururu
Tel: 254 365 32179
email: nyahu_dc@africaonline.co.ke

SOUTHERN NYANZA
Bishop Rt Revd James Kenneth Ochiel, PO Box 65, 40300 Homa Bay
Tel: 254 385 22127
Fax: 254 385 22056
email: acksnyanza@swiftkenya.com

TAITA TAVETA
Bishop Rt Revd Samson M. Mwaluda, PO Box 75, 80300 Voi
Tel: 254 147 30096
Fax: 254 147 30364
email: acktaita@swiftmombasa.com

THIKA
Bishop Rt Revd Gideon G. Githiga, PO Box 214, 01000 Thika
Tel: 254 151 21735/31654
Fax: 254 151 31544
email: ackthika@swiftkenya.com

The Anglican Church in Korea

Members 14,558

From the time when Bishop John Corfe arrived in Korea in 1890 until 1965, the Diocese of Korea has had English bishops. In 1993 the Archbishop of Canterbury installed the newly elected Primate and handed jurisdiction to him, making the Anglican Church of Korea a province of the Anglican Communion. There are four religious communities in the country as well as an Anglican university.

Primate Most Revd Solomon Jong Mo Yoon (*Bishop of Pusan*)

Provincial Offices 3 Chong-dong, Chung-ku, Seoul 100–120
Tel: 82 2 738 8952
Fax: 82 2 737 4210
email: yoonsjm@hanmail.net

Secretary-General Revd Gwang Joon Kim (*same address*)
Tel: 82 2 738 8952
Fax: 82 2 737 4210
email: abgwk@hanmail.net
Web: www.skh.or.kr

ANGLICAN UNIVERSITY
(*Songkonghoe Daehak*) # 1 Hand-dong, Kuro-ku, Seoul 152–140 (*President* Revd Jeremiah K. S. Kim)
Tel: 82 2610 4100
Fax: 82 2 737 4210
email: ksyang@mail.skhu.ac.kr

CHURCH PAPER
Daehan Songgonghoesinmun This fortnightly paper of the Anglican Church of Korea is the joint concern of all three dioceses. Newspaper format. Printed in Korean. Contains regular liturgical and doctrinal features as well as local, national and international church news.
Tel: 82 2 736 6990
Fax: 82 2 738 1208

PUSAN
Bishop Rt Revd Solomon Jong Mo Yoon (*Archbishop of the Province*), Anglican Diocese of Pusan, 18 Daechengdong-2ga, Chung-Ku, Pusan 600–092
Tel: 82 51 463 5742
Fax: 82 51 463 5957
email: yoonsjm@hanmail.net

SEOUL
Bishop Most Revd Paul Keun Sang Kim, Anglican Diocese of Seoul, 3 Chong-Dong, Chung-Ku, Seoul 100–120
Tel: 82 2 735 6157
Fax: 82 2 723 2640
email: paulkim7@hitel.net

TAEJON
Bishop Most Revd Michael Hi Yeon Kwon, Anglican Diocese of Taejon, 87–6 Sunwha 2don, Chung-Ku, Taejon 302–823
Tel: 82 42 256 9987
Fax: 82 42 255 8918
email: tdio@unitel.co.kr

The Church of the Province of Melanesia

Members 250,000

After 118 years of missionary association with the Church of the Province of New Zealand, the Church of the Province of Melanesia was formed in 1975. The province encompasses the Republic of Vanuatu and the Solomon Islands, both sovereign island nations in the South Pacific, and the French Trust Territory of New Caledonia.

Archbishop of the Province David Vunagi (*Bishop of Central Melanesia*)

General Secretary Mr George Kiriau (*same address*)
Tel: 677 20470
email: kiriau_g@comphq.org.sb

ANGLICAN THEOLOGICAL COLLEGE
Bishop Patteson Theological College, Kohimarama, PO Box 19, Honiara, Solomon Islands (trains students up to degree standard) (*Principal* Revd Revd Ben Seka)
Tel: 677 29124
Fax: 677 21098

BANKS AND TORRES
Bishop Rt Revd Nathan Tome, PO Box 19, Sola, Vanualava, Torba Province, Republic of Vanuatu
Tel and Fax: 678 38520

CENTRAL MELANESIA
Bishop Most Revd David Vunagi, PO Box 19, Honiara, Solomon Islands
Tel: 677 21137
Fax: 677 21435
email: dvunagi@comphq.org.sb

CENTRAL SOLOMONS
Bishop Most Revd David Vunagi (Ag), PO Box 52, Tulagi, CIP, Solomon Islands
Tel: 677 32006
Fax: 677 32113

HANUATO'O
Bishop Rt Revd Alfred Karibongi, PO Box 20, Kira Kira, Makira Province, Solomon Islands
Tel: 677 50012
email: ebiscobal@solomon.com.sb

MALAITA
Bishop Rt Revd Samuel Sahu, Bishop's House, PO Box 7, Auki Malaita Province, Solomon Islands
Tel: 677 40125
email: domauki@solomon.com.sb

TEMOTU
Bishop Rt Revd George Angus Takeli, Bishop's House, Lata, Santa Cruz, Temotu Province, Solomon Islands
Tel: 677 53080

VANUATU
Bishop Rt Revd James Marvin Ligo, Bishop's House, PO Box 238, Luganville, Santo, Republic of Vanuatu   *Tel* and *Fax*: 678 37065/36631
        email: diocese_of_vanuatu@ecunet.org/
        comdov@vanuatu.com.vu

YSABEL
Bishop Rt Revd Richard Naramana, Bishop's House, PO Box 6, Buala, Jejevo, Ysabel Province, Solomon Islands   *Tel*: 677 35124
        email: episcopal@solomon.com.sb

The Anglican Church of Mexico

Members 21,000
The Mexican Episcopal Church began with the political reform in 1857, which secured freedom of religion, separating the Roman Catholic Church from the government and politics. Some priests organized a National Church and contacted the Episcopal Church in the United States, seeking the ordination of bishops for the new church. They adopted the name 'Mexican Episcopal Church'. The Mexican Church became an autonomous province of the Anglican Communion in 1995 with the name Iglesia Anglicana de Mexico.

Archbishop Rt Revd Carlos Touché-Porter (*Bishop of Mexico*)

Provincial Secretary Revd Canon Habacuc Ramos Huerta, Calle La Otra Banda # 40, Col. San Angel, Delegación Alvaro Obregón, 01000 México
        Tel: 52 55 5616 2490/5550 4073
        Fax: 52 55 5616 4063
email:ofipam@att.net.mx / habacuc_mx@yahoo.es
        Web: www.iglesiaanglicanademexico.org

Provincial Treasurer C. P. Edgar Gómez-González (*same address*)   *email*: ofipam@att.net.mx

CUERNAVACA
Bishop Rt Revd Ramiro Delgado-Vera, Calle Minerva No 1, Col. Delicias, CP 62330 Cuernavaca, Morelos, México

Tel and *Fax*: 52 777 315 2870/322 8035 (Office)
        52 777 322 2559 (Home)
        email: adoc@cableonline.com.mx

MEXICO
Bishop Most Revd Carlos Touché Porter (*Archbishop of the Province*), Ave San Jerónimo 117, Col. San Ángel, Delegación Álvaro Obregón, 01000 México, D.F.   *Tel*: 52 55 5616 3193
        Fax: 52 55 5616 2205
        email: diomex@netvoice.com.mx

NORTHERN MEXICO
Bishop Rt Revd Marcelino Rivera Delgado, Simón Bolivar 2005 Norte, Col. Mitras Centro, CP 64460, Monterrey, NL   *Tel*: 52 81 8333 0992
        Fax: 52 81 8348 7362
        email: diocesisdelnorte@prodigy.net.mx

SOUTHEASTERN MEXICO
Bishop Rt Revd Benito Juárez-Martínez, Avenida de Las Américas #73, Col. Aguacatal, 91130 Xalapa, Veracruz   *Tel*: 52 228 814 6951
        Fax: 52 228 814 4387
        email: dioste99@aol.com

WESTERN MEXICO
Bishop Rt Revd Lino Rodríguez-Amaro, Francisco Javier Gamboa #255, Col. Sector Juárez, 44100 Guadalajara, Jalisco
        Tel: 52 33 3560 4726
        Fax: 52 33 3616 4413
        email: iamoccidente@prodigy.net.mx

The Church of the Province of Myanmar (Burma)

Members 63,845
Anglican chaplains and missionaries worked in Burma in the early and mid-nineteenth century. The Province of Myanmar was formed in 1970, nine years after the declaration of Buddhism as the state religion and four years after all foreign missionaries were forced to leave.

Archbishop of the Province Most Revd Stephen Than Myint Oo (*Bishop of Yangon*)

Provincial Secretary Mr Kenneth Saw, PO Box 11191, 140 Pyidaungsu Yeiktha Rd, Dagon, Yangon   *Tel*: 95 1 395279
        Tel: 95 1 395350
        email: cpm.140@mptmail.net.mm

Provincial Treasurer Daw Myint Htwe Ye (*same address*)

Secretary and Treasurer, Yangon Diocesan Trust Association Daw Pin Lone Soe (*same address*)

ANGLICAN THEOLOGICAL COLLEGES
Holy Cross Theological College, 104 Inya Rd, University PO (11041), Yangon (*Principal* Samuel San Myat Shwe)

Emmanuel Theological College, Mohnyin, Kachin State (*Principal* Bishop David Than Lwin)

CHURCH NEWSLETTER
The province publishes a monthly 36-page *Newsletter*. *Editor and Manager* Mr Saw Peter Aye,

ANGLICAN AND PORVOO COMMUNIONS

PO Box 11191, Bishopscourt, 140 Pyidaungsu Yeiktha Rd, Dagon, Yangon

HPA-AN
Bishop Rt Revd Saw Stylo, No (4) Block, Bishop Gone, Diocesan Office, Hpa-an, Kayin State
Tel: 95 58 21696

MANDALAY
Bishop Rt Revd Noel Nay Lin, Bishopscourt, 22nd St, 'C' Rd (between 85–86 Rd), Mandalay
Tel: 95 2 34110

MYITKYINA
Bishop Rt Revd David Than Lwin, Diocesan Office, Tha Kin Nat Pe Rd, Thida Ya, Myitkyina
Tel: 95 74 23104

Assistant Bishop Rt Revd Gam Dee (*same address*)

SITTWE
Bishop Rt Revd James Min Dein, St John's Church, Paletwa, Southern Chin State, Via Sittwe

TOUNGOO
Bishop Rt Revd Saw (John) Wilme, Diocesan Office, Nat Shin Naung Rd, Toungoo
Tel: 95 54 23 519 (office)
95 54 24216 (home)

YANGON
Bishop Most Revd Stephen Than Myint Oo (*Archbishop of the Province*), PO Box 11191, 140 Pyidaungsu-Yeiktha Rd, Dagon, Yangon
Tel: 95 1 395279/395350 (office)
95 1 381909 (home)

Assistant Bishop Samuel Htan Oak, 44 Pyi Road, Dagon, Yangon
Tel: 95 1 372300

The Church of Nigeria

(Anglican Communion)

Members 17,500,000
The rebirth of Christianity began with the arrival of Christian freed slaves in Nigeria in the middle of the nineteenth century. The Church Missionary Society established an evangelistic ministry, particularly in the south. The division of the Province of West Africa in 1979 formed the Province of Nigeria and the Province of West Africa. In the 1990s, nine missionary bishops consecrated themselves to evangelism in northern Nigeria. Membership growth has dictated the need for new dioceses year by year. In 1997 the Church of Nigeria was divided into three provinces to enable more effective management. In 1999 another twelve dioceses were created, and in January 2003 the Church was re-organized into ten provinces.
  A large number of new dioceses have been created in the Church of Nigeria. At the time of going to press, some details were unavailable, so this list is incomplete.

Primate of All Nigeria Most Revd Peter Jasper Akinola (*Archbishop of the Province of Abuja and Bishop of Abuja*)

General Secretary Ven Oluranti Odubogun, Episcopal House, PO Box 212, AD CP, Abuja
Tel: 234 9 523 6950
email: abuja@anglican.skannet.com.ng
Web: www.anglican-nig.org

Provincial Treasurer Mr J. N. Aziagba (*same address*)
email: treasurer@anglican-nig.org

THEOLOGICAL COLLEGES
Immanuel College (Ecumenical), PO Box 515, Ibadan

Trinity College (Ecumenical), Umuahia, Imo State

Vining College, Akure, Ondo State

St Francis of Assisi College, Wusasa, Zaria

Crowther College of Theology, Okene, Kogi State

Ezekiel College of Theology, Ujoelen, Ekpoma, Edo State

Please note: The Church of Nigeria is growing very fast. The compilers are aware that there are new dioceses that are not listed here, but at the time of going to press insufficient information was available to include these. Please refer to the Church of Nigeria web site for further information:
www.anglican-nig.org

PROVINCE OF ABUJA
Archbishop Most Revd Peter Jasper Akinola (*Primate of All Nigeria and Bishop of Abuja*)

ABUJA
Bishop Most Revd Peter Jasper Akinola (*Primate of All Nigeria and Archbishop of the Province of Abuja*), Archbishop's Palace, PO Box 212, ADCP, Abuja
Tel: 234 9 524 0496
email: primate@anglican-nig.org

BIDA
Bishop Rt Revd Jonah Kolo, Bishop's House, St John's Mission Compound, PO Box 14, Bida
Tel: 234 66 460 178
email: bida@anglican-nig.org

GWAGWALADA
Bishop Rt Revd Tanimu Samari Aduda, PO Box 287, Gwagwalada, F.C.T., Abuja
Tel: 234 9 882 2083
email: gwagwalada@anglican-nig.org

IDAH
Bishop Rt Revd Joseph N. Musa, Bishop's Lodge, PO Box 25, Idah, Kogi State
Tel: 234 803 385 4463 (Mobile)
email: idah@anglican-nig.org

IJUMU
Bishop Rt Revd Ezekiel Ikupolati

KAFANCHAN
Bishop Rt Revd William Diya, PO Box 29, Kafanchan, Kaduna State   *Tel:* 234 61 20 634

KOTANGORA
Bishop Rt Revd Jonah N. Ibrahim, Bishop's House, PO Box 1, Kontagora, Niger State
Tel: 234 803 625 2325 (Mobile)
email: jonaibrahim@yahoo.co.uk

KUBWA
Bishop Rt Revd Duke Akamisoko St. Andrew's Church, Opposite Julius Berger Camp, Gado Nasko Road, Phase II Site I,   *Tel:* 234 9 672 4063
email: kubwa@anglican-nig.org

KUTIGI
Bishop Rt Revd Jeremiah Ndana Kolo

KWOI
Bishop Rt Revd Paul Samuel Zamani

LAFIA
Bishop Rt Revd Miller Kangdim Maza, PO Box 560, Lafia, Nasarawa State   *Tel:* 234 47 221 329

LOKOJA
Bishop Rt Revd Emmanuel Egbunu, PO Box 11, Lokoja, Kogi State   *Tel:* 234 58 220 588
Fax: 234 58 221 788
email: lokoja@anglican-nig.org

MAKURDI
Bishop Rt Revd Nathaniel Inyom, Bishopscourt, PO Box 1, Makurdi, Benue State
Tel: 234 44 533 349
email: makurdi@anglican-nig.org/
makurdi@anglican.skannet.com.ng

MINNA
Bishop Rt Revd Nathaniel Yisa, PO Box 2469, Minna, Niger State   *Tel:* 234 66 220 035 (Office)
234 66 220 515 (Home)

OKENE
Bishop Rt Revd Emmanuel Bayo Ajulo

OTUKPO
Bishop Rt Revd David K. Bello, St John's

Cathedral, Sgt Ugbade Ave, PO Box 0360, Otukpo, Benue State   *Tel:* 234 44 662 312
email: anglicandioceseofotukpo@yahoo.com/
bishopdkbello@yahoo.com

ZONKWA (Missionary diocese)
Bishop Rt Revd Praise Omole-Ekun, Bishop's Residence, PO Box 26, Zonkwa, Kaduna State 802002   *email:* zonkwa@anglican-nig.org

PROVINCE OF BENDEL
Archbishop Most Revd Nicholas D. Okoh (*Bishop of Asaba*)

AKOKO-EDO
Bishop Rt Revd Gabriel Akinbiyi

ASABA
Bishop Most Revd Nicholas D. Okoh (*Archbishop of the Province of Bendel*), Bishopscourt, PO Box 216, Cable Point, Asaba, Delta State
Tel: 234 56 280 682
email: asaba@anglican-nig.org

BENIN
Bishop Rt Revd P. O. J. Imasuen, Bishopscourt, PO Box 82, Benin City, Edo State
Tel: 234 803 079 9560 (Mobile)
email: petglad2002@yahoo.com

ESAN
Bishop Rt Revd Friday John Imakhai, Bishopscourt, Ujoelen, PO Box 921, Ekpoma, *email:* Edo State   *Tel:* 234 55 981 29
email: bishopfriday@hotmail.com

IKA
Bishop Rt Revd Peter Onekpe, St John's Cathedral, PO Box 1063, Agbor, 321001 Delta State   *Tel:* 234 55 250-14
email: ika@anglican-nig.org/bishoppeter@
yahoo.com

NDOKWA
Bishop Rt Revd David Obiosa

OLEH
Bishop Rt Revd Jonathan F. E. Edewor, JP, PO Box 8, Oleh, Delta State
Tel: 234 803 549 4215 (Mobile)
email: oleh@anglican-nig.org/angoleh2000@
yahoo.com

SABONGIDDA-ORA
Bishop Rt Revd John Akao, Bishopscourt, PO Box 13, Sabongidda-Ora, Edo State
Tel: 234 57 54 049
email: akao@cashette.com

UGHELLI
Bishop Rt Revd Vincent O. Muoghereh, Bishopscourt, Ovurodawanre, PO Box 760, Ughelli, Delta State   *Tel:* 234 53 258 307
234 802 302 9906 (Mobile)

WARRI

Bishop Rt Revd Christian Ideh, Bishopscourt, 17 Mabiaku Rd, GRA, PO Box 4571, Warri, Delta State *Tel:* 234 53 255 857
email: warri@anglican-nig.org

WESTERN IZON (Missionary diocese)

Bishop Rt Revd Edafe Emamezi, Bishopscourt, PO Box 56, Sagbama, River State
Tel: 234 806 357 2263 (Mobile)
email: anglizon@yahoo.co.uk

PROVINCE OF IBADAN

Archbishop Most Revd Joseph Akinfenwa (*Bishop of Ibadan*)

AJAYI CROWTHER

Bishop Rt Revd Olukemi Oduntan, Bishopscourt, Iseyin, PO Box 430, Iseyin, Oyo State
Tel: 234 837 198 182 (Mobile)
email: ajayicrowtherdiocese@yahoo.com

ETIKI KWARA

Bishop Rt Revd Andrew Ajayi

IBADAN

Bishop Most Revd Joseph Akinfenwa (*Archbishop of the Province of Ibadan*), PO Box 3075, Mapo, Ibadan *Tel:* 234 2 810 1400
Fax: 234 2 810 1413
email: ibadan@anglican-nig.org/
bishop@skannet.com

IBADAN-NORTH

Bishop Rt Revd Dr Segun Okubadejo, Bishopscourt, Moyede, PO Box 28961, Agodi, Ibadan *Tel:* 234 2 8107 482
email: angibn@skannet.com

IBADAN-SOUTH

Bishop Rt Revd Jacob Ademola Ajetunmobi, Bishopscourt, PO Box 166, Dugbe, Ibadan
Tel and *Fax:* 234 2 231 6464
email: ibadan-south@anglican-nig.org/
jacajet@skannet.com

IFE

Bishop Rt Revd Oluranti Odubogun, Bishopscourt, PO Box 312, Ile-Ife, Osun State
Tel: 234 36 232 255
email: stphilipscathayetoroife@yahoo.com

IFE EAST

Bishop Rt Revd Rufus Okeremi

IGBOMINA

Bishop Rt Revd Michael O. Akinyemi, Bishopscourt, Esie, PO Box 102, Oro P.A, Kwara State
Tel: 234 31 700 0025
email: igbomina@anglican-nig.org

ILESA

Bishop Rt Revd Dr Samuel O. Sowale, Bishopscourt, Oke-Ooye, PO Box 237, Ilesa
Tel: 234 36 460 138
email: ilesha@anglican-nig.org/
bishop-solwale@yahoo.com

JEBBA

Bishop Rt Revd Timothy S. Adewole, Bishopscourt, PO Box 2, Kwara State
Tel: 234 803 572 5298 (Mobile)

KWARA

Bishop Rt Revd Dr Olusegun Adeyemi, Bishopscourt, Fate Rd, PO Box 1884, Ilorin, Kwara State *Tel:* 234 31 220 879
email: angkwa@skannet.com

NEW BUSSA

Bishop Rt Revd Israel Amoo, Bishopscourt, off Kanji Road, PO Box 208, New Bussa, Niger State
Tel: 234 31 220 125
email: anglicannewbussa@yahoo.com

OFFA

Bishop Rt Revd Gabriel A. Akinbiyi, PO Box 21, Offa, Kwara State *Tel:* 234 31 801 011
email: offa@anglican-nig.org

OGBOMOSO (Missionary diocese)

Bishop Rt Revd Dr Matthew Osunade, Bishop's House, PO Box 1909, Ogbomoso, Osun State
Tel: 234 803 524 4606 (Mobile)
email: ogbomoso@anglican-nig.org/
maaosunade@yahoo.com

OKE-OGUN

Bishop Rt Revd Solomon Amusan, Bishopscourt, Apinnite, PO Box 30, Saki, Oyo State
Tel: 234 802 323 3365 (Mobile)

OKE-OSUN

Bishop Rt Revd Nathaniel Fasogbon, Bishopscourt, PO Box 251, Gbongan, Osun State

OMU-ARAN

Bishop Rt Revd Philip Adeyemo, Bishop's House, Expressway, PO Box 224, Omu-Aran, Kwara State *Tel:* 234 05 673 7052

OSUN

Bishop Rt Revd James Afolabi Popoola, Bishopscourt, Isale-Aro, PO Box 285, Osogbo
Tel: 234 35 240 325
email: osun@anglican-nig.org

OYO

Bishop Rt Revd Jacob Ola Fasipe, Bishopscourt, PO Box 23, Oyo *Tel:* 234 803 857 2120 (Mobile)
email: oyo@anglican-nig.org

PROVINCE OF JOS

Archbishop Most Revd Benjamin A. Kwashi (*Bishop of Jos*)

BAUCHI
Bishop Rt Revd Musa Tula, Bishop's House, 2 Hospital Rd, PO Box 2450, Bauchi
Tel: 234 77 546 066
email: bauchi@anglican-nig.org

BUKURU
Bishop Rt Revd Jawn Zhumbes, Bishopscourt, Citrus Estate Sabon Bariki, PO Box 605, Plateau State
Tel: 234 803 397 9906 (Mobile)

DAMATURU
Bishop Rt Revd Abiodun Ogunyemi, PO Box 312, Damaturu, Yobe State
Tel: 234 74 522 142
email: damaturu@anglican-nig.org

GOMBE
Bishop Rt Revd Henry C. Ndukuba, Bishops-court, PO Box 1509, Gombe, Gombe State, 760001 Nigeria
Tel: 234 72 221 212
email: gombe@anglican-nig.org/
ndukubah@yahoo.com

JALINGO
Bishop Rt Revd Timothy Yahaya, PO Box 4, Jalingo, Taraba State 660001
Tel and *Fax:* 234 79 223 812
email: jalingo@anglican.skannet.com.ng

JOS
Bishop Most Revd Benjamin A. Kwashi (*Archbishop of the Province of Jos*), Bishopscourt, PO Box 6283, Jos, 930001, Plateau State
Tel: 234 73 464 325
234 803 701 7928 (Mobile)
email: jos@anglican-nig.org

LANGTANG
Bishop Rt Revd Stanley Fube

MAIDUGURI
Bishop Rt Revd Emmanuel K. Mani, Bishopscourt, Off Lagos St, GRA PO Box 1693, Maiduguri, Borno State
Tel and *Fax:* 234 76 234 010
234 802 374 7463 (Mobile)
email: maiduguri@anglican-nig.org

PANKSHIN
Bishop Rt Revd Olumuyiwa Ajayi, Diocesan Secretariat, PO Box 24, Pankshin, Plateau State
Tel: 234 803 344 7318 (Mobile)
email: olumijayi@yahoo.com

YOLA
Bishop Rt Revd Markus A. Ibrahim, PO Box 601, Jimeta-Yola, Adamawa State
Tel: 234 75 624 303
234 805 175 9508 (Mobile)
email: yola@anglican-nig.org/
marcusibrahim2002@yahoo.com

PROVINCE OF KADUNA
Archbishop Most Revd Edmund E. Akanya (*Bishop of Kebbi*)

BARI
Bishop Rt Revd Idris Zubairu

DUTSE
Bishop Rt Revd Yusuf Ibrahim Lumu, PO Box 6, Yadi, Dutse, Jigawa State
Tel: 234 64 721 379
234 803 583 9381 (Mobile)
email: dutse@anglican-nig.org

GUSAU
Bishop Rt Revd John G. Danbinta, PO Box 64, Gusau, Zamfara State
Tel: 234 63 204 747
email: gusau@anglican-nig.org

KADUNA
Bishop Rt Revd Josiah Idowu-Fearon, PO Box 72, Kaduna
Tel: 234 62 240 085
Fax: 234 62 244 408
email: kaduna@anglican-nig.org

KANO
Bishop Rt Revd Zakka Lalle Nyam, Bishopscourt, PO Box 362, Kano
Tel and *Fax:* 234 64 647 816
email: kano@anglican-nig.org

KATSINA
Bishop Rt Revd Jonathan Bamaiyi, Bishop's Lodge, PO Box 904, Katsina
Tel: 234 65 432 718
234 803 601 5584 (Mobile)
email: bpjonathanbamaiyi@yahoo.co.uk

KEBBI
Bishop Most Revd Edmund E. Akanya (*Archbishop of the Province of Kaduna*), PO Box 701, Birnin Kebbi, Kebbi State
Tel and *Fax:* 234 68 321 179
email: kebbi@anglican-nig.org/
kebbi@anglican.skannet.com

SOKOTO
Bishop Rt Revd Augustine Omole, Bishop's Lodge, 68 Shuni Road, PO Box 3489, Sokoto
Tel: 234 60 234 639/234 60 232 323
email: sokoto@anglican-nig.org

WUSASA
Bishop Rt Revd Ali Buba Lamido, PO Box 28, Wusasa, Zaria, Kaduna State
Tel: 234 69 334 594
email: wusasa@anglican.skannet.com.ng

ZARIA
Bishop Rt Revd Cornelius Bello, Bishopscourt, St George's Cathedral, PO Box 28, Zaria, Kaduna State
Tel: 234 69 335 033
email: cssbello@hotmail.com

PROVINCE OF LAGOS
Archbishop Most Revd Ephraim Adebola Ademowo (*Bishop of Lagos*)

AWORI
Bishop Rt Revd Johnson Akinwamide Atere

BADAGRY (Missionary diocese)
Bishop Rt Revd Babatunde J. Adeyemi, Bishops-court, Kunle Gardens, Seme Road, Iyaafin Junction, PO Box 7, Badagry, Lagos State
Tel: 234 1 773 5546
234 803 306 4601 (Mobile)
email: badagry@anglican-nig.org

EGBA
Bishop Rt Revd Dr Matthew O. Owadayo, Bishopscourt, Onikolobo, PO Box 267, Ibara, Abeokuta *Tel:* 234 39 240 933
234 803 319 2799 (Mobile)
Fax: 234 39 240 933
*email:*egba@anglican-nig.org/
mowadayo@yahoo.com

EGBA WEST
Bishop Rt Revd Samuel Ajani, Bishopscourt, Oke-Ata Housing Estate, PO Box 6204, Sapon, Abeokuta *Tel:* 234 805 518 4822 (Mobile)
email: samuelajani@yahoo.com

IFO
Bishop Rt Revd Akin Odejide, Bishopscourt, Trinity House KM1, Ibogun Rd, PO Box 104, Ifo, Ogun State *Tel:* 234 1 763 6335
email: jaodejide@yahoo.com

IJEBU
Bishop Rt Revd Ezekiel Awosoga, Bishopscourt, Ejinrin Rd, PO Box 112, Ijebu-Ode
Tel: 234 37 432 886
email: ijebu@anglican-nig.org/
bishop@ang-ijebudiocese.com

IJEBU NORTH
Bishop Rt Revd Solomon Kuponu, Bishopscourt, PO Box 6, Ijebu-Igbo, Ogun State
Tel: 234 803 457 8506 (Mobile)
email: dioceseofijebunorth@yahoo.com

LAGOS
Bishop Most Revd Ephraim Adebola Ademowo (*Archbishop of the Province of Lagos*), 29 Marina, PO Box 13, Lagos *Tel:* 234 1 263 5930
email: lagos@anglican.skannet.com.ng/
diocesan@dioceseoflagos.org

LAGOS MAINLAND
Bishop Rt Revd Adebayo Akinde, PO Box 45, Ebute-Metta, Lagos

LAGOS WEST
Bishop Rt Revd Peter A. Adebiyi, PO Box 506, Ikeja, Lagos State *Tel:* 234 1 493 7336/7/8
email: lagoswest@anglican-nig.org/
dioceseoflagoswest@yahoo.com

ON THE COAST
Bishop Rt Revd Joshua Ogunele, Bishopscourt, Ikoya Rd, P. M. B. 3, Ilutitun-Osooro, Ondo State
Tel: 234 805 634 5496 (*Mobile*)

REMO
Bishop Rt Revd Michael O. Fape, Bishopscourt, Ewusi St, PO Box 522, Sagamu, Ogun State
Tel: 234 37 640 598
email: remo@anglican-nig.org/
mofape@skannet.com

YEWA
Bishop Rt Revd Simeon O. M. Adebola, Bishopscourt, PO Box 484, Ilaro, Ogun State
Tel: 234 1 7924 0696

MISSIONS PROVINCE
NOMADIC MISSION
Bishop Rt Revd Simon P. Mutum, PO Box 381, Bukuru Jos, Plateau State
Tel: 234 803 623 4030 (mobile)
email: anglicannomadic@yahoo.co.uk /
angnomadic@yahoo.com

PROVINCE OF THE NIGER
Archbishop Most Revd Maxwell S. C. Anikwenwa (*Bishop of Awka*)

ABAKALIKI
Bishop Rt Revd Benson C. B. Onyeibor, All Saints' Cathedral, PO Box 112, Abakaliki, Ebonyi State *Tel:* 234 43 220 762
234 803 501 3083 (Mobile)
email: abakaliki@anglican-nig.org

AFIKPO
Bishop Rt Revd Paul Udogu, Bishop's House, Uwana, PO Box 699, Afikpo, Ebonyi State
Tel: 234 803 344 6534 (Mobile)
email: udogupaul@yahoo.com

AGUATA
Bishop Rt Revd Christian Ogochukwo Efobi, Bishopscourt, PO Box 1128, Ekwulobia, Anambra State *Tel:* 234 803 750 1077 (Mobile)
email: aguata@anglican-nig.com

AWGU-ANINRI
Bishop Rt Revd Emmanuel Agwu, Bishopscourt, PO Box 305, Awgu, Enugu State
Tel: 234 803 334 9360 / 805 731 4775 (Mobile)

AWKA
Bishop Most Revd Maxwell S. C. Anikwenwa (*Archbishop of the Province of The Niger*), Bishopscourt, Ifite Rd, PO Box 130, Awka, Anambra State *Tel:* 234 48 550 058
email: awka@anglican-nig.org/
anglawka@infoweb.com.ng

ENUGU
Bishop Rt Revd Dr Emmanuel O. Chukwuma, Bishop's House, PO Box 418, Enugu, Enugu State *Tel:* 234 42 453 804
email: enugu@anglican-nig.org

ENUGU NORTH
Bishop Rt Revd Sosthenes Eze, Bishopscourt, St Mary's Cathedral, Ngwo-Enugu
Tel: 234 802 370 9362 (Mobile)
email: venzoseze@yahoo.com

IHIALA
Bishop Rt Revd Ralph Okafor

IKWO
Bishop Rt Revd Kenneth Ifemene, Bishop's Residence, Agubia Ikwo, PO Box 998, Abakaliki, Ebonyi State   *Tel:* 234 805 853 4849 (Mobile)
email: bishopikwoanglican@yahoo.com

MBAMMILI
Bishop Rt Revd Henry Okeke

NGBO
Bishop Rt Revd Christian I. Ebisike, Bishop's House, Ezillo, PO Box 93, Abakaliki, Ebonyi State   *Tel:* 234 806 779 4899 (Mobile)
email: ngbodio@yahoo.com

NIGER WEST
Bishop Rt Revd Anthony O. Nkwoka
Tel: 234 803 384 3339 (Mobile)
email: ankwoka@yahoo.com

NIKE
Bishop Rt Revd Evans Ibeagha, Bishopscourt, Off Hill View Avenue, Trans-Ekulu, PO Box 2416, Enugu, Enugu State
Tel: 234 803 324 1387 (Mobile)
email: pnibeagha@yahoo.com

NNEWI
Bishop Rt Revd Godwin I. N. Okpala, Bishopscourt, PO Box 2630, Nnewi, Anambra State   *Tel:* 234 46 311 253/308 580
email: nnewi@anglican-nig.org/
nnewianglican@infoweb.abs.net

NSUKKA
Bishop Rt Revd Alloysius Agbo, PO Box 516, Nsukka, Enugu State
email: nsukka@anglican-nig.org

OGBARU
Bishop Rt Revd Samuel Ezeofor, Bishopscourt, PO Box 46, Atani, Anambra State
Tel: 234 46 306 587
email: ezechukwunyere@yahoo.com

OJI RIVER
Bishop Rt Revd Amos A. Madu, PO Box 213, Oji River, Enugu State   *Tel:* 234 42 882 219
234 803 670 4888 (Mobile)
email: ojiriver@anglican-nig.org

ON THE NIGER
Bishop Rt Revd Ken Okeke, Bishopscourt, PO Box 42, Onitsha, Anambra State
Tel: 234 46 410 337
email: niger@anglican-nig.org/
kengoziokeke@yahoo.com

PROVINCE OF NIGER DELTA
Archbishop Most Revd Ugochuckwu U. Ezuoke (*Bishop of Aba*)

ABA
Bishop Most Revd Ugochuckwu U. Ezuoke, Bishopscourt, 70/72 St Michael's Rd, PO Box 212, Aba, Abia State   *Tel:* 234 82 308 431
email: aba@anglican-nig.org/
abanglifoserve@hotmail.com

ABA NGWA NORTH
Bishop Rt Revd Nathan C. Kanu, Bishopscourt, PO Box 43, Aba, Abia State
Tel: 234 803 822 4623
email: odinathnfe@sbcglobal.net

AHOADA
Bishop Rt Revd Clement Nathan Ekpeye, Bishopscourt, St Paul's Cathedral, PO Box 4, Ahoada East L.G.A., Rivers State
Tel: 234 803 542 2847 (Mobile)
email: ahoada@anglican-nig.org

AROCHUKWU-OHAFIA (Missionary diocese)
Bishop Rt Revd Johnson C. Onuoha, Bishopscourt, PO Box 193, Arochukwu, Abia State
Tel: 234 803 717 0234 (Mobile)
email: arooha@anglican-nig.org/
johnchiobishop@yahoo.com

CALABAR
Bishop Rt Revd Tunde Adeleye, Bishopscourt, PO Box 74, Calabar, Cross River State
Tel: 234 98 232 812
234 803 337 3120 (Mobile)
email: calabar@anglican-nig.org/
bishoptunde@yahoo.com

ETCHE
Bishop Rt Revd Okechukwu Precious Nwala, Bishopscourt, PO Box 89, Okehi, Etche Rivers State   *Tel*: 234 807 525 2842 (Mobile)
email: etchediocese@yahoo.com/
precious_model5@yahoo.com

IKWERRE
Bishop Rt Revd Blessing Enyindah, Bishopscourt, PO Box 14229, Port Harcourt, Rivers State
Tel: 234 802 321 2824 (Mobile)
email: blessingenyindah@yahoo.com

IKWUANO
Bishop Rt Revd Chigozirim Onyegbule, Bishopscourt, PO Box 5, Oloko, Ikwuano, Abia State   *Tel:* 234 803 085 9310 (Mobile)
email: ikwuano@anglican-nig.org

ISIALA NGWA
Bishop Rt Revd Owen N. Azubuike, Bishops-court, St George's Cathedral Compound, Umuomainta Mbawsi P.M.B., Mbawsi, Abia State   *Tel:* 234 805 467 0528 (Mobile)
email: bpowenazubuike@yahoo.com

ISIALA NGWA SOUTH
Bishop Rt Revd Isaac Nwaobia, St Peter's Cathedral, PO Box 15, Owerrinta, Abia State
Tel: 234 805 787 1100
email: bishopisaacnwaobia@priest.com

ISIUKWUATO (Missionary diocese)
Bishop Rt Revd Samuel C. Chukuka, Bishop's House, PO Box 350, Ovim, Abia State
Tel: 234 803 338 6221 (Mobile)
email: isiukwuato@anglican-nig.org/
rootedword@yahoo.com

NIGER DELTA
Bishop Rt Revd Gabriel Pepple, PO Box 115, Port Harcourt, Rivers State   *Tel:* 234 84 233 308
email: nigerdelta@anglican-nig.org

NIGER DELTA NORTH
Bishop Rt Revd Ignatius Kattey, PO Box 53, Diobu, Port Harcourt, Rivers State
Tel: 234 84 231 338
email: niger-delta-north@anglican-nig.org/
nigerdeltanorth@yahoo.com

NIGER DELTA WEST
Bishop Rt Revd Adolphus Amabebe, Bishopscourt, PO Box 10, Yenagoa, Bayelsa State
Tel: 234 803 372 5982 (Mobile)
email: niger-delta-west@anglican-nig.org

NORTHERN IZON
Bishop Rt Revd Anga Fred Nyanabo

OGBIA
Bishop Rt Revd James Oruwori

OGONI (Missionary diocese)
Bishop Rt Revd Solomon S. Gberegbara, Bishopscourt, PO Box 73, Bori-Ogoni, Rivers State   *Tel:* 234 803 339 2545 (Mobile)
email: ogoni@anglican-nig.org/
ogoniangdiocese@yahoo.com

OKRIKA
Bishop Rt Revd Tubokosemie Abere, Bishopscourt, PO Box 11, Okrika, Rivers State
Tel: 234 84 575 003
234 803 312 5226 (Mobile)
email: dioceseofokrika@yahoo.com

UKWA
Bishop Rt Revd Samuel K. Eze, PO Box 20468, Aba, Abia State   *Tel:* 234 803 789 2431 (Mobile)
email: ukwa@anglican-nig.org/
kelerem53787@yahoo.com

UMUAHIA
Bishop Rt Revd Ikechi N. Nwosu, Bishopscourt, PO Box 96, Umuahia, Abia State
Tel: 234 88 220 311
email: umuahia@anglican-nig.org

UYO
Bishop Rt Revd Isaac Orama, Bishopscourt, PO Box 70, Uyo, Akwa Ibom State
Tel: 234 85 202 440
234 803 710 7894
email: uyo@anglican-nig.org

PROVINCE OF ONDO
Archbishop Most Revd Samuel Adedayo Abe (*Bishop of Ekiti*)

AKOKO
Bishop Rt Revd Gabriel Akinbiyi, PO Box 572, Ikare-Akoko, Ondo State   *Tel:* 234 50 670 209
email: akoko@anglican.skannet.com.ng

AKURE
Bishop Rt Revd Michael O. Ipinmoye, Bishopscourt, PO Box 1622, Akure, Ondo State
Tel and *Fax:* 234 34 231 012
234 803 717 4561 (Mobile)
email: angdak@gannetcity.net/
akure@anglican-nig.org

EKITI
Bishop Most Revd Samuel A. Abe (*Archbishop the Province of Ondo*), Bishopscourt, PO Box 12, Ado-Ekiti, Ekiti State   *Tel:* 234 30 250 305
234 802 225 9389 (Mobile)
email: ekiti@anglican.skannet.com.ng/
ekiti@anglican-nig.org

EKITI-OKE
Bishop Rt Revd Isaac O. Olubowale, Bishopscourt, PO Box 207, Usi-Ekiti, Ekiti State
Tel: 234 803 600 9582 (Mobile)
email: ekitioke@anglican-nig.org

EKITI-WEST
Bishop Rt Revd Samuel O. Oke, Bishop's Residence, 6 Ifaki St, PO Box 477, Ijero-Ekiti
Tel: 234 803 429 2823 (Mobile)
email: ekitiwest@anglican-nig.org

KABBA
Bishop Rt Revd Samuel O. Olayanju, Bishopscourt, Obaro Way, PO Box 62, Kabba, Kogi State
Tel: 234 58 300 633
234 803 653 0180 (Mobile)

ONDO
Bishop Rt Revd George L. Lasebikan, Bishopscourt, College Rd, PO Box 265, Ondo
Tel: 234 34 610 718
234 803 472 1813 (Mobile)
email: ondo@anglican-nig.org/
angond@skannet.com

OWO
Bishop Rt Revd James A. Oladunjoye, Bishopscourt, PO Box 472, Owo, Ondo State
Tel: 234 51 241 463
email: owo@anglican-nig.org

PROVINCE OF OWERRI
Archbishop Most Revd Bennett C. I. Okoro (*Bishop of Orlu*)

EGBU
Bishop Rt Revd Emmanuel U. Iheagwam, All Saints' Cathedral, PO Box 1967, Owerri, Imo State
Tel: 234 83 231 797
234 803 491 1090 (Mobile)
email: egbu@anglican-nig.org

IDEATO
Bishop Rt Revd Caleb A. Maduomo, Bishopscourt, PO Box 2, Arondizuogu, Imo State
Tel: 234 803 745 4503 (Mobile)
email: ideato@anglican-nig.org/
bpomacal@hotmail.com

MBAISE
Bishop Rt Revd Bright J. E. Ogu, Bishopscourt, PO Box 10, Ife, Ezinihitte Mbaise, Imo State
Tel: 234 782 441 483
234 803 553 4762 (Mobile)
email: mbaise@anglican-nig.org/
bjeogu@yahoo.com

OJAHI-EGBEMA
Bishop Rt Revd Chidi Oparaojiaku

OKIGWE NORTH
Bishop Rt Revd Godson Ukanwa, PO Box 156, Okigwe, Imo State *Tel:* 234 806 475 8139 (Mobile)
email: okigwenorth@anglican-nig.org

OKIGWE SOUTH
Bishop Rt Revd David Onuoha, Bishopscourt, Ezeoke Nsu, PO Box 235, Nsu, Ehime Mbano LGA, Imo State *Tel:* 234 8037 454 510 (Mobile)
email: okigwe-south@anglican-nig.org/
okisouth@yahoo.com

ORLU
Bishop Most Revd Bennett C. I. Okoro (*Archbishop of the Province of Owerri*), Bishopscourt, PO Box 260, Nkwerre, Imo State *Tel:* 234 82 440 538
234 803 671 1271 (Mobile)

ORU
Bishop Rt Revd Geoffrey Chukwunenye, Emmanuel Cathedral Church, Mgbidi, Imo State
Tel: 234 803 308 1270 (Mobile)
email: geoinlagos@yahoo.com

OWERRI
Bishop Rt Revd Dr Cyril C. Okorocha, No. 1 Mission Crescent, PMB 1063, Owerri, Imo State
Tel: 234 83 230 784
email: owerri@anglican-nig.org/
adowe@phca.linkserve.com

ON THE LAKE
Bishop Rt Revd Chijioke Oti

The Anglican Church of Papua New Guinea

Members 166,046
Organized as a missionary diocese of Australia in 1898, the Church was part of the Australian province of Queensland until 1977. The first indigenous priest was ordained in 1914. The Anglican Church functions mostly in rural areas where mountains and rainforest provide natural barriers to travel. Some 60 per cent of the funding is raised internally; most of the balance comes from grants from Australia, New Zealand, Canada and the UK-based Papua New Guinea Church Partnership.

Archbishop Most Revd James Simon Ayong (*Bishop of Aipo Rongo*)

General Secretary Mr Richard Rabiafi, PO Box 673, Lae, Morobe Province *Tel:* 675 472 4111
Fax: 675 472 1852
email: acpnggensec@global.net.pg

Provincial Registrar Mrs Winifred Kamit, PO Box 1569, Port Moresby, National Capital District
Tel: 675 321 1033
Fax: 675 321 1885
email: wkamit@gadens.com.pg

THEOLOGICAL COLLEGE
Newton Theological College, PO Box 162, Popondetta, Oro Province (*Principal* Br Justus Van Houten, SSF) *Tel:* 675 329 7421
Fax: 675 329 7476
email: acpngntc@global.net.pg
Web: www.newtoncollege-png.org/support.htm

CHURCH PAPER
Family Magazine. Published three times a year. *Editors* Mr and Mrs Hugh Dormer, PO Box 2476, Lae, Morobe Province 411
Tel and *Fax:* 675 472 0537
email: dormer@global.net.pg

AIPO RONGO
Bishop Most Revd James Simon Ayong (*Archbishop of the Church of Papua New Guinea*), PO Box 893, Mt Hagen, Western Highlands Province *Tel:* 675 542 1131/3727
Fax: 675 542 1181
email: acpngair@global.net.pg/
archbishopjayong@hotmail.com

Suffragan Bishops
Rt Revd Nathan Ingen (*same address*)
Rt Revd Denys Ririka, PO Box 1178, Goroka, Eastern Highlands Province

DOGURA
Bishop Rt Revd Clyde Igara, PO Box 19, Dogura, MBP
Tel: 675 641 1530
Fax: 675 641 1129

NEW GUINEA ISLANDS
Bishop Rt Revd Allan Migi, Bishop's House, PO Box 806, Kimbe
Tel and *Fax:* 675 9 835 120
email: acpngngi@global.net.pg/
acpngngibishop@global.net.pg

POPONDOTA
Bishop Rt Revd Joe Kopapa, Bishop's House, PO Box 26, Popondetta, Oro Province
Tel: 675 329 7194
Fax: 675 329 7476
email: acpngpop@online.net.pg
Web: http://popondota.anglican.org/

PORT MORESBY
Bishop Rt Revd Peter Ramsden, PO Box 6491, Boroko, NCD
Tel: 675 323 2489
Fax: 675 323 2493
email: acpngpom@global.net.pg/
psramsden.pomanglican@gmail.com
Web: www.portmoresby.anglican.org

The Episcopal Church in the Philippines

Members 170,000
The Philippines is the only Christian nation in Asia. Its 90,000,000 or so population is composed of 75% Roman Catholics while the other 25% are Muslims and other Christian bodies including the Episcopal Church in the Philippines (ECP) which now has six dioceses. The ECP was first established by the Protestant Episcopal Church in the USA (PECUSA) in 1901 and became an autonomous province of the Anglican Communion in 1991. It continues to maintain a close relationship with PECUSA. Its ministry after gaining autonomy is focused not only in the nurture of the faith of the believers and doing evangelism. It is actively involved in community development projects to help eradicate poverty which is hounding the lives of millions of Filipinos today.

National Office The ECP Mission Center, 275 E Rodriguez Sr Ave, 1102 Quezon City

(*Postal address*) PO Box 10321, Broadway Centrum, 1112 Quezon City
Tel: 63 2 722 8478/8481
Fax: 63 2 721 1923
email: ecpnational@yahoo.com.ph

Prime Bishop Most Revd Edward P. Malecdan (*same address*)   *email:* edmalecdan@yahoo.com

Corporate Secretary Ms Laura S. Ocampo (*same address*)   *email:* lbso2@yahoo.com

Administrative Assistant Vacancy

National Finance Officer Ms Bridget T. Lacdao
email: bbalitog@yahoo.com

CENTRAL PHILIPPINES
Bishop Rt Revd Dixie C. Taclobao, 281 E. Rodriguez Sr. Avenue, 1102 Quezon City
Tel: 63 2 412 8561
Fax: 63 2 724 2143
email: dixie_taclobao@yahoo.com.ph

NORTH CENTRAL PHILIPPINES
Bishop Rt Revd Joel A. Pachao, 358 Magsaysay Ave, Baguio City 2600
Tel: 63 74 443 7705
email: bpjoelpachao@yahoo.com

NORTHERN LUZON
Bishop Rt Revd Renato M. Abibico, Bulanao, 3800 Tabuk, Kalinga
Tel: 63 920 271 9999
email: reneabibico@yahoo.com

NORTHERN PHILIPPINES
Bishop Rt Revd Brent Harry W. Alawas, 2616 Bontoc, Mountain Province
Tel: and *Fax:* 63 74 602 1026
email: ednpbrent@hotmail.com

SANTIAGO
Bishop Rt Revd Alexander A. Wandag, Maharlika Highway, 3311 Divisoria Santiago City, Isabela
Tel: 63 78 682 3756
Fax: 63 78 682 1256
email: alexwandageds@yahoo.com

SOUTHERN PHILIPPINES
Bishop Rt Revd Danilo Labacanacruz Bustamante, 186 Sinsuat Ave, Rosario Heights, 9600 Cotabato City
Tel: 63 64 421 2960
Fax: 63 64 421 1703
email: edsp_ecp@yahoo.com

The Church of the Province of Rwanda

Members 1,200,000

In just over 10,170 square miles there are more than one million Anglicans among a fast-growing population, currently 9.5 million. The former Rwanda Mission (now CMS) established its first station at Gahini in 1925 and grew through the revival of the 1930s and 1940s, with the first Rwandan bishop appointed in 1965. Nine dioceses have up to 306 parishes and 379 clergy, organized in 96 deaconries. Like all strata of Rwandan society, the Church suffered, on many levels, through the genocide, and it is a major priority of the Church to replace clergy through training. The Church has a role as a healing ministry to the many traumatized people in Rwanda and to reconciliation, restoration, and rehabilitation. The Church has also been involved in rural development, medical work, vocational training, and education.

Archbishop Most Revd Emmanuel Mbona Kolini (*Bishop of Kigali*)

Dean of the Province Rt Revd Onesphore Rwaje (*Bishop of Byumba*)

Provincial Secretary Revd Emmanuel Gatera, BP 2487, Kigali
Tel: 250 514 160
Fax: 250 516 162
email: egapeer@yahoo.com

Provincial Treasurer Vacancy (*same address*)

BUTARE
Bishop Rt Revd Nathan Gasatura, BP 225, Butare
Tel and Fax: 250 530 504
email: rusodilo@yahoo.fr

BYUMBA
Bishop Rt Revd Onesphore Rwaje, BP 17, Byumba
Tel and Fax: 250 64 242
email: eer@rwanda1.com

CYANGUGU
Bishop Rt Revd Geoffrey Rwubusisi, BP 52, Cyangugu
Tel and Fax: 250 53 7878
email: bishoprwubusisi@yahoo.co.uk

GAHINI
Bishop Rt Revd Alexis Bilindabagabo, BP 22, Kigali
Tel and Fax: 250 567 422

KIBUNGO
Bishop Rt Revd Josias Sendegeya, EER Kibungo Diocese, BP 719, Kibungo
Tel and Fax: 250 566 194
email: bpjosias@yahoo.fr

KIGALI
Bishop Most Revd Emmanuel M. Kolini (*Archbishop of the Province*), BP 61, Kigali
Tel and Fax: 250 573 213
email: ek@terracom.rw

KIGEME
Bishop Rt Revd Augustin Mvunabandi, BP 67, Gikongoro
Tel: 250 535 086 (Office)
250 535 088 (Secretary)
250 535 087 (Home)
email: dkigeme@rwanda1.com

KIVU
Bishop Rt Revd Augustin Ahimana, BP 166 Gisenyi
Tel: 250 788 350 119

SHYIRA
Bishop Rt Revd John Rucyahana Kabango, BP 26, Ruhengeri
Tel and Fax: 250 546 449
email: bpjohnr@rwanda1.com

SHYOGWE
Bishop Rt Revd Jered Kalimba, BP 27, Gitarama
Tel: 250 562 460
Tel and Fax: 250 562 469
email: dsgwegit@yahoo.com

The Scottish Episcopal Church

Members 37,047

The roots of Scottish Christianity go back to St Ninian in the fourth century and St Columba in the sixth. After the Reformation, the Episcopal Church was the established Church of Scotland. It was however replaced as the established Church by the Presbyterians at the Revolution in 1689. Penal statutes in force from 1746 to 1792 weakened the Church, although many congregations remained and the bishops maintained continuity. In 1784 in Aberdeen, the Scottish Church initiated the world-wide expansion of the Anglican Communion with the consecration of the first bishop of the American Church. There was rapid growth in the nineteenth century influenced by the Tractarian movement.

Primus Most Revd David Chillingworth (*Bishop of St Andrews, Dunkeld & Dunblane*)
email: bishop@standrews.anglican.org
Web: www.standrews.anglican.org

Secretary General Mr John Stuart, 21 Grosvenor Crescent, Edinburgh EH12 5EE
Tel: 0131 225 6357
Fax: 0131 346 7247
email: secgen@scotland.anglican.org
Web: www.scotland.anglican.org

MINISTERIAL TRAINING
The Theological Institute of the Scottish Episcopal Church, 21 Grosvenor Crescent, Edinburgh EH12 5EE   *Tel:* 0131 225 6357
Fax: 0131 346 7247
email: tisec@scotland.anglican.org

CHURCH MAGAZINE
Inspires, thirty-two pages, four issues per year. Magazine format. Produced in-house – contact: *Inspires*, 21 Grosvenor Crescent, Edinburgh, EH12 5EE   *email:* inspires@scotland.anglican.org

ABERDEEN AND ORKNEY
Bishop Rt Revd Dr Robert Gillies, Diocesan Office, St Clement's Church House, Mastrick Drive, Aberdeen, AB16 6UF   *Tel:* 01224 662247
Fax: 01224 662168
email: office@aberdeen.anglican.org
Web: www.aberdeen.anglican.org

Dean Very Revd Dr A. E. Nimmo (*same address*)
Tel: 01224 662247
email: alexander306@btinternet.com

ST ANDREW'S CATHEDRAL, Aberdeen
Provost Very Revd Richard Kilgour
Tel: 01224 640119
email: provost@aberdeen.anglican.org

ARGYLL AND THE ISLES
Bishop Vacancy, St Moluag's Diocesan Centre, Croft Avenue, Oban, Argyll, PA34 5JJ
Tel: 01631 570 870
Fax: 01631 570411
email: office@argyll.anglican.org
Web: www.argyllandtheisles.org.uk

Dean Very Revd Norman MacCallum, Rectory, Ardconnel Terrace, Oban PA34 5DJ
Tel: 01631 562323
email: provostOban@argyll.anglican.org

ST JOHN THE DIVINE CATHEDRAL, Oban
(The Cathedral of Argyll)
Provost Very Revd Norman MacCallum, Rectory, Ardconnel Terrace, Oban PA34 5DJ
Tel: 01631 562323

COLLEGIATE CHURCH OF THE HOLY SPIRIT, Cumbrae
(The Cathedral of The Isles)
Warden David Todd   *Tel:* 01475 530353
Fax: 01475 530204
email: Cathedral_Cumbrae@btconnect.com
Web: www.island-retreats.org

BRECHIN
Bishop Rt Revd Dr John Mantle, Diocesan Office. Unit 14 Prospect III, Technology Park, Gemini Crescent, Dundee DD2 1SW   *Tel:* 01382 562244
email: office@brechin.anglican.org
Web: www.thedioceseofbrechin.org

Dean Very Revd David Mumford, St Andrew's Rectory, 9 Castle Street, Brechin, DD9 6JW
Tel: 01356 622708
email: dmumford3@btinternet.com

ST PAUL'S CATHEDRAL, Dundee
Provost Very Revd Jeremy Auld
Tel: 01382 224486
email: email@stpaulscathedraldundee.org

EDINBURGH
Bishop Rt Revd Brian Arthur Smith, Diocesan Centre, 21a Grosvenor Crescent, Edinburgh EH12 5EL   *Tel:* 0131 538 7033
Fax: 0131 538 7088
email: bishop@edinburgh.anglican.org
Web: www.dioceseofedinburgh.org

Dean Very Revd Kevin Pearson (*same address*)
email: pdo@scotland.anglican.org

ST MARY'S CATHEDRAL, Edinburgh
Provost Very Revd Dr Graham John Thomson Forbes, Cathedral Office, Palmerston Place, Edinburgh EH12 5AW   *Tel:* 0131 225 6293
Fax: 0131 225 3181
email: provost@cathedral.net

GLASGOW AND GALLOWAY
Bishop Rt Revd Dr Gregor Duncan, Diocesan Centre, 5 St Vincent Place, Glasgow G1 2DH
Tel: 0141 221 6911
Fax: 0141 221 7014
email: bishop@glasgow.anglican.org
Web: www.glasgow.anglican.org

Dean Very Revd Ian Barcroft, The Rectory, 4c Auchingramont Road, Hamilton ML3 6JT
Tel: 01698 429895
email: rector@stmarysepiscopalhamilton.co.uk

ST MARY THE VIRGIN CATHEDRAL, Glasgow
Provost Very Revd Kelvin Holdsworth, St Mary's Cathedral, 300 Great Western Rd, Glasgow G4 9JB   *Tel:* 0141 339 6691
Fax: 0141 334 5669
email: provost@thecathedral.org.uk

MORAY, ROSS AND CAITHNESS
Bishop Rt Revd Mark Strange, Bishop's House, St John's Rectory, Arpafeelie, North Kessock IV1 1XG   *Tel:* 01463 811333
email: bishop@moray.anglican.org
Web: www.morayrossandcaithness.co.uk

Dean Very Revd Clifford J. Piper, St John's Rectory, Victoria Road, Forres, Moray IV36 3BN
Tel: 01309 672856
email: deanofmoray@tiscali.co.uk

ST ANDREW'S CATHEDRAL, Inverness
Provost Very Revd Alex Gordon, 15 Ardross Street, Inverness, IV3 5NS   *Tel:* 01463 233 535
email: canonalexgordon@btconnect.com

ST ANDREWS, DUNKELD AND DUNBLANE
Bishop Most Revd David Chillingworth (*Primus*), Diocesan Centre, 28a Balhousie Street, Perth, PH1 5HJ
Tel: 01738 443173
Fax: 01738 443174
email: bishop@standrews.anglican.org
Web: www.standrews.anglican.org

Dean Very Revd Kenneth Rathband, 10 Rosemount Park, Blairgowrie PH10 6TZ
Tel: 01250 874 583
email: abcsaints@btinternet.com

ST NINIAN'S CATHEDRAL, Perth
Provost Very Revd Hunter Farquharson, St Ninian's Cathedral, North Methven Street, Perth PH1 5PP
Tel: 01738 850 987
email: provost@perthcathedral.co.uk

The Province of the Anglican Church in South East Asia

Members 224,200
The Anglican Church in South East Asia was originally under the jurisdiction of the Bishop of Calcutta. The first chaplaincy was formed in West Malaysia in 1805; the first bishop was consecrated in 1855. The Diocese of Labuan, Sarawak and Singapore was formed in 1881. A separate Diocese of Singapore was formed in 1909, and in 1962 the Diocese of Jesselton, later renamed Sabah, and the Diocese of Kuching were formed from the former Diocese of Borneo. In 1970 the Diocese of West Malaysia was formed from what had been the Diocese of Malaya and Singapore. Until the inauguration of the Church of the Province of South East Asia, the four dioceses (Kuching, Sabah, Singapore, and West Malaysia) were under the jurisdiction of the Archbishop of Canterbury. Although the province exists under certain social constraints, the Church has experienced much spiritual renewal and has sent out its own mission partners to various parts of the world, especially neighbouring Indonesia, Cambodia, Nepal, Laos, Vietnam and Myanmar.

Primate Most Revd Dr John Chew Hiang Chea (*Bishop of Singapore*)

Provincial Secretary Mr Caldwell David Joseph, No. 16, Jalan Pudu Lama, 50200 Kuala Lumpur, Malaysia
Tel: 60 3 2031 2728
Fax: 60 3 2031 3225
email: anglican@streamyx.com

Provincial Treasurer Mr Keith Chua, 35 Ford Avenue, Singapore 268714, Singapore
Tel: 65 6235 3344
Fax: 65 6736 1201

THEOLOGICAL COLLEGES
House of the Epiphany, PO Box No 347, 93704 Kuching, Sarawak, Malaysia (*Warden* Revd Michael Buma)

Trinity College, 490 Upper Bukit Timah Road, Singapore 678093 (interdenominational)

St Peter's Hall, residential hostel for Anglican students at Trinity College, Singapore (*Warden* Revd Hwa Chih)
Seminari Theoloji Malaysia (STM), Lot 3011, Taman South East, Jalan Tampin Lama, Batu 3, Seremban 70100, Negeri Sembilan, Malaysia (*Principal* Revd Dr Ezra Kok)

KUCHING
Bishop Rt Revd Bolly Anak Lapok, Bishop's House, PO Box 347, 93704 Kuching, Sarawak, Malaysia
Tel: 60 82 240 187
Fax: 60 82 426 488
email: bishopk@streamyx.com

SABAH
Bishop Rt Revd Albert Vun Cheong Fui, PO Box 10811, 88809 Kota Kinabalu, Sabah, Malaysia
Tel: 60 88 245 846
Fax: 60 88 245 942
email: bishopvn@streamyx.com

SINGAPORE
Bishop Most Revd Dr John Chew Hiang Chea (*Primate of the Anglican Church in South East Asia*), St. Andrews Village, No. 1, Francis Thomas Drive, #01–01, Singapore 359340
Tel: 65 6288 7585
Fax: 65 6288 5574
email: bpoffice@anglican.org.sg

Assistant Bishop Rt Revd Rennis Poniah, St John's and St Margaret's Church, 30 Dover Avenue, Singapore 139790, Singapore
Tel: 65 6773 9415
Fax: 65 6778 6264
email: rennis@sjsm.org.sg

WEST MALAYSIA
Bishop Rt Revd Ng Moon Hing, No. 16 Jalan Pudu Lama, 50200 Kuala Lumpur, Malaysia
Tel: 60 3 2031 2728
Fax: 60 3 2031 3225
email: anglican@streamyx.com

ANGLICAN AND PORVOO COMMUNIONS

Assistant Bishops
Rt Revd Dr. S. Batumalai, Christ Church, No. 48, Jalan Gereja, 75000, Melaka, Malaysia
Tel: 60 6 2848804
Fax: 60 6 2848804
email: ccm1753@tm.net.my

Rt Revd Andrew Phang See Yin, Church of Our Redeemer, 306, Jalan Bagan Lebai Tahir, Bagan Ajam, 13050 Butterworth, Penang, Malaysia
Tel: 60 4 3231568
Fax: 60 4 3231568
email: christpg@streamyx.com

The Anglican Church of Southern Africa

Members 2,600,000
The province is the oldest in Africa. British Anglicans met for worship in Cape Town after 1806, with the first bishop appointed in 1847. The twenty-eight dioceses of the province extend beyond the Republic of South Africa and include the Foreign and Commonwealth Office (St Helena and Tristan da Cunha), Mozambique (Lebombo and Niassa), the Republic of Namibia, the Kingdom of Lesotho, and the Kingdom of Swaziland. This Church and its leaders played a significant role in the abolition of apartheid in South Africa and in peace keeping in Mozambique and Angola. A mission diocese was inaugurated in August 2002 in Angola. The Diocese of Ukhahlamba was inaugurated in October 2009 and the Diocese of Mbashe was inaugurated in July 2010

Primate Most Revd Thabo Makgoba (*Archbishop of Cape Town and Metropolitan of the Anglican Church of Southern Africa*)

Provincial Executive Officer Revd Canon Allan Kannemeyer, 20 Bishopscourt Dr, Bishopscourt, Claremont, Western Cape 7708, South Africa
Tel: 27 21 763 1300
Fax: 27 21 797 1329
email: peo@anglicanchurchsa.org.za
Web: www.anglicanchurchsa.org.za

Provincial Treasurer Mr Rob S. Rogerson, PO Box 53014, Kenilworth, 7745, South Africa
Tel: 27 21 763 1300
Fax: 27 21 797 8319
email: rogerson@anglicanchurchsa.org.za

THEOLOGICAL COLLEGE
The College of the Transfiguration, PO Box 77, Grahamstown 6140
Tel: 27 46 622 3332
Fax: 27 46 622 3877
email: office@cott.co.za

ANGOLA (Missionary Diocese)
Bishop Rt Revd Andre Soares, Av. Lenini, Travessa D. Antonia Saldanha N.134, CP 10 341, Luanda, Angola
Tel: 244 2 395 792
Fax: 244 2 396 794
email: anglicana@ebonet.net/
bispo-Soares@hotmail.com

CAPE TOWN
Archbishop Most Revd Thabo Makgoba (*Metropolitan of Southern Africa*), 20 Bishopscourt Dr, Bishopscourt, Claremont, Cape Town 7708, Western Cape, South Africa
Tel: 27 21 763 1300
Fax: 27 21 797 1298/761 4193
email: archpa@anglicanchurchsa.org.za
Web: www.anglicanchurchsa.org

Bishop Suffragan
Rt Revd Garth Counsell (*Bishop of Table Bay*), PO Box 1932, Cape Town 8000
Tel: 27 21 465 1557
Fax: 27 21 465 1571
email: tablebay@ctdiocese.org.za

CHRIST THE KING
Bishop Rt Revd Peter John Lee, PO Box 1653, Rosettenville 2130, South Africa
Tel: 27 11 435 0097
Fax: 27 11 435 2868
email: dckpeter@corpdial.co.za

FALSE BAY
Bishop Rt Revd Merwyn Edwin Castle, PO Box 2804, Somerset West 7129, South Africa
Tel: 27 21 852 5243
Fax: 27 21 852 9430
email: bishopm@falsebaydiocese.org.za

GEORGE
Bishop Vacancy, PO Box 227, George 6530, Cape Province, South Africa
Tel: 27 44 873 5680
Fax: 27 44 873 5680
email: glynis@george.diocese.co.za

GRAHAMSTOWN
Bishop Rt Revd Ebenezer St Mark Ntlali, PO Box 181, Grahamstown 6140, Cape Province, South Africa
Tel: 27 46 636 1996
Fax: 27 46 622 5231
email: bpgtn@intekom.co.za

HIGHVELD
Bishop Rt Revd Hugh Bannerman, PO Box 17462, Benoni West 1503, South Africa
Tel: 27 11 422 2231
Fax: 27 11 420 1336
email: bishophveld@iafrica.com

JOHANNESBURG
Bishop Rt Revd Brian Charles Germond, PO Box 1131, Johannesburg 2000, South Africa
Tel: 27 11 336 8724
Fax: 27 11 333 3053
email: bgermond@cpsajoburg.org.za

KIMBERLEY AND KURUMAN
Bishop Rt Revd Oswald Peter Patrick Swartz, PO Box 45, Kimberley 8300, South Africa
Tel: 27 53 833 2433
Fax: 27 53 831 2730
email: oppswartz@onetel.com

LEBOMBO
Bishop Rt Revd Dinis Salomâo Sengulane, CP 120, Maputo, Mozambique
Tel: 258 1 404 364/405 885
Fax: 258 1 401 093
email: bispo_sengulane@virconn.com

LESOTHO
Bishop Rt Revd Adam Andrease Mallane Taaso, PO Box 87, Maseru 100, Lesotho
Tel: 266 22 31 1974
Fax: 266 22 31 0161
email: diocese@ilesotho.com

MATLOSANE
Bishop Rt Revd Stephen Molopi Diseko, PO Box 11417, Klerksdorp 2570, South Africa
Tel: 27 18 464 2260
Fax: 27 18 462 4939
email: diocesematlosane@telkomsa.net

MPUMALANGA
Bishop Rt Revd Daniel Malasela Kgomosotho, PO Box 4327, White River 1240   *Tel:* 27 13 751 1960
Fax: 27 13 751 3638
email: diompu@telkomsa.net

MTHATHA
Bishop Rt Revd Sitembele Tobela Mzamane, PO Box 25, Umtata, Transkei 5100, South Africa
Tel: 27 47 532 4450
Fax: 27 47 532 4191
email: anglicbspmthatha@intekom.co.za

NAMIBIA
Bishop Rt Revd Nathaniel Ndxuma Nakwatumbah, PO Box 57, Windhoek, Namibia
Tel: 264 61 238 920
Fax: 264 61 225 903
email: bishop@anglicanchurchnamibia.com

NATAL
Bishop Rt Revd Rubin Phillip, PO Box 47439, Greyville, 4023 South Africa   *Tel:* 27 31 309 2066
Fax: 27 31 308 9316
email: bishop@dionatal.org.za

Bishops Suffragan
Rt Revd Hummingfield Charles Nkosinathi

Ndwandwe (*Suffragan Bishop of the South Episcopal Area*) (*same address*)   *Tel:* 27 33 394 1560
email: bishopndwandwe@dionatal.org.za

Rt Revd Funginkosi Mbhele (*Suffragan Bishop of the North West Episcopal Area*), PO Box 123 Escort 3310, South Africa   *Tel:* 27 36 352 2893
Fax: 27 36 352 2810
email: bishopmbhele@dionatal.org.za

NIASSA
Bishop Rt Revd Mark van Koevering, CP 264, Lichinga, Niassa, Mozambique
Tel and *Fax:* 258 712 0735
email: bishop.niassa@gmail.com

PORT ELIZABETH
Bishop Rt Revd Nceba Bethlehem Nopece, PO Box 7109, Newton Park 6055, South Africa
Tel: 27 41 365 1387
Fax: 27 41 365 2049
email: pebishop@iafrica.com

PRETORIA
Bishop Rt Revd Johannes Thomas Seoka, PO Box 1032, Pretoria 0001, South Africa
Tel: 27 12 322 2218
Fax: 27 12 322 9411
email: ptabish@dioceseofpretoria.org

SALDANHA BAY
Bishop The Rt Revd Raphael Bernard Viburt Hess, PO Box 420, Malmesbury 7299, South Africa   *Tel:* 27 22 487 3885
Fax: 27 22 487 3886
email: bishop@dioceseofsaldanhabay.org.za

ST HELENA
Bishop Vacancy, PO Box 62, Island of St Helena, South Atlantic   *Tel:* 290 4471
Fax: 290 4728
email: bishop@cwmail.sh

ST MARK THE EVANGELIST
Bishop Rt Revd Martin Andre Breytenbach, PO Box 643, Polokwane 0700, South Africa
Tel: 27 15 297 3297
Fax: 27 15 297 0408
email: martin@stmark.co.za

SWAZILAND
Bishop Rt Revd Meshack Boy Mabuza, Bishop's House, Muir Street, Mbabane, Swaziland
Tel: 268 404 3624
Fax: 268 404 6759
email: bishopmabuza@africaonline.co.sz

THE FREE STATE
Bishop Rt Revd (Elistan) Patrick Glover, PO Box 411, Bloemfontein, 9300, South Africa
Tel: 27 51 447 6053
Fax: 27 51 447 5874
email: bishoppatrick@dsc.co.za
Web: www.cpsa.org.za/bloemfontein

ANGLICAN AND PORVOO COMMUNIONS

UMZIMVUBU
Bishop Rt Revd Mlibo Mteteleli Ngewu, PO Box 644, Kokstad 4700, South Africa
Tel and *Fax:* 27 39 727 4117
email: mzimvubu@futurenet.co.za

ZULULAND
Bishop Rt Revd Dino Gabriel, PO Box 147, Eshowe 3815, South Africa
Tel and *Fax:* 27 354 742 047
email: bishopdino@netactive.co.za

UKHAHLAMBA
Bishop Rt Revd Mazwi Ernest Tisani, PO Box 1673 Queenstown, 5320 South Africa
Tel: 27 45 858 8673
Fax: 27 45 858 8675
email: ukhahlamba@lantic.net

MBASHE
Bishop Vacancy

The Anglican Church of the Southern Cone of America

(Iglesia Anglicana del Cono Sur de América)

Members 22,490

British immigrants brought Anglicanism to South America in the nineteenth century. The South American Missionary Society continues to work effectively among indigenous peoples and today actively supports diocesan initiatives. In 1974 the Archbishop of Canterbury gave over his metropolitical authority for the dioceses of the Southern Cone, and in 1981 the new province was formed. It includes Argentina, Bolivia, Chile, Northern Argentina, Paraguay, Peru and Uruguay.

Presiding Bishop Most Revd Gregory James Venables (*Bishop of Argentina*)
Web: www.anglicanos.net

Provincial Secretary Mrs Leticia Gomez, A. Gallinal 1852, Montevideo, Uruguay
email: lego@adinet.co.uy

Provincial Treasurer Mrs Margarita Cornejo, Iglesia Anglicana, Cochabamba, Bolivia
Tel and *Fax:* 591 7 226 7356
email: margarita_cornejo@hotmail.com

Executive Secretary Mrs Aída Cuenca de Fernandez, Casilla de Correo 187, CP4400, Salta, Argentina
Tel: 54 387 431 1718
Fax: 54 387 431 26
email: educris@salnet.com.ar

THEOLOGICAL EDUCATION
Planned and carried out by a Theological Education Commission which selects candidates, applies grants and sets courses of study, some of which are led by clergy of the diocese. Some students follow courses of theological training 'by extension' and others attend ecumenical seminaries.

ARGENTINA
Bishop Most Revd Gregory James Venables (*Presiding Bishop of the Province*), Rioja 2995 (1636), Olivos, Provincia de Buenos Aires, Argentina
Tel: 54 11 4342 4618
Fax: 54 11 4331 0234
email: bpgreg@ciudad.com.ar

BOLIVIA
Bishop Rt Revd Francisco Lyons, Iglesia Anglicana, Casilla 848, Cochabamba, Bolivia
Tel and *Fax:* 591 4 440 1168
email: BpFrank@sams-usa.org
Web: www.bolivia.anglican.org

CHILE
Bishop Rt Revd Héctor Zavala Muñoz, Casilla 50675, Correo Central, Santiago, Chile
Tel: 56 2 638 3009
Fax: 56 2 639 4581
email: tzavala@iach.cl
Web: www.iglesiaanglicana.cl

Assistant Bishop Rt Revd Abelino Manuel Apeleo, Casilla de Correo 26-D, Temuco, Chile
Tel and *Fax:* 56 45 910 484
email: aapeleo@iach.cl

NORTHERN ARGENTINA
Bishop Most Revd Gregory James Venables (*Bishop of Argentina*)

Assistant Bishop Rt Revd Nicholas Drayson, Casilla 19, 3636 Ingeniero Juárez, FCNGB Formosa, Argentina
Tel: 54 387 431 1718
Fax: 54 387 431 2622
email: diana.epi@salnet.com.ar

PARAGUAY
Bishop Rt Revd John Alexander Ellison, Iglesia Anglicana de Paraguay, Casilla de Correo 1124, Asunción, Paraguay
Tel: 595 21 200 933
Fax: 595 21 214 328
email: jellison@pla.net.py
Web: www.paraguay.anglican.org

PERU
Bishop Rt Revd Harold William Godfrey, Calle Alcala 336, Urb. La Castellana, Santiago de Surco, Lima 33, Peru
Tel: 51 1 422 9160
Fax: 51 1 440 8540
email: diocesisperu@anglicanperu.org/
wgodfrey@amauta.rcp.net.pe
Web: www.peru.anglican.org

URUGUAY
Bishop Rt Revd Miguel Tamayo, CC 6108, Montevideo, CP11000, Uruguay
Tel: 598 2 915 9627
Fax: 598 2 916 2519
email: mtamayo@netgate.com.uy
Web: www.uruguay.anglican.org

Suffragan Bishop Rt Revd Gilberto Obdulio Porcal Martinez, Reconquista 522, CC 6108, 11000 Montevideo, Uruguay
Tel: 598 2 915 9627
Fax: 598 2 916 2519
email: anglican@netgate.com.uy

The Church of the Province of the Sudan

Members 5,000,000
The Church Missionary Society began work in 1899 in Omdurman; Christianity spread rapidly among black Africans of the southern region. Until 1974, the diocese of Sudan was part of the Jerusalem archbishopric. It reverted to the jurisdiction of the Archbishop of Canterbury until the new province, consisting of four new dioceses, was established in 1976. In 1986 the number of dioceses increased to 11 and in 1992 to 24 dioceses. The doubling of the number of dioceses by 1992 was partly due to leadership crises in the Church and partly due to church growth. Civil and religious strife and a constant flow of refugees have challenged the Church. Its heroic witness to faith in Christ continues to inspire the Anglican Communion and its people.

Archbishop and Primate Most Revd Dr Daniel Deng Bul (*Bishop of Juba*)
Tel and *Fax:* 249 121212607
email: ecsprovince@hotmail.com
archbishopdanieldeng@yahoo.com
Web: www.sudan.anglican.org

Acting Provincial Secretary John Augustino Lumori, PO Box 604, Khartoum, Sudan
Tel: 249 122232176
email: jlumori@yahoo.com/
ecsprovince@hotmail.com
Honorary Provincial Treasurer Mr Evans Sokiri (*same address*) *email:* sokirik@yahoo.co.uk

THEOLOGICAL COLLEGES
Bishop Gwynne College, PO Box 110, Juba, Sudan (*Acting Principal* Revd David V. Bako)
Tel: 249 9124 54933 (Mobile)
email: davidbako7@hotmail.com

Bishop Alison Theological College, PO Box 1076, Arua, Uganda (*Principal* Dr Oliver Duku)
Tel: 254 77 685 554
email: bat_college@yahoo.com

Shokai Bible Training Institute, PO Box 65, Omdurman, 135 Khartoum, Sudan (*Principal* Revd Musa Elgadi)
Tel: 249 187 564944
email: sbti70@yahoo.com

Renk Bible School, PO Box 1532, Khartoum North, Sudan (*Acting Principal* Revd Abraham Noon Jiel)
Tel: 249 918 068 125 (Mobile)
email: joseph_atem@yahoo.com
Bishop Ngalamu Theological College, PO Box 3364, Khartoum, Sudan (*Principal* Revd Paul Issa)
email: leyeonon@hotmail.com

AKOT
Bishop Rt Revd Isaac Dhieu Ater, c/o CMS Office, PO Box 40360, Nairobi, Kenya
BOR
Bishop Rt Revd Nathaniel Garang Anyieth (*Dean of the Province*), c/o NSCC, PO Box 66168, Nairobi, Kenya
Tel: 254 733 855 521/855 675
email: ecs_dioceseofbor@yahoo.co.uk

Assistant Bishop Rt Revd Ezekel Diing Malaangdit, c/o NSCC, PO Box 66168, Kenya

CUEIBET
Bishop Rt Revd Reuben Maciir Makoi, c/o CEAS, PO Box 40870, Nairobi, Kenya *Fax:* 254 2 570 807
email: eapo@cms-africa.org

EL-OBEID
Bishop Rt Revd Ismail Gibriel, PO Box 211, El-Obeid, Sudan
Tel: 249 9122 53459 (Mobile)
email: ismailabudigin2007@yahoo.com

EZO
Bishop Rt Revd John Zawo, c/o ECS Support Office, PO Box 7576, Kampala, Uganda
Tel: 256 41 343 497
email: kereborojohn@yahoo.com

IBBA
Bishop Rt Revd Wilson Elisa Kamani, c/o ECS Support Office, PO Box 7576, Kampala, Uganda
Tel and *Fax:* 256 41 343 497
email: ecs_ibbadiocese@hotmail.com/
ecs-kpa@africaonline.co.ug

JUBA
Bishop Most Revd Dr Daniel Deng Bul (*Archbishop and Primate*), PO Box 604, Khartoum, Sudan
Tel: 249 811 820065
email: dioceseofjuba@yahoo.com
Assistant Bishop Rt Revd Joseph Makor Atot, c/o CMS, PO Box 40360, Nairobi, Kenya

KADUGLI AND NUBA MOUNTAINS
Bishop Rt Revd Andudu Adam Elnail, PO Box 35, Kadugli, Sudan
Tel: 249 631 822898
email: bishandudu@yahoo.com

KAJO-KEJI
Bishop Rt Revd Anthony Poggo, c/o ECS Support Office, PO Box 7576, Kampala, Uganda
Tel: 256 41 343 497
email: bishopkk@gmail.com

KHARTOUM
Bishop Rt Revd Ezekiel Kondo, PO Box 65, Omdurman, 35 Khartoum, Sudan
Tel: 249 187 556931
email: ecs_bishop_Khartoum@kastanet.org

LAINYA
Bishop Rt Revd Peter Amidi, c/o ECS Support Office, PO Box 7576, Kampala, Uganda
Tel and *Fax:* 256 77 658 753
email: petamidi@yahoo.com

LUI
Bishop Rt Revd Bullen A. Dolli, PO Box 60837, Nairobi, Kenya
Tel: 254 2 720 037/56
Fax: 254 2 714 420
email: bishop@luidiocese.org/
cms-nbi@maf.org.ke

MALAKAL
Bishop Rt Revd Hilary Garang Aweer, PO Box 604, Khartoum, Sudan
email: ecs_malak@hotmail.com

MARIDI
Bishop Rt Revd Justin Badi Arama, ECS Support Office, PO Box 7576, Kampala, Uganda
Tel and *Fax:* 256 41 343 497
email: ecsmaridi@hotmail.com

MUNDRI
Bishop Rt Revd Bismark Monday Avokaya, c/o ECS Support Office, PO Box 7576, Kampala, Uganda
Tel and *Fax:* 256 41 343 497
email: ecsmundri@yahoo.com

PACONG
Bishop Rt Revd Joseph Maker
email: ecs.pacongdiocese@yahoo.com

PORT SUDAN
Bishop Rt Revd Yousif Abdalla Kuku, PO Box 278, Port Sudan, Sudan
Tel and *Fax:* 249 311 821224
email: ecsprovince@hotmail.com

REJAF
Bishop Rt Revd Michael Sokiri Lugör, PO Box 110, Juba, Sudan
Tel: 249 1290 76288
email: rejafdioceseecs@yahoo.com

RENK
Bishop Rt Revd Joseph Garang Atem, PO Box 1532, Khartoum North, Sudan
Tel: 249 122 99275 (Mobile)
email: ecs_renk@hotmail.com

ROKON
Bishop Rt Revd Francis Loyo, PO Box 6702, Nairobi 00100 APO, Kenya
Tel: 254 2 568 541/539
Fax: 254 2 560 864
email: bployo@yahoo.co.uk
Web: www.rokon.anglican.org

RUMBEK
Bishop Rt Revd Alapayo Manyang Kuctiel, c/o CMS Nairobi, PO Box 56, Nakuro, Kenya
Tel: 254 37 43186
email: kuctiel@yahoo.com

TEREKEKA
Bishop Rt Revd Micah Dawidi, c/o CMS Nairobi, PO Box 56, Nakuru, Kenya

TORIT
Bishop Rt Revd Bernard Oringa Balmoi, c/o ECS Support Office, PO Box 7576, Kampala, Uganda
Tel: 256 41 343 497
email: ecs_bishop_torit@kastanet.org

WAU
Bishop Rt Revd Henry Cuir Riak, c/o CMS Nairobi, PO Box 56, Nakuro, Kenya
Tel: 254 37 43186
email: riakcuir@yahoo.com /
wauvtc@yahoo.com

YAMBIO
Bishop Rt Revd Peter Munde Yacoub, ECS Support Office, PO Box 7576, Kampala, Uganda
Tel and *Fax:* 256 41 343 497
256 77 622 367 (Mobile)
email: yambio2002@yahoo.com/
ecs-kpa@africaonline.co.ug

YEI
Bishop Rt Revd Hilary Luate Adeba, PO Box 588, Arua, Uganda
Tel: 256 756 561 175
email: hill_sherpherd@yahoo.com/
72wca@techserve.org

YIROL
Bishop Rt Revd Benjamin Mangar Mamur, c/o St Matthew's Church, PO Box 39, Eldoret, Kenya
email: mamurmangar@yahoo.com/
cms-nbi@maf.or.ke

The Anglican Church of Tanzania

Members over 3,000,000

The Universities Mission to Central Africa and the Church Missionary Society began work in 1863 and 1876 in Zanzibar and at Mpwapwa respectively. The province was inaugurated in 1970 following the division of the Province of East Africa into the Province of Kenya and the Province of Tanzania. The 20 dioceses represent both evangelical and Anglo-Catholic Churches.

Archbishop Most Revd Dr Valentino Mokiwa (*Bishop of Dar-es-Salaam*)

Dean Rt Revd Dr Philip Baji (*Bishop of Tanga*)

Provincial Secretary Dr R. Mwita Akiri, PO Box 899, Dodoma   *Tel:* 255 26 232 4574
Fax: 255 26 232 4565
email: akiri@anglican.or.tz
Web: www.anglican.or.tz

Provincial Treasurer Rt Revd Hilkah Omindo Deya (*Bishop of Mara*)

Provincial Registrar Justice Augustino Ramadhani, PO Box 20522, Dar es Salaam
Tel: 255 022 211 5418
email: aslramadhani@yahoo.co.uk

THEOLOGICAL COLLEGES
St Philip's Theological College, PO Box 26, Kongwa (*Principal* Rev John Madinda)
Tel: 255 26 232 0096
email: stphilipstz@yahoo.com

St Mark's Theological College, PO Box 25017, Dar es Salaam (*Principal* Canon John Simalenga)
Tel: 255 22 286 3014
email: st-alban@kicheko.com/
jsimalenga@yahoo.com

CHURCH NEWSLETTER
ACT Forum is issued three times a year (April, August, December) in English containing diocesan, provincial and world church news. *Editor* Vacancy

CENTRAL TANGANYIKA
Bishop Rt Revd Godfrey Mdimi Mhogolo, PO Box 15, Dodoma   *Tel:* 255 26 232 1714
Fax: 255 26 232 4518
email: bishop@dct-tz.org/mhogolo@pnc.com.au

Assistant Bishop Rt Revd Ainea Kusenha (*same address*)   *email:* ngombe2004@kicheko.com

DAR ES SALAAM
Bishop Most Revd Dr Valentino Mokiwa (*Archbishop*), PO Box 25016, Ilala, Dar-es-Salaam   *Tel:* 255 22 286 4426
email: mokiwa_valentine@hotmail.com

KAGERA
Bishop Rt Revd Aaron Kijanjali, PO Box 18, Ngara   *Tel:* 255 28 222 3624
Fax: 255 28 222 2518
email: act-kagera@africaonline.co.tz

KITETO
Bishop Rt Revd Isaiah Chambala, PO Box 74, Kibaya, Kiteto   *Tel:* 255 27 255 2106
email: dkiteto@iwayafrica.com

KONDOA
Bishop Rt Revd Yohana Zakaria Mkavu, PO Box 7, Kondoa   *Tel:* 255 26 236 0312
Fax: 255 26 236 0304/0324
email: d-kondoa@do.ucc.co.tz

LWERU
Bishop Rt Revd Jackton Yeremiah Lugumira, PO Box 12, Muleba   *Tel:* 255 713 274 085
email: jlugumira2@juno.com

MARA
Bishop Rt Revd Hilkiah Deya Omindo Deya, PO Box 131, Musoma   *Tel:* 255 28 262 2376
Fax: 255 28 262 2414
email: actmara@juasun.net

MASASI
Bishop Rt Revd Patrick Mwachiko, Private Bag, PO Masasi, Mtwara Region   *Tel:* 255 23 251 0016
Fax: 255 23 251 0351
email: actmasasi@africaonline.co.tz

MOROGORO
Bishop Rt Revd Dudley Mageni, PO Box 320, Morogoro   *Tel* and *Fax:* 255 23 260 4602
email: act-morogoro@africaonline.co.tz

MOUNT KILIMANJARO
Bishop Rt Revd Simon Elilekia Makundi, PO Box 1057, Arusha   *Tel:* 255 27 254 8396
Fax: 255 27 254 4187
email: dmk@habari.co.tz

MPWAPWA
Bishop Rt Revd Jacob Chimeledya, PO Box 2, Mpwapwa   *Tel:* 255 26 232 0017/0825
Fax: 255 26 232 0063
email: dmp@do.ucc.co.tz

NEWALA
Bishop Rt Revd Oscar Mnunga, c/o Bishop of Masasi

RIFT VALLEY
Bishop Rt Revd John Lupaa, PO Box 16, Manyoni
Tel: 255 26 254 0013
Fax: 255 26 250 3014
email: act-drv@maf.or.tz

RUAHA
Bishop Rt Revd Donald Leo Mtetemela, PO Box 1028, Iringa   *Tel:* 255 26 270 1211
Fax: 255 26 270 2479
email: ruaha@anglican.or.tz

RUVUMA
Bishop Rt Revd Dr Maternus Kapinga, PO Box 1357, Songea, Ruvumu   *Tel:* 255 25 260 0090
Fax: 255 25 260 2987
email: mkkapinga@yahoo.com

SHINYANGA
Bishop Rt Revd Ngusa Charles Kija, PO Box 421, Shinyanga   *Tel:* 255 754 347 746 (Mobile)
email: ckngusa@yahoo.com

SOUTHERN HIGHLANDS
Bishop Rt Revd John Mwela, PO Box 198, Mbeya
Tel: 255 754 266 668 (Mobile)
email: dsh-dev@atma.co.tz

SOUTH-WEST TANGANYIKA
Bishop Vacancy, PO Box 32, Njombe
Tel: 255 26 278 2010
Fax: 255 26 278 2403
email: dswt@africaonline.co.tz

TABORA
Bishop Rt Revd Sadock Makaya, PO Box 1408, Tabora   *Tel:* 255 26 260 4124
Fax: 255 26 260 4899
email: smakaya1@yahoo.co.uk

TANGA
Bishop Rt Revd Dr Philip D. Baji, PO Box 35, Korogwe, Tanga   *Tel:* 255 27 264 0631
Fax: 255 27 264 0568
email: bajipp@anglican.or.tz

VICTORIA NYANZA
Bishop Rt Revd Boniface Kwangu, PO Box 278, Mwanza   *Tel:* 255 28 250 0627
Fax: 255 28 250 0676
email: revkahene1@yahoo.com

WESTERN TANGANYIKA
Bishop Rt Revd Dr Gerard E. Mpango, PO Box 13, Kasulu   *Tel:* 255 28 281 0321
Fax: 255 28 281 0706
email: askofugm@yahoo.com

Assistant Bishops
Rt Revd Naftal Bikaka (*Lake Zone Area of Kigoma District*), PO Box 1378, Kigoma
Tel: 255 28 280 3407
email: bpwbikaka@yahoo.co.uk
Rt Revd Marko Badeleya (*Southern Zone Area of Rukwa Region in Sumbawanga*), PO Box 226, Sumbawanga   *Tel:* 255 25 280 0287
email: bpbadeleya@yahoo.co.uk

ZANZIBAR
Bishop Vacancy, PO Box 5, Mkunazini, Zanzibar
Tel: 255 24 223 5348
Fax: 255 24 223 6772
email: secactznz@zanlink.com

The Church of the Province of Uganda

Members 9,200,000
After its founding in 1877 by the Church Missionary Society, the Church grew through the evangelization of Africa by Africans. The first Ugandan clergy were ordained in 1893 and the Church of Uganda, Rwanda and Burundi became an independent province in 1961. The history of the Church in Uganda has been marked by civil strife and martyrdom. In May 1980 the new Province of Burundi, Rwanda and Zaire was inaugurated; the Province of Uganda has since grown from 17 to 32 dioceses.

Archbishop of the Province Most Revd Henry Luke Orombi (*Bishop of Kampala*)

Primatial and Provincial Secretariat PO Box 14123, Kampala   *Tel:* 256 41 270 218
Fax: 256 41 251 925
email: provinceuganda@yahoo.com

Provincial Secretary Canon Aaron Mwesigye Kafundizeki (*same address*)
email: ankundarev@yahoo.com
Tel: 256 772 455 129 (Mobile)

Provincial Treasurer Mr Richard Obura (*same address*)   *email:* ricobura57@yahoo.com
Tel: 256 41 270 218
Fax: 256 41 251 925

Bishop in charge of continuing education for clergy in service Rt Revd David Sebuhinja (*same address*)
email: sebuhinjadavid@yahoo.co.uk

THEOLOGICAL COLLEGES
Uganda Christian University, Mukono, PO Box 4, Mukono (*Principal* Revd Prof. Stephen Noll)

Bishop Balya College, PO Box 368, Fort-Portal (*Principal* Revd Y. Kule)

Bishop Barham University College (constituent college of Uganda Christian university, Mukono), PO Box 613, Kabale (*Acting Principal* Canon Jovan Turyamureeba)

Archbishop Janani Luwum Theological College, PO Box 232, Gulu (*Principal* Revd Ayela Okot)

Mityana Theological Training College, PO Box 102, Mityana (*Principal* Revd Mukasa-Mutambuze)

Ngora Diocesan Theological College, PO Box 1, Ngora (*Principal* Revd S. Amuret)

Uganda Martyrs Seminary Namugongo, PO Box 31149, Kampala (*Principal* Canon Dr Henry Segawa)

Aduku Diocesan Theological College, PO Aduku, Lira (*Principal* Revd S. O. Obura)

Kabwohe College, PO Kabwohe, Mbarara (*Principal* Revd Y. R. Buremu)

St Paul's Theological College Ringili, PO Box 358, Arua (*Principal* Canon Dr Milton Anguyo)

Bishop Usher Wilson, Buwalasi, Mbale (*Principal* Revd Naphtah Opwata)

Uganda Bible Institute, Mbarara (*Director* Revd Amos Magezi)

Bishop McAllister College, Kyogyera (*Principal* Revd Paul Jefferees)

ANKOLE
Bishop Rt Revd George Tibeesigwa, PO Box 14, Mbarara, Ankole   *Tel:* 256 485 20290

BUKEDI
Bishop Rt Revd Nicodemus Okille, PO Box 170, Tororo   *Tel:* 256 772 542 164 (Mobile)

BUNYORO-KITARA
Bishop Rt Revd Nathan Kyamanywa, PO Box 20, Hoima   *Tel:* 256 464 40 128
256 772 648 232 (Mobile)
email: bkdioces@infocom.co.ug

BUSOGA
Bishop Rt Revd Dr Michael Kyomya, PO Box 1568, Jinja   *Tel:* 256 752 649 102 (Mobile)

CENTRAL BUGANDA
Bishop Rt Revd Jackson Matovu, PO Box 1200, Kinoni-Gomba, Mpigi
Tel: 256 772 475 640 (Mobile)
email: bishopmatovu@yahoo.com

KAMPALA
Bishop Most Revd Henry Luke Orombi (*Archbishop of Uganda*), PO Box 335, Kampala
Tel: 256 414 279 218
256 772 450 178 (Mobile)
Fax: 256 414 251 925
email: kdcou@africaonline.co.ug

Assistant Bishop Rt Revd Dr Zac Niringiye, PO Box 335, Kampala   *Tel:* 256 414 290 231
Fax: 256 414 342 601

KARAMOJA
Bishop Rt Revd Joseph Abura, PO Box 44, Moroto
Tel: 256 782 658 502

KIGEZI
Bishop Rt Revd George Katwesigye, PO Box 3, Kabale   *Tel:* 256 486 22 003

256 772 446 954 (Mobile)
Fax: 256 486 22 802
email: kigezi@infocom.co.ug

KINKIZI
Bishop Rt Revd John Ntegyereize, PO Box 77, Karuhinda, Rukungiri
Tel: 873 761 604 794/5 (Satellite)
256 772 507 163 (Mobile)
Fax: 875 761 604 796/7 (Satellite)

KITGUM
Bishop Rt Revd Benjamin Ojwang, PO Box 187, Kitgum   *Tel:* 256 772 959 924 (Mobile)
email: benojwang2004@yahoo.co.uk

KUMI
Bishop Rt Revd Thomas Edison Irigei, PO Box 18, Kumi   *Tel:* 256 772 659 460 (Mobile)
email: coukumidiocese@yahoo.com

LANGO
Bishop Rt Revd John Charles Odurkami, PO Box 6, Lira   *Tel:* 256 772 614 000 (Mobile)
email: bishoplango@yahoo.com

LUWERO
Bishop Rt Revd Evans Mukasa Kisekka, PO Box 125, Luwero   *Tel:* 256 414 610 048/070
256 772 421 220 (Mobile)
Fax: 256 414 610 132/070
email: kiromas@yahoo.co.uk

MADI / WEST NILE
Bishop Rt Revd Joel Obetia, PO Box 370, Arua
Tel: 256 752 625 414 (Mobile)
email: jobetia@ucu.ac.ug

MASINDI-KITARA
Bishop Rt Revd Stanley Ntagali, PO Box 515, Masindi   *Tel:* 256 772 618 822
email: bishopntagali@yahoo.com

MBALE
Bishop Rt Revd Patrick Gidudu, Bishop's House, PO Box 473, Mbale   *Tel:* 256 45 33 533
256 772 512 051 (Mobile)

MITYANA
Bishop Rt Revd Stephen Samuel Kaziimba, PO Box 102, Mityana   *Tel:* 256 46 2017
email: mtndiocese@hotmail.com

MUHABURA
Bishop Rt Revd Cranmer Mugisha, PO Box 22, Kisoro   *Tel:* 256 486 30 014/058
256 712 195 891 (Mobile)
Fax: 256 486 30 059

MUKONO
Bishop Rt Revd Elia Paul Luzinda Kizito, PO Box 39, Mukono   *Tel:* 256 41 290 229
256 772 603 348 (Mobile)
email: mukodise@utlonline.co.ug

NAMIREMBE
Bishop Rt Revd Samuel Balagadde Ssekkadde, PO Box 14297, Kampala   *Tel:* 256 41 271 682
256 772 500 494 (Mobile)
email: namid@infocom.co.ug

NEBBI
Bishop Rt Revd Alphonse Watho-kudi, PO Box 27, Nebbi   *Tel:* 256 772 650 032 (Mobile)
email: bpalphonse@ekk.org

NORTH ANKOLE
Bishop Rt Revd John Muhanguzi, c/o PO Box 14, Rushere-Mbarara, Ankole
Tel: 256 772 369 947 (Mobile)
email: northankole@gmail.com

NORTH KARAMOJA
Bishop Rt Revd James Nasak, PO Box 26, Kotido
Tel: 256 772 660 228

NORTH KIGEZI
Bishop Rt Revd Edward Muhima, PO Box 23, Rukungiri   *Tel:* 256 486 42 433
256 772 709 387 (Mobile)
email: northkigezi@infocom.co.ug

NORTH MBALE
Bishop Rt Revd Daniel Gimadu, Bishop's House, PO Box 1837, Mbale   *Fax:* 256 752 655 225
email: northmbalediocese@yahoo.com/
petgim2000@yahoo.com

NORTHERN UGANDA
Bishop Rt Revd Nelson Onono-Onweng, PO Box 232, Gulu   *Tel:* 256 772 838 193 (Mobile)
email: ononobp@yahoo.co.uk

RUWENZORI
Bishop Rt Revd Benezeri Kisembo, Bishop's House, PO Box 37, Fort Portal
Tel: 256 772 470 671 (Mobile)
email: bishop@biznas.com

SEBEI
Bishop Rt Revd Augusto Arapyona Salimo, PO Box 23, Kapchorwa   *Tel:* 256 45 51 072
256 772 550 520 (Mobile)
email: augustinesalimo@yahoo.co.uk

SOROTI
Bishop Rt Revd Charles Bernard Obaikol-Ebitu, PO Box 107, Soroti   *Tel:* 256 45 61 795
256 772 557 909 (Mobile)
email: couteddo@infocom.co.ug

SOUTH RUWENZORI
Bishop Rt Revd Jackson T. Nzerebende, PO Box 142, Kasese   *Tel:* 256 772 713 736 (Mobile)
Fax: 256 483 44 450
email: bpbende@yahoo.com

WEST ANKOLE
Bishop Rt Revd Yonah Katoneene, PO Box 140, Bushenyi   *Tel:* 256 753 377 193 (Mobile)
email: wad@westankolediocese.org

WEST BUGANDA
Bishop Rt Revd Dr Samuel Kefa Kamya, PO Box 242, Masaka   *Tel:* 256 772 413 400 (Mobile)
email: wesbug@infocom.co.ug

The Protestant Episcopal Church in the United States of America

(also known as The Episcopal Church)

Members 2,400,000
Anglicanism was brought to the New World by explorers and colonists with the first celebration of the Holy Eucharist in Jamestown, Virginia in 1607. The need for clergy in the colonies was acute and English missionaries provided temporary relief. Though the Bishop of London was responsible for maintaining the church in the colonies, there was no resident bishop for nearly two hundred years, which meant that colonists had to travel to England to be ordained; this caused difficulties when many of the colonial clergy sided with the Crown during the American Revolution. In 1784 the first American bishop (Samuel Seabury of Connecticut) was consecrated in Scotland, and three years later bishops were consecrated in England for the Dioceses of Pennsylvania and New York. In 1785

the first General Convention was held; in 1821 the Domestic and Foreign Missionary Society was formed; and in 1835, by resolution of General Convention, all members of The Episcopal Church were made members of the Missionary Society. The Episcopal Church today maintains 100 dioceses within the United States plus 10 overseas dioceses (Colombia, the Dominican Republic, Central Ecuador, Litoral Ecuador, Haiti, Honduras, Puerto Rico, Taiwan, Venezuela and the Virgin Islands), the Mission Territory of Micronesia (Guam), the Convocation of American Churches in Europe, and, together with the Anglican Church of Canada and the Church in the Province of the West Indies, is a partner in the Metropolitan Council which oversees the Episcopal Church of Cuba; it is governed by the triennial General Convention consisting of a House of Clergy and Lay Deputies, and a House of Bishops, which includes all serving diocesan, suffragan, coadjutor and assisting bishops. Between General Conventions, church affairs are managed by the Executive Council, whose members are elected in part by the two Houses and in part by the nine regional provinces. The Executive Council meets three times each year (except twice during a General Convention year). The province is a strong base of support to the Anglican Communion and has a significant crisis ministry through Episcopal Relief and Development. Episcopalians are also very active in the areas of social justice and ecumenical and interfaith relations, and witness to their faith in all walks of national life.

Presiding Bishop and Primate Most Revd Katharine Jefferts Schori

Offices of the Episcopal Church and its departments Episcopal Church Center, 815 Second Ave, New York, NY 10017, USA   *Tel*: 1 212 716 6000
Fax: 1 212 490 3298
email: pboffice@episcopalchurch.org
Web: www.episcopalchurch.org

President, House of Deputies Ms Bonnie Anderson (*same address*)   *Tel*: 1 212 922 5183
Fax: 1 734 534 6043
email: banderson@episcopalchurch.org

Executive Officer of the General Convention and Secretary of the Executive Council Revd Dr Gregory Straub (*same address*)   *Tel*: 1 212 922 5148
Fax: 1 212 972 9322
email: gcoffice@episcopalchurch.org

Secretary, House of Bishops Rt Revd Kenneth L. Price, The Bishop's Center, 125 East Broad St, Columbus, OH 43215, USA   *Tel*: 1 614 461 8429
Fax: 1 614 461 1015
email: bishopken@aol.com

Bishop Suffragan for Chaplaincies (Armed Forces, Hospital and Prison Ministries) and Bishop in Charge of Micronesia Rt Revd George Elden Packard (*same address*)   *Tel*: 1 212 716 6202
Fax: 1 212 867 1654
email: gpackard@episcopalchurch.org

Deputy to the Presiding Bishop for Ecumenical and Interfaith Relations Rt Revd C. Christopher Epting (*same address*)   *Tel*: 1 212 716 6220
Fax: 1 212 682 5594
email: cepting@episcopalchurch.org

Bishop Suffragan for the Office of Pastoral Development Rt Revd F. Clayton Matthews, 2857 Trent Rd, New Bern, NC, 28562, USA
Tel: 1 252 635 5004
Fax: 1 252 635 5006
email: cmatthews@episcopalchurch.org

Treasurer Mr N. Kurt Barnes (*same address*)
Tel: 1 212 922 5296
Fax: 1 212 867 0395
email: kbarnes@episcopalchurch.org
Web: www.episcopalchurch.org

THEOLOGICAL SEMINARIES
California
Church Divinity School of the Pacific, 2451 Ridge Rd, Berkeley, CA 94709, USA (*Dean* Dr Donn F. Morgan) *Web*: www.cdsp.edu

Connecticut
Berkeley Divinity School at Yale University, 409 Prospect St, New Haven, CT 06511, USA (*Dean* Very Revd Joseph H. Britton) *Web*: http://research.yale.edu/berkeleydivinity

Illinois
Seabury-Western Theological Seminary, 2122 Sheridan Rd, Evanston, IL 60201, USA (*Dean* Very Revd Gary R. Hall) *Web*: www.seabury.edu

Massachusetts
Episcopal Divinity School, 99 Brattle St, Cambridge, MA 02138, USA (*Academic Dean* Revd Sheryl A. Kujawa-Holbrook) *Web*: www.eds.edu

New York
Bexley Hall Episcopal Seminary, 583 Sheridan Ave, Columbus, OH 43209, (*Dean* Very Revd John R. Kevern) *Web*: www.bexley.edu

The General Theological Seminary of The Episcopal Church in the United States, 175 Ninth Ave, New York, NY 10011, USA (*Dean* Very Revd Ward B. Ewing) *Web*: www.gts.edu

Pennsylvania
Trinity Episcopal School for Ministry, 311 Eleventh St, Ambridge, PA 15003, USA (*Interim Dean* Rt Revd John H. Rodgers Jr) *Web*: www.tesm.edu

Tennessee
The School of Theology, The University of the South, 735 University Ave, Sewanee, TN 37383, USA (*Dean* Very Revd William S. Stafford) *Web*: www.sewanee.edu

Texas
The Episcopal Theological Seminary of the Southwest, PO Box 2247, Austin, TX 78768, USA (*Dean* Very Revd Douglas Travis) *Web*: www.etss.edu

Virginia
The Protestant Episcopal Theological Seminary in Virginia, Seminary Post Office, 3737 Seminary Rd, Alexandria, VA 22304, USA (*Dean* Very Revd Ian Markham) *Web*: www.vts.edu

Wisconsin
Nashotah House, 2777 Mission Rd, Nashotah, WI 53058, USA (*Dean* Very Revd Robert S. Munday) *Web*: www.nashotah.edu

CHURCH PAPERS
Episcopal Life An independently edited, officially sponsored monthly newspaper published by the Episcopal Church, 815 Second Ave, New York, NY 10017, USA, upon authority of the General Convention of the Protestant Episcopal Church in the USA. Also see *episcopallife online*, our electronic news service *Web:* www.episcopalchurch.org/episcopal_life.htm

The Living Church Weekly magazine. *Editorial and Business Offices* PO Box 514036, Milwaukee, WI 53203, USA. Contains news and features about Christianity in general and the Episcopal Church in particular.

ALABAMA (Province IV)
Bishop Rt Revd Henry Nutt Parsley Jr, Carpenter House, 521 N 20th St, Birmingham, AL 35203–2611, USA　　　　*Tel:* 1 205 715 2060
Fax: 1 205 715 2066
email: Hparsley@dioala.org
Web: www.dioala.org

Bishop Suffragan Rt Revd John McKee Sloan (*same address*)

ALASKA (Province VIII)
Bishop Vacancy, 1205 Denali Way, Fairbanks, Alaska 99701–4137, USA　　*Tel:* 1 907 452 3040
Fax: 1 907 456 6552
Web: www.episcopalak.org

ALBANY (Province II)
Bishop Rt Revd William H. Love, 68 South Swan St, Albany, NY 12210, USA　　*Tel:* 1 518 465 4737
email: via website
Web: www.albanyepiscopaldiocese.org

ARIZONA (Province VIII)
Bishop Rt Revd Kirk Stevan Smith, 114 West Roosevelt St, Phoenix, AZ 85003–1406, USA
Tel: 1 602 254 0976
Fax: 1 602 495 6603
email: bishop@azdiocese.org
Web: www.azdiocese.org

ARKANSAS (Province VII)
Bishop Rt Revd Larry R. Benfield, PO Box 164668, Little Rock, AR 72216, USA　　*Tel:* 1 501 372 2168
Fax: 1 501 372 2147
email: Lbenfield@arkansas.anglican.org
Web: www.arkansas.anglican.org

ATLANTA (Province IV)
Bishop Rt Revd John Neil Alexander, 2744 Peachtree Rd, Atlanta, GA 30305, USA
Tel: 1 404 601 5320
Fax: 1 404 601 5330
email: bishop@episcopalatlanta.org
Web: www.episcopalatlanta.org

Assistant Bishop Rt Revd Keith B. Whitmore (*same address*)
email: bishopkeith@episcopalatlanta.org

BETHLEHEM (Province III)
Bishop Rt Revd Paul Victor Marshall, 333 Wyandotte St, Bethlehem, PA 18015, USA
Tel: 1 610 691 5655
Fax: 1 610 691 1682
email: bpoffice@diobeth.org
Web: www.diobeth.org

CALIFORNIA (Province VIII)
Bishop Rt Revd Marc Andrus, 1055 Taylor St, San Francisco, CA 94108, USA　　*Tel:* 1 415 673 0606
Fax: 1 415 673 1510
email: bishopmarc@diocal.org
Web: www.diocal.org

CENTRAL ECUADOR (Province IX)
Bishop Rt Revd Wilfrido Ramos-Orench, Centro Diocesano de la ciudad de Quito, calle Francisco Sarmiento No. 39–54 y Portete, sector el Batán, Quito, Ecuador　　*Tel:* 593 2 243 9183
email: wramos@ctdiocese.org
Web: www.ecuadorepiscopal.org

CENTRAL FLORIDA (Province IV)
Bishop Rt Revd John Howe, Diocesan Office, 1017 E Robinson St, Orlando, Florida 32801, USA
Tel: 1 407 423 3567
Fax: 1 407 872 0006
email: jhowe@cfdiocese.org
Web: www.cfdiocese.org

CENTRAL GULF COAST (Province IV)
Bishop Rt Revd Philip Menzie Duncan II, Box 13330, Pensacola, Florida 32591–3330, USA
Tel: 1 850 434 7337
Fax: 1 850 434 8577
email: bishopduncan@diocgc.org
Web: www.centralgulfcoast.anglican.org

CENTRAL NEW YORK (Province II)
Bishop Rt Revd Gladstone 'Skip' Adams, 310 Montgomery St, Suite 200, Syracuse, NY 13202–2093, USA　　*Tel:* 1 315 474 6596
Fax: 1 315 478 1632
email: bishop@cny.anglican.org
Web: www.cny.anglican.org

CENTRAL PENNSYLVANIA (Province III)
Bishop Rt Revd Nathan D. Baxter, PO Box 11937, Harrisburg, PA 17108, USA　　*Tel:* 1 717 236 5959
Fax: 1 717 236 6448
email: via website
Web: www.diocesecpa.org

CHICAGO (Province V)
Bishop Rt Revd Jeffery Lee, 65 E Huron St, Chicago, IL 60611, USA　　*Tel:* 1 312 751 4200
Fax: 1 312 787 4534
email: bishop@episcopalchicago.org
Web: www.epischicago.org

Assistant Bishop Rt Revd Victor A. Scantlebury (*same address*)　　*Tel:* 1 312 751 4216
email: vscantlebury@episcopalchicago.org

COLOMBIA (Province IX)
Bishop Rt Revd Francisco J. Duque Gómez, PO
Box 52964, Bogotá 2, DC Colombia
Tel: 57 1 288 3167
Fax: 57 1 288 3248
email: iec@iglesiaepiscopal.org.co
Web: www.iglesiaepiscopal.org.co

COLORADO (Province VI)
Bishop Rt Revd Robert J. O'Neill, 1300
Washington St, Denver, CO 80203, USA
Tel: 1 303 837 1173
Fax: 1 303 837 1311
email: bishoponeill@coloradodiocese.org
Web: www.coloradodiocese.org

CONNECTICUT (Province I)
Bishop Rt Revd Andrew Donnan Smith, 1335
Asylum Ave, Hartford, CT 06105–2295, USA
Tel: 1 860 233 4481
Fax: 1 860 523 1410
email: adsmith@ctdiocese.org
Web: www.ctdiocese.org

Bishops Suffragan
Rt Revd Laura Ahrens (*same address*)
email: lahrens@ctdiocese.org

Rt Revd James Elliot Curry (*same address*)
email: jcurry@ctdiocese.org

DALLAS (Province VII)
Bishop Rt Revd James Monte Stanton, 1630 North
Garrett Ave, Dallas, TX 75206, USA
Tel: 1 214 826 8310
Fax: 1 214 826 5968
email: jmsdallas@episcopal-dallas.org
Web: www.episcopal-dallas.org

DELAWARE (Province III)
Bishop Rt Revd Wayne Parker Wright, 2020
North Tatnall St, Wilmington, DE 19802, USA
Tel: 1 302 656 5441
Fax: 1 302 656 7342
email: waynewright@dioceseofdelaware.net
Web: www.dioceseofdelaware.net

DOMINICAN REPUBLIC (Province IX)
Bishop Rt Revd Julio Cesar Holguin, Calle
Santiago No 114, Apartado 764, Santo Domingo,
Dominican Republic
Tel: 1 809 688 7493
Fax: 1 809 686 6364
email: iglepidom@codetel.net.do
Web: www.dominicanepiscopalchurch.org

EAST CAROLINA (Province IV)
Bishop Rt Revd Clifton Daniel III, PO Box 1336,
Kinston, NC 28501, USA
Tel: 1 252 522 0885
Fax: 1 252 523 5272
email: cdaniel@diocese-eastcarolina.org
Web: www.diocese-eastcarolina.org

EAST TENNESSEE (Province IV)
Bishop Rt Revd Charles Glen vonRosenberg, 814
Episcopal School Way, Knoxville, Tennessee
37932, USA
Tel: 1 865 966 2110
Fax: 1 865 966 2535
email: cgvonr@etdiocese.net
Web: www.etdiocese.net

EASTERN MICHIGAN (Province V)
Bishop Rt Revd S. Todd Ousley, Diocesan Office,
924 N Niagara St, Saginaw, Michigan 48602, USA
Tel: 1 989 752 6020
Fax: 1 989 752 6120
email: bishop@eastmich.org
Web: www.eastmich.org

EASTERN OREGON (Province VIII)
Bishop Vacancy, PO Box 1548, The Dalles, Oregon
97058, USA
Tel: 1 541 298 4477
Fax: 1 541 296 0939
email: diocese@episdioeo.org
Web: www.episdioeo.org

Assisting Bishop Rt Revd Nedi Rivera (*same
address*)
email: nrivera@episdioeo.org

EASTON (Province III)
Bishop Rt Revd James J. Shand, 314 North St,
Easton, MD 21601, USA
Tel: 1 410 822 1919
Fax: 1 410 763 8259
email: bishopshand@dioceseofeaston.org
Web: www.dioceseofeaston.org

EAU CLAIRE (Province V)
Bishop Vacancy, 510 So. Farwell St, Eau Claire,
WI 54701
Tel: 1 715 835 3331
Fax: 1 715 835 9212
email: deaconjeanne@dioceseofeauclaire.org
Web: www.dioceseofeauclaire.org

EL CAMINO REAL (Province VIII)
Bishop Rt Revd Mary Gray-Reeves, Box 1903
Monterey, CA 93942, USA
Tel: 1 831 394 4465
Fax: 1 831 394 7133
email: Marygrayreeves@earthlink.net
Web: www.edecr.org

**EUROPE, CONVOCATION OF AMERICAN
CHURCHES IN**
Bishop Rt Revd Pierre Welté Whalon, 23 Avenue
George V, 75008 Paris, France
Tel: 33 1 53 23 84 00
Fax: 33 1 47 23 95 30
email: bishops@tec-europe.org
Web: www.tec-europe.org

FLORIDA (Province IV)
Bishop Rt Revd Samuel J. Howard, 325 Market St,
Jacksonville, FL 32202, USA
Tel: 1 904 356 1328
Fax: 1 904 355 1934
email: jhoward@diocesefl.org
Web: www.diocesefl.org

ANGLICAN AND PORVOO
COMMUNIONS

FOND DU LAC (Province V)
Bishop Rt Revd Russell Edward Jacobus, 1047 N.
Lynndale Dr., Suite 1B, Appleton, WI 54914, USA
Tel: 1 920 830 8866
Fax: 1 920 830 8761
email: diofdl@diofdl.org
Web: www.episcopalfonddulac.org

FORT WORTH (Province VII)
Bishop Rt Revd Jack Leo Iker, 2900 Alemeda
Street, Fort Worth, Texas 76108, USA
Tel: 1 817 244 2885
Fax: 1 817 244 3363
email: jliker@fwepiscopal.org
Web: www.fwepiscopal.org

GEORGIA (Province IV)
Bishop Rt Revd Henry Irving Louttit Jr, 611 E Bay
St, Savannah, GA 31401–1296, USA
Tel: 1 912 236 4279
Fax: 1 912 236 2007
email: diocesega@att.net
Web: www.georgia.anglican.org

HAITI (Province II)
Bishop Rt Revd Jean-Zaché Duracin, Église
Épiscopale d'Haiti, Boite Postale 1309, Port-au-
Prince, Haiti
Tel: 509 257 1624
Fax: 509 257 3412
email: epihaiti@hotmail.com

HAWAII (Province VIII)
Bishop Rt Revd Robert L. Fitzpatrick, Diocesan
Office, 229 Queen Emma Sq, Honolulu, HI
96813, USA
Tel: 1 808 536 7776
Fax: 1 808 538 7194
email: rlfitzpatrick@episcopalhawaii.org
Web: www.episcopalhawaii.org

HONDURAS (Province IX)
Bishop Rt Revd Lloyd E. Allen, 23 Av 'C', 21
Calle Colonia, San Pedro Sula, Cortés 21105,
Honduras
Tel: 504 556 6155/6268
Fax: 504 566 6467
email: obispoallen@yahoo.com

IDAHO (Province VIII)
Bishop Rt Revd Brian James Thom, 1858 W. Judith
Lane, Boise, ID 83705
Tel: 1 208 345 4440
Fax: 1 208 345 9735
email: bthom@idahodiocese.org
Web: www.idaho.anglican.org

INDIANAPOLIS (Province V)
Bishop Rt Revd Catherine Elizabeth Maples
Waynick, 1100 W 42nd St, Indianapolis, IN 46208,
USA
Tel: 1 317 926 5454
Fax: 1 317 926 5456
email: bishop@indydio.org
Web: www.indianapolis.anglican.org

IOWA (Province VI)
Bishop Rt Revd Alan Scarfe, 225 37th St, Des
Moines, IA 50312, USA
Tel: 1 515 277 6165
Fax: 1 515 277 0273
email: Ascarfe@iowaepiscopal.org
Web: www.iowaepiscopal.org

KANSAS (Province VII)
Bishop Rt Revd Dean E. Wolfe, Bethany Place,
835 SW Polk St, Topeka, KS 66612–1688, USA
Tel: 1 785 235 9255
Fax: 1 785 235 2449
email: DWolfe@episcopal-ks.org
Web: www.episcopal-ks.org

KENTUCKY (Province IV)
Bishop Rt Revd Edwin Funsten Gulick Jr, 425 S
Second St, Louisville, KY 40202, USA
Tel: 1 502 584 7148
Fax: 1 502 587 8123
email: TedG@episopalky.org
Web: www.episopalky.org

LEXINGTON (Province IV)
Bishop Rt Revd Stacy Fred Sauls, PO Box 610,
Lexington, KY 40586, USA
Tel: 1 859 252 6527
Fax: 1 859 231 9077
email: sfsauls@diolex.org
Web: www.diolex.org

LITORAL ECUADOR (Province IX)
Bishop Rt Revd Alfredo Morante, Box 0901–5250,
Guayaquil-Ecuador
Tel: 593 4 443 050
Fax: 593 4 443 088
email: bishopmorante@hotmail.com /
iedl@gu.pro.ec

LONG ISLAND (Province II)
Bishop Rt Revd Orris G. Walker Jr, 36 Cathedral
Ave, Garden City, NY 11530
Tel: 1 516 248 4800
Fax: 1 516 248 1349
email: owalker@dioceseli.org
Web: www.dioceselongisland.org

LOS ANGELES (Province VIII)
Bishop Rt Revd Joseph Jon Bruno, Box 512164,
Los Angeles, CA 90051, USA
Tel: 1 213 482 2040
Fax: 1 213 482 0844
email: bishop@ladiocese.org
Web: www.ladiocese.org

Bishop Suffragan Rt Revd Chester L. Talton (*same
address*)
email: suffragan@ladiocese.org

LOUISIANA (Province IV)
Bishop Rt Revd Charles Edward Jenkins, 1623
Seventh Street, New Orleans, LA 70115, USA
Tel: 1 504 895 6634
Fax: 1 504 895 6637
email: bishop@edola.org
Web: www.edola.org

MAINE (Province I)
Bishop Rt Revd Stephen T Lane, Loring House,
143 State St, Portland, ME 04101, USA
Tel: 1 207 772 1953
Fax: 1 207 773 0095
email: slane@episcopalmaine.org
Web: www.episcopalmaine.org

MARYLAND (Province III)
Bishop Rt Revd Robert Wilkes Ihloff, 4 East University Parkway, Baltimore, MD 21218, USA
Tel: 1 410 467 1399
Fax: 1 410 554 6387
email: via website
Web: www.ang-md.org

Bishop Suffragan Rt Revd John Leslie Rabb (*same address*)
email: jrabb@ang-md.org

MASSACHUSETTS (Province I)
Bishop Rt Revd M. Thomas Shaw SSJE, 138 Tremont St, Boston, MA 02111, USA
Tel: 1 617 482 5800
Fax: 1 617 482 8431
email: chipbe@diomass.org
Web: www.diomass.org

Bishops Suffragan
Rt Revd Roy F. (Bud) Cederholm, Jr (*same address*)
email: budc@diomass.org

Rt Revd Gayle E. Harris (*same address*)
email: SHP@diomass.org

MICHIGAN (Province V)
Bishop Rt Revd Wendell Nathaniel Gibbs Jr, 4800 Woodward Ave, Detroit, MI 48201, USA
Tel: 1 313 833 4436
Fax: 1 313 831 0259
email: Wgibbs@edomi.org
Web: www.edomi.org

MILWAUKEE (Province V)
Bishop Rt Revd Steven Andrew Miller, 804 E Juneau Ave, Milwaukee, WI 53202–2798
Tel: 1 414 272 3028
Fax: 1 414 272 7790
email: bishop11@diomil.org
Web: www.episcoplamilwaukee.org

MINNESOTA (Province VI)
Bishop Rt Revd James Louis Jelinek, 1730 Clifton Place, Suite 201, Minneapolis, MN 55403-3242, USA
Tel: 1 612 871 5311
Fax: 1 612 871 0552
email: episcopal.centre@episcopalmn.org
Web: www.episcopalmn.org

MISSISSIPPI (Province IV)
Bishop Rt Revd Duncan Montgomery Gray III, PO Box 23107, Jackson, MS 39225–3107, USA
Tel: 1 601 948 5954
Fax: 1 601 354 3401
email: cjohns@dioms.org
Web: www.dioms.org

MISSOURI (Province V)
Bishop Rt Revd George Wayne Smith, 1210 Locust St, St Louis, MO 63103, USA
Tel: 1 314 231 1220
Fax: 1 314 231 3373
email: pensmith@pensmith.net
Web: www.diocesemo.org

MONTANA (Province VI)
Bishop Rt Revd C. Franklin Brookhart, 515 North Park Ave, Helena, MT 59601, USA
Tel: 1 406 442 2230
Fax: 1 406 442 2238
email: cfbmt@qwestoffice.net
Web: www.montana.anglican.org

NAVAJOLAND AREA MISSION (Province VIII)
Bishop Rt Revd Mark MacDonald, PO Box 720, Farmington, NM 87499–0720, USA
Tel: 1 505 327 7549
Fax: 1 505 327 6904
email: mmacdonald@gci.net
Web: www.episcopal-navajo.org

NEBRASKA (Province VI)
Bishop Rt Revd Joe Goodwin Burnett, 109 N 18th St, Omaha, NE 68102, USA
Tel: 1 402 341 5373
Fax: 1 402 341 8683
email: jburnett@episcopal-ne.org
Web: www.episcopal-ne.org

NEVADA (Province VIII)
Bishop Rt Revd Dan T. Edwards, 6135 Harrison Drive, Suite 1, Las Vegas, NV 89120–4076, USA
Tel: 1 702 737 9190
Fax: 1 702 737 6488
email: bishop@nvdiocese.org
Web: www.nvdiocese.org

NEW HAMPSHIRE (Province I)
Bishop Rt Revd V. Gene Robinson, 63 Green St, Concord, NH 03301, USA
Tel: 1 603 224 1914
Fax: 1 603 225 7884
email: GRinNH@aol.com
Web: www.nhepiscopal.org

NEW JERSEY (Province II)
Bishop Rt Revd George E. Councell, 808 West State Street, Trenton, NJ 08618–5326, USA
Tel: 1 609 394 5281
Fax: 1 609 394 9546
email: GCouncell@newjersey.anglican.org
Web: www.newjersey.anglican.org

NEW YORK (Province II)
Bishop Rt Revd Mark Sean Sisk, Synod House, 1047 Amsterdam Ave, Cathedral Heights, New York, NY 10025, USA
Tel: 1 212 316 7400
Fax: 1 212 316 7405
email: bpsisk@dioceseny.org
Web: www.dioceseny.org

Assistant Bishop Rt Revd E. Don Taylor (*same address*)
Tel: 1 212 932 7349
Fax: 1 212 932 7345
email: bptaylor@dioceseny.org

Suffragan Bishop Rt Revd Catherine S. Roskam, Region Two Office, 55 Cedar St, Dobbs Ferry, NY 10522, USA
Tel: 1 914 693 3848
Fax: 1 914 693 0407
email: bproskam@dioceseny.org

NEWARK (Province II)
Bishop Rt Revd Mark Beckwith, 31 Mulberry St,
Newark, NJ 07102, USA   *Tel:* 1 923 430 9900
                             Fax: 1 923 622 3503
email: mbeckwith@dioceseofnewark.org
Web: www.dioceseofnewark.org

NORTH CAROLINA (Province IV)
Bishop Rt Revd Michael Bruce Curry, 200 West
Morgan St, Suite 300, Raleigh, NC 27601, USA
                             Tel: 1 919 834 7474
                             Fax: 1 919 834 7546
                             email: via website
                             Web: www.episdionc.org

NORTH DAKOTA (Province VI)
Bishop Rt Revd Michael G. Smith, 3600 S. 25th St,
Fargo, ND 58104–6861, USA
                             Tel: 1 701 235 6688
                             Fax: 1 701 232 3077
                             email: BpNodak@aol.com
                             Web: www.episcopal-nd.org

NORTHERN CALIFORNIA (Province VIII)
Bishop Rt Revd Barry L. Beisner, Box 161268,
Sacramento, CA 95816–1268
                             Tel: 1 916 442 6918
                             Fax: 1 916 442 6927
                             email: bishopblb@dncweb.org
                             Web: www.dncweb.org

NORTHERN INDIANA (Province V)
Bishop Rt Revd Edward Stuart Little II, 117 N
Lafayette Blvd, South Bend, Indiana 46601, USA
                             Tel: 1 574 233 6489
                             Fax: 1 574 287 7914
email: bishop@ednin.org/info@ednin.org
                             Web: www.ednin.org

NORTHERN MICHIGAN (Province V)
Bishop Vacancy, 131 E Ridge St, Marquette, MI
49855, USA   *Tel:* 1 906 228 7160
                             Fax: 1 906 228 7171
                             email: diocese@upepiscopal.org
                             Web: www.upepiscopal.org

NORTHWEST TEXAS (Province VII)
Bishop Rt Revd C. Wallis Ohl Jr, The Hulsey
Episcopal Center, 1802 Broadway, Lubbock, TX
79401, USA   *Tel:* 1 806 763 1370
                             Fax: 1 806 472 0641
                             email: bishop@nwt.org
                             Web: www.nwt.org

**NORTHWESTERN PENNSYLVANIA
(Province III)**
Bishop Rt Revd Sean W. Rowe, 145 W 6th St, Erie,
PA 16501, USA   *Tel:* 1 814 456 4203
                             Fax: 1 814 454 8703
                             email: seanrowe@dionwpa.org
                             Web: www.dionwpa.org

OHIO (Province V)
Bishop Rt Revd Mark Hollingsworth Jr, 2230
Euclid Ave, Cleveland, OH 44115–2499, USA
                             Tel: 1 216 771 4815
                             Fax: 1 216 623 0735
                             email: mh@dohio.org
                             Web: www.dohio.org

OKLAHOMA (Province VII)
Bishop Rt Revd Edward J. Konieczny, 924 N
Robinson, Oklahoma City, OK 73102, USA
                             Tel: 1 405 232 4820
                             Fax: 1 405 232 4912
                             email: bishopEd@episcopaloklahoma.org
                             Web: www.episcopaloklahoma.org

OLYMPIA (Province VIII)
Bishop Rt Revd Vincent W Warner Jr, PO Box
12126, Seattle, WA 98102, USA
                             Tel: 1 206 325 4200
                             Fax: 1 206 325 4631
                             email: grickel@ecww.org
                             Web: www.ecww.org

Bishop Suffragan Rt Revd Bavi Edna ('Nedi')
Rivera (*same address*)   *email:* nrivera@ecww.org

OREGON (Province VIII)
Bishop Vacancy, 11800 S.W. Military Lane,
Portland, OR 97219, USA   *Tel:* 1 503 636 5613
                             Fax: 1 503 636 5616
                             email: sandyh@diocese-oregon.org
                             Web: www.diocese-oregon.org

Assisting Bishop Rt Revd Sanford ('Sandy')
Hampton (*same address*)

PENNSYLVANIA (Province III)
Bishop Rt Revd Charles Ellsworth Bennison Jr,
240 South Fourth St, Philadelphia, PA 19106, USA
                             Tel: 1 215 627 6434
                             Fax: 1 215 627 2323
                             email: via website
                             Web: www.diopa.org

PITTSBURGH (Province III)
Bishop Vacancy, 900 Oliver Building, 535
Smithfield Street, Pittsburgh, PA 15222, USA
                             Tel: 1 412 281 6131
                             Fax: 1 412 471 5591
                             email: info@pgh.anglican.org
                             Web: www.pgh.anglican.org

Assisting Bishop Rt Revd Robert H. Johnson (*same
address*)

PUERTO RICO (Province IX)
Bishop Rt Revd David Andres Alvarez, PO Box
902, St Just, PR 00978, Puerto Rico
                             Tel: 1 787 761 9800
                             Fax: 1 787 761 0320
                             email: obispoalvarez@spiderlink.net
                             Web: www.episcopalpr.org

QUINCY (Province V)
Bishop Rt Revd Keith Lynn Ackerman, 601 W.
Florence Ave, Peoria, IL 61604–1517, USA
Tel: 1 309 688 8221
Fax: 1 309 688 8229
email: bishop@dioceseofquincy.org
Web: www.dioceseofquincy.org

RHODE ISLAND (Province I)
Bishop Rt Revd Geralyn Wolf, 275 N Main St,
Providence, RI 02903–1298, USA
Tel: 1 401 274 4500
Fax: 1 401 331 9430
email: bishop@episcopalri.org
Web: www.episcopalri.org

RIO GRANDE (Province VII)
Bishop Vacancy, 4304 Carlisle Blvd NE,
Albuquerque, NM 87107–4811, USA
Tel: 1 505 881 0636
Fax: 1 505 883 9048
email: via website
Web: www.riogrande.anglican.org

ROCHESTER (Province II)
Bishop Rt Revd Jack Marston McKelvey, 935 East
Ave, Rochester, NY 14607, USA
Tel: 1 716 473 2977
Fax: 1 716 473 3195
email: BpJackM@aol.com
Web: www.rochesterepiscopaldiocese.org

SAN DIEGO (Province VIII)
Bishop Rt Revd James R. Mathes, 2728 Sixth Ave,
San Diego, CA 92103, USA   Tel: 1 619 291 5947
Fax: 1 619 291 8362
email: bishopmathes@edsd.org
Web: www.sandiego.anglican.org

SAN JOAQUIN (Province VIII)
Bishop Vacant, 4159 E Dakota Ave, Fresno, CA
93726, USA   Tel: 1 559 244 4828
Fax: 1 559 244 4832
Web: www.diosanjoaquin.org

Interim Bishop Jerry A Lamb (*same address*)
email: jerrylamb@diosanjoaquin.org

SOUTH CAROLINA (Province IV)
Bishop Rt Revd Edward L. Salmon Jr, Box 20127,
Charleston, SC 29413–0127, USA
Tel: 1 843 722 4075
Fax: 1 843 723 7628
email: via website
Web: www.dioceseofsc.org

SOUTH DAKOTA (Province VI)
Bishop Rt Revd Creighton L. Robertson, 500 S Main
Avenue, Sioux Falls, South Dakota 57104–6814,
USA   Tel: 1 605 338 9751
Fax: 1 605 336 6243
email: office.diocese@midconetwork.com
Web: www.diocesesd.org

Bishop Coadjutor Rt Revd John T. Tarrant (*same
address*)

SOUTHEAST FLORIDA (Province IV)
Bishop Rt Revd Leopold Frade, 525 NE 15 St,
Miami, FL 33132, USA   Tel: 1 305 373 0881
Fax: 1 305 375 8054
email: bishopfrade@aol.com
Web: www.diosef.org

SOUTHERN OHIO (Province V)
Bishop Rt Revd Thomas E. Breidenthal, 412
Sycamore St, Cincinnati, OH 45202, USA
Tel: 1 513 421 0311
Fax: 1 513 421 0315
email: bishop_breidenthal@episcopal-dso.org
Web: www.episcopal-dso.org

Suffragan Bishop Rt Revd Kenneth Price (*same
address*)   *email:* bishop_price@episcopal-dso.org

SOUTHERN VIRGINIA (Province III)
Bishop Rt Revd Herman 'Holly' Hollerith, 600
Talbot Hall Rd, Norfolk, VA 23505, USA
Tel: 1 757 423 8287
Fax: 1 757 440 5354
email: via website
Web: www.diosova.org

Interim Bishop Rt Revd John C. Buchanan (*same
address*)

SOUTHWEST FLORIDA (Province IV)
Bishop Rt Revd John B. Liscomb, 7313 Merchant
Ct, Sarasota, FL 34240–8437, USA
Tel: 1 941 556 0315
Fax: 1 941 556 0321
email: Jliscomb@episcopalswfla.org
Web: www.episcopalswfla.org

SOUTHWESTERN VIRGINIA (Province III)
Bishop Rt Revd Frank Neff Powell, PO Box 2279,
Roanoke, VA 24009–2279, USA
Tel: 1 540 342 6797
Fax: 1 540 343 9114
email: npowell@dioswva.org
Web: www.dioswva.org

SPOKANE (Province VIII)
Bishop Rt Revd James Edward Waggoner Jr, 245
E 13th Ave, Spokane, WA 99202–1114, USA
Tel: 1 509 624 3191
Fax: 1 509 747 0049
email: jimw@spokanediocese.org
Web: www.spokanediocese.org

SPRINGFIELD (Province V)
Bishop Rt Revd Peter Hess Beckwith, 821 S 2nd
St, Springfield, IL 62704–2694, USA
Tel: 1 217 525 1876
Fax: 1 217 525 1877
email: diocese@episcopalspringfield.org
Web: www.episcopalspringfield.org

ANGLICAN AND PORVOO COMMUNIONS

TAIWAN (Province VIII)
Bishop Rt Revd David J. H. Lai, Friendship House, 7 Lane 105, Hangchow South Rd, Sec. 1, Taipei, Taiwan 10060, Republic of China
Tel: 886 2 2341 1265
Fax: 886 2 2396 2014
email: skh.tpe@msa.hinet.net
Web: www.episcopalchurch.org.tw

TENNESSEE (Province IV)
Bishop Rt Revd John C. Bauernschmidt, 50 Vantage Way, Suite 107, Nashville, TN 37228, USA
Tel: 1 615 251 3322
Fax: 1 615 251 8010
email: info@episcopaldiocese-tn.org
Web: www.episcopaldiocese-tn.org

TEXAS (Province VII)
Bishop Rt Revd Charles Andrew Doyle, 1225 Texas Ave, Houston, TX 77002, USA
Tel: 1 713 353 2100
Fax: 1 713 520 5723
email: dwimberly@epicenter.org
Web: www.epicenter.org

UPPER SOUTH CAROLINA (Province IV)
Bishop Rt Revd Dorsey Felix Henderson Jr, 1115 Marion St, Columbia, SC 29201, USA
Tel: 1 803 771 7800
Fax: 1 803 799 5119
email: dioceseusc@edusc.org
Web: www.edusc.org

UTAH (Province VIII)
Bishop Rt Revd Carolyn Tanner Irish, PO Box 3090, Salt Lake City, UT 84110–3090, USA
Tel: 1 801 322 4131
Fax: 1 801 322 5096
email: CIrish@episcopal-ut.org
Web: www.episcopal-ut.org

VENEZUELA (Province IX)
Bishop Rt Revd Orlando Guerrero-Torres, Apartado 49–143, Avenida Caroni 100, Colinas de Bello Monte, Caracas 1042-A, Venezuela
Tel: 58 212 753 0723
Fax: 58 212 751 3180
email: obispoguerrero@iglesianglicanavzla.org
Web: www.iglesianglicanavzla.org

VERMONT (Province I)
Bishop Rt Revd Thomas C. Ely, 5 Rock Point Road, Burlington, VT 05401–2735, USA
Tel: 1 802 863 3431
Fax: 1 802 860 1562
email: tely@dioceseofvermont.org
Web: www.dioceseofvermont.org

VIRGIN ISLANDS (Province II)
Bishop Rt Revd Ambrose Gumbs, 13 Commandant Gade, Charlotte Amalie, St Thomas, VI 00801, USA
Tel: 1 340 776 1797
Fax: 1 340 777 8485
email: bishop@episcovi.org
Web:
www.episcopaldioceseofthevirginislands.com

VIRGINIA (Province III)
Bishop Rt Revd Peter James Lee, 110 W Franklin St, Richmond, VA 23220
Tel: 1 804 643 8451
Fax: 1 804 644 6928
email: pjlee@thediocese.net
Web: www.thediocese.net

Bishop Coadjutor Rt Revd Shannon S. Johnston (*same address*)
email: kglasco@thediocese.net

Bishop Suffragan
Rt Revd David Colin Jones, Northern Virginia Office, Goodwin House, 4800 Fillmore Avenue, Alexandria, VA 22311, USA
Tel: 1 703 824 1325
Fax: 1 703 824 1348
email: dcjones@thediocese.net

WASHINGTON (Province III)
Bishop John Bryson Chane, Episcopal Church House, Mount St Alban, Washington, DC 20016–5094, USA
Tel: 1 202 537 6555
Fax: 1 202 364 6605
email: jchane@edow.org
Web: www.edow.org

WEST MISSOURI (Province VII)
Bishop Rt Revd Barry Robert Howe, PO Box 413227, Kansas City, MO 64141–3227, USA
Tel: 1 816 471 6161
Fax: 1 816 471 0379
email: bphowe@earthlink.net
Web: www.diowestmo.org

WEST TENNESSEE (Province IV)
Bishop Rt Revd Don Edward Johnson, 692 Poplar Ave, Memphis, TN 38105, USA
Tel: 1 901 526 0023
Fax: 1 901 526 1555
email: info@episwtn.org
Web: www.episwtn.org

WEST TEXAS (Province VII)
Bishop Rt Revd Gary R. Lillibridge, PO Box 6885, San Antonio, TX 78209, USA
Tel: 1 210 824 5387
Fax: 1 210 822 8779
email: gary.lillibridge@dwtx.org
Web: www.dwtx.org

Bishop Suffragan Rt Revd David Reed (*same address*)
email: david.reed@dwtx.org

WEST VIRGINIA (Province III)
Bishop Rt Revd W. Michie Klusmeyer PO Box 5400, Charleston, WV 25361–0400, USA
Tel: 1 304 344 3597
Fax: 1 304 343 3295
email: mklusmeyer@wvdiocese.org
Web: www.wvdiocese.org

WESTERN KANSAS (Province VII)
Bishop Rt Revd James Marshall Adams, Jr, PO Box 2507, Salina, KS 67401–2507
Tel: 1 785 825 1626
Fax: 1 785 825 0974
email: myrnapeterson@sbcglobal.net
Web: www.westernkansas.org

WESTERN LOUISIANA (Province VII)

Bishop Rt Revd D. Bruce MacPherson, PO Box 2031, Alexandria, Louisiana 71309, USA

Tel: 1 318 422 1304
Fax: 1 318 442 8712
email: dbm3wla@aol.com
Web: www.diocesewla.org

WESTERN MASSACHUSETTS (Province I)

Bishop Rt Revd Gordon P. Scruton, 37 Chestnut St, Springfield, MA 01103, USA

Tel: 1 413 737 4786
Fax: 1 413 746 9873
email: JLewis@diocesewma.org
Web: www.diocesewma.org

WESTERN MICHIGAN (Province V)

Bishop Rt Revd Robert R. Gepert, 5220 Lovers Lane, LL100, Portage, MI 49002, USA

Tel: 1 269 381 2710
Fax: 1 269 381 7067
email: rrgsupport@edwm.org
Web: www.edwm.org/

WESTERN NEW YORK (Province II)

Bishop Rt Revd J. Michael Garrison, 1114 Delaware Ave, Buffalo, NY 14209, USA

Tel: 1 716 881 0660
Fax: 1 716 881 1724
email: jmgarrison@episcopalwny.org
Web: www.episcopalwny.org

WESTERN NORTH CAROLINA (Province IV)

Bishop Rt Revd G. Porter Taylor, 900B Centre Park Drive, Asheville, NC 28805, USA

Tel: 1 828 225 6656
Fax: 1 828 225 6657
email: bishop@diocesewnc.org
Web: www.diocesewnc.org

WYOMING (Province VI)

Bishop Rt Revd Bruce Edward Caldwell, 104 South Fourth St, Laramie, WY 82070, USA

Tel: 1 307 742 6606
Fax: 1 307 742 6782
email: bruce@wydiocese.org
Web: www.wydiocese.org

The Church in Wales

Members 66,720

The Church in Wales has been an independent province since its disestablishment and separation from the Church of England in 1920. It is practically coterminous with Wales and is the largest denomination in the country. The major policy-forming body is the Governing Body and the Church's inherited assets, including buildings, are held in trust by the Representative Body.

Archbishop Most Revd Barry Cennydd Morgan (*Bishop of Llandaff*)
Tel: 029 2056 2400
Fax: 029 2056 8410
email: archbishop@churchinwales.org.uk

Provincial Secretary and Archbishop's Registrar Mr John Shirley, 39 Cathedral Rd, Cardiff CF11 9XF
Tel: 029 2034 8218
Fax: 029 2038 7835
email: information@churchinwales.org.uk
Web: www.churchinwales.org.uk

Archbishop's Media Officer Anna Morrell (*same address*)
Tel: 029 2034 8208

THEOLOGICAL COLLEGE

St Michael's Theological College, 54 Cardiff Road, Llandaff, Cardiff CF5 2YJ (*Warden and Principal* Revd Canon Dr Peter H. Sedgwick)
Tel: 029 2056 3379
Fax: 029 2083 8008
email: info@stmichaels.ac.uk

BANGOR

Bishop Rt Revd Andrew Thomas Griffith John, Ty'r Esgob, Ffordd Garth Uchaf Bangor, Gwynedd LL57 2SS
Tel: 01248 362895
Fax: 01248 372454
email: bishop.bangor@churchinwales.org.uk
Web: www.churchinwales.org.uk/bangor

CATHEDRAL CHURCH OF ST DEINIOL, Bangor, Gwynedd

Dean The Very Reverend Alun John Hawkins, The Deanery, Cathedral Precinct, Bangor LL57 1LH
Tel: 01248 362840

LLANDAFF

Bishop Most Revd Dr Barry Cennydd Morgan (*Archbishop of the Province*), Llys Esgob, The Cathedral Green, Llandaff, Cardiff CF5 2YE
Tel: 029 2056 2400
Fax: 029 2056 8410
email: archbishop@churchinwales.org.uk
Web: www.churchinwales.org.uk/llandaff

Assistant Bishop of Llandaff, Rt Revd David Jeffrey Wilbourne, Llys Esgob, The Cathedral Green, Cardiff CF5 2YE
Tel: 029 2920 562400
Fax: 029 2057 7129
email: asstbishop@churchinwales.org.uk

CATHEDRAL CHURCH OF ST PETER AND ST PAUL, Llandaff, Cardiff

Dean Very Revd John Lewis, The Deanery, The Cathedral Green, Llandaff, Cardiff CF5 2YF
Tel: 029 2056 1545

MONMOUTH

Bishop Rt Revd Dominic Walker OGS, Bishopstow, 91a Stow Hill, Newport NP20 4EA
Tel: 01633 263510
Fax: 01633 259946
email: bishop.monmouth@churchinwales.org.uk
Web: www.churchinwales.org.uk/monmouth

CATHEDRAL CHURCH OF ST WOOLOS, Newport
Dean Very Revd Dr Richard Fenwick, The Deanery, Stow Hill, Newport NP20 4ED
Tel: 01633 263338

ST ASAPH

Bishop Rt Revd Gregory Kenneth Cameron, Esgobty, Upper Denbigh Road, St Asaph LL17 0TW
Tel: 01745 583503
Fax: 01745 584301
email: bishop.stasaph@churchinwales.org.uk
Web: www.churchinwales.org.uk/asaph

CATHEDRAL CHURCH OF ST ASAPH, St Asaph, Denbighshire
Dean Very Revd Christopher Potter, The Deanery, Upper Denbigh Road, St Asaph LL17 0RL
Tel: 01745 583597
email: chris_potter@btinternet.com

ST DAVIDS

Bishop Rt Revd J. Wyn Evans, Llys Esgob, Abergwili, Carmarthen SA31 2JG
Tel: 01267 236597
Fax: 01267 237482
email: bishop.stdavids@churchinwales.org.uk
Web: www.churchinwales.org.uk/david

CATHEDRAL CHURCH OF ST DAVID AND ST ANDREW, St Davids, Pembrokeshire
Dean Very Revd David Jonathan Rees Lean, The Deanery, St Davids, Haverfordwest SA62 6RH
Tel: 01437 720456
Fax: 01437 721885

SWANSEA AND BRECON

Bishop Rt Revd John David Edward Davies, Ely Tower, Brecon LD3 9DE
Tel: 01874 622008
Fax: 01874 610927
email: bishop.swanbrec @churchinwales.org.uk
Web: www.churchinwales.org.uk/swanbrec

CATHEDRAL CHURCH OF ST JOHN THE EVANGELIST, Brecon, Powys
Dean Very Revd Geoffrey Marshall, The Deanery, Cathedral Close, Brecon LD3 9DP
Tel: 01874 623344
email: admin@breconcathedral.org.uk

The Church of the Province of West Africa

Members 1,220,000
Church work began in Ghana as early as 1752 and in the Gambia, Guinea, Liberia and Sierra Leone in the nineteenth century. The Province of West Africa was founded in 1951 and was divided to form the Province of Nigeria and the Province of West Africa in 1979. The Church exists in an atmosphere of civil strife and Christians remain a minority.

Archbishop and Primate of the Province of West Africa Most Revd Dr Justice Ofei Akrofi (*Bishop of Accra*)

Dean of the Province of West Africa Rt Revd Albert D. Gomez (*Bishop of Guinea*)

Episcopal Secretary of the Province of West Africa Rt Revd Matthias K. Medadues-Badohu (*Bishop of Ho*)

Provincial Secretary Revd Canon Anthony M. Eiwuley, PO Box Lt 226, Lartebiokorshie, Accra, Ghana
Tel: 233 21 257 370
233 27 720 1538 (Mobile)
email: cpwa@4u.com.gh/
morkeiwuley@gmail.com

Provincial Treasurer Mr Samuel Atuobi Twum (*same address*)
Tel: 233 21 506 208
233 20 201 7969 (Mobile)
email: atlantichousing@yahoo.co.uk

THEOLOGICAL COLLEGES
Ghana
Trinity College (Ecumenical), PO Box 48, Legon, Ghana

St Nicholas Anglican Theological College, PO Box A 162, Cape Coast, Ghana

Liberia
Cuttington University College, Suacoco, PO Box 10–0277, 1000 Monrovia 10, Liberia

Sierra Leone
Theological Hall and Church Training Centre, PO Box 128, Freetown, Sierra Leone

ACCRA

Bishop Most Revd Dr Justice Ofei Akrofi, Bishopscourt, PO Box 8, Accra, Ghana
Tel: 233 21 662 292
Fax: 233 21 668 822
email: cpwa@4u.com.gh/
bishopakrofi@yahoo.com
Web: www.anglicandioceseofaccra.com

BO
Bishop Rt Revd Emmanuel Josie Samuel Tucker,
PO Box 21, Bo, Southern Province, Sierra Leone
Tel: 232 32 648
Fax: 232 32 605
+232 76 677 862 (Mobile)
email: bomission@justice.com/
ejstucker@gmail.com

CAMEROON
Bishop Rt. Revd. Thomas-Babyngton Elango Dibo,
BP 15705, New Bell, Douala, Cameroon
Tel and *Fax:* 237 408 552
email: revdibo2@yahoo.com

CAPE COAST
Bishop Rt Revd Daniel S. A. Allotey,
Bishopscourt, PO Box A 233, Adisadel Estates,
Cape Coast, Ghana
Tel: 233 42 32 502
Fax: 233 42 32 637
email: danallotey@priest.com

Suffragan Bishop Rt Revd Edmund K. Dawson-
Ahmoah (*same address*)
+233 24 464 4764 (Mobile)

FREETOWN
Bishop Rt Revd Julius Olotu Prince Lynch,
Bishop's Court, PO Box 537, Freetown, Sierra
Leone
Tel: 232 22 251 307
232 76 620 690 (Mobile)
email: bertajuls@yahoo.co.uk

GAMBIA
Bishop Rt Revd Dr Tilewa Johnson,
Bishopscourt, PO Box 51, Banjul, The Gambia,
West Africa
Tel: 220 228 405
220 905 227 (Mobile)
email: stilewaj@hotmail.com
Web: www.gambiadiocese.com

GUINEA
Bishop Rt Revd Albert D. Gomez, BP 187,
Conakry, Guinea
Tel: 224 451 323
email: galbertdgomez@yahoo.fr

HO
Bishop Rt Revd Matthias K. Mededues-Badohu,
Bishopslodge, PO Box MA 300, Ho, Volta
Region, Ghana *Tel:* 233 3620 26644 / 233 3620 28606
233 208 162 246 (Mobile)
email: matthoda@ucomgh.com/
matthiaskwab@googlemail.com

KOFORIDUA
Bishop Rt Revd Francis B. Quashie, PO Box 980,
Koforidua, Ghana
Tel: 233 3420 22 329
Fax: 233 81 22 060
email: fbquashie@yahoo.co.uk

KUMASI
Bishop Rt Revd Daniel Yinka Sarfo, Bishop's
House, PO Box 144, Kumasi, Ghana
Tel and *Fax:* 233 51 24 117
233 277 890 411 (Mobile)
email: anglicandioceseofkumasi@yahoo.com /
dysarfo2000@yahoo.co.uk

LIBERIA
Bishop Rt Revd Jonathan B. B. Hart, PO Box
10–0277, 1000 Monrovia 10, Liberia
Tel: 231 224 760
231 651 6343 (Mobile)
Fax: 231 227 519
email: jbbhart@yahoo.com /
bishopecl12@yahoo.com
Web: www.liberia.anglican.org

SEKONDI
Bishop Rt Revd John Kwamina Otoo, PO Box 85,
Sekondi, Ghana
Tel: 233 031 4604
233 208 200887 (Mobile)
email: angdiocesek@yahoo.co.uk

SUNYANI
Bishop Rt Revd Festus Yeboah-Asuamah, PO Box
23, Sunyani, Ghana
Tel: 233 61 23213
233 208 121 670 (Mobile)
Fax: 233 61 712300
email: fyasuamah@yahoo.com

TAMALE
Bishop Rt Revd Emmanuel Anyindana Arongo,
PO Box 110, Tamale, Ghana *Tel:* 233 3720 26639
233 277 890 878 (Mobile)
Fax: 233 3729 22906
email: bishopea2000@yahoo.com

Bishop Coadjutor-Elect Rt Revd Dr Jacob Kofi
Ayeebo
Tel: 233 243 419 864 (Mobile)
email: deanjacob@africaonline.com.gh

WIAWSO
Bishop Rt Revd Abraham Kobina Ackah, PO Box
4, Sefwi, Wiawso, Ghana
Tel: 233 274 005 952 (Mobile)
email: bishopackah@yahoo.com

The Church in the Province of the West Indies

Members 770,000
The West Indies became a self-governing province of the worldwide Anglican Communion in
1883 because of the Church of England missions
in territories that became British colonies. It is
made up of two mainland dioceses, Belize and

Guyana, and six island dioceses including the
Bahamas and Turks and Caicos Islands, Barba-
dos, Jamaica and the Cayman Islands, North
Eastern Caribbean and Aruba, Trinidad and
Tobago, and the Windward Islands. Great
emphasis is being placed on training personnel

for an indigenous ministry as the island locations and scattered settlements make pastoral care difficult and costly.

Archbishop of the Province Vacancy

Administrative Assistant to the Archbishop Ven I. Ranfurly Brown, Church House, PO Box N-7107, Nassau, Bahamas   *Tel:* 1 242 322 3015/6/7
Fax: 1 242 322 7943

Provincial Secretary Mrs Elenor Lawrence, Provincial Secretariat, Bamford House, Society Hill, St John, Barbados, West Indies
Tel: 1246 423 0842/3/8
Fax: 1 246 423 0855
email: bamford@sunbeach.net

THEOLOGICAL SEMINARIES
Codrington College, St John, Barbados (*Principal* Revd Dr Ian Rock)

United Theological College of the West Indies, PO Box 136, Golding Ave, Kingston 7, Jamaica (*Anglican Warden* Revd Garth Minott)

BARBADOS
Bishop Rt Revd Dr John Walder Dunlop Holder, Mandeville House, Collymore Rock, St Michael, Barbados   *Tel:* 1 246 426 2761/2
Fax: 1 246 426 0871
email: jwdh@sunbeach.net
Web: www.anglican.bb

BELIZE
Bishop Rt Revd Philip S. Wright, #25 Bishopsthorpe, PO Box 535, Southern Foreshore, Belize City, Belize, Central America   *Tel:* 501 2 73 029
Fax: 501 2 76 898
email: bzediocese@btl.net
Web: www.belize.anglican.org

GUYANA
Bishop Rt Revd Cornell Moss, The Diocesan Office, PO Box 10949, 49 Barrack St, Georgetown, Guyana, West Indies
Tel: 592 22 64 775
Fax: 592 22 76 091
email: dioofguy@networksgy.com

JAMAICA AND CAYMAN ISLANDS
Bishop Rt Revd Alfred C. Reid, 2 Caledonia Ave, Kingston 5, Jamaica   *Tel:* 1 876 920 2712
Fax: 1 876 960 1774
email: bishopja@anglicandiocese.com
Web: www.jamaica.anglican.org

Bishops Suffragan
Rt Revd Robert McLean Thompson (*Bishop of Kingston*), 3 Duke Street, Kingston, Jamaica, West Indies   *Tel:* 876 926 6692
Fax: 876 960 8463
email: bishop.kingston@anglicandiocese.com

Rt Revd Harold Benjamin Daniel (*Bishop of Mandeville*), Bishop's Residence, 3 Cotton Tree Road, PO Box 84, Mandeville, Jamaica, West Indies
Tel: 1 876 625 6817
Fax: 1 876 625 6819
email: hbdaniel@cwjamaica.com

Rt Revd Dr Howard Gregory (*Bishop of Montego Bay*), PO Box 346, Montego Bay, Jamaica, West Indies   *Tel:* 1 876 952 4963
Fax: 1 876 971 8838
email: hkagregory@hotmail.com

THE BAHAMAS AND THE TURKS AND CAICOS ISLANDS
Bishop Rt Revd Laish Z. Boyd, Church House, PO Box N-7107, Nassau, Bahamas
Tel: 1 242 322 3015/6/7
Fax: 1 242 322 7943
email: primate@batelnet.bs
Web: www.thebahamas.net/cpwi/

Bishop Suffragan Rt Revd Gilbert Arthur Thompson (*New Providence*) (*same address*)

NORTH EAST CARIBBEAN AND ARUBA
Bishop Rt Revd Leroy Errol Brooks, St Mary's Rectory, PO Box 180, The Valley, Anguilla
Tel: 1 264 497 2235
Fax: 1 264 497 8555
email: brookx@anguillanet.com

TRINIDAD AND TOBAGO
Bishop Rt Revd Calvin Wendell Bess, Hayes Court, 21 Maraval Road, Port of Spain, Trinidad, Trinidad and Tobago, West Indies
Tel: 1 868 622 7387
Fax: 1 868 628 1319
email: bessc@tstt.net.tt

WINDWARD ISLANDS
Bishop Rt Revd C. Leopold Friday, Bishop's Court, Montrose, PO Box 502, St Vincent, West Indies   *Tel:* 1 784 456 1895
Fax: 1 784 456 2591
email: diocesewi@vincysurf.com

Other Churches and Extra-Provincial Dioceses

BERMUDA
(Anglican Church of Bermuda)
This extra-provincial diocese is under the metropolitical jurisdiction of the Archbishop of Canterbury.

Bishop Rt Revd Dr Patrick G.H. White, 18 Ferrar's Lane, Pembroke HM08, Bermuda
Tel: 1 441 293 1787
email: bishoppatrick@logic.bm

Diocesan Office, PO Box HM 769, Hamilton HM CX, Bermuda
Tel: 1 441 292 6987
Fax: 1 441 292 5421
email: diocoff@ibl.bm
Web: www.anglican.bm

Archdeacon Ven Andrew Doughty, Warwick Rectory, PO Box WK 530, Warwick, WK BX, Bermuda

THE CHURCH OF CEYLON (SRI LANKA)
Members 52,500
Anglican missionaries commenced their work in Sri Lanka (Ceylon) with the coming of British colonial power in 1796. The Church of Ceylon comprises the Dioceses of Colombo (1845) and Kurunagala (1950). Prior to 1845, the Church in Ceylon was part of the diocese of Madras. The two dioceses belonged to the former Province of India, Pakistan, Burma & Ceylon. Sri Lanka is currently an extra-provincial diocese under the metropolitan authority of the Archbishop of Canterbury, and steps are now being taken for the Church of Ceylon to adopt a new constitution to replace the Provincial Constitution.

Clergy, full-time workers and the laity are trained at the Ecumenical Theological College of Lanka and the Cathedral Institute. Both dioceses are members of the National Christian Council and have cordial working relationships with the Roman Catholic Church and other major faith groups. Through a few private church schools, the dioceses are involved in primary and secondary secular education. The challenges they face include the training and the empowerment of the people of God for mission and witness in the context of poverty, ethnic conflict and a multi-faith environment. Both dioceses are part of an ecumenical journey that seeks organic union with the other older Protestant denominations.

THEOLOGICAL COLLEGE
Theological College of Lanka, Pilimatalawa, nr Kandy

COLOMBO
Bishop Rt Revd Duleep Kamil de Chickera, 368/3A Bauddhaloka Mawatha, Colombo 7
Tel: 94 1 684 810
Fax: 94 1 684 811
email: bishop@eureka.lk

Secretary Mrs Mary Thanja Pereis (*same address*)
email: diocol@eureka.lk

KURUNEGALA
Bishop Rt Revd Kumara Bandara Samuel Illangasinghe, Bishop's Office, Cathedral Close, Kurunegala
Tel: 94 37 22 191/94 37 222 0371
Fax: 94 37 26 806
email: bishopkg@sltnet.lk

EPISCOPAL CHURCH OF CUBA
(Iglesia Episcopal de Cuba)
Members 10,000
The Episcopal Church of Cuba is under a Metropolitan Council in matters of faith and order. Council members include the Primate of Canada, the Archbishop of the West Indies, and the Presiding Bishop of the Episcopal Church of the United States of America or a Bishop appointed by him.

Interim Diocesan Bishop Rt Revd Miguel Tamayo, Calle 6 # 273, Vedado, Ciudad de la Habana 4, C.P. 10400, Cuba
Tel: 537 32 11 20
Fax: 537 33 32 93
Web: www.cuba.anglican.org

THEOLOGICAL COLLEGE
Seminario Evangelico de Teologica, Aptdo. 149, Matanzas (Interdenominational, run in cooperation with the Methodist and Presbyterian Churches)

CHURCH PAPER
Heraldo Episcopal Published bimonthly. Contains diocesan, provincial and world news, homiletics, devotional and historical articles.

FALKLAND ISLANDS
In 1977 the Archbishop of Canterbury resumed episcopal jurisdiction over the Falkland Islands and South Georgia which had been relinquished in 1974 to the Church of the Southern Cone of America. In 2006 he appointed Bishop Stephen Venner, the Bishop of Dover, as his commissary, with the title Bishop for the Falkland Islands. The whole parish covers the Falkland Islands, South Georgia, and the South Sandwich Islands and British Antarctic Territory. Christ Church Cathedral is the most southerly cathedral in the world.

Bishop for the Falkland Islands Rt Revd Dr Stephen Venner (*Bishop to HM Forces*), 83 Hathaway Court, Rochester ME1 1QY
Tel: 01634 838787
email: stephen@venner.org.uk

Rector Revd Dr Richard Hines, The Deanery, PO Box 160, Stanley, Falkland Islands, South Atlantic FIQQ 1ZZ
Tel: 00 500 21100
Fax: 00 500 21100
email: christchurch@horizon.co.fk

Associate Minister Revd Kathy Biles (c/o *same address*)   *email:* k.biles@horizon.co.fk

LUSITANIAN CHURCH
(Portuguese Episcopal Church)
Members 5,000

Founded in 1880 by a group of local Roman Catholic priests and lay people as a reaction to a number of dogmas from the first Vatican Council. The Church consisted of Roman Catholic priests who formed congregations in and around Lisbon using a translation of the 1662 English Prayer Book. Its own first Prayer Book of Common Prayer was issued in 1884. A Lusitanian bishop was consecrated in 1958 and in the early 1960s many provinces of the Anglican Communion established full communion with the Church in Portugal. Full integration occurred in 1980 when the Church became an extra-provincial diocese under the metropolitical authority of the Archbishop of Canterbury. It takes seriously its role in the emerging Europe and has a commitment to helping the poor. It has a strong mission emphasis for the many unchurched people in the country, specially by its two diaconal institutions providing services and help to children and the elderly. The Church and its leaders cooperate fully with the Diocese in Europe (Church of England) and the Convocation of American Churches in Europe, assisting in each other's congregation and being a united Anglican voice in an increasingly secular Europe. In 1998 the diocesan synod of the Lusitanian Church approved and accepted the Porvoo Declaration, expressing its desire to be involved in the life of the Porvoo Communion and to cooperate, with interchangeable ministries, with the congregations of the Porvoo Churches in Portugal.

Bishop Rt Revd Dr Fernando da Luz Soares, Secretaria Diocesana, Apartado 392, P-4431-905 Vila Nova de Gaia, Portugal   *Tel:* 351 22 375 4018
                        Fax: 351 22 375 2016
email: centrodiocesano@igreja-lusitana.org
       Web: www.igreja-lusitana.org

Treasurer Senhor António Vaz Pinto dos Santos, Tesouraria Diocesana (*same address*)

SPANISH EPISCOPAL REFORMED CHURCH
Members 5,000

Parishes: 22 self supported, plus a similar number of congregations.

The Spanish Church covers the whole country and is divided into three archdiaconates, with three archdeacons:

Archdiaconate I: Catalonia, Valencia and Balearic islands

Archdiaconate II: Andalusia and Canary islands

Archdiaconate III: Central and Northern Spain

Under the leadership of some former Roman Catholic priests, in 1868 the Spanish Reformed Episcopal Church was established in Gibraltar and was for some years under the pastoral care of the Church of Ireland. The first Bishop was appointed in 1880 and consecrated in 1894 by the Bishop of Meath along with two other Bishops, and the Church of Ireland accepted metropolitan authority. The same year the Church adopted the Mozarabic Liturgy, which was the liturgy of the early Spanish Church. The Church was fully integrated into the Anglican Communion in 1980 under the metropolitical authority of the Archbishop of Canterbury. It has a strong evangelistic and mission commitment and it is organized into departments: youth, women, ecumenism, Christian education, mission and evangelization. The Church also has a very important social programme for immigrants, which was established in many parishes by helping with clothes and food for over 10,000 people per year. The history of the Church has been one of persecution and difficulties, especially during Franco's dictatorship, but it is firm in its cooperation with the Diocese in Europe and the Convocation of American Churches in Europe for a stronger Anglican presence throughout Europe.

Bishop Rt Revd Carlos López Lozano (*Bishop of Madrid*), Spanish Reformed Episcopal Church, Calle Beneficencia 18, 28004 Madrid
                      Tel: 34 91 445 2560
                      Fax: 34 91 594 4572
         email: eclesiae@arrakis.es
            Web: www.iere.cjb.net

Treasurer Señor Jesus Diaz Barragan (*same address*)

Regional Councils

COUNCIL OF THE ANGLICAN PROVINCES OF AFRICA

The Council of Anglican Provinces of Africa (CAPA) was established in 1979 in Chilema, Malawi, by Anglican Primates in Africa who saw the need to form a coordinating body that would help to bring the Anglican Communion in Africa together and to articulate issues affecting the Church. The organization was set up with the following aims and objectives:

- to help the Anglican churches in Africa develop beneficial relationships between themselves and with the wider Anglican Communion;
- to provide a forum for the Church in Africa to share experiences, consult and support each other;
- to confer about common responsibilities on the African continent;
- to establish opportunities for collaboration and joint activities;

- to maintain and develop relationships between the Anglican Church in Africa, partners, other denominations, fellowships, national and regional councils.

Today CAPA works with 12 Anglican provinces in Africa and the Diocese of Egypt. These provinces include Nigeria, West Africa, Sudan, Kenya, Uganda, Tanzania, Congo, Rwanda, Burundi, Central Africa, Southern Africa and Indian Ocean.

Chairman Most Revd Ian Ernest (*Primate of Indian Ocean*)

General Secretary The Rev Canon Grace Kaiso, PO Box 10329, 00100 Nairobi, Kenya
Tel: 254 20 3873 283/700
Fax: 254 20 3870 876
email: Generalsec@capa-hq.org
Web: www.capa-hq.org

Administrative Officer Mrs Elizabeth Gichovi (*same address*) *email:* info@capa-hq.org

HIV/AIDS TB & Malaria Programme Coordinator Mr Emmanuel Olatunji (*same address*)
email: olatunji@capa-hq.org/otunuel@yahoo.com

THE COUNCIL OF THE CHURCHES OF EAST ASIA
This Council, whose history began in 1954, has gone through an evolution. With most of the dioceses forming into provinces, the Council is now a fellowship for common action. Its membership includes dioceses in the Province of South East Asia, the Church of Korea, the Philippine Episcopal Church, Hong Kong Sheng Kung Hui, the Diocese of Taiwan (which is associated with the Episcopal Church of the USA), the Province of Myanmar, Nippon Sei Ko Kai (the Holy Catholic Church in Japan), the Philippine Independent Church and the Anglican Church of Australia who are members as a national Church or province.

Chairman Most Revd Dr John Chew Hiang Chea (*Archbishop of the Province of South East Asia*) Diocese of Singapore, St. Andrew's Village, 1, Francis Thomas Drive, 01–01 Singapore 359340.
Tel: 65 6288 7585
Fax: 65 6288 5574
email: bpoffice@anglican.org.sg
anglican@streamyx.com

THE SOUTH PACIFIC ANGLICAN COUNCIL
The Council now comprises the Province of Melanesia, the Province of Papua New Guinea, and the Diocese of Polynesia.

Chairman Rt Revd Elison Pogo (*Primate of the Church of Melanesia*), Archbishop's House, PO Box 19, Honiara, Solomon Islands *Tel:* 677 26 601
Fax: 677 21 098

Secretary Rt Revd Jabez Bryce (*Bishop of Polynesia*), PO Box 35, Suva, Fiji *Tel:* 679 3304 716
Fax: 679 3302 687
email: episcopus@connect.com.fj

ANGLICAN AND PORVOO COMMUNIONS

UNITED CHURCHES IN FULL COMMUNION

CHURCHES RESULTING FROM THE UNION OF ANGLICANS WITH CHRISTIANS OF OTHER TRADITIONS

The population of the countries of South Asia is over 1,000 million and these Churches cover the whole area. The total Christian population is around 22–3 million and Christians of many different traditions, ranging from ancient oriental to pentecostal, are to be found here. The region is undergoing rapid social, economic and political change. There is also a resurgence of some of the great world religions. Although there is a great deal of industrialization and there have been 'green revolutions' in the agricultural sector in many countries, there is still a tremendous inequality in the distribution of wealth and income. In spite of the relatively small numbers of Christians, the Churches have grown steadily and have been responsible for many initiatives in education, medical work and community development. Their influence is out of all proportion to their size. The Church of England continues to relate to these Churches mainly through its mission agencies: CMS, USPG, SPCK and Crosslinks. In addition, the Oxford Mission, the Dublin University Mission to Chota Nagpur and the Religious Communities are doing valuable work. Support in money and personnel also comes from Churches in Canada, from CMS in Australia and New Zealand, from the USA, Holland, Germany, Scandinavia, Japan and Singapore. The Churches themselves are involved in the training and sending of mission personnel both inside and outside India, including the sending of mission partners to the UK. Mission partners from the Church of England work under the authority of the local church or institution to which they have been sent. The Church of North India, the Church of South India and Mar Thoma Syrian Church of Malenkara are in full communion with each other and are members of a joint council to further and deepen their unity. Since 1988, these Churches have become full members of the Lambeth Conference and the Anglican Consultative Council. Their moderators also attend the meetings of Anglican Primates.

The Church of Bangladesh

Members 15,623
Congregations/Pastorates 72
Bangladesh was part of the State of Pakistan which was partitioned from India in 1947. After the civil war between East and West Pakistan ended in 1971, East Pakistan became Bangladesh. The Church of Bangladesh is one of the United Churches, formed by a union of Anglicans with Christians of other traditions.

Moderator Rt Revd Paul S. Sakar (*Bishop of Kushtia*)

General Secretary Mr Augustin Dipok Karmokar, St Thomas' Church, 54 Johnson Road, Dhaka – 1100   *Tel:* 880 2 711 6546
Fax: 880 2 712 1632
email: cbdacdio@bangla.net

Treasurer Mr Joel Mondal (*same address*)

THEOLOGICAL COLLEGE
St Andrew's Theological College, 54/1 Barobag, Mirpur 2, Dhaka – 1216, Bangladesh (*Principal* Revd Sourav Folia)   *Tel:* 880 2 802 0876

DHAKA
Bishop Rt Revd Michael S. Baroi (*Bishop of Dhaka and Moderator of the Church of Bangladesh*), St Thomas's Church, 54 Johnson Rd, Dhaka – 1100
Tel: 880 2 711 6546
Fax: 880 2 712 1632
email: cbdacdio@bangla.net

KUSHTIA
Bishop Rt Revd Paul S. Sarkar, 94 N.S. Road, Thanapara, Kushtia   *Tel* and *Fax:* 880 71 54618
email: cob@citechco.net

The Church of North India

Members 1,250,000

The Church was inaugurated in 1970 after many years of preparation. It includes the Anglican Church, the United Church of Northern India (Congregationalist and Presbyterian), the Methodist Church (British and Australian Conferences), the Council of Baptist Churches in Northern India, the Church of the Brethren in India, and the Disciples of Christ. Along with the Church of South India, the Church of Pakistan and the Church of Bangladesh, it is one of the four United Churches.

Moderator Most Revd Joel V. Mal (*Bishop of Chandigarh*)

Deputy Moderator The Rt Revd Purely Lyngdoh (*Bishop of North East India*)

General Secretary and Acting Treasurer Revd Dr Enos Das Pradhan, CNI Bhavan, 16 Pandit Pant Marg, New Delhi 110 001   *Tel:* 91 11 2371 6513
email: gscni@ndb.vsnl.net.in/enos@cnisynod.org
Web: www.cnisynod.org

Treasurer Mr Kosala (*same address*)
email: cnitr@cnisynod.org

CHURCH PAPER
The North India Church Review The official monthly magazine of the CNI. Contains articles, reports, diocesan news, world news and letters. *Editor/Editorial Office* (*same address*)

AGRA
Bishop Rt Revd S. R. Cutting, Bishop's House, 4/116-B Church Rd, Civil Lines, Agra 282 002, UP
Tel: 91 562 2854 845
Fax: 91 562 2520 074
email: doacni@sancharnet.in

AMRITSAR
Bishop Rt Revd Pradeep Kumar Samantaroy, 26 R. B. Prakash Chand Rd, Opp Police Ground, Amritsar 143 001, Punjab
Tel and Fax: 91 183 222 2910
email: bunu13@rediffmail.com
Web: www.amritsardiocese.org

ANDAMAN AND NICOBAR ISLANDS
Bishop Rt Revd Christopher Paul, Bishop's House, 21 Church Lane, Goal Ghar, Port Blair 744 101, Andaman and Nicobar Islands
Tel and Fax: 91 3192 231 362
email: cniportblair@yahoo.co.in

BARRACKPORE
Bishop Rt Revd Brojen Malakar, Bishop's Lodge, 86 Middle Rd, Barrackpore, Kolkata 700120, West Bengal
Tel: 91 33 2592 0147
Fax: 91 33 2593 1852

BHOPAL
Bishop Rt Revd Laxman L. Maida, Bishop's House, 57, Rseidency Area, Behind Narmada Water Tank, Indore 452 001 (MP)
Tel: 91 731 270 0232
91 98270 34737 (Mobile)
email: bhopal_diocese@rediffmail.com

CHANDIGARH
Bishop Most Revd Joel Vidyasagar Mal (*Moderator CNI*), Bishop's House, Mission Compound, Brown Rd, Ludhiana 141 001, Punjab
Tel and Fax: 91 161 222 5707
email: bishopdoc@yahoo.com/
joelvmal@yahoo.com

CHOTA NAGPUR
Bishop Rt Revd B. B. Baskey, Bishop's Lodge, PO Box 1, Church Rd, Ranchi 834 001, Jharkhand
Tel and Fax: 91 651 235 1184
email: rch_cndta@sancharnet.in

CUTTACK
Bishop Rt Revd Dr Samson Das, Bishop's House, Mission Rd, Cuttack 753 001, Orissa
Tel: 91 671 230 0102
email: diocese@vsnl.net

DELHI
Bishop Rt Revd Sunil Singh, Bishop's House, 1 Church Lane, Off North Ave, New Delhi 110 001
Tel: 91 11 2371 7471
email: stmartin@dels.vsnl.net.in

DURGAPUR
Bishop Rt Revd Probal Kanto Dutta, Bishop's House, St Michael's Church Compound, Aldrin Path, Bidhan Nagar, Dugapur 713 212
Tel: 91 343 253 4552
email: probal_dutta@yahoo.com

EASTERN HIMALAYA
Bishop Rt Revd Dr Naresh Ambala, Bishop's Lodge, PO Box 4, Darjeeling 734 101, W Bengal
Tel: 91 354 225 8183
email: bpambala@yahoo.com

GUJARAT
Bishop Rt Revd Vinodkumar Mathushellah Malaviya, Bishop's House, I.P. Mission Compound, Ellisbridge, Ahmedabad 380 006, Gujarat   *Tel and Fax:* 91 79 2656 1950
email: gujdio@yahoo.co.in

JABALPUR
Bishop Rt Revd Prem Chand Singh, Bishop's House, 2131 Napier Town, Jabalpur 482 001, MP
Tel: 91 761 2622 109
email: bishoppcsingh@yahoo.co.in

KOLHAPUR

Bishop Rt Revd Bathuel Ramchandra Tiwade, Bishop's House, EP School Compound, Kolhapur 416 001, MS
Tel and *Fax:* 91 231 2654 832
email: kdccni@vsnl.com

KOLKATA

Bishop Rt Revd Ashok Biwas, Bishop's House, 51 Chowringhee Rd, Calcutta 700 071, WB
Tel: 91 33 6534 7770
Fax: 91 33 2822 6340
email: samrajubh@vsnl.net

LUCKNOW

Bishop Rt Revd Anil Stephen, Bishop's House, 25/11 Mahatma Gandhi Marg, Allahabad 211 011, UP
Tel: 91 532 242 7053
Fax: 91 532 256 0713

MARATHWADA

Bishop Rt Revd M. U. Kasab, Bungalow 28 / A, Mission Compound, Cantonment, Aurangabad 431 002, MS
Tel and *Fax:* 91 240 237 3136
email: revmukasab@yahoo.co.in

MUMBAI

Bishop Rt Revd Prakash Dinkar Patole, 19 Hazarimal Somani Marg, Fort Mumbai 400 001
Tel: 91 22 2206 0248
email: bishopbomcni@rediffmail.com

NAGPUR

Bishop Rt Rev Paul Dupare, Cathedral House, Opp. Indian Coffee House, Sadar, Nagpur 440 001, MS
Tel: 91 712 562 1737
Fax: 91 712 309 7310
email: bishop@nagpur.dot.org.in

NASIK

Bishop Rt Revd Pradip Lemuel Kamble, Bishop's House, 1 Outram Rd, Tarakpur, Ahmednagar 414 001, MS
Tel: 91 241 241 1806
Fax: 91 241 242 2314
email: bishopofnasik@rediffmail.com

NORTH EAST INDIA

Bishop Rt Revd Purely Lyngdoh (*Deputy Moderator, CNI*), Bishop's Kuti, Shillong, Meghalaya 793 001
Tel: 91 364 2223 155
Fax: 91 364 2501 178
email: bishopnei15@hotmail.com

PATNA

Bishop Rt Revd Philip Phembuar Marandih, Bishop's House, Christ Church Compound, Bhagalpur 812 001, Bihar
Tel: 91 641 2400 033/2300 714
Fax: 91 641 2300 714
email: cnipatna@rediffmail.com

PHULBANI

Bishop Rt Revd Bijay Kumar Nayak, Bishop's House, Mission Compound, Gudripori, G-udaigiri, Phulbani 762 100, Kandhamal, Orissa 762 001
Tel: 91 6847 260569
email: bp.bkn@rediffmail.com

PUNE

Bishop Rt Revd Vijay Bapurao Sathe, Pune Diocesan Office, 1 Stevely Road (General Bhagat Marg), Red Bungalow, Pune 411 001, MS
Tel: 91 20 2633 4374
email: punediocese@yahoo.co.in

RAJASTHAN

Bishop Rt Revd Collin Theodore, 2/10 CNI Social Centre, Civil Lines, Opp. Bus Stand, Jaipur Rd, Ajmer 305 001
Tel: 91 145 2420 633
Fax: 91 145 2621 627

SAMBALPUR

Bishop Rt Revd Christ Kiron Das, Mission Compound, Bolangir 767 001, Orissa
Tel and *Fax:* 91 6652 230625
email: bishop_ckdas@rediffmail.com

The Church of Pakistan

Members 800,000
One of four United Churches in the Anglican Communion, the Church of Pakistan comprises the Anglican Church of Pakistan, the dioceses of Lahore and Karachi, two conferences of the United Methodist Church, the Scottish Presbyterian Church in Pakistan, and the Pakistan Lutheran Church.

Moderator Rt Revd Dr Alexander John Malik (*Bishop of Lahore*)

Deputy Moderator Rt Revd Sadiq Daniel (*Bishop of Karachi*)

General Secretary Mr Humphrey Peters, St John's Cathedral, 1 Sir Syed Road, Peshawar
Tel: 92 91 278 916/270 812
Tel: 92 91 5270 916/5270 812
Fax: 92 91 277 499
Web: www.churchofpakistan.org.pk

Treasurer Mr John Wilson, 27 Liaquat Road, Civil Lines, Hyderabad
Tel: 92 221 861 187/92 222 780 221

FAISALABAD

Bishop Rt Revd John Samuel, Bishop's House, PO Box 27, Mission Rd, Gojra, Distt Toba Tek Sing
Tel: 92 46 351 4689
92 300 655 0074 (Mobile)
email: jsamuel@brain.net.pk

HYDERABAD

Bishop Rt Revd Raffique Masih, 27 Liaquat Rd, Civil Lines, Hyderabad 71000, Sind
Tel: 92 22 2780 221
Fax: 92 22 2785 879
email: dohcop@yahoo.com

KARACHI

Bishop Rt Revd Saddiq Daniel (*Deputy Moderator, COP*), Holy Trinity Cathedral, Fatima Jinnah Rd, Karachi 75530
Tel: 92 521 6843
email: sadiqdaniel@hotmail.com

LAHORE

Bishop Rt Revd Dr Alexander John Malik (*Moderator, COP*), Bishopsbourne, Cathedral Close, The Mall, Lahore 54000
Tel: 92 42 723 3560 (Office)
92 42 7120 766 (Home)
Fax: 92 42 722 1270
email: bishop_Lahore@hotmail.com

MULTAN

Bishop Vacancy, 113 Qasim Rd, PO Box 204, Multan Cantt
Tel and Fax: 92 61 8799

PESHAWAR

Bishop Rt Revd Munawar Kenneth Rumalshah, Diocesan Centre, 1 Sir-Syed Rd, Peshawar 2500, North West Frontier Province *Tel:* 92 91 5276 519
email: bishopdop@hotmail.com

RAIWIND

Bishop Rt Revd Samuel Azariah, 17 Warris Rd, PO Box 2319, Lahore 54000
Tel: 92 42 758 8950
Fax: 92 42 757 7255
email: sammyazariah49@yahoo.com

SIALKOT

Bishop Rt Revd Samuel Pervez, Lal Kothi, Barah Patthar, Sialkot 2, Punjab
Tel: 92 432 264 895
Fax: 92 432 264 828/92 300 8615 828
email: chs_sialkot@yahoo.com

ARABIAN GULF

Bishop for Rt Revd Azad Marshall (*Area Bishop within the Diocese of Cyprus*), PO Box 688, Lahore, Punjab 54000, Pakistan
Tel: 92 42 542 0452
email: bishop@saintthomascenter.org

The Church of South India

Members 4,000,000

The Church was inaugurated in 1947 by the union of the South India United Church (itself a union of Congregational and Presbyterian/ Reformed traditions), the southern Anglican dioceses of the Church of India, and Burma, and the Methodist Church in South India. It is one of the four United Churches in the Anglican Communion.

Moderator Most Revd Dr J. W. Gladstone (*Bishop in South Kerala*)

Deputy Moderator Rt Revd Dr A. Christopher Asir (*Bishop in Madurai-Ramnad*)

General Secretary Revd Moses Jayakumar, CSI Centre 5 Whites Rd, Royapettah, Chennai 600 014, India
Tel: 91 44 2852 1566/4166 (office)
2852 3763 (home)
email: csi@vsnl.com

Honorary Treasurer Mr T. Devasahayam FCA, Tsoudury Nilayam, 2–5–211, Nakkalaguta, Hanamkonda, 506 001, Andhra Pradesh
Tel: 91 44 2852 4166 (Office)
91 870 225 2938 (Home)
Fax: 91 44 2858 4163
email: csisnd_tr@satyam.net.in

OFFICIAL MAGAZINE

CSI Life English Monthly Magazine. Contains articles, reports and news from the dioceses. *Editor:* The General Secretary CSI; *Managing Editor:* Rev. R. Mohanraj, Director, Dept of Communication, 5 Whites Road, Royapettah, Chennai 600 014; Yearly subscription Rs.150/- (£25 in UK, $30 in USA, $ 35 in Australia, $35 in New Zealand, sent by Air Mail).

CHENNAI (*formerly* MADRAS)

Bishop in Rt Revd Dr V. Devasahayam, Diocesan Office, PO Box 4914, 226 Cathedral Rd, Chennai 600 086, Tamil Nadu
Tel: 91 44 2811 3929/3933/7629
Fax: 91 44 2811 0608
email: bishopdeva@hotmail.com
Web: www.csimadrasdiocese.org

COIMBATORE

Bishop in Rt Revd Dr Manikam Dorai, Diocesan Office, 256 Race Course Rd, Coimbatore 641 018, Tamil Nadu
Tel: 91 422 221 3605
Fax: 91 442 200 0400
email: bishopdorai@presidency.com

DORNAKAL

Bishop in Rt Revd Dr B. S. Devamani, Bishop's Office S. C. RLY, Cathedral Compound, Dornakal 506 381, Warangal Dist., Andhra Pradesh
Tel: 91 8719 227 752 (Home)
227 535 (Office)
email: bshpindk@yahoo.co.in

EAST KERALA

Bishop in Rt Revd Dr K. G. Daniel, Bishop's House, Melukavumattom, Kottayam 686 652, Kerala State
Tel: 91 4822 291 044 (Home)
91 4822 220 001 (Office)
Fax: 91 4822 291 044
email: bishopkgdaniel@rediffmail.com

JAFFNA
Bishop in Rt Revd Daniel S. Thiagarajah, Bishop's office in Colombo, 36 5/2 Sinsapa Road, Colombo 6, Sri Lanka   *Tel:* 94 60 21495 0795 (Office)
Fax: 94 11 250 5805
email: dsthiagarajah@yahoo.com

KANYAKUMARI
Bishop in Rt Revd G. Devakadasham, CSI Diocesan Office, 71A Dennis St, Nagercoil 629 001, Tamil Nadu   *Tel:* 91 4652 231 539
Fax: 91 4652 226 560
email: csikkd@vsnl.in

KARIMNAGAR
Bishop in Rt Revd Dr P. Surya Prakash, Bishop's House, 2–8–95 CVRN Road, PO Box 40, Makarampura post, Karimnagar 505 001, Andhra Pradesh   *Tel:* 91 878 22 62229
email: suryaprakash@yahoo.com/
bishopsuryaprakash@yahoo.com

KARNATAKA CENTRAL
Bishop in Rt Revd S. Vasanthkumar, Diocesan Office, 20 Third Cross, CSI Compound, Bangalore 560 027, Karnataka
Tel: 91 80 2222 3766/4941
email: csikcd@vsnl.com

KARNATAKA NORTH
Bishop in Rt Revd J. Prabhakara Rao, Bishop's House, All Saints' Church Compound, Dharwad 580 008, Karnataka   *Tel:* 91 836 244 7733
Fax: 91 836 274 5461
email: bishopprabhakar@yahoo.co.in

KARNATAKA SOUTH
Bishop in Rt Revd Devaraj Bangera, Bishop's House, Balmatta, Mangalore 575 001, Karnataka
Tel: 91 824 243 2657/242 1802
Fax: 91 824 242 1802
email: bishopbangera@rediffmail.com

KRISHNA-GODAVARI
Bishop in Rt Revd Dr G. Dyvasirvadam, CSI St Andrew's Cathedral Compound, Main Rd, Machilipatnam 521 002, AP   *Tel:* 91 8672 220 623
email: bishopkrishna@yahoo.com

MADHYA KERALA
Bishop in Rt Revd Thomas Samuel, CSI Bishop's House, Cathedral Rd, Kottayam 686 018, Kerala
Tel: 91 481 2566 536
Fax: 91 481 566 531
email: csimkdbishop@sancharnet.in/
csimkdbishop@bsnl.in/bishopthomassamuel@
yahoo.com

MADURAI-RAMNAD
Bishop in Rt Revd Dr A. Christopher Asir (*Deputy Moderator, CSI*), 5 Bhulabai Desai Rd, Chockikulam, Madurai 625 002, Tamil Nadu
Tel: 91 452 256 3196/0541
Fax: 91 452 256 0864
email: bishop@csidmr.net

MEDAK
Bishop in Rt Revd Kanak Prasad, Bishop's Annexe, 145, MacIntyre Road, Secunderabad, Andhra Pradesh 500 003   *Tel:* 94 40 2783 3151
Fax: 94 40 2784 4215

NANDYAL
Bishop in Rt Revd Dr P. J. Lawrence, Bishop's House, Nandyal RS 518 502, Kurnool Dist., Andhra Pradesh   *Tel:* 91 8514 222 477
Fax: 91 8514 242 255
email: lawrencejoba@yahoo.com

NORTH KERALA
Bishop in Rt Revd Dr K. P. Kuruvilla, PO Box 104, Shoranur 679 121, Kerala   *Tel:* 91 466 2224 454
Fax: 91 466 2222 545
email: csinkd@md5.vsnl.net

RAYALASEEMA
Bishop in Rt Revd K. B. Yesuvaraprasad, Bishop's House, CSI Compound, Gooty 515 401, Ananthapur Dist, AP   *Tel:* 91 8662 325 320
Fax: 91 8562 275 200

SOUTH KERALA
Bishop in Rt Revd J. W. Gladstone (*Moderator, CSI*), Bishop's House, LMS Compound, Trivandrum 695 033, Kerala State
Tel: 91 471 231 5490
Fax: 91 471 231 6439
email: bishopgladstone@yahoo.com

THOOTHUKUDI-NAZARETH
Bishop in Charge Rt Revd J. A. D. Jebachandran, Bishop's House, 111/32T, Polpettai Extension, State Bank Colony, Thoothukudi 628 002, Tamil Nadu   *Tel:* 91 461 2345 430
Fax: 91 431 2346 911
email: bishoptnd@dataone.in
Web: http://csitnd.org

TIRUNELVELI
Bishop in Rt Revd Dr S. Jeyapaul David, Bishopstowe, PO Box 118, 16, North High Ground Rd, Tirunelveli 627 002, Tamil Nadu
Tel: 91 462 257 8744
Fax: 91 462 257 4525
email: bishop@csitirunelveli.org
Web: www.csitirunelveli.org

TRICHY-TANJORE
Bishop in Rt Revd Dr G. Paul Vasanthakumar, PO Box 31, 17 VOC Rd, Cantonment, Tiruchiarapalli 620 017, Tamil Nadu   *Tel:* 91 431 2771 254
Fax: 91 431 2418 485
email: csittd@tr.net.in

VELLORE
Bishop in Rt Revd Dr Yesurathnam William, CSI Diocesan Office, 1/A Officer's Lane, Vellore 632 001, Tamil Nadu   *Tel:* 91 416 2232 160
Fax: 91 416 2223 835
email: bishopwilliam@sify.com

THE HOLY CATHOLIC CHURCH IN CHINA

(Chung Hua Sheng Kung Hui)

The Chung Hua Sheng Kung Hui was an important denomination in China and its history dates back to the mid-nineteenth century. Today the CHSKU, as a separate denomination, no longer exists in the People's Republic of China, except for Hong Kong which returned to Chinese sovereignty on 1 July 1997. Under the formula 'one country – two systems' Hong Kong keeps its autonomy for 50 years, including the religious situation. The same applies to Macao which was returned by Portugal to China at the end of 1999. On the Chinese mainland the Protestant Churches, with few exceptions, have entered into a post-denominational phase under the China Christian Council. A United Church is in the process of being created and Christians of Anglican inspiration are very much a part of this process. Bishop K. H. Ting, now in his old age, has retired from active leadership of the China Christian Council and the Nanjing Union Theological Seminary.

Although the CHSKU is no longer in existence, many former Anglicans still share a strong spiritual affinity with other Anglican Churches on matters of belief and liturgical tradition. As the Chinese Protestant Church develops its own ecclesiology and forms of worship, the Anglican traditions will no doubt contribute to a richer synthesis.

The relations between the Church in China and the Churches in Britain are facilitated by the China Desk of the Churches Together in Britain and Ireland (CTBI). It provides advice to government, churches and media, and publishes the *China Study Journal*, a documentary review of Chinese religions and government policy. The China Desk is a continuation of the ecumenical China Study Project which was established in 1972 by the leading missionary societies, including Anglican organizations such as the CMS, USPG and the Archbishop's China Appeal Fund.

The Friends of the Church in China, an ecumenical association which works closely with the China Desk of CTBI, takes a more grass-roots approach in relation to Christians in China. It publishes a popular newsletter on China and organizes visits to Chinese churches. China Desk/CTBI, Bastille Court, 2 Paris Garden, London SE1 8ND. The contact is Mr Lawrence Braschi, Director of China Desk (*email:* Lawrence. braschi@ctbi.org.uk, *Tel:* 020 7901 4886).

Friends of the Church in China, c/o Seagulls, Pinmill, Chelmondiston, Ipswich IP9 1JN. Its Chairman is Canon Simon Brown.

ANGLICAN AND PORVOO COMMUNIONS

OTHER CHURCHES IN COMMUNION WITH THE CHURCH OF ENGLAND

Old Catholic Churches of the Union of Utrecht

The Old Catholic Churches are a family of nationally organized churches which bound themselves together in the Union of Utrecht in 1889. Most of them owe their origin to Roman Catholics who were unable to accept the decrees of the First Vatican Council in 1870 and left the communion of that Church. The Archbishopric of Utrecht, however (from which the other Old Catholic Churches derived their episcopal orders), has been independent of Rome since the eighteenth century following a complex dispute involving papal and capitular rights of nomination and accusations of Jansenism (until 1910 in the Netherlands only). The Latin Mass continued in use, though all the Old Catholic Churches now worship in the vernacular. Their rites stand within the Western tradition, with various 'Eastern' features.

By the acceptance of the Bonn Agreement on 20 and 22 January 1932, the Convocation of Canterbury established full communion with the Old Catholic Churches by means of the following resolutions:

'That this House approves of the following statements agreed on between the representatives of the Old Catholic Churches and the Churches of the Anglican Communion at a Conference held at Bonn on 2 July 1931:

1. Each Communion recognises the catholicity and independence of the other and maintains its own.
2. Each Communion agrees to admit members of the other Communion to participate in the sacraments.
3. Intercommunion does not require from either Communion the acceptance of all doctrinal opinion, sacramental devotion, or liturgical practice characteristic of the other, but implies that each believes the other to hold all the essentials of the Christian Faith.

'And this House agrees to the establishment of Intercommunion between the Church of England and the Old Catholics on these terms.'

An Anglican–Old Catholic International Coordinating Council was established in 1998.

AUSTRIA
Bishop Rt Revd John Ekemezie Okoro, Schottenring 17/ 1/3/12, A–1010 Vienna
email: b.dilekci@altkatholiken.at
Web: www.altkatholiken.at

CROATIA
Bishop Vacancy, *under the care of Rt Revd Bernhard Heitz* (Bishop Emeritus of Austria), Etrichstraße 40 / 2/ 12, 1110 Vienna *email:* bischof.heitz@altkatholiken.at

CZECH REPUBLIC
Bishop Rt Revd Dušan Hejbal, Na Bateriich 27, CZ–162 00 Prague 6 *email:* stkat@starokatolici.cz
Web: www.starokatolici.cz

FRANCE
Bishop Delegate Most Revd Joris Vercammen (*Archbishop of Utrecht*)
Mission de France, 15 rue de Douai, 75009 Paris, France *email:* bishof@christkath.ch
Web: www.vieux-catholique-alsace.com

GERMANY
Bishop Rt Revd Joachim Vobbe, Gregor–Mendel-Strasse 28, 53115 Bonn, Germany
email: ordinariat@alt-katholisch.de
Web: www.alt-katholisch.de

ITALY
Mission in Italy Revd Petr Živný, Viale Caterina da Forli, 58, 1–201146, Milano, Italy *Tel:* 39 2 48 70 94 43 *email:* altkatholischekircheitalien@guarigione-liberazione-org
Web: www.chiesaveterocattolica.org

NETHERLANDS
Archbishop Most Revd Dr Joris Vercammen (*Archbishop of Utrecht and President of the International Bishops' Conference*), Kon Wilhelminalaan, 3, NL–3818 HN Amersfoort
email: buro@okkn.nl
Web: www.okkn.nl/welkom

POLAND (The Polish National Catholic Church)
Prime Bishop Most Revd Wiktor Wysoczanski, ul. Wilcza 31/16c, PL–002–544 Warsaw
email: polskokatolicki@pnet.pl
Web: www.polskokatolicki.pl

SWEDEN AND DENMARK
Bishop Delegate Rt Revd Dirk Jan Schoon, Ruysdaelstraat 37, NL–1070 XA Amsterdam, Netherlands   *email:* bvh@okkn.nl

SWITZERLAND
Bishop Rt Revd Harald Rein, Willadingweg 39, CH–3006 Bern   *email:* bischof@christkath.ch
Web: www.christkath.ch

Philippine Independent Church

The Philippine Independent Church is in part the result of the Philippine revolution against Spain in 1896 for religious emancipation and Filipino identity. It was formally established in 1902, declaring its independence from the Roman Catholic Church but seeking to remain loyal to the Catholic Faith. It now derives its succession from the Protestant Episcopal Church in the United States of America (and therefore from Anglican sources), with which full communion was established in September 1961. It has a membership of approximately seven million followers, 34 dioceses with 50 bishops, 600 regular church buildings and 2,000 village chapels served by about 600 priests.

Following the report of a Commission appointed by the Archbishop of Canterbury, full communion on the basis of the Bonn Agreement was established between the Church of England and the Philippine Independent Church in 1963 by the Convocations of Canterbury and York. It is in full communion with all the member Churches in the Anglican Communion.

The Philippine Independent Church is very active in its ecumenical relations. It is the most senior member in the National Council of the Churches in the Philippines, a member of Council of Churches in East Asia, a member of the Christian Churches in Asia, and an active member of the World Council of Churches.

Supreme Bishop (*Obisbo Maximo*) Most Revd Tomas A. Millamena, 1500 Taft Avenue, Ermita, Manila, Philippines 2801.
Tel: 63 2 523 72 42
Fax: 63 2 521 39 32
email: ifiphil@hotmail.com

Mar Thoma Syrian Church of Malabar

The Christian community in South India is very ancient and is believed by its members to have been founded by the Apostle Thomas (Mar Thoma). Over the centuries contact with Christian bodies from outside India has led to the fragmentation of the original community into a number of jurisdictions. During the latter part of the nineteenth century the Christians of the West Syrian (Syrian Orthodox) tradition divided into two over the issue of the removal of non-biblical features from teaching and worship of the Church. The influence of Anglican missionaries of the Church Missionary Society who had been working in Malabar since the beginning of the nineteenth century accelerated the new stance in the Church. The larger section (which itself has subsequently divided into the Indian Orthodox and Jacobite Churches) chose closer links with Antioch and remained 'unreformed'; the smaller group, which eventually adopted the name of Mar Thoma Syrian Church of Malabar, undertook a conservative revision of its rites, removing elements (such as the invocation of saints and prayers for the dead) that were not scriptural practices but had given room for misunderstanding of the gospel. The general form of Mar Thoma worship remains eastern. Its episcopal succession derives from the Patriarchate of Antioch.

The former CIPBC (Church of India, Pakistan, Burma and Ceylon) had partial intercommunion with the Mar Thoma Church from 1937 until 1961 when a Concordat of Full Communion was established. The Mar Thoma Syrian Church of Malabar is now in full communion with the Churches of South India and North India. The union of these three churches is now known as the Communion of Churches in India (CCI), which fosters cooperation in mission, theological training, and formulations and involvement in social issues. The Mar Thoma Church has stated its desire to preserve its eastern traditions and is not willing to merge with the two Western United Churches. A number of Anglican Provinces are in full communion with the Mar Thoma Church, the Church of England having become so in 1974.

The Malabar Independent Syrian Church of Thozhiyoor occupies a unique position in the complex history of the Church in South India. At various times in the past its bishops have consecrated bishops for both the Orthodox and Mar Thoma Churches when the episcopal succession in those churches has died out. The MISC is fully Orthodox in rite and faith. It is in communion with the Mar Thoma Church and its current practice is to extend eucharistic hospitality to Christians of other traditions. The former Metropolitan was an ecumenical participant at the 1998 Lambeth Conference.

ANGLICAN AND PORVOO COMMUNIONS

THE MAR THOMA SYRIAN CHURCH OF MALABAR

Metropolitan Most Revd Dr Philipose Mar Chrysostom Mar Thoma, Poolatheen, Tiruvalla 689 101, Kerala, South India

Tel: 91 469 263 0313
Fax: 91 469 260 2626
email: pulathen@md3.vsnl.net.in

Sabha Secretary Revd Dr Cherian Thomas, Mar Thoma Church Headquarters, Sabha Office, SCS Campus, Tiruvalla 689 101, Kerala, South India

Tel: 91 469 263 0449
Fax: 91 469 263 0327
email: marthoma@vsnl.com

THE MALABAR INDEPENDENT SYRIAN CHURCH

Most Revd Cyril Mar Basilios, St George's Cathedral, Thozhiyoor, Thrissur Dt 680 520, Kerala, South India

Maps of the Churches and Provinces of the Anglican Communion

The maps of the Anglican Communion which follow have been supplied by Nicola Lawrence of The Mothers' Union. She will be happy to hear of any changes which need to be made.

© *The Mothers' Union 2008*

ANGLICAN AND PORVOO COMMUNIONS

MAP 1

The Scottish Episcopal Church
1 Moray, Ross and Caithness
2 Argyll and the Isles
3 St Andrews, Dunkeld and Dunblane
4 Aberdeen and Orkney
5 Brechin
6 Glasgow and Galloway
7 Edinburgh

.... Diocesan Boundary

━ ━ ━ ━ Provincial Boundary

The Isles of Scilly are included
in the Diocese of Truro

The Channel Islands are annexed
to the Diocese of Winchester

The Church of Ireland
Province of Armagh
8 Derry and Raphoe
9 Connor
10 Tuam, Killala and Achonry
11 Kilmore, Elphin and Ardagh
12 Clogher
13 Armagh
14 Down and Dromore

Province of Dublin
15 Limerick and Killaloe
16 Meath and Kildare
17 Cork, Cloyne and Ross
18 Cashel and Ossory
19 Dublin and Glendalough

The Church in Wales
20 Bangor
21 St Asaph
22 St Davids
23 Swansea and Brecon
24 Llandaff
25 Monmouth

The Church of England
Province of York
26 Carlisle
27 Newcastle
28 Durham
29 Ripon and Leeds
30 Bradford
31 Blackburn
32 York
33 Wakefield
34 Manchester
35 Liverpool
36 Chester
37 Sheffield
38 Southwell and Nottingham
39 Sodor and Man

Province of Canterbury
40 Lichfield
41 Derby
42 Lincoln
43 Hereford
44 Worcester
45 Birmingham
46 Coventry
47 Leicester
48 Peterborough
49 Ely
50 Norwich
51 St Edmundsbury and Ipswich
52 Gloucester
53 Bristol
54 Oxford
55 St Albans
56 London
57 Chelmsford
58 Truro
59 Exeter
60 Bath and Wells
61 Salisbury
62 Winchester
63 Portsmouth
64 Guildford
65 Southwark
66 Rochester
67 Chichester
68 Canterbury
Diocese in Europe

Extra-Provincial Dioceses
Bermuda
Lusitanian Church
Spanish Episcopal Reformed Church
The Church of Ceylon
Falkland Islands

ANGLICAN AND PORVOO COMMUNIONS

MAP 2

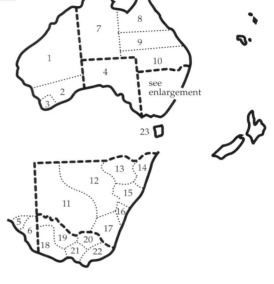

PAPUA NEW GUINEA

The Anglican Church of Australia

Province of Western Australia
1 North West Australia
2 Perth
3 Bunbury

Province of South Australia
4 Willochra
5 Adelaide
6 The Murray

Province of Queensland
7 The Northern Territory
8 North Queensland
9 Rockhampton
10 Brisbane

Province of New South Wales
11 Riverina
12 Bathurst
13 Armidale
14 Grafton
15 Newcastle
16 Sydney
17 Canberra and Goulburn

Province of Victoria
18 Ballarat
19 Bendigo
20 Wangaratta
21 Melbourne
22 Gippsland

23 Tasmania *(extra-provincial)*

The Anglican Church of Papua New Guinea
24 Aipo Rongo
25 Dogura
26 New Guinea Islands
27 Popondota
28 Port Moresby

MAP 3

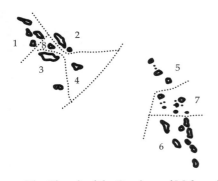

FIJI

16

TONGA

The Church of the Province of Melanesia
  1 Ysabel
  2 Malaita
  3 Central Melanesia
  4 Hanuato'o
  5 Temotu
  6 Vanuatu and New Caledonia
  7 Banks and Torres
  8 Central Solomons

The Anglican Church in Aotearoa,
New Zealand and Polynesia
  9 Auckland
  10 Waikato
  11 Waiapu
  12 Wellington
  13 Nelson
  14 Christchurch
  15 Dunedin
  16 Polynesia

Bishopric of Aotearoa
A Hui Amorangi ki te Tai Tokerau
B Hui Amorangi ki te Manawa o te Wheke
C Hui Amorangi ki te Tairawhiti
D Hui Amorangi ki te Upoko o te Ika
E Hui Amorangi ki te Waipounamu

– – – – – – – –   Bishopric of Aotearoa

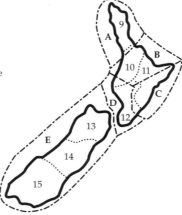

The Episcopal Church in the United States of America

Province I
1 Connecticut
2 Maine
3 Massachusetts
4 New Hampshire
5 Rhode Island
6 Vermont
7 Western Massachusetts

Province II
8 Albany
9 Central New York
10 Long Island
11 New Jersey
12 New York
13 Newark
14 Rochester
15 Western New York
Haiti *(see Map 5)*
Virgin Islands *(see Map 5)*
Convocation of American Churches
   in Europe

Province III
16 Bethlehem
17 Central Pennsylvania
18 Delaware
19 Easton
20 Maryland
21 Northwestern Pennsylvania
22 Pennsylvania
23 Pittsburgh
24 Southern Virginia
25 Southwestern Virginia
26 Virginia
27 Washington
28 West Virginia

Province IV
29 Alabama
30 Atlanta
31 Central Florida
32 Central Gulf Coast
33 East Carolina

34 East Tennessee
35 Florida
36 Georgia
37 Kentucky
38 Lexington
39 Louisiana
40 Mississippi
41 North Carolina
42 South Carolina
43 Southeast Florida
44 Southwest Florida
45 Tennessee
46 Upper South Carolina
47 West Tennessee
48 Western North Carolina

Province V
49 Chicago
50 Eau Claire
51 Fond du Lac
52 Indianapolis
53 Michigan
54 Milwaukee
55 Missouri
56 Northern Indiana
57 Northern Michigan
58 Ohio
59 Quincy
60 Southern Ohio
61 Springfield
62 Western Michigan
63 Eastern Michigan

Province VI
64 Colorado
65 Iowa
66 Minnesota
67 Montana
68 Nebraska
69 North Dakota
70 South Dakota
71 Wyoming

Province VII
72 Arkansas
73 Dallas
74 Fort Worth
75 Kansas
76 Northwest Texas
77 Oklahoma
78 Rio Grande
79 Texas
80 West Missouri
81 West Texas
82 Western Kansas
83 Western Louisiana

Province VIII
84 Arizona
85 California
86 Eastern Oregon
87 El Camino Real
88 Idaho
89 Los Angeles
90 Navajoland Area Mission
91 Nevada
92 Northern California
93 Olympia
94 Oregon
95 San Diego
96 San Joaquin
97 Spokane
98 Utah
Hawaii
Alaska *(see Map 6)*
Taiwan *(see Map 14)*
Micronesia

Anglican and Porvoo Communions

MAP 4

ANGLICAN AND PORVOO COMMUNIONS

MAP 5

The Church in the Province of the West Indies
32 Belize
33 Jamaica and the Cayman Islands
34 North Eastern Caribbean & Aruba
35 Windward Islands
36 Barbados
37 Trinidad and Tobago
38 Guyana
46 Suriname (part of the Diocese of Guyana)
47 Cayenne (part of the Diocese of Guyana)
39 The Bahamas and the Turks and Caicos Islands

Province IX
2 Honduras
6 Litoral Ecuador
7 Central Ecuador
8 Colombia
9 Dominican Republic
11 Puerto Rico
12 Venezuela

The Anglican Church of Mexico
13 Western Mexico
14 Northern Mexico
15 Mexico
16 Cuernavaca
17 Southeastern Mexico

The Anglican Church of the Central American Region
1 Guatemala
3 El Salvador
4 Nicaragua
5 Panama
10 Costa Rica

The Episcopal Anglican Church of Brazil
18 Rio de Janeiro
19 Recife
20 Southern Brazil
21 São Paulo
22 Southwestern Brazil
23 Brasilia
24 Pelotas
44 Curitiba
45 Amazon
48 Missionary District of Oesle-Brasil

Anglican Church of the Southern Cone of America
25 Argentina
26 Chile
27 Northern Argentina
28 Paraguay
29 Peru
30 Uruguay
31 Bolivia

The Episcopal Church of Cuba
(Autonomous diocese)
40 Cuba

41 Bermuda (*extra-provincial to Canterbury*)
42 Haiti (Province II ECUSA – *see Map 4*)
43 Virgin Islands (Province II ECUSA – *see Map 4*)

MAP 6

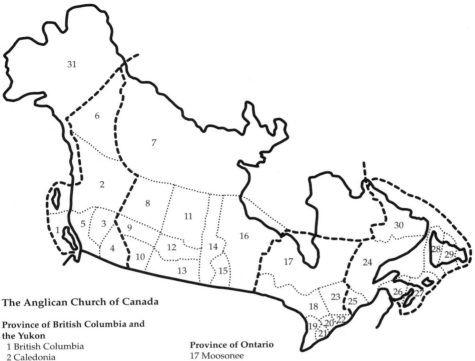

The Anglican Church of Canada

Province of British Columbia and the Yukon
1 British Columbia
2 Caledonia
3 Anglican Parishes of the Central Interior
4 Kootenay
5 New Westminster
6 Yukon

Province of Rupert's Land
7 The Arctic
8 Athabasca
9 Edmonton
10 Calgary
11 Saskatchewan
12 Saskatoon
13 Qu'Appelle
14 Brandon
15 Rupert's Land
16 Keewatin

Province of Ontario
17 Moosonee
18 Algoma
19 Huron
20 Toronto
21 Niagara
22 Ontario
23 Ottawa

Province of Canada
24 Quebec
25 Montreal
26 Fredericton
27 Nova Scotia and Prince Edward Island
28 Western Newfoundland
29 Central Newfoundland
30 Eastern Newfoundland and Labrador

31 Alaska *(in Province VIII of ECUSA)*

MAP 7

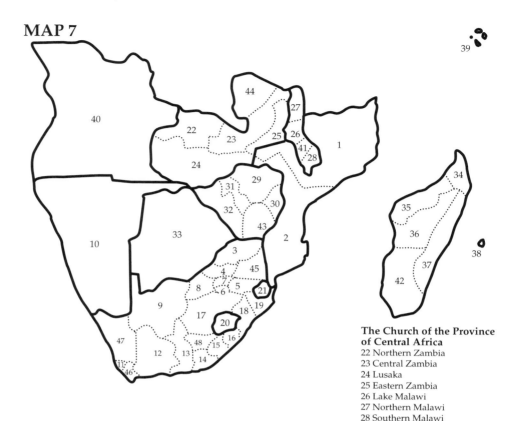

The Church of the Province
of Central Africa
22 Northern Zambia
23 Central Zambia
24 Lusaka
25 Eastern Zambia
26 Lake Malawi
27 Northern Malawi
28 Southern Malawi
29 Harare
30 Manicaland
31 Central Zimbabwe
32 Matabeleland
33 Botswana
41 Upper Shire
43 Masvingo
44 Luapula

The Church of the Province
of the Indian Ocean
34 Antsiranana
35 Mahajanga
36 Antananarivo
37 Toamasina
38 Mauritius
39 Seychelles
42 Fianarantsoa

The Church of the Province
of Southern Africa
 1 Niassa
 2 Lebombo
 3 St Mark the Evangelist
 4 Pretoria
 5 Highveld
 6 Christ the King
 7 Johannesburg
 8 Matlosane
 9 Kimberley and Kuruman
10 Namibia
11 Cape Town
12 George
13 Port Elizabeth
14 Grahamstown

15 Mthatha
16 Umzimvubu
17 Free State
18 Natal
19 Zululand
20 Lesotho
21 Swaziland
40 Angola
45 Mpumalanga
46 False Bay
47 Saldanha Bay
48 Ukhahlamba

St Helena

MAP 8

Anglican Church of Kenya
1 Nambale
2 Bungoma
3 Katakwa
4 Maseno North
5 Maseno West
6 Maseno South
7 Southern Nyanza
8 Butere
9 Mumias
10 Nairobi
11 Mount Kenya South
12 Mount Kenya West
13 Nakuru
14 Nyahururu
15 Embu
16 Mbeere
17 Mount Kenya Central
18 Eldoret
19 Kitale
20 Kirinyaga
21 Meru
22 Machakos
23 Kajiado
24 Mombasa
25 Taita Taveta
26 Kitui
44 Thika
45 Bondo
48 All Saints Cathedral
51 Kericho

Anglican Church of Tanzania
27 Morogoro
28 Tanga
29 Zanzibar
30 Ruaha
31 Rift Valley
32 Tabora
33 Western Tanganyika
34 South West Tanganyika
35 Ruvuma
36 Masasi
37 Kagera

38 Victoria Nyanza
39 Mara
40 Mount Kilimanjaro
41 Central Tanganyika
42 Mpwapwa
43 Southern Highlands
46 Kondoa
47 Dar-es-Salaam
49 Shinyanga
50 Lweru
52 Kiteto

see enlargement

10 and 48

MAP 9

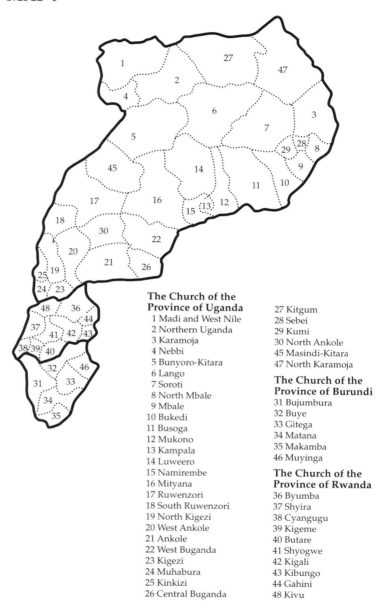

The Church of the Province of Uganda
1 Madi and West Nile
2 Northern Uganda
3 Karamoja
4 Nebbi
5 Bunyoro-Kitara
6 Lango
7 Soroti
8 North Mbale
9 Mbale
10 Bukedi
11 Busoga
12 Mukono
13 Kampala
14 Luweero
15 Namirembe
16 Mityana
17 Ruwenzori
18 South Ruwenzori
19 North Kigezi
20 West Ankole
21 Ankole
22 West Buganda
23 Kigezi
24 Muhabura
25 Kinkizi
26 Central Buganda

27 Kitgum
28 Sebei
29 Kumi
30 North Ankole
45 Masindi-Kitara
47 North Karamoja

The Church of the Province of Burundi
31 Bujumbura
32 Buye
33 Gitega
34 Matana
35 Makamba
46 Muyinga

The Church of the Province of Rwanda
36 Byumba
37 Shyira
38 Cyangugu
39 Kigeme
40 Butare
41 Shyogwe
42 Kigali
43 Kibungo
44 Gahini
48 Kivu

Anglican and Porvoo Communions

MAP 10

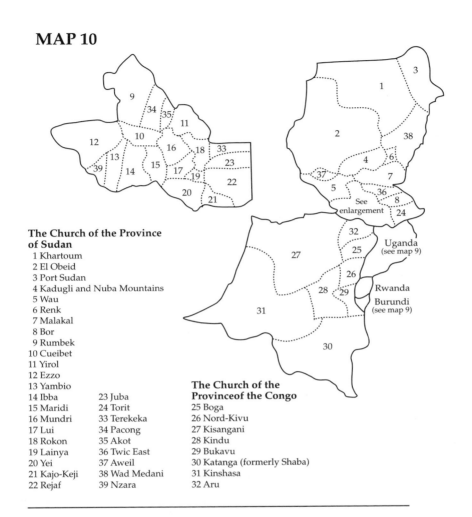

The Church of the Province of Sudan
1 Khartoum
2 El Obeid
3 Port Sudan
4 Kadugli and Nuba Mountains
5 Wau
6 Renk
7 Malakal
8 Bor
9 Rumbek
10 Cueibet
11 Yirol
12 Ezzo
13 Yambio
14 Ibba
15 Maridi
16 Mundri
17 Lui
18 Rokon
19 Lainya
20 Yei
21 Kajo-Keji
22 Rejaf
23 Juba
24 Torit
33 Terekeka
34 Pacong
35 Akot
36 Twic East
37 Aweil
38 Wad Medani
39 Nzara

The Church of the Province of the Congo
25 Boga
26 Nord-Kivu
27 Kisangani
28 Kindu
29 Bukavu
30 Katanga (formerly Shaba)
31 Kinshasa
32 Aru

The Church of Nigeria
(Anglican Communion) *(see map overleaf)*

Province of Abuja
7 Minna
9 Abuja
10 Kafanchan
13 Makurdi
48 Lokoja
57 Oturkpo
66 Bida
70 Gwagwalada
71 Lafia
Idah
Kubwa
Zonkwa
Ijumu
Kutigi
Kwoi
Okene
Kotangora

Province of Bendel
19 Benin
26 Asaba
36 Warri
45 Sabongidda-Ora
74 Oleh
75 Ughelli
76 Esan
78 Ikka
Western Izon
Akoko-Edo
Ndokwa

Province of Ibadan
8 Kwara
14 Ibadan
15 Osun
16 Ilesa

30 Ife
46 Oke-Osun
61 Ibadan-North
62 Ibadan-South
64 Offa
65 Igbomina
Ajayi Crowther
New Bussa
Ogbomoso
Oke-Ogun
Oyo
Ekiti Kwara
Ife East
Jebba
Omu-Aran

MAP 11

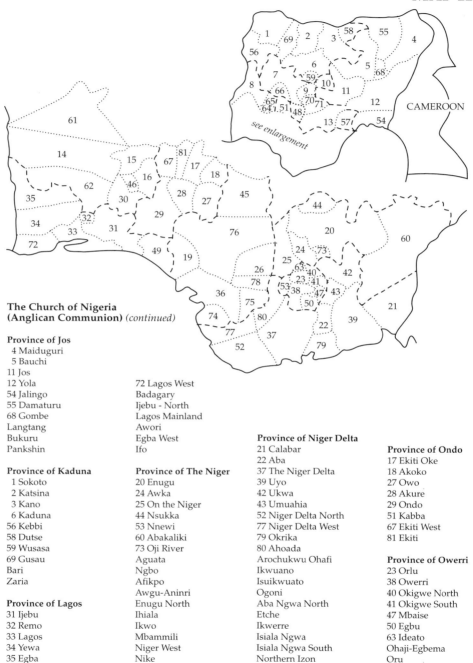

The Church of Nigeria (Anglican Communion) *(continued)*

Province of Jos
4 Maiduguri
5 Bauchi
11 Jos
12 Yola
54 Jalingo
55 Damaturu
68 Gombe
Langtang
Bukuru
Pankshin

72 Lagos West
Badagary
Ijebu - North
Lagos Mainland
Awori
Egba West
Ifo

Province of Kaduna
1 Sokoto
2 Katsina
3 Kano
6 Kaduna
56 Kebbi
58 Dutse
59 Wusasa
69 Gusau
Bari
Zaria

Province of The Niger
20 Enugu
24 Awka
25 On the Niger
44 Nsukka
53 Nnewi
60 Abakaliki
73 Oji River
Aguata
Ngbo
Afikpo
Awgu-Aninri
Enugu North
Ihiala
Ikwo
Mbammili
Niger West
Nike
Ogbaru

Province of Lagos
31 Ijebu
32 Remo
33 Lagos
34 Yewa
35 Egba
49 Diocese On The Coast

Province of Niger Delta
21 Calabar
22 Aba
37 The Niger Delta
39 Uyo
42 Ukwa
43 Umuahia
52 Niger Delta North
77 Niger Delta West
79 Okrika
80 Ahoada
Arochukwu Ohafi
Ikwuano
Isuikwuato
Ogoni
Aba Ngwa North
Etche
Ikwerre
Isiala Ngwa
Isiala Ngwa South
Northern Izon
Ogbia

Province of Ondo
17 Ekiti Oke
18 Akoko
27 Owo
28 Akure
29 Ondo
51 Kabba
67 Ekiti West
81 Ekiti

Province of Owerri
23 Orlu
38 Owerri
40 Okigwe North
41 Okigwe South
47 Mbaise
50 Egbu
63 Ideato
Ohaji-Egbema
Oru
On the Lake

A large number of new dioceses have been created in the Church of Nigeria. These are listed above (unnumbered) but unfortunately at the time of going to press it was not possible to confirm the geographical position of these dioceses and so they are not yet represented on the map.

MAP 12

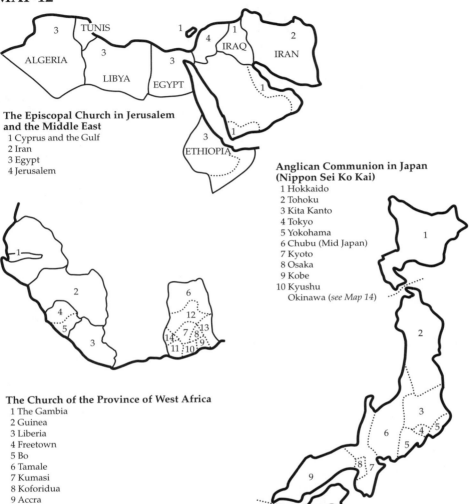

The Episcopal Church in Jerusalem and the Middle East
1 Cyprus and the Gulf
2 Iran
3 Egypt
4 Jerusalem

Anglican Communion in Japan (Nippon Sei Ko Kai)
1 Hokkaido
2 Tohoku
3 Kita Kanto
4 Tokyo
5 Yokohama
6 Chubu (Mid Japan)
7 Kyoto
8 Osaka
9 Kobe
10 Kyushu
  Okinawa (*see Map 14*)

The Church of the Province of West Africa
1 The Gambia
2 Guinea
3 Liberia
4 Freetown
5 Bo
6 Tamale
7 Kumasi
8 Koforidua
9 Accra
10 Cape Coast
11 Sekondi
12 Sunyani
13 Ho
14 Wiawso
Cameroon (*see Map 11*)

MAP 13

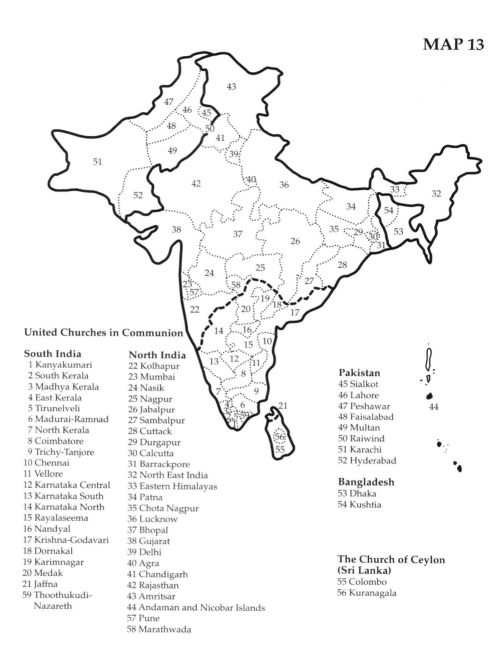

United Churches in Communion

South India
1 Kanyakumari
2 South Kerala
3 Madhya Kerala
4 East Kerala
5 Tirunelveli
6 Madurai-Ramnad
7 North Kerala
8 Coimbatore
9 Trichy-Tanjore
10 Chennai
11 Vellore
12 Karnataka Central
13 Karnataka South
14 Karnataka North
15 Rayalaseema
16 Nandyal
17 Krishna-Godavari
18 Dornakal
19 Karimnagar
20 Medak
21 Jaffna
59 Thoothukudi-
    Nazareth

North India
22 Kolhapur
23 Mumbai
24 Nasik
25 Nagpur
26 Jabalpur
27 Sambalpur
28 Cuttack
29 Durgapur
30 Calcutta
31 Barrackpore
32 North East India
33 Eastern Himalayas
34 Patna
35 Chota Nagpur
36 Lucknow
37 Bhopal
38 Gujarat
39 Delhi
40 Agra
41 Chandigarh
42 Rajasthan
43 Amritsar
44 Andaman and Nicobar Islands
57 Pune
58 Marathwada

Pakistan
45 Sialkot
46 Lahore
47 Peshawar
48 Faisalabad
49 Multan
50 Raiwind
51 Karachi
52 Hyderabad

Bangladesh
53 Dhaka
54 Kushtia

**The Church of Ceylon
(Sri Lanka)**
55 Colombo
56 Kuranagala

MAP 14

Chung Hua Sheng Kung Hui (China)

Contact is only with the Diocese of Hong Kong and Macao, which is under the temporary Metropolitan Authority of the Council of the Churches of East Asia.

The Anglican Church of Korea
1 Pusan
2 Seoul
3 Taejon

The Province of Myanmar
4 Myitkyina
5 Mandalay
6 Sittwe
7 Yangon
8 Toungoo
9 Hpa-an

The Episcopal Church in the Philippines
10 Northern Luzon
11 North Central Philippines
12 Northern Philippines
13 Central Philippines
14 Southern Philippines

The Province of the Anglican Church in South East Asia
15 Kuching
16 Sabah
17 Singapore
18 West Malaysia

22 Okinawa
(Diocese in the Anglican Communion in Japan)

23 Taiwan
(Diocese in Province VIII of ECUSA)

Hong Kong Sheng Kung Hui
(Hong Kong Anglican Church)
19 Hong Kong Island
20 Eastern Kowloon
21 Western Kowloon

ANGLICAN AND PORVOO COMMUNIONS

THE COMMUNION OF PORVOO CHURCHES

In October 1992 representatives of the four British and Irish Anglican Churches, the five Nordic Lutheran Churches and the three Baltic Lutheran Churches met in Finland for the fourth and final plenary session of their formal Conversations, which had commenced in 1989. They agreed *The Porvoo Common Statement*, named after Porvoo Cathedral, in which they had celebrated the Eucharist together.

The Common Statement recommended that the participating churches jointly make the Porvoo Declaration, bringing them into communion with each other. This involves common membership, a single, interchangeable ministry and structures to enable the Churches to consult each other on significant matters of faith and order, life and work. The implementation of the commitments contained in the Declaration is coordinated by the Porvoo Agreement Contact Group. The Porvoo Panel of the Church of England was established in 2000 to monitor and develop the implementation of the Porvoo commitments in dioceses and sector ministries.

In 1994 and 1995 the Declaration was approved by the four Anglican Churches, four of the Nordic Lutheran Churches and two of the Baltic Lutheran Churches. The General Synod's final approval of the Declaration in July 1995, following a reference to the diocesan synods, was by overwhelming majorities in each House. The Declaration was signed in the autumn of 1996 at services in Trondheim (Norway), Tallinn (Estonia) and Westminster Abbey.

In 1980 the Lusitanian Church (Portuguese Episcopal Church) became an extra-provincial diocese under the metropolitical authority of the Archbishop of Canterbury and in 1998 the diocesan synod of the Lusitanian Church approved and accepted the Porvoo Declaration. Furthermore in 1980 the Spanish Reformed Episcopal Church fully integrated into the Anglican Communion also coming under the metropolitical authority of the Archbishop of Canterbury. Both churches by virtue of coming under the Archbishop of Canterbury's metropolitical authority and accepting the Porvoo Declaration were integrated into the Porvoo Communion (see also page 398).

The Evangelical Lutheran Chuch in Denmark decided to sign the Porvoo Declaration in December 2009. The Evangelical–Lutheran Church of Latvia has not yet reached its decision.

Along with the Evangelical Lutheran Church of Latvia, the Porvoo Communion is represented by two additional Churches with observer status. They are the Lutheran Church in Great Britain and the Latvian Evangelical Lutheran Church Abroad. The Porvoo Contact Group took the decision to invite both these Churches at its meeting in Madrid in October 2010.

The Nordic Lutheran Churches are the historic national Churches of their respective countries. At the Reformation, when they adhered to Lutheranism, they continued to be episcopally ordered, retaining the historic sees. In Sweden and Finland the succession of the laying on of hands at episcopal consecration was unbroken, whereas in Denmark, Norway and Iceland this was not the case. The Estonian and Latvian Lutheran Churches are similarly their countries' historic national Churches, which became Lutheran at the Reformation. Only in the northern part of Estonia was episcopacy retained, and there only until 1710, but it was restored in both Estonia and Latvia in the twentieth century, the bishops being consecrated in the historic succession. The Lithuanian Lutheran Church, which is now a small minority Church, adopted episcopacy in historic succession in 1976.

The Porvoo Agreement supersedes earlier separate agreements dating from the 1920s, 1930s and 1950s with the Churches concerned (except the Lithuanian Lutheran Church). These provided for mutual eucharistic hospitality and (with the Swedish, Finnish, Estonian and Latvian Churches) mutual participation in episcopal consecrations. Because of the Soviet occupation of the Baltic States, however, it was only in 1989 and 1992 respectively that it was possible for an Anglican bishop to participate in a Latvian and an Estonian consecration for the first time.

The Porvoo Declaration commits the signatory Churches 'to regard baptized members of all of our Churches as members of our own'. It also means that clergy ordained by bishops of the signatory Churches are placed in the same position with regard to ministry in the Church of England as those ordained by Anglican bishops overseas.

Further information can be found on the Porvoo website: www.porvoochurches.org, or is available from the European Secretary at the Council for Christian Unity at Church House, Westminster.

The Porvoo Agreement Contact Group

Co-Chairmen
Rt Revd Martin Wharton (*Bishop of Newcastle*)
 email: bishop@newcastle.anglican.org
Rt Revd Karl Sigurbjörnsson (*Bishop of Iceland*)
 email: biskup@biskup.is

Co-Secretaries
Ms Beate Fagerli (Nordic and Baltic Churches)
    email: beate.fagerli@kirken.no
Revd Dr Leslie Nathaniel (Church of England
Council for Christian Unity – *see* page 172)
    email: leslie.nathaniel@c-of-e.org.uk

The Porvoo Panel
Chairman Rt Revd David Hamid (*Diocese in Europe*)

Porvoo Chaplains in England

Estonia
The Very Revd Lagle Heinla, Estonian House, 18
Chepstow Villas, London W11 2RB
    Tel: 020 7229 6700

Finland
The Revd Teemu Hälli, The Finnish Church in
London, 33 Albion Street, London SE16 7JG
    Tel: 020 7237 1261

Iceland
*Chaplaincy being carried out by visits at regular
intervals from Revd Adda Björnsdottie*

Norway
The Revd Torbjørn Holt, 1 St Olav's Square,
Albion Street, London SE16 7JB
    Tel: 020 7740 3900
The Revd Just Salvesen (*same address*)

Sweden
The Very Revd Michael Persson, 6 Harcourt
Street, London W1H 2BD   *Tel:* 020 7616 0271
The Revd Göran Capron Lundqvist

Churches in the Communion of Porvoo Churches

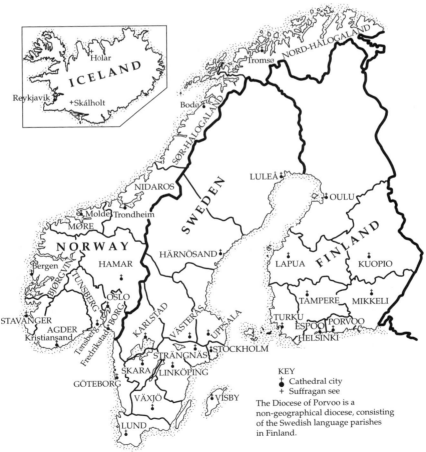

KEY
♦ Cathedral city
+ Suffragan see
The Diocese of Porvoo is a non-geographical diocese, consisting of the Swedish language parishes in Finland.

Note: An updated version reflecting all recent changes in the Porvoo Communion is in preparation

NORDIC LUTHERAN CHURCHES

The Evangelical–Lutheran Church in Denmark

The Evangelical-Lutheran Church in Denmark signed the Porvoo Declaration at a ceremony in Copenhagen Cathedral on 3 October 2010. Full Church details will be included in the next edition.

Porvoo Agreement Contact
Revd Jan Nilsson, Council on International Relations of the Evangelical–Lutheran Church in

Denmark, Peter Bangs Vej 1 D, DK-2000 Frederiksberg
Tel: 45 33 11 44 88
Fax: 45 33 11 95 88
email: jn@interchurch.dk

Bishop of Copenhagen Rt Revd Peter Skov-Jakobsen, Nørregade 11, DK-1165 Copenhagen K
Tel: 45 33 47 65 00
Fax: 45 33 14 39 69
email: kmkbh@km.dk
Web: www.folkekirken.dk

The Evangelical–Lutheran Church of Finland

The first bishop in the Finnish Church was St Henrik, the Apostle of Finland. According to tradition, St Henrik was an Englishman who accompanied King Erik II of Sweden on a military expedition to south-western Finland in 1155 and was martyred there the following year. From the middle of the thirteenth century until 1809 Finland was part of Sweden, and until the Reformation it formed a single diocese (Turku) in the Province of Uppsala.

In 1554 the Swedish king appointed the Finnish Lutheran Reformer Mikael Agricola (d. 1557) as Bishop of Turku, at the same time founding a second Finnish see, Viipuri (eventually transferred to Tampere). In addition to translating the New Testament and parts of the Old into Finnish, Mikael Agricola compiled the first catechism, liturgy and ritual in Finnish. He is regarded as the father of Finnish as a written language.

A wave of revivals, beginning in the eighteenth century, gave rise in the nineteenth to four mass movements. These remained within the Church of Finland and are still influential on its life today.

In 1809 Finland was annexed by Russia. As a result, the Finnish Church became entirely independent of the Church of Sweden, and from 1817 the Bishop of Turku was styled Archbishop. Finland finally gained its independence in 1917.

Today, roughly 80 per cent of Finns are members of the Evangelical–Lutheran Church of Finland, while only 4 per cent are members of other Churches. The ELCF is a 'folk church' (as is the Orthodox Church). The framework for its life is set by the Ecclesiastical Act. Amendments to this state law can only be proposed by the Synod, and

Parliament can accept or reject but not amend such proposals. The Church is governed by the Synod, the Church Council and the Bishops' Conference. Although the Archbishop is only *primus inter pares* of the Finnish bishops, he is the President of the Synod and chairs both the Bishops' Conference and the Church Council.

The Church is organized in nine dioceses, one of which consists of the Swedish-speaking parishes (Porvoo). The diocese of Helsinki has recently divided into two, giving rise to the new see of Espoo.

Porvoo Agreement Contact Executive Secretary for Theology Tomi Karttunen, Department for International Relations, Satamakatu 11, Box 185, FI-00161 Helsinki
Tel: 358 9 1802 290
Fax: 358 9 1802 230
email: tomi.karttunen@evl.fi
Web: www.evl.fi/english/index.html

HELSINKI
Bishop Rt Revd Irja Askola, Diocesan Chapter, PO Box 142, FI-00121 Helsinki
Tel: 358 9 2340 3010
Fax: 358 9 2340 3050
email: irja.askola@evl.fi
Web: www.helsinginhiippakunta.evl.fi/

ESPOO
Bishop Rt Revd Dr Mikko Heikka, Diocesan Chapter, PO Box 203, FI-02771 Espoo
Tel: 358 9 8050 8832
Fax: 358 9 8050 8848
email: mikko.heikka@evl.fi
Web: http://espoonhiippakunta.evl.fi/english/

KUOPIO
Bishop Rt Revd Dr Wille Riekkinen, Diocesan Chapter, PO Box 42, FI-70101 Kuopio   *Tel:* 358 17 288 8414
Fax: 358 17 288 8420
email: wille.riekkinen@evl.fi

LAPUA
Bishop Rt Revd Dr Simo Peura, Diocesan Chapter, PO Box 60, FI-62101 Lapua   *Tel:* 358 6 4339 325
Fax: 358 6 4339 320
email: simo.peura@evl.fi

MIKKELI
Bishop Rt Revd Dr Seppo Häkkinen, Diocesan Chapter, PO Box 122, FI-50101 Mikkeli
Tel: 358 15 3216 011
Fax: 358 15 3216 016
email: seppo.hakkinen@evl.fi

OULU
Bishop Rt Revd Dr Samuel Salmi, Diocesan Chapter, PO Box 85, FI-90101 Oulu   *Tel:* 358 8 311 4654
Fax: 358 8 311 0659
email: samuel.salmi@evl.fi

PORVOO
(The Diocese of Porvoo (Borgå) is a non-geographical Swedish-language diocese.)

Bishop Rt Revd Dr Björn Vikström, Diocesan Chapter, PO Box 30, FI-06101 Borgå
Tel: 358 19 529 7716
Fax: 358 19 585 705
email: bjorn.vikstrom@evl.fi
Web: http://borgastift.planeetta.com

TAMPERE
Bishop Rt Revd Dr Matti Repo, Diocesan Chapter, Eteläpuisto 2C, FI-33200 Tampere
Tel: 358 3 238 1130
Fax: 358 3 238 1150
email: matti.repo@evl.fi
Web: www.tampereenhiippakunta.fi/in_english

TURKU
Archbishop of Turku and Finland Rt Revd Kari Mäkinen, PO Box 60, FI-20501 Turku
Tel: 358 2 279 7031
Fax: 358 2 279 7002
email: Arkkipiispa@evl.fi

Bishop of Turku Vacancy (*same address*)
Tel: 358 2 279 7033
Fax: 358 2 2797 001

The Evangelical–Lutheran Church of Iceland

Christianity was adopted at Thingvellir by decree of the legislature in the year 1000. The ancient Icelandic sees of Skálholt and Hólar were founded in 1055 and 1106, respectively. Having previously been under the jurisdiction of Bremen and Lund, from 1153 Iceland belonged to the Province of Nidaros (Trondheim). Part of the Kingdom of Norway from 1262, Iceland eventually came under Danish rule. The Lutheran Reformation was introduced in 1541. From this time onwards until 1908 (with one exception in the late eighteenth century), Icelandic bishops were consecrated by the Bishops of Sealand (Copenhagen).

The two Icelandic sees were united in 1801, but in 1909 they were revived as suffragan sees. Iceland gained its independence from Denmark in 1918, becoming a republic in 1944.

A new Church law came into effect on 1 January 1998, granting the Church considerable autonomy from the state. The Church Assembly is the highest organ of the Church. Today, around 90 per cent of the Icelandic population are members of the Church of Iceland.

Porvoo Agreement Contact Revd Dr Sigurdur Arni Thordarson, Neskirkja, Hagatorgi, 107 Reykjavik, Iceland   *Tel:* 354 511 1561
email: s@biskup.is

The Church of Iceland comprises a single diocese, with two suffragan bishops in the ancient sees of Hólar and Skálholt.

Bishop of Iceland Most Revd Karl Sigurbjörnsson, Laugavegur 31, 101 Reykjavík
Tel: 354 535 1500
Fax: 354 551 3284
email: biskup@biskup.is
Web: www.kirkjan.is/?english

Bishop of Skálholt Rt Revd Sigurdur Sigurdarson, Skálholt, Biskupshús, Skálholti, 801 Selfoss
Tel: 354 486 8972
Fax: 354 486 8975
email: srsigsig@eyjar.is

Bishop of Hólar Rt Revd Jón Adalsteinn Baldvinsson, Biskupssetur, Hólar, 551 Saudárkrókur   *Tel:* 354 453 6300
Fax: 354 453 6301
email: jon.a.baldvinsson@kirkjan.is

Contact for ecumenical affairs Ms Steinunn A. Björnsdóttir, Ecumenical Secretary, Bishop's office, Laugavegur 31, 150 Reykjavík, Iceland
Tel: 354 535 1500
Fax: 354 551 3284
email: steinunn.bjornsdottir@biskup.is

The Church of Norway

From around AD 1000 Christianity was brought to Norway by missionaries both from the British Isles and from Germany. Central to the Christianizing of Norway was King Olav Haraldsson. After his death in 1030 he was venerated as St Olave, and his shrine in Nidaros Cathedral (Trondheim) was a centre of pilgrimage. Episcopal sees were established in Nidaros, Bergen, Oslo (by 1100), and in Stavanger (1125) and Hamar (1153). Part of the Province of Lund from 1103, Norway became a separate province when Nidaros was raised to an archiepiscopal see in 1153. In addition to the five Norwegian sees, the Province of Nidaros also included six further dioceses covering Iceland, the Faeroes, Greenland, the Shetland and Orkney Islands, the Hebrides and the Isle of Man. Under Olav IV (1380–87) Norway was united with Denmark.

The Norwegian Reformation of 1537 was imposed by the new King of Denmark, Christian III, with little evidence of popular enthusiasm. New bishops ('superintendents') were ordained to the sees of Nidaros, Bergen and Stavanger by Johannes Bugenhagen, the Superintendent of Wittenberg, in 1537, and Bugenhagen's Danish Church Order was extended to Norway in 1539. Of the pre-Reformation bishops, Bishop Hans Rev of Oslo alone accepted the Reformation, and returned to his see (to which that of Hamar had been united) as Superintendent in 1541. The diocesan structure had been retained, with four of the five historic sees, and the term 'bishop' soon replaced its Latin synonym 'superintendent', but until recent years neither Bishop Rev nor any other bishop consecrated in the historic succession of the laying on of hands participated in the consecration of future bishops. Nidaros ceased to be an archiepiscopal see.

In the eighteenth and nineteenth centuries, pietist movements became influential, but they remained within the Church of Norway, the membership of which still amounts to 86.2 per cent of the population. During the German occupation of 1940–45, the Church was a focus of resistance under the leadership of Bishop Eivind Berggrav of Oslo (1884–1959). In 1993 Rosemarie Köhn became the Church of Norway's first woman bishop, when the Norwegian government appointed her Bishop of Hamar.

The Church of Norway has an 85-member General Synod, consisting of the 80 members of the eleven diocesan councils (including the bishops), three members representing clergy, laity and lay employees, the moderators of the Sami Church Council and the Council on Ecumenical and International Relations, and three non-voting representatives of the theological faculties. Its executive is the 15-member National Council, which has a lay chairman. Related central bodies include the Bishops' Conference, the Council on Foreign Relations, the Sami Church Council and a doctrinal commission. Church legislation still requires parliamentary approval. The King of Norway remains the Church's constitutional head, and the government retains powers over the Church, exercised through the Ministry of the Church, Education and Research.

Porvoo Agreement Contact Revd Dr Beate Fagerli, Council on Ecumenical and International Relations, PB 799 – Sentrum, N-0106 Oslo
Tel: 47 23 08 12 74
Fax: 47 23 08 12 01
email: beate.fagerli@kirken.no

AGDER
Bishop Rt Revd Olav Skjevesland (*Praeses of the Bishops' Conference*), Diocesan Centre, PB 208, 4662 Krisitansand S
Tel: 47 38 10 52 20
Fax: 47 38 10 51 21
email: agder.bdr@kirken.no

BJØRGVIN
Bishop Rt Revd Halvor Nordhaug, Diocesan Centre, Strandgt. 198, PB. 1960 Nordnes, 5018 Bergen
Tel: 47 55 30 64 70
Fax: 47 55 30 64 85
email: bjoergvin.biskop@kirken.no

BORG
Bishop Rt Revd Helga Haugland Byfuglien, Diocesan Centre, Bjarne Aas gt 9, PB 403, N-1601 Fredrikstad
Tel: 47 69 30 79 00
Fax: 47 69 30 79 01
email: borg.bdr@kirken.no

HAMAR
Bishop Rt Revd Solveig Fiske, Diocesan Centre, Folkestadgate 52, PB 172, N-2302 Hamar
Tel: 47 62 55 03 50
Fax: 47 62 55 03 51
email: hamar.bdr@kirken.no

MØRE
Bishop Rt Revd Ingeborg Synøve Midtømme, Diocesan Centre, Moldetrappa 1, N-6415 Molde
Tel: 47 71 25 06 70
Fax: 47 71 25 06 71
email: moere.bdr@kirken.no

NIDAROS
Bishop Rt Revd Tor Singsaas, Diocesan Centre, Archbishop's House, N-7013 Trondheim
Tel: 47 73 53 91 00
Fax: 47 73 53 91 11
email: nidaros.bdr@kirken.no

NORD-HÅLOGALAND
Bishop Rt Revd Per Oskar Kjølaas, Diocesan Centre, Conrad Holmboesvei 20, PB 790, N-9258 Tromsø   *Tel:* 47 77 60 39 60/61
Fax: 47 77 60 39 70
email: nord-haalogaland.bdr@kirken.no

OSLO
Bishop Rt Revd Ole Chr. M. Kvarme, Diocesan Centre, St Halvards plass 3, PB 9307, Gronland, N-0135 Oslo   *Tel:* 47 23 30 11 60
Fax: 47 23 30 11 99
email: oslo.bdr@kirken.no

SØR-HÅLOGALAND
Bishop Rt Revd Tor Berger Jørgensen, Diocesan Centre, Tolder Holmersvei 11, N-8003 Bodø
Tel: 47 75 54 85 50
Fax: 47 75 54 85 60
email: soer-haalogaland.bdr@kirken.no

STAVANGER
Bishop Rt Revd Erling J. Petterson, Diocesan Centre, Domkirkeplasson 2, PB 629, N-4003 Stavanger   *Tel:* 47 51 84 62 70
Fax: 47 51 84 62 71
email: stavanger.bdr@kirken.no

TUNSBERG
Bishop Rt Revd Laila Riksaasen Dahl,Diocesan Centre, Håkon 5.s gt, PB 1253, N-3105
Tel: 47 33 35 43 00
Fax: 47 33 35 43 01
email: tunsberg.bdr@kirken.no

The Church of Sweden

The first to preach the gospel in Sweden was St Ansgar (801–65), the first Archbishop of Hamburg-Bremen, but it was in the eleventh century that the systematic conversion of Sweden was begun, largely by missionaries from England. From 1104 the new Swedish dioceses formed part of the Nordic Province of Lund (which was Danish until 1658), but only until 1164, when Uppsala was raised to an archiepiscopal see. The most celebrated figure of the medieval Swedish Church is St Birgitta of Vadstena (1303–73), foundress of the Brigittine Order.

Under the Lutheran Reformers Olaus Petri (1493–1552) and his brother Laurentius (d. 1573), who became the first Lutheran archbishop in 1531, the Swedish Reformation was gradual, and moderate in character. The Augsburg Confession was adopted in 1593.

The eighteenth and nineteenth centuries saw both latitudinarian and pietist movements, and in the early twentieth century a strong high-church movement developed. Archbishop Nathan Söderblom (1866–1931), one of the leading figures of the Ecumenical Movement, used the concept of 'evangelical catholicity' to describe the Church of Sweden's position. The Conference of Bishops of the Anglican Communion adopted a resolution of altar and pulpit fellowship with the Church of Sweden in 1920. In 1997 Christina Odenberg became the Church of Sweden's first woman bishop, when she was appointed Bishop of Lund.

The Church of Sweden is governed by a General Synod with 251 members and a 15-member Central Board (chaired by the archbishop), together with the Bishops' Conference. The bishops attend the Synod, but are not members of it, although they have all the rights of members except the right to vote. They are *ex-officio* members of the Synod Committee on Church Doctrine.

A separation of Church and State was effected in the year 2000, a year which also was marked by the 1000-year celebration of Christian faith in Sweden at the well of Husaby in the Diocese of Skara.

Porvoo Agreement Contact Revd Dr Christopher Meakin, Ecumenical Officer, Church of Sweden, S-751 70 Uppsala   *Tel:* 46 18 16 98 68
Fax: 46 18 16 95 38
email: christopher.meakin@svenskakyrkan.se

Archbishop's Chaplain Revd Dr Ann-Cathrin Jarl, S-751 70 Uppsala   *Tel:* 46 18 16 96 23
Fax: 46 18 16 96 25
email: ann-cathrin.jarl@svenskakyrkan.se

(**Note:** *The dioceses here are arranged alphabetically. The order traditionally used in Sweden reflects the chronological seniority of the Swedish dioceses.*)

GÖTEBORG
Bishop Rt Revd Dr Carl Axel Aurelius, Stiftskansliet, Box 11937, SE-404 39 Göteborg
Tel: 46 31 771 30 00
Fax: 46 31 771 30 30
email: carlaxel.aurelius@svenskakyrkan.se

HÄRNÖSAND
Bishop Rt Revd Dr Tuulikki Koivunen Bylund), Stiftskansliet, Box 94, SE-871 22 Härnösand
Tel: 46 611 254 00
Fax: 46 611 134 75
email: tuulikki.bylund@svenskakyrkan.se

KARLSTAD
Bishop Rt Revd Esbjörn Hagberg, Stiftskansliet, Box 186, SE-651 05 Karlstad   *Tel:* 46 54 17 24 00
Fax: 46 54 17 24 70
email: esbjorn.hagberg@svenskakyrkan.se

LINKÖPING

Bishop Rt Revd Dr Martin Lind, (from March 2011 there will be a new bishop), Stiftskansliet, Box 1367, SE-581 31 Linköping
Tel: 46 13 24 26 00
Fax: 46 13 14 90 95
email: martin.lind@svenskakyrkan.se

LULEÅ

Bishop Rt Revd Hans Stiglund, Stiftskansliet, Stationsgatan 40, SE-972 32 Luleå
Tel: 46 920 26 47 00
Fax: 46 920 26 47 21
email: hans.stiglund@svenskakyrkan.se

LUND

Bishop Rt Revd Dr Antje Jackelén, Stiftskansliet, Box 32, SE-221 00 Lund   *Tel:* 46 46 35 87 00
Fax: 46 46 18 49 48
email: antje.jackelen@svenskakyrkan.se

SKARA

Bishop Rt Revd Dr Erik Aurelius, Malmgatan 14, SE-532 32 Skara   *Tel:* 46 511 262 00
Fax: 46 511 262 70
email: erik.aurelius@svenskakyrkan.se

STOCKHOLM

Bishop Rt Revd Eva Brunne, Stiftskansliet, Box 16306, SE-103 25 Stockholm
Tel: 46 8 508 940 00
Fax: 46 8 24 75 75
email: eva.brunne@svenskakyrkan.se

STRÄNGNÄS

Bishop Rt Revd Dr Hans-Erik Nordin, Stiftskansliet, Box 84, SE-645 22 Strängnäs
Tel: 46 152 234 00
Fax: 46 152 234 56
email: hans-erik.nordin@svenskakyrkan.se

UPPSALA

Archbishop Most Revd Anders Wejryd, SE-751 70 Uppsala   *Tel:* 46 18 16 95 00
Fax: 46 18 16 96 25
email: archbishop@svenskakyrkan.se

Bishop Rt Revd Dr Ragnar Persenius, Box 1314, SE-751 43 Uppsala   *Tel:* 46 18 68 07 00
Fax: 46 18 12 87 62
email: ragnar.persenius@svenskakyrkan.se

VÄSTERÅS

Bishop Rt Revd Thomas Söderberg, Stiftskansliet, V Kyrkogatan 9, SE-722 15 Västerås
Tel: 46 21 17 85 00
Fax: 46 21 12 93 10
email: thomas.soderberg@svenskakyrkan.se

VÄXJÖ

Bishop Vacancy, Box 527, SE-351 06 Växjö
Tel: 46 470 77 38 00
Fax: 46 470 72 95 50
email: biskop.vaxjo@svenskakyrkan.se

VISBY

Bishop Rt Revd Dr Lennart Koskinen (from March 2011 there will be a new bishop), Stiftskansliet, Box 1334, SE-621 24 Visby
Tel: 46 498 40 49 00
Fax: 46 498 21 01 03
email: lennart.koskinen@svenskakyrkan.se
Further information about the history of the Nordic Lutheran Churches and of their relations with the Church of England can be found in Lars Österlin, *Churches of Northern Europe in Profile. A Thousand Years of Anglo-Nordic Relations* (Norwich, 1995).

BALTIC LUTHERAN CHURCHES

The Estonian Evangelical–Lutheran Church

The conversion of Estonia to Christianity began at the end of the tenth century, and the first known bishop was consecrated in 1165. The mission was prosecuted by the Brethren of the Sword, an order founded in 1202 which merged with the Teutonic Order in 1237. In 1219 the Danes conquered the northern area and founded the capital Reval (Tallinn), which became an episcopal see within the Province of Lund. Further sees were established at Dorpat (Tartu) in 1224 and Hapsal (Saare-Lääne) in 1227, within the Province of Riga, the capital of Livonia, which included the southern part of modern Estonia. In some areas secular authority was in the hands of the bishops, while in others the Teutonic Order held sway. The entire area was very much under German dominance.

The Lutheran movement reached Estonia in 1523, and as early as the following year an assembly in Reval decided to adhere to the Reformation. Later in the century, however, the twin provinces of Estonia and Livonia became divided between neighbouring powers. Most of Estonia placed itself under Swedish rule in 1561, but Denmark ruled the island of Oesel (Saarema) from 1560 to 1645 and Livonia was annexed by Poland from 1561 to 1621. In Swedish Estonia, the Church was governed by a bishop and consistory, but Danish ecclesiastical law was introduced in Oesel, while Livonia came under the influence of the Counter-Reformation. Superintendents, rather than bishops, were appointed for these areas after they came under Swedish rule (in 1621 and 1645).

In 1710 both provinces came under Russian rule. In Estonia the office of bishop was replaced with that of superintendent. The consistories were chaired by laymen. In 1832 the Lutheran Churches of all three Baltic provinces were united with Russia's German-speaking Lutheran Church into a Russian Lutheran Church, with a General Consistory in St Petersburg. Each province (and – until 1890 – Reval, Oesel and Riga separately) had its own general superintendent and consistory. The University of Dorpat (Tartu), originally founded in 1632, was refounded in 1802. As the only Protestant theological faculty in the Russian Empire, it was of great importance. Throughout the period up to 1918 the clergy were German, like the ruling elite. The Moravian Church, which was active in Estonia and Livonia from 1736, enjoyed considerable influence over the Estonian peasantry, and by 1854 there were 276 Moravian prayer halls. However, the Moravian authorities blocked the development of this movement into a separate Moravian Church, and the Moravians' adherents remained within the Lutheran Church.

In 1918 Estonia and the Estonian northern part of Livonia became an independent state. The Church too became independent. It remained united, having both German and Estonian clergy and members. The office of bishop was immediately restored, the first bishop being consecrated in 1921 by the Archbishop of Uppsala and a Finnish bishop.

Estonia's independent existence lasted little more than 20 years, however. In 1940 it was occupied by the Red Army. German occupation followed, but Soviet rule was restored in 1944. Archbishop Kõpp, who had remained unconsecrated because the war prevented bishops from other countries travelling to Estonia, went into exile with 70 other clergy and tens of thousands of church members. As a result of this the Estonian Evangelical–Lutheran Church Abroad was born. Of the clergy who remained, one-third were eventually deported to Siberia. Not until 1968 was it possible for an archbishop to be consecrated, although the first post-war Archbishop had already been elected in 1949.

In 1988, Estonia began to move towards independence, which was achieved in 1991. This was accompanied by a remarkable blossoming of church life. The Theological Faculty at Tartu, which had been dissolved by the Soviet authorities, was reopened. The Theological Institute of the EELC in Tallinn, which was set up after the war, also continues its work.

The Estonian Evangelical–Lutheran Church still forms one diocese, headed by an Archbishop and a Suffragan Bishop. It is governed by a General Synod, the executive organ of which is the six-member Consistory.

Porvoo Agreement Contact Very Revd Veiko Vihuri, Karja kirikla, 94201 Pärsama, Saaremaa
Tel: 372 45 73 65
email: veiko.vihuri@eelk.ee

Archbishop of Estonia Most Revd Andres Põder, Consistory of the EELC, Kirikuplats 3, 10130 Tallinn
Tel: 372 6 27 73 50
Fax: 372 6 27 73 52
email: konsistoorium@eelk.ee
Web www.eelk.ee

ANGLICAN AND PORVOO COMMUNIONS

The Evangelical–Lutheran Church of Lithuania

Not until 1387 was an episcopal see established in Vilnius, following the baptism the previous year of Grand Duke Jogaila (whose coronation as King of Poland inaugurated a union lasting until 1795), and it was 1418 before the inhabitants of German-dominated Samogitia (covering much of present-day Lithuania) were forced to accept baptism.

A Lutheran congregation was founded in Vilnius as early as 1521, but persecution forced the Lithuanian Reformer Martin Mazvydas to flee to Königsberg. In time the Lithuanian nobility established the Reformed faith on their estates, while the numerous German merchants and craftsmen established Lutheran congregations in the towns from the 1550s. Until the early nineteenth century, the Lutheran Church continued to be a German and urban minority Church.

Sigismund Vasa (1587–1632) successfully restored Roman Catholicism as the religion of the people, and subsequent anti-Protestant policies meant that by 1775, when religious freedom was granted, just 30 Reformed and five Lutheran congregations remained (except those in Prussian-ruled Tauragé/Tauroggen).

In 1795 most of Lithuania was ceded to Russia, and Lithuania's Lutheran congregations were placed under the Consistory of Courland (now southern Latvia). Immigration of Lutheran Letts, Germans and Lithuanians from East Prussia produced new Lutheran congregations, especially in the countryside. The pastors (only nine in 1918) were all Germans.

At independence in 1918, Lithuania's population included 75,000 Lutherans, of whom roughly 30,000 were Germans, 30,000 Lithuanians and 15,000 Letts. In 1920 separate synods had to be formed for the three linguistic groups, and for much of the inter-war period tension between them paralysed the Lutheran Church. By 1939, however, there were 55 congregations with 33 pastors. To these should be added the separate Lutheran Church of the Prussian *Memelgebiet*, which Lithuania annexed in 1923. By 1939 this had 135,000 members (the majority German) in 32 parishes, served by 39 pastors.

Lithuanian Lutheranism was soon to be decimated. In 1941, following the 1940 Soviet annexation of Lithuania, most of the German population, together with a large number of Lithuanian Lutherans, emigrated to Germany. In Memelland and the Vilnius area, both reintegrated into Lithuania and thus the Soviet Union in 1945, the picture was even more stark. All but 30,000 inhabitants fled, while the pastor of the historic Lutheran church in Vilnius emigrated with his entire congregation.

A provisional Lutheran Consistory found itself responsible for 20,000 Lithuanians and Letts in Lithuania proper, together with just 15,000 Lithuanians in Klaipéda (Memelland). There were no pastors in Klaipéda and only six in the rest of the country, three of whom were soon banished to Siberia. After Stalin's death in 1953 and a first post-war synod in 1955, the structures of church life were gradually restored, but several thousand more Protestants emigrated between 1957 and 1965. At a second synod in 1970, Jonas Kalvanas, the only pastor left who had studied theology at university (he was ordained in 1940), was elected to chair the Consistory. It was with his consecration as Bishop by the Archbishop of Estonia in 1976 that his church gained the historic episcopate. He was succeeded in 1995 by his son and namesake, whose early death in 2003 left the see vacant until the consecration in June 2004 of Bishop Mindaugas Sebutis.

In 2003 the Lutheran Church had 54 congregations, with about 20,000 communicant members and twenty-four clergy.

Porvoo Agreement Contact Revd Darius Petkunas, Simonaitytes 18–21, LT-5814 Klaipéda
Tel: 370 6 220 409
email: darius.petkunas@liuteronai.lt

Bishop of the Evangelical–Lutheran Church of Lithuania Rt Revd Mindaugas Sebutis, Vokieciu 20, LT-01130 Vilnius   *Tel* and *Fax:* 370 5 212 3792
email: sabutis@times.lt
Web: www.liuteronai.lt/index_ang.html

NON-SIGNATORY CHURCHES

The Evangelical–Lutheran Church of Latvia

The Church of Latvia has not yet voted on the Porvoo Declaration.

Archbishop of Riga and Latvia Most Revd Janis Vanags, M.Pils 4, LV 1050, Riga

Tel: 371 6 225406
Fax: 371 6 225436
email: lelb@lelb.lv / archbishop@ lelb.lv

Porvoo Agreement Contact Dr Sandra Gintere *(same address)* *email:* sandra.gintere@ lelb.lv

---

There are also Anglican chaplaincies in most of the countries covered by the Porvoo Agreement. These belong to the Archdeaconry of Scandinavia and Germany within the Diocese in Europe. A leaflet giving details is available from the Diocesan Office of the Diocese in Europe, *see below.*

The *Directory of English-speaking Churches Abroad* (£4.00 as at 1 May 2009) lists English-speaking churches of Anglican and many other denominations in countries where English is not the first language, and is available from Intercontinental Church Society, 1 Athena Drive, Tachbrook Park, Warwick CV34 6NL

Tel: 01926 430 347
Fax: 01926 888 092
email: enquiries@ics-uk.org
Web: www.ics-uk.org

Credit card orders accepted by telephone or on the web site.

Continental Anglican churches are listed in the *Diocesan Directory* of the Diocese of Gibraltar in Europe, available from the Diocesan Office, 14 Tufton St, Westminster, London SW1P 3QZ   *Tel:* 020 7976 8001
Fax: 020 7976 8002

ANGLICAN AND PORVOO COMMUNIONS

Ecumenical | **PART 6**

PART 6 CONTENTS

ECUMENICAL

The Church of England is committed to the search for the full, visible unity of the Christian Church, and to the bodies which promote this at the local, intermediate, national, European and world levels. The Council for Christian Unity advises the General Synod and the Archbishops' Council on inter-church relations and acts as the principal channel of communication between the General Synod and the churches and ecumenical bodies, at the national and international levels. The CCU engages in informal ecumenical dialogue and implements any decisions of the General Synod regarding formal conversations.

ECUMENICAL CANONS
Canon B 43 (Of Relations with Other Churches) and Canon B 44 (Of Local Ecumenical Projects) make provision for sharing in worship and ministry with other churches. Full background information is given in *The Ecumenical Relations Code of Practice* (Church House, 1989). This paper, with its supplements, is now available electronically from ccu@c-of-e.org.uk. A range of useful introductory resource papers is also available from the same address.

CHURCHES DESIGNATED UNDER THE ECUMENICAL RELATIONS MEASURE
The Church of England's legal office maintains the list of the churches that have been designated by the Archbishops of Canterbury and York as churches to which the Church of England (Ecumenical Relations) Measure, and thus Canons B 43 and B 44, apply. An up-to-date list is maintained on the Church of England web site at www.cofe.anglican.org/about/churchlawlegis/canons/suppindex.pdf, scrolling down to page 203. The following are currently listed: The Baptist Union, the Methodist Church, the Moravian Church, the Roman Catholic Church in England and Wales, the United Reformed Church, the Congregational Federation, the International Ministerial Council of Great Britain, the Lutheran Council of Great Britain, the Greek Orthodox Archdiocese of Thyateira and Great Britain (Ecumenical Patriarchate), the Council of African and Afro-Caribbean Churches, the Free Church of England, the Southam Road Evangelical Church Banbury, Member Churches of the Evangelical Church in Germany (EKD), the Assemblies of God in Great Britain and Ireland, the New Testament Church of God, the Russian Patriarchal Church of Great Britain being the Orthodox Diocese of Sourozh (Moscow Patriarchate), the Independent Methodist Churches, the Church of the Augsburg Confession of Alsace and Lorraine, the Evangelical–Lutheran Church of France, the Reformed Church of Alsace and Lorraine, the Reformed Church of France.

Churches Together in England

Churches Together in England is in association with Churches Together in Britain and Ireland. Its basis is as follows:

> Churches Together in England unites in pilgrimage those Churches in England which, acknowledging God's revelation in Christ, confess the Lord Jesus Christ as God and Saviour according to the Scriptures, and, in obedience to God's will and in the power of the Holy Spirit, commit themselves:
> – to seek a deepening of their communion with Christ and with one another in the Church, which is his body; and
> – to fulfil their mission to proclaim the Gospel by common witness and service in the world to the glory of the one God, Father, Son and Holy Spirit.

The Presidents of Churches Together in England are: The Archbishop of Canterbury, the Archbishop of Westminster and Commissioner Elizabeth Matear, who meet together quarterly.

It has 33 Member Churches: Antiochian Orthodox Church, Baptist Union of Great Britain, Cherubim and Seraphim Council of Churches, Church of England, Church of God of Prophecy, Church of Scotland (in England), Congregational Federation, Coptic Orthodox Church, Council for African and Caribbean Churches, Council of Oriental Orthodox Christian Churches, Elim Pentecostal Church, Ichthus Christian Fellowship, Evangelische Synod Deutscher Sprache in Grossbritannien, Independent Methodist Churches, International Ministerial Council of Great Britain, Joint Council for Anglo-Caribbean Churches, Lutheran Council of Great Britain, Mar Thoma Church, Methodist Church, Moravian Church, New Testament Assembly, New Testament Church of God, Oecumenical Patriarchate (Archdiocese of Thyateira and GB), Redeemed Christian Church of God, Religious Society of Friends, Roman Catholic Church, Russian Orthodox Church, Salvation Army, Seventh Day Adventists, Transatlantic and Pacific Alliance of

Churches, United Reformed Church, Wesleyan Holiness Church.

The Religious Society of Friends has membership under a clause designed for 'any Church or Association of Churches which on principle has no credal statements in its tradition'.

All substantive decisions are taken by these Member Churches.

Churches Together in England encourages its Member Churches to work together nationally, and provides various means for this purpose. There is an *Enabling Group*, which meets two times a year. Its Convenor is Revd Peter Whittaker and its Deputy Convenor Pauline Johnson. There is a *Forum* of 300 members, which meets every three years. Its Moderator is Janet Scott and its Deputy Moderator Bishop Doye Agama.

There are 16 *Coordinating Groups* (*see below*).

There are also a large number of informal or as yet not formally recognized groups and networks.

Churches Together in England encourages its Member Churches to work together locally. To enable this most counties and metropolitan areas have established ecumenical councils and officers, whose task is to foster and encourage all sorts of ecumenical work locally within their areas. The main task of the two Field Officers (*see below*) is to support those working in counties and metropolitan areas.

Churches Together in England publishes an ecumenical e-news monthly, with a paper version, *CTE Digest*, available quarterly.

General Secretary Revd Dr David Cornick, Churches Together in England, 27 Tavistock Square, London WC1H 9HH   *Tel:* 020 7529 8133   *Web:* www.churches-together.net

Field Officer South Revd John Bradley (*same address*)

Executive Secretary (*Free Churches*) Revd Mark Fisher (*same address*)

Finance Officer Mr Michael Wood (*same address*)

Executive Officer and Secretary of Health Care Chaplaincy Steering Committee Revd Debbie Hodge (*same address*)

Free Church Education Officer Miss Sarah Lane (*same address*)

Field Officer North & Midlands Jenny Bond (*same address*)   *Tel:* 07805 380699

Minority Ethnic Christian Affairs Secretary Bishop Joe Aldred, 269 Kingsbury Rd, Birmingham B24 8RD   *Tel:* 0777 563 2288   *email:* joe.aldred@cte.org.uk

COORDINATING GROUPS

GROUP FOR LOCAL UNITY
Secretary Revd John Bradley (*CTE address see above*)   *Tel:* 020 7529 8144   *email:* john.bradley@cte.org.uk

GROUP FOR EVANGELIZATION
Secretary Captain Jim Currin (*address see above*)   *Tel:* 024 7626 1895   *email:* jim.currin@cte.org.uk

CHURCHES JOINT EDUCATION POLICY COMMITTEE
Miss Sarah Lane (*CTE address see above*)   *Tel:* 020 7529 8130   *email:* sarah.lane@cte.org.uk

CHURCHES CRIMINAL JUSTICE FORUM
Secretary Stuart Dew, Catholic Bishops' Conference of England and Wales, 39 Eccleston Square, London SW1V 1BX   *Tel:* 020 7901 4878   *email:* dews@cbcew.org.uk

CHURCHES COMMITTEE FOR HOSPITAL CHAPLAINCY
Secretary Revd Debbie Hodge (*CTE address as above*)   *Tel:* 020 7529 8136   *email:* debbie.hodge@cte.org.uk

CHURCHES COMMUNITY WORK ALLIANCE
Secretary Nils Chittenden, St Chad's College, North Bailey, Durham DH1 3RH   *Tel:* 0191 374 7342   *email:* nilsc@ccwa.org.uk

YOUTH WORK MATTERS
Contact Carole Golden (*CTE address as above*)   *Tel:* 020 7529 8133   *email:* carole.golden@cte.org.uk

PRISON CHAPLAINCY HEADQUARTERS TEAM
Secretary Revd Alan Ogier, Prison Chaplaincy Headquarters, Room 624 Horseferry House, Dean Ryle St, London SW1P 2AW   *Tel:* 020 7217 8048   *email:* chaplaincy@prisons-chap-hq.demon.co.uk

ECUMENICAL STRATEGY GROUP FOR MINISTERIAL TRAINING
Secretary Tony Milner, Catholic Bishops' Conference of England and Wales, 39 Eccleston Square, London SW1V 1BX   *email:* tony.milner@dabnet.org

THEOLOGY AND UNITY GROUP
Secretary Revd Dr David Cornick (*CTE address see above*)   *Tel:* 020 7529 8133   *email:* david.cornick@cte.org.uk

CHURCHES RURAL GROUP
Convenor Canon Andrew Bowden, Arthur Rank Centre, The National Agricultural Centre, Stoneleigh Park, Warks. CV8 2LZ   *Tel:* 024 7685 3060   *email:* info@arthurrankcentre.org.uk

CHURCHES TOGETHER FOR HEALING
Secretary Revd Elsie Howell, 60 Andrew Allan Rd, Rockwell Green, Wellington, Som. TA21 9DY   *Tel:* 01823 664529
                email: revelsie@howell.freeserve.co.uk

INDEM (Group for Mission in Industry and the Economy)
Mr David Wrighton, INDEM, 34 Chalvington Rd, Chandlers Ford, Eastleigh, Hants. SO53 3DX
                              Tel: 023 8026 1146
                email: wrcgdgshim@cs.com

SPIRITUALITY GROUP
Secretary Revd Dr David Cornick (*CTE address as above*)   *Tel:* 020 7529 8133
                email: david.cornick@cte.org.uk

WOMEN'S COORDINATING GROUP
Secretary Revd Debbie Hodge (*CTE address as above*)   *Tel:* 020 7529 8132
                email: debbie.hodge@cte.org.uk

There are also four *Agencies*:

CHURCHES' MEDIA COUNCIL
(Formerly Churches' Advisory Council for Local Broadcasting)
Administrator Patricia Flynn, Christian Enquiry Agency, Freepost WC2947, South Croydon CR2 8UZ   *Tel:* 020 8144 7177
                email: cea@deogloria.co.uk

CHRISTIAN ENQUIRY AGENCY
Administrator Patricia Flynn, Christian Enquiry Agency, Freepost WC2947, South Croydon CR2 8UZ   *Tel:* 020 8144 7177
                email: cea@deogloria.co.uk

CHRISTIAN AID
PO Box 100, London SE1 7RL   *Tel:* 020 7620 4444
                email: info@christian-aid.org

CAFOD
Director Mr Chris Bain, 2 Romero Close, Stockwell Rd, London SW9 9TY
                              Tel: 020 7733 7900
                email: hqcafod@cafod.org.uk

The following are *Bodies in Association* with Churches Together in England: Action by Christians Against Torture, Association of Centres of Adult Theological Education, Association of Inter-Church Families, Bible Society, Christian Council on Ageing, Christian Council on Approaches to Defence and Disarmament, Christian Education, Christians Aware, Church Action on Poverty, Churches Alert to Sex Trafficking Across Europe (CHASTE), Churches Community Work Alliance (CCWA), Churches East–West Europe Relations Network (CEWERN), Churches for All, College of Preachers, Community of Aidan and Hilda, Corrymeela Community, Ecumenical Council for Corporate Responsibility, Ecumenical Society of the Blessed Virgin Mary, Faith in Europe, Feed the Minds, Fellowship of St Alban and St Sergius, Fellowship of Reconciliation, Focolare Movement, Housing Justice, Industrial Mission Association, International Ecumenical Fellowship, Iona Community, Irish School of Ecumenics, L'Arche, Living Stones, MODEM, Oikocredit, Retreat Association, Society for Ecumenical Studies, Student Christian Movement, William Temple Foundation, Women's World Day of Prayer, Young Men's Christian Association, Y Care International.
     For addresses, *see* page 447 (under CTBI) or the **List of Organizations** (pages 259–263).

ECUMENICAL

Intermediate County Bodies and Area Ecumenical Councils

Bedfordshire Churches Together in Bedfordshire	Vacancy	**Birmingham** (*see also* **West Midlands**) Birmingham Churches Together	Revd Dr Colin Marsh St George's Community Hub Great Hampton Row Newtown, Birmingham B19 3JG *Tel:* 0121 236 3966 *email:* office@ birminghamchurches. org.uk
Berkshire Churches Together in Berkshire	Mrs Honor Alleyne CT Berkshire Office Park URC Hall Palmer Park Avenue Reading Berkshire RG6 1DN *Tel:* 0118 926 1062 *email:* ctberks@tesco.net		

Black Country (*see also* **Staffordshire**)
Black Country Churches Engaged (BCCE)

Mr Mike Topliss
18 Selman's Hill
Bloxwich
Walsall
Staffs. WS3 3RJ
Tel: 01922 475932
email: jmtopliss@
talktalk.net

Bristol, Greater
Churches Together in Greater Bristol

Jon Doble
162 Pennywell Lane
Bristol BS5 0TX
Tel: 0117 956 5447
email: jon@ccisr.org.uk

Buckinghamshire
Churches Together in Buckinghamshire
(Except Milton Keynes)

Major David Scott
3 Criss Grove
Chalfont St Peter
Bucks SL9 9HG
Tel: 020 7367 4751
email: davidscott5@
talktalk.net

Cambridgeshire
Cambridgeshire Ecumenical Council

Mrs Priscilla Barlow
Silverlands, Church St
Litlington
Royston
Herts SG8 0QB
Tel: 01763 852841
email:
priscilla.barlow@
easynet.co.uk

Cheshire
Churches Together in Cheshire

Mark Thompson
81 Forge Fields
Sandbach
Cheshire
CW11 3RD
Tel: 01270 750431
email: ceo@cheshire-churches-together.org.uk

Cornwall
Churches Together in Cornwall

Canon Martin Boxall
Goonhilland
Farmhouse
Bunthouse, St Gluvias
Penryn
Cornwall
TR10 9AS
Tel: 01872 863241

Coventry *See* **Warwickshire**

Cumbria
Churches Together in Cumbria

Vacancy
See
www.churches
togethercumbria.
co.uk

Derbyshire and Nottinghamshire
Churches Together in Derbyshire & Nottinghamshire

Revd Philip Webb
Dovedale
52 South Avenue
Chellaston
Derbyshire
DE73 1RS
Tel: 01332 705078
email: dovedale.revs@
virgin.net

Devon
Churches Together in Devon

Sabrina Groeschel
Tel: 01626 773 577
email:
Sabrina_groeschel@
yahoo.co.uk

Dorset
Churches Together in Dorset

Mrs Val Potter
22 D'Urberville Close
Dorchester
Dorset DT1 2JT
Tel: 01305 264416
email: ctdorset@
clara.net

Durham *see* **North-East England**

Essex and London, East
Churches Together in Essex & East London CLG

Revd Lee Batson
The Vicarage
Church Road
Boreham
Chelmsford CM3 3EG
Tel: 01245 451087
email: lbatson@
chelmsford.
anglican.org

Gloucestershire
Gloucestershire Churches Together

Revd Dr Alison Evans
Britannia Cottage
High Street
Kings Stanley
Stonehouse
GL10 3JD
Tel: 01453 824034
email:
malcolm.alison@
btinternet.com

Guernsey
Churches Together in Guernsey

Mr Roy Sarre
Le Campère
Les Villets
Forest
Guernsey
Channel Islands
GY8 0HP
Tel: 01481 265004

Hampshire and Isle of Wight
Churches Together in Hampshire & the Island

Dr Paul Rolph
71 Andover Road
Winchester
SO22 6AU
Tel: 01962 862574
email: cthi@
  rolph.freeuk.com

Herefordshire
Churches Together in Herefordshire

Andrew Harter
Upper House
Grosmont
Abergavenny
NP7 8EP
Tel: 01981 241383
email: ctih@
  harter.co.uk

Hertfordshire
Churches Together in Hertfordshire

Major Gerald Peacock
83 Cromer Way
Luton
Bedfordshire
LU2 7EE
Tel: 01582 492993
email:
  geraldpeacock39@
  btinternet.com

Isle of Man
Churches Together in Man

Mrs Mavis Matthewman
Tarnalforn
12 Ballagarey Rd
Glen Vine
Isle of Man
IM4 4EA
Tel: 01624 851692

Isle of Wight *see* **Hampshire**

Jersey
Christians Together in Jersey

Martin Dryden
Monte Urbe House
La Rue de la Blinerie
St Clements
Jersey JE2 6QT
email: martin@
  mont-ube.net

Kent
Churches Together in Kent

Revd David Vannerley
(Researcher)
email: moderator@
  urcsouthern.org.uk /
  ctk-7@ctkent.org.uk

Lancashire
Churches Together in Lancashire

Revd Debbie Peatman
  (Ecumenical
  Development
  Officer)
Rectory,
  Church Walk,
  Morecambe
  LA4 5PR
Tel: 07806 643 097
email:
  debbie.peatman@
  ctlancashire.org.uk
Revd Steven Hughes
  (Inter Faith Officer)
69 Liverpool Old Rd
Much Hoole
Preston Lancs
PR4 4RB
Tel: 01772 612267
email:
  steven.hughes@
  ctlancashire.org.uk

Leicestershire
Churches Together in Leicestershire

Vacancy
email: cedo.ctil@
  fsmail.net

Lincolnshire
Churches Together in All Lincolnshire

Simon Dean
  (administrator)
c/o Church House
The Old Palace
Lincoln
LN2 1PU
Tel: 01522 504070
email:
  office@ctal.org.uk

London, East *see* **Essex**
East London Church Leaders Group

Revd Lee Batson
Vicarage, Church Rd
Boreham, Chelmsford
CM3 3EG
Tel: 01245 451087
email: lbatsom@
  chelmsford.
  anglican.org

London, North *see* **North Thames**

London, North Thames
Churches Together North Thames

Revd Bernie Collins
Ickenham United
  Reformed Church
Swakeleys Road
Ickenham
Uxbridge UB10 8BE
Tel: 07982 186 301
email: Revbcollins@
  aol.com

London, South
Churches Together in
South London

John Richardson
c/o St John's Vicarage
Secker Street
London SE1 9UF
Tel: 01462 422502
email: john@
ctslondon.org.uk

London, West
Churchlink West
London

Fr William Taylor
25 Ladbroke Grove
London W11 3PD
Tel: 020 7727 3439
email: vicar@stjohns
nottinghill.com

Manchester, Greater
Greater Manchester
Churches Together

Revd Graham
Kent
St Peter's House
Precinct Centre
Oxford Road
Manchester
M13 9GH
Tel: 0161 273 5508
Fax: 0161 272 7172
email:
sph.gmct@
man.ac.uk

Merseyside
Churches Together in
the Merseyside
Region

Revd Ian Smith
Quaker Meeting
House
22 School Lane
Liverpool L1 3BT
Tel: 0151 709 0125
email: office@
ctmr.org.uk

Milton Keynes
Mission Partnership of
the Milton Keynes
Christian Council

Revd Dr Mary Cotes
c/o Christian
Foundation
The Square
Aylesbury Street
Wolverton
MK12 5HX
Tel: 01908 311310
email:
missionpartnership
@tiscali.co.uk

Norfolk
Norfolk and Waveney
Churches Together

Vacancy
Contact: Bishop
Graham Jones
email: bishop@bishop
ofnorwich.org

North-East England
North East Christian
Churches Together
(NECCT)

Revd John Durell
4 Wearside Drive
Durham
DH1 1LE
Tel: 0191 384 1475
email: john.durell@
urc-northernsynod.
org.uk

Nottinghamshire (*see*
Derbyshire)

Oxfordshire
Churches Together in
Oxfordshire

Mr Bede Gerrard
c/o Cowley Road
Methodist Church
Jeune Street
Oxford OX4 1BN
Tel: 01865 723801
email: bjg1@
waitrose.com

Peterborough (*see*
Shire and Soke)

Shire and Soke
Churches Together in
Northamptonshire &
Peterborough

Teresa Brown
Tel: 01832 293535
email: teresabrown@
shireandsoke.org.uk

Shropshire (Except
Telford)
Churches Together in
Shropshire

Mr Ged Cliffe
Fern Villa
Four Crosses
Llanymynech
Powys SY22 6PR
Tel: 01691 831374
email: gedcliffe@
tiscali.co.uk

Somerset
Somerset Churches
Together in Somerset

Vacancy
Contact: Tim Richards
email: richardstime@
hotmail.com

Staffordshire
Churches Linked Across
Staffs & the Potteries
(CLASP) (*as* **Black
Country**)

Mike Topliss
Tel: 01922 475 932
email: jmtopliss@
talktalk.net

Suffolk
Churches Together in
Suffolk

Julie Mansfield
Applegarth
Wilmslow Avenue
Woodbridge
Suffolk
IP12 4HW
Tel: 01394 384370
email:
ctsuffolkjmmansfield
@homecall.co.uk

Surrey
Churches Together in
Surrey

Revd Susan Loveday
10 Abbey Gardens
Chertsey
Surrey KT16 8RQ
Tel: 01932 566920
email: sue.loveday.
ctsurrey@
lineone.net

Ecumenical

Sussex
Churches Together in
  Sussex

Mr Ian Chisnall
85 Hollingbury
  Rise
Brighton
BN1 7HH
Tel: 07976 811654
  (Mobile)
email: ianpchisnall@
  aol.com

Swindon
Swindon Churches
  Together

Revd Lee Rayfield
Tel: 01793 523 810
email: bishop.
  swindon@
  bristoldiocese.org

Telford
Telford Christian
  Council

Rebecca Higgs
Meeting Point
  House
Southwater Square
Town Centre
Telford TF3 4HS
Tel: 01952 291904
email: rebeccahiggs@
  staytelford.co.uk

Warwickshire
Churches Together
  in Coventry &
  Warwickshire

Kay Dyer
6 Sycamore Close
Stratford-upon-Avon
CV37 0DZ
Tel: 01789 298299
email: ctcw@fish.co.uk

Waveney *see* **Norfolk**

Wiltshire
Wiltshire Churches
  Together

Liz Overthrow
email: roy.overthrow@
  btinternet.com

Worcestershire
Churches Together
  in Worcestershire

Revd David Ryan
4 Daty Croft
Home Meadow
Worcester
WR4 0JB
Tel: 01905 616109
email: dpryangb@
  aol.com

**Yorkshire, East
  and Hull**
Kingston upon Hull &
  East Yorkshire
  Churches Together

Mrs Cathy Crumpton
Key Churches
  Together
Methodist Central
  Hall
King Edward St
Hull
HU1 3SQ
Tel: 01482 328196
email: cathy@
  keyct.karoo.co.uk

**Yorkshire, North York
  Moors**
North York Moors
  Churches Together

Barbara Burke
York & Hull District
  Office
28 The Green
Acomb, York
YO26 5LR
Tel: 01904 786 275
email: admin@
  yorkhullmethodist.
  org.uk

Yorkshire, South
Churches Together in
  South Yorkshire

Val Higgins
CTSY Office
Victoria Hall
  Methodist Church
Norfolk St
Sheffield S1 2JB
Tel: 0114 278 8308
email:
  admin@
  ctsouthyorkshire.
  plus.com

Yorkshire, Vale of York
ENVOY (Ecumenical
  Network in the Vale
  of York)

Nigel Currey
17 Mayfield Drive
Brayton
Selby
North Yorkshire
YO8 9JZ
Tel: 01347 838593
email: ncurrey1@
  talktalk.net

Yorkshire, West
West Yorkshire
  Ecumenical Council

Clive Barrett
Hinsley Hall
62 Headingley Lane
Leeds LS6 2BX
Tel: 0113 261 8053
Fax: 0113 261 8054
email: office@
  wyec.co.uk

Churches Together in Britain and Ireland

Office 39 Ecclestone Square, London SW1V 1BX
Tel: 08456 806851
Fax: 08456 806852
email: gensec@ctbi.org.uk
Web: www.ctbi.org.uk

Churches Together in Britain and Ireland (CTBI) is an umbrella body through which the Churches co-operate on common issues. It works closely with the other 'Churches Together' bodies, which focus separately on England, Wales, Scotland and Ireland. Together they have an important role to witness to the essential unity of the Christian movement. CTBI's core tasks are providing 'structured ecumenical space' for meeting and encounter, facilitating shared study on common issues and fostering relationships – among the Churches and between the Churches and the wider world.

Churches Together in Britain and Ireland (formerly the Council of Churches for Britain and Ireland and the direct successor of the British Council of Churches) was established by its member Churches to enable them to work together for the advancement of the Christian religion, the relief of poverty, the advancement of education and any other charitable purpose. It seeks to further these objects by providing opportunities for representatives of the Churches from the four nations to meet together and to share some of their resources in the pursuance of jointly agreed activities.

Following a review of its work, Churches Together in Britain and Ireland has become an agency serving the churches through the four National Ecumenical Instruments. As a separate charitable company, limited by guarantee, CTBI now relates to the churches, as members, through the ecumenical structures of the nations. It is now more relational and its focus is on working agreed common themes across the different work areas described below. The current themes are:

– environment/climate change
– migration and the movements of people
– culture, identity and the public space

Our principal activities and Networks are:

- Witnessing to and working towards the visible unity of the Christian Churches and providing opportunities for representatives of the Churches to meet and to plan their work together. A **Senior Representatives Forum**, attended by delegates from all member churches and bodies in association, is held in the spring of each year. An annual **Networking Conference** brings together the various Networks which comprise members of the member Chruches, Agencies and Bodies in Association.

- Working on the Churches' behalf on issues of racial justice through the **Churches Racial Justice Network** (formerly known as CCRJ, the Churches' Commission for Racial Justice). The Racial Justice Network is a major vehicle for the Churches' engagement with the complex work of racial justice throughout Ireland, Scotland, Wales and England. Central to the work is the Racial Justice Fund, which supports a wide range of grass-roots organizations. These funded groups are invited into a dynamic partnership designed to build their capacity for effective action and to provide first rate information and experience for use in education, lobbying and campaigning. **Racial Justice Sunday,** celebrated ecumenically on the second Sunday in September, gives an opportunity for vital educational work with churches and congregations and raises the media profile of the work of racial justice. Other projects include Capacity Building for Black Churches, the Bail Circle and the Peers project. The recent publication of *Migration Principles*, which in turn is building on the work of *Asylum Principles*, seeks to promote an active discussion and programme around the complex issue of migration. Working with other departments within CTBI, the Racial Justice team are taking forward Migration as a major theme.

- Through the **Churches Network for Mission (CNM),** seeking to serve and assist churches, agencies and the four national ecumenical instruments in our common task of participating in God's mission in the world. GMN is a key point of contact with world ecumenical mission bodies, particularly the World Council of Churches and the Council of European Churches. GMN's current projects include:

  – Preparation for and follow up to the **Edinburgh 2010 Mission Conference**
  – **Mission Theology Advisory Group,** offering expertise from around the four nations in Mission theology. Publications and web resources are being produced to support the ongoing work of the churches' mission in new contexts.
  – **China** – the China Desk provides a dedicated expert centre maintaining a wide range of relationships in China and undertaking research and analysis on Chinese affairs. It co-ordinates the work of the China Forum which acts as a bridge to Chinese Christians, both Catholic and Protestant, with partnership maintained through a variety of on-going projects.

- Through the **Churches Inter Religious Network,** working with the Churches to engage effectively in relations and dialogue with other faiths in Britain and Ireland. The Network is a point of reference for the Churches which facilitates an exchange of information and experience among Christians about inter faith relations, whilst enabling critical reflection on the religiously and socially plural society of the four nations. In Scotland, it works through the Churches' Agency for Inter Faith Relations in Scotland. The Network seeks to fulfil its aims by responding to requests by the Churches on inter faith issues, monitoring inter faith relations in the four nations, nurturing links between Christians working in this field, pooling the theological resources of the Churches for ministry and witness in this area, and producing appropriate written or other material to help the Churches. In addition CTBI is a member body, on behalf of the Churches, of the Inter Faith Network for the United Kingdom, which provides a national forum for people from the main faith communities to meet, discuss and share.

- Through the **Churches International Student Network**, supporting international students by networking, education and communication among the Churches and between them, government and other agencies specializing in international students' affairs. The Network seeks to link the varied work of the many church agencies among students and supports the Churches in their response to the needs of international students. It initiated and maintains co-funding from the Foreign Office for denominational and ecumenical scholarships, administers World Council of Churches scholarships in Britain and Ireland and operates a hardship fund for international students for which it raises funding.
- Developing and publishing for the Churches **resources for study and prayer**. This includes printed and web based materials for the Week of Prayer for Christian Unity, which is observed each year from 18 to 25 January, as well as a Lent study programme.
- Through the **Church and Public Issues Network**, supporting and resourcing the Churches in their work on political, social and ethical issues, paying particular attention to:

– public policy agendas of Westminster, and also Cardiff, Edinburgh, Belfast, Dublin and Brussels
– the churches' engagement with contemporary social issues
– moral/ethical issues, especially where there is a distinctive Christian contribution to be made

The Church and Society Forum takes a lead in networking those who work on church and society issues across the four nations, and in sharing and disseminating information and expertise. It represents the Churches jointly, where appropriate, to Government bodies, other agencies and elsewhere. It has one main residential meeting each year, with others as the need arises.

STAFF
Canon Robert Fyffe, *General Secretary*

Mr Stephen Cutler, *Director of Business and Finance*
Mrs Mary Gandy, *Resources Manager*
Lawrence Braschi, *China Desk Director*
Revd Peter Colwell, *Director of Programmes*
Mr Dave Chadwick, *Web Manager*

CTBI MEMBER CHURCHES AND BODIES OF CHURCHES
ANTIOCHIAN ORTHODOX CHURCH
Father George Hackney
Little Portion, Back Lane, Barnby, Newark NG24 2SD   *Tel:* 01636 626417
email: fathergeorge@macace.net

BAPTIST UNION OF GREAT BRITAIN
Revd Jonathan Edwards *General Secretary*
Baptist House, 129 Broadway, Didcot OX11 8RT
Tel: 01235 517700
Fax: 01235 517715
email: info@baptist.org.uk
Web: www.baptist.org.uk

CATHOLIC BISHOPS' CONFERENCE OF ENGLAND AND WALES
Fr Marcus Stock *General Secretary*
39 Eccleston Square, London SW1V 1BX
Tel: 020 7630 8220
Fax: 020 7901 4821
email: secretariat@cbcew.org.uk
Web: www.catholic-ew.org.uk

CATHOLIC BISHOPS' CONFERENCE OF SCOTLAND
Revd Paul Conroy *General Secretary*
64 Aitken St, Airdrie ML6 6LT   *Tel:* 01236 764061
Fax: 01236 762489
email: GenSec@BpsConfScot.com
Web:
www.scmo.org/_titles/bishops_conference.htm

CHURCH IN WALES
John Shirley *Provincial Secretary*
39 Cathedral Rd, Cardiff CF11 9XF
Tel: 029 2034 8200
Fax: 029 2038 7835
email: johnshirley@churchinwales.org.uk
Web: www.churchinwales.org.uk

CHURCH OF ENGLAND
Mr William Fittall *Secretary General of the General Synod and the Archbishops' Council*
Church House, Great Smith St, London SW1P 3AZ   *Tel:* 020 7898 1000
Fax: 020 7898 1369
email: cofe.comms@c-of-e.org.uk
Web: www.cofe.anglican.org

CHURCH OF GOD OF PROPHECY
Bishop Wilton R. Powell *National Overseer*
6 Beacon Court, Birmingham Rd, Great Barr, Birmingham B43 6NN   *Tel:* 0121 358 2231
Fax: 0121 358 8617
email: admin@cogop.org.uk
Web: www.cogop.org.uk

CHURCH OF IRELAND
Mrs Janet Maxwell *Head of Synod Services and Communications*
Church of Ireland House, Church Avenue, Rathmines, Dublin 6, RoI   *Tel:* ++ 353 (0)1 4125621
Fax: ++ 353 (0)1 4978821
email: janet.maxwell@rcbdub.org
Web: www.ireland.anglican.org

CHURCH OF SCOTLAND
Revd John Chalmers *Principal Clerk (from July 2010)*
Principal Clerk's Office, 121 George St, Edinburgh EH2 4YN   *Tel:* 0131 240 2240
Fax: 0131 240 2239
email: pracproc@cofscotland.org.uk
Web: www.churchofscotland.org.uk

CONGREGATIONAL FEDERATION
Revd Michael Heaney *General Secretary*
8 Castle Gate, Nottingham NG1 7AS
Tel: 0115 911 1460
Fax: 0115 911 1462
email: admin@congregational.org.uk
Web: www.congregational.org.uk

COPTIC ORTHODOX CHURCH
Bishop Angaelos
Coptic Orthodox Church Centre, Shephalbury Manor, Broadhall Way, Stevenage SG2 8RH
Tel: 01438 745232
Fax: 01438 313879
email: admin@CopticCentre.com
Web: www.CopticCentre.com

COUNCIL OF ORIENTAL ORTHODOX CHURCHES
Bishop Angaelos *President*
c/o Coptic Orthodox Church Centre (*as above*)
email: admin@CopticCentre.com

GERMAN-SPEAKING CONGREGATION
Mr Georg Staab
Council for German Church Work, 35 Craven Terrace, London W2 3EL   *Tel:* 020 7706 8589
Fax: 020 7706 2870
email: office@ev-synode.org.uk
Web: www.ev-synode.org.uk

INDEPENDENT METHODIST CHURCHES
Mr William Gabb *General Secretary*
Independent Methodist Resource Centre & Registered Office
Fleet St, Pemberton, Wigan WN5 0DS
Tel: 01942 223526
Fax: 01942 227768
email: resourcecentre@imcgb.org.uk
Web: www.imcgb.org.uk

INTERNATIONAL MINISTERIAL COUNCIL OF GREAT BRITAIN (IMCGB)
Bishop Onye Obika
217 Langhedge Lane, London N18 2TG
Tel: 020 8345 5376
email: imcgb@aol.com
Web: www.imcgb.com

JOINT COUNCIL FOR ANGLO AND AFRICAN-CARIBBEAN CHURCHES
Revd Esme Beswick *President*
141 Railton Rd, London SE24 0LT
Tel and Fax: 020 7737 6542

LUTHERAN COUNCIL OF GREAT BRITAIN
Revd Thomas Bruch *General Secretary*
30 Thanet St, London WC1H 9QH
Tel: 020 7554 2900
Fax: 020 7383 3081
email: enquiries@lutheran.org.uk
Web: www.lutheran.org.uk

MAR THOMAS CHURCH
Dr Zac Varghese *Ecumenical Officer*
3 Rose Garden Close, Edgware, London HA8 7RF
Tel: 020 8951 5273
email: zacvarghese@aol.co.uk

METHODIST CHURCH
Revd Dr Martin Atkins *General Secretary*
25 Marylebone Rd, London NW1 5JR
Tel: 020 7467 5143
Fax: 020 7467 5226
email: generalsecretary@methodistchurch.org.uk
Web: www.methodist.org.uk

METHODIST CHURCH IN IRELAND
Revd Donald Ker *General Secretary*
1 Fountainville Ave, Belfast BT9 6AN
Tel: 028 9032 4554
Fax: 028 9023 9467
email: secretary@irishmethodist.org
Web: www.irishmethodist.org

MORAVIAN CHURCH
Jackie Morten
Moravian Church House, 5 Muswell Hill,
London N10 3TJ   *Tel:* 020 8883 3409
                        Fax: 020 8365 3371
             email: office@moravian.org.uk
             Web: www.moravian.org.uk

NEW TESTAMENT ASSEMBLY
Revd Nezlin Sterling *General Secretary*
5 Woodstock Ave, London W13 9UQ
                        Tel: 020 8579 3841
                        Fax: 020 8537 9253
             email: njsterlnta@aol.com

NEW TESTAMENT CHURCH OF GOD
Bishop Donald Bolt
3 Cheyne Walk, Northampton NN1 5PT
                        Tel: 01604 643311
                        Fax: 01604 790254
             email: bigmove@ntcg.org.uk
             Web: www.ntcg.org.uk

**OECUMENICAL PATRIARCHATE (ARCHDIOCESE OF
THYATEIRA AND GREAT BRITAIN)**
His Eminence Archbishop Gregorios
5 Craven Hill, London W2 3EN
                        Tel: 020 7723 4787
                        Fax: 020 7224 9301
             email: thyateiragb@yahoo.com
             Web: www.nostos.com/church/

PRESBYTERIAN CHURCH OF WALES
Revd Ifan Roberts *General Secretary*
Tabernacle Chapel, 81 Merthyr Road, Whitchurch, Cardiff CF14 1DD   *Tel:* 029 2062 7465
                        Fax: 029 2061 6188
   email: swyddfa.office@ebcpcw.org.uk
             Web: www.ebcpcw.org.uk

RELIGIOUS SOCIETY OF FRIENDS
Gillian Ashmore *Chief Recording Clerk*
Friends House, 173 Euston Rd, London NW1 2BJ
                        Tel: 020 7663 1000
                        Fax: 020 7663 1001
             email: enquiries@quaker.org.uk
             Web: www.quaker.org.uk

RELIGIOUS SOCIETY OF FRIENDS IN IRELAND
Mr Ian Woods
40 Castle Grove, Swords, Co Dublin

**RUSSIAN ORTHODOX CHURCH (ECUMENICAL
PATRIARCHATE)**
Mrs Gillian Crow
6 Maiden Place, London NW5 1HZ
             email: gillian@crow.co.uk
             Web www.exarchate-uk.org

SALVATION ARMY
Commissioner John Matear *Territorial Commander
UK and RoI*
101 Newington Causeway, London SE1 6BN
                        Tel: 020 7367 4500
                        Fax: 020 7367 4728
             email: info@salvationarmy.org.uk
             Web: www.salvationarmy.org.uk

SCOTTISH EPISCOPAL CHURCH
Mr John Stuart *Secretary General for Synod Office*
21 Grosvenor Crescent, Edinburgh EH12 5EE
                        Tel: 0131 225 6357
                        Fax: 0131 346 7247
             email: office@scotland.anglican.org
             Web: www.scottishepiscopal.com

**TRANS-ATLANTIC & PACIFIC ALLIANCE OF
CHURCHES**
Archbishop Paul Hackman *President*
281-283 Rye Lane, London SE15 4UA
                     Tel and Fax: 020 7639 4058
             email: tapacglobal@aol.com

**UNDEB YR ANNIBYNWYR CYMRAEG/UNION OF
WELSH INDEPENDENTS**
Revd Dr Geraint Tudor *General Secretary*
Tŷ John Penri, 5 Axis Court, Riverside Business
Park, Swansea Vale, Swansea SA7 0AJ
                        Tel: 01792 795888
                        Fax: 01792 795376
             email: Undeb@annibynwyr.org
             Web: www.annibynwyr.org

UNITED FREE CHURCH OF SCOTLAND
Revd Andrew McMillan
11 Newton Place, Glasgow G3 7PR
                        Tel: 0141 332 3435
                        Fax: 0141 333 1973
             email: office@ufcos.org.uk
             Web: www.ufcos.org.uk

UNITED REFORMED CHURCH
Revd Roberta Rominger *General Secretary*
86 Tavistock Place, London WC1H 9RT
                        Tel: 020 7916 2020
                        Fax: 020 7916 2021
             email: urc@urc.org.uk
             Web: www.urc.org.uk

ASSOCIATE MEMBER
ROMAN CATHOLIC CHURCH OF IRELAND
Revd Aidan O'Boyle *Executive Secretary*
The Irish Episcopal Conference, Columba Centre,
Maynooth, Co Kildare, Republic of Ireland
                        Tel: 00 353 1 505 3020
                        Fax: 00 353 1 629 2360
             email: ex.sec@iecon.ie

ECUMENICAL

BODIES IN ASSOCIATION

Chas Raws, 38 The Mount, Heswello, Wirral CH60 4RA
email: uk.acat@googlemail.com
Web: www.acatuk.org.uk

ASSOCIATION OF INTER-CHURCH FAMILIES
Mr Keith Lander (*Executive Officer*), 27 Tavistock Square, London WC1H 9HH
Tel: 020 7529 8131
Fax: 020 7529 8134
email: info@interchurchfamilies.org.uk
Web: www.interchurchfamilies.org.uk

BIBLE READING FELLOWSHIP
Richard Fisher, 15 The Chambers, Vineyard, Abingdon OX14 3FE
Tel: 01865 319 700
email: enquiries@brf.org.uk
Web: www.brf.org.uk

BIBLE SOCIETY
James Catford (*Chief Executive*), Stonehill Green, Westlea, Swindon SN5 7DG
Tel: 01793 418 100
Web: www.biblesociety.org.uk

CHRISTIAN COUNCIL ON AGEING
Mrs Christine Hodgson, 6 The Ridgeway, Market Harborough LE16 7HQ
Tel: 01858 432771
email: info@ccoa.org.uk
Web: www.ccoa.org.uk

CHRISTIAN EDUCATION
Peter Fishpool (*Chief Executive*), 1020 Bristol Rd, Selly Oak, Birmingham B29 6LB
Tel: 0121 472 4242
Fax: 0121 472 7575
email: admin@christianeducation.org.uk
Web: www.christianeducation.org.uk

CHRISTIANS AWARE
Mrs Barbara Butler, 2 Saxby St, Leicester LE2 0ND
Tel and *Fax:* 0116 254 0770
email: barbarabutler@christiansaware.co.uk
Web: www.christiansaware.co.uk

CHURCH ACTION ON POVERTY
Mr Niall Cooper (*National Coordinator*), Dale House, 35 Dale St, Manchester M1 2HF
Tel: 0161 236 9321
Fax: 0161 237 5359
email: info@church-poverty.org.uk
Web: www.church-poverty.org.uk

CHURCHES' ALERT TO SEX TRAFFICKING ACROSS EUROPE
Angela Deavall (*Chief Executive*), PO Box 983, Cambridge CB3 8WY
Tel: 0845 456 9335
email: contact@chaste.org.uk
Web: www.chaste.org.uk

COLLEGE OF PREACHERS
Ms Marfa Jones (*Administrator*), Chester House, Pages Lane, Muswell Hill, London N10 1PR
Tel: 020 8883 7850
email: administrator@collegeofpreachers.org.uk
Web: www.collegeofpreachers.org.uk

COMMUNITY OF AIDAN AND HILDA
Lindisfarne Retreat, The Open Gate, Holy Island, Berwick-upon-Tweed TD15 2SD
Tel: 01289 389222
email: ca-and-h@demon.co.uk
Web: www.aidanandhilda.org.uk

CORRYMEELA COMMUNITY
Corrymeela House, 8 Upper Crescent, Belfast BT7 1NT
Tel: 028 9050 8080
Fax: 028 9050 8070
email: annemcdonagh@corrymeela.org
Web: www.corrymeela.org

ECUMENICAL COUNCIL FOR CORPORATE RESPONSIBILITY
Miles Litvinoff (*Coordinator*), PO Box 500, Oxford OX1 1ZL
Tel: 020 8965 9682
email: info@eccr.org.uk
Web: www.eccr.org.uk

ECUMENICAL SOCIETY OF THE BLESSED VIRGIN MARY
Paul Paniccia, 1 Badgers Glade, Burghfield Common, Reading RG7 3RG

FAITH IN EUROPE
Dr Philip Walters (*General Secretary*), 81 Thorney Leys, Witney OX28 5BY
Tel: 01993 771778
email: philip.walters@waltfam.freeserve.co.uk
Web: www.faithineurope.org.uk

FEED THE MINDS
Josephine Carlssen (*Director*), Park Place, 12 Lawn Lane, London SW8 1UD
Tel: 020 7592 3900
Fax: 020 7592 3939
email: info@feedtheminds.org
Web: www.feedtheminds.org

FELLOWSHIP OF RECONCILIATION
Revd John Johansen-Berg (*Director*), St James' Church Centre, Beauchamp Lane, Oxford OX4 3LF
Tel: 01865 748796
email: office@for.org.uk
Web: www.for.org.uk

FELLOWSHIP OF ST ALBAN AND ST SERGIUS
Revd Stephen Platt, 1 Canterbury Rd, Oxford OX2 6LU
Tel: 01865 52991
Fax: 01865 316700
email: gensec@sobornost.org
Web: www.sobornost.org

Ecumenical

FOCOLARE MOVEMENT
Celia Blackden, 11 Drummond Avenue, Leeds
LS16 5JZ
email: celiablackden@yahoo.co.uk
Web: www.focolare.org.uk

HOUSING JUSTICE
Ms Alison Gelder (*Chief Executive*), 209 Old
Marylebone Rd, London NW1 5QT
Tel: 020 7723 7273
Fax: 020 7723 5943
email: info@housingjustice.org.uk
Web: www.housingjustice.org.uk

INDUSTRIAL MISSION ASSOCIATION
Revd Stephen Hazlett, Northumbrian Industrial
Mission, 14 The Oaks West, Sunderland SR2 8HZ
Tel: 07900 231360
Web: www.industrialmission.org.uk

INTERNATIONAL ECUMENICAL FELLOWSHIP
David Hardiman, 59 Old St, Headington, Oxford
OX3 9HT
Tel: 0191 4566 1643
email: davidhardiman@blueyonder.com
Web: www.uk-ief.co.uk

IONA COMMUNITY
Revd Peter Macdonald, 4th Floor, Savoy House,
140 Sauchiehall St, Glasgow G2 3DH
Tel: 0141 332 6343
Fax: 0141 332 1090
email: admin@iona.org.uk
Web: www.iona.org.uk

IRISH SCHOOL OF ECUMENICS
Prof Linda Hogan, 683 Antrim Rd, Belfast BT15
4EG *and* Bea House, Milltown Park, Dublin 6, RoI
Tel: +44 (0) 28 9077 5010
Fax: +44 (0) 28 9037 3986
email: lhogan2@tcd.ie
Web: www.tcd.ie/ise

L'ARCHE
Ms Lal Keenan, L'Arche Community, 15 North-
wood High St, London SE27 9JU
Tel: 020 8670 6714
Fax: 020 8670 0818
email: info@larche.org.uk
Web: www.larche.org.uk

LIVING STONES
Dr Aziz Nour, 77 Exeter Rd, Southgate, London
N14 5JU
Web: www.livingstonesonline.org.uk

MAGNET RESOURCES
Lynne Ling, PO Box 10378, Bishop's Stortford
CM23 9FT
Tel: 0844 7362524
Web: www.ourmagnet.co.uk

MODEM
Mr John Nelson (*National Secretary and Publica-
tions Editor*), 24 Rostron Crescent, Formby L37
2ET
Tel: 01704 873973
Fax: 01704 871273
email: jrn24rcf2003@yahoo.co.uk
Web: www.modem.uk.com

**OIKOCREDIT, ECUMENICAL DEVELOPMENT
COOPERATIVE SOCIETY**
Patrick Hynes, UK Support Office, PO Box 809,
Garstang, Preston PR3 1TU
Web: www.oikocredit.org

OPERATION NOAH
Anne Pettifor, Grayston Centre, 28 Charles
Square, London N1 6HT
Tel: 0207 324 4761
email: admin@operationnoah.org
Web: www.operationnoah.org

PRISON FELLOWSHIP ENGLAND AND WALES
Tim Diaper, PO Box 945, Maldon, Essex CM9
4EW
Tel: 01621 843232
Web: www.prisonfellowship.org

RETREAT ASSOCIATION
Alison MacTier, The Central Hall, 256 Bermond-
sey St, London SE1 3UJ
Tel: 020 7357 7736
Fax: 020 7357 7724
email: info@retreats.org.uk
Web: www.retreats.org.uk

SOCIETY OF ECUMENICAL STUDIES
Revd Mark Woodruff (*Secretary*), 26 Daysbrook
Rd, London SW2 3TD
Tel: 020 8678 8195
email: ecumenicalstudies@btinternet.com
Web: www.ecumenicalstudies.org.uk

STUDENT CHRISTIAN MOVEMENT
Revd Martin Thompson, Unit 308F, The Big
Peg, 120 Vyse St, Jewellery Quarter, Birmingham
B18 6NF
Tel: 0121 200 3355
email: co@movement.org.uk
Web: www.movement.org.uk

WOMEN'S WORLD DAY OF PRAYER MOVEMENT
Jean Hackett, National Office, Commercial Rd,
Tunbridge Wells TN1 2RR
Tel: 01892 541411
Fax: 01892 541745
email: office@wwdp-natcomm.org
Web: www.wwdp-natcomm.org

YOUNG MEN'S CHRISTIAN ASSOCIATION (YMCA)
Ms Helen Dennis (*Policy and Parliamentary
Officer*), 53 Parker St, London WC2B 5PT
Tel: 0845 873 6633
email: enquiries@ymca.org.uk
Web: www.ymca.org.uk

ECUMENICAL

Churches Together in Britain and Ireland 451

Scotland, Wales and Ireland

ACTION OF CHURCHES TOGETHER IN SCOTLAND
7 Forrester Lodge, Inglewood House, Alloa FK10
2HU   *Tel:* 01259 216980
                                           Fax: 01259 215964
              email: ecumenical@acts-scotland.org

General Secretary Brother Stephen Smyth

*Convenor of the Trustees and ACTS Members'
Meeting* Rt Revd Philip Kerr

ACTS is the national ecumenical body for
Scotland, the expression of the Churches' commitment to cooperation with one another in the
service of Christ. ACTS works closely with its
partners in England, Wales and Ireland. Its
principal body is the Members' Meeting, composed of representatives from the member
churches. The work of ACTS is forwarded by
four Networks: Church and Society, Church Life,
Mission, and Faith Studies. In addition to the core
staff ACTS employs the Scottish Churches Racial
Justice Officer.

Member Churches Church of Scotland,
Congregational Federation, Methodist Church,
Religious Society of Friends, Roman Catholic
Church, Salvation Army, Scottish Episcopal
Church, United Free Church, United Reformed
Church.

**CYTÛN: EGLWYSI YNGHYD YNG
NGHYMRU
CHURCHES TOGETHER IN WALES**
58 Richmond Rd, Cardiff, South Wales CF24 3UR
              Tel (main office): 029 2046 4204
                  Web: www.cytun.org.uk

Chief Executive Revd Aled Edwards OBE
                          Tel: 029 2046 4375
                  *email:*aled@cytun.org.uk

Bilingual Office Administrator to Chief Executive
Mrs Sasha Perriam   *Tel:* 029 2046 4204
                  email: post@cytun.org.uk

National Assembly Policy Officer Mr Geraint
Hopkins   *Tel:* 029 2046 4378
                  email: geraint@cytun.org.uk

Faith Order and Witness Officer Rhian Linecar
                          Tel: 029 2046 4371
                  email: rhian@cytun.org.uk

Cytun's Basis and Commitment:
Cytun unites in pilgrimage those churches in
Wales, which acknowledging God's revelation in
Christ, confess the Lord Jesus Christ as God and

Saviour according to the Scriptures, and in
obedience to God's will and in the power of the
Holy Spirit, commit ourselves.

To seek a deepening of their communion with
Christ with one another and in the church which
is his body, and to fulfil the mission to proclaim
the gospel by common witness and service in the
world, to the glory of the one God, Father, Son
and Holy Spirit.

Member Denominations The Baptist Union of
Wales, the Roman Catholic Church, the Church
in Wales, the Congregational Federation, the
Covenanted Baptist Churches, the German
Speaking Lutheran, the Methodist Church, the
Presbyterian Church of Wales, the Quakers,
the Salvation Army, the Union of Welsh
Independents, the United Reformed Church and
the South Wales Baptist Association.

Aligned Groupings The Covenanted Churches in
Wales, the Free Church Council of Wales.

CYTÛN also works in close collaboration with
the Commission of the Covenanted Church in
Wales and the Free Church Council of Wales.

THE IRISH COUNCIL OF CHURCHES
Inter-Church Centre, 48 Elmwood Ave, Belfast
BT9 6AZ   *Tel:* 028 9066 3145
                                   Fax: 028 9066 4160
                  email: info@irishchurches.org
                  Web: www.irishchurches.org

President Most Revd Richard Clarke

Vice-President Revd Fr Godrey O'Donnell

Hon Treasurer Mr Robert Cochran

Executive Officer Mr Mervyn McCullagh

Administrator Mrs Karen Kelly

History From 1906 the Presbyterian and Methodist Churches had a joint committee for united
efforts. In 1910 the General Assembly of the Presbyterian Church invited other evangelical
Churches to set up similar joint committees with
it. The Church of Ireland accepted and by 1911
the joint committee of these two Churches was in
action. Following a recommendation of the 1920
Lambeth Conference, these joint committees
developed in 1922 into the United Council of
Christian Churches and Religious Communions
in Ireland including six of the present member
churches. In 1966 the United Council changed its
name to the Irish Council of Churches. The
Council employed its first full-time secretary in
April 1972.

Aims The Irish Council of Churches is constituted by Christian Communions in Ireland willing to join in united efforts to promote the spiritual, physical, moral and social welfare of the people and the extension of the rule of Christ among all nations and over every region of life.

Member Churches (*14*) Antiochian Orthodox Church in Ireland, Greek Orthodox Church, Lifelink Network of Churches, Lutheran Church in Ireland, Methodist Church in Ireland, Irish District of the Moravian Church, Non-Subscribing Presbyterian Church of Ireland, Presbyterian Church in Ireland, Religious Society of Friends in Ireland, Rock of Ages Cherubim and Seraphim Church, Romanian Orthodox Church in Ireland, Russian Orthodox Church in Ireland, Salvation Army (Ireland Division).

Structure The Council consists of 83 members appointed by the member Churches, together with the Heads of the member Churches and up to ten co-opted members, the General Secretary, Treasurer and immediate Past President of the Council. There is an Annual Meeting and occasional gatherings. The member Churches appoint an Executive Committee, which meets quarterly and is responsible for the oversight of the work of the Council.

The Council continues to serve both jurisdictions (Northern Ireland and the Republic of Ireland) and comprises 14 member churches (see below). It is an associate member of Churches Together in Britain and Ireland and the Conference of European Churches and has links with the World Council of Churches.

(a) It is currently re-assessing its purpose and direction in the rapidly changing contexts both sides of the border; its ecumenical witness across the island and relationships between and beyond its member churches, and its international links through its Board of Overseas Affairs.

(b) It meets quarterly with the Roman Catholic Church in Ireland through the Irish Inter-Church Committee and every 18 months as the Irish Inter-Church Meeting. The last Meeting was held in Dublin in in October 2010, taking the focus of Baptism.

(c) The Inter-Church Committee on Social Issues (ICCSI), a forum of the Irish Inter-Church Committee, currently employs a Project Officer to working on a parish-based integration programme in the Republic.

(d) It is represented on various regional, national and CTBI bodies concerned with regional equality panels, inter-faith, international, mission, overseas aid, racial justice and TV and radio affairs, and the Week of Prayer for Christian Unity.

(e) It is currently serviced by 2 staff based in the Belfast office (Executive Officer and Administrator) and 1 part-time Ecumenical Officer based in Dublin.

More information about the Council's work can be obtained from www.irishchurches.org which includes the most recent Annual Report.

Meissen Agreement with the Evangelical Church in Germany

The Evangelical Church in Germany (Evangelische Kirche in Deutschland – EKD) is a Communion of 23 member churches (mostly *Landeskirchen* or territorial churches). Of these, ten are Lutheran (eight of them forming the United Evangelical Lutheran Church – VELKD), one is purely Reformed, one is predominantly Reformed and twelve are United (seven forming the Evangelical Church of the Union – EKU). In many of the United churches the Lutheran tradition predominates.

In November 1988 the General Synod welcomed the Meissen Common Statement, *On the Way to Visible Unity*, which called for a closer relationship between the Church of England and the German Evangelical Churches. The Meissen Declaration, which it recommended, was approved by the General Synod in July 1990 without dissent, and solemnly affirmed and proclaimed an Act of Synod on 29 January 1991. The Meissen Declaration makes provision for the Church of England and the Evangelical Church in Germany to live in closer fellowship with one another (though not yet with interchangeable ministries) and commits them to work towards the goal of full visible unity. The member churches of the EKD have been designated as churches to which the Ecumenical Canons apply (*see* **Ecumenical Canons**).

The Meissen Commission (the Sponsoring Body for the Church of England–EKD Relations) exists to oversee and encourage relationships (*see* Council for Christian Unity). Fuller information is contained in *The German Evangelical Churches* (CCU Occasional Paper No 1 £2.95 + 35p p&p) and *Anglo-German Ecumenical Links: An Information Pack* (£1 inc. p&p). The text of the Meissen Agreement can be found in *The Meissen Agreement: Texts* (CCU Occasional Paper No 2 £2.10 inc. p&p). These are all available from the Council for Christian Unity. Most of this material is downloadable from the CCU web site at www.cofe.anglican.org/info/ccu.

Co-Chairmen of the Meissen Commission Bishop Dr Friedrich Weber (*EKD*), Rt Revd Nicholas Baines (*Church of England*)

English Co-Secretary of the Meissen Commission
Revd Dr Leslie Nathaniel, Council for Christian
Unity, Church House, Great Smith St, London
SW1P 3AZ   *Tel:* 020 7898 1474

German Co-Secretary of the Meissen Commission
OKR Christoph Ernst, EKD Kirchenamt, Postfach
21 02 20, D – 30402 Hannover, Germany
                             Tel: 00 49 511 2796 127
                             Fax: 00 49 511 2796 725
                    email: christoph.ernst@ekd.de
                                   Web: www.ekd.de

The Reuilly Common Statement: Relations with the French Lutheran and Reformed Churches

Encouraged by the positive reception of the Meissen and Porvoo Agreements, the Anglican Churches of Britain and Ireland engaged in dialogue with the French Reformed and Lutheran Churches, with formal conversations beginning in 1994. These Churches had signalled their desire to enter into closer fellowship with Anglican Churches on the model of the Meissen Agreement, which the Church of England had concluded with the Evangelical Church in Germany (EKD).

The relations between the Anglican and French Churches are steeped in history. Contacts go back to the Middle Ages and took on a new character through the impetus of the Reformation. In later years, at times of turbulence and persecution, churches on both sides of the Channel welcomed those persecuted for their faith.

The conversations involved four participating churches from each side: the four Anglican Churches of the British Isles (the Church of England, the Church of Ireland, the Scottish Episcopal Church and the Church in Wales) and the four French Churches of the Lutheran and Reformed traditions (the Church of the Augsburg Confession of Alsace and Lorraine, the Evangelical Lutheran Church of France, the Reformed Church of Alsace and Lorraine and the Reformed Church of France).

The Reuilly Common Statement which forms the outcome of these conversations takes its name from a community of deaconesses, committed to prayer and meditation. The Statement was approved by the General Synod of the Church of England in November 1999, and the Statement was signed by the participatory Churches in Canterbury and Paris during the summer of 2001.

In common with other ecumenical statements, the Reuilly document first sets the scene, with the history and present context of the participants, and then moves on to current theological issues: the Church as Sign, Instrument and Foretaste of the Kingdom of God; the Church as Communion (*koinonia*); Growth towards Visible Unity; Agreement in Faith and the Apostolicity of the Church and its Ministry.

The Churches declare that they have found a high degree of unity and faith, and outline three areas of future work together: common efforts in witness and service; continuing theological work, particularly on questions of oversight, authority, eucharistic ministry and formally uniting ministries; the practical consequences of the Agreement: prayer, sharing of worship, partnership, and joint ventures across a range of areas.

The implementation of the Agreement is coordinated by a Contact Group. The Anglican Co-Chairman is the Bishop of Guildford and the French Co-Chairman is Pasteur Geoffroy Goetz.

For information on current links and initiatives, contact:
Revd Dr Leslie Nathaniel, The Council for Christian Unity, Church House, Great Smith Street, London SW1P 3AZ

The full text of the Reuilly Declaration, together with background articles on the theological issues and the participating Churches, can be found in *Called to Witness and Service*, Church House Publishing (1999), ISBN 0 7151 5757 4.

Conference of European Churches

General Secretary Ven Colin Williams, PO Box 2100, 150 Route de Ferney, 1211 Geneva 2, Switzerland
                             Tel: 41 22 791 61 11
                             Fax: 41 22 791 62 27
                    email: cec@cec-kek.org
                              Web: ceceurope.org

Born in the era of the 'cold war' some 50 years ago, the CEC emerged into a fragmented and divided continent. Thus it was that Churches of Eastern and Western Europe felt one priority of their work to be promoting international understanding – building bridges. This the CEC has consistently tried to do, always insisting that no 'iron curtain' exists among the Churches.

The supreme governing body of the Conference is the Assembly. Here all 120 member

Churches are represented. The first Assembly was in 1959 and further Assemblies were held in 1960, 1962, 1964, 1967, 1971, 1974, 1979, 1986, 1992, 1997 and 2003. The last assembly was held in Lyon, France, from 15–21 July 2009. It was an opportunity to celebrate the 50th anniversary of CEC.

The CEC initiated the European Ecumenical Assembly 'Peace with Justice' held in Basel in May 1989, co-sponsored with the Council of European Bishops' Conferences (CCEE, Roman Catholic). A second European Ecumenical Assembly was held in Graz, Austria, in 1997 with the theme 'Reconciliation: Gift of God and Source of New Life'. In 2001, CEC and CCEE launched the 'Charta Oecumenica – guidelines for the growing cooperation among the Churches in Europe'. A third European Ecumenical Assembly was held in Sibiu, Romania, in 2007 with the theme 'The light of Christ shines upon all – Hope for renewal and unity in Europe'.

The 40-member Central Committee oversees the implementation of the decisions of the Assembly. A Presidium, drawn from the Central Committee, acts as the Executive Council of the Conference.

Since 1 January 1999 the European Ecumenical Commission on Church and Society (EECCS) with offices in Brussels and Strasbourg integrated with CEC, and, together with CEC's existing work, created the new Church and Society Commission of the CEC. A merger is also planned between CEC and the Brussels-based Churches' Commission for Migrants in Europe (CCME).

The Secretariat in Geneva and offices in Brussels and Strasbourg ensure the continuity of the activities. There are 20.25 staff positions. These include the General Secretary and Secretaries responsible for finance and administration, the Churches in Dialogue Commission and the Church and Society Commission.

Publications include occasional papers, and *Monitor,* a quarterly newsletter.

World Council of Churches

The Church of England has taken its full share in the international ecumenical movement since the Edinburgh Conference of 1910. In 2009 the General Synod made a grant of £108,000 to the General Budget of the World Council of Churches.

Presidium Archbishop Dr Anastasios of Tirana and All Albania (Orthodox Autocephalous Church of Albania), Mr John Taroanui Doom (Maòhi Protestant Church, French Polynesia), Revd Dr Simon Dossou (Protestant Methodist Church in Benin), Revd Dr Soritua Nababan (Protestant Christian Batak Church (HKBP), Indonesia), Revd Dr Ofelia Ortega (Presbyterian-Reformed Church in Cuba), Patriarch Abune Paulos (Ethiopian Orthodox Tewahedo Church), Revd Dr Bernice Powell Jackson (United Church of Christ, USA), Dr Mary Tanner (Church of England)

Moderator of Central Committee Revd Dr Walter Altmann (Evangelical Church of the Lutheran Confession in Brazil)

Vice-Moderators
Metropolitan Prof Dr Gennadios of Sassima (Limouris) (Ecumenical Patriarchate of Constantinople)
Revd Dr Margaretha M. Hendriks-Ririmasse (Protestant Church in the Moluccas, Indonesia)

General Secretary Revd Dr Olav Fykse Tveit (Church of Norway)

Office PO Box 2100, 150 route de Ferney, 1211 Geneva 2, Switzerland   *Tel:* 00 41 22 791 61 11
Fax: 00 41 22 791 03 61
Web: www.oikoumene.com
Cable: Oikoumene Geneva
email: infowcc@wcc-coe.org

The World Council of Churches was brought into formal existence by a resolution of its first Assembly at Amsterdam in 1948.

Member Churches agree to the following basis:

> The World Council of Churches is a fellowship of churches which confess the Lord Jesus Christ as God and Saviour according to the Scriptures and therefore seek to fulfil together their common calling to the glory of the one God, Father, Son and Holy Spirit.

Extract from the Constitution
The primary purpose of the fellowship of churches in the WCC is to call one another to visible unity in one faith and in one eucharistic fellowship, expressed in worship and common life in Christ, through witness and service to the world, and to advance towards that unity in order that the world may believe.

In seeking *koinonia* in faith and life, witness and service, the churches through the Council will:

1. promote the prayerful search for forgiveness and reconciliation in a spirit of mutual

accountability, the development of deeper relationships through theological dialogue, and the sharing of human, spiritual and material resources with one another;
2. facilitate common witness in each place and in all places, and support each other in their work for mission and evangelism;
3. express their commitment to *diakonia* in serving human need, breaking down barriers between people, promoting one human family in justice and peace, and upholding the integrity of creation, so that all may experience the fullness of life;
4. nurture the growth of an ecumenical consciousness through processes of education and a vision of life in community rooted in each particular cultural context;
5. assist each other in their relationships to and with people of other faith communities;
6. foster renewal and growth in unity, worship, mission and service.
In order to strengthen the one ecumenical movement, the Council will:

1. nurture relations with and among churches, especially within but also beyond its membership;
2. establish and maintain relations with national councils, regional conferences of churches, organizations of Christian World Communions and other ecumenical bodies;
3. support ecumenical initiatives at regional, national and local levels;
4. facilitate the creation of networks among ecumenical organizations;
5. work towards maintaining the coherence of the one ecumenical movement in its diverse manifestations.
The World Council shall offer counsel and provide opportunity for united action in matters of common interest.
It may take action on behalf of constituent churches only in such matters as one or more of them may commit to it and only on behalf of such churches.

The World Council shall not legislate for the churches; nor shall it act for them in any manner except as indicated or as may hereafter be specified by the constituent churches.

The WCC is governed by an Assembly of Member Churches, a Central Committee, and by an Executive Committee and other subordinate bodies as may be established. Assemblies are held every six to eight years and have been as follows:

1. AMSTERDAM, 1948 – theme: 'Man's Disorder and God's Design'
2. EVANSTON, 1954 – theme: 'Christ the Hope of the World'
3. NEW DELHI, 1961– theme: 'Jesus Christ, the Light of the World'
4. UPPSALA, 1968 – theme: 'Behold, I Make All Things New'
5. NAIROBI, 1975 – theme: 'Jesus Christ Frees and Unites'
6. VANCOUVER, 1983 – theme: 'Jesus Christ the Life of the World'
7. CANBERRA, 1991– theme: 'Come, Holy Spirit – Renew the Whole Creation'
8. HARARE 1998 – theme: 'Turn to God – Rejoice in Hope'
9. PORTO ALEGRE 2006 – theme: 'God, in your grace, transform the world'

The Central Committee elected by the Ninth Assembly includes two members of the Church of England: the Rt Revd Thomas Frederick Butler, Bishop of Southwark (now retired), and Dr Mary Tanner, one of the WCC presidents.

The WCC has 349 member churches, including 38 which are associated. Almost every Church of the Anglican Communion is included, together with most of the Orthodox Churches and all the main Protestant traditions. The Roman Catholic Church is not a member but has sent official observers to all main WCC meetings since 1960. It is a full member of the Faith and Order Commission of the WCC.

Regional Conferences

CONFERENCE OF EUROPEAN CHURCHES
See page 454.

Who's Who   **PART 7**

Abbreviations used in the biographies

AABM ..... Archbishops' Adviser for Bishops' Ministry
ABIST .... Associate, British Institute of Surgical
Technology
ABM .... Advisory Board of Ministry (now
Ministry Division)
AC .... Archbishops' Council
ACA ..... Associate, Institute of Chartered Accountants
ACC .... Anglican Consultative Council
ACCM .... Advisory Council for the Church's Ministry
(now Ministry Division)
ACE .... Associateship of the College of Education
Member, Association of Conference Executives
ACGI ... Associate, City and Guilds of London Institute
ACIB .... Associate, Chartered Institute of Bankers
(formerly AIB)
ACII .... Associate, Chartered Insurance Institute
ACIS .. Associate, Institute of Chartered Secretaries and
Administrators
ACMA .. Associate, Chartered Institute of Management
Accountants (formerly ACWA)
ACORA ..... Archbishops' Commission on Rural Areas
ACP .... Associate, College of Preceptors
ACS .... Additional Curates Society
ACertCM .... Archbishop of Canterbury's Certificate in
Church Music
AD .... Area Dean
ADipR .... Archbishop's Diploma for Readers
AHA .... Area Health Authority
AIA .... Associate, Institute of Actuaries
AKC .... Associate, King's College London
ALA .... Associate, Library Association
ALCD .... Associate, London College of Divinity
ALCM .... Associate, London College of Music
APR .... Association for Promoting Retreats
ARC .... Anglican-Roman Catholic
ARCIC .... Anglican-Roman Catholic International
Commission
ARCM .... Associate, Royal College of Music
ARCO .... Associate, Royal College of Organists
ARCO(CHM) .... Associate, Royal College of Organists
with Diploma in Choir Training
ARCS .... Associate, Royal College of Science
ARMIT .... Associate, Royal Melbourne Institute of
Technology
ASWA .... Anglican Society for the Welfare of Animals
ATCL ...... Associate, Trinity College of Music London
ATII .... Associate Member, Institute of Taxation
Aberd .... Aberdeen
Abp .... Archbishop
Aberw .... Aberystwyth
Acad .... Academy
AdDipEd .... Advanced Diploma in Education
Admin . Administration, Administrative, Administrator
Adn .... Archdeacon
Adnry .... Archdeaconry
Adv .... Adviser, Advisory
Agric .... Agricultural, Agriculture
Aid .... Aidan('s)
Alb .... Alban('s)
Andr .... Andrew('s), Andrews
Angl .... Anglican(s)
Ant .... Anthony('s)
Appt .... Appointment(s), appointed
Ascen .... Ascension
Assoc .... Associate, Association
Asst .... Assistant
Assur .... Assurance

Aug .... Augustine('s)
Auth .... Authority
b .... Born
B & W .... (Diocese of) Bath and Wells
BA .... Bachelor of Arts
BAGUPA .... Bishop's Advisory Group on UPAs
BBC .... British Broadcasting Corporation
BCC .... British Council of Churches (now see CCBI)
BCh or BChir Bachelor of Surgery (also see BS and ChB)
BD .... Bachelor of Divinity
BDS .... Bachelor of Dental Surgery
BEd .... Bachelor of Education
BFBS .... British and Foreign Bible Society
BLitt .... Bachelor of Letters
BM .... Board of Mission
BMU .... Board for Mission and Unity
Bmet .... Bachelor of Metallurgy
BMus .... Bachelor of Music (also see MusB or MusBac)
BNC .... Brasenose College
BPS .... British Pharmacological Society
BRF .... Bible Reading Fellowship
BS .... Bachelor of Science (also see BSc), Bachelor of
Surgery (also see BCh, BChir and ChB)
BSR .... Board for Social Responsibility
BSc .... Bachelor of Science (also see BS)
BSocSc .... Bachelor of Social Science (also see BSSc)
BTh Btheol .... Bachelor of Theology (also see STB)
BVM&S . Bachelor of Veterinary Medicine and Surgery
BVSc .... Bachelor of Veterinary Science
BYFC .... British Youth for Christ
Bapt .... Baptist('s)
Barn .... Barnabas('s)
Bart .... Bartholomew('s)
Bd .... Board
Bedf .... Bedford
Bibl .... Biblical
Birm .... (Diocese of) Birmingham
Blackb .... (Diocese of) Blackburn
Boro .... Borough
Bp .... Bishop
Br .... British
Bradf .... (Diocese of) Bradford
Bris .... (Diocese of) Bristol
Bucks .... Buckingham(shire)
C .... Curate
C of E .... Church of England
C of I .... Church of Ireland
C-in-c .... Curate-in-charge
CA .... Church Army Member, Institute of Chartered
Accountants of Scotland
CAB .... Citizens Advice Bureau
CAC .... Crown Appointments Commission
(now Crown Nominations Commission)
CACLB .... Churches Advisory Council for Local
Broadcasting (now Churches' Media Council)
CB .... Companion, Order of the Bath
CBE .... Commander, Order of the British Empire
CBF .... Central Board of Finance
CBI .... Confederation of British Industry
CCC .... Corpus Christi College, Council for the Care of
Churches
CCCS Commonwealth and Continental Church Society
CCHH .... Churches Council for Health and Healing
CCLA .... Churches, Charities and Local Authorities
CCOM .... Churches' Commission on Mission
CCRJ .... Churches' Commission for Racial Justice
CCU .... Council for Christian Unity

CCYW .... Certificate in Community Youth Work
CD .... Canadian Forces Decoration, Conventional District
CDC .... Clergy Discipline Commission
CEC .... Conference of European Churches
CECC .... Church of England Committee for Communications
CEDR .... Centre for Dispute Resolution
CEEC .... Church of England Evangelical Council
CEIG .... Christian Ethical Investment Group
CEM .... Christian Education Movement
CERT TH .... Certificate in Theology
CF .... Chaplain to the Forces
CFE .... College of Further Education
CHRISM .... Christians in Secular Ministry
CJGS ...... Community of the Companions of Jesus the Good Shepherd
CLASP .. Churches Linked Across Staffs & the Potteries
CME .... Continuing Ministerial Education
CMEAC ...... Committee for Minority Ethnic Anglican Concerns
CMS ... Church Mission Society, Church Music Society
CNC .... Crown Nominations Commission
CPA .... Chartered Patent Attorney
CPAS .... Church Pastoral Aid Society
CPC ...... Certificate of Professional Competence (Road Transport)
CQSW .... Certificate of Qualification in Social Work
CR .... Community of the Resurrection (Mirfield)
CRAC ... Central Religious Advisory Committee of the BBC and ITA
CRC .... Central Readers Council
CSC .... Community of the Servants of the Cross
CSEM .... Certificate in Special Education Management
CSO .... Central Statistical Office
CSR .... Council for Social Responsibility
CSWG .... Community of the Servants of the Will of God
CTBI .... Churches Together in Britain and Ireland
CTE .... Churches Together in England
CTH .... Certificate in Theology
CTM .... Certificate in Theology for Ministry
CU .... Church Union
CUF .... Church Urban Fund
CYCW ...... Certificate in Youth and Community Work
CYFA .... Church Youth Fellowships Association
Cam .... Cambridge
Cambs .... Cambridgeshire
Can .... Canon
Cant .... (Diocese of) Canterbury
Carl .... (Diocese of) Carlisle
Cath .... Catharine('s)/Catherine('s)
Cathl .... Cathedral
Cchem .... Certified/Chartered Chemist
CdipAF . Certified Diploma in Accounting and Finance
Cen .... Centre, Center, Central
Ceng .... Chartered Engineer
Cert CT .... Certificate in Ceramic Technology
CertEd .... Certificate of Education
CertMBiol .... Certificate of Microbiology
Ch .... Christ('s), Church(es)
Chair .... Chairman, Chairwoman
Chan .... Chancellor
Chapl .... Chaplain(s), Chaplaincy(ies)
ChB .... Bachelor of Surgery (also see BCh, BChir and BS)
Ch Ch .... Christ Church
Chelmsf .... (Diocese of) Chelmsford
Ches .... (Diocese of) Chester
Chich .... (Diocese of) Chichester
Chr .... Christian(s)
Chris .... Christopher('s)
Chu .... Churchill

Cl-in-c .... Cleric-in-charge
Clem .... Clement('s)
Cllr .... Councillor/Counsellor
Cmaths .... Chartered Mathematician
Co .... Company, County(ies)
Co-ord .... Coordinator, Coordinating
Coll .... College
Colleg .... Collegiate
Com .... Community
Commn .... Commission
Commr .... Commissioner
Comp .... Comprehensive
Conf .... Confederation, Conference
Consult .... Consultant/Consultancy
Corp .... Corporation
Coun .... Council
Conv .... Convocation
Cphys ... Chartered Physicist of the Institute of Physics
Cov .... (Diocese of) Coventry
Cstat .... Chartered Statistician
Ctee .... Committee
Cuth .... Cuthbert('s)
DAC Diocesan Advisory Committee, Diploma in Adult Counselling
DBE .... Diocesan Board of Education
DBF .... Diocesan Board of Finance
DCH .... Diploma in Child Health
DCL .... Doctor of Civil Law
DCO .... Diocesan Communications Officer
DD .... Doctor of Divinity
DDO .... Diocesan Director of Ordinands
DDS .... Doctor of Dental Surgery
DHSM .... Diploma in Health Service Management
DHSS .... Department of Health and Social Security
DIC .... Diploma of Membership of Imperial College London
DL .... Deputy Lieutenant
DLC .... Diploma of Loughborough College
DMS .... Diploma in Management Studies
DN .... Diploma in Nursing
DOE .... Department of the Environment
DPA .... Diploma in Public Administration
DPS .... Diploma in Pastoral Studies
DMin .... Doctor of Ministry
DPhil .... Doctor of Philosophy (also see PhD)
DProf .... Doctor in Professional Studies
DRACSC . Deployment, Remuneration and Conditions of Service Committee
DSPT .... Diploma in Social and Pastoral Theology
DSS ... Diploma in Social Studies Department of Social Security
DSc .... Doctor of Science (also see ScD)
DTI .... Department of Trade and Industry
DTS .... Diploma in Theological Studies
DTh .... Doctor of Theology (also see ThD)
DUniv .... Doctor of the University
Dav .... David('s)
Dep .... Deputy
Dept .... Department
Devel .... Development
Dio .... Diocese
Dioc .... Diocesan
Dip .... Diploma
DipAdEd .... Diploma in Advanced Education
DipBA .... Diploma in Business Administration
DipC .... Diploma in Counselling
DipChemEng .... Diploma in Chemical Engineering
DipEd .... Diploma in Education
DipHE .... Diploma in Higher Education
DipLA .... Diploma in Liturgy and Architecture
DipLRM .... Diploma in Leadership, Renewal and Mission Studies
DipMin .... Diploma in Ministry

DipN .... Diploma in Nursing
DipPallMed .... Diploma in Palliative Medicine
DipRJ .... Diploma in Retail Jewellery
DipSE .... Diploma in Special Education
DipSW .... Diploma in Social Work
DipSocSc .... Diploma in Social Sciences
DipTh .... Diploma in Theology
Dip UEM .... Diploma in Urban Estate Management
Dir .... Director
Distr .... District
Div .... Divinity, Division
Dn .... Deacon
Dny .... Deanery
Doct .... Doctrinal, Doctrine
Dom .... Domestic
Down .... Downing
Dr .... Doctor
Dss .... Deaconess
Dub .... Dublin
Dur .... (Diocese of) Durham
E .... East, Eastern
EAMTC ...... East Anglian Ministerial Training Course
ECUSA .... Episcopal Church of the United States of
                                                    America
EFAC .... Evangelical Fellowship in the Anglican
                                                 Communion
EIG . Ecclesiastical Insurance Group (now Ecclesiastical
                                                  Insurance)
EJM(RC) .... Ecclesiastical Jurisdiction Measure
                                         (Revision Committee)
EKD .... Evangelische Kirche Deutschland
EPA .... European Patent Attorney
ERMC .... Eastern Region Ministry Course
Eccl .... Ecclesiastical
Ecum .... Ecumenical
Ed .... Editor, Editorial
Edin .... (Diocese of) Edinburgh
Edm .... Edmund('s)
Eds .... Edmundsbury
Educ .... Education
Educl .... Educational
Edw .... Edward('s)
Eliz .... Elizabeth('s)
Em .... Emmanuel('s)
Emer .... Emeritus
Eng .... Engineering
Environ .... Environmental
Engl .... English
Episc .... Episcopal Episcopalian
Eur . (Diocese of) Gibraltar in Europe Europe, European
EurIng .... European Engineer
Eur Phys .... European Physicist
Ev .... Evangelist('s), Evangelists
Evang .... Evangelical, Evangelism
Ex .... (Diocese of) Exeter
Exam .... Examining
Exec .... Executive
FAC .... Fabric Advisory Committee
FASC .... Fellow, Academy of St Cecilia
FBA .... Fellow, British Academy
FBCS .... Fellow, British Computer Society
FCA .... Fellow, Institute of Chartered Accountants
FCAA .... Fellow, Cyprus Association of Actuaries
FCCA .... Fellow, Chartered Association of Certified
                      Accountants (formerly FACCA)
FCEM .... Fellow, College of Emergency Medicine
FCIM .... Fellow, Chartered Institute of Marketing
                                         (formerly FInstM)
FC INST M ... Fellow, Chartered Institute of Marketing
FCIOB .... Fellow, Chartered Institute of Building
FCIPD .... Fellow, Chartered Institute of Personnel and
                      Development (formerly FIPD)
FCP .... Fellow, College of Preceptors

FDSRCS .... Fellow in Dental Surgery, Royal College of
                              Surgeons of England
FE .... Further Education
FGMS .... Fellow, Guild of Musicians and Singers
F&GP .... Finance and General Purposes
FIA .... Fellow, Institute of Actuaries
FIBMS .... Fellow, Institute of Biomedical Sciences
FIHT .... Fellow of the Institution of Highways and
                              Transportation
FIMA .... Fellow, Institute of Mathematics and its
                              Applications
FIMgt .... Fellow, Institute of Management
FJMU .... Fellow, Liverpool John Moores University
FKC .... Fellow, King's College London
FLAME .... Family Life and Marriage Education
FOAG .... Faith and Order Advisory Group
FPMI .... Fellow, Pensions Management Institute
FRAI .... Fellow, Royal Anthropological Institute
FRAeS .... Fellow, Royal Aeronautical Society
FRAS .... Fellow, Royal Astronomical Society
FRCO .... Fellow, Royal College of Organists
FRCOG ..... Fellow, Royal College of Obstetricians and
                              Gynaecologists
FRCOphth . Fellow, Royal College of Ophthalmologists
FRCS .... Fellow, Royal College of Physicians and
                              Surgeons of England
FRCSE or FRCSEd .. Fellow, Royal College of Surgeons
                              of Edinburgh
FRHistS .... Fellow, Royal Historical Society
FRICS .... Fellow, Royal Institution of Chartered
                      Surveyors (formerly FLAS and FSI)
FRIPHH .... Fellow, Royal Institute of Public Health
                              and Hygiene
FRGS .... Fellow, Royal Geographical Society
FRS .... Fellow, Royal Society
FRSA .... Fellow, Royal Society of Arts
FRSC .... Fellow, Royal Society of Chemistry
                              (formerly FRIC)
FRSL .... Fellow, Royal Society of Literature
FRSM .... Fellow, Royal Society of Medicine
FSA .... Fellow, Society of Antiquaries
FSCA .... Fellow, Royal Society of Company and
                      Commercial Accountants
FTII .... Fellow, Institute of Taxation
Fell(s) .... Fellow(s), Fellowship
Fest .... Festival
Fin .... Financial
Fitzw .... Fitzwilliam
Foundn .... Foundation
Fran .... Francis(')
G&C .... Gonville and Caius
GAD .... Government Actuary's Department
GEC .... General Electric Company
GLC .... Greater London Council
GOE .... General Ordination Examination
GP .... General Practitioner
GS .... General Synod
Gabr .... Gabriel('s)
Gd .... Good
Gen .... General
Geo .... George('s)
Gib .... Gibraltar
Glas ..... (Diocese of) Glasgow and Galloway, Glasgow
Glos .... Gloucestershire
Glouc .... (Diocese of) Gloucester
Gov .... Governor
Grp .... Group
Gr .... Grammar
Greg .... Gregorian
Gt .... Great
Guildf .... (Diocese of) Guildford
H .... Holy
H&FE .... Higher and Further Education

HA	Health Authority
HCC	Hospital Chaplaincies Council
HDipEd	Higher Diploma in Education
HE	Higher Education
HM	Her (or His) Majesty('s)
HMP	Her Majesty's Prison(s)
HNC	Higher National Certificate
HND	Higher National Diploma
HRH	Her/His Royal Highness
Hatf	Hatfield
Hd	Head
Heref	(Diocese of) Hereford
Hertf	Hertford
Herts	Hertfordshire
Hist	History
Ho	House
Hon	Honorary, Honourable
Hosp(s)	Hospital(s)
IARCCUM	International Anglican – Roman Catholic Commission on Unity and Mission
IBA	Independent Broadcasting Authority
ICI	Imperial Chemical Industries
ICS	Intercontinental Church Society
IDC	Inter-Diocesan Certificate
IMEC	Initial Ministerial Education Committee
IOM	Isle of Man
IPR	Institute of Public Relations
ITV	Independent Television
Imp	Imperial
Inc, Incorp	Incorporated
Incumb	Incumbent
Ind	Industry, Industrial
Info	Information
Insp	Inspector, Inspectorate
Inst	Institute, Institution
Intercon	Intercontinental
Internat	International
Ips	Ipswich
JP	Justice of the Peace
Jas	James('s)
Jasp	Jasper('s)
Jes	Jesus
Jo	John('s)
Jos	Joseph('s)
Jt or jt	Joint
Jun	Junior
K	King('s)
KA	Knight of St Andrew, Order of Barbados
KCVO	Knight Commander, Royal Victorian Order
KHS	Knight of the Holy Sepulchre
Kath	Katharine('s), Katherine('s)
LDSRCS(Eng)	Licentiate in Dental Surgery of the Royal College of Surgeons (of England)
LEA	Local Education Authority
LEP	Local Ecumenical Project
LICeram	Licenciate, Institute of Ceramics
LLAM	Licentiate, London Academy of Music and Dramatic Art
LLB	Bachelor of Laws
LLD	Doctor of Laws
LLM	Master of Laws
LMH	Lady Margaret Hall
LNSM	Local Non-stipendiary Minister (or Ministry)
LRAM	Licentiate, Royal Academy of Music
LRCP	Licentiate, Royal College of Physicians
LRPS	Licentiate, Royal Photographic Society
LRSC	Licentiate, Royal Society of Chemistry
LSE	London School of Economics and Political Science
LTCL	Licentiate, Trinity College of Music, London
LTh	Licentiate in Theology (also see LST)
LVO	Lieutenant, Royal Victorian Order
Lab	Laboratory
Lamp	Lampeter

Lanc	Lancaster
Lancs	Lancashire
Laur	Laurence('s)
Lawr	Lawrence('s)
Lect	Lecturer
Leic	(Diocese of) Leicester
Leics	Leicestershire
Leon	Leonard('s)
Legis	Legislative
Lib	Librarian, Library
Lic	Licence, Licensed, Licentiate
Lich	(Diocese of) Lichfield
Linc	(Diocese of) Lincoln
Lincs	Lincolnshire
Liturg	Liturgical
Liv	(Diocese of) Liverpool
Llan	(Diocese of) Llandaff
Lon	(Diocese of) London
Loughb	Loughborough
Lt	Little
Ltd	Limited
M	Member
M&AA	Michael and All Angels
MA	Master of Arts
MB,BS &MB,ChB	Conjoint degree of Bachelor of Medicine, Bachelor of Surgery
MBC	Metropolitan (or Municipal) Borough Council
MBCS	Member, British Computer Society
MBE	Member, Order of the British Empire
MCIH	Corporate Member, Chartered Institute of Housing
MCIJ	Member, Chartered Institute of Journalists
MCIM	Member, Chartered Institute of Marketing (formerly MInstM)
MCIPD	Member, Chartered Institute of Personnel and Development (formerly MIPD)
MCLIP	Member, Chartered Institute of Library and Information Professionals
MCS	Master of Christian Studies
MCSP	Member, Chartered Society of Physiotherapy
MCST	Member, College of Speech Therapists
MCT	Member, Association of Corporate Treasurers
MDCT	Manager's Diploma in Ceramic Technology
MDiv	Master of Divinity
MEd	Master of Education
MIBC	Member, Institute of Business Counsellors
MICE	Member, Institution of Civil Engineers (formerly AMICE)
MIChemE	Member, Institution of Chemical Engineers
MIEE	Member, Institution of Electrical Engineers (formerly AMIEE MIERE)
MIMA	Member, Institute of Management Accountants
MIMgt	Member, Institute of Management
MIOT	Member, Institute of Operating Theatre Technicians
MIPD	Member, Institute of Personnel and Development (now see MCIPD)
MIPR	Member, Institute of Public Relations
MIStructE	Member, Institute of Structural Engineers
MInstD	Member, Institute of Directors
MInstGA	Member, Institute of Group Analysis
MInstP	Member, Institute of Physics
MLitt	Master of Letters
MOD	Ministry of Defence
MOW	Movement for the Ordination of Women
MP	Member of Parliament
MPA	Mission and Public Affairs
MPhil	Master of Philosophy
MRCGP	Member, Royal College of General Practitioners
MRCS	Member, Royal College of Surgeons
MRCVS	Member, Royal College of Veterinary Surgeons

MRSC .... Member, Royal Society of Chemistry	P .... Patron(s), Priest
MSc .... Master of Science	P in O .... Priest in Ordinary
MTech .... Master of Technology	P-in-c .... Priest-in-charge
MTh or MTheol .... Master of Theology (also see	PACTA .... Professional Associate, Clinical Theology
STM and ThM)	Association
MU .... Mothers' Union	PCC .... Parochial Church Council
Magd .... Magdalen('s)/Magdalene('s)	PGCE .... Postgraduate Certificate in Education
Man .... (Diocese of) Manchester	PNG .... Papua New Guinea
Man Dir .... Managing Director	POT .... Post Ordination Training
Mansf .... Mansfield	PPS .... Parliamentary Private Secretary
Marg .... Margaret('s)	PR .... Public Relations
Mart .... Martin('s)	PRCC .. Policy and Resources Coordinating Committee
Marlboro .... Marlborough	PRO .... Public Relations Officer
Matt .... Matthew('s)	PV .... Priest Vicar
Mert .... Merton	PWM .... Partnership for World Mission
Meth .... Methodist	Par .... Parish(es)
Metrop .... Metropolitan	Parl .... Parliamentary
Mgr .... Manager	Pastl .... Pastoral
Mgt .... Management	Patr .... Patrick('s), Patronage
Mich .... Michael('s), Michael and All Angels	Pemb .... Pembroke(shire)
Mil .... Military	Perm .... Permission
Min .... Minister, Ministries, Ministry, Minor	Pet .... Peter('s)
Minl .... Ministerial	Peterb .... (Diocese of) Peterborough
Miss .... Mission('s), Missionary	Peterho .... Peterhouse
Missr .... Missioner	PhD .... Doctor of Philosophy (also see DPhil)
Mod .... Moderator	Phil .... Phil(l)ip('s)
Movt .... Movement	Pk .... Park
Mss .... Manuscripts	plc .... public limited company
Mt .... Mount	Poly .... Polytechnic
Mus .... Music	Portsm .... (Diocese of) Portsmouth
MusB or MusBac .... Bachelor of Music (also see BMus)	Prchr .... Preacher
N .... North	Preb .... Prebendary
NACRO .... National Association for the Care and	Prec .... Precentor
Rehabilitation of Offenders	Prep .... Preparatory
NAHT .... National Association of Headteachers	Pres .... President
NCA .... National Certificate in Agriculture	Prin .... Principal
NCIs .... National Church Institutions	Pris .... Prison(s)
NDA .... National Diploma in Agriculture	Priv .... Private
NDD .... National Diploma in Design	Prof .... Professor, Professorial
NEOC ..... North East Oecumenical Course North East	Prov .... Provost, Provisions
Ordination Course	Ptnr .... Partner
NHS .... National Health Service	Pty .... Party
NNEB .... National Nursery Examination Board	pt .... part-time
NSM .... Non-stipendiary Minister (or Ministry)	QC .... Queen's Counsel
NSW .... New South Wales (Australia)	QHC .... Queen's Honorary Chaplain
NT .... New Testament	Qu .... Queen('s), Queens'
NTMTC .... North Thames Ministerial Training Course	R .... Rector, Royal
NW .... North West/Northwestern	RAMC .... Royal Army Medical Corps
NZ .... New Zealand	RCHME . Royal Commission on Historical Monuments
Nat .... National	of England
Newc .... (Diocese of) Newcastle	RAF .... Royal Air Force
Nic .... Nicholas('s)/Nicolas('s)	RC .... Roman Catholic
Nn .... Northern	RCO .... Royal College of Organists
Norf .... Norfolk	RD .... Royal Navy Reserve Decoration, Rural Dean
Norw .... (Diocese of) Norwich	RE .... Religious Education
Northn .... Northampton	RGN .... Registered General Nurse
Nottm .... Nottingham	RHM .... Rank Hovis McDougall
Notts .... Nottinghamshire	RIBA .... (Member) Royal Institute of British Architects
Nuff .... Nuffield	(formerly ARIBA)
OAM .... Order of Australia Medal	RICS .... Royal Institute of Chartered Surveyors
OBE .... Officer, Order of the British Empire	RM .... Registered Midwife
OCF .... Officiating Chaplain to the Forces	RMA or RMC .... Royal Military Academy (formerly
OGS .... Oratory of the Good Shepherd	College), Sandhurst
OLM .... Ordained Local Minister (or Ministry)	RMN .... Registered Mental Nurse
ONC .... Ordinary National Certificate	RN .... Royal Navy
OStJ ... Officer, Most Venerable Order of the Hospital of	RSA .... Royal Society of Arts, Republic of South Africa
St John of Jerusalem	RSCM .... Royal School of Church Music
OT .... Old Testament	RSIN .... Rural Stress Information Network
OTC .... Open Theology College	Raph .... Raphael('s)
OU, Open Univ .... Open University	Rdr(s) .... Reader(s)
Ord .... Ordinand(s), Ordination	Red .... Redundant
Ox .... (Diocese of) Oxford	Relig .... Religious
Oxon .... Oxfordshire	Relns .... Relations

Rep(s) .... Representative(s)
Res .... Residential, Residentiary
Resp .... Responsibility
Resurr .... Resurrection
Rev .... Review
Revd .... Reverend
Rich .... Richard('s)
Ripon .... Ripon and Leeds
Roch .... (Diocese of) Rochester
Rsch .... Research
Rt .... Right
Rtd or rtd .... Retired
S .... South, Southern
S&Man .... (Diocese of) Sodor and Man
SAMS .... South American Mission Society
SAOMC .... St Albans and Oxford Ministry Course
SASRA .... Soldiers' and Airmen's Scripture Readers
Association
SBL .... Society of Biblical Literature
SCM .... State Certified Midwife, Student Christian
Movement
SDMTS .... Southern Dioceses Ministerial
Training Scheme
SE .... South East
SEITE ... South East Institute for Theological Education
SOAS .... School of Oriental and African Studies
SOSc .... Society of Ordained Scientists
SPCK ...... Society for Promoting Christian Knowledge
SPI .... Society of Practitioners of Insolvency
SRN .... State Registered Nurse
SRP .... State Registered Physiotherapist
SS .... Saints/Saints', Sidney Sussex
SSC ..... Secretarial Studies Certificate, Societas Sanctae
Crucis (Society of the Holy Cross)
SSF .... Society of St Francis
SSM .... Society of the Sacred Mission
SST .... Society for the Study of Theology
STB .... Bachelor of Theology (also see BTh)
STETS ... Southern Theological Education and Training
Scheme
STh .... Scholar in Theology (also see ThSchol)
STL .... Reader (or Professor) of Sacred Theology
STM ..... Master of Theology (also see MTh or MTheol
and ThM)
SU .... Scripture Union
SW .... South West
Sacr .... Sacrist, Sacristan
Salis .... Salisbury
Sarum .... (Diocese of) Salisbury
Sav .... Saviour('s)
ScD .... Doctor of Science (also see DSc)
Sch(s) .... School(s)
Sec(s) .... Secretary(ies)
Secdry .... Secondary
Selw .... Selwyn
Sem .... Seminary
Sen .... Senior
Sheff .... (Diocese of) Sheffield
Shep .... Shepherd
Shrops .... Shropshire
So .... Souls, Souls'
Soc .... Social, Society
Som .... Somerset
Southn .... Southampton
Sq .... Square
St .... Saint
St Alb .... (Diocese of) St Albans
St And .... (Diocese of) St Andrews, Dunkeld and
Dunblane
St As .... (Diocese of) St Asaph
St D .... (Diocese of) St Davids
St E&I .... (Diocese of) St Edmundsbury and Ipswich

Ste .... Sainte
Steph .... Stephen('s)
Stg .... Standing
Strg .... Steering
Suff .... Suffragan
Supt .... Superintendent
S'wark .... Southwark
S'well .... Southwell
Syn .... Synod
TCert .... Teacher's Certificate
TEFL .... Teacher of English as a Foreign Language
TETC .. Theological Education and Training Committee
TM .... Team Minister (or Ministry)
TR .... Team Rector
TV .... Team Vicar, Television
Tchr .... Teacher
Tdip .... Teacher's Diploma
Tech .... Technical, Technology
Techn .... Technician
Th, Theol .... Theological
ThD .... Doctorate in Theology (also see DTh)
ThM ..... Master of Theology (also see MTh or MTheol
and STM)
Thos .... Thomas('s)
Tm .... Team
Tr .... Trainer
Treas .... Treasurer('s)
Trg .... Training
Trin .... Trinity
UCCF .. Universities and Colleges Christian Fellowship
of Evangelical Unions (formerly IVF)
UCE .... University of Central England
UCL .... University College London
UEA .... University of East Anglia
UMIST ... University of Manchester Institute of Science
and Technology
UPA .... Urban Priority Area (or Areas)
URC .... United Reformed Church
USCL .... United Society for Christian Literature
USPG .... United Society for the Propagation of the
Gospel (formerly SPG, UMCA, and CMD)
UWE .... University of the West of England
UWIST .... University of Wales Institute of Science
and Technology
Univ .... University
V .... Vicar, Virgin('s)
VRSC .... Vocations, Recruitment and Selection
Committee
Vc .... Vice
Ven .... Venerable
Vis .... Visiting
Voc .... Vocational, Vocations
Vol .... Voluntary
W .... West, Western
w .... with
WATCH .... Women and the Church
WCC .... World Council of Churches
WEA .... Workers' Educational Association
WEMTC .. West of England Ministerial Training Course
Wadh .... Wadham
Wakef .... (Diocese of) Wakefield
Warw .... Warwickshire
Westf .... Westfield
Westmr .... Westminster
Wilf .... Wilfred('s), Wilfrid('s)
Wilts .... Wiltshire
Winch .... (Diocese of) Winchester
Wkg .... Working
Worc .... (Diocese of) Worcester
Wrdn .... Warden
YMCA .... Young Men's Christian Association

WHO'S WHO

A Directory of General Synod members, together with those suffragan bishops, deans and archdeacons who are not members of General Synod, and principal staff members of the General Synod, the Archbishops' Council, the Church Commissioners, the Pensions Board and Lambeth Palace, and Church Commissioners who are not members of General Synod. General Synod members are distinguished by the date of their membership, printed at the end of their entry, following the letters GS. Current membership of the General Synod is denoted by the lack of a closing date. The information contained here is supplied by the individuals concerned and no warranty is given as to its accuracy.

ADCOCK, Mrs Isabel Ruth, LLB
47 East Street Tollesbury Maldon Essex CM9 8QD [CHELMSFORD] *b* 1949 *educ* Gillingham Sch; Mid-Essex Tech Coll; Inns of Court Sch; *CV* Barrister 1975–81; 6th Form Tchr 1996–99; Tcher 1999–2000; Lect Legal practice 2000; Legal Aid Cttee 2000–05 GS 2000–05; 2010– *Tel:* 01621 860326
email: Adcocki@hotmail.co.uk

AINSWORTH, Revd Janina Helen Margaret, BEd, MA
Church House Great Smith St London SW1P 3AZ [CHIEF EDUCATION OFFICER, GENERAL SECRETARY, EDUCATION DIVISION AND NATIONAL SOCIETY] *b* 1950 *educ* Nottm High Sch for Girls; Homerton Coll Cam; Univ of Lanc; Ripon Coll Cuddesdon; *CV* Tchr-in-c RE Manor Sch Arbury Cambs 1974–75; Tchr-in-c RE Greaves Sch Lanc 1975–79; Pt Lect St Mart Coll Lanc 1979–82; Educ Liaison Worker Tameside Coun for Racial Equality 1983–84; RE Adv Man DBE 1986–98; Dioc Dir of Educ Man Dioc 1998–2006; deacon 2005, p 2006, NSM E Farnsworth and Kearsley, Man 2005–07; Chief Educ Officer and Gen Sec Nat Soc from 2007
Tel: 020 7898 1500
Fax: 020 7898 1520
email: janina.ainsworth@c-of-e.org.uk

ALBAN JONES, Revd Timothy Morris, BA, MBE
The Vicarage Cross Green Soham, Ely Cambridgeshire, CB7 5DU [ELY] *b* 1964 *educ* Wycliffe Coll; Warwich Univ; Ripon Coll Cuddesdon;; *CV* Asst C, Tupsley 1988–93;Chapl of St Michael's Hospice, Hereford 1990–92; TV Ross Team Ministry 1993–2000; Chapl with Deaf People 1994–2000; Dioc Voc Adv 1995–1999; V Soham and Wicken from 2000; POT Tutor from 2006; M Dioc Voc Panel from 2007; M Dioc Board of Patronage from 2009; Rural Dean of Fordham and Quy from 2010; Selection Off Board of Readers from 2010 GS 2010– *Tel:* 01353720423
email: vicar@soham.org.uk

ALDERTON-FORD, Revd Jonathan Laurence, B Th
Church Office Christ Church Moreton Hall Symonds Rd Bury St Edmunds IP32 7EW [ST EDMUNDSBURY AND IPSWICH] *b* 1957 *educ* Denes High Sch Lowestoft; Nottm Univ; St Jo Coll Nottm; *CV* C St Faith Gaywood Norw 1985–87; C St Andr Herne Bay 1987–90; Min Ch Ch LEP Moreton Hall from

1990; Chair Mid Anglia New Wine Network; Chair Passion Play for Bury St Edm; Elected M Dioc Commn from 2008; Trustee Premier Christian Radio; Can St Eds Cath from 2008 GS 1999– *Tel:* 01284 769956 (Home)
01284 725391 (Office)
Fax: 01284 725391
email: minister@ccmh.org.uk

ALEXANDER, Mrs April Rosemary, BA, Cert Ed
59 High Street Bletchingley Redhill Surrey RH1 4PB [SOUTHWARK] *b* 1943 *educ* R Masonic Sch Rickmansworth; Open Univ; Homerton Coll Cam; *CV* Various teaching posts 1964–84; Financial Services Industry 1984–92; Financial Services Authority (formerly Securities and Investments Bd) 1992–99; Exec Dir Occupational Pensions Regulatory Authority 1999–2005; Lay Chair Dioc Syn 1996–2006; Head of Trustee Educ, The Pensions Regulator 2005–07; Consult The Pensions Regulator and Pensions Ind 2007; M DRACSC; M GS Legis Cttee; M Ch Commn Bd of Govs 2009; M Audt Cttee of Ch Commns; M Rev Cttee Bps & Ps (Consecration and Ord of Women) Measure 2009 GS 2000– *Tel:* 01883 743421
07867 977823
email: april@abalexander.co.uk

ALI, Canon Linda, BA, MA
51 Thief Lane York YO10 3HQ [YORK] *b* 1943 *educ* Bp Anstey Gr Sch Trinidad; Univ of York; *CV* Trade Marks Co-ord, Colgate Palmolive Eur 1970–89; Trade Marks Mgr, Unilever Plc UK 1989–97; Researcher/writer, Nat Archives, Lon from 2002; M York Forum for Racial Concerns; M CMEAC from 2006; Chair of Trustees USPG: Anglicans in World Mission from 2009; M Derwent Dny Syn; M Soc Resp Coun, N Yorks GS 2005– *Tel:* 01904 413698
07966 363721 (Mobile)
email: linda@jj26.fsnet.co.uk

ALLAIN-CHAPMAN, Dr Thomas Joseph, BA, MA, Ph D
Church House Great Smith St London SW1P 3AZ [PUBLISHING MANAGER, ARCHBISHOPS' COUNCIL] *b* 1969 *educ* Mount St Mary's Coll Sheff; K Coll Lon; *CV* Inglis Fell, K Coll Lon 1991–92; freelance writer and ed 1994–95; Ed, HarperCollins Relig 1995–97; Asst Commissioning Ed, Collins Educ

1997–2000, Commissioning Ed 2000, Publishing Mgr 2000–05; Head of Publishing, Church Ho Publishing 2005–09; Publishing Mgr AC from 2009 *Tel:* 020 7898 1450
Fax: 020 78981449
email: thomas.allain-chapman@c-of-e.org.uk

ALLEN, Mrs (Penelope) Penny,
12 Cranbrook Grove Perton Wolverhampton WV6 7RY [LICHFIELD] *b* 1950 *educ* Kibworth Beauchamp Gr; Oadby Beauchamp Upper Sch; Leic City Coll of Ed; *CV* Tchr, Leic 1971–74; Tchr Staffordshire 1974–77; Supply tcher 1985–88; Head of dept 1988–2009; M South Staffs District Counc 1989–91; M Perton Parish Counc from 1987; M Lichf Dioc; Lay Chair Trysull Deanery.
GS 2010– *Tel:* 01902 756125
email: mrspennyallen@yahoo.co.uk

ALLEN, Mr Timothy Edward, MA
Bell House Quay St Orford Woodbridge IP12 2NU [ST EDMUNDSBURY AND IPSWICH] *b* 1944 *educ* Framlingham Coll;Trin Coll Cam; *CV* Bank of England 1966–86; M Haringey Coun Lon 1972–78; Sec to Securities and Investments Bd 1986–97; Sec to Bd of Fin Services Authority 1997–98; M Dioc Syn; M Bp's Coun/DBF; M Agenda Plan and Business Cttee; Chair DAC; M Coun St Eds Cathl; M CNC St E and I vacancy 2006–07; M CCC 2006–08; M CBC from 2008; Chair CBC Sculpture and Furnishings Ctee; M Cathl and Ch Bldgs Div Grp; M Fees Advisory Commn; M Min Div Fin Panel; Chair Revision Cttee on draft Stipends (Cessation of Special Payments) Measure 2004; Chair Revision Cttee on draft Pastl (Amendment) Measure 2004; M Revision Cttee draft Diocs, Pastl and Mission Measure 2006; Chair Revision Cttee on Draft Eccl Fees (Amendment) Measure 2009; Lay Elder Par of Orford from 2001
GS 2000– *Tel:* 01394 450789
email: tim@bellhouseorford.com

ALLISTER, Ven Donald Spargo, MA
Bishop's Lodging The Palace Peterborough PE1 1YB [BISHOP OF PETERBOROUGH] *b* 1952 *educ* Birkenhead Sch; Peterho Cam; Trinity Th Coll Bris; *CV* C St Geo Hyde, Ches 1976–79; C St Nic Sevenoaks, Roch 1979–83; V Ch Ch Birkenhead, Ches 1983–89; R St Mary Cheadle, Ches 1989–2002; RD Cheadle 1999–2002; Adn of Chester 2002–09; Bp of Chester 2009–10; M numerous dioc cttees; Chair Dioc Houses and Glebe Cttee; Chair Dioc Par Share Grp; Bp's Adv for healthcare chapl; M CCU; Bp of Peterborough from 2010
GS 2005–2010 *Tel:* 01733 562492
Fax: 01733 890077
email: bishop@peterborough-diocese.org.uk

ALLSOPP, Ven Christine, B Sc
Westbrook 11 The Drive Northampton NN1 4RZ [ARCHDEACON OF NORTHAMPTON; PETERBOROUGH] *b* 1947 *educ* St Alb Girls' Gr Sch; Univ of

Aston; Salis and Wells (SDMTS); *CV* C St Pet Caversham and St Marg Mapledurham 1989–94; TV Bracknell Tm Min 1994–98; TR Bourne Valley 1998–2005; RD Alderbury 1999–2005; Non-res Can Salis Cathl 2002–05; Chair Dioc Ho of Clergy 2000–04; M Bd of Min 1998–2004; Non-res Can Peterb Cathl from 2005; Chair Peterb DBE from 2005
GS 2005– *Tel:* 01604 714015
Fax: 01604 792016
email: archdeacon@aofn.wanadoo.co.uk

ALLSOPP, Dr Dennis, BSc PhD CBiol FSB MCLIP
Westbrook 11 The Drive Northampton NN1 4RZ [PETERBOROUGH] *b* 1946 *educ* Rotherham Gr Sch; Aston Univ; *CV* Rsrch Fellow, Info & Service Mgr, Biodeterioration Info Centre, Bio Sc Dept, Aston Univ 1970–83; Industrial Mycologist & Head of Genetic Resources & Industrial Services Division, Commonwealth Mycological Institute 1983–94; CAB International Biodiversity Co-ord 1994–96; Private Consult Bio, from 1996; M Provincial Panel for the Province of Cant, Clergy Discipline Measure, from 2009; Eucharistic Asst Peterb from 2006; M House of Laity, GS from 2010; M Parochial Ch Counc 1971–2005; Lay Pstrl Asst Salis Dioc, 2000–05; M Sarum Archdnry Prop Cttee 1998–2004; Churchwarden, Birm & Lon,1970–1989; Deanery Prison Link Rep Reading Prison, Ox, 1980
GS 2010– *Tel:* 01604 792354
Fax: 01604 792016
email: dennis.allsopp@yahoo.com

ANGUS, Dr Christopher John, MA, PhD
Burtholme East Lanercost Brampton Cumbria CA8 2HH [CARLISLE] *b* 1949 *educ* Hampton Sch; Trin Hall, Cam Univ; Newcastle Univ; *CV* Senior Systems Analyst, ICL 1970–75; Consult, Mancos 1975–78; Application Develop Manager, CAD-Centre, Cam 1978–83; Tech Dir, Prosys Technology 1983–89; Dir, Angus Assoc 1989–2000; Software Architect, Shell 2002–03; Chief Architect, Kalido 2003; M Bp's Counc 2006; M Adnry Mapping Cttee from 2001
GS 2010– *Tel:* 016977 41504
email: chris.angus@btinternet.com

ANNAS, Rt Revd Geoff,
Ash Garth Broughton Crescent Barlaston Stoke-on-Trent ST12 9DD [AREA BISHOP OF STAFFORD] *b* 1953 *CV* Area Bp of Stafford from 2010
Tel: 01782 373308

APPLEBY, Revd Jane Elizabeth, BSc, MSc, BA, BA
Battle Hill Vicarage Berwick Drive Wallsend NE28 9ED [NEWCASTLE] *b* 1958 *educ* Bris Univ; Newcastle Poly; Cranmer Hall, Dur; *CV* OU Tutor Mathematics 1991–94; AC Holy Cross, Fenham 2003–06; TV, Ch of the Good Shepherd LEP, Battle Hill, Wallsend from 2006
GS 2010– *Tel:* 01912627518
email: janeteappleby@yahoo.com

APPLEGATE, Ven John, Ph D
Southern North West Training Partnership Aiken Hall, University of Chester Crab Lane, Padgate Warrington WA2 0DB [MANCHESTER] *educ* Bris Univ; Trin Coll Bris; *CV* C Collyhurst, Man 1984–87; C Broughton 1987–94; C Higher Broughton 1987–92; C St Clem w St Matthias Lower Broughton 1987–92; C St Jas w St Clem and St Matthias Broughton 1992–94; R Broughton 1994–96; TR Broughton 1996–2002; AD Salford 1997–2002; Hon Rsch Fell and p-t Lect Man Univ from 2000; Adn of Bolton 2002–08; Course Prin Southern Northwest Trg Ptnrship from 2008
GS 2002–   *Tel:* 01925 534303
            email: snwtpprincipal@chester.ac.uk

ARDRON, Mrs (Yvonne) Shayne, BSc
93 Letchworth Road Leicester LE3 6FN [LEICESTER] *b* 1966 *educ* Laurence Jackson Sch; Prior Pursglove Coll; Leicester Polytech; *CV* Quality Control Tester 1988-95; Lay Rdr from 2005
GS 2010–   *email:* shayne.ardron@btinternet.com

ARMITSTEAD, Col Edward Bradley Lawrence, CBE
Pendomer House Pendomer Yeovil BA22 9PB [BATH AND WELLS] *b* 1946 *educ* Shrewsbury Sch; R Military Academy Sandhurst; Defence Services Staff Coll India; *CV* Army Officer 1967–2001, Rtd from 2001; Preacher and Tchr; M Coun SASRA; Rdr; Chair Oak Hill Th Coll Coun
GS 2000–   *Tel:* 01935 862785
            email: e.armitstead@btinternet.com

ARMSTRONG, Very Revd Christopher John, Cert Ed, B Th
The Deanery Preston New Rd Blackburn BB2 6PS [DEAN OF BLACKBURN] *b* 1947 *educ* Dunstable Gr Sch; Dur Univ; Kelham Th Coll; Nottm Univ; *CV* Tchr Dunstable 1969–72; Asst C All SS Maidstone 1975–79; Chapl Coll of St Hild & St Bede Dur 1979–85; Dom Chapl to Abp of York and DDO 1985–91; Incumb St Mart Scarboro 1991–2001; Dean of Blackburn from 2001
GS 2003–05   *Tel:* 01254 52502
                            01254 503090 (Office)
                            Fax: 01254 689666
            email: dean@blackburn.anglican.org

ASHCROFT, Ven Mark David, BA, MA
14 Moorgate Avenue Withington Manchester M20 1HE [ARCHDEACON OF MANCHESTER] *b* 1954 *educ* Rugby; Worc Coll Ox; Fitzwilliam Coll Cam; Ridley Hall; *CV* Asst C Burnage St Margaret 1982–85; Tutor St Paul Sch of Divinity Kapsabet Kenya 1986–90; Prin St Paul Theol Coll Kapsabet Kenya 1990–95; R Ch Ch Man 1996–2009; AD N Man 2000–2006; Adn of Man from 2009
                            Tel: 0161 448 1976
            email: Archdeaconmanchester@
                     manchester.anglican.org

ASHE, Ven (Francis) John, B Met, Cert Th
Hollytree House Whitwell Rd Sparham Norwich NR9 5PN [ARCHDEACON OF LYNN; NORWICH] *b* 1953 *educ* Ch Hosp; Sheff Univ; Ridley Hall Cam; *CV* C Ashtead, Guild 1979–82; P-in-c St Faith Plumstead, Cape Town 1982–87; R Wisley-w-Pyrford, Guild 1987–93; V Godalming, Guild 1993–2001; RD Godalming 1996–2002; TR Godalming 2001–09; M Bp's Coun; Bp's Adv BAP (Pastl) 2002–2009; Hon Can Guild Cathl 2003–2009; Warden of Rdrs, Norw from 2009; Adn of Lynn from 2009
                            Tel: 01362 688032
            email: archdeacon.lynn@norwich.anglican.org

ASHENDEN, Canon Dr Gavin Roy Pelham, LLB, BA, MTL, D Phil
Sussex Place Horsebridge Common Ashurst Steyning W Sussex BN44 3AL [UNIVERSITIES, SOUTHERN] *b* 1954 *educ* K Sch Cant; Bris Univ; Oak Hill Coll; Heythrop Coll, Lon Univ; Sussex Univ; *CV* C St Jas Bermondsey 1980–82; TV St Ant Hamsey Green, Sanderstead, S'wark 1982–89; Univ Chapl and Lect Sussex Univ from 1989; Dir Aid to Russian Christians 1982–94; M of Coun and Vc-Chair Keston College 1982–95; M CCU 1995–2000; Dioc Adv on new relig movements; Exam Chapl to Bp of Chich; Preb of Hampstead, Chich Cathl 2003, Bursalis Preb 2005
GS 1995–2000, 2004–   *Tel:* 01273 877123
                            07879 493491 (Mobile)
                            Fax: 01273 678918
            email: g.ashenden@sussex.ac.uk

ASHTON, Rt Revd Cyril Guy, MA
Bishop's House 3 Farrington Court Wickersley Rotherham S66 1JQ [SUFFRAGAN BISHOP OF DONCASTER; SHEFFIELD] *b* 1942 *educ* Lanc Univ; Oak Hill Th Coll; *CV* C Blackpool St Thos 1967–70; Voc Sec CPAS 1970–74; V Lancaster St Thos 1974–91; Lanc Almshouses 1976–90; Dioc Dir of Trg Blackb 1991–99; Hon Can Blackb Cathl 1991–99; Bp Doncaster from 2000   *Tel:* 01709 730130
                            Fax: 01709 730230
            email: cyril.ashton@sheffield.anglican.org

ASHTON, Mr David,
2 Manor Drive Battyeford Mirfield WF14 0ER [WAKEFIELD] *b* 1941 *educ* Warw Rd Junior Sch; Dewsbury and Batley Tech Sch; Kitson Eng Coll; *CV* Br Telecom Integrity Mgr; M GS Stg Orders Cttee; M Bp's Coun
GS 1972–   *Tel:* 01924 497996
            email: david_ashton@hotmail.com

ASHWIN, Mr John Basil Edward Hamilton, MA, PGCE, FRSA
31 Wellington Rd Chichester PO19 6BB [CHICHESTER] *b* 1937 *educ* St Olave's and St Saviour's Sch S'wark; Selwyn Coll Cam; Cam Inst of Educ; *CV* Tchr of Engl then Head of Engl Dept, Emanuel Sch SW Lon 1963–69; Head of Engl Dept then Sen Master, William Morris Sen High Sch, Walthamstow 1969–75; Head, St Dav and St Kath Comp

Sch, Hornsey 1975-81; Head, Bp Luffa Sch, Chich 1981–2000; Chair W Sussex Secdry Heads 1995–98; rtd: pt External Adv and Threshold Assessor for schools, Cam Educ Associates; Accredited Section 23 Insp; Mod Rdrs' Trg Chich Dio; Lay Chair Chich Dny Syn; Vc-Chair Govs, Univ Coll Chich; Consult for Secdry Heads
GS 2002–
Tel: 01243 786501 07939 333858 (Mobile)
email: johnashwin@31wellington.fsnet.co.uk

ASHWORTH, Mrs Lorna,
28 Desmond Rd Eastbourne BN22 7LF [CHICHESTER] *b* 1970 *CV* Elected to GS 2005
GS 2005–   *email:* ashko@tiscali.co.uk

ASTIN, Revd Moira Anne Elizabeth, BA, MA, Dip Min
23 Kingfisher Drive Woodley Reading RG5 3LG [OXFORD] *b* 1965 *educ* City of Lon Sch for Girls; Sir William Perkins Sch; Clare Coll Cam; Wycliffe Hall Th Coll; *CV* C Newbury 1995–99; Min Dunston Park LEP and C Thatcham from 1999; TV Thatcham 2001–05; TV Southlake St Jas Woodley from 2005; Ecum Officer Berks from 2003; Tm Leader Ecum Officers Ox Dioc from 2008; V Southlake St James Woodley from 2009; M Brd Miss, 2000–02; M Misson-shaped Ch 2002–04; M Legal Aid Comm 2005–10; M Fees Review Grp 2007–09; M Standing Cttee, Conv Cant & House of Clergy 2005–10; M Ox Miss & Pstrl Cttee 2003–10
GS 2000–   *Tel:* 0118 954 5669
email: moira.astin@ntlworld.com

ASTON, Archdeacon of. See RUSSELL, Ven Brian Kenneth

ASTON, Suffragan Bishop of. See WATSON, Rt Revd Andrew John

ATKINSON, Very Revd Peter Gordon, MA, FRSA
The Deanery 10 College Green Worcester WR1 2LH [DEAN OF WORCESTER] *b* 1952 *educ* Maidstone Gr Sch; St Jo Coll Ox; Westcott Ho Cam; *CV* C Clapham Old Town TM 1979–83; P-in-C Tatsfield 1983–90; R H Trin Bath 1990–91; Prin Chich Th Coll 1991–94; Bursalis Preb Chich Cathl 1991–97; R Lavant 1994–97; Chan Chich Cathl 1997–2007; Dean of Worcester from 2007; M Dioc Syn 2000–05; Master St Oswald's Hosp Worc from 2007
GS 2000–05   *Tel:* 01905 732909 (Office)
01905 732939 (Study)
Fax: 01905 732906
email: peteratkinson@worcestercathedral.org.uk

ATKINSON, Ven Richard William Bryant, MA, MA, OBE
46 Southernhay Rd Stoneygate Leicester LE2 3TJ [ARCHDEACON OF LEICESTER] *b* 1958 *educ* St Paul's Sch Lon; Magd Coll Cam; Cuddesdon Th Coll; Birm Univ; *CV* C Abingdon w Shippon 1984–87; TV Sheff Manor Par 1987–91; Hon M of Staff

Cuddesdon Th Coll 1987–92; TR Sheff Manor Par 1991–96; V All SS Rotherham 1996–2002; Hon Can Sheff Cathl 1998–2002; Adn of Leicester from 2002; Chair Open Syn Grp 1996–2001; M CTE and CTBI 1997–2002; Ch Commr 2001–08; M Cen Ch Fund Cttee 1997–2002; CUF Trustee 2003–08; Dep Chair Places for People 1997–2005; Chair Phoenix Enterprises (Rotherham) Ltd 1998–2002; Chair Braunstone New Deal for Communities Programme 2003–06; Chair St Phil Cen for Study and Engagement in Multi Faith Society; Chair Launde Abbey Mgt Cttee 2002–08; M Carnegie Trust UK Enquiry into the Future of Civil Society in Britain and Ireland; M Presence and Engagement Task Gp
GS 1991–   *Tel:* 0116 270 4441 (Home)
0116 248 7419 (Office)
07718 656229 (Mobile)
Fax: 0116 270 4441 (Home)
0116 253 2889 (Office)
email: richard.atkinson@leccofe.org

ATWELL, Very Revd James Edgar, MA, Th M, BD
The Deanery The Close Winchester SO23 9LS [DEAN OF WINCHESTER] *b* 1946 *educ* Dauntsey's Sch; Ex Coll Ox; Harvard Univ; Cuddesdon Th Coll; *CV* C St Jo E Dulwich 1970–74; C Gt St Mary Cam 1974–77; Chapl Jes Coll Cam 1977–81; V Towcester w Easton Neston 1981–95; RD Towcester 1983–91; Prov of St Eds 1995–2000; Dean 2000–06; Dean of Winchester from 2006
Tel: 01962 853738 (Home)
01962 857205 (Office)
Fax: 01962 857264
email: the.dean@winchester-cathedral.org.uk

ATWELL, Rt Revd Robert Ronald, BA (Hons), M.Litt
Bishop's Lodge Back Lane Dunham Town, Altrincham Cheshire WA14 4SG [BISHOP OF STOCKPORT] *b* 1954 *educ* Wanstead High Sch; St John's Coll Dur; Westcott Ho Cam; *CV* Asst C John Keble Ch Mill Hill 1978–81; Chapl Trinity Coll Cam 1981–87; Benedictine Monk Burford Priory 1987–98; V Par of St Mary-the-Virgin Primrose Hill 1998–2008; Bp Stockport from 2008; Chair Min Cttee Chester Dioc; Trustee SNWTP   *Tel:* 0161 928 5611
Fax: 0161 929 0692
email: bpstockport@chester.anglican.org

AUCKLAND, Archdeacon of. See BARKER, Ven Nicholas John Willoughby

AUSTEN, Dr Simon Neil, BSc, MA, DipMin
12 Brunstock Close Lowry Hill Carlisle CA3 0HL [CARLISLE] *b* 1967 *educ* City of Lon Freemen's Sch; Warwick Univ; Wycliffe Hall Th Coll; *CV* Science master, Monkton Combe Junior Sch, 1988–89; Lay Asst, St. Michael's Bath 1990–91; Asst C, Great Chesam TM Dioc Ox 1994–98; Chapl, Stowe Sch, Buckingham 1998–2002; V, St. John's w St. Peter's, Carlisle from 2002; M C of E Evang Counc from 2004
GS 2010–   *Tel:* 01228 810076
email: simon@hkchurch.org.uk

AVIS, Canon Paul David Loup, BD, Ph D
Church House Great Smith St London SW1P 3AZ
[GENERAL SECRETARY, COUNCIL FOR CHRISTIAN
UNITY] *b* 1947 *educ* St Geo Monoux Gr Sch
Walthamstow; Lon Univ; Westcott Ho Th Coll;
CV C S Molton Grp 1975–80; V Stoke Canon, Pol-
timore w Huxham, Rewe w Netherexe 1980–98;
Sub Dean Ex Cathl 1997–2008; Dir Centre for
Study of the Christian Church from 1997; Sec
CCU from 1998; Vc Chair FOAG 1994–98; Chair
Ho of Clergy Ex Dioc Syn 1996–98; ed *Ecclesiology*
from 2004; Canon Theologian of Ex from 2008;
Chapl to the Qu from 2008; Hon Visiting Prof
Univ of Exeter from 2009
GS 1990–95   *Tel:* 020 7898 1470
                                  07974 696615 (Mobile)
                                   Fax: 020 7898 1483
         email: paul.avis@c-of-e.org.uk

AYERS, Revd Paul Nicholas, MA
Vicarage Vicarage Drive Pudsey LS28 7RL [BRAD-
FORD] *b* 1961 *educ* Bradf Gr Sch; St Pet Coll Ox;
Trin Coll Bris; *CV* C St Jo Bapt Clayton 1985–88; C
St Andr Keighley 1988–91; V St Cuth Wrose 1991–
97; V St Lawr and St Paul Pudsey from 1997
GS 1995–   *Tel:* 0113 256 4197
         email: paul.ayers@tiscali.co.uk

BACK, Mr Robin Philip, AIB, FRSA
*The Old Manse Church Lane Guestwick Norfolk
NR20 5QJ* [NORWICH] *b* 1946 *educ* Uppingham;
Geneva Univ; *CV* Standard Chartered Bank in
Middle East, India, Indonesia, Thailand and USA
1967–88; MD Backs Electronic Publishing Ltd
from 1989; Prime Wdn, Worshipful Co of Dyers
of City of Lon 2002–03; M Bp's Coun from 2003;
Lay Chair, Dioc Syn from 2003; Lay Chair,
Sparham Dny Syn 1996–2001; M DBF from 2003;
Chair Friends of Scott Polar Research Inst, Univ
of Cam 2007–10
GS 2005–   *Tel:* 01362 683281
                                          01326 683835
             email: robin@bepl.co.uk

BAILEY, Ven David Charles, MA, M Sc, BA
14 Springside Rd Walmersley Bury BL9 5JE [ARCH-
DEACON OF BOLTON] *b* 1952 *educ* Bradf Gr Sch;
Linc Coll Oxf; Nottm Univ; St Jo Coll Nottm; *CV*
C St Jo Worksop 1980–83; C Edgware, P-in-c St
Andr Broadfields 1983–87; V S Cave and Ellerker
w Broomfleet 1987–97; RD Howden 1991–97;
Hon Can York Minster 1998–2008; V Beverley
Minster 1997–2008; Adn Bolton from 2008
                                   Tel: 0161 761 6117
                                  07944 518765 (Mobile)
  email: archbolton@manchester.anglican.org

BAIN, Ven (John) Stuart, BA
*St Nicholas' Vicarage Hedworth Lane Boldon Colliery
NE35 9JA* [ARCHDEACON OF SUNDERLAND; DUR-
HAM] *b* 1955 *educ* Blaydon Sec Sch; Durham Univ;
Westcott Ho Cam; *CV* C H Trin Washington
1980–84; C St Nic Dunston 1984–86; V St Oswald

Shiney Row and St Aid Herrington 1986–92; P-in-
c St Paul Spennymoor and Whitworth 1992–97;
P-in-c St Jo Merrington 1994–97; AD Auckland
1996–2002; Hon Can Dur 1998; V St Paul Spennymoor, Whitworth and St Jo Merrington 1997–
2002; Chair DFW Adoption from 1999; Asst P St
Nic Hedworth 2002; P-in-c St Nic Hedworth from
2003; P-in-c St Geo E Boldon from 2009; P-in-C St
Nics Boldon from 2010; Adn of Sunderland from
2002   *Tel:* 0191 536 2300
                                   Fax: 0191 519 3369
        email: Archdeacon.of.Sunderland@
                  durham.anglican.org

BAINES, Rt Revd Nicholas, BA (Hons)
53 Stanhope Road Croydon CRO 5NS [BISHOP OF
CROYDON; SOUTHWARK] *b* 1957 *educ* Holt Comp
Sch Liv; Bradf Univ; Trin Coll Bris; *CV* C St Thos
Kendal 1987–91; C H Trin Leic 1991–92; V Roth-
ley 1992–2000; RD Goscote 1995–2000; Adn of
Lambeth 2000–03; Broadcaster; Dir EIG 2002–10;
Bp of Croydon from 2003; Angl Co-Chair
Meissen Comm; Chair Sandford St Mart Trust
from 2009
GS 1995–2003, 2004–05
                                Tel: 020 8256 9630 (Office)
                                   020 8686 1822 (Home)
                                  07974 194735 (Mobile)
                                Fax: 020 8256 9631 (Office)
                                   020 8649 7658 (Home)
  email: bishop.nick@southwark.anglican.org

BAKER, Revd Jonathan Mark Richard, MA,
M Phil, Hon DD
Pusey House Oxford OX1 3LZ [OXFORD] *b* 1966
educ Merchant Taylors' Sch Northwood; St Jo
Coll Ox; St Steph Ho Th Coll; *CV* C All SS
Ascot Heath 1993–96; P-in-c St Mark and H
Trin Reading 1996–99; V St Mark and H Trin
Reading 1999–2002; Prin Pusey Ho, Ox from
2003
GS 2000–   *Tel:* 01865 278415
                                          01865 288023
     email: jonathan.baker@stx.ox.ac.uk

BALLARD, Ven Peter James, B Ed, Dip Th
Wheatfield 7 Dallas Rd Lancaster LA1 1TN [ARCH-
DEACON OF LANCASTER; BLACKBURN] *b* 1955 *educ*
Chadderton Gr Sch for Boys; Bede Coll Dur; Lon
Univ; Sarum and Wells Th Coll; *CV* C Grantham
1987–91; Asst Chapl Grantham and Kesteven
Gen Hosp 1989–91; R St Pet and St Paul Port Pirie
S Australia 1991; V Ch Ch Lancaster 1991–98;
RD Lancaster 1995–98; Can Res and Dioc Dir of
Educ 1998–2006; Dir of Educ from 1998; Adn of
Lancaster from 2006; Pro Chan Univ of Cumbria
from 2007
GS 2000–2010   ·   *Tel:* 01524 32897 (Home)
                                   01254 503070(Office)
                                  07970 923141 (Mobile)
                                Fax: 01524 66095 (Home)
                                   01254 699963 (Office)
   email: peter.ballard@blackburn.anglican.org

BARBER, Mr John Stephen, BSc
16 Launceston Close, Cherry Tree Gardens Oldham OL8 2XE [MANCHESTER] *b* 1971 *educ* The Blue Coat C o fE, Oldham; Oldham Coll, Bolton Univ; *CV* Joiner/Carpenter, Oldham MBC, 1988–96; Bldg Surveyor, Oldham MBC, 1997–2004; Senior Renewal Surveyor, Tameside MBC from 2004
GS 2010–   *Tel:* 0161 620 0668
                    email: johnsbarber@btinternet.com

BARBER, Revd Neil Andrew Austin, BA
St Giles' Vicarage 16 Browning Street Normanton Derby DE23 8DN [DERBY] *b* 1963 *educ* Ealing Coll of H Ed; Oakhill Coll; NTMTC; *CV* Systems Eng/Project Mgr, IBM UK, 1986–95; Lay Assoc Min, St Mary's Basingstoke, Winc 1995–98; C St Mary's Basingstoke, Winc 1998–2001; Incumb, St Giles' Normanton by Derby
GS 2010–   *Tel:* 01332–767483
        email: neil.barber@stgiles-derby.org.uk

BARKER, Ven Nicholas John Willoughby, MA
Holy Trinity Vicarage 45 Milbank Rd Darlington DL3 9NL [ARCHDEACON OF AUCKLAND] *b* 1949 *educ* Sedbergh Sch; Oriel Coll Ox; Trin Coll Bris; *CV* C St Mary Watford 1977–80; TV St Jas and Em Didsbury 1980–86; TR St Geo Kidderminster 1986–2007; RD Kidderminster 2001–07; Adn of Auckland from 2007; Hon Can Dur Cathl from 2007
GS 2005–07   *Tel:* 01325 480444
                    07912 269 364 (Mobile)
                    Fax: 01325 354027
        email: archdeacon.of.auckland@
                    durham.anglican.org

BARKER, Ven Timothy Reed, MA
Archdeacon's House 1A Northfield Rd Quarrington Sleaford NG34 8RT [ARCHDEACON OF LINCOLN; LINCOLN] *b* 1956 *educ* Man Gr Sch; Queen's Coll Cam; Westcott Ho; *CV* C Nantwich 1980–83; V Norton St Berteline and St Christopher 1983–88; V Runcorn All Saints 1988–94; Urban Officer Ches 1990–98; Bp of Chester's Chap 1994–98; P assoc, Ches Cath 1994–98; V Spalding St Mary and Nicholas 1998–2009; Rural Dean Elloe West 2000–09; M Linc Cathl Chap 2000–09; Can and Preb of Linc from 2003; Rural Dean Elloe East 2008–09; P-in-C Spalding St Paul 2007–09; M DRACS Cttee 2001–05; M CME Panel 2003–06; M Clergy Terms of Service Implementation Group 2005–07; M Marriage Law Working Party 2006; M Dioc Syn from 1999; Trustee Alcuin Club from 1990; Adn Linc from 2009
GS 2000–05; 2008–   *Tel:* 01529 304348 (Office)
                    07590 950041 (Mobile)
    email: archdeacon.lincoln@lincoln.anglican.org

BARKING, Area Bishop of. See HAWKINS, Rt Revd David John Leader

BARLEY, Revd Preb Lynda Mary, BA, M Sc, PGCE
Church House Great Smith Street London SW1P 3AZ [HEAD OF RESEARCH AND STATISTICS, ARCHBISHOPS' COUNCIL] *b* 1953 *educ* Tiffin Girls' Sch Kingston-upon-Thames; York Univ; Univ Coll Lon; S'wark Ord Course; *CV* Statistician Bank of England 1976–79; Rsch Mgr Bible Soc 1979–87; Rsch Consult 1987–98; Tutor Open Univ from 1992; OFSTED and Section 23 Sch Insp 1993–2006; Ho for Duty Priest Dunsford & Doddiscombsleigh 1998–2000; Hd of Rsch & Statistics, AC, from 2000; Asst Min (NSM) Culm Valley Tm Min from 2003; Chapl S'wark Cathl from 2007; Vis Lect, K Coll Lon from 2006; Preb Exeter Cathl from 2009   *Tel:* 020 7898 1542
                    Fax: 020 7898 1532
        email: lynda.barley@c-of-e.org.uk

BARNEY, Mr Stephen George, B Sc, MBA
The Dower House 77 Brook St Wymeswold LE12 6TT [LEICESTER] *b* 1950 *educ* Cranfield Univ; *CV* Main Bd Dir public companies rtd; Rdr; Chair DBF; Trustee Launde Abbey; Dir SMCP
GS 2005–   *Tel:* 01509 881160
                    07767 320320 (Mobile)
        email: stephen@barney4747@fsnet.co.uk

BARNSTAPLE, Archdeacon of. See GUNN-JOHNSON, Ven David Allan

BARRELL, Mrs Anneliese Gledhill, MCSP, Grad Dip Phys, DSA
47 Whitleigh Ave Crownhill Plymouth PL5 3AU [EXETER] *b* 1938 *educ* Burlington Sch Lon; Prince of Wales Gen Hosp Sch of Physiotherapy, Lon; *CV* Rtd NHS physiotherapy mgr; pt lect, Plymouth Coll FE; M Dioc Coun for Work with Children and Young People, Chair of Youth and FE Cttee; Chair Devon Trefoil Guild
GS 2000–   *Tel:* 01752 777053
                    07713 147828 (Mobile)
        email: annagb@blueyonder.co.uk

BARTON, Mrs Jennifer Diane,
Noumena Little Green Broadwas on Teme Worcestershire WR6 5NH [WORCESTER] *b* 1942 *educ* Challney Secondary Sch, Luton; *CV* Computer Punch Card Operator, 1958–65; Worc Ed Dept, Spec needs Children 1986–93; M Dioc Brd Ed 1996–2006; M Worc Dioc Syn from 1998; M Martley & Worc West Deanery Syn from 1995
GS 2010–   *Tel:* 01886 821581 07758957841
        email: JDNOUMENA@AOL.COM

BASHFORTH, Revd Alan George, MA, B Th
Vicarage 6 Penwinnick Parc St Agnes TR5 0UQ [TRURO] *b* 1964 *educ* Humphrey Davy Gr Sch; Ox Univ; Ex Univ; Ripon Coll Cuddesdon; *CV* Police officer, S Yorks Police 1983–90; nursing auxiliary 1990–93; C Calstock, Truro 1996–98; C St Ives, Truro 1998–2001; V St Agnes and Mithian w. Mount Hawke from 2001; RD Powder from 2004;

M Bp's Coun; M DBF; M Dioc Pastl Cttee; Chair Ho of Clergy from 2009
GS 2005– *Tel:* 01872 553391
email: onepaw@btinternet.com

BASINGSTOKE, Suffragan Bishop of.
See HANCOCK, Rt Revd Peter

BASTON, Ven Caroline Jane, BSc, PGCE, Cert Theol
5 The Boltons Wootton Bridge Ryde Isle of Wight PO33 4PB [ARCHDEACON OF THE ISLE OF WIGHT; PORTSMOUTH] *b* 1956 *educ* Godolphin Sch Salis; Birm Univ; City of Birm Poly; Ripon Coll Cuddesdon; *CV* C St Chris Thornhill, Southn, Winch 1989–94; R All SS Winch w. St Andr Chilcomb w. St Pet Chesil 1995–2006; Dioc Communications Officer 1995–98; DDO 1999–2006; Hon Can Winch Cathl from 2000; Adn of Isle of Wight from 2006; M Dioc Syn, Miss and Soc Forum, Bp's Coun, DAC, DBE *Tel:* 01983 884432
email: adiow@portsmouth.anglican.org

BATH AND WELLS, Bishop of. See PRICE, Rt Revd Peter Bryan

BATH, Archdeacon of. See PIGGOTT, Ven Andy (Andrew John)

BAYES, Rt Revd Paul,
Bishopswood 3 Stobarts Close Knebworth SG3 6ND [SUFFRAGAN BISHOP OF HERTFORD] *b* 1953 *CV* C Tynemouth Cullercoats St Paul Newc 1979–82; Chapl Qu Eliz Coll Lon 1982–87; Chapl Chelsea Coll 1985–87; TV High Wycombe Ox 1987–90; TR 1990–94; TR Totton Win 1995–04; AD Lyndhurst 2000–04; Nat Miss and Evang Adv Abps' Coun from 2004; Hon Can Worc Cathl 2007–10; Bp of Hertford from 2010
email: bishophertford@stalbans.anglican.org

BAYLIS, Revd Sally Anne, BA,MA, PGCE
Daybrook Vicarage 241 Oxclose Lane Daybrook Nottingham NG5 6FB [SOUTHWELL & NOTT] *b* 1955 *educ* Herts & Essex H Sch, Bishop's Stortford; Queen's Coll Lon Univ of Kent; St John's Coll Nott; *CV* Bookseller 1978–85; Freelance editor/translator 1990–2003; Secondary School Tchr 1993–2001; AC All Hallows Gedling 2003–07 P-in-C St Paul's w St Timothy's Daybrook from 2007; M Dioc Syn from 2005
GS 2010– *Tel:* 0115 9262686 07506441634
email: sally504@btinternet.com

BAYNES, Canon Matthew Thomas Crispin, MA
The Rectory Bredon Tewkesbury GL20 7LT [WORCESTER] *b* 1962 *educ* Orange Hill H Sch, Edgware; MIddx UEA; Cam Univ; Westcott Ho Th Coll; *CV* Nursing Auxillary, St Christopher's Hospice, Sydenham 1983–84; C Ch Ch, Southgate1987–90; Chapl Southgate Tech Coll 1987–90; P-in-C, All Saints' Berkhamsted 1990–95; Chapl St. Francis Hospice, Berkhamsted 1990–95; V Ch Ch Coseley,1995–99; Assoc Dioc Chapl Agriculture &

Rural Life 2002–09; R, Bredon w Bredon's Norton 1999; Rural Dean of Pershore 2005; P-in-C Beckford Grp P 2009; Can Worc 2010; St Alb Dioc Syn; Worc Dioc Syn; Worc Dioc Brd Ed; Worc Dioc Pstrl Cttee
GS 2010– *Tel:* 01684 772237
email: mbaynes@toucansurf.com

BAYNES, Mr Simon Henry Crews, BSc, C Eng, FBCS
4 Pilgrim Close St Albans AL2 2JD [ST ALBANS] *b* 1958 *educ* Orange Hill Boys' Gr Sch; Sheff Univ; *CV* Logica from 1979, Chartered Eng from 1990; Chair of Pension Trustees from 1997; Trustee, Life Academy (The Pre-Retirement Assoc) from 2007; M St Alb Dioc Syn from 2003; M St Alb DBF from 2003; M Dny Syn from 2001; M St Alb Cathl Fin Cttee 1997–2007; M Inter-Dioc Fin Forum from 2005; M Bp's Coun from 2007; Trustee Cam Univ Press Sen Staff Pension Scheme from 2008; M CNC (St Alb Vacancy-in-See) 2008–09
GS 2005– *Tel:* 01727 875524 (Home)
07860 828711 (Mobile)
email: simon@simonbaynes.fsnet.co.uk

BEACH, Revd Mark Howard Francis, BA, MA
The Rectory Church St Rugby CV21 3PH [COVENTRY] *b* 1962 *educ* Ellesmore Coll Shropshire; Univ of Kent; Univ of Nottm; St Stephen's Ho; *CV* C Beeston S'well 1987–90; C Hucknall 1990–93; R Gedling 1993–2001; R Netherfield 1996–2001; Bp's Chapl Wakef 2001–03; TR Rugby Cov from 2003; M Bp's Coun and Dioc Syn Cov
GS 2008– *Tel:* 01788 542936 (Home)
01788 565609 (Office)
07930 577 248 (Mobile)
email: rector@rugbyteam.org.uk

BEAKE, Ven Stuart Alexander, MA
Archdeacon's House Lime Grove West Clandon Guildford GU4 7UT [ARCHDEACON OF SURREY; GUILDFORD] *b* 1949 *educ* K Coll Sch Wimbledon; Em Coll Cam; Cuddesdon Coll Ox; *CV* C St Mary Hitchin 1974–79; TV St Mary Hemel Hempstead 1979–85; Dom Chapl to Bp of Southwell 1985–87; V Shottery St Andr 1987–2000; RD Fosse Dny 1992–99; DDO Cov Dioc 1995–2000; Hon Can Cov Cathl 1999–2000; Can Res and Sub-Dean Cov Cathl 2000–05; Adn of Surrey from 2005
GS 1980–85 *Tel:* 01483 790352 (Office)
01483 211924 (Home)
Fax: 01483 790333 (Office)
01483 223397 (Home)
email: stuart.beake@cofeguildford.org.uk

BEAL, Dr John Frank, PhD, BDS, MFDS(RCSEng), HonMFPH, FRSPH
Oakroyd 4 North Park Road Leeds LS8 1JD [RIPON AND LEEDS] *educ* Finchley County Gr Sch; Royal Dental Hospital of London; *CV* House Surgeon, Royal Dental Hosp of Lon 1965–66; Lect in Dental Public Health, Birm Univ 1966–76; Senior Dental Officer, Avon Area Health Authority (Teaching)

1977–79; Area Dental Officer, Birm Area Health Authority (Teaching) 1979–83; Consult in Dental Public Health, Leeds Health Authority, 1983–2008; Regional Dental Officer, Yorkshire Regional Health Authority, 1990–2009; Locum Consult in Dental Public Health, Wakefield District Primary Care Trust from 2010; Hospital Chapls Counc 1995–2000; M Bp's Counc, Ripon Dioc from 1990; Vice-chair Brd of Miss and Unity, Ripon Dioc 1987–89
GS 1995–2005; 2010–   Tel: 0113–2948795
            email: johnfbeal@hotmail.co.uk

BECK, Miss Rachel Gillian, BA
21 Cecil Street Lincoln LN1 3AU [LINCOLN] *b* 1980 *educ* Wales High Sch; Bp Grosseteste Coll; *CV* Receptionist Sheff Dioc Ch Ho 1999–2000; Admin Rotherham Youth Service 2000–01; PA to Asst Dir of Educ, Rotherham 2001–02; Primary Tchr, Linc from 2005
GS 2000–   Tel: 07753634477
            email: rgbeck@btinternet.com

BEDFORD, Archdeacon of. See HUGHES, Ven Paul Vernon

BEDFORD, Suffragan Bishop of. See INWOOD, Rt Revd Richard Neil

BEER, Ven John Stuart, MA Oxon, MA Cantab
St Botolph's Rectory 1a Summerfield Cambridge CB3 9HE [ARCHDEACON OF CAMBRIDGE; ELY] *b* 1944 *educ* Roundhay Sch Leeds; Pemb Coll Ox; Westcott Ho Th Coll; *CV* C St Jo Knaresborough 1971–74; Fell and Chapl Fitzw Coll and New Hall Cam 1974–80; R Toft w Caldecote and Childerley and Harwick 1980–87; V Grantchester 1987–97; DDO, Dir of POT and Rdr Trg 1987-97; Hon Can Ely Cathl from 1989; Chair Cathl Pilgrims Assoc Conference 1986–96; M Ethics Cttee Dunn Nutrition Unit 1985–2001; Adn of Huntingdon 1997–2004; acting Adn of Wisbech 2002–04; Co-DDO and Dir POT 1997–2002; Bye-Fell Fitzw Coll from 2001; M Bp's Coun; Chair Liturg Cttee; M Fin Cttee; Bps' Selection Adv from 2002; Adn of Ely 2004–07; Adn of Cambridge from 2007
GS 2003–2010   Tel: 01223 350424
                                      Fax: 01223 360929
    email: archdeacon.cambridge@ely.anglican.org

BELCHER, Dr William Peter Argent, BSc, PhD
39 Redgrove Park Cheltenham Gloucestershire GL51 6QY [GLOUCESTER] *b* 1949 *educ* Framlingham Coll, Suffolk; Leeds Univ; Cam Univ; *CV* Materials Eng in Nuclear Electricity Generating Industry, Nuclear Electric Plc 1988–95; British Energy Generation Ltd. 1995–2009; Chwrdn, Lay Chair of PCC; Leadership Team of St Mary w St Matthew Ch, Cheltenham 2002–08; Materials Eng in Nuclear Electricity Generating Industry, EDF-Energy 2009
GS 2010–   Tel: 01242228690
        email: williambelcher@btinternet.com

BELL, Rt Revd James Harold, MA, BA, Cert Theol
Thistledown Main St Exelby Bedale DL8 2HD [SUFFRAGAN BISHOP OF KNARESBOROUGH; RIPON AND LEEDS] *b* 1950 *educ* Appleby Gr Sch; St Jo Coll Dur; Wycliffe Hall Ox; *CV* Hon C St Mich at the Northgate, Ox 1975–76; Chapl and lect BNC Ox 1976–82, Fell 1979–82; R St Mary Northolt, Lon 1982–93; Area Dean Ealing 1991–93; Adv for Min, Willesden Area 1993–97; Dir of Min and Tr, Ripon Dioc 1997–99; Res Can Ripon Cathl 1997–99; Dir of Mission Ripon Dioc 1999–2004; Hon Can Ripon Cathl 1999–2004; Bp of Knaresborough from 2004; M Dioc Syn, DBF, DBE (ex officio), Dioc Coun for Mission, Rural Affairs Gp of the GS; Dir Meth Chapel Aid; M Harrogate Coll Consult Cttee; Gov York St Jo Univ Coll
GS 2010–   Tel: 01677 423525
                                      01677 424392
                                      Fax: 01677 423525
        email: bishop.knaresb@btinternet.com

BELL, Sir Stuart, MP
Church House Great Smith St London SW1P 3AZ [SECOND CHURCH ESTATES COMMISSIONER] *b* 1938 *educ* Hookergate Gr Sch Durham; Gray's Inn Lon; *CV* Barrister-at-Law; MP for Middlesbrough from 1983; PPS to Rt Hon Roy Hattersley 1983–84; Front Bench Spokesperson N Ireland 1984–87; Vc Chair Inter-Parliamentary Br Grp 1991–94; Vc Chair Br Irish Inter-Parliamentary Body 1990–92; Front Bench Spokesperson Trade and Industry 1992–97; M House of Commons Commn from 2000; Chair Fin and Services Cttee from 2008; Second Ch Estates Commr from 1997; Freeman of City of Lon from 2003; Chair Franco-Br Parliamentary Grp; Chevalier de la Legion d'Honneur 2006
GS 1997–   Tel: 020 7898 1623
                                      Fax: 020 7898 1131

BENFIELD, Revd Paul John, LLB, B Th
St Nicholas Vicarage Highbury Ave Fleetwood FY7 7DJ [BLACKBURN] *b* 1956 *educ* Cam Gr Sch for Boys; Newc Univ; Coll of Law, Chancery Lane, Lon; Chich Th Coll; *CV* Chancery barrister 1978–86; C Shiremoor, Newc 1989–92; C Hexham, Newc 1992–93; TV All SS, St Anne, St Mich & St Thos Lewes, Chich 1993–97; R Pulborough, Chich 1997–2000; V St Nich Fleetwood, Blackb from 2000; M Legal Aid Commn from 2006; M Rev Cttee on Draft Vacancies in Suffragan Sees and Other Eccl Offices Meas; M Rev Cttee on Draft Crown Benefices (Par Representatives) Meas 2008; M Revd Cttee for Draft Pastl and Miss Meas from 2009; M Steering Cttee for Draft Care of Caths Meas from 2009; M Fleetwood Town Coun from 2009
GS 2005–   Tel: 01253 874402
        email: benfield@btinternet.com

BENN, Rt Revd Wallace Parke, BA, Dip Th
Bishop's Lodge 16A Prideaux Rd Eastbourne BN21 2NB [AREA BISHOP OF LEWES; CHICHESTER] *b* 1947

educ St Andr Coll Dub; Univ Coll Dub; Univ of Lon; Trin Coll Bris; *CV* C St Mark New Ferry, Wirral 1972–76; C St Mary Cheadle 1976–82; V St Jas the Great Audley 1982–87; V St Pet Harold Wood 1987–97; pt Chapl Harold Wood Hosp 1987–96; Bp of Lewes from 1997; M Dioc Syn; M Dioc Staff Tm; Bp's Coun; M DBF; Bp w Oversight for Youth and Children's Work; Pres C of E Evang Coun; Pres Fellowship of Word and Spirit; Chair Bible by the Beach

Tel: 01323 648462   *Fax:* 01323 641514
email: bishop.lewes@diochi.org.uk

BENNETT, Dr Anthony John, BEd, MA, PhD
1 Merriefield Close, Broadstone Dorset BH18 8DG [WINCHESTER] *b* 1950 *educ* Nottingham Coll; Univ of Essex; *CV* Tchr History & US Politics, Royal Hospital Sch, Ipswich 1974–89; Tchr of US Politics, Charterhouse, 1989–2009; Under Master, Charterhouse 1997–2004; Deputy Headmaster, Charterhouse 2004–09; Bournemouth Deanery Syn M from 2010
GS 2010–

Tel: 01202 252523
email: ajb44@ymail.com

BENYON, Mr Thomas, DipTh, OBE
Rectory Farm House 2 Church St Bladon Oxon OX2O 1RS [OXFORD] *b* 1942 *educ* Wellington Sch; RMA Sandhurst; Wycliffe Hall Ox; *CV* Lieut Scots Guards 1963–67; District Coun AVDC; Contested Heyton 1974; MP Abingdon 1979–83; Chair Milton Keynes Health Auth 1989–92; Dir Buckingham Health Auth 1992–94; Founder ZANE: Zimbabwe A National Emergency
GS 2005–

Tel: 01993 811722
07831 859085
email: tom.benyon@btinternet.com

BERKSHIRE, Archdeacon of. See RUSSELL, Ven Norman Atkinson

BERRY, Professor Anthony John, B Sc, M Phil, Ph D, DIC
24 Leafield Rd Disley Stockport SK12 2JF [CHESTER] *b* 1939 *educ* Bath Univ; Imp Coll Lon; Seattle Univ; Man Univ; *CV* Aerodynamicist Br Aircraft Corp 1962; Aerodynamics Engineer The Boeing Co Seattle 1965–69; Rsch Fell 1971–73, Lect 1973–86, Sen Lect 1986–95 in Mgt Devel Man Univ; Prof Sheff Hallam Univ 1995–2002; Prof emeritus 2002; M Dioc Syn; Rdr
GS 1994–

Tel: 01663 762393
07759 492318
email: anthonyberry@btinternet.com

BESSANT, Canon Simon, B Mus, MA
Eccleshall Vicarage Ringinglow Rd Sheffield S11 7PQ [SHEFFIELD] *b* 1956 *educ* Francis Combe Comp Watford; Sheff Univ; St Jo Coll Nottm; *CV* C St Jo and St Jas Bootle 1981–84; C Em Holloway 1984–85, P-in-c 1985–81; Ecum Adv for Bp of Stepney 1990–91; V Ch of the Redeemer Blackburn 1991–98; RD of Blackburn 1997–98; Dioc Dir for Miss

and Evang and Officer for Dioc Bd for Miss and Unity 1998–2007; Dioc Dir for CME 1–4 2002–05; V All Saints Ecclesall, Sheff from 2007; M Lon Dioc Bd of Educ 1989–91; M Blackb Dioc Bd of Min 1995–2002; M Blackb Dioc Liturg Cttee 1998–2007; Sec to Blackb Dioc, Lancs Coun of Mosques Dialogue Grp 1998–2007; initiator and M Churches Together in Lancs Inter-Faith Forum 1999–2007, Chair 1999–2003; initiator and M Lancs Inter-Faith Forum 2000–2007, Chair 2001–03; GS rep on NEOC Bd 2001–05; M MPA Coun 2003–05; M Presence and Engagement Strg Grp 2004–05; M Follow-up Grp, Strg Cttee and Rev Cttee, Rev of Diocs Pastl and Miss Measure 2004–06; Chair Wkg Party creating code of practice on Miss Initiatives under Diocs, Pastl and Miss Measure from 2006; M Bradf Chs for Dialogue and Diversity Adv Grp from 2006; M AC 2006–07; M C of E Appts Cttee 2006–07; Hon Can Blackb Cath 2006–07; Can Emer Blackb Cath from 2006
GS 2001–07, 2008–

Tel: 0114 236 0084
07957 211319 (Mobile)
email: simon.bessant@
ecclesall.parishchurch.org.uk

BESWICK, Mr David Terence,
6 Sheriffs Way Eccleshall Stafford ST21 6BQ [LICHFIELD] *b* 1933 *educ* Tarporley C of E Sch; *CV* Chwdn, St Helen Tarporley 1972–77; chwdn, H Trin Eccleshall 1984–2003, lay chair PCC 2003–04; lay chair Eccleshall Dny Syn from 2003; M Lich Dioc Syn from 2002, Pastl Cttee from 2004
GS 2005–

Tel: 01785 850622
Fax: 01785 851249

BETTS, Revd Canon Steven James, B Sc, Cert Th
Emmaus House 65 The Close Norwich NR1 4DH [NORWICH] *b* 1964 *educ* Nottm Bluecoat Gr Sch; York Univ; Cuddesdon Th Coll; *CV* C Bearsted w Thurnham 1990–94; Chapl to Bp of Norw 1994–97; V Old Catton Norw 1997–2005; RD Norw N 2001–05; M Dioc Commn 2001–09; Chair Dioc Ho of Clergy from 2003; M Bp's Coun from 2003; M DBF Exec from 2003; Bp's Officer for Ord and Initial Trg from 2005; Hon Can Norw Cathl from 2008; M Par Fin Gp Dioc of Norw from 2009
GS 2000–   *Tel:* 01603 729816 (Office)

email: steven.betts@norwich.anglican.org

BEVERLEY, Bishop of. See JARRETT, Rt Revd Martyn William

BIRKENHEAD, Suffragan Bishop of. See SINCLAIR, Rt Revd (Gordon) Keith

BIRMINGHAM, Archdeacon of. See OSBORNE, Ven Hayward John

BIRMINGHAM, Bishop of. See URQUHART, Rt Revd David Andrew

WHO'S WHO

BIRMINGHAM, Dean of. See OGLE, Very Revd Catherine

BISHOP, Ven Ian Gregory, BA, BSc ARICS
Poplar Fell Nantwich Road Middlewich Chester CW10 9HG [ARCHDEACON OF MACCLESFIELD/ CHESTER] *b* 1962 *educ* Devizes Sch; Portsm Poly; Oak Hill Th Coll; *CV* Surveyor Croydon Counc 1984–86; Estate Mgr Gatwick Airport 1986–88; C Ch Ch Purley S'wark 1991–95; R Tas Valley Team Ministry 1995–2001; R Middlewich & Byley 2001– 10; Rural Dean of Middlewich 2004–10; Archdn of Macclesfield from 2011; Dioc Syn 1997–2001; M Parsonages Cttee 1997–2001; Dioc Syn 2004–09; Dioc Adv Cttee 2004–09
GS 2010–   *Tel:* 07794389118
            email: ian.bishop@chester.anglican.org

BISHOP, Mrs Pamela Elizabeth, BSc, PGCE
250 Nottingham Road Mansfield Notts NG18 4SH [SOUTHWELL & NOTT] *b* 1944 *educ* Staveley Netherthorpe Gr Sch; Nott Univ; *CV* Science Tchr, The Latymer Sch 1967–70; Head of Biology, The Brunts Sch, 1970–77; Deputy Head, The Manor Sch 1977–79; Lect Ed, Nott Univ 1989–2001; Independent Ed Consult & Ofsted Sch Inspector from 2001; Dioc Chair Ho of Laity from 2008; M Bp's Counc from 2006; Deanery Lay Chair from 2007
GS 2010–   *Tel:* 01623 633494
            email: pandpbishop@btopenworld.com

BISSON, Mrs Jane Victoria, FSI, ACIS, MSc
Glenhaven La Rocque Grouville Jersey JE3 9BB [WINCHESTER [CHANNEL ISLANDS]] *b* 1949 *educ* Blancheland Coll; *CV* Legal Trustees (Jersey) Ltd 1988–91; Integro Trust Co 1991–94; Fin Services Commn 1994; Royal Bank of Scotland Internat 1994–2000; Mourant Internat Fin Admin, Legal and Risk Dept from 2005; Regional Mgr KYCOS Ltd, Jersey and Guernsey; M AC Audit Cttee; M Dioc Syn
GS 1995–
        Tel: 01534 853162 07797 750896 (Mobile)
            email: jane_bisson@googlemail.com

BLACKBURN, Rt Revd Richard Finn, BA, MA
34 Wilson Rd Botanical Gardens Sheffield S11 8RN [BISHOP OF WARRINGTON; LIVERPOOL] *b* 1952 *educ* Aysgarth Sch; Eastbourne Coll; St Jo Coll Dur; Hull Univ; Westcott Ho Th Coll; *CV* NatWest Bank 1976–81; C St Dunstan and All SS Stepney 1983–87; P-in-c St Jo Bapt Isleworth 1987–92; V St Mark Mosborough w Em Waterthorpe 1992–99; RD Attercliffe 1996–99; Hon Can Sheff Cathl 1998–99; Can Res Sheff Cathl 1999–2005; M Pensions Bd 2004–09, Vc-Chair from 2006; Adn of Sheff and Rotherham 1999–2009; Bp of Warrington from 2009
GS 2000–05
        Tel: 0114 266 6009 (Home) 01709 309110 (Office)
                            07714 329638 (Mobile)
                        Fax: 01709 309107 (Office)

email: archdeacons.office@sheffield.anglican.org

BLACKBURN, Archdeacon of. See HAWLEY, Ven John Andrew

BLACKBURN, Bishop of. See READE, Rt Revd Nicholas Stewart

BLACKBURN, Dean of. See ARMSTRONG, Very Revd Christopher John

BOARDMAN, Ven Jonathan Thomas, MA
Via del Babuino 153 00187 Rome Italy [ARCHDEACON OF ITALY AND MALTA; EUROPE] *b* 1963 *educ* Bolton Sch; Magd Coll Ox; Magd Coll Cam; Westcott Ho; *CV* C St Mary W Derby, Liv 1990– 93; Prec St Alb Abbey 1993–96; TR Catford and Downham, S'wark 1996–99; RD E Lewisham 1998–99; Chapl All SS Rome from 1999; Sen tutor, Angl Cen Rome from 2001; M S'wark Dioc Syn and Bp's Coun 1996–99; M Eur Dioc Syn and Bp's Coun 2004–07; Area Dean Italy and Malta from 2007; Can Dioc Cath Chapter from 2007; Adn Italy and Malta from 2009
GS 2005–09   *Tel:* +39 06 3600 1881
                        +39 349 655 8844 (Mobile)
                        Fax: +39 06 3600 1881
                    email: office@allsaintsrome.org

BOARDMAN, Preb Philippa Jane, MA
Vicarage St Stephen's Rd London E3 5JL [LONDON] *b* 1963 *educ* Haberdashers' Aske's Sch for Girls; Jes Coll Cam; Ridley Hall Th Coll; *CV* C St Mary and St Steph Walthamstow 1990–93; Asst Pr St Mary of Eton Hackney Wick 1993–96; P-in-c St Paul w St Mark Old Ford 1996–2003, V from 2003; Preb St Paul's Cathl from 2002
GS 1994–   *Tel:* 020 8980 9020
                            Fax: 020 8981 5055

BODDINGTON, Ms Caroline Elizabeth, MA
(Oxon), MCIPD
The Wash House Lambeth Palace London SE1 7JU [ARCHBISHOPS' SECRETARY FOR APPOINTMENTS] *b* 1964 *educ* Malvern Girls' Coll; Keble Coll Ox; *CV* BG Grp 1986–2003: HR Strategy and Devel Mgr 1997–99, Hd of Learning and Devel 2000, Hd of HR Operations 2001–03; Abps' Sec for Appts from 2004   *Tel:* 020 7898 1876
                            020 7898 1877
            email: caroline.boddington@c-of-e.org.uk

BODMIN, Archdeacon of. See COHEN, Ven Clive Ronald Franklin

BODY, Mrs Debra Jane, CTABRSM
Linden Lea Bushley 2 Church St Bladon Oxon OX20 1RS [EXETER] *b* 1966 *educ* Hayesfield Sch, Bath; Newton Park; Bath Coll of HE; *CV* Underwriter/ claims assessor, Royal Insurance 1988–92; music tchr from 1995; M PCC; M dny syn, dioc syn
GS 2005–   *Tel:* 01684 275 963
            email: timanddebbody@phonecoop.coop

BOLTON, Archdeacon of. See **BAILEY, Ven David Charles**

BOLTON, Suffragan Bishop of. See **EDMONDSON, Rt Revd Christopher Paul**

BOOKER, Revd Michael Paul Montague, BA, MA, PGCE
92 Swaynes Lane Comberton Cambridge CB23 7EF [ELY] *b* 1957 *educ* Cambridgeshire County High Sch; Jesus Coll, Ox; Bris Univ; Trin Coll, Bris; *CV* Tchr, Purley Boys' High Sch 1980–84; C, St Mary Bredin, Cant 1987–91; V, St Mary, Leamington Priors 1991–96; Dir of Miss & Pstrl Studies, Ridley Hall, Cam 1996–2005; P-in-C, Comberton and Toft 2005–10; TR, Lordsbridge Team Ministry from 2010; Chair Dioc Children's Counc 2006–2010
GS 2010–   *Tel*: 01223 260095
          email: mikebooker@lordsbridge.org

BOOTH, Mr John David Sebastian, MA, FRSA
Simon's Lee Amberley West Sussex BN18 9NR [CHICHESTER] *b* 1958 *educ* Huish's Gr Sch Taunton; Mert Coll Ox; *CV* Vc Pres Merrill Lynch 198386; Sen Vc Pres Prudential Bache 198893; Man Dir Bankers Trust Internat 199396; Chair Luther Pendragon Ltd from 1992; Maintel Holdings PLC from 1996; Integrated Asset Mgt PLC from 1998, Jazz FM from 2009; Dir Herald Investment Mgmt Ltd; Oldfield and Partners Ltd; Staffcare Ltd; Chair Link ICAP (subs. of ICAP plc); M AC Fin Cttee 1999–2010 and Investment Review Group 2009–; M CAC; M DBF; Chair Pensions Measure Review Cttee 2001–2; Guardian Nat Shrine of Our Lady of Walsingham; M Chancellor's Court, University of Oxford; M Chancellors Forum, Univ of the Arts Lon; Hon. Fellow and M Coun St Steph Ho, Ox; Gov Pusey Ho, Ox; M Canterbury Cathedral Campaign Board
GS 1999–   *Tel*: 01798 831344
          07767 474343 (Mobile)
          email: j@johnbooth.com

BOOYS, Revd Canon Sue (Susan) Elizabeth, BA, Cert Th, PGCE, MA
Rectory Manor Farm Rd Dorchester-on-Thames Wallingford OX10 7HZ [OXFORD] *b* 1956 *educ* Harrow County Girls' Sch; Bristol Univ; Ox Min Course; Heythrop, Lon Univ; *CV* C Kidlington Tm Ox 1995–99; TV Dorchester Tm Ox from 1999, TR from 2005; M Bp's Coun; M GS Business Cttee; Gov Ripon Coll Cuddesdon from 2006; AD Aston and Cuddesdon from 2007
GS 2002–   *Tel*: 01865 340007
          07815 609602 (Mobile)
          Fax: 01865 341192
          email: rector@dorchester-abbey.org.uk

BOURNEMOUTH, Archdeacon of. (NOT APPOINTED AT TIME OF GOING TO PRESS)

BOYD-LEE, Mr Paul Winston Michael, BA, Dip Th
Manor Barn Horsington Templecombe BA8 0ET [SALISBURY] *b* 1941 *educ* Brighton Coll; Open Univ; Ex Univ; *CV* Theatre Mgr Rank Organization 1963–66; Credit Controller Internat Factors Ltd 1966–72; Dir Bible Truth Publishers from 1972; a Dir of Ch Army from 1999; M Ch Army Investment and Remuneration Cttees; M AC from 2005; M Audit Cttee from 2006; M Ethical Investment Adv Gp
GS 1991–   *Tel*: 01963 371137
          07710 604777 (Mobile)
          email: paulbl@btinternet.com

BOYLING, Very Revd Mark Christopher, MA
The Deanery Carlisle CA3 8TZ [DEAN OF CARLISLE] *b* 1952 *educ* K Jas Gr Sch Almondbury, W Yorks; Keble Coll Ox; Cuddesdon Th Coll; *CV* C St Mark Northwood, Kirkby 1977–79; TV 1979–85; Chapl to Bp of Liv 1985–89; V St Pet Formby, Liv 1989–94; Can Res and Prec Liv Cathl 1994–2004; Dean of Carlisle from 2004   *Tel*: 01228 523335
          Fax: 01228 547049
          email: dean@carlislecathedral.org.uk

BRACKLEY, Rt Revd Ian James, MA
Dayspring 13 Pilgrims Way Guildford GU4 8AD [SUFFRAGAN BISHOP OF DORKING; GUILDFORD] *b* 1947 *educ* Westcliff High Sch; Keble Coll Ox; Cuddesdon Th Coll; Ecum Inst Geneva; *CV* C St Mary Magd w St Fran Lockleaze Bris 1971–74; Asst Chapl Bryanston Sch 1974–77; Chapl 1977–80; V St Mary E Preston Chich 1980–88; RD Arundel and Bognor 1982–87; TR St Wilf Haywards Heath 1988–96; RD Cuckfield 1989–95; Bp of Dorking from 1996; M Ho of Bps CME Cttee from 2001; M Bd of Ch Army 2002; M CCU 2006; Chair Bd of Govs of STETS 1999; Commissary Bp for Portsm Dioc 2009–10
GS 1990–95, 2001, 2005   *Tel*: 01483 570829
          Fax: 01483 567268
          email: bishop.ian@cofeguildford.org.uk

BRADFORD, Archdeacon of. See **LEE, Ven David John**

BRADFORD, Bishop of. (NOT APPOINTED AT TIME OF GOING TO PRESS)

BRADFORD, Dean of. See **ISON, Very Revd David John**

BRADLEY, Ven Peter David Douglas, B Th
Rectory 1A College Rd Up Holland Skelmersdale WN8 0PY [ARCHDEACON OF WARRINGTON; LIVERPOOL] *b* 1949 *educ* Brookfield Comp Sch; Nottm Univ; Ian Ramsey Coll; Linc Th Coll; *CV* C Up Holland 1979–83; V H Spirit Dovecot 1983–94; Sec Dioc Bd of Min 1983–88; Sec Grp for Urban Min and Leadership 1984–88; Asst Dir In-Service Trg 1988–89; Dir CME from 1989; TR St Tho Up Holland from 1994; M BM Mission at Home

Who does **Christ's work today** in the Holy Land?

Bible*Lands* seeks to improve the lives of vulnerable and disadvantaged people in the Middle East.

We do this in partnership with local Christians, focusing on education, healthcare and community development.

For further information, resources, or to invite a guest speaker, please contact us on **01494 897950 www.biblelands.org.uk**

Cttee; M Dioc Bd of Min; Hon Can Liv Cathl from 2000; Adn of Warrington from 2001/2
GS 1990–2010   *Tel:* 01695 622936
                               Fax: 01695 625865
email: archdeacon@peterbradley.fsnet.co.uk

BRADLEY, Very Revd Peter Edward, MA
Sheffield Cathedral Church St Sheffield S1 1HA [DEAN OF SHEFFIELD] *b* 1964 *educ* R Belfast Academical Inst; Trin Hall Cam; Ripon Coll Cuddesdon; *CV* C St Mich & All A w St Edm Northampton 1988–90; Chapl Gonville & Caius Coll Cam 1990–95; TV St Mich Abingdon 1995–98; TV All SS High Wycombe 1998–2003, TR 2003; Dean of Sheffield from 2003; Fell Coll of Prchrs, Washington DC from 2006   *Tel:* 0114 275 3434
                               0114 263 6063
                               Fax: 0114 279 7412
email: dean@sheffield-cathedral.org.uk

BRADWELL, Area Bishop of. See GREEN, Rt Revd Laurie (Laurence Alexander)

BRANDON, Revd Beatrice, MA, DMS, FRSA, FRSM
Clopton Manor Clopton Northants NN14 3DZ [ARCHBISHOP'S ADVISER FOR THE HEALING MINISTRY] *b* 1955 *educ* Heythrop Coll Lon; *CV* M Dioc Past Ctee 1992–2005; M Abps Millenium Adv Gp 1996–2000; Dioc Vacancy-in-See Ctee 1996–2003; Chair Ho Laity and Lay Vc Chair Dioc Syn Peterb 1997–2003; Convener Ho Bps Healing Min Strg Gp 2000–07; Chair Chs Together for Healing 2004–08; Trustee Abp York Youth Trust from 2008; Abps' Adv for Healing Min from 2008
GS 1995–2005   *Tel:* 01832 720346
                               Fax: 01832 720446
email: beatrice@healingministry.org.uk

BRETT, Mr Justin Edward, MA, PGCE
Roedean School Brighton BN2 5RQ [CHICHESTER] *b* 1971 *educ* Cheltenham Coll; Ex Coll Ox; *CV* Tchr Caldicott Sch 1995–2001; Head of English and RS, Brockhurst Sch 2001–2002; Policy Exec West Berkshire Counc 2003–04; Tchr, St Gabriel's Sch 2004–08; Head of Classics, St Aubyns Sch from 2008; Lay Chair Newbury Deanery 2006–08
GS 2005–   *Tel:* 07876 746074
email: justin.brett@yahoo.co.uk

BREWER, Mrs Rosalind Patricia Anne, BA, RGN
37 Greenstead Road Newby Scarborough YO12 6HN [YORK] *b* 1947 *CV* Qualified RGN 1968; Staff Nurse 1968–70; Night Sister 1972–78; Practice Nursing Sister 1982–90; Family Planning Sister 1984–2006; Senior Practice Nursing Sister/Mgr 1990–2006; Cytology Adv to Primary Care Trust 1995–2006; Nurse Tutor and Assessor 1998–2006; Dioc Prop Sub Cttee from 2010; Archbp's Counc from 2006; Patronage Brd from 2006; Vice Chair Dioc Pstrl & Miss Sub Cttee from 2004;York Dioc Syn from 2006; Lay Chair Scarborough Deanery Syn from 2005
GS 2010–   *Tel:* 01723369731
email: ros.brewer@btinternet.com

BRIDEN, Rt Worshipful Timothy John, MA, LLB
Lamb Chambers Lamb Building Temple London EC4Y 7AS [VICAR-GENERAL OF CANTERBURY] *b* 1951 *educ* Ipswich Sch; Downing Coll Cam; *CV* Chancellor of Dioc of B&W from 1993; Chancellor of Dioc of Truro from 1998; Vicar-General of Canterbury from 2005; M Legal Adv Commn
GS 2005–   *Tel:* 020 7797 8300
                               Fax: 020 7797 8308
email: info@lambchambers.co.uk

BRIERLEY, Ven David James, BA Hons
Sudbury Lodge Stanningfield Rd Great Whelnetham Bury St Edmunds IP30 0TL [ARCHDEACON OF SUDBURY; ST EDMUNDSBURY AND IPSWICH] *b* 1953 *educ* Fearns Co Secdry; Bacup and Rawtenstall Gr Sch; Bristol Univ; Oak Hill Th Coll; *CV* C St Mary Balderstone, Rochdale, Manch 1977–80; TV Eccles 1980–85; Manch Dioc Ecum Officer 1981–88; V Harwood 1985–95; Chair Decade of Evang, Manch 1991–99; V and RD Walmsley 1995–2002; Dioc Missr, Bradf 2002–06; Res Can Bradf 2002–04; Adn of Sudbury from 2006
                               Tel and Fax: 01284 386942
                               email: archdeacon.david@
                               stedmundsbury.anglican.org

BRINDLEY, Very Revd David Charles, BD, M Th, M Phil, AKC
The Deanery 13 Pembroke Rd Portsmouth PO1 2NS [DEAN OF PORTSMOUTH] *b* 1953 *educ* Wednesfield Gr Sch; K Coll Lon; *CV* C Epping, Chelms 1976–79; Lect, Coll of St Paul and St Mary, Cheltenham 1979–82; V Quorn and Dir of Clergy Trg, Leic 1982–86; Prin W of Eng Minl Trg Course 1987–94; TR Warwick 1994–2002; Dean of Portsm from 2002; Chair Portsm DAC from 2003; Sec and Treas Assoc of Engl Cathls from 2005
GS 1985–87, 2004–   *Tel:* 023 9282 4400 (Home)
                               023 9234 7605 (Office)
                               Fax: 023 9229 5480
                               email: david.brindley@
                               portsmouthcathedral.org.uk

BRISTOL, Archdeacon of. See McCLURE, Ven Tim (Timothy Elston)

BRISTOL, Bishop of. See HILL, Rt Revd Michael Arthur

BRISTOL, Dean of, see HOYLE, Very Revd Dr David Michael

BRITTON, Mr Andrew James Christie, BA, MSc
2 Shabden Park High Rd, Chipstead Coulsdon, Surrey CR5 3SF [ARCHBISHOPS' COUNCIL] *b* 1940 *educ* R Gr Sch, Newc-upon-Tyne; Oriel Coll Ox; Lon Sch of Economics; *CV* Economist HM Treasury 1968–82; Dir Nat Institute of Economic and Social Research 1982–95; Exec Sec Ch's Enquiry into Unemployment and the Future of Work 1995–97; Chair S'wark Dioc Bd of Fin 2000–2007; Chair Abps' Coun Fin Cttee from 2007

Chair S'wark Dioc Bd of Fin 2000–2007; Chair Abps' Coun Fin Cttee from 2007
GS 2007– *Tel:* 01737 553 678

BRIXWORTH, Suffragan Bishop of. (NOT APPOINTED AT TIME OF GOING TO PRESS)

BROADBENT, Rt Revd Pete (Peter Alan), MA
173 Willesden Lane Brondesbury London NW6 7YN [AREA BISHOP OF WILLESDEN AND ACTING BISHOP OF STEPNEY; LONDON] *b* 1952 *educ* Merchant Taylors Sch Northwood; Jes Coll Cam; St Jo Coll Nottm; *CV* C St Nic Dur City 1977–80; C Em Holloway 1980–83; Chapl to N Lon Poly and Hon C St Mary Islington 1983–89; Bp's Chapl for Miss in Stepney 1980–89; Councillor and Chair of Planning Lon Boro of Islington 1982–89; V Trin St Mich Harrow 1989–95; AD Harrow 1994; Adn of Northolt 1995–2001; Bp of Willesden from 2001; M Dioc Commn 1989–92; M Panel of Chairmen GS 1990-92, from 2009; M C of E Evang Coun 1984–95, from 2006; Chair Vacancy-in-See Cttee Regulation Wkg Pty 1991–93; M GS Stg Orders Cttee 1991–95; M Appts Sub-Cttee 1992–95; M CBF 1991–98; M GS Stg Cttee 1992–98; Chair GS Business Sub-Cttee 1996–98; Chair Elections Review Grp 1996–2000; Chair Lon Dioc Bd for Schs 1996–2006; Chair Memralife Gp (Spring Harvest/ICC); Chair Business Cttee 1999–2000; M AC 1999–2000; M City Parochial Foundn 1999–2003; M Urban Bps Panel from 2001; Trustee CUF from 2002; Chair Coun St Jo Coll Nottm 2002–10; Pres W Lon YMCA from 2004; Chair Standards Cttee, Lon Boro Harrow 2006–2010; Chair Eden Greater Lon Network from 2010; Chair Bless Network from 2004; Vc Pres CPAS from 2009; Chair Dioc Strategic Policy Cttee from 2009
GS 1985–2001; 2004– *Tel:* 020 8451 0189
07957 144674 (Mobile)
Fax: 020 8451 4606
email: bishop.willesden@btinternet.com

BROMILOW, Dr Ian Geoffrey, BSc, MSc, Phd
The Old School Hilton Blandford Forum Dorset DT11 0DB [SALISBURY] *b* 1956 *educ* Tower Coll, Rainhill & Scarisbrick Hall Sch, Southport; UCL; ICL; Bris Univ; *CV* Country Chair, Shell Companies in Jordan & Iraq, Amman, Jordan, 2006–09; Country Chair, Shell Iraq, Dubai,UAE, 2005–06; Mging Dir, Shell/BP Kenya Ltd and Shell Tanzania, Nairobi, Kenya 2002–05; Gen Mgr, Shell Uganda and Shell Rwanda, 2000–02; Head Consumer Lubricants, Shell International, London, 1998–2000; Brand Mgr, Shell International, London, 1995–98; Marketing and Sales Mgr, SASLUCO (Shell Joint Venture), Jeddah, Saudi Arabia, 1991–95; Base oil Supply, Demand & Trading, Shell International, 1989–91; Oil Market Analyst, Shell International London, 1986–89; Math, Shell Rsrch, Amsterdam, The Netherlands, 1982–86; Lay Minister Training
GS 2010– *Tel:* 01258880044
email: igbromilow@gmail.com

BROMLEY AND BEXLEY, Archdeacon of. See WRIGHT, Ven Paul

BROOKE, Revd David Martin, MA, PGCE
The Rectory Church Lane Redmarshall Stockton-on-Tees TS21 1ES [DURHAM] *b* 1958 *educ* Ferryhill Comp Sch; Selwyn Coll Cam; ULIE; SAOMC; *CV* Asst Master, Bedford Sch 1981–85; Marketing Mngr, Epson UK 1985–92; Marketing Mngr, Dell UK 1992–99; C Luton Lewsey St Hugh St Alb 1999–00; NSM Sunnyside w Bourne End 2000–02; C 2002–04 V Bishopton w Gt Stainton Dur from 2004; R Redmarshall from 2004; R Grindon, Stillington and Wolviston from 2004; P-in-c Billingham St Mary from 2010; AD Stockton from 2007
GS 2010– *Tel:* 01740 630810 07967 326085
email: david@revd.co.uk

BROWN, Mr Andrew Charles, B Sc, FRICS
Church House Great Smith St London SW1P 3AZ [SECRETARY, CHURCH COMMISSIONERS] *b* 1957 *educ* Ashmole Comp Sch; S Bank Poly; *CV* Healey & Baker 1981–84; St Quintin 1984–94; Dep Sec and Chief Surveyor Ch Commrs 1994–2003, Sec from 2003; M Fin and Invest Ctee, Lionheart from 2007; M Allchurches Trust from 2008; Trustee and Chair the2:67project 2007–10; Trustee William Leech (Foundn) and Dir William Leech (Invest) from 2007
Tel: 020 7898 1785
Fax: 020 7898 1131
email: andrew.brown@c-of-e.org.uk

BROWN, Revd Dr Malcolm Arthur, MA, PhD, FHEA
Church House Great Smith St London SW1P 3AZ [DIRECTOR, MISSION AND PUBLIC AFFAIRS DIVISION, ARCHBISHOPS' COUNCIL] *b* 1954 *educ* Eltham Coll; Oriel Coll Ox; Man Univ; Westcott Ho Cam; *CV* C Riverhead w. Dunton Green, Roch 1979–83; TV and Ind Missioner, Southn City Centre, Winch 1983–91; Exec Sec William Temple Foundn 1991–2000; Hon C St Paul Heaton Moor, Man 1993–2000; Prin EAMTC 2000–05; Prin ERMC 2005–07; Dir MPA from 2007; M BSR Ind and Economic Affairs Cttee 1987–91; M BSR Soc, Economic and Ind Affairs Cttee 1997–2002; Th Consult Rev of Diocs, Pastl and Related Measures 2001–04; M Min Div Th Educ and Trg Cttee; M Min Div Fin Panel 2006–07
Tel: 020 7898 1468
email: malcolm.brown@c-of-e.org.uk

BROWN, Mr Philip Charles, MA
75 Dells Lane Biggleswade SG18 8LH [ST ALBANS] *b* 1946 *educ* Bedford Modern School, Emmanuel College Cambridge; *CV* M St Albans Bishop's Council; Board of Finance; Board for Church Society from 2006; Lay Chair Biggleswade Deanery Synod from 2005 *Tel:* 01767 312576
email: phil@gableend.me.uk

BROWN, Mr Richard Alexander Hamilton,
Glebe House Ingleby Arncliffe Northallerton York-shire DL6 3JX [YORK] *b* 1974 *educ* Stokesley Sch; Univ of Humberside; YMC; *CV* Comp Dir from 2005; Elected GS 2010
GS 2010–   *Tel:* 01609 882141
                    email: richard.brown@yorksj.ac.uk

BRUINVELS, Canon Peter Nigel Edward, LLB, FRSA, FCIM, MCIJ, MCIPR
14 High Meadow Close St Paul's Rd West Dorking RH4 2LG [GUILDFORD] *b* 1950 *educ* St Jo Sch Leatherhead; Lon Univ; Inns of Court Sch of Law; *CV* MP Leic E 1983–87; Party Candidate The Wrekin 1997; Prin Peter Bruinvels Associates, Media Mgt and Public Affairs Consults; M Dioc Syn and Dorking Dny Syn from 1974; Freeman of City of Lon 1980; M Dios Commn 1991–96; M Legislative Cttee 1991–96 and from 2000; News Broadcaster, Political Commentator and Free-lance Journalist; Ch Commr from 1992, Pastl Cttee from 1993, Gov Ch Cmmrs from 1992; Mgt Adv Cttee 1999–2009; Ofsted and Section 48 SIAS RE Sch Insp from 1994; M DSS Child Support and Soc Security Appeals Tribunal 1994–99; Man Ed Bruinvels News & Media, Press and Broadcasting Agents; M Dioc Bd of Educ from 1994; M GS Bd of Educ 1996–2006; Co-opted M Surrey LEA 1997–2007; Gov Univ of York St Jo 1999–2007; Dir Ch Army and Chair Remuneration Cttee 1999–2004; Independent Lay Chair NHS Complaints Tribunal 1999–2004; M Clergy Discipline Review Grp from 1999; Chair Surrey Schs Organization Cttee 2000–07; Court Member Univ of Sussex 2000–08; M Dearing Implementation Grp from 2001; County Field Officer (Surrey) Royal Br Legion from 2002; Dir E Elmbridge and Mid Surrey Primary Care Trust 2002–07; M Mgt Adv Cttee 1999–2009; Lay Can Guildf Cathl from 2002; Vc-Pres and Chair Ho of Laity, Dioc Syn from 2003; Guild CNC from 2003; M SE War Pensions Cttee from 2003; Chair Surrey Joint Services Charities Cttee from 2004; Chair Guildf Dioc Bd of Educ 2005–08; Hon Sec Surrey County Appeals Cttee form 2002; M Guildf Coll of Cans from 2002; M Cathls Fabric Commn for Eng from 2006; M Guildf Cathl Coun from 2006; Gov Whitelands Coll (Roehampton Univ) from 2007, Chair from 2009; Dep Chair Nominations & Gov-ernance Cttee (Ch Commissioners) from 2009
GS 1985–   *Tel:* 01306 887082 (Home)
                    01372 386500 (Office)
                    07721 411688 (Mobile)
                    Fax: 0870 133 1756
                    01372 375843
email: canonpeterbruinvels@talk21.com / pba@ supanet.com (Office)

BRYANT, Rt Revd Mark Watts, BA
Bishop's House 25 Ivy Lane Gateshead NE9 6QD [SUFFRAGAN BISHOP OF JARROW] *b* 1949 *educ* St Jo Sch Leatherhead; St Jo Coll Dur; Cuddesdon Th Coll; *CV* C Addlestone 1975–79; C St Jo Studley,

Trowbridge 1979–83, V 1983–88; Chapl Trow-bridge CFE 1979–83; DDO and Dir Vocations and Tr, Cov 1988–96; Hon Can Cov Cathl 1993–2001; TR Cov Caludon 1996–2001; AD Cov E 1999–2001; Adn of Coventry 2001–07; Can Res Cov Cathl 2006–07; Bp of Jarrow from 2007
GS 1998–2008   *Tel:* 0191 491 0917
                    Fax: 0191 491 5116
email: bishop.of.jarrow@durham.anglican.org

BUCKINGHAM, Archdeacon of. See GORHAM, Ven Karen Marisa

BUCKINGHAM, Area Bishop of. See WILSON, Rt Revd Alan Thomas Lawrence

BUCKLER, Very Revd Philip John Warr, MA
The Deanery 11 Minster Yard Lincoln LN2 1PJ [DEAN OF LINCOLN] *b* 1949 *educ* Highgate Sch; St Pet Coll Ox; Cuddesdon Coll; *CV* C St Pet Bushey Heath 1972–75; Chapl Trin Coll Cam 1975–81; Sacr and Min Can St Paul's Cathl 1981–86; V Hampstead 1987–99; AD N Camden 1993–98; Can Res St Paul's Cathl 1999–2007, Treas 2000–07; Dean of Lincoln from 2007   *Tel:* 01522 561611
                    Fax: 01522 561603
                    email: dean@lincolncathedral.com

BULL, Dr John W, B Sc, Ph D, D Sc, Eur Ing, C Eng, FIHT, FIStructE, FIWSC, FICE
Gable Ends 11 Glebe Mews Bedlington NE22 6LJ [NEWCASTLE] *b* 1944 *educ* Farnborough Gr Sch; Ches Coll of Educ; Univ Coll Cardiff; *CV* Tchr ILEA 1966–68; Engineer/Chartered Engineer Dur Co Coun 1974–79; Lect in Structural Engineering Newc Univ 1979–2002, sen lect from 2002; Author and Ed of Engineering textbooks; M Dioc Syn from 1988; M Bp's Coun from 1988; Vc Pres Dioc Syn 1994–2006; Chair Dioc Bd of Educ 1991–97; Lay Chair Bedlington Dny Syn 1990–97; Dioc Bd of Educ from 2004
GS 1995–
                    Tel: 0191 222 7924 (Office) 0191 222 6418
                    07710 200416 (Mobile)
                    Fax: 0191 222 5322
                    email: John.Bull@newcastle.ac.uk

BULLOCK, Revd Canon Sarah Ruth, BA Dip
St Edmunds Rectory 1 Range Road Whalley Range Manchester M16 8FS [MANCHESTER] *b* 1964 *educ* Fallowfield C of E Sch; Univ of Surrey; Cranmer Hall, St. John's Coll, Dur; *CV* English Tchr, Chea-dle Hulme Sch 1986–90; Asst Dioc Yth Off, Man 1986–90; AC St. Paul, Kersal Moor w St Andrew, Man, 1993–98; P-in-C St Edmund, Whalley Range 1998–2004; P-in-C St. James' w St. Clement, Moss Side, 19999–2004; R United Benefice of St. Edmund, Whalley Range & St. James' w St. Clement, Man from 2004; Hon Can Man Cathl 2007; Bps Adv Womans Min, Man 2009; Dean City & Borough Man 2010; M Man Urban Regen & Sem Grp Commiss Urban Life & Faith, 1999–2009; M Discipleship & Min Training Cttee, Man,

2003–06; M Bps Adv Grp Sexuality 2004; Chair Discipleship & Min Training Cttee, Man, 2005; Bps Adv Womens Min, Man 2009; M Man Syn & DBF 2009; M Bps Counc 2010; M Min Devlp Review T, Man, 2010
GS 2010– *Tel and Fax:* 0161 226 1291
email: REVSBULLOCK@aol.com

BURNLEY, Suffragan Bishop of. See GODDARD, Rt Revd John William

BURRAGE, Mr Paul, BSc, FCA
Church House Great Smith St London SW1P 3AZ [DIRECTOR OF ACCOUNTING SERVICES, NATIONAL CHURCH INSTITUTIONS] *b* 1952 *educ* Reading Sch; Sir William Borlase's Sch; Newcastle Univ; *CV* Fin Man to Fin Dir in various internat Freight Forwarding Companies 1979–91; Fin Dir Heating Oil and Petroleum Distributor 1991–92; Consult, Dir of Fin and Resources British Red Cross 1993–2004; Head of Fin Refugee Coun 2005–05; Chief Accountant NCIs 2005–07; (Acting) Dir of Fin Accounting NCIs 2008–09; Dir Accounting Services from 2009 *Tel:* 020 7898 1677
Fax: 020 7898 1770
email: paul.burrage@c-of-e.org.uk

BURRIDGE, Revd Prof Richard Alan, MA, Ph D, PGCE, Dip Th, FKC
King's College London Strand London WC2R 2LS [UNIVERSITIES, LONDON] *b* 1955 *educ* Bris Cathl Sch; Univ Coll Ox; Nottm Univ; St Jo Coll Nottm; *CV* Classics Master and Ho Tutor Sevenoaks Sch 1978–82; C SS Pet and Paul Bromley 1985–87; Chapl and pt Lect in Depts of Th and Classics & Ancient History Univ of Ex 1987–94; Dean of K Coll Lon from 1994; M Academic Bd NTMTC 1994–2008; Chair Chr Evidence Soc from 1994; Chair Eric Symes Abbott Memorial Fund from 1994; M Studiorum Novi Testamenti Societas from 1995; M SST from 1995; M SBL from 1995; ABM External Moderator to SW Min Tr Course 1995–99; Chair Min Div Educ Validatory Panel 1998–2004; M Min Div TETC 1998–2004; M CECC; Commr to Bp of High Veld from 1996; GS Rep PIM Consultation to Province of W Africa 1997; Adv and Writer for Nat Millennium Experience Co and Greenwich Dome 1998–99; M Vote 1 Min Div Wkg Party 1999–2000; M Review Grp on Structure and Funding of Ordination Tr 2000–03; FKC 2002; Chair Bp of S'wark's Theol Grp 2004–2009; rep Abp of Cant and Angl Communion at Second World Congress for Pastl Care of Catholic Foreign Students, Rome, Dec 2005; M Academic Board St Mellitus College from 2008; M Ethical Investment Adv Gp (Ch Commns' rep) from 2008; Prof of Bibl Interpretation at K Coll Lon from 2008; Woods Fell (Visiting Prof) at Virginia Theol Seminary, Alexandria VA, USA 2009; Dep Chr Ethical Investment Adv Gp from 2010
GS 1994– *Tel:* 020 7848 2333
Fax: 020 7848 2344
email: richard.burridge@kcl.ac.uk

BURROWS, Mr Gerald David, B Sc, M Sc, T Cert
3 Hall Rd Fulwood Preston PR2 9QD [BLACKBURN] *b* 1942 *educ* Wellington Gr Sch; Univ Coll of N Wales, Bangor; *CV* Scientific Officer Rutherford High Energy Lab 1967–69; Lect Grimsby Coll of Tech 1969–71; Sen Lect Blackb Coll from 1971
GS 1990– *Tel:* 01772 719159
email: gerald.burrows@talk21.com

BURROWS, Ven Peter, B Th
Archdeacon's Lodge 3 West Park Grove Roundhay Leeds LS8 2HQ [ARCHDEACON OF LEEDS] *b* 1955 *educ* Spondon Ho Sec Sch; Derby Coll of FE; Sarum and Wells Th Coll; *CV* C Baildon 1983–87; R Broughton Astley 1993–93; P-in-c Stoney Stanton w Croft 1993–95; TR Broughton Astley and Croft w Stoney Stanton 1995–2000; RD Guthlaxton I 1994–2000; DDO and Par Development Officer 1996–2000; M Dioc Syn; M Vacancy-in-See Cttee; M DAC; Coord Dioc Tm Forum; M Bp's Coun; Hon Can Leic Cathl; Dep Dir Min from 2002; Dir Min 2003–05; Adn Leeds from 2005; Hon Can Ripon Cathl from 2005; Chair Min and Training Devel Grp; Chair One City Projects and Oastler Centre; Trustee Children's Internat Summer Villages; M Inst of Directors
GS 2010– *Tel:* 0113 269 0594
email: peterb@riponleeds-diocese.org.uk

BURTON-JONES, Ven Simon David, MA (Hons); BTh; MA
The Archdeaconry Kings Orchard, The Precinct Rochester, Kent ME1 1TG [ARCHDEACON OF ROCHESTER] *b* 1962 *educ* Fleetwood High Sch; Emmanuel Coll Cam; St John's Coll Nottm; *CV* TC St Peter's Darwen w St Paul's Hoddlesdon 1993–96; C St Mark's Biggin Hill 1996–98; V St Mary's Bromley 1998–2005; R St Nic Chislehurst 2005–10; Adn of Roch from 2010
Tel: 01634 813533 (Home)
01634 560000 (Office)
email: simonburtonjones@btinternet.com
web: www.simonburton-jones.com

BUSH, Ven Roger Charles, BA
Westwood House Tremorvah Crescent Truro TR1 1NL [ARCHDEACON OF CORNWALL; TRURO] *b* 1956 *educ* Fakenham Gr Sch; K Coll Lon; Coll of the Resurr, Mirfield; *CV* C Newbold, Derby 1986–90; TV Parish of the Resurr, Leic 1990–94; TR Redruth w. Lanner & Treleigh, Truro 1994–2004; Can Chan, Truro Cathl 2004–06; Adn of Cornwall from 2006
GS 2004– *Tel:* 01872 225630
01872 274351
email: roger@truro.anglican.org

BUTCHER, Dr Jackie (Jacqueline Anne), MA, M Sc, Ph D
10 Vernon Rd Totley Rise Sheffield S17 3QE [SHEFFIELD] *b* 1965 *educ* Wootton Upper Sch; Newnham Coll Cam; Sussex Univ; Leic Univ; *CV* Rsch Associate 1992–95; full-time mother 1995–2000;

M Dioc Bd Faith & Justice; Bp's Adv in World Development Issues
GS 2000–   Tel: 0114 262 1293
                    email: ja_butcher@yahoo.co.uk

BUTLER, Rt Revd Paul Roger,
Bishop's Manor Bishop's Drive Southwell NG25 0JR [BISHOP OF SOUTHWELL AND NOTTINGHAM] *b* 1955 *educ* Kingston Grammar Sch; Nottm Univ; Wycliffe Hall; *CV* C All Saints w Holy Trinity, Wandsworth 1983–87; Scripture Union Inner Lon Evang 1987–92; Dep Head of Miss 1992–94; NSM St Paul's, East Ham (Chelmsford) 1988–94; P-in-C St Mary w St Stephen Walthamstow (Chelmsford) 1994–97; P-in-C St Luke, Walthamstow 1994–97; TR of Walthamstow 1997–2004; AD Walthamstow Forest 2000–04; Can St Paul's Byumba, Rwanda from 2001; Bp of Southampton 2004–2009; Bp of Southwell and Nottm from 2009; Chair of CMS 2008–10 Bp of Southwell and Nottingham from 2009   Tel: 01636 812112
                email: bishop@southwell.anglican.org

BUTLER, Canon Simon, BSc, DTS, MA
Rectory 1 Addington Rd Sanderstead South Croydon CR2 8RE [SOUTHWARK] *b* 1964 *educ* Bournemouth Sch; UEA; Britannia R Naval Coll; St Jo Coll Nottm; *CV* C Chandler's Ford, Winch 1992–94; C St Jos Worker Northolt, Lon 1994–97; V Immanuel and St Andr Streatham, S'wark 1997–2004; AD Streatham 2002–04; P-in-c and acting TR Sanderstead TM, S'wark from 2004, TR from 2006; M S'wark Dioc Liturg Cttee
GS 2005–   Tel: 020 8657 1366
            email: rector@sanderstead-parish.org.uk

BUTTERFIELD, Ven David John, B Mus, Dip Th, DPS
Brimley Lodge 27 Molescroft Rd Beverley HU17 7DX [ARCHDEACON OF THE EAST RIDING; YORK] *b* 1952 *educ* Belle Vue Boys Gr Sch Bradf; R Holloway Coll Lon Univ; St Jo Coll Nottm; *CV* C Ch Ch Southport 1977–81; Min St Thos CD Aldridge 1981–91; V St Mich Lilleshall w. St Mary Sheriffhales 1991–2002; V St Mich Lilleshall w. St Jo Muxton and St Mary Sheriffhales 2002–07; M BM 1995–96; RD Edgmond 1997–98; RD Edgmond and Shifnal 1999–2006; M Bp's Coun (Lich) 1994–2006; Chair Dioc Syn Ho of Clergy 2003–06; Adn of E Riding from 2007
GS 1990–2005   Tel and Fax: 01482 881659
        email: archdeacon.of.eastriding@yorkdiocese.org

BUTTERY, Revd Graeme, BA, MA
St Oswald's Clergy House Brougham Terrace Hartlepool TS24 8EY [DURHAM] *b* 1962 *educ* Dame Allan's Boys Sch Newc; York Univ; Newc Univ; St Steph Ho Th Coll; *CV* C Peterlee 1988–91; C Sunderland, TM 1991–92; TV Sunderland, TM 1992–94; V St Lawr the Martyr Horsley Hill 1994–2005; V St Oswald Hartlepool from 2005
GS 1995–   Tel: 01429 273201
                    email: G_BUTTERY@sky.com

CALVER, Revd Canon Gill, B Sc
New Rectory High St Staplehurst TN12 0BJ [CANTERBURY] *b* 1947 *educ* Sydenham High Sch; Q Eliz Coll, Univ of Lon; *CV* Chapl to the Queen from 2008
GS 2005–2010   Tel and Fax: 01580 891258
                email: gill.calver@btinternet.com

CAMBRIDGE, Archdeacon of. See BEER, Ven John Stuart

CAMERON, Rt Worshipful Dr Sheila Morag Clark, CBE, QC, DCL, MA, LLM
Bayleaves Bepton Midhurst GU29 9RB [DEAN OF THE ARCHES AND AUDITOR] *b* 1934 *educ* Commonweal Lodge Sch Purley; St Hugh's Coll Ox; Univ of Cardiff; *CV* Barrister-at-Law; Official Prin Adnry of Hampstead 1968–86; Chan Chelms Dioc 1969–2001; Chan Lon Dioc 1992–2001; Chair Eccl Judges Assoc 1997–2004; M Legal Adv Commn from 1975; M Marriage Commn 1975–78; Chair Abps' Grp on the Episcopate 1986–90; Boundary Commr for England 1989–96; Vic-Gen Province of Cant 1983–2005; Recorder of Crown Court 1985–99; M Coun on Tribunals 1986–90
GS 1983–   Tel: 020 7828 0770
                                               01730 813971
            Fax: 020 7828 0770 01730 716300

CAMPBELL, Dr (John) Graham, Ph D, B Sc, FCA
18 Eaglesfield Hartford Northwich CW8 1NQ [CHESTER] *b* 1942 *educ* Man Gr Sch, Birm Univ; *CV* Birm Univ Rsch Chemist ICI 1966–71; Student Accountant Worth & Co 1971–74; Audit Sen Spicer & Pegler 1974–76; Accountant then Commercial Mgr Br Nuclear Fuels plc 1976–2003; M Bp's Coun from 1998; M Dioc Fin and Cen Services Cttee from 1997; M Foxhill Dioc Conf Cen Coun from 1998; M C of E Pensions Bd from 2004; Treas C of E Evang Coun from 2005
GS 2000–   Tel: 01606 75849
            email: j.graham.campbell@googlemail.com

CANTERBURY, Archbishop of. See WILLIAMS, Most Revd and Rt Hon Rowan Douglas

CANTERBURY, Archdeacon of. See WATSON, Ven Sheila Anne

CANTERBURY, Dean of. See WILLIS, Very Revd Robert Andrew

CAPON, Dr Peter Charles, B Sc, Ph D
137 Birchfields Rd Manchester M14 6PJ [MANCHESTER] *b* 1944 *educ* Kimbolton Sch; Southn Univ; Cam Univ; Man Univ; *CV* Sen Lect in Computer Science Man Univ 1976–2004; rtd; Rdr at H Trin Rusholme, Manch from 1991
GS 1995–   Tel: 0161 225 5970
                email: peter.capon@cs.man.ac.uk

CARLISLE, Archdeacon of. See PRATT Richard David

CARLISLE, Bishop of. See NEWCOME, Rt Revd James William Scobie

CARLISLE, Dean of. See BOYLING, Very Revd Mark Christopher

CARR, Mrs Katherine Mary, BA, PGCE
Old Post Office Marrick Richmond DL11 7LQ [RIPON AND LEEDS] *b* 1932 *educ* Richmond High Sch·for Girls; Westf Coll Lon; Lon Univ Inst of Educ; *CV* Asst Mistress Burghley Primary Sch Lon 1953–55; Asst Mistress Parliament Hill Comp Sch 1955–59; Lect Darlington Coll of Educ 1959–60, 1969–72; Dep Hd Sedgefield Comp Sch 1972–80; Hd Woodham Comp Sch Newton Aycliffe 1980–90; Rtd; JP; M Dioc Syn; Lay Chair Richmond Dny Syn; M Bp's Coun; Talking Newspaper; Life Pres Richmondshire Concert Soc
GS 1995–2010
email: katherinecarr@btinternet.com

CARTWRIGHT, Revd Paul, BA, PGCE
Priory House 24 Kirkland Gardens Monk Bretton Barnsley S71 2GD [WAKEFIELD] *b* 1971 *educ* Hemsworth H Sch; Leeds Met Univ; Univ of Huddersfield; Leeds Univ; Coll of the Resurrection, Mirfield; *CV* Police Officer, West Yorkshire Police,1990–2006; Major Incident/Crime Family Liasion Officer, West Yorkshire Police 2002–06; Equalities & Diversity Trainer, West Yorkshire Police 2003–06; Barnsley Deanery Vocations Off from 2010; AC St Helen's Church, Athersley from 2008
GS 2010–   *Tel:* 01226 285209 07852 174303
email: fr.paul.cartwright@gmail.com

CASSIDY, Rt Revd George Henry, B Sc, M Phil
Bishop's Manor Southwell NG25 0JR [BISHOP OF SOUTHWELL AND NOTTINGHAM] *b* 1942 *educ* Belfast High Sch; Qu Univ Belfast; Univ Coll Lon; Oak Hill Th Coll; *CV* C Ch Ch Clifton Bris 1972–75; V St Edyth Sea Mills Bris 1975–82; V St Paul Portman Sq Lon 1982–87; Adn of Lon and Can Res St Paul's Cathl 1987–99; Bp of S'well and Nottm from 1999; entered Ho of Lords 2003
GS 1995–   *Tel:* 01636 812112
Fax: 01636 815401
email: bishop@southwell.anglican.org

CASTLE, Rt Revd Dr Brian Colin, BA, MA, Ph D
Bishop's Lodge 48 St Botolph's Road Sevenoaks TN13 3AG [SUFFRAGAN BISHOP OF TONBRIDGE; ROCHESTER] *b* 1949 *educ* Wilson's Gr Sch, Camberwell; Univ Coll London; Cuddesdon Coll Ox; Univ of Birm; *CV* Asst C St Nic Sutton 1977; Asst C St Pet Limpsfield, S'wark 1977–81; P-in-c Chingola, Chililabombwe and Solwezi, N Zambia 1981–4; Vis Lect Ecum Inst, Bossey, Switzerland 1984–5; V N Petherton and Northmoor Green 1985–92; Vc Prin and Dir of Pastl Studies Ripon Coll Cud-

desdon 1992–2001; Hon Can Roch Cathl and Bp of Tonbridge from 2002; Abps' Adv for Alternative Spiritualities and New Relig Movts; Co-chair Miss Thel Adv Grp   *Tel:* 01732 456070
Fax: 01732 741449
email: bishop.tonbridge@rochester.anglican.org

CAWDELL, Revd Simon Howard, BA, MA CTM
The Rectory 16 East Castle Street Bridgnorth Shropshire WV16 4AL [HEREFORD] *b* 1965 *educ* Kings Sch, Worcester; Univ Coll Dur; Kings Coll, Lon; Ridley Hall, Cam; *CV* Investment Analyst; Coast Securities Ltd, Lon 1987–91; C St. Philip, Cheam Common S'wark 1994–98; V Claverley & Tuck Hill 1998–2010; TR Bridgnorth & P-in-C Morville w Aston Ayre, Acton Round& Monkhopton w Upton Cresset from 2010; Rural Dean of Bridgnorth from 2009; Dioc Syn from 2000–06, from 2009; Dioc Brd Fin from 1999 (Exec M 2007–10), Vice Chair Benefice Bldgs Cttee 2001–7, Chair Dioc Investment Cttee 2007–10
GS 2010–   *Tel:* 01746 761573
email: s.h.cawdell@btinternet.com

CHALONER, Mr Mark Daniel Dawson, MA
Church House Great Smith St London SW1P 3AZ [CHIEF INVESTMENT OFFICER, CHURCH COMMISSIONERS] *b* 1961 *educ* K Sch Roch; Jes Coll Cam; *CV* On staff of Ch Commrs from 1988; Chief Investment Officer, Ch Commrs from 2000
Tel: 020 7898 1126
Fax: 020 7898 1111
email: mark.chaloner@c-of-e.org.uk

CHANDLER, Ven Ian Nigel, BD, AKC, CMTh
St Mark's House 46a Cambridge Road Ford Plymouth PL2 1PU [ARCHDEACON OF PLYMOUTH] *b* 1965 *educ* Bishopsgarth Sch Stockton-on-Tees; Stockton Sixth Form Coll; K Coll Lon; Chich Th Coll; *CV* C All SS Hove 1992–96; Dom Chapl to Bp of Chich 1996–2000; V St Rich Haywards Heath from 2000; RD Cuckfield from 2004; M Dioc Syn from 2000; M Dioc Fin Cttee from 2004; Adn of Plymouth from 2010   *Tel:* 01752 793397
email: archdeacon.of.plymouth@
exeter.anglican.org

CHANDLER, Very Revd Dr Michael John, Dip Th, S Th, Ph D
The Deanery Ely CB7 4DN [DEAN OF ELY] *b* 1945 *educ* K Coll Lond; Brasted Place Coll: Linc Th Coll; *CV* C St Dunstan, Cant 1972–75; C St Jo Bapt Margate 1975–78; V Newington 1978–88; RD Sittingbourne 1984–88; R St Steph Hackington 1988–95; RD Cant 1994–95; Can Treas Cant Cathl 1995–2003; Dean of Ely from 2003   *Tel:* 01353 667735
Fax: 01353 665658
email: dean@cathedral.ely.anglican.org

CHAPMAN, Prof Mark David, MA, DipTh, DPhil
1 Church Close Cuddesdon Oxford OX44 9HD [OXFORD] *b* 1960 *educ* St Bartholomew's Sch; Trin Coll Ox; Munich Univ; OMC; *CV* Sir Henry

Stephenson Fellow, Univ Sheffield 1989–91; NSM Dorchester Team Ministry, 1994–99; Lect Systematic Th Ripon Coll Cuddesdon from 1992; Vice-Prin, Ripon Coll Cuddesdon from 2001; Visiting Prof, Oxford Brookes Univ from 2009; Rdr Modern Th, Ox Univ from 2008; NSM Assoc P Wheatley Team Ministry w spec respons Cuddesdon, Garsington & Horspath from 1999
GS 2010–   *Tel:* 01865 874310
       Fax: 01865 874310
email: MChapman@ripon-cuddesdon.ac.uk

CHAPMAN, Revd Sarah Jean, Dip COT, GME
Bitterne Park Vicarage 7 Thorold Rd Southampton SO18 1HZ [WINCHESTER] *b* 1955 *educ* Cheltenham Ladies' Coll; Lon Coll of Occupational Therapy; SDMTS; *CV* C (NSM) Rogate w. Terwick and Trotton w. Chithurst, Chich 1989–94; C (NSM) Easebourne, Chich 1994–96; Dioc Lic to Officiate, Portsm 1996–97; NSM St Phil Cosham; V St Mary Magd Sheet, Portsm 1997–2002; V Bitterne Park, Winch from 2002; M Winch Dioc Healing and Wholeness Cttee 2003–05; Bp's Exam Chapl from 2003; M VRSC from 2006
GS 2003–05; 2005–10   *Tel:* 023 8055 1560
email: revsarah@sargil.co.uk

CHARING CROSS, Archdeacon of. See
JACOB, Ven William Mungo

CHARMAN, Canon Jane Ellen Elizabeth, MA
4 The Sidings Downton Salisbury SP5 3QZ [SALIS-BURY] *b* 1960 *educ* Newtead Wood Sch, Orpington; St John's Coll Dur; Selwyn Coll Cam; Westcott House Th Coll; *CV* C, St George's Tuffley w St Margaret's Whaddon, Glouc, 1985–90; Chapl, Clare Coll Cam, 1990–95; R Duxford St Peter & V St Mary & St John Hinxton & St Mary Magdalene Ickleton, Ely, 1995–2004; Rural Dean Shelford Deanery, Ely, 2003–04; Dir Lrning for Discipleship and Ministry, Salisbury, from 2004; Dioc Rep South Central Regional Training Partnership Management Brd from 2006; Chair South Central Regional Training Partnership CMD Co-ord Grp from 2006; M National CMD panel from 2009; M STETS Brd of Studies from 2009
GS 2010–   *Tel:* 01725 512620   07814 899657
email: jane.charman@salisbury.anglican.org

CHARTRES, Rt Revd and Rt Hon Richard John Carew, KCVO, DD, FSA
The Old Deanery Dean's Court London EC4V 5AA [BISHOP OF LONDON] *b* 1947 *educ* Hertf Gr Sch; Trin Coll Cam; Cuddesdon Th Coll; Linc Th Coll; *CV* C St Andr Bedford 1973–75; Bp's Dom Chapl 1975–80; Chapl to Abp of Cant 1980–84; P-in-c St Steph w St Jo Westmr 1984–85; V 1986–92; DDO 1985–92; Prof Div Gresham Coll 1986–92; Six Preacher Cant Cathl 1991–96; Bp of Stepney 1992–95; Bp of Lon from 1995; Dean of HM Chapels Royal and PC 1996; Chair Ch Heritage Forum; Ch Commrs from 1999; M Centr Cttee

CEC; M Jt Liaison Grp between CEC and Coun of Eur Catholic Bps' Confs; Chair Ch Buildings Cttee from 2003; Acting Chair Ch Commrs Bd from 1999; Chair Shrink the Footprint from 2004
GS 1995–   *Tel:* 020 7248 6233
       Fax: 020 7248 9721
email: bishop@londin.clara.co.uk

CHAVE, Preb Brian Philip, BA (OU)
The Vicarage Vowles Close Hereford HR4 0DF [HER-EFORD] *b* 1951 *educ* Winslade Sch Ex; Seale-Hayne Agric Coll Devon; Trinity Coll Bris; *CV* C Cullompton w Kentisbeare and Blackborough, Ex 1984–87; TV Oakmoor Tm Min, Ex 1987–93; C for Agric, Heref 1993–96; Comms Officer and Bp's Staff Officer (Dom Chapl), Heref 1997–2001; TV W Heref Tm Min from 2001; Vc Pres Heref Dioc Syn and Chair Ho of C; M Bp's Coun; Chair Bd of Govs Whitecross High Sch, Heref
GS 2008–   *Tel:* 01432 273086 (Office)
email: brianchave@btinternet.com

CHEESEMAN, Mr James Reginald,
25 Lambarde Drive Sevenoaks TN13 3HX [ROCHES-TER] *b* 1934 *educ* Sevenoaks Sch; Coll of St Mark and St Jo; *CV* Supply Staff Kent Educ Cttee 1954–55; Asst Tchr Midfield Prim Sch 1957–68; Dep Hdmaster Edgebury Prim Sch 1968–69; Chair Ho of Laity Roch Dioc Syn 1976–79; M GS Bd of Educ 1981–91; Hdmaster Pet Hills' Sch Rotherhithe 1969–97; Co-Chair Sevenoaks Dny Syn 1976–96; Sec Sevenoaks Dny Syn; Trustee Guild of All So; Treas Qu Victoria Clergy Fund from 1991; Lay Chair Forward In Faith Roch; Chair Dioc Bd of Patronage; Sec Kent Cricket Bd
GS 1975–   *Tel:* 01732 455718

CHEETHAM, Rt Revd Dr Richard Ian, MA, PGCE, Cert Theol, Ph D
Kingston Episcopal Area Office 620 Kingston Rd Raynes Park SW20 8DN [AREA BISHOP OF KING-STON; SOUTHWARK] *b* 1955 *educ* Kingston Gr Sch; CCC Ox; Ripon Coll Cuddesdon; K Coll Lon; *CV* C H Cross Fenham 1987–90; V St Aug of Cant Limbury, Luton 1990–99; RD Luton 1995–98; Adn of St Alb 1999–2002; Bp of Kingston from 2002; Chair Nat Chr Muslim Forum; M Roehampton Univ Coun; Chair C of E Continuing Ministerial Devel; Chair S'wark Dioc Bd of Educ
       Tel: 020 8545 2440
       Fax: 020 8545 2441
email: bishop.richard@southwark.anglican.org

**CHELMSFORD, Bishop of, see COTTRELL,
Rt Revd Stephen Geoffrey**

**CHELMSFORD, Dean of. See JUDD, Very Revd
Peter Somerset Margesson**

**CHELTENHAM, Archdeacon of, see
SPRINGETT, Ven Robert**

CHESSUN, Rt Revd Christopher Thomas James, MA
37 South Rd Forest Hill London SE23 2UJ [AREA BISHOP OF WOOLWICH; SOUTHWARK] *b* 1956 *educ* Hampton Gr Sch; Univ Coll Ox; Westcott Ho Cam; *CV* Asst C St Mich and AA Sandhurst 1983–87; Sen C St Mary Portsea 1987–99; Chapl and Min Can St Paul's Cathl 1989–93; R Stepney, St Dunstan and All SS 1993–2001; AD Tower Hamlets 1997–2001; Adn of Northolt from 2001; M Dioc Syn 2001–05; Bp of Woolwich 2005–11; Bp of S'wark from 2011   *Tel:* 020 7939 9407 (Office)
020 8699 7771 (Home)
Fax: 020 8699 7949
email: bishop.christopher@
southwark.anglican.org

CHESTER, Revd Philip Anthony Edwin, LLB,
Dip Th
St Matthew's House 20 Great Peter St London SW1P 2BU [LONDON] *b* 1955 *educ* Calday Grange; Birm Univ; St Jo Coll Dur; *CV* Asst P St Chad Shrewsbury 1980–85; Asst P St Martin-in-the-Fields Lon 1985–88; Chapl K Coll Lon 1988–95; PV Westmr Abbey from 1990; V St Matt Westmr from 1995
GS 2005–2010   *Tel:* 020 7222 3704
Fax: 020 7233 0255
email: office@stmw.org

CHESTER, Archdeacon of, see GILBERTSON, Ven Michael Robert

CHESTER, Bishop of. See FORSTER, Rt Revd Peter Robert

CHESTER, Dean of. See McPHATE, Very Revd Prof Gordon Ferguson

CHESTERFIELD, Archdeacon of. (NOT APPOINTED AT TIME OF GOING TO PRESS)

CHICHESTER, Archdeacon of. See McKITTRICK, Ven Douglas Henry

CHICHESTER, Bishop of. See HIND, Rt Revd John William

CHICHESTER, Dean of. See FRAYLING, Very Revd Nicholas Arthur

CLARK, Revd Jonathan Dunnett, BA, M Litt, MA
St Mary's Rectory Stoke Newington Church St London N16 9ES [LONDON] *educ* Ex Univ; Bris Univ; Southn Univ; Trin Coll Bris; *CV* C Stanwix, Carl 1988–92; Chapl Bris Univ 1992–93; Dir of Studies S Diocs Minl Tr Scheme 1994–97; Chapl Univ of N Lon 1997–2002; Chapl Lon Metrop Univ 2002–03; AD Islington 1999–2003; R St Mary Stoke Newington from 2003; P-in-c Brownswood Park from 2004
GS 2005–2010   *Tel:* 020 7254 6072
07968 845698 (Mobile)
Fax: 020 7923 4135
email: rector@stmaryn16.org

CLARK, Mr John Guthrie,
12 Ash Drive Haughton Stafford ST18 9EU [LICHFIELD] *b* 1938 *educ* Slough Gr Sch; Wrekin Coll; Ches Dio Tr Coll; *CV* Tchr Dawley Sec Mod Sch 1960–65; Phoenix Comp Sch 1965–67; Hd of RE, Wobaston Sec Mod Sch 1967–68; Hd of Religious, Social and Moral Educ, Aelfgar Comp Sch 1968–86 and Hagley Pk Comp Sch Rugeley 1986–93; M Dioc Pastl Cttee, Bp's Coun and Bd of Educ; Local Min Consult; Rdr
GS 1970–2010   *Tel:* 01785 780689

CLARK, Revd Jonathan Jackson, MA
St George's Church Great George Street Leeds LS1 3BR [RIPON AND LEEDS] *b* 1957 *educ* St Peters Sch, York; Linc Coll, Ox; Ridley, Cam; *CV* C, St Lukes, Princess Drive, Liv 1984–87; C, St Johns and St Marks, Clacton-on-sea 1987–92; V, St Simon, Shepherds Bush, London 1993–2003; Area Dean, Hammersmith and Fulham 1996–2001; R St George's Leeds from 2003; Chair of St George's Crypt Trustees from 2005
GS 2010–   *Tel:* 01132438498
email: jonathan.clark@stgeorgesleeds.org.uk

CLARKE, Very Revd John Martin, MA, BD
The Dean's Lodgings 25 The Liberty Wells BA5 2SZ [DEAN OF WELLS; BATH AND WELLS] *b* 1952 *educ* W Buckland Sch; Hertf Coll Ox; New Coll Edin; Edin Th Coll; *CV* C Ascen Kenton, Newc 1976–79; Prec St Ninian's Cathl, Perth 1979–82; Info Officer and Communications Adv to GS of Scottish Episcopal Ch 1982–87; Philip Usher Memorial Sch, Greece 1987–88; V St Mary Battersea 1989–96; Prin Ripon Coll Cuddesdon 1997–2004; Dean of Wells from 2004   *Tel:* 01749 670278
email: dean@wellscathedral.uk.net

CLARKE, Canon Prof Michael Gilbert, CBE, BA,
MA, DLitt, DL
Millington House 15 Lansdowne Crescent Worcester WR3 8JE [WORCESTER] *b* 1944 *educ* Qu Eliz Gr Sch Wakef; Sussex Univ; *CV* Lect in Politics Edin Univ 1969–75; Dep Dir Policy Planning Lothian Regional Coun 1975–81; Dir Local Government Tr Bd 1981–90; Chief Exec Local Government Mgt Bd 1990–93; Hd of Sch of Public Policy Birm Univ 1993–98; Pro-Vc Chan Birm Univ from 1998, Vc-Prin 2003–08; Lay Can and Chapter Member Worc Cathl 2001–10; Canon Emeritus 2010; Gov Qu Foundn, Birm from 2000 and WMTC from 2008; M Diocs Commn from 2008; M Panel of Chairs from 2009
GS 1990–93, 1995–   *Tel:* 01905 617634
email: michael.clarkeinworcester@btinternet.com

CLEVELAND, Archdeacon of. See FERGUSON, Ven Paul John

COCHRANE, Revd Philip Andrew, BA
The Parish Office West Street Fareham PO16 0EL [PORTSMOUTH] *b* 1970 *educ* Coleraine Acd Insti; Reading Univ; Trin Coll Bris; *CV* Customer ser-

vice & sales w Equitable Life & Clerical Medl, 1992–2001; Buckinghamshire County Councillor, 1997–2001; Pensions Consult & Head of Reward Consulting w Jardine Lloyd Thompson Benefit Solutions, 2002–2004; AC, Parish of Holy Trin w St Columba, Fareham 2007–09; Bp Portsm's Adv Porvoo, from 2008; TV Parish of Holy Trin w St Columba, Fareham from 2009; M Dioc Litt & Worship Adv Grp from 2008; M Dioc Syn from 2009; M Bp's Counc from 2010
GS 2010–   Tel: 01329 318665
        email: Philip@scfareham.org.uk

COCKETT, Ven Elwin Wesley, BA
86 Aldersbrook Rd Manor Park London E12 5DH [ARCHDEACON OF WEST HAM; CHELMSFORD] *b* 1959 *educ* St Paul's Cathl Choir Sch; Forest Sch, Snaresbrook; Aston Trg Scheme; Oak Hill Coll; *CV* C St Chad, Chadwell Heath 1991–94; C-in-c St Paul, Harold Hill 1994–95, P-in-c 1995–97, V 1997–2000; TR Billericay and Little Burstead TM 2000–07; RD Basildon 2004–07; Adn of West Ham from 2007; Club Chapl West Ham United Football Club from 1992   Tel: 020 8989 8557
                                   Fax: 020 8530 1311
        email: a.westham@chelmsford.anglican.org

COCKSWORTH, Rt Revd Dr Christopher John, BA (Hons), PhD, PGCE, Hon DD
Bishop's House 23 Davenport Rd Coventry CV5 6PW [BISHOP OF COVENTRY] *b* 1959 *educ* Forest Sch for boys, Horsham; Univ of Man; Didsbury Sch of Educ; St John's Coll, Nottm; *CV* Asst C Ch Ch Epsom 1988–92; Chapl Royal Holloway Univ of Lon 1992–96; Dir S Theol Educ and Training Scheme 1996–2001; Prin Ridley Hall Cam 2001–08; Bp Cov from 2008
GS 2008–   Tel: 024 7667 2244
                                   Fax: 024 2671 3271
        email: bishcov@btconnect.com

COHEN, Ven Clive Ronald Franklin, ACIB
Archdeacon's House Cardinham Bodmin PL30 4BL [ARCHDEACON OF BODMIN; TRURO] *b* 1946 *educ* Tonbridge Sch; Sarum and Wells Th Coll; *CV* C Esher 1981–85; R Winterslow 1985–2000; RD Alderbury 1989–93; Non Res Can and Preb Sarum Cathl 1992–2000; Adn of Bodmin from 2000   Tel and Fax: 01208 821614
        email: clive@truro.anglican.org

COLCHESTER, Archdeacon of. See COOPER, Ven Annette Joy

COLCHESTER, Area Bishop of. See MORGAN, Rt Revd Christopher Heudebourck

COLES, Revd Stephen Richard, MA, BA
The Cardinal's Hat 25 Romilly Rd Finsbury Park London N4 2QY [LONDON] *b* 1949 *educ* Latymer Upper Sch Hammersmith; Univ Coll Ox; Trin Hall Cam; Leeds Univ; Coll of the Resurrection, Mirfield; *CV* C St Mary Stoke Newington 1981–

84; Chapl K Coll Cam 1984–89; V St Thos Finsbury Park from 1989
GS 2000–   Tel: 020 7359 5741
        email: cardinal.jeoffry@btconnect.com

COMBES, Ven Roger Matthew, LLB
3 Danehurst Crescent Horsham RH13 5HS [ARCHDEACON OF HORSHAM; CHICHESTER] *b* 1947 *educ* Sherborne Sch; K Coll Lon; Ridley Hall Th Coll; *CV* C St Paul Onslow Sq Lon 1974–77; C H Trin Brompton Lon 1976–77; C H Sepulchre Cam 1977–86; R St Matt St Leonards-on-Sea 1986–2003; M Bp's Coun from 1998; RD Hastings 1998–2002; Adn of Horsham from 2003
GS 1995–2005   Tel: 01403 262710
        email: archhorsham@diochi.org.uk

CONDICK, Mrs Margaret, B Sc, Cert Ed
34 Rectory Lane Kirton Ipswich IP10 0PY [ST EDMUNDSBURY AND IPSWICH] *b* 1944 *educ* Sutton High Sch GPDST; Manch Univ; *CV* Tchr of Physics, Stockport 1967–70; pt tchr of maths, Suffolk 1985–97; Communications Officer, Chs Together in Suffolk 1998–2000; County Ecum Officer for Suffolk 2000–09
GS 2003–   Tel: 01394 448576
        email: margaret.condick@btopenworld.com

CONNER, Rt Revd David John, MA
The Deanery Windsor Castle Windsor SL4 1NJ [DEAN OF WINDSOR] *b* 1947 *educ* Ex Coll Ox; St Steph Ho Th Coll; *CV* Hon C Summertown Ox 1971–76; Asst Chapl St Edw Sch Ox 1971–73; Chapl 1973–80; TV Wolvercote w Summertown 1976–80; Chapl Win Coll 1980–87; V Gt St Mary w St Mich Cam 1987–94; RD Cam 1989–94; Bp of Lynn 1994–98; Dean of Windsor from 1998; Bp to HM Forces 2001–09   Tel: 01753 865561
                                   Fax: 01753 819002
        email: david.conner@stgeorges-windsor.org

CONWAY, Rt Revd Stephen David, MA, MA
Bishop's Croft Winterbourne Earls Salisbury SP4 6HJ [AREA BISHOP OF RAMSBURY; SALISBURY] *b* 1957 *educ* Abp Tenison's Gr Sch Lon; Keble Coll Ox; Selw Coll Cam; Westcott Ho; *CV* C St Mary Heworth 1986–89; C St Mich and AA Bishopwearmouth 1989–90; DDO 1989–94; Hon C St Marg Dur 1990–94; P-in-c then V St Mary Cockerton 1994–98; Sen Chapl to Bp of Dur and Dioc Communications Officer 1998–2002; Adn of Dur and Can Res Dur Cathl 2002–06; Area Bp of Ramsbury from 2006; M Bps Insp of Th Colls and Courses 1997–2006; Chair of Mental Health Matters from 2004–2010; GS 1995–2000; Chair Dioc Learning, Discipleship and Min Coun from 2006; Warden of Lay Mins from 2006–2010; Trustee Affirming Catholicism 2001–08, Vc-Pres from 2008; Anglican Bishop for LArche from 2010
GS 1995–2000   Tel: 01380 729808
                                   Fax: 01380 738096
        email: sramsbury@salisbury.anglican.org

The Kingdom of God belongs to such as these...

The Children's Society

The Children's Society transforms the lives of over 44,000 children and young people each year.

Founded in 1881 by a Sunday school teacher, our Christian values of love, justice and forgiveness underpin the way we work with children and young people.

God's unconditional love, as seen in the life and ministry of Jesus, inspires us to work with all children and young people. We show God's love through our work with children at risk on the streets, disabled children, young refugees, young carers and those within the youth justice system.

Our resources will help your church reach out to children and young people in your community and help you to support the work of The Children's Society through prayer and worship, fundraising and volunteering.

For more information on free resources and how to get involved visit **www.childrenssociety.org.uk** or call our Supporter Care team on **0845 300 1148.**

Charity Registration No. 221124 | Photograph modelled for The Children's Society | © Laurence Dutton

A better childhood. For every child.   www.childrenssociety.org.uk

COOK, Revd Canon James Christopher Donald, MA
St Agne's Vicarage 1 Buckingham Avenue Liverpool L17 3BA [LIVERPOOL] *b* 1949 *educ* Bournemouth Sch; Chr Ch Coll, Ox; St Stephen's House Th Coll; *CV* Regimental Officer, 5th Royal Inniskilling Dragoon Guards, 1973–78; Asst C Witney, Oxon, 1980–83; Chapl to the Forces, 1983–2004; P-in-C, St Agnes & St Pancras, Toxteth Park, Liv, 2004–06; V, St Agnes & St Pancras, Toxteth Park, Liv from 2006
GS 2010–   *Tel:* 0151 733 1742
                    email: leoclericus@aol.com

COOK, Revd John Richard Millward, BA
The Vicarage Station Road, Wargrave Reading Berkshire RG10 8EU [OXFORD] *b* 1961 *educ* Repton Sch; St Jo Coll Dur; Wycliffe Hall Th Coll; *CV* C St Peter's Farnborough 1989–92; C and Dir of Tr All Souls, Langham Place, London 1992–98; V of St John w St Andrew, Chelsea 1998–2008; V of St Mary, Wargrave w St Peter's, Knowl Hill, Ox Dico, from 2008
GS 1995–2007; 2010–
                    Tel: 01189402202 01189402300
                    Fax: 01189401470
                    email: johnrmcook@btconnect.com

COOPER, Ven Annette Joy, BA, CQSW, Dip RS
63 Powers Hall End Witham CM8 1NH [ARCHDEACON OF COLCHESTER; CHELMSFORD] *b* 1953 *educ* Lilley and Stone Newark Girls High Sch; Open Univ; Lon Univ Extra-mural Dept; S'wark Ord Course; *CV* Local Auth Social Worker; Asst Chapl Tunbridge Wells Health Auth 1988–91; NSM Dn St Pet Pembury 1988; Chapl Bassetlaw Hosp and Community Services NHS Trust 1991–96; Chapl to Center Parcs Sherwood Village 1996–99; Chapl to S'well Dioc MU 1996–99; P-in-c Edwinstowe 1996–2004; AD Worksop 1999–2004; Hon Can S'well Minster 2002–04; M Dioc Bd of Educ 1994–97; M Bp's Coun from 1999; Vc-Pres/ Chair Dioc Ho of Clergy 2001–04; M GS Panel of Chairmen 2003–04, 2006–; M Discipline Commn from 2003; Adn of Colchester from 2004; M Nat Stewardship Cttee from 2007; Dir Allchurches Trust from 2008
GS 2000–2004; 2005–   *Tel:* 01376 513130
                    Fax: 01376 500789
email: a.colchester@chelmsford.anglican.org

COOPER, Ms Susan Margaret, B Sc, FIA, DPS, FCAA
28 Headstone Lane Harrow HA2 6HG [LONDON] *b* 1947 *educ* Harrow Weald Co Gr Sch; Univ Coll of Wales Aberystwyth; Birm Univ; *CV* Legal and Gen Assurance Soc 1969–80; Corporate Business Actuary BUPA 1980–90; Consultant Actuary 1992–2002; Consulting Actuary, GAD from 2002; Rdr St Jo Bapt Pinner from 1995; M Strg Cttee for Draft Stipends (Cessation of Special Payments) Measure 2003–04; M Br Regional Cttee St Geo Coll Jerusalem from 2003; Hon Sec CHRISM from

2006; M Strg Ctee for Draft C of E Pensions (Amendment) Measure 2007–08
GS 2000–   *Tel:* 020 8863 2094 (Home)
                    020 7211 2626 (Office)
                    Fax: 08700 516752
                    email: scooper@hedstone.demon.co.uk

CORNWALL, Archdeacon of. See BUSH, Ven Roger Charles

CORTEEN, Mrs Christine,
21 Hillside Road Wool Wareham Dorset BH20 6DY [SALISBURY] *b* 1956 *educ* Merchant Taylors' Sch, Liv; Liv Univ; *CV* Local Government Off from 1977; Income and Payments Man, Poole Borough Counc from 1990; Counc Miss, Sarum; St Aldhelm's Miss Fund, Sarum; Learning for Discipleship and Ministry, Sarum
GS 2010–   *Tel:* 01929462642
                    email: c.corteen@poole.gov.uk

COTTON, Canon Robert Lloyd, MA, Dip Th
Holy Trinity Rectory 9 Eastgate Gardens Guildford GU1 4AZ [GUILDFORD] *b* 1958 *educ* Uppingham; Merton Coll Ox; Westcott Ho Cam; *CV* C St Mary Bromley 1983-85; C Bisley & W End 1987–89; P-in-c St Paul E Molesey 1989–96; Prin Guildf Dioc Min Course 1989–96; R H Trin & St Mary Guildf from 1996; Chair Ho of Clergy from 2004; Can Dioc of Highveld, S Africa from 2006
GS 2004–   *Tel:* 01483 575489
                    email: rector@holytrinityguildford.org.uk

COTTRELL, Rt Revd Stephen Geoffrey, BA
Bishopscourt Main Rd Margaretting Ingatestone Essex CM4 0HD [BISHOP OF CHELMSFORD] *b* 1958 *educ* Belfairs High Sch for Boys; Poly of Central Lon; St Steph Ho; *CV* C Ch Ch & St Paul Forest Hill, S'wark 1984–88; P-in-c St Wilf Parklands, Chich and Asst Dir of Pastl Studies, Chich Th Coll 1988–93; Dioc Missr, Wakef 1993–98; Springboard Missr 1998–2001; Can Pastor Peterb Cathl 2001–04; Bp of Reading 2004–10; Bp of Chelmsford from 2010   *Tel:* 01277 352001
                    Fax: 01277 355374
email: bishopscourt@chelmsford.anglican.org

COVENTRY, Archdeacon Missioner of. See RODHAM, Ven Morris

COVENTRY, Archdeacon of. (NOT APPOINTED AT TIME OF GOING TO PRESS)

COVENTRY, Bishop of. See COCKSWORTH, Rt Revd Dr Christopher John

COVENTRY, Dean of. See IRVINE, Very Revd John Dudley

COX, Revd Alison, BTh, MHort
St Mark's Vicarage 2 Church Square Railway Street Dukinfield SK16 4PX [CHESTER] *b* 1963 *educ*

Westville Girls' Sch; Weymouth Gr Sch; Pershore Coll Horticulture; Ripon Coll Cuddesdon; *CV* Asst Garden Centre mgr; Journalist; C St Mary's & St Nicolas, Spalding 2003–07; P-in-c St Mark's Dukinfield from 2007
GS 2010–   *Tel:* 0161 330 2783
                                        email: alisoncox19@hotmail.com

COX, Canon Simon John, MA, MA, BSc, PhD
All Hallows Rectory 86 All Hallows Rd Bispham Blackpool FY2 0AY [BLACKBURN] *b* 1953 *educ* Roxeth Manor CSM, South Harrow; Montgomery of Alamein CSM Sch Winchester; Eastleigh Tech Coll; Q Mary Coll London; Univ Liverpool; Ridley Hall Cam; Selwyn Coll Cam; Univ Lancaster; *CV* C Livesey St Andrew 1982–85; C Cheadle Hulme St Andrew i/c Emmanuel 1985–89; V Disley St Mary 1989–94; R Bispham All Hallows from 1994; P-in-C Blackpool South Shore St Peter 2005–07; AD Blackpool from 2004; Hon Can Blackburn from 2008; Vc Chair Dioc Ho of Clergy; M Bp's Counc; Bd Finance Exec, Pastl & Miss Comm; Bd of Min, Property Commn; Chair Dioc Patronage Bd; Vc Chair DEF
GS 2002–2005, 2009–   *Tel and Fax:* 01253 351886
                                        email: Drsjcox@yahoo.co.uk

CRAVEN, Prof John Anthony George, MA Cantab, Hon D Sc
Fyning Cross Rogate Petersfield GU31 5EF [APPOINTED MEMBER, ARCHBISHOPS' COUNCIL] *b* 1949 *educ* Pinner Gr Sch; K Coll Cam; Kennedy Memorial Scholar, Massachusetts Inst of Tech; *CV* Univ of Kent (Cant) Lect in Mathematical Economics 1971, Sen Lect 1976; Reader in Economics 1980, Prof of Economics 1986; elected Dean of Social Sciences 1987, re-elected 1990; Pro Vc-Chan 1991, Dep Vc-Chan 1993; Vc-Chan Univ of Ports from 1997; 1977–96 in Cant Dioc, at various times M and Treas Eastry PCC, M Dny and Dioc Syns, M CUF Dioc Cttee, Chair St Mart Trust for Homeless in Deal and Dover; in Ports Dioc, Foundn Gov St Luke's C of E Vol Aided Sch from 2002, Chair from 2003; M Ports Cathl Coun from 2003; Lay Can Ports Cathl from 2006; Gov S Kent Coll of FE 1991–96; Gov Highbury Coll of FE 1997–2002
GS 2006–   *Tel:* 01730 821392 (Home)
                                        023 9284 3190 (Office)
                                        Fax: 023 9284 3400
                                        email: john.craven@port.ac.uk

CRAVEN, Archdeacon of. See SLATER, Ven Paul John

CRAY, Rt Revd Graham Alan, BA
The Rectory Church Road Harrietsham Maidstone Kent ME17 1AP [ARCHBISHOPS' MISSIONER] *b* 1947 *educ* Trinity Sch of John Whitgift, Croydon; Leeds Univ; St Jo Coll Nottm; *CV* C St Mark Gillingham, Roch 1971–75; N Co-ord Ch Pastl Aid Soc 1975–78; V St Mich-le-Belfrey 1978–92; Prin Rid-

ley Hall Cam 1992–2000; Six Prchr of Cant Cathl 1997–2002; Bp of Maidstone 2001–2009; Archbishops' Missioner from 2009; Leader Fresh Expressions Tm; Assistant Bp Cant Dioc; Assistant Bp York Dioc
GS 1985–92   *Tel:* 01622 851170
                              email: graham.cray@freshexpressions.org.uk

CREDITON, Suffragan Bishop of. See EVENS, Rt Revd Robert John Scott

CROFT, Rt Revd Dr Steven John Lindsey,
Bishopscroft Snaithing Lane Sheffield S10 3LG [BISHOP OF SHEFFIELD] *b* 1957 *educ* Heath Sch Halifax; Worc Coll Ox; Cranmer Hall, St Jo Coll Dur; *CV* C St Andrew Enfield 1983–1987; V St George's Ovenden 1987–1996; Warden Cranmer Hall 1996–2004; Abps' Missioner and Team Ldr of Fresh Expressions 2004–09; Bp of Sheffield from 2009   *Tel:* 0114 230170
                                        Fax: 0114 2630110
                              email: bishop@sheffield.anglican.org

CROFT, Canon William Stuart, MA, BA, MTh
315 Thorpe Road Longthorpe Peterborough PE3 6LU [PETERBOROUGH] *b* 1953 *educ* King Edward VI Sch; Trin Hall, Cam; King's Coll Lon; Ripon Col lCuddesdon; *CV* AC, St James Friern Barnet 1981–83; Tutor Chich Th Coll 1983–92; V, St Margaret of Antioch Fernhurst 1992–98; Prec Peterb Cathl 1998–2004; Dioc Dir Ord, Peterb, 1998–2002; P-in-C, St Botolph's, Longthorpe, Peterb from 2004; M Joint Implementation Comm Ang Meth Covenant from 2003
GS 2010–   *Tel:* 01733 263016
                              email: williamsbill_croft@hotmail.com

CROW, Mr Timothy, LLB
Legal Office Church House Great Smith St London SW1P 3AZ [DEPUTY OFFICIAL SOLICITOR TO THE CHURCH COMMISSIONERS] *b* 1954 *educ* Barnard Castle Sch; Mid-Essex Technical Coll and Sch of Art; *CV* Solicitor in private practice, Sussex 1979–95; Official Solicitor's Dept, Church Commissioners 1995–2000; Legal Office of the NCIs from 2000; Deputy Official Solicitor to the Church Commissioners from 2000   *Tel:* 020 7898 1717
                                        email: tim.crow@c-of-e.org.uk

CROYDON, Archdeacon of. See DAVIES, Ven Tony (Vincent Anthony)

CROYDON, Area Bishop of. See BAINES, Rt Revd Nicholas

CRUMPLER, Mr Peter George, FCIPR, Dip Cam
Church House Great Smith St London SW1P 3AZ [DIRECTOR OF COMMUNICATIONS FOR THE ARCHBISHOPS' COUNCIL, CHURCH OF ENGLAND] *b* 1956 *educ* Chiswick Sch, Lon; Harlow Coll; *CV* Communications posts within British Gas plc 1982–91; Internat Public Affairs Mgr, British Gas plc 1991–97; Hd of External Affairs Internat, BG plc 1997–

2000; Hd of Communications, BG Group plc 2000–01; Communications Officer, St Alb Dioc 2001–04; Dir of Communications for Abp's Coun, C of E from 2004; Admitted as Rdr, St Alb dioc 2008; Fell, Chartered Inst of Public Relations from 2000

Tel: 020 7898 1462
Fax: 020 7222 6672
email: peter.crumpler@c-of-e.org.uk

CUMBERLAND, Archdeacon of West. See HILL, Ven Colin

CUNLIFFE, Ven Dr Christopher John, MA, D Phil, MA, A R Hist S
Derby Church House Full St Derby DE1 3DR [ARCHDEACON OF DERBY] *b* 1955 *educ* Charterhouse; Ch Ch Ox; Trin Coll Cam; Westcott Ho Cam; *CV* C Chesterfield Par Ch 1983–85; Chapl and Jun Rsch Fell, Linc Coll Ox 1985–89; Chapl City Univ and Guildhall Sch of Music and Drama 1989–91; Selection Sec and Voc Officer, Adv Bd of Min 1991–96; Bp of Lon's Adv for Ord Min 1996–2003; Clerk, All SS Educ Trust 2004; Chapl to Bp of Bradwell 2004–06; Adn of Derby from 2006; Chair Derby Dioc Communications Cttee; Can Res Derby Cathl 2006–08   Tel: 01332 388676
Fax: 01332 292969
email: archderby@derby.anglican.org

CURRAN, Ven Patrick Martin Stanley, BA, B Th
British Embassy Jauresgasse 12 Vienna 1030 Austria [ARCHDEACON OF THE EASTERN ARCHDEACONRY; EUROPE] *b* 1956 *educ* Ostsee Gymnasium, Timmendorfer Strand, Germany; Univ of K Coll Halifax, Nova Scotia, Canada; Southampton Univ; Chich Th Coll; *CV* C Heavitree with Ex St Paul Ex 1984–87; Bp's Chapl to Students, Bradf 1987–93; Chapl Bonn with Cologne, Eur 1993–2000; Can Malta Cathl 2000; Chapl Ch Ch Vienna from 2000; Adn of the Eastern Archdeaconry from 2002
Tel: 00 43 1 7148900
00 43 1 7185902
Fax: 00 43 1 7148900
email: office@christchurchvienna.org

CURRIE, Canon Stuart William, MA, PGCE
St Stephen's Vicarage 1 Beech Avenue Worcester WR3 8PZ [WORCESTER] *b* 1953 *educ* Boteler Gr Sch, Warrington; Hertford Coll Ox; Univ Coll Dur; Fitzwilliam Coll Cam; Westcott Ho; *CV* C Ch Ch Reading 1985–89; V in Banbury TM 1989–94; V Barbourne St Stephen from 1994; Chair Worc Dioc Ho of Clergy; Chair Worc DBE
GS 2008–   Tel: 01905 452169
email: sw.currie@virgin.net

CUTTING, Revd Alastair Murray, B Ed, MA, L Th, DPS
Henfield Vicarage Church Rd Copthorne Crawley RH10 3RD [CHICHESTER] *b* 1960 *educ* Geo Watson's Coll Edin; Lushington Sch Ooty, S India; Watford Boy's Gr Sch; Westhill Coll Birm; Heythrop Coll Lon; St Jo Coll Nottm; *CV* C All SS

Woodlands, Sheff 1987–88; C Wadsley, Sheff 1989–91; Chapl to Nave and Town Cen, Uxbridge, Lon 1991–96; V Copthorne, Chich 1996–2010; M Bp's Coun from 1998; Asst RD E Grinstead 2002–10; Chair Ho of Clergy from 2009
GS 2005–   Tel: 01273 492017 (Home)
01273 495532 (Office)
07736 676106 (Mobile)
Fax: 01342 712063
email: acutting@mac.com

DAILEY, Miss Prudence Mary Prior, MA
15 Northfield Rd Headington Oxford OX3 9EW [OXFORD] *b* 1965 *educ* Simon Langton Gr Sch for Girls Cant; K Sch Cant; Mert Coll Ox; *CV* NHS Gen Mgt Trainee and various admin posts in NHS 1988–97; Ox City Coun 1992–96; Sen Business Systems Analyst, Toys 'R' Us 1998–2009; Chair Prayer Book Soc
GS 2000–   Tel: 01865 766023
07730 516620 (Mobile)
email: prudence.dailey@tiscali.co.uk

DAKIN, Canon Timothy John, BA, MTh
3 Highgrove Place Ruscombe Reading RG10 9LF [OXFORD] *b* 1958 *educ* Priory Sch Shrewsbury; St Mary's Sch Nairobi; Henley Sixth Form Coll; St Mark's and St Jo Coll Plymouth; K Coll Lon; Ch Ch Ox; Carlile Coll Nairobi; *CV* Prin Carlile Coll, Nairobi 1993–2000; Hon C Nairobi Cathedral 1994–2000; Gen Sec CMS from 2000; Can Theol Cov Cathl from 2001; Assoc P St James Ruscombe & St Marys Twyford from 2000; M MPA Coun; M PWM Panel
GS 2005–   Tel: 0118 934 3909
email: timjdakin@googlemail.com

DALES, Mr Martin Paul,
Priory Cottage Old Malton YO17 7HB [YORK] *b* 1955 *educ* St Dunstan's Coll; Bretton Hall; Open Univ; *CV* Dep Hd, Housemaster and Dir of Music various schs 1976–94; Freelance musician, tchr and composer from 1994; Organist and Choirmaster from 1976, All Saints, Thornton-le-Dale from 2007; freelance broadcaster from 1976, BBC Radio York from 1994; music publisher from 1981; Media Relations Officer RSCM NE Yorks Area (Sec 2000–02); media and PR Adv various inc FindClaudia.co.uk and DontDrainUs.org; Coun Malton Town Coun 1989–99, 2003– (Mayor 1991–92, 1996–97); Secretary, Ryedale Cameras in Action; Chairman Amotherby Sch Govs; M Dioc Syn from 1995; M Coun for Min and Trg 1998–2000; past M Abp's Coun; M Revision Cttee Draft Amending Canon No 22; past M Appts Cttee; past M Ho of Laity Stg Cttee; M CCU; past M CMEAC; past M CTE Forum and CTBI Assembly; past Chair Chs Together in S Ryedale; M EKD Delegation 2005;
GS 1995–   Tel: 01653 600990
07764 985009 (Mobile)
Fax: 01653 600990
email: mpd@martindales.me.uk

DALLISTON, Very Revd Christopher Charles, MA
The Deanery 26 Mitchell Avenue Newcastle upon Tyne NE2 3LA [DEAN OF NEWCASTLE] *b* 1956 *educ* Diss Gr Sch; Peterhouse Cam; St Steph Ho Ox; *CV* C St Andr Halsead w H Trin and Greenstead Green 1984–87; Dom Chapl to Bp of Chelms 1987–91; V St Edm Forest Gate, Chelms 1991–95; V St Botolp w St Chris Boston 1995–2003; Dean of Newcastle from 2003   *Tel:* 0191 281 6554
0191 232 1939
email: dean@stnicnewcastle.co.uk

DALLOW, Revd Gillian Margaret, BA, M Ed, PGCE, CEM
57 The High St Northwood Middlesex HA6 1EB [SYNODICAL SECRETARY, CONVOCATION OF CANTERBURY] *b* 1945 *educ* Cathays High Sch Cardiff; Univ of N Wales Bangor; Bris Univ; Oak Hill Th Coll; W of Eng Univ; *CV* Tchr Mill St Sec Mod Sch Pontypridd 1968–70; Hd of RE Heref High Sch for Girls 1970–73; Hd of RE and Student Counselling Heref Sixth Form Coll 1973–74; Scripture Union Schs Worker S West and Wales 1974–79; Hd of RE Colston's Girls Sch Bris 1979–85; Dioc Educ Adv B & W 1985–91; Dir Tr Lon Bible Coll 1991–98; Adv for Children's Min and P-in-c St Giles Barlestone from 1999; Dioc Dir Under 25s Trg from 2002; Synodical Sec, Conv of Cant from 2006; M C of E Evang Coun from 2006; Sec Eggs (Evangs on GS) from 2009; Perm to Officiate: Dioc of Lon and Dioc of Llandaff
GS 2000–05   *Tel:* 01923 840111
07801 650187 (Mobile)
email: g.dallow@btinternet.com

DAVENPORT, Miss Laura Elizabeth, BA, MA
8 Ashfield Avenue Union Mills Isle of Man IM4 4LN [SODER AND MAN] *b* 1988 *educ* Queen Elizabeth II High Sch, Isle of Man; Cam Univ; Dur Univ; *CV* Dioc Yth Adv, from 2010; Yth Lder, Braddan Ch, from 2010; Business Analyst, Barclays Wealth from 2010; Dioc Comm Forum, from 2010
GS 2010–   *Tel:* 01624852167 07624467232
email: laura.elizabeth.davenport@gmail.com

DAVIES, Mr John, PSC, MBIFM, MCIM
Vicarage Cottages Baughurst Road Ramsdell Tadley RG26 5SH [WINCHESTER] *b* 1951 *educ* King Edward's Sch; RMA; Army Staff Coll; *CV* Regular Army 1969–89; Various commercial appointments 1989–2001; Managing Dir Park Row Consultancy Ltd; Lay Chair Basingstoke Deanery from 2008; Bp's Counc Winc since 2009; Fin Cttee Winc 2006–09
GS 2005–   *Tel:* 01256 851309
email: johndavies@parkrow.fsnet.co.uk

DAVIES, Very Revd Dr John Harverd, MA, M Phil, PhD
Derby Cathedral Centre 18–19 Iron Gate Derby DE1 3GP [DEAN OF DERBY] *b* 1957 *educ* Brentwood Sch; Keble Coll Ox; Corpus Christi Coll Cam; Lancas-

ter Univ; Westcott Ho; *CV* C Liv Par Ch 1984–87; C Peterb Par Ch and Minor Can Peterb Cathl 1987–90; V St Marg Anfield, Liv 1990–94; Chapl, Fell and Dir of Studies in Theol, Keble Coll Ox 1994–99; V Melbourne and DDO Derby Dioc 1999–2009; Dean of Derby from 2010; M Derby Dioc Bd for Min; M Dioc Syn; M GS Theol Educ and Trg Cttee 2006–07; Chair Industrial Miss in Derbyshire from 2009   *Tel:* 01332 341201
Fax: 01332 203991
email: dean@derbycathedral.org

DAVIES, Rt Revd Mark, BA, Cert PS
The Hollies Manchester Rd Rochdale OL11 3QY [SUFFRAGAN BISHOP OF MIDDLETON] *b* 1962 *educ* Hanley High Sch; Stoke-on-Trent Sixth Form Coll; Univ Coll of Ripon and York St Jo; Mirfield Th Coll; *CV* C St Mary Barnsley 1989–92; P-in-c St Paul Old Town Barnsley 1992–95; R Hemsworth from 1995; Asst DDO from 1998; RD Pontefract from 2000; Hon Can Wakef Cathl 2002–06; Adn of Rochdale 2006–08; Bp of Middleton from 2008
GS 2000–06   *Tel:* 01706 358550
email: bishopmark@manchester.anglican.org

DAVIES, Revd Nigel Lawrence, BEd
St Oswald's Vicarage Burneside Kendal Cumbria LA9 6QX [CARLISLE] *b* 1955 *educ* Black Bull Lane Sch; Hutton Gr Sch; St Martin's Coll, Lancaster; Salis and Wells Th Coll; *CV* Dn 1987; P 1988; C St Luke w All Souls, Heywood, Man 1987–91; V Burneside, 1991–07; Tutor Past Studies CBDTI 1992–98; Editor Dioc News 1999–2002; Rural Dean Kendal 2003–08; P-in-C Crosscrake 2004–06; P-in-C Skelsmergh w Selside and Longsleddale, 2006–07; Hon Canon Carlisle Cathl from 06; TR, Beacon Team. Kendal Deanery, Dioc Carlisle from 2007
GS 2009–   *Tel:* 01539 722015
email: canon.nigel@beaconteam.org.uk

DAVIES, Ven Tony (Vincent Anthony), FRSA
St Matthew's House 100 George St Croydon CR0 1PJ [ARCHDEACON OF CROYDON; SOUTHWARK] *b* 1946 *educ* Green Lane Sec Mod Sch Leic; Brasted Th Coll; St Mich Coll Llan; *CV* C St Jas Owton Manor Hartlepool 1973–76; C St Faith Wandsworth 1976–78, V 1978–81; V St Jo Walworth 1981–93; RD S'wark and Newington 1988–93; Adn of Croydon from 1994; Bp's Adv for Healthcare Chapl from 2000   *Tel:* 020 8688 2943 (Home)
020 8256 9630 (Office)
Fax: 020 8256 9631
email: tony.davies@southwark.anglican.org

DE WIT, Ven John, MA
Van Hogendorpstraat 26 Utrecht The Netherlands 3581 KE [ARCHDEACON OF NORTH WEST EUROPE] *b* 1947 *educ* The Leys Sch Cam; Oriel Coll Ox; Clare Coll Cam; Westcott Ho Cam; *CV* Asst C Quinton Birm 1978–81; TV St Michael Solihull 1981–85; V All Saints Kings Heath Birm 1985–94; Area Dean Moseley Birm 1991–94; P-in-C Hampton-in-

Arden Birm 1994–2004; Chap Holy Trin Utrecht from 2004; Sec Birm Dioc Liturg Cttee 1981–87; M Birm DAC 1988–2004 *Tel:* 00 31 30 251 34 24

DERBY, Archdeacon of. See CUNLIFFE, Ven Dr Christopher John

DERBY, Bishop of. See REDFERN, Rt Revd Dr Alastair Llewellyn John

DERBY, Dean of. See CUTTELL, Very Revd Jeffrey

DOBBIE, Brigadier William Ian Cotter, Bsc
5 Richmond Court White Lodge Close Hitchen Hatch Lane, Sevenoaks Kent TN13 3BF [ROCHESTER] *b* 1939 *educ* Wellington Coll; Royal Military Acad Sandhurst; Royal Military Coll of Sc; Army Staff Coll; RAF Staff Coll; *CV* Reg Off 1958–1992; Dep Cheif of Staff 3 Armoured Division 1986–88; Comm Engineer HQ Baor 1988–92; Proj Dir and Adm St Nicholas, Sevenoaks 1992–95; Gen Sec Counc of Vol Welfare Work 1995; Chair Soldiers' and Airmens' Scrip Readers Assoc, 1991; Roch Dioc Bd Patronage
GS 2000–05; 2006– *Tel:* 01732465109
email: gensec@cvww.org.uk

DOBSON, Revd Christopher John, BA, MA
St John's Vicarage Mayfield Park Fishponds Bristol, BS16 3NW [BRISTOL] *b* 1962 *educ* Norwich Sch; Aberystwyth Univ; Wycliffe Hall Th Coll; ; *CV* Manager HMSO Dept, Norwich 1984–85; Youth Worker Shrewsbury House, Everton 1985–86; C, St Mark, Biggin Hill 1989–92; C, St James and St Philip, Tunbridge Wells 1992–95; R, Alls Souls, Mount Pleasant, Harare 1996–2000; V, St Andrew, Paddock Wood, 2000–08; Bp's Adv Links, Rochester 2004–08; Ecumen and Global Partnership Off Bris from 2008
GS 2010– *Tel:* 01179060105 07530821641
email: chris.dobson@bristoldiocese.org

DOCHERTY, Mrs Lucy Clare, BA
33 Southampton Road Fareham Hampshire PO16 7DZ [PORTSMOUTH] *b* 1955 *educ* Tavistock Sch; Nott Univ; *CV* Commercial Retail & marketing posts, 1977–83; Exec Dir & Chair NCT Publ Ltd, 1996–99; Lay Brd M Fareham Pri Care Grp, 1999–2002; Vice Chair National Assoc of Lay People in Pri Care, 2000–03; Chair Fareham & Gosport Pri Care Trust, 2002–06; Non exec Dir Hampshire Probation Trust from 2007; Elected Gov Portsmouth Hosp Foundn Trust from 2007; Chair Govrs 6th Form Coll from 2010; Counc M, Ch House from 2010; Chair House of Laity Ports from 2006; Chair Ports Counc Soc Respons from 2006; Exec M Churches Together in Hampshire, 2000–09; Chair Christians Together in Fareham, Member since 1996
GS 2007– *Tel:* 01329 233602
email: lucy@docherty1.co.uk

DOE, Rt Revd Michael David, BA, LLD (Hon)
USPG: Anglicans in World Mission 200 Great Dover St London SE1 4YB [GENERAL SECRETARY, USPG: ANGLICANS IN WORLD MISSION; HONORARY ASSISTANT BISHOP OF SOUTHWARK] *b* 1947 *educ* Brockenhurst Gr Sch; Dur Univ; Ripon Hall Th Coll; *CV* C St Pet St Helier 1972–76, Hon C 1976–81; Youth Sec BCC 1976–81; V Blackbird Leys LEP Ox 1981–89; RD Cowley 1987–89; Soc Resp Adv Portsm 1989–94; Can Res Portsm Cathl 1989–94; Bp of Swindon 1994–2004; Convenor CTE 1999–2003; Gen Sec USPG from 2004
GS 1990–94, 2000–04
Tel: 020 7378 5661 020 7378 5678
Fax: 020 7378 5650
email: michaeld@uspg.org.uk

DONCASTER, Archdeacon of. See FITZHARRIS, Ven Robert Aidan

DONCASTER, Suffragan Bishop of. See ASHTON, Rt Revd Cyril Guy

DORBER, Very Revd Adrian John, BA, M Th
The Deanery 16 The Close Lichfield WS13 7LD [DEAN OF LICHFIELD] *b* 1952 *educ* St Jo Coll, Dur Univ; K Coll Lon; Westcott Ho Cam; *CV* C Easthampstead, Bracknell, Ox 1979–85; Dny Youth Officer 1982–85; P-in-c St Barn Emmer Green 1985–88; Chapl Portsm Poly 1988–92, Lect 1991–97, Sen Chapl, Public Orator Portsm Univ 1992–97; Hon Chapl Portsm Cathl 1992–97; P-in-c Brancepeth, Dur 1997–2001; Dir Min and Trg 1997–2005; Hon Can Dur Cathl 1997–2005; Dean of Lichfield from 2005; M Dioc Syn and Bp's Coun; Gov Staffordshire Univ; M Ch Leaders' Oversight Grp, W Midlands Regional Trg Partnership; Chair Lich Local Min Scheme Governing Body; Trustee Found for Ch Leadership
Tel: 01543 306294 (Home)
01543 306250 (Office)
Fax: 01543 306251
email: adrian.dorber@lichfield-cathedral.org

DORCHESTER, Area Bishop of. See FLETCHER, Rt Revd Colin William

DORKING, Archdeacon of. See HENDERSON, Ven Julian Tudor

DORKING, Suffragan Bishop of. See BRACKLEY, Rt Revd Ian James

DORMOR, Revd Duncan James, MA, MSc, BA
St John's College Cambridge CB2 1TP [UNIVERSITIES, CAMBRIDGE] *b* 1967 *educ* Sherborne Sch; Magd Coll Ox; Lon Sch of Hygiene and Tropical Medicine; Ripon Coll Cuddesdon; *CV* C Wolverhampton Cen Par, Lich 1995–98; Chapl, St Jo Coll Cam 1998–2002, Dean and Fell from 2002; affiliated lect, Faculty of Div, Cam Univ from 2004; M Coun of Westcott Ho
GS 2005– *Tel:* 01223 338633
email: djd28@cam.ac.uk

DORSET, Archdeacon of. See WAINE, Ven Stephen

DOTCHIN, Revd Andrew Stewart, Dip Th, PG Pstl Th
Whitton Rectory 176 Fircroft Road Ipswich IP1 6PS [ST EDMUNDSBURY AND IPSWICH] *b* 1956 *educ* Royal Hospital School, Nr Ipswich Witwatersrand Technikon - Johannesburg - South Africa Federal Theoligical College - Imbali nr Pietermaritzburg South Africa, Anglia Ruskin University - Cambridge; *CV* C and P-in-C, Parish of Standerton with Evander, Jo'burg 1985–87; Asst P St Martin's in the Veld, Rosebank, Jo'Burg 1987–88; R St John the Divine, Belgravia Jo'burg, 1989–94; Chapl St Martin's School, Rosettenville, Jo'burg 1994–2000; TV: Blyth Valley Team Ministry, Dioc St E&I 2000–04; Editor Third Order Chronicle, Euro Province Third Order Soc St Francis, 2003–10; M House of Clergy, Syn Anglican C of SA 1980–2000; M Prov Elective Assembly Cttee of ACSA, 1993–2000; M ACSA Pub Cttee, 1998–2000; M Exee Cttee SU Independent Sch, 1997–2000; M Dioc HIV/AIDS Cttee, Dioc Jo'burg, 1990–94; R Parish of Whitton w Thurleston and Akenham, Dioc St E&I from 2004 "Member: Board of Education, Diocese of St Edmundsbury and Ipswich 2006–present Member: Diocesan Board of Patronage, Diocese of St Edmundsbury and Ipswich 2006–presentMember: Vacncy in See Committee, Diocese of St Edmundsbury and Ipswich 2006–present Diocesan Chaplain to the Mothers' Union: Diocese of St Edmundsbury and Ipswich 2010–present Chaplain: 188 (Ipswich) Squadron Air Training Corps, 2005–present"
GS 2010–   *Tel:* 01473 742 389   07814 949 828
email: andrew@dotchin.org.,uk

DOVER, Suffragan Bishop of. See WILLMOTT, Rt Revd Trevor

DOWN, Ven Philip Roy, MA, M Th, ARMIT, CCPE
The Old Rectory The Street Pluckley Ashford TN27 0QT [ARCHDEACON OF MAIDSTONE; CANTERBURY] *b* 1953 *educ* Lakeside and Watsonia High Sch, Victoria, Australia; R Melbourne Inst of Tech; Melbourne Coll of Div; Hull Univ; *CV* Parish P Brighton, Victoria (Uniting Ch in Australia) 1982–86; Scunthorpe Circuit (Br Meth Conf) 1986–89; C St Mary and St Jas Gt Grimsby, Linc 1989–91, TV 1991–95; R St Steph Cant 1995–2002; AD Cant 1999–2002; Adn of Maidstone from 2002; M DAC; M Dioc Property and Pastl Cttees; Chair Dioc Bd of Min and Trg, Archbp's Coun, Dioc Syn
GS 2005–   *Tel:* 01233 840291
                Fax: 01233 840759
        email: pdown@archdeacmaid.org

DRIVER, Ven Penny (Penelope May), M Ed, Cert Ed, MA Adult Ed
Emmanuel House Station Rd Ide Exeter EX2 9RS [ARCHDEACON OF EXETER] *b* 1952 *educ* All SS Coll Tottenham; Nn Ord Course; Man Univ; *CV* Dioc Youth Adv Newc 1986–88; C St Geo Cullercoats 1987–88; Dioc Youth Chapl Ripon from 1988–96; Min Can Ripon Cathl from 1996; Dioc Adv for Women's Min from 1991; Asst DDO 1996–98; DDO 1998–2006; Hon Can 1998–2006; M CNC from 2003; Adn of Exeter from 2006
GS 1995–2006, 2010–   *Tel and Fax:* 01392 425577
    email: archdeacon.of.exeter@exeter.anglican.org

DRIVER, Revd Canon Roger John, Dip HE, BA (Hons), MA
The Vicarage 70 Merton Road Bootle Liverpool L20 7AT [LIVERPOOL] *b* 1964 *educ* Broadway Secondary Modern; Weymouth Tech Coll, Liverpool Hope Univ; Trin Coll, Bris; Salis & Wells Th Coll; *CV* AC, St Peter's Much-Woolton, Liv 1990–93; TV, St Paul's, Fazakerley, Liv 1993–2000; TR (designate), Bootle Team Ministry, Liv 2000–03; P-in-C, St Andrew's, Litherland; St Leonard's, Bootle; St Matthew's, Bootle, Liverpool 2000–03; TR, Bootle Team Ministry, Liv from 2003; Civic Link Officer, Sefton Borough from 2004; Area Dean, Bootle, Liv from 2007; Hon Canon, Liv Cathl from 2007; M Bp's Counc, Liv 2001–09
GS 2010–   *Tel and Fax:* 0151 922 3316
        email: rogerdriver@btinternet.com

DUDLEY, Archdeacon of. See TRETHEWEY, Ven Frederick Martyn

DUDLEY, Suffragan Bishop of. See WALKER, Rt Revd David Stuart

Dudley-Smith, Revd James, BA, MA, BTh
The Rectory 41 The Park Yeovil BA20 1DG [BATH AND WELLS] *b* 1966 *educ* Fitzw Coll Cam; Wycliffe Hall Ox; *CV* C New Borough and Leigh Sarum 1997–2001; C Hove Bp Hannington Memorial Ch Chich 2001–06; R Yeovil w Kingston Pitney B and W from 2006
GS 2010–   *Tel:* 01935475352

DUNLOP, Mrs Jennifer Mary, LLB
180a Dowson Rd Hyde SK14 5BW [CHESTER] *b* 1951 *educ* Woking Gr Sch for Girls; Hull Univ; *CV* Solicitor Dukinfield 1975–81; M Dioc Syn from 1988; Family Solicitor in Salford from 1995; Lay Chair Mottram Dny Syn 1990–2000
GS 2000–   *Tel:* 0161 368 2149
        email: jennydunlop2004@yahoo.co.uk

DUNNETT, Revd John Frederick, MA, MSc, BA, CQSW
39 Crescent Rd Warley Brentwood Essex CM14 5JR [CHELMSFORD] *b* 1958 *educ* K Edw Sch Edgbaston; Sidney Sussex Coll Cam; Worc Coll Ox; Trin Coll Bris; *CV* Rsch Asst and Press Officer to Bp of B&W 1987–88; C Kirkheaton Par Ch 1988–93; V St Luke Cranham Park 1993–2006; Gen Dir CPAS from 2006
GS 2005–   *Tel:* 01277 221419
        email: jd@johndunnett.co.uk

DUNWICH, Suffragan Bishop of. See YOUNG, Rt Revd Clive

DURHAM, Archdeacon of. See JAGGER, Ven Ian

DURHAM, Bishop of. (NOT APPOINTED AT TIME OF GOING TO PRESS)

DURHAM, Dean of. See SADGROVE, Very Revd Michael

DURLACHER, Mrs Mary Caroline,
Archdines Chappel Road Fordham Colchester CO6 3LT [CHELMSFORD] *b* 1951 *educ* Cramborne Chase Sch; Kent Univ; Moore Coll; *CV* Churchwarden, All Saints Fordham & Eight Ash Green 1999–2005; Foundn Gov, C o E All Saints Fordham Primary Sch from 2005
GS 2010–   *Tel:* 01206 240 627
        email: marydurlacher@hotmail.com

DYER, Mrs Kay, BA, Cert Ed
6 Sycamore Close Stratford-upon-Avon CV37 0DZ [COVENTRY] *b* 1949 *educ* Blakedown High Sch Leamington Spa; Open Univ; Wolverhampton Univ; *CV* County Ecum Officer, Cov and Warw from 2004; OU tutor from 2003; Chair Cov Dioc Youth Initiative 1997–2001; Children's Work Co-ord, St Andrew Shottery, Stratford-upon-Avon from 2005
GS 2005–   *Tel:* 01789 298299
        email: kay.dyer@ntlworld.com

DYKE, Revd Elizabeth Muriel, B Sc, PGCE, Dip HE
11 Critchley Drive Dunchurch Rugby CV22 6PJ [COVENTRY] *b* 1955 *educ* Harrogate High Sch; Dur Univ; St Mart Coll Lanc; Oak Hill Th Coll; *CV* C St Andr High Wycombe 1994–95; C Bledlow Ridge, Bradenham, Radnage & W Wycombe 1995–97; TV Bedworth 1997–2002; V Dunchurch w. Thurlaston from 2002; Dir of Rdr Initial Trg 2002–08
GS 2004–   *Tel:* 01788 810274
        email: elizabeth.dyke@surefish.co.uk

DZIEGIEL, Mrs Julie Patricia, MA
239 Chartridge Lane Chesham Bucks HP5 2SF [OXFORD] *b* 1963 *educ* Pynton County High Sch; Newham Coll, Cam; *CV* Arthur Andersen, Chartered Accountants, 1984–88; Accountant 1988–94; Accountant & Company Sec from 1994
GS 2010–   *Tel:* 01494 773713
        email: julie@stronglg.demon.co.uk

EAST RIDING, Archdeacon of. See BUTTERFIELD, Ven David John

EASTERN ARCHDEACONRY (Europe). See CURRAN, Ven Patrick Martin Stanley

EBBSFLEET, Bishop of. (NOT APPOINTED AT TIME OF GOING TO PRESS)

EDMONDSON, Rt Revd Christopher Paul, BA, Dip Th, MA, MBII
Bishop's Lodge Walkden Rd Worsley Manchester M28 2WH [SUFFRAGAN BISHOP OF BOLTON] *b* 1950 *educ* Blandford Gr Sch Dorset; Univ of Durham; Cranmer Hall, St John's Coll Dur; *CV* C Kirkheaton Par Ch 1973–79; V Ovenden St George 1979–86; Bp's Adv on Evang 1981–86; Dioc Officer for Evang and P-in-C Bampton, Carl 1986–92; V Shipley St Peter, Bradf 1992–2002; Warden Lee Abbey 2002–08; Bp of Bolton from 2008; Bp's Coun Carl 1989–1992; Chair Bradf Dioc Pastl Cttee 1994–2002; Dir SNWTP from 2008; M Bp's Coun Man from 2008; Chair Scargill Movt Coun from 2009; Chair Greater Man Fresh Expressions Area Strategy Tm from 2009
                                 Tel: 0161 790 8289
                                 Fax: 0161 703 9157
        email: bishopchris@manchester.anglican.org

EDMONDSON, Very Revd Dr John James William, BA, Cert Th, MA, PhD
The Deanery Caldbec Hill Battle TN33 0JY [DEAN OF BATTLE] *b* 1955 *educ* Strode's Sch, Egham; Dur Univ; Cranmer Hall, Dur; *CV* C Gee Cross, Ches 1983–86; C St Paul Camberley, Guildf 1986–88, TV 1988–90; Chapl Elmhurst Ballet Sch, Camberley 1986–90; V Foxton w. Gumley and Laughton and Lubenham, Leic 1990–94; R St Mark Bexhill, Chich 1994–2005; Chich Dioc Vocations Adv 1998–2002; Asst DDO, Chich 2002–05; Dean of Battle, V Battle, Chich from 2005; P-in-c Sedlescombe and Whatlington, Chich 2005–07
                            Tel and Fax: 01424 772693

EDMONTON, Area Bishop of. See WHEATLEY, Rt Revd Peter William

EDWARDS, Canon (Diana) Clare, Bth
22 The Precincts Canterbury CT1 2EP [CANTERBURY] *b* 1956 *educ* Nott Univ; Linc Th Coll; *CV* S Wimbledon H Trin and St Peters S'wark 1986–90; Par Dn 1987–90; Par Dn Lingfield and Crowhurst 1990–94; C 1994–95; Chapl St Piers Hosp Sch Lingfield 1990–95; R Bletchingley S'wark 1995–2004; RD Godstone 1998–2004; Hon Can S'wark Cathl 2001–04; Dean of Women's Min 2003–04; Can Res Cant Cathl from 2004
GS 2010–   *Tel:* 01227865227
        email: canonclare@canterbury-cathedral.org

ELCOCK, Dr Martin, BA, MB, Ch B
The Cottage 3 Digbeth Lane Claverley Wolverhampton WV5 7BP [HEREFORD] *b* 1963 *educ* Oldbury Wells Comp Sch Bridgnorth; Bris Univ; Man Univ; *CV* GP; Chair Good Shepherd Trust (homelessness and social inclusion charity in W Midlands/Derbys); primary sch gov; M Hosp Chapls Counc 2006–10
GS 2000–   *Tel:* 01746 710423
                                 07971 784639 (Mobile)

ELLIS, Rt Revd Tim (Timothy William), D Phil, AKC
Saxonwell Rectory Church St Long Bennington Newark NG23 5ES [SUFFRAGAN BISHOP OF GRANTHAM; LINCOLN] *b* 1953 *educ* City Sch Sheff; K Coll Lon; York Univ; St Aug Cant; *CV* C St Jo Old Trafford 1976–80; V St Tho Pendleton 1980–87; Chapl Salford Coll of Tech 1980–87; V St Leon Norwood, Sheff 1987–2001; P-in-c St Hilda Shiregreen, Sheff 1994–97; Adn of Stow and Lindsey 2001–2006; Vc Chair CCC; FAC York Min, Sheff Cathl, Linc Cathl; Bp of Grantham from 2006
Tel: 01400 283344
Fax: 01400 283321
email: bishop.grantham@lincoln.anglican.org

ELY, Bishop of. (NOT APPOINTED AT TIME OF GOING TO PRESS)

ELY, Dean of. See CHANDLER, Very Revd Dr Michael John

ETHERINGTON, Revd Ferial Mary Gould, BA
The Vicarage Station Road Flookburgh Grange over Sands LA11 7JY [CARLISLE] *b* 1944 *educ* Liskeard Gr Sch; Coll Law; St Albans MTS; *CV* Legal Exec 1976–93; St Alb Child Protection Off 1997– 2004; Selection Conf Secr and Co-ord Ordained Local Min, Min Div, Abps Counc 1997–2004; Carlisle Dioc Ministerial Review Off from 2004; House-for-Duty TV, Cartmel Peninsula from 2010; M Legal Aid Comm 1991–93
GS 1990–93; 2007–
Tel: 015395 58751
email: ferial.etherington@btinternet.com

EUROPE, Archdeacon in North-West. See VAN LEEUWEN, Ven Dirk Willem

EUROPE, Bishop of Gibraltar in. See ROWELL, Rt Revd (Douglas) Geoffrey

EUROPE, Suffragan Bishop in. See HAMID, Rt Revd David

EVENS, Rt Revd Robert John Scott, ACIB, Dip Th
32 The Avenue Tiverton EX16 4HW [SUFFRAGAN BISHOP OF CREDITON; EXETER] *b* 1947 *educ* Maidstone Gr Sch; Trin Coll Bris; *CV* C St Simon Southsea 1977–79; C St Mary Portchester 1979–83; V St Jo Bapt Locks Heath 1983–96; RD Fareham 1993–96; Adn of Bath 1996–2004; Chair Som Chs Together 1996–2000; Suff Bp of Crediton from 2004; Chair Coun for Worship and Min from 2004; Chair Devon Chs Together 2007–09
GS 1994–95, 2000–04
Tel: 01884 250002
Fax: 01884 257454
email: bishop.of.crediton@exeter.anglican.org

EXETER, Archdeacon of. See DRIVER, Ven Penny (Penelope May)

EXETER, Bishop of. See LANGRISH, Rt Revd Michael Laurence

EXETER, Dean of. See MEYRICK, Very Revd (Cyril) Jonathan

FALEY, Revd Monsignor Andrew James,
Catholic Bishops' Conference of England and Wales 39 Eccleston Square London SW1V 1BX [ECUMENICAL REPRESENTATIVE (ROMAN CATHOLIC CHURCH)] *b* 1954
GS 2007– *Tel:* 020 7901 4811 *Fax:* 020 7901 4821
email: andrew.faley@cbcew.org.uk

FARRELL, Mr (Michael Geoffrey) Shaun,
Dip MAN, FCMI, Lic CIPD, OBE
Church House Great Smith St London SW1P 3PS [SECRETARY AND CHIEF EXECUTIVE TO THE CHURCH OF ENGLAND PENSIONS BOARD] *b* 1950 *educ* Gillingham Gr Sch; Open Univ; *CV* On staff of Ch Commrs 1969–98; Commercial Property Mgr 1991–94; Stipends and Allocations Sec 1994–98; Fin Sec AC 1999–2004; Sec and Chief Exec C of E Pensions Bd from 2004 *Tel:* 020 7898 1800
Fax: 020 7898 1801
email: shaun.farrell@c-of-e.org.uk

FARTHING, Revd Paul Andrew, BA, STM, Dip Min
Vicarage Rangemore St Burton-on-Trent DE14 2ED [LICHFIELD] *b* 1958 *educ* Wilsons Gr Sch Camberwell; Vanier Coll Montreal; McGill Univ Montreal; Montreal Dioc Th Coll; *CV* C St Phil Montreal W 1983–85; R St Jo Divine Verdun 1985–96; R St Jo Ev Montreal 1996–99; V St Aidan and St Paul and P-in-c St Modwen Burton-on-Trent from 1999; M Gen Syn Angl Ch of Canada 1989–95; M Doct and Worship Cttee Angl Ch of Canada 1989–92; M Lichf Dioc Syn from 2000; M DBF from 2000
GS 2000–
Tel: 01283 544054
email: p.farthing@ukonline.co.uk

FAULL, Very Revd Vivienne Frances, MA, BA, MBA
21 St Martin's Leicester LE1 5DE [DEAN OF LEICESTER] *b* 1955 *educ* Qu Sch Ches; St Hilda's Coll Ox; Nottm Univ; Open Univ Business Sch; St Jo Coll Nottm; *CV* Dss St Matt and St Jas Mossley Hill 1982–85; Chapl Clare Coll Cam 1985–90; Chapl Glouc Cathl 1990–94; Can Pastor Cov Cathl 1994–2000; Vc Prov Cov Cath 1995–2000; Prov of Leic 2000–02; Dean of Leic from 2002; Chair AEC from 2009
GS 1987–90, 2004– *Tel:* 0116 248 7456 (Office)
0116 270 1630 (Home)
Fax: 0116 2487470
email: viv.faull@LecCofE.org

FELIX, Revd David Rhys, LLB, Cert Th
Vicarage Daresbury Warrington WA4 4AE [CHESTER] *b* 1955 *educ* Calday Grange County Gr Sch; Univ of Wales; Ripon Coll, Cuddesdon; *CV* C St Barn Bromborough 1986–89; V St Andr Grange, Runcorn 1989–99; Chapl Halton Gen Hosp 1995–99; P-in-c H Trin Runcorn 1996–99; RD Frodsham

1998–99; Ind Missr, Halton 1998–99; V All SS Daresbury from 1999; Sen Ind Missr Chester Dio 2000–08; M Dioc Adv Bd for Min 1988–90; M Dioc Adoption Services Cttee 1990–92; Dny Ord Chapl 1990–96; M Dioc Pastl Grp 1994–95; M Dioc Syn from 1994; Dir DBF and M Bp's Coun from 1995; M Dioc Bd of Educ and Schs Cttee 1997–2003; M Archidiaconal Pastl Cttee 1992–94 and from 1998; M Eccl Law Soc from 1987 and of Gen Cttee from 2002; M Dioc Cttee for Miss and Unity 2001–08; Hon Can Ches Cathl 2006
GS 2002–
Tel: 01925 740348 07778 859935 (Mobile)
email: david.felix@btinternet.com

FERGUSON, Ven Paul John, MA, FRCO (CHM), PGCE
48 Langbaurgh Road Hutton Rudby Yarm TS15 0HL [ARCHDEACON OF CLEVELAND; YORK] b 1955 educ Birkenhead Sch; New Coll Ox; Westmr Coll Ox; K Coll Cam; Westcott Ho Th Coll; CV C St Mary Chester 1985–88; Chapl and Sacr Westmr Abbey 1988–92; Prec Westmr Abbey 1992–95; Prec and Res Can York Minster 1995–2001; Adn of Cleveland from 2001; Wrdn of Rdrs from 2004; Sec Ho Bps' Th Grp 1992–2001
GS 2010–
Tel: 01642 706095
07770 592746 (Mobile)
email: archdeacon.of.cleveland@yorkdiocese.org

FIDDES, Revd Prof Paul, MA, D Phil, DD
Regent's Park College Pusey St Oxford OX1 2LB [ECUMENICAL REPRESENTATIVE] b 1947 educ St Pet Coll, Ox; Regent's Park Coll, Ox; CV Principal, Regent's Park Coll, Ox; Prof of Systematic Theol, Ox Univ; Min of Bapt Union of Gt Britain
GS 2005–
Tel: 01865 288134
Fax: 01865 288121
email: paul.fiddes@regents.ox.ac.uk

FINCH, Mrs Sarah Rosemary Ann, BA
97 Englefield Rd Canonbury London N1 3LJ [LONDON] b 1945 educ Godolphin Sch Sarum; Dur Univ; Ox Univ; CV Ed Barrie and Jenkins 1972–75; Trustee BFBS 1978–2005; Chair Exec Cttee BFBS 1991–94; Freelance Non-Fiction Ed from 1986; Gov Sir John Cass's Foundn Primary Sch (C of E) from 1996; M CEEC from 2000; Coun M Latimer Trust from 2003; M Revision Ctee, Common Worship Ordinal; elected M Appts Ctee from 2005; Coun M Oak Hill Theol Coll from 2006; M Angl Mainstream Strg Cttee from 2006; Trustee Latimer Trust from 2007; Dep Chair Latimer Trust Cttee from 2009; M Fin and Gen Purposes Cttee of Oak Hill Theo Coll from 2009
GS 2000–
Tel: 020 7226 2803
Fax: 020 7704 2257
email: sarahrafinch@yahoo.co.uk

FISHER, Ms Alison, CQSW, CMI
[WAKEFIELD] b 1959 educ King Edward VI, Devon; Leeds Univ; Univ Coll Cardiff; CV Probation Officer 1981–90, Senior Probation Officer from 1990; Non Exec Dir Calderdale & Huddersfield Foundn Trust from 2005; Gen Tching Counc, Lay m from 2007; Diversity Mgr, West Yorkshire Probation Trust from 2008
GS 2010–
email: alison.fisher1@ntlworld.com

FITTALL, Mr William Robert, MA
Church House Great Smith St London SW1P 3AZ [SECRETARY GENERAL OF THE GENERAL SYNOD AND THE ARCHBISHOPS' COUNCIL] b 1953 educ Dover Gr Sch; Ch Ch Ox; CV Home Office 1975–80; Ecole Nat d'Administration Paris 1980–81; Home Office 1981–91; Prin Private Sec to N Ireland Sec 1992–93; Home Office 1993–95; Under Sec and Chief of Assessments Staff, Cabinet Office 1995–97; Dir Crime Reduction and Com Programmes, Home Office 1997–2000; Assoc Political Dir, N Ireland Office 2000–02; Sec Gen GS and AC from 2002
Tel: 020 7898 1360
07738 883712 (Mobile)
Fax: 020 7898 1369
email: william.fittall@c-of-e.org.uk

FITZHARRIS, Ven Robert Aidan, BDS
Fairview House 14 Armthorpe Lane Doncaster DN2 5LZ [ARCHDEACON OF DONCASTER; SHEFFIELD] b 1946 educ St Anselm's Coll Birkenhead; Sheff Univ; Linc Th Coll; CV Gen Dental Practitioner 1971–87; pt Clinical Asst Dept Child Dental Health Univ of Sheff 1976–84; Asst C Dinnington St Leonard 1989–1992; V St Pet Bentley 1992–2001; AD Adwick 1995–2001; Hon Can Sheff Cathl from 1998; Substitute Chapl HMP Moorland 1992–2001; Hon Asst Chapl Doncaster R Infirmary from 1995; Eur Link Person from 1997; Adn of Doncaster from 2001; M Bp's Coun from 1995; M Dioc Parsonages Cttee from 1992, Chair from 2001; M Dioc Bd of Educ, Chair from 2001; Chair Dioc Strategy Grp 1999–2001; Surrogate from 2000; Chair Wildwood Project (Bentley) Ltd 1999–2004; Chair Doncaster Cancer Detection Trust from 2003; Chair Doncaster Minster Devel Appeal 2005–07; M Sheff Univ Rsch Ethics Cttee from 2004; Chair Doncaster Re-Furnish Ltd from 2007; M Sheff Univ HR Mgt Cttee from 2006; Chair Together for Regeneration from 2005; Hon Freeman Metrop Boro of Doncaster from 2008
Tel: 01709 309110 (Office)
01302 325787 (Home)
07767 355357 (Mobile)
Fax: 01709 309107 (Office)
01302 760493 (Home)
email: archdeacons.office@sheffield.anglican.org

FITZSIMONS, Canon Kathryn Anne, Cert Th, Cert Ed; MA
52 Newton Court Oakwood Leeds LS8 2PH [RIPON AND LEEDS] b 1957 educ Richmond Sch; Bedford Coll of HE; NEOC; Univ of Leeds; CV NSM C St Jo Bilton, Harrogate 1990–2002; Soc Resp Officer 1992–99; Dioc Urban Officer from 1999; Hon Can

Ripon Cathl from 2004; Pres Diaconal Assoc of the C of E from 2003; Officer, Mission Resourcing Team; M DBF
GS 2004– *Tel:* 0113 248 5011
email: kathrynfitzsimons@hotmail.com

FLACH, Canon Deborah Mary, Dip HE, Dip Counselling
7 rue Leonard de Vinci 59700 Marcq en Baroeul France [EUROPE] *b* 1954 *educ* Beckenham Convent Sch; Trin Coll Bris; Salis and Wells Th Coll; *CV* C St Pet Chantilly, France 1994–96; C H Trin Maisons-Laffitte, France 1996–2004, Asst Chapl 2004–07; M Dioc Syn from 1994; Asst Dir of Ordinands (France) 1997–2010; P-in-c Ch Ch, Lille (Eur) from 2007; Chair House of Clergy from 2007; Bp's Counc from 2007
GS 2005– *Tel:* +333 28526636
email: chaplain@christchurchlille.com

FLETCHER, Rt Revd Colin William, MA, OBE
Arran House Sandy Lane Yarnton Oxford OX5 1PB [AREA BISHOP OF DORCHESTER; OXFORD] *b* 1950 *educ* Marlboro Coll; Tr Coll Ox; Wycliffe Hall Th Coll; *CV* C St Pet Shipley 1975–79; Tutor Wycliffe Hall and C St Andr Ox 1979–84; V H Tr Margate 1984–93; RD Thanet 1989–93; Dom Chapl to Abp of Cant 1993–2000; Canon Dallas Cathl 1993–2000; Bp of Dorchester from 2000
Tel: 01865 208218
Fax: 01865 849003
email: bishopdorchester@oxford.anglican.org

FLETCHER, Mr Ian Jack, FCA
38 Heaton Grove Heaton Bradford BD9 4DZ [BRADFORD] *b* 1952 *educ* Woodhouse Grove Sch; *CV* Articled Clerk, 1970–74; Chartered Accountant from 1975; Director, D J Fletcher (Insurances) Ltd from 1973; Chair Bradf District Community Foundation; Dir Bradford Churches For Dialogue and Diversity; Dir Wellsprings Ltd; Chair Church in the World Dioc Syn Cttee; Chair Dioc Urban Plus Panel; M Dioc Fin Cttee; M Dioc Ministry & Miss Syn Cttee; M Assets Cttee; Lay Canon Bradf Cathl
GS 2010– *Tel:* 01274 492839 01274 729178
Fax: 01274 725470
email: ijf@fgco.com

FLETCHER, Revd Jeremy James, MA
Minster Vicarage Highgate Beverley HU17 0DN [YORK] *b* 1960 *educ* Woodhouse Grove Sch Bradf; Univ Coll Dur; St John's Nott; *CV* Asst C All Saints Stranton, Hartlepool 1988–91; Assoc Min St Nicholas Nottm 1991–94; P-in-C Skegby and Stanton Hill 1994–2000; P-in-C Teversal 1996–2000; Chapl to Bp Southwell 2000–02; Precentor York Minster 2002–09; V Beverley Minster from 2009
GS 1995–2002, 2009– *Tel:* 01482 881434
email: jeremy@jjfletcher.co.uk

FLETCHER, Mr Philip John, CBE, MA
20 Calais St Camberwell London SE5 9LP [APPOINTED MEMBER, ARCHBISHOPS' COUNCIL] *b* 1946 *educ* Marlborough Coll; Trin Coll Ox; *CV* Dir Gen Cities and Countryside Dept of Environment to 1996; Receiver, Metropolitan Police District 1996–2000; Dir Gen Water Services (OFWAT) 2000–06; Chair OFWAT from 2006; Member Ofqual (Qualifications and Examinations Regulator) Bd from 2010
GS 2007– *Tel:* 0121 644 7550
email: philip.fletcher@ofwat.gsi.gov.uk

FOLLETT, Mr Samuel (Joseph),
Christ Church Vicarage 5 High Oaks St Albans AL3 6DJ [ST ALBANS] *b* 1990 *educ* St. George's Sch, Harpenden; Nott Univ; *CV* PA to CE, Church Army 2009–10; Dir, Simplicity from 2007; Elected to GS 2010
GS 2010– *Tel:* 07868 258303
email: sam@samfollett.co.uk

FORD, Revd Mandy (Amanda Kirstine), BA, BTh, MA
10 Parkside Close Leicester LE4 1EP [LEICESTER] *b* 1961 *educ* Cranborne Chase Sch, Wiltshire; Middlesex Univ; Ox Univ; Nott Univ; St Stephen's House Th Coll; *CV* Tchr, Maynard Sch, Exeter 1990–98; C, Parish of the Resurrection, Leic 2000–05; Church Urban Fund Link Officer 2004–09; Vicar, Christ the King, Leic from 2005; Asst Area Dean, City of Leic from 2009; M Abp's Counc Urban Strategy Consult Grp 2004–09; M Cathl Fabric Adv Cttee from 2005; Chair from 2008; Chair of the House of Clergy from 2009
GS 2010– *Tel:* 0116 235 2667
email: mandyford@btinternet.com

FORD, Rt Revd John Frank, MA
31 Riverside Walk Tamerton Foliot Plymouth PL5 4AQ [SUFFRAGAN BISHOP OF PLYMOUTH; EXETER] *b* 1952 *educ* Chich Th Coll; *CV* C Ch Ch Forest Hill 1979–82; V St Aug Lee 1982–91; V Lower Beeding 1991–94; Dom Chapl to Bp of Horsham 1991–94; Dioc Missr from 1994; Can and Preb Chich Cathl from 1997; Prec of Chich Cathl from 2000; Bp of Plymouth from 2005
GS 1999–2005 *Tel:* 01752 769836
email: bishop.of.plymouth@exeter.anglican.org

FOREMAN, Mrs (Antoinette Joan) Anne, CCYW
5 St Leonards Road Exeter Devon EX2 4LA [EXETER] *b* 1943 *educ* Teignmouth Gr Sch; Bradf & Ilkley Comm Coll; *CV* Yth & Comm Worker, Sutton 1983–85; Senior Yth & Comm Worker, Kingston 1985–88; Asst Prin Yth Off, Sutton 1988–91; National Yth Off Genl Syn Brd Ed 1991–95; Ch House; M GS Brd Miss 2001–03; Lay Chair Okehampton Deanery; M Dioc Syn; M Bps Counc; Vice Chair Dioc Miss & Pstrl Cttee; M Vacancy in See Cttee; Bps Adv from 2008; External Exam BEd Fieldwork Placements St. Martins Coll Lan 1992–94; M Adv Counc Comm & Yth Work

Course Goldsmiths Coll 1991–94; Dir & Trustee Guildford YMCA 2002–05; M Counc Mngment Univ Coll St. Mark & St. John 2006–10
GS 1999–2005; 2010–   Tel: 01392 279859
        email: anne@anneforeman.co.uk

FORSTER, Rt Revd Dr Peter Robert, MA, BD, Ph D
Bishop's House Abbey Square Chester CH1 2JD [BISHOP OF CHESTER] *b* 1950 *educ* Tudor Grange Gr Sch Solihull; Merton Coll Ox; Edin Univ; Edin Th Coll; *CV* C St Matt and St Jas Mossley Hill Liv 1980–82; Sen Tutor St Jo Coll Dur 1983–91; V Beverley Minster 1991–96; Bp of Ches from 1996; Ch Commr 1999–2004, from 2009
GS 1985–91,1996–   Tel: 01244 350864
        Fax: 01244 314187
    email: bpchester@chester.anglican.org

FORWARD, Miss Emma Joy, BA
24 Whitchurch Ave Exeter EX2 5NT [EXETER] *b* 1984 *educ* St Pet C of E High Sch Ex; St Hugh's Coll Ox; *CV* Trainee tchr from 2005; full time tchr from 2006
GS 2005–   Tel: 01392 251617
    email: emmaforward@yahoo.co.uk

FOSTER, Rt Revd Christopher Richard James,
BA, MA (ECON), MA
Bishopsgrove 26 Osborn Rd Fareham PO16 7DQ [BISHOP OF PORTSMOUTH] *b* 1953 *educ* R Gr Sch Guildf; Dur Univ; Manch Univ; Trinity Hall Cam, Wescott Ho Cam; *CV* Lect in Economics Univ of Dur 1976–77; Asst C Tettenhall Regis TM Wolverhampton 1980–82; Chapl Wadham Col Ox and Asst P St Mary w St Cross and St Pet in the East Ox 1982–86; V Ch Ch Southgate 1986–94; CME Dir Edmonton Area 1988–94; Sub Dean and Res Can St Alb1994–2001; Bp of Hertford 2001–2010; Bp of Portsmouth from 2010   Tel: 01329 280247
        Fax: 01329 231538
    email: bishports@portsmouth.anglican.org

FRAIS, Revd Jonthan Jeremy, LLB BA DipTh
The Rectory 11 Coverdale Avenue Little Common East Sussex TN39 4TY [CHICHESTER] *b* 1965 *educ* Judd Gr Sch; Tonbridge Kingston Poly; Oak Hill Coll; *CV* AC Ch Ch, Orpington 1992–96; Asst Chapl, St Andrew's, Moscow 1996–99; Chapl, Ch Ch, Kyiv, Ukraine 1999–2005; R, St Mark's, Bexhill, from 2005; M Adv Grp Ch Soc 2007–10
GS 2000–05; 2010–   Tel and Fax: 01424 843733
        email: frais@tiscali.co.uk

FRANCE, Revd Stephen Mark, Bth (Oxon)
Rectory Rectory Close Burwash Essex Sussex, TN19 7BH [CHICHESTER] *b* 1966 *educ* Tapton School; Wycliffe Hall Th Coll;; *CV* Whitehall Civil Servant 1986–97; Ox Univ 1997–2000; C Newbold w Dunston, Derby 2000–03; Independant Lay Member of Derbyshire C C Standard's Cttee 2001–05; Dioc Duty Press Officer; P-in-C Derby 2003–05; P-in-C Chich 2005–06; Rector, Burwash, Chich from 2006; Rector, Society of Catholic

Priests, Chich from 2008; M Chesterfield Daycentre for the Homeless Cttee 2001–03; M Dioc Syn Derby 2002–05; M Dioc Comm Cttee, Derby 2002–05; M Coun for Developing Discipleship and Ministry 2002–05; Derbyshire CC Emergency Chapl 2004–05; Gov Walter Evans Sch 2003–05; M Soc of Catholic Priests, Chich from 2005; Gov Burwash Sch from 2005; Chair Barnsley Trust from 2005; M Dioc Syn, Chich from 2005; M Dioc and Adnry Pastoral and Miss Cttees from 2006; M Bp's Coun, Chich from 2008; Emergency Chapl, Chich from 2010;   Tel: 01435 882301
        email: revfrance@tiscali.co.uk

FRANCE, Archdeacon of. See LETTS, Ven Kenneth John

FRANKLIN, Revd Canon Richard Heighway,
BA, MPhil
Holy Trinity Vicarage 7 Glebe Close Weymouth Dorset DT4 9RL [SALISBURY] *b* 1954 *educ* Warwick Sch; Southampton Univ; Salis & Wells Th Coll; *CV* C Thame w Towersey 1978–81; Asst chapl Univ of Southampton 1981–83; Tutor & Dir of Studies Chich Th Coll 1983–89; P-in-C Stalbridge 1989–94; V Holy Trinity Weymouth from 1994; Ed journal 'Studies in Christian Ethics' 1987–91; M Dioc Brd of Ch & Soc 1996–2006; Euro Off Bp of Salisbury from 1998; Rural Dean of Weymouth 2004–2008
GS 2003–25; 2010–   Tel: 01305 760354
    email: richardfranklin@iname.com

FRASER, Revd Dr Giles,
45 St John's Avenue Putney London SW15 6AL [SOUTHWARK] *CV* M GS from 2000
GS 2000–10   Tel:

FRAYLING, Very Revd Nicholas Arthur, BA,
Hon LLD, FJMU
The Deanery Canon Lane Chichester PO19 1PX [DEAN OF CHICHESTER] *b* 1944 *educ* Repton; Ex Univ; Cuddesdon; *CV* Mgt trg retail trade 1962–64; prison welfare 1964–66 and part-time 1966–71; C St Jo Peckham 1971–74; V All SS Tooting Graveney 1974–83; Can Res and Prec Liv Cathl 1983–87; R Liv 1987–2002; Dean of Chich from 2002; Chair S'wark DAC 1980–83; M Liv Dioc Syn and Bishop's Coun   Tel: 01243 812485 (Office)
        01243 812494 (Home)
        Fax: 01243 812499
    email: dean@chichestercathedral.org.uk

FREAR, Mrs Jacqueline, T Cert
Kirk Braddan Vicarage Saddle Rd Braddan Isle of Man IM4 4LB [SODOR AND MAN] *b* 1942 *educ* Annecy Convent Seaford; St Gabr Coll Lon; *CV* Teaching posts in Beds, Wilts and Avon
GS 2000–10   Tel: 01624 675523

FREEMAN, Mr John, BA, Ad Dip Ed Mgt, DMS,
Cert Ed, JP
The Smiths' House 99 High St Barwell LE9 8DS [LEICESTER] *b* 1947 *educ* Hinckley Gr Sch; Open

Univ; De Montfort Univ, Garnett Coll; Birm Coll of Food; *CV* Lect South Fields Coll Leic 1972–82; Dir Faculty of Arts, N Herts Coll 1982–99; Ptnr, The Grove Tavern, Lon 1999–2003; Mgt Consult, Leic Univ from 2005
GS 2005–2010   *Tel:* 01455 842548
     email: j.freeman5@btinternet.com

FREEMAN, Mr John Jeremy Collier, Eur Ing, DLC, B Sc, MIChemE, C ENG
Stable Court 20a Leigh Way Weaverham Northwich CW8 3PR [CHESTER] *b* 1937 *educ* Embley Park Sch; Loughb Univ; *CV* Graduate Chemical Engineer ICI 1961–94 inc Asst to Gen Mgr Magadi Soda Co, Kenya 1975–77; Rtd 1994, now very active in vol sector; M Local Agenda 21 Forum; Par Coun from 1980; Sch Gov from 1980; M Dioc Fin and Central Services Cttee from 1994; M Exec Chs Together in Cheshire from 1995; Chair Dioc PWM Cttee; M Dioc CSR Cttee; Chr Aid activist; Sec Dioc Justice and Devel Educ Grp; M Bp's Coun; M Dioc Syn; Dioc World Devel Adv; M Core Grp Angl World Devel Advs; Treas Open Syn Grp; Companion of the Melanesian Brotherhood
GS 2000–   *Tel:* 01606 852872
        Fax: 01606 854140
     email: jjcfreeman@tiscali.co.uk

FREEMAN, Ven Robert John, B Sc, MA
2 Vicarage Gardens Brighouse HD6 3HD [ARCH-DEACON OF HALIFAX; WAKEFIELD] *b* 1952 *educ* Cambs High Sch; St Jo Coll Dur; Fitzw Coll Cam; Ridley Hall Cam; *CV* C St Jo Blackpool 1977–81; TV St Winifred Chigwell 1981–85; V Ch of the Martyrs Leic 1985–99; RD Christianity S (Leic) 1994–98; Hon Can Leic 1994–2003; Nat Evang Adv, AC from 1999; Chair Agenda and Support Cttee of Grp for Evangelisation (CTE) 2000–03; Sec Miss, Evang and Renewal in Eng Cttee, Bd of Mission, AC 1999–2003; Chair rejesus.co.uk from 2000; Dir Just Fairtrade Ltd 2000–03; Adn of Halifax from 2003; M Chs Regional Commn for Yorkshire and Humberside 2004; Chair Chr Enquiry Agency from 2006; Trustee Simeon and Hyndman's from 2007; Chair Wakefield Dioc Bd of Finance from 2008
GS 1997–99, 2008–
     Tel: 01484 714553 07980 751902 (Mobile)
        Fax: 01484 711897
     email: archdeacon.halifax@
        wakefield.anglican.org

FRENCH, Mr Philip Colin, MA, MIET, CPhys, MInstP
Arden Five Oak Green Rd Five Oak Green Tonbridge TN12 6TJ [ROCHESTER] *b* 1960 *educ* R Gr Sch Newc; Br Sch Brussels; Churchill Coll Cam; *CV* Rsch Asst, Univ Coll Lon 1984–87; Overseas Career Service Officer, Br Coun 1987–96; (First Sec (Educ & Science), Calcutta 1988–91); Sen Consult, Hewlett-Packard Ltd 1996–99; Tech Dir, Software.com, later Openwave Systems Inc 1999–2003; IT mgt posts in HM Prison Service and Nat

Offender Mgt Service 2003–2008; Chief Technology Officer, Min of Justice from 2009; M Bp's Coun, Roch Dioc
GS 1985–88, 2005–   *Tel:* 01892 838713 (Home)
        020 3334 4848 (Office)
        07952 273253 (Mobile)
     email: philip.c.french@btinternet.com

FRITH, Rt Revd Richard Michael Cokayne, MA
Hullen House Woodfield Lane Hessle HU13 0ES [SUFFRAGAN BISHOP OF HULL; YORK] *b* 1949 *educ* Marlboro Coll; Fitzw Coll Cam; St Jo Coll Nottm; *CV* C Mortlake w E Sheen 1974–78; TV Thamesmead 1978–83; TR Keynsham 1983–92; Adn of Taunton 1992–98; Bp of Hull from 1998
GS 1995–98   *Tel:* 01482 649019
        Fax: 01482 647449
     email: richard@bishop.karoo.co.uk

FROUDE, Canon David Colin, ACIB
St Mary's Vicarage 8 Priory Gardens Shirehampton Bristol BS11 0BZ [BRISTOL] *b* 1949 *educ* Colston's Sch, Bris; Senior Manager, HSBC 2004;; *CV* Par Clerk, St Mary's, Bris from 200; Chair Bris Dioc Brd Finance Ltd from 2004; M C of E Pensions Brd from 2009; M Bris Cathl Coun from 2002; M Provincial Panel Clergy Discipline Measure from 2003; Chair Bris DBF Finance Cttee from 2004; Chair Bris DBF Budget Cttee from 2004; Chair Bris DBF Remuneration Cttee from 2004; M Bris DBF Audit Cttee from 2004; M Bris Dioc Syn Agenda Ctee from 2004; M Bp's Coun from 2004; Chair Trustees Bris DBF Staff Retirement Benefit Scheme from 2004; SW Region DBF Chair, M from 2004, Convenor from 2006; C of E Consultative Grp of DBF Chairs and Dioc Secs, M from 2006, Chair from 2009 Member, Administrative Costs Working/Procurement Group from 2007 Member, Bishop of Bristol Senior Staff from 2007 Member, Bristol Diocese Strategic Policy Group 2007–2009 Yes, I am happy for my data to be published in both print and electronic formats
GS 2010–   *Tel:* 07768 958704
     email: davidfroude@lineone.net

FRY, Mrs Christine Ann, BA, PG Dip
25 St Leonards Avenue, Chineham Basingstoke RG24 8RD [WINCHESTER] *b* 1964 *educ* Arden Sch;. Solihull Sixth Form Coll; Southampton Univ; Middlesex Poly; *CV* Probation Service Off, Middlesex Probation Area,1986–88; Trainee Probation Off, Middlesex Probation Area, 1988–90; Probation Off, Hampshire Probation Area 1990–93; Youth and Comm Worker, St Mary's Ch, Eastrop, Basingstoke 1993–95; Court Welfare Off, Hampshire Probation Area 1995–98; Probation Off, Hampshire Probation Area, 1998–2001; Senior Probation Off, Hampshire Probation Area 2001–08; Area Mgr, Hampshire Proabtion Area 2008–09; Business Change Mgr, Hampshire Probation Trust from 2010
GS 1995–2000; 2010–   *Tel:* 01256 474466
     email: chrisfry01@yahoo.co.uk

FRY, Dr Roger Gordon, BD, AKC, D Litt, FRSA, CBE
Avda Pio XII 92 28036 Madrid Spain [EUROPE] *b*
1943 *educ* Portsm Gr Sch; Lon Univ; *CV* Chair
King's Grp from 1981; Chair Coun of Br
Independent Schs in the Eur Com from 1996;
Chair Coun of Br Internat Schs from 2006; Dir
Independent Schs Coun from 2008
GS 1990–95; 2005–2010   *Tel:* +34 91 3598800
                               Fax: +34 91 3592767
          email: roger.fry@kingsgroup.org

FULHAM, Suffragan Bishop of. (NOT
APPOINTED AT TIME OF GOING TO PRESS)

FULLARTON, Mr Derek, FRSA
Lambeth Palace London SE1 7JU [PATRONAGE
SECRETARY TO THE ARCHBISHOP OF CANTERBURY] *b*
1952 *educ* Camphill Sch Paisley; Glasgow Univ;
CV On staff of Ch Commrs from 1974; on
secondment as Private Sec to the Sec-General of
GS 1985–89; M Engl Cttee, Friends of Angl Cen in
Rome from 1990; Sec Palace Trustees Wells 1992–
99; Sec Lambeth Palace Library Trustees 1996–
2006; Admin Sec Lambeth Palace 1999–2006; Dir
Lambeth Projects (2000) Ltd; Abp's Patronage Sec
from 2006   *Tel:* 020 7898 1252
                            07525 492758 (Mobile)
     email: derek.fullarton@lambethpalace.org.uk

GARNETT, Ven David Christopher, BA, MA
The Vicarage Edensor Bakewell Derbys DE45 1PH
[ARCHDEACON OF CHESTERFIELD; DERBY] *b* 1945
educ Giggleswick Sch; Nottm Univ; Fitzw Coll
Cam; Westcott Ho Th Coll; *CV* C Cottingham
1969–72; Chapl, Fell and Tutor Selw Coll Cam
1972–77; Pastl Adv Newnham Coll Cam 1972–77;
R Patterdale 1977–80; DDO Carlisle 1977–80; V
Heald Green 1980–87; Chapl St Ann's Hospice
1980–87; R Christleton 1987–92; TR Ellesmere
Port 1992–96; Adn of Chesterfield from 1996;
Chair Bp's Th Adv Grp 1987–93; Chair Assoc of
Ch Fells 1987–92; V Edensor and Beeley from
2007
GS 1990–96, 2000–05   *Tel:* 01246 582130
     email: davidcgarnett@yahoo.co.uk

GAY, Canon Perran Russell, MA, BA, PGCE, FRGS
Cathedral Office 14 St Mary's Street, Truro TR1 2AF
[TRURO] *b* 1959 *educ* Truro Sch; Cam Univ; Ex
Univ; Ox Univ; Ripon Coll Cuddesdon; *CV* AC
Bodmin w Lanhydrock & Lanivet 1987–90; Bp
Truro's Domestic Chapl 90–94; Truro Dioc Ecum
Offr 1990–93; Dir Ministerial Training, Truro
1993–2001; Can Chan, Truro Cathl 1994–2001;
Can Prec, Truro Cathl from 2001; Dioc Lit Adv,
Truro from 2001; Chapl Epiphany Ho, Truro from
2007; M Dioc Brd Ed 1988–90; M Dioc Decade of
Evan Steering Cttee 1990–94; Exec M of Churches
Together Cornwall 1990–94; M CTE Enabling Grp
1992–94; M Praxis Counc from 1996; County
Chapl, Royal British Legion from 1998; Chair,
Dioc Deaf Ministry Support Grp 1996–2001;
Chair, Dioc Lit Cttee from 2001; M Dioc Forma-
tion Grp from 2004; Chair, Dioc Porvoo Link
Cttee from 2009
GS 2010–   *Tel:* 01872 245003
                       Fax: 01872 277788
          email: perran@perrangay.com

GEORGE, Rt Worshipful Charles Richard, MA,
QC
*Francis Taylor Building Inner Temple London EC4Y
7BY* [DEAN OF THE ARCHES] *b* 1945 *educ* Bradfield
Coll Magdalen Coll Ox; Corpus Christi Coll Cam;
CV Asst master Eton College 1967–72; Barrister,
Francis Taylor Building, Inner Temple (formerly 2
Harcourt Buildings) from 1975; Chancellor Dioc
of S'wark 1996–2009; M of Panel of Chairmen of
Bps' Disciplinary Tribunals for Provinces of
Canterbury and York from 2007; M of Ho Coun,
St Stephen's Ho, Ox from 1999; Visiting Lecturer
in Environmental Law, KCL from 2006; Dean of
the Arches, Auditor of the Chancery Court of
York, Master of the Faculties from 2009
GS 2009–2010   *Tel:* 020 7353 8415
                             Fax: 020 73537622
          email: charles.george@ftb.eu.com

GERMANY AND NORTHERN EUROPE,
Archdeacon of. See LLOYD, Ven Jonathan
Wilford

GIBBS, Revd Dr Jonathan Robert, MA PhDe
*The Rectory Village Road Heswall, Wirral, Mersey-
side CH60 0DZ* [CHESTER] *b* 1961 *educ* The King's
Sch; Chester Jesus Coll Ox; Jesus College, Cam;
Ridley Hall, Cam; *CV* AC Stalybridge, Holy Trin
1989–92; Chapl, Basel, Switzerland w Freiburg,
Germany 1992–98; R, Heswall from 1998; M Bp's
Counc from 1999; M Fin & Central Services Cot-
tee from 1999; Chair of Ho of Clergy, Dioc Syn
from 2006.
GS 1995–98; 2010–   *Tel:* 01513423471
          email: jgibbs@heswallparish.co.uk

GIBRALTAR IN EUROPE, Bishop of. See
ROWELL, Rt Revd (Douglas) Geoffrey

GIBRALTAR, Archdeacon of. See SUTCH, Ven
David

GIBRALTAR, Dean of. See PADDOCK, Very
Revd Dr John

GIDDINGS, Dr Philip James, MA, D Phil
5 Clifton Park Rd Caversham Reading RG4 7PD
[OXFORD] *b* 1946 *educ* Sir Thos Rich's Sch Glouc;
Worc and Nuff Colls Ox; *CV* Lect in Public
Admin Ex Univ 1970–72; Hd, Sch of Politics and
Intl Relations, Reading Univ; Rdr; M Dioc Syn
from 1974; M Bp's Coun 1979–2006; Lay Vc Pres
Dioc Syn 1989–2000; M BSR 1991–96, Exec Cttee
1992–96; M CAC 1992–97; M GS Panel of Chair-
men 1995–96; Vc Chair GS Ho of Laity 1995–2000,
2005–; M AC from 1999; Chair Ch and World Div
AC 1999–2002; M Crown Appts Commn Review

Grp 1999–2001; Elected M AC from 2000; Chair Coun of MPA from 2003; Convenor, Angl Mainstream UK from 2003; Dep Chair GS Legislative Cttee from 2005
GS 1985–   *Tel:* 0118 954 3892 (Home)
                           0118 378 8207 (Office)
                           Fax: 0118 975 3833
email: P.J.Giddings@reading.ac.uk

GILBERTSON, Ven Michael Robert, MA, BA, PhD
Church House Lower Lane Aldford Chester CH3 6HP [ARCHDEACON OF CHESTER] *b* 1961 *educ* Stockport Grammar Sch; New Coll Ox; Cranmer Hall Dur; *CV* Dept of Trade and Industry 1982–1991; C St Matthew's Surbiton 1997–2000; V All Saints Stranton 2000–2010; AD of Hartlepool 2002–2010; Hon Can Durham Cathedral 2008–2010; Adn of Chester from 2010   *Tel:* 01244 681973
email: michael.gilbertson@chester.anglican.org

GILLEY, Revd Dr Margaret (Meg) Mary, MTheol, PhD
Vicarage Bourne Terrace Annfield Plain Stanley Co Durham DH9 8QS [DURHAM] *b* 1954 *educ* Nelson Gr Sch; St And Univ; Dur Univ; NEOC; *CV* Primary Care Devel rsch, Sunderland Health Commn 1991–94; Programmes Mgr, Sunderland Health Auth 1994–96; Locality Dir, Co Durham Health Auth 1996–98; Chief Exec, Darlington Primary Care Grp 1998–2000; C St Jo Birtley 2000–03; V St Mark Stockton & St Jo Elton 2003–2009; Assoc P Lancaster Deanery from 2009; M AC Fin Cttee
GS 2005–   *Tel:* 01207 236 974
                           07752 432366 (Mobile)
email: meg.gilley@durham.anglican.org

GILLINGS, Ven Richard John, BA
5 Robins Lane Bramhall Stockpot SK7 2PE [ARCHDEACON OF MACCLESFIELD; CHESTER] *b* 1945 *educ* Sale Co Gr Sch; St Chad's Coll Dur; Linc Th Coll; *CV* C St Geo Altrincham 1970–75; P-in-c St Thos Stockport 1975–77; R St Thos Stockport 1977–83 and P-in-c St Pet Stockport 1978–83; R Priory Tm Par Birkenhead 1983–93; RD Birkenhead 1985–93; Hon Can Ches Cathl 1992–94; V St Mich Bramhall 1993–2005; Adn of Macclesfield from 1994
GS 1980–2005   *Tel:* 0161 439 2254
                           Fax: 0161 439 0878
email: richard.gillings@chester.anglican.org

GILLIVER, Miss Joy Alison, MA, PGCE
3 Wadhurst Rise Brighton BN2 5PW [CHICHESTER] *b* 1961 *educ* Bishop Stopford Sch; Enfield Regent's Park Coll; Ox Univ; Selwyn Coll Cam, Heythrop Coll, LU; *CV* RE Tchr, Sch of S. Helen & S. Katharine, Abingdon. 1983–95; Head of RE, Hemel Hempstead Sch. 1995–97; RE Tchr, The Queen's Sch, Bushey 1997–98; Ed consult Birm 1997–98; Comm Develp worker, Kingstanding, Birm 1998–99; Adv ed & training of adults, Chich 1999–2009; Adv for Min & Adult Christian Ed,

Chich from 2009; M Chich Dioc Rdrs Cttee from 1999
GS 2010–   *Tel:* 07884 180545
email: joy@gilliver37.freeserve.co.uk

GLEDHILL, Rt Revd Jonathan Michael, BA, MA, BCTS, D Univ (Keele)
Bishop's House 22 The Close Lichfield WS13 7LG [BISHOP OF LICHFIELD] *b* 1949 *educ* Strode's Sch Egham; Keele Univ; Bris Univ; Trin Coll Bris; *CV* C All SS Marple 1975–78; P-in-c St Geo Folkestone 1978–83; V St Mary Bredin Cant 1983–96; Tutor/Lect Cant Sch of Min 1983–94; Tutor/Lect SE Inst for Th Educ 1994–96; RD Cant 1988–94; Hon Can Cant Cathl 1992–96; Bp of Southn 1996–2003; M Meissen Commn 1993–96; Chair Angl Old Catholic Internat Co-ordinating Council Coun from 1998; Chair Nat Coll of Evangelists 1998–2010; Bp of Lichfield from 2003; Keele Univ Hon Dr Univ 2007
GS 1995–96, 2003–   *Tel:* 01543 306000
                           Fax: 01543 306009
email: bishop.lichfield@lichfield.anglican.org

GLOUCESTER, Archdeacon of. See SIDAWAY, Ven Geoffrey Harold

GLOUCESTER, Bishop of. See PERHAM, Rt Revd Michael Francis

GLOUCESTER, Dean of. (NOT APPOINTED AT TIME OF GOING TO PRESS)

GNANADOSS, Miss Vasantha Berla Kirubaibai, B Sc
242 Links Rd London SW17 9ER [SOUTHWARK] *b* 1951 *educ* Portsm Gr Sch; Birkbeck Coll Lon; *CV* Commissioner's Secretariat, Metropolitan Police Service
GS 1990–   *Tel:* 020 8769 3515
                           020 7230 5017
                           07803 590610 (Mobile)
email: vasanthi.gnanadoss@met.police.uk

GODDARD, Rt Revd John William, BA
Dean House 449 Padiham Rd Burnley BB12 6TE [SUFFRAGAN BISHOP OF BURNLEY; BLACKBURN] *b* 1947 *educ* St Chad's Coll Dur Univ; *CV* C S Bank 1970–74; C Cayton w Eastfield 1974–75; V Ascen Middlesbrough 1975–82; RD Middlesbrough 1981–87; V All SS Middlesbrough 1982–88; Can and Preb York Minster 1987–88; Can Emer York from 1988; Vc Prin Edin Th Coll 1988–92; TR Ribbleton 1992–2000; Bp of Burnley from 2000
GS 2008–   *Tel:* 01282 470360
                           07779 786114 (Mobile)
                           Fax: 01282 470361
email: bishop.burnley@ntlworld.com

GODDARD, Mrs Madelaine, BSc, SRD
35 Princes Drive Littleover Derby DE23 6DX [DERBY] *b* 1944 *educ* Lewis Sch for Girls; Lon Univ; *CV* Sen Dietitian, Bethnal Green 1967–69; District

Dietitian, N Gwent HMC 1969–77; pt tchr, Derby High Sch from 1986; Dioc Pres MU; Tax Commr GS 2003–
    Tel: 01332 348077
    07817 043257 (Mobile)
    email: goddard35@btinternet.com

GODDARD, Mrs Vivienne, BA, PGCE
39 Kearsley Ave Tarleton Preston PR4 6BP [BLACK-BURN] *b* 1948 *educ* Roch Girls' Gr Sch; Dur Univ; *CV* RE Tchr, Cleveland Girls Grammar School 1970–74 Supply Tchr 1974–76; DirCleveland Lay Training & Foundn Scheme for York Dioc; RE Tchr Bydales School, Marske, 1984–88; Acting Head of Dept, 1988–92; Publishing Manager, Rutherford House, Edinburgh, 1994–95; RE Tchr 1996–97; Local Non-Stipendiary Ministry Officer, Black b1998; OLM Officer, Blackb 2004; Bp's Officer for LM 1996–2007
GS 1980–88; 2000–
    Tel: 01772 812532
    07779 786141 (Mobile)
    email: viviennegoddard@talktalk.net

GODSALL, Revd Andrew Paul, BA
12 Cathedral Close Exeter Devon EX1 1EZ [EXETER] *b* 1959 *educ* Tudor Grange Gr Sch; Birm Univ; Ripon Coll Cuddesdon; *CV* Mgr 1981–86; BBC Radio Pro 1984–86; AC, St John's Great Stanmore, 1988–91; Assoc V, All Saints Ealing Comm, 1991–94; V, All Saints Hillingdon, 1994–2001; DDO, Willesden Area, Lon, 1999–2001; Asst & Chapl Bp Ex, 2001–06; Dir, Councl Worship & Min, 2006; Can Chan, Ex Cathl, 2006; Chair, Willesden Area Litt Resources Grp, 1995–99; Sec, Patterns of Ministry Working party, Ex, 2002–03
GS 2010–
    Tel: 01392 294920
    email: andrew.godsall@exeter.anglican.org

GOODER, Dr Paula Ruth, MA, D Phil
61 Linden Rd Bournville Birmingham B30 1JT [BIR-MINGHAM] *b* 1969 *educ* Fallowfield C of E H Sch, Loreto Sixth Form Coll, Manch; Worc Coll Ox; Qu Coll Ox; *CV* Tutor in Biblical Studies, Ripon Coll Cuddesdon 1995–2001; Tutor in NT Studies, Qu Foundn 2001–2007; Freelance Writer and Lec-turer Biblical Studies from 2007; Can Theol Birm Cathl from 2005–; Canon Theol Guildf Cathl from 2010; Lay Can Salis Cathl from 2010
GS 2005–
    Tel: 0121 744 0260
    email: prgooder@gmail.com

GOODING, Canon Ian Eric, B Com, BSc, LTh, Dip PS, C Eng
Rectory Stanhope St Stanton-by-Dale Ilkeston Derby-shire DE7 4QA [DERBY] *b* 1942 *educ* Nottm H Sch; Leeds Univ; St Jo Coll Nottm; *CV* Devel/Produc-tion Engineer Turner & Newhall 1965–67, PA to Works Dir 1967–68, Systems Analyst 1968–70; Rdr, Manch Dioc 1968–70; C Wandsworth S'wark 1973–75; C with charge of All SS Wandsworth 1975–77; R Stanton-by-Dale w. Dale Abbey, Derby from 1977, R Risley, Derby from 1994; sen industrial chapl from 1977; RD Erewash from 1997; Hon Can Derby Cathl from 2002; M DBF

and Exec Coun DBF; M Bp's Coun; M Derbyshire Ecum Industrial Cttee; Chair Trustees Chr Broad-casting Coun from 1988; Bd M Erewash Local Strategic Ptnrship from 2004; M C of E Pensions Bd from 2006; Chair Stanton-by-Dale Par Coun from 2007 GS 2005–2010
    Tel: 0115 932 4584
    07974 370330 (Mobile)
    Fax: 0115 932 4584
    email: ian.e.gooding@gmail.com

GORE, Mr Philip, BA, MIMgt, FRSA
12 Ellesmere Rd Morris Green Bolton BL3 3JT [MANCHESTER] *b* 1957 *educ* Smithills Gr Sch Bol-ton; Hull Univ; *CV* Chair Philip Gore (Bolton) Ltd from 1981; Dir Silverwood Forestry Ltd from 1991; pt Tutor and Lect; M Bp's Coun; DBF, Dioc Fin Cttee; M Dioc Bd of Min; M Dioc Bd of Patronage; M Ch Soc Trust; Lay Chair Deane Dny Syn from 1990; M Coun Ch Soc; JP GS 1985–
    Tel: 01204 63798 (Home)
    01204 62126 (Office)
    Fax: 01204 659750
    email: philipgore@compuserve.com

GORHAM, Ven Karen Marisa, BA
Rectory Stone Aylesbury HP17 8RZ [ARCHDEACON OF BUCKINGHAM; OXFORD] *b* 1964 *educ* Mayflower Sch, Billericay; Trin Th Coll Bris; *CV* C North-allerton w Kirby Sigston 1995–99; P-in-c St Paul Maidstone, Asst DDO and RD Maidstone 1999–2007; Hon Can Cant 2006–07; Adn of Bucking-ham from 2007
GS 2003–07, 2010
    Tel: 01865 208264 01865 208266
    email: archdbuc@oxford.anglican.org

GOUDIE, Dr Richard Angus, MB BChir MRCGP
197 Gilesgate Durham DH1 1QN [DURHAM] *b* 1951 *educ* Barnard Castle Sch; St John's Coll Cam; Kings Coll Hosp Lon; Newcastle GP Vocational Training Scheme; *CV* GP, Cartington Terrace Medical Grp, Newcastle 1982–1991; GP, Kepier Medical Practice, Tyne and Wear, 1991; PCC m St Nicholas Church Dur & Dur Deanery Syn from 1996; M D Dioc Syn from 2006; M Dur Dioc Syn Miss Cttee 2006–10; M Dur Bps Counc 2010
GS 2010–
    Tel: 0191 3840013
    Fax: 0191 5849493
    email: angus.goudie@virgin.net

GOVENDER, Very Revd Rogers Morgan, BTh, Dip Th
Manchester Cathedral Cathedral Yard, Victoria St Manchester M3 1SX [DEAN OF MANCHESTER] *b* 1960 *educ* Glenover High Sch, Durban, S Africa; Univ of Natal (Pietermaritzburg), S Africa; St Paul's Coll, Grahamstown, S Africa; *CV* C Ch Ch Overport, S Africa 1985–87; R St Mary Greyville, Durban, S Africa 1988–92; R St Matt Hayfields, Pietermaritzburg, S Africa 1993–99; Adn of Pietermaritzburg 1997–99; R St Thos Berea, Durban 1999–2000; P-in-c Ch Ch Didsbury, Man 2001–05; P-in-c St Chris Withington, Man 2003–05; AD Withington 2003–05; Dean of Man from

2006; M Dioc Syn; M Bp's Coun; M AC CMEAC from 2006; M AC Liturg Commn from 2006; Chair Dioc Pastl Cttee
GS 2008–2010
Tel: 0161 833 2220
0161 792 2801 (Home)
07983 978346 (Mobile)
Fax: 0161 839 6218
email: dean@manchestercathedral.org

GRANTHAM, Suffragan Bishop of. See ELLIS, Rt Revd Dr Tim (Timothy William)

GREEN, Ven John, QHC, BCS
RN Chaplaincy Service MP 1.2 Leach Building Whale Island Portsmouth PO2 8BY [CHAPLAIN OF THE FLEET AND ARCHDEACON FOR THE ROYAL NAVY; ARMED FORCES SYNOD] b 1953 educ SW Ham County Tech Sch; Hendon Coll of Science and Tech; NE Lon Poly; Linc Th Coll; CV Project Eng, Thorn Lighting 1974–77, Sen Eng 1977–80; C St Mich and All Angels, Watford 1983–86; C St Steph w. St Julian, St Alb 1986–91; Chapl RN 1991; Chapl of the Fleet and Adn for RN from Mar 2006; Hon Can Portsmouth Cath from 2006
GS 2005–
Tel: 023 9262 5055
Fax: 023 9262 5134
email: john.green107@mod.uk

GREEN, Rt Revd Laurie (Laurence Alexander),
BD, AKC, STM, D Min
Bishop's House Orsett Rd Horndon-on-the-Hill SS17 8NS [AREA BISHOP OF BRADWELL; CHELMSFORD] b 1945 educ East Ham Gr Sch; K Coll Lon; New York State Univ; New York Th Seminary; St Aug Coll Cant; CV C St Mark Kingstanding Birm 1970–73; V St Chad Erdington 1973–83; Prin Aston Tr Scheme 1983–89; Hon C H Trin Birchfield 1984–89; TR All SS Poplar Lon 1989–93; Bp of Bradwell from 1993
Tel: 01375 673806
Fax: 01375 674222
email: b.bradwell@chelmsford.anglican.org

GREENER, Very Revd Jonathan Desmond Francis, MA
The Deanery 1 Cathedral Close Margaret St, Wakefield WF1 2DP [DEAN OF WAKEFIELD] b 1961 educ Reigate Gr Sch; Trin Coll Cam; Coll of Resurrection Mirfield; CV C H Trin w St Matt, Southwark 1991–94; Dom Chapl to Bp of Truro 1994–96; V Ch of Good Shepherd, Brighton 1996–2003; Adn of Pontefract 2003–07; Dean Wakefield from 2007
GS 2003–07
Tel: 01924 239308 (Home)
01924 373923 (Office)
Fax: 01924 215054
email: jonathan.greener@wakefield-cathedral.org.uk

GREENWOOD, Mr Adrian Douglas Crispin,
MA, MCIH
91 Lynton Rd Bermondsey London SE1 5QT [SOUTHWARK] b 1951 educ Judd Sch Tonbridge; Jes Coll Cam; Coll of Law Lon; CV Chwrdn St James Bermondsey 1983–92, 1995–2004; Lay Chair St

James Bermondsey 1982–2010; Chief Exec Gateway Housing Assoc (formerly Bethnal Green and Victoria Park Housing Assoc Ltd) 1992–2010; Trustee Salmon Youth Centre Bermondsey 2000–10; Trustee Isle of Dogs Community Foundation 1998–2010 M Dioc Syn 1994–2010, Lay Chair 2006–10; M Tower Hamlets Local Strategic Ptnrship 2002–10; Lay Chair Bermondsey Dny Syn 2004–10
GS 2000–
Tel: 020 7237 6920
email: amgreenwood@tiscali.co.uk

GREENWOOD, Mr Nigel Desmond, M Phil, M Ed, C CHEM, FRSC, FIBMS, FRIPH
47 Broomfield Adel Leeds LS16 7AD [RIPON AND LEEDS] b 1944 educ Leeds Gr Sch; Leeds Univ; Leic Univ; CV Leeds Public Health Dept 1962–68; Tobacco Rsch Coun 1968–69; United Leeds Hosps 1969–74; Wigston CFE 1974–77; Keighley Tech Coll 1978–80; Airedale and Wharfedale Coll 1981–95; Educ and Trg Consult 1995–99; Dir One City Projects from 1999; Chair Dioc Bd of Educ; Convenor W Yorks Faith in F.E. Chapl Gp; Gov Yorks Min Course; Hon Lay Can Ripon Cath from 2009; Trustee Changing Attitude; Trustee Leeds Asylum-Seekers Support Network
GS 1990–
Tel: 0113 261 1438
07940 587618 (Mobile)
email: greenwoodnd@aol.com

GREGORY, Rt Revd Clive Malcolm, BA, MA
61 Richmond Rd Wolverhampton WV3 9JH [AREA BISHOP OF WOLVERHAMPTON; LICHFIELD] b 1961 educ Sevenoaks Sch; Lanc Univ; Qu Coll Cam; Westcott Ho Cam; CV C St Jo Bapt Margate 1988–92; Sen Chapl Univ of Warwick 1992–98; TR Coventry East 1998–2007; Hon MA, Univ of Warwick 1999; Assoc DDO Coventry 2001–07; Area Bp of Wolverhampton from 2007
Tel: 01902 824503
Fax: 01902 824504
email: bishop.wolverhampton@lichfield.anglican.org

GRIMSBY, Suffragan Bishop of. See ROSSDALE, Rt Revd David Douglas James

GRYLLS, Revd Catherine Anne, MA, MTh, PGCE
15 Raglan Road Edgbaston Birmingham B5 7RA [BIRMINGHAM] b 1970 educ John Hanson Sch, Andover; Marlborough Coll; Cam Univ, Birm Univ, Ox Univ; Ripon Coll Cuddesdon; CV Tm, S'wark Dioc Retreat House 1991–92; Maths and RE Teacher, Saltley Sch, Birmingham, 1993–95; Maths Teacher, Holyhead Sch, Birmingham, 1995–97; Asst C, St Peter's Hall Green Birm 2000–04; P-in-C St Paul Balsall Heath and St Mary & St Ambrose Edgbaston, Birm 2004–05; P-in-C, Balsall Heath and Edgbaston (SS Mary & Ambrose), Birm 2006–08; Incumbent, Balsall Heath and Edgbaston, Birm from 2008
GS 2010–
Tel: 0121 440 2196
email: gryllsc@btinternet.com

GUERNSEY, Dean of. See MELLOR, Very Revd (Kenneth) Paul

GUILDFORD, Bishop of. See HILL, Rt Revd Christopher John

GUILDFORD, Dean of. See STOCK, Very Revd Victor Andrew

GUILLE, Very Revd John Arthur, MA, B Th, Cert Ed
The Residence Vicars Court Southwell NG25 0HP [DEAN OF SOUTHWELL; SOUTHWELL AND NOTTINGHAM] *b* 1949 *educ* Guernsey Gr Sch; Ch Ch Coll Cant; Southn Univ; Sarum and Wells Th Coll; *CV* C Chandlers Ford 1976–80; P-in-c St Jo Bournemouth 1980–83; P-in-c St Mich Bournemouth 1983–84; V St Jo w St Mich Bournemouth 1984–89; R St Andre de la Pommeraye Guernsey 1989–99; Vc Dean Guernsey 1996–99; Adn of Basingstoke 1999–2000; Can Res Win Cathl from 1999; Adn of Win 2000–07; M Dioc Syn from 1977; Vc-Dean Win Cathl 2006–07; Dean of S'well from 2007
GS 1990–2000   *Tel:* 01636 817282
        email: dean@southwellminster.org.uk

GUNN-JOHNSON, Ven David Allan, S Th, MA
Stage Cross Sanders Lane Bishop's Tawton Barnstaple EX32 0BE [ARCHDEACON OF BARNSTAPLE; EXETER] *b* 1949 *educ* Stratton Gr Sch Biggleswade; St Steph Ho Ox; *CV* C St Matt Oxhey, St Albans 1981–84; C Cheshunt, St Albans 1984–88; TR Colyton, Exeter 1988–2003; RD Honiton 1990–96; Preb Ex Cathl 1999–2003; M Dioc Coun for Worship and Min; Adn Barnstaple from 2003; Dioc Wrdn of Rdrs from 2004; Episc V for the Diaconate from 2009
    Tel: 01271 375475 07921 150428 (Mobile)
                           Fax: 01271 377934
        email: archdeacon.of.barnstaple@
                               exeter.anglican.org

HACKNEY, Archdeacon of. (NOT APPOINTED AT TIME OF GOING TO PRESS)

HACKWOOD, Ven Paul, B Sc Dip Theol, MBA
The Archdeaconry 21 Church Rd Glenfield LE3 8DP [ARCHDEACON OF LOUGHBOROUGH; LEICESTER] *b* 1961 *educ* Darlaston Comp Sch; Bradf Coll; Huddersfield Univ; Birm Univ; Bradf Sch of Mgt; Qu Coll Birm; *CV* C All SS Horton Bradf 1989–93; C St Oswald Chapel Green 1991–93; Soc Resp Adv St Alb Dioc 1993–97; V St Marg Thornbury Bradf 1997–2005; Adn Loughborough from 2005; Trustee CUF, M Funding Cttee from 2004; M W Yorks Police Auth 2003–05   *Tel:* 0116 248 7421
                                   0116 231 1632
                           Fax: 0116 253 2889
        email: paul.hackwood@leccofe.org

HADDOCK, Mr Peter,
43 Woodland Way Morden SM4 4DS [SOUTHWARK]
CV Elected to GS 2005
GS 2005–

HALIFAX, Archdeacon of. See FREEMAN, Ven Robert John

HALL, Sergeant Frances Mary,
SNCO RAF Continuous Improvement Team Air Command RAF High Wycombe HP14 4UE [REPRESENTATIVE, ARMED FORCES SYNOD] *b* 1970 *educ* Whitecross High Sch Heref; Heref Sixth Form Coll; *CV* HM Forces from 1992; M RAF Adny Syn from 1999, Sec 2003–05; M Forces Synodical Coun from 2003, Asst Sec from 2004; Sec Armed Forces Syn from 2005
GS 2005–   *Tel:* 01494 562842 (Home)
                               01494 497785 (Office)
                           Fax: 01494 496830
        email: fran.hall865@mod.uk

HALL, Ven John Barrie,
Tong Vicarage Shifnal TF11 8PW [ARCHDEACON OF SALOP; LICHFIELD] *b* 1941 *educ* Sarum and Wells Th Coll; *CV* C St Edw Cheddleton 1984–88; V Rocester 1988–94; V Rocester and Croxden w Hollington 1994–98; RD Uttoxeter 1991–98; Adn of Salop and V Tong from 1998; Vc-Chair DBF; M DAC; Chair Dioc Pastl Cttee; M Ch Buildings Cttee; M Benefice Buildings Cttee; M Dioc Trust; Chair Lich Dioc Red Chs Uses Cttee; Chair Shrops Hist Chs Trust; Chair Dioc Child Protection Grp; Pres Telford Chr Coun
GS 2002–2010   *Tel:* 01902 372622
                           Fax: 01902 374021
        email: archdeacon.salop@lichfield.anglican.org

HALL, Canon John Michael, BA Hons, MA
49 Mount Rd Fleetwood FY7 6QZ [BLACKBURN] *b* 1962 *educ* St Michael's CE High Sch Chorley; Runshaw Sixth Form Coll Leyland; Leeds Univ; Lanc Univ; Mirfield Theol Coll; *CV* Can Bloemfontein from 2000; Can Blackb from 2009; Chair Ho of Clergy Blackb from 2003; V Fleetwood, St David and St Peter
GS 2000–05, 2008–2010   *Tel:* 01253 876176
        email: johnbloem@aol.com

HALL, Very Revd John Robert, BA, FRSA, hon DD, hon DTheol, FRSA, hon FCollT
The Deanery Westminster London SW1P 3PA [DEAN OF WESTMINSTER] *b* 1949 *educ* St Dunstan's Coll Catford; St Chad's Coll Dur; Cuddesdon Th Coll; *CV* Head of RE Malet Lambert High Sch Hull 1971–73; C St Jo Divine Kennington 1975–78; P-in-c All SS S Wimbledon 1978–84; V St Pet Streatham 1984–92; Exam Chapl to Bp of S'wark 1988–92; M GS Bd of Educ 1991–92; Chair FCP 1990–93; Dioc Dir of Educ Blackb 1992–98; Fell Woodard Corp from 1992; M Gov Body, St Mart's Coll Lanc 1992–98; Hon Can Blackb Cathl 1992–94 and 1998–2000; Res Can Blackb Cathl 1994–98; Can Emer from 2000; M Nat Soc Coun 1999–2006; Trustee St Gabr's Trust 1998–2006; M Gov Body Cant Ch Ch Univ Coll 1999–2006; Trustee Urban Learning Found 1999–2002; M Gen Teaching Coun 2000–04; Gen Sec Bd of Educ and Nat Soc

1998–2002; CEO, Educ Division and Gen Sec Nat Soc 2003–06; Hon Asst C St Alban S Norwood 2003–06; Gov St Dunstan's Coll from 2003; Chair of Govs Westmr Sch from 2006; Hon Fell Cant Ch Ch Univ; Hon Fell Coll of Teachers from 2009; Hon Fell St Chad's Coll, Dur from 2009; Dean of Westmr from 2006; Dean of the Order of the Bath from 2006
GS 1984–92
Tel: 020 7654 4801
07973 418859 (Mobile)
Fax: 020 7654 4883
email: john.hall@westminster-abbey.org

HALL, Mr Robin Michael, LLB, MCIPR
44 St Margaret's Square Adelaide Avenue London SE4 1YR [SOUTHWARK] b 1979 educ Emmanuel Gr Sch; Gorseinon Tertiary Coll; Univ Coll, Dur Univ; CV Comm Mgr, London Underground 2007–10; Head of Labour Grp Off, London Borough of Islington, 2003–07; Caseworker & Parliamentary Asst, Office of Oona King MP, 2001–03; Ed & Welfare Off, Dur SU 2000–01; Public Affairs Mgr, Transport for London, from 2010; GS from 2010
GS 2010–
Tel: 07779241322
email: robinhall79@googlemail.com

HALLIDAY, Mr Malcolm Keith,
7 Kirkstall Gardens Keighley BD21 5PN [BRADFORD] b 1944 educ Rutlish Sch, Merton;; CV Inland Revenue 1963–1985; Bradf Dioc Sec 1985–2010; Bradf Dioc Dir Edu 1999–2003; Rdr from 1979; Lay Canon Bradf Cathl 1999–2010
GS 2010–
Tel: 01535 606048
email: malcolm.halliday@btinternet.com

HAM, Archdeacon of West. See COCKETT, Ven Elwin Wesley

HAMID, Rt Revd David, B Sc, M Div, DD
14 Tufton St London SW1P 3QZ [SUFFRAGAN BISHOP IN EUROPE] b 1955 educ Nelson High Sch, Burlington, Canada; McMaster Univ Canada; Univ of Trin Coll, Toronto, Canada; CV C St Chris Burlington Canada 1981–83; R St Jo Burlington Canada 1983–87; Miss Co-ord for Latin America/Caribbean, GS of Angl Ch of Canada 1987–96; Dir of Ecum Affairs and Studies, Angl Ch of Canada 1996–2002; Suff Bp in Europe from 2002; ex officio M FOAG (C of E) 1996–2002; Co-Sec ARCIC 1996–2002; Co-Sec Angl-Orthodox Theol Dialogue 1996–2002; Co-Sec Angl-Lutheran Internat Wkg Grp 1999–2002; Co-Sec Angl-RC Commn on Unity and Miss 2001–02; Co-Sec Angl-Baptist Internat Conversations 1999–2002; Co-Sec Angl-Old Catholic Internat Co-ord Coun 1998–2002; Co-Sec Angl-Oriental Orthodox Dialogue 2001–02; Sec Inter-Angl Theol and Doct Commn 2001–02; Sec Inter-Angl Stg Cttee on Ecum Relns 2000–02; Consult to Jt Wkg Grp of WCC and RC Church 2000–06; Consult to Angl-RC Commn on Unity and Miss from 2002; M Angl-Old Catholic Internat Co-ord Coun from 2005; Chair Porvoo

Panel; Abp of Cant's Link Bp for Common Word Dialogue w Muslims
Tel: 020 7898 1160
07801 449113 (Mobile)
Fax: 020 7898 1166
email: david.hamid@c-of-e.org.uk
web: www.eurobishop.blogspot.com

HAMMOND, Sir Anthony Hilgrove, KCB, QC, MA, LLM
The White Cottage Blackheath Guildford GU4 8RB [STANDING COUNSEL TO THE GENERAL SYNOD] b 1940 educ Malvern Coll; Em Coll Cam; CV Solicitor GLC 1965–68; Legal Asst Home Office 1968; Sen Legal Asst 1970; Asst Legal Adv 1974; Prin Asst Legal Adv 1980; Legal Adv and Dep Under-Sec of State and Legal Adv Nn Ireland Office 1988; Solicitor and Dir Gen Legal Services DTI 1992; Treasury Solicitor HM Procurator Gen and Hd of Government Legal Service 1997–2000; Stg Counsel to the GS from 2000; M Legal Adv Commn
Tel: 01483 892607 /
01726 833156 (Home)
020 7898 1799 (Office)
Fax: 01483 890667
01726 833156

HAMMOND, Mr Robert Ian, BA, MA, AIWS, FRSA
22 South Primrose Hill Chelmsford CM1 2RG [CHELMSFORD] b 1966 educ Hylands Sch Chelmsf; Open Univ; Heythrop Coll, Lon Univ; CV NatWest Bank 1985–87; HM Customs and Excise 1987–2005; HM Revenue and Customs from 2005, Senior Prin - Strategic Organisation Design Manager; Freelance Wine and Spirit Educator and Judge from 2009; Chelms Dioc Syn from 1996; M Bp's Coun from 2003; M Chelms Cathl Coun from 2003; M MPA Coun from 2006; M Dioc Bd of Patr 2007–2010; M Dioc Pastl Ctee 2007–2010; M C of E (Eccl Fees) Measure: Steering Ctee 2008–2010; Chair of Govs Cathl Sch Chelmsf
GS 2000–
Tel: 01245 269105
07711 672308 (Mobile)
email: rihammond@me.com

HAMPSTEAD, Archdeacon of. (NOT APPOINTED AT TIME OF GOING TO PRESS)

HANCOCK, Rt Revd Peter, MA, BA
Bishop's Lodge Colden Lane Old Alfresford SO24 9DY [SUFFRAGAN BISHOP OF BASINGSTOKE] b 1955 educ Price's Sch Fareham; Selw Coll Cam; Oak Hill Th Coll; St Jo Coll Nottm; CV C Ch Ch Portsdown 1980–83; C Radipole and Melcombe Regis TM 1983–87; V St Wilf Cowplain 1987–99; RD Havant 1993–98; Hon Can Portsm Cathl 1997–99; Adn of The Meon 1999–2010; Bp of Basingstoke from 2010; Acting Warden of Rdrs 1999–2000; Acting RD Gosport 2002–03; Dir of Mission 1999–2006; Chair CPAS Trustees 2004–2010
Tel: 01962 737330 (Office)
email: bishop.peter@winchester.anglican.org

HANCOCK, Mr Paul, BDS, MSc, Dip HSM, MHSM, FRSH
Mamre 3 Arncliffe Drive Burtonwood Warrington WA5 4NB [LIVERPOOL] *b* 1946 *educ* K Edw VI Sch Lich; Man Univ; *CV* Gen dental practitioner 1968–74; Com Dental Officer 1974; Sen Dental Officer 1974–93; Asst District Dental Officer 1993–97; Asst Dir Dental Services 1997–99; Asst Clinical Dir Dental Services from 1999; M Liv Dioc Syn 1997–2003; M Bd of Miss and Unity 1998–2003; Lay Swanwick Conference Cttee Sec and Treas 1998–2003; Par Treas from 2004; M Dny Syn from 2005; M Dioc Syn from 2008
GS 2005–   *Tel:* 01925 292559
                                  Fax: 01925 295988
                          email: hancockpa1@aol.com

HAND, Revd Nigel, Lth Th
Birmingham Cathedral Colmore Row Birmingham B3 2QB [BIRMINGHAM] *b* 1954 *educ* St John's Th Coll, Nott; *CV* Asst C St Luke Birm, 1984–88; Asst C and TV Walton, 1988–97; Asst C Sellypark 1997–2004; Adn Moseley 2004–07; P-in-C Selly Park, 2001–08; Canon Residentiary and Canon Missioner Birm Cathl from 2008
GS 2010–   *Tel:* 01212621856
                                  Fax: 01212621860
                         email: canonmissioner@
                         birminghamcathedral.com

HAND, Revd Nigel Arthur, Lth Th
Birmingham Cathedral Colmore Row Birmingham B3 2QB [BIRMINGHAM] *b* 1954 *educ* St John's Th Coll, Nott; *CV* Asst C St Luke 1984–88; Asst C and TV Walton 1988–97; Asst C Selly Park 1997–2004; Adn Moseley 2004–07; P-in-C Selly Park 2004–08; Canon Residentiary and Canon Missioner, Birm Cathl from 2008
GS 2010–   *Tel:* 01212621856
                                  Fax: 01212621860
                         email: canonmissioner@
                         birminghamcathedral.com

HANSON, Dr Charles Goring, MA, PhD
Longlands House Ashgate Lane Wetheral Carlisle, CA4 8HE [CARLISLE] *b* 1934 *educ* Felsted Sch, Essex; Trin Hall Cam; *CV* Lect and Senior Lect Economic, Univ of Newcastle upon Tyne, 1962–95; Retired
GS 2010–   *Tel:* 01228560337
                    email: charleshansonecon@yahoo.co.uk

HARBORD, Canon (Paul) Geoffrey, MA
4 Clarke Drive Sheffield S10 2NS [SHEFFIELD] *b* 1956 *educ* Thornbridge Gr Sch Sheff; Keble Coll Ox; Chich Th Coll; *CV* C Rawmarsh w Parkgate 1983–86; C St Geo Doncaster 1986–90; P-in-c St Edm Sprotbrough 1990–95; V Masbrough 1995–2003; JP from 1999; M Legal Aid Commn; M DAC; M Dioc Worship and Liturg Cttee; Dom Chapl to Bp of Sheff from 2003; M Coun Coll of

Resurrection, Mirfield; M CDC 2003–06; Hon Can Sheff Cathl 2007
GS 2000–   *Tel:* 0114 266 1932
                                  0114 230 2170
                                  Fax: 0114 263 0110
                 email: geoffrey@bishopofsheffield.org.uk

HARDING, Mr Nick (Nicholas) Andrew, B Ed
8 Belmont Close Mansfield Woodhouse NG19 9GD [SOUTHWELL AND NOTTINGHAM] *b* 1964 *educ* St Philip's RC Coll Birm; Ex Univ; *CV* Primary sch tchr 1985–88; Dir ICIS Trust 1989–94; Educ Officer, S'well Minster 1995–2002; S'well Dioc Children's Officer from 2002; M GS Bd of Educ Children's Panel; M Dioc Liturg Cttee, Bd of Educ, Lay Min Grp; magistrate
GS 2005–   *Tel:* 01636 817234 (Work)
                               07827 291694 (Mobile)
                                  Fax: 01623 622272
                 email: nick@southwell.anglican.org

HARDMAN, Ven Christine Elizabeth, B Sc (Econ), M Th
129A Honor Oak Park Forest Hill London SE23 3LD [ARCHDEACON OF LEWISHAM AND GREENWICH; SOUTHWARK] *b* 1951 *educ* Qu Eliz Girls' Gr Sch Barnet; City of Lon Poly; Westmr Coll Ox; St Alb Dioc Minl Trg Scheme; *CV* Dss St Jo Bapt Markyate 1984–87; C 1987–88; Course Dir St Alb Minl Trg Scheme 1988–96; V H Trin Stevenage from 1996; RD Stevenage from 1999; Adn of Lewisham and Greenwich from 2001; M Dioc Syn; M Bp's Coun
GS 1998–2001, 2004–   *Tel:* 020 8699 8207 (Home)
                      020 7939 9400 (Office)
                      Fax: 020 7939 9465
                      email: christine.hardman@
                      southwark.anglican.org

HARDWICK, Very Revd Dr Christopher George, MA, Ph D, ACIB
The Deanery The Avenue Truro TR1 1HR [DEAN OF TRURO] *b* 1957 *educ* K Edw VI Sch Lich; Open Univ; Birm Univ; Cuddesdon Ox; *CV* C Worc SE Tm 1992–95; pt Chapl St Rich Hospice Worc and RNIB New Coll Worc 1992–95; R Ripple, Earls Croome w. Hill Croome & Strensham 1995–2005; RD Upton 1997–2005; R Upton-upon-Severn 2000–2005; Worc Dioc Trg Incumbent 2000–03; Chair Worc Dioc Ho of Clergy 2002–05; Hon Can Worc Cathl 2003–05; Dean of Truro from 2005; M Ch Commrs Pastl Cttee from 2002–07; GS Proctor in Conv 2004–05; M SST from 2001; Ch Commr from 2007; M Ch Commn Bishoprics and Cathls Ctee from 2007   *Tel:* 01872 245006
                                  01872 276782
                                  Fax: 01872 277788
                 email: dean@trurocathedral.org.uk

HARGREAVES-SMITH, Mr Aiden Richard, MA, LLM, FRSA
23 Battlebridge Court Wharfdale Rd London N1 9UA [LONDON] *b* 1968 *educ* Batley Gr Sch; Man Univ;

Europeenne de Formation Professionnelle, Paris; Univ of Westminster; Man Metropolitan Univ; Coll of Law; *CV* Civil Service 1992–95; Tutor St Anselm Hall 1991–93, Sen Tutor 1993–98, M SCR from 1991; Trainee Solicitor Winckworth and Pemberton 1998–2000; Solicitor Winckworth Sherwood from 2000, Partner from 2007, Head Eccl, Educ and Charities Dep from 2010; Registrar Dioc in Eur and Bp's Legal Sec from 2009; Assoc Fell, Soc for Advanced Legal Studies from 1998; M Eccl Law Soc from 2002, M Gen Cttee from 2005; M Charity Law Assoc; M Soc for the Maintenance of the Faith from 2002; M Coun Qu Victoria Clergy Fund from 2003; Gov Pusey Ho, Ox from 2003; M Sen Appts Review Grp; Assoc M Ecum Coun for Corporate Responsibility from 2005; M C of E Appts Cttee from 2005; M Fees Adv Commn (appt by Pres of Law Soc) from 2005; M Stg Cttee Ho of Laity; M CNC; M Pastl Measure Appeals Panel
GS 2000–   *Tel:* 020 7833 9182 (Home)
020 7593 5064 (Office
email: arhs1@tiscali.co.uk

HARLEY, Ven Michael, AKC, Cert Ed, S Th, M Phil
22 St John's Sr Winchester Hants SO23 0HF [WINCHESTER] *b* 1950 *educ* Qu Eliz Gr Sch Crediton; K Coll Lon; Ch Ch Coll Cant; St Aug Coll Cant; Lambeth; Univ of Kent at Cant; *CV* C St William Walderslade, Roch 1975–78; C-incharge St Barn Weeke, Winch 1978–81; V Pear Tree, Southn 1981–86; V Hurstbourne Tarrant 1986–99; V Chandler's Ford 1999–2009; Winch Dioc Rural Officer 1991–97; RD Andover 1994–99; Chair Winch Dioc Ho of Clergy 2005–09; STETS tutor 2003–06; Hon Can Winch Cath from 2007; Par P St Faith Winch, Master St Cross Winch from 2009; Adn Winch from 2009
GS 2005–   *Tel:* 01962 869442
email: michael.harley@winchester.anglican.org

HARLOW, Archdeacon of. See WEBSTER, Ven Martin Duncan

HARPER, Revd (Rosemary Elizabeth) Rosie, BA, MA LRAM, DipRAM
The Rectory Church Street Amersham Bucks HP7 0DB [OXFORD] *b* 1955 *educ* Blyth G Sch; Birm Univ; Royal Academy of Music, Lon; Heythrop Coll; NTMTC; *CV* Singer & lect vocal studies; Chapl High Sheriff of Buckingham 2009–10; Acting P-in-c St Leonard's Chesham Bois, 2002–03; AC St Mary's w Coleshill, Amersham, 1990–2002; V Great Missenden w Ballinger & Little Hampden 2003; Chapl Bp Buckingham 2005; Bp's Counc 2006; Dioc Brd Patronage 2006
GS 2010–   *Tel:* 01494728988   07743679651
email: rosie51619@aol.com

HARRISON, Prof Glynn, MD, FRCPsych
2 Harley Place Clifton Bristol BS8 3JT [BRISTOL] *b* 1949 *educ* Havelock Sch Grimsby; Dundee Univ; *CV* Consult psychiatrist, Nottm 1982–94; Foundation Chair of Com Mental Health, Nottm Univ

1994–97; Norah Cooke Hurle Prof of Mental Health, Bris Univ 1997–2009; Hon Consult Psychiatrist, AWP Trust, Bath 1997–2009; Prof Emeritus of Psychiatry, Bris Univ from 2009; Pres Internat Federation of Psychiatric Epidemiology from 2007; M CNC from 2007
GS 2005–   *Tel:* 0117 970 6430
email: glynn.harrison9@gmail.com

HARRISON, Dr Jamie (James Herbert), MB, BS, FRCGP, MA
5 Dunelm Court South St Durham DH1 4QX [DURHAM] *b* 1953 *educ* Stockport Gr Sch; Magd Coll Ox; K Coll Hosp Medical Sch Lon; *CV* GP Durham City from 1990; Pres SCR St Jo Coll Dur; Rdr; Lay Chair, Dur Dioc Syn; Dep GP Dean Dir, Northern Deanery, North East SHA
GS 1995–   *Tel:* 0191 384 8643
Fax: 0191 386 5934
email: dunelm5@btinternet.com

HART, Mr Peter David, Cert. Ed
10 Ashbank Place Crewe Cheshire CW1 3FR [CHESTER] *b* 1949 *educ* Crewe Grammar Sch; Madeley Coll of Edu; *CV* Primary Sch Teacher 1971–2004; Lay Chair Nantwich Deanery Syn; M Archdiaconal Miss and Pastoral Cttee; Lay Chair Foward in Faith Ches Dioc
GS 2010–   *Tel:* 01270216248   07857500115

HASLAM, Mrs (Agnes) Lois, Dip Ad Ed, Cert Ed
3 Poplar Close Gatley Cheadle SK8 4LU [CHESTER] *b* 1938 *educ* Whalley Range High Sch Man; Man Univ; Totley Hall Coll of Educ; *CV* Tchr St Marg C of E Secdry Sch Man 1959–60; tchr Cheadle Adult Educ Cen 1961–70, 1972–75, Prin 1975–84; tchr Gatley Playgroup 1970–72; Stockport Boro Co-ord for Adult Basic Educ 1984–95; retd 1995; Lay Chair Stockport Dny Syn; Dioc Selector for Ordinands; Spiritual Dir; M Melanesian Wkg Grp; past M Dioc Bd of Educ, Adult Educ and Lay Trg, Cathls Meas 1999 Transitional Coun, Round Tables Future of Educ and Trg; nat Bp's Selector for 4 years
GS 2005–   *Tel and Fax:* 0161 428 2164
email: loishaslam@btinternet.com

HAWKINS, Revd Canon Clive, MA, Dip Th, DHSM
Eastrop Rectory 2A Wallis Rd Basingstoke RG21 3DW [WINCHESTER] *b* 1953 *educ* Simon Langton Gr Sch for Boys, Cant; St Pet Coll Ox; Trin Th Coll Bris; *CV* C Ch Ch Winch 1982–86; R St Mary Eastrop, Basingstoke from 1986; AD Basingstoke 2000–08; M Bp's Coun, Dioc Stg Cttee, Dioc Syn, N Area Team 2000–08, N Area Pastl Cttee 2000–08; M Strg Cttee Eccl Offices (Terms of Service) Measure
GS 2005–   *Tel:* 01256 830021 (Home)
01256 464249 (Church)
Fax: 01256 330305
email: clive.hawkins@ stmarys-basingstoke.org.uk

HAWKINS, Rt Revd David John Leader, B Th, L Th, ALCD
Barking Lodge 35 Verulam Ave Walthamstow London E17 8ES [AREA BISHOP OF BARKING; CHELMSFORD] *b* 1949 *educ* Wrekin Coll Shrops; Nottm Univ; Lon Coll of Div; St Jo Coll Nottm; *CV* C St Andr Bebington 1973–76; Wrdn Bida Bible Trg Cen, Nigeria 1976–82; Can Emer Kaduna, Nigeria 1982; P-in-c St Matt with St Luke Ox 1983–86; V St Geo Leeds 1986–99, TR 1999–2002; Exec Trustee, St Geo's Crypt 1986–2002; Chair Dioc Communications Cttee, Ripon and Leeds 1998–2002; Chapl Yorks Country Cricket Club 1986–2002; Chair of Trustees Leeds Faith in Schs 1993–2002; Dir Ashlar Ho 1986–2002; Area Bp of Barking from 2003; Dioc Hd Bp Miss and Par Devel from 2004; Dioc Hd Bp Youth and Children from 2004; Apb's Hd Bp on Black Majority Ch from 2006; Pres Bardsey Bird and Field Observatory from 2007; Chair Lon Global Day of Prayer 2007   *Tel:* 020 8509 7377
Fax: 020 8521 4097
email: b.barking@chelmsford.anglican.org

HAWKINS, Revd (Patricia Sally) Pat, MA, BPhil, BTh, CQSW
The Vicarage Lymer Road Oxley Wolverhampton WV10 6AA [LICHFIELD] *b* 1959 *educ* Wygeston Girls Gr Sch, Leic; Lady Margaret Hall, Ox; Exeter Univ;St. Stephen's House Th Coll; *CV* Residential Social worker w adolescents 1980–83; LA Social Worker, Devon 1985–86; M Comm of St. Francis 1986–99; C, P of Stafford 2001–04; Incumbent, P of Oxley 2004; Area Dean, Wolverhampton 2008; M Lichf Dioc Syn 2003–4, from 2006
GS 2010–   *Tel:* 01902 783342
email: pathawkins@btinternet.com

HAWLEY, Ven John Andrew, BD, AKC, Cert Theol
19 Clarence Park Blackburn BB2 7FA [ARCHDEACON OF BLACKBURN] *b* 1950 *educ* Ecclesfield Gr Sch; K Coll Lon; Wycliffe Hall Th Coll; *CV* C H Trin Hull 1974–77; C Bradf Cathl 1977–80; V All SS Woodlands, Doncaster 1980–91; TR Dewsbury 1991–2002; Chair Mission Doncaster 1985–2001; M Bp's Coun 1985–91; Vc Chair Wakef Dioc BMU 1991–96; M Action Partners Coun 1992–99; Chair Wakef Dioc Communications 1996–2002; Chair Wakef Dioc Red Chs Uses 1999–2002; Chair Wakef Dioc Ho of Clergy 2000–02; M Pastl Measure Review Grp from 2001; M Misc Provisions Measure Revision Grp from 2000; Adn of Blackburn from 2002; Acting Adn of Lanc from 2010
GS 1996–2002   *Tel:* 01254 262571 01254 503074
(Secretary) 07980 945035 (Mobile)
Fax: 01254 667309
email: archdeacon.blackburn@gmail.com

HAYDEN, Ven David Frank, Dip Th, BD
8 Boulton Rd Thorpe St Andrew Norwich NR7 0DF [ARCHDEACON OF NORFOLK; NORWICH] *b* 1947 *educ* Langley Sch Norwich; Tyndale Hall Bris; *CV* C St Matt Silverhill, Chich 1971–75; C Galleywood

Common, Chelms 1975–79; R Redgrave cum Botesdale with Rickinghall, St E & I 1979–1984; RD Hartismere 1981–84; P-in-c Gresham, Norw 1984–98; V Cromer, Norw 1984–2002; pt hosp chapl 1984–2000; RD Repps 1995–2002; Hon Can Norw Cathl 1996–2002; Adn of Norfolk from 2002; M Bp's Coun; M DAC; Bp's Staff Rep Church and Tourism and New Ways of Being Church; Fresh Expressions; Creative Use of Ch Buildings   *Tel and Fax:* 01603 702477
email: archdeacon.norfolk@norwich.anglican.org

HEALD, Mrs Victoria Mary,
9 West Street Geddington Kettering North Hants NN14 1BD [PETERBOROUGH] *b* 1949 *educ* Barnsley Girs High Sch; Barnsley Tech Coll; *CV* NHS Sec from 2009; Elected GS 2010
GS 2010–   *Tel:* 01536744276
email: vheald@talktalk.net

HENDERSON, Ven Janet, BA, RGN
Hoppus House Smith Lane, Hutton Conyers Ripon HG4 5DX [ARCHDEACON OF RICHMOND; RIPON AND LEEDS] *b* 1957 *educ* Ardwyn Gr Sch, Aberw; Dur Univ; Addenbrooke's Sch of Nursing, Cam; Cranmer Hall Dur; *CV* C SS Pet and Paul Wisbech 1988–90; Par Deacon, Bestwood TM Nottm 1990–93; Lect, St Jo Coll Nottm 1993–97; Lect, Cam Theol Federation 1997–2001; P-in-c St Patr Nuthall and Dean of Women's Min, S'well and Nottm Dioc 2001–07; Adn of Richmond and Res Can Ripon Cathl from 2007   *Tel:* 01765 601316
email: janeth@riponleeds-diocese.org.uk

HENDERSON, Ven Julian Tudor, MA
The Old Cricketers Portsmouth Rd Ripley Woking GU23 6ER [ARCHDEACON OF DORKING; GUILDFORD] *b* 1954 *educ* Radley Coll; Keble Coll Ox; Ridley Hall Cam; *CV* C St Mary Islington 1979–83; V Em and St Mary in the Castle, Hastings 1983–92; V H Trin Claygate 1992–2005; RD 1996–2001; Chair Dioc Evangelical Fellowship 1997–2001; Hon Can Guild Cathl 2002; Tutor Dioc Min Course from 2003; Adn of Dorking from 2005
GS 2004–   *Tel:* 01483 479300 (Office)
01483 479568 (Home)
email: julian.henderson@cofeguildford.org.uk

HEPPLESTON, Mr Michael,
Turnpike House 1 Turnpike Newchurch Lancashire BB4 9DU [MANCHESTER] *b* 1957 *CV* Man Dioc Syn; Man Min & Pstrl Cttee; Regional Operations Mgr, Media on the Move from 2005
GS 2010–   *Tel:* 01706 220349
email: mheppleston@mediaotm.com

HERBERT, Revd Clare Marguerite, BA, MTh, CQSW
37 Sydenham Hill London SE26 6SH [LONDON] *b* 1954 *educ* Okehampton Sch; St Hild's Coll, Dur Univ; New Coll, Edinb Univ; Social Work Dept, Bris Univ; Linc Th Coll; *CV* Parish Worker and Asst Univ Chapl, St Paul's Univ Ch, Bris 1981–85;

WHO'S WHO

Child and Family Social Worker, North Bris, 1986–89; Paediatric Renal Social Worker, Southmead Hosp, Bris 1989–92; Pastoral Care Adv, Lay Ministry Dept Lon Dioc, 1992–95; C, St Martin-in-the-Fields, 1995–98; R, St Anne w St Thomas and St Peter Soho, 1998–2007; National Coord of Inclusive Church, 2007–10; Lect Inclusive Th at St Martin-in-the-Fields, from 2010; Bp's Staff and Area Counc of the Two Cities Area of the Lon Dioc, 2000–05; Dean of Women for the Two Cities Area.
GS 2010   Tel: 0208 761 3616
                       0207 766 1143 07504 577210
                             Fax: 0207 839 5163
             email: herbert.clare@googlemail.com

HEREFORD, Archdeacon of. (NOT APPOINTED AT TIME OF GOING TO PRESS)

HEREFORD, Bishop of. See PRIDDIS, Rt Revd Anthony Martin

HEREFORD, Dean of. See TAVINOR, Very Revd Michael Edward

HERTFORD, Archdeacon of. See JONES, Ven Trevor Pryce

HERTFORD, Suffragan Bishop of. See BAYES, Rt Revd Paul

HESKETT, Mr Robert William, B Sc, FRICS
5 Strand London WC2N 5AF [CHURCH COMMISSIONER] *b* 1953 *educ* St Edw Sch Ox; Univ of S Bank; *CV* With Land Securities plc from 1978, currently Portfolio Dir for Lon; Dep ChairAssets Cttee and Chair Property Grp; Ch Commr from 1998   Tel: 020 7024 3857
                             Fax: 020 7024 3770
          email: robert.heskett@landsecurities.com

HIBBERT, Revd Richard Charles, BA
Christ Church Vicarage 115 Denmark St Bedford MK40 3TJ [ST ALBANS] *b* 1962 *educ* Merchant Taylors' Sch Northwood; Trin Coll Bris; *CV* C St Mary Luton 1996–2000; V Ch Ch Bedford from 2000; asst RD Bedford 2004–2010; RD Bedford from 2010; M CEEC 2006–2010
GS 2005–   Tel and Fax: 01234 359342
           email: vicar@christchurchbedford.org.uk

HILL, Ven Colin, Ph D, B Sc
50 Stainburn Rd Workington CA14 1SN [ARCHDEACON OF WEST CUMBERLAND; CARLISLE] *educ* Blakey Moor Sch, Blackb; Blackb Tech and Gr Sch; Leic Univ; Open Univ; Ripon Hall Ox; *CV* C Ch of the Martyrs Leic 1966–69; C with Special Resp for St Crispin Braunstone, Leic 1969–71; Lect Ecum Inst Teesside 1971–72; V St Thos & St Jas Worsbrough, Sheff 1972–78; Chs Devel Officer for Miss and Min, Lich and Heref Diocs 1978–96; RD Telford Severn Gorge, Heref 1980–96; RD Telford, Lich 1980–96; Preb Heref Cathl 1983–96;

Can Res Carl Cathl 1996–2004; Dioc Sec Carl 1996–2004; Can Treas Carl Cathl 1997–2004; Vc-Dean Carl Cathl 2004; Chair Dioc Bd for Soc Resp; Nat Chair Ch Ho Deaneries Grp; Adn of W Cumberland from 2004   Tel: 01900 66190
                             Fax: 01900 603534
           email: archdeacon.west@carlislediocese.org.uk

HILL, Rt Revd Christopher John, BD, AKC, M Th
Willow Grange Woking Rd Guildford GU4 7QS [BISHOP OF GUILDFORD] *b* 1945 *educ* Sebright Sch Worcs; K Coll Lon; *CV* C Tividale Lich 1969–73; C Codsall 1973–74; Abp's Asst Chapl on Foreign Relations 1974–81; Abp's Sec for Ecum Affairs 1981–89; Angl Sec ARCIC I and II 1974–91; Hon Can Cant Cathl 1982–89; Chapl to HM The Queen 1987–96; Can Res and Prec St Paul's Cathl 1989–96; M C of E-German Chs Conversations 1987–89; C of E Nordic-Baltic Conversations 1989–93; Vc Chair Eccl Law Soc 1993–2002, Chair from 2002; Chair Cathl Precs Conf 1994–96; Co-Chair C of E-French Protestant Conversations 1993–98; M Legal Adv Cttee from 1991; Co-Chair Lon Soc Jews and Chrs 1991–96; M CCU 1991–96, Chair from 2008; Bp of Stafford 1996–2004; M FOAG 1997–2008, Vc Chair from 1998 (now known as Faith and Order Commission - FAOC); Co-Chair Meissen Th Conversations from 1998; Vc-Chair Ho of Bps' Wkg Pty on Women in the Episcopate 2000–04; M Wkg Pty on Review of Bps' legal costs, Fees Adv Commn 2003; M Liturg Commn 2003–05; M Ordinal Revision Grp from 2004; M CDC from 2004; Chair Wkg Pty on Women Bps 2005–06; M Ho of Bps Theol Grp from 2005; Clerk of the Closet from 2005; Bp of Guildford from 2004; Chair CCU from 2008; Chair Bps' Eur Grp from 2008; M King's Coll Lon Coun from 2009; Vc Pres Coun of European Ch from 2009; M Ho of Lords (Lords Spiritual) from 2010
GS 2000–   Tel: 01483 590500
                             Fax: 01483 590501
     email: bishop.christopher@cofeguildford.org.uk

HILL, Rt Revd Michael Arthur,
58a High St Winterbourne Bristol BS36 1JQ [BISHOP OF BRISTOL] *b* 1949 *educ* Wilmslow Gr Sch; NW Cheshire CFE; Man Coll of Commerce; Ridley Hall Cam; Fitzw Coll Cam; *CV* C St Mary Magd Addiscombe 1977–80; C St Paul Slough 1980–83; P-in-c St Leon Chesham Bois 1983–90, R 1990–92; RD Amersham 1989–92; Adn of Berks 1992–98; Bp of Buckingham 1998–2003; Bp of Bristol from 2003
GS 1995–98, 2003–   Tel: 01454 777728
                       07808 290908 (Mobile)
                             Fax: 01454 777814
           email: bishop@bristoldiocese.org

HILL, Ven Peter, BSc, MTh
4 Victoria Crescent Sherwood Nottingham NG5 4DA [ARCHDEACON OF NOTTINGHAM; SOUTHWELL AND NOTTINGHAM] *b* 1950 *educ* Man Univ; Nottm Univ; Wycliffe Hall, Ox; *CV* C Porchester, S'well

1983–86; V Huthwaite 1986–95; P-in-c Calverton 1995–2004; RD S'well 1997–2001; Chair Dioc Bd of Educ 2001–2004; Dioc Chief Exec 2004–07; Hon Can S'well Minster from 2001; Adn of Nottingham from 2007
GS 2010–   *Tel:* 0115 985 8641 (Home)
                         01636 817206 (Office)
                     Fax: 01636 815882 (Office)
email: archdeacon-nottm@southwell.anglican.org

HILLS, Mr Nicholas Paul, BA
Church House Westminster London SW1P 3AZ [ADMINISTRATIVE SECRETARY, CENTRAL SECRETARIAT] *b* 1964 *educ* Sir Joseph Williamson's Mathematical Sch, Roch; Leic Univ; *CV* 1987–99 Teacher; on staff of Abps' Coun from 1999; Fin Div from 1999; Central Secretariat from 2002; Sec Appts Cttee; Sec Ho of Laity and Ho of Laity Stg Cttee; Asst Sec Abps' Coun   *Tel:* 020 7898 1363
                         Fax: 020 7989 1369
email: nicholas.hills@c-of-e.org.uk

HIND, Rt Revd John William, BA, DD
The Palace Chichester PO19 1PY [BISHOP OF CHICHESTER] *b* 1945 *educ* Watford Gr Sch; Leeds Univ; Cuddesdon Th Coll; *CV* Asst Master Leeds Modern Sch 1966–69; Asst Lect K Alfred's Coll Win 1969–70; C Catford, Southend and Downham 1972–76; V Ch Ch Forest Hill 1976–82; P-in-c St Paul Forest Hill 1981–82; Prin Chich Th Coll 1982–91; Bursalis Preb Chich Cathl 1982–91; Bp of Horsham 1991–93; Chair FOAG 1999–2010; Bp of Gib in Eur 1993–2001; Bp of Chich from 2001; Consult to CCU; M Faith and Order Commn of WCC; M Inter Angl Stg Commn on Ecum Relns 2000–08; M Ho of Lords from 2008; Chair Faith and Order Commn of C of E from 2010
GS 1993–   *Tel:* 01243 782161
                          Fax: 01243 531332
email: bishop.chichester@diochi.org.uk

HIND, Mr Timothy Charles, MA, FCII
Plowman's Corner The Square Westbury-sub-Mendip Wells BA5 1HJ [BATH AND WELLS] *b* 1950 *educ* Watford Boys Gr Sch; St Jo Coll Cam; *CV* Various posts at Sun Life (now AXA) from 1972; Quality Mgr, AXA UK; Chartered Insurer; M Bp's Coun; Chair Dioc Vacancy-in-See Cttee 1996–98; M Dioc Bd of Educ 1995–97; M Bd of Educ (Schs and Colls) 1995–97; M C of E Pensions Bd 1996–; M C of E Pensions Bd Investment and Fin Cttee 1996–97; M ABM 1998; M DRACSC 1999–2008; Lay Vc-Chair Dioc Syn from 1999–2009; Lay Chair Axbridge Dny Syn 1984–91; M Dioc Bd of Patr 1986–94; Vc-Chair Bd of Govs Kings of Wessex Com Sch 1996–99; Churchwarden St Jo Bapt Axbridge 2001–05; Sec OSG 2001–04; Chair OSG from 2004–11; Vc Chair C of E Pensions Bd from 2010
GS 1995–2000, 2001–   *Tel:* 01749 870356 (Home)
                    07977 917434 (Mobile, Office)
                          07977 580374 (Mobile)
                     email: tim@hind.org.uk

HINE, Mr Peter Geoffrey, BA
Chapel Howe Sour Nook Sebergham Carlisle CA5 7DY [CARLISLE] *b* 1949 *educ* Wallasey Tech Gr Sch; Dur Univ; *CV* Various posts w Financial Services sector 1972–98; Vol ch and ed worker 1998–2002; Trustee C of E Pension Scheme 1998–2001; Trustee and Dir Worldshare from1999; Finance Resources Off Dioc Carlisle from 2002
GS 2010–   *Tel:* 01228 815401
                 email: ghine@carlislediocese.org.uk

HM FORCES, Bishop to. See VENNER, Rt Revd Stephen Squires

HOBBS, Revd Christopher John Pearson, BA, BD, Dip.Ed., AKC
St Thomas's Vicarage 2 Sheringham Ave Southgate London N14 4UE [LONDON] *b* 1960 *educ* St Andrew's Cathl Sch, Sydney; Sydney Univ; King's Coll Lon; Wycliffe Hall Th Coll; *CV* Tchr, Hill House International Junior Sch 1983–86; C, Christ Church Barnet 1991–94; Asst Minister, Jesmond Parish Church 1994–97; V St Thomas's Oakwood from 1997
GS 2010–   *Tel and Fax:* 02083601749
          email: christopher.hobbs@blueyonder.co.uk

HOBBS, Revd Maureen Patricia, BSc, Dip Bus Admin, CTM
Vicarage 20 Dartmouth Ave Pattingham WV6 7DP [LICHFIELD] *b* 1954 *educ* Wanstead High Sc Lon; Surrey Univ; Warwick Univ; Westcott Ho Cam; *CV* Asst linguist specialist, GCHQ 1976–78; recruitment and mgt consult 1978–95; C St Chad w. St Mary, Shrewsbury 1997–2001; R Baschurch and Weston Lullingfield w. Hordley from 2001; P-in-C Pattingham w Patshull from 2009; RD Tryshull from 2009; Min Dev Adv fro Wolverhampton Episcopal Area; Dioc Adv for Women in Min from 2003
GS 2005–
           Tel: 01902 700257 07812 805371 (Mobile)
               email: hobbsmaureen@yahoo.co.uk

HOLGATE, Mr Robert Geoffrey, BA, FCA
66 Purnells Way Knowle Solihull B93 9EE [BIRMINGHAM] *b* 1952 *educ* Lawrence Sheriff Sch, Rugby; Leeds Univ;; *CV* C Accountant trainee 1973–76; Audit Asst 1976–78; Tax Asst and Manager 1978–89; Senior Tax Manager KPMG from 1989; Dioc Birm Bp's Counc 1998–2010; Fin Sub-cttee 1998–2010; Vice Chair Dioc Brd Fin 2001–10; Acting Chair Dioc Brd Fin 2008–09; M Inter Dioc Fin Forum 2008–10; M Dioc Vacancy in See Cttee from 2000
GS 2010–   *Tel:* 0121 232 3406 01564 776573
               email: rands.holgate@btinternet.com

HOLMES, Mrs Madeleine Ratcliffe,
Le Peladis Rte Pommier 24350 Lisle Dordogne France [EUROPE] *b* 1942 *educ* Knutsford Secondary Sch; Wimslow Eve Class; St John's, Nott; *CV* PA to Dir Gen Royal Institute of Public Administration

1989–91; Odgers & Co London PA to Management Consult 1989–97; PA and PR customers of Software House, Actiontech Ltd., High Wycombe, 1987; Sales & Production Co-ord Communications Direct High Wycombe, 1985–86; Admin/Direct Mail copywriting and PRPerferap Ltd, High Wycombe 1980–86; Fashion Model 1976–80; Dioc Environment Off 2010; Prayer Chain Coord Chapl 2008; Rder 2006; Local Radio Programme for Chapl 2007; Contribtr Chapl Bp's Counc 2006–09; Archdeaconry sub-cttee 'Building Together in France' 2007
GS 2010–   *Tel:* 00335 53 04 85 44
     email: madeleine@peladis.plus.com

HORSHAM, Archdeacon of. See COMBES, Ven Roger Matthew

HORSHAM, Area Bishop of. See SOWERBY, Rt Revd Mark

HOUGHTON, Revd James Robert, AKC, Cert Ed
St Michael's Vicarage 15 Long Acre Close Eastbourne BN21 1UF [CHICHESTER] *b* 1944 *educ* Highgate Sch; K Coll Lon; St Luke's, Ex; *CV* C St Chad E Herrington, Sunderland, Dur 1968–70; Asst Youth Chapl, Bris 1970–72; C St Lawr Heavitree, Ex 1973–78; Mgr Yiewsley and W Drayton Com Cen and Hon C St Mart W Drayton, Lon 1978–80; Chapl and Head of Relig Studies Grey Coat Hosp, Westmr, Lon 1980–88; Chapl and Head of Relig Studies Stonar Sch, Melksham, Salis 1988–96; Chapl and Head of Relig Studies Sch of St Mary and St Anne, Abbots Bromley, Lich 1996–99; R Buxted and Hadlow Down, Chich 1999–2002; V St Mich and All Angels, Eastbourne, Chich from 2002
GS 2005–   *Tel:* 01323 645740
     email: fatherjamie@btopenworld.com

HOULDING, Preb David Nigel Christopher, AKC, DD(hc)
All Hallows' House 52 Courthope Rd London NW3 2LD [LONDON] *b* 1953 *educ* K Sch Cant; K Coll Lon; St Aug Coll Cant; *CV* Lay Chapl Chr Medical Coll Vellore, S India 1976–77; C All SS Hillingdon 1977–81; C St Alb Holborn w St Pet Saffron Hill 1981–85; V St Steph w All Hallows Hampstead from 1985; Preb St Paul's Cath from 2004; Pro-Prolocutor Conv of Cant form 1998; Chair Dioc Ho of Clergy and Vc-Chair Dioc Syn from 2000; AD of N Camden 2001–03; Master SSC from 1997; M Dioc Syn from 1991; M Bp's Coun from 1997; M Edmonton Coun; M Dioc Liturg Grp; M Coun ACS; M Coun of St Steph Ho, Ox from 2001; Ldr, Cath Grp in GS 2000 07; M Adv Panel for Vocations 1997–2002; M Weekday Lectionary and Rules to Order the Service Revision Cttees 1999; M CCRJ 2000–01; M GS Appts Cttee from 2001; M CAC Perry Review Strg Grp 2002–03; M Conv Wkg Grp on Clergy Code of Practice 2000–03; M Clergy Employment Review Grp 2003–05 and Follow-up Grp from 2005; M Meth

Cov Impl Grp from 2003; Chair C of E Appts Cttee from 2004, reappointed 2006, 2009; M AC 2004–05, re-elected 2007; Fell Nashotah Ho from 2005; M CCU from 2006; M strg ctee, Clergy Terms of Service
GS 1995–   *Tel:* 020 7267 7833
     020 7267 6317(Office)
     07710 403294 (Mobile)
     Fax: 020 7267 6317 (Office)
     email: fr.houlding@lineone.net

HOWARD, Father Andrew, BA, MA
45 Lothian Rd Middlesbrough TS4 2HS [YORK] *b* 1963 *educ* Allestree Woodlands Sch Derby; High Peak Coll of FE Buxton; Man Poly; Man Univ; Leeds Univ; Coll of the Resurr Mirfield; *CV* Asst C Worksop Priory 1997–2001; V St Timothy of Ephesus, Hemlington 2001–05; Chapl Univ of Teesside, Assoc P St Jo and St Columba Middlesbrough from 2005
GS 2009–   *Tel:* 01642 242926
     email: a.howard@tees.ac.uk

HOWE, Ven George Alexander, BA
Vicarage Windermere Rd Lindale-in-Cartmel Grange-over-Sands LA11 6LB [ARCHDEACON OF WESTMORLAND AND FURNESS; CARLISLE] *b* 1952 *educ* Liv Inst High Sch; St Jo Coll Dur; Westcott Ho Th Coll; *CV* C St Cuth Peterlee 1975–79; C St Mary Norton-on-Tees 1979–81; V Hart w Elwick Hall 1981–85; R Sedgefield 1985–91; RD Sedgefield 1988–91; V H Trin Kendal 1991–2000; RD Kendal 1994–99; Dioc Ecum Officer; Adn of Westmorland and Furness from 2000; Chair Ch and Com Fund from 2007
GS 2001–   *Tel:* 01539 534717
     Fax: 01539 535090
     email: archdeacon.south@carlislediocese.org.uk

HOYLE, Very Revd Dr David Michael, MA, PhD
Bristol Cathedral College Green Bristol BS1 5TJ [DEAN OF BRISTOL] *b* 1957 *educ* Watford Boys Grammar Sch; Corpus Christi Coll Cam; Ripon Coll Cuddesdon; *CV* Asst C Good Shepherd Cam1986–1988; Chapl and Fell Magdalene College Cam1988–1991; Dean and Fell Magadalene Coll Cam 1991–1995; Dir of Studies Magadalene Coll Cam from 1995; V Ch Ch Southgate 1995–2002; Dir POT Edmonton Area 2000–2002; Dir of Mini Dioc of Glos and Can Res Glos Cathl 2002–2010; Dean of Bristol Cathl from 2010; Secretary Ho of Bps Theol Gp 2002–2007
     Tel: 0117 926 4879
     Fax: 0117 925 3678
     email: dean@bristol-cathedral.co.uk

HUBBARD, Ven Julian Richard Hawes, MA (Cantab, Oxon)
Archdeacon's Lodging Christ Church Oxford OX1 1DP [ARCHDEACON OF OXFORD] *b* 1955 *educ* K Edw VI Gr Sch Chelms; Em Coll Cam; Wycliffe Hall Ox; *CV* C St Dionis Parsons Green Lon 1981–84; Chapl Jesus Coll Ox 1984–89; Tutor Wycliffe Hall

Ox 1984–89; Selection Sec ACCM 1989–91; Sen
Selection Sec ABM 1991–93; V St Thos on the
Bourne Guildf 1993–99; RD Farnham 1996–99;
Guildf Dioc FE Officer 1993–97; Dir Minl Trg
Guildf Dioc 1999–2005; Res Can Guildf Cathl
1999–2005; Adn Oxf and Res Can Ch Ch from
2005   *Tel:* 01865 208245
                                             01865 208263
                                      Fax: 01865 849003
   email: archdoxf@oxford.anglican.org

HUGHES, Ven Paul Vernon, Dip UEM,
Cert Theol Oxon
17 Lansdowne Rd Luton LU3 1EE [ARCHDEACON OF
BEDFORD; ST ALBANS] *b* 1953 *educ* Pocklington Sch,
E Yorks; Poly Cen Lon; Ripon Coll Cuddesdon;
CV Res Property Surveyor, Chestertons 1974–79;
C Chipping Barnet w Arkley 1982–86; TV Dun-
stable Tm Min 1986–93; V Boxmoor 1993–2003;
RD Hemel Hempstead 1996–2003; Adn of Bed-
ford from 2003; M DBF Cttees, DAC, Dioc Pastl
and Miss Cttee, Closed Chs Uses Cttee, Com-
munications Adv Grp, Bd for Ch and Soc, New
Devel Areas, Bp's Staff, Bp's Staff Deployment
Grp   *Tel:* 01582 730722
                                      Fax: 01582 877354
   email: archdbedf@stalbans.anglican.org

HULL, Suffragan Bishop of. See FRITH, Rt
Revd Richard Michael Cokayne

HUMPHREYS, Mrs Jennifer Ann, BA
34 Riverside Banwell North Somerset BS29 6EE
[BATH AND WELLS] *b* 1951 *educ* Wesley Coll Bristol;
CV Gov Banwell Primary School; World Mission
Adviser Bath and Wells from 1998; Dioc Syn Rep
for Locking Deanery;
GS 2010–   *Tel:* 01934 822052
   email: rodjen@humphreys.eclipse.co.uk

HUMPHREYS, Ms Jacqueline Louise, MA, LLM
St John's Chambers 101 Victoria St Bristol BS1 6PU
[BRISTOL] *b* 1970 *educ* Churchill Comp Sch; Worc
Coll Ox; Inns of Court Sch of Law; Cardiff Univ;
CV Barrister from 1994; M Family Law Bar Assoc
from 1998; M Eccles Law Soc from 1999; M Legis
Cttee from 2000; M Legal Adv Commn from
2000; M Rules Cttee from 2004, M Legal Aid Cttee
from 2006
GS 2000–   *Tel:* 0117 921 3456
                                      Fax: 0117 929 4821
   email: jacqueline.humphreys@
                                   stjohnschambers.co.uk

HUNT, Ven Judy (Judith Mary), BVSC, MA, Ph D,
Dip C, MRCVS, FRSM
*Glebe House The Street Ashfield Stowmarket IP14
6LX* [ARCHDEAON OF SUFFOLK] *b* 1957 *educ* Bolton
Sch; Bris Univ Veterinary Sch; R Veterinary Coll
Lon Univ, Fitzw Coll Cam; Chester Coll; Ridley
Hall Th Coll; *CV* Par Dn St Pet Heswall 1991–94,
C 1994–95; P-in-c St Mary Tilston w St Edith
Shocklach 1995–2003; Malpas Dny Officer for

Min Amongst Children and Young People 1995–
98; Adv for Women in Min 1996–2000; Dny Sub-
warden of Rdrs 1998–2001; Archdny Vocations
Officer (Asst DDO) 1999–2003; M Dioc Cttee for
Min, Educ and Tr; M Rural Min Grp; Min
Reviewer; Dioc Dir of Min 2003–06; Dioc Dir of
Miss and Min 2006–09; Res Can Chester 2003–09;
M nat CME and Devel Panel 2003–06; M CDC
2004–07; Adn Suffolk from 2009
                                      Tel: 01728 685497
                                      Fax: 01728 685969
                                email: archdeacon.judy@
                              stedmundsbury.anglican.org

HUNT, Revd Vera Susan Henrietta, SDMTC, MBE
54 Highway Avenue Maidenhead Berks SL6 5AQ
[REPRESENTATIVE, DEAF ANGLICANS TOGETHER] *b*
1933 *educ* Oak Lodge Residential Sch; Salis and
Wells Th Coll; *CV* Pres and Cttee M Deaf Anglicans Together; Hon Chapl Ox Dioc Deaf Ch
GS 2005–   *Fax:* 01628 623909
                         email: vera.hunt@yahoo.co.uk

**HUNTINGDON AND WISBECH, Archdeacon
of.** See McCURDY, Ven Hugh Kyle

HUNTINGDON, Suffragan Bishop of. See
THOMSON, Rt Revd David

HURLEY, Mr Robert Michael, BA
*Nursery House 38 Furlong Road Bourne End Bucks
SL8 5AA* [OXFORD] *b* 1987 *educ* John Hampden Gr
Sch; Sir William Borlase's Gr Sch; Nott Univ;
CV Info Analyst, Enfield Pri Care Trust; Senior
Comm Analyst, North West Lon Hosp NHS Trust
GS 2008–   *Tel:* 01628 524214 07845 564464
                             email: rmh@rmhurley.com

**HUTCHINSON CERVANTES, Revd Ian
Charles,** BSc, MSc, MA, GDip Th
*St George's Anglican Church Calle Nunez de Balboa
43 Madrid Spain 28001* [EUROPE] *b* 1962 *educ* St
Thomas' Sch, Malaysia; St Paul's Coll NZ;
Amazon Valley Acad, Brazil; Cant Univ NZ;
Reading Univ; Cam Univ; Cardiff Univ; Westcott
House Th Coll; *CV* Assit C, St Mary the V, Ox,
1989–92; LT St Marys Pro-Cathl, Dioc Venezuela
1993; P-in-C St Andrews w St Barnabbas, Dioc
Belize, 1993–97; Miss Personnel Prog Off Latin
America and Caribbean, USPG 1997–2004; Chapl
St George's Ch, Madrid, Dioc Euro from 2004;
Bp's Nom USPG Counc; Bp's Rep PWM; Dioc
Obs Iere Syn
GS 2010–   *Tel:* +34915765109
         email: chaplain@stgeorgesmadrid.com

INESON, Revd Dr Emma Gwynneth, BA, MPhil,
PhD
11 Glentworth Rd Redland Bristol BS6 7EG [BRIS-
TOL] *b* 1969 *educ* Bryntirion Comp Schl, Bridgend,
Wales; Birm Univ; Trin Coll Bris; *CV* Tching Asst
Eng Lang, Birm Univ, 1993–97; Asst C, Dore,
Sheffield 2000–03; Chapl, Lee Abbey Devon

2003–06; Tutor Prac Th, Trin Coll Bris from 2007; NS Assit C and Assoc Min from 2010, St Matthew and St Nathanael, Kingsdown, Bris from 2006; M Bris Dioc Remun Cttee from 2008
GS 2010– *Tel:* 01179424186

INGE, Rt Revd Dr John Geoffrey, B Sc, PGCE, MA, Ph D
Bishop's Office The Old Palace Deansway Worcester WR1 2JE [BISHOP OF WORCESTER] *b* 1955 *educ* Kent Coll Cant; Dur Univ; Keble Coll Ox; Coll of the Resurrection Mirfield; *CV* Asst Chapl Lancing Coll 1984–86; Jun Chapl Harrow Sch 1986–89, Sen Chap 1989–90; V Wallsend St Luke, Newc 1990–96; Res Can Ely Cathl 1996–2003, Vice Dean 1999–2003; Bp of Huntingdon 2003–07; M Coun Ridley Hall from 2004; Trustee, Common Purpose from 2005; Bp of Worcester from 2007; Visitor, Com of the Holy Name from 2007; Visitor Mucknell Com from 2009; Chair Coll of Evangelists from 2010; M Faith and Order Commn from 2010
Tel: 01905 731599
Fax: 01905 739382
email: bishop.worcester@cofe-worcester.org.uk

INWOOD, Rt Revd Richard Neil, MA, B Sc, BA
Bishop's Lodge Bedford Rd Cardington Bedford MK44 3SS [BISHOP OF BEDFORD; ST ALBANS] *b* 1946 *educ* Burton-on-Trent Gr Sch; Univ Coll Ox; St Jo Coll Nottm; *CV* C Ch Ch Fulwood Sheff 1974–78; C (Dir of Pastoring) All So Langham Place 1978–81; V St Luke Bath 1981–89; R Yeovil w Kingston Pitney 1989–95; Preb Wells Cathl 1990–95; Ch Commr 1991–95; Hon Treas Simeon's Trustees/Hyndman Trust 1986–2003; Adn of Halifax 1995–2003; Chair Coun St Jo Coll Nottm 1998–2002; Bp of Bedford from 2003; Cen Chapl MU 2004–09
GS 1985–95,1997–2000 *Tel:* 01234 831432
Fax: 01234 831484
email: bishopbedford@stalbans.anglican.org

IPGRAVE, Ven Dr Michael Geoffrey, PhD, MA
Trinity House 4 Chapel Court Borough High St London SE1 1HW [ARCHDEACON OF SOUTHWARK] *b* 1958 *educ* Magd Coll Sch, Brackley; Oriel Coll Ox; St Chad's Coll Dur; SOAS, Lon Univ; Ripon Coll Cuddesdon; *CV* Dn 1982; P 1983 (Peterb); C All SS Oakham w. Hambleton and Egleton, and Braunston w. Brooke, Peterb 1982–85; Asst P The Resurrection, Chiba, Yokohama, Japan 1985–87; TV The Ascension, Leic 1987–90; TV The Holy Spirit, Leic 1990–94; P-in-c St Mary de Castro, Leic 1994–95; TR The Holy Spirit, Leic 1995–99; Dioc Adv on Inter Faith Relns 1990–99; Bp's Chapl 1990–99; Hon Asst P The Presentation, Leic 1999–2004; Hon Can Leic Cathl 1994–2004; Inter Faith Relns Adv, AC 1999–2004; Sec Chs Commn on Inter Faith Relns 1999–2004; Adn of Southwark from 2004; Can Miss S'wark Cathl from 2010
Tel: 020 7939 9409
020 7928 4866
Fax: 020 7939 9465
email: michael.ipgrave@southwark.anglican.org

IRELAND, Revd Mark Campbell, M Theol, MA
35 Crescent Rd Wellington Telford TF1 3DW [LICHFIELD] *b* 1960 *educ* Bromsgrove High Sch; Oban High Sch; St Jo Sch Marlborough; St Andr Univ; Wycliffe Hall Ox; Cliff Coll, Sheff Univ; *CV* Tchr, Murree Chr Sch, Pakistan 1981–82; C St Gabriel Blackb 1984–87; C Lancaster Priory 1987–89; Chapl HM Prison, Lancaster 1987–89; V Baxenden, Accrington 1989–97; Dioc Missr, Lich 1998–2007; TV St Matt Walsall 1998–2007; Tm Leader, Miss Div, Lich Dioc 2002–06; M Bp's Coun 2000–03; V All SS Wellington w. St Cath Eyton from 2007
GS 1995–98; 2005– *Tel:* 01952 641251 (Home)
01952 248554 (Office)
email: vicar@allsaints-wellington.org

IRVINE, Very Revd John Dudley, BA, MA
The Deanery 11 Priory Row Coventry CV1 5EX [DEAN OF COVENTRY] *b* 1949 *educ* Haileybury Coll; Sussex Univ; Ox Univ; Wycliffe Hall Th Coll; *CV* C H Trin Brompton 1981–85; V St Barn Kensington 1985–2001; Dean of Cov from 2001
Tel: 024 7663 1448
024 7652 1200
Fax: 024 7652 1220
email: john.irvine@coventrycathedral.org.uk

ISLE OF MAN, Archdeacon of. See SMITH, Ven Brian

ISLE OF WIGHT, Archdeacon of the. See BASTON, Ven Caroline Jane

ISON, Very Revd David John, BA, PhD, DPS
The Deanery 1 Cathedral Close Bradford BD1 4EG [DEAN OF BRADFORD] *b* 1954 *educ* Brentwood Sch; Leic Univ; Nottm Univ; K Coll Lon; St Jo Coll Nottm; *CV* C St Nic w. St Luke Deptford, S'wark 1979–85; Tutor, Ch Army Trg Coll 1985–88; V St Phil Potters Green, Cov 1988–93; Dioc Officer for CME, Ex 1993–2005; Res Can Ex 1995–2005; Dean of Bradf from 2005 GS 1990–93
Tel: 01274 777720
01274 777727
Fax: 01274 777730
email: david.ison@bradfordcathedral.org

ITALY AND MALTA, Archdeacon of. See BOARDMAN, Ven Jonathan Thomas

JACKSON, Revd Richard Charles, MA, MSc, DipHE
The Vicarage Cowfold Road Bolney, Haywards Heath East Sussex RH17 5QR [CHICHESTER] *b* 1961 *educ* Latymer Upper Sch; Ch Ch, Ox; Cranfield Univ; Trin Coll Bris; *CV* Rural Dean of Horsham, 2004–09; Archdnry Warden of Rdrs 1999–2004; V Rudgwick 1998–2009; C All Saints, Lindfield 1994–98; Senior Agronomist, Cleanacres Ltd 1985–92; Dioc Adv Miss & Renewal from 2009; Dioc Rdrs Cttee 1999–2004
GS 2010– *Tel:* 01444 881301 01273 421021
email: richard.jackson@diochi.org.uk

JACKSON, Ven Robert William, MA (Cantab), MA (Econ), Dip Th, DPS
55B Highgate Rd Walsall WS1 3JE [ARCHDEACON OF WALSALL; LICHFIELD] *b* 1949 *educ* High Storrs Gr Sch Sheff; K Coll Cam; Manch Univ; St Jo Coll Nottm; *CV* Govt Economic Adv 1972–78; C Ch Ch Fulwood, Sheff 1981–84; V St Mark Grenoside, Sheff 1984–92; V St Mary Scarborough, York 1992–2001; Springboard Missr 2001–04; Adn of Walsall from 2004   *Tel:* 01922 620153
email: archdeacon.walsall@lichfield.anglican.org

JACOB, Ven William Mungo, LLB, MA, Ph D
15a Gower Street London WC1E 6HW [ARCHDEACON OF CHARING CROSS; LONDON] *b* 1944 *educ* K Edw VII Sch King's Lynn; Hull Univ; Linacre Coll Ox; Edin Univ; Ex Univ; St Steph Ho Th Coll; *CV* C Wymondham 1970–73; Asst Chapl Ex Univ 1973–75; Dir of Pastl Studies Sarum and Wells Th Coll 1975–80; Vc-Prin 1977–80; Sec Cttee for Th Educ ACCM 1980–86; Warden Linc Th Coll 1986–96; Adn at The Old Deanery 1996–2000; Adn of Charing Cross from 1996; R St Giles-in-the-Fields from 2000
GS 1999–2000   *Tel:* 020 7636 4646 (Home)
          020 7323 1992 (Office)
          Fax: 020 7323 4102 (Office)
email: archdeacon.charingcross@
          london.anglican.org

JAGGER, Ven Ian, MA, MA
15 The College Durham DH1 3EQ [ARCHDEACON OF DURHAM] *b* 1955 *educ* Huddersfield New Coll; K Coll Cam; St Jo Coll Dur; *CV* C St Mary Virgin Twickenham Lon 1982–85; P-in-c Willen, Milton Keynes Ox 1985–87; TV Willen, Stantonbury LEP 1987–94; Chapl Willen Hospice 1985–94; Dir Milton Keynes Chr Trg Scheme 1986–94; TR Fareham H Trin Portsm 1994–98; Ecum Officer Portsm Dio 1994–96; RD Fareham 1996–98; Can Res Portsm Cathl and Dioc Missr 1998–2001; Adn of Auckland 2001–06; Adn of Durham and Can Res Dur Cathl from 2006
GS 2002–   *Tel:* 0191 384 7534
          Fax: 0191 386 6915
email: archdeacon.of.durham@
          durham.anglican.org

JAGO, Mr Derek, ONC
21 Clarence Gdns Bishop Auckland DL14 7RB [DURHAM] *b* 1949 *educ* Willington Sec Sch; Bp Auckland Coll; New Coll Dur; Gateshead Coll; *CV* Rdr to pars of Witton Park, Etherley and Escomb from 1999; pt Broadcaster; LibDem District Coun Wear Valley; M Auckland Dny Syn
GS 1998–   *Tel and Fax:* 01388 458358
email: Derek_Jago@btclick.com

JAMES, Rt Revd Graham Richard, BA
Bishop's House Norwich NR3 1SB [BISHOP OF NORWICH] *b* 1951 *educ* Northampton Gr Sch; Lanc Univ; Cuddesdon Th Coll; *CV* C Christ Carpenter Peterb 1975–78; C Digswell 1978–82; TR Digswell

1982–83; Selection Sec and Sec for CME ACCM 1983–85; Sen Selection Sec 1985–87; Chapl to Abp of Cant 1987–93; Bp of St Germans 1993–99; Bp of Norw from 1999; M Bd of Countryside Agency 2001–06; Chair Rural Bps Panel 2001–06; Chair CRAC, BBC and Ofcom 2004–08; M AC from 2006; Chair Min Div from 2006; Chair Stg Conf on Relig and Belief, BBC from 2009
GS 1995–   *Tel:* 01603 629001
          Fax: 01603 761613
email: bishop@bishopofnorwich.org

JAMES, Mr Philip John, B SocSc
Church House Great Smith St London SW1P 3AZ [HEAD OF (RESOURCE) STRATEGY AND DEVELOPMENT UNIT, CHURCH COMMISSIONERS AND ARCHBISHOPS' COUNCIL] *b* 1967 *educ* Bris Gr Sch; Birm Univ; *CV* On staff of Ch Commrs from 1988; Hd of Policy Unit from 1999; Head of (Resource) Strategy and Development Unit, Ch Commrs and AC from 2009   *Tel:* 020 7898 1671
email: philip.james@c-of-e.org.uk

JARRETT, Rt Revd Martyn William, BD, AKC, M Phil
3 North Lane Roundhay Leeds LS8 2QJ [BISHOP OF BEVERLEY; PROVINCIAL EPISCOPAL VISITOR: YORK] *b* 1944 *educ* Cotham Gr Sch Bris; K Coll Lon; St Boniface Th Coll Warminster; Hull Univ; *CV* C St Geo East Bristol 1968–70; C Swindon New Town 1970–74; P-in-c St Jos the Worker Northolt 1974–76, V 1976–81; V St And Uxbridge 1981–85; Selection Sec ACCM 1985–88; Sen Selection Sec ACCM 1989–91; V Our Lady and All SS Chesterfield 1991–94; Bp of Burnley 1994–2000; Bp of Beverley from 2000; Asst Bp Dur from 2000; Asst Bp Ripon and Leeds from 2000; Asst Bp Sheff from 2000; Asst Bp S'well and Nottm from 2000; Asst Bp Man from 2001; Asst Bp Wakef from 2001; Asst Bp Bradf from 2002; Asst Bp Liv from 2003; M Chs Commn for Inter-Faith Rels 2000–05; M CCU from 2001; Patr Coll of Rdrs from 2003; M Urban Bps' Panel from 1998; Chair Revision Cttee on Lectionary 2004; M Revision Ctte on Canon 28 2008; M Revision Cttee on Bps and Ps (Consecration and Ord of Women) from 2009
GS 2000–   *Tel:* 0113 265 4280
          Fax: 0113 265 4281
email: bishop-of-beverley@3–north-
          lane.fsnet.co.uk

JARROW, Suffragan Bishop of. See BRYANT, Rt Revd Mark Watts

JEANS, Ven Alan Paul, B Th, MIAS, MIBC, MA
Herbert House 118 Lower Rd Salisbury SP2 9NW [ARCHDEACON OF SARUM; SALISBURY] *b* 1958 *educ* Bournemouth Sch; Dorset Inst of HE; Southn Univ; Sarum and Wells Th Coll; Univ Wales Lamp; *CV* C Parkstone Team 1989–93; P-in-c Bp Cannings, All Cannings and Etchilhampton 1993–98; Dioc Adv for Par Develt 1998–2005; M

The Church and Community Fund

The CCF can offer grants in support of exciting and innovative parish or Diocesan community projects. Projects that show imagination in responding to need and can help to bridge the gap between the Church and the local community are particularly welcome.

- We award £400,000+ every year to exciting church and community projects! We have a strong focus on current initiatives in the Church and regularly support projects in line with the Church's focus on Fresh Expressions, developing the use of Church Buildings, Social Outreach and Youth Evangelism;

- We have helped employ Youth Workers, renovate old Church halls for use as lively community centres, reordered Church buildings to enable them to be used more flexibly and have helped Churches provide hot meals for the homeless;

- We also give an annual grant to the Archbishops' Council in support of the national functions of the Church.

We warmly welcome donations and legacies in support of our work. We support the local Church in responding to the needs of their community throughout the country in both rural and urban areas, bringing about lasting change in some of the neediest parts of England.

Please go to www.churchandcommunityfund.org.uk, call 020 7898 1541/1767 or email us at ccf@c-of-e.org.uk

The Church and Community Fund, Church House, Great Smith Street, London, SW1P 3AZ

The Church and Community Fund is an exempted charity under the trusteeship of The Archbishops' Council of the Church of England (1074857). It exists to support the mission of the Church of England.

CCf The Church and Community Fund
Supporting the Church of England's
mission in the whole community
REGISTERED CHARITY NO. 1074857

✠ THE CHURCH OF ENGLAND

DAC; Adn of Sarum from 2003; Asst DDO from 2005; RD Alderbury 2005–07; DDO from 2007 GS 2000–05, 2010   *Tel:* 01722 336290 (Home)
01380 729808 (Office)
Fax: 01380 738096
email: adsarum@salisbury.anglican.org

JENKINS, Ven Dr David Harold, MA, PhD
Sudbury Lodge Stanningfield Road Bury St Edmunds IP30 0TL [ARCHDEACON OF SUDBURY] *b* 1961 *educ* Belfast Royal Academy; Sidney Sussex Coll Cam; Ripon Coll Cuddesdon; *CV* Asst C Good Shepherd Cambridge 1989–1991; Asst C St Peter's Earley Reading 1991–1994; V St Michael & All Angels Blackpool 1994–1999; V St John Baptist Broughton Preston 1999–2004; DDE Dioc of Carlisle 2004–2010; Residentiary Can Carlisle Cathl 2004–2010; Adn of Sudbury from 2010
Tel: 01284 386942
email: archdeacon.david@
stedmundsbury.anglican.org

JENKINS, Canon Gary John, BA, PGCE, BA, MTh
4 Carlton Road Redhill Surrey RH1 2BX [SOUTHWARK] *b* 1959 *educ* Sir Walter St John's School, Battersea University of York Oak Hill; *CV* C St Luke's, West Norwood 1989–94; V St Peter's, St Helier, 1994–2001; V, Holy Trin, Redhill from 2001; M Bps S'wark Th Issues Grp, 2005–10; M S'wark Dioc Syn, from 2001
GS 2010–   *Tel:* 01737 779917
email: gary@htredhill.com

JEPSON, Dr Rachel Margaret Elizabeth, B Ed (Hons), MA, PhD, TEFL, FIMA
56a Upland Rd Selly Park Birmingham B29 7JS [BIRMINGHAM] *b* 1967 *educ* Edgbaston CE Coll for Girls; Univ Coll of St Mart Lanc; Univ of Glos w Trin Coll Bris; St Jo Coll Dur; *CV* Tchr Grove Sch Handsworth 1993–98; Res Tutor St Jo Coll Dur 1998–2002; M Dioc Bd of Educ to 2006; GS Rep, CTE Forum and CTBI Assembly; Appt M Revision Cttee Care of Cathls Measure 2002; Appt M Additional Collects Revision Cttee 2003; M Birm Dioc Bp's Coun; M Birm Stg Adv Coun for Relig Educ; Tchr (TLR Resp, RE Co-ord), Rookery Sch, Handsworth from 2007; Appt Revision Cttee C of E (Misc Provisions) Meas 2008; Vc-Chair PCC St Martin-in-the-Bull Ring Birm Par Ch from 2008
GS 2000–   *Tel:* 0121 472 2064
email: rachel.jepson@tiscali.co.uk

JERSEY, Dean of. See KEY, Very Revd Robert Frederick

JESSIMAN, Revd Timothy Edward, MA
61 Hart Plain Avenue Waterlooville Hampshire PO8 8RG [PORTSMOUTH] *b* 1958 *educ* Portsm Tech High Sch; Trent Poly; Ox Poly; Portsm Univ; York St John Univ; Oak Hill Th Coll; *CV* Chapl North Devon NHS 1995–2000; Chapl Grenville Sch 1996–99; TV St Peter's in the Torridge Estuary

Team Ministry Ex 1995–2000; Minster The Beacon Church Ecum Ch Plant 1999–2000; M Ex Dioc Sy 1996–2000; V Hart Plain Ch, Joint Methodist and Anglican Local Ecum Partnership from 2000; M Dioc Syn; M Dioc Miss & Soc Forum; M Dioc Evan Working Grp; Dioc 'Back to Church Sunday' Co-ord; M Urban Min Grp; M Fresh Expressions Southern Regional Training Partnership
GS 2010–   *Tel:* 02392264551
email: im.jessiman@ntlworld.com

JOHN, Very Revd Jeffrey Philip Hywel, MA, D Phil
The Deanery Sumpter Yard St Albans AL1 1BY [DEAN OF ST ALBANS] *b* 1953 *educ* Tonyrefail Gr Sch; Hertf Coll Ox; BNC Ox; Magd Coll Ox; St Steph Ho; *CV* C St Aug Penarth 1978–80; Asst Chapl Magd Coll Ox 1980–82; Chapl and lect BNC Ox 1982–84; Fell and Dean of Divinity Magd Coll Ox 1984–91; V H Trin Eltham 1991–97; Dir of Trg S'wark Dioc and Can Theol and Chanc S'wark Cathl 1997–2004; M GS Stg Cttee 1996–2000; M GS Appts Cttee 1995–2000; M S'wark Dioc Syn, Bp's Coun 1997–2004; Dean of St Alb from 2004   *Tel:* 01727 890202
Fax: 01727 890227
email: dean@stalbanscathedral.org.uk

JOHNS, Mrs Sue (Susan Margaret), HNC, M Phil
8 Dragonfly Lane Norwich NR4 7JR [NORWICH] *b* 1955 *educ* Thorpe Gr Sch; Norw City Coll; Leeds Univ; *CV* Analytical Chemist, Public Analyst's Lab 1973–80; Housewife and Mother; Food Scientist MAFF CSL Food Science Lab Norw 1991–98; Joint Food Safety and Standards Grp 1998–2000; Food Standards Agency 2000–09, Health & Safety Exec, currently Priv Sec to Chair and Bd Sec
GS 1990–   *Tel:* 020 7276 8000
Fax: 01603 507609 (Home)
email: sue.johns@hse.gsi.gov.uk

JOHNSTON, Mrs Mary Geraldine, BA, AKC, MCIPD
56 Fairlawn Grove Chiswick London W4 5EH [LONDON] *b* 1939 *educ* Barking Abbey Sch; K Coll Lon; *CV* Personnel Dept ICI 1961–66; Personnel Admin and Employee Relations Singer Co New York 1966–68; American Express New York 1968–70; Asst Personnel Mgr and Staff Devel Mgr Guinness Overseas 1970–80; M Lon and S'wark Dioc Jt Prisons and Penal Concerns Grp; Dir of Affirming Catholicism; Convenor of Affirming Catholics in Synod; M CNC
GS 1995–   *Tel:* 020 8995 6427
email: marygjohnston@btinternet.com

JONES, Canon Joyce Rosemary, MA
Oakfield 206 Barnsley Road, Denby Dale Huddersfield HD8 8TS [WAKEFIELD] *b* 1954 *educ* King Edward VI H Sch; Cam Univ; Newnham Coll; NOC; *CV* AC All Saints Pontefract 1997–2000; Vocations Adv, Asst Chapl Kirkwood Hospice &

AC Cumberworth Denby and Denby Dale 2000–0; P-in-cShelley and Shepley from 2001; Bp's Adv for Prayer and Spirituality from 2005
GS 2010–   *Tel:* 01484 862350
                    Fax: 01484 862350
          email: joycerjones@aol.com

JONES, Rt Revd James Stuart, BA, PGCE, DD
Bishop's Lodge Woolton Park Liverpool L25 6DT [BISHOP OF LIVERPOOL] *b* 1948 *educ* Duke of York's Military Sch Dover; Ex Univ; Wycliffe Hall Th Coll; *CV* C Ch Ch Clifton 1982–90; V Em S Croydon 1990–94; Bp of Hull 1994–98; Bp of Liv from 1998
GS 1995–   *Tel:* 0151 421 0831
                    Fax: 0151 428 3055
    email: bishopslodge@liverpool.anglican.org

JONES, Very Revd Keith Brynmor, MA
The Deanery York YO1 7JQ [DEAN OF YORK] *b* 1944 *educ* Ludlow Gr Sch; Selw Coll Cam; Cuddesdon Th Coll; *CV* C Limpsfield w Titsey 1969–72; Dean's V St Alb Abbey 1972–76; P-in-c St Mich Borehamwood 1976–79; TV 1979–82; V St Mary le Tower Ipswich 1982–96; RD Ipswich 1993–95; Dean of Ex 1996–2004; Dean of York from 2004
GS 1999–2005   *Tel:* 01904 557202 (Office)
                    01904 557260 (Home)
          email: dean@yorkminster.org

JONES, Ven Philip Hugh, Dip Chr Theol & Min, Solicitor
27 The Avenue Lewes BN7 1QT [ARCHDEACON OF LEWES AND HASTINGS; CHICHESTER] *b* 1951 *educ* Leys Sch Cam; Chich Theol Coll; *CV* C St Mary V Horsham 1994–97; V H Innocents Southwater 1997–2005; RD Horsham 2002–05; Adn of Lewes & Hastings from 2005   *Tel:* 01273 479530
                    Fax: 01273 476529
        email: archlandh@diochi.org.uk

JONES, Revd Rhiannon Elizabeth, BA, MA, MA
Rectory 2 Apthorpe St Fulbourn Cambridge CB21 5EY [ELY] *b* 1972 *educ* Ox High Sch; Ex Univ; Lon Sch of Theol; Ridley Hall, Cam; *CV* Co-ord of Jubilee Cen, Cam 1995–98; C Huntingdon Team Min 2000–04; R Fulbourn, Great Wilbraham, Little Wilbraham and Six Mile Bottom from 2004; M Ely Bp's Coun from 2005; M Lit Com from 2006
GS 2005–2010   *Tel:* 01223 880337
          email: rhiannonejones@me.com.

JONES, Ven Trevor Pryce, B Ed, B Th, LL M, Cert Ed, ACP
Glebe House St Mary's Lane Hertingfordbury Hertford SG14 2LE [ARCHDEACON OF HERTFORD; ST ALBAN'S] *b* 1948 *educ* Dial Stone Sch Stockport; St Luke's Coll Ex; Southn Univ; Sarum and Wells Th Coll; Univ of Wales, Cardiff Law Sch; St Jo Coll Dur; *CV* C St Geo Glouc 1976–79; Warden Bp Mascall Centre Ludlow and M Heref Dioc Educ Tm 1979–84; DCO 1981–96; Sec Heref-Nurnberg Eur Ecum Partnership 1982–87; M Bp's Coun 1987–87; M Dioc Ecum Cttee 1985–87, Chair

1996–97; TR Heref S Wye TM 1984–97; OCF 1985–97; Preb Heref Cathl 1993–97; M Dioc Pastl/Minl Cttee 1996–97; Adn of Hertford from 1997; Hon Can St Alb Cathl 1997; Chair St Alb and Ox Min Course 1998–2007; Chair Reach Out Projects Mgt Coun from 1998, Reach Out Plus from 2010; Bp's Selector 2001–08; Chair Rural Strategy Grp from 2001; Vc-Chair ERMC from 2004; Chair Hockerill Educ Foundn 2005; M Legal Adv Commn 2006
GS 2000–05; 2005–10   *Tel:* 01992 581629
                    Fax: 01992 535349
        email: archdhert@stalbans.anglican.org

JUDD, Very Revd Peter Somerset Margesson, MA, DL
The Dean's House 3 Harlings Grove Waterloo Lane Chelmsford CM1 1YQ [DEAN OF CHELMSFORD] *b* 1949 *educ* Charterhouse Sch; Trin Hall Cam; Cuddesdon Th Coll; *CV* C St Phil w St Steph Salford 1974–76; Chapl Clare Coll Cam 1976–81; Acting Dean Clare Coll 1980–81; TV Burnham w Dropmore, Hitcham and Taplow 1981–88; V St Mary V Iffley 1988–97; RD Cowley 1995–97; R and Prov of Chelmsf from 1997, Dean from 2000
GS 2003–05   *Tel:* 01245 354318 (Home)
                    01245 294492 (Office)
                    07740 456844 (Mobile)
                    Fax: 01245 294499
     email: dean@chelmsfordcathedral.org.uk

JUDKINS, Mrs Mary, BA, PGCE, MA
Old Vicarage 3 Church Lane East Ardsley Wakefield WF3 2LJ [WAKEFIELD] *b* 1951 *educ* Leominster Gr Sch; Bris Univ; St Mary's Coll Cheltenham; Open Univ; *CV* Tchr in Bris and E Grinstead 1984–94; Supply Tchr; Homemaker/Mother; Lay Chair Dioc Syn; GS Rep SAMS 1995–2005; M CCU; M CMEAC 2000–05; delegate WCC 9th Assembly 2006; vol co-ord N Kirklees Chr Faith Cen, Dewsbury Minster from 2005; Educ Officer Interfaith Kirklees (Schools) from 2007
GS 1995–   *Tel:* 01924 826802
          email: elephantmj@aol.com

JUKES, Very Revd Keith Michael, BA
Minster House Bedern Bank Ripon HG4 1PE [DEAN OF RIPON; RIPON AND LEEDS] *b* 1954 *educ* Leeds Univ; Linc Th Coll; *CV* C H Trin Wordsley, Lich 1978–81; C Wolverhampton 1981–83; C-in-c Stoneydelph St Martin CD 1983–90; TR Glascote and Stoneydelph 1990–91; RD Tamworth 1990–91; TR Cannock and V Hatherton 1991–97; Preb Lich Cathl 1996–97; P-in-c Selby Abbey, York 1997–99; V 1999–2007; Dean of Ripon from 2007
                    Tel: 01765 602609
                    01765 603462
                    07890 956004 (Mobile)
                    Fax: 01765 690398
     email: deankeith@riponcathedral.org.uk

KAJUMBA, Ven Daniel Steven Kimbugwe, BA, HND, Dip Th, Dip IMBM, LAMDA
84 Higher Drive Purley CR8 2HJ [ARCHDEACON OF

REIGATE; SOUTHWARK] *b* 1952 *educ* Christian Life Coll; Bournemouth Univ; Open Univ; S'wark Ord Course; Lond Univ; *CV* C St Alb Goldington 1985–87; pt Chapl Bedford Prison; Uganda 1987–98: Man Dir Transocean; Gen Man Rio Holdings Internat; Kingdom of Buganda Sec Gen, Cabinet Min PR, Functions and Protocol, Min Foreign Affairs; TV St Fran Horley 1999–2001; Adn of Reigate from 2001; M Dioc Syn; M Bp's Coun; M Business Cttee; M Fin Cttee; M Exec and Glebe Cttee; M Stipends and Budget Cttee; M Parsonages and Property Maintenance Cttee; M Fairer Shares Cttee; M Sites/Advisory and Red Churches Uses Cttee; M CMEAC; M Croydon Area Coun   *Tel:* 020 8660 9276 (Home)
020 8681 5496 (Work) 07949 594460 (Mobile)
Fax: 020 8660 9276 (Home)
020 8686 2074 (Work)
email: daniel.kajumba@southwark.anglican.org

KEARON, Canon Kenneth Arthur, BA, MA, M Phil, DD
Anglican Communion Office St Andrew's House 16 Tavistock Crescent London W11 1AP [SECRETARY GENERAL, ANGLICAN COMMUNION] *b* 1953 *educ* Mountjoy Sch Dub; Trin Coll Dub; Cam Univ; Irish Sch of Ecumenics; *CV* Dn 1981; P 1982; C All SS Raheny and St Jo Coolock, Dioc of Dublin and Glendalough 1981–84; Dean of Residence Trin Coll Dub 1984–91; R Tullow, Dub 1991–99; Dir Irish Sch of Ecumenics 1999–2004; M Chapter of Ch Ch Cathl, Dub from 1995, Chan 2002–04; Sec Gen Angl Communion from 2005; Hon Can St Paul's Cathl Lon, St Geo Cathl Jerusalem, Ch Ch Cathl Cant   *Tel:* 020 7313 3905
Fax: 020 7313 3999
email: kenneth.kearon@anglicancommunion.org

KELLY, Mr Declan Gerard, MSc, BSc, MCLIP
Church House Great Smith St London SW1P 3AZ [DIRECTOR OF LIBRARIES, ARCHIVES AND IT, CHURCH COMMISSIONERS] *b* 1960 *educ* St Hugh's Coll Nottm; Qu Mary Coll Lon; Sheffield Univ; *CV* Rsch Centre Mgr, BBC World Service 1993–97; Intake and Acquisitions Mgr, BBC Archives 1997–99, Rsch Services Mgr 2000–03, Output Services Mgr 2003–05; Dir of Libraries, Archives and IT, Ch Commrs from 2005
Tel: 020 7898 1432
email: declan.kelly@c-of-e.org.uk

KEMP, Mr David Stephen,
11 Ham Shades Lane Whitstable Kent CT5 1NT [CANTERBURY] *b* 1974 *educ* Simon Langton Gr Sch, Cant; ; *CV* Sec Herne Bay Bldg Soc 1978–86; Dep CEO, Kent Reliance Bldg Soc 1986–90; Dioc Sec, Cant 1990–2007; Non-Exec Dir, Kent Reliance Bldg Soc, 1986; Govr, Cant Christ Church Univ 2006; Chair Cant Dioc Child Protection Management Gp from 2007
GS 2010–   *Tel:* 01227 272470
email: kemps11@btinternet.com

**KENSINGTON, Area Bishop of. See
WILLIAMS, Rt Revd Paul Gavin**

KENT, Mr Ian David,
Brightmanshayes Petrockstowe Okehampton EX20 3EY [EXETER] *b* 1980 *educ* Gt Torrington Sch; Plymouth Coll of Art and Design; *CV* Printer from 1996; M Dioc Syn from 2000
GS 2000–2010   *Tel and Fax:* 01409 281281
email: ian.kent@brightmanshayes.freeserve.co.uk

KEY, Very Revd Robert Frederick, BA, DPS
The Deanery David Place St Helier Jersey JE2 4TE [DEAN OF JERSEY; WINCHESTER] *b* 1952 *educ* Alleyn's Sch Dulwich; Bris Univ; Oak Hill Th Coll; *CV* C St Ebbe Ox 1976–80; Min St Patr Wallington 1980–85; V Eynsham and Cassington 1985–91; V St Andr Ox 1991–2001; M Coun Wycliffe Hall from 1985; M Coll of Evangelists; Gen Dir CPAS 2001–05; M Defence Select Cttee 2005–10; M Eccl Cttee of Parliament 2005–10; Dean of Jersey from 2005
GS 1995–2005, 2010–   *Tel:* 01534 720001
email: robert_f_key@yahoo.com

KEY, Mr Simon Robert, MA, Cert Ed
4 Old St Salisbury SP2 8JL [SALISBURY] *b* 1945 *educ* Salis Cathl Sch; Sherborne Sch; Clare Coll Cam; *CV* Master, Loretto Sch Edin 1967–69; Harrow Sch 1969–83; Min for Local Government and Inner Cities 1990–92, for Nat Heritage 1992–93, for Transport 1993–94; Shadow Min for Defence 1997–99, for Internat Devel 1999–2001, for Science 2003–05; M Defence Select Cttee; MP for Salis from 1983; M Salis Dioc Syn from 2003; M Coun of Salis Cathl from 2002; M Eccl Cttee of Parliament from 2005; Fellow Soc of Antiquaries from 2006; Lay Can Salis Cath from 2008; M Defence Select Cttee 2005–10; M Eccl Cttee of Parliament 2005–10
GS 2005–   *Tel:* 01722 326622
email: srobertkey@hotmail.com

KIDDLE, Canon John, MA, MTh
19 Stanbury Avenue Watford Herts WD17 3HW [ST ALBANS] *b* 1958 *educ* Monkton Combe Sch; Queens' Coll Cam; Heythrop Coll UL; Ridley Hall, Cam; *CV* AC, Ormskirk Parish Church, 1982–86; V, St Gabriel's Church Huyton Quarry, 1986–91; V, St Luke's Church Watford, 1991–08; Rural Dean of Watford, 1999–04 Hon Can St Alb Cathl 2005–10; Off Miss and Devlp, St Alb from 2008; Residentiary Can St Alb Cathl from 2010; M Dioc Syn 1986–89; Sec Brd Miss and Unity 1986–89; M Dioc Syn 1997–00; M Dioc Pstrl Cttee 1997–00; M Bedford Deanery Review 1999–00; Chair Luton Deanery Review Grp 2003–04; Chair Dioc Vision for Action Grp 2004–06; Exec Off Brd Ch and Soc from 2008
GS 2010–   *Tel:* 01923 460083, 01727 818146
email: john.kiddle@stalbans.anglican.org

KILLWICK, Canon Simon David Andrew, BD, AKC, Cert Th
Christ Church Rectory Monton St Moss Side Manchester M14 4GP [MANCHESTER] *b* 1956 *educ* Westmr Sch; K Coll Lon; St Steph Ho Th Coll; *CV* C St Mark Worsley 1981–84; TV St Mary Ellenbrook 1984–97; P-in-c Ch Ch Moss Side from 1997, R from 2006; Exam Chapl to Bp of Man 2002–07; Hon Can Manch from 2004; AD Hulme from 2007
GS 1998–   *Tel:* 0161 226 2476
                          email: frskillwick@btinternet.com

KINGS, Rt Revd Graham Ralph, MA, DipTh, PhD
Sherborne House Tower Hill Iwerne Minster Blandford Forum DT11 8NH [AREA BISHOP OF SHERBORNE; SALISBURY] *b* 1953 *educ* Buckhurst Hill County Sch; RMA Sandhurst; Hertford Coll Ox; Ridley Hall Cam; Selwyn Coll Cam; *CV* Asst C St Mark Harlesden 1980–84; CMS Mission Partner Kenya 1985–91; Dir Studies and Vc Prin St Andrew's Coll Kabare 1985–91; Hon Can St Andrew's Cath Kerugoya Kenya 1991; Overseas Advr Henry Martyn Trust Cam 1992–95; Lect Mission Stud 1992–2000; Dir Henry Martyn Centre for Mission studies in World Christianity 1995–2000, Cambridge Theological Federation; V St Mary Islington 2000–09; M MTAG 1996–2005; Trustee Anvil 1998–2004; M Lit Comm from 2002; Manager Ang Comm Network for Inter faith Concerns from 2007; Theol Sec Fulcrum from 2003; Area Bp of Sherborne from 2009
                                             Tel: 01202 659427
                                             Fax: 01202 691418
            email: gsherborne@salisbury.anglican.org

KINGSTON, Area Bishop of. See CHEETHAM, Rt Revd Richard Ian

KIRK, Revd Gavin John, BTh, MA
The Precentory Minster Yard Lincoln LN2 1PX [LINCOLN] *b* 1961 *CV* Asst C, Seaford-cum-Sutton 1986–89; Succentor Rochester Cathl 1989–91; Head of Classics and Asst Chapl, The King's Schl, Rochester, 1991–98; Can Res & Precentor Portsmouth Cathl 1998–2003; Canon Residentiary & Precentor, Lincoln Cathl from 2003; Chair Portsmouth Bp's Adv Grp for Worship 1998–2003; Trustee NTMTS 2001–03; Chair Lincoln Dioc Lit Cttee from 2008
GS 2000–03; 2010–   *Tel:* 01522 561632
            email: precentor@lincolncathedral.com

KNARESBOROUGH, Suffragan Bishop of. See BELL, Rt Revd James Harold

KNOWLES, Rt Revd Graeme Paul, AKC, RNR
The Deanery 9 Amen Court London EC4M 7BU [DEAN OF ST PAUL'S; LONDON] *b* 1951 *educ* Dunstable Gr Sch; K Coll Lon; St Aug Coll Cant; *CV* C St Peter-in-Thanet 1974–79; C and Prec Leeds Par Ch 1979–81; Chapl Prec Portsm Cathl 1981–87; V Leigh Park 1987–93; RD Havant 1990–

93; Adn of Portsm 1993–99; Dean of Carl 1999–2003; M CCC 1995–2001, Vc-Chair 1996–2001; Chair CCC from 2003; Bp of Sodor and Man 2003–07; Dean of St Paul's from 2007; Chair CCC 2003–08; Chair CBC 2008–09
GS 1995–98, 2003–07   *Tel:* 020 7236 2827
                                 Fax: 020 7332 0298
            email: thedean@stpaulscathedral.org.uk

LAKE, Canon Stephen David, B Th
Old Rectory Sumpter Yard St Albans AL1 1BY [ST ALBANS] *b* 1963 *educ* Homefield Sch; Chich Th Coll; *CV* C Sherborne w. Castleton & Lillington 1988–92; P-in-c St Aldhelm Branksome 1992–96, V 1996–2001; Asst RD Poole 1996–2000; RD Poole 2000–01; Can Res and Sub Dean Cathl and Abbey Ch of St Alb from 2001, Acting Dean 2003–04; Chair Dioc Liturg Cttee; Chair Easter Monday Pilgrimage Cttee; Chair Bd for Christian Development
GS 2004–   *Tel:* 01727 890201
                                  07900 988646 (Mobile)
            email: subdean@stalbanscathedral.org

LAMBETH, Archdeacon of. See SKILTON, Ven Christopher John

LANCASTER, Archdeacon of. See BALLARD, Ven Peter James

LANCASTER, Suffragan Bishop of. See PEARSON, Rt Revd Geoffrey Seagrave

LANGRISH, Rt Revd Michael Laurence, B Soc Sc, BA, MA, Hon DD (Birm), Hon DD (Ex)
The Palace Exeter EX1 1HY [BISHOP OF EXETER] *b* 1946 *educ* K Edw Sch Southn; Birm Univ; Fitzw Coll Cam; Ridley Hall Th Coll; *CV* C Stratford-upon-Avon 1973–76; Chapl Rugby Sch 1976–81; V Offchurch and DDO 1981–87; Exam Chapl to Bp of Cov 1982–89; Chair ACCM Vocations Cttee 1984–91; TR Rugby 1987–93; Chair Ho of Clergy Dioc Syn 1988–93; Hon Can Cov Cathl 1990–93; Bp of Birkenhead 1993–2000; M BAGUPA 1996–98; M Urban Bps' Panel 1996–2000; M BSR Community and Urban Affairs Cttee 1998–2001; Bp of Exeter from 2000; Chair Rural Affairs Cttee, M BM 2001–06; M Ch Commrs Bishoprics and Cathls Cttee 2002–06; Chair Melanesian Mission 2002–09; M Bd of Chr Aid from 2003; Chair Toyne Follow-up Grp 2004–06; M Ho of Lords from 2005; Chair Diocs Pastl and Miss Measure Grp 2006–08; Chair Rural Strategy Grp 2006–09; Chair Ch Legislation Adv Cttee from 2009
GS 1985–93, 1999–   *Tel:* 01392 272362
                                   Fax: 01392 430923
         email: bishop.of.exeter@exeter.anglican.org

LANGSTAFF, Rt Revd James Henry, MA (Oxon), BA (Nottm)
Bishopscourt St Margaret's Street Rochester ME1 1TS [BISHOP OF ROCHESTER] *b* 1956 *educ* Cheltenham Coll; Ox Univ; Nottm Univ; St Jo Coll

Nottm; *CV* C St Pet Farnborough, Guildf 1981–86, P-in-c 1985–86; P-in-c St Matt Duddeston & St Clem Nechells, Birm 1986, V 1987–96; RD Birm City 1995–96; Chapl to Bp of Birm 1996–2000; R H Trin Sutton Coldfield, Birm 2000–04; Area Dean of Sutton Coldfield 2002–04; Bp of Lynn 2004–10; Bp of Rochester from 2010; Chair Flagship Housing Grp from 2006; M E of England Regional Assembly from 2007; Chair Housing Justice from 2008
Tel: 01634 842471
07989 330582 (Mobile)
Fax: 01634 831136
email: bishop.rochester@rochester.anglican.org

LASH, Very Revd Archimandrite Ephrem, MA, STB
18 Tuffnell Park Mansions London N7 6HS [ECUMENICAL REPRESENTATIVE (ORTHODOX CHURCHES)] *b* 1930 *educ* Downside Sch; St Jo Coll Ox; Seminaire St Sulpice, Paris; Ecole Pratique des Hautes Etudes (Diplom) Paris; *CV* Lect in Bibl and Patristic Studies Univ of Newc 1978–84; rtd
GS 1995–
Tel: 0203 218 8007
07932 191789 (Mobile)
email: ephrem@chorlton.com

LAW-JONES, Revd Peter Deniston, MA, PGCE
The Vicarage St Thomas Road Lytham St Annes FY8 1JL [BLACKBURN] *b* 1955 *educ* Greenhill Sch, Rochdale; Newcastle Univ; Man Univ; Lanc University; Linc Th Coll; *CV* Teacher, John Leggott 6th Form Coll 1981–84; Asst C St Lawrence Chorley 1987–91; V St Francis Feniscliffe 1991–96; Hon. Tutor Lancashire and Cumbria Th Partnership 1999–2009; V St Thomas St Annes on the Sea from 1996; Area Dean of Kirkham from 2009; M DiocPastoral and Miss Cttee from 2009; M Bp's Counc from 2009; M Dioc Bd Miss from 2009
GS 2010–
Tel: 01253 723750
email: law-jones@peter11.orangehome.co.uk

LEAFE, Mrs Susannah Mary, BSc PGCE
6 Troy Court Daglands Road Fowey PL23 1JX [TRURO] *b* 1971 *educ* Wimbledon H Sch; Bris Univ; Nott Univ; *CV* Head of Geography, Clifton H Sch 1996–2008; Tchr Geography, Queen Elizabeth's Hosp 2008; FLAME coord, Truro Dioc 2009–10; Women's Ministry Facilitator, Fowey Parish Ch from 2008
GS 2010–
Tel: 07753690120
email: dands.leafe@blueyonder.co.uk

LEATHARD, Prof Helen Louise, B Sc, Ph D, F B Pharmacol S, MA
29 Coronation Way Lancaster LA1 2TQ [BLACKBURN] *b* 1947 *educ* Kirkby Stephen Gr Sch Westmorland; Chelsea Coll Lon; K Coll Hosp Medical Sch; St Mart Coll Lancaster; *CV* Rsch Fell K Coll Hosp Medical Sch 1974–76; Lect in Pharmacology; Charing Cross and Westmr Medical Sch 1977–92; Sen Lect in Physiology St Martin's Coll

Lanc 1992–94; Rdr in Pharmacology and Human Physiology St Martin's Coll Lanc (now Univ of Cumbria) 1994–2001; Prof of Healing Science and Pharmacology from 2001, Prof Emerita, in retirement 2010; M Dioc Syn; Guild of St Raph Coun; Editor Chrism; M Order of St Luke from 2003; Consult Cen for Study of Theol and Health; M Tunstall Dny Syn; Rdr
GS 2000–
Tel: 01524 849495 (Home)
email: helenleathard@btinternet.com

LEE, Ven David John, B Sc, MA, PhD, Dip Theol, Dip Miss Studies
47 Kirkgate Shipley W Yorkshire BD18 3EH [ARCHDEACON OF BRADFORD] *b* 1946 *educ* Wolverhampton Gr Sch; Bris Univ; All Nations Chr Coll; Lon Univ; Cam Univ; Birm Univ; Ridley Hall, Cam; *CV* Sch Master, Lesotho 1967–68; Sch Master, Walsall 1968–77; C St Marg Putney, S'wark 1977–80; Lect in NT and Theol, Bp Tucker Coll Uganda 1980–86; Lect in Biblical Studies and Missiology, Selly Oak Colls, Tutor Crowther Hall, Selly Oak 1986–91; R Middleton and Wishaw 1991–96; Dir for Miss and Res Can Birm Cathl 1996–2004; Adn of Bradford from 2004; involvement with Angl Ch Planting Initiatives, Nat Coun for Chr Unity (Local Unity Panel), Grace Houses, Birm (internat student work), Chaplaincy Plus, Birm (work-based chaplaincy and mission), Samuel White Charities, Middleton (almshouse trust); Bradf Chs for Dialogue and Diversity (miss educ); Gov Imm C of E Com Coll, Idle, Bradf
GS 2005
Tel: 01274 200698
07711 671351 (Mobile)
Fax: 01274 200698
email: david.lee@bradford.anglican.org

LEE, Revd John, B Sc, M Sc, MInstGA
The Wash House Lambeth Palace London SE1 7JU [CLERGY APPOINTMENTS ADVISER] *b* 1947 *educ* St Dunstan's Coll Catford; Univ Coll Swansea; Inst of Grp Analysis Lon; Ripon Hall Th Coll; *CV* Experimental Officer R Australian Navy Rsch Laboratory Sydney 1971–73; pt Nursing Auxiliary Chu Hosp Ox 1973–75; C Cockett 1975–78; P-in-c St Teilo Cockett 1976–78; Pr/Counsellor St Botoloph Aldgate 1978–84; Hon Psychotherapist Dept of Psychological Medicine St Bart's Hosp Lon 1980–86; Course Consultant St Alb Minl Tr Scheme 1980–85; P-in-c Chiddingstone w Chiddingstone Causeway 1984–89; R 1989–98; Tutor in Individual and Grp Psychotherapy Dept of Psychological Medicine St Bart's Medical Sch 1987–92; Staff Consult Richmond Fell 1989–98; Psychotherapist and Grp Analyst in private practice 1987–98; Clergy Appointments Adv from 1998
Tel: 020 7898 1898
Fax: 020 7898 1899
email: admin.caa@c-of-e.org.uk

LEE, Revd (John Charles) Hugh Mellanby, MA, M Tech, FRSA
12 Walton St Oxford OX1 2HG [OXFORD] *b* 1944

educ Marlboro Coll; Trin Hall Cam; Brunel Univ; Ox NSM Course; *CV* Operational Rsch Scientist Nat Coal Bd 1966–76; Coal Supply Tm Leader Internat Energy Agency 1976–84; Dep Hd of Economics Br Coal 1984–91; Dir Coal and Electricity Consulting WEFA Energy 1992–95; NSM Amersham-on-the-Hill 1981–88; NSM St Aldate Ox 1988–93; NSM Wheatley 1993–95; pt Work and Economic Life Missr Berks, Bucks and Oxon 1995–2002; NSM House for Duty P-in-c, St Mich at the North Gate, Ox and City R 2002–09; pt Consult Energy Economist from 1995; Treas and Trustee Chs Media Trust 1994–2001; Dir Equigas and Equipower from 1998, Chair from 2003; Moderator CHRISM 1998–2001; married Anne Mellanby 1967; children Kate born 1971, Alexander born 1973; founding trustee Ox Industrial Chapl from 1998; M DRASCS 2004–06
GS 2000– *Tel:* 01865 316245
07879 426625 (Mobile)
Fax: 01865 316245
email: hugh.lee@btinternet.com

LEEDS, Archdeacon of. See BURROWS, Ven Peter

LEICESTER, Archdeacon of. See ATKINSON, Ven Richard William Bryant

LEICESTER, Bishop of. See STEVENS, Rt Revd Timothy John

LEICESTER, Dean of. See FAULL, Very Revd Vivienne Frances

LENNOX, Mr Lionel Patrick Madill, LLB
Provincial and Diocesan Registry Stamford House Piccadilly York YO1 9PP [REGISTRAR OF PROVINCE AND DIOCESE OF YORK; REGISTRAR OF CONVOCATION OF YORK; REGISTRAR OF TRIBUNALS FOR PROVINCE OF YORK] *educ* St Jo Sch Leatherhead; Birm Univ; Leeds Metropolitan Univ; *CV* Solicitor from 1973; In private practice 1973–80; Asst Legal Adv GS 1981–87; Sec Abp of Cant's Grp on Affinity 1982–84; Sec Bp of Lon's Grp on Blasphemy 1981–87; Sec Legal Adv Commn 1986–89; Registrar Province and Dioc York, Legal Secretary to the Archbp of York, Registrar York Conv and Eccl Notary from 1987 and Ptnr Denison Till (York) Solicitors from 1987; M Legal Adv Commn from 1987; Notary Public from 1992; M Eccll Rule Cttee from 1992; Registrar of Tribunals from 2006; Trustee Yorks Hist Chs Trust; Trustee St Leon Hospice York 2000–09; City of York Under Sheriff 2006–07; Pres Yorkshire Law Soc 2007–08
Tel: 01904 623487
01904 611411
Fax: 01904 561470

LEROY, Mr Peter John, MA, PGCE
8 Brook Cottage Lower Barton Corston Bath BA2 9BA [BATH AND WELLS] *b* 1944 *educ* Monkton Combe Sch; Qu Coll Cam; *CV* History tchr and House-master Radley Coll 1967-84; Hdmaster Monkton Combe Jun Sch and Relig Studies tchr 1984–94; Vc-Chair Incorp Assoc of Prep Schs 1993–94; Sec Studylink EFAC Internat Tr Partnership 1995–2002; M Bd of Educ 1997–2005; M Dioc Bd of Educ from 1997; Sch Gov; Scripture Union Bd and Coun 1997–2006; Chair Trustees, Open the Book from 2007; Rdr from 1997
GS 1975–85, 1995–2010 *Tel:* 01225 873023
email: panda@leroy.com

LETTS, Ven Kenneth John, BA, Dip Ed
11 rue de la Buffa 06000 Nice France [ARCHDEACON OF FRANCE; EUROPE] *b* 1942 *educ* Coll of Resurr Mirfield; *CV* C St Steph Mt Waverley (Australia) 1971–74; Chapl Melbourne C of E Gr Sch 1974–81; P-in-c Albert Park 1981–94; Sen Chapl St Mich Sch 1982–94; Chapl Nice w Vence from 1994; Can Gib Cathl from 2004; Adn of France from 2007
Tel: 00 33 4 93 87 19 83
Fax: 00 33 4 93 82 25 09
email: anglican@free.fr

LEWES AND HASTINGS, Archdeacon of. See JONES, Ven Philip Hugh

LEWES, Area Bishop of. See BENN, Rt Revd Wallace Parke

LEWIS, Very Revd Christopher Andrew, MA, Ph D
The Deanery Christ Church Oxford OX1 1DP [DEAN OF CHRIST CHURCH, OXFORD] *b* 1944 *educ* Marlboro Coll; Bris Univ; CCC Cam; Westcott Ho Th Coll; Episc Th Sch Cam Mass; *CV* Royal Navy 1961–66; C Barnard Castle 1973–76; Tutor Ripon Coll Cuddesdon 1976–81; Dir Ox Inst for Ch and Soc 1976–79; P-in-c Aston Rowant and Crowell 1978–81; Vc Prin Ripon Coll Cuddesdon 1981–82; V Spalding 1982–87; Can Res Cant Cathl 1987–94; Dir Minl Tr Cant dio 1989–94; Sen Insp Theol Colls and Courses from 1991; Dean of St Alb 1994–2003; Chair Inspections Wkg Pty, Ho of Bp's Cttee for Min 1996–2003; TETC 1996–2003; Chair Assoc of Engl Cathls 2000–09; Dean Ch Ch Ox from 2003
GS 1985–88, 1995–2005 *Tel:* 01865 276161
Fax: 01865 276238
email: rachel.perham@chch.ox.ac.uk

LEWIS, Revd Edward John, JP, BA, B Ed, MA, FRSA, M Inst D
Church House Great Smith St London SW1P 3AZ [CHIEF EXECUTIVE AND DIRECTOR OF TRAINING, HOSPITAL CHAPLAINCIES COUNCIL] *b* 1958 *educ* Penlan Sch Swansea; Univ of Wales; Chich Th Col; Univ of Surrey; *CV* C Llangiwg 1983–85; Sen C Morriston and Asst Chapl Morriston Hosp 1985–87; V Tregaron, Strata Florida and Ystradmeurig and Chapl Tregaron Hosp 1987–89; Sen Chapl Walsall Hosps NHS Trust, Walsall Com Trust and District Chapl Walsall HA 1989–2000; Asst RD Walsall 1995–2000; Sec and Dir Tr HCC

from 2000; Visiting Lect, St Mary's Univ Coll Twickenham from 2003; Chair City of Westmr Magistrates' Trg Ctee from 2007; Chaplain to HMQ from 2008   *Tel:* 020 7898 1892
07957 529646 (Mobile)
Fax: 020 7898 1891
email: edward.lewis@c-of-e.org.uk

LEWIS, Mr Paul, BA, Postgrad Dip (Environmental Planning)
Church House Great Smith St London SW1P 3AZ [PASTORAL AND CLOSED CHURCHES SECRETARY, BISHOPRICS AND CATHEDRALS SECRETARY, CHURCH COMMISSIONERS] *b* 1952 *educ* Cantonian High Sch, Cardiff; Liv Univ; *CV* Asst Planner Chorley Borough Coun 1974–85; Appeals Officer Monmouth Borough Coun 1985–91; Asst Borough Planning Officer Hastings Borough Coun 1991–95, Borough Planning Officer/Chief Planner 1995–2004; Pastl and Closed Chs Sec Ch Commrs from 2004; Bishoprics and Closed Chs Sec Ch Commrs from 2009   *Tel:* 020 7898 1741
07894 930474 (Mobile)
Fax: 020 7898 1873
email: paul.lewis@c-of-e.org.uk

LEWISHAM, Archdeacon of. See HARDMAN, Ven Christine Elizabeth

LICHFIELD, Archdeacon of. See LILEY, Ven Christopher Frank

LICHFIELD, Bishop of. See GLEDHILL, Rt Revd Jonathan Michael

LICHFIELD, Dean of. See DORBER, Very Revd Adrian John

LILEY, Ven Christopher Frank, B Ed
24 The Close Lichfield WS13 7LD [ARCHDEACON OF LICHFIELD] *b* 1947 *educ* Bp Lonsdale Coll of Educ, Derby; Linc Th Coll; *CV* C Kingswinford 1974–79; TV Ch Ch Stafford 1979–84; V Norton, Letchworth 1984–96; RD Hitchin 1990–96; P-in-c St Alkmund Shrewsbury 1996–2001; V St Chad w St Mary Shrewsbury 1996–2001; Adn of Lich from 2001; Chair Bd of Min to 2002   *Tel:* 01543 306145
01543 306146
Fax: 01543 306147
email: archdeacon.lichfield@lichfield.anglican.org

LILLEY, Canon Christopher Howard, Dip CM, FTII
The Chrysalis 12 Hillside Ave Sutton on Sea Mablethorpe LN12 2JH [LINCOLN] *b* 1951 *educ* K Sch Grantham; St Jo Coll Nottm; *CV* Hon C Skegness and Winthorpe 1985–93; C Gt Limber w Brocklesby 1993–96; P-in-c Middle Rasen Grp 1996–97; R Middle Rasen Grp 1997–2002; V Scawby with Redbourne and Hibaldstow and P-in-c Waddingham, Snitterby and Bishop Norton 2002–2010; RD Yarborough 2002–2009; M Bp's Coun 2001–2009; Dioc Ecum Officer 2001–2009; Ch Commr 1997–98; M AC Fin Cttee

1999–2001 and 2004–07; M Ch Commrs Bishoprics and Cathls Cttee 1999–2006; P-in-c Kirton w. Lindsey and Grayingham 2006–2010; M CCU from 2007; Miss Enabler (NSM) Mablethorpe and Sutton on Sea Gps of Par from 2010
GS 1996–   *Tel:* 01507 440039
email: c.lilley@btinternet.com

LINCOLN, Archdeacon of. See BARKER, Ven Timothy Reed

LINCOLN, Bishop of. See SAXBEE, Rt Revd John Charles

LINCOLN, Dean of. See BUCKLER, Very Revd Philip John Warr

LINDISFARNE, Archdeacon of. See ROBINSON, Ven Peter John Alan

LINDSEY, Archdeacon of Stow and. See SINCLAIR, Ven Jane Elizabeth Margaret

LIVERPOOL, Archdeacon of. See PANTER, Ven Ricky (Richard) James Graham

LIVERPOOL, Bishop of. See JONES, Rt Revd James Stuart

LIVERPOOL, Dean of. See WELBY, Very Revd Justin Portal

LIVESEY, Mr Timothy Peter Nicholas, BA
Lambeth Palace London SE1 7JU [ARCHBISHOP OF CANTERBURY'S SECRETARY FOR PUBLIC AFFAIRS] *b* 1959 *educ* Stonyhurst Coll; New Coll Ox; *CV* 2nd Lieut, R Irish Rangers 1977–78; Asst Registrar and Dep Sec UMDS, Guy's and St Thos Hosps 1984–87; Foreign and Commonwealth Office 1987–2006; First Sec (Aid), Lagos 1989–93; Hd, Press and Public Affairs, Paris 1996–2000; Asst Press Sec, 10 Downing St 2000–02; on secondment as Princ Adv for Public Affairs to Cardinal Abp of Westmr 2002–04; Asst Dir, Information and Strategy, FCO 2004–06; Abp of Cant's Sec for Public Affairs from 2006   *Tel:* 020 7898 1274
Fax: 020 7898 1210
email: tim.livesey@lambethpalace.org.uk

LLOYD, Ven Jonathan Wilford, B Sc, MA, Dip Applied Social Studies, CQSW
Tuborgvej 82 2900 Hellerup Copenhagen Denmark [ARCHDEACON OF GERMANY AND NORTHERN EUROPE] *b* 1956 *educ* Lancing Coll; Surrey Univ; City of Lon Poly; Goldsmiths Coll Lon Univ; North Lon Poly; S'wark Ord Course; *CV* PA to Bp of Namibia-in-Exile 1975–78; Rsch IDAF 1978–80; Com Wkr Lewisham 1980–81; Soc Wkr Lon Boro of S'wark 1982–84; Family Soc Wkr and Practice Tchr, Newham FWA 1984–86; Prin Soc Wkr St Chris Hospice Lond 1986–91; Help the Hospices Intl Fell (Sloan Kettering Meml Hosp, New York) 1991; Peace Monitor Kwa Zulu Natal (EMPSA)

1993; hon C St Bart Sydenham 1990–93, hon P-in-c 1993–94; Dir of Soc Resp, S'wark dioc 1991–95; M Lambeth Millennium Gp 1996–99; Priest V S'wark Cathl 1991–97; Chair Lond and S'wark Diocs Prisons and Criminal Justice Gp 1992–96; Bp's Officer for Ch and Society, S'wark 1995–97; M S'wark Dioc Miss Team 1995–97; M Bd of Dirs S Lon Industrial Miss 1991–95; S'wark Dioc Eur Link Officer 1991–97; Univ Chapl and Ecum Chaplaincy Team Leader, Univ of Bath 1997–2004; M Dioc Bd of Ed 1998–2003; Trustee Dorothy Ho Hospice Care 1998–2001; Chair Conf of Eur Univ Chapls 1998–2002; P-in-c Charlcombe w. Bath St Steph 2004–09; Co-Vc-Chair B & W Dioc Coun for Miss 2004–06; Non-Exec Dir R United Hosp Bath NHS Trust 2002–09; Chair B & W Dioc Soc Resp Grp 2004–09; M Bp's Coun 2008–09; M Inter-Dioc Fin Forum 2006–09; Chapl St Alban Copenhagen with Aarhus (Dioc in Eur) from 2009; Adn Germany and N Eur from 2010; Hon Can Holy Trin Pro-Cath Brussels from 2010
GS 1995–97, 2005–09   *Tel:* 00 45 39 62 77 36
email: jlloyd.uk@btinternet.com

LLOYD, Canon Nigel James Clifford, B Th, S Th
19 Springfield Rd Parkstone Poole BH14 0LG [SALISBURY] *b* 1951 *educ* Lancing Coll; Nottm Univ; Linc Th Coll; *CV* C Sherborne Abbey 1981–84; R Lytchett Matravers 1984–92; TR Lower Parkstone from 1992; Area Ecum Officer 1994–99; Dioc Ecum Officer 1999–2001; Asst RD Poole 2000–01, RD 2001–09; non-res Can and Preb of Salis Cathl from 2002; M CCU 2001–05; M Bp's Coun 2000–05
GS 2000–   *Tel:* 01202 748860 (Home)
01202 749085 (Office)
07940 348776 (Mobile)
email: nigel.lloyd@dsl.pipex.com

LONDON (ST PAUL'S), Dean of. See KNOWLES, Rt Revd Graeme Paul

LONDON, Archdeacon of. See MEARA, Ven David Gwynne

LONDON, Bishop of. See CHARTRES, Rt Revd and Rt Hon Richard John Carew

LONDON, Hon. Assistant Bishop of. See MARSHALL, Rt Revd Michael Eric

LORDING, Mrs Rosemary Kathleen, BA
93 Kings Acre Rd Hereford HR4 0RQ [HEREFORD] *b* 1947 *educ* Eliz Newcomen Sch, Lon; Mid Essex Tech Coll, Chelms; Herefordshire Coll of Tech; *CV* Catering mgt 1968–73; Personnel and trg mgr, retail 1988–96; Gen Mgr, Three Counties Trg 1996–99; Trg and Devel Mgr, Herefordshire Primary Care Trust 1999–2001; voluntary worker; M Bp's Coun, Dioc Policy and Resources Cttee; DBF Revenue Cttee; additional M Heref Cathl Chapter; Chair Ho of Laity Heref Dioc
GS 2004–   *Tel:* 01432 340050
email: rk.lording@virgin.net

LOUGHBOROUGH, Archdeacon of. See NEWMAN, Ven David Maurice Frederick

LOWMAN, Ven David Walter, BD, AKC
The Archdeacon's Lodge 136 Broomfield Road Chelmsford CM1 1RN [ARCHDEACON OF SOUTHEND; CHELMSFORD] *b* 1948 *educ* Crewkerne Gr Sch; K Coll Lon; St Aug Coll Cant; *CV* Civil Servant 1966–70; C Notting Hill TM 1975–78; C St Aug w St Jo Kilburn 1978–81; Selection Sec and Voc Adv ACCM 1981–86; TR Wickford and Runwell 1986–93; DDO, Lay Min Adv and NSM Officer 1993–2001; Hon Can Chelmsf Cathl from 1993; M Dioc Syn from 1986; Vc Chair St Mellitus Coll 2008; Gov Brentwood Sch; Sen Selector, Bps' Selection Confs; M Marriage Law Reform Group
GS 1995–2005   *Tel:* 01245 258257
Fax: 01245 250845
email: a.southend@chelmsford.anglican.org

LOWSON, Ven Christopher, M Th, STM, LLM, AKC
Church House Great Smith St London SW1P 3AZ [DIRECTOR OF MINISTRY, ARCHBISHOPS' COUNCIL] *b* 1953 *educ* Newc Cathl Sch; Consett Gr Sch; K Coll Lon; St Aug Coll Cant; Pacific Sch of Religion Berkeley California (WCC Scholar); Heythrop Coll Lon; Cardiff Law Sch; *CV* C St Mary Richmond 1977–82; P-in-c H Trin Eltham 1982–83, V 1983–91; Chapl Avery Hill Coll 1982–85; Chapl Thames Poly 1985–91; V Petersfield and R Buriton 1991–99; RD Petersfield 1995–99; Vis Lect Portsm Univ 1998–2006; Adn of Portsm Jan–Nov 1999; Adn of Portsdown 1999–2006; Chair Bd of Min; Bp of Portsm's Adv to Hosp Chaplaincy; Dioc Rep on Inter-Diocesan Fin Forum 1999–2006; Dir of Min, AC from 2006; PV Westmr Abbey from 2006
GS 2000–05   *Tel:* 020 7898 1390
07957 657312 (Mobile)
Fax: 020 7898 1421
email: christopher.lowson@c-of-e.org.uk

LUDLOW, Archdeacon of. See MAGOWAN, Rt Revd Alistair James

LUDLOW, Suffragan Bishop of. See MAGOWAN, Rt Revd Alistair James

LUNN, Councillor Robin Christopher, BA
Little Hambledon 10 Malthouse Crescent Inkberrow WR7 4EF [WORCESTER] *b* 1968 *educ* Ditcham Park Sch; Univ of Kent; *CV* Business Devel Mgr from 2005; County Councillor for Redditch N from 2005
GS 2004–   *Tel:* 01386 792073
07785 305849 (Mobile)
Fax: 01386 791531
email: rlunn@worcestershire.gov.uk

LYNAS, Revd Stephen Brian, B Th, MBE, PGCE
Bishops' Office The Palace Wells Somerset BA5 2PD [BATH AND WELLS] *b* 1952 *educ* Borden Gr Sch,

Kent; St Jo Coll Nottm; Trin Hall Cam; *CV* C Penn, Lich 1978–81; Relig Progr Org BBC Radio Stoke-on-Trent 1981–84; C Hanley 1981–82; C Edensor 1982–84; Relig Progr Producer BBC Bris 1985–88; Relig Progr Sen Producer BBC S and W Eng 1988–91; Hd Relig Progr TV South 1991–92; Com and Relig Affairs Ed Westcountry TV from 1992; Abps' Officer for Millennium 1996–2001; P Resources Adv, B&W Dioc 2001–07; Sen Chapl and Adv to Bps of B & W and Taunton from 2007 GS 2005–   *Tel:* 01749 672341
Fax: 01749 679355
email: chaplain@bathwells.anglican.org

LYNN, Archdeacon of. See ASHE, Ven (Francis) John

LYNN, Suffragan Bishop of. (NOT APPOINTED AT TIME OF GOING TO PRESS)

LYON, Mrs Rosemary Jane, BA, MA, PGCE
13 New Acres Newburgh Wigan WN8 7TU [BLACKBURN] *b* 1962 *educ* Ormskirk Grammar Sch; St Aidan's Coll Dur Univ; York Univ; Lon Univ; *CV* Teacher Cardinal Vaugh Mem Sch 1985–88; Vol Pastoral Asst Dioc Argentina 1988–89; Cowley High Sch 1989–90; Chester Catholic High Sch 1990–92; Tarporley County Sch 1992–93; Ormskirk Grammar Sch 1993–94; Maricourt Catholic High Sch from 2002; St Mary's Catholic Pri Sch from 2002; M W Dev Gp Blackb; Elected to GS 2010
GS 2010–   *Tel:* 01257464541
email: Rosie.jl46@yahoo.co.uk

MACCLESFIELD, Archdeacon of. See Bishop, Ven Ian Gregory

MacLEAY, Revd Angus Murdo, MA, M Phil
Rectory Rectory Lane Sevenoaks TN13 1JA [ROCHESTER] *b* 1959 *educ* The Vyne Basingstoke; Qu Mary's Sixth Form Coll Basingstoke; Univ Coll Ox; Wycliffe Hall Ox; *CV* C H Trin Platt, Man 1988–92; V St Jo Houghton w. St Pet Kingmoor, Carl 1992–2001; R St Nich Sevenoaks from 2001; M Angl-Meth Formal Conversations 1998–2001; M Dioc Syn; M Revision Cttee for Consecration and Ordination of Women Measure
GS 1995–2001; 2005–   *Tel:* 01732 740340
Fax: 01732 742810
email: office@stnicholas-sevenoaks.org

MAGOWAN, Rt Revd Alistair James, B Sc, Dip HE, M Th (Oxon)
Bishop's House Corvedale Road Craven Arms SY7 9BT [SUFFRAGAN BISHOP OF LUDLOW, HEREFORD] *b* 1955 *educ* K Sch Worc; Leeds Univ; Trin Coll Bris; Westmr Coll Ox; *CV* C St Jo Bapt Owlerton 1981–84; C St Nic Dur 1984–89; Chapl St Aid Coll Dur 1984–89; V St Jo Bapt Egham 1989–2000; RD Runnymede 1993–2000; Chair Guidf Dioc Bd of Educ 1996–2000; Adn of Dorset 2000–09; Suff Bp of

Ludlow from 2009; Adn of Ludlow from 2009; Chair Salis DBE 2004–09
GS 1995–2000, 2004–10   *Tel:* 01588 673571
Fax: 01588 673671
email: bishopofludlow@btinternet.com

MAIDSTONE, Archdeacon of. See DOWN, Ven Philip Roy

MAIDSTONE, Suffragan Bishop of. (NOT APPOINTED AT TIME OF GOING TO PRESS)

MALCOURONNE, Mr Keith Robert, MA, FCA, CF
20 Riverside Rd Staines TW18 2LE [GUILDFORD] *b* 1959 *educ* Sutton Manor Gr Sch; New Coll Ox; *CV* Chair Insight Management & Systems Consultants Ltd from 2005; Dir Globus Energy plc from 2007; Fin Dir The Specialist Washing Company Ltd from 2007; Managing ptnr, Bolton Colby Chartered Accountants 1993–2005; Fin ptnr BC technologies LLP from 2000; Man Dir Heathrow Corporate Consulting Ltd from 2005; Dir and Chair Bd Fin and Audit Ctee, World Vision UK; Chartered Accountant, corporate financier and bus consult from 1983; Nat Chair of Crusaders 1991–97; Chair Berega Relief Equipment and Devel Trust from 2001; Treas Ox Cen for Miss Studies; Vc-Chair AC Audit Cttee from 2006; Chair Fin and Audit Ctee Urban Saints; M Guildf Dioc Bp's Coun and DBF exec, Dioc Audit Cttee; Lay Chair Runnymede Dny
GS 2005–   *Tel:* 01784 455501
07990 511905 (Mobile)
email: keith@bc-group.co.uk

MALLARD, Mrs Zahida, Dip Mgt Studies
17 The Crescent Crossflatts Bingley BD16 2EU [BRADFORD] *b* 1968 *educ* Westborough High Sch Dewsbury; Dewsbury and Batley Tech and Art Coll; Wulfrun Coll Wolverhampton; Wolverhampton Poly; Bradf Univ; Queen's Birm Th Coll; *CV* Welfare Rights Officer from 1992; Welfare Rights Manager from 2000; M DBE; M Dioc Bd for Ch in Society; Dioc Link Person to CMEAC; M MPA Coun; M Bradf Com Legal Services Advice Partnership Bd; Common Purpose Graduate; Bp's Counc Bradf from 2003; Brd Edu 2006–09; Lay Canon from 2010
GS 2000–   *Tel:* 01274 562640 (Home)
01274 435174 (Office)
07931 761202 (Mobile)
email: zahidamallard@yahoo.co.uk

MALLETT, Revd Dr Marlene Rosemarie, BA, PhD
St John's Vicarage 49 Wiltshire Road London SW9 7NE [SOUTHWARK] *b* 1959 *educ* Foxford Comp Sch; Sussex Univ; Warwick Univ; SEITE; *CV* AC Ch Ch North Brixton 2004–07; C Exec Off, Brent Mental Health Consortium 200204; Rsrch Sociologist, Med Rsrch Counc 1991–2002; Academic Co-ord, Centre for Caribbean Med, Guys, Kings & St. Thomas' Med Sch, 2001–02; Hon. Lect, Dept. of Legal, Political & Social Sciences, South

Bank Univ 1995–97; Rsrch Fellow Institute of Social & Economic Rsrch, Univ of the West Indies, Cave Hill Campus, 1989–90; Rsrch Consult, Swedish International Development Agency, Addis Ababa 1988; Project Admin Rsrch Co-op Adv Grp, 1987–88; Rsrch Consult Women & Development Project, Commonwealth Secr HQ, 1986–87; Rsrch Asst, Institute of Development Studies, 1985–86; Rsrch Admin, Institute of Development Studies, 1983–85; Rsrcher/Admin Eastern & Southern African Universities Rsrch Project, ESAURP, Univ of Dar es Salaam, 1982–83; P-in-C St. John the Evan, Angell Town from 2007; M Dioc Syn from 205; Convenor of Kingston Area Minority Ethnic Anglican Concerns Cttee 2006; M Dioc Minority Ethnic Anglican Concerns Cttee 2006; M Kingston Area Forum 2007;'M Dioc Litt Cttee from 2008
GS 2010–   *Tel:* 0207 733 0585
     email: rosemarie.mallett@btinternet.com

MALMESBURY, Archdeacon of. (NOT APPOINTED AT TIME OF GOING TO PRESS)

MAN, Archdeacon of. See SMITH, Ven Brian

MANCHESTER, Archdeacon of. See ASHCROFT, Ven Mark

MANCHESTER, Bishop of. See McCULLOCH, Rt Revd Nigel Simeon

MANCHESTER, Dean of. See GOVENDER, Very Revd Rogers Morgan

MANDELBROTE, Mr Giles Howard, MA, FSA
Lambeth Palace Library London SE1 7JU [LIBRARIAN AND ARCHIVIST, LAMBETH PALACE LIBRARY] *b* 1961 *educ* Eton Coll; St John's Coll Ox; *CV* Editor Quiller Press (publishers) 1989–92; Curatorial Officer, Royal Commission on Historical Manuscripts 1992–95; Curator, British Collections 1501–1800, British Library 1995–2010; Librarian and Archivist, Lambeth Palace Library from 2010   *Tel:* 020 7898 1266
                   Fax: 020 7898 7932
   email: giles.mandelbrote@c-of-e.org.uk

MANSELL, Ven Clive Neville Ross, LLB, Dip HE
3 The Ridings Blackhurst Lane Tunbridge Wells TN2 4RU [ARCHDEACON OF TONBRIDGE; ROCHESTER] *b* 1953 *educ* City of Lon Sch; Leic Univ; Coll of Law; Trin Coll Bris; *CV* Solicitor (no longer practising); C Gt Malvern Priory 1982–85; Min Can Ripon Cathl 1985–89; R Kirklington w Burneston, Wath and Pickhill 1989–2002; AD Wensley 1998–2002; Archdeacon of Tonbridge from 2002; M Revision Cttee on the Draft Churchwardens Measure; M Legal Aid Commn from 1996; Ch Commr from 1997–2008 (M Ch Commissioners' Assets Cttee, Red Chs Cttee); M Revision Cttee on Draft Amending Canon No 22; M Revision Cttee on

Draft C of E (Misc Provisions) Measure and Draft Amending Canon No 23; Chair Strg Cttee C of E Pensions (Amendment) Measure; M Strg Cttee, Common Worship Ordinal,M Dioc Bd of Educ; M Dioc Bd of Patronage; M Dioc Rural Adv Grp; Chair Ch in Society; M Bp's Coun; formerly Chair of Dioc Bd for Mission, Ecumenism and Parish Devt, M Eccl Law Soc; Dep Prolocutor N Province/Prov of York 2001–02; M Appeal Panel for Internal Syn Elections and Elections of Convocations; M GS Panel of Chairmen (2003–2010,; Ch Revision Cttee on Draft Bps and Ps (Consecration and Ord of Women) Measure; M Nat Adns Forum 2003–2010; Chair of Adns on GS; Simeon's Trustee 2003–08; Foundation Fell Univ of Gloucestershire
GS 1995–   *Tel:* 01892 520660
     email: archdeacon.tonbridge@
                rochester.anglican.org

MANTLE, Dr Richard John, FRSA
Cleveland House Barrowby Lane Kirkby Overblow Yorkshire HG3 1HQ [RIPON AND LEEDS] *b* 1947 *educ* Tiffin Sch; Ealing Coll of Higher Ed; *CV* Deputy Managing Dir, ENO 1979–85; Managing Dir Scottish Opera 1985–91; Gen Dir Edmonton Opera Canada, 1991–94; Guardian of the Holy House, Shrine of Our Lady of Walsingham from 1999; Gen Dir Opera North from 1994
GS 2010–   *Tel:* 01423 81592
     email: richard.mantle@operanorth.co.uk

MARRIOTT, Major General Patrick Claude, PSC, HCSC, CBE
Government House Royal Military Academy Sandhurst Camberley GU15 4PE [REPRESENTATIVE, ARMED FORCES SYNOD] *b* 1958 *educ* Gresham's Sch, Holt; *CV* Military service in Germany, UK inc N Ireland, Canada, Israel, Egypt, Bosnia, Kosovo, Norway, USA, Hong Kong, Oman, Kuwait, Iraq; Commanding Officer The Queen's Royal Lancers 1998–2000; Chief of Staff HQ 1 (UK) Armoured Division (invasion of Iraq); Commander 7th Armoured Brigade 2005–07; Asst Unit of Staff (operations) Joint Headquarters, Northwood; Commandant Royal Military Academy Sandhurst from 2009
GS 2005–   *Tel:* 01276 412206
     email: marriottpckh@hotmail.com

MARSHALL, Dr Edmund Ian, MA, Ph D
37 Roundwood Lane Harpenden Herts AL5 3BP [ST ALBANS] *b* 1940 *educ* Humberstone Foundn Sch Clee; Magd Coll Ox; Liv Univ; *CV* Univ Lect Liv and Hull 1962–66; Mathematician in Industry 1967–71; MP Goole 1971–83; Lect in Management Science Bradf Univ 1984–2000; Vc-Pres Meth Conf 1992–93; M Dioc Syn from 1996; M Bp's Coun 1997–2007; M Dioc Pastl Cttee 1998–2007; Bp's Adv for Ecum Affairs Wakef 1998–2007; Chair Wakef Cathl Com Cttee 2000–07; Rdr 1994–2007; M Wakef Cathl Chap 2003–07; M CCU from

2006; Chair Rev Ctee for Diocs Pastl and Miss Measure 2006; Reader St Alb Dioc from 2008 GS 2000–   Tel: 01582 461236
email: edmund.marshall@btinternet.com

MARTIN, Mrs (Bridget Elizabeth) Anne, B Ed, M Mus, M Phil, LTCL
8 Woodberry Close Chiddingfold GU8 4SF [GUILD-FORD] *b* 1949 *educ* Whyteleafe Gr Sch; Homerton Coll Cam; Lon Univ Inst of Educ; Surrey Univ; Trin Coll of Music; *CV* Primary sch music special-ist in state (inc ch schs) and private sectors in Suffolk, Cambs and Germany 1972–79; lect in music, Basford Hall FE Coll Nottm 1982–84; head of music, St Ives Prep Sch, Haslemere 1988–96; rsch Renaissance music Surrey Univ 1996–98; music tchr, Tormead Sch Guildf 1998–2001; head of music, St Teresa's Prep Sch 2001–04; presently working as specialist recorder tchr in state and private sectors; arranger, writer, adjudicator and conductor; M Godalming Dny Syn and Guildf DBE from 2006; long serving M of ch choir; involved with Chr Aid locally for 20 yrs
GS 2005–   Tel: 01428 683854
email: be_anne_martin@hotmail.com

MASON, Canon Dr John Philip, MA PhD CChem FRSC
3 Flaxyards Eaton Lane Tarporley CW6 9GL [CHES-TER] *b* 1959 *educ* King George V Sch; Ch Coll Cam; Birm Univ; *CV* Rsrch Scientist, Harwell Labora-tory 1980–85; Rsrch & Business Mgr, AEA Tech-nology 1986–94; Programme/Business Mgr, Laboratory of the Government Chemist (LGC) 1994–2002; Dir LGC Grp Holdings plc 2002–06; Dioc Sec, Chester 2006–10
GS 2010–   Tel: 01829 733971
email: johnpmason@gmail.com

MAURICE, Rt Revd Peter David, BA, Dip Th
The Palace Wells BA5 2SU [SUFFRAGAN BISHOP OF TAUNTON; BATH AND WELLS] *b* 1951 *educ* Purley Gr Sch; St Chad's Coll Dur; Mirfield Th Coll; Westmr Coll Ox; *CV* C St Paul Wimbledon Park 1975–79; TV All SS East Sheen 1979–85; V H Trin Rother-hithe 1985–96; RD Bermondsey 1991–96; V All SS Tooting 1996–2003; Adn of Wells 2003–06; Bp of Taunton from 2006   Tel: 01749 672341
Fax: 01749 679355
email: bishop.taunton@bathwells.anglican.org

McCLURE, Ven Tim (Timothy Elston), BA
10 Great Brockeridge Bristol BS9 3TY [ARCHDEACON OF BRISTOL] *b* 1946 *educ* Kingston Gr Sch; St Jo Coll Dur; Ridley Hall Th Coll; *CV* C Kirkheaton 1970–73; Marketing Mgr Agrofax L.I.P. Ltd 1973–74; C St Ambrose Chorlton-on-Medlock 1974–79; TR Whitworth Man and Presiding Chapl 1979–82; Chapl Man Poly 1974–82; Gen Sec SCM 1982–92; Dir Chs Coun for Ind and Social Resp 1992–99; Lord Mayor's Chapl Bris 1996–99; Hon Can Bris Cathl from 1992; Adn of Bris from 1999;

Chair Traidcraft plc 1990–97; Chair Chr Conf Trust 1998–2003; Chair Social Enterprise Works from 2000   Tel: 0117 962 2438 (Home)
0117 962 1433 (Office)
07725 047318 (Mobile)
Fax: 0117 962 9438
email: tim.mcclure@bristoldiocese.org

McCULLOCH, Rt Revd Nigel Simeon, MA; Hon DCL
Bishopscourt Bury New Rd Manchester M7 4LE [BISHOP OF MANCHESTER] *b* 1942 *educ* Liv Coll; Selw Coll Cam; Cuddesdon Th Coll; *CV* C Elles-mere Port 1966–70; Chapl Ch Coll Cam 1970–73; Dir of Th Studies Ch Coll Cam 1970–75; Dioc Missr Norw Dioc 1973–78; R SS Thos & Edm Sarum 1978–86; Adn of Sarum 1979–86; Chair ABM Finance Cttee 1987–92; Bp of Taunton 1986–92; Bp of Wakef 1992–2002; Chair Dec of Evang Stg Grp 1989–98; Chair Communications Cttee 1993–98; Lord High Almoner from 1997; Chair BM Miss, Evang and Renewal Cttee 1998–99; Chair Statistics Rev Grp 1998–2000; Chair Sand-ford St Mart Trust and Relig in Broadcasting Grp 1999–2008; Bp of Manchester from 2002; M Ho of Lords Cttees on BBC and Communications from 2005; Chair Coun of Chr and Jews from 2007; Chair Women in the Episcopate Legislation Grp 2006–09; Chair Steering Gp for Women in the Episcopate Legis Revision from 2009
GS 1990–   Tel: 0161 792 2096 (Office)
Fax: 0161 792 6826
email: bishop@
bishopscourt.manchester.anglican.org

McCURDY, Ven Hugh Kyle,
Whitgift House The College Ely CB7 4DL [ARCH-DEACON OF HUNTINGDON AND WISBECH; ELY] *b* 1958 *educ* Geo Abbot Sch Guild; Portsm Poly; Cardiff Univ; Trin Coll Bris; *CV* C St Jo Egham 1985–88; C St Jo Woking 1988–91; V St Andr His-ton 1991–2005; P-in-c St Andr Impington 1998–2005; RD N Stowe 1994–2005; Adn of Hunting-don and Wisbech from 2005; M DAC, Pastl Cttee, Bp's Coun; Acting Dir of Miss; Trustee Cam-bridgeshire ACRE; Gov Wisbech Grammar Sch; M Cam Theol Federation Coun; M Coun Ridley Hall Th Coll; M CPAS Coun of Reference
GS 2010–
Tel: 01353 658404 01353 652709 (Office)
email: archdeacon.handw@ely.anglican.org

McDONALD, Very Revd Alan Douglas, LLB, BD, MTH, DLitt, DD
1 Cairnhill Gardens St Andrews Fife KY16 8QY [CHURCH OF SCOTLAND] *b* 1951 *educ* Glas Acad-emy; Strathclyde Univ; Edin Univ; St Andrews Univ; New Coll Edin; *CV* Comm Min, Edin 1979–83; P Min Holburn Central, Aberdeen 1983–98; P Min St Leonards, St Andrews from 1998;

Convener Ch and Nation Cttee 2000–04; Moderator Gen Ass C of S from 2006
GS 2010–   *Tel:* 01334472793
          email: alan.d.mcdonald@talk21.com

McDONOUGH, Canon Philip Michael James,
B Sc
28 Washbrook Close Barton-le-Clay MK45 4LF [ST ALBANS] *b* 1939 *educ* Wandsworth Tech Coll Lon; Imp Coll Lon; *CV* Asst Chapl Luton and Dunstable Hosp 1996–2004; Rdr from 1985; Sec St Alb Dioc Rdrs Assoc 1995–2004; M CRC Exec 1999–2004; M AC Min Div VRSC 2000–05; M C of E Hosp Chapl Coun, Coun St Alb Cathl from 2001; Lay Chair Ampthill Dny Syn from 2002; Hon Can St Alb Cathl from 2002; Hon Can St Alb Cathl 2002–09, Emeritus 2009; Associate Sec CRC 2004–05; Trustee Br Red Cross Soc Staff Pension Fund from 2006
GS 2000–   *Tel:* 01582 881772
                        07759 444879 (Mobile)
     email: canonpmcdonough@btinternet.com

McFARLANE, Ven Janet (Jan) Elizabeth,
B Med Sci, BA, Dip Min Std
31 Bracondale Norwich NR1 2AT [ARCHDEACON OF NORWICH] *b* 1964 *educ* Blythe Bridge High Sch Stoke-on-Trent; Sheff Univ; Dur Univ; Cranmer Hall Dur; *CV* Speech therapist 1987–90; C Stafford TM, Lich 1993–96; Chapl and Min Can, Ely Cathl 1996–99; Norw Dioc Communications Officer 1999–2009; Chapl to Bp of Norw 2001–09; Hon PV Nor Cath 2000–09; M Bp's Coun, Dioc Syn, Dioc Communications Cttee; Adn Norwich from 2009; Dioc Dir of Communications from 2009
GS 2005–   *Tel:* 01603 620007
          email: archdeacon.norwich@
                   norwich.anglican.org

McGINLEY, Revd John Charles, BSc, BA
5 Ratcliffe Road Leicester LE23TE [LEICESTER] *b* 1969 *educ* Hewett Comp Sch, Norwich; Birm Univ; Trinity Coll Bris; *CV* Asst Buyer, Harrods Ltd, 1990–93; Asst C, Holy Trinity w St Paul, Hounslow 1996–2000; TV Holy Trinity w St John, Hinckley 2000–05; TR Holy Trinity w St John, Hinckley 2005–09; V Holy Trinity Leic from 2009;
GS 2010–   *Tel:* 0116 2548981
     email: vicar@holytrinityleicester.org

MCGREGOR, Revd Alexander Scott, MA
Legal Office Church House Great Smith St London SW1P 3AZ [DEPUTY LEGAL ADVISER TO THE ARCHBISHOPS' COUNCIL and the GENERAL SYNOD] *b* 1972 *educ* John Lyon Sch Harrow; Ch Ch Ox; Coll of Law; Inns of Court Sch of Law; St Albans and Ox Min Course; *CV* Barrister in independent practice 1996–2005; Legal Adviser in the Legal Office of the NCIs 2006–08; Deputy Legal Adviser to the Archbishops' Coun and the GS from 2009; M The Honourable Soc of Lincoln's Inn from 1994; M Dacorum Boro Coun 1999–

2007; Assistant C (NSM) St Mary Harrow 2006–09; Assistant C (NSM) St Barnabas Pimlico and St Mary Bourne Street from 2009; Deputy Chancellor Dioc of Ox from 2007   *Tel:* 020 7898 1748
     email: alexander.mcgregor@c-of-e.org.uk

MCINTYRE, Revd Eva, MA (Oxon)
The Vicarage Church Avenue Stourport on Severn DY13 9DD [WORCESTER] *b* 1960 *educ* Parkstone Grammar School for Girls; Worcester Colleg oxford; St Stephen's House; *CV* Dss St James Devizes 1984–6; Dn Oakdale team Ministry 1986–8; Producer Religious Programmes BBC Radio Leeds 1988–90; Producer BBC 1990–1; Area Co-ordinator Christian Aid 1992–8; Freelance writer; R Bangor Monachorum and Worthenbury, Church in Wales 1998–2003; Co-ordinating Chaplain HMP Brockhill 2003–06; V Stourport on Severn and Wilden from 2006   *Tel:* 01299 822041
          email: evacymm@btinternet.com

McISSAC, Mrs Debra, BA, LLB/D. Jur. Law Soc of Eng & Wales
Parsonage Farm House White Way Pitton Wiltshire SP5 1DT [SALISBURY] *b* 1953 *educ* Marian High Sch, Saskatchewan; Canada Univ of Saskatchewan; Osgoode Hall, York Univ, Canada; Wycliffe Hall; Ripon Coll Cuddesdon; *CV* Adv, Off of the Ombudsman, Province of Saskatchewan, 1973; Spec Adv, Minister of Justice, Ottawa, 1975; Barrister and Solicitor, Edmonton, Alberta, Canada 1976–83; Barrister and Solicitor, Toronto, Canada 1983–85; Solicitor, Durrant Piesse, London, England 1985–86; Solicitor, Freshfields, Lon 1986–88; Dir Prof Devlp, Lovells, Lon, 1989–2000; Chief Monitor,Training Contracts, Law Soc of Eng & Wales, 2000–06; Principal, D Ball Consulting 2000–10; Legal Ed and Training Grp; Treasurer,1994–96; Chair, 1996–98; Lord Chancellor's Adv Cttee Ed & Conduct Standing Conf, 1994–99; Advocacy Sub-cttee of Law Soc's Training Cttee, 1998–2008; Counc of the Law Soc of Eng & Wales; Counc M, 2005–08; Chair, Ed & Training Cttee, 2005-08; M, Regulatory Affairs Grp, 2005–07; M, Regulatory Affairs Brd, 2007–08; Adv Sarum Archdeaconry Miss &Pstrl Cttee, Salis from 2010; Lay Chair, Alderbury Deanery Syn, Salis Dioc from 2010; Alderbury Deanery Standing & Pstrl Cttee, from 2005
GS 2010–
     Tel: 01722712758, 02073738742 07879662188
                        email: db@dball.com

McKITTRICK, Ven Douglas Henry,
2 Yorklands Dyke Rd Avenue Hove BN3 6RW [ARCHDEACON OF CHICHESTER] *b* 1953 *educ* John Marley Comp Sch, Newcastle-upon-Tyne; St Steph Ho Ox; *CV* C St Paul Deptford, S'wark 1977–80; C St Jo Tuebrook, Liv 1980–81; TV St Steph Grove St, Liv 1981–89; V St Agnes Toxteth Pk, Liv 1989–97; V St Pet with Chapel Royal Brighton, Chich from 1997; RD of Brighton from 1998; Can and Preb of Chich Cathl from 1998;

Archdeacon of Chichester from 2002; M DAC, Bd of Educ, DBF, Pastl Cttee, Parsonages Cttee; Bp's Adv Hosp Chaplaincy; Coun M Additional Curates Soc 2005; M Hosp Chapl Coun 2006; Bp's Adv on Ecumenism
GS 2004–   *Tel:* 01273 505330 (Home)
                                        01273 421021 (Office)
                                        Fax: 01273 421041
email: archchichester@diochi.org.uk

McLEAN, Revd (Margaret Anne) Maggie, MA
Battyeford Vicarage 107A Stocks Bank Road Mirfield WF14 9QT [WAKEFIELD] *b* 1962 *educ* Greenhead Gr Sch; Birm Univ; Heythrop Coll; Cranmer Hall Dur; Queens Th Coll; *CV* C All Saints Church, Bedford 1991–94; Chapl St.Albans High Sch for Girls 1994–98; Assoc P St.Alb Abbey; Asst Social Responsibility Adv 1998–99; Anglican Chapl, Univ of Huddersfield 1999–2002; P-in-C St.Philip and St.James, Scholes and St.Luke and Whitechapel, Cleckheaton 2002–09; P-in-C Christ the King, Battyeford 2009; DiocTraining Off
GS 2010–   *Tel:* 01924493277
email: m.a.mclean@btinternet.com

McMULLEN, Mrs Christine Elizabeth, BA,
Dip Ad Ed, MA
Farm Cottage Montpelier Place Buxton SK17 7EJ [DERBY] *b* 1943 *educ* Homelands Sch Derby; R Holloway Coll Lon; Nott Univ; Derby Univ; *CV* Rdr from 1986; Dir of Pastl Studies Nn Ord Course from 1994, Vc-Prin from 2005; Lay Chair Buxton Dny from 2005; M DRACS from 2000; Lay M Derby Cathl Chapter from 2000; M Ch Commrs Pastl Cttee from 2001
GS 1990–   *Tel:* 01298 73997
                                        0161 249 2511
email: christine@thenoc.org.uk

McPHATE, Very Revd Prof Gordon Ferguson,
BA, MA, M Th, M Sc, MB, Ch B, MD, FRCP
The Deanery 7 Abbey St Chester CH1 2JF [DEAN OF CHESTER] *b* 1950 *educ* Perth Gr Sch; Cam Univ; Aberd Univ; Edin Univ; Surrey Univ; Westcott Ho Cam; *CV* Lect in Physiology, Guy's Hosp Lon 1979–84; Hon C Sanderstead, S'wark 1978–80; Hon PV and Sacrist, S'wark Cathl 1980–86; Registrar in Chemical Pathology, Guildf Hosps 1984–86; Lect and Sen Lect in Pathology, Univ of St Andr 1986–2002; Hon Angl Chapl, Univ of St Andr 1986–2002; Consult Chemical Pathologist, Fife Hosps 1993–2002; Dean of Chester from 2002; Vis Prof of Theol, Univ of Chester from 2003
GS 2004–05   *Tel:* 01244 500971
email: dean@chestercathedral.com

McPHERSON, Mrs Katherine, MBA, BA
59 Mycenae Rd London SE3 7SE [APPOINTED MEMBER, ARCHBISHOPS' COUNCIL] *b* 1964 *educ* P. L. Meth Girls' Sch Singapore; Temasek Jun Coll Singapore; Nat Univ of Singapore; Univ of Kent; *CV* Exec Consult, Ernst and Young Singapore 1987–92; Sen Mgr, Ernst and Young Lon 1992–95;

Lon Hd of Sales and Marketing (Media & Resources), Ernst and Young 1996–98; Nat Hd of Sales and Marketing (Telecoms, Media & Entertainment), Ernst and Young 1998–99; Project Dir (secondment), BBC Mar-Nov 1999; Managing Consult, Cap Gemini Ernst and Young 1999–2001; Operations Dir, YMCA Lambeth, Lewisham and S'wark 2001–2002; Dir Business Devel and Marketing, EMEA, White and Case 2002–04; Apptd M AC 2003–09; Head of Bus Devel, Corporate Div, Herbert Smith 2004–05; Head of Bus Devel, Europe, Herbert Smith 2005–07; Head Winning Business, Global Markets, KPMG from 2007
GS 2003–   *Tel:* 020 8858 1856 (Home)
                                        07984 046149 (Mobile)
email: katherine.mcpherson@kpmg.co.uk

MEARA, Ven David Gwynne, MA, S.Th, FSA
Rectory St Brides Church Fleet St London EC4Y 8AU [ARCHDEACON OF LONDON] *b* 1947 *educ* Merchant Taylor's Sch Northwood; Oriel Coll Ox; Cuddesdon Theol Coll; *CV* C Ch Ch Reading 1973–77; Chapl Univ of Reading 1977–82; V Basildon Aldworth and Ashampstead 1982–94; RD Bradfield 1990–94; R Buckinham 1994–2000; AD Buckingham 1994–2000; Chair Ox Dioc Adv Gp on Miss 1990–2000; R St Bride's Fleet St from 2000; Adn of Lon from 2009; Hon Can Ch Ch Ox; M Lon DAC from 2009; M Dioc Syn from 2009
                                        Tel: 020 7427 0133
                                        020 7236 7891
                                        Fax: 020 7583 4867
email: archdeacon.london@london.anglican.org

MELLOR, Very Revd (Kenneth) Paul, BA, MA
The Deanery Cornet St St Peter Port Guernsey GY1 1BZ [DEAN OF GUERNSEY; WINCHESTER] *b* 1949 *educ* Ashfield Sch, Kirkby-in-Ashfield; Southn Univ; Leeds Univ; Mirfield Th Coll; Cuddesdon Th Coll; *CV* C St Mary V Cottingham 1973–76; C All SS Ascot 1976–80; V St Mary Magd Tilehurst 1980–85; V Menheniot 1985–94; RD E Wivelshire 1990–94; Hon Can Truro Cathl 1990–94; Chair Dioc Bd of Miss and Unity 1990–95; CFCE 1996–2000; Can Treas Truro Cathl 1994–2003; Dean of Guernsey from 2003
GS 1994–2003; 2005–   *Tel:* 01481 720036
                                        07720 506863 (Mobile)
                                        Fax: 01481 722948
email: paul@townchurch.org.gg

MEON, Archdeacon of The. (NOT APPOINTED AT TIME OF GOING TO PRESS)

MESSHAM, Canon Barbara Lynn, Cert Ed
18 Vicarage Gate Guildford Surrey GU2 7QJ [GUILDFORD] *b* 1952 *educ* Christ's Hosp Girls' High Sch; Nott Univ; Bretton Hall Coll; STETS; *CV* Maths Tchr, 1975–96; AC St Thomas-on-the-Bourne, Farnham 1999–2003; V, All Saints' Church, Guildford from 2003; Rural Dean of Guildford, from

WHO'S WHO

2006; Hon Can Guild Cathl from 2010; M Guild Dioc Syn
GS 2010–   Tel: 01483 572006
          email: barbara@messhams.co.uk

MEYRICK, Very Revd (Cyril) Jonathan, MA
(Oxon)
The Deanery 10 Cathedral Close Exeter EX1 1EZ
[DEAN OF EXETER] *b* 1952 *educ* Lancing Coll; St Jo Coll Ox; Salis & Well Th Coll; *CV* C Bicester, Ox 1976–78; Bp's Chapl, Ox 1978–81; OT tutor, Codrington Coll, Barbados 1981–84; TV Burnham Team, Ox 1984–90; TR Tisbury, Salis 1990–98; RD Chalke, Sarum 1997–98; Res Can Roch 1998–2005; acting Dean of Roch 2002–04; Dean of Exeter from 2005; Chair Coun for Miss & Unity from 2005   Tel: 01392 273509
                                            01392 431266
                                   Fax: 01392 285986
     email: dean@exeter-cathedral.org.uk

MIDDLESEX, Archdeacon of. See WELCH, Ven Stephan John

MIDDLETON, Suffragan Bishop of. See DAVIES, Rt Revd Mark

MILLAR, Revd Dr Sandra, BA; MA; PhD; DipTh; DipMin
18 Overbury Road Gloucester GL1 4EA [GLOUCESTER] *b* 1957 *educ* Rugby High Sch for Girls; Univ Coll, Cardiff; Warwick Univ; Ripon Coll, Cuddesdon; *CV* Product mgr, Boots Company, 1979–84; Product mgr, Coop 1984–88; Sales/Marketing Mgr, Windsor Foods 1989–91; Sales/Marketing Mgr, SU 1991–93; National Dir Kings Kids England 1994–98; AC, Chipping Barnet w Arkley 2000–03; TV, Dorchester Team and tutor at Ripon Coll Cuddesdon 2003–07; Children's Off, Glouc from 2007; Brd for Christian Devlp, St Alb 2000–03; Dioc Syn, St. Alb 2000–03; Gov of SAOMC 2001–06; M Miss Initiatives Grp, from 2007; M Bps Worship, Prayer and Spirituality Grp from 2007
GS 2010–   Tel: 01452 835554 07976 823986
                email: smillar@glosdioc.org.uk

MILLER, Ven Geoff (Geoffrey Vincent), B Ed, MA
80 Moorside North Fenham Newcastle-upon-Tyne NE4 9DU [ARCHDEACON OF NORTHUMBERLAND; NEWCASTLE] *b* 1956 *educ* Sharston High Sch, Manch; Dur Univ; St Jo Coll Nottm; Newc Univ; *CV* C Jarrow 1983–86; TV St Aidan Billingham 1986–92; Dioc Urban Devel Officer 1991–99; Com Chapl Stockton-on-Tees 1992–94; P-in-c St Cuth Darlington 1994–96, V 1996–99; Dioc Urban Officer and Res Can Newc Cathl 1999–2005; Adn of Northumberland from 2005; M DAC; M Dioc Pastl Cttee; M Fin, Pastl, Parsonages, Priorities & Planning cttees and Strat Dev Gp of Bp's Coun; M Dioc Child Protection Cttee; M Shepherd's Dene, Sons of Clergy, Ch Inst, Hosp of God at

Greatham, Lord Crewe Trust; Chair Br Cttee of French Protestant Industrial Miss
                                   Tel: 0191 273 8245
                                   Fax: 0191 226 0286
        email: g.miller@newcastle.anglican.org

MILLS, Mr David John, MBE
51 Greenways Over Kellet Carnforth LA6 1DE [CARLISLE] *b* 1937 *CV* Senior Probation Officer (Rtd); Rdr; Bp's Selector Min Div; M Dioc Bd of Educ
GS 1985–   Tel: 01524 732194

MONCKTON, Mrs Joanna Mary,
Horsebrook Hall Brewood Stafford ST19 9LP [LICHFIELD] *b* 1941 *educ* Oxton Ho Sch Kenton Ex; *CV* High Sheriff of Staffordshire 1995–96; Dir Penk (Holdings) Ltd and Penk Ltd; Farm Partner; Housewife; Chairman Lichf Branch Prayer Book Soc 1982–2001; Shannon Trust rep for HMYOI Brinsford
GS 1990–   Tel: 01902 850288

MORGAN, Rt Revd Christopher Heudebourck,
Dip Th, BA, M Th
1 Fitzwalter Rd Lexden Colchester CO3 3SS [AREA BISHOP OF COLCHESTER; CHELMSFORD] *b* 1947 *educ* City of Bath Boys Sch; Lanc Univ; Heythrop Coll Lon; Kelham Th Coll; *CV* C Birstall 1973–76; Asst Chap Brussels 1976–80; P-in-c Redditch St Geo 1980–81; TV Redditch, The Ridge 1981–85; V Sonning 1985–96; Prin Berks Chr Tr Scheme 1985–89; Dir Pastl Studies St Alb and Ox Min Course 1992–95; Glouc Dioc Officer for Min 1996–2001; Dioc Can Res Glouc Cathl 1996–2001; Bp of Colchester from 2001   Tel: 01206 576648
                                   Fax: 01206 763868
    email: b.colchester@chelmsford.anglican.org

MORGAN, Mr David Geoffrey Llewelyn,
25 Newbiggen St Thaxted CM6 2QS [CHELMSFORD] *b* 1935 *educ* St Jo Sch Leatherhead; *CV* Rtd Solicitor; Company Dir; Chair Dioc Bd of Patr; M Dioc Fin Cttee from 1988; Trustee Victoria Clergy Fund from 1989; Chair Nat CU Coun from 1998; Gen Sec Guild of All Souls from 2003
GS 1990–   Tel: 01371 830132
                                   Fax: 01371 831430

MORGAN, Mrs Susan Deirdre, BA (Hons),
Chartered FCIPD, MHSM, FRSA
Church House Great Smith St London SW1P 3AZ [DIRECTOR OF HUMAN RESOURCES, ARCHBISHOPS' COUNCIL] *b* 1956 *educ* The Dame Alice Harpur Sch Bedford; N Lon Poly; *CV* Dir of Personnel Essex and Herts Health Services 1991–94; Dir Human Resources and Commercial Services Princess Alexandra Hosp NHS Trust Harlow 1994–97; Employers' rep on the Employment Tribunals for Engl and Wales from 1992; Personnel Dir CBF 1997–98; Dir of Human Resources to AC from 1998, serving all of the Nat Church Insts; M Race Panel of Employment Tribunals from 2002; Chair

Staff Cttee, Chelmsf Dioc from 2005; M Staff Sttee WHCM Counselling and Support from 2009
Tel: 020 7898 1565
email: su.morgan@c-of-e.org.uk

MORRIS, Revd Jane Elizabeth, BA, MSc, PGCE
156 Anson Road London NW2 6BH [LONDON] *b* 1960 *educ* Ealing Gr Sch; York Univ; NEOC; *CV* Tchr, Science at Tadcaster Gr Sch 1972–74; Head of Science at the Mount Sch, York 1974–92; Head of Science and Chapl, Queen Margaret's Sch, Escrick 1992–95; AC St Michael-le-Belfrey Church, York 1992–95; Assoc V St George's Church, Leeds 1995–2005; Brd of Studies, NEOC 1998–2002; Lder of West Yorkshire New Wine Network 2003–05; M of New Wine North Leadership 2003–05; TV of St Gabriel's Church, Cricklewood from 2005; Healing Ministry Adv in the Willesden Episcopal Area; M of the New Wine Leadership Team for Lon and the South East; Resource Church Leader for the Alpha Course
GS 2010–   Tel: 02084526305
email: jane.morris@st-gabriels.org

MORRIS, Ven Roger Anthony Brett, BSc (Hons), ARCS, MA (Cantab)
The Archdeacon's House Walkers Lane Whittington Worcester WR5 2RE [ARCHDEACON OF WORCESTER] *b* 1968 *educ* Chipping Sodbury Sch; Filton Tech Coll; Imperial Coll Lon; Trin Coll Cam; Ridley Hall Cam; *CV* Asst C of Northleach, W Hampnett and Farmington, Cold Aston, W Notgrove and Turkdean 1993–96; R of Sevenhampton w Charlton Abbotts, Hawling and Whittington, Dowdeswell w Andoversford, The Shiptons and Salperton, and Withington 1996–2003; Dir Par Devel and Evang, Cov 2003–08; Adn of Worc from 2008
email: rmorris@cofe-worcester.org.uk

MUGGERIDGE, Miss (Sara Ann) Sally, BA, MBA, Cert Th, FCIM, FCIPD, FRSA, MIOD
The Old Farm House Pike Road, Eythorne Dover Kent CT15 4DJ [CANTERBURY] *b* 1949 *educ* South Hampstead High Sch; Guildhall Sch Music and Drama; Westfield Coll, Lon Univ; Henley Management Coll; SE Inst Th Ed; *CV* "Chief Executive Industry and Parliament Trust 2003–2010 Development Director, Pearson plc 1999–2003 HR Director, Cable & Wireless (Asia Pacific) 1996–1999 Management Developm't Director, Cable & Wireless plc 1992–1996 Marketing Director Mercury Communications Ltd. 1990–1992" Trustee Foundn Ch Leadership 2003; Trustee Tutu Foundn UK 2003; M Counc, Kent Univ 2006; M Chartered Institute of Marketing Academic Senate 2005; M Chartered Dir Cttee IOD 2007; International President, The Malcolm Muggeridge Soc 2003; Middle Warden, The Worshipful Company of Marketors 1992; Lay M Sandwich Deanery Syn
GS 2010–   Tel: 01304 831964 07770 381911
email: sally@sallymuggeridge.com

MUNRO, Revd Dr Robert Speight, B Sc, BA, Dip Ap Th, PGCE, D Min
Rectory 1 Depleach Rd Cheadle SK8 1DZ [CHESTER] *b* 1963 *educ* William Hulme's Gr Sch Man; Bris Univ; All Souls Coll Lon; Man Univ; Oak Hill Th Coll; Refrmd Th Sem US; *CV* Teach Math and PE Hazel Grove HS 1987–1990; C St Jo Bapt Hartford 1993–97; R St Wilf Davenham 1997–2003; R St Mary Cheadle from 2003; M Bp's Coun from 2000
GS 2005–   Tel: 0161 428 3440 0161 428 8050
Fax: 0161 428 3440 0161 428 8050
email: rob@munro.org.uk

NAGEL, Mrs Mary Philippa, B Ed
Aldwick Vicarage 25 Gossamer Lane Bognor Regis PO21 3AT [CHICHESTER] *b* 1954 *educ* Worthing High Sch; Lon Univ; *CV* Section 23 Insp of Schs until 2005
GS 1990–   Tel: 01243 262049
email: nagel@aldwick.demon.co.uk

NEIL-SMITH, Mr (Noel) Jonathan, MA
Church House Great Smith St London SW1P 3AZ [ADMINISTRATIVE SECRETARY, CENTRAL SECRETARIAT] *b* 1959 *educ* Marlboro Coll; St Jo Coll Cam; *CV* On staff of Ch Commrs from 1981; Bishoprics Officer 1994–96; Seconded to GS from 1997; Asst Sec Ho of Bps 1997–98; Sec Ho of Bps from 1998; Hon Lay Can Guildf Cathl from 2002   Tel: 020 7898 1373
Fax: 020 7898 1369
email: jonathan.neil-smith@c-of-e.org.uk

NEWARK, Archdeacon of. See PEYTON, Ven Nigel

NEWCASTLE, Assistant Bishop of . See WHITE, Rt Revd Frank (Francis)

NEWCASTLE, Bishop of. See WHARTON, Rt Revd (John) Martin

NEWCASTLE, Dean of. See DALLISTON, Very Revd Christopher Charles

NEWCOME, Rt Revd James William Scobie, MA, FRSA
Holm Croft 13 Castle Rd Kendal LA9 7AU [BISHOP OF CARLISLE] *b* 1953 *educ* Marlboro Coll; Trin Coll Ox; Selw Coll Cam; Ridley Hall Th Coll; *CV* C All SS Leavesden 1978–82; Min Bar Hill LEP Ely 1982–94; Tutor Ridley Hall Cam 1983–88; V Dry Drayton 1990–94; RD N Stowe 1993–94; DDO Ches 1994–2000; Res Can Ches Cathl 1994–2002; Dioc Dir of Min 1996–2002; Suff Bp of Penrith 2002–09; Bp Carlisle from 2009; Chairman Dioc Bd of Min and Trg; Pres Chs Together in Cumbria; M Rural Bps Panel; M Bps CME Cttee; Chair Nat Stewardship Cttee
GS 2000–02   Tel: 01539 727836
Fax: 01539 734380
email: bishop.carlisle@carlislediocese.org.uk

NEWEY, Mr (Sidney) Brian, MA
Chestnut Cottage The Green South Warborough OX10 7DN [OXFORD] *b* 1937 *educ* Burton-upon-Trent Gr Sch; Worc Coll Ox; *CV* With Br Rail from 1960, Gen Mgr W Region 1984–87; Dir Regional Railways 1987–90; Asst to Chief Exec Br Rail 1990–93; Consult in transport 1993–96; rtd; M AC Fin Cttee; M AC Audit Cttee; M DRACSC; M Nat Soc Investment Cttee; Chair Ox DBF and assoc cttees
GS 2005–   *Tel:* 01865 858322
                                  Fax: 01865 858043

NEWMAN, Very Revd Adrian, B Sc, Dip Th, M Phil
The Deanery Priors Gate House Rochester ME1 1SR [DEAN OF ROCHESTER] *b* 1958 *educ* Rickmansworth Comp Sch; Bris Univ; Trin Coll Bris; *CV* C St Mark Forest Gate 1985–89; V Hillsborough and Wadsley Bridge, Sheff 1989–96; R St Mart in the Bull Ring, Birm 1996–2004; Dean of Roch from 2005; Hon Fell Cant Ch Ch Univ
                                  Tel: 01634 843366
                                       01634 202183
                               07963 066629 (Mobile)
                                  Fax: 01634 401410
            email: dean@rochestercathedral.org

NEWMAN, Ven David Maurice Frederick, BA, MA
Church House St Martin's East Leicester LE1 5FX [ARCHDEACON OF LOUGHBOROUGH; LEICESTER] *b* 1954 *educ* The Leys Sch Cam; Hertf Coll Ox; St John's Notts; *CV* Asst C Christ Church Orpington 1979–83; Asst C St Mary's Bushbury 1983–86; V All Saints Ockbrook and St Stephen's Borrowash 1986–1997; TR Emmanuel Loughborough and St Mary-in-Charnwood, Nanpanton 1997–2009; AD Akeley East deanery 1999–2006; Chair Ho Clergy Leic Dioc 2006–09; Adn of Loughborough from 2009   *Tel:* 0116 248 7421
            email: dmfnewman@talktalk.net

NOBLETT, Ven William Alexander, B Th, M Th
Room 310 Abell House John Islip St London SW1P 4LH [CHAPLAIN GENERAL OF THE NATIONAL OFFENDER MANAGEMENT SERVICE SCHEME] *b* 1953 *educ* High Sch Dub; Southn Univ; Ox Univ; Sarum and Wells Th Coll; *CV* C Sholing, Win 1978–80; Incumbent Ardamine, Kiltennel & Glascarrig 1980–82; Chapl RAF 1982–84; V St Thos Middlesbrough 1984–87; Dep Chapl HMP Wakefield 1987–89, Chapl 1989–92; Chapl HMP Norwich 1992–97; Chapl HMP Full Sutton 1997–2001; Chapl Gen HM Prisons from 2001; Can York Min from 2001; Chapl to the Queen 2005; Hon Can Liv Cath from 2009
GS 2001–   *Tel:* 020 7217 8997
                                       020 7217 8201
                                  Fax: 020 7217 8980
        email: william.noblett@noms.gsi.gov.uk

NORFOLK, Archdeacon of. See HAYDEN, Ven David Frank

NORTH, Revd Philip John, MA
The Rectory 191 St Pancras Way London NW1 9NH [LONDON] *b* 1966 *educ* The Latymer Sch, Edmonton; York Uni; St Stephen's House, Ox; *CV* AC S Mary and S Peter, Sunderland 1992–96; V Holy Trin, Hartlepool 1996–2002; Area Dean of Hartlepool 2000–02; P Administrator of the Shrine of Our Lady of Walsingham 2002–08; T R of the Parish of Old St Pancras from 2008
GS 2010–   *Tel:* 020 7485 5791
                        email: philip.north@mac.com

NORTH-WEST EUROPE, Archdeacon in. See DE WIT, Ven John

NORTHAMPTON, Archdeacon of. See ALLSOPP, Ven Christine

NORTHOLT, Archdeacon of. See TREWEEK, Ven Rachel

NORTHUMBERLAND, Archdeacon of. See MILLER, Ven Geoff (Geoffrey Vincent)

NORWICH, Archdeacon of. See McFARLANE, Ven Janet Elizabeth

NORWICH, Bishop of. See JAMES, Rt Revd Graham Richard

NORWICH, Dean of. See SMITH, Very Revd Graham Charles Morell

NOTTINGHAM, Archdeacon of. See HILL, Ven Peter

NUNN, Canon Andrew Peter, BA, BA
Southwark Cathedral London Bridge London SE1 9DA [SOUTHWARK] *b* 1957 *educ* Guthlaxton Upper Sch Wigston, Leic; Leic Poly; Leeds Univ; Coll of Resurr Mirfield; *CV* C St Jas Manston, Ripon 1983–87; C Leeds Richmond Hill 1987–91, V 1991–95; Chapl Agnes Stewart C of E High Sch, Leeds 1987–91; Personal Asst to Bp of S'wark 1995–99; Sub-Dean, Prec and Can Res S'wark Cathl from 1999; Wrdn of Rdrs, S'wark; Chair Dioc Liturg Cttee; Bp's Selector; M Dioc Syn; M S'wark Min and Trg Cttee
GS 2005–   *Tel:* 020 7367 6727
                                  Fax: 020 7367 6725
    email: andrew.nunn@southwark.anglican.org

O'BRIEN, Mr Gerald Michael, B Sc, DMS
Chestnuts 14 Oakhill Rd Sevenoaks Kent TN13 1NP [ROCHESTER] *b* 1948 *educ* Dulwich Coll; Bris Univ; *CV* Promotions Sec, ICS 1994–97; Dir of Communications, Crosslinks 1997–2002; M CEEC 1988–92, from 1996; M CPAS Coun 1999–2004
GS 1980–85, 1987–
                                  Tel: 01732 453894
                               07711 938517 (Mobile)
                      email: gmobrien@btinternet.com

OAKHAM, Archdeacon of. See PAINTER, Ven David Scott

OGLE, Very Revd Catherine, BA, MPhil, MA, MA
38 Goodby Road Moseley Birmingham B13 8NJ [DEAN OF BIRMINGHAM] *b* 1961 *educ* Perse Sch for Girls, Cam; Univ of Leeds; Fitzwilliam Coll Cam; Westcott Ho Cam; *CV* AC St Mary Middleton, Leeds 1988–91; Relig Programmes Ed BBC Leeds 1991–95; NSM St Margaret & All Hallows, Leeds 1991–95; P-in-C Woolley w W Bretton 1995–2001; Ed Wakef Dioc Magazine 1995–2001; V Huddersfield 2001–2010; Dean of Birmingham from 2010; M Wakef Dioc Liturgy Gp, Communications Gp, Dioc Syn; M Coun Coll of the Resurrection, Mirfield 2008–10; Hon Can Wakef Cathl from 2008   *Tel:* 0121 262 1840
          Fax: 0121 262 1860
email: dean@birminghamcathedral.com

OLDHAM, Mr Gavin David Redvers, MA (Cantab)
Ashfield House St Leonards Tring HP23 6NP [OXFORD; CHURCH COMMISSIONER] *b* 1949 *educ* Eton; Trin Coll Cam; *CV* Wedd Durlacher Mordaunt 1975–86, Partner 1984–86; Secretariat Barclays De Zoete Wedd (BZW) 1984–88; Chief Exec Barclayshare Ltd 1986–89, Chair 1989–90; Chair/Chief Exec The Share Cen Ltd from 1990; Chief Exec Share plc from 2000; Chair The Share Foundn from 2005; Ch Commr from 1999; M Fin Cttee AC from 2001; M Ethical Investment Adv Grp from 1999
GS 1995–   *Tel:* 01494 758348 (Home)
          01296 439100 (Office)
          07767 337696 (Mobile)
          Fax: 01296 414410
email: ceo@share.co.uk

OLIVER, Canon Thomas Gordon, L Th, B Th, Dip Ad Ed
The Rectory Shipley Hills Road, Meopham, Gravesend Kent DA13 0AD [ROCHESTER] *b* 1948 *educ* Whinney Hill Sec Mod Sch Dur; Dur Johnson Gr Tech Sch; Lon Coll of Div; St Jo Coll Nottm; *CV* C St Jo the Divine Thorpe Edge 1972–76; C St Mark Woodthorpe 1976–80; V All SS Huthwaite 1980–85; Dir Pastl Studies St Jo Coll Nottm 1985–94; Dioc Dir of Tr 1994–99; Bp's Officer for Min and Trg from 1999; Hind Report' follow- up Task Forces for IME and CMD 2006–08; Continuing Min Ed Devlp Panel 2006–09
GS 1995–   *Tel:* 01474 812068
          Fax: 01474 812970
email: canongordon.oliver@gmail.com

OSBORNE, Mrs Emma Charlotte, MA
Lawn Farm Milton Lilbourne Pewsey SN9 5LQ [CHURCH COMMISSIONER] *b* 1964 *educ* Redland High Sch, Bris; Ch Ch Ox; *CV* County NatWest 1985–89; Lloyds Investment Mgrs 1989–91; Credit Suisse/CSFB 1991–97; Investment Mgr, Chubb Insurance from 1997   *Tel:* 01672 563459
          020 7956 5362
email: emma.osborne@lawnfarm.co.uk

OSBORNE, Ven Hayward John, MA, PGCE
Birmingham Diocesan Office 175 Harborne Park Rd Birmingham B17 0BH [ARCHDEACON OF BIRMINGHAM] *b* 1948 *educ* Sevenoaks Sch; New Coll Ox; Westcott Ho Th Coll; *CV* C St Pet and St Paul Bromley 1973–77; C Halesowen 1977–80, TV 1980–83; TR St Barnabas Worc 1983–88; V St Mary Moseley 1988–2001; AD Moseley 1994–2001; Hon Can Birm Cathl from 2000; Adn of Birm from 2001
GS 1998–   *Tel:* 0121 426 0441 (Office)
email: hs.osborne@btinternet.com

OSBORNE, Very Revd June, BA (Econ) Hons, M Phil, Cert Theol, DL
The Deanery 7 The Close Salisbury SP12EF [DEAN OF SALISBURY] *b* 1953 *educ* Whalley Range Gr Sch, Manch; Manch Univ; Birm Univ; St Jo Coll Nottm; Wycliffe Hall Ox; *CV* C St Mart-in-the-Bullring and Chapl, Birm Children's Hosp 1980–84; St Mark Old Ford 1984–89; St Paul w. St Steph and St Mark Old Ford 1989–95; Can Treas Salis Cathl 1995–2004; Dean of Salis from 2004; M Bd of Soc Resp 1985–90; M Stg Cttee GS 1990–95; Sen Insp of Theol Educ 1994–2004; Chair DAC 2003–07; Deputy Lieut of Wilts from 2006
GS 1985–95; 2004–05   *Tel:* 01722 555110
          Fax: 01722 555155
email: thedean@salcath.co.uk

OXFORD (CHRIST CHURCH), Dean of. See LEWIS, Very Revd Christopher Andrew

OXFORD, Archdeacon of. See HUBBARD, Ven Julian Richard Hawes

OXFORD, Bishop of. See PRITCHARD, Rt Revd John Lawrence

PACKER, Rt Revd John Richard, MA
Hollin House Weetwood Avenue Leeds LS16 5NG [BISHOP OF RIPON AND LEEDS] *b* 1946 *educ* Man Gr Sch; Keble Coll Ox; Ripon Hall Th Coll; *CV* C St Pet St Helier 1970–73; Dir Pastl Studies Ripon Hall 1973–75 and Ripon Coll Cuddesdon 1975–77; Chapl St Nic Abingdon 1973–77; V Wath upon Dearne w Adwick upon Dearne 1977–86; RD Wath 1983–86; R Sheff Manor 1986–91; RD Attercliffe 1990–1991; Adn of W Cumberland 1991–96; P-in-c Bridekirk 1995–96; Bp of Warrington 1996–2000; Bp of Ripon and Leeds from 2000
GS 1985–91, 1992–96, 2000–10
          Tel: 0113 244 2789 (Office)
          0113 274 2395 (Home)
          Fax: 0113 230 5471
email: bishop@riponleeds-diocese.org.uk

PADDOCK, Very Revd Dr John Alllan Barnes, BA, MA, PhD, PGCE, FRSA
The Deanery Bomb House Lane Gibraltar [DEAN OF GIBRALTAR; EUROPE] *b* 1951 *CV* Dean of Gibraltar from 2008   *Tel:* 00350 200 78377
          Fax: 00350 78463
email: deangib@gibraltar.gi

PAINTER, Ven David Scott, MA, LTCL, Cert Ed
Diocesan Office Peterborough PE1 1YB [ARCH-
DEACON OF OAKHAM; PETERBOROUGH] *b* 1944 *educ*
Qu Eliz Sch Crediton; Trin Coll of Music; Worc
Coll Ox; Cuddesdon Th Coll; *CV* C St Andr
Plymouth 1970–73; C All SS Marg St 1973–76;
Dom Chapl to Abp of Cant and DDO 1976–80; V
Roehampton 1980–91; RD Wandsworth 1985–90;
Can Res and Treas S'wark Cathl and DDO 1991–
2000; Adn of Oakham and Can Res Peterb Cathl
from 2000, Vc-Dean 2004–05; M Panel of Bps'
Selectors from 1997
GS 2000–05   *Tel:* 01733 887019
                                        01733 891360
                               Fax: 01733 555271
                               email: david.painter@
                               peterborough-diocese.org.uk

PALMER, Dr Richard John, BA, Ph D, RMSA, MCLIP,
FSA
Lambeth Palace Library London SE1 7JU [LIBRARIAN
AND ARCHIVIST, LAMBETH PALACE LIBRARY] *b* 1949
educ Canton High Sch Cardiff; Univ of Kent; *CV*
Asst Lib Lon Boro Hounslow 1970–73; Rsch Asst
Royal Commn on Historical Mss 1976–80; Post-
Doctoral Rsch Fell Wellcome Inst 1980–83; Cur-
ator Western Mss, Wellcome Inst for the History
of Medicine and Hon Lect in History of Medicine
at UCL 1983–91; Librarian and Archivist Lam-
beth Palace Library from 1991
                               Tel: 020 7898 1400
                               Fax: 020 7928 7932
                     email: richard.palmer@c-of-e.org.uk

PANTER, Ven Ricky (Richard) James Graham,
Cert Ed, GOE
2a Monfa Rd Bootle L20 6BQ [ARCHDEACON OF
LIVERPOOL] *b* 1948 *educ* Monkton Combe Sch
Bath; Worc Coll of Educ; Oak Hill Th Coll; *CV* RE
tchr, Chatham Tech High Sch for Boys 1970–71;
primary tchr, Boscombe C of E Primary 1971–73;
C H Trin Rusholme, Man 1976–80; Asst V St
Cyprian w Ch Ch Toxteth 1980–85; V St Andr
Clubmoor 1985–96; V St Jo and St Jas Orrell Hey,
Bootle from 1996; AD Bootle 1999–2002; Arch-
deacon of Liverpool from 2002; M Dioc BMU
Ecumenism Cttee 1985–90; M Dioc Pastl Cttee
1991–96   *Tel:* 0151 922 3758 (Home)
                           0151 705 2154 (Office)
                           Fax: 0151 922 3758
       email: ricky.panter@liverpool.anglican.org

PARKER, Mr Peter William, TD, MA, FIA
1 Turner Drive London NW11 6TX [CHURCH COM-
MISSIONER] *b* 1933 *educ* Win Coll: New Coll Ox;
CV Ptnr, Phillips & Drew 1962–85; Vc-Pres, Inst
of Actuaries 1988–91; M Abps' Rev of Bps' Needs
and Resources 1999–2002; M C of E Pensions Bd
from 2003; M Assets Cttee 2003–08; M Bishoprics
& Cathls Cttee from 2004; Ch Commr and M Bd
of Govs from 2003   *Tel:* 020 8458 2646
                             Fax: 020 8455 8498

PARSONS, Revd Dr Michael William Semper,
MA, DPhil
6 Spa Villas Montpellier Gloucester GL1 1LB
[GLOUCESTER] *b* 1947 *educ* Hul GS St Catherine's
Coll; Ox Selwyn Coll; Ridley Hall Cam; *CV* Prin
Lect Th, Univ Glouc 2009–10); DDO and Dir C
Training, Glouc 2000–04; DDO & P-in-C, Hemp-
sted,Glouc 1996–2000; TR, Walbrook Epiphany,
Derby 1995–96; P-in-C, Derby St Augustine,
Derby 1985–95; Vocations Adv, Derby 1987–96;
SPCK Fellow, NEICE & Hon Lect Th, Univ Dur
1984–85; SPCK Viewdata Fellow, Dept Th, Univ
Dur 1981–84; AC, Edmonton All Saints, Lon
1978–81; Univ Tching Fellow, Dept Physics, Univ
Nott 1973–75; Lect Physics, St Catherine's Coll,
Ox 1972–73; Prin, WEMTC 2004; Exec Dir, Ian
Ramsey Centre, Th Fac, Ox Univ 1999
GS 2003–05; 2010–   *Tel and Fax:* 01452 524550
                               email: mwsp@btinternet

PATERSON, Rt Revd Robert Mar Eskine, BA,
MA, DipTh
*Thie Yn Aspick 4 The Falls Tromode Rd, Douglas Isle
of Man, IM4 4P2* [BISHOP OF SODOR AND MAN] *b*
1949 *educ* King Henry VIII Sch, Cov; St John's
Coll Dur Univ; Cranmer Hall Dur; *CV* C Harpur-
hey Man 1972–73; C Sketty Swansea 1973–78; R
Llangattock and Llangynidr 1978–83; V Ga Balfa
Cardiff 1983–94; TR Cowbridge, Llandaff 1994–
2000; Prin Officer Ch in Wales Coun for Miss and
Min 2000–06; Chapl and Researcher to Abp of
York 2006–08; Bp Sodor and Man from 2008; Vc
Chair Liturg Commn; Vc Chair Theol Educ for
the Angl Communion   *Tel:* 01624 622108
                    email: bishop-sodor@iommail.com

PAVER, Canon Elizabeth Caroline, FRSA
*113 Warning Tongue Lane Bessacar Doncaster DN4
6TB* [SHEFFIELD] *b* 1944 *educ* Doncaster Girls High
Sch; St Mary's Coll Cheltenham; *CV* In Primary
Educ 28 years; Hdtchr Crags Rd Nurs/Inf Sch
1976–80; Hdtchr Askern Nurs/Inf Sch Littlemoor
1980–86; Hdtchr Intake Nursery and First Sch
Doncaster from 1986; M Nat Coun NAHT from
1991; Centenary Nat Pres 1997–97; NAHT
Appointee to Gen Teaching Coun from 2000; past
M Panel of Chairmen GS; Lay Chair Dioc Syn; M
Bp's Coun; M Dioc Bd of Educ Tr Cttee; apptd M
AC 1999–2002; Lay Can Sheff Cathl from 2000;
Ch Commr from 2004
GS 1991–   *Tel:* 01302 530706
                             Fax: 01302 360811
               email: ecp@intake.doncaster.sch.uk

PAYNE, Canon Mark James Townsend, BA
Vicarage Vicarage Lane Scaynes Hill RH17 7PB
[CHICHESTER] *b* 1969 *educ* Heref Cathl Sch; Dur
Univ; Ridley Hall; *CV* C St Marg Angmering
1995–99; Dioc Evangelist 1999–2004; Adv for
work with children and young people 2001–04;
P-in-c St Aug Scaynes Hill and Dioc World Miss
Officer from 2004; M Dioc Overseas Coun; M
Inter-dioc W Africa Link; Sec Dioc Overseas

40/4 stacking chair

Design: David Rowland

HOWE

First produced in 1964, and in continuous production ever since, **40/4** is renowned for its unsurpassed stacking and handling capabilities and its elegant and spare aesthetic. Winner of many design awards over the years, our famous chair is in the permanent collection of the Museum of Modern Art, New York.

40/4 was supplied to St Paul's Cathedral in 1973 and most recently Rochester Cathedral in 2010. In between times, Canterbury, Salisbury, Ely, Gloucester, Leicester, Leeds and Southwark, and many large and small churches across the country.

020 8673 9777 • info@howeuk.co.uk • www.howe.com

535

Coun; Preb of Colworth from 2008; M C of E Angl Communion Panel from 2008
GS 2005–
Tel: 01444 831265
07880 728800 (Mobile)
email: markjtpayne@tesco.net

PEARSON, Rt Revd Geoffrey Seagrave, BA
Shireshead Vicarage Whinney Brow Forton Preston PR3 0AE [SUFFRAGAN BISHOP OF LANCASTER; BLACKBURN] *b* 1951 *educ* St Jo Coll Dur; Cranmer Hall Dur; *CV* C Kirkheaton, Wakef 1974–77; C-in-c Redeemer, Blackb 1977–82, V 1982–85; Asst Home Sec GS Bd for Miss and Unity 1985–89; Hon C Forty Hill, Lon 1985–89; Exec Sec BCC Evang Cttee 1986–89; V Roby, Liv 1989–2006; AD Huyton 2002–06; Hon Can Liv Cathl 2003–06; Bp of Lancaster from 2006
Tel: 01524 799900
07809 618385 (Mobile)
Fax: 01524 799901
email: bishoplancaster@btconnect.com

PENFOLD, Revd Susan, BA, MA, PhD
The Vicarage Church Lane Great Harwood BB6 7PU [BLACKBURN] *b* 1952 *educ* York Univ; Bris Univ; Selwyn Coll Cam Univ; Cuddesdon Th Coll; *CV* Rsrch Asst, Dept Biochemistry, Bris Univ, 1976–77; Travelling Sec, Universities and Colleges Christian Fellowship, 1977–81; Deaconess, Buckhurst Hill, Chelmsf 1984–87; C, Parish of Greenside, Dur 1987–90; C Cononley w Bradley, Bradf 1990–97; Assoc DDO, Bradf 1996–2001; Dioc Dir Ordinands and Dean of Ministry, Wakef 2001–08; Dir Ministry and Residentiary Canon, Blackb from 2008; M Adv, Mirfield, 2001–08; M Ministry Division FinPanel 2003–08; Assessor for the Lower House of the Convocation of York 2005–08
GS 2005–08; 2010–
Tel: 01254 503085
email: Sue.penfold@blackburn.anglican.org

PENRITH, Suffragan Bishop of. (NOT APPOINTED AT TIME OF GOING TO PRESS)

PENTLAND, Ven Raymond Jackson, QHC, BA, MTh
Chaplaincy Services (RAF) HQ AIR CMD, Royal Air Force High Wycombe HP14 4UE [ARCHDEACON FOR THE ROYAL AIR FORCE] *b* 1957 *educ* Cowdenknowes High Sch Greenock; William Booth Memorial Coll; Open Univ; Ox Univ; St Jo Coll Nottm; *CV* C St Jude Mapperley, S'well 1988–90; Chapl RAF 1990–2005; Command Chapl 2005–06; Archdeacon for the RAF from 2006; Hon Can and Preb Linc Cathl from 2006; Chaplain-in-Chief RAF from 2009
GS 2005–
Tel: 01494 496800
email: ray.pentland929@mod.uk

PERHAM, Rt Revd Michael Francis, MA, FRSCM, Hon DPhil
2 College Green Gloucester GL1 2LR [BISHOP OF GLOUCESTER] *b* 1947 *educ* Hardye's Sch Dorchester; Keble Coll Ox; Cuddesdon Th Coll; *CV* C St Mary Addington 1976–81; Chapl to Bp of Win 1981–84; TR Oakdale, Poole 1984–92; Can Res and Prec Norw Cathl 1992–98; Vc Dean 1995–98; Prov of Derby 1998–2000; Dean of Derby 2000–04; M Liturg Commn 1986–2001; M Cathls Fabric Commn 1996–2001; M AC 1999–2004; Chair GS Business Cttee 2001–04; Bp of Gloucester from 2004; Chair SPCK from 2003; Bp Protector Soc of St Francis from 2005; Chair Hosp Chapl Coun from 2007; Vc-Chair MPA Coun from 2007; Chair Govs of Ripon Coll Cuddesdon from 2009; Author
GS 1989–92, 1993–
Tel: 01452 410022 ext. 271
01452 524598
Fax: 01452 308324
email: bshpglos@glosdioc.org.uk

PERUMBALATH, Revd Dr John, MA, MTh, PhD
Vicarage Perry Street North Fleet, Gravesend Kent DA11 8RD [ROCHESTER] *b* 1966 *educ* Government High Sch, Meenangadi; Osmania Univ; North West Univ; Serampore Th Coll; *CV* Lect in New Testament, Serampore Coll 1993–95; V, St James' Church, Calcutta 1995–2000; V, St Thomas' Church, Calcutta 2000–01; Asst P, St George's Church, Beckenham 2002–05, TV, Northfleet and Roserville 2005–08; V, All Saints Church, Gravesend from 2008; Dioc Urban Officer from 2008; M Bp's Counc from 2007; M Adv Counc for Ministry and Training 2007–2010
GS 2010–
Tel: 01474 534398
email: jperumbalath@btopenworld.com

PETERBOROUGH, Bishop of. See ALLISTER, Rt Revd Donal Spargo

PETERBOROUGH, Dean of. See TAYLOR, Very Revd Charles William

PEYTON, Ven Nigel, MA, BD, STM
4 The Woodwards Balderton Newark NG24 3GG [ARCHDEACON OF NEWARK] *b* 1951 *educ* Latymer Upper Sch Lon; Edin Univ; Edin Th Coll; Scottish Fell Union Th Seminary New York; Lanc Univ; *CV* Chapl St Paul's Cathl Dundee 1976–82; P-in-c All So Invergowrie 1979–85; V All SS Nottm 1985–91; P-in-c H Trin Lambley 1991–99; Dioc Min Devel Adv 1991–99; Adn of Newark and Hon Canon of Southwell from 1999; JP 1987–2003; Bps' Vocational Adv 1992–; M Bp's Coun 1999–; Chair Dioc Bd of Min and Pastl Cttee 2000–03; M Min Div DRACSC 2001–2010; M Legal Aid Commn 2001–06; M Provincial Panel, Clergy Discipline Commn 2006–10, Assessor 2010–; Dir EIG from 2005; M Cathl Coun 2008–; Hon Teaching Fell Lanc Univ 2010–; GS 1995–2010
Tel: 01636 612249 (Home)
01636 817206 (Office)
07917 690576 (Mobile)
email: archdeacon-newark@ southwell.anglican.org

PHILPOTT, Preb Sam (Samuel),
21, Plaistow Crescent Plymouth PL5 2EA [EXETER] *b* 1941 *educ* R Naval Hosp Sch Holbrook; Kelham

Th Coll; *CV* C St Mark Swindon 1965–70; C St Martin Torquay 1970–73; TV All SS Exmouth 1973–76; V Shaldon 1976–78; P-in-c St Pet Plymouth 1978–80, V from 1980; RD Plymouth Devonport 1985–91 and 1995–2001; Preb of Ex Cathl from 1991; Acting P-in-c St Thomas N Keyham from 1997, P-in-c from 1999; Chair Dioc Ho of Clergy from 2000; M Bp's Coun; M Dioc Bd of Educ; M Dioc Budget Assess Grp; M DBF Stg Cttee; M Dioc Vacancy-in-See Cttee; M Bp of Plymouth's Adv Grp for Plymouth city; Chair Ship Hostel Plymouth; M Drake Foundn Plymouth; Chair Grants Cttee, Grass Roots Panel; Dir and Chair Millfields Comm Economic Devel Trust Plymouth; M Plymouth Scrutiny Panel for Children's Services; Bp of Ebbsfleet's Coun of Priests; M Nat Coun and Exec Cttee Forward in Faith; Regional Dn Tamar, Forward in Faith
GS 1990–   *Tel:* 01752 298502
                              Fax: 01752 222007
              email: frphilpott@aol.com

PIGGOTT, Ven Andy (Andrew John), B Sc (Econ), Dip Th, PGCE
56 Grange Rd Saltford Bristol BS31 3AG [ARCH-DEACON OF BATH; BATH AND WELLS] *b* 1951 *educ* Thornes Ho Gr Sch Wakef; Holly Lodge Gr Sch Smethwick; Q Mary Coll Lon; Nottm Univ; St Jo Coll Nottm; *CV* C St Phil w. St Jas Dorridge, Birm 1986–89; TV St Chad Kidderminster w. St Geo Team, Worc 1989–94; V St Lawr Biddulph, Lich 1994–99; CPAS Min & Vocations Adv 1999–2001, acting Gen Dir 2000–01, Patr Sec 2001–05; Adn of Bath from 2005; GS 2010–
GS 2010–   *Tel:* 01225 873609
                              Fax: 01225 874610
        email: adbath@bathwells.anglican.org

PILGRIM, Revd (Colin) Mark, BA, MA, CertEs
St Peter's Vicarage 17 The Drive Henleaze Bristol BS9 4LD [BRISTOL] *b* 1956 *educ* St John's Sch, Leatherhead; Kingston Poly; Geneva Univ; W of Eng Univ; Westcott House Th Coll; *CV* C, Chorlton-cum-Hardy, Man 1984–87; C, Ecum P Whitchurch, 1987–89; V, St Oswald's, Bedminster Down 1989–95; Dioc Child and Y Off, Bris 1995–2001; V, St Peter, Henleaze from 2001; Area Dean, Bris West Deanery from 2006; Chair Dioc Lit and Wor Cttee 2004–08; M Bp's Counc from 2010
GS 2009–   *Tel:* 0117 962 0636
              email: markpilgrimis@aol.com

PLATTEN, Rt Revd Stephen George, B Ed, Dip Theol, BD, D Litt
Bishop's Lodge Woodthorpe Lane Wakefield WF2 6JL [BISHOP OF WAKEFIELD] *b* 1947 *educ* Stationers' Company's Sch; Lon Univ Inst of Educ; Trin Coll Ox; Cuddesdon Th Coll; *CV* C Headington 1975–78; Chapl and Tutor Linc Th Coll 1978–82; DDO and Minl Tr and Can Res Portsm Cathl 1982–89; Sec for Ecum Affairs to Abp of Cant 1990–95; Dean of Norw 1995–2003; Bp of Wakefield from 2003; Chair SCM Cant Press from 2001; Chair

Govs Angl Centre in Rome from 2002; Chair Liturg Commn from 2005; M Ho of Lords from 2009
GS 1997–   *Tel:* 01924 255349
                              Fax: 01924 250202
      email: bishop@bishopofwakefield.org.uk

PLYMING, Revd Dr Philip James John, BA, MA, PhD
The Vicarage Church Road Claygate Esher KT10 0JP [GUILDFORD] *b* 1974 *educ* Oakmeeds Comm Sch; Haywards Heath VIth Form Coll; Cam Univ; Dur Univ; Edin Univ; Cranmer Hall Dur; *CV* C Ch Ch Chineham 2001–06; V, Holy Trin Claygate from 2006; M Guildf Dioc Syn from 2007
GS 2009–   *Tel:* 01372 463603
        email: philipplyming@holytrinityclaygate

PLYMOUTH, Archdeacon of. See CHANDLER, Ven Ian Nigel

PLYMOUTH, Suffragan Bishop of. See FORD, Rt Revd John Frank

PODMORE, Dr Colin John, MA, D Phil, F R Hist S
Church House Great Smith St London SW1P 3AZ [ADMINISTRATIVE SECRETARY, CENTRAL SECRE-TARIAT] *b* 1960 *educ* Bodmin Gr Sch; Bodmin Sch; Keble Coll Ox; Selw Coll Cam; *CV* Tchr St Mich C of E High Sch Chorley 1983–85; Asst Sec BMU, CCU 1988–97; Dep Sec CCU 1998–99; Sec IFCG 1988–91; Co-Sec Meissen Commn 1991–99; Co-Sec Porvoo Contact Grp 1996–99; Cen Secretariat from 1999; Sec Liturg Publ Grp 1999–2002; Sec Liturg Commn 2002–09; Sec CAC Rev Grp 1999–2001; Sec Sen Appts Rev Grp 2005–07; Sec Ho of Clergy; Sec Diocs Commn; Trustee Nikaean Ecum Trust, Cleaver Trust   *Tel:* 020 7898 1385
              email: colin.podmore@c-of-e.org.uk

PONTEFRACT, Archdeacon of. See TOWNLEY, Ven Peter Kenneth

PONTEFRACT, Suffragan Bishop of. See ROBINSON, Rt Revd Anthony William

PORTER, Rt Revd Anthony, MA (Oxon), MA (Cantab)
Dunham House 8 Westgate Southwell NG25 0JL [SUFFRAGAN BISHOP OF SHERWOOD; SOUTHWELL AND NOTTINGHAM] *b* 1952 *educ* Aire Boro Gr Sch; Don Valley High Sch; Gravesend Sch for Boys; Hertford Coll Ox; Ridley Hall Cam; *CV* C Edg-ware, Lon 1977–80; C St Mary Haughton, Manch 1980–83; P-in-c Ch Ch Bacup 1983–87, V 1987–91; R Rusholme 1991–2006; Bp of Sherwood from 2006; M Dioc Syn, Bp's Coun; M Coll of Evangs 2009   *Tel:* 01636 819133
                              Fax: 01636 819085
    email: bishopsherwood@southwell.anglican.org

PORTSDOWN, Archdeacon of. See READER, Ven Dr Trevor Alan John

PORTSMOUTH, Bishop of. See FOSTER, Rt Revd Christopher Richard James

PORTSMOUTH, Dean of. See BRINDLEY, Very Revd David Charles

POTTER, Ven Peter Maxwell, MA
St Ursula's Church Jubilaumsplatz 2 3000 Bern 6 Switzerland [ARCHDEACON OF SWITZERLAND; EUROPE] *b* 1946 *educ* County Grammar Sch Crewe; Univ Coll Swansea; Univ of British Columbia; Salisbury and Wells Theol Coll; *CV* C Bradford-on-Avon 1985–88; C Harnham 1988–91; P-in-c N Bradley, Southwick and Heywood 1991–96; V St Anne's Sale 1996–2000; R St Columba's Largs 2000–08; Chapl St Ursula's Berne w Neuchatel from 2008; Adn of Switzerland from 2009
Tel: 0041 31 351 0343
email: berne@anglican.ch

POUNDS, Mrs Sylvia Lyn, RGN, RDN
3 Woodlands Louth Lincolnshire LN11 0WS [LINCOLN] *b* 1950 *educ* Cheadle County Gr Sch; Trent Polytech; Coll of St Mark and St John Plymouth, Lincoln Sch of Th and Min Studies; *CV* Head of Specialist Child and Adolescent Mental Health, 2000-10; Gen Manager Adult and Older Peoples Mental Health 1994–2000; Nurse Non-Exec Dir 1992–95; Dir Goole Development Trust 1997–98; Sector Manager Comm Health Care NHS 1992–94; Dir of Nursing and Health Visiting 1990–92; Nursing and Nurse Management Posts 1976–1990
GS 2010–
Tel: 07771549947
email: spounds@btconnect.com

PRATT, Ven Richard David, MA (Oxon), BCS, PhD (Birmingham)
50 Stainburn Road Workington Cumbria CA14 1SN *b* 1955 *educ* Ranelagh School, Bracknell; Lincoln Coll, Ox; Nottingham Univ; Lincoln Theol Coll; *CV* C All Hallows Wellingborough 1984–87; TV Kingsthorpe 1987–92; V St Benedict's Hunsbury 1992–7, P-in-C St Cuthbert's Carlisle and DCO Carlisle Diocese 1997–2008; Adn West Cumbria from 2009
Tel: 01900 66190
email: archdeacon.west@carlislediocese.org.uk

PRATT, Revd Stephen Samuel, BA, DipH.E, BA, PGCE
The Rectory 203 St Michaels Road Chell Stoke on Trent ST6 6JT [LICHFIELD] *b* 1967 *educ* St Margarets Aigburth Liv; Univ Coll Chester, Keele Univ; Oak Hill Th Coll; *CV* Maths Tchr & Head of Year at St Edwards C of E, Romford 1989–98; C All Saints, Goodmayes 2000–03; TV Chell Team Ministry 2003–07; P-in-C St Michael Chell w Ch of the Saviour Chell Heath 2007–08; V St Michael Chell w Ch of the Saviour Chell Heath from 2008; Chapl to TA Forces from 2005; Lichf Dioc Local Ministry Governing Body repr Syn
GS 2010–
Tel: 01782 838708   07951027290
email: stephen_pratt@sky.com

PRESLAND, Mr Andrew Roy, B Sc
58 Harborough Rd Rushden NN10 0LP [PETERBOROUGH] *b* 1966 *educ* Rushden Boys' Sch; Leic Univ; *CV* Asst Statistician, DOE 1989–95; Statistician DOE, later DETR 1995–99; Sen Lib Clerk (Statistics), Ho of Commons Lib (secondment) 1999–2001; Statistician, Office of Dep Prime Min (local govt finance) 2001–06, DCLG from 2006 (strategy and performance); Lay Chair, Higham Dny Syn; Treas E Northants Faith Gp from 2005; M Bp's Coun from 2006; M AC Fin Cttee from 2006; M DBF 2006–08;
GS 2003–
Tel: 01933 316927
email: andrewpresland@
harboroughroad58.freeserve.co.uk

PRESTON, Dr John Philip Harry, BSc, PHD
Church House Great Smith St London SW1P 3AZ [NATIONAL STEWARDSHIP AND RESOURCES OFFICER, ARCHBISHOPS' COUNCIL] *b* 1965 *educ* Lakes Sch; Exeter Sch; Lancs Univ; *CV* Marketing Mgr Procter and Gamble 1989–2000; Grp Marketing Dir S Staffordshire Grp 2000–02; Marketing, Sales and NPD Mgr, Freshway Foods 2002–05; Nat Stewardship and Resources Officer from 2005
Tel: 020 7898 1540
email: john.preston@c-of-e.org.uk

PRICE, Rt Revd Peter Bryan, Cert Ed, DPS
The Palace Wells BA5 2PD [BISHOP OF BATH AND WELLS] *b* 1944 *educ* Glastonbury Sch Morden; Redland Coll of Educ Bris; Oak Hill Th Coll; Heythrop Coll Lon; *CV* Asst Tchr Ashton Park Sch Bris 1966–70; Sen Tutor Lindley Lodge Young People's Cen 1970; Head of RE Cordeaux High Sch Louth 1970–72; Com Chapl and C Ch Ch Portsdown 1974–78; Chapl Scargill Ho 1978–80; V St Mary Magd Addiscombe 1980–88; Can Chan S'wark Cathl 1988–91; Gen Sec USPG 1992–97; M Miss Agencies Wkg Grp 1992–93; M Angl Commn on Miss 1993–96; Bp of Kingston 1997–2002; M BM; M PWM; M Ch Commn on Miss; M Miss Th Adv Grp; M Gov Body SPCK; Chair S'wark Dioc Bd of Educ; Chair The Manna Soc 1997–2001; Chair Bp's Palace Trust from 2002; Bp of Bath and Wells from 2002; M Ho of Lords from 2008; Chair Angl Communion Pastl Visitors Programme from 2008
GS 2002–
Tel: 01749 672341
Fax: 01749 679355
email: bishop@bathwells.anglican.org

PRIDDIS, Rt Revd Anthony Martin, MA, Dip Theol, FCEM
The Bishop's House Hereford HR4 9BN [BISHOP OF HEREFORD] *b* 1948 *educ* Watford Gr Sch; CCC Cam; New Coll Ox; Cuddesdon Th Coll; *CV* C New Addington 1972–75; Chapl Ch Ch Ox 1975–80; TV St Jo High Wycombe 1980–86; P-in-c Amersham 1986–90, R 1990–96; RD Amersham 1992–96; Hon Can Ch Ch Ox from 1995; Bp of Warwick 1996–2004; Bp of Hereford from 2004; Trustee Cov Relate 2001–03; Trustee FLAME Network 2001–06, Co-Chair 2003–06; Lay M Bd

Coll of Emergency Medicine 2002–08; Central Safeguarding Liaison Grp from 2002; W Midlands Cultural Consortium 2002–05; Trustee Eveson Charitable Trust from 2004; Hon Fell Coll of Emergency Medicine from 2004; Chair Rural Bps' Panel 2006–9; Rural Affairs Group from 2009; House of Lords from 2009
GS 2004–   Tel: 01432 271355
                      Fax: 01432 373346
    email: bishop@hereford.anglican.org

PRITCHARD, Rt Revd John Lawrence, MA,
M Litt
Diocesan Church House North Hinksey Lane Oxford OX2 0NB [BISHOP OF OXFORD] *b* 1948 *educ* Arnold Sch Blackpool; St Pet Coll Ox; Ridley Hall Th Coll; St Jo Coll Dur; *CV* C St Mart-in-the-Bull-Ring Birm 1972–76; Dioc Youth Officer B and W 1976–79; P-in-c St Geo Wilton 1980–88; Dir Pastl Studies Cranmer Hall, St Jo Coll Dur 1989–93; Warden Cranmer Hall 1993–96; Adn of Cant and Can Res Cant Cathl 1996–2001; Bp of Jarrow 2002–07; Bp of Oxford from 2007
GS 1999–2002, 2007–   Tel: 01865 208222 (Office)
                      Fax: 01865 790470
   email: bishopoxon@oxford.anglican.org

PWAISIHO, Rt Revd William Alaha, OBE,
SECONDARY CERT, Dip Th
Rectory Church Lane Gawsworth Macclesfield SK11 9RJ [HONORARY ASSISTANT BISHOP OF CHESTER] *b* 1948 *educ* Alangaula Sch, Pawa and Selwyn Coll, Bp Patteson Theol Centre Kohimarama, Honiara, all in Solomon Islands; *CV* Chapl to Abp of Melanesia 1976–77; C Kohimarama Par Auckland NZ 1977–78; Chapl/Tutor Bp Patteson Theol Cen Kohimarama 1978–79; Dean St Barn Cathl Honiara 1980–81; Bp of Malaita Solomon Islands 1981–89; Gen Sec Melanesian DM 1990–95; Industrial Mgr and Chapl to Kumagai Gumi Ltd, Solomon Islands 1995–96; Asst Bp and C in Sale from 1997; Asst Bp and R Gawsworth from 1999; M Dioc Syn; M Ho Bps Dioc Minority Ethnic Cttee; Melanesian Miss Engl Cttee; M ChsTogether UK Pacific Forum; first missionary Bp from Melanesia to UK since 1849; first Pacific islander to hold office of Rector in UK and to be appointed Chapl to High Sheriff; awarded OBE 2004; M Cheshire Constabulary Ethnic Minority Independent Adv Grp; Hon Chapl to Crimebeat Eng and Wales; M Rotary Club of Macclesfield
GS 1997–   Tel and Fax: 01260 223201
   email: bishop.gawsworth@virgin.net

PYE, Mr Christopher Charles, BA, M Sc
140 Hinckley Rd St Helens WA11 9JY [LIVERPOOL] *b* 1946 *educ* Grange Park Sch St Helens; Open Univ; Manchester Univ; *CV* Technologist in Glass Industry from 1963; Rtd Occupational Hygiene Mgr; Lay Chair St Helens Dny Syn from 1986; Lay Chair Dioc Syn 1991–2003; Rdr
GS 1985–90, 1992–   Tel: 01744 609506
   email: chrispye@blueyonder.co.uk

RAMSBURY, Area Bishop of. See CONWAY, Rt Revd Stephen David

RANDALL, Canon Samuel Paul, MA
The Vicarage, Morton Lane, East Morton, Keighley, BD20 5RS [BRADFORD] *b* 1959 *educ* Leeds Univ MA90; Ridley Hall Cam 84; *CV* C Kingston Upon Hull St Nic York 1987-89; CF 1989–93; Dioc Ecum Officer Dur 1997–2001; P-in-c Holmside 1997–2001; Bp's Officer for Ch in the World Bradford from 2002; Hon Can Bradf Cathl from 04;
GS 2010–   Tel: 01274 561640   079671200710
   email: sam.randall@bradford.anglican.org

RAWLINGS, Ven John Edmund Frank, AKC
Blue Hills Bradley Rd Bovey Tracey Newton Abbot TQ13 9EU [ARCHDEACON OF TOTNES; EXETER] *b* 1947 *educ* Godalming Gr Sch; K Coll Lon; St Aug Coll Cant; *CV* C Rainham 1970–73; C Tattenham Corner w. Burgh Heath 1973–76; Chapl RN 1976–92; V Tavistock w. Gulworthy 1992–2006; RD Tavistock 1997–2002; Preb of Ex 1999–2006; Adn of Totnes and Min Devel Trg Officer from 2006; Chapl to Melanesian Brotherhood Companions from 2006   Tel: 01626 832064
                     Fax: 01626 834947
   email: archdeacon.of.totnes@exeter.anglican.org

RAYFIELD, Rt Revd Dr Lee Stephen, B Sc (Hons),
PhD, CTM
Mark House Field Rise Swindon SN1 4HP [SUFFRAGAN BISHOP OF SWINDON; BRISTOL] *b* 1955 *educ* Thos Bennett Comp Sch, Crawley; Crawley Coll of Tech; Southn Univ; St Mary's Hosp Medical Sch, Lon Univ; Ridley Hall, Cam; *CV* C All SS w. St Andr Woodford Wells, Chelmsf 1993–97; P-in-c St Pet w. St Mark Hosp Ch Furze Platt, Ox 1997–2004, V 2004–05; AD Maidenhead & Windsor, Ox 2000–05; Bp of Swindon from 2005; M UK Gene Therapy Adv Cttee 2000–09; M Soc of Ordained Scientists from 1995; M Fell of Par Evang from 1995; Coun M Evang Alliance from 2007; M Ho of Bps CME Cttee from 2007; M Ethical Investment Adv Grp from 2007   Tel: 01793 538654
                     Fax: 01793 525181
   email: bishop.swindon@bristoldiocese.org

RAZZALL, Revd Charles Humphrey, MA
St Michael's Rectory 198 Ford Lane Crewe CW1 3TN [CHESTER] *b* 1905 *educ* St Paul's Sch, Lon; Worcester Coll Ox; Westcott House Th Coll; *CV* Asst C Catford and Downham T, 1979–83; V St Hilda w St Cyprian, Crofton Park 1983–87; TV Oldham 1987–2001; Area Dean Oldham 1992–99; Hon Can Man Cathl 1998–2001; R St Michael Coppenhall, Crewe from 2001
GS 1995–2000; 2010–   Tel: 01270215151
   email: razzall@angelfields.eclipse.co.uk

READ, Revd Charles William,
42 Heigham Road Norwich NR2 3AU [NORWICH] *b* 1960 *educ* King Edward VI Sch, Lichfield; Man

Univ; Man Poly; St John's Coll, Nott; *CV* Head of RS, Audenshaw High School 1982–86; C, Oldham Team Ministry, 1988–90; C, St.Clement Urmston 1990–93; Goodshaw & Crawshawbooth 1993–94; P-in-C & TV Broughton Team Ministry 1994–99; Lect Lit & Doc, Cranmer Hall, Dur 1999–2006; Vice-Prin & Dir Studies Norwich Dioc Ministry Course from 2007; Eucharistic Prayers Steering Cttee 1998–2000; Thl Ed & Training Cttee 2005–06 GS 1997–2000; 2005–06; 2010–

Tel: 01603 729813
email: charlesread@norwich.anglican.org

READE, Rt Revd Nicholas Stewart, BA, Dip Th
Bishop's House Ribchester Rd Blackburn BB1 9EF [BISHOP OF BLACKBURN] *b* 1946 *educ* Eliz Coll Guernsey; Leeds Univ; Coll of the Resurrection, Mirfield; *CV* C St Chad Coseley 1973–75; C-in-c H Cross Bilbrook and C Codsall 1975–78; V St Pet Upper Gornal and Chapl Burton Rd Hosp Dudley 1978–82; V Mayfield 1982–88; RD Dallington 1982–88; V and RD Eastbourne 1988–97; Chair Dioc Liturg Cttee 1989–97; Can and Preb Chich Cathl from 1990; Pres Eastbourne Police Court Miss from 1994; Adn of Lewes and Hastings 1997–2004; Chair Dioc Bd of Patr 1992–97; Vc-Pres Dioc Syn and Chair Ho of Clergy 1997–2000; Patron Sussex Heritage Trust from 1998; M Dioceses Commn from 2000; Pres Crowhurst Chr Healing Cen from 2000; Bp of Blackburn from 2004; M Ho of Bps Healing Min Strg Grp from 2004; Patron Rosemere Cancer Foundn from 2005; Vc-Pres Disabled Living from 2005; Patron Helping Hands from 2005; Patron SELRAP from 2006; Patron Derian House Children's Hospice from 2006; Chair Ctee for Min of and among Deaf and Disabled People from 2008; M SAG(E) from 2008; M Urban Bishops Panel from 2010; Fell Royal Soc of Arts from 2009; Pres Coll of St Barnabas, Lingfield from 2009; Warden Guild of St Raphael from 2009; Patron Blackb Cathl Appeal Fund from 2010
GS 1995–2000, 2002–   *Tel:* 01254 248234
Fax: 01254 246668
email: bishop@bishopofblackburn.org.uk

READER, Ven Dr Trevor Alan John, B Sc, M Sc, Ph D, SOSc
5 Brading Ave Southsea PO4 9QJ [ARCHDEACON OF PORTSDOWN; PORTSMOUTH] *b* 1946 *educ* Haverfordwest Gr Sch; Portsm Poly; S Diocs Min Trg Scheme, Salis & Wells Th Coll; *CV* Rsch Asst biological sciences Ports Poly 1968–72, Sen Lect 1972–86; C St Mary, Alverstoke 1986–89; P-in-c, then V St Mary, Hook w Warsash 1989–98; P-in-c Blendworth, H Trin w Chalton St Mich & All Angels w Idsworth St Hubert and Ports Dioc Dir of NSM 1998–2003; Adn of Isle of Wight 2003–06; Adn of Portsdown from 2006; Chair Dioc Bd of Educ 2003–10; M DAC for Care of Chs; M Dioc Parsonages and Property Cttee; Bp's Liaison

Officer for Prisons 2003–06; Bp's Adv to Hosp Chapl from 2006   *Tel:* 023 9243 2693
07737 180384 (Mobile)
Fax: 023 9229 8788
email: adportsdown@portsmouth.anglican.org

READING, Area Bishop of. (NOT APPOINTED AT TIME OF GOING TO PRESS)

REDFERN, Rt Revd Dr Alastair Llewellyn John, MA, MA, Ph D
The Bishop's House 6 King St Duffield Belper DE56 4EU [BISHOP OF DERBY] *b* 1948 *educ* Bicester Sch; Ch Ch Ox; Trin Coll Cam; Westcott Ho Th Coll; Bris Univ; *CV* C Tettenhall 1976–79; Lect in Ch Hist, Dir of Pastl Studies and Vc-Prin Cuddesdon Th Coll 1979–87; C All SS Cuddesdon 1983–87; Can Res Bris Cathl 1987–97; Can Theologian and Dir of Tr 1987–97; Mod of Par Resource Tm 1995–97; M ABM Initial Minl Educ Cttee; Mod Abps Dip for Rdrs; Bp of Grantham 1997–2005; Dean of Stamford 1998–2005; Chair Fin Panel, Min Div; M Theol, Educ and Trg Cttee; M Bp's Cttee for Min; M Bp's CME Cttee; M Legal Aid Commn; Bp of Derby from 2005; M Ho of Bps Th Gp
GS 2005–   *Tel:* 01332 840132
Fax: 01332 840397
email: bishop@bishopofderby.org

REED, Ven John Peter Cyril, BD, AKC, Cert Th (Oxon)
2 Monkton Heights West Monkton Taunton TA2 8LU [ARCHDEACON OF TAUNTON; BATH & WELLS] *b* 1951 *educ* Monkton Combe Sch; K Coll Lon; Cuddesdon Th Coll; *CV* Asst C Croydon Par Ch 1979–82; Prec St Alb 1982–86; R Timsbury and Priston 1986–93; Chapl for Rural Affairs Bath Adnry 1987–93; TR Ilminster and District TM 1993–99; Adn Taunton from 1999; Dioc Warden of Rdrs   *Tel:* 01823 413315
Fax: 01823 413384
email: adtaunton@bathwells.anglican.org

REES, Mrs Christina (Henking Muller), BA, MA, FRSA
Churchfield Pudding Lane Barley Royston Herts SG8 8JX [ST ALBANS] *b* 1953 *educ* Hampton Day Sch; Pomona Coll; Wheaton Graduate Sch; K Coll Lon; *CV* Researcher IBA 1980; Asst Public Relns Officer The Children's Society 1985–87; Writer from 1980; Broadcaster from 1990; M Strg Cttee and Initiation Services Revision Cttee 1996–98; M CECC 1996–98; M ABM 1996–98; Chair WATCH 1996–2010; Trustee, Li Tim-Oi Foundn from 1997; Elected M AC 1999–2000; Trustee, Chr Evidence Soc 2000–05; M Theol Educ and Trg Cttee 2000–05; GS rep, Bd Govs Ripon Coll Cuddesdon from 2000; co-opted Bd Govs Tr Coll Bris 2000–05; M CMEAC 1999–2004; Dir Churchfield Trust; M CRAC; Dip in Coaching (Coaching Futures/

OCR); elected M AC from 2005; Trustee Chr Assoc of Business Execs
GS 1990–

Tel: 01763 848472
01763 848822
Fax: 01763 848774
email: christina@mediamaxima.com

REES, Canon (Vivian) John (Howard), MA, LLB, M Phil
16 Beaumont St Oxford OX1 2LZ [JOINT REGISTRAR, PROVINCE OF CANTERBURY] *b* 1951 *educ* Skinners' Sch Tunbridge Wells; Southn Univ; Ox Univ; Leeds Univ; Wycliffe Hall Th Coll; *CV* Solicitor and Eccl Notary (Admitted 1975); C Moor Allerton TM 1979–82; Chapl and Tutor Sierra Leone Th Hall, Freetown 1983–86; Ptnr Winckworth Sherwood Solicitors from 1986; Treas Eccl Law Soc from 1995; Jt Registrar Ox Dioc from 1998; Jt Registrar Prov of Cant from 2000; Legal Adv ACC from 1998; Vc-Chair Legal Adv Commn from 2001; Provincial Can Cant Cathl from 2001; Registrar, Clergy Discipline Tribunals Prov of Cant from 2006
GS 1995–2000

Tel: 01865 865875 (Home)
01865 297200 (Office)
07973 327417 (Mobile)
Fax: 01865 726274
email: vjhrees@btinternet.com / jrees@wslaw.co.uk

REID, Canon Jennifer, BA
Healam 9 Poplars Rd Linthorpe Middlesbrough TS5 6RL [YORK] *b* 1943 *CV* University lecturer, rtd
GS 2000–

Tel: 01642 823127 (Home)
01642 782095 (Office)
email: jennyreid@ntlworld.com

REIGATE, Archdeacon of. See KAJUMBA, Ven Daniel Steven Kimbugwe

REPTON, Suffragan Bishop of. See SOUTHERN, Rt Revd Humphrey Ivo John

RICE, Dr Philip, BSc MSc, PhD,MICE C.Eng, MEI
23 Christchurch Square Homerton London E9 7HU [LONDON] *b* 1949 *educ* Doncaster Gr Sch; LSE, UCL; *CV* Rsrch Fellow Transport Section, Imperial Coll 1978–85; Direct Entrant Economist Civil service, 1985; Economic Adv, Dept of Energy, Energy Forecasts and Oil Prices, 1985–91; Economic Adv, Inland Revenue, Statistics and Economics Division, Oil & Financial Sector and Capital Gains Tax 1991–98; Senior Economist, Inland Revenue, Team Leader, Direct Business Taxes & Anti-Avoidance, from 1998; Lay Chair of Hackney Deanery, Lon Dioc 2000–06; M Bp's Counc Lon Dioc from 2006
GS 2010–

Tel: 02089851914
email: phillip@christopherrice.orangehome.co.uk

RICHBOROUGH, Bishop of. (NOT APPOINTED AT TIME OF GOING TO PRESS)

RICHMOND, Revd Dr Patrick Henry, MA, DPhil
161 Newmarket Road Norwich NR4 6SY [NORWICH] *b* 1969 *educ* Marlborough Coll; Wiltshire Balliol Coll; Green Coll, Ox; Wycliffe Hall Th Coll; *CV* C, Church of the Martyrs, Leic 1997–2001; Chapl & Fellow, St Catharines Coll, Cam 2001–06; Dean of Chapel, St Catharines Coll, Came 2006–07; V, Ch Ch, Eaton, Norwich from 2007
GS 2010–

Tel: 01603 2508449 07982785765
email: phr@eatonparish.com

RICHMOND, Archdeacon of. See HENDERSON, Ven Janet

RIPON AND LEEDS, Bishop of. See PACKER, Rt Revd John Richard

RIPON, Dean of. See JUKES, Very Revd Keith Michael

ROBBINS, Ven Stephen, QHC, BD, AKC
MoD Chaps (A) Trenchard Lines Upavon Pewsey SN9 6BE [ARCHDEACON FOR THE ARMY] *b* 1953 *educ* Jarrow Gr Sch; K Coll Lon; St Aug Coll Cant; *CV* C St Andr Tudhoe Grange, Dur 1976–80; C-in-c St Ninian Harlow Green, Dur 1980 84, V 1984–87; R Army Chapls' Dept from 1987; Dir Trg MOD Chapls (Army) and Adn for the Army from 2004; Dep Chapl Gen 2007–08; Chapl Gen from 2008
GS 2004–

Tel: 01980 615801
01980 615809 07747 100993 (Mobile)
Fax: 01980 615800
email: lf-chapsa-cg-pa@mod.uk

ROBERTS, Canon (John) Mark Arnott, AKC, PGCE
Rectory Knightrider St Sandwich CT13 9ER [CANTERBURY] *b* 1954 *educ* Caterham Sch; K Coll Lon Univ; Ch Ch Coll Cant; Chich Th Coll; *CV* C St Mary V, Ashford, Kent 1977–82; V and R St Mary's Bay, St Mary in the Marsh, Ivychurch 1982–91; R Sandwich from 1991; P-in-C Worth from 2004; Area Dean of Sandwich 2000–06; M Dioc Syn; M Abp's Coun; Hon Can Cant Cathl from 2003; Chair Dioc Syn Ho of Clergy from 2006
GS 2003–

Tel: 01304 613138
email: revdmarkroberts@supanet.com

ROBERTS, Ven Kevin Thomas, MA, BA
2 The Abbey Carlisle CA3 8TZ [ARCHDEACON OF CARLISLE] *b* 1955 *educ* Guisborough Grammar Sch; Prior Pursglove Coll; Queens' Coll Cam; Univ Nottm; St John's Coll Nottm; *CV* C Beverley Minster 1983–86; C St James Woodley 1986–91; V Meole Brace 1991–2009; RD Shrewsbury 1998–2008; Preb Lichfield Cathl 2002–09; Res Can Carlisle Cathl; Adn Carlisle from 2009; Ox Dioc Syn 1988–91; Lich Dioc Syn 1992–2009; Bps Coun Lich 1997–2006; Lich Vacancy-in-See Comm 1998–2003
Tel: 01228 523026 07833 478520 (Mobile)
email: archdeacon.north@carlisle diocese.org.uk

ROBERTS, Ven Stephen John, BD, MTh
2 Alma Rd Wandsworth London SW18 1AB [ARCH-DEACON OF WANDSWORTH; SOUTHWARK] *b* 1958 *educ* Newcastle-under-Lyme High Sch; K Coll Lon; Westcott Ho Cam; Heythrop Coll Lon; *CV* C St Mary Riverhead w. St Jo Dunton Green, Roch 1983–86; C St Martin-in-the-Fields, S'wark 1986–89; V St Geo Camberwell and Wrdn Trin Coll Centre, S'wark 1989–2000; Sen DDO and Can Res, S'wark Cathl 2000–05; Adn of Wandsworth from 2005   *Tel:* 020 8874 8567 (Home)
020 8785 1985 (Work)
Fax: 020 8785 1981
email: stephen.roberts@southwark.anglican.org

ROBERTS, Revd Dr Vaughan Simon, BA, MA, PhD
The Rectory The Butts Warwick CV34 4SS [COVEN-TRY] *b* 1959 *educ* Montgomery of Alamein Comp Sch; Winch and Peter Symonds Coll; Univ Coll of N Wales, Bangor; Univ of Bath; McCormick Theol Sem, Chicago; Westcott Ho Cam; *CV* C St Thomas-on-the-Bourne Farnham 1985–89; Chapl Phyllis Tuckwell Hosp Farnham 1988–89; Univ Chapl Univ of Bath 1989–96; P-in-c Ch Ch Proprietory Chapel Bath 1992–96; Dir Ords and Vocations Adv Bath and Wells 1996–2003; P-in-c Chewton Mendip Benefice 1996–2003; M Coun for WEMTC 1998–2003; M Coun for STETS 1999–2003; TR Warwick and V Collegiate Ch of St Mary from 2003; M AAR from 2008
GS 2009–2010   *Tel and Fax:* 01926 492909
email: vaughan.roberts@btinternet.com

ROBILLIARD, Mr David John,
Le Petit Gree Torteval Guernsey GY8 0RD [WIN-CHESTER (CHANNEL ISLANDS)] *b* 1952 *educ* Guern-sey Gr Sch for Boys; *CV* Clearing and Internat Banking 1969–82; HM Dep Greffier 1982–87; Prin Asst Chief Exec Guernsey Civil Service 1987–94; Hd of Constitutional Affairs States of Guernsey 1994–2007; Prin Officer States Assembly and Constitution Ctee from 2008; M Dioc Stg Cttee; Treas Guernsey Dny Syn; chwdn of Torteval
GS 1998–   *Tel:* 01481 264344 (Home)
01481 717027 (Office)
07781 164344 (Mobile)
Fax: 01481 264543 (Home)
01481 713884 (Office)
email: villula@cwgsy.net

ROBINSON, Rt Revd Anthony William, Cert Ed
Pontefract House 181a Manygates Lane Wakefield WF2 7DR [SUFFRAGAN BISHOP OF PONTEFRACT; WAKEFIELD] *b* 1956 *educ* Bedf Modern Sch; Bedf Coll of HE; Sarum and Wells Th Coll; *CV* C St Paul Tottenham 1982–85; TV Resurr Leic 1985–89; TR 1989–97; RD Christianity N 1992–97; Hon Can Leic Cathl from 1994; M CBF 1995–97; M CMEAC 1996–97; Adn of Pontefract 1997–2003; Bishop of Pontefract from 2002
GS 1995–97, 2000–02   *Tel:* 01924 250781
Fax: 01924 240490
email: bishop.pontefract@wakefield.anglican.org

ROBINSON, Ven Peter John Alan, BA, MA, PhD
4 Acomb Close Morpeth NE61 2YH [ARCHDEACON OF LINDISFARNE; NEWCASTLE] *b* 1961 *CV* Adn of Lindisfarne from 2008   *Tel:* 01670 503810
email: p.robinson@newcastle.anglican.org

ROCHDALE, Archdeacon of. See VANN, Cherry Elizabeth

ROCHESTER, Archdeacon of. See BURTON-JONES, Ven Simon David

ROCHESTER, Bishop of. See LANGSTAFF, Rt Revd James Henry

ROCHESTER, Dean of. See NEWMAN, Very Revd Adrian

RODGERS, Mrs Sue (Susan Elizabeth),
13 Rowlands Ave Waterlooville PO7 7RT [PORT-SMOUTH] *b* 1954 *educ* Haywards Heath Sec Sch; *CV* WRNS 1971–79; Night Staff St Mary's Hosp Portsm; Bereavement Cllr; Co-ord Bereavement Grp; Par Asst/Administrator St Wilf Cowplain until 2001; Lay Can Portsm Cath from 2008
GS 2000–   *Tel:* 023 9225 3091
07974 570414 (Mobile)
Fax: 023 9223 3367
email: Sue@Rodgersuk.com

RODHAM, Ven Morris, MA, PGCE, BA, DipHE
3 The Gardens Thurlaston Rugby CV23 9LS [ARCH-DEACON MISSIONER, DIOCESE OF COVENTRY] *b* 1959 *educ* RGS Newcastle; Durham Univ Hatfield College; Bristol Univ; Trinity Coll Bristol; *CV* Regular Army (Royal Artillery) 1978, 1981–84; TR Warwick Schl (Classics, CCF, Hockey) 1985–90; C St Mark's Leamington 1993–1997; V St Mary's Leamington 1997–2010; RD Warwick and Leamington 2006–10; Adn Missioner from 2010
Tel: 02476 521337
email: morris.rodham@covcofe.org

ROSE, Revd Susan Margaret, B Ed
The Vicarage Station Road Cheddar Somerset BS27 3AH [BATH AND WELLS] *b* 1959 *educ* Stoud Girls High Sch; Keswick Grammar Sch; Westminster Coll Higher Ed; SAOMC;; *CV* Teacher, 1981–98; C,North Petherton w Moorland, 1998–2000; Rec-tor, The Alfred Jewel Benefice, 2000–09; P-in-C, Cheddar; Rodney Stoke w Draycott, 2009; Sec Cttee Ministerial Review, 2000–04; Design team Bps Course for Rdrs, 2003–05; Vocations Chapl 2004–06; Rural Dean 2006–09; M Dioc Patronage Brd, from 2009
GS 2010–   *Tel:* 01934 740394
email: rev.suerose@virgin.net

ROSEMARY CHN, Sister, MA, MA, Dip Pastl Th (APU)
Convent of the Holy Name Morley Rd Oakwood Derby DE21 4QZ [RELIGIOUS COMMUNITIES (SOUTH)] *b* 1944 *educ* Barr's Hill Sch Cov; Newn-

ham Coll Cam; St Mary's Coll Dur Univ; Westcott Ho Cam; *CV* Various teaching posts, 1967–76; Community of the Holy Name from 1976; Dn 1998; P 1999 (Derby Dioc); C St Osmund, Derby 1998–2001; Perm to officiate, Derby and S'well Diocs from 2001; Assoc P, Morley, Smalley and Loscoe (Derby) from 2010
GS 2003–   *Tel:* 0115 978 5101
                    email: rosemarychn@yahoo.co.uk

ROSSDALE, Rt Revd David Douglas James, MA, M Sc
Bishop's House Church Lane Irby-on-Humber Grimsby DN37 7JR [SUFFRAGAN BISHOP OF GRIMSBY; LINCOLN] *b* 1953 *educ* St Jo Sch Leatherhead; K Coll Lon; Westmr Coll Ox; Roehampton Inst; Chich Th Coll; *CV* C St Laur Upminster 1981–86; V St Luke Moulsham 1986–90; V H Trin Cookham 1990–2000; AD Maidenhead 1994–2000; Hon Can Ch Ch Ox 1999–2000; Bp of Grimsby from 2000; Hon Can and Preb Lincoln from 2000   *Tel:* 01472 371715
                                  Fax: 01472 371716
                  email: rossdale@btinternet.com

ROWELL, Rt Revd (Douglas) Geoffrey, MA, Ph D, D Phil, DD, Hon DD
Bishop's Lodge Worth Crawley RH10 7RT [BISHOP OF GIBRALTAR IN EUROPE] *b* 1943 *educ* Eggar's Gr Sch Alton; Win Coll; CCC Cam; Cuddesdon Th Coll; *CV* Asst Chapl and Hastings Rashdall Student New Coll Ox 1968–72; Hon C St Andr Headington 1968–72; Fell, Chapl and Tutor in Th Keble Coll Ox 1972–94, Emer Fell from 1994; Univ Lect in Th 1977–94; M Liturg Commn 1980–90; Gov Pusey Ho Ox 1979–2009, Pres from 1995; M Gov Body SPCK 1984–94 and from 1997; Hon Dir Abp's Exam in Th 1986–2001; Can and Preb Chich Cathl 1981–2001; M Angl-Oriental Orthodox Internat Forum from 1985, Angl Co-Chair from 1996; Conservator Mirfield Cert in Pastl Th 1987–93; M Coun Mgt St Steph Ho Th Coll from 1988, Chairman from 2004; M Doct Commn 1990–95, Consult 1996–99, M 1999–2004; Bp of Basingstoke 1994–2001; C of E Rep on CTBI 1995–2001; Vis Prof Univ Coll Chich (Sch of Religion and Theol) 1996–2003; Chair Chs Funerals Grp from 1997; M Inter Angl Stg Commn on Ecum Relns 2000–2008, Vc-Chairman from 2003; Hon Can Win Cathl 2000–2001; Ho Bps Theol Grp from 1999; M Clergy Discipline (Theol and Liturg) Wkg Pty 2000–03; M Ho of Bps' Wkg Pty on Women in the Episcopate 2000–04; Bp of Gib in Eur from 2001
GS 2001–   *Tel:* 01293 883051
                                  Fax: 01293 884479
            email: bishop@dioceseineurope.org.uk

ROY, Mr Anirban, BA, CIMA Adv Dip
11 Longton Grove London SE26 6QQ [LONDON] *b* 1977 *educ* Tiffin Sch; Trin Coll, Cam; ; *CV* Head of Regulatory Compliance, Office of Comm Ofcom, 2007–10; Policy Manager, Ofcom 2004–07;

Strategy Consult Solving International, 2002–04; Corporate Finance Consult, Arthur D. Little, 1999–2002; Principal, Ofcom from 2010
GS 2010–   *Tel:* 07968 173 213
                      email: urbanroy@gmail.com

RUOFF, Mrs Alison Laura, SRN, SCM, DN
The White House 75 Crossbrook St Cheshunt EN8 8LU [LONDON] *b* 1942 *educ* Sutton Coldfield Girls High Sch; Nightingale Sch of Nursing, St Thos Hosp; Br Hosp for Mothers and Babies; Nursing Inst Worc; RCN; *CV* VSO India 1961–62; Night Sister St Thos Hosp 1966–67; Asst Dir of Nursing Internat Grenfell Assoc Newfoundland 1968–70; Admin Sister St Thos Hosp Grp 1970–72; Nursing Officer/Sen Nursing Officer Univ Coll Hosp 1972–74; Housewife and mother; JP 1979–2003; M Dioc Bp's Coun; CEEC Exec; Lay Chair Lon DEF; M UK Coun Girl Crusaders' Union; speaker and broadcaster
GS 1995–   *Tel:* 01992 623113
                              07956 569323 (Mobile)
                  email: alison_ruoff@hotmail.com

RUSSELL, Ven Brian Kenneth, MA, PhD
26 George Rd Edgbarton Birmingham B15 1PJ [ARCHDEACON OF ASTON; BIRMINGHAM] *b* 1950 *educ* Bris Gr Sch; Trin Hall Cam; Birm Univ; Cuddesdon Ox; *CV* C St Matt Redhill 1976–79; P-in-c St Jo Kirk Merrington, Dur and Dir of Studies NEOC 1979–83; Dir of Studies and Lect in Chr Doct, Linc Theol Coll 1983–86; Sec Cttee for Theol Educ and Selection Sec, ACCM/ABM 1986–93; Bp's Dir for Min, Birm Dioc 1993–2005; sch gov; Hon Can Birm Cathl from 1999; M Vol and Continuing Educ Cttee, GS Bd of Educ 1994–99; Bp's Sen Selector from 1998; Bp's Sen Insp for Theol Colls and Courses from 2001; M Bps' Inspections Wkg Pty from 2003; Bp's Exam Chapl, Birm from 1996; Chair Birm Dioc Ministries Forum from 2005; Gov Q Foundn for Theol Educ, Birm from 1994; Adn of Aston from 2005
                                  Tel: 0121 426 0428
                                       0121 454 5525
                                  Fax: 0121 428 1114
            email: b.russell@birmingham.anglican.org

RUSSELL, Mr Mark Kenneth, LLB
Church Army Marlowe House 109 Station Rd Sidcup DA15 7AD [APPOINTED MEMBER, ARCHBISHOPS' COUNCIL] *b* 1974 *educ* Portadown Coll; Q Univ Belfast; *CV* Project exec, W. D. Irwin & Sons Ltd, Portadown 1995–97; youth pastor, High St Meth Ch, Lurgan 1997–2000; youth min, Ch Ch Chorleywood 2000–06; Chief Exec Ch Army from 2006; appt M AC from 2005; M Coll of Evs from 2008; M Coun Evang Alliance from 2008; M C of E Evang Coun from 2009   *Tel:* 020 8309 3505
                                  Fax: 020 8309 3500
                 email: m.russell@churcharmy.org.uk

RUSSELL, Ven Norman Atkinson, MA, BD
Foxglove House Love Lane Donnington Newbury RG14 2JG [ARCHDEACON OF BERKSHIRE; OXFORD] *b*

1943 *educ* R Belfast Academical Inst; Chu Coll Cam; Lon Coll of Div; *CV* C Ch Ch w Em Clifton 1970–74; C Ch Ch Trent Park Enfield 1974–77; R Harwell w Chilton 1977–84; P-in-c Gerrards Cross 1984–88; P-in-c Fulmer 1985–88; R Gerrards Cross and Fulmer 1988–98; Hon Can Ch Ch Ox 1995–98; RD Amersham 1996–98; Adn of Berks from 1998; Prolocutor Lower Ho Conv of Cant 2005–10; M Abp's Coun 2005–10; M Appts Cttee 2006–10; M Ch Heritage Forum 2006–10; Vc-Chair Ecum Coun for Corporate Resp 1999–2002; M Clergy Terms of Service Implementation Grp/Panel 2005–10

Tel: 01635 552820 07776 180991 (Mobile)
Fax: 01635 522165
email: archdber@oxford.anglican.org

RUSSELL, Mrs Victoria Christine, Cert Ed
Foxglove House Love Lane Donnington Newbury RG14 2JG [OXFORD] *b* 1948 *educ* Badminton Sch; Whitelands Coll of Ed; *CV* Tchr, 1970–76; Head of RE & Geography, Gateway School, Bucks, 1989–1996; Head of RE & Geography, Maltman's Green School, Bucks, 1996–2006; M Ox Healing Team
GS 2010–   *Tel:* 01635 552 820 07765 951 021
Fax: 01635 522 165
email: vcrussell@googlemail.com

RUTHERFORD, Revd Rosalind Elizabeth,
BA PGCE
45 Beaconsfield Road Basingstoke Hampshire RG21 3DG [WINCHESTER] *b* 1952 *educ* King's H Sch for Girls; Warwick St Hugh's Coll, Ox; Goldsmiths' Coll, UL; STETS; *CV* Field Officer, Third World First 1974–76; Toy Library Organiser, Manchester Youth and Community Service1976–77; Tchr, Parliament Hill Sch for Girls 1998–80; Tchr Burlington Danes Sch 1980–84; Adult Education tutor Reading Adult Coll 1987–2003; C St Peter's Earley 2003–06; TV Basingstoke Team Ministry from 2006
GS 2010–   *Tel:* 01256 464616
email: vicar@allsaintsbasingstoke.org.uk

RYLANDS, Rt Revd Mark James, BA
Athlone House 68 London Road Shrewsbury SY2 6PG [AREA BISHOP OF SHREWSBURY] *b* 1961 *CV* Area Bp of Shrewsbury from 2009
Tel: 01743 235867
email: bishop.shrewsbury@lichfield.anglican.org

SADGROVE, Very Revd Michael, MA, FRSA
The Deanery Durham DH1 3EQ [DEAN OF DURHAM] *b* 1950 *educ* Univ Coll Sch Lon; Ball Coll Ox; Trin Coll Bris; *CV* Lic to Offic Ox dio 1975–76; Lect OT Sarum & Wells Th Coll 1977–82; Vc-Prin 1980–82; V Alnwick 1982–87; Can Res, Prec and Vc-Provost Cov Cathl 1987–95; Provost of Sheff 1995–2000, Dean 2000–03; Dean of Durham from 2003; M Min Coun; M TETC; Chair Dur Dioc Adv

Cttee; Chair Dur Univ Ethics Adv Cttee; M Dur Univ Coun; R St Chad's Coll Dur
Tel: 0191 384 7500
Fax: 0191 386 4267
email: michael.sadgrove@durhamcathedral.co.uk

SAGE, Mrs Hilary Charlotte,
32 Nathans Rd North Wembley HA0 3RX [REPRESENTATIVE, DEAF ANGLICANS TOGETHER] *b* 1944 *educ* Thomasson Memorial Sch; *CV* M Cttee Deaf Anglicans Together
GS 2005–   *Fax:* 020 8904 0494
email: hilary.sage@btinternet.com

SALFORD, Archdeacon of, see SHARPLES, Ven David

SALISBURY, Bishop of. (NOT APPOINTED AT TIME OF GOING TO PRESS)

SALISBURY, Dean of. See OSBORNE, Very Revd June

SALOP, Archdeacon of. See HALL, Ven John Barrie

SANDIFORD, Mrs Christine Krogh, BA, MA, PGCE
330 Lapwing Lane Manchester M20 6UW [MANCHESTER] *b* 1944 *educ* Baldwin High Sch (Pittsburgh PA); Smith Coll; Wesleyan Univ; Man Univ; Man Dio Rdr Training Course; *CV* Par Admin Didsbury 1989–1995; Volunteer Adv Withington Citizens Advice from 1982; Sub-warden of Rdrs Man Dioc from 2008
GS 2009–   *Tel:* 0161 434 1343
email: christine@sandiford.info

SARGENT, Lieutenant Commander Philippa Mary, MA, PGCert
31 Launceston Close Priddy's Hard Gosport PO12 4GE [REPRESENTATIVE, ARMED FORCES SYNOD] *b* 1968 *educ* Bennett Memorial Sch for Girls; Ox Univ; Portsm Univ; *CV* Naval Officer from 1991
GS 2005–   *Tel:* 023 9258 3080
email: philippa.sargent@virgin.net

SARUM, Archdeacon of. See JEANS, Ven Alan Paul

SAXBEE, Rt Revd John Charles, BA, Ph D
Bishop's House Eastgate Lincoln LN2 1QQ [BISHOP OF LINCOLN] *b* 1946 *educ* Cotham Gr Sch Bris; Bris Univ; Dur Univ; St Jo Coll Dur; *CV* C Em w St Paul Plymouth 1972–76; V St Phil Weston Mill 1976–81; TV Cen Ex 1981–87; Dir SW Minl Tr Course 1981–92; Preb of Ex Cathl 1988–92; Adn of Ludlow 1992–2002; Warden of Rdrs 1992–2002; Bp of Ludlow 1994–2002; Bp of Lincoln from 2001; Pres Modern Churchpeople's Union from 1997; Relig Adv to Carlton TV 1997–2006; M Coll of Evang from 1999; M Pastl and Dioc Measures Rev Grp; M Bps' Cttee for Min; M Insp Wkg Pty

1999–2007; Chair Bd of Educ and Nat Soc from 2008
GS 1985–94, 2000–   *Tel:* 01522 534701
Fax: 01522 511095
email: bishop.lincoln@lincoln.anglican.org

SAXBY, Revd Martin Peter, BA, DipTh
St Matthews Vicarage 7 Vicarage Road Rugby CV22 7AJ [COVENTRY] *b* 1952 *educ* Wandsworth Comp Sch; St. John's Coll, Dur; Cranmer Hall; *CV* AC St. Mary Magdalene, Peckham 1978–81; AC Ramsey w St Peter's Upwood & Ramsey St. Mary's 1981–84; Incumb Mattishall w Mattishall Burgh, Welborne and Yaxham 1984–90; Incumb St. Matthew's Rugby1990–2007; Incumb St. Matthew's & St. Oswald's Rugby 2008; Area Dean of Rugby 2005; M Bp's Counc from 2004; Joint Chair Dioc Miss Fund from 2010
GS 2010–   *Tel:* 01788 330442
Fax: 07053 480 079
email: martinpa@m2o.org.uk

SCOTT, Mrs Angela Mary, MTh, Cert Ed
The Stead Willow Grove Chislehurst Kent BR7 5BU [ROCHESTER] *b* 1950 *educ* Portsmouth High Sch; Bedord Coll of Phys Ed; Spurgeon's Th Coll; *CV* Tchr, Stratford House Sch, Kent 1972–75; Home Maker 1975–99; Part-time Tchr, Marjory McClure Sch, Kent 1984–87; Supply Tching, Bromley 1987–92; Church Admin, 1992–98; Dioc Pastoral Asst from 2000; Dioc Tutor, 2000–08
GS 2000–05; 2010–
Tel: 020 8467 3589   07809 438737

SCOTT-JOYNT, Rt Revd Michael Charles, MA
Wolvesey Winchester SO23 9ND [BISHOP OF WIN-CHESTER] *b* 1943 *educ* Bradfield Coll; K Coll Cam; Cuddesdon Th Coll; *CV* C Cuddesdon 1967–70; Tutor Cuddesdon Th Coll 1967–72; TV Newbury 1972–75; R Bicester 1975–81; Can Res St Alb Cathl, DDO and POT 1982–87; Bp of Stafford 1987–95; Bp of Win from 1995; M Legislative Cttee; Visitor Alton Abbey
GS 1993–   *Tel:* 01962 854050
Fax: 01962 897088
email: michael.scott-joynt@dsl.pipex.com

SCOWEN, Mr Clive Richard, LLB
69 Brooke Ave Harrow HA2 0ND [LONDON] *b* 1958 *educ* John Lyon Sch Harrow; Bris Univ; Inns of Court Sch of Law; *CV* Called to bar (Inner Temple) 1981; law reporter, Incorporated Coun of Law Reporting 1983–90; Dep Ed Weekly Law Reports 1990–2000; Joint Ed, Law Reports Consolidated Index from 2000; Man Ed, Weekly Law Reports 2006–07; Ed Law Reports and Weekly Law Reports from 2008; Councillor, Lon Boro of Harrow 1990–2002; Rdr from 1991; M Bris Univ Court from 1980; Dir Glencoe Trust Ltd; Dir Soul Survivor Harrow; Trustee, Charles Gardner Meml Fund; Trustee, Maseno Project Trust; M MPA Coun; M GS Stg Orders Cttee; M Lon Dioc Bp's Coun; Dir Lon Dioc Fund; M Willesden Area Coun; M Bp of Lon's Miss Fund Bd; M Harrow Dny Stg Cttee
GS 2005–   *Tel:* 020 8422 1329
07771 780805 (Mobile)
email: clivescowen@onetel.com

SCREECH, Rt Revd Royden, BD, AKC
32 Falmouth Rd Truro TR1 2HX [SUFFRAGAN BISHOP OF ST GERMANS; TRURO] *b* 1953 *educ* Cotham Gr Sch Bris; K Coll Lon; St Aug Coll Cant; *CV* C St Cath Hatcham 1976–80; V St Ant Nunhead 1980–87; P-in-c St Silas Nunhead 1983–87; RD Camberwell 1983–87; V St Edw New Addington 1987–94; ABM Selection Sec and LNSM Co-ord 1994–96; Sen Selection Sec ABM 1997–98; Sen Selection Sec Min Div 1999–2000; Staff M Min Div; Sec to VRSC; Bp of St Germans from 2000
Tel: 01872 273190
Fax: 01872 277883
email: bishop@stgermans.truro.anglican.org

SEARLE, Revd Jacqueline Ann, MA, BEd, Dip Th
35 Church Street Littleover Derby DE23 6GF [DERBY] *b* 1960 *educ* Talbot Heath, Bournemouth; Whitelands Coll, Lon; Trin Coll Bris; *CV* Tchr 1982–90; C Ch Ch Roxeth 1992–94; C St Stephen's Ealing 1994–96; Tutor Applied Th & Dean of Women Trin Coll Bris 1996–2003; Dean of Women's Ministry Derby 2007–10; Incumb St Peter's, Littleover, Derby from 2003; Rural Dean of Derby South from 2010
GS 2010–   *Tel:* 01332 767802
email: jackie@stpeterlittleover.org.uk

SEDDON, Mr (William Trevor) Bill, BSc, ASIP
20 Carpenters Wood Drive Chorleywood Rickmansworth Herts WD3 5RJ [ST ALBANS] *b* 1952 *educ* Grove Park Boys' Gr Sch, Wrexham; UCL; *CV* Asst Investment Man, Central Fin Brd Methodist Ch, 1985–87; Investment Man, Dominion Insurance 1980–85; Asset Manager Paine Webber 1977–80; Asst Investment Man, White Weld 1975–77; Trainee Investment Man, Central Brd Fin C of E 1973–75; Investment M & CE, Central Fin Brd Methodist Ch and Epworth Investment Management Ltd from 1987.
GS 2010–   *Tel:* 01923 285727
Fax: 0207 496 3631
email: bill.seddon@cfbmethodistchurch

SEED, Ven Richard Murray Crosland, MA
Holy Trinity Rectory 81 Micklegate York YO1 6LE [ARCHDEACON OF YORK] *b* 1949 *educ* St Phil Sch Burley-in-Wharfedale; Leeds Univ; Edin Th Coll; *CV* C Ch Ch Skipton 1972–75; C Baildon 1975–77; TV Kidlington Ox 1977–80; P-in-c Clifford 1989–99; V Boston Spa 1980–99; P-in-c Thorp Arch w Walton 1998–99; RD of New Ainsty York 1997–99; R Holy Trin Micklegate from 1999; Adn of York from 1999; Chairman Martin Ho Children's Hospice; Chairman Dioc Pastl Cttee and Dioc Red Chs Users Cttee   *Tel:* 01904 623798
Fax: 01904 628155
email: archdeacon.of.york@yorkdiocese.org

SELBY, Suffragan Bishop of. See WALLACE, Rt Revd Martin William

SELVARATNAM, Revd Christian Nathan, BSc
52 The Gallops York YO24 3NF [YORK] *b* 1968 *educ* Wolfreton Sch; Univ of Warwick; Cranmer Hall Th Coll; *CV* York City Ch, Senior pastor, 1999–2004; Comm Ch, Bishop's Stortford, Asst Pastor 1994–99; Copyzone Printers, Bishop's Stortford, Mgr & Graphic designer 1992–96; Holy Trin Ch, Coventry, Head Verger 1990–92; Alpha International, Dirof Alpha in the North of England from 2004; G2 (Fresh Expression of Church), P-in-C from 2008; St Michael le Belfrey, Head of Discipleship and New Initiatives from 2010
GS 2010–   *Tel:* 01904 624190
          email: christian.selvaratnam@gmail.com

SENTAMU, Most Revd and Rt Hon Dr John Tucker Mugabi, LLB, MA, Ph D, LLD (Hon), DD (Hon), FRSA, Privy Counsellor
Bishopthorpe Palace Bishopthorpe York YO23 2GE [ARCHBISHOP OF YORK] *b* 1949 *educ* Makerere Univ Kampala; Selw Coll Cam; Ridley Hall Th Coll; *CV* Asst Chapl Selw Coll Cam 1979; Chapl HM Remand Cen Latchmere Ho 1979–82; C St Andr Ham 1979–82; C St Paul Herne Hill 1982–83; P-in-c H Trin Tulse Hill; Par Priest St Matthias 1983–84; V H Trin and St Matthias Tulse Hill 1984–96; P-in-c St Sav Brixton 1987–89; Bp of Stepney 1996–2002; M NACRO Young Offenders Cttee 1986–95; M Abp's Adv Grp on UPAs 1986–92; M ABM Coun from 1985; M Stg Cttee GS Ho of Clergy 1985–96; M GS Stg Cttee 1988–96; M GS Policy Cttee 1990–96; Chair Dioc Ho of Clergy 1992–96; M Decade of Evang Strg Grp and Springboard Exec 1991–96; M Turnbull Proposals Strg Grp; M Strg Grp Women (Priests) Ordination Measure; Pro-Prolocutor Conv of Cant 1990–94; Chair CMEAC 1990–99; Prolocutor Conv of Cant 1994–96; M The Stephen Lawrence Judicial Inquiry 1997–99; Pres and Chair Lon Marriage Guidance Coun 2000–04; Chair Damilola Taylor Murder Review 2002; Fell Univ Coll Ch Ch Cant 2001; Fell Qu Mary Coll Univ of Lon 2001; Hon Dr OU 2001; D Phil (Hon) Univ of Glos 2002; DD (Hon) Univ of Birm 2003; Chair ECI NDC 2002–04; Chair NHS Sickle Cell and Thalassaemia Screening Programme from 2001; Bp of Birmingham 2002–05; Midlander of the Year 2003; Vc-Chair Commn on Urban Life and Faith; Pres Youth for Christ, Eng and Nat YMCA; Abp of York from 2005; LLD (Hon), Univ of Leic 2005; Hon Fell Selw Coll Cam 2005; Chan York St Jo Univ from 2006; Freeman City of Lon 2000; DD (Hon) Univ of Hull 2007; DL (Hon) Univ of Sheff 2007; Yorkshire Man of the Year 2007; Speaker of the Year 2007; Master Bencher (Hon) Gray's Inn 2007; Freeman City of Montego Bay 2007; Chan Univ of Cumbria from 2007; Hon Dr Birm City Univ 2008; DD (Hon) Univ of Cam 2008; DCL (Hon) Northubria Univ 2008; DD (Hon) Univ of Nottm 2008; DD (Hon) Wycliffe Coll Toronto

2009; LLD (Hon) Teesside University 2009; York Tourism Awards "York Ambassador" 2010
GS 1985–96; 2002–   *Tel:* 01904 707021
                                  Fax: 01904 709204
          email: office@archbishopofyork.org

SEVILLE, Revd Thomas Christopher John, CR
House of the Resurrection Mirfield WF14 0BN [RELIGIOUS COMMUNITIES IN CONVOCATION, NORTH] *CV* Elected to GS 2005
GS 2005–

SHAND, Mr John Alexander Ogilvie, MA, LIB (Cant), MA (Birm)
1 Old Barhouse Mews Hill Top Longdon Green, Rugeley Staffordshire, WS15 4GA [LICHFIELD] *b* 1942 *educ* Nottingham High Sch; Queen's Coll Cam; Centre for Reformation and Early Modern Studies Univ Birm; *CV* Barrister Midland and Ox Circuit, 1965–69, 1972–81; Tutor and Fellow Queen's Coll Cam 1969–72; Chair Ind Tribunal 1981–88; Circuit Judge 1988–2005; Chan Dioc of Lich and S'well
GS 2010–   *Tel:* 01543492662
          email: jaoshand@yahoo.co.uk

SHARPLES, Ven David,
2 The Walled Gardens Ewhurst Avenue Swinton M7 0FR [ARCHDEACON OF SALFORD] *b* 1958 *CV* Adn of Salford from 2010   *Tel:* 0161 794 2331
                              0161 708 9366
          email: archdeaconsalford@
                  manchester.anglican.org

SHEFFIELD AND ROTHERHAM, Archdeacon of. See SNOW, Ven Martyn

SHEFFIELD, Bishop of. See CROFT, Rt Revd Dr Steven John Lindsey

SHEFFIELD, Dean of. See BRADLEY, Very Revd Peter Edward

SHELLEY, Dr (John Richard) Jack, MA, MB BChir, MRCGP
Shobrooke Park Crediton Devon EX17 1DG [EXETER] *b* 1943 *educ* King's Sch, Cam Univ; St Mary's Univ; Ex Univ; SWMTC Rdr Cert; *CV* Chair Devon Local Med Cttee 1999–2002; Partner South Molton Health Centre 1974–2003; Farmer 1974; Med Prac 1967; Rdr Ex 2009; M Ex Dioc Syn from 2002; M Counc Worship & Min Ex from 2003; Lay Chair Cadbury Deanery from 2005; Rdr from 2009
GS 2009–   *Tel:* 01363775153 07971136901
          email: jack@shobrookepark.com

SHERBORNE, Archdeacon of. See TAYLOR, Ven Paul Stanley

SHERBORNE, Area Bishop of. See KINGS, Rt Revd Graham Ralph

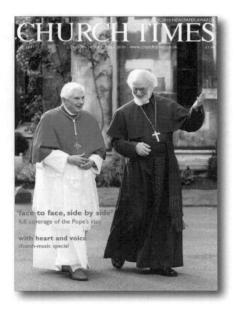

SHERIFF, Canon Suzanne, BA
78 Station Rd Tadcaster LS24 9JR [YORK] *b* 1963 *educ* Dorchester Gr Sch for Girls; Trin Coll Bris; *CV* Par Dn St Nich Hull 1987–91; Par Dn/C St Aidan Hull 1991–96; TV Marfleet 1996–2000; TR Marfleet 2000–07; M York Dioc Syn; M Coll of Cans York Minster from 2001; V Tadcaster and Newton Kyme from 2007
GS 2005–   *Tel:* 01937 833394
                          email: sue.sheriff@virgin.net

SHERWOOD, Suffragan Bishop of. See PORTER, Rt Revd Anthony

SHOREY, Mr Kenneth, BA, Cert Ed
30 Pool Road Hartley Wintney Hook RG27 8RD [WINCHESTER] *b* 1947 *educ* Greenford Gr Sch; Borough Road Coll; OU; *CV* Headteacher, Court Moor Sch, Hampshire, 1987–2005; Chief Exec Positive Parenting Publ & Programmes, 2006–09; Project Dir Care for the Family, 2009–10 Sessional Consultant for Hampshire County Counc from 2005
GS 2010–   *Tel:* 01252 843803
                          email: ken@shoreyfamily.co.uk

SHREWSBURY, Area Bishop of. See RYLANDS, Rt Revd Mark

SIDAWAY, Ven Geoffrey Harold,
Glebe House Church Lane Maisemore Gloucester GL2 8EY [ARCHDEACON OF GLOUCESTER] *b* 1942 *educ* Kelham Th Coll; *CV* C Beighton 1966–70; C All SS Chesterfield 1970–72; V St Bart Derby 1972–77; V St Mart Maidstone 1977–86; V Bearsted and Thurnham 1986–2000; RD Sutton 1992–2000; Hon Can Cant Cathl 1994–2000; Commr for Bp of Kinkizzi Uganda from 1995; Adn of Glos from 2000; Reserved Can Glos Cathl from 2000, Res Can from 2007
GS 1995–2000, 2005–07   *Tel:* 01452 528500
                          Fax: 01452 381528
                          email: archdglos@star.co.uk

SIMS, Ven Christopher Sidney,
1a Small Street, Walsall W Midlands WS1 3PR [ARCHDEACON OF WALSALL] *b* 1949 *educ* Bramcote Hills Gr Sch; Chester Coll of Ed; Wycliffe Hall; *CV* AC St Jo the Evang Walmley 1977–80; V St Cyprian w St Chad Hay Mill Birm 1980–88; V St Michael Stanwix w St Mark Belah Carl 1988–96; Rd Carl 1990–95; Hon Can Carl Cath 1991–96; P-in-C Allhallows and Torpenhow, Boltongate w Ireby and Uldale, Bassenthwaite w Isel and Setmurthy 1996–2001; TR Binsey TM 2001–03; V Shrewsbury Abbey and St Peter Monkmoor 2003–09; RD Shrewsbury 2008–09; Adn of Walsall from 2009
GS 2010–   *Tel:* 01922 707861
                   01922 709092 07527252752
                          Fax: 01922 700951
email: archdeacon.walsall@lichfield.anglican.org

SINCLAIR, Rt Revd (Gordon) Keith, MA, BA
Bishop's Lodge 67 Bidston Rd Prenton CH43 6TR [SUFFRAGAN BISHOP OF BIRKENHEAD; CHESTER] *b* 1952 *educ* Trin Sch Croydon; Ch Ch Ox; Cranmer Hall Dur; *CV* C Ch Ch Summerfield 1984–88; pt Chapl, Children's Hosp Birm; V SS Pet & Paul Aston juxta Birm 1988–2001; AD Aston 2000–01; V H Trin Cov 2001–06; Bp of Birkenhead from 2007; M Bp's Coun and Dioc Syn, Ches; Trustee/ Chair Ches DBE; Gov Bp's High Sch Ches; Trustee Historic Cheshire Chs Preservation Trust; Trustee Chs Together in Merseyside; Chair Gov Body for Bp's High Sch; Chair CPAS Coun of Reference   *Tel:* 0151 652 2741
                          Fax: 0151 651 2330
email: bpbirkenhead@chester.anglican.org

SINCLAIR, Ven Jane Elizabeth Margaret, MA, BA
Sanderlings Willingham Rd Market Rasen LN8 3RE [ARCHDEACON OF STOW AND LINDSEY; LINCOLN] *b* 1956 *educ* Westonbirt Sch Tetbury; St Hugh's Coll Ox; Nottm Univ; St Jo Coll Nottm; *CV* Dss St Paul w St Jo Herne Hill and St Sav Ruskin Park 1983– 86; Lect in Liturg and Chapl St Jo Coll Nottm 1986–93; Can Res and Prec Sheff Cathl 1993–2003; M Liturg Commn 1986–2001; M Archbishops' Commn on Ch Music 1989–1992; M Cathl Fabric Commn for Eng from 2001; V Rotherham Minster (All SS) 2003–07; Adn of Stow and Lindsey from 2007
GS 1995–2007   *Tel:* 01673 849896
                       07809 521995 (Mobile)
                email: archdeacon.stowlindsey@
                          lincoln.anglican.org

SINCLAIR, Revd John Robert,
The Vicarage High Street Newburn Newcastle NE15 8LQ [NEWCASTLE] *b* 1958 *educ* Walbottle High Sch; Oak Hill Th Coll; *CV* C, Ponteland S Mary Newcastle 1992–96; V Longbenton St Mary Magdalene Newcastle 1996–2001; V Newburn St Michael & All Angels Newcastle from 2001; Area Dean Newcastle West from 2007; Hon Can Newcastle Cathl from 2008; Chair House of Clergy from 2009; M Evang Task Group 2001; M Dioc Fin Strategy Grp 2009
GS 2010–   *Tel:* 01912290522 07746743857
                   email: johnsinclair247@aol.com

SKILTON, Ven Christopher John, MA, Cert Theol, MA (Miss & Min)
7 Hoadly Rd London SW16 1AE [ARCHDEACON OF LAMBETH; SOUTHWARK] *b* 1955 *educ* Latymer Upper Sch Hammersmith; Magd Coll Cam; Wycliffe Hall Ox; *CV* C St Mary Ealing 1980–84; C Newborough w Leigh St Jo Wimborne 1984–88; TV St Paul Gt Baddow 1988–95; TR Sanderstead 1995–2003; RD Croydon S 2000–03; Adn of Lambeth from 2004   *Tel:* 020 8545 2440 (Office)
                   020 8769 4384 (Home)
                   07903 704506 (Mobile)
                   Fax: 020 8545 2441 (Office)
email: chris.skilton@southwark.anglican.org

SLACK, Mr Stephen, MA
Church House Great Smith Street London SW1P 3AZ
[REGISTRAR AND CHIEF LEGAL ADVISER TO THE
GENERAL SYNOD, JOINT REGISTRAR OF THE PROV-
INCES OF CANTERBURY AND YORK, CHIEF LEGAL
ADVISER TO THE ARCHBISHOPS' COUNCIL AND
OFFICIAL SOLICITOR TO THE CHURCH COMMIS-
SIONERS] *b* 1954 *educ* Aylesbury Gr Sch; Ch Ch
Ox; *CV* Solicitor in private practice 1979–84; Sen
Lawyer Charity Commn Liv 1984–89; Hd Legal
Section Charity Commn Taunton 1989–2001; Hd
Legal Office and Chief Legal Adv to AC and GS
from 2001, Registrar GS, Jt Registrar Provinces
Cant and York, M Legal Adv Commn from 2001;
Official Solicitor to Ch Commrs from 2009
Tel: 020 7898 1366
Fax: 020 7898 1718
020 7898 1721
email: stephen.slack@c-of-e.org.uk

SLATER, Mr Colin Stuart, MBE
11 Muriel Rd Beeston Nottingham NG9 2HH
[SOUTHWELL AND NOTTINGHAM] *b* 1934 *educ* Belle
Vue Gr Sch Bradf; *CV* Chief PRO Notts Co Coun
1969–87, Severn Trent Water 1987–89, Notts Co
Cricket Club 1989–95; Chair BBC Radio Nottm
Adv Coun 1975–79; former Chair Soc of Co PROs
and IPR Local Govt Grp; M Coun Inst of PR
1986–90; JP 1977–2004; Chair Nottingham
Magistrates 2003 and 2004; Chair Notts Courts
Bd 2005–07; Chair Notts-Derbys Courts Bd from
2007; PR Consult and freelance broadcaster from
1995; M Bp's Coun, Fin Cttee; Vc-Chair Chr
Stewardship Cttee of AC from 1999; M Coun St Jo
(Nottm) Coll from 2006 and its Stg Cttee from
2008, Vc Chair from 2010
GS 1990– *Tel:* 0115 925 7532
07919 008788 (Mobile)
Fax: 0115 925 7532
email: colinslater@mac.com

SLATER, Ven Paul John, MA, BA
*Woodlands Netherghyll Lane Cononley Keighley
BD20 8PB* [ARCHDEACON OF CRAVEN; BRADFORD] *b*
1958 *educ* Bradf Gr Sch; Corpus Christi Ox; St Jo
Coll Dur; *CV* C St Andr Keighley 1984–88; P-in-c
St Jo Cullingworth 1988–93; Dir Lay Trg Foundn
Course 1988–93; PA to Bp of Bradf 1993–95; Wrdn
of Rdrs 1992–96; R St Mich Haworth 1995–2001;
Bp's Officer for Min from 2001; Adn of Craven
from 2005 *Tel and Fax:* 01535 635113
email: paulj.slater@dial.pipex.com

SLATER, Mrs Susan Gay, Cert Ed, DGA
3 Church St Spalding PE11 2PB [LINCOLN] *b* 1944
educ Ox High Sch; Homerton Coll Cam; *CV*
Admin trainee/Higher Exec Officer, DHSS 1967–
74; domestic admin and voluntary work 1974–94;
PA to Nat Dir Leprosy Mission England and
Wales 1994–2005; rtd 2005; Gen Adv S Holland
CAB; M Linc Dioc HR Cttee; Sec Elloe W Dny

Syn; M Ch & Com Fund Cttee; Chair S Holland
Fairtrade Steering Gp
GS 2005– *Tel:* 01775 768286
email: sueslater@d-lweb.net

SLEE, Very Revd Colin Bruce, OBE, FKC, BD, AKC
Provost's Lodging London SE1 9JE [DEAN OF
SOUTHWARK] *b* 1945 *educ* Ealing Gr Sch; K Coll
Lon; St Aug Coll Cant; *CV* C St Fran Heartsease
Norw 1970-73; C Gt St Mary Cam 1973–76; Chapl
Girton Coll Cam 1973–76; Chapl and Tutor K Coll
Lon 1976–82; Sub Dean and Can Res St Alb 1982–
94; Provost of S'wark from 1994, Dean from 2000
GS 1995– *Tel:* 020 7928 6414 (Home)
020 7367 6731 (Office)
07831 627090 (Mobile)
Fax: 020 7928 6414 (Home)
020 7367 6725 (Office)
email: Colin.Slee@dswark.org.uk (Office)
/ SleeBanks@aol.com (Home)

SLOMAN, Mrs Anne, BA, OBE
All Saints Cottage Bale Rd Sharrington NR24 2PF
[CHAIR, CHURCH BUILDINGS COUNCIL] *b* 1944 *educ*
Farlington, Horsham; St Hilda's Coll Ox; *CV* BBC
journalist 1967–2003; ed five gen election pro-
grammes 1974–92; asst ed Today Programme
1981–82; ed Special Current Affairs 1983–93; dep
hd weekly TV and radio programmes 1994–96; M
Coun RIIA 1992–2002; BBC's Chief Political Adv
1996–2003; OBE 2004; M McLean Wkg Pty,
Clergy Terms of Service from 2003; M C of E
Broadcasting Grp 2004–09; M Communications
Panel from 2004; Trustee Norfolk Com Foundn
from 2005; Vc-Chair Norfolk Com Foundn from
2006; Co-ord Ch Buildings Campaign 2006–09;
Appt M Abp's Coun 2002–09; Chair Ch Buildings
Coun from 2009 *Tel:* 01263 862291 (Norfolk)
020 77402 0576 (London)
07717 772174 (Mobile)
Fax: 01263 862291 (Home)
email: annesloman@hotmail.com

SMITH, Rt Revd Dr Alan Gregory Clayton, BA,
MA, Ph D, Hon DD (Birm)
*Abbey Gate House Abbey Mill Lane St Albans AL3
4HD* [BISHOP OF ST ALBANS] *b* 1957 *educ* Trow-
bridge High Sch for Boys; Birm Univ; Wycliffe
Hall Th Coll; Univ of Wales, Bangor; *CV* C St
Lawr Pudsey 1981–82, w St Paul 82–84; Chapl
Lee Abbey 1984–90; Dioc Missr and Exec Sec
Lichf Dioc BMU 1990–97; TV St Matt Walsall
1990–97; Adn of Stoke-upon-Trent 1997–2001;
Canon of Lichfield Cathedral, 1997–2009; Bp of
Shrewsbury 2001–09; Chair Shrops Strategic
Ptnrship 2006–09; M Rural Bps Panel from 2006–
09; Joint Chair Angl Meth Working Party on the
Ecclesiology of Emerging Expressions of Ch from
2009; Bp of St Albans from 2009
GS 1999–2001, 2009– *Tel:* 01727 853305
Fax: 01727 846715
email: bishop@stalbans.anglican.org

SMITH, Ven Brian, MTh (Oxon), Cert Th
*St George's Vicarage 16 Devonshire Rd Douglas IM2
3RB* [ARCHDEACON OF THE ISLE OF MAN; SODOR
AND MAN] *b* 1944 *educ* Preston Gr Sch, Barton
Peveril Gr Sch, Eastleigh; Westmr Coll Ox; Salis &
Wells Th Coll; *CV* C St Thos w. St Oswald Pen-
nywell, Sunderland, Dur 1974–77; Chapl RAF
1977–95; V St Jo Keswick, Carl 1995–2005; P-in-c
St Bridget Bridekirk, Carl 2002–04; RD Derwent
1997–2005; Hon Can Carl Cath 1999–2005; Adn of
Isle of Man and V St Geo Douglas from 2005; M
GS, Dioc Syn, Chair DAC, IOM Ch Commrs,
DBF, Soc Resp Cttee, Legislative Cttee, Vacancy-
in-see Cttee, Communications Cttee from 2005;
Trustee K William's Coll IOM
GS 2010– *Tel:* 01624 675430
email: arch-sodor@mcb.net

SMITH, Mr Christopher John Addison, BA, FCA
Lambeth Palace London SE1 7JU [CHIEF OF STAFF,
LAMBETH PALACE] *b* 1949 *educ* St Pet Sch York;
Univ of E Anglia; *CV* Price Waterhouse 1970–93,
various trainee and mgmt posts 1970–89, Human
Resources Ptnr 1989–93; Gen Sec Dioc of Lon
1993–99; Gen Mgr C. Hoare & Co. Bankers 1999–
2003; M CBF, Exec, Staff Cttee, AC Fin Cttee
1995–2000; Chief of Staff, Lambeth Palace from
2003
GS 1995–2000 *Tel:* 020 7898 1200
email: chris.smith@lambethpalace.org.uk

SMITH, Very Revd Graham Charles Morell, BA
The Deanery The Close Norwich NR1 4 EG [DEAN OF
NORWICH] *b* 1947 *educ* Whitgift Sch Croydon; Dur
Univ; Westcott Ho Cam; *CV* C All SS Tooting
Graveney, S'wark 1976–80; TV Thamesmead
Ecum Par, S'wark 1980–87; TR Kidlington w.
Hampton Poyle, Ox 1987–97; R Leeds 1997–2004;
Dean of Norwich from 2004 *Tel:* 01603 218308
Fax: 01603 766032
email: dean@cathedral.org.uk

SMITH, Mr Graham William, BSc, DMS
20 Parklands Wotton-under-Edge GL12 7LT
[GLOUCESTER] *b* 1943 *educ* Mundella Gr Sch;
Aston Univ; *CV* Principal Eng, Project Manage-
ment Dept, Nat Power plc until 1992; Bursar and
Clerk to Govs, Katharine Lady Berkeley's Sch
1993–96; rtd 1996; M Bp's Coun; M Dioc Syn; M
IDFF
GS 2005– *Tel:* 01453 842618
email: smithgra@supanet.com

SMITH, Ven Jonathan Peter,
6 Sopwell Lane St Albans Herts AL1 1RR [ARCH-
DEACON OF ST ALBANS] *b* 1955 *educ* Ipswich Sch;
King's Coll London; Queens' Coll Cam; Westcott
Ho Cam; *CV* Asst C All Saints' Gosforth 1980–82;
Asst C Waltham Abbey 1982–85; Chapl The City
Univ 1985–88; R Harrold and Carlton w Chel-
lington 1988–97; V St John's Harpenden 1997–
2008; Rural Dean Wheathampstead 1999–2008;
Adn St Alb from 2008; St Alb Bp's Counc; St Alb

Brd Patronage; St Alb Brd Fin; St Alb Miss & Pstrl
Cttee; St Alb Brd Ed; St Alb Adv Cttee; St Alb
Urban Forum; Residentiary Can Cathl and
Abbey Ch of St Alb
GS 2010– *Tel:* 01727 818121
Fax: 01727 844469
email: archdstalbans@stalbans.anglican.org

SMITH, Mr Peter Reg, FRICS
*Lusaka House Great Glemham Saxmundham IP17
2DH* [ST EDMUNDSBURY AND IPSWICH] *b* 1946 *educ*
K Edw VI Sch Southn; Coll of Estate Mgt; *CV* M
Coun USPG from 1991; Chair Dioc Overseas
Miss Grp 1997–2004; Chair Dioc Ho of Laity
1997–2000; M Bd of Miss 2001–03; M Bp's Coun
and Pastl Cttee; M Vacancy-in-See Cttee; M Revision Cttee, Common Worship Ordinal; M Revision Cttee, Pastl (Amendment) Measure; M CFCE
from 2006; Lay Can St Eds Cathl from 2005;
Trustee, Queen Victoria Clergy Fund
GS 1993– *Tel:* 01728 663466
07790 596502 (Mobile)
email: happyhackers@usa.net

**SODOR AND MAN, Bishop of. See
PATERSON, Rt Revd Robert Mar Erskine**

SOUTHAMPTON, Suffragan Bishop of. (NOT
APPOINTED AT TIME OF GOING TO PRESS)

**SOUTHEND, Archdeacon of. See LOWMAN,
Ven David Walter**

SOUTHERN, Rt Revd Humphrey Ivo John, MA
Repton House Church St, Lea Matlock DE4 5JP [SUF-
FRAGAN BISHOP OF REPTON; DERBY] *b* 1960 *educ*
Harrow Sch; Ch Ch Ox; Ripon Coll Cuddesdon;
CV C St Marg Rainham, Roch 1986–89; C Walton-
on-the-Hill, Liv 1989–92; V Hale, TR Hale w. Bad-
shot Lea, Guild 1992–99; Guild Dioc Ecum Officer
1993–99; TR Tisbury, TR Nadder Valley Tm Min,
Sarum 1999–2007; RD Chalke 2000–07; Hon Can
Salis Cathl 2006–07; Bp of Repton from 2007; M
Guild Dioc Syn 1992–99; M Sarum Dioc Syn
2000–07; Chair Ho of Clergy, Sarum Dioc Syn
2004–07; M Sarum Dioc Pastl Cttee 2000–07;
Chair Derby Dioc Pastl Cttee from 2007
Tel: 01629 534644
Fax: 01629 534003
email: bishop@repton.free-online.co.uk

**SOUTHWARK, Archdeacon of. See IPGRAVE,
Ven Dr Michael Geoffrey**

**SOUTHWARK, Bishop of, See CHESSUN,
Rt Revd Christopher Thomas James**

**SOUTHWARK, Dean of. See SLEE, Very Revd
Colin Bruce**

**SOUTHWELL AND NOTTINGHAM, Bishop
of. See BUTLER, Rt Revd Paul Roger**

SOUTHWELL AND NOTTINGHAM, Dean of.
See GUILLE, Very Revd John Arthur

SOWERBY, Rt Revd Mark Crispin Rake, BD, AKC, MA
Bishop's House 21 Guildford Rd Horsham W Sussex RH12 1LU [BISHOP OF HORSHAM] *b* 1963 *educ* Barnard Castle Sch; St Aidan & St Jo Fisher's United Sixth Form Harrogate; K Coll Lon; Lanc Univ, Coll of Resurrection, Mirfield; *CV* C Knaresborough 1987–90; C St Cuth Darwen w. St Steph Tockholes 1990–92; V St Mary Magd Accrington 1992–97; Chapl St Christopher's CE Hich Schl Accrington 1992–97; Chapl Accrington Victoria Hosp 1992–97; Asst DDO Blackb 1993–96; M Blackburn Dioc Syn; Selection Sec/Vocations Officer ABM/Min Div of AC 1997–2001; Sec Vocations Adv Sub-Cttee (ABM) then Voc Panel (Min Div); Staff M VRSC and Candidates Cttee/Panel 1997–2001; V St Wilf Harrogate 2001–04, TR from 2004; M Ripon Dioc Syn; Asst DDO Ripon 2005–09; Dio Minl Rev Adv from 2008; M Mirfield/NOC Jt Monitoring Body; Bp's Insp of Colls and Courses; M Coun Coll of Ressurection, Mirfield; Frere Trustee (Mirfield); M VRSC 2006–07; M Min Coun from 2008; TR St Wilfrid's Harrogate; M Ripon Dioc Dyn 2002–09; M Mirfield/NOC Jt Monitoring Body 2001–09; M Coun Coll of Resurrection Mirfield 2005–09; Area Bp of Horsham from 2009
GS 2005–09   *Tel:* 01403 211139
                              Fax: 01403 217349
       email: bishop.horsham@diochi.org.uk

SPENCER, Mrs Caroline Sarah, BA, PGCE
Little Eggarton Godmersham Canterbury CT4 7DY [CANTERBURY] *b* 1953 *educ* Wycombe Abbey Sch; St Hilda's Coll Ox; Lon Univ Inst of Educ; *CV* Asst Tchr Hist Sydenham High Sch 1976–80; pt Tutor Westmr Tutors Ltd 1981–84; Mother and Vol Worker for Ch and Com from 1980; M Abp's Coun; Chair Dioc Ho of Laity; Lay Member, Chapter of Cant Cathl
GS 1995–   *Tel:* 01227 731170
                       07947 045025 (Mobile)
                              Fax: 01227 731170
       email: caroline@eggarton.eclipse.co.uk

SPENCER, Dr Jonathan Page, MA DPhil
Little Eggarton, Eggarton Lane Godmersham Canterbury CT4 7DY [CHAIR, CHURCH OF ENGLAND PENSIONS BOARD] *b* 1949 *educ* Bournemouth Sch; Cambridge Univ; Oxford Univ; *CV* Chair Church of England Pensions Board
                              Tel: 01227 731170
       email: jspencer@eggarton.eclipse.co.uk

SPIERS, Canon Peter Hendry, BA, Cert Th
St Luke's Vicarage 71 Liverpool Rd Crosby Liverpool L23 5SE [LIVERPOOL] *b* 1961 *educ* Liv Coll; St Jo Coll Dur; Ridley Hall Th Coll; *CV* C St Luke Princess Drive 1986–90; TV St Pet Everton 1990–95; V

St Geo Everton 1995–2005; P-in-c St Luke Crosby from 2005
GS 2000–   *Tel:* 0151 924 1737
       email: pete@spiersfamily.eclipse.co.uk

SPRINGETT, Ven Robert, BTh, MA
Abbey Cottage Stables 1 Gloucester Rd Tewkesbury Gloucestershire GL20 5SS [ARCHDEACON OF CHELTENHAM] *b* 1962 *educ* Brentwood Sch; Nottm Univ; Kings Coll Lon; Lincoln Theol Coll; *CV* C St James Colchester 1989–92; C St Martin Basildon 1992–94; P-in-C South Ockendon and Belhus Park 1994–2001; AD Thurrock 1998–2001; R Wanstead 2001–10; Area Dean of Redbridge 2008–10; Adn of Cheltenham from 2010; M DAC Bd of Educ   *Tel:* 01684 300067
       email: archdchelt@glosdioc.org.uk

ST ALBANS, Archdeacon of. See SMITH, Ven Jonathan Peter

ST ALBANS, Bishop of. See SMITH, Rt Revd Alan Gregory Clayton

ST ALBANS, Dean of. See JOHN, Very Revd Jeffrey Philip Hywel

ST EDMUNDSBURY AND IPSWICH, Bishop of. See STOCK, Rt Revd (William) Nigel

ST EDMUNDSBURY, Dean of. See WARD, Very Revd Dr Frances Elizabeth Fearn

ST GERMANS, Suffragan Bishop of. See SCREECH, Rt Revd Royden

ST PAUL'S, Dean of. (NOT APPOINTED AT TIME OF GOING TO PRESS)

STAFFORD, Area Bishop of. See ANNAS, Rt Revd Geoff

STEADMAN, Revd Mark John, LLB, MA
St Philip's Vicarage Avondale Square London SE1 5PD [SOUTHWARK] *b* 1974 *educ* Horndean Comm Sch; Univ of Southampton; Inns of Court Sch of Law; Cam Univ; Westcott Ho Th Coll; *CV* AC S. Mary's Portsea 2002–05; P-in-C S. Philip with S. Mark Camberwell from 2005; Area Dean Bermondsey from 2008; Acting Area Dean Camberwell from 2009; M Dioc IME Staff Team from 2005; M Dioc Brd Fin from 2010; M Dioc Exec & Glebe Cttee from 2010
GS 2010–   *Tel:* 0207 237 3239
       email: frmark.steadman@yahoo.co.uk

STEPNEY, Area Bishop of. (NOT APPOINTED AT TIME OF GOING TO PRESS)

STEVENS, Canon Anne, BA, MA, MTh
93 Bolingbroke Grove London SW11 6HA [SOUTHWARK] *b* 1961 *CV* Elected to GS 2005
GS 2005–   *Tel:* 020 7228 1990
       email: anne.stevens@southwark.anglican.org

STEVENS, Mr Robin Michael, B Sc
3 Aldeburgh Way Chelmsford CM1 7PB [CHELMS-
FORD] *b* 1945 *educ* Chigwell Sch; Birm Univ; *CV*
Eng Marconi Communication Systems 1967–79;
eng Thames Television 1979–91; Nat Stewardship
Officer, AC 1992–2005; Chelmsford Borough
councillor from 2005; Rdr from 1990
GS 2005–   *Tel:* 01245 268042
                        email: rms@ukgateway.net

STEVENS, Rt Revd Timothy John, MA, DCL, DLitt
Bishop's Lodge 10 Springfield Rd Leicester LE2 3BD
[BISHOP OF LEICESTER] *b* 1946 *educ* Chigwell Sch;
Selw Coll Cam; Ripon Coll Cuddesdon; *CV* C E
Ham TM 1976–79; TV St Alb Upton Park 1979–80;
TR Canvey Island 1980–88; Bp of Chelmsf's
Urban Officer 1988–91; Adn of West Ham 1991–
95; Bp of Dunwich 1995–99; Bp of Leic from 1999;
Chair Urban Bps Panel 2001–06; Chair Children's
Soc from 2004; M AC from 2006; M Ho of Bps
Standing Cttee from 2006
GS 1987–95, 1999–   *Tel:* 0116 270 8985
                                   07860 692258
                              Fax: 0116 270 3288
                     email: bishop.tim@leccofe.org

STOBAR, Revd Brenda Jacqueline, BSc, BA, PGCE
28 Elswick Green Marshside Southport PR9 9XT
[LIVERPOOL] *b* 1957 *educ* Childwall Valley High
Sch; Liv Univ; Lanc Univ; Leeds Univ; Northern
Ordination Course; *CV* Biology tchr, Liv 1981–86;
Day-care provider 1992–98; Science and Music
Co-ord, Sefton, 1999–06; Special Needs tchr,
Sefton,2006-07; Stipendiary C, Emmanuel P Ch,
Southport from 2007"
GS 2010–   *Tel:* 01704227294
                     email: ukjacquel@yahoo.co.uk

STOBART, Dr Cherida Dawn, BSc, BVSc, PhD, MRCVS
*Fern Cottage 31 Pauls Causeway Congresbury North
Somerset* [BATH AND WELLS] *b* 1962 *educ* St Clare's
Convent Sch, Glamorgan; Bryntirion Comp,
Glamorgan; Bris Univ; Open Univ; Trin Coll, Bris;
Vet Surgeon, Hereford, 1986–87;; *CV* Rsch Asst,
Vet Med, Bris Univ 1987–88; PhD Vet Med Bris
Univ 1988–1991; Post Doc Rsch Assoc, Vet Med
Bris Univ 1992–93; Rsch Assoc, Social Med, 1994;
Rsch Fell, Health Services Rsch, 1995–98; Rsch
Manager, Med Rsch Coun (MRC) Health Services
Rsch Unit, Bris Univ 1998–2000; Finance and HR
Manager, MRC Health Services Rsch Unit, Bris
Univl 2000–2007; MRC Clinical Trial Manager,
Primary Care, Bris Uni from 2008
GS 2010–   *Tel:* 01934 832188

STOCK, Very Revd Victor Andrew, OAM, AKC,
FRSA
The Deanery 1 Cathedral Close Guildford GU2 7TL
[DEAN OF GUILDFORD] *b* 1944 *educ* Christopher
Wren Sch; K Coll Lon; St Boniface Coll Warmin-
ster; *CV* C Pinner, Lon 1969–73; Res Chapl Lon
Univ 1973–79; R Friern Barnet 1979–86; R St

Mary-le-Bow, City of Lon 1986–2002; Dean of
Guildford from 2002
GS 1980–86   *Tel:* 01483 560328 (Home)
                              01483 547862 (Office)
                              Fax: 01483 303350
              email: dean@guildford-cathedral.org

STOCK, Rt Revd (William) Nigel, BA, Dip Theol
Bishop's House 4 Park Rd Ipswich IP1 3ST [BISHOP
OF ST EDMUNDSBURY AND IPSWICH] *b* 1950 *educ*
Dur Sch; Dur Univ; Ripon Coll Cuddesdon; *CV* C
St Pet Stockton 1976–79; P-in-c St Pet Taraka,
PNG 1979–84; V St Mark Shiremoor 1985–91; TR
N Shields 1991–98; RD Tynemouth 1992–98; Hon
Can Newc Cathl 1997–98; Res Can Dur Cathl
1998–2000; Bp of Stockport 2000–07; Bp of St E & I
from 2007; M Ho of Bps CME Cttee 2002–09; M
Appts Cttee of C of E from 2003; Chair Local
Unity Panel (CCU) 2007–09; M Min Coun from
2008; M Dioc Commn from 2008; Co-Chair Meth
Angl Panel for Unity in Miss from 2009; Chair
Melanesian Miss from 2009
GS 2003–   *Tel:* 01473 252829
                             Fax: 01473 232552

STOCKPORT, Suffragan Bishop of. (NOT
APPOINTED AT TIME OF GOING TO PRESS)

**STOKE-UPON-TRENT, Archdeacon of. See
STONE, Ven Godfrey Owen**

STOKOE, Father (Wayne) Jeffrey, Dip HE
17 Heaton Gardens Edlington DN12 1SY [SHEF-
FIELD] *b* 1956 *educ* Trin Ho Navigation Sch, Hull;
Coll of the Resurrection, Mirfield; *CV* C St Cath-
erine of Siena Sheff 1996–98; V St Jo the Baptist
Edlington from 1999; Hon Chapl 103 (Doncaster)
sqdrn ATC from 2003
GS 2009–   *Tel:* 01709 858358
              email: wjs@stokoej.freeserve.co.uk

STONE, Ven Godfrey Owen, MA, PGCE, Dip LRM
*39 The Brackens Clayton Newcastle-under-Lyme
ST5 4JL* [ARCHDEACON OF STOKE-UPON-TRENT;
LICHFIELD] *b* 1949 *educ* St Bart Gr Sch Newbury;
Ex Coll Ox; Wycliffe Hall Ox; *CV* C Rushden with
Newton Bromswold, Peterb 1981–87; Dir of Pastl
Studies, Wycliffe Hall Ox 1987–92; TR Bucknall
Tm Min, Lich 1992–2002; RD Stoke-upon-Trent
1998–2002; Adn of Stoke-on-Trent from 2002
                             Tel: 01782 663066
                                   07786 447115
                              Fax: 01782 711165
    email: archdeacon.stoke@lichfield.anglican.org

STORKEY, Dr Elaine, BA, MA, DD, Ph D (Hon)
*The Old School High St Coton Cambridgeshire CB23
7PL* [ELY] *educ* Ossett Gr Sch; Univ Coll of Wales
Abth; McMaster Univ Ontario; York Univ; *CV*
Tutor in Philosophy Man Coll Ox 1967–68; Rsch
Fell in Sociology Stirling Univ 1968–69; Tutor
Open Univ 1976–80; Vis Lect Calvin Coll USA
1980–81; Covenant Coll USA 1981–82; Lect in

Philosophy Oak Hill Th Coll 1982–87; Lect in Faculty of Social Science Open Univ 1987–91; Dir Inst for Contemporary Christianity 1992–98; Vis Lect in Theol K Coll Lon 1996–2001; Ext Mod Birkbeck Coll Lon from 1998; Scriptwriter for BBC OU; Assoc Ed 'Third Way' from 1984; Broadcaster BBC from 1987; M ACORA 1988–90; M Crown Appts Commn 1990; Vc-Pres UCCF 1987–93; M Abps' Commn on Cathl 1992–94; M Lausanne Wkg Pty on Th 1992–97; M CRAC 1993–98; Examiner Sociology of Religion Lon Univ from 1993; Trustee C of E Newspaper from 1994; Vc-Pres Cheltenham and Glouc Coll of HE from 1994; M Forum for the Future 1995–98; M Orthodox-Evang Dialogue WCC from 1996; New Coll Scholar Univ of NSW Sydney 1997; Pres Tear Fund from 1997; M Wkg Pty on Chr-Jewish Relns from 1998; Lambeth DD 1998; M John Ray Inst from 1999; Sen Rsch Fell Wycliffe Hall, Ox 2003–07; M CNC 2002–07; Visiting Prof Messiah Coll, Pennsylvania, USA summer 2005; Chair Fulcrum from 2006; columnist for Swedish newspaper 'Dagen' from 2006; Chair Ch Army Ord and Commn Review Gp 2007–08; Examiner Univ of Wales 2008
GS 1987–
> *Tel:* 01954 212381 07969 354673 (Mobile)
> *email:* elaine@storkey.com

STOW AND LINDSEY, Archdeacon of. See SINCLAIR, Ven Jane Elizabeth Margaret

STRAIN, Revd Christopher Malcolm, LLB,
Solicitor, Cert Theol
St Luke's Vicarage 2 Birchwood Rd Parkstone Poole BH14 9NP [SALISBURY] *b* 1956 *educ* Aldwickbury Prep Sch; Bedford Sch; Southn Univ; Guildf Coll of Law; Wycliffe Hall; *CV* C St Jo w. Em Werrington, Peterb 1986–89; C-in-charge St Steph Broadwater, Worthing, Chich 1989–1994; TV Hampreston and Stapehill, Wimborne, Salis 1994–2000; V St Luke Parkstone from 2000; Sch gov; Chapl to Scouts and Cubs, Poole; Surrogate for Marriages; Chair Ch Together in Poole
GS 2005–
> *Tel:* 01202 741030
> *email:* cmstrain@tiscali.co.uk

STRATFORD, Revd Dr Timothy Richard, B Sc,
PhD
Rectory Old Hall Lane Kirkby L32 5TH [LIVERPOOL] *b* 1961 *educ* Knowsley Hey Comp Sch; York Univ; Wycliffe Hall Th Coll; Univ of Sheff; *CV* C Mossley Hill 1986–89; C St Helens St Helen 1989–91; Chapl to Bp of Liv 1991–94; V Gd Shep W Derby 1994–2003; TR Kirkby and TV St Chad Kirkby from 2003; M Liturg Commn from 2006
GS 2000–
> *Tel:* 0151 547 2155
> 078855 734914 (Mobile)
> *Fax:* 08701 673589
> *email:* tim.stratford@btinternet.com

STROYAN, Rt Revd John Ronald Angus,
M Theol, MA
Warwick House 139 Kenilworth Rd Coventry CV4

7AP [SUFFRAGAN BISHOP OF WARWICK; COVENTRY] *b* 1955 *educ* Harrow Sch; St Andr Univ; Q Coll Birm; Ecum Inst, Bossey, Switzerland; Univ of Wales; *CV* C St Pet Hillfields, Cov E Tm 1983–87; V St Matt w. St Chad Smethwick, Birm 1987–94; V Bloxham, Milcombe & S Newington, Ox 1994–2005; AD Deddington, Ox 2002–05; Bp of Warwick from 2005; Pres Com of the Cross of Nails UK from 2007; Sec W Midlands Regional Gp from 2008; M Rural Bps' Panel from 2009; Co-Moderator Chs Together in Cov and Warwickshire from 2009; M Internat Commn for Angl-Orthodox Theol Dialogue from 2009
> *Tel:* 024 7641 2627
> *Fax:* 024 7641 5254
> *email:* bishop.warwick@CovCofE.org

STUART, Rt Revd Ian Campbell, MA, BA, Cert Ed,
Dip Ed Admin
Pro Vice-Chancellor's Office Liverpool Hope University Hope Park Taggart Avenue Liverpool L16 9JD [ASSISTANT BISHOP, LIVERPOOL] *educ* New England Univ (NSW); Melbourne Univ; St Barn Coll of Min, Townsville; *CV* Australia 85–99; Asst Bp and Bp Administrator N Queensland 1992–99; Chapl Liv Hope 1999–2001; Asst Bp Liv from 1999; Provost Hope Park 2001–05; Asst Vc-Chan Liv Hope Univ from 2005   *Tel:* 0151 291 3547
> *Fax:* 0151 291 3669
> *email:* Stuarti@hope.ac.uk

STURGESS, Mrs Sheridan Jane, MA, FCA
Holywell Pengover Road Liskeard Cornwall PL14 3NW [TRURO] *b* 1955 *educ* Kidderminster H Sch; Newnham Coll, Cam; *CV* Dioc Sec, Truro, 2002–10; Stewardship Adv, Truro 1997–2002; Parish Admin, St Martins Ch, Liskeard 1994–97; Self-employed Chartered Accountant, Sheridan Sturgess & Co 1983–94; M Fin Cttee 2008–10; M Ch & Comm Fund 2005–09; M Inter-Dioc Fin Forum 2002–10
GS 2010–
> *Tel:* 01579 346411
> *email:* sheri.sturgess@googlemail.com

SUDBURY, Archdeacon of, JENKINS, Ven Dr David Harold

SUFFOLK, Archdeacon of. See HUNT, Ven Judy (Judith Mary)

SULLIVAN, Ven Nicola Ann, BTh, SRN, RM
6 The Liberty Wells BA5 2SU [ARCHDEACON OF WELLS; BATH AND WELLS] *b* 1958 *educ* Ips Convent of Jesus and Mary; Mills Gr Sch, Framlingham; St Bart's Hosp; Bris Maternity Hosp; Wycliffe Hall Ox; *CV* C St Anne Earlham, Norw 1995–99; Assoc V Bath Abbey 1999–2002; Subdean Wells Cathl 2003–07; Bp's Chapl and Pastl Asst 2002–07; Adn of Wells and Res Can Wells Cathl from 2007; M Norw Dioc Syn 1997–99; M B & W Dioc Syn, Bp's Coun, DBF   *Tel:* 01749 685147
> *Fax:* 01749 679755
> *email:* adwells@bathwells.anglican.org

SUNDERLAND, Archdeacon of. See BAIN, Ven (John) Stuart

SURREY, Archdeacon of. See BEAKE, Ven Stuart Alexander

SUTCH, Ven (Christopher) David, AKC, TD
St Andrew's Chaplaincy, Oficina 1 Edf Jupiter, Avda Nuestro Padre Jesus Cautivo 74 Los Boliches Fuengirola 29640 [ARCHDEACON OF GIBRALTAR] *b* 1947 *educ* St John's Sch Leatherhead; King's Coll Lon; St Augustine's Theo Coll Cant; *CV* C Hartcliffe 1970–75; T V Dorcan 1975–79; V Alveston 1979–89; V Cainscross w Selsley 1999–2007; Chapl Costa Del Sol (East) 2007–08; Adn Gibraltar from 2008   *Tel:* 0034 952 580 600
Fax: 0034 952 472 140
email: frdavid@standrews-cofe-spain.com

SUTCLIFFE, Mr Tom (James Thomas), MA
12 Polworth Rd Streatham London SW16 2EU [SOUTHWARK] *b* 1943 *educ* Prebendal Sch Chich; Hurstpierpoint Coll; Magd Coll Ox; *CV* Engl tchr Purcell Sch 1964–65; Countertenor lay-clerk Westmr Cathl 1966–70; Mgr Musica Reservata 1966–69; performer with Schola Polyphonica, Pro Cantione Antiqua, Concentus Musicus, Vienna and Darmstadt Opera 1966–70; Advertisement Mgr and Ed 'Music and Musicians' magazine 1968–73; Sub-ed, opera critic, dep arts ed, dep obits ed 'Guardian' 1973–96; Opera Critic 'Evening Standard' 1996–2002; Leverhulme Fell 1991, 2005; Hon Fell Rose Bruford Coll from 2006; M Exec Cttee Affirming Catholicism 1996–2002; Chair Music Section of Critics' Circle 1999–2009; Vc-Pres of Critic's Circle from 2008; dramaturg in Brussels, Vienna and Dresden from 1998; M Cathls Fabric Commn for Eng from 2002
GS 1990–   *Tel:* 020 8677 5849
07815 101314 (Mobile)
Fax: 020 8677 7939
email: tomsutcliffe@email.msn.com

SUTTON, Mrs Debbie (Deborah Margaret), BSc, PG Dip Dietetics
2 Taswell Rd Southsea PO5 2RG [PORTSMOUTH] *b* 1957 *educ* Walthamstow Hall, Sevenoaks; Chelsea Coll, Lon Univ; *CV* Dietitian, Portsm Hosps NHS Trust 1981–98; Project Dietician from 2008
GS 2005–   *Tel:* 023 9275 6926
email: deb2tas@hotmail.com

SWINDON, Suffragan Bishop of. See RAYFIELD, Rt Revd Dr Lee Stephen

SWINSON, Mrs Margaret Anne, MA, ACA, CTA
46 Glenmore Ave Liverpool L18 4QF [LIVERPOOL] *b* 1957 *educ* Alice Ottley Sch Worc; Liv Univ; *CV* Accountant (Tax Specialist); GS Stg Cttee 1991–97; M BSR 1990–95; Chair Race and Com Relns Cttee 1990–95; Trustee CUF 1987–97; M CTBI; C

of E Delegate to WCC Canberra 1991; M CBF 1996–98; M Bd of Miss 2001–03; M CCU from 2006; Mod CTBI from 2006
GS 1985–   *Tel and Fax:* 0151 724 3533
email: maggie@swinsonfamily.net

SWITZERLAND, Archdeacon in. See POTTER, Ven Peter Maxwell

SYKES, Revd Clare Mary, BA
The Vicarage 28 Church Lane Bromyard Herefordshire HR7 4DZ [HEREFORD] *b* 1961 *educ* Beaconsfield Sch; St. John's Th Coll; WEMTC; *CV* M&S Mgmnt trainee 1980–83; Tear Fund, PA, 1983–87; The Benefice of Tupsley w Hampton Bp, Dioc Heref, Stipendiary AC, 1996–2001; The Benefice of Bromyard & Stoke Lacy, Self-Supporting Assoc Min from 2001; NHS Chapl Bromyard Comm Hosp from 2001; Rural Dean of Bromyard from 2005
GS 2010–   *Tel:* 01885 482438
email: clare@thesykes.plus.com

SYKES, Mr John Nicholas, MA
Tower Place West London EC3R 5BU [CHURCH COMMISSIONER] *b* 1959 *educ* Bradford Gr Sch; Jes Coll Ox; *CV* Investment Consult; Baillie, Gifford & Co Ltd 1980–84; Baring Asset Mgt 1984–97; Sen Consult William M Mercer Investment from 1997; Ch Commr from 2001; M Assets Cttee and Securities Grp   *Tel and Fax:* 020 7178 3268
email: nick.sykes@mercer.com

SYKES, Rt Revd Stephen Whitefield, MA, DD (Cam), Hon DD (Zurich), Hon DD (Virginia Theol Sem)
Ingleside Whinney Hill Durham DH1 3BE [HONORARY ASSISTANT BISHOP, DURHAM] *b* 1939 *educ* Bris Gr Sch; Monkton Combe Sch; St Jo Coll Cam; Harvard Univ; Ripon Hall Th Coll; *CV* Asst Lect Div Cam Univ 1964–68; Fell and Dean St Jo Coll Cam 1964–74; Lect 1968–74; Van Mildert Prof Dur Univ 1974–85; Can Res Dur Cathl 1974–85; Regius Prof Div Cam Univ 1985–90; Bp of Ely 1990–99; Prin St Jo Coll Dur 1999–2006; Prof Theol Dur Univ; Asst Bp Dur; Chair Doct Commn 1997–2005
GS 1990–99   *Tel:* 0191 384 6465
Fax: 0191 375 0637

TAN, Dr Chik Kaw, B Pharm, MSc, PhD, MRPharmS, PGCMedEd
12 Montfort Place Westlands Newcastle-under-Lyme ST5 2HE [LICHFIELD] *b* 1956 *educ* Anglo-Chinese Sch, Ipoh, Malaysia; Bath Univ; Aston Univ; Keele Univ; *CV* Pres Bath Univ Chr Union 1979–80; Adv Bris Chinese Chr Fellowship 1981–86; Prayer Grp leader, Newcastle-under-Lyme OMF Prayer Grp 1986–95; M OMF Internat 1996–2002; Assoc Pastor, Surabaya (Indonesia) Internat Chr Fellowship 2001–02; M Preaching Tm, St Jas Audley from 1987; Hon Sen Lect Keele Univ from 2005; M Newc Dny Syn; M Lich Dioc Syn; M N

Staffs Local Rsch Ethics Cttee 2202–2008; GS 2008–2010
GS 2005– Tel: 01782 441604
email: ck11x@yahoo.ie

TANN, Prof Jennifer, BA; PhD
Thanet House High Street Chalford Stroud GL6 8DH [GLOUCESTER] *b* 1939 *educ* Badminton Sch; Man Univ; Birm Univ; *CV* Prof Innovation, Birm Univ, 1989–2008; Dir Continuing Ed, Univ Newcastle 1986–89; R Aston Univ 1974–86; Lec Aston Univ 1969–74; Prof Emerita, Birm Univ from 2008; Management Consultant, Caret Ltd from 1992
GS 2010– Tel: 01453884142

TATTERSALL, Mr Geoffrey Frank, MA, QC
2 The Woodlands Lostock Bolton BL6 4JD [MAN-CHESTER] *b* 1947 *educ* Man Gr Sch; Ch Ch Ox; *CV* Barrister; Called to Bar Lincoln's Inn 1970; Bencher 1997; In practice Nn Circuit from 1970; Recorder Crown Court from 1989; QC from 1992; Called to Bar NSW 1992; SC from 1995; Judge of Appeal IOM from 1997; Deputy High Court Judge from 2003; Lay Chair Bolton Dny Syn 1993–2002; Chair Ho of Laity Dioc Syn 1994–2003; M Fees Adv Commn from 1995; M Strg Cttee Clergy Discipline Measure from 1996; M Bp's Coun; M DBF and Trust and Fin Cttee till 2004; Chair Stg Orders Cttee GS from 1999; Chan of Carl Dioc from 2003; Hon Lay Can Manch Cathl 2003; Chan Manch Dioc from 2004; Dep V-Gen S & Man 2004–08; External Reviewer of decisions of Dir of Fair Access from 2005; Chair Disciplinary Tribunals, Clergy Discipline Measure from 2006; Chair Revision Cttee, draft C of E Marriage Measure 2006–07; Chair Revision Cttee, draft Eccl Officer (Terms of Service) Measure 2007–08; M Strg and Revisions Cttee for draft C of E Bps and Ps (Consecration and Ord of Women) Measure from 2009; M Worshipful Co of Par Clerks from 2009; Par Clerk St George-in-the-East
GS 1995– Tel: 01204 846265
Fax: 01204 849863
email: gftqc@hotmail.co.uk

TAUNTON, Archdeacon of. See REED, Ven John Peter Cyril

TAUNTON, Suffragan Bishop of. See MAURICE, Rt Revd Peter David

TAVINOR, Very Revd Michael Edward, MA, M Mus, ARCO, PGCE
The Deanery College Cloisters Cathedral Close Hereford HR1 2NG [DEAN OF HEREFORD] *b* 1953 *educ* Bishopshalt Sch Hillingdon, Middx; Univ Coll Dur; Em Coll Cam; K Coll Lon; Ripon Coll Cuddesdon; *CV* C St Pet Ealing Lon 1982–85; Prec, Sacrist and Min Can Ely Cathl 1985–90; P-in-c Stuntney Ely 1987–90; V Tewkesbury with Walton Cardiff Glouc 1990–2002; V Twyning Glos 1999–2002; Hon Can Glouc Cathl 1997–2002;

Dean of Hereford from 2002; M Dioc Syn from 2002; Pres Ch Music Soc 2005; Hon Fell Guild of Ch Musicians from 2006 Tel: 01432 374203
Fax: 01432 374220
email: dean@herefordcathedral.org

TAYLOR, Very Revd Charles William, BA, MA, Hon FGCM
The Deanery Minster Precincts Peterborough PE1 1XS [DEAN OF PETERBOROUGH] *b* 1953 *educ* St Paul's Cathl Choir Sch; Marlborough Coll; Selwyn Coll Cam; Cuddesdon Coll Ox; Ch Divinity Sch of Pacific, Graduate Theol Union, Berkeley, Calif USA; *CV* C Cen Wolverhampton TM 1976–79; Chapl Westmr Abbey (Minor Can) 1979–84; V Stanmore w. Oliver's Battery, Winch 1984–90; R N Stoneham & Bassett, Southn 1990–95; Can Res and Prec, Lich Cathl 1995–2007; Dean of Peterb from 2007; M Lich Dioc Liturg Cttee 1976–79; M Winch Dioc Liturg Cttee 1984–95; Chair Lich Dioc Worship Team 1995–2006; M Cathls Liturg and Music Cttee 1996–2007; Gov King's Sch Peterb, Oakham Sch, Uppingham Sch from 2007; M Peterb City Com Cohesion Bd from 2008; Dir Peterb Culture & Leisure Trust from 2010 Tel: 01733 562780
email: charles.taylor@
peterborough-cathedral.org.uk

TAYLOR, Ven Paul Stanley, B Ed, M Th
Aldhelm House Rectory Lane West Stafford Dorchester DT2 8AB [ARCHDEACON OF SHERBORNE; SALISBURY] *b* 1953 *educ* Lodge Farm Co Sec Sch; Redditch Co High Sch; Westmr Coll Ox; Westcott Ho Cam; *CV* C St Steph Bush Hill Park 1984–88; V St Andr Southgate 1988–97; Asst Dir POT 1987–94, Dir 1994–2000, 2002–04; V St Mary & Ch Ch Hendon 1997–2004; AD W Barnet 2000–04; Assoc Tutor NTMTC 2001–04; Adn of Sherborne from 2004 Tel: 01305 269074
07796 691203 (Mobile)
Fax: 01305 269074
email: adsherborne@salisbury.anglican.org

TERRETT, Group Captain Paul Everard, OBE, LLB
Idle Cottage Sharptor Liskeard PL14 5AT [TRURO] *b* 1934 *educ* Cotham Gr Sch; Bris Univ; *CV* Dny lay Chair from 1996; Can Emer Truro Cathl; Chair Truro DBF 2003–06, Vc-Chair from 2006; M Bp's Coun, DBF, Patr, Pastl and Glebe Ctees
GS 2005– Tel: 01579 362741
email: terretts@sharptor.co.uk

TEWKESBURY, Suffragan Bishop of. See WENT, Rt Revd John Stewart

THEODORESON, Mr Ian, FCA
Church House Great Smith St London SW1P 3AZ [CHIEF FINANCE OFFICER, NATIONAL CHURCH INSTITUTIONS] *educ* Sen Mgr Ernst & Young 1977–87; Fin Dir Save the Children 1987–95; Dir Cor-

porate Resources Barnardo's 1995–2009; Chief Finance Officer, NCIs from 2009;

Tel: 020 7898 1795
email: ian.theodoreson@c-of-e.org.uk

THETFORD, Suffragan Bishop of. See WINTON, Rt Revd Alan Peter

THOMAS, Revd Rod (Roderick Charles Howell), B Sc, Cert Th
St Matthew's Vicarage 3 Sherford Rd Elburton Plymouth PL9 8DQ [EXETER] *b* 1954 *educ* Ealing Gr Sch for Boys; LSE; Wycliffe Hall Th Coll ; *CV* Dir Employment Affairs CBI 1987–91; C St Paul Stonehouse Plymouth 1993–95; C St Andr Plymouth 1995–99; P-in-c St Matt Elburton 1999–2005, V from 2005; Chair Reform; M BM 2001–03; M Wkg Pty on Sen Ch Appts from 2005; M CPAS Coun of Reference from 2005
GS 2000–   Tel: 01752 402771
email: rod.thomas@elburtonchurch.com

THOMAS-BETTS, Dr Anna, MA, Ph D, MBE
68 Halkingcroft Langley Slough SL3 7AY [OXFORD] *b* 1941 *educ* Christava Mahilalayam, Alwaye, S India; Madras Chr Coll, Madras Univ; Keele Univ; *CV* Lect in Physics Madras Chr Coll 1960–62; Post-Doctoral Rsch Asst Imp Coll Lon 1966–74; Lect in Geophysics Imp Coll Lon 1974–92, Sen Lect from 1992; Coll Tutor from 1998; M CCU 1991–96; M CBF 1996–99; M BSR 2000–02; M MPA from 2003; M Gov Body of Ripon Coll Cuddesdon from 2006; Chair Independent Monitoring Bd, Colnbrook Immigration Removal Cen from 2004; Chair Forum of Chairs of Independent Monitoring Bds at Immigration Removal Cen from 2007
GS 1990–   Tel: 01753 822013 (Home)
                                  020 7594 6430 (Office)
email: a.thomas-bts@ic.ac.uk

THOMSON, Canon Celia Stephana Margaret, MA
3 Miller's Green Gloucester GL1 2BN [GLOUCESTER] *b* 1955 *educ* St Swithun's Winch 1967–71; Ox Univ; Salisbury and Wells Theol Coll; *CV* C St Barnabas Southfields, S'wark 1991–95; V Ch Ch W Wimbledon, S'wark 1995–2003; Tutor in Ethics, SEITE 1995–2000; Vocations Adv Lambeth Adnry 1995–2000; Bp's Adv from 2007; Can Pastor Glouc Cath from 2003
GS 2008–   Tel: 01452 415824
email: cthomson@gloucestercathedral.org.uk

THOMSON, Rt Revd David, MA, D Phil, FRSA, FSA, FRHistS
14 Lynn Road Ely CB6 1DA [BISHOP OF HUNTINGDON] *b* 1952 *educ* K Edw VII Sch Sheffield; Keble Coll Ox; Selwyn Coll Cam; Westcott Ho Cam; *CV* C Maltby 1981–84; TV Banbury 1984–94; TR Cockermouth 1994–2002; Chair Dioc Children and Young People's Cttee; Bp's Adv for Healthcare Chapl, Team and Grp Mins and Deliverance

Min; Archdeacon of Carlisle and Can Res Carl Cathl 2002–08; Bp Huntingdon from 2008; Hon Can Ely Cathl from 2008   Tel: 01353 662137
                                   07771 864550 (Mobile)
                                  Fax: 01353 669357
email: bishop.huntingdon@ely.anglican.org

THORNTON, Rt Revd Tim (Timothy) Martin, BA, MA
Lis Escop Feock Truro TR3 6QQ [BISHOP OF TRURO] *b* 1957 *educ* Devonport High Sch for Boys; Southn Univ; St Steph Ho Ox; K Coll Lond; *CV* C Todmorden 1980–82; P-in-c Walsden 1982–85; Lect Univ of Wales (Cardiff) 1985–87; Chapl 1985–86; Sen Chapl 1986–87; Bp's Chapl Wakef 1987–91; DDO Wakef 1988–91; Bp's Chapl Lon 1991–94; Dep P in O 1992–2001; Prin N Thames Minl Tr Course 1994–98; V Kensington St Mary Abbots w S Geo, Gov St Mary Abbots C of E Primary Sch, Chair Campden Charities 1998–2001; AD Kensington 2000–01; K Coll Theol Trustee; Area Bp of Sherborne 2001–08; Trustee BRF; Bp Truro from 2009; Chair The Children's Society
                                   Tel: 01872 862657
                                  Fax: 01872 862037
email: bishop@truro.anglican.org

TICEHURST, Mrs Carol Ann,
25 South Park Lincoln LN5 8ER [LINCOLN] *b* 1938 *educ* Sincil Girls' Sch Lincoln; Lincoln Coll; *CV* Medical Sec; hdmaster's PA; Pres R Br Legion Lincs Women's Section and caseworker from 1998; M GS Catholic Grp; M Forward in Faith
GS 1995–   Tel: 01522 580728
email: xxcaticehurst@virginmedia.com

TONBRIDGE, Archdeacon of. See MANSELL, Ven Clive Neville Ross

TONBRIDGE, Suffragan Bishop of. See CASTLE, Rt Revd Dr Brian Colin

TOOKE, Mr Stephen Edgar,
The Haven 21 Wisbech Road March Cambridgeshire PE15 8ED [ELY] *b* 1946 *educ* Queen's Sch; Isle of Ely Coll; *CV* Police Superintendent 1989–96; National Co-ord SPCK Worldwide 1996–99; Area Fundraising Mgr The Children's Soc 1999–2001; Lay Chair Ely Dioc Syn 1996– 2009; Rdr from 1997; Lay Chair Deanery Syn from 2002; M Ely Dioc Bp's Counc; M Vacancy in See Cttee & C.N.C. 2001 & 2010
GS 1995–2005; 2010–   Tel: 01354652844
email: stooke@havenmarch.plus.com

TOTNES, Archdeacon of. See RAWLINGS, Ven John Edmund Frank

TOWNLEY, Ven Peter Kenneth, BA, DSPT
The Vicarage Kirkthorpe Wakefield WF1 5SZ [ARCHDEACON OF PONTEFRACT] *b* 1955 *educ* Moston Brook High Sch Man; Sheff Univ; Man Univ; Ridley Hall Th Coll; *CV* C Ch Ch Ashton-under-

Lyne 1980–83; P-in-c St Hugh's CD Oldham 1983–88; R All SS Stretford 1988–96; V St Mary-le-Tower Ipswich 1996–2008; M Meissen Commn 1991–2001; RD of Ipswich from 2001; Hon Can from 2003; M Porvoo Panel from 2003; M Inter-dioc Fin Forum; Adn Pontefract from 2008 GS 1992–95, 2000–08   *Tel:* 01924 434459 (Office)
01924 896327 (Home)
Fax: 01924 364834 (Office)
01924 896327 (Home)
email: archdeacon.pontefract@
wakefield.anglican.org

TOWNSEND, Mr James Edward, BA, PGCE
46 Tuscany House 19 Dickinson St Manchester M1 4LX [MANCHESTER] *b* 1987 *educ* Dean Close Sch; York Univ; *CV* Maths Tchr, Copley High Sch Stalybridge from 2009; GS 2010
GS 2010–   *Tel:* 07816 779635
email: james@jamestownsend.org

TRETHEWEY, Ven Frederick Martyn, BA, Dip Th, S Th
15 Worcester Rd Droitwich WR9 8AA [ARCH-DEACON OF DUDLEY; WORCESTER] *b* 1949 *educ* St Austell Gr Sch; Lon Univ; Oak Hill Th Coll; *CV* C Tollington Pk St Mark w St Anne 1978–82; C Whitehall Pk St Andr Hornsey Lane 1982–87; TV Hornsey Rise Whitehall Pk Tm 1987–88; V Brockmoor, Lich 1988–93; V Brockmoor, Worc 1993–2001; Chapl Russells Hall Hosp Dudley 1988–94; Chapl Dudley Grp of Hosps NHS Trust 1994–2001; RD Himley 1996–2001; Hon Can Worc Cathl 1999–2001; Adn Dudley from 2001; Rep Dudley Com Ptnrship 2001–05; Chair Black Country Chs Engaged Enabling Grp 2003–05
Tel and Fax: 01905 773301
email: ftrethewey@cofe-worcester.org.uk

TREWEEK (nee Montgomery), Ven Rachel, BA, BTh
16 Baldwyn Gardens Acton London W3 6HL [ARCH-DEACON OF NORTHOLT; LONDON] *b* 1963 *educ* Broxbourne Sch; Reading Univ; Wycliffe Hall Ox; *CV* Paediatric Speech and Language Therapist, Gospel Oak Health Cen, Hampstead Health Auth 1985–87; Speech and Language Therapist, Child Devel Team, Hampstead Health Auth 1987–89; Clinical Mgr for Paediatric Speech and Language Therapists in Health Cens, Bloomsbury, Hampstead & Islington Health Auths 1989–91; C St Geo Tufnell Park, Lon 1994–97, Assoc V 1997–99; V St Jas the Less Bethnal Green, Lon 1999–2006; Adn of Northolt from 2006; CME Officer, Stepney Area, Lon Dioc 1999–2001; Bp's Visitor, Stepney Area 2004–06; GS 2010–
GS 2010–   *Tel:* 020 8993 6415
email: archdeacon.northolt@london.anglican.org

TROTT, Revd Stephen, BA, MA, LLM
Rectory 41 Humfrey Lane Boughton Northampton NN2 8RQ [PETERBOROUGH] *b* 1957 *educ* Bp Vesey's

Gr Sch Sutton Coldfield; Hull Univ; Fitzw Coll Cam; Cardiff Univ; Westcott Ho Th Coll (Cam Federation of Th Colls); *CV* C Hessle 1984–87; C St Alb Hull 1987–88; R Pitsford w Boughton from 1988; Sec CME 1988–93; Vis Chapl Northants Gr Sch from 1991, Gov and Dir from 2001; Surrogate for Marriage Licences from 2001; M Legis Cttee 1995–2000, from 2005; M Legal Adv Commn 1996–2006; M CCBI and CTE 1996–99; M Revision Cttee on Calendar, Lectionary and Collects 1996; Ch Commr and M Pastl Cttee from 1997, Closed Chs Cttee 1999–2001, from 2004, Dep Chair from 2009; Bd of Govs from 1999; M Nom-inations and Governance Cttee from 2009; M DRACSC 1999–2001; M Revision Cttee on Clergy Discipline Measure 1999–2000; GS Rep on Gov Body of SAOMC 2001–06; C of E Delegate to Conf of Eur Chs, Trondheim, 2003; M Eccl Law Soc from 1988; M Dioc Syn from 1990; M Vacancy-in-See Cttee from 1995; Clerical Vc-Pres Dioc Syn and Chair Dioc Ho of Clergy 2000–03; M Peterb Cathl Coun 2001–04; M of DBF and Bishop's Council from 2010; M Pastl (Amend-ment) Measure Revision Cttee from 2004; M Follow-up Grp, Review of Diocs, Pastl & Related Measures from 2004; M Panel of Reference, Angl Communion from 2005; M Strg Cttee Diocs Pastl and Miss Measure 2005–06; Stg Cttee, Conv of Cant from 2006; M Nominations and Governance Cttee from 2009; M Revision Cttee, Eccl Fees Meas; Synodical Sec, Convocation of Cant from 2010
GS 1995–   *Tel:* 01604 845655
07712 863000 (Mobile)
email: revstrott@btinternet.com

TRURO, Bishop of. See THORNTON, Rt Revd Tim Martin

TRURO, Dean of. See HARDWICK, Very Revd Dr Christopher George

TURNER, Canon (Thelma) Ann, B Sc
Grote Steenweg 47/42 2600 Berchem Belgium [EUROPE] *b* 1948 *educ* Wintringham Gr Sch, Grimsby; Univ of Kent at Cant; *CV* Hd of Science, Upminster Comp Sch 1972–78; Scientific Engl trainer 1985–91; written communication trainer from 1991; M Adnry of NW Eur Stg Cttee; Vc-Chair Ho of Laity, Dioc in Eur; M Dioc Com-munications Cttee, Dioc OLM Wkg Party, Dioc PIM Consultation, Bp's Coun; Lay Can (Gibraltar) from 2009
GS 2005–   *Tel:* 0032 3440 2581
0032 477 626 184 (Mobile)
email: ann@turner.be

URQUHART, Rt Revd David Andrew, BA
Bishop's Croft Harborne Birmingham B17 0BG [BISHOP OF BIRMINGHAM] *b* 1952 *educ* Rugby Sch; Ealing Business Sch; Wycliffe Hall Th Coll; *CV* C St Nic Hull 1984-87; TV Drypool Hull 1987–92; V H Trin Cov 1992–2000; Bp of Birkenhead 2000–06;

**Corporation of the
Sons of the Clergy**

**The Friends of the
Clergy Corporation**

Charities working together to support the clergy

The two leading clergy charities now work together in their grant administration and operate a unified grant-making system. Applications are considered by a common body of trustees, who are responsible for the affairs of both corporations. It is only necessary to complete a single application form and this is used by both organisations when considering an applicant's needs.

Grants are available for a wide range of purposes, including:

- ◆ **school clothing and school trips**
- ◆ **clerical clothing, holidays and resettlement**
- ◆ **heating and home maintenance for the retired**
- ◆ **bereavement expenses and some of the expenses arising from separation and divorce**

We can also help in cases of emergency, illness and misfortune. Our combined grants during 2009 of some £1.75m formed the largest source of charitable assistance to the clergy family nationwide.

More than ever, donations and legacies are needed to help us maintain this level of support.

For more information please contact us at:

**1 Dean Trench Street, London SW1P 3HB Tel: 020 7799 3696
Email: enquiries@clergycharities.org.uk www.clergycharities.org.uk**

Charity No. 207736   Both registered in England and Wales   Charity No. 264724

Chair CMS Trustees 1994–2007; Prelate of Order of St Mich and St Geo from 2005; Abp of Cant's Episcopal Link with China from 2006; Bp of Birm from 2006
GS 2006– *Tel:* 0121 427 1163
email: bishop@birmingham.anglican.org

VANN, Ven Cherry Elizabeth, GRSM, ARCM, Dip RS, Cert in Counselling, Br Sign Lang Level 3
57 Melling Rd Oldham OL4 1PN [ARCHDEACON OF ROCHDALE; MANCHESTER] *b* 1958 *educ* Lutterworth Upper Sch; R Coll of Music; Westcott Ho; *CV* C St Mich, Flixton 1989–92; Chapl Bolton Coll of HE and FE and C Bolton Par Ch 1992–98; Chapl among Deaf People and TV E Farnworth and Kearsley 1998–2004; TR E. Farnworth & Kearsley 2004–08; Bp's Adv in Women's Min 2004–09; AD Farnworth 2005–08; Hon Can Man Cathl 2007; Adn Rochdale from 2008
GS 2003– *Tel:* 0161 678 1454
07803 139274 (Mobile)
email: archrochdale@manchester.anglican.org

VENNER, Rt Revd Stephen Squires, BA, MA, DD, DL
83 Hathaway Court The Esplanade Rochester ME1 1QY [BISHOP TO HM FORCES] *b* 1944 *educ* Hardye's Sch Dorchester; Birm Univ; Linacre Coll Ox; Lon Inst of Educ; St Steph Ho Th Coll; *CV* C St Pet Streatham 1968–71; Hon C St Marg Streatham Hill 1971–72; Hon C Ascen Balham 1972–74; V St Pet Clapham and Bp's Chapl to Overseas Students 1974–76; V St Jo Trowbridge 1976–82; V H Trin Weymouth 1982–94; M Dorset LEA 1982–94; Chair Dioc Bd of Educ Sarum 1989–94; RD Weymouth 1988–94; Non-Res Can Sarum Cathl 1989–94; Chair Ho of Clergy Dioc Syn 1993–94; M GS Bd of Educ from 1985, Chair VCE Cttee from 1997; Bp of Middleton 1994–99; Chair Dioc Bd of Educ 1994–99; Bp of Dover (Bp in Cant) 1999–2009; Co-Chair C of E/Moravian Contact Grp 1994–99; Pres Woodard Corp 1999–2002; Vc-Chair Gov Ch Ch Univ Coll Cant 2000–05; Vc-Chair C of E Bd of Educ 2001–09; Chapl to Lord Warden of the Cinque Ports 2004–09; Chair of Govs (Pro-Chan) Cant Ch Ch Univ 2005–09; Bp for the Falklands from 2006; Bp to HM Forces from 2009; Deputy Lieutenant of Kent from 2010; Hon Asst Bp Rochester from 2010
GS 1985–94, 2000–09 *Tel:* 01634 838787 (Home)
07980 743628 (Mobile)
email: stephen@venner.org.uk

VINCE, Mr Jacob Peter, MA, DBA, MRICS
3 High St Horam Heathfield TN21 0EJ [CHICHESTER] *b* 1960 *educ* Latymer Upper Sch; Univ of Wales; City Univ; *CV* Dir and Charterer Surveyor from 1996; M Bp's Coun; Ch Commr; M Ch Buildings (Uses and Disposals) Cttee
GS 2005– *Tel:* 01453 812623
01435 813700
Fax: 01435 813732
email: jvince@caxtons.com /
jacob.vince@btconnect

VINCENT, Mr Adrian, BA, MA
16 Faris Barn Drive Woodham Surrey KT15 3DZ [GUILDFORD] *b* 1970 *educ* George Abbot Sch; Dur Univ; Kings' Coll Lon; *CV* ITT Lon and Edinb Insurance Grp 1993–95; Asst Grants Sec, Adv Brd Min 1995–97; Archbps' Commission on the Organisation of the C of E 1997–98; Statistics Unit, Archbps' Counc 1999–2000; Exec Off, House of Bps Dept of the Central Sec 2000–07; Policy Off, The Gen Counc of the Bar 2007–08; Head of Remuneration and Policy, The Gen Counc of the Bar from 2008
GS 2010– *Tel:* 01932 349335
email: avwebsite@hotmail.co.uk

WAINE, Ven Stephen,
28 Merriefield Drive Broadstone BH18 8BP [ARCHDEACON OF DORSET] *b* 1959 *CV* Adn of Dorset from 2010 *Tel:* 01202 659427
Fax: 01202 691418
email: addorset@salisbury.anglican.org

WAKEFIELD, Bishop of. See PLATTEN, Rt Revd Stephen George

WAKEFIELD, Dean of. See GREENER, Very Revd Jonathan

WALKER, Canon Anthony (Tony) Charles St John, MA
St Saviour's Vicarage 31 Richmond Rd Retford DN22 6SJ [SOUTHWELL AND NOTTINGHAM] *b* 1955 *educ* Brentwood Sch; Tr Coll Ox; Wycliffe Hall Ox; *CV* C Bradf Cathl 1981–84; C St Ann w. Em Nottm 1984–88; V St Saviour Retford 1988–2001; P-in-c St Swithun E Retford 2001; TR Retford from 2002; AD Retford 2000–09; Hon Can S'well Minster from 2004; M Dioc Syn, Cathl Coun, Bp's Coun
GS 2004– *Tel and Fax:* 01777 703800
email: tony@tonywalker.f9.co.uk

WALKER, Dr Brian, Ph D, MA, BA (Hons), BSc (Hons), C.Eng, FCMI, FIET, MIoF (Cert)
63–67 Church Street, Micheldever Winchester SO21 3DB [WINCHESTER] *b* 1944 *educ* Southfield Sch, Ox; Univ of Winch; Univ of Southn; Open Univ; *CV* Dir Fundraising Naomi Ho Children's Hospice from 1992, Vc-P from 1997; Dir Customer Services Southern Electric 1993–94; Regional Mgr Southern Electric PLC 1996–96; Customer Service and Operations Dir MBP Utility Services 1996–97; Sen Devel Mgr Sabre Power 1998–99; Consult Cohort Ltd, Sierra Leone 2001–04; Exec Dir Religions for Peace (UK) from 2004; M Newc Ptnrship Panel; M Overseas Ch Panel; M Eur Ptnrship Panel; M Dioc Ecum Panel; Dir Cen of Religions for Reconciliation and Peace, Univ of Winch from 2009; Hon Research Fell Univ of Winch from 2009
GS 2007– *Tel:* 01962 774221
email: hopeis@btinternet.com

WALKER, Rt Revd David Stuart, MA, FRSA
Bishop's House Bishops Walk Cradley Heath B64 7RH [SUFFRAGAN BISHOP OF DUDLEY; WORCESTER] *b* 1957 *educ* Man Gr Sch; K Coll Cam; Qu Th Coll Birm; *CV* C Handsworth 1983–86; TV Maltby 1986–91; Ind Chapl Maltby 1986–91; V Bramley and Ravenfield 1991–95; TR Bramley and Ravenfield w Hooton Roberts and Braithwell 1995–2000; Hon Can Sheff Cathl 2000; Bp of Dudley from 2000; M Adv Coun on Relns of Bps and Relig Coms from 2002; Chair Housing Justice 2003–07; Sec W Midlands Regional Bps Grp 2003–08; Chair Housing Assoc Charitable Trust from 2004; M Bps' Urban Panel from 2004; M NPIA Independent Adv Panel from 2009; M C of E Pensions Bd from 2006, Dep Vc Chair from 2010; M CMEAC from 2006; M CUF from 2008; M Equality and DIversity Bd Adv Gp (Homes and Cttees Agency) from 2009; Chair C of E Pensions Bd Housing Cttee from 2009
GS 2005–   *Tel:* 0121 550 3407
                          Fax: 0121 550 7340
          email: bishop.david@cofe-worcester.org.uk

WALKER, Mrs (Pauline) Debra, B Pharm, MRPharmS
Willow Lodge Church Lane Lydiate L31 4HL [LIVERPOOL] *b* 1960 *educ* Ormskirk Gr Sch; Bradf Univ; *CV* Pharmacist qualified 1982; Elected to GS 2010
GS 2010–   *Tel:* 0151 520 2496
          email: debrawalker@btinternet.com

WALKER, Revd Ruth Elizabeth, BA, PGCE
The Vicarage 5 Howard Close Bidford-on-Avon Warwickshire B50 4EL [COVENTRY] *b* 1958 *educ* Hayes Sch; St.John's Coll, Dur; Hughes Hall,Cam; St.John's Coll Nott; *CV* RE Tchr The Embrook School, Wokingham, Berks 1980–83; RE Tchr, Ranelagh School, Bracknell, Berks 1983–86; Parish Dn St. Mary's Princes Risborough w Ilmer, Ox 1988–90; AC & Congregational Chapl Bradf Cathl 1990–93; AC P of West Swindon & the Lydiards, Bris1993–94; NSM P of West Swindon & the Lydiards, Bris 1994–96; AC St. John the Baptist & St. Andrew Parks & Walcot, Bris 1996–98; Hon.Ce PTO P of Ch Ch Swindon, Bris 1999; Assoc Minr Keresley w Coundon & C-in-C Keresley Village Comm Ch, Cov 1999–2010; Area Dean Cov North Deanery 2004–10; Assoc Min Heart of England Parishes, Cov 2010
GS 2010–   *Tel and Fax:* 01789 772217
          email: ruth@heartparishes.org.uk

WALKER, Mr Timothy Edward Hanson, CB, MA, D Phil, D Sc (Hon), FIET, FRSA
Church House Great Smith St London SW1P 3AZ [THIRD CHURCH ESTATES COMMISSIONER] *b* 1945 *educ* Tonbridge Sch; Brasenose Coll Ox; *CV* Dir Gen Immigration, Home Office 1995–98; Dep Chair HM Customs and Excise, 1998–2000; Dir Gen Health and Safety Exec 2000–05; Non Exec Dir Lon Strategic Health Auth, 2006–2009; Third Ch Estates Commr from 2006; Chair Ch Commrs

Bishoprics and Caths, Pastl and Closed Chs Ctees; Trustee Prostate Cancer Charity from 2006; Chair Accountancy and Actuarial Discipline Bd from 2008; Dir Fin Reporting Coun from 2008; Trustee De Morgan Foundn   *Tel:* 020 7898 1624
          email: timothy.walker@c-of-e.org.uk

WALLACE, Rt Revd Martin William, BD, AKC
Bishop's House Barton-le-Street Malton YO17 6PL [SUFFRAGAN BISHOP OF SELBY; YORK] *b* 1948 *educ* Varndean Gr Sch for Boys Brighton; Tauntons Sch Southn; K Coll Lon; St Aug Coll Cant; *CV* C Attercliffe Sheff 1971–74; C New Malden 1974–77; V St Mark Forest Gate 1977–93; Chapl Forest Gate Hosp 1977–80; RD Newham 1982–91; P-in-c Em Forest Gate 1985–89; P-in-c All SS Forest Gate 1991–93; Dioc Urban Officer 1991–93; Hon Can Chelmsf Cathl 1989–97; P-in-c St Thos Bradwell and St Lawr 1993–97; Ind Chapl Maldon and Dengie 1993–97; Adn of Colchester 1997–2003; Suff Bp of Selby from 2003   *Tel:* 01653 627191
                          Fax: 01653 627193
          email: bishselby@clara.net

WALSALL, Archdeacon of. See SIMS, Ven Christopher Sidney

WANDSWORTH, Archdeacon of. See ROBERTS, Ven Stephen John

WARD, Very Revd Dr Frances Elizabeth Fearn, M Theol; PhD
Deanery The Great Churchyard Bury St Edmunds Suffolk IP33 1RS [DEAN OF ST EDMUNDSBURY] *b* 1959 *educ* King's Sch Ely; Univ of St Andrews; Royal Lon Hospital; Univ of Cam; Univ of Man; Univ of Bradf; Westcott Ho Cam; *CV* Par Deacon St Bartholomew, Westhoughton 1989–93; Tutor Practical Theol, Northern Coll (URC & Cong. Fed) 1993–98; Hon C St George, Unsworth 1998–99; V St Peter, Bury 1999–2005; Bp's Advisor on Women's Min 2002–04; Hon C St Stephen and all Martyrs' Leverbridge 2005–06; Residentiary Can Bradf Cathl 2006–2010; Dean of St Edmundsbury from 2010   *Tel:* 01284 748722
                          Fax: 01284 768655
          email: dean@stedscathedral.org

WARD, Mr John Selwyn, LLB
Flat 7 18 Holmdale Rd London NW6 1BN [LONDON] *b* 1971 *educ* Abbey Gate Coll Ches; Bris Univ; Katholieke Universiteit Leuven; Coll of Law, Ches; *CV* Solicitor; trainee solicitor, S J Berwin, Lon 1994–96; Stagiaire, Directorate Gen for Competition, Eur Commn 1996–97; asst solicitor, S J Berwin, Brussels 1997; Sen Legal Adv, Office of Fair Trading 1997–2003; Sen Legal Adv, DEFRA 2003–07; Legal Sec to the Advocate Gen for Scotland from 2007; M PCC Emm Ch W Hampstead from 1999; M N Camden Dny Syn from 2002; Convener GS Human Sexuality Grp from 2006;
GS 2005–   *Tel:* 07734 080573 (Mobile)
          email: jward.anglican@zen.co.uk

WARD, Revd Dr Kevin, MA, Ph D
School of Theology & Religious Studies University of Leeds Leeds LS2 9JT [UNIVERSITIES, NORTHERN] *b* 1947 *educ* Pudsey Gr Sch; Edin Univ; Trin Coll Cam; Bp Tucker Th Coll, Mukono, Uganda; *CV* CMS Miss Ptnr (Tutor Bp Tucker Th Coll, Ch of Uganda) 1975–91; Tutor Qu Coll Birm 1991; Par Min Halifax, Wakef Dio 1991–95; Sen Lect in African Studies, Sch of Th and Relig Studies, Leeds Univ from 1995; NSM St Mich Headingley, Ripon Dio; M Ripon Dioc Wkg Grp in Human Sexuality; Trustee CMS
GS 2003–05; 2005   *Tel:* 0113 343 3641
              email: trskw@leeds.ac.uk

WARNER, Mr David Hugh, Dip Ed, GOE
41 Ox Lane Harpenden AL5 4HF [ST ALBANS] *b* 1932 *educ* St Jo Sch Leatherhead; St Mark and St Jo Coll Chelsea; Cam Inst of Educ; St Alb Min Tr Scheme; *CV* Dep Head St Nic Harpenden C of E JMI Sch 1964–71; Head Wigginton C of E JMI Sch 1972–73; Head St Helen's Wheathampstead C of E JMI Sch 1974–93; Rtd
GS 1995–   *Tel and Fax:* 01582 762379
              email: dhwarner@tiscali.co.uk

WARNER, Rt Revd Martin Clive, BA, MA, PhD
60 West Green Stokesley Middlesbrough TS9 5BD [BISHOP OF WHITBY] *b* 1958 *educ* K St Roch; Maidstone Gr Sch; St Chad's Coll Dur; St Steph Ho; *CV* C St Pet Plymouth 1984–88; TV Resurr Leic 1988–93; P Admin Shrine of Our Lady of Walsingham 1993–2002; Can Pastor, St Paul's Cathl from 2003; Treasurer, St Paul's Cathl 2008–09; Bp of Whitby from 2009   *Tel:* 01642 714475
                            Fax: 01642 714472
       email: bishopofwhitby@yorkdiocese.org

WARREN, Dr Yvonne, MA, PhD, UKCP, BACP
Cornerston 6 Hillview Stratford Upon Avon Warwickshire CV37 9AY [COVENTRY] *b* 1938 *educ* Beford High Sch; *CV* Nurse 1957–61; Relate Supervisor 1980–95; Psychotherapist from 1996; Bp's Adv from 1990; Candidates Panel from 1994; R from 1996; Bp's Visitor 1990–2006; Lay Rep GS Ridley Hall Th Coll 2000–07; Act Dioc Adv Pastoral Care and Counselling
GS 2000–05; 2005–07; 2010–   *Tel:* 01789414255
              email: ywarren@hotmail.co.uk

WARRINGTON, Archdeacon of. See BRADLEY, Ven Peter David Douglas

WARRINGTON, Suffragan Bishop of. See BLACKBURN, Rt Revd Richard Finn

WARWICK, Suffragan Bishop of. See STROYAN, Rt Revd John Ronald Angus

WATSON, Rt Revd Andrew John, MA
16 Coleshill St Sutton Coldfield W Midlands B72 1SH [SUFFRAGAN BISHOP OF ASTON; BIRMINGHAM] *b* 1961 *educ* Win Coll; CCC Cam; Ridley Hall Th Coll; *CV* C St Pet Ipsley 1987–90; C St Jo and St

Pet Notting Hill 1990–95; V St Steph E Twickenham from 1995; M Bp's Coun; M MPA Coun from 2006; AD Hampton 2003–08; Bp of Aston from 2008
GS 2000–08   *Tel:* 020 426 0406 (Office)
                            0121 354 6632 (Home)
  email: bishopofaston@birmingham.anglican.org

WATSON, Ven Ian Leslie Stewart, CTH, GOE
9 Armorial Rd Coventry CV3 6GH [ARCHDEACON OF COVENTRY] *b* 1950 *educ* Nottm High Sch; Britannia R Naval Coll; Army Staff Coll; Joint Warfare Establishment; Wycliffe Hall Ox; *CV* C St Andrew Plymouth w St George w St Paul Stonehouse 1981–85; TV Ipsley, Meth Min Matchborough 1985–89; V Woodley 1989–92; TR Woodley 1992–95; Chapl Amsterdam, Heiloo and Dan Helder 1995–2001; DDO Benelux 1997–2001; Chief Exec Intercontinental Ch Soc 2001–07; Can Gib Cathl 2001–07 (Emer from 2007); Adn Cov from 2007; Adv on Deliverance Min (Worc) 1987–89; M Meth Syn 1985–89; M Bp's Coun (Eur) 2001–07; M Dioc Syn (Cov) from 2007
              Tel: 024 7652 1337 (Office)
                     024 7641 7750 (Home)
                     07714 214790 (Mobile)
              Fax: 024 7652 1330
       email: ian.watson@covcofe.org /
              i.watson440@btinternet.com

WATSON, Ven Sheila Anne, MA, M Phil
29 The Precincts Canterbury CT1 2EP [ARCHDEACON OF CANTERBURY] *b* 1953 *educ* Ayr Acad; St And Univ; Corpus Christi Coll Ox; Coates Hall Th Coll Edin; *CV* Dss St Sav Bridge of Allan and St Jo Alloa, St And 1979–80; Dss St Mary Monkseaton Newc 1980–84; Officer for Miss and Min Kensington Episc Area Lon 1984–87; Hon C St Luke and Ch Ch Chelsea Lon 1987–96; Selection Sec ABM 1992–93, Senior Selection Sec 1993–96; Adv in CME Salis 1997–2002; Dioc Dir of Min Salis 1998–2002; Hon Can Salis 2000; Adn of Buckingham 2002–07; Adn of Canterbury from 2007   *Tel:* 01227 865238
                            Fax: 01227 785209
   email: archdeacon@canterbury-cathedral.org

WEBSTER, Canon Glyn Hamilton, SRN
4 Minster Yard York YO1 7JD [YORK] *b* 1951 *educ* Darwen Sec Tech (Gr) Sch; St Jo Coll Dur; *CV* C All SS Huntington York 1977–81; V St Luke Ev York and Sen Chapl York District Hosp 1981–92; Sen Chapl York Health Services NHS Trust 1992–99; Can and Preb York Minster 1994–99; RD York 1997–2004; Can Res and Treas York Minster from 1999; Can Pastor from 2000; Prolocutor of York from 2000; M AC from 2000; Chair Dioc Ho of Clergy; Chan York Minster from 2004; Assoc DDO from 2005; M GS Business Cttee from 2005; M Hosp Chapl Coun from 2005
GS 1995–   *Tel:* 01904 620877 (Home)
                            01904 557207 (Office)
                            Fax: 01904 557204
       email: chancellor@yorkminster.org

WEBSTER, Ven Martin Duncan, BSc, Dip Th
Glebe House Church Lane Sheering Bishops Stortford CM22 7NR [ARCHDEACON OF HARLOW; CHELMS-FORD] *b* 1952 *educ* Durn Falls Sec Modern Sch; Abbs Cross Tech High Sch; Nottm Univ; Linc Th Coll; *CV* C St Pet and St Mich Thundersley, Chelmsf 1978–81; TV Canvey Island 1981–86; V All SS and St Giles Nazeing 1986–99; AD Harlow 1989–99; NSM Officer 1995–99; TR Waltham Abbey 1999–2009; Adn Harlow from 2009
GS 2005–2010   *Tel:* 01297 734524
     email: a.harlow@chelmsford.anglican.org

WELBY, Very Revd Justin Portal, MA, BA
Liverpool Cathedral St James' Mount Liverpool L1 7AZ [DEAN OF LIVERPOOL] *b* 1956 *educ* Eton Coll; Trin Coll Cam; St Jo Coll Dur; Cranmer Hall; *CV* Mgr Project Finance, Soc Nationale Elf Aquitaine, Paris 1978–83; Treas Elf UK plc, Lon 1983–84; Grp Treas Enterprise Oil plc, Lon 1984–89; C All SS Chilvers Coton and St Mary V, Astley, Nuneaton, Cov 1992–95; R St Jas Southam and St Mich & All Angels Ufton, Cov 1995–2002; Dir of Internat Min and Res Can Cov Cathl 2002–05; Sub-Dean and Can for Reconciliation Min, Cov Cathl 2005–07; P-in-c H Trin Cov 2007; Dean of Liv from 2007
                              Tel: 0151 709 6271
                              Fax: 0151 702 7292
     email: dean@liverpoolcathedral.org.uk

WELCH, Ven Stephan John, BA, DipTheol, MTh
98 Dukes Ave Chiswick London W4 2AF [ARCH-DEACON OF MIDDLESEX; LONDON] *b* 1950 *educ* Luton Gr Sch; Luton Sixth Form Coll; Hull Univ; Birm Univ; Heythrop Coll, Lon Univ; Qu Coll Birm; *CV* C Ch Ch Waltham Cross, St Alb 1977–80; P-in-c and V St Mary Reculver & St Bart Herne Bay, Cant 1980–92; V St Mary Hurley & St Jas the Less Stubbings, Ox 1992–2000; V St Pet Hammersmith, Lon 2000–06; AD Hammersmith and Fulham 2001–06; Adn of Middlesex from 2006; Chair Lon Dioc Bd for Schs; M DAC, DBF, Bp's Coun
     Tel: 020 8742 8308 07780 704059 (Mobile)
          email: archdeacon.middlesex@
                              london.anglican.org

WELLS, Archdeacon of. See SULLIVAN, Ven Nicola Ann

WELLS, Dean of. See CLARKE, Very Revd John Martin

WENT, Rt Revd John Stewart, MA
Bishop's House Church Rd Staverton Cheltenham GL51 0TW [SUFFRAGAN BISHOP OF TEWKESBURY; GLOUCESTER] *b* 1944 *educ* Colchester R Gr Sch; Cam Univ; Oak Hill Th Coll; *CV* C Em North-wood 1969–75; V H Trin Margate 1975–83; Vc Prin Wycliffe Hall Ox 1983–89; Adn of Surrey 1989–96; Bp of Tewkesbury from 1996
GS 1990–95   *Tel:* 01242 680188
                              Fax: 01242 680233
          email: bshptewk@star.co.uk

WEST CUMBERLAND, Archdeacon of. See PRATT, Ven Richard

WEST HAM, Archdeacon of. See COCKETT, Ven Elwin Wesley

WESTMINSTER, Dean of. See HALL, Very Revd John Robert

WESTMORLAND AND FURNESS, Archdeacon of. See HOWE, Ven George Alexander

WHARTON, Rt Revd (John) Martin, MA
Bishop's House 29 Moor Rd South Newcastle-upon-Tyne NE3 1PA [BISHOP OF NEWCASTLE] *b* 1944 *educ* Ulverston Gr Sch; Dur Univ; Linacre Coll Ox; Ripon Hall Th Coll; *CV* C St Pet Birm 1972–75; C St Jo Bapt Croydon 1975–77; Dir of Pastl Studies Ripon Coll Cuddesdon 1977–83; Exec Sec Bd of Min and Tr Bradf Dio 1983–91; Can Res Bradf Cathl and Bp's Officer for Min and Tr 1992; Bp of Kingston-upon-Thames 1992–97; Bp of Newc from 1997
GS 1998–   *Tel:* 0191 285 2220
                              Fax: 0191 284 6933
     email: bishop@newcastle.anglican.org

WHEATLEY, Rt Revd Peter William, MA
27 Thurlow Rd London NW3 5PP [AREA BISHOP OF EDMONTON; LONDON] *b* 1947 *educ* Ipswich Sch; Qu Coll Ox; Pemb Coll Cam; Mirfield Th Coll; Ripon Hall Th Coll; *CV* C All SS Fulham 1973–78; V H Cross, Cromer St, St Pancras 1978–82; V St Jas W Hampstead, P-in-c St Mary w All So Kilburn 1982–95; Chair Chr Concern for S Africa 1992–95; Dir POT Edmonton Area 1985–95; M BSR Inter-nat Affairs Cttee 1981–96; Adn of Hampstead 1995–99; Bp of Edmonton from 1999
GS 1975–95   *Tel:* 020 7435 5890
                              Fax: 020 7435 6049
     email: bishop.edmonton@london.anglican.org

WHITBY, Suffragan Bishop of. See WARNER, Rt Revd Martin Clive

WHITE, Mr David Peter, B Sc, FCMA, DChA
Church House Great Smith St London SW1P 3AZ [HEAD OF FINANCIAL POLICY AND PLANNING, FINANCE AND RESOURCES, ARCHBISHOPS' COUNCIL AND CHURCH COMMISSIONERS] *b* 1966 *educ* Dart-ford Gr Sch; LSE; *CV* On staff of Church Com-missioners since 1990, Head of Fin Planning, Ch Crs 2002–07, Head of Fin Policy and Planning, AC and Ch Crs from 2007.   *Tel:* 020 7898 1684
                              Fax: 020 7898 1131
          email: david.white@c-of-e.org.uk

WHITE, Rt Revd Frank (Francis), B Sc, Dip Th
Bishop's House 29 Moor Rd South Newcastle Upon Tyne NE3 1PA [ASSISTANT BISHOP OF NEWCASTLE] *b* 1949 *educ* St Cuth Gr Sch Newc; Consett Tech Coll; UWIST Cardiff; Univ Coll Cardiff; St Jo Coll Nottm; *CV* Dir Youth Action York 1971–73;

Who's Who

Detached Youth Worker Man Catacombs Trust 1973–77; C St Nic Dur 1980–84; C St Mary and St Cuth Chester-le-Street 1984–87; Chapl to Dur HA Hosps 1987–89; V St Jo Ev Birtley 1989–97; RD Chester-le-Street 1993–97; Hon Can Dur Cathl 1997–2002; Adn of Sunderland 1997–2002; Bp of Brixworth from 2002–2010; Hon Can Peterb Cathl from 2002–2010; Fell Univ of Northampton from 2010; Assistant Bp of Newcastle from 2010
GS 1987–2000   *Tel:* 0191 285 2220
     Fax: 0191 284 6933
     email: bishopfrank@newcastle.anglican.org

WHITE, Mrs Margaret Joan, CQSW
The White House 6 Blayney Row Heddon Station Newcastle NE158QD [NEWCASTLE] *b* 1933 *educ* Skerry's Coll; Walbottle Gr Sch; Rutherford Coll of F Ed; Sunderland Poly; *CV* Shorthand Typist 1948–52; Sec Thos. Cook 1952–54; Secy Lon & Lanc Insurance Co. 1954–56; Sec Assoc Anaesthetists, Winnipeg, 1956–60; Sec Chipman Chemicals, Winnipeg 1960–61; Sec Med Rsrch Counc, Newcastle 1961–62; Sec Transport & Genl Workers' Union 1962–65; Sec Westlands Special Sch 1965–74; Ed Welfare Off, Newcastle LEA, 1974–92; Dioc Apptmt, AFIA Rep MU from 1990
GS 2010–   *Tel:* 0191 2674569
     email: heddonstation@btinternet.com

WHITE, Canon Bob (Robert Charles), MA, Cert Th
St Mary's Vicarage Fratton Rd Portsmouth PO1 5PA [PORTSMOUTH] *b* 1961 *educ* Portsmouth Gr Sch; Mansfield Coll Ox; St Steph Ho Ox; *CV* C St Jo Forton 1985–88; C St Mark North End with special responsibility for St Fran Hilsea 1988–92; V St Clare Warren Park 1992–2000; V St Fran Leigh Park 1994–2000; RD Havant 1998–2000; V St Mary Portsea from 2000; M Bp's Coun; Dioc Adv on Urban Ministry; CUF Link Officer; Chair Dioc Ho of Clergy
GS 1995–2000, 2004–   *Tel:* 023 9282 2687
     email: revrcwhite@aol.com

WHITEHEAD, Hazel, BD, AKC, MA, D. MIN TEFL
The Rectory 5 The Spinning Walk Shere Surrey GU5 9HN [GUILDFORD] *b* 1954 *educ* Fryerns Gr; King's Coll Lon; NTMTC, Lambeth; *CV* Prin Guild Dioc Min 1994–2005; AC St MAry Oatlands 1993–1997; Tchr 1989–95; Dioc Dir Mini Training 2005; Archbp's CMD Assesor BAP Adv; Co-Chair South Central Regional Training Partnership from 2008; Chair CAEIMT 2003–05; M TETC and EVP 1994–2004
GS 2010–   *Tel:* 01483 709307
     Fax: 01483 790333
     email: hazel.whitehead@cofeguildford.org.uk

WHITTAM SMITH, Mr Andreas, MA, CBE
154 Campden Hill Rd London W8 7AS [FIRST CHURCH ESTATES COMMISSIONER] *b* 1937 *educ* Birkenhead Sch; Keble Coll Ox; *CV* Founder & Ed 'The Independent' 1986–94; Dir Independent Print Limited); Pres Br Bd of Film Classification

1997–2002; Chair Fin Ombudsman Service Ltd 1999–2003; Chair The Children's Mutual; Vc-Pres Nat Coun for One-Parent Families; Chair Ch Commrs Assets Cttee; M Ch Commrs Bd of Govs; M AC from 2002
GS 2002–   *Tel:* 020 7221 8354
     email: andreasws@mac.com

WHITWORTH, Mrs Ruth,
Green End Melmerby Ripon HG4 5HL [CHELMSFORD] *b* 1952
GS 1990–99; 2005–10; 2010–   *Tel:* 01765 640922

WIGHT, Archdeacon of the Isle of. See BASTON, Ven Caroline Jane

WILLESDEN, Area Bishop of. See BROADBENT, Rt Revd Pete (Peter Alan)

WILLIAMS, Sister Anne, Dip EvS
Good Shepherd Clergy House Forest Rd Ford Estate Sunderland SR4 0DX [DURHAM] *b* 1946 *educ* A J Dawson Gr Sch Wellfield; Wilson Carlile Coll of Evang; *CV* Civil Servant 1964–70; Fin Office Admin 1971–93; Communications/PR Support for Third World charity 1993–96; Dep Bursar Dur High Sch for Girls 1996–2002; Vc-Chairman Forward in Faith from 1994; Ch Army Ev in trg 2003–04; Com Missioner from 2004; Miss Enabler pt-time 2004–09; Regional Devel Officer CLCGB from 2009
GS 1990–   *Tel:* 0191 5656 870 (Home)
     07715 178654 (Mobile)
     email: sranneca@aol.com

WILLIAMS, Mr Tony (Anthony) James, B Sc, ARCS, FPMI
29 Great Smith St London SW1P 3PS [PENSIONS MANAGER, CHURCH OF ENGLAND PENSIONS BOARD] *b* 1953 *educ* Grove Park Gr Sch Wrexham; Imp Coll Lon Univ; *CV* Post Office 1975–89; Dep Pensions Mgr, C of E Pensions Bd 1989–2003, Pensions Mgr from 2003   *Tel:* 020 7898 1839
     Fax: 020 7898 1801
     email: tony.williams@c-of-e.org.uk

WILLIAMS, Revd David Grant, BSc
Christ Church Vicarage Sleepers Hill Winchester SO22 4ND [WINCHESTER] *b* 1961 *educ* Newport Gr Sch; Bris Univ; Crowther Hall, Birm; Wycliffe Hall Th Coll; *CV* Deputy Headteacher (CMS Mission Partner), Kitui District, Kenya 1983–85; Lay Asst, Christ Ch Clifton, Bris 1985–1986; AC Ecclesall, Sheffield Dioc 1989–92; V Ch Ch Dore, Sheffield Dic 1992–2002; Area Dean, Eccesall Deanery, Sheffield Dioc 1997–2002; Chapl,Aldine House Secure Unit, Sheffield 1998–2002; V Ch Ch Winc from 2002; M Dioc Pstrl Cttee 1997–2002; Chair Dioc Stewardship Grp 2000–02; M Bps Counc & Dioc Standing Cttee from 2010; M Dioc Brd Ed from 2010
GS 2010–   *Tel:* 01962 862414
     07889547095
     email: david.williams@ccwinch.org.uk

English Clergy Association

www.clergyassoc.co.uk

The Association seeks to be a Church of England mutual resource for clergy, patrons and churchwardens requiring information or insight. Members include male and female clergy, private patrons and other lay people concerned to maintain an authentic Church of England.

Annual Address in London: 16th May 2011
previous speakers include
the Bishops of London and Rochester, the Marquess of Salisbury,
Chancellor Dr. James Behrens, Dr. Brian Hanson, Professor Norman
Doe and Sir Patrick Cormack.

Donations to the Benefit Fund provide Clergy Holidays:
Gifts, Legacies, Church Collections much appreciated.
Registered Charity No. 258559

Benoporto-eca@yahoo.co.uk for Membership enquiries.
The Old School House, Norton Hawkfield, Bristol BS39 4HB
Chairman: The Rev'd John Masding, M.A., LL.M.

The 2009 Annual Address by the Rt. Rev'd Dr. Michael Nazir-Ali entitled
Double Jeopardy: Secularism, Militant Islam and the Christian Faith
is fully reported in No. 169 of the Members' journal Parson & Parish.

WILLIAMS, Revd David Michael, MA, Dip LIB, Dip Th, FSA, FRSA
Church House Great Smith St London SW1P 3AZ [CLERK TO THE GENERAL SYNOD AND HEAD OF CENTRAL SECRETARIAT, ARCHBISHOPS' COUNCIL] *b* 1950 *educ* Glyn Gr Sch Ewell; Ex Univ; Lon Univ; Univ of Kent; *CV* Employed at CCC 1972–73 and 1974–87; Dep Sec CCC 1982–87; Employed by CBF from 1987; Dep Sec CBF 1991–94; Sec CBF 1994–98; Clerk to GS and Dir Central Services, AC 1999–2002; Clerk to GS and Head of Central Secretariat, AC from 2002; JP   *Tel:* 020 7898 1559
Fax: 020 7898 1369
email: david.williams@c-of-e.org.uk

WILLIAMS, Rt Revd Paul Gavin, BA
Dial House Riverside Twickenham TW1 3DT [AREA BISHOP OF KENSINGTON; LONDON] *b* 1968 *educ* Court Fields Sch Wellington; Grey Coll Univ Dur; Wycliffe Hall Ox; *CV* C St James Muswell Hill 1992–95; Asst V Christ Ch Clifton 1996–99; R St James Gerrards Cross w Fulmer 1999–2009; Area Bp of Kensington from 2009   *Tel:* 020 8892 7781
email: bishop.kensington@london.anglican.org

WILLIAMS, Most Revd and Rt Hon Rowan Douglas, MA, D Phil, DD, FBA
Lambeth Palace London SE1 7JU [ARCHBISHOP OF CANTERBURY] *b* 1950 *educ* Dynevor Sec Sch; Ch Coll Cam; Wadham Coll Ox; Coll of Resurrection Mirfield; *CV* Tutor, Westcott Ho Cam 1977–80; Hon C St Geo Chesterton, Ely 1980–83; Lect in Div, Cam 1980–86; Dean and Chapl, Clare Coll Cam 1984–86; Can Theologian, Leic Cathl 1981–92; Can Res, Ch Ch Ox 1986–92; Lady Margaret Prof of Div, Ox 1986–92; Bp of Monmouth 1992–2002; Abp of Wales 2000–02; Abp of Canterbury from 2002
GS 2002–   *Tel:* 020 7898 1200

WILLIAMS, Mrs Shirley-Ann, LRAM, LLAM, Hon FLAM, Cert Th
2 Katherine's Lane Ridgeway Ottery St Mary EX11 1FB [EXETER] *educ* Barr's Hill Sch Cov; Leeds Univ; Ex Univ; *CV* Freelance Tutor and Examiner in Speech and Drama, Public Speaking and Communication Skills; Tutor, Coll of Preachers; Broadcaster; M GS Appts Cttee; M GS Ho of Laity Stg Cttee; Chair Dioc Bd of Patr; M Bp's Dioc Coun; M Dioc Syn; M Dioc Coun for Worship and Ministry; M Dioc Liturg Grp; M Dioc Coun for Work with Children and Young People; Lay Chair Ottery Dny Syn; Vc Pres Dioc Syn and Chair Dioc Ho of Laity 1982–2003; Dir/Exec Trustee Rural Com Coun of Devon 1990–2005; MU Trustee, Ex Dioc, rep, Com Coun of Devon; Chair Nat Wkg Pty Ecum Decade of Chs in Solidarity w Women 1995–98; Chair Ch Working for Women Grp 1999–2003; M Review of Diocs, Pastl and Related Measures; M CTE and CTBI; Ed Open Syn Grp magazine
GS 1985–2010   *Tel and Fax:* 01404 811064
email: shanwill@tinyonline.co.uk

WILLIS, Very Revd Robert Andrew, BA
The Deanery The Precincts Canterbury CT1 2EP [DEAN OF CANTERBURY] *b* 1947 *educ* Kingswood Gr Sch; Warw Univ; Worc Coll Ox; Cuddesdon Th Coll; *CV* C St Chad Shrewsbury 1972–75; V Choral Sarum Cathl 1975–78; TR Tisbury and RD Chalke 1978–89; V Sherborne 1987–92; RD Sherborne 1991–92; Dean of Heref 1992–2001; Dean of Cant from 2001; M PWM Cttee 1990–2001; M Cathls Fabric Commn from 1993; M Liturg Commn 1994–98; Chair Deans' Conf from 1999
GS 1985–92, 1994–   *Tel:* 01227 762862
Fax: 01227 865250
email: dean@canterbury-cathedral.org

WILLMOTT, Rt Revd Trevor, MA, Dip Theol
The Bishop's Office Old Palace Canterbury [SUFFRAGAN BISHOP OF DOVER] *b* 1950 *educ* Plymouth Coll; St Pet Coll Ox; Fitzw Coll Cam; Westcott Ho Th Coll; *CV* C St Geo Norton 1974–77; Asst Chapl Oslo w Trondheim 1978–79; Chapl Naples w Capri, Bari and Sorrento 1979–83; R Ecton and Wdn Peterb Dioc Retreat Ho 1983–89; DDO and Dir of POT 1986–97; Can Res and Prec Peterb Cathl 1989–97; Adn of Dur and Can Res Dur Cathl 1997–2002; Suff Bp of Basingstoke 2002–2010; Bp of Dover from 2010; M GS Business Sub-cttee from 2005; M Ho of Bps Stg Cttee from 2005; Trustee Foundn for Chr Leadership; M Rural Bps Panel from 2004; Patr Cross Borders YMCA from 2005; Trustee St Michael's Coll, Llandaff; Visitor to the Sisters of Bethany
GS 2000–   *Tel:* 01227 459382 *Fax:* 01227 784985
email: trevor.willmott@bishcant.org

WILSON, Rt Revd Alan Thomas Lawrence, MA, D Phil
Sheridan Grimms Hill Great Missenden HP16 9BG [AREA BISHOP OF BUCKINGHAM; OXFORD] *b* 1955 *educ* St Jo Coll Cam; Ball Col Ox; Wycliffe Hall Ox; *CV* Hon C Eynsham, Ox 1979–81, C 1981–82; C Caversham and Mapledurham 1982–89; V St Jo Caversham 1989–92; Angl substitute Chapl, HMP Reading, 1990–1992; R Sandhurst 1992–2003; RD Sonning 1998–2003; Area Bp of Buckingham from 2003; M Coun, Wycombe Abbey Sch from 2008; Chair Ox Dioc Bd of Educ from 2010; Univ of Buckingham Visiting Prof in Theol from 2010   *Tel:* 01494 862173
07525 655756 (Mobile)
Fax: 01494 890508
email: bishopbucks@oxford.anglican.org /
alan.wilson49@btopenworld.com

WILSON, Mr Brian Kenneth, MA FIA
84 Albert Road Epsom Surrey KT17 4EL [SOUTHWARK] *b* 1947 *educ* Lewes County Grammar School for Boys University of Oxford; *CV* Sch Master, Dulwich Coll 1971–74; Sch Master, King's Sch Cant 1974–76; Asst Actuary, Bacon & Woodrow 1976–83; Partner, Bacon & Woodrow 1983–2002; Prin, Hewitt Assoc 2002–10; Prin, Aon

Hewitt from 2010; Dir & Trustee, South London Church Fund & S'wark Dioc Brd Fin from 2008
GS 2010–   *Tel:* 01372 740155
           email: brian.k.wilson@btinternet.com

WILSON, Ven Christine Louise, Dip Th
The Old Vicarage Baslow Derbyshire DE45 1RY [ARCHDEACON OF CHESTERFIELD] *b* 1958 *educ* Margaret Hardy Sch, Brighton; SDMTS; *CV* C Henfield w. Shermanbury and Woodmancate, Chich 1997–2002; TV Hove 2002–08; V Goring by Sea 2008–10; Adn Chesterfield from 2010; Chich Dioc Overseas Cttee 2007–09; Adv Cttee, Derby from 2010; Bd of Finance, Derby from 2010; Bd of Edu, Derby from 2010; Pastoral Cttee, Derby from 2010; Parsonages Cttee, Derby from 2010
GS 2010–   *Tel:* 01246 583023
        email: archchesterfield@derby.anglican.org

WILSON, Mr John, MIH, MIF
49 Oakhurst Lichfield WS14 9AL [LICHFIELD] *educ* Polytechnic of North London; ; *CV* HM Forces 1961–76; Deputy Area School Meals Advisor, Cambridgeshire County Council 1977–78; Regional Sales and marketing Manager, Bateman Catering 1978–83; Dir of Training, Mantislight Ltd, 1983–87; Dir Operations, Deansbury Ltd, 1987–92; Charity Management Consult, Charity Support Services, 1992–97; National Fundraising and Marketing Advisor, Age Concern England, 1997–2001; Charity Management Consult, Charity Support Services, 2001–06; Chief Exec, Line Line, 2006–10; M Dioc Syn from 1989; M Dioc Pastoral Cttee from 2000; M Bp's Counc from 2000; M Brd of Partonage from 2003; Dioc Chair of House of Laity from 2009; Lay Chair of Lichf Deanery from 1987; Treasurer Church House Deaneries Group (The National Deaneries Network) from 2003
GS 2005–   *Tel:* 01543 268678
                        Fax: 01543 411685
           email: charity.services@btclick.com

WILSON-RUDD, Miss Fay (Felicity),
3 Old School Place North Grove Wells BA5 2TD [BATH AND WELLS] *b* 1941 *educ* Filton High Sch; *CV* Asst Stewardship Adv St Alb Dio 1981–84; Resources Adv B & W 1984–2001; pt Chapl Co-ord Somerset NHS Ptnrship and Soc Care Trust from 1999
GS 1993–   *Tel and Fax:* 01749 677286 (Home)
                        07712 581903 (Mobile)
           email: faywilsonrudd@msn.com

WILTS, Archdeacon of. See WRAW, Ven John Michael

WINCHESTER, Archdeacon of. See HARLEY, Ven Michael

WINCHESTER, Bishop of. See SCOTT-JOYNT, Rt Revd Michael Charles

WINCHESTER, Dean of. See ATWELL, Very Revd James Edgar

WINDSOR, Dean of. See CONNER, Rt Revd David John

WINSTANLEY, Rt Revd Alan Leslie, B Th
Vicarage Preston Rd Whittle-le-Woods Chorley PR6 7PS [HONORARY ASSISTANT BISHOP OF BLACKBURN] *b* 1949 *educ* Leigh Boys' Gr Sch, Lancs; St Jo Coll Nottm; *CV* C St Andr Livesey, Blackb 1972–75; C St Mary Gt Sankey Liv 1975–78; V Penketh Liv 1978–81; SAMS Miss Lima, Peru 1982–85, Arequipa 1986–87; Bp of Peru and Bolivia 1988–93; V Eastham and Hon Asst Bp of Chester 1994–2003; V St Jo Ev, Whittle-le-Woods and Hon Asst Bp of Blackburn from 2003
                    Tel and Fax: 01257 241291
           email: alan.winstanley@talktalk.net

WINTER, Revd Dr Dagmar, Dr Theol
Vicarage Kirkwhelpington Newcastle upon Tyne NE19 2RT [NEWCASTLE] *b* 1963 *educ* Gesamtschule Oberursel; Erlangen Univ; Aberd Univ; Heidelberg Univ; Herborn Th Coll; *CV* C St Mark Bromley 1996–99; Assoc V and Dny Trg Officer Hexham Abbey 1999–2006; P-in-c Kirkwhelpington, Kirkharle, Kirkheaton and Cambo and Dioc Officer for Rural Affairs from 2006; AD of Morpeth from 2010
GS 2005–

WINTON, Rt Revd Alan Peter, BA, PhD
The Red House 53 Norwich Rd Stoke Holy Cross Norwich NR14 8AB [BISHOP OF THETFORD] *b* 1958 *educ* Chislehurst and Sidcup Gr Sch; Trin Coll Bristol; Univ Sheff; Linc Theol Coll; *CV* Asst C Christ Ch Southgate 1991–95; P-in-C St Paul's Walden w Preston 1995–99; CME Officer Dioc St Albans 1995–99; R Welwyn w Ayot St Peter 1999–2005; TR Welwyn 2005–09; Bp of Thetford from 2009; Chair Discipleship and Min Forum Siod Norw; Chair Norw Dioc Ministry Course Governing Body   *Tel:* 01508 491014
                        Fax: 01508 492105
     email: bishop.thetford@norwich.anglican.org

WISBECH, Archdeacon of, [NOT APPOINTED AT TIME OF GOING TO PRESS],

WITCOMBE, Revd Canon John Julian, MA, MPhil
Department of Ministry 4 College Green Gloucester GL1 2LR [GLOUCESTER] *b* 1959 *educ* Bramcote Hills Gr Sch; Nott High Sch; Emman Colle, Cam; Nott Univ; St. John's Coll, Nott; *CV* C, St John's Birtley, Dur 1984–87; C-in-C, St. Barnabas' Inham Nook, S'well 1987–91; V, St. Luke's Lodge Moor, Sheff, 1991–95; TR, Uxbridge, Lon, 1995–98; Dean, St John's Coll Nott, 1998–2005; Off Min & Dir of Ordinands, Glouc, 2005–2010; Dir, Dept of

Disicipleship and Ministry, Glouc from 2010; Residentiary Can, Glouc Cathl from 2010
GS 2010–   *Tel:* 01452 835549
    email: jwitcombe@glosdioc

WITTS, Mrs Susan Anne, BA
20 Amber Drive Chorley PR6 0LA [BLACKBURN] *b* 1958 *educ* Mather Colll Man; Edge Hill Univ; Church Coll Cert Sch Work St Martin's Lanc;; CV Primary Sch Tchr 1979–2005; Asst Dir Children's Work, Bd Edu; Blackb Dioc from 2005; Dioc Blackb bd Edu Liturg Ctee; Elected to GS 2010
GS 2010–   *Tel:* 01254 503070
    email: Susan.witts@blackburn.anglican.org

WOLSTENHOLME, Ms Carol, OBE, FCIPD
12 Ashleigh Crescent Denton Newcsatle upon Tyne NE5 2AE [NEWCASTLE] *b* 1943 *educ* Rutherford High Sch Newc; CV Dept Work and Pensions Human Resources 1960–2003; Mgt Consult from 2000; Chair Newc Dioc Miss and Pastl Ctee from 2006; M Newc Dioc Strategical Devel Gp from 2007
GS 2009–   *Tel:* 0191 2745144
    email: carol43@aol.com

WOLVERHAMPTON, Area Bishop of. See GREGORY, Rt Revd Clive Malcolm

WOLVERSON, Revd Marc Ali Morad, BA, Dip Min
Vicarage 85 Buxton Rd High Lane Stockport SK6 8DS [CHESTER] *b* 1968 *educ* St Louis Country Day Sch, USA; Loyola Univ, USA; Kansas Univ, USA; Ripon Coll Cuddesdon; CV C St Mary Nantwich 1996–99; Asst R and sch Chapl, St Luke's Episcopal Ch and Sch, Baton Rouge, Louisiana 1999–2000; Assoc V St Mich and All Angels Bramhall 2000–04; V St Thos High Lane from 2004; M Ches Dioc Syn; Dioc Spiritual Dir, Cursillo
GS 2005–   *Tel:* 01663 762627
    email: frmarc@onetel.com

WOOD, Canon (Nicholas) Martin, AKC, MTh
101 London Road Bowers Gifford Basildon Essex SS13 2DU [CHELMSFORD] *b* 1951 *educ* Brentwood Sch; Mid Essex Tech Coll; Kings Coll Lon; Univ of Wales Lampeter; St Augustine's Coll, Cant; CV C East Ham Team Ministry 1975–78; C in C, St. Luke, Leyton 1978–81; V Rush Green 1981–91; Chapl Barking Coll 1981–91; TR Elland 1991–2005; Rural Dean of Brighouse & Elland 1996–2005; Hon can Wakef Cathl 2001–05; P Develp Adv Bradwell Episcopal Area of Chelms from 2005; Hon can Chelms Cathl from 2008; Chelms Dioc Brd Miss 1983–84; Chelms Dioc Pstrl support & develp grp 1985–88; Wakef Dioc Syn 1991–05; Wakef Bp's Counc 1997–2005; Wakef Dioc Brd Min & Training sub cttee 1991–94; Wakef Dioc clergy ed and training grp 1994–98; Wakef Min Scheme Counc & ed sub grp 1996–2005; Wakef Min Adv Grp 1994–2005; Chair Wakef Dioc Family Life grp FLAME 1998–2005; Chelms Miss and

P Develop Adv Grp from 2005; Chelms Dioc Syn from 2009
GS 2010–   *Tel:* 01268 552219
    email: mwood@chelmsford.anglican.org

WOOLWICH, Area Bishop of. See CHESSUN, Rt Revd Christopher Thomas James

WORCESTER, Archdeacon of. See MORRIS, Ven Roger Anthony Brett

WORCESTER, Bishop of. See INGE, Rt Revd Dr John Geoffrey

WORCESTER, Dean of. See ATKINSON, Very Revd Peter Gordon

WRAW, Ven John Michael, BA
Southbroom House London Rd Devizes SN10 1LT [ARCHDEACON OF WILTS; SALISBURY] *b* 1959 *educ* K Sch Chester; Lincoln Coll Ox; Fitzwilliam Coll Cam; Ridley Hall Cam; CV C St Pet Bromyard, Heref 1985–88; TV Sheff Manor Team 1988–92; V Clifton St Jas, Sheff 1992–2001; P-in-c Wickersley St Alb, Sheff 2001–04; Adn of Wilts from 2004
    Tel: 01380 729808
    Fax: 01380 738096
    email: adwilts@salisbury.anglican.org

WRIGHT, Ven Dr Paul, BD, MTh, DMin, AKC
The Archdeaconry The Glebe Chislehurst BR7 5PX [ARCHDEACON OF BROMLEY AND BEXLEY; ROCHESTER] *b* 1954 *educ* Crayford Sch; K Coll Lon; Heythrop Coll Lon; Ripon Coll, Cuddesdon; Lampeter Univ of Wales; CV C St Geo Beckenham, Roch 1979–83; C St Mary w St Matthias & St Jo, S'wark 1983–85; Chapl Ch Sch Richmond, S'wark 1983–85; V St Aug Gillingham, Roch 1985–90; R St Paulinus Crayford, Roch 1990–99; RD Erith 1993–97; Hon Can Roch Cathl 1998–2003; V St Jo Evang Sidcup, Roch 1999–2003; Adn of Bromley and Bexley from 2003; M Bp's Coun; M Dioc Bd of Patr; Chair Adv Bd for Miss and Unity; M Eccl Law Soc; Bp's Insp of Theol Colls
    Tel: 020 8467 8743
    07985 902601 (Mobile)
    Fax: 020 8467 8743
    email: archdeacon.bromley@
    rochester.anglican.org

WYNBURNE, Revd John Paterson Barry, BA, M.Div
The Vicarage 84a High St Long Crendon Bucks HP18 9AL [OXFORD] *b* 1948 *educ* St Jo School Leatherhead, Surrey; Univ of Dur; Univ of Toronto; Ridley Hall Cam; CV C St Jo Ch Stanmore 1973–76; Chapl Bucharest w Sofia 1976–77; Asst P St Martin's Dorking 1978–80; V St Mary's Send, Surrey 1980–88; V St Michael's Camberley 1988–95; TR Beaconsfield 1995–2009; V United Benefice Long Crendon, Cheersley, Nether Winchendon from 2009
GS 1985–1990; 2009–2010   *Tel:* 01844 201424
    email: revwynburne@btinternet.com

WYNNE, Mrs Alison,
88 Balcarres Rd Leyland PR25 3ED [BLACKBURN] *b* 1961 *educ* Pleckgate High Sch, Blackb; *CV* Wages clerk, MOD 1979–83; Computer Programmer, MOD 1983–86; Computer Applications Programmer, Lancs Constabulary 1986–87; IT Systems Programmer, Lancs Constabulary 1987–89; Chr outreach worker from 2001; Orthopaedic support worker Lancashire Teaching Hospitals from 2009
GS 2005–   *Tel:* 01772 454209
                                         07719 727527 (Mobile)
                              email: alison@wynne.org.uk

WYTHE, Mr John Michael, BSc, FRICS
Woodpeckers Ashwood Rd Woking GU22 7JN [CHURCH COMMISSIONER] *b* 1956 *educ* Woking Gr Sch for Boys; Reading Univ; *CV* Dir Prudential Property Investment Mgrs; Hd of Fund Mgt; Ch Commr from 2007; M Assets Cttee
                                   Tel: 020 7548 6721
                       email: john.wythe@prupim.com

YEOMAN, Revd Ruth Jane, MA, BSc, MSc
Vicarage 12 Fairfax Gardens Menston Ilkley LS29 6ET [BRADFORD] *b* 1960 *educ* Nottm Bluecoat Sch; Sheff Univ; Ripon Coll Cuddesdon; *CV* C St Pet and St Paul Coleshill w. Maxstoke, Birm 1991–95; Asst P St Phil and St Jas Hodge Hill and Adv for Children's Work, Birm Dioc 1995–2000; House-leader, L'Arch Lambeth Com 2001–02; V St Jo Divine Menston w. Woodhead from 2003; Assoc DDO Bradf from 2006; NADAWM representative Bradf from 2009
GS 2005–   *Tel:* 01943 877739
                                         07752 912646 (Mobile)
                              email: ruthjyeoman@hotmail.com

YORK, Archbishop of. See SENTAMU, Most Revd and Rt Hon Dr John Tucker Mugabi

YORK, Archdeacon of. See SEED, Ven Richard Murray Crosland

YORK, Dean of. See JONES, Very Revd Keith Brynmor

YOUNG, Rt Revd Clive, BA
28 Westerfield Rd Ipswich IP4 2UJ [SUFFRAGAN BISHOP OF DUNWICH; ST EDMUNDSBURY AND IPSWICH] *b* 1948 *educ* K Edw VI Gr Sch Chelmsf; Dur Univ; Ridley Hall Cam; *CV* C Neasden cum Kingsbury 1972–75; C St Paul Hammersmith 1975–79; P-in-c St Paul w St Steph Old Ford 1979–82; V 1982–92; AD Tower Hamlets 1988–92; Adn of Hackney 1992–99; V St Andr Holborn 1992–99; Bp of Dunwich from 1999   *Tel:* 01473 222276
                                         Fax: 01473 210303

INDEX

Note: Names of dioceses appear in *italics*; page references in **bold** type indicate maps. Names beginning 'St' are filed as if spelled 'Saint'. Hyphens and apostrophes are ignored for filing purposes.

Index